Blackstone's

Environmental Legislation

Sixth Edition

Edited by

Donald McGillivray

Senior Lecturer in Law, Kent Law School,
University of Kent

OXFORD
UNIVERSITY PRESS

OXFORD
UNIVERSITY PRESS

Great Clarendon Street, Oxford OX2 6DP

Oxford University Press is a department of the University of Oxford.
It furthers the University's objective of excellence in research, scholarship,
and education by publishing worldwide in

Oxford New York

Auckland Cape Town Dar es Salaam Hong Kong Karachi
Kuala Lumpur Madrid Melbourne Mexico City Nairobi
New Delhi Shanghai Taipei Toronto

With offices in

Argentina Austria Brazil Chile Czech Republic France Greece
Guatemala Hungary Italy Japan Poland Portugal Singapore
South Korea Switzerland Thailand Turkey Ukraine Vietnam

Oxford is a registered trade mark of Oxford University Press
in the UK and in certain other countries

Published in the United States
by Oxford University Press Inc., New York

First published 1994
Second edition 1995
Third edition 2000
Fourth edition 2002
Fifth edition 2004
Sixth edition 2006

British Library Cataloguing in Publication Data

Data available

Typeset by Newgen Imaging Systems (P) Ltd., Chennai, India
Printed in Great Britain
on acid-free paper by
CPI Bath

ISBN 0–19–928825–9 978–0–19–928825–0

1 3 5 7 9 10 8 6 4 2

CONTENTS

ALPHABETICAL CONTENTS

EDITOR'S PREFACE TO THE SIXTH EDITION

This is the first edition of Blackstone's Environmental Legislation that has not been edited by Bob Duxbury and Sandra Morton. I should first thank them for their efforts in establishing and keeping up to date (and most importantly keeping to a manageable size) previous editions.

For my own part I have sought to include those provisions which, in my opinion, are most likely to be considered on the majority of environmental law modules. I have been helped in this by the UK Centre for Legal Education subject survey on environmental law (www.ukcle.ac.uk/research/projects/environmental.html), and I am grateful to my co-authors for the work they put into this survey.

Accordingly, provisions mainly concerned with landscape conservation (in particular the planning regime relating to listed buildings and conservation areas) have been omitted, but coverage of nature conservation law has been enhanced, most notably by the return of key provisions of Part 2 of the Wildlife and Countryside Act 1981 as now amended by the Countryside and Rights of Way Act 2000. In the interests of space I have also tried to avoid coverage of special regimes or regimes controlling specific pollutants. As a result I have excluded coverage of things like nitrate vulnerable zones, distinct provisions on abandoned mines and water pollution, and rules about specific waste streams like end of life vehicles. I appreciate that this may have a certain distorting effect, and may result in some particular legal responses and tools not being covered. But I am very conscious that many students' contact with environmental law is relatively brief—perhaps a one term or one semester module—where only general provisions can be studied. I have also omitted Part I of the Environmental Protection Act 1990 on integrated pollution control on the grounds that, with IPC coming to a rest by 2007, and Local Authority Air Pollution Control having now been transferred over to IPPC, the successor integrated pollution prevention and control regime ought now to be universally taught in this area.

I have also tried to be ruthless at omitting material that I consider need not trouble the student user—procedural or substantive detail which in my opinion it is simply not useful to reproduce because it does not speak to the student about law and the environment. In some instances where it is important for the student—in understanding the shape of the provisions—to know that a certain provision exists but where the precise details are of little relevance then I have either put in the title of the section and omitted the details, or included the first couple of subsections or provisions of a regulation to give the general flavour and made it clear that the rest has been omitted. In terms of format, I have continued with the abbreviations used previously. So [...] indicates provisions repealed, while... indicates omitted material. In a couple of places I have included the start of a highly technical annex or schedule to illustrate the approach of the law to standard setting but excluded the bulk of the provisions. In these and a very few other places I have felt it necessary to add an 'Editor's note' but, these aside, this edition is not annotated.

In terms of new material, I have included the key provisions of the Human Rights Act. The extent to which human rights law under the Convention does or should influence environmental regulation is not just of practical importance; discussing the environment through a human rights lens can be a particularly valuable way of posing some of the tensions in environmental regulation. I am also conscious that environmental law is taught as much to non-law students who are very unlikely to have encountered this in earlier study. In terms of national law, other notable developments include the Clean Neighbourhoods and Environment Act 2005 (though most of this amends existing legislation on things like waste), the Environmental Information Regulations 2004, the misleadingly titled Hazardous

Waste (England and Wales) Regulations 2005 (which do cover what used to be called 'special waste' but which do not apply to Wales), and the Environmental Assessment of Plans and Programmes Regulations 2004 implementing the Strategic Environmental Assessment Directive. Quite a number of the other newcomers to this book are included for their sustainable development duties, or for their (often minor, it must be said) contribution to the law on reducing greenhouse gas emissions.

Some key international documents are also included for the first time. It is difficult to imagine an environmental law module which, even if it did not specifically tackle international environmental law, did not, in some way, consider the Rio Declaration or the Aarhus Convention in relation to the development of environmental law and policy generally. I have also included extracts from the UN Framework Convention on Climate Change and its Kyoto Protocol (together with the recent Compliance rules), reflecting the extent to which 'carbon law' is emerging at the very core of—and perhaps even supplanting—environmental law as traditionally conceived.

In terms of EC law, I have generally continued the practice of including only implementing legislation. Two directives are, nevertheless, included: the Environmental Liability Directive because of its centrality and because there are as yet no implementing regulations, and the Water Framework Directive because, although there are certain implementing regulations, these provide almost no insight on what this hugely important directive aims to achieve.

Finally, in terms of content, I have tried to give as equal coverage as is possible to the law in Wales as to the law in England, though in a few cases where Welsh provisions are analogous to their English counterparts I have omitted the details. In some areas covered by Regulations, however, the law in the two countries is diverging. In these cases I have given the relevant English provision and students in Wales may need specific direction on this.

It is a little difficult to say exactly when the law is stated as at. The work in updating these statutes was completed in mid-April 2006 using, as the main research tool, a mix of LexisNexisButterworths and, to a lesser degree, Westlaw. These stated the law as at anything from mid February to mid March 2006. In addition, I have included provisions such as the Natural Environment and Rural Communities Act 2006 which, although most of it is to come into force by commencement order after this preface is written, I have assumed is fully in force. I have also gone through the statutes and statutory instruments enacted up to mid-April 2006 and incorporated any changes that these are due to make by the time this edition is published. The same goes for other provisions which are being brought into force over time by commencement order. There are still isolated pockets where trying to say what the law will be by the date of publication remains tricky, for example in relation to planning obligations and contributions, and I hope that teachers will keep students on the right track in areas like these. Unfortunately it has not been possible, for this edition, to footnote those provisions which are not yet in force.

In terms of keeping up to date between editions, there is an accompanying Online Resource Centre at www.oxfordtextbooks.co.uk/orc/statutes/, where significant developments and amendments to the law will be posted.

Many thanks go to the following. To OUP for asking me to take over as editor (a particularly brave move given the delays in producing other work for them). To Melanie Jackson for her efficiency and courtesy in working on this, and to the anonymous reviewers for their assistance. To Sarah Carter, the outgoing (and much valued) Law Librarian at Kent, without whose vision in securing for Kent such an impressive array of electronic legal resources this project would have been so much more difficult. To Stuart and Loz, for their last minute guidance and suggestions as we played fantasy statutes via email (sorry the Weeds Act never made the final squad). To the present (at the time of writing) government, without whose intransigence over the appalling state of academic pay this project might never have been agreed to or, because of the current assessment boycott, finished with relatively little interruption. And finally to Jane, both for my good fortune in having as a partner a much better environmental lawyer to take soundings from, and for doing the early shifts in particular on those occasions when I worked longer into the night on this than is sensible.

Comments on this edition and on what to include in future editions are of course welcome, and can be emailed to d.mcgillivray@kent.ac.uk.

Donald McGillivray
Barcombe, May 2006

EDITORS' PREFACE TO THE FIRST EDITION

Although laws relating to the environment have been studied for many years in one form or another, the appearance of a subject called 'environmental law' is a relatively new phenomenon. It no doubt reflects a fashionable concern with the so-called 'green' agenda but it also owes much to the introduction, at the beginning of the decade, of comprehensive legislation dealing with pollution and waste management with its 'integrated' approach to environment. A further factor has been the gradual coalescing of the well-established planning system with wider environmental considerations, prompted in large measure by the impetus of European environmental law and policy.

In 1991 the editors of this book introduced an Environmental Law course on the LLB degree at Nottingham Law School. The need for a readily accessible collection of statutes and statutory instruments—for teaching, private study and examining—was obvious. Having decided to put together our own selection, as it were, 'in-house', we approached Blackstone Press to see if commercial publication was a possibility. They responded with characteristic enthusiasm.

We realise, however, that we have set ourselves a daunting task. Unlike courses, on, say, contract law, environmental law programmes differ greatly from institution to institution in coverage, emphasis and approach. Our aim has been to bring together what we feel to be the most important and widely referred-to sections of statutes and statutory instruments in the field of environmental law. Given the inevitable limitations of space set by our publishers we have had to make some difficult decisions a to what to include and what to leave out. In particular, and with regret, we felt that there would be no room for reference to many other EC directives, UK statutory instruments or to government circulars and policy guidance. Provisions relating to Scotland or Northern Ireland have also been omitted. Readers will need to look elsewhere for these.

The extracts are set out in chronological order. Subsequent amendments to statutes are denoted by square brackets ([]) with no reference to the amending statute. Thus the extensive changes to the Town and Country Planning Act 1990 made by the Planning and Compensation Act 1991 are indicated in this way. In those very few cases where we have not cited a section in full, the omitted material is denoted by three dots (. . .) and sub-sections which have been repealed are indicated thus, ([. . .]). With the exception of the footnotes, the recently issued Waste Management Licensing Regulations have been reproduced in full because of their impact on the implementation of Part II of the Environmental Protection Act and the requirements relating to 'Directive waste'.

We would like to thank those colleagues at other institutions who, when approached by the publishers as to the potential coverage of this book, gave most helpful advice. A debt of gratitude is also owed to our publishers for their support and encouragement. We sincerely hope that those concerned with environmental law will find the book of some use.

Robert Duxbury
Sandra Morton

PART I

UK Legislation

European Communities Act 1972

(1972, c. 68)

2.—(1) All such rights, powers, liabilities, obligations and restrictions from time to time created or arising by or under the Treaties, and all such remedies and procedures from time to time provided for by or under the Treaties, as in accordance with the Treaties are without further enactment to be given legal effect or used in the United Kingdom shall be recognised and available in law, and be enforced, allowed and followed accordingly; and the expression 'enforceable Community right' and similar expressions shall be read as referring to one to which this subsection applies.

(2) Subject to Schedule 2 to this Act, at any time after its passing Her Majesty may by Order in Council, and any designated Minister or department may by regulations, make provision—

(a) for the purpose of implementing any Community obligation of the United Kingdom, or enabling any such obligation to be implemented, or of enabling any rights enjoyed or to be enjoyed by the United Kingdom under or by virtue of the Treaties to be exercised; or

(b) for the purpose of dealing with matters arising out of or related to any such obligation or rights or the coming into force, or the operation from time to time, of subsection (1) above;

and in the exercise of any statutory power or duty, including any power to give directions or to legislate by means of orders, rules, regulations or other subordinate instrument, the person entrusted with the power or duty may have regard to the objects of the Communities and to any such obligation or rights as aforesaid.

In this subsection 'designated Minister or department' means such Minister of the Crown or government department as may from time to time be designated by Order in Council in relation to any matter or for any purpose, but subject to such restrictions or conditions (if any) as may be specified by the Order in Council.

(3) ...

(4) The provision that may be made under subsection (2) above includes, subject to Schedule 2 to this Act, any such provision (of any such extent) as might be made by Act of Parliament, and any enactment passed or to be passed, other than one contained in this part of this Act, shall be construed and have effect subject to the foregoing provisions of this sections; but, except as may be provided by any Act passed after this Act, Schedule 2 shall have effect in connection with the powers conferred by this and the following sections of this Act to make Orders in Council and regulations.

(5) ...

(6) ...

3.—(1) For the purposes of all legal proceedings any question as to the meaning or effect of any of the Treaties, or as to the validity, meaning or effect of any Community instrument, shall be treated as a question of law (and, if not referred to the European Court, be for determination as such in accordance with the principles laid down by and any relevant [decision of the European Court or any court attached thereto)].

(2) Judicial notice shall be taken of the Treaties, of the Official Journal of the Communities and of any decision of, or expression of opinion by, the European Court [or any court attached thereto] on any such question as aforesaid; and the Official Journal shall be admissible as evidence of any instrument or other act thereby communicated of any of the Communities or of any Community institution.

SCHEDULE 2 PROVISIONS AS TO SUBORDINATE LEGISLATION

2.—(1) . . . where a provision contained in any section of this Act confers power to make regulations (otherwise than by modification or extension of an existing power), the power shall be exercisable by statutory instrument.

(2) Any statutory instrument containing an Order in Council or regulations made in the exercise of a power so conferred, if made without a draft having been approved by resolution of each House of Parliament, shall be subject to annulment in pursuance of a resolution of either House.

. . .

Building Act 1984

(1984, c. 55)

PART I BUILDING REGULATIONS[1]

Power to make building regulations

1 Power to make building regulations

(1) The Secretary of State may, for any of the purposes of—

(a) securing the health, safety, welfare and convenience of persons in or about buildings and of others who may be affected by buildings or matters connected with buildings,

[(b) furthering the conservation of fuel and power,

(c) preventing waste, undue consumption, misuse or contamination of water,

(b) furthering the protection or enhancement of the environment,

(c) facilitating sustainable development, or

(d) furthering the prevention or detection of crime,]

make regulations with respect to the [matters mentioned in subsection (1A) below].

[(1A) Those matters are—

(a) the design and construction of buildings;

(b) the demolition of buildings;

(c) services, fittings and equipment provided in or in connection with buildings.]

(2) Regulations made under subsection (1) above are known as building regulations.

(3) Schedule 1 to this Act has effect with respect to the matters as to which building regulations may provide.

(4) The power to make building regulations is exercisable by statutory instrument. . . .

. . .

2 Continuing requirements

(1) Building regulations may impose on owners and occupiers of buildings to which building regulations are applicable such continuing requirements as the Secretary of State considers appropriate for securing, with respect to any provision of building regulations designated in the regulations as a provision to which those requirements relate, that the

[1] Editor's note: section 1(1) and Schedule 1 amended by, and section 1(1A) and section 2A added by, the Sustainable and Secure Buildings Act 2004.

purposes of that provision are not frustrated; but a continuing requirement imposed by virtue of this subsection does not apply in relation to a building unless a provision of building regulations so designated as one to which the requirement relates applies to that building.

(2) Building regulations may impose on owners and occupiers of buildings of a prescribed class (whenever erected, and whether or not any building regulations were applicable to them at the time of their erection) continuing requirements with respect to all or any of the following matters—

(a) the conditions subject to which any services, fittings or equipment provided in or in connection with a building of that class may be used,
(b) the inspection and maintenance of any services, fittings or equipment so provided,
(c) the making of reports to a prescribed authority on the condition of any services, fittings or equipment so provided,

and so much of paragraph 8 of Schedule 1 to this Act as restricts the application of building regulations does not apply to regulations made by virtue of this subsection.

(3) If a person contravenes a continuing requirement imposed by virtue of this section, the local authority, without prejudice to their right to take proceedings for a fine in respect of the contravention, may—

(a) execute any work or take any other action required to remedy the contravention, and
(b) recover from that person the expenses reasonably incurred by them in so doing.

(4) Where a local authority have power under subsection (3) above to execute any work or take any other action, they may, instead of exercising that power, by notice require the owner or the occupier of the building to which the contravention referred to in that subsection relates to execute that work or take that action.

...

[2A Continuing requirements in relation to fuel, power and emissions]

[(1) Building regulations may impose, on owners and occupiers of buildings, continuing requirements that fall within subsection (2) below.

(2) A continuing requirement falls within this subsection if—

(a) it requires the inspection and testing of a building—
   (i) as respects the use of fuel and power in or in connection with the building; or
   (ii) as respects its contribution to or effect on emissions (whether or not from the building) of smoke, gases, vapours or fumes;
(b) it requires the inspection and testing of any service, fitting or equipment provided in or in connection with a building—
   (i) as respects the use of fuel and power in or in connection with the service, fitting or equipment; or
   (ii) as respects its contribution to or effect on emissions (whether or not from it or the building) of smoke, gases, vapours or fumes;
(c) it requires the implementation, in relation to a building, or any service, fitting or equipment provided in or in connection with a building, of—
   (i) measures for the purpose mentioned in section 1(1)(b) above; or
   (ii) measures (otherwise than for that purpose) that are calculated to secure, or to contribute to, the prevention or reduction of emissions (whether or not from the building in question or a thing provided in or in connection with it) of smoke, gases, vapours or fumes;
(d) it requires the keeping of records in relation to matters within paragraph (a), (b) or (c); or
(e) it requires the making of reports in relation to any of those matters to a prescribed authority.

(3) Those requirements may be imposed in the case of buildings, or in the case of services, fittings and equipment provided in or in connection with buildings, irrespective of both—

(a) when the buildings were erected; and

(b) whether building regulations were applicable to them at the time of their erection.

(4) Subsections (3) to (6) of section 2 above apply in relation to continuing requirements imposed by virtue of this section as they apply in relation to continuing requirements imposed by virtue of that section.

(5) Paragraph 8(2) of Schedule 1 to this Act does not impose any restriction on the building regulations that may be made by virtue of this section.]

Section 1(3)

SCHEDULE 1

BUILDING REGULATIONS

7 Without prejudice to the generality of section 1(1) of this Act, building regulations may—

(a) for any of the purposes mentioned in section 1(1) of this Act, make provision with respect to any of the following matters—

...

(ii) suitability, durability[, use and reuse] of materials and components (including surface finishes),

...

(vi) measures affecting the transmission of heat,

(vii) measures affecting the transmission of sound,

...

(ix) measures affecting the emission of smoke, gases, [vapours,] fumes, grit or dust or other noxious or offensive substances,

...

(xii) storage, treatment and removal of waste,

(xiii) installations utilising solid fuel, oil, gas, electricity or any other fuel or power (including appliances, storage tanks, heat exchangers, ducts, fans and other equipment),

...

(xviii) standards of heating, artificial lighting, mechanical ventilation and air-conditioning and provision of power outlets,

(xix) open space about buildings and the natural lighting and ventilation of buildings,

[(xxiib) measures affecting the use of fuel or power,

(xxiic) equipment for monitoring and measuring supplies of fuel, power or heat,

(xxiid) recycling facilities (including facilities for composting),]

(xxiii) matters connected with or ancillary to any of the foregoing matters,

(b) require things to be provided or done in connection with buildings (as well as regulating the provision or doing of things in or in connection with buildings),

(c) prescribe the manner in which work is to be carried out.

8 ...

[(2) Subject to subparagraphs (3) to (6) below and to sections 2(2) and 2A of this Act, building regulations shall not apply to or in connection with buildings erected before the date on which the regulations come into force.

...

Gas Act 1986

(1986, c. 44)

[4AA The principal objective and general duties of the Secretary of State and the Authority]

[(1) The principal objective of the Secretary of State and the Gas and Electricity Markets Authority (in this Act referred to as 'the Authority') in carrying out their respective functions under this Part is to protect the interests of consumers in relation to gas conveyed through pipes, wherever appropriate by promoting effective competition between persons engaged in, or in commercial activities connected with, the shipping, transportation or supply of gas so conveyed.

(2) The Secretary of State and the Authority shall carry out those functions in the manner which he or it considers is best calculated to further the principal objective, having regard to—

(a) the need to secure that, so far as it is economical to meet them, all reasonable demands in Great Britain for gas conveyed through pipes are met; and

(b) the need to secure that licence holders are able to finance the activities which are the subject of obligations imposed by or under this Part or the Utilities Act 2000.

...

(5) Subject to subsection (2), the Secretary of State and the Authority shall carry out their respective functions under this Part in the manner which he or it considers is best calculated—

(a) to promote efficiency and economy on the part of persons authorised by licences or exemptions to carry on any activity, and the efficient use of gas conveyed through pipes;

(b) to protect the public from dangers arising from the conveyance of gas through pipes or from the use of gas conveyed through pipes;

[(ba) to contribute to the achievement of sustainable development[2]; and]

(c) to secure a diverse and viable longterm energy supply, [and (so far as not otherwise required to do so by this subsection) shall] have regard, in carrying out those functions, to the effect on the environment of activities connected with the conveyance of gas through pipes.

[(5A) In carrying out their respective functions under this Part in accordance with the preceding provisions of this section the Secretary of State and the Authority must each have regard to—

(a) the principles under which regulatory activities should be transparent, accountable, proportionate, consistent and targeted only at cases in which action is needed; and

(b) any other principles appearing to him or, as the case may be, it to represent the best regulatory practice.]

(6) In this section 'consumers' includes both existing and future consumers.

...

Control of Pollution (Amendment) Act 1989

(1989, c. 14)

1 Offence of transporting controlled waste without registering

(1) Subject to the following provisions of this section, it shall be an offence for any person who is not a registered carrier of controlled waste, in the course of any business of his

[2] Editor's note: subsection 5(ba) added by s. 83 Energy Act 2004.

or otherwise with a view to profit, to transport any controlled waste to or from any place in Great Britain.

(2) A person shall not be guilty of an offence under this section in respect of—

(a) the transport of controlled waste within the same premises between different places in those premises;

(b) the transport to a place in Great Britain of controlled waste which has been brought from a country or territory outside Great Britain and is not landed in Great Britain until it arrives at that place;

(c) the transport by air or sea of controlled waste from a place in Great Britain to a place outside Great Britain.

(3) The Secretary of State may by regulations provide that a person shall not be required for the purposes of this section to be a registered carrier of controlled waste if—

(a) he is a prescribed person or a person of such a description as may be prescribed; or

(b) without prejudice to paragraph (a) above, he is a person in relation to whom the prescribed requirements under the law of any other member State are satisfied.

(4) In proceedings against any person for an offence under this section in respect of the transport of any controlled waste it shall be a defence for that person to show—

(a) that the waste was transported in an emergency of which notice was given, as soon as practicable after it occurred, to the [regulation authority] in whose area the emergency occurred; or

(b) that he neither knew nor had reasonable grounds for suspecting that what was being transported was controlled waste and took all such steps as it was reasonable to take for ascertaining whether it was such waste.

(5) A person guilty of an offence under this section shall be liable on summary conviction to a fine not exceeding level 5 on the standard scale.

(6) In this section 'emergency', in relation to the transport of any controlled waste, means any circumstances in which, in order to avoid, remove or reduce any serious danger to the public or serious risk of damage to the environment, it is necessary for the waste to be transported from one place to another without the use of a registered carrier of such waste.

2 Registration of carriers

(1) Subject to section 3 below, the Secretary of State may by regulations make provision for the registration of persons with [regulation authorities] as carriers of controlled waste and, for that purpose, for the establishment and maintenance by such authorities, in accordance with the regulations, of such registers as may be prescribed.

(2) Regulations under this section may—

(a) make provision with respect to applications for registration;

(b) impose requirements with respect to the manner in which [regulation authorities] maintain registers of carriers of controlled waste;

(c) provide for the issue of a certificate of registration to a registered carrier of controlled waste both on his registration and on the making of any alteration of any entry relating to him in a register of such carriers;

[...]

(e) provide that the provision by a [regulation authority] to a registered carrier of such copies of a certificate of registration as are provided in addition to the certificate provided in pursuance of provision made by virtue of paragraph (c) above is to be made subject to the payment of a charge imposed under the regulations.

(3) Provision contained in any regulations under this section by virtue of subsection (2)(a) above may, in particular, include provision which—

(a) prescribes the manner of determining the [regulation] authority to which an application is to be made;

(b) [...]

(c) prescribes the period within which an application for the renewal of any registration which is due to expire is to be made;

(d) imposes requirements with respect to the information which is to be provided by an applicant to the authority to which his application is made;

(e) [...]

[(3A) Without prejudice to the generality of paragraph (d) of subsection (3) above—

(a) [...]

(b) The power to impose requirements with respect to information under paragraph (d) of that subsection includes power to make provision requiring an application to be accompanied by such information as may reasonably be required by the regulation authority to which it is to be made.]

(4) Provision contained in any regulations under this section by virtue of subsection (2)(b) above may, in particular, include provision—

(a) specifying or describing the information to be incorporated in any register maintained by a [regulation] authority in pursuance of any such regulations;

(b) requiring a registered carrier of controlled waste to notify a [regulation] authority which maintains such a register of any change of circumstances affecting information contained in the entry relating to that carrier in that register;

(c) requiring a [regulation] authority, to such extent and in such manner as may be prescribed, to make the contents of any such register available for public inspection free of charge; and

(d) requiring such an authority, on payment of such charges as may be imposed under the regulations, to provide such copies of the contents of any such register to any person applying for a copy as may be prescribed.

[(4A) Regulations under this section may include provision for—

(a) the registration of a person as a carrier of controlled waste to be subject to conditions relating to the vehicles used by him in transporting such waste; or

(b) the revocation by a regulation authority of the registration of a carrier of controlled waste who has breached a condition imposed on him under paragraph (a) above.

(4B) Provision contained in any regulations under this section by virtue of subsection (4A) above may, in particular, include provision—

(a) for inspection by a regulation authority of the vehicles of registered carriers of controlled waste for the purpose of ensuring compliance with conditions imposed under subsection (4A)(a) above;

(b) for a regulation authority to impose charges on registered carriers of controlled waste in respect of such inspections.]

(5) Subsections (2) to (4B) above are without prejudice to the generality of subsection (1) above.

3 Restrictions on power under section 2

(1) Nothing in any regulations under section 2 above shall authorise a [regulation] authority to refuse an application for registration except where—

(a) there has, in relation to that application, been a contravention of the requirements of any regulations made by virtue of subsection (2)(a) of that section; or

(b) the applicant or another relevant person has been convicted of a prescribed offence and, in the opinion of the authority, it is undesirable for the applicant to be authorised to transport controlled waste.

(2) Nothing in any regulations under section 2 above shall authorise any [regulation authority] to revoke any person's registration as a carrier of controlled waste except in accordance with regulations under subsection (4A) of that section, or where—

(a) that person or another relevant person has been convicted of a prescribed offence; and

(b) in the opinion of the authority, it is undesirable for the registered carrier to continue to be authorised to transport controlled waste; but registration in accordance with any regulations under that section shall cease to have effect after such period as may be prescribed or if the registered carrier gives written notice requiring the removal of his name from the register.

(3) Regulations under section 2 above may require every registration in respect of a business which is or is to be carried on by a partnership to be a registration of all the partners and to cease to have effect if any of the partners ceases to be registered or if any person who is not registered becomes a partner.

(4) Nothing in any regulations under section 2 above shall have the effect of bringing the revocation of any person's registration as a carrier of controlled waste into force except—

(a) after the end of such period as may be prescribed for appealing against the revocation under section 4 below; or

(b) where that person has indicated, within that period, that he does not intend to make or continue with an appeal.

(5) In relation to any applicant for registration or registered carrier, another relevant person shall be treated for the purposes of any provision made by virtue of subsection (1) or (2) above as having been convicted of a prescribed offence if—

(a) any person has been convicted of a prescribed offence committed by him in the course of his employment by the applicant or registered carrier or in the course of the carrying on of any business by a partnership one of the members of which was the applicant or registered carrier;

(b) a body corporate has been convicted of a prescribed offence committed at a time when the applicant or registered carrier was a director, manager, secretary or other similar officer of that body corporate; or

(c) where the applicant or registered carrier is a body corporate, a person who is a director, manager, secretary or other similar officer of that body corporate—

(i) has been convicted of a prescribed offence; or

(ii) was a director, manager, secretary or other similar officer of another body corporate at a time when a prescribed offence for which that other body corporate has been convicted was committed.

(6) In determining for the purposes of any provision made by virtue of subsection (1) or (2) above whether it is desirable for any individual to be or to continue to be authorised to transport controlled waste, a [regulation] authority shall have regard, in a case in which a person other than the individual has been convicted of a prescribed offence, to whether that individual has been a party to the carrying on of a business in a manner involving the commission of prescribed offences.

4 Appeals against refusal of registration etc

(1) Where a person has applied to a [regulation] authority to be registered in accordance with any regulations under section 2 above, he may appeal to the Secretary of State if—

(a) his application is refused; or

(b) the relevant period from the making of the application has expired without his having been registered;

and for the purposes of this subsection the relevant period is two months or, except in the case of an application for the renewal of his registration by a person who is already registered, such longer period as may be agreed between the applicant and the [regulation] authority in question.

(2) A person whose registration as a carrier of controlled waste has been revoked may appeal against the revocation to the Secretary of State.

(3) On an appeal under this section the Secretary of State may, as he thinks fit, either dismiss the appeal or give the [regulation] authority in question a direction to register the appellant or, as the case may be, to cancel the revocation.

(4) Where on an appeal made by virtue of subsection (1)(b) above the Secretary of State dismisses an appeal, he shall direct the [regulation] authority in question not to register the appellant.

(5) It shall be the duty of a [regulation] authority to comply with any direction under this section.

(6) The Secretary of State may by regulations make provision as to the manner in which and time within which an appeal under this section is to be made and as to the procedure to be followed on any such appeal.

(7) Where an appeal under this section is made in accordance with regulations under this section—

(a) by a person whose appeal is in respect of such an application for the renewal of his registration as was made, in accordance with regulations under section 2 above, at a time when he was already registered; or

(b) by a person whose registration has been revoked, that registration shall continue in force, notwithstanding the expiry of the prescribed period or the revocation, until the appeal is disposed of.

(8) For the purposes of subsection (7) above an appeal is disposed of when any of the following occurs, that is to say—

(a) the appeal is withdrawn;

(b) the appellant is notified by the Secretary of State or the [regulation] authority in question that his appeal has been dismissed; or

(c) the [regulation] authority comply with any direction of the Secretary of State to renew the appellant's registration or to cancel the revocation.

[(9) This section is subject to section 114 of the Environment Act 1995 (delegation or reference of appeals etc).]

[5 Power to require production of authority, stop and search etc]

[(1) This section applies where an authorised officer of a regulation authority or a constable reasonably believes that controlled waste has been, is being or is about to be transported in contravention of section 1(1) above.

(2) The authorised officer or constable may—

(a) require any person appearing to him to be or to have been engaged in transporting that waste to produce his (or, as the case may be, his employer's) authority to do so;

(b) search any vehicle that appears to him to be a vehicle that has been, is being or is about to be used for transporting that waste;

(c) carry out tests on anything found in any such vehicle (including by taking away samples for testing of anything so found);

(d) seize any such vehicle and any of its contents.

(3) For the purposes of subsection (2)(a) above, a person's authority for transporting controlled waste is—

(a) his certificate of registration as a carrier of controlled waste;

(b) such copy of that certificate as satisfies requirements specified in regulations made by the appropriate person; or

(c) such evidence as may be so specified that he is not required to be registered as a carrier of controlled waste.

(4) Where an authorised officer or constable has required a person to produce an authority under subsection (2)(a) above, the person must do so—

(a) by producing it forthwith to the authorised officer or constable;

(b) by producing it at a place and within a period specified in regulations made by the appropriate person; or

(c) by sending it to that place and within that period.

(5) In acting under subsection (2) above an authorised officer or constable may—

(a) stop any vehicle as referred to in paragraph (b) of that subsection (but only a constable in uniform may stop a vehicle on any road);

(b) enter any premises for the purpose specified in paragraph (b) or (d) of that subsection.

...

(7) A person commits an offence if—

(a) he fails without reasonable excuse to comply with a requirement imposed under paragraph (a) of subsection (2) above;

(b) he fails without reasonable excuse to give any assistance that an authorised officer or constable may reasonably request in the exercise of a power under that subsection;

(c) he otherwise intentionally obstructs an authorised officer or constable in the exercise of a power under that subsection.

(8) A person is not guilty of an offence by virtue of subsection (7)(a) above unless it is shown—

(a) that the waste in question was controlled waste; and

(b) that the waste was or was being transported to or from a place in Great Britain.

(9) Where an authorised officer or constable has stopped a vehicle under subsection (5) above, he may (in addition to any requirement that may be imposed under paragraph (a) of subsection (2) above) require any occupant of the vehicle to give him—

(a) the occupant's name and address;

(b) the name and address of the registered owner of the vehicle;

(c) any other information he may reasonably request.

(10) A person commits an offence if—

(a) he fails without reasonable excuse to comply with a requirement under subsection (9) above;

(b) he gives information required under that subsection that is—

(i) to his knowledge false or misleading in a material way, or

(ii) given recklessly and is false or misleading in a material way.

(11) A person guilty of an offence under this section is liable on summary conviction to a fine not exceeding level 5 on the standard scale.]

[5A Seizure of vehicles etc: supplementary]

...

[5B Fixed penalty notices for offences under section 5]

[(1) This section applies where it appears to a regulation authority that a person has failed without reasonable excuse to comply with a requirement under section 5(2)(a) above (requirement to produce authority to transport waste).

(2) The regulation authority may give that person a notice offering him the opportunity of discharging any liability to conviction for an offence under section 5(7)(a) above by payment of a fixed penalty.

...

(9) The fixed penalty payable to a regulation authority under this section is, subject to subsection (10) below, £300.

(10) The appropriate person may by order substitute a different amount for the amount for the time being specified in subsection (9) above.

...]

[5C Use of fixed penalties under section 5B]

[(1) This section applies in relation to amounts paid to a regulation authority in pursuance of notices under section 5B above (its 'fixed penalty receipts').

(2) Fixed penalty receipts—

(a) where received by the Environment Agency, must be paid to the Secretary of State;

(b) where received by a waste collection authority, must be used in accordance with the following provisions of this section.

(3) A waste collection authority may use its fixed penalty receipts only for the purposes of—

(a) its functions under section 5 above (including functions relating to the enforcement of offences under that section);

(b) such other of its functions as may be specified in regulations made by the appropriate person.

(4) Regulations under subsection (3)(b) above may in particular have the effect that an authority may use its fixed penalty receipts for the purposes of any of its functions.

. . .]

6 [. . .]

7 Further enforcement provisions

(1) Subject to subsection (2) below, the provisions of [section 71] of the [Environmental Protection Act 1990 (powers of entry, of dealing with imminent pollution or to obtain information)] shall have effect as if the provisions of this Act were provisions of that Act and as if, in those sections, references to a [waste regulation] authority were references to a [regulation] authority.

(2) [. . .]

(3) A person shall be guilty of an offence under this subsection if he—

(a) fails, without reasonable excuse, to comply with any requirement in pursuance of regulations under this Act to provide information to the Secretary of State or a [regulation] authority; or

(b) in complying with any such requirement, provides information which he knows to be false [or misleading] in a material particular or recklessly provides information which is false [or misleading] in a material particular;

and in paragraph (a) above the words 'without reasonable excuse' shall be construed in their application to . . . England and Wales, as making it a defence for a person against whom proceedings for the failure are brought to show that there was a reasonable excuse for the failure, rather than as requiring the person bringing the proceedings to show that there was no such excuse.

(4) A person guilty of an offence under subsection (3) above shall be liable on summary conviction to a fine not exceeding level 5 on the standard scale.

(5) Where the commission by any person of an offence under this Act is due to the act or default of some other person, that other person shall also be guilty of the offence; and a person may be charged with and convicted of an offence by virtue of this subsection whether or not proceedings for the offence are taken against any other person.

(6) Where a body corporate is guilty of an offence under this Act (including where it is so guilty by virtue of subsection (5) above) in respect of any act or omission which is shown to have been committed with the consent or connivance of, or to be attributable to any neglect on the part of, any director, manager, secretary or other similar officer of the body corporate or any person who was purporting to act in any such capacity, he, as well as the body corporate, shall be guilty of that offence and shall be liable to be proceeded against and punished accordingly.

(7) Where the affairs of a body corporate are managed by its members, subsection (6) above shall apply in relation to the acts and defaults of a member in connection with his functions of management as if he were a director of the body corporate.

(8) [. . .]

8 Regulations

. . .

9 Interpretation

(1) In this Act—

['appropriate person' means—

(a) the Secretary of State, in relation to England;

(b) the National Assembly for Wales, in relation to Wales.]

'controlled waste' has, [at any time], the same meaning as [for the purposes of Part II of the Environmental Protection Act 1990];

[...]

'prescribed' means prescribed by regulations made by the Secretary of State;

['regulation authority' means—

(a) in relation to England and Wales, the Environment Agency; and

(b) ...

and any reference to the area of a regulation authority shall accordingly be construed as a reference to any area in England and Wales...]

'road' has the same meaning as in the Road Traffic Act 1988;

'transport', in relation to any controlled waste, includes the transport of that waste by road or rail or by air, sea or inland waterway but does not include moving that waste from one place to another by means of any pipe or other apparatus that joins those two places.

'vehicle' means any motor vehicle or trailer within the meaning of the Road Traffic Regulation Act 1984.

[(1A) In sections 5 to 7 above 'regulation authority' also means a waste collection authority falling within section 30(3)(a), (b) or (bb) of the Environmental Protection Act 1990.]

[(1B) For the purposes of any provision of this Act, 'authorised officer' in relation to any authority means an officer of the authority who is authorised in writing by the authority for the purposes of that provision.]

(2) ...

Electricity Act 1989

(1989, c. 29)

[3A The principal objective and general duties of the Secretary of State and the Authority]

[(1) The principal objective of the Secretary of State and the Gas and Electricity Markets Authority (in this Act referred to as 'the Authority') in carrying out their respective functions under this Part is to protect the interests of consumers in relation to electricity conveyed by distribution systems [or transmission systems], wherever appropriate by promoting effective competition between persons engaged in, or in commercial activities connected with, the generation, transmission, distribution or supply of electricity [or the provision or use of electricity interconnectors].

(2) The Secretary of State and the Authority shall carry out those functions in the manner which he or it considers is best calculated to further the principal objective, having regard to—

(a) the need to secure that all reasonable demands for electricity are met; and

(b) the need to secure that licence holders are able to finance the activities which are the subject of obligations imposed by or under this Part[, the Utilities Act 2000 or Part 2 or 3 of the Energy Act 2004].

...

(5) Subject to subsection (2), the Secretary of State and the Authority shall carry out their respective functions under this Part in the manner which he or it considers is best calculated—

(a) to promote efficiency and economy on the part of persons authorised by licences or exemptions to [distribute, supply or participate in the transmission of] electricity [or to participate in the operation of electricity interconnectors] and the efficient use of electricity conveyed by distribution systems [or transmission systems];

(b) to protect the public from dangers arising from the generation, transmission, distribution or supply of electricity;

[(ba) to contribute to the achievement of sustainable development;[1] and]

(c) to secure a diverse and viable long-term energy supply,

[and (so far as not otherwise required to do so by this subsection) shall], in carrying out those functions, have regard to the effect on the environment of activities connected with the generation, transmission, distribution or supply of electricity.]

[(5A) In carrying out their respective functions under this Part in accordance with the preceding provisions of this section the Secretary of State and the Authority must each have regard to—

(a) the principles under which regulatory activities should be transparent, accountable, proportionate, consistent and targeted only at cases in which action is needed; and

(b) any other principles appearing to him or, as the case may be, it to represent the best regulatory practice.]

(6) In this section 'consumers' includes both existing and future consumers.

...

Town and Country Planning Act 1990

(1990, c. 8)

PART I PLANNING AUTHORITIES

1 Local planning authorities: general

(1) In a non-metropolitan county—

(a) the council of a county is the county planning authority for the county, and

(b) the council of a district is the district planning authority for the district, and references in the planning Acts to a local planning authority in relation to a non-metropolitan county shall be construed, subject to any express provision to the contrary, as references to both the county planning authority and the district planning authorities.

[(1A) Subsection (1) does not apply in relation to Wales.]

[(1B) In Wales—

(a) the local planning authority for a county is the county council; and

(b) the local planning authority for a county borough is the county borough council.]

(2) The council of a metropolitan district is the local planning authority for the district and the council of a London borough is the local planning authority for the borough.

(3) In England (exclusive of the metropolitan counties, Greater London and the Isles of Scilly) [...] all functions conferred on local planning authorities by or under the planning Acts shall be exercisable both by county planning authorities and district planning authorities.

(4) In this Act 'mineral planning authority' means—

(a) in respect of a site in a non-metropolitan county, the county planning authority; and

[1] Editor's note: subsection 5(ba) added by s. 83 Energy Act 2004.

(b) in respect of a site in a metropolitan district or London borough, the local planning authority.

[(4A) Subsection (4) does not apply in relation to Wales.]

[(4B) As to any site in Wales, the local planning authority is also the mineral planning authority.]

(5) This section has effect subject to any express provision to the contrary in the planning Acts and, in particular—

(a) [this section has] effect subject to [sections 4A to] [8A] of this Act [and] [...]
(b) subsections (1) to (2) have effect subject to sections 2 and 9; and
(c) subsection (3) has effect subject to [...] Schedule 1 (which contains provisions as to the exercise of certain functions under this Act by particular authorities and liaison between them).

[(6) The exercise, in relation to Wales, of functions conferred on local planning authorities is subject to [...] Schedule 1A.]

[4A National Parks with National Park authorities

(1) Where a National Park authority has been established for any area, this section, [...] shall apply, as from such time as may be specified for the purposes of this section in the order establishing that authority, in relation to the Park for which it is the authority.

(2) Subject to subsections (4) and (5) below, the National Park authority for the Park shall be the sole local planning authority for the area of the Park and, accordingly—

(a) functions conferred by or under the planning Acts on a planning authority of any description (including the functions of a mineral planning authority under those Acts and under the Planning and Compensation Act 1991) shall, in relation to the Park, be functions of the National Park authority, and not of any other authority; and
(b) so much of the area of any other authority as is included in the Park shall be treated as excluded from any area for which that other authority is a planning authority of any description.

(3) For the purposes of subsection (2) above functions under the planning Acts which (apart from this section) are conferred—

(a) in relation to some areas on the county or district planning authorities for those areas, and
(b) in relation to other areas on the councils for those areas, shall be treated, in relation to those other areas, as conferred on each of those councils as the local planning authority for their area.

(4) The functions of a local planning authority by virtue of sections 198 to 201, 206 to 209 and 211 to 215, so far as they are functions of a National Park authority by virtue of this section, shall be exercisable as respects any area which is or is included in an area for which there is a district council, concurrently with the National Park authority, by that council.

(5) For the purposes of any enactment relating to the functions of a district planning authority, the functions of a district council by virtue of subsection (4) above shall be deemed to be conferred on them as a district planning authority and as if the district were the area for which they are such an authority.]

PART III CONTROL OVER DEVELOPMENT

55 Meaning of 'development' and 'new development'

(1) Subject to the following provisions of this section, in this Act, except where the context otherwise requires, 'development,' means the carrying out of building, engineering, mining or other operations in, on, over or under land, or the making of any material change in the use of any buildings or other land.

[(1A) For the purposes of this Act 'building operations' includes—
(a) demolition of buildings;
(b) rebuilding;
(c) structural alterations of or additions to buildings; and
(d) other operations normally undertaken by a person carrying on business as a builder.]

(2) The following operations or uses of land shall not be taken for the purposes of this Act to involve development of the land—
(a) the carrying out for the maintenance, improvement or other alteration of any building of works which—
(i) affect only the interior of the building, or
(ii) do not materially affect the external appearance of the building, and are not works for making good war damage or works begun after 5th December 1968 for the alteration of a building by providing additional space in it underground;
(b) the carrying out on land within the boundaries of a road by a [...] highway authority of any works required for the maintenance or improvement of the road; [but, in the case of any such works which are not exclusively for the maintenance of the road, not including any works which may have significant adverse effects on the environment.]
(c) the carrying out by a local authority or statutory undertakers of any works for the purpose of inspecting, repairing or renewing any sewers, mains, pipes, cables or other apparatus, including the breaking open of any street or other land for that purpose;
(d) the use of any buildings or other land within the curtilage of a dwellinghouse for any purpose incidental to the enjoyment of the dwellinghouse as such;
(e) the use of any land for the purposes of agriculture or forestry (including afforestation) and the use for any of those purposes of any building occupied together with land so used;
(f) in the case of buildings or other land which are used for a purpose of any class specified in an order made by the Secretary of State under this section, the use of the buildings or other land or, subject to the provisions of the order, of any part of the buildings or the other land, for any other purpose of the same class.
[(g) the demolition of any description of building specified in a direction given by the Secretary of State to local planning authorities generally or to a particular local planning authority.]

[(2A) The Secretary of State may in a development order specify any circumstances or description of circumstances in which subsection (2) does not apply to operations mentioned in paragraph (a) of that subsection which have the effect of increasing the gross floor space of the building by such amount or percentage amount as is so specified.

(2B) The development order may make different provision for different purposes.]

(3) For the avoidance of doubt it is hereby declared that for the purpose of this section—
(a) the use as two or more separate dwellinghouses of any building previously used as a single dwellinghouse involves a material change in the use of the building and of each part of it which is so used;
(b) the deposit of refuse or waste materials on land involves a material change in its use, notwithstanding that the land is comprised in a site already used for that purpose, if—
(i) the superficial area of the deposit is extended, or
(ii) the height of the deposit is extended and exceeds the level of the land adjoining the site.

(4) For the purposes of this Act mining operations include—

(a) the removal of material of any description—
(i) from a mineral-working deposit;
(ii) from a deposit of pulverised fuel ash or other furnace ash or clinker; or
(iii) from a deposit of iron, steel or other metallic slags; and
(b) the extraction of minerals from a disused railway embankment.

[(4A) Where the placing or assembly of any tank in any part of any inland waters for the purpose of fish farming there would not, apart from this subsection, involve development of the land below, this Act shall have effect as if the tank resulted from carrying out engineering operations over that land; and in this subsection—

'fish farming' means the breeding, rearing or keeping of fish or shellfish (which includes any kind of crustacean and mollusc);

'inland waters' means waters which do not form part of the sea or of any creek, bay or estuary or of any river as far as the tide flows; and

'tank' includes any cage and any other structure for use in fish farming.]

(5) Without prejudice to any regulations made under the provisions of this Act relating to the control of advertisements, the use for the display of advertisements of any external part of a building which is not normally used for that purpose shall be treated for the purposes of this section as involving a material change in the use of that part of the building.

56 Time when development begun

(1) Subject to the following provisions of this section, for the purposes of this Act development of land shall be taken to be initiated—
(a) if the development consists of the carrying out of operations, at the time when those operations are begun;
(b) if the development consists of a change in use, at the time when the new use is instituted;
(c) if the development consists both of the carrying out of operations and of a change in use, at the earlier of the times mentioned in paragraphs (a) and (b).

(2) For the purposes of the provisions of this Part mentioned in subsection (3) development shall be taken to be begun on the earliest date on which any material operation comprised in the development begins to be carried out.

(3) The provisions referred to in subsection (2) are sections 85(2), 86(6), 87(4), [89,] 91, 92 and 94.

(4) In subsection (2) 'material operation' means—
(a) any work of construction in the course of the erection of a building;
[(aa) any work of demolition of a building;]
(b) the digging of a trench which is to contain the foundations, or part of the foundations, of a building;
(c) the laying of any underground main or pipe to the foundations, or part of the foundations, of a building or to any such trench as is mentioned in paragraph (b);
(d) any operation in the course of laying out or constructing a road or part of a road;
(e) any change in the use of any land which constitutes material development.

(5) In subsection (4)(e) 'material development' means any development other than—
(a) development for which planning permission is granted by a general development order [or a local development order] for the time being in force and which is carried out so as to comply with any condition or limitation subject to which planning permission is so granted;
[(b) development of a class specified in paragraph 1 or 2 of Schedule 3;]
(c) development of any class prescribed for the purposes of this subsection.

(6) In subsection (5) 'general development order' means a development order (within the meaning of section 59) made as a general order applicable (subject to such exceptions as may be specified in it) to all land in England and Wales.

57 Planning permission required for development

(1) Subject to the following provisions of this section, planning permission is required for the carrying out of any development of land.

(2) Where planning permission to develop land has been granted for a limited period, planning permission is not required for the resumption, at the end of that period, of its use for the purpose for which it was normally used before the permission was granted.

(3) Where by a development order [or a local development order] planning permission to develop land has been granted subject to limitations, planning permission is not required for the use of that land which (apart from its use in accordance with that permission) is its normal use.

(4) Where an enforcement notice has been issued in respect of any development of land, planning permission is not required for its use for the purpose for which (in accordance with the provisions of this Part of this Act) it could lawfully have been used if that development had not been carried out.

(5) In determining for the purposes of subsections (2) and (3) what is or was the normal use of land, no account shall be taken of any use begun in contravention of this Part or of previous planning control.

(6) For the purposes of this section a use of land shall be taken to have been begun in contravention of previous planning control if it was begun in contravention of Part III of the 1947 Act, Part III of the 1962 Act or Part III of the 1971 Act.

(7) Subsection (1) has effect subject to Schedule 4 (which makes special provision about use of land on 1st July 1948).

58 Granting of planning permission: general

(1) Planning permission may be granted—

(a) by a development order [or a local development order];

(b) by the local planning authority (or, in the cases provided in this Part, by the Secretary of State) on application to the authority in accordance with a development order;

(c) on the adoption or approval of a simplified planning zone scheme or alterations to such a scheme in accordance with section 82 or, as the case may be, section 86; or

(d) on the designation of an enterprise zone or the approval of a modified scheme under Schedule 32 to the Local Government, Planning and Land Act 1980 in accordance with section 88 of this Act.

(2) Planning permission may also be deemed to be granted under section 90 (development with government authorisation).

(3) This section is without prejudice to any other provisions of this Act providing for the granting of permission.

[61A Local development orders

(1) A local planning authority may by order (a local development order) make provision to implement policies—

(a) in one or more development plan documents (within the meaning of Part 2 of the Planning and Compulsory Purchase Act 2004);

(b) in a local development plan (within the meaning of Part 6 of that Act).

(2) A local development order may grant planning permission—

(a) for development specified in the order;

(b) for development of any class so specified.

(3) A local development order may relate to—

(a) all land in the area of the relevant authority;

(b) any part of that land;

(c) a site specified in the order.

(4) A local development order may make different provision for different descriptions of land.

(5) But a development order may specify any area or class of development in respect of which a local development order must not be made.

(6) A local planning authority may revoke a local development order at any time.

(7) Schedule 4A makes provision in connection with local development orders.

61B Intervention by secretary of state or national assembly

(1) At any time before a local development order is adopted by a local planning authority the appropriate authority may direct that the order (or any part of it) is submitted to it for its approval.

(2) If the appropriate authority gives a direction under subsection (1)—

(a) the authority must not take any step in connection with the adoption of the order until the appropriate authority gives its decision;

(b) the order has no effect unless it (or, if the direction relates to only part of an order, the part) has been approved by the appropriate authority.

(3) In considering an order or part of an order submitted under subsection (1) the appropriate authority may take account of any matter which it thinks is relevant.

(4) It is immaterial whether any such matter was taken account of by the local planning authority.

(5) The appropriate authority—

(a) may approve or reject an order or part of an order submitted to it under subsection (1);

(b) must give reasons for its decision under paragraph (a).

(6) If the appropriate authority thinks that a local development order is unsatisfactory—

(a) it may at any time before the order is adopted by the local planning authority direct them to modify it in accordance with the direction;

(b) if it gives such a direction it must state its reasons for doing so.

(7) The local planning authority—

(a) must comply with the direction;

(b) must not adopt the order unless the appropriate authority gives notice that it is satisfied that they have complied with the direction.

(8) The appropriate authority—

(a) may at any time by order revoke a local development order if it thinks it is expedient to do so;

(b) must, if it revokes a local development order, state its reasons for doing so.

(9) Subsections (3) to (6) of section 100 apply to an order under subsection (8) above as they apply to an order under subsection (1) of that section and for that purpose references to the Secretary of State must be construed as references to the appropriate authority.

(10) The appropriate authority is—

(a) the Secretary of State in relation to England;

(b) the National Assembly for Wales in relation to Wales.

61C Permission granted by local development order

(1) Planning permission granted by a local development order may be granted—

(a) unconditionally, or

(b) subject to such conditions or limitations as are specified in the order.

(2) If the permission is granted for development of a specified description the order may enable the local planning authority to direct that the permission does not apply in relation to—

(a) development in a particular area, or

(b) any particular development.

61D Effect of revision or revocation of development order on incomplete development

(1) A development order or local development order may include provision permitting the completion of development if—

(a) planning permission is granted by the order in respect of the development, and

(b) the planning permission is withdrawn at a time after the development is started but before it is completed.

(2) Planning permission granted by a development order is withdrawn—

(a) if the order is revoked;

(b) if the order is amended so that it ceases to grant planning permission in respect of the development or materially changes any condition or limitation to which the grant of permission is subject;

(c) by the issue of a direction under powers conferred by the order.

(3) Planning permission granted by a local development order is withdrawn—

(a) if the order is revoked under section 61A(6) or 61B(8);

(b) if the order is revised in pursuance of paragraph 2 of Schedule 4A so that it ceases to grant planning permission in respect of the development or materially changes any condition or limitation to which the grant of permission is subject;

(c) by the issue of a direction under powers conferred by the order.

(4) The power under this section to include provision in a development order or a local development order may be exercised differently for different purposes.]

69 Register of applications etc

(1) The local planning authority must keep a register containing such information as is prescribed as to—

(a) applications for planning permission;

(b) requests for statements of development principles (within the meaning of section 61E)[1];

(c) local development orders;

(d) simplified planning zone schemes.

(2) The register must contain—

(a) information as to the manner in which applications mentioned in subsection (1)(a) and requests mentioned in subsection (1)(b) have been dealt with;

(b) such information as is prescribed with respect to any local development order or simplified planning zone scheme in relation to the authority's area.

(3) A development order may require the register to be kept in two or more parts.

(4) Each part must contain such information as is prescribed relating to the matters mentioned in subsection (1)(a) and (b).

(5) A development order may also make provision—

(a) for a specified part of the register to contain copies of applications or requests and of any other documents or material submitted with them;

(b) for the entry relating to an application or request (and everything relating to it) to be removed from that part of the register when the application (including any appeal arising out of it) or the request (as the case may be) has been finally disposed of.

(6) Provision made under subsection (5)(b) does not prevent the inclusion of a different entry relating to the application or request in another part of the register.

(7) The register must be kept in such manner as is prescribed.

(8) The register must be kept available for inspection by the public at all reasonable hours.

(9) Anything prescribed under this section must be prescribed by development order.

70 Determination of applications: general considerations

(1) Where an application is made to a local planning authority for planning permission—

1 Editor's note: no s. 61E has ever been enacted.

(a) subject to sections 91 and 92, they may grant planning permission, either unconditionally or subject to such conditions as they think fit; or
(b) they may refuse planning permission.

(2) In dealing with such an application the authority shall have regard to the provisions of the development plan, so far as material to the application, and to any other material considerations.

(3) Subsection (1) has effect subject to [section 65] and to the following provisions of this Act, to sections 66, 67, 72 and 73 of the Planning (Listed Buildings and Conservation Areas) Act 1990 and to section 15 of the Health Services Act 1976.

[71A Assessment of environmental effects

(1) The Secretary of State may by regulations make provision about the consideration to be given, before planning permission for development of any class specified in the regulations is granted, to the likely environmental effects of the proposed development.

(2) The regulations—
(a) may make the same provision as, or provision similar or corresponding to, any provision made, for the purposes of any Community obligation of the United Kingdom about the assessment of the likely effects of development on the environment, under section 2(2) of the European Communities Act 1972; and
(b) may make different provision for different classes of development.

(3) Where a draft of regulations made in exercise both of the power conferred by this section and the power conferred by section 2(2) of the European Communities Act 1972 is approved by resolution of each House of Parliament, section 333(3) shall not apply.]

72 Conditional grant of planning permission

(1) Without prejudice to the generality of section 70(1), conditions may be imposed on the grant of planning permission under that section—
(a) for regulating the development or use of any land under the control of the applicant (whether or not it is land in respect of which the application was made) or requiring the carrying out of works on any such land, so far as appears to the local planning authority to be expedient for the purposes of or in connection with the development authorised by the permission;
(b) for requiring the removal of any buildings or works authorised by the permission, or the discontinuance of any use of land so authorised, at the end of a specified period, and the carrying out of any works required for the reinstatement of land at the end of that period.

(2) A planning permission granted subject to such a condition as is mentioned in subsection (1)(b) is in this Act referred to as 'planning permission granted for a limited period'.

...

73 Determination of applications to develop land without compliance with conditions previously attached

(1) This section applies, subject to subsection (4), to applications for planning permission for the development of land without complying with conditions subject to which a previous planning permission was granted.

(2) On such an application the local planning authority shall consider only the question of the conditions subject to which planning permission should be granted, and—
(a) if they decide that planning permission should be granted subject to conditions differing from those subject to which the previous permission was granted, or that it should be granted unconditionally, they shall grant planning permission accordingly, and
(b) if they decide that planning permission should be granted subject to the same conditions as those subject to which the previous permission was granted, they shall refuse the application.

...

[(5) Planning permission must not be granted under this section to the extent that it has effect to change a condition subject to which a previous planning permission was granted by extending the time within which—

(a) a development must be started;

(b) an application for approval of reserved matters (within the meaning of section 92) must be made.]

73A Planning permission for development already carried out

(1) On an application made to a local planning authority, the planning permission which may be granted includes planning permission for development carried out before the date of the application.

(2) Subsection (1) applies to development carried out—

(a) without planning permission;

(b) in accordance with planning permission granted for a limited period; or

(c) without complying with some condition subject to which planning permission was granted.

(3) Planning permission for such development may be granted so as to have effect from—

(a) the date on which the development was carried out; or

(b) if it was carried out in accordance with planning permission granted for a limited period, the end of that period.

75 Effect of planning permission

(1) Without prejudice to the provisions of this Part as to the duration, revocation or modification of planning permission, any grant of planning permission to develop land shall (except in so far as the permission otherwise provides) enure for the benefit of the land and of all persons for the time being interested in it.

(2) Where planning permission is granted for the erection of a building, the grant of permission may specify the purposes for which the building may be used.

(3) If no purpose is so specified, the permission shall be construed as including permission to use the building for the purpose for which it is designed.

[76A Major infrastructure projects

(1) This section applies to—

(a) an application for planning permission;

(b) an application for the approval of a local planning authority required under a development order,

if the Secretary of State thinks that the development to which the application relates is of national or regional importance.

(2) The Secretary of State may direct that the application must be referred to him instead of being dealt with by the local planning authority.

(3) If the Secretary of State gives a direction under subsection (2) he may also direct that any application—

(a) under or for the purposes of the planning Acts, and

(b) which he thinks is connected with the application mentioned in subsection (1), must also be referred to him instead of being dealt with by the local planning authority.

(4) If the Secretary of State gives a direction under this section—

(a) the application must be referred to him;

(b) he must appoint an inspector to consider the application.

(5) If the Secretary of State gives a direction under subsection (2) the applicant must prepare an economic impact report which must—

(a) be in such form and contain such matter as is prescribed by development order;

(b) be submitted to the Secretary of State in accordance with such provision as is so prescribed.

(6) For the purposes of subsection (5) the Secretary of State may, by development order, prescribe such requirements as to publicity and notice as he thinks appropriate.

(7) A direction under this section or section 76B may be varied or revoked by a subsequent direction.

(8) The decision of the Secretary of State on any application referred to him under this section is final.

(9) Regional relates to a region listed in Schedule 1 to the Regional Development Agencies Act 1998 (c 45).

(10) The following provisions of this Act apply (with any necessary modifications) to an application referred to the Secretary of State under this section as they apply to an application which falls to be determined by a local planning authority—

(a) section 70;

(b) section 72(1) and (5);

(c) section 73;

(d) section 73A.

(11) A development order may apply (with or without modifications) any requirements imposed by the order by virtue of section 65 or 71 to an application referred to the Secretary of State under this section.

(12) This section does not apply to an application which relates to the development of land in Wales.

76B Major infrastructure projects: inspectors

(1) This section applies if the Secretary of State appoints an inspector under section 76A(4)(b) (the lead inspector).

(2) The Secretary of State may direct the lead inspector—

(a) to consider such matters relating to the application as are prescribed;

(b) to make recommendations to the Secretary of State on those matters.

(3) After considering any recommendations of the lead inspector the Secretary of State may—

(a) appoint such number of additional inspectors as he thinks appropriate;

(b) direct that each of the additional inspectors must consider such matters relating to the application as the lead inspector decides.

. . .]

77 Reference of applications to Secretary of State

(1) The Secretary of State may give directions requiring applications for planning permission, or for the approval of any local planning authority required under a development order [or a local development order] to be referred to him instead of being dealt with by local planning authorities.

(2) A direction under this section—

(a) may be given either to a particular local planning authority or to local planning authorities generally; and

(b) may relate either to a particular application or to applications of a class specified in the direction.

(3) Any application in respect of which a direction under this section has effect shall be referred to the Secretary of State accordingly.

(4) Subject to subsection (5), where an application for planning permission is referred to the Secretary of State under this section, sections [70, 72(1) and (5), 73 and 73A] shall apply, with any necessary modifications, as they apply to such an application which falls to be determined by the local planning authority [and a development order may apply, with or without modifications, to an application so referred any requirements imposed by such an order by virtue of section 65 or 71.]

(5) Before determining an application referred to him under this section, the Secretary of State shall, if either the applicant or the local planning authority wish, give each of them an

opportunity of appearing before, and being heard by, a person appointed by the Secretary of State for the purpose.

(6) Subsection (5) does not apply to an application for planning permission referred to a Planning Inquiry Commission under section 101.

(7) The decision of the Secretary of State on any application referred to him under this section shall be final.

78 Right to appeal against planning decisions and failure to take such decisions

(1) Where a local planning authority—

(a) refuse an application for planning permission or grant it subject to conditions;

(b) refuse an application for any consent, agreement or approval of that authority required by a condition imposed on a grant of planning permission or grant it subject to conditions; or

(c) refuse an application for any approval of that authority required under a development order [or a local development order] or grant it subject to conditions,

the applicant may by notice appeal to the Secretary of State.

(2) A person who has made such an application may also appeal to the Secretary of State if the local planning authority have [done none of the following]

(a) given notice to the applicant of their decision on the application;

[(aa) given notice to the applicant that they have exercised their power under section 70A [or 70B] to decline to determine the application;]

(b) given notice to him that the application has been referred to the Secretary of State in accordance with directions given under section 77,

within such period as may be prescribed by the development order or within such extended period as may at any time be agreed upon in writing between the applicant and the authority.

. . .

[78A Appeal made: functions of local planning authorities

(1) This section applies if a person who has made an application mentioned in section 78(1)(a) appeals to the Secretary of State under section 78(2).

(2) At any time before the end of the additional period the local planning authority may give the notice referred to in section 78(2).

(3) If the local planning authority give notice as mentioned in subsection (2) that their decision is to refuse the application—

(a) the appeal must be treated as an appeal under section 78(1) against the refusal;

(b) the Secretary of State must give the person making the appeal an opportunity to revise the grounds of the appeal;

(c) the Secretary of State must give such a person an opportunity to change any option the person has chosen relating to the procedure for the appeal.

(4) If the local planning authority give notice as mentioned in subsection (2) that their decision is to grant the application subject to conditions the Secretary of State must give the person making the appeal the opportunity—

(a) to proceed with the appeal as an appeal under section 78(1) against the grant of the application subject to conditions;

(b) to revise the grounds of the appeal;

(c) to change any option the person has chosen relating to the procedure for the appeal.

(5) The Secretary of State must not issue his decision on the appeal before the end of the additional period.

(6) The additional period is the period prescribed by development order for the purposes of this section and which starts on the day on which the person appeals under section 78(2).]

79 Determination of appeals

(1) On an appeal under section 78 the Secretary of State may—

(a) allow or dismiss the appeal, or

(b) reverse or vary any part of the decision of the local planning authority (whether the appeal relates to that part of it or not),

and may deal with the application as if it had been made to him in the first instance.

(2) Before determining an appeal under section 78 the Secretary of State shall, if either the appellant or the local planning authority so wish, give each of them an opportunity of appearing before and being heard by a person appointed by the Secretary of State for the purpose.

(3) Subsection (2) does not apply to an appeal referred to a Planning Inquiry Commission under section 101.

(4) Subject to subsection (2), the provisions of sections [70, 72(1) and (5), 73 and 73A] and Part I of Schedule 5 shall apply, with any necessary modifications, in relation to an appeal to the Secretary of State under section 78 as they apply in relation to an application for planning permission which falls to be determined by the local planning authority [and a development order may apply, with or without modifications, to such an appeal any requirements imposed by a development order by virtue of section 65 or 71].

(5) The decision of the Secretary of State on such an appeal shall be final.

(6) If, before or during the determination of such an appeal in respect of an application for planning permission to develop land, the Secretary of State forms the opinion that, having regard to the provisions of sections 70 and 72(1), the development order and any directions given under that order, planning permission for that development—

(a) could not have been granted by the local planning authority; or

(b) could not have been granted otherwise than subject to the conditions imposed,

he may decline to determine the appeal or to proceed with the determination.

[(6A) If at any time before or during the determination of such an appeal it appears to the Secretary of State that the appellant is responsible for undue delay in the progress of the appeal, he may—

(a) give the appellant notice that the appeal will be dismissed unless the appellant takes, within the period specified in the notice, such steps as are specified in the notice for the expedition of the appeal; and

(b) if the appellant fails to take those steps within that period, dismiss the appeal accordingly.]

. . .

91 General condition limiting duration of planning permission

(1) Subject to the provisions of this section, every planning permission granted or deemed to be granted shall be granted or, as the case may be, be deemed to be granted, subject to the condition that the development to which it relates must be begun not later than the expiration of—

(a) [three] years beginning with the date on which the permission is granted or, as the case may be, deemed to be granted; or

(b) such other period (whether longer or shorter) beginning with that date as the authority concerned with the terms of planning permission may direct.

(2) The period mentioned in subsection (1)(b) shall be a period which the authority consider appropriate having regard to the provisions of the development plan and to any other material considerations [and any of the matter which the authority consider relevant].

(3) If planning permission is granted without the condition required by subsection (1), it shall be deemed to have been granted subject to the condition that the development to which it relates must be begun not later than the expiration of [three] years beginning with the date of the grant.

[(3A) Subsection (3B) applies if any proceedings are begun to challenge the validity of a grant of planning permission or of a deemed grant of planning permission.

(3B) The period before the end of which the development to which the planning permission relates is required to be begun in pursuance of subsection (1) or (3) must be taken to be extended by one year.

(3C) Nothing in this section prevents the development being begun from the time the permission is granted or deemed to be granted.]

(4) Nothing in this section applies—

(a) to any planning permission granted by a development order [or a local development order];

(b) to any planning permission granted [for development carried out before the grant of that permission];

(c) to any planning permission granted for a limited period;

[(d) to any planning permission for development consisting of the winning and working of minerals or involving the depositing of mineral waste which is granted (or deemed to be granted) subject to a condition that the development to which it relates must be begun before the expiration of a specified period after—

(i) the completion of other development consisting of the winning and working of minerals already being carried out by the applicant for the planning permission; or

(ii) the cessation of depositing of mineral waste already being carried out by the applicant for the planning permission;]

(e) to any planning permission granted by an enterprise zone scheme;

(f) to any planning permission granted by a simplified planning zone scheme; or

(g) to any outline planning permission, as defined by section 92.

92 Outline planning permission

(1) In this section and section 91 'outline planning permission' means planning permission granted, in accordance with the provisions of a development order, with the reservation for subsequent approval by the local planning authority or the Secretary of State of matters not particularised in the application ('reserved matters').

(2) Subject to the following provisions of this section, where outline planning permission is granted for development consisting in or including the carrying out of building or other operations, it shall be granted subject to conditions to the effect—

(a) that, in the case of any reserved matter, application for approval must be made not later than the expiration of three years beginning with the date of the grant of outline planning permission; and

(b) that the development to which the permission relates must be begun not later than—

(i) the expiration of five years from the date of the grant of outline planning permission; or

(ii) if later, the expiration of two years from the final approval of the reserved matters or, in the case of approval on different dates, the final approval of the last such matter to be approved.

(3) If outline planning permission is granted without the conditions required by subsection (2), it shall be deemed to have been granted subject to those conditions.

(4) The authority concerned with the terms of an outline planning permission may, in applying subsection (2), substitute, or direct that there be substituted, for the periods of three years, five years or two years referred to in that subsection such other periods respectively (whether longer or shorter) as they consider appropriate.

(5) They may also specify, or direct that there be specified, separate periods under paragraph (a) of subsection (2) in relation to separate parts of the development to which the planning permission relates; and, if they do so, the condition required by paragraph (b) of that subsection shall then be framed correspondingly by reference to those parts, instead of by reference to the development as a whole.

(6) In considering whether to exercise their powers under subsections (4) and (5), the authority shall have regard to the provisions of the development plan and to any other material considerations.

106 Planning obligations[2]

(1) Any person interested in land in the area of a local planning authority may, by agreement or otherwise, enter into an obligation (referred to in this section and sections 106A and 106B as 'a planning obligation'), enforceable to the extent mentioned in subsection (3)—

(a) restricting the development or use of the land in any specified way;

(b) requiring specified operations or activities to be carried out in, on, under or over the land;

(c) requiring the land to be used in any specified way; or

(d) requiring a sum or sums to be paid to the authority on a specified date or dates or periodically.

(2) A planning obligation may—

(a) be unconditional or subject to conditions;

(b) impose any restriction or requirement mentioned in subsection (1)(a) to (c) either indefinitely or for such period or periods as may be specified; and

(c) if it requires a sum or sums to be paid, require the payment of a specified amount or an amount determined in accordance with the instrument by which the obligation is entered into and, if it requires the payment of periodical sums, require them to be paid indefinitely or for a specified period.

(3) Subject to subsection (4) a planning obligation is enforceable by the authority identified in accordance with subsection (9)(d)—

(a) against the person entering into the obligation; and

(b) against any person deriving title from that person.

(4) The instrument by which a planning obligation is entered into may provide that a person shall not be bound by the obligation in respect of any period during which he no longer has an interest in the land.

(5) A restriction or requirement imposed under a planning obligation is enforceable by injunction.

(6) Without prejudice to subsection (5), if there is a breach of a requirement in a planning obligation to carry out any operations in, on, under or over the land to which the obligation relates, the authority by whom the obligation is enforceable may—

(a) enter the land and carry out the operations; and

(b) recover from the person or persons against whom the obligation is enforceable any expenses reasonably incurred by them in doing so.

(7) Before an authority exercise their power under subsection (6)(a) they shall give not less than twenty-one days' notice of their intention to do so to any person against whom the planning obligation is enforceable.

(8) Any person who wilfully obstructs a person acting in the exercise of a power under subsection (6)(a) shall be guilty of an offence and liable on summary conviction to a fine not exceeding level 3 on the standard scale.

(9) A planning obligation may not be entered into except by an instrument executed as a deed which—

(a) states that the obligation is a planning obligation for the purposes of this section;

(b) identifies the land in which the person entering into the obligation is interested;

(c) identifies the person entering into the obligation and states what his interest in the land is; and

(d) identifies the local planning authority by whom the obligation is enforceable.

(10) A copy of any such instrument shall be given to the authority so identified.

(11) A planning obligation shall be a local land charge...

...

[2] Editor's note: ss. 106–106B are to be repealed by the Planning and Compulsory Purchase Act 2004, ss. 118(1), 120, Sch. 6, paras 1, 5, Sch. 9. But no date for this has been set.

106A Modification and discharge of planning obligations

(1) A planning obligation may not be modified or discharged except—

(a) by agreement between the authority by whom the obligation is enforceable and the person or persons against whom the obligation is enforceable; or

(b) in accordance with this section and section 106B.

(2) An agreement falling within subsection (1)(a) shall not be entered into except by an instrument executed as a deed.

(3) A person against whom a planning obligation is enforceable may, at any time after the expiry of the relevant period, apply to the local planning authority by whom the obligation is enforceable for the obligation—

(a) to have effect subject to such modifications as may be specified in the application; or

(b) to be discharged.

(4) In subsection (3) 'the relevant period' means—

(a) such period as may be prescribed; or

(b) if no period is prescribed, the period of five years beginning with the date on which the obligation is entered into.

(5) An application under subsection (3) for the modification of a planning obligation may not specify a modification imposing an obligation on any other person against whom the obligation is enforceable.

(6) Where an application is made to an authority under subsection (3), the authority may determine—

(a) that the planning obligation shall continue to have effect without modification;

(b) if the obligation no longer serves a useful purpose, that it shall be discharged; or

(c) if the obligation continues to serve a useful purpose, but would serve that purpose equally well if it had effect subject to the modifications specified in the application, that it shall have effect subject to those modifications.

(7) The authority shall give notice of their determination to the applicant within such period as may be prescribed.

. . .

(10) Section 84 of the Law of Property Act 1925 (power to discharge or modify restrictive covenants affecting land) does not apply to a planning obligation.

106B Appeals

(1) Where a local planning authority—

(a) fail to give notice as mentioned in section 106A(7); or

(b) determine that a planning obligation shall continue to have effect without modification,

the applicant may appeal to the Secretary of State.

(2) For the purposes of an appeal under subsection (1)(a), it shall be assumed that the authority have determined that the planning obligation shall continue to have effect without modification.

(3) An appeal under this section shall be made by notice served within such period and in such manner as may be prescribed.

(4) Subsections (6) to (9) of section 106A apply in relation to appeals to the Secretary of State under this section as they apply in relation to applications to authorities under that section.

. . .

PART VII ENFORCEMENT

Introductory

[171A Expressions used in connection with enforcement

(1) For the purposes of this Act—

(a) carrying out development without the required planning permission; or

(b) failing to comply with any condition or limitation subject to which planning permission has been granted,

constitutes a breach of planning control.

(2) For the purposes of this Act—

(a) the issue of an enforcement notice (defined in section 172); or

(b) the service of a breach of condition notice (defined in section 187A),

constitutes taking enforcement action.

(3) In this Part 'planning permission' includes permission under Part III of the 1947 Act, of the 1962 Act or of the 1971 Act.]

171B Time limits

(1) Where there has been a breach of planning control consisting in the carrying out without planning permission of building, engineering, mining or other operations in, on, over or under land, no enforcement action may be taken after the end of the period of four years beginning with the date on which the operations were substantially completed.

(2) Where there has been a breach of planning control consisting in the change of use of any building to use as a single dwellinghouse, no enforcement action may be taken after the end of the period of four years beginning with the date of the breach.

(3) In the case of any other breach of planning control, no enforcement action may be taken after the end of the period of ten years beginning with the date of the breach.

(4) The preceding subsections do not prevent—

(a) the service of a breach of condition notice in respect of any breach of planning control if an enforcement notice in respect of the breach is in effect; or

(b) taking further enforcement action in respect of any breach of planning control if, during the period of four years ending with that action being taken, the local planning authority have taken or purported to take enforcement action in respect of that breach.

171C Power to require information about activities on land

(1) Where it appears to the local planning authority that there may have been a breach of planning control in respect of any land, they may serve notice to that effect (referred to in this Act as a 'planning contravention notice') on any person who—

(a) is the owner or occupier of the land or has any other interest in it; or

(b) is carrying out operations on the land or is using it for any purpose.

(2) A planning contravention notice may require the person on whom it is served to give such information as to—

(a) any operations being carried out on the land, any use of the land and any other activities being carried out on the land; and

(b) any matter relating to the conditions or limitations subject to which any planning permission in respect of the land has been granted,

as may be specified in the notice.

(3) Without prejudice to the generality of subsection (2), the notice may require the person on whom it is served, so far as he is able—

(a) to state whether or not the land is being used for any purpose specified in the notice or any operations or activities specified in the notice are being or have been carried out on the land;

(b) to state when any use, operations or activities began;

(c) to give the name and [postal] address of any person known to him to use or have used the land for any purpose or to be carrying out, or have carried out, any operations or activities on the land;

(d) to give any information he holds as to any planning permission for any use or operations or any reason for planning permission not being required for any use or operations;

(e) to state the nature of his interest (if any) in the land and the name and [postal] address of any other person known to him to have an interest in the land.

(4) A planning contravention notice may give notice of a time and place at which—

(a) any offer which the person on whom the notice is served may wish to make to apply for planning permission, to refrain from carrying out any operations or activities or to undertake remedial works; and

(b) any representations which he may wish to make about the notice, will be considered by the authority, and the authority shall give him an opportunity to make in person any such offer or representations at that time and place.

(5) A planning contravention notice must inform the person on whom it is served—

(a) of the likely consequences of his failing to respond to the notice and, in particular, that enforcement action may be taken; and

(b) of the effect of section 186(5)(b).

(6) Any requirement of a planning contravention notice shall be complied with by giving information in writing to the local planning authority.

(7) The service of a planning contravention notice does not affect any other power exercisable in respect of any breach of planning control.

(8) In this section references to operations or activities on land include operations or activities in, under or over the land.

171D Penalties for non-compliance with planning contravention notice

(1) If, at any time after the end of the period of twenty-one days beginning with the day on which a planning contravention notice has been served on any person, he has not complied with any requirement of the notice, he shall be guilty of an offence.

(2) An offence under subsection (1) may be charged by reference to any day or longer period of time and a person may be convicted of a second or subsequent offence under that subsection by reference to any period of time following the preceding conviction for such an offence.

(3) It shall be a defence for a person charged with an offence under subsection (1) to prove that he had a reasonable excuse for failing to comply with the requirement.

(4) A person guilty of an offence under subsection (1) shall be liable on summary conviction to a fine not exceeding level 3 on the standard scale.

(5) If any person—

(a) makes any statement purporting to comply with a requirement of a planning contravention notice which he knows to be false or misleading in a material particular; or

(b) recklessly makes such a statement which is false or misleading in a material particular,

he shall be guilty of an offence.

(6) A person guilty of an offence under subsection (5) shall be liable on summary conviction to a fine not exceeding level 5 on the standard scale.

Temporary stop notices

171E Temporary stop notice

(1) This section applies if the local planning authority think—

(a) that there has been a breach of planning control in relation to any land, and

(b) that it is expedient that the activity (or any part of the activity) which amounts to the breach is stopped immediately.

(2) The authority may issue a temporary stop notice.

(3) The notice must be in writing and must—

(a) specify the activity which the authority think amounts to the breach;

(b) prohibit the carrying on of the activity (or of so much of the activity as is specified in the notice);

(c) set out the authority's reasons for issuing the notice.

(4) A temporary stop notice may be served on any of the following—
(a) the person who the authority think is carrying on the activity;
(b) a person who the authority think is an occupier of the land;
(c) a person who the authority think has an interest in the land.

(5) The authority must display on the land—
(a) a copy of the notice;
(b) a statement of the effect of the notice and of section 171G.

(6) A temporary stop notice has effect from the time a copy of it is first displayed in pursuance of subsection (5).

(7) A temporary stop notice ceases to have effect—
(a) at the end of the period of 28 days starting on the day the copy notice is so displayed,
(b) at the end of such shorter period starting on that day as is specified in the notice, or
(c) if it is withdrawn by the local planning authority.

171F Temporary stop notice: restrictions

(1) A temporary stop notice does not prohibit—
(a) the use of a building as a dwelling house;
(b) the carrying out of an activity of such description or in such circumstances as is prescribed.

(2) A temporary stop notice does not prohibit the carrying out of any activity which has been carried out (whether or not continuously) for a period of four years ending with the day on which the copy of the notice is first displayed as mentioned in section 171E(6).

(3) Subsection (2) does not prevent a temporary stop notice prohibiting—
(a) activity consisting of or incidental to building, engineering, mining or other operations, or
(b) the deposit of refuse or waste materials.

(4) For the purposes of subsection (2) any period during which the activity is authorised by planning permission must be ignored.

(5) A second or subsequent temporary stop notice must not be issued in respect of the same activity unless the local planning authority has first taken some other enforcement action in relation to the breach of planning control which is constituted by the activity.

(6) In subsection (5) enforcement action includes obtaining the grant of an injunction under section 187B.

171G Temporary stop notice: offences

(1) A person commits an offence if he contravenes a temporary stop notice—
(a) which has been served on him, or
(b) a copy of which has been displayed in accordance with section 171E(5).

(2) Contravention of a temporary stop notice includes causing or permitting the contravention of the notice.

(3) An offence under this section may be charged by reference to a day or a longer period of time.

(4) A person may be convicted of more than one such offence in relation to the same temporary stop notice by reference to different days or periods of time.

(5) A person does not commit an offence under this section if he proves—
(a) that the temporary stop notice was not served on him, and
(b) that he did not know, and could not reasonably have been expected to know, of its existence.

(6) A person convicted of an offence under this section is liable—
(a) on summary conviction, to a fine not exceeding £20,000;
(b) on conviction on indictment, to a fine.

(7) In determining the amount of the fine the court must have regard in particular to any financial benefit which has accured or has appeared to accrue to the person convicted in consequence of the offence.

171H Temporary stop notice: compensation

(1) This section applies if and only if a temporary stop notice is issued and at least one of the following paragraphs applies—

(a) the activity which is specified in the notice is authorised by planning permission or a development order or local development order;

(b) a certificate in respect of the activity is issued under section 191 or granted under that section by virtue of section 195;

(c) the authority withdraws the notice.

(2) Subsection (1)(a) does not apply if the planning permission is granted on or after the date on which a copy of the notice is first displayed as mentioned in section 171E(6).

(3) Subsection (1)(c) does not apply if the notice is withdrawn following the grant of planning permission as mentioned in subsection (2).

(4) A person who at the time the notice is served has an interest in the land to which the notice relates is entitled to be compensated by the local planning authority in respect of any loss or damage directly attributable to the prohibition effected by the notice.

(5) Subsections (3) to (7) of section 186 apply to compensation payable under this section as they apply to compensation payable under that section; and for that purpose references in those subsections to a stop notice must be taken to be references to a temporary stop notice.]

172 Issue of enforcement notice

(1) The local planning authority may issue a notice (in this Act referred to as an 'enforcement notice') where it appears to them—

(a) that there has been a breach of planning control; and

(b) that it is expedient to issue the notice, having regard to the provisions of the development plan and to any other material considerations.

(2) A copy of an enforcement notice shall be served—

(a) on the owner and on the occupier of the land to which it relates; and

(b) on any other person having an interest in the land, being an interest which, in the opinion of the authority, is materially affected by the notice.

(3) The service of the notice shall take place—

(a) not more than twenty-eight days after its date of issue; and

(b) not less than twenty-eight days before the date specified in it as the date on which it is to take effect.

173 Contents and effect of notice

(1) An enforcement notice shall state—

(a) the matters which appear to the local planning authority to constitute the breach of planning control; and

(b) the paragraph of section 171A(1) within which, in the opinion of the authority, the breach falls.

(2) A notice complies with subsection (1)(a) if it enables any person on whom a copy of it is served to know what those matters are.

(3) An enforcement notice shall specify the steps which the authority require to be taken, or the activities which the authority require to cease, in order to achieve, wholly or partly, any of the following purposes.

(4) Those purposes are—

(a) remedying the breach by making any development comply with the terms (including conditions and limitations) of any planning permission which has been granted in respect of the land, by discontinuing any use of the land or by restoring the land to its condition before the breach took place; or

(b) remedying any injury to amenity which has been caused by the breach.

(5) An enforcement notice may, for example, require—
(a) the alteration or removal of any buildings or works;
(b) the carrying out of any building or other operations;
(c) any activity on the land not to be carried on except to the extent specified in the notice; or
(d) the contour of a deposit of refuse or waste materials on land to be modified by altering the gradient or gradients of its sides.

(6) Where an enforcement notice is issued in respect of a breach of planning control consisting of demolition of a building, the notice may require the construction of a building (in this section referred to as a 'replacement building') which, subject to subsection (7), is as similar as possible to the demolished building.

(7) A replacement building—
(a) must comply with any requirement imposed by any enactment applicable to the construction of buildings;
(b) may differ from the demolished building in any respect which, if the demolished building had been altered in that respect, would not have constituted a breach of planning control;
(c) must comply with any regulations made for the purposes of this subsection (including regulations modifying paragraphs (a) and (b)).

(8) An enforcement notice shall specify the date on which it is to take effect and, subject to sections 175(4) and 289(4A), shall take effect on that date.

(9) An enforcement notice shall specify the period at the end of which any steps are required to have been taken or any activities are required to have ceased and may specify different periods for different steps or activities; and, where different periods apply to different steps or activities, references in this Part to the period for compliance with an enforcement notice, in relation to any step or activity, are to the period at the end of which the step is required to have been taken or the activity is required to have ceased.

(10) An enforcement notice shall specify such additional matters as may be prescribed, and regulations may require every copy of an enforcement notice served under section 172 to be accompanied by an explanatory note giving prescribed information as to the right of appeal under section 174.

(11) Where—
(a) an enforcement notice in respect of any breach of planning control could have required any buildings or works to be removed or any activity to cease, but does not do so; and
(b) all the requirements of the notice have been complied with, then, so far as the notice did not so require, planning permission shall be treated as having been granted by virtue of section 73A in respect of development consisting of the construction of the buildings or works or, as the case may be, the carrying out of the activities.

(12) Where—
(a) an enforcement notice requires the construction of a replacement building;
(b) all the requirements of the notice with respect to that construction have been complied with,

planning permission shall be treated as having been granted by virtue of section 73A in respect of development consisting of that construction.

[173A Variation and withdrawal of enforcement notices

(1) The local planning authority may—
(a) withdraw an enforcement notice issued by them; or
(b) waive or relax any requirement of such a notice and, in particular, may extend any period specified in accordance with section 173(9).

(2) The powers conferred by subsection (1) may be exercised whether or not the notice has taken effect.

(3) The local planning authority shall, immediately after exercising the powers conferred by subsection (1), give notice of the exercise to every person who has been served with a copy of the enforcement notice or would, if the notice were re-issued, be served with a copy of it.

(4) The withdrawal of an enforcement notice does not affect the power of the local planning authority to issue a further enforcement notice.]

174 Appeal against enforcement notice

(1) A person having an interest in the land to which an enforcement notice relates or a relevant occupier may appeal to the Secretary of State against the notice, whether or not a copy of it has been served on him.

[(2) An appeal may be brought on any of the following grounds—

(a) that, in respect of any breach of planning control which may be constituted by the matters stated in the notice, planning permission ought to be granted or, as the case may be, the condition or limitation concerned ought to be discharged;

(b) that those matters have not occurred;

(c) that those matters (if they occurred) do not constitute a breach of planning control;

(d) that, at the date when the notice was issued, no enforcement action could be taken in respect of any breach of planning control which may be constituted by those matters;

(e) that copies of the enforcement notice were not served as required by section 172;

(f) that the steps required by the notice to be taken, or the activities required by the notice to cease, exceed what is necessary to remedy any breach of planning control which may be constituted by those matters or, as the case may be, to remedy any injury to amenity which has been caused by any such breach;

(g) that any period specified in the notice in accordance with section 173(9) falls short of what should reasonably be allowed.

(3) An appeal under this section shall be made [. . .]—

(a) by giving written notice of the appeal to the Secretary of State before the date specified in the enforcement notice as the date on which it is to take effect; or

(b) by sending such notice to him in a properly addressed and pre-paid letter posted to him at such time that, in the ordinary course of post, it would be delivered to him before that date]; [or

(c) by sending such notice to him using electronic communications at such time that, in the ordinary course of transmission, it would be delivered to him before that date].

(4) A person who gives notice under subsection (3) shall submit to the Secretary of State, either when giving the notice or within the prescribed time, a statement in writing—

(a) specifying the grounds on which he is appealing against the enforcement notice; and

(b) giving such further information as may be prescribed.

(5) If, where more than one ground is specified in that statement, the appellant does not give information required under subsection (4)(b) in relation to each of those grounds within the prescribed time, the Secretary of State may determine the appeal without considering any ground as to which the appellant has failed to give such information within that time.

(6) In this section 'relevant occupier' means a person who—

(a) on the date on which the enforcement notice is issued occupies the land to which the notice relates by virtue of a licence; and

(b) continues so to occupy the land when the appeal is brought.

176 General provisions relating to determination of appeals

(1) On an appeal under section 174 the Secretary of State may—

(a) correct any defect, error or misdescription in the enforcement notice; or

(b) vary the terms of the enforcement notice, if he is satisfied that the correction or variation will not cause injustice to the appellant or the local planning authority.

[(2) Where the Secretary of State determines to allow the appeal, he may quash the notice.]

[(2A) The Secretary of State shall give any directions necessary to give effect to his determination on the appeal.]

(3) The Secretary of State—

(a) may dismiss an appeal if the appellant fails to comply with section 174(4) within the prescribed time; and

(b) may allow an appeal and quash the enforcement notice if the local planning authority fail to comply with any requirement of regulations made by virtue of paragraph (a), (b), or (d) of section 175(1) within the prescribed period.

(4) If the Secretary of State proposes to dismiss an appeal under paragraph (a) of subsection (3) or to allow an appeal and quash the enforcement notice under paragraph (b) of that subsection, he need not comply with section 175(3).

(5) Where it would otherwise be a ground for determining an appeal under section 174 in favour of the appellant that a person required to be served with a copy of the enforcement notice was not served, the Secretary of State may disregard that fact if neither the appellant nor that person has been substantially prejudiced by the failure to serve him.

177 Grant or modification of planning permission on appeals against enforcement notices

(1) On the determination of an appeal under section 174, the Secretary of State may—

[(a) grant planning permission in respect of the matters stated in the enforcement notice as constituting a breach of planning control, whether in relation to the whole or any part of those matters or in relation to the whole or any part of the land to which the notice relates;]

(b) discharge any condition or limitation subject to which planning permission was granted;

[(c) determine whether, on the date on which the appeal was made, any existing use of the land was lawful, any operations which had been carried out in, on, over or under the land were lawful or any matter constituting a failure to comply with any condition or limitation subject to which planning permission was granted was lawful and, if so, issue a certificate under section 191.

(1A) The provisions of sections 191 to 194 mentioned in subsection (1B) shall apply for the purposes of subsection (1)(c) as they apply for the purposes of section 191, but as if—

(a) any reference to an application for a certificate were a reference to the appeal and any reference to the date of such an application were a reference to the date on which the appeal is made; and

(b) references to the local planning authority were references to the Secretary of State.

(1B) Those provisions are: sections 191(5) to (7), 193(4) (so far as it relates to the form of the certificate), (6) and (7) and 194].

(2) In considering whether to grant planning permission under subsection (1), the Secretary of State shall have regard to the provisions of the development plan, so far as material to the subject matter of the enforcement notice, and to any other material considerations.

[(3) The planning permission that may be granted under subsection (1) is any planning permission that might be granted on an application under Part III.]

(4) Where under subsection (1) the Secretary of State discharges a condition or limitation, he may substitute another condition or limitation for it, whether more or less onerous.

(5) Where an appeal against an enforcement notice is brought under section 174, the appellant shall be deemed to have made an application for planning permission [in respect of the matters stated in the enforcement notice as constituting a breach of planning control].

...

(6) Any planning permission granted under subsection (1) on an appeal shall be treated as granted on the application deemed to have been made by the appellant.

(7) In relation to a grant of planning permission or a determination under subsection (1) the Secretary of State's decision shall be final.

(8) For the purposes of section 69 the Secretary of State's decision shall be treated as having been given by him in dealing with an application for planning permission made to the local planning authority.

178 Execution and cost of works required by enforcement notice

[(1) Where any steps required by an enforcement notice to be taken are not taken within the period for compliance with the notice, the local planning authority may—

(a) enter the land and take the steps; and

(b) recover from the person who is then the owner of the land any expenses reasonably incurred by them in doing so.]

(2) Where a copy of an enforcement notice has been served in respect of any breach of planning control . . . —

(a) any expenses incurred by the owner or occupier of any land for the purpose of complying with the notice, and

(b) any sums paid by the owner of any land under subsection (1) in respect of expenses incurred by the local planning authority in taking steps required by such a notice to be taken,

shall be deemed to be incurred or paid for the use and at the request of the person by whom the breach of planning control was committed.

. . .

(5) Regulations under subsection (3) may also provide for the charging on the land of any expenses recoverable by a local planning authority under subsection (1).

[(6) Any person who wilfully obstructs a person acting in the exercise of powers under subsection (1) shall be guilty of an offence and liable on summary conviction to a fine not exceeding level 3 on the standard scale.]

179 [Offence where enforcement notice not complied with

(1) Where, at any time after the end of the period for compliance with an enforcement notice, any step required by the notice to be taken has not been taken or any activity required by the notice to cease is being carried on, the person who is then the owner of the land is in breach of the notice.

(2) Where the owner of the land is in breach of an enforcement notice he shall be guilty of an offence.

(3) In proceedings against any person for an offence under subsection (2), it shall be a defence for him to show that he did everything he could be expected to do to secure compliance with the notice.

(4) A person who has control of or an interest in the land to which an enforcement notice relates (other than the owner) must not carry on any activity which is required by the notice to cease or cause or permit such an activity to be carried on.

(5) A person who, at any time after the end of the period for compliance with the notice, contravenes subsection (4) shall be guilty of an offence.

(6) An offence under subsection (2) or (5) may be charged by reference to any day or longer period of time and a person may be convicted of a second or subsequent offence under the subsection in question by reference to any period of time following the preceding conviction for such an offence.

(7) Where—

(a) a person charged with an offence under this section has not been served with a copy of the enforcement notice; and

(b) the notice is not contained in the appropriate register kept under section it shall be a defence for him to show that he was not aware of the existence of the notice.

(8) A person guilty of an offence under this section shall be liable—

(a) on summary conviction, to a fine not exceeding £20,000; and

(b) on conviction on indictment, to a fine.

(9) In determining the amount of any fine to be imposed on a person convicted of an offence under this section, the court shall in particular have regard to any financial benefit which has accrued or appears likely to accrue to him in consequence of the offence.]

183 Stop notices

[(1) Where the local planning authority consider it expedient that any relevant activity should cease before the expiry of the period for compliance with an enforcement notice, they may, when they serve the copy of the enforcement notice or afterwards, serve a notice (in this Act referred to as a 'stop notice') prohibiting the carrying out of that activity on the land to which the enforcement notice relates, or any part of that land specified in the stop notice.]

[(2) In this section and sections 184 and 186 'relevant activity' means any activity specified in the enforcement notice as an activity which the local planning authority require to cease and any activity carried out as part of that activity or associated with that activity.]

[(3) A stop notice may not be served where the enforcement notice has taken effect.]

[(4) A stop notice shall not prohibit the use of any building as a dwellinghouse.]

[(5) A stop notice shall not prohibit the carrying out of any activity if the activity has been carried out (whether continuously or not) for a period of more than four years ending with the service of the notice; and for the purposes of this subsection no account is to be taken of any period during which the activity was authorised by planning permission.]

[(5A) Subsection (5) does not prevent a stop notice prohibiting any activity consisting of, or incidental to, building, engineering, mining or other operations or the deposit of refuse or waste materials.]

(6) A stop notice may be served by the local planning authority on any person who appears to them to have an interest in the land or to be engaged in any activity prohibited by the notice.

(7) The local planning authority may at any time withdraw a stop notice (without prejudice to their power to serve another) by serving notice to that effect on persons served with the stop notice.

184 Stop notices: supplementary provisions

(1) A stop notice must refer to the enforcement notice to which it relates and have a copy of that notice annexed to it.

(2) A stop notice must specify the date on which it will take effect (and it cannot be contravened until that date).

[(3) That date—

(a) must not be earlier than three days after the date when the notice is served, unless the local planning authority consider that there are special reasons for specifying an earlier date and a statement of those reasons is served with the stop notice; and

(b) must not be later than twenty-eight days from the date when the notice is first served on any person.]

(4) A stop notice shall cease to have effect when—

(a) the enforcement notice to which it relates is withdrawn or quashed; or

(b) the [period for compliance with the enforcement notice] expires; or

(c) notice of the withdrawal of the stop notice is first served under section 183(7).

(5) A stop notice shall also cease to have effect if or to the extent that the activities prohibited by it cease, on a variation of the enforcement notice, to be included [relevant activities].

(6) Where a stop notice has been served in respect of any land, the local planning authority may display there a notice (in this section and section 187 referred to as a 'site notice')—

(a) stating that a stop notice has been served and that any person contravening it may be prosecuted for an offence under section 187,
(b) giving the date when the stop notice takes effect, and
(c) indicating its requirements.

(7) If under section 183(7) the local planning authority withdraw a stop notice in respect of which a site notice was displayed, they must display a notice of the withdrawal in place of the site notice.

(8) A stop notice shall not be invalid by reason that a copy of the enforcement notice to which it relates was not served as required by section [172] if it is shown that the local planning authority took all such steps as were reasonably practicable to effect proper service.

186 Compensation for loss due to stop notice

(1) Where a stop notice is served under section 183 compensation may be payable under this section in respect of a prohibition contained in the notice only if—
(a) the enforcement notice is quashed on grounds other than those mentioned in paragraph (a) of section 174(2);
(b) the enforcement notice is varied (otherwise than on the grounds mentioned in that paragraph) so that [any activity the carrying out of which is prohibited by the stop notice ceases to be a relevant activity];
(c) the enforcement notice is withdrawn by the local planning authority otherwise than in consequence of the grant by them of planning permission for the development to which the notice relates; or
(d) the stop notice is withdrawn.

(2) A person who, when the stop notice is first served, has an interest in or occupies the land to which the notice relates shall be entitled to be compensated by the local planning authority in respect of any loss or damage directly attributable to the prohibition contained in the notice or, in a case within subsection (1)(b), [the prohibition of such of the activities prohibited by the stop notice as cease to be relevant activities].

(3) A claim for compensation under this section shall be made to the local planning authority within the prescribed time and in the prescribed manner.

(4) The loss or damage in respect of which compensation is payable under this section in respect of a prohibition shall include any sum payable in respect of a breach of contract caused by the taking of action necessary to comply with the prohibition.

[(5) No compensation is payable under this section—
(a) in respect of the prohibition in a stop notice of any activity which, at any time when the notice is in force, constitutes or contributes to a breach of planning control; or
(b) in the case of a claimant who was required to provide information under section 171C or 330 or section 16 of the Local Government (Miscellaneous Provisions) Act 1976, in respect of any loss or damage suffered by him which could have been avoided if he had provided the information or had otherwise co-operated with the local planning authority when responding to the notice.]

(6) Except in so far as may be otherwise provided by any regulations made under this Act, any question of disputed compensation under this Part shall be referred to and determined by the Lands Tribunal.

(7) In relation to the determination of any such question, the provisions of sections 2 and 4 of the Land Compensation Act 1961 shall apply subject to any necessary modifications and to the provisions of any regulations made under this Act.

187 Penalties for contravention of stop notice

[(1) If any person contravenes a stop notice after a site notice has been displayed or the stop notice has been served on him he shall be guilty of an offence.]

[(1A) An offence under this section may be charged by reference to any day or longer period of time and a person may be convicted of a second or subsequent offence under this section by reference to any period of time following the preceding conviction for such an offence.]

[(1B) References in this section to contravening a stop notice include causing or permitting its contravention.]

[(2) A person guilty of an offence under this section shall be liable—

(a) on summary conviction, to a fine not exceeding £20,000; and

(b) on conviction on indictment, to a fine.]

[(2A) In determining the amount of any fine to be imposed on a person convicted of an offence under this section, the court shall in particular have regard to any financial benefit which has accrued or appears likely to accrue to him in consequence of the offence.]

(3) In proceedings for an offence under this section it shall be a defence for the accused to prove—

(a) that the stop notice was not served on him, and

(b) that he did not know, and could not reasonably have been expected to know, of its existence.

187A [Enforcement of conditions

(1) This section applies where planning permission for carrying out any development of land has been granted subject to conditions.

(2) The local planning authority may, if any of the conditions is not complied with, serve a notice (in this Act referred to as a 'breach of condition notice') on—

(a) any person who is carrying out or has carried out the development; or

(b) any person having control of the land,

requiring him to secure compliance with such of the conditions as are specified in the notice.

(3) References in this section to the person responsible are to the person on whom the breach of condition notice has been served.

(4) The conditions which may be specified in a notice served by virtue of subsection (2)(b) are any of the conditions regulating the use of the land.

(5) A breach of condition notice shall specify the steps which the authority consider ought to be taken, or the activities which the authority consider ought to cease, to secure compliance with the conditions specified in the notice.

(6) The authority may by notice served on the person responsible withdraw the breach of condition notice, but its withdrawal shall not affect the power to serve on him a further breach of condition notice in respect of the conditions specified in the earlier notice or any other conditions.

(7) The period allowed for compliance with the notice is—

(a) such period of not less than twenty-eight days beginning with the date of service of the notice as may be specified in the notice; or

(b) that period as extended by a further notice served by the local planning authority on the person responsible.

(8) If, at any time after the end of the period allowed for compliance with the notice—

(a) any of the conditions specified in the notice is not complied with; and

(b) the steps specified in the notice have not been taken or, as the case may be, the activities specified in the notice have not ceased,

the person responsible is in breach of the notice.

(9) If the person responsible is in breach of the notice he shall be guilty of an offence.

(10) An offence under subsection (9) may be charged by reference to any day or longer period of time and a person may be convicted of a second or subsequent offence under that subsection by reference to any period of time following the preceding conviction for such an offence.

(11) It shall be a defence for a person charged with an offence under subsection (9) to prove—

(a) that he took all reasonable measures to secure compliance with the conditions specified in the notice; or

(b) where the notice was served on him by virtue of subsection (2)(b), that he no longer had control of the land.

(12) A person who is guilty of an offence under subsection (9) shall be liable on summary conviction to a fine not exceeding level 3 on the standard scale.

(13) In this section—

(a) 'conditions' includes limitations; and

(b) references to carrying out any development include causing or permitting another to do so.]

187B [Injunctions restraining breaches of planning control

(1) Where a local planning authority consider it necessary or expedient for any actual or apprehended breach of planning control to be restrained by injunction, they may apply to the court for an injunction, whether or not they have exercised or are proposing to exercise any of their other powers under this Part.

(2) On an application under subsection (1) the court may grant such an injunction as the court thinks appropriate for the purpose of restraining the breach.

(3) Rules of court may provide for such an injunction to be issued against a person whose identity is unknown.

(4) In this section 'the court' means the High Court or the county court.]

188 Register of enforcement and stop notices

...

191 [Certificate of lawfulness of existing use or development

(1) If any person wishes to ascertain whether—

(a) any existing use of buildings or other land is lawful;

(b) any operations which have been carried out in, on, over or under land are lawful; or

(c) any other matter constituting a failure to comply with any condition or limitation subject to which planning permission has been granted is lawful,

he may make an application for the purpose to the local planning authority specifying the land and describing the use, operations or other matter.

(2) For the purposes of this Act uses and operations are lawful at any time if—

(a) no enforcement action may then be taken in respect of them (whether because they did not involve development or require planning permission or because the time for enforcement action has expired or for any other reason); and

(b) they do not constitute a contravention of any of the requirements of any enforcement notice then in force.

(3) For the purposes of this Act any matter constituting a failure to comply with any condition or limitation subject to which planning permission has been granted is lawful at any time if—

(a) the time for taking enforcement action in respect of the failure has then expired; and

(b) it does not constitute a contravention of any of the requirements of any enforcement notice or breach of condition notice then in force.

(4) If, on an application under this section, the local planning authority are provided with information satisfying them of the lawfulness at the time of the application of the use, operations or other matter described in the application, or that description as modified by the local planning authority or a description substituted by them, they shall issue a certificate to that effect; and in any other case they shall refuse the application.

(5) A certificate under this section shall—

(a) specify the land to which it relates;

(b) describe the use, operations or other matter in question (in the case of any use falling within one of the classes specified in an order under section 55(2)(f), identifying it by reference to that class);

(c) give the reasons for determining the use, operations or other matter to be lawful; and

(d) specify the date of the application for the certificate.

(6) The lawfulness of any use, operations or other matter for which a certificate is in force under this section shall be conclusively presumed.

(7) A certificate under this section in respect of any use shall also have effect, for the purposes of the following enactments, as if it were a grant of planning permission—

(a) section 3(3) of the Caravan Sites and Control of Development Act 1960;

(b) section 5(2) of the Control of Pollution Act 1974; and

(c) section 36(2)(a) of the Environmental Protection Act 1990.]

192 [Certificate of lawfulness of proposed use or development

(1) If any person wishes to ascertain whether—

(a) any proposed use of buildings or other land; or

(b) any operations proposed to be carried out in, on, over or under land, would be lawful, he may make an application for the purpose to the local planning authority specifying the land and describing the use or operations in question.

(2) If, on an application under this section, the local planning authority are provided with information satisfying them that the use or operations described in the application would be lawful if instituted or begun at the time of the application, they shall issue a certificate to that effect; and in any other case they shall refuse the application.

(3) A certificate under this section shall—

(a) specify the land to which it relates;

(b) describe the use or operations in question (in the case of any use falling within one of the classes specified in an order under section 55(2)(f), identifying it by reference to that class);

(c) give the reasons for determining the use or operations to be lawful; and

(d) specify the date of the application for the certificate.

(4) The lawfulness of any use or operations for which a certificate is in force under this section shall be conclusively presumed unless there is a material change, before the use is instituted or the operations are begun, in any of the matters relevant to determining such lawfulness.]

193 [Certificates under sections 191 and 192: supplementary provisions

(1) An application for a certificate under section 191 or 192 shall be made in such manner as may be prescribed by a development order and shall include such particulars, and be verified by such evidence, as may be required by such an order or by any directions given under such an order or by the local planning authority.

(2) Provision may be made by a development order for regulating the manner in which applications for certificates under those sections are to be dealt with by local planning authorities.

(3) In particular, such an order may provide for requiring the authority—

(a) to give to any applicant within such time as may be prescribed by the order such notice as may be so prescribed as to the manner in which his application has been dealt with; and

(b) to give to the Secretary of State and to such other persons as may be prescribed by or under the order, such information as may be so prescribed with respect to such applications made to the authority, including information as to the manner in which any application has been dealt with.

(4) A certificate under either of those sections may be issued—

(a) for the whole or part of the land specified in the application; and

(b) where the application specifies two or more uses, operations or other matters, for all of them or some one or more of them;

and shall be in such form as may be prescribed by a development order.

(5) A certificate under section 191 or 192 shall not affect any matter constituting a failure to comply with any condition or limitation subject to which planning permission has been granted unless that matter is described in the certificate.

(6) In section 69 references to applications for planning permission shall include references to applications for certificates under section 191 or 192.

(7) A local planning authority may revoke a certificate under either of those sections if, on the application for the certificate—

(a) a statement was made or document used which was false in a material particular; or

(b) any material information was withheld.

(8) Provision may be made by a development order for regulating the manner in which certificates may be revoked and the notice to be given of such revocation.]

194 [Offences

(1) If any person, for the purpose of procuring a particular decision on an application (whether by himself or another) for the issue of a certificate under section 191 or 192—

(a) knowingly or recklessly makes a statement which is false or misleading in a material particular;

(b) with intent to deceive, uses any document which is false or misleading in a material particular; or

(c) with intent to deceive, withholds any material information, he shall be guilty of an offence.

(2) A person guilty of an offence under subsection (1) shall be liable—

(a) on summary conviction, to a fine not exceeding the statutory maximum; or

(b) on conviction on indictment, to imprisonment for a term not exceeding two years, or a fine, or both.

(3) Notwithstanding section 127 of the Magistrates' Courts Act 1980, a magistrates' court may try an information in respect of an offence under subsection (1) whenever laid.]

PART VIII SPECIAL CONTROLS

CHAPTER ONE TREES

197 Planning permission to include appropriate provision for preservation and planting of trees

It shall be the duty of the local planning authority—

(a) to ensure, whenever it is appropriate, that in granting planning permission for any development adequate provision is made, by the imposition of conditions, for the preservation or planting of trees; and

(b) to make such orders under section 198 as appear to the authority to be necessary in connection with the grant of such permission, whether for giving effect to such conditions or otherwise.

198 Power to make tree preservation orders

(1) If it appears to a local planning authority that it is expedient in the interests of amenity to make provision for the preservation of trees or woodlands in their area, they may for that purpose make an order with respect to such trees, groups of trees or woodlands as may be specified in the order.

(2) An order under subsection (1) is in this Act referred to as a 'tree preservation order'.

(3) A tree preservation order may, in particular, make provision—

(a) for prohibiting (subject to any exemptions for which provision may be made by the order) the cutting down, topping, lopping, uprooting, wilful damage or wilful destruction of trees except with the consent of the local planning authority, and for enabling that authority to give their consent subject to conditions;

(b) for securing the replanting, in such manner as may be prescribed by or under the order, of any part of a woodland area which is felled in the course of forestry operations permitted by or under the order;

(c) for applying, in relation to any consent under the order, and to applications for such consent, any of the provisions of this Act mentioned in subsection (4), subject to such adaptations and modifications as may be specified in the order.

(4) The provisions referred to in subsection (3)(c) are—

(a) the provisions of Part III relating to planning permission and to applications for planning permission, except sections 56, 62, 65, 69(3) and (4), 71, 91 to 96, 100 and 101 and Schedule 8; and

(b) sections 137 to 141, 143 and 144 (except so far as they relate to purchase notices served in consequence of such orders as are mentioned in section 137(1)(b) or (c));

(c) section 316.

(5) A tree preservation order may be made so as to apply, in relation to trees to be planted pursuant to any such conditions as are mentioned in section 197(a), as from the time when those trees are planted.

(6) Without prejudice to any other exemptions for which provision may be made by a tree preservation order, no such order shall apply—

(a) to the cutting down, uprooting, topping or lopping of trees which are dying or dead or have become dangerous, or

(b) to the cutting down, uprooting, topping or lopping of any trees in compliance with any obligations imposed by or under an Act of Parliament or so far as may be necessary for the prevention or abatement of a nuisance.

(7) This section shall have effect subject to—

(a) section 39(2) of the Housing and Planning Act 1986 (saving for effect of section 2(4) of the Opencast Coal Act 1958 on land affected by a tree preservation order despite its repeal); and

(b) section 15 of the Forestry Act 1967 (licences under that Act to fell trees comprised in a tree preservation order).

[(8) In relation to an application for consent under a tree preservation order the appropriate authority may by regulations make provision as to—

(a) the form and manner in which the application must be made;

(b) particulars of such matters as are to be included in the application;

(c) the documents or other materials as are to accompany the application.

(9) The appropriate authority is—

(a) the Secretary of State in relation to England;

(b) the National Assembly for Wales in relation to Wales,

and in the case of regulations made by the National Assembly for Wales section 333(3) must be ignored.]

[200 Tree preservation orders: Forestry Commissioners

(1) A tree preservation order does not have effect in respect of anything done—

(a) by or on behalf of the Forestry Commissioners on land placed at their disposal in pursuance of the Forestry Act 1967 or otherwise under their management or supervision;

(b) by or on behalf of any other person in accordance with a relevant plan which is for the time being in force.

(2) A relevant plan is a plan of operations or other working plan approved by the Forestry Commissioners under—

(a) a forestry dedication covenant within the meaning of section 5 of the Forestry Act 1967, or

(b) conditions of a grant or loan made under section 1 of the Forestry Act 1979.

(3) A reference to a provision of the Forestry Act 1967 or the Forestry Act 1979 includes a reference to a corresponding provision replaced by that provision or any earlier corresponding provision.]

CHAPTER TWO LAND ADVERSELY AFFECTING AMENITY OF NEIGHBOURHOOD

215 Power to require proper maintenance of land

(1) If it appears to the local planning authority that the amenity of a part of their area, or of an adjoining area, is adversely affected by the condition of land in their area, they may serve on the owner and occupier of the land a notice under this section.

(2) The notice shall require such steps for remedying the condition of the land as may be specified in the notice to be taken within such period as may be so specified.

(3) Subject to the following provisions of this Chapter, the notice shall take effect at the end of such period as may be specified in the notice.

(4) That period shall not be less than 28 days after the service of the notice.

PART XII VALIDITY

288 Proceedings for questioning the validity of other orders, decisions and directions

(1) If any person—

(a) is aggrieved by any order to which this section applies and wishes to question the validity of that order on the grounds—

(i) that the order is not within the powers of this Act, or

(ii) that any of the relevant requirements have not been complied with in relation to that order; or

(b) is aggrieved by any action on the part of the Secretary of State to which this section applies and wishes to question the validity of that action on the grounds—

(i) that the action is not within the powers of this Act, or

(ii) that any of the relevant requirements have not been complied with in relation to that action,

he may make an application to the High Court under this section.

(2) Without prejudice to subsection (1), if the authority directly concerned with any order to which this section applies, or with any action on the part of the Secretary of State to which this section applies, wish to question the validity of that order or action on any of the grounds mentioned in subsection (1), the authority may make an application to the High Court under this section.

(3) An application under this section must be made within six weeks from the date on which the order is confirmed (or, in the case of an order under section 97 which takes effect under section 99 without confirmation, the date on which it takes effect) or, as the case may be, the date on which the action is taken.

(4) This section applies to any such order as is mentioned in subsection (2) of section 284 and to any such action on the part of the Secretary of State as is mentioned in subsection (3) of that section.

(5) On any application under this section the High Court—

(a) may, subject to subsection (6), by interim order suspend the operation of the order or action, the validity of which is questioned by the application, until the final determination of the proceedings;

(b) if satisfied that the order or action in question is not within the powers of this Act, or that the interests of the applicant have been substantially prejudiced by a failure to comply with any of the relevant requirements in relation to it, may quash that order or action.

(6) Paragraph (a) of subsection (5) shall not apply to applications questioning the validity of tree preservation orders.

(7) In relation to a tree preservation order, or to an order made in pursuance of section 221(5), the powers conferred on the High Court by subsection (5) shall be exercisable by way of quashing or (where applicable) suspending the operation of the order either in whole or in part, as the court may determine.

(8) References in this section to the confirmation of an order include the confirmation of an order subject to modifications as well as the confirmation of an order in the form in which it was made.

(9) In this section 'the relevant requirements', in relation to any order or action to which this section applies, means any requirements of this Act or of the Tribunals and Inquiries Act [1992], or of any order, regulations or rules made under this Act or under that Act which are applicable to that order or action.

(10) Any reference in this section to the authority directly concerned with any order or action to which this section applies—

(a) in relation to any such decision as is mentioned in section 284(3)(f), is a reference to the council on whom the notice in question was served and, in a case where the Secretary of State has modified such a notice, wholly or in part, by substituting another local authority or statutory undertakers for that council, includes a reference to that local authority or those statutory undertakers;

(b) in any other case, is a reference to the authority who made the order in question or made the decision or served the notice to which the proceedings in question relate, or who referred the matter to the Secretary of State, or, where the order or notice in question was made or served by him, the authority named in the order or notice.

PART XV MISCELLANEOUS AND GENERAL PROVISIONS

336 Interpretation

(1) In this Act, except in so far as the context otherwise requires and subject to the following provisions of this section and to any transitional provision made by the Planning (Consequential Provisions) Act 1990—

...

'agriculture' includes horticulture, fruit growing, seed growing, dairy farming, the breeding and keeping of livestock (including any creature kept for the production of food, wool, skins or fur, or for the purpose of its use in the farming of land), the use of land as grazing land, meadow land, osier land, market gardens and nursery grounds, and the use of land for woodlands where that use is ancillary to the farming of land for other agricultural purposes, and 'agricultural' shall be construed accordingly;

...

'building' includes any structure or erection, and any part of a building, as so defined, but does not include plant or machinery comprised in a building;

...

['building operations' has the meaning given by section 55]

'buildings or works' includes waste materials, refuse and other matters deposited on land, and references to the erection or construction of buildings or works shall be construed accordingly [and references to the removal of buildings or works include demolition of buildings and filling in of trenches];

...

'engineering operations' includes the formation or laying out of means of access to highways;

...

'land' means any corporeal hereditament, including a building, and, in relation to the acquisition of land under Part IX, includes any interest in or right over land;

'means of access' includes any means of access, whether private or public, for vehicles or for foot passengers, and includes a street;

...

'minerals' includes all minerals and substances in or under land of a kind ordinarily worked for removal by underground or surface working, except that it does not include peat cut for purposes other than sale;

...

'open space' means any land laid out as a public garden, or used for the purposes of public recreation, or land which is a disused burial ground;

...

'owner', in relation to any land, means a person, other than a mortgagee not in possession, who, whether in his own right or as trustee for any other person, is entitled to receive the rack rent of the land or, where the land is not let at a rack rent, would be so entitled if it were so let;

...

'the planning Acts' means this Act, the Planning (Listed Buildings and Conservation Areas) Act 1990, the Planning (Hazardous Substances) Act 1990 and the Planning (Consequential Provisions) Act 1990;

...

'use', in relation to land, does not include the use of land for the carrying out of any building or other operations on it;

...

Environmental Protection Act 1990

(1990, c.43)

PART II WASTE ON LAND

29 Preliminary

(1) The following provisions have effect for the interpretation of this Part.

[(1A) 'Appropriate person' means—

(a) in relation to England, the Secretary of State;

(b) in relation to Wales, the National Assembly for Wales.]

(2) The 'environment' consists of all, or any, of the following media, namely land, water and the air.

(3) 'Pollution of the environment' means pollution of the environment due to the release or escape (into any environmental medium) from—

(a) the land on which controlled waste is treated,

(b) the land on which controlled waste is kept,

(c) the land in or on which controlled waste is deposited,

(d) fixed plant by means of which controlled waste is treated, kept or disposed of,

of substances or articles constituting or resulting from the waste and capable (by reason of the quantity or concentrations involved) of causing harm to man or any other living organisms supported by the environment.

(4) Subsection (3) above applies in relation to mobile plant by means of which controlled waste is treated or disposed of as it applies to plant on land by means of which controlled waste is treated or disposed of.

(5) For the purposes of subsections (3) and (4) above 'harm' means harm to the health of living organisms or other interference with the ecological systems of which they form part and in the case of man includes offence to any of his senses or harm to his property; and 'harmless' has a corresponding meaning.

(6) The 'disposal' of waste includes its disposal by way of deposit in or on land and, subject to subsection (7) below, waste is 'treated' when it is subjected to any process, including making it re-usable or reclaiming substances from it and 'recycle' (and cognate expressions) shall be construed accordingly.

(7) Regulations made by the Secretary of State may prescribe activities as activities which constitute the treatment of waste for the purposes of this Part or any provision of this Part prescribed in the regulations.

(8) 'Land' includes land covered by waters where the land is above the low water mark of ordinary spring tides and references to land on which controlled waste is treated, kept or deposited are references to the surface of the land (including any structure set into the surface).

(9) 'Mobile plant' means, subject to subsection (10) below, plant which is designed to move or be moved whether on roads or other land.

(10) Regulations made by the Secretary of State may prescribe descriptions of plant which are to be treated as being, or as not being, mobile plant for the purposes of this Part.

(11) 'Substance' means any natural or artificial substance, whether in solid or liquid form or in the form of a gas or vapour.

30 Authorities for purposes of this Part

[(1) Any reference in this Part to a waste regulation authority—

(a) in relation to England and Wales, is a reference to the Environment Agency; and

(b) ...

and any reference in this Part to the area of a waste regulation authority shall accordingly be taken as a reference to the area over which the Environment Agency ... exercises its functions or, in the case of any particular function, the function in question.]

(2) For the purposes of this Part the following authorities are waste disposal authorities, namely—

(a) for any non-metropolitan county in England, the county council;

(b) in Greater London, the following—

(i) for the area of a London waste disposal authority, the authority constituted as the waste disposal authority for that area;

(ii) for the City of London, the Common Council;

(iii) for any other London borough, the council of the borough;

(c) in the metropolitan county of Greater Manchester, the following—

(i) for the metropolitan district of Wigan, the district council;

(ii) for all other areas in the county, the authority constituted as the Greater Manchester Waste Disposal Authority;

(d) for the metropolitan county of Merseyside, the authority constituted as the Merseyside Waste Disposal Authority;

(e) for any district in any other metropolitan county in England, the council of the district;

(f) for any district in Wales, the council of the district;

(g) ...

(3) For the purposes of this Part the following authorities are waste collection authorities—

(a) for any district in England and Wales not within Greater London, the council of the district;

(b) in Greater London, the following—

(i) for any London borough, the council of the borough;

(ii) for the City of London, the Common Council;
(iii) for the Temples, the Sub-Treasurer of the Inner Temple and the Under Treasurer of the Middle Temple respectively;

(c) ...

(4) In this section references to particular authorities having been constituted as waste disposal [...] or regulation authorities are references to their having been so constituted by the Waste Regulation and Disposal (Authorities) Order 1985 made by the Secretary of State under section 10 of the Local Government Act 1985 and the reference to London waste disposal authorities is a reference to the authorities named in Parts I, II, III, IV and V of Schedule 1 to that Order and this section has effect subject to any order made under the said section 10 [...].

(5)–(8) [...]

33 Prohibition on unauthorised or harmful deposit, treatment or disposal etc. of waste

(1) Subject to subsection (2) and (3) below... a person shall not—

(a) deposit controlled waste, or knowingly cause or knowingly permit controlled waste to be deposited in or on any land unless a waste management licence authorising the deposit is in force and the deposit is in accordance with the licence;
(b) treat, keep or dispose of controlled waste, or knowingly cause or knowingly permit controlled waste to be treated, kept or disposed of—
(i) in or on any land, or
(ii) by means of any mobile plant,
except under and in accordance with a waste management licence;
(c) treat, keep or dispose of controlled waste in a manner likely to cause pollution of the environment or harm to human health.

(2) Subject to subsection (2A) below, paragraphs (a) and (b) of subsection (1) above does not apply in relation to household waste from a domestic property which is treated, kept or disposed of within the curtilage of the property.

(2A) Subsection (2) above does not apply to the treatment, keeping or disposal of household waste by an establishment or undertaking.

(3) Subsection (1)(a), (b) or (c) above do not apply in cases prescribed in regulations made by the Secretary of State and the regulations may make different exceptions for different areas.

(4) The Secretary of State, in exercising his power under subsection (3) above, shall have regard in particular to the expediency of excluding from the controls imposed by waste management licences—

(a) any deposits which are small enough or of such a temporary nature that they may be so excluded;
(b) any means of treatment or disposal which are innocuous enough to be so excluded;
(c) cases for which adequate controls are provided by another enactment than this section.

(5) Where controlled waste is carried in and deposited from a motor vehicle, the person who controls or is in a position to control the use of the vehicle shall, for the purposes of subsection (1)(a) above, be treated as knowingly causing the waste to be deposited whether or not he gave any instructions for this to be done.

(6) A person who contravenes subsection (1) above or any condition of a waste management licence commits an offence.

(7) It shall be a defence for a person charged with an offence under this section to prove—

(a) that he took all reasonable precautions and exercised all due diligence to avoid the commission of the offence; or

(b) that he acted under instructions from his employer and neither knew nor had reason to suppose that the acts done by him constituted a contravention of subsection (1) above; or

[(c) that the acts alleged to constitute the contravention were done in an emergency in order to avoid danger to human health in a case where—

(i) he took all such steps as were reasonably practicable in the circumstances for minimising pollution of the environment and harm to human health; and

(ii) particulars of the acts were furnished to the waste regulation authority as soon as reasonably practicable after they were done.]

(8) Except in a case falling within subsection (9) or (10) below, a person who commits an offence under this section shall be liable—

(a) on summary conviction, to imprisonment for a term not exceeding six months or a fine not exceeding £40,000 or both; and

(b) on conviction on indictment, to imprisonment for a term not exceeding two years or a fine or both.

(9) A person who commits an offence under this section in relation to [hazardous] waste (other than household waste of the description specified in subsection (10) below) shall be liable—

(a) on summary conviction, to imprisonment for a term not exceeding six months or a fine not exceeding £40,000 or both;

(b) on conviction on indictment, to imprisonment for a term not exceeding five years or a fine or both.

(10) A person who commits an offence under subsection (1)(c) above in relation to household waste from a domestic property within the curtilage of the dwelling shall be liable—

(a) on summary conviction, to imprisonment for a term not exceeding three months or a fine not exceeding the statutory maximum or both;

(b) on conviction on indictment, to imprisonment for a term not exceeding two years or a fine or both.

[33A Section 33 offences: investigation and enforcement costs

(1) This section applies where a person is convicted of an offence under section 33 above in respect of a contravention of subsection (1) of that section.

(2) The court by or before which the offender is convicted may make an order requiring him to pay to an enforcement authority a sum which appears to the court not to exceed the costs arising from—

(a) investigations of the enforcement authority which resulted in the conviction; and

(b) the seizure by the enforcement authority under section 34B below of a vehicle involved in the offence.

(3) The costs arising from the seizure of a vehicle as specified in subsection (2)(b) above may include the cost of disposing of the contents of the vehicle.

(4) The power of a court to make an order under this section is in addition to its power to make an order under section 18 of the Prosecution of Offences Act 1985 (award of costs against accused).

(5) In this section 'enforcement authority' means the Environment Agency or a waste collection authority.]

[33B Section 33 offences: clean-up costs

(1) This section applies where a person is convicted of an offence under section 33 above in respect of a contravention of subsection (1) of that section consisting of the deposit or disposal of controlled waste.

(2) The reference in section 130(1)(a) of the Powers of Criminal Courts (Sentencing) Act 2000 (compensation orders) to loss or damage resulting from the offence includes costs incurred or to be incurred by a relevant person in—

(a) removing the waste deposited or disposed of in or on the land;
(b) taking other steps to eliminate or reduce the consequences of the deposit or disposal; or
(c) both.

(3) In subsection (2) above 'relevant person' means—
(a) the Environment Agency;
(b) a waste collection authority;
(c) the occupier of the land;
(d) the owner of the land (within the meaning of section 78A(9) below).

(4) The reference in subsection (2) above to costs incurred does not, in the case of the Environment Agency or a waste collection authority, include any costs which the Agency or authority has already recovered under section 59(8) below.

(5) In relation to the costs referred to in subsection (2) above, the reference in section 131(1) of the Powers of Criminal Courts (Sentencing) Act 2000 (limit on amount payable) to £5000 is instead to be construed as a reference to the amount of those costs (or, if the costs have not yet been incurred, the likely amount).]

[33C Section 33 offences: forfeiture of vehicles

(1) This section applies where a person is convicted of an offence under section 33 above in respect of a contravention of subsection (1) of that section consisting of the deposit or disposal of controlled waste.

(2) The court by or before which the offender is convicted may make an order under this section if—
(a) the court is satisfied that a vehicle was used in or for the purposes of the commission of the offence; and
(b) at the time of his conviction the offender has rights in the vehicle.

(3) An order under this section operates to deprive the offender of his rights in the vehicle (including its fuel) at the time of his conviction and to vest those rights in the relevant enforcement authority.

...

(10) In this section—

'relevant enforcement authority' means—
(a) the Environment Agency, where the proceedings in respect of the offence have been brought by or on behalf of the Agency, or
(b) in any other case, the waste collection authority in whose area the offence was committed;

'vehicle' means any motor vehicle or trailer within the meaning of the Road Traffic Regulation Act 1984 or any mobile plant.]

34 Duty of care etc. as respects waste

(1) Subject to subsection (2) below, it shall be the duty of any person who imports, produces, carries, keeps, treats or disposes of controlled waste or, as a broker, has control of such waste, to take all such measures applicable to him in that capacity as are reasonable in the circumstances—
(a) to prevent any contravention by any other person of section 33 above;
[(aa) to prevent any contravention by any other person of regulation 9 of the Pollution Prevention and Control (England and Wales) Regulations 2000 or of a condition of a permit granted under regulation 10 of those Regulations;]
(b) to prevent the escape of the waste from his control or that of any other person; and
(c) on the transfer of the waste, to secure—
(i) that the transfer is only to an authorised person or to a person for authorised transport purposes; and

(ii) that there is transferred such a written description of the waste as will enable other persons to avoid a contravention of that section [or any condition of a permit granted under regulation 10 of those Regulations] and to comply with the duty under this subsection as respects the escape of waste.

(2) The duty imposed by subsection (1) above does not apply to an occupier of domestic property as respects the household waste produced on the property.

[(2A) It shall be the duty of the occupier of any domestic property in England [or Wales] to take all such measures available to him as are reasonable in the circumstances to secure that any transfer by him of household waste produced on the property is only to an authorised person or to a person for authorised transport purposes.]

(3) The following are authorised persons for the purpose of subsection (1)(c) and (2A) above—

(a) any authority which is a waste collection authority for the purposes of this Part;
(b) any person who is the holder of a waste management licence under section 35 below [...]
(c) any person to whom section 33(1) above does not apply by virtue of regulations under subsection (3) of that section;
(d) any person registered as a carrier of controlled waste under section 2 of the Control of Pollution (Amendment) Act 1989;
(e) any person who is not required to be so registered by virtue of regulations under section 1(3) of that Act; and
(f) ...

[(3A) The Secretary of State may by regulations amend subsection (3) above so as to add, whether generally or in such circumstances as may be prescribed in the regulations, any person specified in the regulations, or any description of person so specified, to the persons who are authorised persons for the purposes of subsection (1)(c) and (2A) above.]

(4) The following are authorised transport purposes for the purposes of subsection (1)(c) and (2A) above—

(a) the transport of controlled waste within the same premises between different places in those premises;
(b) the transport to a place in Great Britain of controlled waste which has been brought from a country or territory outside Great Britain not having been landed in Great Britain until it arrives at that place; and
(c) the transport by air or sea of controlled waste from a place in Great Britain to a place outside Great Britain;

and 'transport' has the same meaning in this subsection as in the Control of Pollution (Amendment) Act 1989.

[(4A) For the purposes of subsection (1)(c)(ii) above—

(a) a transfer of waste in stages shall be treated as taking place when the first stage of the transfer takes place, and
(b) a series of transfers between the same parties of waste of the same description shall be treated as a single transfer taking place when the first of the transfers in the series takes place.]

(5) The Secretary of State may, by regulations, make provision imposing requirements on any person who is subject to the duty imposed by subsection (1) above as respects the making and retention of documents and the furnishing of documents or copies of documents.

(6) Any person who fails to comply with the duty imposed by subsection (1) or (2A) above or with any requirement imposed under subsection (5) above shall be liable—

(a) on summary conviction, to a fine not exceeding the statutory maximum; and
(b) on conviction on indictment, to a fine.

(7) The Secretary of State shall, after consultation with such persons or bodies as appear to him representative of the interests concerned, prepare and issue a code of practice for

the purpose of providing to persons practical guidance on how to discharge the duty imposed on them by subsection (1) above.

(8) The Secretary of State may from time to time revise a code of practice issued under subsection (7) above by revoking, amending or adding to the provisions of the code.

(9) A code of practice prepared in pursuance of subsection (7) above shall be laid

(a) before both Houses of Parliament; [...].

(10) A code of practice issued under subsection (7) above shall be admissible in evidence and if any provision of such a code appears to the court to be relevant to any question arising in the proceedings it shall be taken into account in determining that question.

(11) Different codes of practice may be prepared and issued under subsection (7) above for different areas.

[34A Fixed penalty notices for certain offences under section 34

(1) This section applies where it appears to an enforcement authority that a person has failed to comply with a duty to furnish documents to that authority imposed under regulations made at any time under section 34(5) above.

(2) The authority may serve on that person a notice offering him the opportunity of discharging any liability to conviction for an offence under section 34(6) above by payment of a fixed penalty.

...

(9) The fixed penalty payable to an enforcement authority under this section is, subject to subsection (10) below, £300.

(10) The appropriate person may by order substitute a different amount for the amount for the time being specified in subsection (9) above.

...

(14) In this section—

...

'enforcement authority' means the Environment Agency or a waste collection authority.]

[34B Power to search and seize vehicles etc

(1) This section applies where an authorised officer of an enforcement authority or a constable reasonably believes that the grounds in subsection (2) or (3) below exist.

(2) The grounds in this subsection are that—

(a) a relevant offence has been committed,

(b) a vehicle was used in the commission of the offence, and

(c) proceedings for the offence have not yet been brought against any person.

(3) The grounds in this subsection are that—

(a) a relevant offence is being or is about to be committed, and

(b) a vehicle is being or is about to be used in the commission of the offence.

(4) The authorised officer or constable may—

(a) search the vehicle;

(b) seize the vehicle and any of its contents.

...

(7) A person commits an offence if—

(a) he fails without reasonable excuse to give any assistance that an authorised officer or constable may reasonably request in the exercise of a power under subsection (4) or (5) above;

(b) he otherwise intentionally obstructs an authorised officer or constable in exercising that power.

(8) Where an authorised officer or constable has stopped a vehicle under subsection (5)(a) above, he may require any occupant of the vehicle to give him—

(a) the occupant's name and address;

(b) the name and address of the registered owner of the vehicle;

(c) any other information he may reasonably request.

(9) A person commits an offence if—

(a) he fails without reasonable excuse to comply with a requirement under subsection (8) above;

(b) he gives information required under that subsection that is—

(i) to his knowledge false or misleading in a material way, or

(ii) given recklessly and is false or misleading in a material way.

(10) A person guilty of an offence under this section is liable on summary conviction to a fine not exceeding level 5 on the standard scale.

(11) In this section and section 34C below—

'authorised officer' means an officer of an enforcement authority who is authorised in writing by the authority for the purposes of this section;

'enforcement authority' means—

(a) the Environment Agency, or

(b) a waste collection authority;

'relevant offence' means—

(a) an offence under section 33 above, or

(b) an offence under section 34 above consisting of a failure to comply with the duty imposed by subsection (1) of that section;

'road' has the same meaning as in the Road Traffic Regulation Act 1984;

'vehicle' means any motor vehicle or trailer within the meaning of that Act or any mobile plant.]

[34C Seizure of vehicles etc: supplementary

...]

35 Waste management licences: general

(1) A waste management licence is a licence granted by a waste regulation authority authorising the treatment, keeping or disposal of any specified description of controlled waste in or on specified land or the treatment or disposal of any specified description of controlled waste by means of specified mobile plant.

(2) A licence shall be granted to the following person, that is to say—

(a) in the case of a licence relating to the treatment, keeping or disposal of waste in or on land, to the person who is in occupation of the land; and

(b) in the case of a licence relating to the treatment or disposal of waste by means of mobile plant, to the person who operates the plant.

(3) A licence shall be granted on such terms and subject to such conditions as appear to the waste regulation authority to be appropriate and the conditions may relate—

(a) to the activities which the licence authorises, and

(b) to the precautions to be taken and works to be carried out in connection with or in consequence of those activities:

and accordingly requirements may be imposed in the licence which are to be complied with before the activities which the licence authorises have begun or after the activities which the licence authorises have ceased.

(4) Conditions may require the holder of a licence to carry out works or do other things notwithstanding that he is not entitled to carry out the works or do the thing and any person whose consent would be required shall grant, or join in granting, the holder of the licence such rights in relation to the land as will enable the holder of the licence to comply with any requirements imposed on him by the licence.

(5) Conditions may relate, where waste other than controlled waste is to be treated, kept or disposed of, to the treatment, keeping or disposal of that other waste.

(6) The Secretary of State may, by regulations, make provision as to the conditions which are, or are not, to be included in a licence; and regulations under this subsection may make different provision for different circumstances.

(7) The Secretary of State may, as respects any licence for which an application is made to a waste regulation authority, give to the authority directions as to the terms and conditions

which are, or are not, to be included in the licence; and it shall be the duty of the authority to give effect to the directions.

[(7A) In any case where—

(a) an entry is required under this section to be made in any record as to the observance of any condition of a licence, and

(b) the entry has not been made, that fact shall be admissible as evidence that that condition has not been observed.

(7B) Any person who—

(a) intentionally makes a false entry in any record required to be kept under any condition of a licence, or

(b) with intent to deceive, forges or uses a licence or makes or has in his possession a document so closely resembling a licence as to be likely to deceive, shall be guilty of an offence.

(7C) A person guilty of an offence under subsection (7B) above shall be liable—

(a) on summary conviction, to a fine not exceeding the statutory maximum;

(b) on conviction on indictment, to a fine or to imprisonment for a term not exceeding two years, or to both.]

(8) It shall be the duty of waste regulation authorities to have regard to any guidance issued to them by the Secretary of State with respect to the discharge of their functions in relation to licences.

(9) A licence may not be surrendered by the holder except in accordance with section 39 below.

(10) A licence is not transferable by the holder but the waste regulation authority may transfer it to another person under section 40 below.

(11) A licence shall continue in force until [it ceases to have effect under subsection (11A) below,] it is revoked entirely by the waste regulation authority under section 38 below or it is surrendered or its surrender is accepted under section 39 below.

[(11A) A licence shall cease to have effect if and to the extent that the treatment, keeping or disposal of waste authorised by the licence is authorised by a permit granted under regulations under section 2 of the Pollution Prevention and Control Act 1999.]

(12) In this Part 'licence' means a waste management licence and 'site licence' and 'mobile plant licence' mean, respectively, a licence authorising the treatment, keeping or disposal of waste in or on land and a licence authorising the treatment or disposal of waste by means of mobile plant.

[35A Compensation where rights granted pursuant to section 35(4) or 38(9A)

(1) This section applies in any case where—

(a) the holder of a licence is required—

(i) by the conditions of the licence; or

(ii) by a requirement imposed under section 38(9) below,

to carry out any works or do any other thing which he is not entitled to carry out or do;

(b) a person whose consent would be required has, pursuant to the requirements of section 35(4) above or 38(9A) below, granted, or joined in granting, to the holder of the licence any rights in relation to any land; and

(c) those rights, or those rights together with other rights, are such as will enable the holder of the licence to comply with any requirements imposed on him by the licence or, as the case may be, under section 38(9) below.

(2) In a case where this section applies, any person who has granted, or joined in granting, the rights in question shall be entitled to be paid compensation under this section by the holder of the licence.

(3) The Secretary of State shall by regulations provide for the discriptions of loss and damage for which compensation is payable under this section.

(4) The Secretary of State may by regulations—

(a) provide for the basis on which any amount to be paid by way of compensation under this section is to be assessed;

(b) without prejudice to the generality of subsection (3) and paragraph (a) above provide for compensation under this section to be payable in respect of—

(i) any effect of any rights being granted, or

(ii) any consequence of the exercise of any rights which have been granted;

(c) provide for the times at which any entitlement to compensation under this secton is to arise or at which any such compensation is to become payable;

(d) provide for the persons or bodies by whom, and the manner in which, any dispute—

(i) as to whether any, and (if so) how much and when, compensation under this section is payable; or

(ii) as to the person to or by whom it shall be paid, is to be determined;

(e) provide for when or how applications may be made for compensation under this section;

(f) without prejudice to the generality of paragraph (d) above, provide for when or how applications may be made for the determination of any such disputes as are mentioned in that paragraph;

(g) without prejudice to the generality of paragraphs (e) and (f) above, prescribe the form in which any such applications as are mentioned in those paragraphs are to be made;

(h) make provision similar to any provision made by paragraph 8 or Schedule 19 to the Water Resources Act 1991;

(j) make different provision for different cases, including different provision in relation to different persons or circumstances;

(k) include such incidental, supplemental, consequential or transitional provision as the Secretary of State considers appropriate.]

36 Grant of licences

(1) An application for a licence shall be made—

(a) in the case of an application for a site licence, to the waste regulation authority in whose area the land is situated; and

(b) in the case of an application for a mobile plant licence, to the waste regulation authority in whose area the operator of the plant has his principal place of business; [and shall be made on a form provided for the purpose by the waste regulation authority and accompanied by such information as that authority reasonably requires and the charge prescribed for the purpose by a charging scheme under section 41 of the Environment Act 1995.

(1A) Where an applicant for a licence fails to provide the waste regulation authority with any information required under subsection (1) above, the authority may refuse to proceed with the application, or refuse to proceed with it until the information is provided.]

(2) A licence shall not be issued for a use of land for which planning permission is required in pursuance of the Town and Country Planning Act 1990 . . . unless—

(a) such planning permission is in force in relation to that use of the land, or

(b) an established use certificate is in force under section 192 of the said Act of 1990 . . . in relation to that use of the land.

(3) Subject to subsection (2) above and subsection (4) below, a waste regulation authority to which an application for a licence has been duly made shall not reject the application if it is satisfied that the applicant is a fit and proper person unless it is satisfied that its rejection is necessary for the purpose of preventing—

(a) pollution of the environment;

(b) harm to human health; or

(c) serious detriment to the amenities of the locality; but paragraph (c) above is inapplicable where planning permission is in force in relation to the use to which the land will be put under the licence.

(4) Where the waste regulation authority proposes to issue a licence, the authority must, before it does so—

(a) refer the proposal to [the appropriate planning authority] and the Health and Safety Executive; and

(b) consider any representations about the proposal which the [authority] or the Executive makes to it during the allowed period.

(5) [...]

(6) [...]

(7) Where any part of the land to be used is within a site of special scientific interest (within the meaning of the Wildlife and Countryside Act 1981) and the waste regulation authority proposes to issue a licence, the authority must, before it does so—

(a) refer the proposal to the appropriate nature conservation body; and

(b) consider any representations about the proposal which the body makes to it during the allowed period;

and in this section any reference to the appropriate nature conservation body is a reference to Natural England . . . or the Countryside Council for Wales, according as the land is situated in England . . . or Wales.

(8) [...]

(9) If within the period of four months beginning with the date on which a waste regulation authority received an application for the grant of a licence, or within such longer period as the authority and the applicant may at any time agree in writing, the authority has neither granted the licence in consequence of the application nor given notice to the applicant that the authority has rejected the application, the authority shall be deemed to have rejected the application.

[(9A) Subsection (9) above—

(a) shall not have effect in any case where, by virtue of subsection (1A) above, the waste regulation authority refuses to proceed with the application in question, and

(b) shall have effect in any case where, by virtue of subsection (1A) above, the waste regulation authority refuses to proceed with it until the required information is provided, with the substitution for the period of four months there mentioned of the period of four months beginning with the date on which the authority received the information.

(10) The period allowed to the appropriate planning authority, the Health and Safety Executive or the appropriate nature conservancy body for the making of representations under subsection (4) or (7) above about a proposal is the period of twenty-eight days beginning with the day on which the proposal is received by the waste regulation authority or such longer period as the waste regulation authority, the appropriate planning authority, the Executive or the body, as the case may be, agree in writing.

(11) In this section—

'the appropriate planning authority' means—

(a) where the relevant land is situated in the area of a London borough council, that London borough council;

(b) where the relevant land is situated in the City of London, the Common Council of the City of London;

(c) where the relevant land is situated in a non-metropolitan county in England, the council of that county;

(d) where the relevant land is situated in a National Park or the Broads, the National Park authority for that National Park or, as the case may be, the Broads Authority;

(e) where the relevant land is situated elsewhere in England or Wales, the council of the district or, in Wales, the county or county borough, in which the land is situated;

(f) ...

'the Broads' has the same meaning as in the Norfolk and Suffolk Broads Act 1988;

'National Park authority', [...] means a National Park authority established under section 63 of the Environment Act 1995 which has become the local planning authority for the National Park in question;

'the relevant land' means—

(a) in relation to a site licence, the land to which the licence relates; and

(b) in relation to a mobile plant licence, the principal place of business of the operator of the plant to which the licence relates.

(12) [...]

(13) The Secretary of State may by regulations amend the definition of 'appropriate planning authority' in subsection (11) above.

(14) This section shall have effect subject to section 36A below.]

[36A Consultation before the grant of certain licences

(1) This section applies where an application for a licence has been duly made to a waste regulation authority, and the authority proposes to issue a licence subject (by virtue of section 35(4) above) to any condition which might require the holder of the licence to—

(a) carry out any works, or

(b) do any other thing, which he might not be entitled to carry out or do.

(2) Before issuing the licence, the waste regulation authority shall serve on every person appearing to the authority to be a person failing within subsection (3) below a notice which complies with the requirements set out in subsection (4) below.

(3) A person falls within this subsection if—

(a) he is the owner, lessee or occupier of any land; and

(b) that land is land in relation to which it is likely that, as a consequence of the licence being issued subject to the condition in question, rights will have to be granted by virtue of section 35(4) above to the holder of the licence.

(4) A notice served under subsection (2) above shall—

(a) set out the condition in question;

(b) indicate the nature of the works or other things which that condition might require the holder of the licence to carry out or do; and

(c) specify the date by which, and the manner in which, any representations relating to the condition or its possible effects are to be made to the waste regulation authority by the person on whom the notice is served.

(5) The date which, pursuant to subsection (4)(c) above, is specified in a notice shall be a date not earlier than the date on which expires the period—

(a) beginning with the date on which the notice is served, and

(b) of such length as may be prescribed in regulations made by the Secretary of State.

(6) Before the waste regulation authority issues the licence it must, subject to subsection (7) below, consider any representations made in relation to the condition in question, or its possible effects, by any person on whom a notice has been served under subsection (2) above.

(7) Subsection (6) above does not require the waste regulation authority to consider any representations made by a person after the date specified in the notice served on him under subsection (2) above as the date by which his representations in relation to the condition or its possible effects are to be made.

(8) In subsection (3) above

'owner', in relation to any land in England and Wales, means the person who—

(a) is for the time being receiving the rack-rent of the land, whether on his own account or as agent or trustee for another person; or

(b) would receive the rack-rent if the land were let at a rack-rent, but does not include a mortgagee not in possession; and

...]

37 Variation of licences

(1) While a licence issued by a waste regulation authority is in force, the authority may, subject to regulations under section 35(6) above and to subsection (3) below,—

(a) on its own initiative, modify the conditions of the licence to any extent which, in the opinion of the authority, is desirable and is unlikely to require unreasonable expense on the part of the holder; and

(b) on the application of the licence holder accompanied by [the charge prescribed for the purpose by a charging scheme under section 41 of the Environment Act 1995,] modify the conditions of his licence to the extent requested in the application.

(2) While a licence issued by a waste regulation authority is in force, the authority shall, except where it revokes the licence entirely under section 38 below, modify the conditions of the licence—

(a) to the extent which in the opinion of the authority is required for the purpose of ensuring that the activities authorised by the licence do not cause pollution of the environment or harm to human health or become seriously detrimental to the amenities of the locality affected by the activities; and

(b) to the extent required by any regulations in force under section 35(6) above.

(3) The Secretary of State may, as respects any licence issued by a waste regulation authority, give to the authority directions as to the modifications which are to be made in the conditions of the licence under subsection (1)(a) or (2)(a) above; and it shall be the duty of the authority to give effect to the directions.

(4) Any modification of a licence under this section shall be effected by notice served on the holder of the licence and the notice shall state the time at which the modification is to take effect.

(5) Section 36(4), [...] (7), [...] and (10) above shall with the necessary modifications apply to a proposal by a waste regulation authority to modify a licence under subsection (1) or (2)(a) above as they apply to a proposal to issue a licence, except that—

(a) the authority may postpone the reference so far as the authority considers that by reason of an emergency it is appropriate to do so; and

(b) the authority need not consider any representations as respects a modification which, in the opinion of the waste regulation authority, will not affect any authority mentioned in the subsections so applied.

(6) If within the period of two months beginning with the date on which a waste regulation authority received an application by the holder of a licence for a modification of it, or within such longer period as the authority and the applicant may at any time agree in writing, the authority has neither granted a modification of the licence in consequence of the application nor given notice to the applicant that the authority has rejected the application, the authority shall be deemed to have rejected the application.

[(7) This section shall have effect subject to section 37A below.]

[37A Consultation before certain variations

(1) This section applies where—

(a) a waste regulation authority proposes to modify a licence under section 37(1) or (2)(a) above; and

(b) the licence, if modified as proposed, would be subject to a relevant new condition.

(2) For the purposes of this section, a 'relevant new condition' is any condition by virtue of which the holder of the licence might be required to carry out any works or do any other thing—

(a) which he might not be entitled to carry out or do, and

(b) which he could not be required to carry out or do by virtue of the conditions to which, prior to the modification, the licence is subject.

(3) Before modifying the licence, the waste regulation authority shall serve on every person appearing to the authority to be a person failing within subsection (4) below a notice which complies with the requirements set out in subsection (5) below.

(4) A person falls within this subsection if—

(a) he is the owner, lessee or occupier of any land; and

(b) that land is land in relation to which it is likely that, as a consequence of the licence being modified so as to be subject to the relevant new condition in question, rights will have to be granted by virtue of section 35(4) above to the holder of the licence.

(5) A notice served under subsection (3) above shall—

(a) set out the relevant new condition in question;

(b) indicate the nature of the works or other things which that condition might require the holder of the licence to carry out or do but which he could not be required to carry out or do by virtue of the conditions (if any) to which, prior to the modification, the licence is subject; and

(c) specify the date by which, and the manner in which, any representations relating to the condition or its possible effects are to be made to the waste regulation authority by the person on whom the notice is served.

(6) The date which, pursuant to subsection (5)(c) above, is specified in a notice shall be a date not earlier than the date on which expires the period—

(a) beginning with the date on which the notice is served, and

(b) of such length as may be prescribed in regulations made by the Secretary of State.

(7) Before the waste regulation authority issues the licence it must, subject to subsection (8) below, consider any representations made in relation to the condition in question, or its possible effects, by any person on whom a notice has been served under subsection (3) above.

(8) Subsection (7) above does not require the waste regulation authority to consider any representations made by a person after the date specified in the notice served on him under subsection (3) above as the date by which his representations in relation to the condition or its possible effects are to be made.

(9) A waste regulation authority may postpone the service of any notice or the consideration of any representations required under the foregoing provisions of this section so far as the authority considers that by reason of an emergency it is appropriate to do so.

(10) In subsection (3) above, 'owner' has the same meaning as it has in subsection (3) of section 36A above by virtue of subsection (8) of that section.]

38 Revocation and suspension of licences

(1) Where a licence granted by a waste regulation authority is in force and it appears to the authority—

(a) that the holder of the licence has ceased to be a fit and proper person by reason of his having been convicted of a relevant offence; or

(b) that the continuation of the activities authorised by the licence would cause pollution of the environment or harm to human health or would be seriously detrimental to the amenities of the locality affected; and

(c) that the pollution, harm or detriment cannot be avoided by modifying the conditions of the licence;

the authority may exercise, as it thinks fit, either of the powers conferred by subsections (3) and (4) below.

(2) Where a licence granted by a waste regulation authority is in force and it appears to the authority that the holder of the licence has ceased to be a fit and proper person by reason of the management of the activities authorised by the licence having ceased to be in the

hands of a technically competent person, the authority may exercise the power conferred by subsection (3) below.

(3) The authority may, under this subsection, revoke the licence so far as it authorises the carrying on of the activities specified in the licence or such of them as the authority specifies in revoking the licence.

(4) The authority may, under this subsection, revoke the licence entirely.

(5) A licence revoked under subsection (3) above shall cease to have effect to authorise the carrying on of the activities specified in the licence or, as the case may be, the activities specified by the authority in revoking the licence but shall not affect the requirements imposed by the licence which the authority, in revoking the licence, specify as requirements which are to continue to bind the licence holder.

(6) Where a licence granted by a waste regulation authority is in force and it appears to the authority—

(a) that the holder of the licence has ceased to be a fit and proper person by reason of the management of the activities authorised by the licence having ceased to be in the hands of a technically competent person; or

(b) that serious pollution of the environment or serious harm to human health has resulted from, or is about to be caused by, the activities to which the licence relates or the happening or threatened happening of an event affecting those activities; and

(c) that the continuing to carry on those activities, or any of those activities, in the circumstances will continue or, as the case may be, cause serious pollution of the environment or serious harm to human health;

the authority may suspend the licence so far as it authorises the carrying on of the activities specified in the licence or such of them as the authority specifies in suspending the licence.

(7) The Secretary of State may, if he thinks fit in relation to a licence granted by a waste regulation authority, give to the authority directions as to whether and in what manner the authority should exercise its powers under this section; and it shall be the duty of the authority to give effect to the directions.

(8) A licence suspended under subsection (6) above shall, while the suspension has effect, be of no effect to authorise the carrying on of the activities specified in the licence or, as the case may be, the activities specified by the authority in suspending the licence.

(9) Where a licence is suspended under subsection (6) above, the authority, in suspending it or at any time while it is suspended, may require the holder of the licence to take such measures to deal with or avert the pollution or harm as the authority considers necessary.

[(9A) A requirement imposed under subsection (9) above may require the holder of a licence to carry out works or do other things notwithstanding that he is not entitled to carry out the works or do the thing and any person whose consent would be required shall grant, or join in granting, the holder of the licence such rights in relation to the land as will enable the holder of the licence to comply with any requirements imposed on him under that subsection.

(9B) Subsections (2) to (8) of section 36A above shall, with the necessary modifications, apply where the authority proposes to impose a requirement under subsection (9) above which may require the holder of a licence to carry out any such works or do any such thing as is mentioned in subsection (9A) above as they apply where the authority proposes to issue a licence subject to any such condition as is mentioned in subsection (1) of that section, but as if—

(a) the reference in subsection (3) of that section to section 35(4) above were a reference to subsection (9A) above; and

(b) any reference in those subsections—

(i) to the condition, or the condition in question, were a reference to the requirement; and

(ii) to issuing a licence were a reference to serving a notice, under subsection (12) below, effecting the requirement.

(9C) The authority may postpone the service of any notice or the consideration of any representations required under section 36A above, as applied by subsection (9B) above, so far as the authority considers that by reason of an emergency it is appropriate to do so.]

(10) A person who, without reasonable excuse, fails to comply with any requirement imposed under subsection (9) above otherwise than in relation to hazardous waste shall be liable—

(a) on summary conviction, to a fine of an amount not exceeding the statutory maximum; and

(b) on conviction on indictment, to imprisonment for a term not exceeding two years or a fine or both.

(11) A person who, without reasonable excuse, fails to comply with any requirement imposed under subsection (9) above in relation to hazardous waste shall be liable—

(a) on summary conviction, to imprisonment for a term not exceeding six months or a fine not exceeding the statutory maximum or both; and

(b) on conviction on indictment, to imprisonment for a term not exceeding five years or a fine or both.

(12) Any revocation or suspension of a licence or requirement imposed during the suspension of a licence under this section shall be effected by notice served on the holder of the licence and the notice shall state the time at which the revocation or suspension or the requirement is to take effect and, in the case of suspension, the period at the end of which, or the event on the occurrence of which, the suspension is to cease.

[(13) If a waste regulation authority is of the opinion that proceedings for an offence under subsection (10) or (11) above would afford an ineffectual remedy against a person who has failed to comply with any requirement imposed under subsection (9) above, the authority may take proceedings in the High Court . . .]

39 Surrender of licences

(1) A licence may be surrendered by its holder to the authority which granted it but, in the case of a site licence, only if the authority accepts the surrender.

(2) The following provisions apply to the surrender and acceptance of the surrender of a site licence.

(3) The holder of a site licence who desires to surrender it shall make an application for that purpose to the authority [on a form provided by the authority for the purpose, giving such information and accompanied by such evidence as the authority reasonably requires and accompanied by the charge prescribed for the purpose by a charging scheme under section 41 of the Environment Act 1995.]

(4) An authority which receives an application for the surrender of a site licence—

(a) shall inspect the land to which the licence relates, and

(b) may require the holder of the licence to furnish to it further information or further evidence.

(5) The authority shall determine whether it is likely or unlikely that the condition of the land, so far as that condition is the result of the use of the land for the treatment, keeping or disposal of waste (whether or not in pursuance of the licence), will cause pollution of the environment or harm to human health.

(6) If the authority is satisfied that the condition of the land is unlikely to cause the pollution or harm mentioned in subsection (5) above, the authority shall, subject to subsection (7) below, accept the surrender of the licence; but otherwise the authority shall refuse to accept it.

(7) Where the authority proposes to accept the surrender of a site licence, the authority must, before it does so,—

(a) refer the proposal to [the appropriate planning authority]; and

(b) consider any representations about the proposal which [the appropriate planning authority] makes to it during the allowed period;

[...]

(8) [...]

(9) Where the surrender of a licence is accepted under this section the authority shall issue to the applicant, with the notice of its determination, a certificate (a 'certificate of completion') stating that it is satisfied as mentioned in subsection (6) above and, on the issue of that certificate, the licence shall cease to have effect.

(10) If within the period of three months beginning with the date on which an authority receives an application to surrender a licence, or within such longer period as the authority and the applicant may at any time agree in writing, the authority has neither issued a certificate of completion nor given notice to the applicant that the authority has rejected the application, the authority shall be deemed to have rejected the application.

(11) Section 36(10) above applies for the interpretation of the 'allowed period' in [subsection (7) above].

[(12) In this section—

'the appropriate planning authority' means—

(a) where the relevant land is situated in the area of a London borough council, that London borough council;

(b) where the relevant land is situated in the City of London, the Common Council of the City of London;

(c) where the relevant land is situated in a non-metropolitan county in England, the council of that county;

(d) where the relevant land is situated in a National Park or the Broads, the National Park authority for that National Park or, as the case may be, the Broads Authority;

(e) where the relevant land is situated elsewhere in England or Wales, the council of the district or, in Wales, the county or county borough, in which the land is situated;

(f) ...

'the Broads' has the same meaning as in the Norfolk and Suffolk Broads Act 1988;

'National Park authority', subject to subsection (13) below, means a National Park authority established under section 63 of the Environment Act 1995 which has become the local planning authority for the National Park in question;

'the relevant land', in the case of any site licence, means the land to which the licence relates.

(13) As respects any period before a National Park authority established under section 63 of the Environment Act 1995 in relation to a National Park becomes the local planning authority for that National Park, any reference in this section to a National Park authority shall be taken as a reference to the National Park Committee or joint or special planning board for that National Park.

(14) The Secretary of State may by regulations amend the definition of 'appropriate planning authority' in subsection (12) above.]

40 Transfer of licences

(1) A licence may be transferred to another person in accordance with subsections (2) to (6) below and may be so transferred whether or not the licence is partly revoked or suspended under any provision of this Part.

(2) Where the holder of a licence desires that the licence be transferred to another person ('the proposed transferee') the licence holder and the proposed transferee shall jointly make an application to the waste regulation authority which granted the licence for a transfer of it.

(3) An application under subsection (2) above for the transfer of a licence shall be made [on a form provided by the authority for the purpose, accompanied by such information as the authority may reasonably require, the charge prescribed for the purpose by a charging scheme under section 41 of the Environment Act 1995] and the licence.

(4) If, on such an application, the authority is satisfied that the proposed transferee is a fit and proper person the authority shall effect a transfer of the licence to the proposed transferee.

(5) The authority shall effect a transfer of a licence under the foregoing provisions of this section by causing the licence to be endorsed with the name and other particulars of the proposed transferee as the holder of the licence from such date specified in the endorsement as may be agreed with the applicants.

(6) If within the period of two months beginning with the date on which the authority receives an application for the transfer of a licence, or within such longer period as the authority and the applicants may at any time agree in writing, the authority has neither effected a transfer of the licence nor given notice to the applicants that the authority has rejected the application, the authority shall be deemed to have rejected the application.

42 Supervision of licensed activities

(1) While a licence is in force it shall be the duty of the waste regulation authority which granted the licence to take the steps needed—

(a) for the purpose of ensuring that the activities authorised by the licence do not cause pollution of the environment or harm to human health or become seriously detrimental to the amenities of the locality affected by the activities; and

(b) for the purpose of ensuring that the conditions of the licence are complied with.

(2) [...]

(3) For the purpose of performing the duty imposed on it by subsection (1) above, any officer of the authority authorised in writing for the purpose by the authority may, if it appears to him that by reason of an emergency it is necessary to do so, carry out work on the land or in relation to plant or equipment on the land to which the licence relates or, as the case may be, in relation to the mobile plant to which the licence relates.

(4) Where a waste regulation authority incurs any expenditure by virtue of subsection (3) above, the authority may recover the amount of the expenditure from [the holder, or (as the case may be) the former holder, of the licence] except where the holder or former holder of the licence shows that there was no emergency requiring any work or except such of the expenditure as he shows was unnecessary.

(5) Where it appears to a waste regulation authority that a condition of a licence granted by it is not being complied with, [or is likely not to be complied with,] then, without prejudice to any proceedings under section 33(6) above, the authority may—

[(a) serve on the holder of the licence a notice—

(i) stating that the authority is of the opinion that a condition of the licence is not being complied with or, as the case may be, is likely not to be complied with;

(ii) specifying the matters which constitute the non-compliance or, as the case may be, which make the anticipated non-compliance likely;

(iii) specifying the steps which must be taken to remedy the non-compliance or, as the case may be, to prevent the anticipated non-compliance from occurring; and

(iv) specifying the period within which those steps must be taken; and]

(b) if in the opinion of the authority the licence holder [has not taken the steps specified in the notice within the period so specified,] exercise any of the powers specified in subsection (6) below.

(6) The powers which become exercisable in the event mentioned in subsection (5)(b) above are the following—

(a) to revoke the licence so far as it authorises the carrying on of the activities specified in the licence or such of them as the authority specifies in revoking the licence;

(b) to revoke the licence entirely; and

(c) to suspend the licence so far as it authorises the carrying on of the activities specified in the licence or, as the case may be, the activities specified by the authority in suspending the licence.

[(6A) If a waste regulation authority is of the opinion that revocation or suspension of the licence, whether entirely or to any extent, under subsection (6) above would afford an ineffectual remedy against a person who has failed to comply with any requirement imposed under subsection (5)(a) above, the authority may take proceedings in the High Court... for the purpose of securing compliance with the requirement.]

(7) Where a licence is revoked or suspended under subsection (6) above, [subsections (5) and (12) or, as the case may be, subsections (8) to (12) of section 38] above shall apply with the necessary modifications as they respectively apply to revocations or suspensions of licences under that section; [...]

(8) The Secretary of State may, if he thinks fit in relation to a licence granted by a waste regulation authority, give to the authority directions as to whether and in what manner the authority should exercise its powers under this section; and it shall be the duty of the authority to give effect to the directions.

43 Appeals to Secretary of State from decisions with respect to licences

(1) Where, except in pursuance of a direction given by the Secretary of State,—

(a) an application for a licence or a modification of the conditions of a licence is rejected;

(b) a licence is granted subject to conditions;

(c) the conditions of a licence are modified;

(d) a licence is suspended;

(e) a licence is revoked under section 38 or 42 above;

(f) an application to surrender a licence is rejected; or

(g) an application for the transfer of a licence is rejected;

then, except in the case of an application for a transfer, the applicant for the licence or, as the case may be, the holder or former holder of it may appeal from the decision to the Secretary of State and, in the case of an application for a transfer, the proposed transferee may do so.

(2) Where an appeal is made to the Secretary of State—

[...]

(a) [...]

(b) [...]

(c) if a party to the appeal so requests, or the Secretary of State so decides, the appeal shall be or continue in the form of a hearing (which may, if the person hearing the appeal so decides, be held or held to any extent in private).

[(2A) This section is subject to section 114 of the Environment Act 1995 (delegation or reference of appeals etc).]

(3) Where, on such an appeal, the Secretary of State or other person determining the appeal determines that the decision of the authority shall be altered it shall be the duty of the authority to give effect to the determination.

(4) While an appeal is pending in a case falling within subsection (1)(c) or (e) above, the decision in question shall, subject to subsection (6) below, be ineffective; and if the appeal is dismissed or withdrawn the decision shall become effective from the end of the day on which the appeal is dismissed or withdrawn.

(5) Where an appeal is made in a case falling within subsection (1)(d) above, the bringing of the appeal shall have no effect on the decision in question.

(6) Subsection (4) above shall not apply to a decision modifying the conditions of a licence under section 37 above or revoking a licence under section 38 or 42 above in the case of which the notice effecting the modification or revocation includes a statement that in the opinion of the authority it is necessary for the purpose of preventing or, where that is not

practicable, minimising pollution of the environment or harm to human health that that subsection should not apply.

(7) Where the decision under appeal is one falling within subsection (6) above or is a decision to suspend a licence, if, on the application of the holder or former holder of the licence, the Secretary of State or other person determining the appeal determines that the authority acted unreasonably in excluding the application of subsection (4) above or, as the case may be, in suspending the licence, then—

(a) if the appeal is still pending at the end of the day on which the determination is made, subsection (4) above shall apply to the decision from the end of that day; and

(b) the holder or former holder of the licence shall be entitled to recover compensation from the authority in respect of any loss suffered by him in consequence of the exclusion of the application of that subsection or the suspension of the licence;

and any dispute as to a person's entitlement to such compensation or as to the amount of it shall be determined by arbitration or in Scotland by a single arbiter appointed, in default of agreement between the parties concerned, by the Secretary of State on the application of any of the parties.

(8) Provision may be made by the Secretary of State by regulations with respect to appeals under this section and in particular—

(a) as to the period within which and the manner in which appeals are to be brought; and

(b) as to the manner in which appeals are to be considered.

[44 Offences of making false or misleading statements or false entries

(1) A person who—

(a) in purported compliance with a requirement to furnish any information imposed by or under any provision of this Part, or

(b) for the purpose of obtaining for himself or another any grant of a licence, any modification of the conditions of a licence, any acceptance of the surrender of a licence or any transfer of a licence,

makes a statement which he knows to be false or misleading in a material particular, or recklessly makes any statement which is false or misleading in a material particular, commits an offence.

(2) A person who intentionally makes a false entry in any record required to be kept by virtue of a licence commits an offence.

(3) A person who commits an offence under this section shall be liable—

(a) on summary conviction, to a fine not exceeding the statutory maximum;

(b) on conviction on indictment, to a fine or to imprisonment for a term not exceeding two years, or to both.]

[44A National waste strategy: England and Wales

(1) The Secretary of State shall as soon as possible prepare a statement ('the strategy') containing his policies in relation to the recovery and disposal of waste in England and Wales.

(2) The strategy shall consist of or include—

(a) a statement which relates to the whole of England and Wales; or

(b) two or more statements which between them relate to the whole of England and Wales.

(3) The Secretary of State may from time to time modify the strategy.

(4) Without prejudice to the generality of what may be included in the strategy, the strategy must include—

(a) a statement of the Secretary of State's policies for attaining the objectives specified in Schedule 2A to this Act;

(b) provisions relating to each of the following, that is to say—
(i) the type, quantity and origin of waste to be recovered or disposed of;
(ii) general technical requirements; and
(iii) any special requirements for particular wastes.

(5) In preparing the strategy or any modification of it, the Secretary of State—
(a) shall consult the Environment Agency,
(b) shall consult—
(i) such bodies or persons appearing to him to be representative of the interests of local government, and
(ii) such bodies or persons appearing to him to be representative of the interests of industry,
as he may consider appropriate, and
(c) may consult such other bodies or persons as he considers appropriate,

(6) Without prejudice to any power to give directions conferred by section 38 of the Environment Act 1995, the Secretary of State may give directions to the Environment Agency requiring it—
(a) to advise him on the policies which are to be included in the strategy;
(b) to carry out a survey of or investigation into—
(i) the kinds or quantities of waste which it appears to that Agency is likely to be situated in England and Wales,
(ii) the facilities which are or appear to that Agency likely to be available or needed in England and Wales for recovering or disposing of any such waste,
(iii) any other matter upon which the Secretary of State wishes to be informed in connection with his preparation of the strategy or any modification of it,
and to report its findings to him.

(7) A direction under subsection (6)(b) above—
(a) shall specify or describe the matters or the areas which are to be the subject of the survey or investigation; and
(b) may make provision in relation to the manner in which—
(i) the survey or investigation is to be carried out, or
(ii) the findings are to be reported or made available to other persons.

(8) Where a direction is given under subsection (6)(b), the Environment Agency shall, in accordance with any requirement of the direction,—
(a) before carrying out the survey or investigation, consult—
(i) such bodies or persons appearing to it to be representative of local planning authorities, and
(ii) such bodies or persons appearing to it to be representative of the interests of industry,
as it may consider appropriate; and
(b) make its findings available to those authorities.

(9) In this section—
'local planning authority' has the same meaning as in the Town and Country Planning Act 1990;
'strategy' includes the strategy as modified from time to time and 'statement' shall be construed accordingly.

(10) This section makes provision for the purpose of implementing Article 7 of the directive of the Council of the European Communities, dated 15th July 1975, on waste, as amended by—
(a) the directive of that Council, dated 18th March 1991, amending directive 75/442/EEC on waste; and
(b) the directive of that Council, dated 23rd December 1991, standardising and rationalising reports on the implementation of certain Directives relating to the environment.

44B ...]

45 Collection of controlled waste

(1) It shall be the duty of each waste collection authority—

(a) to arrange for the collection of household waste in its area except waste

(i) which is situated at a place which in the opinion of the authority is so isolated or inaccessible that the cost of collecting it would be unreasonably high, and

(ii) as to which the authority is satisfied that adequate arrangements for its disposal have been or can reasonably be expected to be made by a person who controls the waste; and

(b) if requested by the occupier of premises in its area to collect any commercial waste from the premises, to arrange for the collection of the waste.

(2) Each waste collection authority may, if requested by the occupier of premises in its area to collect any industrial waste from the premises, arrange for the collection of the waste; but a collection authority in England and Wales shall not exercise the power except with the consent of the waste disposal authority whose area includes the area of the waste collection authority.

(3) No charge shall be made for the collection of household waste except in cases prescribed in regulations made by the Secretary of State; and in any of those cases—

(a) the duty to arrange for the collection of the waste shall not arise until a person who controls the waste requests the authority to collect it; and

(b) the authority may recover a reasonable charge for the collection of the waste from the person who made the request.

(4) A person at whose request waste other than household waste is collected under this section shall be liable to pay a reasonable charge for the collection and disposal of the waste to the authority which arranged for its collection; and it shall be the duty of that authority to recover the charge unless in the case of a charge in respect of commercial waste the authority considers it inappropriate to do so.

(5) It shall be the duty of each waste collection authority—

(a) to make such arrangements for the emptying, without charge, of privies serving one or more private dwellings in its area as the authority considers appropriate;

(b) if requested by the person who controls a cesspool serving only one or more private dwellings in its area to empty the cesspool, to remove such of the contents of the cesspool as the authority considers appropriate on payment, if the authority so requires, of a reasonable charge.

(6) A waste collection authority may, if requested by the person who controls any other privy or cesspool in its area to empty the privy or cesspool, empty the privy or, as the case may be, remove from the cesspool such of its contents as the authority consider appropriate on payment, if the authority so requires, of a reasonable charge.

(7) A waste collection authority may—

(a) construct, lay and maintain, within or outside its area, pipes and associated works for the purpose of collecting waste;

(b) contribute towards the cost incurred by another person in providing or maintaining pipes or associated works connecting with pipes provided by the authority under paragraph (a) above.

(8) A waste collection authority may contribute towards the cost incurred by another person in providing or maintaining plant or equipment intended to deal with commercial or industrial waste before it is collected under arrangements made by the authority under subsection (1)(b) or (2) above.

(9) Subject to section 48(1) below, anything collected under arrangements made by a waste collection authority under this section shall belong to the authority and may be dealt with accordingly.

(10) ...

(11) ...

(12) In this section 'privy' means a latrine which has a moveable receptacle and 'cesspool' includes a settlement tank or other tank for the reception or disposal of foul matter from buildings.

[45A Arrangements for separate collection of recyclable waste

(1) This section applies to any waste collection authority whose area is in England (an 'English waste collection authority').

(2) Where an English waste collection authority has a duty by virtue of section 45(1)(a) above to arrange for the collection of household waste from any premises, the authority shall ensure that the arrangements it makes in relation to those premises include the arrangements mentioned in subsection (3) below, unless it is satisfied that (in that case)—

(a) the cost of doing so would be unreasonably high; or

(b) comparable alternative arrangements are available.

(3) The arrangements are arrangements for the collection of at least two types of recyclable waste together or individually separated from the rest of the household waste.

(4) The requirement in subsection (2) above shall apply from 31st December 2010.

(5) The Secretary of State may, if requested to do so by an English waste collection authority, direct the authority that subsection (4) above shall have effect in relation to that authority as if the date mentioned there were such later date as may be specified in the direction (being a date no later than 31st December 2015).

(6) In this section, 'recyclable waste means household waste which is capable of being recycled or composted.'

45B ...]

46 Receptacles for household waste

(1) Where a waste collection authority has a duty by virtue of section 45(1)(a) above to arrange for the collection of household waste from any premises, the authority may, by notice served on him, require the occupier to place the waste for collection in receptacles of a kind and number specified.

(2) The kind and number of the receptacles required under subsection (1) above to be used shall be such only as are reasonable but, subject to that, separate receptacles or compartments of receptacles may be required to be used for waste which is to be recycled and waste which is not.

(3) In making requirements under subsection (1) above the authority may, as respects the provision of the receptacles—

(a) determine that they be provided by the authority free of charge;

(b) propose that they be provided, if the occupier agrees, by the authority on payment by him of such a single payment or such periodical payments as he agrees with the authority;

(c) require the occupier to provide them if he does not enter into an agreement under paragraph (b) above within a specified period; or

(d) require the occupier to provide them.

(4) In making requirements as respects receptacles under subsection (1) above, the authority may, by the notice under that subsection, make provision with respect to—

(a) the size, construction and maintenance of the receptacles;

(b) the placing of the receptacles for the purpose of facilitating the emptying of them, and access to the receptacles for that purpose;

(c) the placing of the receptacles for that purpose on highways ...

(d) the substances or articles which may or may not be put into the receptacles or compartments of receptacles of any description and the precautions to be taken where particular substances or articles are put into them; and

(e) the steps to be taken by occupiers of premises to facilitate the collection of waste from the receptacles.

(5) No requirement shall be made under subsection (1) above for receptacles to be placed on a highway or, as the case may be, road, unless—

(a) the relevant highway authority or roads authority have given their consent to their being so placed; and

(b) arrangements have been made as to the liability for any damage arising out of their being so placed.

(6) person who fails, without reasonable excuse, to comply with any requirements imposed under subsection (1), (3)(c) or (d) or (4) above shall be liable on summary conviction to a fine not exceeding level 3 on the standard scale.

(7) Where an occupier is required under subsection (1) above to provide any receptacles he may, within the period allowed by subsection (8) below, appeal to a magistrates' court . . . against any requirement imposed under subsection (1), subsection (3)(c) or (d) or (4) above on the ground that—

(a) the requirement is unreasonable; or

(b) the receptacles in which household waste is placed for collection from the premises are adequate.

(8) The period allowed to the occupier of premises for appealing against such a requirement is the period of twenty-one days beginning—

(a) in a case where a period was specified under subsection (3)(c) above, with the end of that period; and

(b) where no period was specified, with the day on which the notice making the requirement was served on him.

(9) Where an appeal against a requirement is brought under subsection (7) above—

(a) the requirement shall be of no effect pending the determination of the appeal;

(b) the court shall either quash or modify the requirement or dismiss the appeal; and

(c) no question as to whether the requirement is, in any respect, unreasonable shall be entertained in any proceedings for an offence under subsection (6) above.

(10) In this section—

'receptacle' includes a holder for receptacles; and

'specified' means specified in a notice under subsection (1) above.

47 Receptacles for commercial or industrial waste

(1) A waste collection authority may, at the request of any person, supply him with receptacles for commercial or industrial waste which he has requested the authority to arrange to collect and shall make a reasonable charge for any receptacle supplied unless in the case of a receptacle for commercial waste the authority considers it appropriate not to make a charge.

(2) If it appears to a waste collection authority that there is likely to be situated, on any premises in its area, commercial waste or industrial waste of a kind which, if the waste is not stored in receptacles of a particular kind, is likely to cause a nuisance or to be detrimental to the amenities of the locality, the authority may, by notice served on him, require the occupier of the premises to provide at the premises receptacles for the storage of such waste of a kind and number specified.

(3) The kind and number of the receptacles required under subsection (2) above to be used shall be such only as are reasonable.

(4) In making requirements as respects receptacles under subsection (2) above, the authority may, by the notice under that subsection, make provision with respect to—

(a) the size, construction and maintenance of the receptacles;

(b) the placing of the receptacles for the purpose of facilitating the emptying of them, and access to the receptacles for that purpose;

(c) the placing of the receptacles for that purpose on highways . . .

(d) the substances or articles which may or may not be put into the receptacles and the precautions to be taken where particular substances or articles are put into them; and

(e) the steps to be taken by occupiers of premises to facilitate the collection of waste from the receptacles.

(5) No requirement shall be made under subsection (2) above for receptacles to be placed on a highway . . . unless—

(a) the relevant highway authority . . . have given their consent to their being so placed; and

(b) arrangements have been made as to the liability for any damage arising out of their being so placed.

(6) A person who fails, without reasonable excuse, to comply with any requirements imposed under subsection (2) or (4) above shall be liable on summary conviction to a fine not exceeding level 3 on the standard scale.

(7) Where an occupier is required under subsection (2) above to provide any receptacles he may, within the period allowed by subsection (8) below, appeal to a magistrates' court . . . against any requirement imposed under subsection (2) or (4) above on the ground that—

(a) the requirement is unreasonable; or

(b) the waste is not likely to cause a nuisance or be detrimental to the amenities of the locality.

(8) The period allowed to the occupier of premises for appealing against such a requirement is the period of twenty-one days beginning with the day on which the notice making the requirement was served on him.

(9) Where an appeal against a requirement is brought under subsection (7) above—

(a) the requirement shall be of no effect pending the determination of the appeal; and

(b) the court shall either quash or modify the requirement or dismiss the appeal; and

(c) no question as to whether the requirement is, in any respect, unreasonable shall be entertained in any proceedings for an offence under subsection (6) above.

(10) In this section—

'receptacle' includes a holder for receptacles; and

'specified' means specified in a notice under subsection (2) above.

[47ZA Fixed penalty notices for offences under sections 46 and 47

(1) This section applies where on any occasion an authorised officer of a waste collection authority has reason to believe that a person has committed an offence under section 46 or 47 above in the area of that authority.

(2) The authorised officer may give that person a notice offering him the opportunity of discharging any liability to conviction for the offence by payment of a fixed penalty to the waste collection authority.

. . .]

[47ZB Amount of fixed penalty under section 47ZA

(1) This section applies in relation to a fixed penalty payable to a waste collection authority in pursuance of a notice under section 47ZA above.

(2) The amount of the fixed penalty—

(a) is the amount specified by the waste collection authority in relation to the authority's area, or

(b) if no amount is so specified, is £100.

. . .

(6) The appropriate person may by order substitute a different amount for the amount for the time being specified in subsection (2)(b) above.]

[47A Recycling and composting: duty to report to Parliament

(1) Not later than 31st October 2004, the Secretary of State shall lay before each House of Parliament a report of the performance—

(a) of each English waste authority in meeting its recycling and composting standards (if any); and

(b) of each English waste collection authority towards meeting the requirement imposed by section 45A(2) above.

(2) In this section—

'English waste authority' means a waste collection authority or a waste disposal authority whose area is in England;

'English waste collection authority' means a waste collection authority whose area is in England; and

'recycling and composting standards' means, in relation to an English waste authority, such performance standards and performance indicators (if any) as may be specified for that authority in an order made under section 4 of the Local Government Act 1999 in connection with the recycling and composting of household waste.]

48 Duties of waste collection authorities as respects disposal of waste collected

(1) Subject to subsections (2) and (6) below, it shall be the duty of each waste collection authority to deliver for disposal all waste which is collected by the authority under section 45 above to such places as the waste disposal authority for its area directs.

[(1A) A waste collection authority in England which is not also a waste disposal authority must discharge its duty under subsection (1) above in accordance with any directions about separation of waste given by the waste disposal authority for its area.]

(2) The duty imposed on a waste collection authority by subsection (1) above does not, except in cases falling within subsection (4) below, apply as respects household waste or commercial waste for which the authority decides to make arrangements for recycling the waste; and the authority shall have regard, in deciding what recycling arrangements to make, to its waste recycling plan under section 49 below.

(3) A waste collection authority which decides to make arrangements under subsection (2) above for recycling waste collected by it shall, as soon as reasonably practicable, by notice in writing, inform the waste disposal authority for the area which includes its area of the arrangements which it proposes to make.

(4) Where a waste disposal authority has made arrangements, as respects household waste or commercial waste in its area or any part of its area, to recycle the waste, or any of it, the waste disposal authority may, by notice served on the waste collection authority, object to the waste collection authority having the waste recycled; and the objection may be made as respects all the waste, part only of the waste or specified descriptions of the waste.

(5) Where an objection is made under subsection (4) above, subsection (2) above shall not be available to the waste collection authority to the extent objected to.

(6) A waste collection authority may provide plant and equipment for the sorting and baling of waste retained by the authority under subsection (2) above.

(8) A waste collection authority may permit another person to use facilities provided by the authority under subsection (6) above and may provide for the use of another person any such facilities as the authority has power to provide under that subsection; and—

(a) subject to paragraph (b) below, it shall be the duty of the authority to make a reasonable charge in respect of the use by another person of the facilities, unless the authority considers it appropriate not to make a charge;

(b) no charge shall be made under this subsection in respect of household waste; and

(c) anything delivered to the authority by another person in the course of using the facilities shall belong to the authority and may be dealt with accordingly.

(9) . . .

49 [...]

51 Functions of waste disposal authorities

(1) It shall be the duty of each waste disposal authority to arrange—

(a) for the disposal of the controlled waste collected in its area by the waste collection authorities; and

(b) for places to be provided at which persons resident in its area may deposit their household waste and for the disposal of waste so deposited.

(2) The arrangements made by a waste disposal authority under subsection (1)(b) above shall be such as to secure that—

(a) each place is situated either within the area of the authority or so as to be reasonably accessible to persons resident in its area;

(b) each place is available for the deposit of waste at all reasonable times (including at least one period on the Saturday or following day of each week except a week in which the Saturday is 25th December or 1st January);

(c) each place is available for the deposit of waste free of charge by persons resident in the area;

but the arrangements may restrict the availability of specified places to specified descriptions of waste.

(3) A waste disposal authority may include in arrangements made under subsection (1)(b) above arrangements for the places provided for its area for the deposit of household waste free of charge by residents in its area to be available for the deposit of household or other controlled waste by other persons on such terms as to payment (if any) as the authority determines.

(4) For the purpose of discharging its duty under subsection (1)(a) above as respects controlled waste collected as mentioned in that paragraph a waste disposal authority—

(a) shall give directions to the waste collection authorities within its area as to the persons to whom and places at which such waste is to be delivered;

(b)–(d) [...]

(e) may contribute towards the cost incurred by persons who produce commercial or industrial waste in providing and maintaining plant or equipment intended to deal with such waste before it is collected; and

(f) may contribute towards the cost incurred by persons who produce commercial or industrial waste in providing or maintaining pipes or associated works connecting with pipes provided by a waste collection authority within the area of the waste disposal authority.

[(4A) A waste disposal authority in England which is not also a waste collection authority may in directions under subsection (4)(a) above include requirements about separation that relate to waste as delivered, but may do so only if it considers it necessary for assisting it to comply with any obligation imposed on it by or under any enactment.

(4B) Before exercising its power to include requirements about separation in directions under subsection (4)(a) above, a a waste disposal authority shall consult the waste collection authorities within its area.

(4C) In exercising its power to include requirements about separation in directions under subsection (4)(a) above, a waste disposal authority shall have regard to any guidance given by the Secretary of State as to the exercise of that power.

(4D) A waste disposal authority which includes requirements about separation in directions given under subsection (4)(a) above shall notify the waste collection authorities to which the directions are given of its reasons for including the requirements.]

(5)–(6) [...]

(7) Subsection (1) above is subject to section 77.

(8) ...

52 Payments for recycling and disposal etc. of waste

(1) Where, under section 48(2) above, a waste collection authority retains for recycling waste collected by it under section 45 above, the waste disposal authority for the area which includes the area of the waste collection authority shall make to that authority payments, in respect of the waste so retained—

[(a) in the case of a waste disposal authority in England, of such amounts as may be determined in accordance with regulations made by the Secretary of State; and

(b) in the case of a waste disposal authority in Wales],

of such amounts representing its net saving of expenditure on the disposal of the waste as the authority determines.

[(1A) The Secretary of State may by order disapply subsection (1) above in relation to any waste disposal authority constituted under section 10 of the Local Government Act 1985 (joint arrangements for waste disposal in London and metropolitan counties).]

[(1B) A waste disposal authority is not required to make payments to a waste collection authority under subsection (1) above where, on the basis of arrangements involving the two authorities, the waste collection authority has agreed that such payments need not be made.]

(2) Where, by reason of the discharge by a waste disposal authority of its functions, waste arising in its area does not fall to be collected by a waste collection authority under section 45 above, the waste collection authority shall make to the waste disposal authority payments, in respect of the waste not falling to be so collected—

[(a) in the case of a waste collection authority in England, of such amounts as may be determined in accordance with regulations made by the Secretary of State; and

(b) in the case of a waste collection authority in Wales],

of such amounts representing its net saving of expenditure on the collection of the waste as the authority determines.

(3) Where a person other than a waste collection authority, for the purpose of recycling it, collects waste arising in the area of a waste disposal authority which would fall to be collected under section 45 above, the waste disposal authority may make to that person payments, in respect of the waste so collected—

[(a) in the case of a waste disposal authority in England, of such amounts as may be determined in accordance with regulations made by the Secretary of State; and

(b) in the case of a waste disposal authority in Wales],

of such amounts representing its net saving of expenditure on the disposal of the waste as the authority determines.

(4) Where a person other than a waste collection authority, for the purpose of recycling it, collects waste which would fall to be collected under section 45 above, the waste collection authority may make to that person payments, in respect of the waste so collected—

[(a) in the case of a waste collection authority in England, of such amounts as may be determined in accordance with regulations made by the Secretary of State; and

(b) in the case of a waste collection authority in Wales],

of such amounts representing its net saving of expenditure on the collection of the waste as the authority determines.

[(4A) The Secretary of State may by regulations impose on waste disposal authorities in England a duty to make payments corresponding to the payments which are authorised by subsection (3)(a) above to such persons in such circumstances and in respect of such descriptions or quantities of waste as are specified in the regulations.]

(5) The Secretary of State may, by regulations, impose on waste disposal authorities [in Wales] a duty to make payments corresponding to the payments which are authorised by [subsection (3)(b)] above to such persons in such circumstances and in respect of such descriptions or quantities of waste as are specified in the regulations.

(6) For the purposes of [subsections (1)(b), (3)(b)] and (5) above the net saving of expenditure of a waste disposal authority on the disposal of any waste retained or collected

for recycling is the amount of the expenditure which the authority would, but for the retention or collection, have incurred in having it disposed of less any amount payable by the authority to any person in consequence of the retention or collection for recycling (instead of the disposal) of the waste.

(7) For the purposes of [subsections (2)(b) and (4)(b)] above the net saving of expenditure of a waste collection authority on the collection of any waste not falling to be collected by it is the amount of the expenditure which the authority would, if it had had to collect the waste, have incurred in collecting it.

(8) The Secretary of State shall, by regulations, make provision for the determination of the net saving of expenditure for the purposes of subsections [subsections (1)(b), (2)(b), (3)(b), (4)(b)] and (5) above.

[(8A) The Secretary of State may give guidance—

(a) to a waste disposal authority in England, for the purposes of determining whether to exercise the power in subsection (3) above;

(b) to a waste collection authority in England, for the purposes of determining whether to exercise the power in subsection (4) above.]

(9) A waste disposal authority shall be entitled to receive from a waste collection authority such sums as are needed to reimburse the waste disposal authority the reasonable cost of making arrangements under section 51(1) above for the disposal of commercial and industrial waste collected in the area of the waste disposal authority.

(10) A waste disposal authority shall pay to a waste collection authority a reasonable contribution towards expenditure reasonably incurred by the waste collection authority in delivering waste, in pursuance of a direction under section 51(4)(a) above, to a place which is unreasonably far from the waste collection authority's area.

(11) Any question arising under subsection (9) or (10) above shall, in default of agreement between the two authorities in question, be determined by arbitration.

[(12) In this section, references to recycling waste include re-using it (whether or not the waste is subjected to any process).]

[52A Payments for delivering waste pre-separated

(1) A waste disposal authority in England which is not also a waste collection authority shall pay to a waste collection authority within its area such amounts as are needed to ensure that the collection authority is not financially worse off as a result of having to comply with any separation requirements.

(2) A waste disposal authority in England which is not also a waste collection authority may pay to a waste collection authority within its area—

(a) which performs its duty under section 48(1) above by delivering waste in a state of separation, but

(b) which is not subject to any separation requirements as respects the delivery of that waste,

contributions of such amounts as the disposal authority may determine towards expenditure of the collection authority that is attributable to its delivering the waste in that state.

(3) The Secretary of State may by regulations make provision about how amounts to be paid under subsection (1) above are to be determined.

(4) Regulations under subsection (3) above may include provision for amounts to be less than they would otherwise be (or to be nil) if conditions specified in the regulations are not satisfied.

(5) Any question arising under subsection (1) above shall, in default of agreement between the paying and receiving authorities, be determined by arbitration.

(6) A waste collection authority in England which is not also a waste disposal authority shall supply the waste disposal authority for its area with such information as the disposal authority may reasonably require—

(a) for the purpose of determining amounts under this section, or

(b) for the purpose of estimating any amounts that would fall to be determined under this section were the collection authority to be subject to particular separation requirements.

(7) In this section 'separation requirements', in relation to a waste collection authority, means requirements about separation included in directions given to it under section 51 (4)(a) above.]

55 Powers for recycling waste

(1) This section has effect for conferring on waste disposal authorities and waste collection authorities powers for the purposes of recycling waste.

(2) A waste disposal authority may—

(a) make arrangements to recycle waste as respects which the authority has duties under section 51(1) above or agrees with another person for its disposal or treatment;

(b) make arrangements to use waste for the purpose of producing from it heat or electricity or both;

(c) buy or otherwise acquire waste with a view to its being recycled;

(d) use, sell or otherwise dispose of waste as respects which the authority has duties under section 51(1) above or anything produced from such waste.

(3) A waste collection authority may—

(a) buy or otherwise acquire waste with a view to recycling it;

(b) use, or dispose of by way of sale or otherwise to another person, waste belonging to the authority or anything produced from such waste.

(4)...

57 Power of Secretary of State to require waste to be accepted, treated, disposed of or delivered

(1) The Secretary of State may, by notice in writing, direct the holder of any waste management licence or waste permit to accept and keep, or accept and treat or dispose of, waste at specified places on specified terms.

(2) The Secretary of State may, by notice in writing, direct any person who is keeping waste on any land to deliver the waste to a specified person on specified terms with a view to its being treated or disposed of by that other person.

(3) A direction under this section may impose a requirement as respects waste of any specified kind or as respects any specified consignment of waste.

(4) A direction under subsection (2) above may require the person who is directed to deliver the waste to pay to the specified person his reasonable costs of treating or disposing of the waste.

(5) A person who fails, without reasonable excuse, to comply with a direction under this section shall be liable on summary conviction to a fine not exceeding level 5 on the standard scale.

(6) A person shall not be guilty of an offence under any other enactment prescribed by the Secretary of State by regulations made for the purposes of this subsection by reason only of anything necessarily done or omitted in order to comply with a direction under this section.

(7) The Secretary of State may, where the costs of the treatment or disposal of waste are not paid or not fully paid in pursuance of subsection (4) above to the person treating or disposing of the waste, pay the costs or the unpaid costs, as the case may be, to that person.

[(7A) In subsection (1) 'waste permit' means a permit under the Pollution Prevention and Control (England and Wales) Regulations 2000 which authorises the disposal or recovery of waste; and for this purpose 'disposal or recovery' means an operation listed in Annex IIA or Annex IIB of Council Directive 75/442/EEC on waste (as amended by Commission Decision 96/350/EEC).]

[(8) In this section—

'specified' means specified in a direction under this section; and

'waste' means anything which is waste as defined in Article 1 of, and Annex 1 to, Directive 75/442/EEC (as amended by Directive 91/156/EEC) including anything which is excluded from the scope of that Directive by Article 2(1)(b)(iii) of that Directive, but not including anything excluded by the remainder of that Article.]

59 Powers to require removal of waste unlawfully deposited

(1) If any controlled waste is deposited in or on any land in the area of a waste regulation authority or waste collection authority in contravention of section 33(1) above, the authority may, by notice served on him, require the occupier to do either or both of the following, that is—

(a) to remove the waste from the land within a specified period not less than a period of twenty-one days beginning with the service of the notice;

(b) to take within such a period specified steps with a view to eliminating or reducing the consequences of the deposit of the waste.

(2) A person on whom any requirements are imposed under subsection (1) above may, within the period of twenty-one days mentioned in that subsection, appeal against the requirement to a magistrates' court...

(3) On any appeal under subsection (2) above the court shall quash the requirement if it is satisfied that—

(a) the appellant neither deposited nor knowingly caused nor knowingly permitted the deposit of the waste; or

(b) there is a material defect in the notice; and in any other case shall either modify the requirement or dismiss the appeal.

(4) Where a person appeals against any requirement imposed under subsection (1) above, the requirement shall be of no effect pending the determination of the appeal; and where the court modifies the requirement or dismisses the appeal it may extend the period specified in the notice.

(5) If a person on whom a requirement imposed under subsection (1) above fails, without reasonable excuse, to comply with the requirement he shall be liable, on summary conviction, to a fine not exceeding level 5 on the standard scale and to a further fine of an amount equal to one-tenth of level 5 on the standard scale for each day on which the failure continues after conviction of the offence and before the authority has begun to exercise its powers under subsection (6) below.

(6) Where a person on whom a requirement has been imposed under subsection (1) above by an authority fails to comply with the requirement the authority may do what that person was required to do and may recover from him any expenses reasonably incurred by the authority in doing it.

(7) If it appears to a waste regulation authority or waste collection authority that waste has been deposited in or on any land in contravention of section 33(1) above and that—

(a) in order to remove or prevent pollution of land, water or air or harm to human health it is necessary that the waste be forthwith removed or other steps taken to eliminate or reduce the consequences of the deposit or both; or

(b) there is no occupier of the land or the occupier cannot be found without incurring unreasonable expense; or

(c) the occupier neither made nor knowingly permitted the deposit of the waste; the authority may remove the waste from the land or take other steps to eliminate or reduce the consequences of the deposit or, as the case may require, to remove the waste and take those steps.

(8) Where an authority exercises any of the powers conferred on it by subsection (7) above it shall be entitled to recover the cost incurred by it in removing the waste or taking the steps or both and in disposing of the waste—

(a) in a case falling within subsection (7)(a) above, from the occupier of the land unless he proves that he neither made nor knowingly caused nor knowingly permitted the deposit of the waste;

(b) in any case, from any person who deposited or knowingly caused or knowingly permitted the deposit of any of the waste;

[(8A) An authority may not recover costs under subsection (8) above if a compensation order has been made under section 130 of the Powers of Criminal Courts (Sentencing) Act 2000 in favour of the authority in respect of any part of those costs.

(8B) Subsection (8A) does not apply if the order is set aside on appeal.]

except such of the cost as the occupier or that person shows was incurred unnecessarily.

(9) Any waste removed by an authority under subsection (7) above shall belong to that authority and may be dealt with accordingly.

[59ZA Section 59: supplementary power in relation to owner of land

(1) Where the grounds in subsection (2), (3) or (4) below are met, a waste regulation authority or waste collection authority may, by notice served on him, require the owner of any land in its area to comply with either or both of the requirements mentioned in subsection (1)(a) and (b) of section 59 above.

(2) The grounds in this subsection are that it appears to the authority that waste has been deposited in or on the land in contravention of section 33(1) above and—

(a) there is no occupier of the land, or

(b) the occupier cannot be found without the authority incurring unreasonable expense.

(3) The grounds in this subsection are that—

(a) the authority has served a notice under subsection (1) of section 59 above imposing a requirement on the occupier of the land,

(b) the occupier of the land is not the same person as the owner of the land, and(c) the occupier has failed to comply with the requirement mentioned in paragraph (a) above within the period specified in the notice.

(4) The grounds in this subsection are that—

(a) the authority has served a notice under subsection (1) of section 59 above imposing a requirement on the occupier of the land,

(b) the occupier of the land is not the same person as the owner of the land, and

(c) the requirement mentioned in paragraph (a) above has been quashed on the ground specified in subsection (3)(a) of that section.

(5) Subsections (2) to (6) of section 59 above apply in relation to requirements imposed under this section on the owner of the land as they apply in relation to requirements imposed under that section on the occupier of the land but as if in subsection (3) there were inserted after paragraph (a)—

'(aa) in order to comply with the requirement the appellant would be required to enter the land unlawfully; or'

(6) In this section 'owner' has the meaning given to it in section 78A(9) below.]

[59A Directions in relation to exercise of powers under section 59

(1) The Secretary of State may issue directions setting out categories of waste to which a waste regulation authority or waste collection authority in England and Wales should give priority for the purposes of exercising its powers under section 59 above.

(2) Priorities set out in directions under subsection (1) above may be different for different authorities or areas.

(3) But nothing in this section or in any directions issued under it affects any power of an authority under section 59 above.]

60 Interference with waste sites and receptacles for waste

(1) No person shall sort over or disturb—

(a) anything deposited at a place for the deposit of waste provided by or under arrangements made with a waste disposal authority or by any other local authority or person.

(b) anything deposited in a receptacle for waste, whether for public or private use, provided by a waste collection authority, by a waste disposal contractor under arrangements made with a waste disposal authority, by a parish or community council or by a holder of a waste management licence or...

(c) the contents of any receptacle for waste which, in accordance with a requirement under section 46 or 47 above, is placed on any highway... or in any other place with a view to its being emptied;

unless he has the relevant consent or right to do so specified in subsection (2) below.

(2) The consent or right that is relevant for the purposes of subsection (1)(a), (b) or (c) above is—

(a) in the case of paragraph (a), the consent of the authority or other person who provides the place for the deposit of the waste;

(b) in the case of paragraph (b), the consent of the authority or other person who provides the receptacle for the deposit of the waste;

(c) in the case of paragraph (c), the right to the custody of the receptacle, the consent of the person having the right to the custody of the receptacle or the right conferred by the function by or under this Part of emptying such receptacles.

(3) A person who contravenes subsection (1) above shall be liable on summary conviction to a fine of an amount not exceeding level 3 on the standard scale.

[62A Lists of wastes displaying hazardous properties

(1) The Secretary of State shall by regulations list any controlled waste in England which—

(a) is not listed as a hazardous waste in the Hazardous Waste List; and

(b) appears to him to display any of the properties listed in Annex III to Council Directive 91/689/EEC

(2) The National Assembly for Wales shall by regulations list any controlled waste in Wales which—

(a) is not listed as a hazardous waste in the Hazardous Waste List; and

(b) appears to it to display any of the properties listed in Annex III to Council Directive 91/689/EEC

(3) In this section 'the Hazardous Waste List' means the list referred to in the first indent of Article 1(4) of Council Directive 91/689/EEC

(4) Regulations under subsection (2) shall be made by statutory instrument but section 161(2) shall not apply to regulations under that subsection.]

63 Waste other than controlled waste

(1) The Secretary of State may, after consultation with such bodies as he considers appropriate, make regulations providing that prescribed provisions of this Part shall have effect in a prescribed area—

(a) as if references in those provisions to controlled waste or controlled waste of a kind specified in the regulations included references to such waste as is mentioned in section 75(7)(c) below which is of a kind so specified; and

(b) with such modifications as may be prescribed; and the regulations may make such modifications of other enactments as the Secretary of State considers appropriate.

[(2)–(3) [...]

(4) Section 45(2) and section 47(1) above shall apply to waste other than controlled waste as they apply to controlled waste.

[63A Power to take steps to minimise generation of controlled waste

(1) A relevant authority may do, or arrange for the doing of, or contribute towards the expenses of the doing of, anything which in its opinion is necessary or expedient for the

purpose of minimising the quantities of controlled waste, or controlled waste of any description, generated in its area.

(2) Where a relevant authority in England ('the first authority') proposes to exercise any of its powers under subsection (1), it shall before doing so consult about the proposal every other relevant authority whose area includes all or part of the area of the first authority.

(3) In this section 'relevant authority' means a waste collection authority or a waste disposal authority.]

64 Public registers

(1) Subject to sections 65 and 66 below, it shall be the duty of each waste regulation authority to maintain a register containing prescribed particulars of or relating to—

(a) current or recently current licences ('licences') granted by the authority;
(b) current or recently current applications to the authority for licences;
(c) applications made to the authority under section 37 above for the modification of licences;
(d) notices issued by the authority under section 37 above effecting the modification of licences;
(e) notices issued by the authority under section 38 above effecting the revocation or suspension of licences or imposing requirements on the holders of licences;
(f) appeals under section 43 above relating to decisions of the authority;
(g) certificates of completion issued by the authority under section 39(9) above;
(h) notices issued by the authority imposing requirements on the holders of licences under section 42(5) above;
(i) convictions of the holders of licences granted by the authority for any offence under this Part (whether in relation to a licence so granted or not);
(j) the occasions on which the authority has discharged any function under section 42 or 61 above;
(k) directions given to the authority under any provision of this Part by the Secretary of State;
(l) [...]
(m) such matters relating to the treatment, keeping or disposal of waste in the area of the authority or any pollution of the environment caused thereby as may be prescribed;

and any other document or information required to be kept in the register under any provision of this Act.

(2) Where information of any description is excluded from any register by virtue of section 66 below, a statement shall be entered in the register indicating the existence of information of that description.

[(2A) The Secretary of State may give to a waste regulation authority directions requiring the removal from any register of its of any specified information not prescribed for inclusion under subsection (1) above or which, by virtue of section 65 or 66 below, ought to be excluded from the register.]

(3) For the purposes of subsection (1) above licences are 'recently' current for the period of twelve months after they cease to be in force and applications for licences are 'recently' current if they relate to a licence which is current or recently current or, in the case of an application which is rejected, for the period of twelve months beginning with the date on which the waste regulation authority gives notice of rejection or, as the case may be, on which the application is deemed by section 36(9) above to have been rejected.

(4) It shall be the duty of each waste collection authority in England [or Wales] [...] to maintain a register containing prescribed particulars of such information contained in any register maintained under subsection (1) above as relates to the treatment, keeping or disposal of controlled waste in the area of the authority.

[(5) The waste regulation authority in relation to England and Wales shall furnish any waste collection authorities in its area with the particulars necessary to enable them to discharge their duty under subsection (4) above.]

(6) Each waste regulation authority and waste collection authority

[(a)] shall secure that any register maintained under this section is open to inspection [...] by members of the public free of charge at all reasonable hours; and

[(b)] shall afford to members of the public reasonable facilities for obtaining, on payment of reasonable charges, copies of entries in the register

[and, for the purposes of this subsection, places may be prescribed by the Secretary of State at which any such registers or facilities as are mentioned in paragraph (a) or (b) above are to be available or afforded to the public in pursuance of the paragraph in question.]

(7) Registers under this section may be kept in any form.

(8) In this section 'prescribed' means prescribed in regulations by the Secretary of State.

65 Exclusion from registers of information affecting national security

(1) No information shall be included in a register maintained under section 64 above (a 'register') if and so long as, in the opinion of the Secretary of State, the inclusion in the register of that information, or information of that description, would be contrary to the interests of national security.

...

66 Exclusion from registers of certain confidential information

(1) No information relating to the affairs of any individual or business shall be included in a register maintained under section 64 above (a 'register'), without the consent of that individual or the person for the time being carrying on that business, if and so long as the information—

(a) is, in relation to him, commercially confidential; and

(b) is not required to be included in the register in pursuance of directions under subsection (7) below;

but information is not commercially confidential for the purposes of this section unless it is determined under this section to be so by the authority maintaining the register or, on appeal, by the Secretary of State.

(2) Where information is furnished to an authority maintaining a register for the purpose of—

(a) an application for, or for the modification of, a licence;

(b) complying with any condition of a licence; or

(c) complying with a notice under section 71(2) below;

then, if the person furnishing it applies to the authority to have the information excluded from the register on the ground that it is commercially confidential (as regards himself or another person), the authority shall determine whether the information is or is not commercially confidential.

...

71 Obtaining of information from persons and authorities

(1) [...]

(2) For the purpose of the discharge of their respective functions under this Part—

(a) the Secretary of State, and

(b) a waste regulation authority,

may, by notice in writing served on him, require any person to furnish such information specified in the notice as the Secretary of State or the authority, as the case may be, reasonably considers he or it needs, in such form and within such period following service of the notice [or at such time,] as is so specified.

[(2A) A waste collection authority has the power referred to in subsection (2) for the purpose of the discharge of its functions under sections 34B and 34C above.]

(3) A person who—

(a) fails, without reasonable excuse, to comply with a requirement imposed under subsection (2) or (24) above; [...]

(b) [...]

shall be liable—

(i) on summary conviction, to a fine not exceeding the statutory maximum;

(ii) on conviction on indictment, to a fine or to imprisonment for a term not exceeding two years, or to both.

[(4) The Secretary of State may, by notice in writing, require a waste regulation authority or waste collection authority in England and Wales to supply to him, or to such other person as may be specified in the notice, such information as may be so specified in respect of—

(a) cases where the authority has exercised any powers under section 59 above, and

(b) cases where the authority has taken action under any other enactment in respect of any deposit or other disposal of controlled waste in contravention of section 33(1) above.]

73 Appeals and other provisions relating to legal proceedings and civil liability

(1) An appeal against any decision of a magistrates' court under this Part (other than a decision made in criminal proceedings) shall lie to the Crown Court at the instance of any party to the proceedings in which the decision was given if such an appeal does not lie to the Crown Court by virtue of any other enactment.

(2) ...

(3) Where a person appeals to the Crown Court...against a decision of a magistrates' court...dismissing an appeal against any requirement imposed under this Part which was suspended pending determination of that appeal, the requirement shall again be suspended pending the determination of the appeal to the Crown Court...

(4) Where an appeal against a decision of any authority lies to a magistrates' court...by virtue of any provision of this Part, it shall be the duty of the authority to include in any document by which it notifies the decision to the person concerned a statement indicating that such an appeal lies and specifying the time within which it must be brought.

(5) Where on an appeal to any court against or arising out of a decision of any authority under this Part the court varies or reverses the decision it shall be the duty of the authority to act in accordance with the court's decision.

(6) Where any damage is caused by waste which has been deposited in or on land, any person who deposited it, or knowingly caused or knowingly permitted it to be deposited, in either case so as to commit an offence under section 33(1) or 63(2) above, is liable for the damage except where the damage—

(a) was due wholly to the fault of the person who suffered it; or

(b) was suffered by a person who voluntarily accepted the risk of the damage being caused;

but without prejudice to any liability arising otherwise than under this subsection.

(7) The matters which may be proved by way of defence under section 33(7) above may be proved also by way of defence to an action brought under subsection (6) above.

(8) In subsection (6) above—

'damage' includes the death of, or injury to, any person (including any disease and any impairment of physical or mental condition); and

'fault' has the same meaning as in the Law Reform (Contributory Negligence) Act 1945.

(9) For the purposes of the following enactments—

(a) the Fatal Accidents Act 1976;

(b) the Law Reform (Contributory Negligence) Act 1945; and

(c) the Limitation Act 1980;

. . . any damage for which a person is liable under subsection (6) shall be treated as due to his fault.

[73A Use of fixed penalty receipts

(1) The Environment Agency must pay amounts received by it under section 34A above to the Secretary of State.

(2) A waste collection authority may use amounts received by it under section 34A or 47ZA above (its 'fixed penalty receipts') only for the purposes of—

(a) its functions under this Part (including functions relating to the enforcement of offences under this Part); and

(b) such other of its functions as may be specified in regulations made by the appropriate person.

(3) Regulations under subsection (2)(b) above may (in particular) have the effect that a waste collection authority may use its fixed penalty receipts for the purposes of any of its functions.

(4) A waste collection authority must supply the appropriate person with such information relating to its use of its fixed penalty receipts as the appropriate person may require.

(5) The appropriate person may by regulations—

(a) make provision for what a waste collection authority is to do with its fixed penalty receipts—

(i) pending their being used for the purposes of functions of the authority referred to in subsection (2) above;

(ii) if they are not so used before such time after their receipt as may be specified by the regulations;

(b) make provision for accounting arrangements in respect of a waste collection authority's fixed penalty receipts.

(6) The provision that may be made under subsection (5)(a)(ii) above includes (in particular) provision for the payment of sums to a person (including the appropriate person) other than the waste collection authority.

(7) Before making regulations under this section, the appropriate person must consult—

(a) the waste collection authorities to which the regulations are to apply;

(b) such other persons as the appropriate person thinks fit.

(8) Regulations under this section may make different provision for different purposes (including different provision in relation to different authorities or different descriptions of authority).

(9) The powers to make regulations conferred by this section are, for the purposes of subsection (1) of section 100 of the Local Government Act 2003, to be regarded as included among the powers mentioned in subsection (2) of that section.]

74 Meaning of 'fit and proper person'

(1) The following provisions apply for the purposes of the discharge by a waste regulation authority of any function under this Part which requires the authority to determine whether a person is or is not a fit and proper person to hold a waste management licence.

(2) Whether a person is or is not a fit and proper person to hold a licence is to be determined by reference to the carrying on by him of the activities which are or are to be authorised by the licence and the fulfilment of the requirements of the licence.

(3) Subject to subsection (4) below, a person shall be treated as not being a fit and proper person if it appears to the authority—

(a) that he or another relevant person has been convicted of a relevant offence;

(b) that the management of the activities which are or are to be authorised by the licence are not or will not be in the hands of a technically competent person; or

(c) that the person who holds or is to hold the licence has not made and either has no intention of making or is in no position to make financial provision adequate to discharge the obligations arising from the licence.

(4) The authority may, if it considers it proper to do so in any particular case, treat a person as a fit and proper person notwithstanding that subsection (3)(a) above applies in his case.

(5) It shall be the duty of waste regulation authorities to have regard to any guidance issued to them by the Secretary of State with respect to the discharge of their functions of making the determinations to which this section applies.

(6) The Secretary of State may, by regulations, prescribe the offences that are relevant for the purposes of subsection (3)(a) above and the qualifications and experience required of a person for the purposes of subsection (3)(b) above.

(7) For the purposes of subsection (3)(a) above, another relevant person shall be treated, in relation to the licence holder or proposed licence holder, as the case may be, as having been convicted of a relevant offence if—

(a) any person has been convicted of a relevant offence committed by him in the course of his employment by the holder or, as the case may be, the proposed holder of the licence or in the course of the carrying on of any business by a partnership one of the members of which was the holder or, as the case may be, the proposed holder of the licence;

(b) a body corporate has been convicted of a relevant offence committed when the holder or, as the case may be, the proposed holder of the licence was a director, manager, secretary or other similar officer of that body corporate; or

(c) where the holder or, as the case may be, the proposed holder of the licence is a body corporate, a person who is a director, manager, secretary or other similar officer of that body corporate—

(i) has been convicted of a relevant offence; or

(ii) was a director, manager, secretary or other similar officer of another body corporate at a time when a relevant offence for which that other body corporate has been convicted was committed.

75 Meaning of 'waste' and household, commercial and industrial waste and hazardous waste

(1) The following provisions apply for the interpretation of this Part.

[(2) 'Waste' means any substance or object in the categories set out in Schedule 2B to this Act which the holder discards or intends or is required to discard; and for the purposes of this definition—

'holder' means the producer of the waste or the person who is in possession of it; and

'producer' means any person whose activities produce waste or any person who carries out pre-processing, mixing or other operations resulting in a change in the nature or composition of this waste.]

(3) [...]

(4) 'Controlled waste' means household, industrial and commercial waste or any such waste.

(5) Subject to subsection (8) below, 'household waste' means waste from—

(a) domestic property, that is to say, a building or self-contained part of a building which is used wholly for the purposes of living accommodation;

(b) a caravan (as defined in section 29(1) of the Caravan Sites and Control of Development Act 1960) which usually and for the time being is situated on a caravan site (within the meaning of that Act);

(c) a residential home;

(d) premises forming part of a university or school or other educational establishment;

(e) premises forming part of a hospital or nursing home.

(6) Subject to subsection (8) below, 'industrial waste' means waste from any of the following premises—

(a) any factory (within the meaning of the Factories Act 1961);
(b) any premises used for the purposes of, or in connection with, the provision to the public of transport services by land, water or air;
(c) any premises used for the purposes of, or in connection with, the supply to the public of gas, water or electricity or the provision of sewerage services; or
(d) any premises used for the purposes of, or in connection with, the provision to the public of postal or telecommunications services.

(7) Subject to subsection (8) below, 'commercial waste' means waste from premises used wholly or mainly for the purposes of a trade or business or the purposes of sport, recreation or entertainment excluding—
(a) household waste;
(b) industrial waste;
(c) waste from any mine or quarry and waste from premises used for agriculture within the meaning of the Agriculture Act 1947 . . . and
(d) waste of any other description prescribed by regulations made by the Secretary of State for the purposes of this paragraph.

(8) Regulations made by the Secretary of State may provide that waste of a description prescribed in the regulations shall be treated for the purposes of provisions of this Part prescribed in the regulations as being or not being household waste or industrial waste or commercial waste; but no regulations shall be made in respect of such waste as is mentioned in subsection (7)(c) above and references to waste in subsection (7) above and this subsection do not include sewage (including matter in or from a privy) except so far as the regulations provide otherwise.

[(8A) 'Hazardous waste'—
(a) in the application of this Part to England, means any waste which is a hazardous waste for the purposes of the Hazardous Waste (England and Wales) Regulations 2005;
(b) in the application of this Part to Wales, means any waste which is a hazardous waste for the purposes of the Hazardous Waste (Wales) Regulations 2005.]

(8B) . . .]

(9) [. . .]

[(10) Schedule 2B to this Act (which reproduces Annex I to the Waste Directive) shall have effect.

(11) Subsection (2) above is substituted, and Schedule 2B to this Act is inserted, for the purpose of assigning to 'waste' in this Part the meaning which it has in the Waste Directive by virtue of paragraphs (a) to (c) of Article 1 of, and Annex I to, that Directive, and those provisions shall be construed accordingly.

(12) In this section 'the Waste Directive' means the directive of the Council of the European Communities, dated 15th July 1975, on waste, as amended by—
(a) the directive of that Council, dated 18th March 1991, amending directive 75/442/EEC on waste; and
(b) the directive of that Council, dated 23rd December 1991, standardising and rationalising reports on the implementation of certain Directives relating to the environment; and]
(c) the decision of the European Commission, dated 24 May 1996, adopting Annexes IIA and IIB to Directive 75/442/EEC on waste.

78 This Part and radioactive substances

Except as provided by regulations made by the Secretary of State under this section, nothing in this Part applies to radioactive waste within the meaning of the Radioactive Substances Act [1993]; but regulations may—
(a) provide for prescribed provisions of this Part to have effect with such modifications as the Secretary of State considers appropriate for the purposes of dealing with such radioactive waste;

(b) make such modifications of the Radioactive Substances Act [1993] and any other Act as the Secretary of State considers appropriate.

[PART IIA CONTAMINATED LAND

78A Preliminary

(1) The following provisions have effect for the interpretation of this Part.

(2) 'Contaminated land' is any land which appears to the local authority in whose area it is situated to be in such a condition, by reason of substances in, on or under the land, that—

(a) significant harm is being caused or there is a significant possibility of such harm being caused; or

[(b) significant pollution of controlled waters is being caused or there is a significant possibility of such pollution being caused;]

(3) A 'special site' is any contaminated land—

(a) which has been designated as such a site by virtue of section 78C(7) or 78D(6) below; and

(b) whose designation as such has not been terminated by the appropriate Agency under section 78Q(4) below.

(4) 'Harm' means harm to the health of living organisms or other interference with the ecological systems of which they form part and, in the case of man, includes harm to his property.

(5) The questions—

(a) what harm ['or pollution of controlled waters'] is to be regarded as 'significant',

(b) whether the possibility of significant harm [or of significant pollution of controlled waters] being caused is 'significant',

(c) [...]

shall be determined in accordance with guidance issued for the purpose by the Secretary of State in accordance with section 78YA below.

(6) Without prejudice to the guidance that may be issued under subsection (5) above, guidance under paragraph (a) of that subsection may make provision for different degrees of importance to be assigned to, or for the disregard of,—

(a) different descriptions of living organisms or ecological systems [or of poisonous, noxious or polluting matter or solid waste matter];

(b) different descriptions of places [or controlled waters, or different degrees of pollution]; or

(c) different descriptions of harm to health or property, or other interference;

and guidance under paragraph (b) of that subsection may make provision for different degrees of possibility to be regarded as 'significant' (or as not being 'significant') in relation to different descriptions of significant harm [or of significant pollution].

(7) 'Remediation' means—

(a) the doing of anything for the purpose of assessing the condition of—

(i) the contaminated land in question;

(ii) any controlled waters affected by that land; or

(iii) any land adjoining or adjacent to that land;

(b) the doing of any works, the carrying out of any operations or the taking of any steps in relation to any such land or waters for the purpose—

(i) of preventing or minimising, or remedying or mitigating the effects of, any significant harm, or any [significant] pollution of controlled waters, by reason of which the contaminated land is such land; or

(ii) of restoring the land or waters to their former state; or

(c) the making of subsequent inspections from time to time for the purpose of keeping under review the condition of the land or waters;

and cognate expressions shall be construed accordingly.

(8) Controlled waters are 'affected by' contaminated land if (and only if) it appears to the enforcing authority that the contaminated land in question is, for the purposes of subsection (2) above, in such a condition, by reason of substances in, on or under the land, that [significant pollution of those waters is being caused or there is a significant possibility of such pollution being caused].

(9) The following expressions have the meaning respectively assigned to them—'the appropriate Agency' means—

(a) in relation to England and Wales, the Environment Agency;

(b) . . .

'appropriate person' means any person who is an appropriate person, determined in accordance with section 78F below, to bear responsibility for any thing which is to be done by way of remediation in any particular case;

'charging notice' has the meaning given by section 78P(3)(b) below;

'controlled waters'—

(a) in relation to England and Wales, has the same meaning as in Part III of the Water Resources Act 1991 [except that 'ground waters' does not include waters contained in underground strata but above the saturation zone]; and

(b) . . .

. . .

'enforcing authority' means—

(a) in relation to a special site, the appropriate Agency;

(b) in relation to contaminated land other than a special site, the local authority in whose area the land is situated;

. . .

'local authority' in relation to England and Wales means—

(a) any unitary authority;

(b) any district council, so far as it is not a unitary authority;

(c) the Common Council of the City of London and, as respects the Temples, the Sub-Treasurer of the Inner Temple and the Under-Treasurer of the Middle Temple respectively;

. . .

'notice' means notice in writing;

'notification' means notification in writing;

'owner', in relation to any land in England and Wales, means a person (other than a mortgagee not in possession) who, whether in his own right or as trustee for any other person, is entitled to receive the rack rent of the land, or, where the land is not let at a rack rent, would be so entitled if it were so let;

. . .

'pollution of controlled waters' means the entry into controlled waters of any poisonous, noxious or polluting matter or any solid waste matter;

'prescribed' means prescribed by regulations;

'regulations' means regulations made by the Secretary of State;

'remediation declaration' has the meaning given by section 78H(6) below;

'remediation notice' has the meaning given by section 78E(1) below;

'remediation statement' has the meaning given by section 78H(7) below;

'required to be designated as a special site' shall be construed in accordance with section 78C(8) below;

'substance' means any natural or artificial substance, whether in solid or liquid form or in the form of a gas or vapour;

'unitary authority' means—

(a) the council of a county, so far as it is the council of an area for which there are no district councils;
(b) the council of any district comprised in an area for which there is no county council;
(c) the council of a London borough;
(d) the council of a county borough in Wales.

78B Identification of contaminated land

(1) Every local authority shall cause its area to be inspected from time to time for the purpose—
(a) of identifying contaminated land; and
(b) of enabling the authority to decide whether any such land is land which is required to be designated as a special site.

(2) In performing its functions under subsection (1) above a local authority shall act in accordance with any guidance issued for the purpose by the Secretary of State in accordance with section 78R below.

(3) If a local authority identifies any contaminated land in its area, it shall give notice of that fact to—
(a) the appropriate Agency;
(b) the owner of the land;
(c) any person who appears to the authority to be in occupation of the whole or any part of the land; and
(d) each person who appears to the authority to be an appropriate person; and any notice given under this subsection shall state by virtue of which of paragraphs (a) to (d) above it is given.

(4) If, at any time after a local authority has given any person a notice pursuant to subsection (3)(d) above in respect of any land, it appears to the enforcing authority that another person is an appropriate person, the enforcing authority shall give notice to that other person—
(a) of the fact that the local authority has identified the land in question as contaminated land; and
(b) that he appears to the enforcing authority to be an appropriate person.

78C Identification and designation of special sites

(1) If at any time it appears to a local authority that any contaminated land in its area might be land which is required to be designated as a special site, the authority—
(a) shall decide whether or not the land is land which is required to be so designated; and
(b) if the authority decides that the land is land which is required to be so designated, shall give notice of that decision to the relevant persons.

(2) For the purposes of this section 'the relevant persons' at any time in the case of any land are the persons who at that time fall within paragraphs (a) to (d) below that is to say—
(a) the appropriate Agency;
(b) the owner of the land;
(c) any person who appears to the local authority concerned to be in occupation of the whole or any part of the land; and
(d) each person who appears to that authority to be an appropriate person.

(3) Before making a decision under paragraph (a) of subsection (1) above in any particular case, a local authority shall request the advice of the appropriate Agency, and in making its decision shall have regard to any advice given by that Agency in response to the request.

(4) If at any time the appropriate Agency considers that any contaminated land is land which is required to be designated as a special site, that Agency may give notice of that fact to the local authority in whose area the land is situated.

(5) Where notice under subsection (4) above is given to a local authority, the authority shall decide whether the land in question—

(a) is land which is required to be designated as a special site, or

(b) is not land which is required to be so designated, and shall give notice of that decision to the relevant persons.

(6) Where a local authority makes a decision falling within subsection (1)(b) or 5(a) above, the decision shall, subject to section 78D below, take effect on the day after whichever of the following events first occurs, that is to say—

(a) the expiration of the period of twenty-one days beginning with the day on which the notice required by virtue of subsection (1)(b) or, as the case may be, (5)(a) above is given to the appropriate Agency; or

(b) if the appropriate Agency gives notification to the local authority in question that it agrees with the decision, the giving of that notification;

and where a decision takes effect by virtue of this subsection, the local authority shall give notice of that fact to the relevant persons.

(7) Where a decision that any land is land which is required to be designated as a special site takes effect in accordance with subsection (6) above, the notice given under subsection (1)(b) or, as the case may be, (5)(a) above shall have effect, as from the time when the decision takes effect, as the designation of that land as such a site.

(8) For the purposes of this Part, land is required to be designated as a special site if, and only if, it is land of a description prescribed for the purposes of this subsection.

(9) Regulations under subsection (8) above may make different provision for different cases or circumstances or different areas or localities and may, in particular, describe land by reference to the area or locality in which it is situated.

(10) Without prejudice to the generality of his power to prescribe any description of land for the purposes of subsection (8) above, the Secretary of State, in deciding whether to prescribe a particlar description of contaminated land for those purposes, may, in particular, have regard to—

(a) whether land of the description in question appears to him to be land which is likely to be in such a condition, by reason of substances in, on or under the land that—

(i) serious harm would or might be caused, or

(ii) serious pollution of controlled waters would [or might be caused]; or caused; or

(b) whether the appropriate Agency is likely to have expertise in dealing with the kind of significant harm, or [significant] pollution of controlled waters, by reason of which land of the description in question is contaminated land.

78D Referral of special site decisions to the Secretary of State

(1) In any case where—

(a) a local authority gives notice of a decision to the appropriate Agency pursuant to subsection (1)(b) or (5)(b) of section 78C above, but

(b) before the expiration of the period of twenty-one days beginning with the day on which that notice is so given,

that Agency gives the local authority notice that it disagrees with the decision, together with a statement of its reasons for disagreeing, the authority shall refer the decision to the Secretary of State and shall send to him a statement of its reasons for reaching the decision.

(2) Where the appropriate Agency gives notice to a local authority under paragraph (b) of subsection (1) above, it shall also send to the Secretary of State a copy of the notice and of the statement given under that paragraph.

(3) Where a local authority refers a decision to the Secretary of State under subsection (1) above, it shall give notice of that fact to the relevant persons.

(4) Where a decision of a local authority is referred to the Secretary of State under subsection (1) above, he—

(a) may confirm or reverse the decision with respect to the whole or any part of the land to which it relates; and

(b) shall give notice of this decision on the referral—

(i) to the relevant persons; and

(ii) to the local authority.

(5) Where a decision of a local authority is referred to the Secretary of State under subsection (1) above, the decision shall not take effect until the day after that on which the Secretary of State gives the notice required by subsection (4) above to the persons there mentioned and shall then take effect as confirmed or reversed by him.

(6) Where a decision which takes effect in accordance with subsection (5) above is to the effect that at least some land is land which is required to be designated as a special site, the notice given under subsection (4)(b) above shall have effect, as from the time when the decision takes effect, as the designation of that land as such a site.

(7) In this section 'the relevant persons' has the same meaning as in section 78C above.

78E Duty of enforcing authority to require remediation of contaminated land etc.

(1) In any case where—

(a) any land has been designated as a special site by virtue of section 78C(7) or 78D(6) above, or

(b) a local authority has identified any contaminated land (other than a special site) in its area,

the enforcing authority shall, in accordance with such procedure as may be prescribed and subject to the following provisions of this Part, serve on each person who is an appropriate person a notice (in this Part referred to as a 'remediation notice') specifying what that person is to do by way of remediation and the periods within which he is required to do each of the things so specified.

(2) Different remediation notices requiring the doing of different things by way of remediation may be served on different persons in consequence of the presence of different substances in, on or under any land or waters.

(3) Where two or more persons are appropriate persons in relation to any particular thing which is to be done by way of remediation, the remediation notice served on each of them shall state the proportion, determined under section 78F(7) below, of the cost of doing that thing which each of them respectively is liable to bear.

(4) The only things by way of remediation which the enforcing authority may do, or require to be done, under or by virtue of this Part are things which it considers reasonable, having regard to—

(a) the cost which is likely to be involved; and

(b) the seriousness of the harm, or [of the] pollution of controlled waters, in question.

(5) In determining for any purpose of this Part—

(a) what is to be done (whether by an appropriate person, the enforcing authority or any other person) by way of remediation in any particular case,

(b) the standard to which any land is, or waters are, to be remediated pursuant to the notice, or

(c) what is, or is not, to be regarded as reasonable for the purposes of subsection (4) above,

the enforcing authority shall have regard to any guidance issued for the purpose by the Secretary of State.

(6) Regulations may make provision for or in connection with—

(a) the form or content of remediation notices; or

(b) any steps of a procedural nature which are to be taken in connection with, or in consequence of, the service of a remediation notice.

78F Determination of the appropriate person to bear responsibility for remediation

(1) This section has effect for the purpose of determining who is the appropriate person to bear responsibility for any particular thing which the enforcing authority determines is to be done by way of remediation in any particular case.

(2) Subject to the following provisions of this section, any person, or any of the persons, who caused or knowingly permitted the substances, or any of the substances, by reason of which the contaminated land in question is such land to be in, on or under that land is an appropriate person.

(3) A person shall only be an appropriate person by virtue of subsection (2) above in relation to things which are to be done by way of remediation which are to any extent referable to substances which he caused or knowingly permitted to be present in, on or under the contaminated land in question.

(4) If no person has, after reasonable inquiry, been found who is by virtue of subsection (2) above an appropriate person to bear responsibility for the things which are to be done by way of remediation, the owner or occupier for the time being of the contaminated land in question is an appropriate person.

(5) If, in consequence of subsection (3) above, there are things which are to be done by way of remediation in relation to which no person has, after reasonable inquiry, been found who is an appropriate person by virtue of subsection (2) above, the owner or occupier for the time being of the contaminated land in question is an appropriate person in relation to those things.

(6) Where two or more persons would, apart from this subsection, be appropriate persons in relation to any particular thing which is to be done by way of remediation, the enforcing authority shall determine in accordance with guidance issued for the purpose by the Secretary of State whether any, and if so which, of them is to be treated as not being an appropriate person in relation to that thing.

(7) Where two or more persons are appropriate persons in relation to any particular thing which is to be done by way of remediation, they shall be liable to bear the cost of doing that thing in proportions determined by the enforcing authority in accordance with guidance issued for the purpose by the Secretary of State.

(8) Any guidance issued for the purposes of subsection (6) or (7) above shall be issued in accordance with section 78YA below.

(9) A person who has caused or knowingly permitted any substance ('substance A') to be in, or under any land shall also be taken for the purposes of this section to have caused or knowingly permitted there to be in, on or under that land any substance which is there as a result of a chemical reaction or biological process affecting substance A.

(10) A thing which is to be done by way of remediation may be regarded for the purposes of this Part as referable to the presence of any substance notwithstanding that the thing in question would not have to be done—

(a) in consequence only of the presence of that substance in any quantity; or

(b) in consequence only of the quantity of that substance which any particular person caused or knowingly permitted to be present.

78G Grant of, and compensation for, rights of entry etc.

(1) A remediation notice may require an appropriate person to do things by way of remediation, notwithstanding that he is not entitled to do those things.

(2) Any person whose consent is required before any thing required by a remediation notice may be done shall grant, or join in granting, such rights in relation to any of the relevant land or waters as will enable the appropriate person to comply with any requirements imposed by the remediation notice.

(3) Before serving a remediation notice, the enforcing authority shall reasonably endeavour to consult every person who appears to the authority—

(a) to be the owner or occupier of any of the relevant land or waters, and

(b) to be a person who might be required by subsection (2) above to grant, or join in granting, any rights,

concerning the rights which that person may be so required to grant.

(4) Subsection (3) above shall not preclude the service of a remediation notice in any case where it appears to the enforcing authority that the contaminated land in question is in such a condition, by reason of substances in, on or under the land, that there is imminent danger of serious harm or serious pollution of controlled waters, being caused.

(5) A person who grants, or joins in granting, any rights pursuant to subsection (2) above shall be entitled, on making an application within such period as may be prescribed and in such manner as may be prescribed to such person as may be prescribed, to be paid by the appropriate person compensation of such amount as may be determined in such manner as may be prescribed.

(6) Without prejudice to the generality of the regulations that may be made by virtue of subsection (5) above regulations by virtue of that subsection may make such provision in relation to compensation under this section as may be made by regulations by virtue of subsection (4) of section 35A above in relation to compensation under that section.

(7) In this section, 'relevant land or waters' means—

(a) the contaminated land in question;

(b) any controlled waters affected by that land; or

(c) any land adjoining or adjacent to that land or those waters.

78H Restrictions and prohibitions on serving remediation notices

(1) Before serving a remediation notice, the enforcing authority shall reasonably endeavour to consult—

(a) the person on whom the notice is to be served,

(b) the owner of any land to which the notice relates,

(c) any person who appears to that authority to be in occupation of the whole or any part of the land, and

(d) any person of such other description as may be prescribed, concerning what is to be done by way of remediation.

(2) Regulations may make provision for, or in connection with, steps to be taken for the purposes of subsection (1) above.

(3) No remediation notice shall be served on any person by reference to any contaminated land during any of the following periods, that is to say—

(a) the period—

(i) beginning with the identification of the contaminated land in question pursuant to section 78B(1) above, and

(ii) ending with the expiration of the period of three months beginning with the day on which the notice required by subsection (3)(d) or, as the case may be, (4) of section 78B above is given that person in respect of that land;

(b) if a decision falling within paragraph (b) of section 78C(1) above is made in relation to the contaminated land in question, the period beginning with the making of the decision and ending with the expiration of the perod of three months beginning with—

(i) in a case where the decision is not referred to the Secretary of State under section 78D above, the day on which the notice required by section 78C(6) above is given, or

(ii) in a case where the decision is referred to the Secretary of State under section 78D above, the day on which he gives the notice required by subsection (4)(b) of that section;

(c) if the appropriate Agency gives a notice under subsection (4) of section 78C above to a local authority in relation to the contaminated land in question, the period beginning with the day on which that notice is given and endng with the expiration of the period of three months beginning with—
   (i) in a case where notice is given under subsection (6) of that section, the day on which that notice is given;
   (ii) in a case where the authority makes a decision falling within subsection (5)(b) of that section and the appropriate Agency fails to give notice under paragraph (b) of section 78D(1) above, the day following the expiration of the period of twenty-one days mentioned in that paragraph; or
   (iii) in a case where the authority makes a decision falling within section 78C(5)(b) above which is referred to the Secretary of State under section 78D above, the day on which the Secretary of State gives the notice required by subsection (4)(b) of that section.

(4) Neither subsection (1) nor subsection (3) above shall preclude the service of a remediation notice in any case where it appears to the enforcing authority that th land in question is in such a condition, by reason of substances in, on or under the land, that there is imminent danger of serious harm, or serious pollution of controlled waters, being caused.

(5) The enforcing authority shall not serve a remediation notice on a person if and so long as any one or more of the following conditions is for the time being satisfied in the particular case, that is to say—

(a) the authority is satisfied, in consequence of section 78E(4) and (5) above, that there is nothing by way of remediation which could be specified in a remediation notice served on that person;
(b) the authority is satisfied that appropriate things are being, or will be, done by way of remediation without the service of a remediation notice on that person;
(c) it appears to the authority that the person on whom the notice would be served is the authority itself; or
(d) the authority is satisfied that the powers conferred on it by section 78N below to do what is appropriate by way of remediation are exercisable.

(6) Where the enforcing authority is precluded by virtue of section 78E(4) or (5) above from specifying in a remediation notice any particular thing by way of remediation which it would otherwise have specified in such a notice, the authority shall prepare and publish a document (in this Part referred to as a 'remediation declaration') which shall record—

(a) the reasons why the authority would have specified that thing; and
(b) the grounds on which the authority is satisfied that it is precluded from specifying that thing in such a notice.

(7) In any case where the enforcing authority is precluded, by virtue of paragraph (b), (c) or (d) of subsection (5) above, from serving a remediation notice, the responsible person shall prepare and publish a document (in this Part referred to as a 'remediation statement') which shall record—

(a) the things which are being, have been, or are expected to be, done by way of remediation in the particular case;
(b) the name and address of the person who is doing, has done, or is expected to do, each of those things; and
(c) the periods within which each of those things is being, or is expected to be, done.

(8) For the purposes of subsection (7) above, the 'responsible person' is—

(a) in a case where the condition in paragraph (b) of subsection (5) above is satisfied, the person who is doing or has done, or who the enforcing authority is satisfied will do, the things there mentioned; or
(b) in a case where the condition in paragraph (c) or (d) of that subsection is satisfied, the enforcing authority.

(9) If a person who is required by virtue of subsection (8)(a) above to pepare and publish a remediation statement fails to do so within a reasonable time after the date on which a remediation notice specifying the things there mentioned could, apart from subsection (5) above, have been served, the enforcing authority may itself prepare and publish the statement and may recover its reasonable costs of doing so from that person.

(10) Where the enforcing authority has been precluded by virtue only of subsection (5) above from serving a remediation notice on an appropriate person but—

(a) none of the conditions in that subsection is for the time being satisified in the particular case, and

(b) the authority is not precluded by any other provison of this Part from serving a remediation notice on that appropriate person,

the authority shall serve a remediation notice on that person; and any such notice may be so served without any further endeavours by the authority to consult persons pursuant to subsection (1) above, if and to the extent that that person has been consulted pursuant to that subsection concerning the things which will be specified in the notice.

78J Restrictions on liability relating to the pollution of controlled waters

(1) This section applies where any land is contaminated land by virtue of paragraph (b) of subsection (2) of section 78A above (whether or not the land is also contaminated land by virtue of paragraph (a) of that subsection).

(2) Where this section applies, no remediation notice given in consequence of the land in question being contaminated land shall require a person who is an appropriate person by virtue of section 78F(4) or (5) above to do anything by way of remediation to that or any other land, or any waters, which he could not have been required to do by such a notice had paragraph (b) of section 78A(2) above (and all other references to pollution of controlled waters) been omitted from this Part.

(3) If, in a case where this section applies, a person permits, has permitted, or might permit, water from an abandoned mine or part of a mine—

(a) to enter any controlled waters, or

(b) to reach a place from which it is or, as the case may be, was likely, in the opinion of the enforcing authority, to enter such waters,

no remediation notice shall require him in consequence to do anything by way of remediation (whether to the contaminated land in question or to any other land or waters) which he could not have been required to do by such a notice had paragraph (b) of section 78A(2) above (and all other references to pollution of controlled waters) been omitted from this Part.

(4) Subsection (3) above shall not apply to the owner or former operator of any mine or part of a mine if the mine or part in question became abandoned after 31st December 1999.

(5) In determining for the purposes of subsection (4) above whether a mine or part of a mine became abandoned before, on or after 31st December 1999 in a case where the mine or part has become abandoned on two or more occasions, of which—

(a) at least one falls on or before that date, and

(b) at least one falls after that date,

the mine or part shall be regarded as becoming abandoned after that date (but without prejudice to the operation of subsection (3) above in relation to that mine or part at, or in relation to, any time before the first of those occasions which fall after that date).

(6) Where, immediately before a part of a mine becomes abandoned, that part is the only part of the mine not falling to be regarded as abandoned for the time being, the abandonment of that part shall not be regarded for the purposes of subsection (4) or (5) above as constituting the abandonment of the mine, but only of that part of it.

(7) Nothing in subsection (2) or (3) above prevents the enforcing authority from doing anything by way of remediation under section 78N below which it could have done apart from that subsection, but the authority shall not be entitled under section 78P below to recover from any person any part of the cost incurred by the authority in doing by way of

remediation anything which it is precluded by subsection (2) or (3) above from requiring that person to do.

(8) In this section 'mine' has the same meaning as in the Mines and Quarries Act 1954.

78K Liability in respect of contaminating substances which escape to other land

(1) A person who has caused or knowingly permitted any substances to be in, on or under any land shall also be taken for the purposes of this Part to have caused or, as the case may be, knowingly permitted those substances to be in, on or under any other land to which they appear to have escaped.

(2) Subsections (3) and (4) below apply in any case where it appears that any substances are or have been in, on or under any land (in this section referred to as 'land A') as a result of their escape, whether directly or indirectly from other land in, on or under which a person caused or knowingly permitted them to be.

(3) Where this subsection applies, no remediation notice shall require a person—

(a) who is the owner or occupier of land A, and

(b) who has not caused or knowingly permitted the substances in question to be in, on or under that land,

to do anything by way of remediation to any land or waters (other than land or waters of which he is the owner or occupier) in consequence of land A appearing to be in such a condition, by reason of the presence of those substances in, on or under it, that significant harm[, or significant pollution of controlled waters, is being caused, or there is a significant possibility of such harm or pollution being caused].

(4) Where this subsection applies, no remediation notice shall require a person—

(a) who is the owner or occupier of land A, and

(b) who has not caused or knowingly permitted the substances in question to be in, on or under that land,

to do anything by way of remediation in consequence of any further land in, on or under which those substances or any of them appear to be or to have been present as a result of their escape from land A ('land B') appearing to be in such a condition, by reason of the presence of those substances in, on or under it, that significant harm[, or significant pollution of controlled waters, is being caused, or there is a significant possibility of such harm or pollution being caused] unless he is also the owner or occupier of land B.

(5) In any case where—

(a) a person ('person A') has caused or knowingly permitted any substances to be in, on, or under any land,

(b) another person ('person B') who has not caused or knowingly permitted those substances to be in, or under that land becomes the owner or occupier of that land, and

(c) the substances, or any of the substances, mentioned in paragraph (a) above appear to have escaped to other land,

no remediation notice shall require person B to do anything by way of remediation to that other land in consequence of the apparent acts or omissions of person A, except to the extent that person B caused or knowingly permitted the escape.

(6) Nothing in subsection (3), (4) or (5) above prevents the enforcing authority from doing anything by way of remediation under section 78N below which it could have done apart from that subsection, but the authority shall not be entitled under section 78P below to recover from any person any part of the cost incurred by the authority in doing by way of remediation anything which it is precluded by subsection (3), (4) or (5) above from requiring that person to do.

(7) In this section, 'appear' means appear to the enforcing authority, and cognate expressions shall be construed accordingly.

78L Appeals against remediation notices

(1) A person on whom a remediation notice is served may, within the period of twenty-one days beginning with the day on which the notice is served, appeal against the notice—

[(a) if it was served by a local authority in England, or served by the Environment Agency in relation to land in England, to the Secretary of State;

(b) if it was served by a local authority in Wales, or served by the Environment Agency in relation to land in Wales, to the National Assembly for Wales;

and in the following provisions of this section 'the appellate authority' means . . . [the Secretary of State or the National Assembly for Wales, as the case may be].

(2) On any appeal under subsection (1) above the appellate authority—

(a) shall quash the notice, if it is satisfied that there is a material defect in the notice; but

(b) subject to that, may confirm the remediation notice, with or without modification, or quash it.

(3) Where an appellate authority confirms a remediation notice, with or without modification, it may extend the period specified in the notice for doing what the notice requires to be done.

(4) Regulations may make provision with respect to—

(a) the grounds on which appeals under subsection (1) above may be made;

(b) [. . .]; or

(c) the procedure on an appeal under subsection (1) above.

(5) Regulations under subsection (4) above may (among other things)—

(a) include provisions comparable to those in section 290 of the Public Health Act 1936 (appeals againt notices requiring the execution of works);

(b) prescribe the cases in which a remediation notice is, or is not, to be suspended until the appeal is decided, or until some other stage in proceedings;

(c) prescribe the cases in which the decision on an appeal may in some respects be less favourable to the appellant than the remediation notice against which he is appealing;

(d) prescribe the cases in which the appellant may claim that a remediation notice should have been served on some other person and prescribe the procedure to be followed in those cases;

(e) make provision as respects—

(i) the particulars to be included in the notice of appeal;

(ii) the persons on whom notice of appeal is to be served and the particulars, if any, which are to accompany the notice; and

(iii) the abandonment of an appeal;

(f) make different provision for different cases or classes of case.

(6) This section is subject to section 114 of the Environment Act 1995 (delegation or reference of appeals etc).

78M Offences of not complying with a remediation notice

(1) If a person on whom an enforcing authority serves a remediation notice fails, without reasonable excuse, to comply with any of the requirements of the notice, he shall be guilty of an offence.

(2) Where the remediation notice in question is one which was required by section 78E(3) above to state, in relation to the requirement which has not been complied with, the proportion of the cost involved which the person charged with the offence is liable to bear, it shall be a defence for that person to prove that the only reason why he has not complied with the requirement is that one or more of the other persons who are liable to bear a proportion of that cost refused, or was not able, to comply with the requirement.

(3) Except in a case falling within subsection (4) below, a person who commits an offence under subsection (1) above shall be liable, on summary conviction, to a fine not exceeding

level 5 on the standard scale and to a further fine of an amount equal to one-tenth of level 5 on the standard scale for each day on which the failure continues after conviction of the offence and before the enforcing authority has begun to exercise its powers by virtue of section 78N(3)(c) below.

(4) A person who commits an offence under subsection (1) above in a case where the contaminated land to which the remediation notice relates is industrial, trade or business premises shall be liable on summary conviction to a fine not exceeding £20,000 or such greater sum as the Secretary of State may from time to time by order substitute and to a further fine of an amount equal to one-tenth of that sum for each day on which the failure continues after conviction of the offence and before the enforcing authority has begun to exercise its powers by virtue of section 78N(3)(c) below.

(5) If the enforcing authority is of the opinion that proceedings for an offence under this section would afford an ineffectual remedy against a person who has failed to comply with any of the requirements of a remediation notice which that authority has served on him, that authority may take proceedings in the High Court . . . for the purpose of securing compliance with the remediation notice.

(6) In this section 'industrial, trade or business premises' means premises used for any industrial, trade or business purposes or premises not so used on which matter is burnt in connection with any industrial, trade or business process, and premises are used for industrial purposes where they are used for the purposes of any treatment or process as well as where they are used for the purpose of manufacturing.

(7) No order shall be made under subsection (4) above unless a draft of the order has been laid before, and approved by a resolution of, each House of Parliament.

78N Powers of the enforcing authority to carry out remediation

(1) Where this section applies, the enforcing authority shall itself have power, in a case falling within paragraph (a) or (b) of section 78E(1) above, to do what is appropriate by way of remediation to the relevant land or waters.

(2) Subsection (1) above shall not confer power on the enforcing authority to do anything by way of remediation if the authority would, in the particular case, be precluded by section 78YB below from serving a remediation notice requiring that thing to be done.

(3) This section applies in each of the following cases, that is to say—

(a) where the enforcing authority considers it necessary to do anything itself by way of remediation for the purpose of preventing the occurrence of any serious harm, or serious pollution of controlled waters, of which there is imminent danger;

(b) where an appropriate person has entered into a written agreement with the enforcing authority for that authority to do, at the cost of that person, that which he would otherwise be required to do under this Part by way of remediation;

(c) where a person on whom the enforcing authority serves a remediation notice fails to comply with any of the requirements of the notice;

(d) where the enforcing authority is precluded by section 78J or 78K above from including something by way of remediation in a remediation notice;

(e) where the enforcing authority considers that, were it to do some particular thing by way of remediation, it would decide, by virtue of subsection (2) of section 78P below or any guidance issued under that subsection,—

(i) not to seek to recover under subsection (1) of that section any of the reasonable cost incurred by it in doing that thing; or

(ii) to seek so to recover only a portion of that cost;

(f) where no person has, after reasonable inquiry, been found who is an appropriate person in relation to any particular thing.

(4) Subject to section 78E(4) and (5) above, for the purposes of this section, the things which it is appropriate for the enforcing authority to do by way of remediation are—

(a) in a case falling within paragraph (a) of subsection (3) above, anything by way of remediation which the enforcing authority considers necessary for the purpose mentioned in that paragraph;

(b) in a case falling within paragraph (b) of that subsection, anything specified in, or determined under, the agreement mentioned in that paragraph;

(c) in a case falling within paragraph (c) of that subsection, anything which the person mentioned in that paragraph was required to do by virtue of the remediation notice;

(d) in a case falling within paragraph (d) of that subsection, anything by way of remediation which the enforcing authority is precluded by section 78J or 78K above from including in a remediation notice;

(e) in a case falling within paragraph (e) or (f) of that subsection, the particular thing mentioned in the paragraph in question.

(5) In this section 'the relevant land or waters' means—

(a) the contaminated land in question;

(b) any controlled waters affected by that land; or

(c) any land adjoining or adjacent to that land or those waters.

78P Recovery of, and security for, the cost of remediation by the enforcing authority

(1) Where, by virtue of section 78N(3)(a), (c), (e) or (f) above, the enforcing authority does any particular thing by way of remediation, it shall be entitled, subject to section 78J(7) and 78K(6) above, to recover the reasonable cost incurred in doing it from the appropriate person or, if there are two or more appropriate persons in proportions determined pursuant to section 78F(7) above.

(2) In deciding whether to recover the cost, and, if so, how much of the cost, which it is entitled to recover under subsection (1) above, the enforcing authority shall have regard—

(a) to any hardship which the recovery may cause to the person from whom the cost is recoverable; and

(b) to any guidance issued by the Secretary of State for the purposes of this subsection.

(3) Subsection (4) below shall apply in any case where—

(a) any cost is recoverable under subsection (1) above from a person—

(i) who is the owner of any premises which consist of or include the contaminated land in question; and

(ii) who caused or knowingly permitted the substances, or any of the substances, by reason of which the land is contaminated land to be in, on or under the land; and

(b) the enforcing authority serves a notice under this subsection (in this Part referred to as a 'charging notice') on that person.

(4) Where this subsection applies—

(a) the cost shall carry interest, at such reasonable rate as the enforcing authority may determine, from the date of service of the notice until the whole amount is paid; and

(b) subject to the following provisions of this section, the cost and accrued interest shall be a charge on the premises mentioned in subsection (3)(a)(i) above.

(5) A charging notice shall—

(a) specify the amount of the cost which the enforcing authority claims is irrecoverable;

(b) state the effect of subsection (4) above and the rate of interest determined by the authority under that subsection; and

(c) state the effect of subsections (7) and (8) below.

(6) On the date on which an enforcing authority serves a charging notice on a person, the authority shall also serve a copy of the notice on every other person who, to the knowledge of the authority, has an interest in the premises capable of being affected by the charge.

(7) Subject to any order under subsection (9)(b) or (c) below, the amount of any cost specified in a charging notice and the accrued interest shall be a charge on the premises—

(a) as from the end of the period of twenty-one days beginning with the service of the charging notice, or

(b) where an appeal is brought under subsection (8) below, as from the final determination or (as the case may be) the withdrawal, of the appeal,

until the cost and interest are recovered.

(8) A person served with a charging notice or a copy of a charging notice may appeal against the notice to a county court within the period of twenty-one days beginning with the date of service.

(9) On an appeal under subsection (8) above, the court may—

(a) confirm the notice without modification;

(b) order that the notice is to have effect with the substitution of a different amount for the amount originally specified in it; or

(c) order that the notice is to be of no effect.

(10) Regulations may make provision with respect to—

(a) the grounds on which appeals under this section may be made; or

(b) the procedure on any such appeal.

(11) An enforcing authority shall, for the purpose of enforcing a charge under this section, have all the same powers and remedies under the Law of Property Act 1925, and otherwise, as if it were a mortgagee by deed having powers of sale and lease, of accepting surrenders of leases and of appointing a receiver.

(12) Where any cost is a charge on premises under this section, the enforcing authority may by order declare the cost to be payable with interest by instalments within the specified period until the whole amount is paid.

(13) In subsection (12) above—

'interest' means interest at the rate determined by the enforcing authority under subsection (4) above; and

'the specified period' means such period of thirty years or less from the date of service of the charging notice as is specified in the order.

(14) ...

78Q Special sites

(1) If, in a case where a local authority has served a remediation notice, the contaminated land in question becomes a special site, the appropriate Agency may adopt the remediation notice and, if it does so,—

(a) it shall give notice of its decision to adopt the remediation notice to the appropriate person and to the local authority;

(b) the remediation notice shall have effect, as from the time at which the appropriate Agency decides to adopt it, as a remediation notice given by that Agency; and

(c) the validity of the remediation notice shall not be affected by—

(i) the contaminated land having become a special site;

(ii) the adoption of the remediation notice by the appropriate Agency; or

(iii) anything in paragraph (b) above.

(2) Where a local authority has, by virtue of section 78N above, begun to do anything, or any series of things, by way of remediation—

(a) the authority may continue doing that thing, or that series of things, by virtue of that section, notwithstanding that the contaminated land in question becomes a special site; and

(b) section 78P above shall apply in relation to the reasonable cost incurred by the authority in doing that thing or those things as if that authority were the enforcing authority.

(3) If and so long as any land is a special site, the appropriate Agency may from time to time inspect that land for the purpose of keeping its condition under review.

(4) If it appears to the appropriate Agency that a special site is no longer land which is required to be designated as such a site, the appropriate Agency may give notice—

(a) to the Secretary of State, and

(b) to the local authority in whose area the site is situated,

terminating the designation of the land in question as a special site as from such date as may be specified in the notice.

(5) A notice under subsection (4) above shall not prevent the land, or any of the land, to which the notice relates beng designated as a special site on a subsequent occasion.

(6) In exercising its functions under subsection (3) or (4) above, the appropriate Agency shall act in accordance with any guidance given for the purpose by the Secretary of State.

78R Registers

(1) Every enforcing authority shall maintain a register containing prescribed particulars of or relating to—

(a) remediation notices served by that authority;

(b) appeals against any such remediation notices;

(c) remediation statements or remediation declarations prepared and published under section 78H above;

(d) in relation to an enforcing authority in England and Wales, appeals against charging notices served by that authority;

(e) notices under subsection (1)(b) or (5)(a) of section 78C above which have effect by virtue of subsection (7) of that section as the designation of any land as a special site;

(f) notices under subsection (4)(b) of section 78D above which have effect by virtue of subsection (6) of that section as the designation of any land as a special site;

(g) notices given by or to the enforcing authority under section 78Q(4) above terminating the designation of any land as a special site;

(h) notifications given to that authority by persons—

(i) on whom a remediation notice has been served, or

(ii) who are or were required by virtue of section 78H(8)(a) above to prepare and publish a remediation statement,

of what they claim has been done by them by way of remediation;

(j) notifications given to that authority by owners or occupiers of land—

(i) in respect of which a remediation notice has been served, or

(ii) in respect of which a remediation statement has been prepared and published,

of what they claim has been done on the land in question by way of remediation;

(k) convictions for such offences under section 78M above as may be prescribed;

(l) such other matters relating to contaminated land as may be prescribed; but that duty is subject to sections 78S and 78T below.

(2) The form of, and the descriptions of information to be contained in, notifications for the purposes of subsection (1)(h) or (j) above may be prescribed by the Secretary of State.

(3) No entry made in a register by virtue of subsection (1)(h) or (j) above constitutes a repesentation by the body maintaining the register or, in a case where the entry is made by virtue of subsection (6) below, the authority which sent the copy of the particulars in question pursuant to subsection (4) or (5) below—

(a) that what is stated in the entry to have been done has in fact been done; or

(b) as to the manner in which it has been done.

(4) Where any particulars are entered on a register maintained under this section by the appropriate Agency, the appropriate Agency shall send a copy of those particulars to the local authority in whose area is situated the land to which the particulars relate.

(5) In any case where—

(a) any land is treated by virtue of section 78X(2) below as situated in the area of a local authority other than the local authority in whose area it is in fact situated, and

(b) any particulars relating to that land are entered on the register maintained under this section by the local authority in whose area the land is so treated as situated, that authority shall send a copy of those particulars to the local authority in whose area the land is in fact situated.

(6) Where a local authority receives a copy of any particulars sent to it pursuant to subsection (4) or (5) above, it shall enter those particulars on the register maintained by it under this section.

(7) Where information of any description is excluded by virtue of section 78T below from any register maintained under this section, a statement shall be entered in the register indicating the existence of information of that description.

(8) It shall be the duty of each enforcing authority—

(a) to secure that the registers maintained by it under this section are available, at all reasonable times, for inspection by the public free of charge; and

(b) to afford to members of the public facilities for obtaining copies of entries, on payment of reasonable charges;

and, for the purposes of this subsection, places may be prescribed by the Secretary of State at which any such registers or facilities as are mentioned in paragraph (a) or (b) above are to be available or afforded to the public in pursuance of the paragraph in question.

(9) Registers under this section may be kept in any form.

78S Exclusion from registers of information affecting national security

(1) No information shall be included in a register maintained under section 78R above if and so long as, in the opinion of the Secretary of State, the inclusion in the register of that information, or information of that description, would be contrary to the interests of national security.

(2)–(4) [. . .]

78T Exclusion from registers of certain confidential information

(1) No information relating to the affairs of any individual or business shall be included in a register maintained under section 78R above, without the consent of that individual or the person for the time being carrying on that business, if and so long as the information—

(a) is, in relation to him, commercially confidential; and

(b) is not required to be included in the register in pursuance of directions under subsection (7) below;

but information is not commercially confidential for the purposes of this section unless it is determined under this section to be so by the enforcing authority or, on appeal, by the Secretary of State.

(2) Where it appears to an enforcing authority that any information which has been obtained by the authority under or by virtue of any provision of this Part might be commercially confidential, the authority shall—

(a) give to the person to whom or whose business it relates notice that that information is required to be included in the register unless excluded under this section; and

(b) give him a reasonable opportunity—

(i) of objecting to the inclusion of the information on the ground that it is commercially confidential; and

(ii) of making representations to the authority for the purpose of justifying any such objection;

and, if any representations are made, the enforcing authority shall, having taken the representations into account, determine whether the information is or is not commercially confidential.

(3) Where, under subsection (2) above, an authority determines that information is not commercially confidential—

(a) the information shall not be entered in the register until the end of the period of twenty-one days beginning with the date on which the determination is notified to the person concerned;

(b) that person may appeal to the Secretary of State against the decision;

and, where an appeal is brought in respect of any information, the information shall not be entered in the register until the end of the period of seven days following the day on which the appeal is finally determined or withdrawn.

(4) An appeal under subsection (3) above shall, if either party to the appeal so requests or the Secretary of State so decides, take or continue in the form of a hearing (which must be held in private).

(5) Subsection (10) of section 15 above shall apply in relation to an appeal under subsection (3) above as it applies in relation to an appeal under that section.

(6) Subsection (3) above is subject to section 114 of the Environment Act 1995 (delegation or reference of appeals etc).

(7) The Secretary of State may give to the enforcing authorities directions as to specified information, or descriptions of information, which the public interest requires to be included in registers maintained under section 78R above notwithstanding that the information may be commercially confidential.

(8) Information excluded from a register shall be treated as ceasing to be commercially confidential for the purposes of this section at the expiry of the period of four years beginning with the date of the determination by virtue of which it was excluded; but the person who furnished it may apply to the authority for the information to remain excluded from the register on the ground that it is still commercially confidential and the authority shall determine whether or not that is the case.

(9) Subsections (3) to (6) above shall apply in relation to a determination under subsection (8) above as they apply in relation to a determination under subsection (2) above.

(10) Information is, for the purposes of any determination under this section, commercially confidential, in relation to any individual or person, if its being contained in the register would prejudice to an unreasonable degree the commercial interests of that individual or person.

(11) For the purposes of subsection (10) above, there shall be disregarded any prejudice to the commercial interests of any individual or person so far as relating only to the value of the contaminated land in question or otherwise to the ownership or occupation of that land.

78U Reports by the appropriate Agency on the state of contaminated land

(1) The appropriate Agency shall—

(a) from time to time, or

(b) if the Secretary of State at any time so requests,

prepare and publish a report on the state of contaminated land in England and Wales . . . as the case may be.

(2) A local authority shall, at the written request of the appropriate Agency, furnish the appropriate Agency with such information to which this subsection applies as the appropriate Agency may require for the purpose of enabling it to perform its functions under subsection (1) above.

(3) The information to which subsection (2) above applies is such information as the local authority may have, or may reasonably be expected to obtain, with respect to the condition of contaminated land in its area, being information which the authority has acquired or may acquire in the exercise of its functions under this Part.

78V Site-specific guidance by the appropriate Agency concerning contaminated land

(1) The appropriate Agency may issue guidance to any local authority with respect to the exercise or performance of the authority's powers or duties under this Part in relation to any particular contaminated land; and in exercising or performing those powers or duties in relation to that land the authority shall have regard to any such guidance so issued.

(2) If and to the extent that any guidance issued under subsection (1) above to a local authority is inconsistent with any guidance issued under this Part by the Secretary of State, the local authority shall disregard the guidance under that subsection.

(3) A local authority shall, at the written request of the appropriate Agency, furnish the appropriate Agency with such information to which this subsection applies as the approprate Agency may require for the purpose of enabling it to issue guidance for the purposes of subsection (1) above.

(4) The information to which subsection (3) above applies is such information as the local authority may have, or may reasonably be expected to obtain, with respect to any contaminated land in its area, being information which the authority has acquired, or may acquire, in the exercise of its functions under this Part.

78W The appropriate Agency to have regard to guidance given by the Secretary of State

(1) The Secretary of State may issue guidance to the appropriate Agency with respect to the exercise or performance of that Agency's powers or duties under this Part; and in exercising or performing those powers or duties the appropriate Agency shall have regard to any such guidance so issued.

(2) The duty imposed on the appropriate Agency by subsection (1) above is without prejudice to any duty imposed by any other provision of this Part on that Agency to act in accordance with guidance issued by the Secretary of State.

78X Supplementary provisions

(1) Where it appears to a local authority that two or more different sites, when considered together, are in such a condition, by reason of substances in, on or under the land, that—

- (a) significant harm is being caused or there is a significant possibility of such harm being caused, or
- [(b) significant pollution of controlled waters is being caused or there is a significant possibility of such pollution being caused,]

this Part shall apply in relation to each of those sites, whether or not the condition of the land at any of them, when considered alone, appears to the authority to be such that significant harm[, or significant pollution of controlled waters, is being caused, or there is a significant possibility of such harm or pollution being caused].

(2) Where it appears to a local authority that any land outside, but adjoining or adjacent to, its area is in such a condition, by reason of substances in, on or under the land, that significant harm[, or significant pollution of controlled waters, is being caused, or there is a significant possibility of such harm or pollution being caused], within its area—

- (a) the authority may, in exercising its functions under this Part, treat that land as if it were land situated within its area; and
- (b) except in this subsection, any reference—
  - (i) to land within the area of a local authority, or
  - (ii) to the local authority in whose area any land is situated,

  shall be construed accordingly;

but this subsection is without prejudice to the functions of the local authority in whose area the land is in fact situated.

(3) A person acting in a relevant capacity—

(a) shall not thereby be personally liable, under this Part, to bear the whole or any part of the cost of doing any thing by way of remediation, unless that thing is to any extent referable to substances whose presence in, on or under the contaminated land in question is a result of any act done or omission made by him which it was unreasonable for a person acting in that capacity to do or make; and

(b) shall not thereby be guilty of an offence under or by virtue of section 78M above unless the requirement which has not been complied with is a requirement to do some particular thing for which he is personally liable to bear the whole or any part of the cost.

(4) In subsection (3) above, 'person acting in a relevant capacity' means—

(a) a person acting as an insolvency practitioner, within the meaning of section 388 of the Insolvency Act 1986 (includng that section as it applies in relation to an insolvent partnership by virtue of any order made under section 421 of that Act);

(b) the official receiver acting in a capacity in which he would be regarded as acting as an insolvency practitioner within the meaning of section 388 of the Insolvency Act 1986 if subsection (5) of that section were disregarded;

(c) the official receiver acting as receiver or manager;

(d) a person acting as a special manager under section 177 or 370 of the Insolvency Act 1986;

(e) . . .

(f) a person acting as a receiver or receiver and manager—

(i) under or by virtue of any enactment; or

(ii) by virtue of his appointment as such by an order of a court or by any other instrument.

(5) Regulations may make different provision for different cases or circumstances.

78YA Supplementary provisions with respect to guidance by the Secretary of State

(1) Any power of the Secretary of State to issue guidance under this Part shall only be exercisable after consultation with the appropriate Agency and such other bodies or persons as he may consider it appropriate to consult in relation to the guidance in question.

(2) A draft of any guidance proposed to be issued under section 78A(2) or (5), 78B(2) or 78F(6) or (7) above shall be laid before each House of Parliament and the guidance shall not be issued until after the period of 40 days beginning with the day on which the draft was so laid or, if the draft is laid on different days, the later of the two days.

(3) If, within the period mentioned in subsection (2) above, either House resolves that the guidance, the draft of which was laid before it, should not be issued, the Secretary of State shall not issue that guidance.

(4) In reckoning any period of 40 days for the purposes of subsection (2) or (3) above, no account shall be taken of any time during which Parliament is dissolved or prorogued or during which both Houses are adjourned for more than four days.

(5) The Secretary of State shall arrange for any guidance issued by him under this Part to be published in such manner as he considers appropriate.

78YB Interaction of this Part with other enactments

(1) A remediation notice shall not be served if and to the extent that it appears to the enforcing authority that the powers of the appropriate Agency under section 27 above may be exercised in relation to—

(a) the significant harm (if any), and

(b) the [significant] pollution of controlled waters (if any), by reason of which the contaminated land in question is such land.

(2) Nothing in this Part shall apply in relation to any land in respect of which there is for the time being in force a site licence under Part II above, except to the extent that any significant harm, or [significant] pollution of controlled waters, by reason of which that land would otherwise fall to be regarded as contaminated land is attributable to causes other

than—

(a) breach of the conditions of the licence; or

(b) the carrying on, in accordance with the conditions of the licence, of any activity authorised by the licence.

[(2A) This Part shall not apply if and to the extent that—

(a) any significant harm, or pollution of controlled waters, by reason of which the land would otherwise fall to be regarded as contaminated, is attributable to the final disposal by deposit in or on land of controlled waste, and

(b) enforcement action may be taken in relation to that disposal.

(2B) A remediation notice shall not be served in respect of contaminated land if and to the extent that—

(a) the significant harm, or pollution of controlled waters, by reason of which the contaminated land is such land is attributable to an activity other than the final disposal by deposit in or on land of controlled waste, and

(b) enforcement action may be taken in relation to that activity.

(2C) In subsections (2A) and (2B) above—

'controlled waste' has the meaning given in section 75(4) of this Act; and

'enforcement action' means action under regulation 24 (enforcement notices) or regulation 26(2) (power of regulator to remedy pollution) of the Pollution Prevention and Control (England and Wales) Regulations 2000.]

(3) If, in a case falling within subsection (1) or (7) of section 59 above, the land in question is contaminated land, or becomes such land by reason of the deposit of the controlled waste in question, a remediation notice shall not be served in respect of that land by reason of that waste or any consequences of its deposit, if and to the extent that it appears to the enforcing authority that the powers of a waste regulation authority or waste collection authority under that section may be exercised in relation to that waste or the consequences of its deposit.

(4) No remediation notice shall require a person to do anything the effect of which would be to impede or prevent the making of a discharge in pursuance of a consent given under Chapter II of Part III of the Water Resources Act 1991 (pollution offences)....

78YC This Part and radioactivity*

Except as provided by regulations, nothing in this Part applies in relation to harm, or pollution of controlled waters, so far as attributable to any radioactivity possessed by any substance; but regulations may—

(a) provide for prescribed provisions of this Part to have effect with such modifications as the Secretary of State considers appropriate for the purpose of dealing with harm, or pollution of controlled waters, so far as attributable to any radioactivity possessed by any substances; or

(b) make such modifications of the Radioactive Substances Act 1993 or any other Act as the Secretary of State considers appropriate.]

PART III STATUTORY NUISANCES AND CLEAN AIR

79 Statutory nuisances and inspections therefor

(1) [Subject to subsections (1A) to (6A)] below, the following matters constitute 'statutory nuisances' for the purposes of this Part, that is to say—

(a) any premises in such a state as to be prejudicial to health or a nuisance;

(b) smoke emitted from premises so as to be prejudicial to health or a nuisance;

* Editor's note: see the Radioactive Contaminated Land (Enabling Powers) (England) Regulations 2005 (SI 2005, No. 3467).

(c) fumes or gases emitted from premises so as to be prejudicial to health or a nuisance;

(d) any dust, steam, smell or other effluvia arising on industrial, trade or business premises and being prejudicial to health or a nuisance;

(e) any accumulation or deposit which is prejudicial to health or a nuisance;

(f) any animal kept in such a place or manner as to be prejudicial to health or a nuisance;

[(fa) any insects emanating from relevant industrial, trade or business premises and being prejudicial to health or a nuisance;

(fb) artificial light emitted from premises so as to be prejudicial to health or a nuisance;]

(g) noise emitted from premises so as to be prejudicial to health or a nuisance;

[(ga) noise that is prejudicial to health or a nuisance and is emitted from or caused by a vehicle, machinery or equipment in a street...]

(h) any other matter declared by any enactment to be a statutory nuisance;

and it shall be the duty of every local authority to cause its area to be inspected from time to time to detect any statutory nuisances which ought to be dealt with under sections 80 [or sections 80 and 80A below] and, where a complaint of a statutory nuisance is made to it by a person living within its area, to take such steps as are reasonably practicable to investigate the complaint.

[(1A) No matter shall constitute a statutory nuisance to the extent that it consists of, or is caused by, any land being in a contaminated state.

(1B) Land is in a 'contaminated state' for the purposes of subsection (1A) above if, and only if, it is in such a condition, by reason of substances in, on or under the land, that—

(a) harm is being caused or there is a possibility of harm being caused; or

(b) pollution of controlled waters is being, or is likely to be, caused;

and in this subsection 'harm', 'pollution of controlled waters' and 'substance' have the same meaning as in Part IIA of this Act.]

(2) Subsection (1)(b), (fb) and (g) above do not apply in relation to premises—

(a) occupied on behalf of the Crown for naval, military or air force purposes or for the purposes of the department of the Secretary of State having responsibility for defence, or

(b) occupied by or for the purposes of a visiting force;

and 'visiting force' means any such body, contingent or detachment of the forces of any country as is a visiting force for the purposes of any of the provisions of the Visiting Forces Act 1952.

(3) Subsection (1)(b) above does not apply to—

(i) smoke emitted from a chimney of a private dwelling within a smoke control area,

(ii) dark smoke emitted from a chimney of a building or a chimney serving the furnace of a boiler or industrial plant attached to a building or for the time being fixed to or installed on any land,

(iii) smoke emitted from a railway locomotive steam engine, or

(iv) dark smoke emitted otherwise than as mentioned above from industrial or trade premises.

(4) Subsection (1)(c) above does not apply in relation to premises other than private dwellings.

(5) Subsection (1)(d) above does not apply to steam emitted from a railway locomotive engine.

[(5A) Subsection (1)(fa) does not apply to insects that are wild animals included in Schedule 5 to the Wildlife and Countryside Act 1981 (animals which are protected), unless they are included in respect of section 9(5) of that Act only.

[(5B) Subsection (1)(fb) does not apply to artificial light emitted from—

(a) an airport;

(b) harbour premises;
(c) railway premises, not being relevant separate railway premises;
(d) tramway premises;
(e) a bus station and any associated facilities;
(f) a public service vehicle operating centre;
(g) a goods vehicle operating centre;
(h) a lighthouse;
(i) a prison.]

(6) Subsection (1)(g) above does not apply to noise caused by aircraft other than model aircraft.

[(6A) Subsection (1)(ga) above does not apply to noise made—

(a) by traffic,
(b) by any naval, military or air force of the Crown or by a visiting force (as defined in subsection (2) above), or
(c) by a political demonstration or a demonstration supporting or opposing a cause or campaign.]

(7) In this Part—

['airport' has the meaning given by section 95 of the Transport Act 2000;

'appropriate person' means—

(a) in relation to England, the Secretary of State;
(b) in relation to Wales, the National Assembly for Wales;

'associated facilities', in relation to a bus station, has the meaning given by section 83 of the Transport Act 1985;

'bus station' has the meaning given by section 83 of the Transport Act 1985;]

'chimney' includes structures and openings of any kind from or through which smoke may be emitted;

'dust' does not include dust emitted from a chimney as an ingredient of smoke;

['equipment' includes a musical instrument;]

'fumes' means any airborne solid matter smaller than dust;

'gas' includes vapour and moisture precipitated from vapour;

['goods vehicle operating centre', in relation to vehicles used under an operator's licence, means a place which is specified in the licence as an operating centre for those vehicles, and for the purposes of this definition 'operating centre' and 'operator's licence' have the same meaning as in the Goods Vehicles (Licensing of Operators) Act 1995;

'harbour premises' means premises which form part of a harbour area and which are occupied wholly or mainly for the purposes of harbour operations, and for the purposes of this definition 'harbour area' and 'harbour operations' have the same meaning as in Part 3 of the Aviation and Maritime Security Act 1990;]

'industrial, trade or business premises' means premises used for any industrial, trade or business purposes or premises not so used on which matter is burnt in connection with any industrial, trade or business process, and premises are used for industrial purposes where they are used for the purposes of any treatment or process as well as where they are used for the purposes of manufacturing;

['lighthouse' has the same meaning as in Part 8 of the Merchant Shipping Act 1995;]

'local authority' means, subject to subsection (8) below;—

(a) in Greater London, a London borough council, the Common Council of the City of London and, as respects the Temples, the Sub-Treasurer of the Inner Temple and the Under-Treasurer of the Middle Temple respectively;
(b) [in England and Wales] outside Greater London, a district council; [...]
(c) the Council of the Isles of Scilly;
(d) ...

'noise' includes vibration;

['person responsible'—

(a) in relation to a statutory nuisance, means the person to whose act, default or sufferance the nuisance is attributable;
(b) in relation to a vehicle, includes the person in whose name the vehicle is for the time being registered under the vehicle Excise and Registration Act 1994 and any other person who is for the time being the driver of the vehicle;
(c) in relation to machinery or equipment, includes any person who is for the time being the operator of the machinery or equipment;]

['prison' includes a young offender institution;]

'prejudicial to health' means injurious, or likely to cause injury, to health;

'premises' includes land and, subject to subsection (12) [and [in relation to England and Wales] section 81A(9)] below, any vessel;

'private dwelling' means any building, or part of a building, used or intended to be used, as a dwelling;

['public service vehicle operating centre', in relation to public service vehicles used under a PSV operator's licence, means a place which is an operating centre of those vehicles, and for the purposes of this definition 'operating centre', 'PSV operator's licence' and 'public service vehicle' have the same meaning as in the Public Passenger Vehicles Act 1981;

'railway premises' means any premises which fall within the definition of 'light maintenance depot', 'network', 'station' or 'track' in section 83 of the Railways Act 1993;

'relevant separate railway premises' has the meaning given by subsection (7A);]

['road' has the same meaning as in Part IV of the New Roads and Street Works Act 1991:]

'smoke' includes soot, ash, grit and gritty particles emitted in smoke;

['street' means a highway and any other road, footway, square or court that is for the time being open to the public;]

['tramway premises' means any premises which, in relation to a tramway, are the equivalent of the premises which, in relation to a railway, fall within the definition of 'light maintenance depot', 'network', 'station' or 'track' in section 83 of the Railways Act 1993;]

and any expressions used in this section and in [the Clean Air Act 1993] have the same meaning in this section as in that Act and [section 3 of the Clean Air Act 1993] shall apply for the interpretation of the expression 'dark smoke' and the operation of this Part in relation to it.

[(7A) Railway premises are relevant separate railway premises if—
(a) they are situated within—
(i) premises used as a museum or other place of cultural, scientific or historical interest, or
(ii) premises used for the purposes of a funfair or other entertainment, recreation or amusement, and
(b) they are not associated with any other railway premises.

(7B) For the purposes of subsection (7A)—
(a) a network situated as described in subsection (7A)(a) is associated with other railway premises if it is connected to another network (not being a network situated as described in subsection (7A)(a));
(b) track that is situated as described in subsection (7A)(a) but is not part of a network is associated with other railway premises if it is connected to track that forms part of a network (not being a network situated as described in subsection (7A)(a));
(c) a station or light maintenance depot situated as described in subsection (7A)(a) is associated with other railway premises if it is used in connection with the provision of railway services other than services provided wholly within the premises where it is situated.

In this subsection 'light maintenance depot', 'network', 'railway services', 'station' and 'track' have the same meaning as in Part 1 of the Railways Act 1993.]

[(7C) In this Part 'relevant industrial, trade or business premises' means premises that are industrial, trade or business premises as defined in subsection (7), but excluding—
(a) land used as arable, grazing, meadow or pasture land,

(b) land used as osier land, reed beds or woodland,
(c) land used for market gardens, nursery grounds or orchards,
(d) land forming part of an agricultural unit, not being land falling within any of paragraphs (a) to (c), where the land is of a description prescribed by regulations made by the appropriate person, and
(e) land included in a site of special scientific interest (as defined in section 52(1) of the Wildlife and Countryside Act 1981),

and excluding land covered by, and the waters of, any river or watercourse, that is neither a sewer nor a drain, or any lake or pond.

(7D) For the purposes of subsection (7C)—

'agricultural' has the same meaning as in section 109 of the Agriculture Act 1947;

'agricultural unit' means land which is occupied as a unit for agricultural purposes;

'drain' has the same meaning as in the Water Resources Act 1991;

'lake or pond' has the same meaning as in section 104 of that Act;

'sewer' has the same meaning as in that Act.]

(8) Where, by an order under section 2 of the Public Health (Control of Disease) Act 1984, a port health authority... has been constituted for any port health district, the port health authority... shall have by virtue of this subsection, as respects its district, the functions conferred or imposed by this Part in relation to statutory nuisances other than a nuisance falling within paragraph (fb), (g) [or (ga)] of subsection (1) above and no such order shall be made assigning those functions; and 'local authority' and 'area' shall be construed accordingly.

(9) In this Part 'best practicable means' is to be interpreted by reference to the following provisions—

(a) 'practicable' means reasonably practicable having regard among other things to local conditions and circumstances, to the current state of technical knowledge and to the financial implications;
(b) the means to be employed include the design, installation, maintenance and manner and periods of operation of plant and machinery, and the design. construction and maintenance of buildings and structures;
(c) the test is to apply only so far as compatible with any duty imposed by law;
(d) the test is to apply only so far as compatible with safety and safe working conditions, and with the exigencies of any emergency or unforeseeable circumstances;

and, in circumstances where a code of practice under section 71 of the Control of Pollution Act 1974 (noise minimisation) is applicable, regard shall also be had to guidance given in it.

(10) A local authority shall not without the consent of the Secretary of State institute summary proceedings under this Part in respect of a nuisance falling within paragraph (b), (d) [(e), (fb) or (g)] ... of subsection (1) above if proceedings in respect thereof might be instituted under Part I [or under regulations under section 2 of the Pollution Prevention and Control Act 1999.]

(11) The area of a local authority which includes part of the seashore shall also include for the purposes of this Part the territorial sea lying seawards from that part of the shore; and subject to subsection (12) [and in relation to England and Wales, section 81A] below, this Part shall have effect, in relation to any area included in the area of a local authority by virtue of this subsection—

(a) as if references to premises and the occupier of premises included respectively a vessel and the master of a vessel; and
(b) with such other modifications, if any, as are prescribed in regulations made by the Secretary of State.

(12) A vessel powered by steam reciprocating machinery is not a vessel to which this Part of this Act applies.

80 Summary proceedings for statutory nuisances

(1) Subject to subsection (2A) where a local authority is satisfied that a statutory nuisance exists, or is likely to occur or recur, in the area of the authority, the local authority shall serve a notice ('an abatement notice') imposing all or any of the following requirements—

(a) requiring the abatement of the nuisance or prohibiting or restricting its occurrence or recurrence;

(b) requiring the execution of such works, and the taking of such other steps, as may be necessary for any of those purposes,

and the notice shall specify the time or times within which the requirements of the notice are to be complied with.

(2) [Subject to section 80A(1) below,] the abatement notice shall be served—

(a) except in a case falling within paragraph (b) or (c) below, on the person responsible for the nuisance;

(b) where the nuisance arises from any defect of a structural character, on the owner of the premises;

(c) where the person responsible for the nuisance cannot be found or the nuisance has not yet occurred, on the owner or occupier of the premises.

[(2A) Where a local authority is satisfied that a statutory nuisance falling within paragraph (g) of section 79(1) above exists, or is likely to occur or recur, in the area of the authority, the authority shall—

(a) serve an abatement notice in respect of the nuisance in accordance with subsections (1) and (2) above; or

(b) take such other steps as it thinks appropriate for the purpose of persuading the appropriate person to abate the nuisance or prohibit or restrict its occurrence or recurrence.

(2B) If a local authority has taken steps under subsection (2A)(b) above and either of the conditions in subsection (2C) below is satisfied, the authority shall serve an abatement notice in respect of the nuisance.

(2C) The conditions are—

(a) that the authority is satisfied at any time before the end of the relevant period that the steps taken will not be successful in persuading the appropriate person to abate the nuisance or prohibit or restrict its occurrence or recurrence;

(b) that the authority is satisfied at the end of the relevant period that the nuisance continues to exist, or continues to be likely to occur or recur, in the area of the authority.

(2D) The relevant period is the period of seven days starting with the day on which the authority was first satisfied that the nuisance existed, or was likely to occur or recur.

(2E) The appropriate person is the person on whom the authority would otherwise be required under subsection (2A)(a) above to serve an abatement notice in respect of the nuisance.]

[(3) A person served with an abatement notice] may appeal against the notice to a magistrates' court . . . within the period of twenty-one days beginning with the date on which he was served with the notice.

(4) If a person on whom an abatement notice is served, without reasonable excuse, contravenes or fails to comply with any requirement or prohibition imposed by the notice, he shall be guilty of an offence.

(5) Except in a case falling within subsection (6) below, a person who commits an offence under subsection (4) above shall be liable on summary conviction to a fine not exceeding level 5 on the standard scale together with a further fine of an amount equal to one-tenth of that level for each day on which the offence continues after the conviction.

(6) A person who commits an offence under subsection (4) above on industrial, trade or business premises shall be liable on summary conviction to a fine not exceeding £20,000.

(7) Subject to subsection (8) below, in any proceedings for an offence under subsection (4) above in respect of a statutory nuisance it shall be a defence to prove that the best practicable means were used to prevent, or to counteract the effects of, the nuisance.

(8) The defence under subsection (7) above is not available—

(a) in the case of a nuisance falling within paragraph (a), (d), (e), (f), (fa) or (g) of section 79(1) above except where the nuisance arises on industrial, trade or business premises;

[(aza) in the case of a nuisance falling within paragraph (fb) of section 79(1) above except where—

(i) the artificial light is emitted from industrial, trade or business premises, or

(ii) the artificial light (not being light to which sub-paragraph (i) applies) is emitted by lights used for the purpose only of illuminating an outdoor relevant sports facility;]

[(aa) in the case of a nuisance falling within paragraph (ga) of section 79(1) above except where the noise is emitted from or caused by a vehicle, machinery or equipment being used for industrial, trade or business purposes;]

(b) in the case of a nuisance falling within paragraph (b) of section 79(1) above except where the smoke is emitted from a chimney; and

(c) in the case of a nuisance falling within paragraph (c) or (h) of section 79(1) above.

[(8A) For the purposes of subsection (8)(aza) a relevant sports facility is an area, with or without structures, that is used when participating in a relevant sport, but does not include such an area comprised in domestic premises.

(8B) For the purposes of subsection (8A) 'relevant sport' means a sport that is designated for those purposes by order made by the Secretary of State, in relation to England, or the National Assembly for Wales, in relation to Wales. A sport may be so designated by reference to its appearing in a list maintained by a body specified in the order.(8C) In subsection (8A) 'domestic premises' means—

(a) premises used wholly or mainly as a private dwelling, or

(b) land or other premises belonging to, or enjoyed with, premises so used.]

(9) In proceedings for an offence under subsection (4) above in respect of a statutory nuisance falling within paragraph (g) [or (ga)] of section 79(1) above where the offence consists in contravening requirements imposed by virtue of subsection (1)(a) above it shall be a defence to prove—

(a) that the alleged offence was covered by a notice served under section 60 or a consent given under section 61 or 65 of the Control of Pollution Act 1974 (construction sites, etc); or

(b) where the alleged offence was committed at a time when the premises were subject to a notice under section 66 of that Act (noise reduction notice), that the level of noise emitted from the premises at that time was not such as to a constitute a contravention of the notice under that section; or

(c) where the alleged offence was committed at a time when the premises were not subject to a notice under section 66 of that Act, and when a level fixed under section 67 of that Act (new buildings liable to abatement order) applied to the premises, that the level of noise emitted from the premises at that time did not exceed that level.

(10) Paragraphs (b) and (c) of subsection (9) above apply whether or not the relevant notice was subject to appeal at the time when the offence was alleged to have been committed.

80A [Abatement notice in respect of noise in street

(1) In the case of a statutory nuisance within section 79(1)(ga) above that—

(a) has not yet occurred, or

(b) arises from noise emitted from or caused by an unattended vehicle or unattended machinery or equipment,

the abatement notice shall be served in accordance with subsection (2) below.

(2) The notice shall be served—

(a) where the person responsible for the vehicle, machinery or equipment can be found, on that person;

(b) where that person cannot be found or where the local authority determines that this paragraph should apply, by fixing the notice to the vehicle, machinery or equipment.

(3) Where—

(a) an abatement notice is served in accordance with subsection (2)(b) above by virtue of a determination of the local authority, and

(b) the person responsible for the vehicle, machinery or equipment can be found and served with a copy of the notice within an hour of the notice being fixed to the vehicle, machinery or equipment,

a copy of the notice shall be served on that person accordingly.

(4) Where an abatement notice is served in accordance with subsection (2)(b) above by virtue of a determination of the local authority, the notice shall state that, if a copy of the notice is subsequently served under subsection (3) above, the time specified in the notice as the time within which its requirements are to be complied with is extended by such further period as is specified in the notice.

(5) Where an abatement notice is served in accordance with subsection (2)(b) above, the person responsible for the vehicle, machinery or equipment may appeal against the notice under section 80(3) above as if he had been served with the notice on the date on which it was fixed to the vehicle, machinery or equipment.

(6) Section 80(4) above shall apply in relation to a person on whom a copy of an abatement notice is served under subsection (3) above as if the copy were the notice itself.

(7) A person who removes or interferes with a notice fixed to a vehicle, machinery or equipment in accordance with subsection (2)(b) above shall be guilty of an offence, unless he is the person responsible for the vehicle, machinery or equipment or he does so with the authority of that person.

(8) A person who commits an offence under subsection (7) above shall be liable on summary conviction to a fine not exceeding level 3 on the standard scale.]

81 Supplementary provisions

(1) [Subject to subsection (1A) below, where] more than one person is responsible for a statutory nuisance section 80 above shall apply to each of those persons whether or not what any one of them is responsible for would by itself amount to a nuisance.

[(1A) In relation to a statutory nuisance within section 79(1)(ga) above for which more than one person is responsible (whether or not what any one of those persons is responsible for would by itself amount to such a nuisance), section 80(2)(a) above shall apply with the substitution of 'any one of the persons' for 'the person'.

(1B) In relation to a statutory nuisance within section 79(1)(ga) above caused by noise emitted from or caused by an unattended vehicle or unattended machinery or equipment for which more than one person is responsible, section 80A above shall apply with the substitution—

(a) in subsection (2)(a), of 'any of the persons' for 'the person' and of 'one such person' for 'that person',

(b) in subsection (2)(b), of 'such a person' for 'that person',

(c) in subsection (3), of 'any of the persons' for 'the person' and of 'one such person' for 'that person',

(d) in subsection (5), of 'any person' for 'the person', and

(e) in subsection (7), of 'a person' for 'the person' and of 'such a person' for 'that person'.]

(2) Where a statutory nuisance which exists or has occurred within the area of a local authority, or which has affected any part of that area, appears to the local authority to be wholly or partly caused by some act or default committed or taking place outside the area, the local authority may act under section 80 above as if the act or default were wholly within that area, except that any appeal shall be heard by a magistrates' court... having jurisdiction where the act or default is alleged to have taken place.

(3) Where an abatement notice has not been complied with the local authority may, whether or not they take proceedings for an offence... under section 80(4) above, abate the nuisance and do whatever may be necessary in execution of the notice.

(4) Any expenses reasonably incurred by a local authority in abating, or preventing the recurrence of, a statutory nuisance under subsection (3) above may be recovered by them from the person by whose act or default the nuisance was caused and, if that person is the owner of the premises, from any person who is for the time being the owner thereof; and the court... may apportion the expenses between persons by whose acts or defaults the nuisance is caused in such manner as the court consider... fair and reasonable.

(5) If a local authority is of opinion that proceedings for an offence under section 80(4) above would afford an inadequate remedy in the case of any statutory nuisance, they may, subject to subsection (6) below, take proceedings in the High Court... for the purpose of securing the abatement, prohibition or restriction of the nuisance, and the proceedings shall be maintainable notwithstanding the local authority have suffered no damage from the nuisance.

(6) In any proceedings under subsection (5) above in respect of a nuisance falling within paragraph (g) [or (ga)] of section 79(1) above, it shall be a defence to prove that the noise was authorised by a notice under section 60 or a consent under section 61 (construction sites) of the Control of Pollution Act 1974.

(7) The further supplementary provisions in Schedule 3 to this Act shall have effect.

[81A Expenses recoverable from owner to be a charge on premises

(1) Where any expenses are recoverable under section 81(4) above from a person who is the owner of the premises there mentioned and the local authority serves a notice on him under this section—

(a) the expenses shall carry interest, at such reasonable rate as the local authority may determine, from the date of service of the notice until the whole amount is paid, and

(b) subject to the following provisions of this section, the expenses and accrued interest shall be a charge on the premises.

(2)–(10)...

81B Payment of expenses by instalments

(1) Where any expenses are a charge on premises under section 81A above, the local authority may by order declare the expenses to be payable with interest by instalments within the specified period, until the whole amount is paid.

(2)–(6)...]

82 Summary proceedings by persons aggrieved by statutory nuisances

(1) A magistrates' court may act under this section on a complaint... made by any person on the ground that he is aggrieved by the existence of a statutory nuisance.

(2) If the magistrates' court... is satisfied that the alleged nuisance exists, or that although abated it is likely to recur on the same premises [or, in the case of a nuisance within section 79(1)(ga) above, in the same street...], the court... shall make an order for either or both of the following purposes—

(a) requiring the defendant . . . to abate the nuisance, within a time specified in the order, and to execute any works necessary for that purpose;

(b) prohibiting a recurrence of the nuisance, and requiring the defendant . . . within a time specified in the order, to execute any works necessary to prevent the recurrence;

and may also impose on the defendant a fine not exceeding level 5 on the standard scale.

(3) If the magistrates' court . . . is satisfied that the alleged nuisance exists and is such as, in the opinion of the court . . . torender premises unfit for human habitation, an order under subsection (2) above may prohibit the use of the premises for human habitation until the premises are, to the satisfaction of the court . . ., rendered fit for that purpose.

(4) Proceedings for an order under subsection (2) above shall be brought—

(a) except in a case falling within [paragraph (b), (c) or (d) below], against the person responsible for the nuisance;

(b) where the nuisance arises from any defect of a structural character, against the owner of the premises;

(c) where the person responsible for the nuisance cannot be found, against the owner or occupier of the premises.

[(d) in the case of a statutory nuisance within section 79(1)(ga) above caused by noise emitted from or caused by an unattended vehicle or unattended machinery or equipment, against the person responsible for the vehicle, machinery or equipment.]

[(5) Subject to subsection (5A) below, where] more than one person is responsible for a statutory nuisance, subsections (1) to (4) above shall apply to each of those persons whether or not what any one of them is responsible for would by itself amount to a nuisance.

[(5A) In relation to a statutory nuisance within section 79(1)(ga) above for which more than one person is responsible (whether or not what any one of those persons is responsible for would by itself amount to such a nuisance), subsection (4)(a) above shall apply with the substitution of 'each person responsible for the nuisance who can be found' for 'the person responsible for the nuisance'.

(5B) In relation to a statutory nuisance within section 79(1)(ga) above caused by noise emitted from or caused by an unattended vehicle or unattended machinery or equipment for which more than one person is responsible, subsection (4)(d) above shall apply with the substitution of 'any person' for 'the person'.]

(6) Before instituting proceedings for an order under subsection (2) above against any person, the person aggrieved by the nuisance shall give to that person such notice in writing of his intention to bring the proceedings as is applicable to proceedings in respect of a nuisance of that description and the notice shall specify the matter complained of.

(7) The notice of the bringing of proceedings in respect of a statutory nuisance required by subsection (6) above which is applicable is—

(a) in the case of a nuisance falling within paragraph (g) [or (ga)] of section 79(1) above, not less than three days' notice; and

(b) in the case of a nuisance of any other description, not less than twenty-one days' notice;

but the Secretary of State may, by order, provide that this subsection shall have effect as if such period as is specified in the order were the minimum period of notice applicable to any description of statutory nuisance specified in the order.

(8) A person who, without reasonable excuse, contravenes any requirement or prohibition imposed by an order under subsection (2) above shall be guilty of an offence and liable on summary conviction to a fine not exceeding level 5 on the standard scale together with a further fine of an amount equal to one-tenth of that level for each day on which the offence continues after the conviction.

(9) Subject to subsection (10) below, in any proceedings for an offence under subsection (8) above in respect of a statutory nuisance it shall be a defence to prove that the best practicable means were used to prevent, or to counteract the effects of, the nuisance.

(10) The defence under subsection (9) above is not available—

(a) in the case of a nuisance falling within paragraph (a), (d), (e), (f), (fa) or (g) of section 79(1) above except where the nuisance arises on industrial, trade or business premises;

[(aza) in the case of a nuisance falling within paragraph (fb) of section 79(1) above except where—

(i) the artificial light is emitted from industrial, trade or business premises, or

(ii) the artificial light (not being light to which sub-paragraph (i) applies) is emitted by lights used for the purpose only of illuminating an outdoor relevant sports facility];

[(aa) in the case of a nuisance falling within paragraph (ga) of section 79(1) above except where the noise is emitted from or caused by a vehicle, machinery or equipment being used for industrial, trade or business purposes;]

(b) in the case of a nuisance falling within paragraph (b) of section 79(1) above except where the smoke is emitted from a chimney;

(c) in the case of a nuisance falling within paragraph (c) or (h) of section 79(1) above; and

(d) in the case of a nuisance which is such as to render the premises unfit for human habitation.

[(10A) For the purposes of subsection (10)(aza) 'relevant sports facility' has the same meaning as it has for the purposes of section 80(8)(aza).]

(11) If a person is convicted of an offence under subsection (8) above, a magistrates' court . . . may, after giving the local authority in whose area the nuisance has occurred an opportunity of being heard, direct the authority to do anything which the person convicted was required to do by the order to which the conviction relates.

(12) Where on the hearing of proceedings for an order under subsection (2) above it is proved that the alleged nuisance existed at the date of the making of the complaint . . . , then, whether or not at the date of the hearing it still exists or is likely to recur, the court . . . shall order the defendant . . . (or defendants . . . in such proportions as appears fair and reasonable) to pay to the person bringing the proceedings such amount as the court . . . considers reasonably sufficient to compensate him for any expenses properly incurred by him in the proceedings.

(13) If it appears to the magistrates' court . . . that neither the person responsible for the nuisance nor the owner or occupier of the premises [or (as the case may be) the person responsible for the vehicle, machinery or equipment] can be found the court . . . may, after giving the local authority in whose area the nuisance has occurred an opportunity of being heard, direct the authority to do anything which the court . . . would have ordered that person to do.

PART VI GENETICALLY MODIFIED ORGANISMS

106 Purpose of Part VI and meaning of 'genetically modified organisms' and related expressions

[(1) This Part has effect for the purpose of ensuring that all appropriate measures are taken to avoid damage to the environment which may arise from the escape or release from human control of genetically modified organisms.]

(2) In this Part the term 'organism' means any acellular, unicellular or multicellular entity (in any form), other than humans or human embryos; and, unless the context otherwise requires, the term also includes any article or substance consisting of or including biological matter.

(3) For the purpose of subsection (2) above 'biological matter' means anything (other than an entity mentioned in that subsection) which consists of or includes—

(a) tissue or cells (including gametes or propagules) or subcellular entities, of any kind, capable of replication or of transferring genetic material, or

(b) genes or other genetic material, in any form, which are so capable,

and it is immaterial, in determining if something is or is not an organism or biological matter, whether it is the product of natural or artificial processes of reproduction and, in the case of biological matter, whether it has ever been part of a whole organism.

(4) For the purposes of this Part[, subject to subsection (4C) below,] an organism is 'genetically modified' if any of the genes or other genetic material in the organism—

[(a) have been artificially modified; or]

(b) are inherited or otherwise derived, through any number of replications, from genes or other genetic material (from any source) which were so modified.

[(4A) Genes or other genetic material in an organism are 'artificially modified' for the purposes of subsection (4) above if they are altered otherwise than by a process which occurs naturally in mating or natural recombination.

This subsection is subject to subsections (4B) and (4C) below.

(4B) For the purposes of subsection (4) above—

(a) genes or other genetic material shall be taken to be artificially modified if they are altered using such techniques as may be prescribed for the purposes of this paragraph;

(b) genes or other genetic material shall not be regarded as artificially modified by reason only of being altered by the use of such techniques as may be prescribed for the purposes of this paragraph.

(4C) An organism shall be taken not to be a genetically modified organism for the purposes of this Part if it is an organism of a prescribed description.

(4D) In subsections (4B) and (4C) above 'prescribed' means prescribed by regulations made by the Secretary of State.]

(5) . . .

(6) . . .

(7) In this Part, where the context permits, a reference to 'reproduction', in relation to an organism, includes a reference to its replication or its transferring genetic material.

107 Meaning of 'damage to the environment', 'control' and related expressions in Part VI

(1) The following provisions have effect for the interpretation of this Part.

[(2) The 'environment' includes land, air and water and living organisms supported by any of those media.]

(3) 'Damage to the environment' is caused by the presence in the environment of genetically modified organisms which have (or of a single such organism which has) escaped or been released from a person's control and are (or is) capable of causing harm . . .

(4) An organism shall be regarded as present in the environment notwithstanding that it is present in or on any human or other organism, or any other thing, which is itself present in the environment.

(5) Genetically modified organisms present in the environment are capable of causing harm if—

(a) they are individually capable, or are present in numbers such that together they are capable, of causing harm; or

(b) they are able to produce descendants which will be capable, or which will be present in numbers such that together they will be capable, of causing harm;

and a single organism is capable of causing harm either if it is itself capable of causing harm or if it is able to produce descendants which will be so capable.

[(6) 'Harm' means adverse effects as regards the health of humans or the environment.]

(7) 'Harmful' and 'harmless' mean respectively, in relation to genetically modified organisms, their being capable or their being incapable of causing harm.

(8) The Secretary of State may by regulations provide, in relation to genetically modified organisms of any description specified in the regulations, that—

(a) the capacity of those organisms for causing harm of any description so specified, or

(b) harm of any description so specified,

shall be disregarded for such purposes of this Part as may be so specified.

[(9) Organisms of any description are under the 'control' of a person where he keeps them contained by measures designed to limit their contact with humans and the environment and to prevent or minimise the risk of harm.]

(10) An organism under a person's control is 'released' if he deliberately causes or permits it to cease to be under his control or the control of any other person and to enter the environment; and such an organism 'escapes' if, otherwise than by being released, it ceases to be under his control or that of any other person and enters the environment.

[(11) Genetically modified organisms of any description are 'marketed' by a person when products consisting of or including such organisms are placed on the market by being made available to other persons, whether or not for consideration.]

108 Risk assessment and notification requirements

(1) Subject to subsections (2) and (7) below, no person shall import or acquire, release or market any genetically modified organisms unless, before doing that act—

(a) he has carried out an assessment of any risks there are (by reference to the nature of the organisms and the manner in which he intends to keep them after their importation or acquisition or, as the case may be, to release or market them) of damage to the environment being caused as a result of doing that act; and

(b) in such cases and circumstances as may be prescribed, he has given the Secretary of State such notice of his intention of doing that act and such information as may be prescribed.

(2) Subsection (1) above does not apply to a person proposing to do an act mentioned in that subsection who is required under section 111(1)(a) below to have a consent before doing that act.

(3) Subject to subsections (4) and (7) below, a person who is keeping genetically modified organisms shall, in such cases or circumstances and at such times or intervals as may be prescribed—

(a) carry out an assessment of any risks there are of damage to the environment being caused as a result of his continuing to keep them;

(b) give the Secretary of State notice of the fact that he is keeping the organisms and such information as may be prescribed.

(4) Subsection (3) above does not apply to a person who is keeping genetically modified organisms and is required under section 111(2) below to have a consent authorising him to continue to keep the organisms.

(5) It shall be the duty of a person who carries out an assessment under subsection (1)(a) or (3)(a) above to keep, for the prescribed period, such a record of the assessment as may be prescribed.

(6) A person required by subsection (1)(b) or (3)(b) above to give notice to the Secretary of State shall give the Secretary of State such further information as the Secretary of State may by notice in writing require.

(7) Regulations under this section may provide for exemptions, or for the granting by the Secretary of State[, or by the Secretary of State and the Food Standards Agency acting jointly,] of exemptions to particular persons or classes of person, from the requirements of subsection (1) or (3) above in such cases or circumstances, and to such extent, as may be prescribed.

(8) The Secretary of State may at any time—

(a) give directions to a person falling within subsection (1) above requiring that person to apply for a consent before doing the act in question; or

(b) give directions to a person falling within subsection (3) above requiring that person, before such date as may be specified in the direction, to apply for a consent authorising him to continue keeping the organisms in question;

and a person given directions under paragraph (a) above shall then, and a person given directions under paragraph (b) above shall from the specified date, be subject to section 111 below in place of the requirements of this section.

(9) Regulations under this section may—

(a) prescribe the manner in which assessments under subsection (1) or (3) above are to be carried out and the matters which must be investigated and assessed;

(b) prescribe minimum periods of notice between the giving of a notice under subsection (1)(b) above and the doing of the act in question;

(c) make provision allowing the Secretary of State to shorten or to extend any such period;

(d) prescribe maximum intervals at which assessments under subsection (3)(a) above must be carried out;

and the regulations may make different provision for different cases and different circumstances.

(10) In this section 'prescribed' means prescribed by the Secretary of State in regulations under this section.

109 General duties relating to importation, acquisition, keeping, release or marketing of organisms

(1) A person who—

(a) is proposing to import or acquire any genetically modified organisms, or

(b) is keeping any such organisms, or

(c) is proposing to release or market any such organisms,

shall, subject to subsection (5) below, be subject to the duties specified in subsection (2), (3) or (4) below, as the case may be.

(2) A person who proposes to import or acquire genetically modified organisms—

(a) shall take all reasonable steps to identify, by reference to the nature of the organisms and the manner in which he intends to keep them (including any precautions to be taken against their escaping or causing damage to the environment), what risks there are of damage to the environment being caused as a result of their importation or acquisition; and

(b) shall not import or acquire the organisms if it appears that, despite any precautions which can be taken, there is a risk of damage to the environment being caused as a result of their importation or acquisition.

(3) A person who is keeping genetically modified organisms—

(a) shall take all reasonable steps to keep himself informed of any damage to the environment which may have been caused as a result of his keeping the organisms and to identify what risks there are of damage to the environment being caused as a result of his continuing to keep them;

(b) shall cease keeping the organisms if, despite any additional precautions which can be taken, it appears, at any time, that there is a risk of damage to the environment being caused as a result of his continuing to keep them; and

(c) shall use the best available techniques not entailing excessive cost for keeping the organisms under his control and for preventing any damage to the environment being caused as a result of his continuing to keep the organisms;

and where a person is required by paragraph (b) above to cease keeping the organisms he shall dispose of them as safely and as quickly as practicable and paragraph (c) above shall continue to apply until he has done so.

(4) A person who proposes to release genetically modified organisms—

(a) shall take all reasonable steps to keep himself informed, by reference to the nature of the organisms and the extent and manner of the release (including any precautions to be taken against their causing damage to the environment), what risks there are of damage to the environment being caused as a result of their being released;

(b) shall not release the organisms if it appears that, despite the precautions which can be taken, there is a risk of damage to the environment being caused as a result of their being released; and

(c) subject to paragraph (b) above, shall use the best available techniques not entailing excessive cost for preventing any damage to the environment being caused as a result of their being released;

and this subsection applies, with the necessary modifications, to a person proposing to market organisms as it applies to a person proposing to release organisms.

(5) This section does not apply—

(a) to persons proposing to import or acquire, to release or to market any genetically modified organisms, in cases or circumstances where, under section 108 above, they are not required to carry out a risk assessment before doing that act;

(b) to persons who are keeping any genetically modified organisms and who—

(i) were not required under section 108 above to carry out a risk assessment before importing or acquiring them;

(ii) have not been required under that section to carry out a risk assessment in respect of the keeping of those organisms since importing or acquiring them;

or

(iii) to holders of consents, in the case of acts authorised by those consents.

110 Prohibition notices

(1) The Secretary of State may serve a notice under this section (a 'prohibition notice') on any person he has reason to believe—

(a) is proposing to import or acquire, release or market any genetically modified organisms; or

(b) is keeping any such organisms;

if he is of the opinion that doing any such act in relation to those organisms or continuing to keep them, as the case may be, would involve a risk of causing damage to the environment.

(2) A prohibition notice may prohibit a person from doing an act mentioned in subsection (1)(a) above in relation to any genetically modified organisms or from continuing to keep them; and the prohibition may apply in all cases or circumstances or in such cases or circumstances as may be specified in the notice.

(3) A prohibition notice shall—

(a) state that the Secretary of State is, in relation to the person on whom it is served, of the opinion mentioned in subsection (1) above;

(b) specify what is, or is to be, prohibited by the notice; and

(c) if the prohibition is not to be effective on being served, specify the date on which the prohibition is to take effect;

and a notice may be served on a person notwithstanding that he may have a consent authorising any act which is, or is to be, prohibited by the notice.

(4) Where a person is prohibited by a prohibition notice from continuing to keep any genetically modified organisms, heshall dispose of them as quickly and safely as practicable or, if the notice so provides, as may be specified in the notice.

(5) The Secretary of State may at any time withdraw a prohibition notice served on any person by notice given to that person.

111 Consents required by certain persons

(1) Subject to subsection (7) below, no person shall import or acquire, release or market any genetically modified organisms—

(a) in such cases or circumstances as may be prescribed in relation to that act, or

(b) in any case where he has been given directions under section 108(8)(a) above,

except in pursuance of a consent granted by the Secretary of State and in accordance with any limitations and conditions to which the consent is subject.

(2) Subject to subsection (7) below, no person who has imported or acquired any genetically modified organisms (whether under a consent or not) shall continue to keep the organisms—

(a) in such cases or circumstances as may be prescribed, after the end of the prescribed period, or

(b) if he has been given directions under section 108(8)(b) above, after the date specified in the directions,

except in pursuance of a consent granted by the Secretary of State and in accordance with any limitations or conditions to which the consent is subject.

(3) A person who is required under subsection (2) above to cease keeping any genetically modified organisms shall dispose of them as quickly and safely as practicable.

(4) An application for a consent must contain such information and be made and advertised in such manner as may be prescribed and shall be accompanied by the fee required under section 113 below.

(5) The applicant shall, in prescribed circumstances, give such notice of his application to such persons as may be prescribed.

(6) The Secretary of State may by notice to the applicant require him to furnish such further information specified in the notice, within such period as may be so specified, as he may require for the purpose of determining the application; and if the applicant fails to furnish the information within the specified period the Secretary of State may refuse to proceed with the application.

[A notice under this subsection must state the reasons for requiring the further information specified in the notice.]

[(6A) Where an applicant for consent for releasing or marketing genetically modified organisms becomes aware, before his application is either granted or rejected, of any new information with regard to any risks there are of damage to the environment being caused as a result of the organisms being released or marketed, he shall notify the Secretary of State of that new information forthwith.]

(7) Regulations under this section may provide for exemptions, or for the granting by the Secretary of State[, or by the Secretary of State and the Food Standards Agency acting jointly,] of exemptions to particular persons or classes of person, from—

(a) any requirement under subsection (1) or (2) above to have a consent, or

(b) any of the requirements to be fulfilled under the regulations by an applicant for a consent,

in such cases or circumstances as may be prescribed.

(8) Where an application for a consent is duly made to him, the Secretary of State may grant the consent subject to such limitations and conditions as may be imposed under section 112 below or he may refuse the application.

(9) The conditions attached to a consent may include conditions which are to continue to have effect notwithstanding that the holder has completed or ceased the act or acts authorised by the consent.

(10) The Secretary of State may at any time, by notice given to the holder of a consent, revoke the consent or vary the consent (whether by attaching new limitations and conditions

or by revoking or varying any limitations and conditions to which it is at thattime subject).

(11) Regulations under this section may make different provision for different cases and different circumstances; and in this section 'prescribed' means prescribed in regulations under this section.

112 Consents: limitations and conditions

(1) The Secretary of State may include in a consent such limitations and conditions as he may think fit... [for the purpose of ensuring that all appropriate measures are taken to avoid damage to the environment which may arise from the activity permitted by the consent].

(2) Without prejudice to the generality of subsection (1) above, the conditions included in a consent may—

(a) require the giving of notice of any fact to the Secretary of State; or

(b) prohibit or restrict the keeping, releasing or marketing of genetically modified organisms under the consent in specified cases or circumstances;

and where, under any condition, the holder of a consent is required to cease keeping any genetically modified organisms, he shall dispose of them, if no manner is specified in the conditions, as quickly and safely as practicable.

(3) Subject to subsection (6) below, there is implied in every consent for the importation or acquisition of genetically modified organisms a general condition that the holder of the consent shall—

(a) take all reasonable steps to keep himself informed (by reference to the nature of the organisms and the manner in which he intends to keep them after their importation or acquisition) of any risks there are of damage to the environment being caused as a result of their importation or acquisition; and

(b) if at any time it appears that any such risks are more serious than were apparent when the consent was granted, notify the Secretary of State forthwith.

(4) Subject to subsection (6) below, there is implied in every consent for keeping genetically modified organisms a general condition that the holder of the consent shall—

(a) take all reasonable steps to keep himself informed of any damage to the environment which may have been caused as a result of his keeping the organisms and of any risks there are of such damage being caused as a result of his continuing to keep them;

(b) if at any time it appears that any such risks are more serious than were apparent when the consent was granted, notify the Secretary of State forthwith; and

(c) use the best available techniques not entailing excessive cost for keeping the organisms under his control and for preventing any damage to the environment being caused as a result of his continuing to keep them.

(5) Subject to subsection (6) below, there is implied in every consent for releasing or marketing genetically modified organisms a general condition that the holder of the consent shall—

(a) take all reasonable steps to keep himself informed (by reference to the nature of the organisms and the extent and manner of the release or marketing) of any risks there are of damage to the environment being caused as a result of their being released or, as the case may be, marketed;

[(b) notify the Secretary of State [forthwith] of—

(i) any new information which becomes available with regard to any risks there are of damage to the environment being so caused, and

(ii) ...

[(iii) any unforeseen event, occurring in connection with a release by him, which might affect the risks there are of damage to the environment being caused as a result of their being released;]]

[(c) take such measures as are necessary to prevent damage to the environment being caused as a result of the release or, as the case may be, the marketing of the organisms;]

[(d) notify the Secretary of State of the measures (if any) taken as a result of new information becoming available or an unforeseen event occurring as described in paragraph (b)(iii) above; and

(e) in a case where new information becomes available or an unforeseen event so occurs, revise the information contained in his application for a consent accordingly and supply the revised information to the Secretary of State].

(6) The general condition implied into a consent under subsection (3), (4) or (5) above has effect subject to any conditions imposed under subsection (1) above; and the obligations imposed by virtue of subsection (4)(c) or (5)(c) above shall not apply to any aspect of an act authorised by a consent which is regulated by such a condition.

(7) There shall be implied in every consent for keeping, releasing or marketing genetically modified organisms of any description a general condition that the holder of the consent—

(a) shall take all reasonable steps to keep himself informed of developments in the techniques which may be available in his case for preventing damage to the environment being caused as a result of the doing of the act authorised by the consent in relation to organisms of that description; and

(b) if it appears at any time that any better techniques are available to him than is required by any condition included in the consent under subsection (1) above, shall notify the Secretary of State of that fact forthwith.

But this general condition shall have effect subject to any conditions imposed under subsection (1) above.

117 Power to deal with cause of imminent danger of damage to the environment

(1) Where, in the case of anything found by him on any premises which he has power to enter, an inspector has reason to believe that it is a genetically modified organism or that it consists of or includes genetically modified organisms and that, in the circumstances in which he finds it, is a cause of imminent danger of damage to the environment, he may seize it and cause it to be rendered harmless (whether by destruction, by bringing it under proper control or otherwise).

(2) Before there is rendered harmless under this section—

(a) any thing that forms part of a batch of similar things, or

(b) any substance,

the inspector shall, if it is practicable and safe for him to do so, take a sample of it and give to a responsible person at the premises a portion of the sample marked in a manner sufficient to identify it.

(3) As soon as may be after anything has been seized and rendered harmless under this section, the inspector shall prepare and sign a written report giving particulars of the circumstances in which it was seized and so dealt with by him, and shall—

(a) give a signed copy of the report to a responsible person at the premises where it was found by him; and

(b) unless that person is the owner of it, also serve a signed copy of the report on the owner;

and if, where paragraph (b) above applies, the inspector cannot after reasonable inquiry ascertain the name or address of the owner, the copy may be served on him by giving it to the person to whom a copy was given under paragraph (a) above.

118 Offences

(1) It is an offence for a person—

(a) to do anything in contravention of section 108(1) above in relation to something which is, and which he knows or has reason to believe is, a genetically modified organism;

(b) to fail to comply with section 108(3) above when keeping something which is, and which he knows or has reason to believe is, a genetically modified organism;
(c) to do anything in contravention of section 111(1) or (2) above in relation to something which is, and which he knows or has reason to believe is, a genetically modified organism;
(d) to fail to comply with any requirement of subsection (2), (3)(a), (b) or (c) or (4) of section 109 above in relation to something which is, and which he knows or has reason to believe is, a genetically modified organism;
(e) to fail, without reasonable excuse, to comply with section 108(5) or (6) [or section 111(6A)] above;
(f) to contravene any prohibition imposed on him by a prohibition notice;
(g) without reasonable excuse, to fail to comply with any requirement imposed under section 115 above;
(h) to prevent any other person from appearing before or from answering any question to which an inspector may, by virtue of section 115(3) above, require an answer;
(i) intentionally to obstruct an inspector in the exercise or performance of his powers or duties, other than his powers or duties under section 117 above;
(j) intentionally to obstruct an inspector in the exercise of his powers or duties under section 117 above;
(k) to fail, without reasonable excuse, to comply with any requirement imposed by a notice under section 116 above;
(l) to make a statement which he knows to be false or misleading in a material particular, or recklessly to make a statement which is false or misleading in a material particular, where the statement is made—
 (i) in purported compliance with a requirement to furnish any information imposed by or under any provision of this Part; or
 (ii) for the purpose of obtaining the grant of a consent to himself or any other person or the variation of a consent;
(m) intentionally to make a false entry in any record required to be kept under section 108 or 111 above;
(n) with intent to deceive, to forge or use a document purporting to be issued under section 111 above or required for any purpose thereunder or to make or have in his possession a document so closely resembling any such document as to be likely to deceive;
(o) falsely to pretend to be an inspector.

(2) It shall be a defence for a person charged with an offence under paragraph (a), (b), (c), (d) or (f) of subsection (1) above to prove that he took all reasonable precautions and exercised all due diligence to avoid the commission of the offence.

(3) A person guilty of an offence under paragraph (c) or (d) of subsection (1) above shall be liable—
(a) on summary conviction, to a fine not exceeding £20,000 or to imprisonment for a term not exceeding six months, or to both;
(b) on conviction on indictment, to a fine or to imprisonment for a term not exceeding five years, or to both.

(4) A person guilty of an offence under paragraph (f) of subsection (1) above shall be liable—
(a) on summary conviction, to a fine not exceeding £20,000 or to imprisonment for a term not exceeding six months, or to both;
(b) on conviction on indictment, to a fine or to imprisonment for a term not exceeding two years, or to both.

(5) A person guilty of an offence under paragraph (a) or (b) of subsection (1) above shall be liable—

(a) on summary conviction, to a fine not exceeding the statutory maximum or to imprisonment for a term not exceeding six months, or to both;

(b) on conviction on indictment, to a fine or to imprisonment for a term not exceeding five years, or to both.

(6) A person guilty of an offence under paragraph (e), (j), (k), (l), (m) or (n) of subsection (1) above shall be liable—

(a) on summary conviction, to a fine not exceeding the statutory maximum or to imprisonment for a term not exceeding six months, or to both;

(b) on conviction on indictment, to a fine or to imprisonment for a term not exceeding two years, or to both.

(7) A person guilty of an offence under paragraph (g), (h) or (i) of subsection (1) above shall be liable on summary conviction to a fine not exceeding the statutory maximum [...].

(8) A person guilty of an offence under paragraph (o) of subsection (1) above shall be liable on summary conviction to a fine not exceeding level 5 on the standard scale.

(9) Where a person is convicted of an offence under paragraph (b) of subsection (1) above in respect of his keeping any genetically modified organism, then, if the contravention in respect of which he was convicted is continued after he was convicted he shall be guilty of a further offence and liable on summary conviction to a fine of one-fifth of level 5 on the standard scale for each day on which the contravention is so continued.

(10) Proceedings in respect of an offence under this section shall not be instituted in England and Wales except by the Secretary of State or with the consent of the Director of Public Prosecutions [...].

119 Onus of proof as regards techniques and evidence

(1) In any proceedings for either of the following offences, that is to say—

(a) an offence under section 118(1)(c) above consisting in a failure to comply with the general condition implied by section 112(4)(c) or (5)(c) above; or

(b) an offence under section 118(1)(d) above consisting in a failure to comply with section 109(3)(c) or (4)(c) above;

it shall be for the accused to prove [the matters described in subsection (1A) below.

(1A) The matters referred to in subsection (1) above are—

(a) in the case of an offence under section 118(1)(c) above consisting in a failure to comply with the general condition implied by section 112(5)(c) above—

(i) that no measures, other than the measures taken by him, were necessary to prevent damage being caused to the environment from the release or, as the case may be, marketing of the organisms, or

(ii) in a case where he took no measures, that no measures were necessary; and

(b) in any other case,]

that there was no better available technique not entailing excessive cost than was in fact used to satisfy the condition or to comply with that section.

(2) Where an entry is required by a condition in a consent to be made in any record as to the observance of any other condition and the entry has not been made, that fact shall be admissible as evidence that that other condition has not been observed.

120 Power of court to order cause of offence to be remedied

(1) Where a person is convicted of an offence under section 118(1)(a), (b), (c), (d), (e) or (f) above in respect of any matters which appear to the court to be matters which it is in his power to remedy, the court may, in addition to or instead of imposing any punishment, order him, within such time as may be fixed by the order, to take such steps as may be specified in the order for remedying those matters.

(2) The time fixed by an order under subsection (1) above may be extended or further extended by order of the court on an application made before the end of the time as originally fixed or as extended under this subsection, as the case may be.

(3) Where a person is ordered under subsection (1) above to remedy any matters, that person shall not be liable under section 118 above in respect of those matters, in so far as they continue during the time fixed by the order or any further time allowed under subsection (2) above.

121 Power of Secretary of State to remedy harm

(1) Where the commission of an offence under section 118(1)(a), (b), (c), (d), (e) or (f) above causes any harm which it is possible to remedy, the Secretary of State may, subject to subsection (2) below—

(a) arrange for any reasonable steps to be taken towards remedying the harm; and

(b) recover the cost of taking those steps from any person convicted of that offence.

(2) The Secretary of State shall not exercise his powers under this section, where any of the steps are to be taken on or will affect land in the occupation of any person other than a person convicted of the offence in question, except with the permission of that person.

122 Public register of information

(1) The Secretary of State shall maintain a register ('the register') containing prescribed particulars of or relating to—

(a) notices given or other information furnished under section 108 above;

(b) directions given under section 108(8) above;

(c) prohibition notices;

(d) applications for consents (and any further information furnished in connection with them) and any advice given by the committee appointed under section 124 below in relation to such applications;

(e) consents granted by the Secretary of State and any information furnished to him in pursuance of consent conditions;

(f) any other information obtained or furnished under any provision of this Part;

(g) convictions for such offences under section 118 above as may be prescribed;

(h) such other matters relating to this Part as may be prescribed; but that duty is subject to section 123 below.

(2) It shall be the duty of the Secretary of State—

(a) to secure that the register is open to inspection by members of the public free of charge at all reasonable hours; and

(b) to afford to members of the public facilities for obtaining copies of entries, on payment of reasonable charges.

(3) The register may be kept in any form.

(4) The Secretary of State may make regulations with respect to the keeping of the register; and in this section 'prescribed' means prescribed in regulations made by the Secretary of State.

123 Exclusion from register of certain information

(1) No information shall be included in the register under section 122 above if and so long as, in the opinion of the Secretary of State, the inclusion of the information would be contrary to the interests of national security.

(2) No information shall be included in the register if and so long as, in the opinion of the Secretary of State, it ought to be excluded on the ground that its inclusion might result in damage to the environment.

(3) No information relating to the affairs of any individual or business shall be included in the register without the consent of that individual or the person for the time being carrying on that business, if the Secretary of State has determined that the information—

(a) is, in relation to him, commercially confidential; and

(b) is not information of a description to which subsection (7) below applies;

unless the Secretary of State is of the opinion that the information is no longer commercially confidential in relation to him.

[...]

127 Definitions

(1) In this Part—

'acquire', in relation to genetically modified organisms, includes any method by which such organisms may come to be in a person's possession, other than by their being imported;

'consent' means a consent granted under section 111 above, and a reference to the limitations or conditions to which a consent is subject is a reference to the limitations or conditions subject to which the consent for the time being has effect;

'descendant', in relation to a genetically modified organism, means any other organism whose genes or other genetic material is derived, through any number of generations, from that organism by any process of reproduction;

'import' means import into the United Kingdom;

'premises' includes any land;

'prohibition notice' means a notice under section 110 above.

(2) This Part, except in so far as it relates to importations of genetically modified organisms, [applies to the territorial sea adjacent to England as it applies in England] [and applies to the territorial sea adjacent to Wales as it applies in Wales], and [applies to any area for the time being designated under section 1(7) of the Continental Shelf Act 1964 as it applies in England].

PART VII NATURE CONSERVATION IN GREAT BRITAIN AND COUNTRYSIDE MATTERS IN WALES

128 Countryside Council for Wales

(1) There shall be a council to be called the Countryside Council for Wales (in this Part referred to as 'the Council').

(2) The Council shall have not less than 8 nor more than 12 members and those members shall be appointed by the National Assembly for Wales.

(3) The National Assembly for Wales may by order made by statutory instrument amend subsection (2) above so as to substitute for the number for the time being specified as the maximum membership of the Council such other number as the Assembly thinks appropriate.

(4) Schedule 6 has effect with respect to the constitution and proceedings of the Council.

130 Countryside functions of Welsh Council

(1) The Countryside Council for Wales shall have such of the functions under the Acts amended by Schedule 8 to this Act (which relates to countryside matters) as are assigned to them in accordance with the amendments effected by that Schedule.

(2) The Countryside Council for Wales shall discharge those functions—

(a) for the conservation and enhancement of natural beauty in Wales and of the natural beauty and amenity of the countryside in Wales, both in the areas designated under the National Parks and Access to the Countryside Act 1949 as National Parks or as areas of outstanding natural beauty and elsewhere;

(b) for encouraging the provision or improvement, for persons resorting to the countryside in Wales, of facilities for the enjoyment thereof and for the enjoyment of the opportunities for open-air recreation and the study of nature afforded thereby; and shall have regard to the social and economic interests of rural areas in Wales.

(3) The reference in subsection (2) above to the conservation of the natural beauty of the countryside includes the conservation of its flora, fauna and geological and physiographical features.

(4) The Countryside Council for Wales shall discharge their functions under those Acts (as amended by Schedule 8) on and after a day to be appointed by an order made by the Secretary of State.

131 Nature conservation functions: preliminary

(1) For the purpose of nature conservation and fostering the understanding of nature conservation, the Council shall have the functions conferred on them by this Part and Part 2 of the Natural Environment and Rural Communities Act 2006.

(2) It shall be the duty of the Councils in discharging their nature conservation functions to take appropriate account of actual or possible ecological changes.

(3) The Councils shall discharge their nature conservation functions on and after a day to be appointed by an order made by the Secretary of State.

(4) The National Assembly for Wales may give the Council general or specific directions with regard to the discharge of any of their nature conservation functions under this Part.

(5) [...]

(6) In this Part 'nature conservation' means the conservation of flora, fauna or geological or physiographical features.

132 General functions of the Council

(1) The Council shall have the following functions, namely—

(a) such of the functions previously discharged by the Nature Conservancy Council under the Acts amended by Schedule 9 to this Act as are assigned to them in accordance with the amendments effected by that Schedule;

(b) the establishment, maintenance and management of nature reserves (within the meaning of section 15 of the National Parks and Access to the Countryside Act 1949) in their area;

(c) the provision of advice for the Secretary of State or any other Minister on the development and implementation of policies for or affecting nature conservation in their area;

(d) the provision of advice and the dissemination of knowledge to any persons about nature conservation in their area or about matters arising from the discharge of their functions under this section or section 134 below;

(e) the commissioning or support (whether by financial means or otherwise) of research which in their opinion is relevant to any of their functions under this section or section 134 below;

(2) The Council shall have power—

(a) to accept any gift or contribution made to them for the purposes of any of the functions conferred on them by subsection (1) above or section 134 below and, subject to the terms of the gift or contribution, to apply it to those purposes;

(b) to initiate and carry out such research directly related to those functions as it is appropriate that they should carry out instead of commissioning or supporting other persons under paragraph (e) of that subsection;

and they may do all such other things as are incidental or conducive to those functions including (without prejudice to the generality of this provision) making charges and holding land or any interest in or right over land.

PART IX GENERAL

156 Power to give effect to Community and other international obligations etc.

(1) The Secretary of State may by regulations provide that the provisions to which this section applies shall have effect with such modifications as may be prescribed for the purpose of enabling Her Majesty's Government in the United Kingdom—

(a) to give effect to any Community obligation or exercise any related right; or

(b) to give effect to any obligation or exercise any related right under any international agreement to which the United Kingdom is for the time being a party.

(2) This section applies to the following provisions of this Act—

(a) Part I;

(b) Part II;

(c) Part VI; and

(d) in Part VIII, sections 140, 141 or 142;

and the provisions of the Radioactive Substances Act 1993.

(3) In this section—

'modifications' includes additions, alterations and omissions;

'prescribed' means prescribed in regulations under this section; and

'related right', in relation to an obligation, includes any derogation or other right to make more onerous provisions available in respect of that obligation.

(4)...

157 Offences by bodies corporate

(1) Where an offence under any provision of this Act committed by a body corporate is proved to have been committed with the consent or connivance of, or to have been attributable to any neglect on the part of, any director, manager, secretary or other similar officer of the body corporate or a person who was purporting to act in any such capacity, he as well as the body corporate shall be guilty of that offence and shall be liable to be proceeded against and punished accordingly.

(2) Where the affairs of a body corporate are managed by its members, subsection (1) above shall apply in relation to the acts or defaults of a member in connection with his functions of management as if he were a director of the body corporate.

158 Offences under Parts I, II, IV, VI, etc. due to fault of others

Where the commission by any person of an offence under Part I, II, IV, or VI, or section 140, 141 or 142 above is due to the act or default of some other person, that other person may be charged with and convicted of the offence by virtue of this section whether or not proceedings for the offence are taken against the first-mentioned person.

159 Application to Crown

(1) Subject to the provisions of this section, the provisions of this Act and of regulations and orders made under it shall bind the Crown.

(2) No contravention by the Crown of any provision of this Act or of any regulations or order made under it shall make the Crown criminally liable; but the High Court... may, on the application of any public or local authority charged with enforcing that provision, declare unlawful any act or omission of the Crown which constitutes such a contravention.

(3)–(7) ...

[Sections 44A and 44B SCHEDULE 2A

OBJECTIVES FOR THE PURPOSES OF THE NATIONAL WASTE STRATEGY

1. Ensuring that waste is recovered or disposed of without endangering human health and without using processes or methods which could harm the environment and, in particular, without—

(a) risk to water, air, soil, plants or animals;

(b) causing nuisance through noise or odours; or

(c) adversely affecting the countryside or places of special interest.

2. Establishing an integrated and adequate network of waste disposal installations, taking account of the best available technology not involving excessive costs.

3. Ensuring that the network referred to in paragraph 2 above enables—

(a) the European Community as a whole to become self-sufficient in waste disposal, and the Member States individually to move towards that aim, taking into account geographical circumstances or the need for specialised installations for certain types of waste; and

(b) waste to be disposed of in one of the nearest appropriate installations, by means of the most appropriate methods and technologies in order to ensure a high level of protection for the environment and public health.

4. Encouraging the prevention or reduction of waste production and its harmfulness, in particular by—

(a) the development of clean technologies more sparing in their use of natural resources;

(b) the technical development and marketing of products designed so as to make no contribution or to make the smallest possible contribution, by the nature of their manufacture, use or final disposal, to increasing the amount or harmfulness of waste and pollution hazards; and

(c) the development of appropriate techniques for the final disposal of dangerous substances contained in waste destined for recovery.

5. Encouraging—

(a) the recovery of waste by means of recycling, re-use or reclamation or any other process with a view to extracting secondary raw materials; and

(b) the use of waste as a source of energy.]

Section 75

[SCHEDULE 2B
CATEGORIES OF WASTE

1. Production or consumption residues not otherwise specified below.

2. Off-specification products.

3. Products whose date for appropriate use has expired.

4. Materials spilled, lost or having undergone other mishap, including any materials, equipment, etc, contaminated as a result of the mishap.

5. Materials contaminated or soiled as a result of planned actions (e.g. residues from cleaning operations, packing materials, containers, etc.).

6. Unusable parts (e.g. reject batteries, exhausted catalysts, etc.).

7. Substances which no longer perform satisfactorily (e.g. contaminated acids, contaminated solvents, exhausted tempering salts, etc.).

8. Residues of industrial processes (e.g. slags, still bottoms, etc.).

9. Residues from pollution abatement processes (e.g. scrubber sludges, baghouse dusts, spent filters, etc.).

10. Machining or finishing residues (e.g. lathe turnings, mill scales, etc.).

11. Residues from raw materials extraction and processing (e.g. mining residues, oil field slops, etc.).

12. Adulterated materials (e.g. oils contaminated with PCBs, etc.).

13. Any materials, substances or products whose use has been banned by law.

14. Products for which the holder has no further use (e.g. agricultural, household, office, commercial and shop discards, etc.).

15. Contaminated materials, substances or products resulting from remedial action with respect to land.

16. Any materials, substances or products which are not contained in the above categories.]

Section 81

SCHEDULE 3
STATUTORY NUISANCES: SUPPLEMENTARY PROVISIONS

Appeals to magistrates' court

1.—(1) This paragraph applies in relation to appeals under section 80(3) against an abatement notice to a magistrates' court.

(2) An appeal to which this paragraph applies shall be by way of complaint for an order and the Magistrates' Courts Act 1980 shall apply to the proceedings.

(3) An appeal against any decision of a magistrates' court in pursuance of an appeal to which this paragraph applies shall lie to the Crown Court at the instance of any party to the proceedings in which the decision was given.

(4) The Secretary of State may make regulations as to appeals to which this paragraph applies and the regulations may in particular—

(a) include provisions comparable to those in section 290 of the Public Health Act 1936 (appeals against notices requiring the execution of works);

(b) prescribe the cases in which an abatement notice is, or is not, to be suspended until the appeal is decided, or until some other stage in the proceedings;

(c) prescribe the cases in which the decision on appeal may in some respects be less favourable to the appellant than the decision from which he is appealing;

(d) prescribe the cases in which the appellant may claim that an abatement notice should have been served on some other person and prescribe the procedure to be followed in those cases.

1A...

Powers of entry etc.

2.—(1) Subject to sub-paragraph (2) below, any person authorised by a local authority may, on production (if so required) of his authority, enter any premises at any reasonable time—

(a) for the purpose of ascertaining whether or not a statutory nuisance exists; or

(b) for the purpose of taking any action, or executing any work, authorised or required by Part III.

(2) Admission by virtue of sub-paragraph (1) above to any premises used wholly or mainly for residential purposes shall not except in an emergency be demanded as of right unless twenty-four hours notice of the intended entry has been given to the occupier.

(3) If it is shown to the satisfaction of a justice of the peace on sworn information in writing—

(a) that admission to any premises has been refused, or that refusal is apprehended, or that the premises are unoccupied or the occupier is temporarily absent, or that the case is one of emergency, or that an application for admission would defeat the object of the entry; and

(b) that there is reasonable ground for entry into the premises for the purpose for which entry is required,

the justice may by warrant under his hand authorise the local authority by any authorised person to enter the premises, if need be by force.

(4) An authorised person entering any premises by virtue of sub-paragraph (1) or a warrant under sub-paragraph (3) above may—

(a) take with him such other persons and such equipment as may be necessary;

(b) carry out such inspections, measurements and tests as he considers necessary for the discharge of any of the local authority's functions under Part III; and

(c) take away such samples or articles as he considers necessary for that purpose.

(5) On leaving any unoccupied premises which he has entered by virtue of sub-paragraph (1) above or a warrant under sub-paragraph (3) above the authorised person shall leave them as effectually secured against trespassers as he found them.

(6) A warrant issued in pursuance of sub-paragraph (3) above shall continue in force until the purpose for which the entry is required has been satisfied.

(7) Any reference in this paragraph to an emergency is a reference to a case where the person requiring entry has reasonable cause to believe that circumstances exist which are

likely to endanger life or health and that immediate entry is necessary to verify the existence of those circumstances or to ascertain their cause and to effect a remedy.

[2A.—(1) Any person authorised by a local authority may on production (if so required) of his authority—

(a) enter or open a vehicle, machinery or equipment, if necessary by force, or

(b) remove a vehicle, machinery or equipment from a street to a secure place,

for the purpose of taking any action, or executing any work, authorised by or required under Part III in relation to a statutory nuisance within section 79(1)(ga) above caused by noise emitted from or caused by the vehicle, machinery or equipment.

(2) On leaving any unattended vehicle, machinery or equipment that he has entered or opened under sub-paragraph (1) above, the authorised person shall (subject to sub-paragraph (3) below) leave it secured against interference or theft in such manner and as effectually as he found it.

(3) If the authorised person is unable to comply with sub-paragraph (2) above, he shall for the purpose of securing the unattended vehicle, machinery or equipment either—

(a) immobilise it by such means as he considers expedient, or

(b) remove it from the street to a secure place.

(4) In carrying out any function under sub-paragraph (1), (2) or (3) above, the authorised person shall not cause more damage than is necessary.

(5) Before a vehicle, machinery or equipment is entered, opened or removed under sub-paragraph (1) above, the local authority shall notify the police of the intention to take action under that sub-paragraph.

(6) After a vehicle, machinery or equipment has been removed under sub-paragraph (1) or (3) above, the local authority shall notify the police of its removal and current location.

(7) Notification under sub-paragraph (5) or (6) above may be given to the police at any police station in the local authority's area or, in the case of the Temples, at any police station of the City of London Police.

(8) For the purposes of section 81(4) above, any expenses reasonably incurred by a local authority under sub-paragraph (2) or (3) above shall be treated as incurred by the authority under section 81(3) above in abating or preventing the recurrence of the statutory nuisance in question.]

Offences relating to entry

3.—(1) A person who wilfully obstructs any person acting in the exercise of any powers conferred by paragraph 2 [or 2A] above shall be liable, on summary conviction, to a fine not exceeding level 3 on the standard scale.

(2) If a person discloses any information relating to any trade secret obtained in the exercise of any powers conferred by paragraph 2 above he shall, unless the disclosure was made in the performance of his duty or with the consent of the person having the right to disclose the information, be liable, on summary conviction, to a fine not exceeding level 5 on the standard scale.

Default powers

4.—(1) This paragraph applies to the following function of a local authority, that is to say its duty under section 79 to cause its area to be inspected to detect any statutory nuisance which ought to be dealt with under [sections 80 and 80A] and its powers under paragraph 2 [or 2A] above.

(2) If the Secretary of State is satisfied that any local authority has failed, in any respect, to discharge the function to which this paragraph applies which it ought to have discharged, he may make an order declaring the authority to be in default.

(3) An order made under sub-paragraph (2) above which declares an authority to be in default may, for the purpose of remedying the default, direct the authority ('the defaulting

authority') to perform the function specified in the order and may specify the manner in which and the time or times within which the function is to be performed by the authority.

(4) If the defaulting authority fails to comply with any direction contained in such an order the Secretary of State may, instead of enforcing the order by mandamus, make an order transferring to himself the function of the authority specified in the order.

(5) Where the function of a defaulting authority is transferred under subparagraph (4) above, the amount of any expenses which the Secretary of State certifies were incurred by him in performing the function shall on demand be paid to him by the defaulting authority.

(6) Any expenses required to be paid by a defaulting authority under subparagraph (5) above shall be defrayed by the authority in like manner, and shall be debited to the like account, as if the function had not been transferred and the expenses had been incurred by the authority in performing them.

(7) The Secretary of State may by order vary or revoke any order previously made by him under this paragraph.

(8) Any order under this paragraph may include such incidental, supplemental and transitional provisions as the Secretary of State considers appropriate.

Protection from personal liability

5. Nothing done by, or by a member of, a local authority or by any officer of or other person authorised by a local authority shall, if done in good faith for the purpose of executing Part III, subject them or any of them personally to any action, liability, claim or demand whatsoever (other than any liability under section 17 and 18 of the Audit Commission Act 1998 (powers of district auditor and court)).

Statement of right of appeal in notices

6. Where an appeal against a notice served by a local authority lies to a magistrates' court by virtue of section 80, it shall be the duty of the authority to include in such a notice a statement indicating that such an appeal lies as aforesaid and specifying the time within which it must be brought.

Water Industry Act 1991

(1991, c. 56)

PART I PRELIMINARY

[Water Services Regulation Authority]

[1A Water Services Regulation Authority

(1) There shall be a body corporate to be known as the Water Services Regulation Authority (in this Act referred to as 'the Authority') for the purpose of carrying out the functions conferred on or transferred to it by this Act or under or by virtue of any other enactment.

(2) The functions of the Authority are performed on behalf of the Crown.

(3) Schedule 1A to this Act shall have effect with respect to the Authority.

(4) In Welsh the Authority may be known as 'Awdurdod Rheoleiddio Gwasanaethau Dwr'.]

General duties

2 General duties with respect to water industry

(1) This section shall have effect for imposing duties on the Secretary of State and on [the Authority] as to when and how they should exercise and perform the following powers and duties, that is to say—

(a) in the case of the Secretary of State, the powers and duties conferred or imposed on him by virtue of the provisions of this Act relating to the regulation of relevant undertakers [and of licensed water suppliers]; and

(b) in the case of [the Authority], the powers and duties conferred or imposed on [*it*] by virtue of any of those provisions, by the provisions relating to the financial conditions of requisitions or by the provisions relating to the movement of certain pipes.

[(2A) The Secretary of State or, as the case may be, the Authority shall exercise and perform the powers and duties mentioned in subsection (1) above in the manner which he or it considers is best calculated—

(a) to further the consumer objective;

(b) to secure that the functions of a water undertaker and of a sewerage undertaker are properly carried out as respects every area of England and Wales;

(c) to secure that companies holding appointments under Chapter 1 of Part 2 of this Act as relevant undertakers are able (in particular, by securing reasonable returns on their capital) to finance the proper carrying out of those functions; and

(d) to secure that the activities authorised by the licence of a licensed water supplier and any statutory functions imposed on it in consequence of the licence are properly carried out.

(2B) The consumer objective mentioned in subsection (2A)(a) above is to protect the interests of consumers, wherever appropriate by promoting effective competition between persons engaged in, or in commercial activities connected with, the provision of water and sewerage services.

. . .

[(3) Subject to subsection (2A) above, the Secretary of State or, as the case may be, the Authority shall exercise and perform the powers and duties mentioned in subsection (1) above in the manner which he or it considers is best calculated—

(a) to promote economy and efficiency on the part of companies holding an appointment under Chapter 1 of Part 2 of this Act in the carrying out of the functions of a relevant undertaker;

(b) to secure that no undue preference is shown, and that there is no undue discrimination in the fixing by such companies of water and drainage charges;

(c) to secure that consumers are protected as respects benefits that could be secured for them by the application in a particular manner of any of the proceeds of any disposal (whenever made) of any of such a company's protected land or of an interest or right in or over any of that land;

(d) to ensure that consumers are also protected as respects any activities of such a company which are not attributable to the exercise of functions of a relevant undertaker, or as respects any activities of any person appearing to the Secretary of State or (as the case may be) the Authority to be connected with the company, and in particular by ensuring—

(i) that any transactions are carried out at arm's length;

(ii) that the company, in relation to the exercise of its functions as a relevant undertaker, maintains and presents accounts in a suitable form and manner;

(iii) that, if the person is a licensed water supplier, its licence does not authorise it to carry on any activities in the area of the company;

(e) to contribute to the achievement of sustainable development.

(4) In exercising any of the powers or performing any of the duties mentioned in subsection (1) above in accordance with the preceding provisions of this section, the Secretary of State and the Authority shall have regard to the principles of best regulatory practice (including the principles under which regulatory activities should be transparent, accountable, proportionate, consistent and targeted only at cases in which action is needed).]

. . .

[(5A) In this section—
'consumers' includes both existing and future consumers; and
'the interests of consumers' means the interests of consumers in relation to—

(a) the supply of water by means of a water undertaker's supply system to premises either by water undertakers or by licensed water suppliers acting in their capacity as such; and
(b) the provision of sewerage services by sewerage undertakers.]

. . .

[(7) The duties imposed by subsections (2A) to (4) above and section 2A below do not affect the obligation of the Authority or, as the case may be, the Secretary of State to perform or comply with any other duty or requirement (whether arising under this Act or another enactment, by virtue of any Community obligation or otherwise).]

. . .

3 General environmental and recreational duties

(1) It shall be the duty of each of the following, that is to say—

(a) the Secretary of State;
(b) . . .
(c) [the Authority]; and
(d) every company holding an appointment as a relevant undertaker,

in formulating or considering any proposals relating to any functions of a relevant undertaker (including, in the case of such a company, any functions which, by virtue of that appointment, are functions of the company itself) to comply with the requirements imposed in relation to the proposals by subsections (2) and (3) below.

(2) The requirements imposed by this subsection in relation to any such proposals as are mentioned in subsection (1) above are—

(a) a requirement, so far as may be consistent—
  (i) with the purposes of any enactment relating to the functions of the undertaker; and
  (ii) in the case of the Secretary of State and [the Authority], with their duties under section 2 above,

  so to exercise any power conferred with respect to the proposals on the person subject to the requirement as to further the conservation and enhancement of natural beauty and the conservation of flora, fauna and geological or physiographical features of special interest [and, in the case of the exercise of such a power by a company holding an appointment as a relevant undertaker, as to further water conservation];
(b) a requirement to have regard to the desirability of protecting and conserving buildings, sites and objects of archaeological, architectural or historic interest; and
(c) a requirement to take into account any effect which the proposals would have on the beauty or amenity of any rural or urban area or on any such flora, fauna, features, buildings, sites or objects.

(3) The requirements imposed by this subsection in relation to any such proposals as are mentioned in subsection (1) above are, subject to the requirements imposed by subsection (2) above—

(a) a requirement to have regard to the desirability of preserving for the public any freedom of access to areas of woodland, mountains, moor, heath, down, cliff or foreshore and other places of natural beauty;
(b) a requirement to have regard to the desirability of maintaining the availability to the public of any facility for visiting or inspecting any building, site or object of archaeological, architectural or historic interest; and

(c) a requirement to take into account any effect which the proposals would have on any such freedom of access or on the availability of any such facility.

(4) Subsections (1) to (3) above shall apply so as to impose duties on [the Authority] and any company holding an appointment as a relevant undertaker in relation to any proposal relating to—

(a) the functions of [the Environment Agency]; or

(b) the functions of an internal drainage board,

as they apply in relation to any proposals relating to the functions of such an undertaker; and for the purposes of this subsection the reference in subsection (2)(a) above to the functions of the undertaker shall have effect as a reference to the functions of [the Environment Agency] or, as the case may be, of the internal drainage board in question.

. . .

4 Environmental duties with respect to sites of special interest

(1) Where [Natural England] or the Countryside Council for Wales are of the opinion that any area of land in England or, as the case may be, in Wales—

(a) is of special interest by reason of its flora, fauna or geological or physiographical features; and

(b) may at any time be affected by schemes, works, operations or activities of a relevant undertaker,

[Natural England (or, as the case may be, the Council)] shall notify the fact that the land is of special interest for that reason to every relevant undertaker whose works, operations or activities may affect the land.

(2) Where a National Park authority or the Broads Authority is of the opinion that any area of land in a National Park or in the Broads—

(a) is land in relation to which the matters for the purposes of which section 3 above has effect are of particular importance; and

(b) may at any time be affected by schemes, works, operations or activities of a relevant undertaker,

the National Park authority or Broads Authority shall notify the fact that the land is such land, and the reasons why those matters are of particular importance in relation to the land, to every relevant undertaker whose works, operations or activities may affect the land.

(3) Where a relevant undertaker has received a notification under subsection (1) or (2) above with respect to any land, that undertaker shall consult the notifying body before carrying out any works, operations or activities which appear to that undertaker to be likely—

(a) to destroy or damage any of the flora, fauna, or geological or physiographical features by reason of which the land is of special interest; or

(b) significantly to prejudice anything the importance of which is one of the reasons why the matters mentioned in subsection (2) above are of particular importance in relation to that land.

(4) Subsection (3) above shall not apply in relation to anything done in an emergency where particulars of what is done and of the emergency are notified to [Natural England], the Countryside Council for Wales, the National Park authority in question or, as the case may be, the Broads Authority as soon as practicable after that thing is done.

(5) The obligations under this section of a relevant undertaker shall be enforceable under section 18 below by the Secretary of State.

(6) In this section—

'the Broads' has the same meaning as in the Norfolk and Suffolk Broads Act 1988;

. . .

and section 3(9) above shall apply, as it applies in relation to that section, for construing (in accordance with section 6 below) any references in this section to a relevant undertaker.

. . .

PART II

CHAPTER II ENFORCEMENT AND INSOLVENCY

Enforcement orders

18 Orders for securing compliance with certain provisions

(1) Subject to subsection (2) and sections 19 and 20 below, where in the case of any company holding an appointment under Chapter I of this Part [or a licence under Chapter 1A of this Part] the Secretary of State or [the Authority] is satisfied—

(a) that that company is contravening—

(i) any condition of the company's appointment [or licence] in relation to which [he or it] is the enforcement authority; or

(ii) any statutory or other requirement which is enforceable under this section and in relation to which [he or it] is the enforcement authority;

or

(b) that that company [is likely to contravene any such condition or requirement], [he or it] shall by a final enforcement order make such provision as is requisite for the purpose of securing compliance with that condition or requirement.

. . .

(2) Subject to section 19 below, where in the case of any company holding an appointment under Chapter I of this Part [or a licence under Chapter 1A of this Part]—

(a) it appears to the Secretary of State or [the Authority] as mentioned in paragraph (a) or (b) of subsection (1) [or (1A)] above; and

(b) it appears to him that it is requisite that a provisional enforcement order be made, he may (instead of taking steps towards the making of a final order) by a provisional enforcement order make such provision as appears to him requisite for the purpose of securing compliance with the condition or requirement in question.

(3) In determining for the purposes of subsection (2)(b) above whether it is requisite that a provisional enforcement order be made, the Secretary of State or, as the case may be, [the Authority] shall have regard, in particular, to the extent to which any person is likely to sustain loss or damage in consequence of anything which, in contravention of any condition or of any statutory or other requirement enforceable under this section, is likely to be done, or omitted to be done, before a final enforcement order may be made.

(4) Subject to sections 19 and 20 below, where the Secretary of State or [the Authority] has made a provisional enforcement order, [he or it] shall confirm it, with or without modifications, if—

(a) [he or it] is satisfied that the company to which the order relates—

(i) is contravening any condition or statutory or other requirement in relation to which [he or it] is the enforcement authority; or

[(ii) is likely to contravene any such condition or requirement;] [or

(iii) is causing or contributing to a contravention of any such condition or requirement; or

(iv) is likely to cause or contribute to any such contravention;] and

(b) the provision made by the order (with any modifications) is requisite for the purpose of securing compliance with that condition or requirement.

(5) An enforcement order—

(a) shall require the company to which it relates (according to the circumstances of the case) to do, or not to do, such things as are specified in the order or are of a description so specified;

(b) shall take effect at such time, being the earliest practicable time, as is determined by or under the order; and

(c) may be revoked at any time by the enforcement authority who made it.

(6) For the purposes of this section and the following provisions of this Act—

(a) the statutory and other requirements which shall be enforceable under this section in relation to a company holding an appointment under Chapter I of this Part [or a licence under Chapter 1A of this Part] shall be such of the requirements of any enactment or of any subordinate legislation as—
(i) are imposed in consequence of that appointment [or licence]; and
(ii) are made so enforceable by that enactment or subordinate legislation;
(b) [the Authority] shall be the enforcement authority in relation to the conditions of an appointment under Chapter I of this Part [or of a licence under Chapter 1A of this Part]; and
(c) the enforcement authority in relation to each of the statutory and other requirements enforceable under this section shall be the Secretary of State, [the Authority] or either of them, according to whatever provision is made by the enactment or subordinate legislation by which the requirement is made so enforceable.

(7) In this section and the following provisions of this Chapter—

'enforcement order' means a final enforcement order or a provisional enforcement order;

'final enforcement order' means an order under this section other than a provisional enforcement order;

'provisional enforcement order' means an order under this section which, if not previously confirmed in accordance with subsection (4) above, will cease to have effect at the end of such period (not exceeding three months) as is determined by or under the order.

[(8) Where any act or omission—
(a) constitutes a contravention of a condition of an appointment under Chapter 1 of this Part or of a condition of a licence under Chapter 1A of this Part or of a statutory or other requirement enforceable under this section; or
(b) causes or contributes to a contravention of any such condition or requirement,

the only remedies for, or for causing or contributing to, that contravention (apart from those available by virtue of this section) shall be those for which express provision is made by or under any enactment and those that are available in respect of that act or omission otherwise than by virtue of its constituting, or causing or contributing to, such a contravention.]

19 Exceptions to duty to enforce

(1) [Subject to the Drinking Water (Undertakings) (England and Wales) Regulations 2000,] neither the Secretary of State nor [the Authority] shall be required to make an enforcement order in relation to any company, or to confirm a provisional enforcement order so made, if [he or it] is satisfied—
(a) that the contraventions were, or the apprehended contraventions are, of a trivial nature;
[(aa) that the extent to which the company caused or contributed to, or was likely to cause or contribute to, a contravention was trivial;]
(b) that the company has given, and is complying with, an undertaking to take all such steps as it appears to [him or it] for the time being to be appropriate for the company to take for the purpose of securing or facilitating compliance with the condition or requirement in question; or
(c) that the duties imposed on [him or it] by Part I of this Act preclude the making or, as the case may be, the confirmation of the order.

. . .

(2) The requirement to comply with an undertaking given for the purposes of subsection (1)(b) above shall be treated as a statutory requirement enforceable under section 18 above—
(a) by the Secretary of State; or

(b) with the consent of or in accordance with a general authorisation given by the Secretary of State, by [the Authority].

(3) Where the Secretary of State or [the Authority], having notified a company that [he or it] is considering the making in relation to the company of an enforcement order or the confirmation of a provisional enforcement order so made, is satisfied as mentioned in paragraph (a), [(aa),] (b) or (c) of subsection (1) above [or, in the case of [the Authority], is satisfied as mentioned in subsection (1A) above], [he or it] shall—

(a) serve notice that [he or it] is so satisfied on the company;

(b) publish a copy of the notice in such manner as [he or it] considers appropriate for the purpose of bringing the matters to which the notice relates to the attention of persons likely to be affected by them; and

(c) in a case where the Secretary of State is satisfied as mentioned in the said paragraph (b), serve a copy of the notice and of the undertaking given for the purposes of that paragraph on [the Authority].

...

20 Procedure for enforcement orders

...

Water Resources Act 1991

(1991, c. 57)

PART III CONTROL OF POLLUTION OF WATER RESOURCES

CHAPTER I QUALITY OBJECTIVES

82 Classification of quality of waters

(1) The Secretary of State may, in relation to any description of controlled waters (being a description applying to some or all of the waters of a particular class or of two or more different classes), by regulations prescribe a system of classifying the quality of those waters according to criteria specified in the regulations.

(2) The criteria specified in regulations under this section in relation to any classification shall consist of one or more of the following, that is to say—

(a) general requirements as to the purposes for which the waters to which the classification is applied are to be suitable;

(b) specific requirements as to the substances that are to be present in or absent from the water and as to the concentrations of substances which are or are required to be present in the water;

(c) specific requirements as to other characteristics of those waters;

and for the purposes of any such classification regulations under this section may provide that the question whether prescribed requirements are satisfied may be determined by reference to such samples as may be prescribed.

83 Water quality objectives

(1) For the purpose of maintaining and improving the quality of controlled waters the Secretary of State may, by serving a notice on the [Agency] specifying—

(a) one or more of the classifications for the time being prescribed under section 82 above; and

(b) in relation to each specified classification, a date,

establish the water quality objectives for any waters which are, or are included in, waters of a description prescribed for the purposes of that section.

(2) The water quality objectives for any waters to which a notice under this section relates shall be the satisfaction by those waters, on and at all times after each date specified in

the notice, of the requirements which at the time of the notice were the requirements for the classification in relation to which that date is so specified.

(3) Where the Secretary of State has established water quality objectives under this section for any waters he may review objectives for those waters if—

(a) five years or more have elapsed since the service of the last notice under subsection (1) or (6) of this section to be served in respect of those waters; or

(b) the [Agency], after consultation with such water undertakers and other persons as it considers appropriate, requests a review;

and the Secretary of State shall not exercise his power to establish objectives for any waters by varying the existing objectives for those waters except in consequence of such a review.

(4) Where the Secretary of State proposes to exercise his power under this section to establish or vary the objectives for any waters he shall—

(a) give notice setting out his proposal and specifying the period (not being less than three months from the date of publication of the notice) within which representations or objections with respect to the proposal may be made; and

(b) consider any representations or objections which are duly made and not withdrawn;

and, if he decides, after considering any such representations or objections, to exercise his power to establish or vary those objectives, he may do so either in accordance with the proposal contained in the notice or in accordance with that proposal as modified in such manner as he considers appropriate.

(5) A notice under subsection (4) above shall be given—

(a) by publishing the notice in such manner as the Secretary of State considers appropriate for bringing it to the attention of persons likely to be affected by it; and

(b) by serving a copy of the notice on the [Agency].

(6) If, on a review under this section or in consequence of any representations or objections made following such a review for the purposes of subsection (4) above, the Secretary of State decides that the water quality objectives for any waters should remain unchanged, he shall serve notice of that decision on the [Agency].

84 General duties to achieve and maintain objectives etc.

(1) It shall be the duty of the Secretary of State and of the [Agency] to exercise the powers conferred on him or it by or under the water pollution provisions of this Act (other than the preceding provisions of this Chapter and sections 104 and 192 below) in such manner as ensures, so far as it is practicable by the exercise of those powers to do so, that the water quality objectives specified for any waters in—

(a) a notice under section 83 above; or

(b) . . .

are achieved at all times.

(2) It shall be the duty of the [Agency], for the purposes of the carrying out of its functions under the water pollution provisions of this Act—

(a) to monitor the extent of pollution in controlled waters; and

(b) to consult, in such cases as it may consider appropriate, with the Scottish Enviornment Protection Agency.

CHAPTER II POLLUTION OFFENCES

85 Offences of polluting controlled waters

(1) A person contravenes this section if he causes or knowingly permits any poisonous, noxious or polluting matter or any solid waste matter to enter any controlled waters.

(2) A person contravenes this section if he causes or knowingly permits any matter, other than trade effluent or sewage effluent, to enter controlled waters by being discharged from a drain or sewer in contravention of a prohibition imposed under section 86 below.

(3) A person contravenes this section if he causes or knowingly permits any trade effluent or sewage effluent to be discharged—

(a) into any controlled waters; or

(b) from land in England and Wales, through a pipe, into the sea outside the seaward limits of controlled waters.

(4) A person contravenes this section if he causes or knowingly permits any trade effluent or sewage effluent to be discharged, in contravention of any prohibition imposed under section 86 below, from a building or from any fixed plant—

(a) on to or into any land; or

(b) into any waters of a lake or pond which are not inland freshwaters.

(5) A person contravenes this section if he causes or knowingly permits any matter whatever to enter any inland freshwaters so as to tend (either directly or in combination with other matter which he or another person causes or permits to enter those waters) to impede the proper flow of the waters in a manner leading, or likely to lead, to a substantial aggravation of—

(a) pollution due to other causes; or

(b) the consequences of such pollution.

(6) Subject to the following provisions of this Chapter, a person who contravenes this section or the conditions of any consent given under this Chapter for the purposes of this section shall be guilty of an offence and liable—

(a) on summary conviction, to imprisonment for a term not exceeding three months or to a fine not exceeding £20,000 or to both;

(b) on conviction on indictment, to imprisonment for a term not exceeding two years or to a fine or to both.

86 Prohibition of certain discharges by notice or regulations

(1) For the purpose of section 85 above a discharge of any effluent or other matter is, in relation to any person, in contravention of a prohibition imposed under this section if, subject to the following provisions of this section—

(a) the [Agency] has given that person notice prohibiting him from making or, as the case may be, continuing the discharge; or

(b) the [Agency] has given that person notice prohibiting him from making or, as the case may be, continuing the discharge unless specified conditions are observed, and those conditions are not observed.

(2) For the purposes of section 85 above a discharge of any effluent or other matter is also in contravention of a prohibition imposed under this section if the effluent or matter discharged—

(a) contains a prescribed substance or a prescribed concentration of such a substance; or

(b) derives from a prescribed process or form a process involving the use of prescribed substances or the use of such substances in quantities which exceed the prescribed amounts.

(3) Nothing in subsection (1) above shall authorise the giving of a notice for the purposes of that subsection in respect of discharges from a vessel; and nothing in any regulations made by virtue of subsection (2) above shall require any discharge from a vessel to be treated as a discharge in contravention of a prohibition imposed under this section.

(4) A notice given for the purposes of subsection (1) above shall expire at such time as may be specified in the notice.

(5) The time specified for the purposes of subsection (4) above shall not be before the end of the period of three months beginning with the day on which the notice is given, except in a case where the [Agency] is satisfied that there is an emergency which requires the prohibition in question to come into force at such time before the end of that period as may be so specified.

(6) Where, in the case of such a notice for the purposes of subsection (1) above as (but for this subsection) would expire at a time at or after the end of the said period of three months, an application is made before that time for a consent under this Chapter in respect of the discharge to which the notice relates, that notice shall be deemed not to expire until the result of the application becomes final—

(a) on the grant or withdrawal of the application;

(b) on the expiration, without the bringing of an appeal with respect to the decision on the application, of any period prescribed as the period within which any such appeal must be brought; or

(c) on the withdrawal or determination of any such appeal.

87 Discharges into and from public sewers etc.

[(1) This section applies for the purpose of determining liability where sewage effluent is discharged as mentioned in subsection (3) or (4) of section 85 above from any sewer or works ('the discharging sewer') vested in a sewerage undertaker ('the discharging undertaker').

(1A) If the discharging undertaker did not cause, or knowingly permit, the discharge it shall nevertheless be deemed to have caused the discharge if—

(a) matter included in the discharge was received by it into the discharging sewer or any other sewer or works vested in it;

(b) it was bound (either unconditionally or subject to conditions which were observed) to receive that matter into that sewer or works; and

(c) subsection (1B) below does not apply.

(1B) This subsection applies where the sewage effluent was, before being discharged from the discharging sewer, discharged through a main connection into that sewer or into any other sewer or works vested in the discharging undertaker by another sewerage undertaker ('the sending undertaker') under an agreement having effect between the discharging undertaker and the sending undertaker under section 110A of the Water Industry Act 1991.

(1C) Where subsection (1B) above applies, the sending undertaker shall be deemed to have caused the discharge if, although it did not cause, or knowingly permit, the sewage effluent to be discharged into the discharging sewer, or into any other sewer or works of the discharging undertaker—

(a) matter included in the discharge was received by it into a sewer or works vested in it; and

(b) it was bound (either unconditionally or subject to conditions which were observed) to receive that matter into that sewer or works.]

(2) A sewerage undertaker shall not be guilty of an offence under section 85 above by reason only of the fact that a discharge from a sewer or works vested in the undertaker contravenes conditions of a consent relating to the discharge if—

(a) the contravention is attributable to a discharge which another person caused or permitted to be made into the sewer or works;

(b) the undertaker either was not bound to receive the discharge into the sewer or works or was bound to receive it there subject to conditions which were not observed; and

(c) the undertaker could not reasonably have been expected to prevent the discharge into the sewer or works.

(3) A person shall not be guilty of an offence under section 85 above in respect of a discharge which he caused or permitted to be made into a sewer or works vested in a sewerage undertaker if the undertaker was bound to receive the discharge there either unconditionally or subject to conditions which were observed.

[(4) In this section 'main connection' has the same meaning as in section 110A of the Water Industry Act 1991.]

88 Defence to principal offences in respect of authorised discharges

(1) Subject to the following provisions of this section, a person shall not be guilty of an offence under section 85 above in respect of the entry of any matter into any waters or any discharge if the entry occurs or the discharge is made under and in accordance with, or as a result of any act or omission under and in accordance with—

(a) a consent given under this Chapter . . . ;

[(aa) a permit granted, under regulations under section 2 of the Pollution Prevention and Control Act 1999, by an authority exercising functions under the regulations that are exercisable for the purpose of preventing or reducing emissions into the air, water and land;]

(b) an authorisation for a prescribed process designated for central control granted under Part I of the Environment Protection Act 1990;

(c) a waste management or disposal licence;

(d) a licence granted under Part II of the Food and Environmental Protection Act 1985;

(e) section 163 below or section 165 of the Water Industry Act 1991 (discharges for works purposes);

(f) any local statutory provision or statutory order which expressly confers power to discharge effluent into water; or

(g) any prescribed enactment.

(2) Schedule 10 to this Act shall have effect, subject to section 91 below, with respect to the making of applications for consents under this Chapter for the purposes of subsection(1)(a) above and with respect to the giving, revocation and modification of such consents.

(3) Nothing in any disposal licence shall be treated for the purposes of subsection (1) above as authorising—

(a) any such entry or discharge as is mentioned in subsections (2) to (4) of section 85 above; or

(b) any act or omission so far as it results in any such entry or discharge.

(4) In this section—

'disposal licence' means a licence issued in pursuance of section 5 of the Control of Pollution Act 1974;

'statutory order' means—

(a) any order under section 168 below or section 167 of the Water Industry Act 1991 (compulsory works orders); or

(b) any order, byelaw, scheme or award made under any other enactment, including an order or scheme confirmed by Parliament or brought into operation in accordance with special parliamentary procedure;

and

'waste management licence' means such a licence granted under Part II of the Environmental Protection Act 1990.

89 Other defences to principal offences

(1) A person shall not be guilty of an offence under section 85 above in respect of the entry of any matter into any waters or any discharge if—

(a) the entry is caused or permitted, or the discharge is made, in an emergency in order to avoid danger to life or health;

(b) that person takes all such steps as are reasonably practicable in the circumstances for minimising the extent of the entry or discharge and of its polluting effects; and

(c) particulars of the entry or discharge are furnished to the [Agency] as soon as reasonably practicable after the entry occurs.

(2) A person shall not be guilty of an offence under section 85 above by reason of his causing or permitting any discharge of trade or sewage effluent from a vessel.

(3) A person shall not be guilty of an offence under section 85 above by reason only of his permitting water from an abandoned mine [or an abandoned part of a mine] to enter controlled waters.

[(3A) Subsection (3) above shall not apply to the owner or former operator of any mine or part of a mine if the mine or part in question became abandoned after 31st December 1999.

(3B) In determining for the purposes of subsection (3A) above whether a mine or part of a mine became abandoned before, on or after 31st December 1999 in a case where the mine or part has become abandoned on two or more occasions, of which—

(a) at least one falls on or before that date, and

(b) at least one falls after that date,

the mine or part shall be regarded as becoming abandoned after that date (but without prejudice to the operation of subsection (3) above in relation to that mine or part at, or in relation to, any time before the first of those occasions which falls after that date).

(3C) Where, immediately before a part of a mine becomes abandoned, that part is the only part of the mine not falling to be regarded as abandoned for the time being, the abandonment of that part shall not be regarded for the purposes of subsection (3A) or (3B) above as constituting the abandonment of the mine, but only of that part of it.]

(4) A person shall not, otherwise than in respect of the entry of any poisonous, noxious or polluting matter into any controlled waters, be guilty of an offence under section 85 above by reason of his depositing the solid refuse of a mine or quarry on any land so that it falls or is carried into inland freshwaters if—

(a) the deposits the refuse on the land with the consent of the [Agency];

(b) no other site for the deposit is reasonably practicable; and

(c) he takes all reasonably practicable steps to prevent the refuse from entering those inland freshwaters.

(5) A highway authority or other person entitled to keep open a drain by virtue of section 100 of the Highways Act 1980 shall not be guilty of an offence under section 85 above by reason of his causing or permitting any discharge to be made from a drain kept open by virtue of that section unless the discharge is made in contravention of a prohibition imposed under section 86 above.

(6) In this section 'mine' and 'quarry' have the same meanings as in the Mines and Quarries Act 1954.

90 Offences in connection with deposits and vegetation in rivers

(1) A person shall be guilty of an offence under this section if, without the consent of the [Agency], he—

(a) removes from any part of the bottom, channel or bed of any inland freshwaters a deposit accumulated by reason of any dam, weir or sluice holding back the waters; and

(b) does so by causing the deposit to be carried away in suspension in the waters.

(2) A person shall be guilty of an offence under this section if, without the consent of the [Agency], he—

(a) causes or permits a substantial amount of vegetation to be cut or uprooted in any inland freshwaters, or to be cut or uprooted so near to any such waters that it falls into them; and

(b) fails to take all reasonable steps to remove the vegetation from those waters.

(3) A person guilty of an offence under this section shall be liable, on summary conviction, to a fine not exceeding level 4 on the standard scale.

(4) Nothing in subsection (1) above applies to anything done in the exercise of any power conferred by or under any enactment relating to land drainage, flood prevention or navigation.

(5) In giving a consent for the purposes of this section the [Agency] may make the consent subject to such conditions as it considers appropriate.

(6) The Secretary of State may by regulations provide that any reference to inland freshwaters in subsection (1) or (2) above shall be construed as including a reference to such coastal waters as may be prescribed.

[Consents for the purposes of sections 88 to 90

90A Applications for consent under section 89 or 90

(1) Any application for a consent for the purposes of section 89(4)(a) or 90(1) or (2) above—

(a) must be made on a form provided for the purpose by the Agency, and

(b) must be advertised in such manner as may be required by regulations made by the Secretary of State,

except that paragraph (b) above shall not have effect in the case of an application of any class or description specified in the regulations as being exempt from the requirements of that paragraph.

(2) The applicant for such a consent must, at the time when he makes his application, provide the Agency—

(a) with all such information as it reasonably requires; and

(b) with all such information as may be prescribed for the purpose by the Secretary of State.

(3) The information required by subsection (2) above must be provided either on, or together with, the form mentioned in subsection (1) above.

(4) The Agency may give the applicant notice requiring him to provide it with all such further information of any description specified in the notice as it may require for the purpose of determining the application.

(5) If the applicant fails to provide the Agency with any information required under subsection (4) above, the Agency may refuse to proceed with the application or refuse to proceed with it until the information is provided.

90B Enforcement notices

(1) If the Agency is of the opinion that the holder of a relevant consent is contravening any condition of the consent, or is likely to contravene any such condition, the Agency may serve on him a notice (an 'enforcement notice').

(2) An enforcement notice shall—

(a) state that the Agency is of the said opinion;

(b) specify the matters constituting the contravention or the matters making it likely that the contravention will arise;

(c) specify the steps that must be taken to remedy the contravention or, as the case may be, to remedy the matters making it likely that the contravention will arise; and

(d) specify the period within which those steps must be taken.

(3) Any person who fails to comply with any requirement imposed by an enforcement notice shall be guilty of an offence and liable—

(a) on summary conviction, to imprisonment for a term not exceeding three months or to a fine not exceeding £20,000 or to both;

(b) on conviction on indictment, to imprisonment for a term not exceeding two years or to a fine or to both.

(4) If the Agency is of the opinion that proceedings for an offence under subsection (3) above would afford an ineffectual remedy against a person who has failed to comply with the requirements of an enforcement notice, the Agency may take proceedings in the High Court for the purpose of securing compliance with the notice.

(5) The Secretary of State may, if he thinks fit in relation to any person, give to the Agency directions as to whether the Agency should exercise its powers under this section and as to the steps which must be taken.

(6) In this section—

'relevant consent' means—

(a) a consent for the purposes of section 89(4)(a) or 90(1) or (2) above; or

(b) a discharge consent, within the meaning of section 91 below; and

'the holder', in relation to a relevant consent, is the person who has the consent in question.]

91 Appeals in respect of consents under Chapter II

(1) This section applies where the [Agency], otherwise than in pursuance of a direction of the Secretary of State—

(a) on an application for a consent under this Chapter for the purposes of section 88(1)(a) above, has refused a consent for any discharges;

(b) in giving a discharge consent, has made that consent subject to conditions;

(c) has revoked a discharge consent, modified the conditions of any such consent or provided that any such consent which was unconditional shall be subject to conditions;

(d) has, for the purposes of paragraph [8(1)] or (2) of Schedule 10 to this Act, specified a period in relation to a discharge consent without the agreement of the person who proposes to make, or makes, discharges in pursuance of that consent;

(e) has refused a consent for the purposes of section 89(4)(a) above for any deposit;

(f) has refused a consent for the purposes of section 90 above for the doing of anything by any person or, in giving any such consent, made that consent subject to conditions.

(2) The person, if any, who applied for the consent [or variation] in question, or any person whose deposits, discharges or other conduct is or would be authorised by the consent [or the person on whom the enforcement notice was served,] may appeal against the decision to the Secretary of State.

[(2A) This section is subject to section 114 of the 1995 Act (delegation or reference of appeals etc).

(2B) An appeal under this section shall, if and to the extent required by regulations under subsection (2K) below, be advertised in such manner as may be prescribed by regulations under that subsection.

(2C) If either party to the appeal so requests or the Secretary of State so decides, an appeal shall be or continue in the form of a hearing (which may, if the person hearing the appeal so decides, be held, or held to any extent, in private).

(2D) On determining an appeal brought by virtue of any of paragraphs (a) to (g) of subsection (1) above against a decision of the Agency, the Secretary of State—

(a) may affirm the decision;

(b) where the decision was a refusal to grant a consent or a variation of a consent, may direct the Agency to grant the consent or to vary the consent, as the case may be;

(c) where the decision was as to the conditions of a consent, may quash all or any of those conditions;

(d) where the decision was to revoke a consent, may quash the decision;

(e) where the decision relates to a period specified for the purposes of paragraph 8(1) or (2) of Schedule 10 to this Act, may modify any provisions specifying that period;

and where he exercises any of the powers in paragraphs (b), (c) or (d) above, he may give directions as to the conditions to which the consent is to be subject.

(2E) On the determination of an appeal brought by virtue of paragraph (h) of subsection (1) above, the Secretary of State may either quash or affirm the enforcement notice and, if he affirms it, may do so either in its original form or with such modifications as he may in the circumstances think fit.

(2F) Subject to subsection (2G) below, where an appeal is brought by virtue of subsection (1)(c) above against a decision—

(a) to revoke a discharge consent,

(b) to modify the conditions of any such consent, or

(c) to provide that any such consent which was unconditional shall be subject to conditions,

the revocation, modification or provision shall not take effect pending the final determination or the withdrawal of the appeal.

(2G) Subsection (2F) above shall not apply to a decision in the case of which the notice affecting the revocation, modification or provision in question includes a statement that in the opinion of the Agency it is necessary for the purpose of preventing or, where that is not practicable, minimising—

(a) the entry into controlled waters of any poisonous, noxious or polluting matter or any solid waste matter, or

(b) harm to human health,

that that subsection should not apply.

(2H) Where the decision under appeal is one falling within subsection (2G) above, if, on the application of the holder or former holder of the consent, the Secretary of State or other person determining the appeal determines that the Agency acted unreasonably in excluding the application of subsection (2F) above, then—

(a) if the appeal is still pending at the end of the day on which the determination is made, subsection (2F) above shall apply to the decision from the end of that day; and

(b) the holder or former holder of the consent shall be entitled to recover compensation from the Agency in respect of any loss suffered by him in consequence of the exclusion of the application of that subsection;

and any dispute as to a person's entitlement to such compensation or as to the amount of it shall be determined by arbitration.

(2J) Where an appeal is brought under this section against an enforcement notice, the bringing of the appeal shall not have the effect of suspending the operation of the notice.

(2K) Provision may be made by the Secretary of State by regulations with respect to appeals under this section and in particular—

(a) as to the period within which and the manner in which appeals are to be brought; and

(b) as to the manner in which appeals are to be considered.]

(3) [...]

(8) In this section 'discharge consent' means such a consent under this Chapter for any discharges or description of discharges as is given for the purposes of section 88(1)(a) above either on an application for a consent or, by virtue of paragraph [6] of Schedule 10 to this Act, without such an application having been made.

CHAPTER III POWERS TO PREVENT AND CONTROL POLLUTION

92 Requirements to take precautions against pollution

(1) The Secretary of State may by regulations make provision—

(a) for prohibiting a person from having custody or control of any poisonous, noxious or polluting matter unless prescribed works and prescribed precautions and other steps have been carried out or taken for the purpose of preventing or controlling the entry of the matter into any controlled waters;

(b) for requiring a person who already has custody or control of, or makes use of, any such matter to carry out such works for that purpose and to take such precautions and other steps for that purpose as may be prescribed.

(2) Without prejudice to the generality of the power conferred by subsection (1) above, regulations under that subsection may—

(a) confer power on the [Agency]—
   (i) to determine for the purposes of the regulations the circumstances in which a person is required to carry out works or to take any precautions or other steps; and
   (ii) by notice to that person, to impose the requirement and to specify or describe the works, precautions or other steps which that person is required to carry out or take;

(b) provide for appeals to the Secretary of State against notices served by the [Agency] in pursuance of provision made by virtue of paragraph (a) above; and

(c) provide that a contravention of the regulations shall be an offence the maximum penalties for which shall not exceed the penalties specified in subsection (6) of section 85 above.

[(3) This section is subject to section 114 of the 1995 Act (delegation or reference of appeals etc).]

93 Water protection zones

(1) Where the Secretary of State considers, after consultation (in the case of an area wholly or partly in England) with the Minister, that subsection (2) below is satisfied in relation to any area, he may be order make provision—

(a) designating that area as a water protection zone; and

(b) prohibiting or restricting the carrying on in the designated area of such activities as may by specified or described in the order.

(2) For the purposes of subsection (1) above this subsection is satisfied in relation to any area if (subject to subsection (3) below) it is appropriate, with a view to preventing or controlling the entry of any poisonous, noxious or polluting matter into controlled waters, to prohibit or restrict the carrying on in that area of activities which the Secretary of State considers are likely to result in the pollution of any such waters.

(3) The reference in subsection (2) above to the entry of poisonous, noxious or polluting matter into controlled waters shall not include a reference to the entry of nitrate into controlled waters as a result of, or of anything done in connection with, the use of any land for agricultural purposes.

(4) Without prejudice to the generality of the power conferred by virtue of subsection (1) above, an order under this section may—

(a) confer power on the [Agency] to determine for the purposes of the order the circumstances in which the carrying on of any activities is prohibited or restricted and to determine the activities to which any such prohibition or restriction applies;

(b) apply a prohibition or restriction in respect of any activities to cases where the activities are carried on without the consent of the [Agency] or in contravention of any conditions subject to which any such consent is given;

(c) provide that a contravention of a prohibition or restriction contained in the order or of a condition of a consent given for the purposes of any such prohibition or restriction shall be an offence the maximum penalties for which shall not exceed the penalties specified in subsection (6) of section 85 above;

(d) provide (subject to any regulations under section 96 below) for anything falling to be determined under the order by the [Agency] to be determined in accordance with such procedure and by reference to such matters and to the opinion of such persons as may be specified in the order;

(e) make different provision for different cases, including different provision in relation to different persons, circumstances or localities; and

(f) contain such supplemental, consequential and transitional provision as the Secretary of State considers appropriate.

(5) The power of the Secretary of State to make an order under this section shall be exercisable by statutory instrument subject to annulment in pursuance of a resolution of either House of Parliament; but the Secretary of State shall not make such an order except on an application made by the [Agency] in accordance with Schedule 11 to this Act and otherwise in accordance with that Schedule.

96 Regulations with respect to consents required by virtue of section 93 or 94

(1) The Secretary of State may, for the purposes of any orders under section 93 above which require the consent of the [Agency] to the carrying on of any activities, by regulations make provision with respect to—

(a) applications for any such consent;
(b) the conditions of any such consent;
(c) the revocation or variation of any such consent;
(d) appeals against determinations on any such application;
(e) the exercise by the Secretary of State of any power conferred on the [Agency] by the orders;
(f) the imposition of charges where such an application has been made, such a consent has been given or anything has been done in pursuance of any such consent; and
(g) the registration of any such application or consent.

(2) . . .

(3) Without prejudice to the generality of the powers conferred by the preceding provisions of this section, regulations under subsection (1) above may apply (with or without modifications) any enactment having effect in relation to consents under Chapter II of this Part.

[(4) This section is subject to section 114 of the 1995 Act (delegation or reference of appeals etc.).]

97 Codes of good agricultural practice

(1) The Ministers may by order made by statutory instrument approve any code of practice issued (whether by either or both of the Ministers or by another person) for the purpose of—

(a) giving practical guidance to persons engaged in agriculture with respect to activities that may affect controlled waters; and
(b) promoting what appear to them to be desirable practices by such person for avoiding or minimising the pollution of any such waters,

and may at any time by such an order approve a modification of such a code or withdraw their approval of such a code or modification.

(2) A contravention of a code of practice as for the time being approved under this section shall not of itself give rise to any criminal or civil liability, but the [Agency] shall take into account whether there has been or is likely to be any such contravention in determining when and how it should exercise—

(a) Its power, by giving a notice under subsection (1) of section 86 above, to impose a prohibition under that section; and
(b) any powers conferred on the [Agency] by regulations under section 92 above.

(3) The Ministers shall not make an order under this section unless they have first consulted the [Agency].

CHAPTER IV SUPPLEMENTAL PROVISIONS WITH RESPECT TO WATER POLLUTION

100 Civil liability in respect of pollution and savings

Except in so far as this Part expressly otherwise provides and subject to the provisions of section 18 of the Interpretation Act 1978 (which relates to offences under two or more laws), nothing in this Part—

(a) confers a right of action in any civil proceedings (other than proceedings for the recovery of a fine) in respect of any contravention of this Part or any subordinate legislation, consent or other instrument made, given or issued under this Part;

(b) derogates from any right of action or other remedy (whether civil or criminal) in proceedings instituted otherwise than under this Part; or

(c) affects any restriction imposed by or under any other enactment, whether public, local or private.

101 Limitation for summary offences under Part III

Notwithstanding anything in section 127 of the Magistrates' Courts Act 1980 (time limit for summary proceedings), a magistrates' court may try any summary offence under this Part, or under any subordinate legislation made under this Part, if the information is laid not more than twelve months after the commission of the offence.

102 Power to give effect to international obligations

The Secretary of State shall have power by regulations to provide that the water pollution provisions of this Act shall have effect with such modifications as may be prescribed for the purpose of enabling Her Majesty's Government in the United Kingdom to give effect—

(a) to any Community obligations; or

(b) to any international agreement to which the United Kingdom is for the time being a party.

104 Meaning of 'controlled waters' etc. in Part III

(1) References in this Part to controlled waters are references to waters of any of the following classes—

(a) relevant territorial waters, that is to say, subject to subsection (4) below, the waters which extend seaward for three miles from the baselines from which the breadth of the territorial sea adjacent to England and Wales is measured;

(b) coastal waters, that is to say, any waters which are within the area which extends landward from those baselines as far as—

(a) the limit of the highest tide; or

(b) in the case of the waters of any relevant river or watercourse, the fresh-water limit of the river or watercourse, together with the waters of any enclosed dock which adjoins waters within that area;

(c) inland freshwaters, that is to say, the waters of any relevant lake or pond or of so much of any relevant river or watercourse as is above the fresh-water limit;

(d) ground waters, that is to say, any waters contained in underground strata;

and, accordingly, in this Part 'coastal waters', 'controlled waters', 'ground waters', 'inland freshwaters' and 'relevant territorial waters' have the meanings given by this subsection.

(2) In this Part any reference to the waters of any lake or pond or of any river or watercourse includes a reference to the bottom, channel or bed of any lake, pond, river or, as the case may be, watercourse which is for the time being dry.

(3) In this section—

'fresh-water limit', in relation to any river or watercourse, means the place for the time being shown as the fresh-water limit of that river or watercourse in the latest map deposited for that river or watercourse under section 192 below;

'miles' means international nautical miles of 1,852 metres;

'lake or pond' includes a reservoir of any description;

'relevant lake or pond' means (subject to subsection (4) below) any lake or pond which (whether it is natural or artificial or above or below ground) discharges into a relevant river or watercourse or into another lake or pond which is itself a relevant lake or pond;

'relevant river or watercourse' means (subject to subsection (4) below) any river or watercourse (including an underground river or watercourse and an artificial river or watercourse) which is neither a public sewer nor a sewer or drain which drains into a public sewer.

(4) The Secretary of State may by order provide—

(a) that any area of the territorial sea adjacent to England and Wales is to be treated as if it were an area of relevant territorial waters for the purposes of this Part and of any other enactment in which any expression is defined by reference to the meanings given by this section;

(b) that any lake or pond which does not discharge into a relevant river or watercourse or into a relevant lake or pond is to be treated for those purposes as a relevant lake or pond;

(c) that a lake or pond which does so discharge and is of a description specified in the order is to be treated for those purposes as if it were not a relevant lake or pond;

(d) that a watercourse of a description so specified is to be treated for those purposes as if it were not a relevant river or watercourse.

(5) An order under this section may—

(a) contain such supplemental, consequential and transitional provision as the Secretary of State considers appropriate; and

(b) make different provision for different cases, including different provision in relation to different persons, circumstances or localities.

(6) The power of the Secretary of State to make an order under this section shall be exercisable by statutory instrument subject to annulment in pursuance of a resolution of either House of Parliament.

PART VII LAND AND WORKS POWERS

CHAPTER I POWERS OF THE AGENCY

161 Anti-pollution works and operations

(1) [Subject to subsections (1A) and (2) below,] where it appears to the [Agency] that any poisonous, noxious or polluting matter or any solid waste matter is likely to enter, or to be or to have been present in, any controlled waters, the [Agency] shall be entitled to carry out the following works and operations, that is to say—

(a) in a case where the matter appears likely to enter any controlled waters, works and operations for the purpose of preventing it from doing so; or

(b) in a case where the matter appears to be or to have been present in any controlled waters, works and operations for the purpose—

(i) of removing or disposing of the matter;

(ii) of remedying or mitigating any pollution caused by its presence in the waters; or

(iii) so far as it is reasonably practicable to do so, of restoring the waters, including any flora and fauna dependent on the aquatic environment of the waters, to their state immediately before the matter became present in the waters

[and, in either case, the Agency shall be entitled to carry out investigations for the purpose of establishing the source of the matter and the identity of the person who has caused or knowingly permitted it to be present in controlled waters or at a place from which it was likely, in the opinion of the Agency, to enter controlled waters.]

[(1A) Without prejudice to the power of the Agency to carry out investigations under subsection (1) above, the power conferred by that subsection to carry out works and operations shall only be exercisable in a case where—

(a) the Agency considers it necessary to carry out forthwith any works or operations failing within paragraph (a) or (b) of that subsection; or

(b) it appears to the Agency, after reasonable inquiry, that no person can be found on whom to serve a works notice under section 161A below.]

(2) Nothing in subsection (1) above shall entitle the [Agency] to impede or prevent the making of any discharge in pursuance of a consent given under Chapter II of Part III of this Act.

(3) Where the [Agency] carries out any such works [operations or investigations] as are mentioned in subsection (1) above, it shall, subject to subsection (4) below, be entitled to recover the expenses reasonably incurred in doing so from any person who, as the case may be—

(a) caused or knowingly permitted the matter in question to be present at the place from which it was likely, in the opinion of the [Agency], to enter any controlled waters; or

(b) caused or knowingly permitted the matter in question to be present in any controlled waters.

(4) No such expenses shall be recoverable from a person for any works [operations or investigations] in respect of water from an abandoned mine [or an abandoned part of a mine] which that person permitted to reach such a place as is mentioned in subsection (3) above or to enter any controlled waters.

[(4A) Subsection (4) above shall not apply to the owner or former operator of any mine or part of a mine if the mine or part in question became abandoned after 31st December 1999.

(4B) Subsections (3B) and (3C) of section 89 above shall apply in relation to subsections (4) and (4A) above as they apply in relation to subsections (3) and (3A) of that section.]

(5) Nothing in this section—

(a) derogates from any right of action or other remedy (whether civil or criminal) in proceedings instituted otherwise than under this section; or

(b) affects any restriction imposed by or under any other enactment, whether public, local or private.

(6) In this section—

'controlled waters' has the same meaning as in Part III of this Act; and

['expenses' includes costs;]

'mine' has the same meaning as in the Mines and Quarries Act 1954.

[161A Notices requiring persons to carry out anti-pollution works and operations

(1) Subject to the following provisions of this section, where it appears to the Agency that any poisonous, noxious or polluting matter or any solid waste matter is likely to enter, or to be or to have been present in, any controlled waters, the Agency shall be entitled to serve a works notice on any person who, as the case may be,—

(a) caused or knowingly permitted the matter in question to be present at the place from which it is likely, in the opinion of the Agency, to enter any controlled waters; or

(b) caused or knowingly permitted the matter in question to be present in any controlled waters.

(2) For the purposes of this section, a 'works notice' is a notice requiring the person on whom it is served to carry out such of the following works or operations as may be specified in the notice, that is to say—

(a) in a case where the matter in question appears likely to enter any controlled waters, works or operations for the purpose of preventing it from doing so; or

(b) in a case where the matter appears to be or to have been present in any controlled waters, works or operations for the purpose—

(i) of removing or disposing of the matter;

(ii) of remedying or mitigating any pollution caused by its presence in the waters; or

(iii) so far as it is reasonably practicable to do so, of restoring the waters, including any flora and fauna dependent on the aquatic environment of the waters, to their state immediately before the matter became present in the waters.

(3) A works notice—

(a) must specify the periods within which the person on whom it is served is required to do each of the things specified in the notice; and

(b) is without prejudice to the powers of the Agency by virtue of section 161(1A)(a) above.

(4) Before serving a works notice on any person, the Agency shall reasonably endeavour to consult that person concerning the works or operations which are to be specified in the notice.

(5) The Secretary of State may by regulations make provision for or in connection with—

(a) the form or content of works notices;

(b) requirements for consultation, before the service of a works notice, with persons other than the person on whom that notice is to be served;

(c) steps to be taken for the purposes of any consultation required under subsection (4) above or regulations made by virtue of paragraph (b) above; or

(d) any other steps of a procedural nature which are to be taken in connection with, or in consequence of, the service of a works notice.

(6) A works notice shall not be regarded as invalid, or as invalidly served, by reason only of any failure to comply with the requirements of subsection (4) above or of regulations made by virtue of paragraph (b) of subsection (5) above.

(7) Nothing in subsection (1) above shall entitle the Agency to require the carrying out of any works or operations which would impede or prevent the making of any discharge in pursuance of a consent given under Chapter II of Part III of this Act.

(8) No works notice shall be served on any person requiring him to carry out any works or operations in respect of water from an abandoned mine or an abandoned part of a mine which that person permitted to reach such a place as is mentioned in subsection (1)(a) above or to enter any controlled waters.

(9) Subsection (8) above shall not apply to the owner or former operator of any mine or part of a mine if the mine or part in question became abandoned after 31st December 1999.

(10) Subsections (3B) and (3C) of section 89 above shall apply in relation to subsections (8) and (9) above as they apply in relation to subsections (3) and (3A) of that section.

(11) Where the Agency—

(a) carries out any such investigations as are mentioned in section 161(1) above, and

(b) serves a works notice on a person in connection with the matter to which the investigations relate,

it shall (unless the notice is quashed or withdrawn) be entitled to recover the costs or expenses reasonably incurred in carrying out those investigations from that person.

(12) The Secretary of State may, if he thinks fit in relation to any person, give directions to the Agency as to whether or how it should exercise its powers under this section.

(13) In this section—

'controlled waters' has the same meaning as in Part III of this Act;

'mine' has the same meaning as in the Mines and Quarries Act 1954.

161B Grant of, and compensation for, rights of entry etc.

(1) A works notice may require a person to carry out works or operations in relation to any land or waters notwithstanding that he is not entitled to carry out those works or operations.

(2) Any person whose consent is required before any works or operations required by a works notice may be carried out shall grant, or join in granting, such rights in relation to any land or waters as will enable the person on whom the works notice is served to comply with any requirements imposed by the works notice.

(3) Before serving a works notice, the Agency shall reasonably endeavour to consult every person who appears to it—

(a) to be the owner or occupier of any relevant land, and

(b) to be a person who might be required by subsection (2) above to grant, or join in granting, any rights, concerning the rights which that person may be so required to grant.

(4) A works notice shall not be regarded as invalid, or as invalidly served, by reason only of any failure to comply with the requirements of subsection (3) above.

(5) A person who grants, or joins in granting, any rights pursuant to subsection (2) above shall be entitled, on making an application within such period as may be prescribed and in such manner as may be prescribed to such person as may be prescribed, to be paid by the person on whom the works notice in question is served compensation of such amount as may be determined in such manner as may be prescribed.

(6) Without prejudice to the generality of the regulations that may be made by virtue of subsection (5) above, regulations by virtue of that subsection may make such provision in relation to compensation under this section as may be made by regulations by virtue of subsection (4) of section 35A of the Environmental Protection Act 1990 in relation to compensation under that section.

(7) In this section—

'prescribed' means prescribed in regulations made by the Secretary of State;

'relevant land' means—

(a) any land or waters in relation to which the works notice in question requires, or may require, works or operations to be carried out; or

(b) any land adjoining or adjacent to that land or those waters; 'works notice' means a works notice under section 161A above.

161C Appeals against works notices

(1) A person on whom a works notice is served may, within the period of twenty-one days beginning with the day on which the notice is served, appeal against the notice to the Secretary of State.

(2) On any appeal under this section the Secretary of State—

(a) shall quash the notice, if he is satisfied that there is a material defect in the notice; but

(b) subject to that, may confirm the notice, with or without modification, or quash it.

(3) The Secretary of State may by regulations make provision with respect to—

(a) the grounds on which appeals under this section may be made; or

(b) the procedure on any such appeal.

(4) Regulations under subsection (3) above may (among other things)—

(a) include provisions comparable to those in section 290 of the Public Health Act 1936 (appeals against notices requiring the execution of works);

(b) prescribe the cases in which a works notice is, or is not, to be suspended until the appeal is decided, or until some other stage in the proceedings;

(c) prescribe the cases in which the decision on an appeal may in some respects be less favourable to the appellant than the works notice against which he is appealing;

(d) prescribe the cases in which the appellant may claim that a works notice should have been served on some other person and prescribe the procedure to be followed in those cases;

(e) make provision as respects—

(i) the particulars to be included in the notice of appeal;

(ii) the persons on whom notice of appeal is to be served and the particulars, if any, which are to accompany the notice; or

(iii) the abandonment of an appeal.

(5) In this section 'works notice' means a works notice under section 161A above.

(6) This section is subject to section 114 of the 1995 Act (delegation or reference of appeals).

161D Consequences of not complying with a works notice

(1) If a person on whom the Agency serves a works notice falls to comply with any of the requirements of the notice, he shall be guilty of an offence.

(2) A person who commits an offence under subsection (1) above shall be liable—

(a) on summary conviction, to imprisonment for a term not exceeding three months or to a fine not exceeding £20,000 or to both;

(b) on conviction on indictment to imprisonment for a term not exceeding two years or to a fine or to both.

(3) If a person on whom a works notice has been served fails to comply with any of the requirements of the notice, the Agency may do what that person was required to do and may recover from him any costs or expenses reasonably incurred by the Agency in doing it.

(4) If the Agency is of the opinion that proceedings for an offence under subsection (1) above would afford an ineffectual remedy against a person who has failed to comply with the requirements of a works notice, the Agency may take proceedings in the High Court for the purpose of securing compliance with the notice.

(5) In this section 'works notice' means a works notice under section 161A above.]

PART VIII INFORMATION PROVISIONS

190 Pollution control register

(1) It shall be the duty of the [Agency] to maintain, in accordance with regulations made by the Secretary of State, registers containing prescribed particulars of [or relating to]—

(a) any notices of water quality objectives or other notices served under section 83 above;

(b) applications made for consents under Chapter II of Part III of this Act;

(c) consents given under that Chapter and the conditions to which the consents are subject;

(d) [...]

(e) the following, that is to say—

(i) samples of water or effluent taken by the [Agency] for the purposes of any of the water pollution provisions of this Act;

(ii) information produced by analyses of those samples;

(iii) such information with respect to samples of water or effluent taken by any other person, and the analyses of those samples, as is acquired by the [Agency] from any person under arrangements made by the [Agency] for the purposes of any of those provisions; and

(iv) the steps taken in consequence of any such information as is mentioned in any of sub-paragraphs (i) to (iii) above;

[...]

[(g) applications made to the Agency for the variation of discharge consents;

(h) enforcement notices served under section 90B above;

(j) revocations, under paragraph 7 of Schedule 10 to this Act, of discharge consents;

(k) appeals under section 91 above;

(l) directions given by the Secretary of State in relation to the Agency's functions under the water pollution provisions of this Act;

(m) convictions, for offences under Part III of this Act, of persons who have the benefit of discharge consents;

(n) information obtained or furnished in pursuance of conditions of discharge consents;

(o) works notices under section 161A above;

(p) appeals under section 161C above;

(q) convictions for offences under section 161D above;

(r) such other matters relating to the quality of water or the pollution of water as may be prescribed by the Secretary of State.

(1A) Where information of any description is excluded from any register by virtue of section 191B below, a statement shall be entered in the register indicating the existence of information of that description.]

(2) It shall be the duty of the [Agency]—

(a) to secure that the contents of registers maintained by the [Agency] under this section are available, at all reasonable times, for inspection by the public free of charge; and

(b) to afford members of the public reasonable facilities for obtaining from the [Agency], on payment of reasonable charges, copies of entries in any of the registers [and, for the purposes of this subsection, places may be prescribed by the Secretary of State at which any such registers or facilities as are mentioned in paragraph (a) or (b) above are to be available or afforded to the public in pursuance of the paragraph in question.]

(3) Section 101 above shall have effect in relation to any regulations under this section as it has effect in relation to any subordinate legislation under Part III of this Act.

[(4) The Secretary of State may give to the Agency directions requiring the removal from any register maintained by it under this section of any specified information which is not prescribed for inclusion under subsection (1) above or which, by virtue of section 191A or 191B below, ought to have been excluded from the register.

(5) In this section 'discharge consent' has the same meaning as in section 91 above.]

[191A Exclusion from registers of information affecting national security

(1) No information shall be included in a register kept or maintained by the Agency under any provision of this Act if and so long as, in the opinion of the Secretary of State, the inclusion in such a register of that information, or information of that description, would be contrary to the interests of national security.

(2)–(4) . . .

191B Exclusion from registers of certain confidential information

(1) No information relating to the affairs of any individual or business shall, without the consent of that individual or the person for the time being carrying on that business, be included in a register kept or maintained by the Agency under any provision of this Act, if and so long as the information—

(a) is, in relation to him, commercially confidential; and

(b) is not required to be included in the register in pursuance of directions under subsection (7) below;

but information is not commercially confidential for the purposes of this section unless it is determined under this section to be so by the Agency or, on appeal, by the Secretary of State.

(2)–(6) . . .

(7) The Secretary of State may give to the Agency directions as to specified information, or descriptions of information, which the public interest requires to be included in registers kept or maintained by the Agency under any provision of this Act notwithstanding that the information may be commercially confidential.

(8)–(10) . . .

(11) Information is, for the purposes of any determination under this section, commercially confidential, in relation to any individual or person, if its being contained in the register would prejudice to any reasonable degree the commercial interests of that individual or person.

(12) . . .

202 Information and assistance required in connection with the control of pollution

(1) It shall be the duty of the [Agency], if and so far as it is requested to do so by either of the Ministers, to give him all such advice and assistance as appears to it to be appropriate for facilitating the carrying out by him of his functions under the water pollution provisions of this Act.

(2) Subject to subsection (3) below, either of the Ministers or the [Agency] may serve on any person a notice requiring that person to furnish him or, as the case may be, it, within a period or at times specified in the notice and in a form and manner so specified, with such information as is reasonably required by the Minister in question or by the [Agency] for the purpose of carrying out any of his or, as the case may be, its functions under the water pollution provisions of this Act.

(3) Each of the Ministers shall have power by regulations to make provision for restricting the information which may be required under subsection (2) above and for determining the form in which the information is to be so required.

(4) A person who fails without reasonable excuse to comply with the requirements of a notice served on him under this section shall be guilty of an offence and [liable—

(a) on summary conviction, to a fine not exceeding the statutory maximum;

(b) on conviction on indictment, to a fine or to imprisonment for a term not exceeding two years, or to both.]

(5) [. . .]

203 Exchange of information with respect to pollution incidents etc.

(1) It shall be the duty of the [Agency] to provide a water undertaker with all such information to which this section applies as is in the possession of the [Agency] and is reasonably requested by the undertaker for purposes connected with the carrying out of its functions.

[(1A) It shall be the duty of the Agency to provide a licensed water supplier with all such information to which this section applies as is in the possession of the Agency and is reasonably requested by the supplier for purposes connected with the carrying on of activities under its licence.]

(2) It shall be the duty of every water undertaker to provide the [Agency] with all such information to which this section applies as is in the possession of the undertaker and is reasonably requested by the [Agency] for purposes connected with the carrying out of any of its functions.

[(2A) It shall be the duty of every licensed water supplier to provide the Agency with all such information to which this section applies as is in the possession of the supplier and is reasonably requested by the Agency for purposes connected with the carrying out of any of its functions.]

[(3) Information provided to a water undertaker, to a licensed water supplier or to the Agency under subsection (1), (1A), (2) or (2A) above shall be provided in such form and in such manner and at such times as the undertaker, the supplier or the Agency, as the case may be, may reasonably require.]

(4) Information provided under [subsection (1), (1A), (2) or (2A)] above to a water undertaker[, to a licensed water supplier], or to the [Agency] shall be provided free of charge.

(5) The duties of

[(a) a water undertaker under subsection (2) above; or

(b) a licensed water supplier under subsection (2A) above,

shall] be enforceable under section 18 of the Water Industry Act 1991 by the Secretary of State.

(6) This section applies to information—

(a) about the quality of any controlled waters or of any other waters; or

(b) about any incident in which any poisonous, noxious or polluting matter or any solid waste matter has entered any controlled waters or other waters.

(7) In this section 'controlled waters' has the same meaning as in Part III of this Act.

[(8) Any reference in this section to a licensed water supplier is a reference to a company holding a licence under Chapter 1A of Part 2 of the Water Industry act 1991.]

204 Restriction on disclosure of information

(1) Subject to the following provisions of this section, no information with respect to any particular business which—

(a) has been obtained by virtue of any of the provisions of this Act; and

(b) relates to the affairs of any individual or to any particular business,

shall, during the lifetime of that individual or so long as that business continues to be carried on, be disclosed without the consent of that individual or the person for the time being carrying on that business.

(2) Subsection (1) above does not apply to any disclosure of information which is made—

(a) for the purpose of facilitating the carrying out by either of the Ministers, [the Agency, . . .] [the Water Services Regulation Authority, the Consumer Council for Water], the Competition Commission or a local authority of any of his, its or, as the case may be, their functions by virtue of this Act, any of the other consolidation Acts [the Water Act 1989, Part I or IIA of the Environmental Protection Act 1990[, the 1995 Act or regulations under section 2 of the Pollution Prevention and Control Act 1999[, or the Water Act 2003].

(b) for the purpose of facilitating the performance by a water undertaker[, sewerage undertaker or company holding a licence under Chapter 1A of Part 2 of the Water Industry Act 1991], of any of the duties imposed on it by or under this Act, any of the other consolidation Acts[, the Water Act 1989 or the Water Act 2003].

(c) in pursuance of any duty imposed by section 197(1)(a) or (2) or [203(1), (1A), (2) or (2A)] or [of any duty imposed by section 27H] of the Water Industry Act 1991;

(d) for the purpose of facilitating the carrying out by any person mentioned in Part I of Schedule 24 to this Act of any of his functions under any of the enactments or instruments specified in Part II of that Schedule;

(e) for the purpose of enabling or assisting the Secretary of State to exercise any powers conferred on him by the Financial Services Act 1986 or by the enactments of relating to companies, insurance companies or insolvency or for the purpose of enabling or assisting any inspector appointed by him under the enactments relating to companies to carry out his functions;

(ee) for the purpose of enabling or assisting any inspector appointed under enactments relating to companies to carry out his functions;

(f) or the purpose of enabling an official receiver to carry out his functions under the enactments relating to insolvency or for the purpose of enabling or assisting a recognised professional body for the purposes of section 391 of the Insolvency Act 1986 to carry out its functions as such;

(g) for the purpose of facilitating the carrying out by the Health and Safety Commission or the Health and Safety Executive of any of its functions under any enactment or of facilitating the carrying out by any enforcing authority, within the meaning of Part I of the Health and Safety at Work etc. Act 1974, of any functions under a relevant statutory provision, within the meaning of that Act;

(h) for the purpose of facilitating the carrying out by the Comptroller and Auditor General of any of his functions under any enactment;

(i) in connection with the investigation of any criminal offence or for the purposes of any criminal proceedings;

(j) for the purposes of any civil proceedings brought under or by virtue of this Act, any of the other consolidation Acts, the Water Act 1989[, the Water Act 2003], or any of the enactments or instruments specified in Part II of Schedule 24 to this Act, or of any arbitration under this Act, any of the other consolidation Acts[, the Water Act 1989 or the Water Act 2003]; or

(k) in pursuance of a Community obligation.

(3) Nothing in subsection (1) above shall be construed—

(a) as limiting the matters which may be included in, or made public as part of, a report of—

(i) the [Agency];

. . .

[(ii) the Water Services Regulation Authority;]

[(iii) the Consumer Council for Water (or any regional committee of that Council established under section 27A of the Water Industry Act 1991); or]
(iv) the Competition Commission,

under any provision of this Act[, Part I or IIA of the Environmental Protection Act 1990, that Act of 1991, or the Environment Act 1995, or regulations under section 2 of the Pollution Prevention and Control Act 1999, or the Water Act 2003].

(b) as limiting the matters which may be published under section 201 of that Act [of 1991]; or
(c) as applying to any information which has been made public as part of such a report or has been so published or to any information exclusively of a statistical nature.

(4) Subject to subsection (5) below, nothing in subsection (1) above shall preclude the disclosure of information—

(a) if the disclosure is of information relating to a matter connected with the carrying out of the functions of a water undertaker or sewerage undertaker[, or with the carrying on by a company holding a licence under Chapter 1A of Part 2 of the Water Industry Act 1991 of activities under its licence,] and is made by one Minister of the Crown or government department to another; or
(b) if the disclosure is for the purpose of enabling or assisting any public or other authority for the time being designated for the purposes of this section by an order made by the Secretary of State to discharge any functions which are specified in the order.

(5) The power to make an order under subsection (4) above shall be exercisable by statutory instrument subject to annulment in pursuance of a resolution of either House of Parliament; and where such an order designates an authority for the purposes of paragraph (b) of that subsection, the order may—

(a) impose conditions subject to which the disclosure of information is permitted by virtue of that paragraph; and
(b) otherwise restrict the circumstances in which disclosure is so permitted.

(6) Any person who discloses any information in contravention of the preceding provisions of this section shall be guilty of an offence and liable—

(a) on summary conviction, to a fine not exceeding the statutory maximum;
(b) on conviction on indictment, to imprisonment for a term not exceeding two years or to a fine or to both.

(7) In this section 'the other consolidation Acts' means the Water Industry Act 1991, the Statutory Water Companies Act 1991, the Land Drainage Act 1991 and the Water Consolidation (Consequential Provisions) Act 1991.

PART IX MISCELLANEOUS AND SUPPLEMENTAL

209 Evidence of samples and abstractions

(1) [...]

(2) [...]

(3) Where, in accordance with the provisions contained in a licence in pursuance of paragraph (b) of subsection (2) of section 46 above, or in pursuance of that paragraph as read with subsection (6) of that section, it has been determined what quantity of water is to be taken—

(a) to have been abstracted during any period from a source of supply by the holder of the licence; or
(b) to have been so abstracted at a particular point or by particular means, or for use for particular purposes,

that determination shall, for the purposes of any proceedings under Chapter II of Part II of this Act or any of the related water resources provisions, be conclusive evidence of the matters to which it relates.

(4) [...]

217 Criminal liabilities of directors and other third parties

(1) Where a body corporate is guilty of an offence under this Act [or under section 4 of the Water Act 2003] and that offence is proved to have been committed with the consent or connivance of, or to be attributable to any neglect on the part of, any director, manager, secretary or other similar officer of the body corporate or any person who was purporting to act in any such capacity, then he, as well as the body corporate, shall be guilty of that offence and shall be liable to be proceeded against and punished accordingly.

(2) Where the affairs of a body corporate are managed by its members, subsection (1) above shall apply in relation to the acts and defaults of a member in connection with his functions of management as if he were a director of the body corporate.

(3) Without prejudice to subsections (1) and (2) above, where the commission by any person of an offence under the water pollution provisions of this Act is due to the act or default of some other person, that other person may be charged with and convicted of the offence whether or not proceedings for the offence are taken against the first-mentioned person.

221 General interpretation

(1) In this Act, except in so far as the context otherwise requires—

['the 1995 Act' means the Environment Act 1995;]

['the Agency' means the Environment Agency;]

...

'watercourse' includes (subject to sections 72(2) and 113(1) above) all rivers, streams, ditches, drains, cuts, culverts, dykes, sluices, sewers and passages through which water flows, except mains and other pipes which—

(a) belong to the [Agency] or a water undertaker; or
(b) are used by a water undertaker or any other person for the purpose only of providing a supply of water to any premises;

...

[222 Crown application

(1) Subject to the provisions of this section, this Act binds the Crown.

(2) No contravention by the Crown of any provision made by or under this Act shall make the Crown criminally liable; but the High Court may, on the application of the Agency, declare unlawful any act or omission of the Crown which constitutes such a contravention.

(3)–(11) ...

[SCHEDULE 10 DISCHARGE CONSENTS

Application for consent

1.—(1) An application for a consent, for the purposes of section 88(1)(a) of this Act, for any discharges—

(a) shall be made to the Agency on a form provided for the purpose by the Agency; and
(b) must be advertised by or on behalf of the applicant in such manner as may be required by regulations made by the Secretary of State.

(2) Regulations made by the Secretary of State may make provision for enabling the Agency to direct or determine that any such advertising of an application as is required under sub-paragraph (1)(b) above may, in any case, be dispensed with if, in that case, it appears to the Agency to be appropriate for that advertising to be dispensed with.

(3) The applicant for such a consent must provide to the Agency, either on, or together with, the form mentioned in sub-paragraph (1) above—

(a) such information as the Agency may reasonably require; and

(b) such information as may be prescribed for the purpose by the Secretary of State;

but, subject to paragraph 3(3) below and without prejudice to the effect (if any) of any other contravention of the requirements of this Schedule in relation to an application under this paragraph, a failure to provide information in pursuance of this sub-paragraph shall not invalidate an application.

(4) The Agency may give the applicant notice requiring him to provide it with such further information of any description specified in the notice as it may require for the purpose of determining the application.

(5) An application made in accordance with this paragraph which relates to proposed discharges at two or more places may be treated by the Agency as separate applications for consents for discharges at each of those places.

Consultation in connection with applications

2.—(1) Subject to sub-paragraph (2) below, the Agency shall give notice of any application under paragraph 1 above, together with a copy of the application, to the persons who are prescribed or directed to be consulted under this paragraph and shall do so within the specified period for notification.

(2) The Secretary of State may, by regulations, exempt any class of application from the requirements of this paragraph or exclude any class of information contained in applications from those requirements, in all cases or as respects specified classes only of persons to be consulted.

(3) Any representations made by the persons so consulted within the period allowed shall be considered by the Agency in determining the application.

(4) For the purposes of sub-paragraph (1) above—

(a) persons are prescribed to be consulted on any description of application if they are persons specified for the purposes of applications of that description in regulations made by the Secretary of State;

(b) persons are directed to be consulted on any particular application if the Secretary of State specifies them in a direction given to the Agency;

and the 'specified period for notification' is the period specified in the regulations or in the direction.

(5) Any representations made by any other persons within the period allowed shall also be considered by the Agency in determining the application.

(6) Subject to sub-paragraph (7) below, the period allowed for making representations is—

(a) in the case of persons prescribed or directed to be consulted, the period of six weeks beginning with the date on which notice of the application was given under sub-paragraph (1) above, and

(b) in the case of other persons, the period of six weeks beginning with the date on which the making of the application was advertised in pursuance of paragraph 1(1)(b) above.

(7) The Secretary of State may, by regulations, substitute for any period for the time being specified in sub-paragraph (6)(a) or (b) above, such other period as he considers appropriate.

Consideration and determination of applications

3.—(1) On an application under paragraph 1 above the Agency shall be under a duty, if the requirements—

(a) of that paragraph, and

(b) of any regulations made under paragraph 1 or 2 above or of any directions under paragraph 2 above,

are complied with, to consider whether to give the consent applied for, either unconditionally or subject to conditions, or to refuse it.

(2) Subject to the following provisions of this Schedule, on an application made in accordance with paragraph 1 above, the applicant may treat the consent applied for as having been refused if it is not given within the period of four months beginning with the day on which the application is received or within such longer period as may be agreed in writing between the Agency and the applicant.

(3) Where any person, having made an application to the Agency for a consent, has failed to comply with his obligation under paragraph 1(3) or (4) above to provide information to the Agency, the Agency may refuse to proceed with the application, or refuse to proceed with it until the information is provided.

(4) The conditions subject to which a consent may be given under this paragraph shall be such conditions as the Agency may think fit and, in particular, may include conditions—

(a) as to the places at which the discharges to which the consent relates may be made and as to the design and construction of any outlets for the discharges;

(b) as to the nature, origin, composition, temperature, volume and rate of the discharges and as to the periods during which the discharges may be made;

(c) as to the steps to be taken, in relation to the discharges or by way of subjecting any substance likely to affect the description of matter discharged to treatment or any other process, for minimising the polluting effects of the discharges on any controlled waters;

(d) as to the provision of facilities for taking samples of the matter discharged and, in particular, as to the provision, maintenance and use of manholes, inspection chambers, observation wells and boreholes in connection with the discharges;

(e) as to the provision, maintenance and testing of meters for measuring or recording the volume and rate of the discharges and apparatus for determining the nature, composition and temperature of the discharges;

(f) as to the keeping of records of the nature, origin, composition, temperature, volume and rate of the discharges and, in particular, of records of readings of meters and other recording apparatus provided in accordance with any other condition attached to the consent; and

(g) as to the making of returns and the giving of other information to the Authority about the nature, origin, composition, temperature, volume and rate of the discharges;

and it is hereby declared that a consent may be given under this paragraph subject to different conditions in respect of different periods.

(5) The Secretary of State may, by regulations, substitute for any period for the time being specified in sub-paragraph (2) above, such other period as he considers appropriate.

4. The Secretary of State may give the Agency a direction with respect to any particular application, or any description of applications, for consent under paragraph 1 above requiring the Agency not to determine or not to proceed with the application or applications of that description until the expiry of any such period as may be specified in the direction, or until directed by the Secretary of State that it may do so, as the case may be.

Reference to Secretary of State of certain applications for consent

5.—(1) The Secretary of State may, either in consequence of representations or objections made to him or otherwise, direct the Agency to transmit to him for determination such applications for consent under paragraph 1 above as are specified in the direction or are of a description so specified.

(2) Where a direction is given to the Agency under this paragraph, the Agency shall comply with the direction and inform every applicant to whose application the direction relates of the transmission of his application to the Secretary of State.

(3) Paragraphs 1(1) and 2 above shall have effect in relation to an application transmitted to the Secretary of State under this paragraph with such modifications as may be prescribed.

(4) Where an application is transmitted to the Secretary of State under this paragraph, the Secretary of State may at any time after the application is transmitted and before it is granted or refused—

(a) cause a local inquiry to be held with respect to the application; or

(b) afford the applicant and the Agency an opportunity of appearing before, and being heard by, a person appointed by the Secretary of State for the purpose.

(5) The Secretary of State shall exercise his power under sub-paragraph (4) above in any case where a request to be heard with respect to the application is made to him in the prescribed manner by the applicant or by the Agency.

(6) It shall be the duty of the Secretary of State, if the requirements of this paragraph and of any regulations made under it are complied with, to determine an application for consent transmitted to him by the Agency under this paragraph by directing the Agency to refuse its consent or to give its consent under paragraph 3 above (either unconditionally or subject to such conditions as are specified in the direction).

(7) Without prejudice to any of the preceding provisions of this paragraph, the Secretary of State may by regulations make provision for the purposes of, and in connection with, the consideration and disposal by him of applications transmitted to him under this paragraph.

Consents without applications

6.—(1) If it appears to the Agency—

(a) that a person has caused or permitted effluent or other matter to be discharged in contravention—

(i) of the obligation imposed by virtue of section 85(3) of this Act; or

(ii) of any prohibition imposed under section 86 of this Act; and

(b) that a similar contravention by that person is likely,

the Agency may, if it thinks fit, serve on him an instrument in writing giving its consent, subject to any conditions specified in the instrument, for discharges of a description so specified.

(2) A consent given under this paragraph shall not relate to any discharge which occurred before the instrument containing the consent was served on the recipient of the instrument.

(3) Sub-paragraph (4) of paragraph 3 above shall have effect in relation to a consent given under this paragraph as it has effect in relation to a consent given under that paragraph.

(4) Where a consent has been given under this paragraph, the Agency shall publish notice of the consent in such manner as may be prescribed by the Secretary of State and send copies of the instrument containing the consent to such bodies or persons as may be so prescribed.

(5) It shall be the duty of the Agency to consider any representations or objections with respect to a consent under this paragraph as are made to it in such manner, and within such period, as may be prescribed by the Secretary of State and have not been withdrawn.

(6) Where notice of a consent is published by the Agency under sub-paragraph (4) above, the Agency shall be entitled to recover the expenses of publication from the person on whom the instrument containing the consent was served.

Revocation of consents and alteration and imposition of conditions

7.—(1) The Agency may from time to time review any consent given under paragraph 3 or 6 above and the conditions (if any) to which the consent is subject.

(2) Subject to such restrictions on the exercise of the power conferred by this sub-paragraph as are imposed under paragraph 8 below, where the Agency has reviewed a

consent under this paragraph, it may by a notice served on the person making a discharge in pursuance of the consent—

(a) revoke the consent;

(b) make modifications of the conditions of the consent; or

(c) in the case of an unconditional consent, provide that it shall be subject to such conditions as may be specified in the notice.

(3) If on a review under sub-paragraph (1) above it appears to the Agency that no discharge has been made in pursuance of the consent to which the review relates at any time during the preceding twelve months, the Agency may revoke the consent by a notice served on the holder of the consent.

(4) If it appears to the Secretary of State appropriate to do so—

(a) for the purpose of enabling Her Majesty's Government in the United Kingdom to give effect to any Community obligation or to any international agreement to which the United Kingdom is for the time being a party;

(b) for the protection of public health or of flora and fauna dependent on an aquatic environment; or

(c) in consequence of any representations or objections made to him or otherwise,

he may, subject to such restrictions on the exercise of the power conferred by virtue of paragraph (c) above as are imposed under paragraph 8 below, at any time direct the Agency, in relation to a consent given under paragraph 3 or 6 above, to do anything mentioned in sub-paragraph (2)(a) to (c) above.

(5) The Agency shall be liable to pay compensation to any person in respect of any loss or damage sustained by that person as a result of the Agency's compliance with a direction given in relation to any consent by virtue of sub-paragraph (4)(b) above if—

(a) in complying with that direction the Agency does anything which, apart from that direction, it would be precluded from doing by a restriction imposed under paragraph 8 below; and

(b) the direction is not shown to have been given in consequence of—

(i) a change of circumstances which could not reasonably have been fore-seen at the beginning of the period to which the restriction relates; or

(ii) consideration by the Secretary of State of material information which was not reasonably available to the Agency at the beginning of that period.

(6) For the purposes of sub-paragraph (5) above information is material, in relation to a consent, if it relates to any discharge made or to be made by virtue of the consent, to the interaction of any such discharge with any other discharge or to the combined effect of the matter discharged and any other matter.

Restriction on variation and revocation of consent and previous variation

8.—(1) Each instrument signifying the consent of the Agency under paragraph 3 or 6 above shall specify a period during which no notice by virtue of paragraph 7(2) or (4)(c) above shall be served in respect of the consent except, in the case of a notice doing anything mentioned in paragraph 7(2)(b) or (c), with the agreement of the holder of the consent.

(2) Each notice served by the Agency by virtue of paragraph 7(2) or (4)(c) above (except a notice which only revokes a consent) shall specify a period during which a subsequent such notice which alters the effect of the first-mentioned notice shall not be served except, in the case of a notice doing anything mentioned in paragraph 7(2)(b) or (c) above, with the agreement of the holder of the consent.

(3) The period specified under sub-paragraph (1) or (2) above in relation to any consent shall not, unless the person who proposes to make or makes discharges in pursuance of the consent otherwise agrees, be less than the period of four years beginning—

(a) in the case of a period specified under sub-paragraph (1) above, with the day on which the consent takes effect; and

(b) in the case of a period specified under sub-paragraph (2) above, with the day on which the notice specifying that period is served.

(4) A restriction imposed under sub-paragraph (1) or (2) above shall not prevent the service by the Agency of a notice by virtue of paragraph 7(2) or (4)(c) above in respect of a consent given under paragraph 6 above if—

(a) the notice is served not more than three months after the beginning of the period prescribed under paragraph 6(5) above for the making of representations and objections with respect to the consent; and

(b) the Agency or, as the case may be, the Secretary of State considers, in consequence of any representations or objections received by it or him within that period, that it is appropriate for the notice to be served.

(5) A restriction imposed under sub-paragraph (1) or (2) above shall not prevent the service by the Agency of a notice by virtue of paragraph 7(2)(b) or (c) or (4)(c) above in respect of a consent given under paragraph 6 above if the holder has applied for a variation under paragraph 10 below.

General review of consents

9.—(1) If it appears appropriate to the Secretary of State to do so he may at any time direct the Agency to review—

(a) the consents given under paragraph 3 or 6 above, or

(b) any description of such consents,

and the conditions (if any) to which those consents are subject.

(2) A direction given by virtue of sub-paragraph (1) above—

(a) shall specify the purpose for which, and

(b) may specify the manner in which,

the review is to be conducted.

(3) After carrying out a review pursuant to a direction given by virtue of sub-paragraph (1) above, the Agency shall submit to the Secretary of State its proposals (if any) for—

(a) the modification of the conditions of any consent reviewed pursuant to the direction, or

(b) in the case of any unconditional consent reviewed pursuant to the direction, subjecting the consent to conditions.

(4) Where the Secretary of State has received any proposals from the Agency under sub-paragraph (3) above in relation to any consent he may, if it appears appropriate to him to do so, direct the Agency to do, in relation to that consent, anything mentioned in paragraph 7(2)(b) or (c) above.

(5) A direction given by virtue of sub-paragraph (4) above may only direct the Agency to do, in relation to any consent,—

(a) any such thing as the Agency has proposed should be done in relation to that consent, or

(b) any such thing with such modifications as appear to the Secretary of State to be appropriate.

Applications for variation

10.—(1) The holder of a consent under paragraph 3 or 6 above may apply to the Agency, on a form provided for the purpose by the Agency, for the variation of be consent.

(2) The provisions of paragraphs 1 to 5 above shall apply (with the necessary modifications) to applications under sub-paragraph (1) above, and to the variation of consents in pursuance of such applications, as they apply to applications for, and the grant of, consents.

Transfer of consents

11.—(1) A consent under paragraph 3 or 6 above may be transferred by the holder to a person who proposes to carry on the discharges in place of the holder.

(2) On the death of the holder of a consent under paragraph 3 or 6 above, the consent shall [...] be regarded as property forming part of the deceased's personal estate, whether or not it would be so regarded apart from this sub-paragraph, and shall accordingly vest in his personal representatives.

(3) If a bankruptcy order is made against the holder of a consent under paragraph 3 or 6 above, the consent shall [...] be regarded for the purposes of any of the Second Group of Parts of the Insolvency Act 1986 (insolvency of individuals; bankruptcy), as property forming part of the bankrupt's estate, whether or not it would be so regarded apart from this sub-paragraph, and shall accordingly vest as such in the trustee in bankruptcy.

(4) [...]

(5) A consent under paragraph 3 or 6 above which is transferred to, or which vests in, a person under this section shall have effect on and after the date of the transfer or vesting as if it had been granted to that person under paragraph 3 or 6 above, subject to the same conditions as were attached to it immediately before that date.

[(6) Where a consent under paragraph 3 or 6 above is to be transferred under sub-paragraph (1) above—

(a) the person from whom and the person to whom the consent is to be transferred shall give joint notice to the Agency of the proposed transfer;
(b) the notice may specify the date on which it is proposed that the transfer should take effect;
(c) within twenty-one days beginning with the date of receipt of the notice duly given in accordance with sub-paragraph (6A) below, the Agency shall—
    (i) arrange to amend the consent by substituting the name of the transferee as holder of the consent; and
    (ii) serve notice on the transferor and the transferee that the amendment has been made; and
(d) the transfer shall take effect from the later of—
    (i) the date on which the Agency amends the consent; and
    (ii) the date (if any) specified in the joint notice under paragraph (a) above.

(6A) A joint notice under sub-paragraph (6)(a) above shall include such information as may be prescribed.

(6B) If the person from whom the consent is to be transferred is a person in whom the consent has vested by virtue of sub-paragraph (2) or (3) above, a joint notice given under sub-paragraph (6)(a) above shall be of no effect unless the notice required by sub-paragraph (7) below has been given.

(6C) A notice or other instrument given by or on behalf of the Agency pursuant to sub-paragraph (6) above shall not constitute an instrument signifying the consent of the Agency for the purposes of paragraph 8 above.]

(7) Where a consent under paragraph 3 or 6 above vests in any person as mentioned in sub-paragraph (2) or (3) above, that person shall give notice of that fact to the Agency not later than the end of the period of fifteen months beginning with the date of the vesting.

(8) If—

(a) a consent under paragraph 3 or 6 above vests in any person as mentioned in sub-paragraph (2) or (3) above, but
(b) that person fails to give the notice required by sub-paragraph (7) above within the period there mentioned,

the consent, to the extent that it permits the making of any discharges, shall cease to have effect.

(9) A person who fails to give a notice which he is required by sub-paragraph [...] (7) above to give shall be guilty of an offence and liable—

(a) on summary conviction, to a fine not exceeding the statutory maximum;

(b) on conviction on indictment, to a fine or to imprisonment for a term not exceeding two years, or to both.]

Clean Air Act 1993

(1993, c. 11)

PART I DARK SMOKE

1 Prohibition of dark smoke from chimneys

(1) Dark smoke shall not be emitted from a chimney of any building, and if, on any day, dark smoke is so emitted, the occupier of the building shall be guilty of an offence.

(2) Dark smoke shall not be emitted from a chimney (not being a chimney of a building) which serves the furnace of any fixed boiler or industrial plant, and if, on any day, dark smoke is so emitted, the person having possession of the boiler or plant shall be guilty of an offence.

(3) This section does not apply to emissions of smoke from any chimney, in such classes of case and subject to such limitations as may be prescribed in regulations made by the Secretary of State, lasting for not longer than such periods as may be so prescribed.

(4) In any proceedings for an offence under this section, it shall be a defence to prove—

(a) that the alleged emission was solely due to the lighting up of a furnace which was cold and that all practicable steps had been taken to prevent or minimise the emission of dark smoke;

(b) that the alleged emission was solely due to some failure of a furnace, or of apparatus used in connection with a furnace, and that—

(i) the failure could not reasonably have been foreseen, or, if foreseen, could not reasonably have been provided against; and

(ii) the alleged emission could not reasonably have been prevented by action taken after the failure occurred; or

(c) that the alleged emission was solely due to the use of unsuitable fuel and that—

(i) suitable fuel was unobtainable and the least unsuitable fuel which was available was used; and

(ii) all practicable steps had been taken to prevent or minimise the emission of dark smoke as the result of the use of that fuel;

or that the alleged emission was due to the combination of two or more of the causes specified in paragraphs (a) to (c) and that the other conditions specified in those paragraphs are satisfied in relation to those causes respectively.

(5) A person guilty of an offence under this section shall be liable on summary conviction—

(a) in the case of a contravention of subsection (1) as respects a chimney of a private dwelling, to a fine not exceeding level 3 on the standard scale; and

(b) in any other case, to a fine not exceeding level 5 on the standard scale.

(6) This section has effect subject to section 51 (duty to notify offences to occupier or other person liable).

2 Prohibition of dark smoke from industrial or trade premises

(1) Dark smoke shall not be emitted from any industrial or trade premises and if, on any day, dark smoke is so emitted the occupier of the premises and any person who causes or permits the emission shall be guilty of an offence.

(2) This section does not apply—
(a) to the emission of dark smoke from any chimney to which section 1 above applies; or
(b) to the emission of dark smoke caused by the burning of any matter prescribed in regulations made by the Secretary of State, subject to compliance with such conditions (if any) as may be so prescribed.

(3) In proceedings for an offence under this section, there shall be taken to have been an emission of dark smoke from industrial or trade premises in any case where—
(a) material is burned on those premises; and
(b) the circumstances are such that the burning would be likely to give rise to the emission of dark smoke,

unless the occupier or any person who caused or permitted the burning shows that no dark smoke was emitted.

(4) In proceedings for an offence under this section, it shall be a defence to prove—
(a) that the alleged emission was inadvertent; and
(b) that all practicable steps had been taken to prevent or minimise the emission of dark smoke.

(5) A person guilty of an offence under this section shall be liable on summary conviction to a fine not exceeding [£20,000].

(6) In this section 'industrial or trade premises' means—
(a) premises used for any industrial or trade purposes; or
(b) premises not so used on which matter is burnt in connection with any industrial or trade process.

(7) This section has effect subject to section 51 (duty to notify offences to occupier or other person liable).

3 Meaning of 'dark smoke'

(1) In this Act 'dark smoke' means smoke which, if compared in the appropriate manner with a chart of the type known on 5th July 1956 (the date of the passing of the Clean Air Act 1956) as the Ringelmann Chart, would appear to be as dark as or darker than shade 2 on the chart.

(2) For the avoidance of doubt it is hereby declared that in proceedings—
(a) for an offence under section 1 or 2 (prohibition of emissions of dark smoke);
(b) [...]

the court may be satisfied that smoke is or is not dark smoke as defined in subsection (1) notwithstanding that there has been no actual comparison of the smoke with a chart of the type mentioned in that subsection.

(3) Without prejudice to the generality of subsections (1) and (2), if the Secretary of State by regulations prescribes any method of ascertaining whether smoke is dark smoke as defined in subsection (1), proof in any such proceedings as are mentioned in subsection (2)—
(a) that that method was properly applied, and
(b) that the smoke was thereby ascertained to be or not to be dark smoke as so defined,

shall be accepted as sufficient.

PART II SMOKE, GRIT, DUST AND FUMES

4 Requirement that new furnaces shall be so far as practicable smokeless

(1) No furnace shall be installed in a building or in any fixed boiler or industrial plant unless notice of the proposal to install it has been given to the local authority.

(2) No furnace shall be installed in a building or in any fixed boiler or industrial plant unless the furnace is so far as practicable capable of being operated continuously without emitting smoke when burning fuel of a type for which the furnace was designed.

(3) Any furnace installed in accordance with plans and specifications submitted to, and approved for the purposes of this section by, the local authority shall be treated as complying with the provisions of subsection (2).

(4) Any person who installs a furnace in contravention of subsection (1) or (2) or on whose instructions a furnace is so installed shall be guilty of an offence and liable on summary conviction—

(a) in the case of a contravention of subsection (1), to a fine not exceeding level 3 on the standard scale; and

(b) in the case of a contravention of subsection (2), to a fine not exceeding level 5 on that scale.

(5) This section does not apply to the installation of domestic furnaces.

(6) This section applies in relation to—

(a) the attachment to a building of a boiler or industrial plant which already contains a furnace; or

(b) the fixing to or installation on any land of any such boiler or plant, as it applies in relation to the installation of a furnace in any fixed boiler or industrial plant.

5 Emission of grit and dust from furnaces

(1) This section applies to any furnace other than a domestic furnace.

(2) The Secretary of State may by regulations prescribe limits on the rates of emission of grit and dust from the chimneys of furnaces to which this section applies.

(3) If on any day grit or dust is emitted from a chimney serving a furnace to which this section applies at a rate exceeding the relevant limit prescribed under subsection (2), the occupier of any building in which the furnace is situated shall be guilty of an offence.

(4) In proceedings for an offence under subsection (3) it shall be a defence to prove that the best practicable means had been used for minimising the alleged emission.

(5) If, in the case of a building containing a furnace to which this section applies and which is served by a chimney to which there is no limit applicable under subsection (2), the occupier fails to use any practicable means there may be for minimising the emission of grit or dust from the chimney, he shall be guilty of an offence.

(6) A person guilty of an offence under this section shall be liable on summary conviction to a fine not exceeding level 5 on the standard scale.

6 Arrestment plant for new non-domestic furnaces

(1) A furnace other than a domestic furnace shall not be used in a building—

(a) to burn pulverised fuel; or

(b) to burn, at a rate of 45.4 kilograms or more an hour, any other solid matter; or

(c) to burn, at a rate equivalent to 366.4 kilowatts or more, any liquid or gaseous matter,

unless the furnace is provided with plant for arresting grit and dust which has been approved by the local authority or which has been installed in accordance with plans and specifications submitted to and approved by the local authority, and that plant is properly maintained and used.

(2) Subsection (1) has effect subject to any exemptions prescribed or granted under section 7.

(3) The Secretary of State may by regulations substitute for any rate mentioned in subsection (1)(b) or (c) such other rate as he thinks fit: but no regulations shall be made so as to reduce any rate unless a draft of the regulations has been laid before and approved by each House of Parliament.

(4) Regulations under subsection (3) reducing any rate shall not apply to a furnace which has been installed, the installation of which has been begun, or an agreement for the purchase or installation of which has been entered into, before the date on which the regulations come into force.

(5) If on any day a furnace is used in contravention of subsection (1), the occupier of the building shall be guilty of an offence and liable on summary conviction to a fine not exceeding level 5 on the standard scale.

7 Exemptions from section 6

(1) The Secretary of State may by regulations provide that furnaces of any class prescribed in the regulations shall, while used for a purpose so prescribed, be exempted from the operation of section 6(1).

(2) If on the application of the occupier of a building a local authority are satisfied that the emission of grit and dust from any chimney serving a furnace in the building will not be prejudicial to health or a nuisance if the furnace is used for a particular purpose without compliance with section 6(1), they may exempt the furnace from the operation of that subsection while used for that purpose.

(3) If a local authority to whom an application is duly made for an exemption under subsection (2) fail to determine the application and to give a written notice of their decision to the applicant within—

(a) eight weeks of receiving the application; or

(b) such longer period as may be agreed in writing between the applicant and the authority,

the furnace shall be treated as having been granted an exemption from the operation of section 6(1) while used for the purpose specified in the application.

(4) If a local authority decide not to grant an exemption under subsection (2), they shall give the applicant a written notification of their decision stating their reasons, and the applicant may within twenty-eight days of receiving the notification appeal against the decision to the Secretary of State.

(5) On an appeal under this section the Secretary of State—

(a) may confirm the decision appealed against; or

(b) may grant the exemption applied for or vary the purpose for which the furnace to which the application relates may be used without compliance with section 6(1);

and shall give the appellant a written notification of his decision, stating his reasons for it.

(6) If on any day a furnace which is exempt from the operation of section 6(1) is used for a purpose other than a prescribed purpose or, as the case may be, a purpose for which the furnace may be used by virtue of subsection (2), (3) or (5), the occupier of the building shall be guilty of an offence and liable on summary conviction to a fine not exceeding level 5 on the standard scale.

8 Requirement to fit arrestment plant for burning solid fuel in other cases

(1) A domestic furnace shall not be used in a building—

(a) to burn pulverised fuel; or

(b) to burn, at a rate of 1.02 tonnes an hour or more, solid fuel in any other form or solid waste,

unless the furnace is provided with plant for arresting grit and dust which has been approved by the local authority or which has been installed in accordance with plans and specifications submitted to and approved by the local authority, and that plant is properly maintained and used.

(2) If a furnace is used in a building in contravention of subsection (1), the occupier of the building shall be guilty of an offence and liable on summary conviction to a fine not exceeding level 5 on the standard scale.

9 Appeal to Secretary of State against refusal of approval

(1) Where a local authority determine an application for approval under section 6 or 8, they shall give the applicant a written notification of their decision and, in the case of a decision not to grant approval, shall state their reasons for not doing so.

(2) A person who—

(a) has made such an application to a local authority; or

(b) is interested in a building with respect to which such an application has been made,

may, if he is dissatisfied with the decision of the authority on the application, appeal within twenty-eight days after he is notified of the decision to the Secretary of State; and the Secretary of State may give any approval which the local authority might have given.

(3) An approval given by the Secretary of State under this section shall have the like effect as an approval of the local authority.

10 Measurement of grit, dust and fumes by occupiers

(1) If a furnace in a building is used—

(a) to burn pulverised fuel;

(b) to burn, at a rate of 45.4 kilograms or more an hour, any other solid matter; or

(c) to burn, at a rate equivalent to 366.4 kilowatts or more, any liquid or gaseous matter,

the local authority may, by notice in writing served on the occupier of the building, direct that the provisions of subsection (2) below shall apply to the furnace, and those provisions shall apply accordingly.

(2) In the case of a furnace to which this subsection for the time being applies, the occupier of the building shall comply with such requirements as may be prescribed as to—

(a) making and recording measurements from time to time of the grit, dust and fumes emitted from the furnace;

(b) making adaptations for that purpose to the chimney serving the furnace;

(c) providing and maintaining apparatus for making and recording the measurements; and

(d) informing the local authority of the results obtained from the measurements or otherwise making those results available to them;

and in this subsection 'prescribed' means prescribed (whether generally or for any class of furnace) by regulations made by the Secretary of State.

(3) If the occupier of the building fails to comply with those requirements, he shall be guilty of an offence and liable on summary conviction—

(a) to a fine not exceeding level 5 on the standard scale; or

(b) to cumulative penalties on continuance in accordance with section 50.

(4) The occupier of a building who by virtue of subsection (2) is under a duty to make and record measurements of grit, dust and fumes emitted from a furnace in the building shall permit the local authority to be represented during the making and recording of those measurements.

(5) The Secretary of State may by regulations substitute for any rate mentioned in subsection (1)(b) or (c) such other rate as he thinks fit; but regulations shall not be made under this subsection so as to reduce any rate unless a draft of the regulations has been laid before and approved by each House of Parliament.

(6) Any direction given by a local authority under subsection (1) with respect to a furnace in a building may be revoked by the local authority by a subsequent notice in writing served on the occupier of the building, without prejudice, however, to their power to give another direction under that subsection.

11 Measurement of grit, dust and fumes by local authorities

(1) This section applies to any furnace to which section 10(2) (duty to comply with prescribed requirements) for the time being applies and which is used—

(a) to burn, at a rate less than 1.02 tonnes an hour, solid matter other than pulverised fuel; or

(b) to burn, at a rate of less than 8.21 Megawatts, any liquid or gaseous matter.

(2) The occupier of the building in which the furnace is situated may, by notice in writing given to the local authority, request that authority to make and record measurements of the grit, dust and fumes emitted from the furnace.

(3) While a notice is in force under subsection (2)—

(a) the local authority shall from time to time make and record measurements of the grit, dust and fumes emitted from the furnace; and

(b) the occupier shall not be under a duty to comply with any requirements of regulations under subsection (2) of section 10 in relation to the furnace, except those imposed by virtue of paragraph (b) of that subsection;

and any such notice given by the occupier of a building may be withdrawn by a subsequent notice in writing given to the local authority by him or any subsequent occupier of that building.

(4) A direction under section 10(1) applying section 10(2) to a furnace which is used as mentioned in subsection (1)(a) or (b) of this section shall contain a statement of the effect of subsections (1) to (3) of this section.

12 Information about furnaces and fuel consumed

(1) For the purpose of enabling the local authority properly to perform their functions under and in connection with sections 5 to 11, the local authority may, by notice in writing served on the occupier of any building, require the occupier to furnish to them, within fourteen days or such longer time as may be limited by the notice, such information as to the furnaces in the building and the fuel or waste burned in those furnaces as they may reasonably require for that purpose.

(2) Any person who, having been duly served with a notice under subsection (1)—

(a) fails to comply with the requirements of the notice within the time limited; or

(b) furnishes any information in reply to the notice which he knows to be false in a material particular,

shall be guilty of an offence and liable on summary conviction to a fine not exceeding level 5 on the standard scale.

13 Grit and dust from outdoor furnaces, etc.

(1) Sections 5 to 12 shall apply in relation to the furnace of any fixed boiler or industrial plant as they apply in relation to a furnace in a building.

(2) References in those sections to the occupier of the building shall, in relation to a furnace falling within subsection (1), be read as references to the person having possession of the boiler or plant.

(3) The reference in section 6(4) (and the reference in paragraph 6(1) and (3) of Schedule 5) to the installation and to the purchase of a furnace shall, in relation to a furnace which is already contained in any fixed boiler or industrial plant, be read as a reference to attaching the boiler or plant to the building or fixing it to or installing it on any land and to purchasing it respectively.

14 Height of chimneys for furnaces

(1) This section applies to any furnace served by a chimney.

(2) An occupier of a building shall not knowingly cause or permit a furnace to be used in the building—

(a) to burn pulverised fuel;

(b) to burn, at a rate of 45.4 kilograms or more an hour, any other solid matter; or

(c) to burn, at a rate equivalent to 366.4 kilowatts or more, any liquid or gaseous matter,

unless the height of the chimney serving the furnace has been approved for the purposes of this section and any conditions subject to which the approval was granted are complied with.

(3) If on any day the occupier of a building contravenes subsection (2), he shall be guilty of an offence.

(4) A person having possession of any fixed boiler or industrial plant, other than an exempted boiler or plant, shall not knowingly cause or permit a furnace of that boiler or plant to be used as mentioned in subsection (2), unless the height of the chimney serving the furnace has been approved for the purposes of this section and any conditions subject to which the approval was granted are complied with.

(5) If on any day a person having possession of any boiler or plant contravenes subsection (3), he shall be guilty of an offence.

(6) A person guilty of an offence under this section shall be liable on summary conviction to a fine not exceeding level 5 on the standard scale.

(7) In this section 'exempted boiler or plant' means a boiler or plant which is used or to be used wholly for any purpose prescribed in regulations made by the Secretary of State; and the height of a chimney is approved for the purposes of this section if approval is granted by the local authority or the Secretary of State under section 15.

15 Applications for approval of height of chimneys of furnaces

(1) This section applies to the granting of approval of the height of a chimney for the purposes of section 14.

(2) Approval shall not be granted by a local authority unless they are satisfied that the height of the chimney will be sufficient to prevent, so far as practicable, the smoke, grit, dust, gases or fumes emitted from the chimney from becoming prejudicial to health or a nuisance having regard to—

(a) the purpose of the chimney;

(b) the position and descriptions of buildings near it;

(c) the levels of the neighbouring ground; and

(d) any other matters requiring consideration in the circumstances.

(3) Approval may be granted without qualification or subject to conditions as to the rate or quality, or the rate and quality, of emissions from the chimney.

(4) If a local authority to whom an application is duly made for approval fail to determine the application and to give a written notification of their decision to the applicant within four weeks of receiving the application or such longer period as may be agreed in writing between the applicant and the authority, the approval applied for shall be treated as having been granted without qualification.

(5) If a local authority decide not to approve the height of a chimney, or to attach conditions to their approval, they shall give the applicant a written notification of their decision which—

(a) states their reasons for that decision; and

(b) in the case of a decision not to approve the height of the chimney, specifies—

(i) the lowest height (if any) which they are prepared to approve without qualification; or

(ii) the lowest height which they are prepared to approve if approval is granted subject to any specified conditions,

or (if they think fit) both.

(6) The applicant may within twenty-eight days of receiving a notification under subsection (5) appeal against the local authority's decision to the Secretary of State.

(7) On an appeal under this section the Secretary of State may confirm the decision appealed against or he may—

(a) approve the height of the chimney without qualification or subject to conditions as to the rate or quality, or the rate and quality, of emissions from the chimney; or

(b) cancel any conditions imposed by the local authority or substitute for any conditions so imposed any other conditions which the authority had power to impose.

(8) The Secretary of State shall give the appellant a written notification of his decision on an appeal under this section which—

(a) states his reasons for the decision; and

(b) in the case of a decision not to approve the height of the chimney, specifies—

(i) the lowest height (if any) which he is prepared to approve without qualification; or

(ii) the lowest height which he is prepared to approve if approval is granted subject to any specified conditions,

or (if he thinks fit) both.

(9) References in this section to 'the applicant' shall, in a case where the original applicant notifies the local authority that his interest in the application has been transferred to another person, be read as references to that other person.

16 Height of other chimneys

(1) This section applies where plans for the erection or extension of a building outside Greater London or in an outer London borough, other than a building used or to be used wholly for one or more of the following purposes, that is to say—

(a) as a residence or residences;

(b) as a shop or shops; or

(c) as an office or offices,

are in accordance with building regulations deposited with the local authority and the plans show that it is proposed to construct a chimney, other than one serving a furnace, for carrying smoke, grit, dust or gases from the building.

(2) The local authority shall reject the plans unless they are satisfied that the height of the chimney as shown on the plans will be sufficient to prevent, so far as practicable, the smoke, grit, dust or gases from becoming prejudicial to health or a nuisance having regard to—

(a) the purpose of the chimney;

(b) the position and descriptions of buildings near it;

(c) the levels of the neighbouring ground; and

(d) any other matters requiring consideration in the circumstances.

(3) If a local authority reject plans under the authority of this section—

(a) the notice given under section 16(6) of the Building Act 1984 shall specify that the plans have been so rejected; and

(b) any person interested in the building may appeal to the Secretary of State.

(4) On an appeal under subsection (3) the Secretary of State may confirm or cancel the rejection and, where he cancels the rejection, may, if he thinks it necessary, direct that the time for rejecting the plans otherwise than under the authority of this section shall be extended so as to run fromthe date on which his decision is notified to the local authority.

(5) ...

PART III SMOKE CONTROL AREAS

18 Declaration of smoke control area by local authority

(1) A local authority may by order declare the whole or any part of the district of the authority to be a smoke control area; and any order made under this section is referred to in this Act as a 'smoke control order'.

(2) A smoke control order—

(a) may make different provision for different parts of the smoke control area;

(b) may limit the operation of section 20 (prohibition of emissions of smoke) to specified classes of building in the area; and

(c) may exempt specified buildings or classes of building or specified fireplaces or classes of fireplace in the area from the operation of that section, upon such conditions as may be specified in the order;

and the reference in paragraph (c) to specified buildings or classes of building include a reference to any specified, or to any specified classes of, fixed boiler or industrial plant.

(3) A smoke control order may be revoked or varied by a subsequent order.

(4) The provisions of Schedule 1 apply to the coming into operation of smoke control orders.

19 Power of Secretary of State to require creation of smoke control areas

(1) If, after consultation with a local authority, the Secretary of State is satisfied—

(a) that it is expedient to abate the pollution of the air by smoke in the district or part of the district of the authority; and

(b) that the authority have not exercised, or have not sufficiently exercised, their powers under section 18 (power to declare smoke control area) to abate the pollution,

he may direct the authority to prepare and submit to him for his approval, within such period not being less than six months from the direction as may be specified in the direction, proposals for making and bringing into operation one or more smoke control orders within such period or periods as the authority think fit.

(2) Any proposals submitted by a local authority in pursuance of a direction under subsection (1) may be varied by further proposals submitted by the authority within the period specified for the making of the original proposals or such longer period as the Secretary of State may allow.

(3) The Secretary of State may reject any proposals submitted to him under this section or may approve them in whole or in part, with or without modifications.

(4) Where a local authority to whom a direction under subsection (1) has been given—

(a) fail to submit proposals to the Secretary of State within the period specified in the direction; or

(b) submit proposals which are rejected in whole or in part,

the Secretary of State may make an order declaring them to be in default and directing them for the purposes of removing the default to exercise their powers under section 18 in such manner and within such period as may be specified in the order.

(5) An order made under subsection (4) may be varied or revoked by a subsequent order so made.

(6) While proposals submitted by a local authority and approved by the Secretary of State under this section are in force, it shall be the duty of the authority to make such order or orders under section 18 as are necessary to carry out the proposals.

20 Prohibition on emission of smoke in smoke control area

(1) If, on any day, smoke is emitted from a chimney of any building within a smoke control area, the occupier of the building shall be guilty of an offence.

(2) If, on any day, smoke is emitted from a chimney (not being a chimney of a building) which serves the furnace of any fixed boiler or industrial plant within a smoke control area, the person having possession of the boiler or plant shall be guilty of an offence.

(3) Subsections (1) and (2) have effect—

(a) subject to any exemptions for the time being in force under section 18, 21 or 22;

(b) subject to section 51 (duty to notify offences to occupier or other person liable).

(4) In proceedings for an offence under this section it shall be a defence to prove that the alleged emission was not caused by the use of any fuel other than an authorised fuel.

(5) A person guilty of an offence under this section shall be liable on summary conviction to a fine not exceeding level 3 on the standard scale.

(6) In this Part 'authorised fuel' means a fuel declared by regulations of the Secretary of State to be an authorised fuel for the purposes of this Part.

21 Power by order to exempt certain fireplaces

The Secretary of State may by order exempt any class of fireplace, upon such conditions as may be specified in the order, from the provisions of section 20 (prohibition of smoke emissions in smoke control area), if he is satisfied that such fireplaces can be used for burning fuel other than authorised fuels without producing any smoke or a substantial quantity of smoke.

22 Exemptions relating to particular areas

(1) The Secretary of State may, if it appears to him to be necessary or expedient so to do, by order suspend or relax the operation of section 20 (prohibition of smoke emissions in smoke control area) in relation to the whole or any part of a smoke control area.

(2) Before making an order under subsection (1) the Secretary of State shall consult with the local authority unless he is satisfied that, on account of urgency, such consultation is impracticable.

(3) As soon as practicable after the making of such an order the local authority shall take such steps as appear to them suitable for bringing the effect of the order to the notice of persons affected.

23 Acquisition and sale of unauthorised fuel in a smoke control area

(1) Any person who

(a) acquires any solid fuel for use in a building in a smoke control area otherwise than in a building or fireplace exempted from the operation of section 20 (prohibition of smoke emissions in smoke control area);

(b) acquires any solid fuel for use in any fixed boiler or industrial plant in a smoke control area, not being a boiler or plant so exempted; or

(c) sells by retail any solid fuel for delivery by him or on his behalf to—

(i) a building in a smoke control area; or

(ii) premises in such an area in which there is any fixed boiler or industrial plant,

shall be guilty of an offence and liable on summary conviction to a fine not exceeding level 3 on the standard scale.

(2) In subsection (1), 'solid fuel' means any solid fuel other than an authorised fuel.

(3) Subsection (1) shall, in its application to a smoke control area in which the operation of section 20 is limited by a smoke control order to specified classes of buildings, boilers or plant, have effect as if references to a building, boiler or plant were references to a building, boiler or plant of a class specified in the order.

(4) The power of the Secretary of State under section 22 (exemptions relating to particular areas) to suspend or relax the operation of section 20 in relation to the whole or any part of a smoke control area includes power to suspend or relax the operation of subsection (1) in relation to the whole or any part of such an area.

(5) In proceedings for an offence under this section consisting of the sale of fuel for delivery to a building or premises, it shall be a defence for the person accused to prove that he believed and had reasonable grounds for believing—

(a) that the building was exempted from the operation of section 20 or, in a case where the operation of that section is limited to specified classes of building, was not of a specified class; or

(b) that the fuel was acquired for use in a fireplace, boiler or plant so exempted or, in a case where the operation of that section is limited to specified classes of boilers or plant, in a boiler or plant not of a specified class.

PART IV CONTROL OF CERTAIN FORMS OF AIR POLLUTION

30 Regulations about motor fuel

(1) For the purpose of limiting or reducing air pollution, the Secretary of State may by regulations—

(a) impose requirements as to the composition and contents of any fuel of a kind used in motor vehicles; and

(b) where such requirements are in force, prevent or restrict the production, treatment, distribution, import, sale or use of any fuel which in any respect fails to comply with the requirements, and which is for use in the United Kingdom.

(2) It shall be the duty of the Secretary of State, before he makes any regulations under this section, to consult—

(a) such persons appearing to him to represent manufacturers and users of motor vehicles;

(b) such persons appearing to him to represent the producers and users of fuel for motor vehicles; and

(c) such persons appearing to him to be conversant with problems of air pollution,

as he considers appropriate.

(3) Regulations under this section—

(a) in imposing requirements as to the composition and contents of any fuel, may apply standards, specifications, descriptions or tests laid down in documents not forming part of the regulations; and

(b) where fuel is subject to such requirements, may, in order that persons to whom the fuel is supplied are afforded information as to its composition or contents, impose requirements for securing that the information is displayed at such places and in such manner as may be prescribed by the regulations.

(4) It shall be duty of every local weights and measures authority to enforce the provisions of regulations under this section within its area; and subsection (2) of section 26 of the Trade Descriptions Act 1968 (reports and inquiries) shall apply as respects those authorities' functions under this subsection as it applies to their functions under that Act.

(5) The following provisions of the Trade Descriptions Act 1968 shall apply in relation to the enforcement of regulations under this section as they apply to the enforcement of that Act, that is to say—

section 27 (power to make test purchases);
section 28 (power to enter premises and inspect and seize goods and documents);
section 29 (obstruction of authorised officers);
section 30 (notice of test);

and section 33 of that Act shall apply to the exercise of powers under section 28 as applied by this subsection.

References to an offence under that Act in those provisions as applied by this sub-section, except the reference in section 30(2) to an offence under section 28(5) or 29 of that Act, shall be construed as references to an offence under section 32 of this Act (provisions supplementary to this section) relating to regulations under this section.

31 Regulations about sulphur content of oil fuel for furnaces or engines

(1) For the purpose of limiting or reducing air pollution, the Secretary of State may by regulations impose limits on the sulphur content of oil fuel which is used in furnaces or engines.

(2) It shall be the duty of the Secretary of State, before he makes any regulations in pursuance of this section, to consult—

(a) such persons appearing to him to represent producers and users of oil fuel;

(b) such persons appearing to him to represent manufacturers and users of plant and equipment for which oil fuel is used; and

(c) such persons appearing to him to be conversant with problems of air pollution,

as he considers appropriate.

(3) Regulations under this section may—

(a) prescribe the kinds of oil fuel, and the kinds of furnaces and engines, to which the regulations are to apply;

(b) apply standards, specifications, descriptions or tests laid down in documents not forming part of the regulations; and

(c) without prejudice to the generality of section 63(1)(a), make different provision for different areas.

(4) It shall be the duty—

(a) of every local authority to enforce the provisions of regulations under this section within its area, except in relation to a furnace which is [...

(i)] part of a process subject to Part I of the Environmental Protection Act 1990[, or

(ii) part of an installation subject to regulation by the Environment Agency under regulations made under section 2 of the Pollution Prevention and Control Act 1999; and]

(b) of the inspectors appointed under that Part to enforce those provisions in relation to [furnaces within sub-paragraph (i) of paragraph (a) above and of the Environment Agency to enforce those provisions in relation to furnaces within sub-paragraph (ii) of that paragraph].

...

(5) In this section 'oil fuel' means any liquid petroleum product produced in a refinery.

32 Provisions supplementary to sections 30 and 31

(1) Regulations under section 30 or 31 (regulation of content of motor fuel and fuel oil) may authorise the Secretary of State to confer exemptions from any provision of the regulations.

(2) A person who contravenes or fails to comply with any provision of regulations under section 30 or 31 shall be guilty of an offence and liable—

(a) on conviction on indictment, to a fine; and

(b) on summary conviction, to a fine not exceeding the statutory maximum; but the regulations may in any case exclude liability to conviction on indictment or reduce the maximum fine on summary conviction.

(3) Regulations under section 30 or 31 shall, subject to any provision to the contrary in the regulations, apply to fuel used for, and to persons in, the public service of the Crown as they apply to fuel used for other purposes and to other persons.

(4) A local authority shall not be entitled by virtue of subsection (3) to exercise, in relation to fuel used for and persons in that service, any power conferred on the authority by virtue of sections 56 to 58 (rights of entry and inspection and other local authority powers).

33 Cable burning

(1) A person who burns insulation from a cable with a view to recovering metal from the cable shall be guilty of an offence unless the burning is part of a process subject to Part I of the Environmental Protection Act 1990 [or or an activity subject to regulations under section 2 of the Pollution Prevention and Control Act 1999.]

(2) A person guilty of an offence under this section shall be liable on summary conviction to a fine not exceeding level 5 on the standard scale.

PART V INFORMATION ABOUT AIR POLLUTION

38 Regulations about local authority functions under sections 34, 35 and 36

(1) The Secretary of State shall by regulations prescribe the manner in which, and the methods by which, local authorities are to perform their functions under sections 34(1)(a) and (b), 35 and 36 (investigation and research etc. into, and the obtaining of information about, air pollution).

(2) It shall be the duty of the Secretary of State, before he makes regulations under this section, to consult—

(a) such persons appearing to him to represent local authorities;

(b) such persons appearing to him to represent industrial interests; and

(c) such persons appearing to him to be conversant with problems of air pollution,

as he considers appropriate.

(3) Regulations under this section may in particular—

(a) prescribe the kinds of emissions to which notices under section 36 (power to require information about air pollution) may relate;

(b) prescribe the kinds of information which may be required by those notices;

(c) prescribe the manner in which any such notice is to be given, and the evidence which is to be sufficient evidence of its having been given, and of its contents and authenticity;

(d) require each local authority to maintain in a prescribed form a register containing—

(i) information obtained by the authority by virtue of section 35(1) (powers of local authorities to obtain information), other than information as to which a direction under section 37(2) (appeals against notices under section 36) provides that the information is not to be disclosed to the public; and

(ii) such information (if any) as the Secretary of State may determine, or as may be determined by or under regulations, with respect to any appeal under section 37 against a notice served by the authority which the Secretary of State did not dismiss;

(e) specify the circumstances in which local authorities may enter into arrangements with owners or occupiers of premises under which they will record and measure emissions on behalf of the local authorities; and

(f) specify the kinds of apparatus which local authorities are to have power to provide and use for measuring and recording emissions, and for other purposes.

(4) Regulations made by virtue of subsection (3)(b) may in particular require returns of—

(a) the total volume of gases, whether pollutant or not, discharged from the premises in question over any period;

(b) the concentration of pollutant in the gases discharged;

(c) the total of the pollutant discharged over any period;

(d) the height or heights at which discharges take place;

(e) the hours during which discharges take place; or

(f) the concentration of pollutants at ground level.

(5) A register maintained by a local authority in pursuance of regulations made by virtue of subsection (3)(d) shall be open to public inspection at the principal office of the authority free of charge at all reasonable hours, and the authority shall afford members of the public reasonable facilities for obtaining from the authority, on payment of reasonable charges, copies of entries in the register.

39 Provision by local authorities of information for Secretary of State

(1) The Secretary of State may, for the purpose of obtaining information about air pollution, direct a local authority to make such arrangements as may be specified in the direction—

(a) for the provision, installation, operation and maintenance by the local authority of apparatus for measuring and recording air pollution; and

(b) for transmitting the information so obtained to the Secretary of State; but before giving the direction under this section the Secretary of State shall consult the local authority.

(2) Where apparatus is provided in pursuance of a direction under this section, the Secretary of State shall defray the whole of the capital expenditure incurred by the local authority in providing and installing the apparatus.

(3) It shall be the duty of the local authority to comply with any direction given under this section.

40 Interpretation of Part V

In this Part—

(a) references to the emission of substances into the atmosphere are to be construed as applying to substances in a gaseous or liquid or solid state, or any combination of those states; and

(b) any reference to measurement includes a reference to the taking of samples.

PART VI SPECIAL CASES

[41A Relation to the Pollution Prevention and Control Act 1999

(1) Where an activity is subject to regulations under section 2 of the Pollution Prevention and Control Act 1999 (regulation of polluting activities), Parts I to III of this Act shall not apply as from the determination date for the activity in question.

(2) The 'determination date', for an activity, is—

(a) in the case of an activity for which a permit is granted, the date on which it is granted, whether in pursuance of the application, or on an appeal, of a direction to grant it;

(b) in the case of an activity for which a permit is refused, the date of refusal or, on appeal, of the affirmation of the refusal.

(3) In subsection (2) 'permit' means a permit under regulations under section 2 of the Pollution Prevention and Control Act 1999 and the reference to an appeal is a reference to an appeal under those regulations.]

45 Exemption for purposes of investigations and research

(1) If the local authority are satisfied, on the application of any person interested, that it is expedient to do so for the purpose of enabling investigations or research relevant to the problem of the pollution of the air to be carried out without rendering the applicant liable to proceedings brought under or by virtue of any of the provisions of this Act or the Environmental Protection Act 1990 mentioned below, the local authority may by notice in writing given to the applicant exempt, wholly or to a limited extent,—

(a) any chimney from the operation of sections 1 (dark smoke), 5 (grit and dust), 20 (smoke in smoke control area) and 43 (railway engines) of this Act and Part III of the Environmental Protection Act 1990 (statutory nuisances);

(b) any furnace, boiler or industrial plant from the operation of section 4(2) (new furnaces to be as far as practicable smokeless);

(c) any premises from the operation of section 2 (emissions of dark smoke);

(d) any furnace from the operation of sections 6 or 8 (arrestment plant) and 10 (measurement of grit, dust and fumes by occupier), and

(e) the acquisition or sale of any fuel specified in the notice from the operation of section 23 (acquisition and sale of unauthorised fuel in smoke control area),

in each case subject to such conditions, if any, and for such period as may be specified in the notice.

(2) Any person who has applied to the local authority for an exemption under this section may, if he is dissatisfied with the decision of the authority on the application, appeal to the Secretary of State; and the Secretary of State may, if he thinks fit, by notice in writing given to the applicant and the local authority, give any exemption which the authority might have given or vary the terms of any exemption which they have given.

46 Crown premises, etc.

(1) It shall be part of the functions of the local authority, in cases where it seems to them proper to do so, to report to the responsible Minister any cases of—

(a) emissions of dark smoke, or of grit or dust, from any premises which are under the control of any Government department and are occupied for the public service of the Crown or for any of the purposes of any Government department;

(b) emissions of smoke, whether dark smoke or not, from any such premises which are within a smoke control area;

(c) emissions of smoke whether dark smoke or not, from any such premises which appear to them to constitute a nuisance to the inhabitants of the neighbourhood; or

(d) emissions of dark smoke from any vessel of Her Majesty's navy, or any Government ship in the service of the Secretary of State while employed for the purposes of Her Majesty's navy, which appear to them to constitute a nuisance to the inhabitants of the neighbourhood,

and on receiving any such report the responsible Minister shall inquire into the circumstances and, if his inquiry reveals that there is cause for complaint, shall employ all practicable means for preventing or minimising the emission of the smoke, grit or dust or for abating the nuisance and preventing a recurrence of it, as the case may be.

(2)–(6) . . .

PART VII MISCELLANEOUS AND GENERAL

47 Application to fumes and gases of certain provisions as to grit, dust and smoke

(1) The Secretary of State may by regulations—

(a) apply all or any of the provisions of sections 5, 6, 7, 42(4) 43(5) 44(6) and 46(1) to fumes or prescribed gases or both as they apply to grit and dust;

(b) apply all or any of the provisions of section 4 to fumes or prescribed gases or both as they apply to smoke; and

(c) apply all or any of the provisions of section 11 to prescribed gases as they apply to grit and dust,

subject, in each case, to such exceptions and modifications as he thinks expedient.

(2) No regulations shall be made under this section unless a draft of the regulations has been laid before and approved by each House of Parliament.

(3) In the application of any provision of this Act to prescribed gases by virtue of regulations under this section, any reference to the rate of emission of any substance shall be construed as a reference to the percentage by volume or by mass of the gas which may be emitted during a period specified in the regulations.

(4) In this section—

'gas' includes vapour and moisture precipitated from vapour; and

'prescribed' means prescribed in regulations under this section.

48 Power to give effect to international agreements

The Secretary of State may by regulations provide that any provision of Parts IV and V, or of this Part (apart from this section) so far as relating to those Parts, shall have effect with such modifications as are prescribed in the regulations with a view to enabling the Government of the United Kingdom to give effect to any provision made by or under any international agreement to which the Government is for the time being a party.

49 Unjustified disclosures of information

(1) If a person discloses any information relating to any trade secret used in carrying on any particular undertaking which has been given to him or obtained by him by virtue of this Act, he shall, subject to subsection (2), be guilty of an offence and liable on summary conviction to a fine not exceeding level 5 on the standard scale.

(2) A person shall not be guilty of an offence under subsection (1) by reason of the disclosure of any information if the disclosure is made—

(a) in the performance of his duty;

(b) in pursuance of section 34(1)(b); or

(c) with the consent of a person having a right to disclose the information.

50 Cumulative penalties on continuance of certain offences

(1) Where—

(a) a person is convicted of an offence which is subject to cumulative penalties on continuance in accordance with this section; and

(b) it is shown to the satisfaction of the court that the offence was substantially a repetition or continuation of an earlier offence by him after he had been convicted of the earlier offence,

the penalty provided by subsection (2) shall apply instead of the penalty otherwise specified for the offence.

(2) Where this subsection applies the person convicted shall be liable on summary conviction to a fine not exceeding—

(a) level 5 on the standard scale; or

(b) £50 for every day on which the earlier offence has been so repeated or continued by him within the three months next following his conviction of that offence,

whichever is the greater.

(3) Where an offence is subject to cumulative penalties in accordance with this section—

(a) the court by which a person is convicted of the original offence may fix a reasonable period from the date of conviction for compliance by the defendant with any directions given by the court; and

(b) where a court has fixed such a period, the daily penalty referred to in subsection (2) is not recoverable in respect of any day before the end of that period.

51 Duty to notify occupiers of offences

(1) If, in the opinion of an authorised officer of the local authority—

(a) an offence is being or has been committed under section 1, 2 or 20 (prohibition of certain emissions of smoke);

(b) [...]

he shall, unless he has reason to believe that notice of it has already been given by or on behalf of the local authority, as soon as may be notify the appropriate person, and, if his notification is not in writing, shall before the end of the four days next following the day on which he became aware of the offence, confirm the notification in writing.

(2) For the purposes of subsection (1), the appropriate person to notify is the occupier of the premises, the person having possession of the boiler or plant, the owner of the railway locomotive engine or the owner or master or other officer or person in charge of the vessel concerned, as the case may be.

(3) In any proceedings for an offence under section 1, 2 or 20 it shall be a defence to prove that the provisions of subsection (1) have not been complied with in the case of the offence; and if no such notification as is required by that subsection has been given before the end of the four days next following the day of the offence, that subsection shall be taken not to have been complied with unless the contrary is proved.

52 Offences committed by bodies corporate

(1) Where an offence under this Act which has been committed by a body corporate is proved to have been committed with the consent or connivance of, or to be attributable to any neglect on the part of, any director, manager, secretary or other similar officer of the body corporate or any person who was purporting to act in any such capacity, he as well as the body corporate shall be guilty of that offence and be liable to be proceeded against and punished accordingly.

(2) Where the affairs of a body corporate are managed by its members this section shall apply in relation to the acts and defaults of a member in connection with his functions of management as if he were a director of the body corporate.

53 Offence due to act or default of another

(1) Where the commission by any person of an offence under this Act is due to the act or default of some other person, that other person shall be guilty of the offence.

(2) A person may be charged with and convicted of an offence by virtue of this section whether or not proceedings for the offence are taken against any other person.

54 Power of county court to authorise works and order payments

(1) If works are reasonably necessary in or in connection with a building in order to enable the building to be used for some purpose without contravention of any of the provisions of this Act (apart from Parts IV and V), the occupier of the building—

(a) may, if by reason of a restriction affecting his interest in the building he is unable to carry out the works without the consent of the owner of the building or some other person interested in the building and is unable to obtain that consent, apply to the county court for an order to enable the works to be carried out by him; and

(b) may, if he considers that the whole or any proportion of the cost of carrying out the works should be borne by the owner of the building or some other person interested in the building, apply to the county court for an order directing the owner or other person to indemnify him, either wholly or in part, in respect of that cost;

and on an application under paragraph (a) or (b) the court may make such order as may appear to the court to be just.

(2) . . .

55 General provisions as to enforcement

(1) It shall be the duty of the local authority to enforce—

(a) the provisions of Parts I to III, section 33 and Part VI; and

(b) the provisions of this Part so far as relating to those provisions;

but nothing in this section shall be taken as extending to the enforcement of any building regulations.

(2) A local authority in England and Wales may institute proceedings for an offence under section 1 or 2 (prohibition of emissions of dark smoke) in the case of any smoke which affects any part of their district notwithstanding, in the case of an offence under section 1, that the smoke is emitted from a chimney outside their district and, in the case of an offence under section 2, that the smoke is emitted from premises outside their district.

(3) . . .

56 Rights of entry and inspection etc.

. . .

57 Provisions supplementary to section 56

. . .

58 Power of local authorities to obtain information

(1) A local authority may serve on any person a notice requiring him to furnish to the authority, within a period or at times specified in the notice and in a form so specified, any information so specified which the authority reasonably considers that it needs for the purposes of any function conferred on the authority by Part IV or V of this Act (or by this Part of this Act so far as relating to those Parts).

(2) The Secretary of State may by regulations provide for restricting the information which may be required in pursuance of subsection (1) and for determining the form in which the information is to be so required.

(3) Any person who—

(a) fails without reasonable excuse to comply with the requirements of a notice served on him in pursuance of this section; or

(b) in furnishing any information in compliance with such a notice, makes any statement which he knows to be false in a material particular or recklessly makes any statement which is false in a material particular,

shall be guilty of an offence and liable on summary conviction to a fine not exceeding level 5 on the standard scale.

60 Default powers

(1) If the Secretary of State is satisfied that any local authority (in this section referred to as the 'defaulting authority') have failed to perform any functions which they ought to have performed, he may make an order—

(a) declaring the authority to be in default; and

(b) directing the authority to perform such of their functions as are specified in the order;

and he may specify the manner in which and the time or times within which those functions are to be performed by the authority.

(2) If the defaulting authority fails to comply with any direction contained in such an order, the Secretary of State may, instead of enforcing the order by mandamus, make an order transferring to himself such of the functions of the authority as he thinks fit.

(3)–(6) . . .

(7) This section does not apply to a failure by a local authority—

(a) to discharge their functions under section 18 (declaration of smoke control areas);

(b) to submit proposals to the Secretary of State in pursuance of a direction under subsection (1) of section 19 (Secretary of State's power to require creation of smoke control area); or

(c) to perform a duty imposed on them by or by virtue of subsection (4) or (6) of that section.

(8) In this section 'functions', in relation to an authority, means functions conferred on the authority by virtue of this Act.

64 General provisions as to interpretation

(1) In this Act, except so far as the context otherwise requires,—

'authorised officer' means any officer of a local authority authorised by them in writing, either generally or specially, to act in matters of any specified kind or in any specified matter;

'chimney' includes structures and openings of any kind from or through which smoke, grit, dust or fumes may be emitted, and, in particular, includes flues, and references to a chimney of a building include references to a chimney which serves the whole or a part of a building but is structurally separate from the building;

'dark smoke' has the meaning given by section 3(1);

'day' means a period of twenty-four hours beginning at midnight;

'domestic furnace' means any furnace which is—

(a) designed solely or mainly for domestic purposes, and

(b) used for heating a boiler with a maximum heating capacity of less than 16.12 kilowatts;

'fireplace' includes any furnace, grate or stove, whether open or closed;

'fixed boiler or industrial plant' means any boiler or industrial plant which is attached to a building or is for the time being fixed to or installed on any land;

'fumes' means any airborne solid matter smaller than dust;

'industrial plant' includes any still, melting pot or other plant used for any industrial or trade purposes, and also any incinerator used for or in connection with any such purposes;

'local authority' means—

(a) in England, the council of a district or a London borough, the Common Council of the City of London, the Sub-Treasurer of the Inner Temple and the Under Treasurer of the Middle Temple;

(aa) in Wales the council of a county or county borough

(b) . . .

'practicable' means reasonably practicable having regard, amongst other things, to local conditions and circumstances, to the financial implications and to the current state of technical knowledge, and 'practicable means' includes the provision and maintenance of plant and its proper use;

'premises' includes land;

'smoke', includes soot, ash, grit and gritty particles emitted in smoke; and

(2) Any reference in this Act to the occupier of a building shall, in relation to any building different parts of which are occupied by different persons, be read as a reference to the occupier or other person in control of the part of the building in which the relevant fireplace is situated.

(3) In this Act any reference to the rate of emission of any substance or any reference which is to be understood as such a reference shall, in relation to any regulations or conditions, be construed as a reference to the quantities of that substance which may be emitted during a period specified in the regulations or conditions.

(4) In this Act, except so far as the context otherwise requires, 'private dwelling' means any building or part of a building used or intended to be used as such, and a building or part of a building is not to be taken for the purposes of this Act to be used or intended to be used otherwise than as a private dwelling by reason that a person who resides or is to reside in it is or is to be required or permitted to reside in it in consequence of his employment or of holding an office.

(5) In considering for the purposes of this Act whether any and, if so, what works are reasonably necessary in order to make suitable provision for heating and cooking in the case of a dwelling or are reasonably necessary in order to enable a building to be used for a purpose without contravention of any of the provisions of this Act, regard shall be had to any difficulty there may be in obtaining, or in obtaining otherwise than at a high price, any fuels which would have to be used but for the execution of the works.

(6) Any furnaces which are in the occupation of the same person and are served by a single chimney shall, for the purposes of sections 5 to 12, 14 and 15, be taken to be one furnace.

Environment Act 1995

(1995, c. 25)

PART I THE ENVIRONMENT AGENCY AND THE SCOTTISH ENVIRONMENT PROTECTION AGENCY

CHAPTER I THE ENVIRONMENT AGENCY

Establishment of the Agency

1 The Environment Agency

(1) There shall be a body corporate to be known as the Environment Agency or, in Welsh, Asiantaeth yr Amgylchedd (in this Act referred to as 'the Agency'), for the purpose of carrying out the functions transferred or assigned to it by or under this Act.

(2) The Agency shall consist of not less than eight nor more than fifteen members of whom—

(a) three shall be appointed by the Minister; and

(b) the others shall be appointed by the Secretary of State.

(3) The Secretary of State shall designate—

(a) one of the members as the chairman of the Agency, and

(b) another of them as the deputy chairman of the Agency.

(4) In appointing a person to be a member of the Agency, the Secretary of State or, as the case may be, the Minister shall have regard to the desirability of appointing a person who has experience of, and has shown capacity in, some matter relevant to the functions of the Agency.

(5) Subject to the provisions of section 36 below, the Agency shall not be regarded—

(a) as the servant or agent of the Crown, or as enjoying any status, immunity or privilege of the Crown; or

(b) by virtue of any connection with the Crown, as exempt from any tax, duty, rate, levy or other charge whatsoever, whether general or local;

and the Agency's property shall not be regarded as property of, or property held on behalf of, the Crown.

(6) ...

Transfer of functions, property etc. to the Agency

2 Transfer of functions to the Agency

(1) On the transfer date there shall by virtue of this section be transferred to the Agency—

(a) the functions of the National Rivers Authority, that is to say—

(i) its functions under or by virtue of Part II (water resources management) of the Water Resources Act 1991 (in this Part referred to as 'the 1991 Act');

(ii) its functions under or by virtue of Part III of that Act (control of pollution of water resources);

(iii) its functions under or by virtue of Part IV of that Act (flood defence) and the Land Drainage Act 1991 and the functions transferred to the Authority by virtue of section 136(8) of the Water Act 1989 and paragraph 1(3) of Schedule 15 to that Act (transfer of land drainage functions under local statutory provisions and subordinate legislation);

(iv) its functions under or by virtue of Part VII of the 1991 Act (land and works powers);

(v) its functions under or by virtue of the Diseases of Fish Act 1937, the Sea Fisheries Regulation Act 1966, the Salmon and Freshwater Fisheries Act 1975, Part V of the 1991 Act or any other enactment relating to fisheries;

(vi) the functions as a navigation authority, harbour authority or conservancy authority which were transferred to the Authority by virtue of Chapter V of Part III of the Water Act 1989 or paragraph 23(3) of Schedule 13 to that Act or which have been transferred to the Authority by any order or agreement under Schedule 2 to the 1991 Act;

(vii) its functions under Schedule 2 to the 1991 Act;

(viii) the functions assigned to the Authority by or under any other enactment, apart from this Act;

(b) the functions of waste regulation authorities, that is to say, the functions conferred or imposed on them by or under—

(i) the Control of Pollution (Amendment) Act 1989, or

(ii) Part II of the Environmental Protection Act 1990 (in this Part referred to as 'the 1990 Act'),

or assigned to them by or under any other enactment, apart from this Act;

(c) the functions of disposal authorities under or by virtue of the waste regulation provisions of the Control of Pollution Act 1974;

(d) the functions of the chief inspector for England and Wales constituted under section 16(3) of the 1990 Act, that is to say, the functions conferred or imposed on him by or under Part I of that Act or assigned to him by or under any other enactment, apart from this Act;

(e) the functions of the chief inspector for England and Wales appointed under section 4(2)(a) of the Radioactive Substances Act 1993, that is to say, the functions conferred or imposed on him by or under that Act or assigned to him by or under any other enactment, apart from this Act;

(f) the functions conferred or imposed by or under the Alkali, &c, Works Regulation Act 1906 (in this section referred to as 'the 1906 Act') on the chief, or any other, inspector (within the meaning of that Act), so far as exercisable in relation to England and Wales;

(g) so far as exercisable in relation to England and Wales, the functions in relation to improvement notices and prohibition notices under Part I of the Health and Safety at Work etc. Act 1974 (in this section referred to as 'the 1974 Act') of inspectors appointed under section 19 of that Act by the Secretary of State in his capacity as the enforcing authority responsible in relation to England and Wales for the enforcement of the 1906 Act and section 5 of the 1974 Act; and

(h) the functions of the Secretary of State specified in subsection (2) below.

(2) The functions of the Secretary of State mentioned in subsection (1)(h) above are the following, that is to say—

(a) so far as exercisable in relation to England and Wales, his functions under section 30(1) of the Radioactive Substances Act 1993 (power to dispose of radioactive waste);

(b) his functions under Chapter III of Part IV of the Water Industry Act 1991 in relation to special category effluent, within the meaning of that Chapter, other than any function of making regulations or of making orders under section 139 of that Act;

(c) so far as exercisable in relation to England and Wales, the functions conferred or imposed on him by virtue of his being, for the purposes of Part I of the 1974 Act, the authority which is by any of the relevant statutory provisions made responsible for the enforcement of the 1906 Act and section 5 of the 1974 Act;

(d) so far as exercisable in relation to England and Wales, his functions under, or under regulations made by virtue of, section 9 of the 1906 Act (registration of works), other than any functions of his as an appellate authority or any function of making regulations;

(e) so far as exercisable in relation to England and Wales, his functions under regulations 7(1) and 8(2) of, and paragraph 2(2)(c) of Schedule 2 to, the Sludge (Use in Agriculture) Regulations 1989 (which relate to the provision of information and the testing of soil).

. . .

4 Principal aim and objectives of the Agency

(1) It shall be the principal aim of the Agency (subject to and in accordance with the provisions of this Act or any other enactment and taking into account any likely costs) in discharging its functions so to protect or enhance the environment, taken as a whole, as to make the contribution towards attaining the objective of achieving sustainable development mentioned in subsection (3) below.

(2) The Ministers shall from time to time give guidance to the Agency with respect to objectives which they consider it appropriate for the Agency to pursue in the discharge of its functions.

(3) The guidance given under subsection (2) above must include guidance with respect to the contribution which, having regard to the Agency's responsibilities and resources, the Ministers consider it appropriate for the Agency to make, by the discharge of its functions, towards attaining the objective of achieving sustainable development.

(4) In discharging its functions, the Agency shall have regard to guidance given under this section.

(5) The power to give guidance to the Agency under this section shall only be exercisable after consultation with

(a) the Agency;

(b) Natural England;

(c) such other persons as the Ministers consider it appropriate to consult in relation to the guidance in question.

(6) A draft of any guidance proposed to be given under this section shall be laid before each House of Parliament and the guidance shall not be given until after the period of 40 days beginning with the day on which the draft was so laid or, if the draft is laid on different days, the later of the two days.

(7) If, within the period mentioned in subsection (6) above, either House resolves that the guidance, the draft of which was laid before it, should not be given, the Ministers shall not give that guidance.

(8) In reckoning any period of 40 days for the purposes of subsection (6) or (7) above, no account shall be taken of any time during which Parliament is dissolved or prorogued or during which both Houses are adjourned for more than four days.

(9) The Ministers shall arrange for any guidance given under this section to be published in such manner as they consider appropriate.

5 General functions with respect to pollution control

(1) The Agency's pollution control powers shall be exercisable for the purpose of preventing or minimising, or remedying or mitigating the effects of, pollution of the environment.

(2) The Agency shall, for the purpose—

(a) of facilitating the carrying out of its pollution control functions, or

(b) of enabling it to form an opinion of the general state of pollution of the environment,

compile information relating to such pollution (whether the information is acquired by the Agency carrying out observations or is obtained in any other way).

(3) If required by either of the Ministers to do so, the Agency shall—

(a) carry out assessments (whether generally or for such particular purpose as may be specified in the requirement) of the effect, or likely effect, on the environment of existing or potential levels of pollution of the environment and report its findings to that Minister; or

(b) prepare and send to that Minister a report identifying—

(i) the options which the Agency considers to be available for preventing or minimising, or remedying or mitigating the effects of, pollution of the environment, whether generally or in cases or circumstances specified in the requirement; and

(ii) the costs and benefits of such options as are identified by the Agency pursuant to sub-paragraph (i) above.

(4) The Agency shall follow developments in technology and techniques for preventing or minimising, or remedying or mitigating the effects of, pollution of the environment.

(5) In this section, 'pollution control powers' and 'pollution control functions', in relation to the Agency, mean respectively its powers or its functions under or by virtue of the following enactments, that is to say—

(a) the Alkali, &c, Works Regulation Act 1906;

(b) Part I of the Health and Safety at Work etc. Act 1974;

(c) Part I of the Control of Pollution Act 1974;

(d) the Control of Pollution (Amendment) Act 1989;

(e) Parts I, II and IIA of the 1990 Act (integrated pollution control etc, waste on land and contaminated land);

(f) Chapter III of Part IV of the Water Industry Act 1991 (special category effluent);

(g) Part III and sections 161 to 161D of the 1991 Act (control of pollution of water resources);

(h) the Radioactive Substances Act 1993;

[(i) regulations under section 2 of the Pollution Prevention and Control Act 1999;]

(j) regulations made by virtue of section 2(2) of the European Communities Act 1972, to the extent that the regulations relate to pollution.

6 General provisions with respect to water

(1) It shall be the duty of the Agency, to such extent as it considers desirable, generally to promote—

(a) the conservation and enhancement of the natural beauty and amenity of inland and coastal waters and of land associated with such waters;

(b) the conservation of flora and fauna which are dependent on an aquatic environment; and

(c) the use of such waters and land for recreational purposes;

and it shall be the duty of the Agency, in determining what steps to take in performance of the duty imposed by virtue of paragraph (c) above, to take into account the needs of persons who are chronically sick or disabled.

This subsection is without prejudice to the duties of the Agency under section 7 below.

(2) It shall be the duty of the Agency to take all such action as it may from time to time consider, in accordance with any directions given under section 38 below, to be necessary or expedient for the purpose—

(a) of conserving, redistributing or otherwise augmenting water resources in England and Wales; and

(b) of securing the proper use of water resources in England and Wales [(including the efficient use of those resources)];

but nothing in this subsection shall be construed as relieving any water undertaker of the obligation to develop water resources for the purpose of performing any duty imposed on it by virtue of section 37 of the Water Industry Act 1991 (general duty to maintain water supply system).

(3) The provisions of the 1991 Act relating to the functions of the Agency under Chapter II of Part II of that Act and the related water resources provisions so far as they relate to other functions of the Agency shall not apply to so much of any inland waters as—

(a) are part of the River Tweed;

(b) are part of the River Esk or River Sark at a point where either of the banks of the river is in Scotland; or

(c) are part of any tributary stream of the River Esk or the River Sark at a point where either of the banks of the tributary stream is in Scotland [except so much of those inland waters as are in England].

[(3A) Subsection (3) above shall apply to—

(a) sections 3 and 4 of the Water Act 2003; and

(b) such of the related water resources provisions as apply in relation to those sections by virtue of section 33(2) of the Water Act 2003,

as it applies to the provisions referred to in that subsection].

(4) Subject to section 106 of the 1991 Act (obligation to carry out flood defence functions through committees), the Agency shall in relation to England and Wales exercise a general supervision over all matters relating to flood defence.

(5) The Agency's flood defence functions shall extend to the territorial sea adjacent to England and Wales in so far as—

(a) the area of any regional flood defence committee includes any area of that territorial sea; or

(b) section 165(2) or (3) of the 1991 Act (drainage works for the purpose of defence against sea water or tidal water, and works etc to secure an adequate outfall for a main river) provides for the exercise of any power in the territorial sea.

(6) It shall be the duty of the Agency to maintain, improve and develop salmon fisheries, trout fisheries, freshwater fisheries and eel fisheries.

(7) . . .

(8) In this section—

'miles' means international nautical miles of 1,852 metres;

'the related water resources provisions' has the same meaning as it has in the 1991 Act;

'the River Tweed' means 'the river' within the meaning of the Tweed Fisheries Amendment Act 1859 as amended by byelaws.

7 General environmental and recreational duties

(1) It shall be the duty of each of the Ministers and of the Agency, in formulating or considering—

(a) any proposals relating to any functions of the Agency other than its pollution control functions, so far as may be consistent—

(i) with the purposes of any enactment relating to the functions of the Agency,

(ii) in the case of each of the Ministers, with the objective of achieving sustainable development,

(iii) in the case of the Agency, with any guidance under section 4 above,

(iv) in the case of the Secretary of State, with his duties under section 2 of the Water Industry Act 1991,

so to exercise any power conferred on him or it with respect to the proposals as to further the conservation and enhancement of natural beauty and the conservation of flora, fauna and geological or physiographical features of special interest;

(b) any proposals relating to pollution control functions of the Agency, to have regard to the desirability of conserving and enhancing natural beauty and of conserving flora, fauna and geological or physiographical features of special interest;

(c) any proposal relating to any functions of the Agency—

(i) to have regard to the desirability of protecting and conserving buildings, sites and objects of archaeological, architectural, engineering or historic interest;

(ii) to take into account any effect which the proposals would have on the beauty or amenity of any rural or urban area or on any such flora, fauna, features, buildings, sites or objects; and

(iii) to have regard to any effect which the proposals would have on the economic and social well-being of local communities in rural areas.

(2) Subject to subsection (1) above, it shall be the duty of each of the Ministers and of the Agency, in formulating or considering any proposals relating to any functions of the Agency,—

(a) to have regard to the desirability of preserving for the public any freedom of access to areas of woodland, mountains, moor, heath, down, cliff or foreshore and other places of natural beauty;

(b) to have regard to the desirability of maintaining the availability to the public of any facility for visiting or inspecting any building, site or object of archaeological, architectural, engineering or historic interest; and

(c) to take into account any effect which the proposals would have on any such freedom of access or on the availability of any such facility.

(3)–(6) . . .

(7) In this section—

'building' includes structure;

'pollution control functions', in relation to the Agency, has the same meaning as in section 5 above.

8 Environmental duties with respect to sites of special interest

(1) Where Natural England or the Countryside Council for Wales is of the opinion that any area of land in England or, as the case may be, in Wales—

(a) is of special interest by reason of its flora, fauna or geological or physiographical features, and

(b) may at any time be affected by schemes, works, operations or activities of the Agency or by an authorisation given by the Agency,

the Agency, or as the case may be the Council, shall notify the fact that the land is of special interest for that reason to the Agency.

(2) Where a National Park authority or the Broads Authority is of the opinion that any area of land in a National Park or in the Broads—

(a) is land in relation to which the matters for the purposes of which sections 6(1) and 7 above (other than section 7(1)(c)(iii) above) have effect are of particular importance, and

(b) may at any time be affected by schemes, works, operations or activities of the Agency or by an authorisation given by the Agency, the National Park authority or Broads Authority shall notify the Agency of the fact that the land is such land, and of the reasons why those matters are of particular importance in relation to the land.

(3) Where the Agency has received a notification under subsection (1) or (2) above with respect to any land, it shall consult the notifying body before carrying out or authorising any works, operations or activities which appear to the Agency to be likely—

(a) to destroy or damage any of the flora, fauna, or geological or physiographical features by reason of which the land is of special interest; or

(b) significantly to prejudice anything the importance of which is one of the reasons why the matters mentioned in subsection (2) above are of particular importance in relation to that land.

(4) Subsection (3) above shall not apply in relation to anything done in an emergency where particulars of what is done and of the emergency are notified to Natural England, the Countryside Council for Wales, the National Park authority in question or, as the case may be, the Broads Authority as soon as practicable after that thing is done.

(5) In this section—

'authorisation' includes any consent or licence;

'the Broads' has the same meaning as in the Norfolk and Suffolk Broads Act 1988; and

'National Park authority', [. . .] means a National Park authority established under section 60 below which has become the local planning authority for the National Park in question.

(6) [. . .]

9 Codes of practice with respect to environmental and recreational duties

(1) Each of the Ministers shall have power by order to approve any code of practice issued (whether by him or by another person) for the purpose of—

(a) giving practical guidance to the agency with respect to any of the matters for the purposes of which sections 6(1), 7 and 8 above have effect, and

(b) promoting what appear to him to be desirable practices by the Agency with respect to those matters,

and may at any time by such an order approve a modification of such a code or withdraw his approval of such a code or modification.

(2) In discharging its duties under section 6(1), 7 or 8 above, the Agency shall have regard to any code of practice, and any modifications of a code of practice, for the time being approved under this section.

(3) Neither of the Ministers shall make an order under this section unless he has first consulted—

(a) the Agency;

(b) Natural England and the Countryside Council for Wales;

(c) the Historic Buildings and Monuments Commission for England;

(d) the Sports Council and the Sports Council for Wales; and

(e) such other persons as he considers it appropriate to consult.

(4) The power of each of the Ministers to make an order under this section shall be exercisable by statutory instrument; and any statutory instrument containing such an order shall be subject to annulment in pursuance of a resolution of either House of Parliament.

10 Incidental functions of the Agency

(1) This section has effect—

(a) for the purposes of section 35(1) below, as it applies in relation to the Agency; and

(b) for the construction of any other enactment which, by reference to the functions of the Agency, confers any power on or in relation to the Agency;

and any reference in this section to 'the relevant purposes' is a reference to the purposes described in paragraphs (a) and (b) above.

(2) For the relevant purposes, the functions of the Agency shall be taken to include the protection against pollution of—

(a) any waters, whether on the surface or underground, which belong to the Agency or any water undertaker or from which the Agency or any water undertaker is authorised to take water;

(b) without prejudice to paragraph (a) above, any reservoir which belongs to or is operated by the Agency or any water undertaker or which the Agency or any water undertaker is proposing to acquire or construct for the purpose of being so operated; and

(c) any underground strata from which the Agency or any water undertaker is for the time being authorised to abstract water in pursuance of a licence under Chapter II of Part II of the 1991 Act (abstraction and impounding).

(3) For the relevant purposes, the functions of the Agency shall be taken to include joining with or acting on behalf of one or more relevant undertakers for the purpose of carrying out any works or acquiring any land which at least one of the undertakers with which it joins, or on whose behalf it acts, is authorised to carry out or acquire for the purposes of—

(a) any function of that undertaker under any enactment; or

(b) any function which is taken to be a function of that undertaker for the purposes to which section 217 of the Water Industry Act 1991 applies.

(4) For the relevant purposes, the functions of the Agency shall be taken to include the provision of supplies of water in bulk, whether or not such supplies are provided for the purposes of, or in connection with, the carrying out of any other function of the Agency.

(5) For the relevant purposes, the functions of the Agency shall be taken to include the provision of houses and other buildings for the use of persons employed by the Agency and the provision of recreation grounds for persons so employed.

(6) In this section—

'relevant undertaker' means a water undertaker or sewerage undertaker; and

'supply of water in bulk' means a supply of water for distribution by a water undertaker taking the supply.

Advisory committees

. . .

CHAPTER III MISCELLANEOUS, GENERAL AND SUPPLEMENTAL PROVISIONS RELATING TO THE NEW AGENCIES

Additional general powers and duties

37 Incidental general functions

(1) Each new Agency (that is to say, in this Part, the Agency . . .—

(a) may do anything which, in its opinion, is calculated to facilitate, or is conducive or incidental to, the carrying out of its functions; and

(b) without prejudice to the generality of that power, may, for the purposes of, or in connection with, the carrying out of those functions, acquire and dispose of land and other property and carry out such engineering or building operations as it considers appropriate;

and the Agency may institute criminal proceedings in England and Wales.

(2) It shall be the duty of each new Agency to provide the Secretary of State or the Minister with such advice and assistance as he may request.

(3) Subject to subsection (4) below, each new Agency may provide for any person, whether in or outside the United Kingdom, advice or assistance, including training facilities, as respects any matter in which that new Agency has skill or experience.

(4) Without prejudice to any power of either new Agency apart from subsection (3) above to provide advice or assistance of the kind mentioned in that subsection, the power conferred

by that subsection shall not be exercised in a case where the person for whom the advice or assistance is provided is outside the United Kingdom, except with the consent in writing of the appropriate Minister which consent may be given subject to such conditions as the Minister giving it thinks fit.

(5) Each new Agency—

(a) shall make arrangements for the carrying out of research and related activities (whether by itself or by others) in respect of matters to which its functions relate; and

(b) may make the results of any such research or related activities available to any person in return for payment of such fee as it considers appropriate.

(6) Subsection (5) above shall not be taken as preventing a new Agency from making the results of any research available to the public free of charge whenever it considers it appropriate to do so.

(7) Each new Agency may by agreement with any person charge that person a fee in respect of work done, or services or facilities provided, as a result of a request made by him for advice or assistance, whether of a general or specific character, in connection with any matter involving or relating to environmental licences.

(8) Subsection (7) above—

(a) is without prejudice to the generality of the powers of either new Agency to make charges; but

(b) is subject to any such express provision with respect to charging by the new Agency in question as is contained in the other provisions of this Part or in any other enactment.

(9) In this section 'engineering or building operations', without prejudice to the generality of that expression, includes—

(a) the construction, alteration, improvement, maintenance or demolition of any building or structure or of any reservoir, watercourse, dam, weir, well, borehole or other works; and

(b) the installation, modification or removal of any machinery or apparatus.

38 Delegation of functions by Ministers etc. to the new Agencies

(1) Agreements may be made between—

(a) any Minister of the Crown, and

(b) a new Agency, authorising the new Agency (or any of its employees) to exercise on behalf of that Minister, with or without payment, any eligible function of his.

(2) An agreement under subsection (1) above shall not authorise the new Agency (or any of its employees) to exercise on behalf of a Minister of the Crown any function which consists of a power to make regulations or other instruments of a legislative character or a power to fix fees or charges.

(3)–(9) ...

(10) In this section—

'eligible function' means any function of a Minister of the Crown which the Secretary of State, having regard to the functions conferred or imposed upon the new Agency in question under or by virtue of this Act or any other enactment, considers can appropriately be exercised by that new Agency (or any of its employees) on behalf of that Minister;

'Minister of the Crown' has the same meaning as in the Ministers of the Crown Act 1975.

39 General duty of the new Agencies to have regard to costs and benefits in exercising powers

(1) Each new Agency—

(a) in considering whether or not to exercise any power conferred upon it by or under any enactment, or

(b) in deciding the manner in which to exercise any such power, shall, unless and to the extent that it is unreasonable for it to do so in view of the nature or purpose of the power or in the circumstances of the particular case, take into account the likely costs and benefits of the exercise or non-exercise of the power or its exercise in the manner in question.

(2) The duty imposed upon a new Agency by subsection (1) above does not affect its obligation, nevertheless, to discharge any duties, comply with any requirements, or pursue any objectives, imposed upon or given to it otherwise than under this section.

40 Ministerial directions to the new Agencies

(1) The appropriate Minister may give a new Agency directions of a general or specific character with respect to the carrying out of any of its functions.

(2) The appropriate Minister may give a new Agency such directions of a general or specific character as he considers appropriate for the implementation of—

(a) any obligations of the United Kingdom under the Community Treaties, or

(b) any international agreement to which the United Kingdom is for the time being a party.

(3) Any direction under subsection (2) above shall be published in such manner as the Minister giving it considers appropriate for the purpose of bringing the matters to which it relates to the attention of persons likely to be affected by them; and—

(a) copies of the direction shall be made available to the public; and

(b) notice shall be given—

(i) in the case of a direction given to the Agency, in the London Gazette, or

(ii) . . . of the giving of the direction and of where a copy of the direction may be obtained.

(4) The provisions of subsection (3) above shall have effect in relation to any direction given to a new Agency under an enactment other than subsection (2) above for the implementation of—

(a) any obligations of the United Kingdom under the Community Treaties, or

(b) any international agreement to which the United Kingdom is for the time being a party,

as those provisions have effect in relation to a direction given under subsection (2) above.

(5) In determining—

(a) any appeal against, or reference or review of, a decision of a new Agency, or

(b) any application transmitted from a new Agency,

the body or person making the determination shall be bound by any direction given by a Minister of the Crown to the new Agency to the same extent as the new Agency.

(6) Any power to give a direction under this section shall be exercisable, except in an emergency, only after consultation with the new Agency concerned.

(7) Any power of the appropriate Minister to give directions to a new Agency otherwise than by virtue of this section shall be without prejudice to any power to give directions conferred by this section.

(8) It is the duty of a new Agency to comply with any direction which is given to that new Agency by a Minister of the Crown under this section or any other enactment.

Charging schemes

41 Power to make schemes imposing charges

(1) Subject to the following provisions of this section and section 40 below—

(a) in the case of any particular licence under Chapter II of Part II of the 1991 Act (abstraction and impounding), the Agency may require the payment to it of such charges as may from time to time be prescribed;

(b) in relation to other environmental licences, there shall be charged by and paid to a new Agency such charges as may from time to time be prescribed; and

(c) as a means of recovering costs incurred by it in performing functions conferred by regulations made for the purpose of implementing Council Directive 91/689/EEC the Agency may require the payment to it of such charges as may from time to time be prescribed;

and in this section 'prescribed' means specified in, or determined under, a scheme (in this section referred to as a 'charging scheme') made under this section by the new Agency in question.

(2) As respects environmental licences, charges may be prescribed in respect of—

(a) the grant or variation of an environmental licence, or any application for, or for a variation of, such a licence;

(b) the subsistence of an environmental licence;

(c) the transfer (where permitted) of an environmental licence to another person, or any application for such a transfer;

(d) the renewal (where permitted) of an environmental licence, or any application for such a renewal;

(e) the surrender (where permitted) of an environmental licence, or any application for such a surrender; or

(f) any application for the revocation (where permitted) of an environmental licence.

(3) A charging scheme may, for the purposes of subsection (2)(b) above, impose—

(a) a single charge in respect of the whole of any relevant licensed period;

(b) separate charges in respect of different parts of any such period; or

(c) both such a single charge and such separate charges,

and in this subsection 'relevant licensed period' means the period during which an environmental licence is in force or such part of that period as may be prescribed.

(4) Without prejudice to subsection (7)(a) below, a charging scheme may, as respects environmental licences, provide for different charges to be payable according to—

(a) the description of environmental licence in question;

(b) the description of authorised activity in question;

(c) the scale on which the authorised activity in question is carried on;

(d) the description or amount of the substance to which the authorised activity in question relates;

(e) the number of different authorised activities carried on by the same person.

(5) A charging scheme—

(a) shall specify, in relation to any charge prescribed by the scheme, the description of person who is liable to pay the charge; and

(b) may provide that it shall be a condition of an environmental licence of any particular description that any charge prescribed by a charging scheme in relation to an environmental licence of that description is paid in accordance with the scheme.

(6) Without prejudice to subsection (5)(b) above, if it appears to a new Agency that any charges due and payable to it in respect of the subsistence of an environmental licence have not been paid, it may, in accordance with the appropriate procedure, suspend or revoke the environmental licence to the extent that it authorises the carrying on of an authorised activity.

(7) A charging scheme may—

(a) make different provision for different cases, including different provision in relation to different persons, circumstances or localities;

(b) provide for the times at which, and the manner in which, the charges prescribed by the scheme are to be paid;

(c) revoke or amend any previous charging scheme;

(d) contain supplemental, incidental, consequential or transitional provision for the purposes of the scheme.

(8) If and to the extent that a charging scheme relates to licences under Chapter II of Part II of the 1991 Act (abstraction and impounding), the scheme shall have effect subject to any

provision made by or under sections 125 to 130 of that Act (exemption from charges, imposition of special charges for spray irrigation in respect of abstraction from waters of the British Waterways Board).

(9) A new Agency shall not make a charging scheme unless the provisions of the scheme have been approved by the Secretary of State under section 42 below.

(10) In this section—

'the appropriate procedure' means such procedure as may be specified or described in regulations made for the purpose by the Secretary of State;

'authorised activity' means any activity to which an environmental licence relates.

(11) Any power to make regulations under this section shall be exercisable by statutory instrument; and a statutory instrument containing any such regulations shall be subject to annulment pursuant to a resolution of either House of Parliament.

[41A Charges in respect of greenhouse gas emissions permits

(1) Without prejudice to subsections (1)(b) and (2) of section 41 above, the following charges may be prescribed under that section as respects permits ('greenhouse gas emissions permits') granted under the Greenhouse Gas Emissions Trading Scheme Regulations 2005 ('the regulations')—

(a) charges in respect of, or in respect of an application for, the allocation of allowances to an operator;

(b) charges in respect of, or in respect of an application for, the retention of allowances by an operator ceasing to carry on an activity to which they relate;

(c) charges in respect of the revocation of a greenhouse gas emissions permit;

(d) charges in respect of the subsistence of an account required to be held in the trading scheme registry by an operator ('operator registry charges').

(2) If the Agency—

(a) proposes to prescribe operator registry charges, or to amend any provision for such charges included in a charging scheme, and

(b) notifies SEPA of its proposals,

the Agency and SEPA shall each include in a charging scheme (subject to approval by the Secretary of State under section 42(2) below) provision giving effect to the proposals.

(3) If the Agency revises any proposals of which it has given notification under subsection (2) above, and notifies SEPA accordingly, the obligations imposed by that subsection apply in relation to the proposals as revised.

(4) A notification under subsection (2) or (3) above shall include details of the amount of the proposed charges.

(5) SEPA shall pass on to the Agency any operator registry charges that it receives.

(6) A charging scheme made by the Agency may require the payment to the Agency of such charges as may from time to time be prescribed in respect of—

(a) the creation of an account in the trading scheme registry, other than one that is required to be held by an operator;

(b) the subsistence of such an account;

(c) the updating of information provided to the Agency in relation to such an account.

(7) In this section—

'allowance' and 'operator' have the same meaning as in the regulations;

'charging scheme' and 'prescribed' have the same meaning as in section 41;

'trading scheme registry' means the registry established under the regulations.]

42 Approval of charging schemes

(1) Before submitting a proposed charging scheme to the Secretary of State for his approval, a new Agency shall, in such manner as it considers appropriate for bringing it to the attention of persons likely to be affected by the scheme, publish a notice—

(a) setting out its proposals; and

(b) specifying the period within which representations or objections with respect to the proposals may be made to the Secretary of State.

(2) Where any proposed charging scheme has been submitted to the Secretary of State for his approval, he shall, in determining whether or not to approve the scheme or to approve it subject to modifications,—

(a) consider any representations or objections duly made to him and not withdrawn; and

(b) have regard to the matter specified in subsection (3) below.

(3) The matter mentioned in subsection (2)(b) above is the desirability of ensuring that, in the case of each of the descriptions of environmental licence specified in the paragraphs of the definition of that expression in section 56 below, the amounts recovered by the new Agency in question by way of charges prescribed by charging schemes are the amounts which, taking one year with another, need to be recovered by that new Agency to meet such of the costs and expenses (whether of a revenue or capital nature)—

(a) which it incurs in carrying out its functions,

(b) in the case of environmental licences which are authorisations under section 13(1) of the Radioactive Substances Act 1993—

(i) which the Food Standards Agency incurs in carrying out its functions under or in consequence of that Act, and

(ii) [...]

as the Secretary of State may consider it appropriate to attribute to the carrying out of those functions in relation to activities to which environmental licences of the description in question relate.

(4) Without prejudice to the generality of the expression 'costs and expenses', in determining for the purposes of subsection (3) above the amounts of the costs and expenses which the Secretary of State considers it appropriate to attribute to the carrying out of a new Agency's or the Food Standards Agency's or the Secretary of State's functions in relation to the activities to which environmental licences of any particular description relate, the Secretary of State—

(a) shall take into account any determination of the new Agency's financial duties under section 44 below; and

(b) may include amounts in respect of the depreciation of, and the provision of a return on, such assets as are held by the new Agency, the Food Standards Agency or the Secretary of State, as the case may be, for purposes connected with the carrying out of the functions in question.

(5)–(6) ...

(7) The consent of the Treasury shall be required for the giving of approval to a charging scheme submitted by the Agency.

(8) It shall be the duty of a new Agency to take such steps as it considers appropriate for bringing the provisions of any charging scheme made by it which is for the time being in force to the attention of persons likely to be affected by them.

(9) If and to the extent that any sums recovered by a new Agency by way of charges prescribed by charging schemes may fairly be regarded as so recovered for the purpose of recovering the amount required to meet (whether in whole or in part)—

(a) [such of the costs and expenses incurred by the Food Standards Agency as fall within subsection (3) above]

those sums shall be paid by that new Agency to the Food Standards Agency.

(10) For the purposes of subsection (9) above, any question as to the extent to which any sums may fairly be regarded as recovered for the purpose of recovering the amount required to meet the costs and expenses falling within that subsection shall be determined by the Secretary of State.

(11) In this section 'charging scheme' has the same meaning as in section 39 above.

Incidental power to impose charges

43 Incidental power of the new Agencies to impose charges

Without prejudice to the generality of its powers by virtue of section 37(1)(a) above and subject to any such express provision with respect to charging by a new Agency as is contained in the preceding provisions of this Chapter or any other enactment, each new Agency shall have the power to fix and recover charges for services and facilities provided in the course of carrying out its functions.

General financial provisions

44 General financial duties

(1) The appropriate Ministers may—

(a) after consultation with a new Agency, and

(b) in the case of the Agency only, with the approval of the Treasury,

determine the financial duties of that new Agency; and different determinations may be made for different functions and activities of the new Agency.

(2) The appropriate Ministers shall give a new Agency notice of every determination of its financial duties under this section, and such a determination may—

(a) relate to a period beginning before, on, or after, the date on which it is made;

(b) contain supplemental provisions; and

(c) be varied by a subsequent determination.

(3) The appropriate Minister may, after consultation with . . . a new Agency, [and, in the case of the Agency only, after consultation with Treasury,] give a direction to that new Agency requiring it to pay to him an amount equal to the whole or such part as may be specified in the direction of any sum, or any sum of a description, so specified which is or has been received by that new Agency.

(4) Where it appears to the appropriate Minister that a new Agency has a surplus, whether on capital or revenue account, he may, after consultation with the Treasury [(in the case of the Agency only)] and the new Agency, direct the new Agency to pay to him such amount not exceeding the amount of that surplus as may be specified in the direction.

(5) . . .

47 Grants to the new Agencies

The appropriate Minister may, [in the case of the Agency only,] with the approval of the Treasury, make to a new Agency grants of such amounts, and on such terms, as he thinks fit.

Information

51 Provision of information by the new Agencies

(1) A new Agency shall furnish the appropriate Minister with all such information as he may reasonably require relating to—

(a) the new Agency's property;

(b) the carrying out and proposed carrying out of its functions; and

(c) its responsibilities generally.

(2) Information required under this section shall be furnished in such form and manner, and be accompanied or supplemented by such explanations, as the appropriate Minister may reasonably require.

(3) The information which a new Agency may be required to furnish to the appropriate Minister under this section shall include information which, although it is not in the possession of the new Agency or would not otherwise come into the possession of the new Agency, is information which it is reasonable to require the new Agency to obtain.

(4) A requirement for the purposes of this section shall be contained in a direction which—

(a) may describe the information to be furnished in such manner as the Minister giving the direction considers appropriate; and

(b) may require the information to be furnished on a particular occasion, in particular circumstances or from time to time.

(5) For the purposes of this section a new Agency shall—

(a) permit any person authorised for the purpose by the appropriate Minister to inspect and make copies of the contents of any accounts or other records of the new Agency; and

(b) give such explanation of them as that person or the appropriate Minister may reasonably require.

52 Annual report

(1) As soon as reasonably practicable after the end of each financial year, each new Agency shall prepare a report on its activities during that year and shall send a copy of that report to each of the appropriate Ministers.

(2) Every such report shall set out any directions under section 40 above which have been given to the new Agency in question during the year to which the report relates, other than directions given under subsection (1) of that section which are identified to that new Agency in writing by the appropriate Minister as being directions the disclosure of which would, in his opinion, be contrary to the interests of national security.

(3) The Secretary of State shall lay a copy of every such report before each House of Parliament and shall arrange for copies of every such report to be published in such manner as he considers appropriate.

(4) A new Agency's annual report shall be in such form and contain such information as may be specified in any direction given to the new Agency by the appropriate Ministers.

Supplemental provisions

53 Inquiries and other hearings

(1) Without prejudice to any other provision of this Act or any other enactment by virtue of which an inquiry or other hearing is authorised or required to be held, the appropriate Minister may cause an inquiry or other hearing to be held if it appears to him expedient to do so—

(a) in connection with any of the functions of a new Agency; or

(b) in connection with any of his functions in relation to a new Agency.

(2) Subsections (2) to (5) of section 250 of the Local Government Act 1972 (which contain supplementary provisions with respect to local inquiries held in pursuance of that section) shall apply to inquiries or other hearings under this section or any other enactment—

(a) in connection with any of the functions of the Agency, or

(b) in connection with any functions of the Secretary of State or the Minister in relation to the Agency,

as they apply to inquiries under that section, but taking the reference in subsection (4) of that section to a local authority as including a reference to the Agency.

(3) . . .

54 Appearance in legal proceedings

In England and Wales, a person who is authorised by the Agency to prosecute on its behalf in proceedings before a magistrates' court shall be entitled to prosecute in any such proceedings although not of counsel or a solicitor.

55 Continuity of exercise of functions: the new Agencies

. . .

56 Interpretation of Part I

(1) In this Part of this Act, except where the context otherwise requires—

. . .

'the 1990 Act' means the Environmental Protection Act 1990;

'the 1991 Act' means the Water Resources Act 1991;

'the appropriate Minister'—

(a) in the case of the Agency, means the Secretary of State or the Minister; and

(b) . . .

'the appropriate Ministers'—

(a) in the case of the Agency, means the Secretary of State and the Minister; and

(b) . . .

'conservancy authority' has the meaning given by section 221 (1) of the 1991 Act;

'costs' includes—

(a) costs to any person; and

(b) costs to the environment;

'disposal authority'—

(a) in the application of this Part in relation to the Agency, has the same meaning as it has in Part I of the Control of Pollution Act 1974 by virtue of section 30(1) of that Act; and

(b) . . .

['the environment' means all, or any, of the following media, namely, the air, water and land (and the medium of air includes the air within buildings and the air within other natural or man-made structures above or below ground);]

'environmental licence', in the application of this Part in relation to the Agency, means any of the following—

(a) registration of a person as a carrier of controlled waste under section 2 of the Control of Pollution (Amendment) Act 1989,

[(aa) a permit granted by the Agency under regulations under section 2 of the Pollution Prevention and Control Act 1999;]

(b) an authorisation under Part I of the 1990 Act, other than any such authorisation granted by a local enforcing authority,

(c) a waste management licence under Part II of that Act,

(d) a licence under Chapter II of Part II of the 1991 Act,

(e) a consent for the purposes of section 88(1)(a), 89(4)(a) or 90 of that Act,

(f) registration under the Radioactive Substances Act 1993,

(g) an authorisation under that Act,

(h) registration of a person as a broker of controlled waste under the Waste Management Licensing Regulations 1994,

(j) registration in respect of [an activity which requires notification under regulation 18AA of those Regulations or] an activity falling within paragraph 45(1) or (2) of Schedule 3 to those Regulations],

[(k) a greenhouse gas emissions permit granted under the Greenhouse Gas Emissions Trading Scheme Regulations 2005,]

so far as having effect in relation to England and Wales;

. . .

'flood defence functions', in relation to the Agency, has the same meaning as in the 1991 Act;

'harbour authority' has the meaning given by section 221(1) of the 1991 Act;

. . .

'the Minister' means the Minister of Agriculture, Fisheries and Food;

'the Ministers' means the Secretary of State and the Minister;

'navigation authority' has the meaning given by section 221(1) of the 1991 Act;

'new Agency' means the Agency . . .

. . .

. . .

'waste regulation authority'—

(a) in the application of this Part in relation to the Agency, means any authority in England or Wales which, by virtue of section 30(1) of the 1990 Act, is a waste regulation authority for the purposes of Part II of that Act; and

(b) . . .

(2) . . .

(3) Where by virtue of any provision of this Part any function of a Minister of the Crown is exercisable concurrently by different Ministers, that function shall also be exercisable jointly by any two or more of those Ministers.

PART III NATIONAL PARKS

Establishment of National Park authorities

63 Establishment of National Park authorities

(1) The Secretary of State may—

(a) in the case of any National Park for which there is an existing authority, or

(b) in connection with the designation of any area as a new such Park,

by order establish an authority (to be known as 'a National Park authority') to carry out in relation to that Park the functions conferred on such an authority by or under this Part.

(2) An order under this section may provide, in relation to any National Park for which there is an existing authority—

(a) for the existing authority to cease to have any functions in relation to that Park as from the time when a National Park authority becomes the local planning authority, for that Park;

(b) for such (if any) of the functions of the existing authority as, by virtue of this Part, are not as from that time to be functions of the National Park authority for that Park to become functions of the person on whom they would be conferred if the area in question were not in a National Park; and

(c) for the winding up of the existing authority and for that authority to cease to exist, or to be dissolved, as from such time as may be specified in the order.

(3) Subject to any order under subsection (4) below, where there is a variation of the area of a National Park for which there is or is to be a National Park authority, the Park for which that authority is or is to be the authority shall be deemed, as from the time when the variation takes effect, to be that area as varied.

(4) Where provision is made for the variation of the area of a National Park for which there is or is to be a National Park authority, the Secretary of State may by order make such transitional provision as he thinks fit with respect to—

(a) any functions which, in relation to any area that becomes part of the National Park, are by virtue of the variation to become functions of that authority; and

(b) any functions which, in relation to any area that ceases to be part of the National Park, are by virtue of the variation to become functions of a person other than that authority.

(5) Schedule 7 to this Act shall have effect with respect to National Park authorities.

64 Natural Park authorities in Wales

. . .

Functions of National Park authorities

65 General purposes and powers

(1) This Part so far as it relates to the establishment and functions of National Park authorities shall have effect for the purposes specified in section 5(1) of the National Parks and Access to the Countryside Act 1949 (purposes of conserving and enhancing the natural beauty, wildlife and cultural heritage of National Parks and of promoting opportunities for the understanding and enjoyment of the special qualities of those Parks by the public).

(2) Sections 37 and 38 of the Countryside Act 1968 (general duties as to the protection of interests of the countryside and the avoidance of pollution) shall apply to National Park authorities as they apply to local authorities.

(3) The functions of a National Park authority in the period (if any) between the time when it is established and the time when it becomes the local planning authority for the relevant Park shall be confined to the taking of such steps as the authority, after consultation with the Secretary of State and any existing authority for that Park, considers appropriate for securing that it is able properly to carry out its functions after that time.

(4) In the application of subsection (3) above in the case of a National Park authority established in relation to a National Park in Wales, the reference to any existing authority for that Park shall have effect as respects consultation carried out during so much of that period as falls before 1st April 1996 as including a reference to any principal council whose area is wholly or partly comprised in that Park.

(5) The powers of a National Park authority shall include power to do anything which, in the opinion of that authority, is calculated to facilitate, or is conducive or incidental to—

(a) the accomplishment of the purposes mentioned in subsection (1) above; or

(b) the carrying out of any functions conferred on it by virtue of any other enactment.

(6) The powers conferred on a National Park authority by subsection (5) above shall not include either—

(a) power to do anything in contravention of any restriction imposed by virtue of this Part in relation to any express power of the authority; or

(b) a power to raise money (whether by borrowing or otherwise) in a manner which is not authorised apart from that subsection;

but the things that may be done in exercise of those powers shall not be treated as excluding anything by reason only that it involves the expenditure, borrowing or lending of money or the acquisition or disposal of any property or rights.

(7) Schedule 8 to this Act shall have effect with respect to the supplemental and incidental powers of a National Park authority.

66 National Park Management Plans

(1) Subject to subsection (2) below, every National Park authority shall, within three years after its operational date, prepare and publish a plan, to be known as a National Park Management Plan, which formulates its policy for the management of the relevant Park and for the carrying out of its functions in relation to that Park.

(2) A National Park authority for a Park wholly or mainly comprising any area which, immediately before the authority's operational date, was or was included in an area for which there was a National Park Plan prepared and published under paragraph 18 of Schedule 17 to the 1972 Act (National Park plans) shall not be required to prepare a Management Plan under subsection (1) above if, within six months of that date, it adopts the existing National Park Plan as its Management Plan and publishes notice that it has done so.

(3) Where a National Park authority is proposing to adopt a plan under subsection (2) above, it may review the plan before adopting it and shall do so if the plan would have fallen to be reviewed under paragraph 18 of Schedule 17 to the 1972 Act in the period of twelve months beginning with the authority's operational date.

(4) A National Park authority shall review its National Park Management Plan within the period of five years of its operational date and, after the first review, at intervals of not more than five years.

(5) Where a National Park authority has adopted a plan under subsection (2) above as its National Park Management Plan and has not reviewed that Plan before adopting it, the first review of that Plan under subsection (4) above shall take place no later than the time when the adopted plan would otherwise have fallen to be reviewed under paragraph 18 of Schedule 17 to the 1972 Act.

(6) Where a National Park authority reviews any plan under this section, it shall—

(a) determine on that review whether it would be expedient to amend the plan and what (if any) amendments would be appropriate;

(b) make any amendments that it considers appropriate; and

(c) publish a report on the review specifying any amendments made.

(7) A National Park authority which is proposing to publish, adopt or review any plan under this section shall—

(a) give notice of the proposal to every principal council whose area is wholly or partly comprised in the relevant Park and, according to whether that Park is in England or in Wales, to Natural England or to the Countryside Council for Wales;

(b) send a copy of the plan, together (where appropriate) with any proposed amendments of the plan, to every body to which notice of the proposal is required to be given by paragraph (a) above; and

(c) take into consideration any observations made by any such body.

(8) A National Park authority shall send to the Secretary of State a copy of every plan, notice or report which it is required to publish under this section.

(9) In this section 'operational date', in relation to a National Park authority, means the date on which the authority becomes the local planning authority for the relevant Park.

69 Planning authority functions under the Wildlife and Countryside Act 1981

(1) A National Park authority which is the local planning authority for any National Park, and not any other authority, shall have all the functions under the Wildlife and Countryside Act 1981 which are conferred as respects that Park on a planning authority of any description.

(2) Accordingly—

(a) a National Park authority shall be the relevant authority for the purposes of sections 39, 41 and 50 of that Act (management agreements and duties of agriculture Ministers in relation to the countryside) as respects any land in any National Park for which that authority is the local planning authority; and

(b) section 52(2) of that Act (construction of references to a local planning authority) shall not apply as respects any National Park for which a National Park authority is the local planning authority.

(3) Section 43 of that Act (maps of National Parks) shall have effect in accordance with the preceding provisions of this section—

(a) in the case of a National Park designated after the commencement of this section, as if the relevant date for the purposes of that section were the date on which a National Park authority becomes the local planning authority for the Park; and

(b) in any other case, as if the function of reviewing and revising any map of a part of the Park in question included a power, in pursuance of the review and revisions, to consolidate that map with other maps prepared under that section as respects other parts of that Park.

PART IV AIR QUALITY

80 National air quality strategy

(1) The Secretary of State shall as soon as possible prepare and publish a statement (in this Part referred to as 'the strategy') containing policies with respect to the assessment or management of the quality of air.

(2) The strategy may also contain policies for implementing—

(a) obligations of the United Kingdom under the Community Treaties, or

(b) international agreements to which the United Kingdom is for the time being a party, so far as relating to the quality of air.

(3) The strategy shall consist of or include—

(a) a statement which relates to the whole of Great Britain; or

(b) two or more statements which between them relate to every part of Great Britain.

(4) The Secretary of State—

(a) shall keep under review his policies with respect to the quality of air; and

(b) may from time to time modify the strategy.

(5) Without prejudice to the generality of what may be included in the strategy, the strategy must include statements with respect to—

(a) standards relating to the quality of air;

(b) objectives for the restriction of the levels at which particular substances are present in the air; and

(c) measures which are to be taken by local authorities and other persons for the purpose of achieving those objectives.

(6) In preparing the strategy or any modification of it, the Secretary of State shall consult—

(a) the appropriate new Agency;

(b) such bodies or persons appearing to him to be representative of the interests of local government as he may consider appropriate;

(c) such bodies or persons appearing to him to be representative of the interests of industry as he may consider appropriate; and

(d) such other bodies or persons as he may consider appropriate.

(7) Before publishing the strategy or any modification of it, the Secretary of State—

(a) shall publish a draft of the proposed strategy or modification, together with notice of a date before which, and an address at which, representations may be made to him concerning the draft so published; and

(b) shall take into account any such representations which are duly made and not withdrawn.

81 Functions of the new Agencies

(1) In discharging its pollution control functions, each new Agency shall have regard to the strategy.

(2) In this section 'pollution control functions', in relation to a new Agency, means—

(a) in the case of the Agency, the functions conferred on it by or under the enactments specified in section 5(5) above; or

(b) . . .

82 Local authority reviews

(1) Every local authority shall from time to time cause a review to be conducted of the quality for the time being, and the likely future quality within the relevant period, of air within the authority's area.

(2) Where a local authority causes a review under subsection (1) above to be conducted, it shall also cause an assessment to be made of whether air quality standards and objectives are being achieved, or are likely to be achieved within the relevant period, within the authority's area.

(3) If, on an assessment under subsection (2) above, it appears that any air quality standards or objectives are not being achieved, or are not likely within the relevant period to be achieved, within the local authority's area, the local authority shall identify any parts of its area in which it appears that those standards or objectives are not likely to be achieved within the relevant period.

83 Designation of air quality management areas

(1) Where, as a result of an air quality review, it appears that nay air quality standards or objectives are not being achieved, or are not likely within the relevant period to be achieved, within the area of a local authority, the local authority shall by order designate as an air quality

management area (in this Part referred to as a 'designated area') any part of its area in which it appears that those standards or objectives are not likely to be achieved within the relevant period.

(2) An order under this section may, as a result of a subsequent air quality review,—

(a) be varied by a subsequent order; or

(b) be revoked by such an order, if it appears on that subsequent air quality review that the air quality standards and objectives are being achieved, and are likely throughout the relevant period to be achieved, within the designated area.

84 Duties of local authorities in relation to designated areas

(1) Where an order under section 83 above comes into operation, the local authority which made the order shall, for the purpose of supplementing such information as it has in relation to the designated area in question, cause an assessment to be made of—

(a) the quality for the time being, and the likely future quality within the relevant period, of air within the designated area to which the order relates; and

(b) the respects (if any) in which it appears that air quality standards or objectives are not being achieved, or are not likely within the relevant period to be achieved, within that designated area.

(2) A local authority which is required by subsection (1) above to cause an assessment to be made shall also be under a duty[1]—

(a) to prepare, before the expiration of the period of twelve months beginning with the coming into operation of the order mentioned in that subsection, a report of the results of that assessment; and

(b) to prepare, in accordance with the following provisions of this Part, a written plan (in this Part referred to as an 'action plan') for the exercise by the authority, in pursuit of the achievement of air quality standards and objectives in the designated area, of any powers exercisable by the authority.

(3) An action plan shall include a statement of the time or times by or within which the local authority in question proposes to implement each of the proposed measures comprised in the plan.

(4) A local authority may from time to time revise an action plan.

(5) This subsection applies in any case where the local authority preparing an action plan or a revision of an action plan is the council of a district in England which is comprised in an area for which there is a county council; and if, in a case where this subsection applies, the county council disagrees with the authority about the contents of the proposed action plan or revision of the action plan—

(a) either of them may refer the matter to the Secretary of State;

(b) on any such reference the Secretary of State may confirm the authority's proposed action plan or revision of the action plan, with or without modifications (whether or not proposed by the county council) or reject it and, if he rejects it, he may also exercise any powers of his under section 85 below; and

(c) the authority shall not finally determine the content of the action plan, or the revision of the action plan, except in accordance with his decision on the reference or in pursuance of directions under section 85 below.

85 Reserve powers of the Secretary of State or SEPA

(1) In this section, 'the appropriate authority' means—

(a) in relation to [local authorities in England and Wales other than local authorities in Greater London, the Secretary of State;]

[(aa) in relation to local authorities in Greater London, the Mayor of London; and]

(b) . . .

[1] Editor's note: s. 84(2)(b) disapplied for 'excellent' local authorities in England by the Local Authorities Plans and Strategies (Disapplication) (England) Order 2005 (SI 2005, No. 157), reg. 8.

(2) The appropriate authority may conduct or make, or cause to be conducted or made,—
(a) a review of the quality for the time being, and the likely future quality within the relevant period, of air within the area of any local authority;
(b) an assessment of whether air quality standards and objectives are being achieved, or are likely to be achieved within the relevant period, within the area of a local authority;
(c) an identification of any parts of the area of a local authority in which it appears that those standards or objectives are not likely to be achieved within the relevant period; or
(d) an assessment of the respects (if any) in which it appears that air quality standards or objectives are not being achieved, or are not likely within the relevant period to be achieved, within the area of a local authority or within a designated area.

(3) If it appears to the appropriate authority—
(a) that air quality standards or objectives are not being achieved, or are not likely within the relevant period to be achieved, within the area of a local authority,
(b) that a local authority has failed to discharge any duty imposed on it under or by virtue of this Part,
(c) that the actions, or proposed actions, of a local authority in purported compliance with the provisions of this Part are inappropriate in all the circumstances of the case, or
(d) that developments in science or technology, or material changes in circumstances, have rendered inappropriate the actions or proposed actions of a local authority in pursuance of this Part,

the appropriate authority may give directions to the local authority requiring it to take such steps as may be specified in the directions.

(4) Without prejudice to the generality of subsection (3) above, directions under that subsection may, in particular, require a local authority[2]—
(a) to cause an air quality review to be conducted under section 82 above in accordance with the directions;
(b) to cause an air quality review under section 82 above to be conducted afresh, whether in whole or in part, or to be so conducted with such differences as may be specified or described in the directions;
(c) to make an order under section 83 above designating as an air quality management area an area specified in, or determined in accordance with, the directions;
(d) to revoke, or modify in accordance with the directions, any order under that section;
(e) to prepare in accordance with the directions an action plan for a designated area;
(f) to modify, in accordance with the directions, any action plan prepared by the authority; or
(g) to implement, in accordance with the directions, any measures in an action plan.

[(4A) The powers of the Mayor of London to give directions under this section to a local authority in Greater London may only be exercised after consultation with the local authority concerned.

(4B) In exercising any function under subsection (2), (3) or (4) above [or (5A) below] the Mayor of London shall have regard to any guidance issued by the Secretary of State to local authorities under section 88(1) below.]

(5) The Secretary of State shall also have power to give directions to local authorities (other than local authorities in Greater London) requiring them to take such steps specified in the directions as he considers appropriate for the implementation of—
(a) any obligations of the United Kingdom under the Community Treaties, or

[2] Editor's note: modified for 'excellent' local authorities in England by the Local Authorities Plans and Strategies (Disapplication) (England) Order 2005 (SI 2005, No. 157), reg. 8.

(b) any international agreement to which the United Kingdom is for the time being a party,

so far as relating to the quality of air.

[(5A) The Mayor of London shall also have the same power to give directions to local authorities in Greater London as the Secretary of State has under subsection (5) above in relation to other local authorities.]

(6) Any direction given under this section shall be published in such manner as the body or person giving it considers appropriate for the purpose of bringing the matters to which it relates to the attention of persons likely to be affected by them; and—

(a) copies of the direction shall be made available to the public; and

(b) notice shall be given—

(i) in the case of a direction given to a local authority in England and Wales, in the London Gazette, or

(ii) . . .

of the giving of the direction and of where a copy of the direction may be obtained.

[(6A) The Mayor of London shall send a copy of any direction he gives under this section to the Secretary of State.]

(7) It is the duty of a local authority to comply with any direction given to it under or by virtue of this Part.

86 Functions of county councils for areas for which there are district councils

(1) This section applies in any case where a district in England for which there is a district council is comprised in an area for which there is a county council; and in this paragraph—

(a) any reference to the county council is a reference to the council of that area; and

(b) any reference to a district council is a reference to the council of a district comprised in that area.

(2) The county council may make recommendations to a district council with respect to the carrying out of—

(a) any particular air quality review,

(b) any particular assessment under section 82 or 84 above, or

(c) the preparation of any particular action plan or revision of an action plan, and the district council shall take into account any such recommendations.

(3) Where a district council is preparing an action plan, the county council shall, within the relevant period, submit to the district council proposals for the exercise (so far as relating to the designated area) by the county council, in pursuit of the achievement of air quality standards and objectives, of any powers exercisable by the county council.

(4) Where the county council submits proposals to a district council in pursuance of subsection (3) above, it shall also submit a statement of the time or times by or within which it proposes to implement each of the proposals.

(5) An action plan shall include a statement of—

(a) any proposals submitted pursuant to subsection (3) above; and

(b) any time or times set out in the statement submitted pursuant to subsection (4) above.

(6) If it appears to the Secretary of State—

(a) that air quality standards or objectives are not being achieved, or are not likely within the relevant period to be achieved, within the area of a district council,

(b) that the county council has failed to discharge any duty imposed on it under or by virtue of this Part,

(c) that the actions, or proposed actions, of the county council in purported compliance with the provisions of this Part are inappropriate in all the circumstances of the case, or

(d) that developments in science or technology, or material changes in circumstances, have rendered inappropriate the actions or proposed actions of the county council in pursuance of this Part,

the Secretary of State may give directions to the county council requiring it to take such steps as may be specified in the directions.

(7) Without prejudice to the generality of subsection (6) above, directions under that subsection may, in particular, require the county council—

(a) to submit, in accordance with the directions, proposals pursuant to subsection (3) above or a statement pursuant to subsection (4) above;

(b) to modify, in accordance with the directions, any proposals or statement submitted by the county council pursuant to subsection (3) or (4) above;

(c) to submit any proposals or statement so modified to the district council in question pursuant to subsection (3) or (4) above; or

(d) to implement, in accordance with the directions, any measures included in an action plan.

(8) The Secretary of State shall also have power to give directions to county councils for areas for which there are district councils requiring them to take such steps specified in the directions as he considers appropriate for the implementation of—

(a) any obligations of the United Kingdom under the Community Treaties, or

(b) any international agreement to which the United Kingdom is for the time being a party,

so far as relating to the quality of air.

(9) Any direction given under this section shall be published in such manner as the Secretary of State considers appropriate for the purpose of bringing the matters to which it relates to the attention of persons likely to be affected by them; and—

(a) copies of the direction shall be made available to the public; and

(b) notice of the giving of the direction, and of where a copy of the direction may be obtained, shall be given in the London Gazette.

(10) It is the duty of a county council for an area for which there are district councils to comply with any direction given to it under or by virtue of this Part.

[86A Functions exercisable by the Mayor of London

(1) Where a local authority in Greater London is preparing an action plan, the Mayor of London (referred to in this section as 'the Mayor') shall, within the relevant period, submit to the authority proposals for the exercise (so far as relating to the designated area) by the Mayor, in pursuit of the achievement of air quality standards and objectives, of any powers exercisable by the Mayor.

(2) Where the Mayor submits proposals to a local authority in pursuance of subsection (1) above, he shall also submit a statement of the time or times by or within which he proposes to implement each of the proposals.

(3) An action plan shall include a statement of—

(a) any proposals submitted pursuant to subsection (1) above; and

(b) any time or times set out in the statement submitted pursuant to subsection (2) above.]

87 Regulations for the purposes of Part IV

(1) Regulations may make provision—

(a) for, or in connection with, implementing the strategy;

(b) for, or in connection with, implementing—

(i) obligations of the United Kingdom under the Community Treaties, or

(ii) international agreements to which the United Kingdom is for the time being a party,

so far as relating to the quality of air; or

(c) otherwise with respect to the assessment or management of the quality of air

(2) Without prejudice to the generality of subsection (1) above, regulations under that subsection may make provision—

(a) prescribing standards relating to the quality of air;

(b) prescribing objectives for the restriction of the levels at which particular substances are present in the air;

(c) conferring powers or imposing duties on local authorities;

(d) for or in connection with—

(i) authorising local authorities (whether by agreements or otherwise) to exercise any functions of a Minister of the Crown on his behalf,

(ii) directing that functions of a Minister of the Crown shall be exercisable concurrently with local authorities; or

(iii) transferring functions of a Minister of the Crown to local authorities;

(e) prohibiting or restricting, or for or in connection with prohibiting or restricting,—

(i) the carrying on of prescribed activities, or

(ii) the access of prescribed vehicles or mobile equipment to prescribed areas,

whether generally or in prescribed circumstances;

(f) for or in connection with the designation of air quality management areas by orders made by local authorities in such cases or circumstances not falling within section 83 above as may be prescribed;

(g) for the application, with or without modifications, of any provisions of this Part in relation to areas designated by virtue of paragraph (f) above or in relation to orders made by virtue of that paragraph;

(h) with respect to—

(i) air quality reviews;

(ii) assessments under this Part;

(iii) orders designating air quality management areas; or

(iv) action plans;

(j) prescribing measures which are to be adopted by local authorities (whether in action plans or otherwise) or other persons in pursuance of the achievement of air quality standards or objectives;

(k) for or in connection with the communication to the public of information relating to quality for the time being, or likely future quality, of the air;

(l) for or in connection with the obtaining by local authorities from any person of information which is reasonably necessary for the discharge of functions conferred or imposed on them under or by virtue of this Part;

(m) for or in connection with the recovery by a local authority from prescribed persons in prescribed circumstances, and in such manner as may be prescribed, of costs incurred by the authority in discharging functions conferred or imposed on the authority under or by virtue of this Part;

(n) for a person who contravenes, or fails to comply with, any prescribed provision of the regulations to be guilty of an offence and liable on summary conviction to a fine not exceeding level 5 on the guilty of an offence and liable on summary conviction to a fine not exceeding level 5 on the standard scale or such lower level on that scale as may be prescribed in relation to the offence;

(o) for or in connection with arrangements under which a person may discharge any liability to conviction for a prescribed offence by payment of a penalty of a prescribed amount;

(p) for or in connection with appeals against determinations or decisions made, notices given or served, or other things done under or by virtue of the regulations.

(3) Without prejudice to the generality of paragraph (h) of subsection (2) above, the provision that may be made by virtue of that paragraph includes provision for or in connection with any of the following, that is to say—

(a) the scope or form of a review or assessment;

(b) the scope, content or form of an action plan;
(c) the time at which, period within which, or manner in which a review or assessment is to be carried out or an action plan is to be prepared;
(d) the methods to be employed—
(i) in carrying out reviews or assessments; or
(ii) in monitoring the effectiveness of action plans;
(e) the factors to be taken into account in preparing action plans;
(f) the actions which must be taken by local authorities or other persons in consequence of reviews, assessments or action plans;
(g) requirements for consultation;
(h) the treatment of representations or objections duly made;
(j) the publication of, or the making available to the public of, or of copies of,—
(i) the results, or reports of the results, of reviews or assessments; or
(ii) orders or action plans;
(k) requirements for—
(i) copies of any such reports, orders or action plans, or
(ii) prescribed information, in such form as may be prescribed, relating to reviews or assessments,
to be sent to the Secretary of State or to the appropriate new Agency.

(4) In determining—
(a) any appeal against, or reference or review of, a decision of a local authority under or by virtue of regulations under this Part, or
(b) any application transmitted from a local authority under or by virtue of any such regulations,
the body or person making the determination shall be bound by any direction given by a Minister of the Crown . . . to the local authority to the same extent as the local authority.

(5) The provisions of any regulations under this Part may include—
(a) provision for anything that may be prescribed by the regulations to be determined under the regulations and for anything falling to be so determined to be determined by such persons, in accordance with such procedure and by reference to such matters, and to the opinion of such persons, as may be prescribed;
(b) different provision for different cases, including different provision in relation to different persons, circumstances, areas or localities; and
(c) such supplemental, consequential, incidental or transitional provision (including provision amending any enactment or any instrument made under any enactment) as the Secretary of State considers appropriate.

(6) Nothing in regulations under this Part shall authorise any person other than a constable in uniform to stop a vehicle on any road.

(7) Before making any regulations under this Part, the Secretary of State shall consult—
(a) the appropriate new Agency;
(b) such bodies or persons appearing to him to be representative of the interests of local government as he may consider appropriate;
(c) such bodies or persons appearing to him to be representative of the interests of industry as he may consider appropriate; and
(d) such other bodies or persons as he may consider appropriate.

(8) Any power conferred by this Part to make regulations shall be exercisable by statutory instrument . . .

88 Guidance for the purposes of Part IV

(1) The Secretary of State may issue guidance to local authorities with respect to, or in connection with, the exercise of any of the powers conferred, or the discharge of any of the duties imposed, on those authorities by or under this Part.

(2) A local authority, in carrying out any of its functions under or by virtue of this Part, shall have regard to any guidance issued by the Secretary of State under this Part.

(3) This section shall apply in relation to county councils for areas for which there are district councils as it applies in relation to local authorities.

89 ...

90 Supplemental provisions

Schedule 11 to this Act shall have effect.

91 Interpretation of Part IV

(1) In this Part—

'action plan' shall be construed in accordance with section 84(2)(b) above;

'air quality objectives' means objectives prescribed by virtue of section 87(2)(b) above;

'air quality review' means a review under section 82 or 85 above;

'air quality standards' means standards prescribed by virtue of section 87(2)(a) above;

'the appropriate new Agency' means—

(a) in relation to England and Wales, the Agency;

(b) ...

'designated area' has the meaning given by section 83(1) above;

'local authority', in relation to England and Wales, means—

(a) any unitary authority,

(b) any district council, so far as it is not a unitary authority,

(c) the Common Council of the City of London and, as respects the Temples, the Sub-Treasurer of the Inner Temple and the Under-Treasurer of the Middle Temple respectively...;

'new Agency' means the Agency...;

'prescribed' means prescribed, or of a description prescribed, by or under regulations;

'regulations' means regulations made by the Secretary of State;

'the relevant period', in the case of any provision of this Part, means such period as may be prescribed for the purposes of that provision;

'the strategy' has the meaning given by section 80(1) above;

'unitary authority' means—

(a) the council of a county, so far as it is the council of an area for which there are no district councils;

(b) the council of any district comprised in an area for which there is no county council;

(c) the council of a London borough;

(d) the council of a county borough in Wales.

(2) Any reference in this Part to it appearing that any air quality standards or objectives are not likely within the relevant period to be achieved includes a reference to it appearing that those standards or objectives are likely within that period not to be achieved.

PART V MISCELLANEOUS, GENERAL AND SUPPLEMENTAL PROVISIONS

Waste

93 Producer responsibility: general

(1) For the purpose of promoting or securing an increase in the re-use, recovery or recycling of products or materials, the Secretary of State may by regulations make provision for imposing producer responsibility obligations on such persons, and in respect of such products or materials, as may be prescribed.

(2) The power of the Secretary of State to make regulations shall be exercisable only after consultation with bodies or persons appearing to him to be representative of bodies or persons whose interests are, or are likely to be, substantially affected by the regulations which he proposes to make.

(3) Except in the case of regulations for the implementation of—

(a) any obligations of the United Kingdom under the Community Treaties, or

(b) any international agreement to which the United Kingdom is for the time being a party,

the power to make regulations shall be exercisable only where the Secretary of State, after such consultation as is required by subsection (2) above, is satisfied as to the matters specified in subsection (6) below.

(4) The powers conferred by subsection (1) above shall also be exercisable, in a case falling within paragraph (a) or (b) of subsection (3) above, for the purpose of sustaining at least a minimum level of (rather than promoting or securing an increase in) re-use, recovery or recycling of products or materials.

(5) In making regulations by virtue of paragraph (a) or (b) of subsection (3) above, the Secretary of State shall have regard to the matters specified in subsection (6) below; and in its application in relation to the power conferred by virtue of subsection (4) above, subsection (6) below shall have effect as if—

(a) any reference to an increase in the re-use, recovery or recycling of products or materials were a reference to the sustaining of at least a minimum level of re-use, recovery or recycling of the products or materials in question, and

(b) any reference to the production of environmental or economic benefits included a reference to the sustaining of at least a minimum level of any such existing benefits,

and any reference in this section or section 94 below to securing or achieving any such benefits shall accordingly include a reference to sustaining at least a minimum level of any such existing benefits.

(6) The matters mentioned in subsections (3) and (5) above are—

(a) that the proposed exercise of the power would be likely to result in an increase in the re-use, recovery or recycling of the products or materials in question;

(b) that any such increase would produce environmental or economic benefits;

(c) that those benefits are significant as against the likely costs resulting from the imposition of the proposed producer responsibility obligation;

(d) that the burdens imposed on businesses by the regulations are the minimum necessary to secure those benefits; and

(e) that those burdens are imposed on persons most able to make a contribution to the achievement of the relevant targets—

(i) having regard to the desirability of acting fairly between persons who manufacture, process, distribute or supply products or materials; and

(ii) taking account of the need to ensure that the proposed producer responsibility obligation is so framed as to be effective in achieving the purposes for which it is to be imposed;

but nothing in sub-paragraph (i) of paragraph (e) above shall be taken to prevent regulations imposing a producer responsibility obligation on any class or description of person to the exclusion of any others.

(7) The Secretary of State shall have a duty to exercise the power to make regulations in the manner which he considers best calculated to secure that the exercise does not have the effect of restricting, distorting or preventing competition or, if it is likely to have any such effect, that the effect is no greater than is necessary for achieving the environmental or economic benefits mentioned in subsection (6) above.

(8) In this section—

'prescribed' means prescribed in regulations;

'product' and 'material' include a reference to any product or material (as the case may be) at a time when it becomes, or has become, waste;

'producer responsibility obligation' means the steps which are required to be taken by relevant persons of the classes or descriptions to which the regulations in question apply in order to secure attainment of the targets specified or described in the regulations;

'recovery', in relation to products or materials, includes—

(a) composting, or any other form of transformation by biological process, of products or materials; or

(b) the obtaining, by any means, of energy from products or materials; 'regulations' means regulations under this section;

'relevant persons', in the case of any regulations or any producer responsibility obligation, means persons of the class or description to which the producer responsibility obligation imposed by the regulations applies;

'relevant targets' means the targets specified or described in the regulations imposing the producer responsibility obligation in question;

and regulations may prescribe, in relation to prescribed products or materials, activities, or the activities, which are to be regarded for the purposes of this section and sections 94 and 95 below or any regulations as re-use, recovery or recycling of those products or materials.

(9) The power to make regulations shall be exercisable by statutory instrument.

(10)–(12) . . .

94 Producer responsibility: supplementary provisions

(1) Without prejudice to the generality of section 93 above, regulations may, in particular, make provision for or with respect to—

(a) the classes or descriptions of person to whom the producer responsibility obligation imposed by the regulations applies;

(b) the classes or descriptions of products or materials in respect of which the obligation applies;

(c) the targets which are to be achieved with respect to the proportion (whether by weight, volume or otherwise) of the products or materials in question which are to be re-used, recovered or recycled, whether generally or in any prescribed way;

(d) particulars of the obligation imposed by the regulations;

(e) the registration of persons who are subject to a producer responsibility obligation and who are not members of registered exemption schemes, the imposition of requirements in connection with such registration, the variation of such requirements, the making of applications for such registration, the period for which any such registration is to remain in force and the cancellation of any such registration;

(f) the approval, or withdrawal of approval, of exemption schemes by the Secretary of State;

(g) the imposition of requirements on persons who are not members of registered exemption schemes to furnish certificates of compliance to the appropriate Agency;

(h) the approval of persons by the appropriate Agency for the purpose of issuing certificates of compliance;

(j) the registration of exemption schemes, the imposition of conditions in connection with such registration, the variation of such conditions, the making of applications for such registration and the period for which any such registration is to remain in force;

(k) the requirements which must be fulfilled, and the criteria which must be met, before an exemption scheme may be registered;
(l) the powers of the appropriate Agency in relation to applications received by it for registration of exemption schemes;
(m) the cancellation of the registration of an exemption scheme;
(n)–(oa) [...]
(p) the fees, or the method of determining the fees, which are to be paid to the appropriate Agency—
 (i) in respect of the approval of persons for the purpose of issuing certificates of compliance;
 (ii) on the making of an application for registration of an exemption scheme;
 (iii) in respect of the subsistence of the registration of that scheme;
 (iv) on submission to the appropriate Agency of a certificate of compliance;
 (v) on the making of an application for, or for the renewal of, registration of a person required to register under the regulations;
 (vi) in respect of the renewal of the registration of that person;
(q) appeals against the refusal of registration, the imposition of conditions in connection with registration, or the cancellation of the registration, of any exemption scheme;
(r) the procedure on any such appeal;
(s) cases, or classes of case—
 (i) in which an exemption scheme is, or is not, to be treated as registered, or
 (ii) in which a person is, or is not, to be treated as a member of a registered exemption scheme,

pending the determination or withdrawal of an appeal, and

otherwise with respect to the position of persons and exemption schemes pending such determination or withdrawal;

(t) the imposition on the appropriate Agency of a duty to monitor compliance with any of the obligations imposed by the regulations;
(u) the imposition on prescribed persons of duties to maintain records, and furnish to the Secretary of State or to the appropriate Agency returns, in such form as may be prescribed of such information as may be prescribed for any purposes of, or for any purposes connected with, or related to, sections 93 to 95 of this Act or any regulations;
(w) the imposition on the appropriate Agency of a duty to maintain, and make available for inspection by the public, a register containing prescribed information relating to registered exemption schemes or persons required to register under the regulations;
(y) the powers of entry and inspection which are exercisable by a new Agency for the purposes of its functions under the regulations;
(ya) [...]

(2) If it appears to the Secretary of State—
(a) that any action proposed to be taken by the operator of a registered exemption scheme would be incompatible with—
 (i) any obligations of the United Kingdom under the Community Treaties, or
 (ii) any international agreement to which the United Kingdom is for the time being a party, or
(b) that any action which the operator of such a scheme has power to take is required for the purpose of implementing any such obligations or agreement,

he may direct that operator not to take or, as the case may be, to take the action in question.

(3) Regulations may make provision as to which of the new Agencies is the appropriate Agency for the purposes of any function conferred or imposed by or under this section or section 93 above, or for the purposes of the exercise of that function in relation to the whole or a prescribed part of Great Britain, and may make provision for things done or omitted to be done by either new Agency in relation to any part of Great Britain to be treated for prescribed purposes as done or omitted to be done by the other of them in relation to some other part of Great Britain.

(4) Persons issuing certificates of compliance shall act in accordance with guidance issued for the purpose by the appropriate Agency, which may include guidance as to matters which are, or are not, to be treated as evidence of compliance or as evidence of non-compliance.

(5) In making any provision in relation to fees, regard shall be had to the desirability of securing that the fees received by each new Agency under the regulations are sufficient to meet the costs and expenses incurred by that Agency in the performance of its functions under the regulations.

(6) In this section—

'the appropriate Agency', subject to regulations made by virtue of subsection (3) above, means—

(a) in relation to England and Wales, the Agency;

(b) ...

'certificate of compliance' means a certificate issued by a person approved for the purpose by the appropriate Agency to the effect that that person is satisfied that the person in respect of whom the certificate is issued is complying with any producer responsibility obligation to which he is subject;

'exemptions scheme' means a scheme which is (or, if it were to be registered in accordance with the regulations, would be) a scheme whose members for the time being are, by virtue of the regulations and their membership of that scheme, exempt from the requirement to comply with the producer responsibility obligation imposed by the regulations;

'new Agency' means the Agency...;

'operator', in relations to an exemption scheme, includes any person responsible for establishing, maintaining or managing the scheme;

'registered exemption scheme' means an exemption scheme which is registered pursuant to regulations;

and expressions used in this section and in section 93 above have the same meaning in this section as they have in that section.

(6A) [...]

(7) Regulations—

(a) may make different provision for different cases;

(b) without prejudice to the generality of paragraph (a) above, may impose different producer responsibility obligations in respect of different classes or descriptions of products or materials and for different classes or descriptions of person or exemption scheme;

(c) may include incidental, consequential, supplemental or transitional provision.

(8) Any direction under this section—

(a) may include such incidental, consequential, supplemental or transitional provision as the Secretary of State considers necessary or expedient; and

(b) shall, on the application of the Secretary of State, be enforceable by injunction...

95 Producer responsibility: offences

(1) Regulations may make provision for a person who contravenes a prescribed requirement of the regulations to be guilty of an offence and liable—

(a) on summary conviction, to a fine not exceeding the statutory maximum;

(b) on conviction on indictment, to a fine.

(2) Where an offence under any provision of the regulations committed by a body corporate is proved to have been committed with the consent or connivance of, or to have been attributable to any neglect on the part of, any director, manager, secretary or other similar officer of the body corporate or a person who was purporting to act in any such capacity, he as well as the body corporate shall be guilty of that offence and shall be liable to be proceeded against and punished accordingly.

(3) Where the affairs of a body corporate are managed by its members, subsection (2) above shall apply in relation to the acts or defaults of a member in connection with his functions of management as if he were a director of the body corporate.

(4) Where the commission by any person of an offence under the regulations is due to the act or default of some other person, that other person may be charged with and convicted of the offence by virtue of this section whether or not proceedings for the offence are taken against the first-mentioned person.

(5) Expressions used in this section and in section 93 or 94 above have the same meaning in this section as they have in that section.

98 Grants for purposes conducive to conservation

(1) The appropriate Minister, with the consent of the Treasury [as respects England and Wales], may by regulations make provision for and in connection with the making of grants to persons who do, or who undertake to that Minister that they will do, anything which in the opinion of that Minister is conducive to—

- (a) the conservation or enhancement of the natural beauty or amenity of the countryside (including its flora and fauna and geological and physiographical features) or of any features of archaeological interest there; or
- (b) the promotion of the enjoyment of the countryside by the public.

(2) Regulations under this section may—

- (a) make different provision for different cases or classes of case or for different areas;
- (b) provide for grants to be made subject to conditions;
- (c) confer power on the appropriate Minister to modify, in any particular case, the conditions to which a grant would otherwise be subject, if he is satisfied that the making of that grant, subject to the conditions as so modified, is consistent with the purposes for which the regulations are made;
- (d) make provision for or in connection with the recovery of any sums paid by way of grant, or the withholding of any further payments of grant, in cases where the applicant for the grant—
  - (i) in making the application, or in furnishing any information in connection with the application, has made a statement which was false or misleading in a material respect;
  - (ii) has failed to do something which he undertook to do if the grant was made; or
  - (iii) is in breach of any condition subject to which the grant was made.

(3) The power to make regulations under this section shall be exercisable by statutory instrument . . .

(4) The powers conferred by this section are in addition to any other powers of the Secretary of State or the Minister of Agriculture, Fisheries and Food.

(5) In this section 'the appropriate Minister' means—

- (a) as respects England, the Minister of Agriculture, Fisheries and Food;
- (b) as respects Wales, the Secretary of State;
- (c) . . .

Powers of entry

108 Powers of enforcing authorities and persons authorised by them

(1) A person who appears suitable to an enforcing authority may be authorised in writing by that authority to exercise, in accordance with the terms of the authorisation, any of the

powers specified in subsection (4) below for the purpose—

(a) of determining whether any provision of the pollution control enactments in the case of that authority is being, or has been, complied with;

(b) of exercising or performing one or more of the pollution control functions of that authority; or

(c) of determining whether and, if so, how such a function should be exercised or performed.

(2) A person who appears suitable to the Agency . . . may be authorised in writing by the Agency . . . to exercise, in accordance with the terms of the authorisation, any of the powers specified in subsection (4) below for the purpose of enabling the Agency . . . to carry out any assessment or prepare any report which the Agency . . . is required to carry out or prepare under section 5(3) or 33(3) above.

(3) Subsection (2) above only applies where the Minister who required the assessment to be carried out, or the report to be prepared, has, whether at the time of making the requirement or at any later time, notified the Agency . . . that the assessment or report appears to him to relate to an incident or possible incident involving or having the potential to involve—

(a) serious pollution of the environment,

(b) serious harm to human health, or

(c) danger to life or health.

(4) The powers which a person may be authorised to exercise under subsection (1) or (2) above are—

(a) to enter at any reasonable time (or, in an emergency, at any time and, if need be, by force) any premises which he has reason to believe it is necessary for him to enter;

(b) on entering any premises by virtue of paragraph (a) above, to take with him—

(i) any other person duly authorised by the enforcing authority and, if the authorised person has reasonable cause to apprehend any serious obstruction in the execution of his duty, a constable; and

(ii) any equipment or materials required for any purpose for which the power of entry is being exercised;

(c) to make such examination and investigation as may in any circumstances be necessary;

(d) as regards any premises which he has power to enter, to direct that those premises or any part of them, or anything in them, shall be left undisturbed (whether generally or in particular respects) for so long as is reasonably necessary for the purpose of any examination or investigation under paragraph (c) above;

(e) to take such measurements and photographs and make such recordings as he considers necessary for the purpose of any examination or investigation under paragraph above;

(f) to take samples, or cause samples to be taken, of any articles or substances found in or on any premises which he has power to enter, and of the air, water or land in, on, or in the vicinity of, the premises;

(g) in the case of any article or substance found in or on any premises which he has power to enter, being an article or substance which appears to him to have caused or to be likely to cause pollution of the environment or harm to human health, to cause it to be dismantled or subjected to any process or test (but not so as to damage or destroy it, unless that is necessary);

(h) in the case of any such article or substance as is mentioned in paragraph (g) above, to take possession of it and detain it for so long as is necessary for all or any of the following purposes, namely—

(i) to examine it, or cause it to be examined, and to do, or cause to be done, to it anything which he has power to do under that paragraph;

(ii) to ensure that it is not tampered with before examination of it is completed;

(iii) to ensure that it is available for use as evidence in any proceedings for an offence under the pollution control enactments in the case of the enforcing authority under whose authorisation he acts or in any other proceedings relating to a variation notice, enforcement notice or prohibition notice under those enactments;

(j) to require any person whom he has reasonable cause to believe to be able to give any information relevant to any examination or investigation under paragraph (c) above to answer (in the absence of persons others than a person nominated by that person to be present and any persons whom the authorised person may allow to be present) such questions as the authorized person thinks fit to ask and to sign a declaration of the truth of his answers;

(k) to require the production of, or where the information is recorded in computerised form, the furnishing of extracts from, any records—

(i) which are required to be kept under the pollution control enactments for the enforcing authority under whose authorisation he acts, or

(ii) which it is necessary for him to see for the purposes of an examination or investigation under paragraph (c) above,

and to inspect and take copies of, or of any entry in, the records;

(l) to require any person to afford him such facilities and assistance with respect to any matters or things within that person's control or in relation to which that person has responsibilities as are necessary to enable the authorised person to exercise any of the powers conferred on him by this section;

(m) any other power for—

(i) a purpose falling within any paragraph of subsection (1) above, or

(ii) any such purpose as is mentioned in subsection (2) above, which is conferred by regulations made by the Secretary of State.

(5) The powers which by virtue of subsections (1) and (4) above are conferred in relation to any premises for the purpose of enabling an enforcing authority to determine whether any provision of the pollution control enactments in the case of that authority is being, or has been, complied with shall include power, in order to obtain the information on which that determination may be made,—

(a) to carry out experimental borings or other works on those premises; and

(b) to install, keep or maintain monitoring and other apparatus there.

(6) Except in an emergency, in any case where it is proposed to enter any premises used for residential purposes, or to take heavy equipment on to any premises which are to be entered, any entry by virtue of this section shall only be effected—

(a) after the expiration of at least seven days' notice of the proposed entry given to a person who appears to the authorised person in question to be in occupation of the premises in question, and

(b) either—

(i) with the consent of a person who is in occupation of those premises; or

(ii) under the authority of a warrant by virtue of Schedule 18 to this Act.

(7) Except in an emergency, where an authorised person proposes to enter any premises and—

(a) entry has been refused and he apprehends on reasonable grounds that the use of force may be necessary to effect entry, or

(b) he apprehends on reasonable grounds that entry is likely to be refused and that the use of force may be necessary to effect entry,

any entry on to those premises by virtue of this section shall only be effected under the authority of a warrant by virtue of Schedule 18 to this Act.

(8) In relation to any premises belonging to or used for the purposes of the United Kingdom Atomic Energy Authority, subsections (1) to (4) above shall have effect subject to

section 6(3) of the Atomic Energy Authority Act 1954 (which restricts entry to such premises where they have been declared to be prohibited places for the purposes of the Official Secrets Act 1911).

(9) The Secretary of State may by regulations make provision as to the procedure to be followed in connection with the taking of, and the dealing with, samples under subsection (4)(f) above.

(10) Where an authorised person proposes to exercise the power conferred by subsection (4)(g) above in the case of an article or substance found on any premises, he shall, if so requested by a person who at the time is present on and has responsibilities in relation to those premises, cause anything which is to be done by virtue of that power to be done in the presence of that person.

(11) Before exercising the power conferred by subsection (4)(g) above in the case of any article or substance, an authorised person shall consult—

(a) such persons having duties on the premises where the article or substance is to be dismantled or subjected to the process or test, and

(b) such other persons,

as appear to him appropriate for the purpose of ascertaining what dangers, if any, there may be in doing anything which he proposes to do or cause to be done under the power.

(12) No answer given by a person in pursuance of a requirement imposed under subsection (4)(j) above shall be admissible in evidence in England and Wales against that person in any proceedings...

(13) Nothing in this section shall be taken to compel the production by any person of a document of which he would on grounds of legal professional privilege be entitled to withhold production on an order for discovery in an action in the High Court...

(14) Schedule 18 to this Act shall have effect with respect to the powers of entry and related powers which are conferred by this section.

(15) In this section—

'authorised person' means a person authorised under subsection (1) or (2) above;

'emergency' means a case in which it appears to the authorised person in question—

(a) that there is an immediate risk of serious pollution of the environment or serious harm to human health, or

(b) that circumstances exist which are likely to endanger life or health,

and that immediate entry to any premises is necessary to verify the existence of that risk or those circumstances or to ascertain the cause of that risk or those circumstances or to effect a remedy;

'enforcing authority' means—

(a) the Secretary of State;

(b) the Agency;

[(ba) a waste collection authority]

(c) ...or

(d) a local enforcing authority;

'local enforcing authority' means—

(a) a local enforcing authority, within the meaning of Part I of the Environmental Protection Act 1990;

(b) a local authority, within the meaning of Part IIA of that Act, in its capacity as an enforcing authority for the purposes of that Part;

(c) a local authority for the purposes of Part IV of this Act or regulations under that Part;

[(d) a local authority for the purposes of regulations under section 2 of the Pollution Prevention and Control Act 1999 extending to England and Wales;]

'mobile plant' means plant which is designed to move or to be moved whether on roads or otherwise;

'pollution control enactments', in relation to an enforcing authority, means the enactments and instruments relating to the pollution control functions of that authority;

'pollution control functions', in relation to the Agency . . . means the functions conferred on it by or under—

(a) the Alkali, &c, Works Regulation Act 1906;
(b) . . .
(c) . . .
(d) Part I of the Health and Safety at Work etc Act 1974;
(e) Parts I, IA and II of the Control of Pollution Act 1974;
(f) the Control of Pollution (Amendment) Act 1989;
(g) Parts I, II and IIA of the Environmental Protection Act 1990 (integrated pollution control, waste on land and contaminated land);
(h) Chapter III of Part IV of the Water Industry Act 1991 (special category effluent);
(j) Part III and sections 161 to 161D of the Water Resources Act 1991;
(k) section 19 of the Clean Air Act 1993;
(l) the Radioactive Substances Act 1993;
(m) regulations made by virtue of section 2(2) of the European Communities Act 1972, to the extent that the regulations relate to pollution;

[and, in relation to the Agency, includes the functions conferred or imposed on, or transferred to, it under section 2 of the Pollution Prevention and Control Act 1999;]

'pollution control functions', in relation to a local enforcing authority, means the functions conferred or imposed on, or transferred to, that authority—

(a) by or under Part I or IIA of the Environmental Protection Act 1990;
(b) by or under regulations made by virtue of Part IV of this Act; or
(c) by or under regulations made by virtue of section 2(2) of the European Communities Act 1972, to the extent that the regulations relate to pollution;

[and, in relation to an authority in England or Wales, includes the functions conferred or imposed on, or transferred to, that authority under section 2 of the Pollution Prevention and Control Act 1999;]

'pollution control functions', in relation to the Secretary of State, means any functions which are conferred or imposed upon him by or under any enactment or instrument and which relate to the control of pollution;

['pollution control functions', in relation to a waste collection authority, means the functions [conferred or imposed on it by or under Part 2] of the Environmental Protection Act 1990;]

'premises' includes any land, vehicle, vessel or mobile plant.

['waste collection authority' shall be construed in accordance with section 30(3)(a), (b) and (bb) of the Environmental Protection Act 1990].

(16) Any power to make regulations under this section shall be exercisable by statutory instrument; and a statutory instrument containing any such regulations shall be subject to annulment pursuant to a resolution of either House of Parliament.

109 Power to deal with cause of imminent danger of serious pollution etc.

(1) Where, in the case of any article or substance found by him on any premises which he has power to enter, an authorised person has reasonable cause to believe that, in the circumstances in which he finds it, the article or substance is a cause of imminent danger of serious pollution of the environment or serious harm to human health, he may seize it and cause it to be rendered harmless (whether by destruction or otherwise).

(2) As soon as may be after any article or substance has been seized and rendered harmless under this section, the authorised person shall prepare and sign a written report giving particulars of the circumstances in which the article or substance was seized and so dealt with by him, and shall—

(a) give a signed copy of the report to a responsible person at the premises where the article or substance was found by him; and
(b) unless that person is the owner of the article or substance, also serve a signed copy of the report on the owner;

and if, where paragraph (b) above applies, the authorised person cannot after reasonable inquiry ascertain the name or address of the owner, the copy may be served on him by giving it to the person to whom a copy was given under paragraph (a) above.

(3) In this section, 'authorised person' has the same meaning as in section 10 above.

110 Offences

(1) It is an offence for a person intentionally to obstruct an authorized person in the exercise or performance of his powers or duties.

(2) It is an offence for a person, without reasonable excuse,—

(a) to fail to comply with any requirement imposed under section 108 above,

(b) to fail or refuse to provide facilities or assistance or any information or to permit any inspection reasonably required by an authorised person in the execution of his powers or duties under or by virtue of that section; or

(c) to prevent any other person from appearing before an authorised person, or answering any question to which an authorised person may require an answer, pursuant to subsection (4) of that section.

(3) It is an offence for a person falsely to pretend to be an authorised person.

(4) A person guilty of an offence under subsection (1) above shall be liable—

(a) in the case of an offence of obstructing an authorised person in the execution of his powers under section 109 above—

(i) on summary conviction, to a fine not exceeding the statutory maximum;

(ii) on conviction on indictment, to a fine or to imprisonment for a term not exceeding two years, or to both;

(b) in any other case, on summary conviction, to a fine not exceeding level 5 on the standard scale.

(5) A person guilty of an offence under subsection (2) or (3) above shall be liable on summary conviction to a fine not exceeding level 5 on the standard scale.

(6) In this section — 'authorised person' means a person authorised under section 108 above and includes a person designated under paragraph 2 of Schedule 18 to this Act; 'powers and duties' includes powers or duties exercisable by virtue of a warrant under Schedule 18 to this Act.

Evidence

111 Evidence in connection with certain pollution offences

(1) [...]

(2) Information provided or obtained pursuant to or by virtue of a condition of a relevant licence (including information so provided or obtained, or recorded, by means of any apparatus) shall be admissible in evidence in any proceedings, whether against the person subject to the condition or any other person.

(3) For the purposes of subsection (2) above, apparatus shall be presumed in any proceedings to register or record accurately, unless the contrary is shown or the relevant licence otherwise provides.

(4) Where—

(a) by virtue of a condition of a relevant licence, an entry is required to be made in any record as to the observance of any condition of the relevant licence, and

(b) the entry has not been made, that fact shall be admissible in any proceedings as evidence that that condition has not been observed.

(5) In this section—

'apparatus' includes any meter or other device for measuring, assessing, determining, recording or enabling to be recorded, the volume, temperature, radioactivity, rate, nature, origin, composition or effect of any substance, flow, discharge, emission, deposit or abstraction;

'condition of a relevant licence' includes any requirement to which a person is subject under, by virtue of or in consequence of a relevant licence;

'environmental licence' has the same meaning as it has in Part I above as it applies in relation to the Agency...;

'relevant licence' means—

(a) any environmental licence;

(b) ...

(c) ...

(d) any consent under Chapter III of Part IV of the Water Industry Act 1991 to make discharges of special category effluent; or

(e) any agreement under section 129 of that Act with respect to, or to any matter connected with, the reception or disposal of such effluent.

Information

113 Disclosure of information

(1) Notwithstanding any prohibition or restriction imposed by or under any enactment or rule of law, information of any description may be disclosed—

(a) by a new Agency to a Minister of the Crown, the other new Agency or a local enforcing authority,

(b) by a Minister of the Crown to a new Agency, another Minister of the Crown or a local enforcing authority, or

(c) by a local enforcing authority to a Minister of the Crown, a new Agency or another local enforcing authority,

for the purpose of facilitating the carrying out by either of the new Agencies of any of its functions, by any such Minister of any of his environmental functions or by any local enforcing authority of any of its relevant functions; and no person shall be subject to any civil or criminal liability in consequence of any disclosure made by virtue of this subsection.

(2) Nothing in this section shall authorise the disclosure to a local enforcing authority by a new Agency or another local enforcing authority of information—

(a) disclosure of which would, in the opinion of a Minister of the Crown, be contrary to the interests of national security; or

(b) which was obtained under or by virtue of the Statistics of Trade Act 1947 and which was disclosed to a new Agency or any of its officers by the Secretary of State.

(3) No information disclosed to any person under or by virtue of this section shall be disclosed by that person to any other person otherwise than in accordance with the provisions of this section, or any provision of any other enactment which authorises or requires the disclosure, if that information is information—

(a) which relates to a trade secret of any person or which otherwise is or might be commercially confidential in relation to any person; or

(b) whose disclosure otherwise than under or by virtue of this section would, in the opinion of a Minister of the Crown, be contrary to the interests of national security.

(4) Any authorisation by or under this section of the disclosure of information by or to any person shall also be taken to authorise the disclosure of that information by or, as the case may be, to any officer of his who is authorised by him to make the disclosure or, as the case may be, to receive the information.

(5) In this section—

'new Agency' means the Agency...;

'the environment' means all, or any, of the following media, namely, the air, water and land (and the medium of air includes the air within buildings and the air within other natural or man-made structures above or below ground);] 'environmental functions', in relation to a Minister of the Crown, means any function of that Minister, whether conferred or imposed under or by virtue of any enactment or otherwise, relating to the environment; and

'local enforcing authority' means—

(a) any local authority within the meaning of Part IIA of the Environmental Protection Act 1990, and the 'relevant functions' of such an authority are its functions under or by virtue of that Part;

[(aa) in relation to England and Wales, any local authority within the meaning of regulations under section 2 of the Pollution Prevention and Control Act 1999;]
(b) any local authority within the meaning of Part IV of this Act, and the 'relevant functions' of such an authority are its functions under or by virtue of that Part; [or]
(c) in relation to England, any county council for an area for which there are district councils, and the 'relevant functions' of such a county council are its functions under or by virtue of Part IV of this Act; or
(d) in relation to England and Wales, any local enforcing authority within the meaning of section 1(7) of the Environmental Protection Act 1990, and the 'relevant functions' of such an authority are its functions under or by virtue of Part I of that Act.

Appeals

114 Power of Secretary of State to delegate his functions of determining, or to refer matters involved in, appeals

(1) The Secretary of State may—
(a) appoint any person to exercise on his behalf, with or without payment, any function to which this paragraph applies; or
(b) refer any item to which this paragraph applies to such person as the Secretary of State may nominate for the purpose, with or without payment.

(2) The functions to which paragraph (a) of subsection (1) above applies are any of the Secretary of State's functions of determining—
(a) an appeal under—
(i) section 31A(2)(b), 42B(5) or 49B of the Control of Pollution Act 1974,
(ii) section 4 of the Control of Pollution (Amendment) Act 1989,
(iii) section 15, 22(5), 43, 62(3)(c), 66(5) or 78G of the Environmental Protection Act 1990,
(iv) . . .
(v) section [36A], 43, [51], 91, 92, 96, 161C[, 191B(5) or 199A] of the Water Resources Act 1991,
(vi) . . .
(vii) paragraph 6 of Schedule 5 to the Waste Management Licensing Regulations 1994,
[(viii) regulations under section 2 of the Pollution Prevention and Control Act 1999 extending to England and Wales,]
[(ix) [section 3 of the Water Act 2003,]
or any matter involved in such an appeal;
(b) the questions, or any of the questions, which fall to be determined by the Secretary of State under section 39(1) or section 49(4) of the Control of Pollution Act 1974.

(3) The items to which paragraph (b) of subsection (1) above applies are—
(a) any matter involved in an appeal falling within subsection (2)(a) above;
(b) any of the questions which fall to be determined by the Secretary of State under section 39(1) or section 49(4) of the Control of Pollution Act 1974.

(4) Schedule 20 to this Act shall have effect with respect to appointments under subsection (1)(a) above.

Crown application

115 Application of this Act to the Crown

(1) Subject to the provisions of this section, this Act shall bind the Crown.

(2) Part III of this Act and any amendments, repeals and revocations made by other provisions of this Act (other than those made by Schedule 21, which shall blind the Crown) bind the Crown to the extent that the enactments to which they relate bind the Crown.

(3) No contravention by the Crown of any provision made by or under this Act shall make the Crown criminally liable; but the High Court . . . may, on the application of the Agency . . . declare unlawful any act or omission of the Crown which constitutes such a contravention.

(4) Notwithstanding anything in subsection (3) above, any provision made by or under this Act shall apply to persons in the public service of the Crown as it applies to other persons.

(5) If the Secretary of State certifies that it appears to him, as respects any Crown premises and any powers of entry exercisable in relation to them specified in the certificate, that it is requisite or expedient that, in the interests of national security, the powers should not be exercisable in relation to those premises, those powers shall not be exercisable in relation to those premises; and in this subsection 'Crown premises' means premises held or used by or on behalf of the Crown.

(6) . . .

124 General interpretation

(1) In this Act, except in so far as the context otherwise requires—

'the Agency' means the Environment Agency;

'financial year' means a period of twelve months ending with 31st March;

'functions' includes powers and duties;

'modifications' includes additions, alterations and omissions and cognate expressions shall be construed accordingly;

'notice' means notice in writing;

'records', without prejudice to the generality of the expression, includes computer records and any other records kept otherwise than in a document . . .

Section 90 SCHEDULE 11

AIR QUALITY: SUPPLEMENTAL PROVISIONS

Consultation requirements

1.—(1) A local authority in carrying out its functions in relation to—

(a) any air quality review,
(b) any assessment under section 82 or 84 of this Act, or
(c) the preparation of an action plan or any revision of an action plan, shall consult such other persons as fall within sub-paragraph (2) below.

(2) Those persons are—

(a) the Secretary of State;
(b) the appropriate new Agency;
(c) in England and Wales, the highway authority for any highway in the area to which the review or, as the case may be, the action plan or revision relates;
(d) every local authority whose area is contiguous to the authority's area;
(e) any county council in England whose area consists of or includes the whole or any part of the authority's area;
(f) any National Park authority for a National Park whose area consists of or includes the whole or any part of the authority's area;
(g) such public authorities exercising functions in, or in the vicinity of, the authority's area as the authority may consider appropriate;
(h) such bodies appearing to the authority to be representative of persons with business interests in the area to which the review or action plan in question relates as the authority may consider appropriate;
(j) such other bodies or persons as the authority considers appropriate.

[(2A) A local authority specified in sub-paragraph (2B) below shall in carrying out the functions falling within sub-paragraph (1)(a) to (c) above also consult the Mayor of London.

(2B) The local authorities mentioned in sub-paragraph (2A) above are—

(a) any local authority in Greater London,

(b) any local authority whose area is contiguous to the area of Greater London.]

(3) ... In this paragraph 'National Park authority', [...] means a National Park authority established under section 63 of this Act which has become the local planning authority for the National Park in question.

(4) [...]

Exchange of information with county councils in England

2.—(1) This paragraph applies in any case where a district in England for which there is a district council is comprised in an area for which there is a county council; and in this paragraph—

(a) any reference to the county council is a reference to the council of that area; and

(b) any reference to a district council is a reference to the council of a district comprised in that area.

(2) It shall be the duty of the county council to provide a district council with all such information as is reasonably requested by the district council for purposes connected with the carrying out of its functions under or by virtue of this Part.

(3) It shall be the duty of a district council to provide the county council with all such information as is reasonably requested by the county council for purposes connected with the carrying out of any of its functions relating to the assessment or management of the quality of air.

(4) Information provided to a district council or county council under sub-paragraph (2) or (3) above shall be provided in such form and in such manner and at such times as the district council or, as the case may be, the county council may reasonably require.

(5) A council which provides information under sub-paragraph (2) or (3) above shall be entitled to recover the reasonable cost of doing so from the council which requested the information.

(6) The information which a council may be required to provide under this paragraph shall include information which, although it is not in the possession of the council or would not otherwise come into the possession of the council, is information which it is reasonable to require the council to obtain.

Joint exercise of local authority functions

3.—(1) The appropriate authority may give directions to any two or more local authorities requiring them to exercise the powers conferred by—

(a) section 101(5) of the Local Government Act 1972 (power of two or more local authorities to discharge functions jointly), or

(b) ...

in relation to functions under or by virtue of this Part in accordance with the directions.

(2) The appropriate authority may give directions to a local authority requiring it—

(a) not to exercise those powers, or

(b) not to exercise those powers in a manner specified in the directions, in relation to functions under or by virtue of this Part.

(3) Where two or more local authorities have exercised those powers in relation to functions under or by virtue of this Part, the appropriate authority may give them directions requiring them to revoke, or modify in accordance with the directions, the arrangements which they have made.

(4) In this paragraph, 'the appropriate authority' means—

(a) in relation to England and Wales, the Secretary of State; and

(b) ...

Public access to information about air quality

4.—(1) It shall be the duty of every local authority—

(a) to secure that there is available at all reasonable times for inspection by the public free of charge a copy of each of the documents specified in sub-paragraph (2) below; and

(b) to afford to members of the public facilities for obtaining copies of those documents on payment of a reasonable charge.

(2) The documents mentioned in sub-paragraph (1)(a) above are—

(a) a report of the results of any air quality review which the authority has caused to be conducted;

(b) a report of the results of any assessment which the authority has caused to be made under section 82 or 84 of this Act;

(c) any order made by the authority under section 83 of this Act;

(d) any action plan prepared by the authority;

(e) any proposals or statements submitted to the authority pursuant to subsection (3) or (4) of section 86 of this Act;

(f) any directions given to the authority under this Part;

(g) in a case where section 86 of this Act applies, any directions given to the county council under this Part.

Fixed penalty offences

5.—(1) Without prejudice to the generality of paragraph (o) of subsection (2) of section 87 of this Act, regulations may, in particular, make provision—

(a) for the qualifications, appointment or authorisation of persons who are to issue fixed penalty notices;

(b) for the offences in connection with which, the cases or circumstances in which, the time or period at or within which, or the manner in which fixed penalty notices may be issued;

(c) prohibiting the institution, before the expiration of the period for paying the fixed penalty, of proceedings against a person for an offence in connection with which a fixed penalty notice has been issued;

(d) prohibiting the conviction of a person for an offence in connection with which a fixed penalty notice has been issued if the fixed penalty is paid before the expiration of the period for paying it;

(e) entitling, in prescribed cases, a person to whom a fixed penalty notice is issued to give, within a prescribed period, notice requesting a hearing in respect of the offence to which the fixed penalty notice relates;

(f) for the amount of the fixed penalty to be increased by a prescribed amount in any case where the person liable to pay the fixed penalty fails to pay it before the expiration of the period for paying it, without having given notice requesting a hearing in respect of the offence to which the fixed penalty notice relates;

(g) for or in connection with the recovery of an unpaid fixed penalty as a fine or as a civil debt or as if it were a sum payable under a county court order;

(h) for or in connection with execution or other enforcement in respect of an unpaid fixed penalty by prescribed persons;

(j) for a fixed penalty notice, and any prescribed proceedings or other prescribed steps taken by reference to the notice, to be rendered void in prescribed cases where a person makes a prescribed statutory declaration, and for the consequences of any notice, proceedings or other steps being so rendered void (including extension of any time limit for instituting criminal proceedings);

(k) for or in connection with the extension, in prescribed cases or circumstances, by a prescribed person of the period for paying a fixed penalty;

(l) for or in connection with the withdrawal, in prescribed circumstances, of a fixed penalty notice, including—
  (i) repayment of any amount paid by way of fixed penalty in pursuance of a fixed penalty notice which is withdrawn; and
  (ii) prohibition of the institution or continuation of proceedings for the offence in connection with which the withdrawn notice was issued;

(m) for or in connection with the disposition of sums received by way of fixed penalty;

(n) for a certificate purporting to be signed by or on behalf of a prescribed person and stating either—
  (i) that payment of a fixed penalty was, or (as the case may be) was not, received on or before a date specified in the certificate, or
  (ii) that an envelope containing an amount sent by post in payment of a fixed penalty was marked as posted on a date specified in the certificate,

to be received as evidence of the matters so stated and to be treated, without further proof, as being so signed unless the contrary is shown;

(o) requiring a fixed penalty notice to give such reasonable particulars of the circumstances alleged to constitute the fixed penalty offence to which the notice relates as are necessary for giving reasonable information of the offence and to state—
  (i) the monetary amount of the fixed penalty which may be paid;
  (ii) the person to whom, and the address at which, the fixed penalty may be paid and any correspondence relating to the fixed penalty notice may be sent;
  (iii) the method or methods by which payment of the fixed penalty may be made;
  (iv) the period for paying the fixed penalty;
  (v) the consequences of the fixed penalty not being paid before the expiration of that period;

(p) similar to any provision made by section 79 of the Road Traffic Offenders Act 1988 (statements by constables in fixed penalty cases);

(q) for presuming, in any proceedings, that any document of a prescribed description purporting to have been signed by a person to whom a fixed penalty notice has been issued has been signed by a person to whom a fixed penalty notice has been issued has been signed by that person;

(r) requiring or authorising a fixed penalty notice to contain prescribed information relating to, or for the purpose of facilitating, the administration of the fixed penalty system;

(s) with respect to the giving of fixed penalty notices, including, in particular, provision with respect to—
  (i) the methods by which,
  (ii) the officers, servants or agents by, to or on whom, and
  (iii) the places at which, fixed penalty notices may be given by, or served on behalf of, a prescribed person;

(t) prescribing the method or methods by which fixed penalties may be paid;

(u) for or with respect to the issue of prescribed documents to persons to whom fixed penalty notices are or have been given;

(w) for a fixed penalty notice to be treated for prescribed purposes as if it were an information or summons or any other document of a prescribed description.

(2) The provision that may be made by regulations prescribing fixed penalty offences includes provision for an offence to be a fixed penalty offence—

(a) only if it is committed in such circumstances or manner as may be prescribed; or

(b) except if it is committed in such circumstances or manner as may be prescribed.

(3) Regulations may provide for any offence which is a fixed penalty offence to cease to be such an offence.

(4) An offence which, in consequence of regulations made by virtue of sub-paragraph (3) above, has ceased to be a fixed penalty offence shall be eligible to be prescribed as such an offence again.

(5) Regulations may make provision for such exceptions, limitations and conditions as the Secretary of State considers necessary or expedient.

(6) In this paragraph—

'fixed penalty' means a penalty of such amount as may be prescribed (whether by being specified in, or made calculable under, regulations);

'fixed penalty notice' means a notice offering a person an opportunity to discharge any liability to conviction for a fixed penalty offence by payment of a penalty of a prescribed amount;

'fixed penalty offence' means, subject to sub-paragraph (2) above, any offence (whether under or by virtue of this Part or any other enactment) which is for the time being prescribed as a fixed penalty offence;

'the fixed penalty system' means the system implementing regulations made under or by virtue of paragraph (o) of subsection (2) of section 87 of this Act; 'the period for paying', in relation to any fixed penalty, means such period as may be prescribed for the purpose;

'regulations' means regulations under or by virtue of paragraph (o) of subsection (2) of section 87 of this Act.

Section 108 SCHEDULE 18

SUPPLEMENTAL PROVISIONS WITH RESPECT TO POWERS OF ENTRY

Interpretation

1.—(1) In this Schedule—

'designated person' means an authorised person, within the meaning of section 91 of this Act and includes a person designated by virtue of paragraph 2 below;

'relevant power' means a power conferred by section 108 of this Act, including a power exercisable by virtue of a warrant under this Schedule.

(2) Expressions used in this Schedule and in section 108 of this Act have the same meaning in this Schedule as they have in that section.

Issue of warrants

2.—(1) If it is shown to the satisfaction of a justice of the peace . . . on sworn information in writing—

(a) that there are reasonable grounds for the exercise in relation to any premises of a relevant power; and

(b) that one or more of the conditions specified in sub-paragraph (2) below is fulfilled in relation to those premises,

the justice . . . may by warrant authorise an enforcing authority to designate a person who shall be authorised to exercise the power in relation to those premises, in accordance with the warrant and, if need be, by force.

(2) The conditions mentioned in sub-paragraph (1)(b) above are—

(a) that the exercise of the power in relation to the premises has been refused;

(b) that such a refusal is reasonably apprehended;

(c) that the premises are unoccupied;

(d) that the occupier is temporarily absent from the premises and the case is one of urgency; or

(e) that an application for admission to the premises would defeat the object of the proposed entry.

(3) In a case where subsection (6) of section 108 of this Act applies, a justice of the peace . . . shall not issue a warrant under this Schedule by virtue only of being satisfied that the exercise of a power in relation to any premises has been refused, or that a refusal is reasonably apprehended, unless he is also satisfied that the notice required by that subsection has been given and that the period of that notice has expired.

(4) Every warrant under this Schedule shall continue in force until the purposes for which the warrant was issued have been fulfilled.

Manner of exercise of powers

3. A person designated as the person who may exercise a relevant power shall produce evidence of this designation and other authority before he exercises the power.

Information obtained to be admissible in evidence

4.—(1) Subject to section 108(12) of this Act, information obtained in consequence of the exercise of a relevant power, with or without the consent of any person, shall be admissible in evidence against that or any other person.

(2) Without prejudice to the generality of sub-paragraph (1) above, information obtained by means of monitoring or other apparatus installed on any premises in the exercise of a relevant power, with or without the consent of any person in occupation of the premises, shall be admissible in evidence in any proceedings against that or any other person.

Noise Act 1996

(1996. c. 37)

Summary procedure for dealing with noise at night

1 Application of sections 2 to 9

(1) Sections 2 to 9 apply to the area of every local authority in England and Wales.

(2)–(4) [. . .]

2 Investigation of complaints of noise at night

[(1) A local authority in England and Wales may, if they receive a complaint of the kind mentioned in subsection (2), arrange for an officer of the authority to take reasonable steps to investigate the complaint.]

(2) The kind of complaint referred to is one made by any individual present in a dwelling during night hours (referred to in this Act as 'the complainant's dwelling') that excessive noise is being emitted from

[(a) another dwelling (referred to in this group of sections as 'the offending dwelling') or

(b) any premises in respect of which a premises licence or a temporary event notice has effect (referred to in this group of sections as 'the offending premises').]

(3) A complaint under subsection (2) may be made by any means.

(4) If an officer of the authority is satisfied, in consequence of an investigation under subsection (1), that—

(a) noise is being emitted from the offending dwelling or the offending premises during night hours, and

(b) the noise, if it were measured from within the complainant's dwelling, would or might exceed the permitted level,

he may serve a notice about the noise under section 3.

(5) For the purposes of subsection (4), it is for the officer of the authority dealing with the particular case—

(a) to decide whether any noise, if it were measured from within the complain-ant's dwelling, would or might exceed the permitted level, and

(b) for the purposes of that decision, to decide whether to assess the noise from within or outside the complainant's dwelling and whether or not to use any device for measuring the noise.

(6) In this group of sections, 'night hours' means the period beginning with 11 p.m. and ending with the following 7 a.m.

(7) Where a local authority receive a complaint under subsection (2) and the offending dwelling is or the offending premises are within the area of another local authority, the first local authority may act under this group of sections as if the offending dwelling or the offending premises were within their area.

[(7A) In this group of sections—

'premises licence' has the same meaning as in the Licensing Act 2003;

'temporary event notice' has the same meaning as in the Licensing Act 2003 (and is to be treated as having effect in accordance with section 171(6) of that Act).]

(8) In this section and sections 3 to 9, 'this group of sections' means that and those sections.

3 Warning notices

(1) A notice under this section (referred to in this Act as 'a warning notice') must—

(a) state that an officer of the authority consider—

(i) that noise is being emitted from the offending dwelling or the offending premises during night hours, and

(ii) that the noise exceeds, or may exceed, the permitted level, as measured from within the complainant's dwelling, and

[(b) give warning—

(i) in a case where the complaint is in respect of a dwelling, that any person who is responsible for noise which is emitted from the offending dwelling in the period specified in the notice and which exceeds the permitted level, as measured from within the complainant's dwelling, may be guilty of an offence;

(ii) in a case where the complaint is in respect of other premises, that the responsible person in relation to the offending premises may be guilty of an offence if noise which exceeds the permitted level, as measured from within the complainant's dwelling, is emitted from the premises in the period specified in the notice.]

(2) The period specified in a warning notice must be a period—

(a) beginning not earlier than ten minutes after the time when the notice is served and

(b) ending with the following 7 a.m.

(3) [In a case where the complaint is in respect of a dwelling], a warning notice must be served—

(a) by delivering it to any person present at or near the offending dwelling and appearing to the officer of the authority to be responsible for the noise, or

(b) if it is not reasonably practicable to identify any person present at or near the dwelling as being a person responsible for the noise on whom the notice may reasonably be served, by leaving it at the offending dwelling.

[(3A) In a case where the complaint is in respect of other premises, a warning notice must be served by delivering it to the person who appears to the officer of the authority to be the responsible person in relation to the offending premises at the time the notice is delivered.]

(4) A warning notice must state the time at which it is served.

(5) For the purposes of this group of sections, a person is responsible for noise emitted from a dwelling if he is a person to whose act, default or sufferance the emission of the noise is wholly or partly attributable.

[(6) For the purposes of this group of sections, the responsible person in relation to premises at a particular time is—

(a) where a premises licence has effect in respect of the premises—

(i) the person who holds the premises licence if he is present at the premises at that time,

(ii) where that person is not present at the premises at that time, the designated premises supervisor under the licence if he is present at the premises at that time, or

(iii) where neither of the persons mentioned in sub-paragraphs (i) and (ii) is present at the premises at that time, any other person present at the premises at that time who is in charge of the premises;

(b) where a temporary event notice has effect in respect of the premises—

(i) the premises user in relation to that notice if he is present at the premises at that time, or

(ii) where the premises user is not present at the premises at that time, any other person present at the premises at that time who is in charge of the premises.]

4 Offence where noise from a dwelling exceeds permitted level after service of notice

(1) If a warning notice has been served in respect of noise emitted from a dwelling, any person who is responsible for noise which—

(a) is emitted from the dwelling in the period specified in the notice, and

(b) exceeds the permitted level, as measured from within the complainant's dwelling,

is guilty of an offence.

(2) It is a defence for a person charged with an offence under this section to show that there was a reasonable excuse for the act, default or sufferance in question.

(3) A person guilty of an offence under this section is liable on summary conviction to a fine not exceeding level 3 on the standard scale.

[4A Offence where noise from other premises exceeds permitted level after service of notice

(1) If—

(a) a warning notice has been served under section 3 in respect of noise emitted from premises,

(b) noise is emitted from the premises in the period specified in the notice, and

(c) the noise exceeds the permitted level, as measured from within the complainant's dwelling,

the responsible person in relation to the offending premises at the time at which the noise referred to in paragraph (c) is emitted is guilty of an offence.

(2) A person guilty of an offence under this section is liable on summary conviction to a fine not exceeding level 5 on the standard scale.]

5 Permitted level of noise

(1) For the purposes of this group of sections, the appropriate person may by directions in writing determine the maximum level of noise (referred to in this group of sections as 'the permitted level') which may be emitted during night hours from any dwelling or other premises.

(2) The permitted level is to be a level applicable to noise as measured from within any other dwelling in the vicinity by an approved device used in accordance with any conditions subject to which the approval was given.

(3) Different permitted levels may be determined for different circumstances, and the permitted level may be determined partly by reference to other levels of noise.

(4) The appropriate person may from time to time vary his directions under this section by further directions in writing.

6 Approval of measuring devices

(1) For the purposes of this group of sections, the appropriate person may approve in writing any type of device used for the measurement of noise; and reference in this group of sections to approved devices are to devices of a type so approved.

(2) Any such approval may be given subject to conditions as to the purposes for which, and the manner and other circumstances in which, devices of the type concerned are to be used.

(3) In proceedings for an offence under section 4 or 4A, a measurement of noise made by a device is not admissible as evidence of the level of noise unless it is an approved device and any conditions subject to which the approval was given are satisfied.

7 Evidence

(1) In proceedings for an offence under section 4 or 4A, evidence—

(a) of a measurement of noise made by a device, or of the circumstances in which it was made, or

(b) that a device was of a type approved for the purposes of section 6, or that any conditions subject to which the approval was given were satisfied,

may be given by the production of a document mentioned in subsection (2).

(2) The document referred to is one which is signed by an officer of the local authority and which (as the case may be)—

(a) gives particulars of the measurement or of the circumstances in which it was made, or

(b) states that the device was of such a type or that, to the best of the knowledge and belief of the person making the statement, all such conditions were satisfied;

and if the document contains evidence of a measurement of noise it may consist partly of a record of the measurement produced automatically by a device.

(3) In proceedings for an offence under section 4, evidence that noise, or noise of any kind, measured by a device at any time was noise emitted from a dwelling may be given by the production of a document—

(a) signed by an officer of the local authority, and

(b) stating that he had identified that dwelling as the source at that time of the noise or, as the case may be, the noise of that kind.

[(3A) In proceedings for an offence under section 4A, evidence that noise, or noise of any kind, measured by a device at any time was noise emitted from any other premises may be given by the production of a document—

(a) signed by an officer of the local authority, and

(b) stating that he had identified those premises as the source at that time of the noise or, as the case may be, noise of that kind.]

(4) For the purposes of this section, a document purporting to be signed as mentioned in subsection (2), (3)(a) or (3A)(a) is to be treated as being so signed unless the contrary is proved.

(5) This section does not make a document admissible as evidence in proceedings for an offence unless a copy of it has, not less than seven days before the hearing or trial, been served on the person charged with the offence.

(6) This section does not make a document admissible as evidence of anything other than the matters shown on a record produced automatically by a device if, not less than three days before the hearing or trial or within such further time as the court may in special circumstance allow, the person charged with the offence serves a notice on the prosecutor requiring attendance at the hearing or trial of the person who signed the document.

8 Fixed penalty notices

(1) Where an officer of a local authority who is authorised for the purposes of this section has reason to believe that a person is committing or has just committed an offence under section 4 or 4A, he may give that person a notice (referred to in this Act as a 'fixed penalty notice') offering him the opportunity of discharging any liability to conviction for that offence by payment of a fixed penalty.

(2) A fixed penalty notice may be given to a person—

(a) by delivering the notice to him, or

(b) if it is not reasonably practicable to deliver it to him, by leaving the notice, addressed to him, at the offending dwelling or the offending premises (as the case may be).

(3) Where a person is given a fixed penalty notice in respect of such an offence—

(a) proceedings for that offence must not be instituted before the end of the period of fourteen days following the date of the notice, and

(b) he cannot be convicted of that offence if he pays the fixed penalty before the end of that period.

(4) A fixed penalty notice must give such particulars of the circumstances alleged to constitute the offence as are necessary for giving reasonable information of the offence.

(5) A fixed penalty notice must state—

(a) the period during which, because of subsection (3)(a), proceedings will not be taken for the offence,

(b) the amount of the fixed penalty, and

(c) the person to whom and the address at which the fixed penalty may be paid.

(6) Payment of the fixed penalty may (among other methods) be made by pre-paying and posting to that person at that address a letter containing the amount of the penalty (in cash or otherwise).

(7) Where a letter containing the amount of the penalty is sent in accordance with subsection (6), payment is to be regarded as having been made at the time at which that letter would be delivered in the ordinary course of post.

[8A Amount of fixed penalty

(1) This section applies in relation to a fixed penalty payable to a local authority in pursuance of a notice under section 8.

(2) In the case of an offence under section 4, the amount of the fixed penalty—

(a) is the amount specified by the local authority in relation to the authority's area, or

(b) if no amount is so specified, is £100.

(2A) In the case of an offence under section 4A the amount of the fixed penalty is £500.

(3) The local authority may make provision for treating the fixed penalty payable in the case of an offence under section 4 as having been paid if a lesser amount is paid before the end of a period specified by the authority.

(4) The appropriate person may by regulations make provision in connection with the powers conferred on local authorities under subsections (2)(a) and (3).

(5) Regulations under subsection (4) may (in particular)—

(a) require an amount specified under subsection (2)(a) to fall within a range prescribed in the regulations;

(b) restrict the extent to which, and the circumstances in which, a local authority can make provision under subsection (3).

(6) The appropriate person may by order substitute a different amount for the amount for the time being specified in subsection (2)(b) or (2A).

8B Fixed penalty notices: power to require name and address

(1) If an officer of a local authority who is authorised for the purposes of section 8 proposes to give a person a fixed penalty notice, the officer may require the person to give him his name and address.

(2) A person commits an offence if—

(a) he fails to give his name and address when required to do so under subsection (1), or

(b) he gives a false or inaccurate name or address in response to a requirement under that subsection.

(3) A person guilty of an offence under subsection (2) is liable on summary conviction to a fine not exceeding level 3 on the standard scale.]

9 Section 8: supplementary

(1) If a form for a fixed penalty notice is specified in an order made by the appropriate person, a fixed penalty notice must be in that form.

(2) If a fixed penalty notice is given to a person in respect of noise emitted from a dwelling in any period specified in a warning notice—

(a) no further fixed penalty notice may be given to that person in respect of noise emitted from the dwelling during that period, but

(b) that person may be convicted of a further offence under section 4 in respect of noise emitted, from the dwelling after the fixed penalty notice is given and before the end of that period.

[(2A) If a fixed penalty notice is given to a person in respect of noise emitted from other premises in any period in a warning notice—

(a) no further fixed penalty notice may be given to that person in respect of noise emitted from the premises during that period, but

(b) that person may be convicted of a further offence under section 4A in respect of noise emitted from the premises after the fixed penalty notice is given and before the end of that period.]

(3) [...]

[(4) A local authority may use any sums it receives under section 8 (its 'penalty receipts') only for the purposes of functions of its that are qualifying functions.

(4A) The following are qualifying functions for the purposes of this section—

(a) functions under this Act, and

(b) functions of a description specified in regulations made by the appropriate person.

(4B) Regulations under subsection (4A)(b) may (in particular) have the effect that a local authority may use its penalty receipts for the purposes of any of its functions.

(4C) A local authority must supply the appropriate person with such information relating to the use of its penalty receipts as the appropriate person may require.

(4D) The appropriate person may by regulations—

(a) make provision for what a local authority is to do with its penalty receipts—

(i) pending their being used for the purposes of qualifying functions of the authority;

(ii) if they are not so used before such time after their receipt as may be specified by the regulations;

(b) make provision for accounting arrangements in respect of a local authority's penalty receipts.

(4E) The provision that may be made under subsection (4D)(a)(ii) includes (in particular) provision for the payment of sums to a person (including the appropriate person) other than the local authority.

(4F) Before making regulations under this section, the appropriate person must consult—

(a) the local authorities to which the regulations are to apply, and

(b) such other persons as the appropriate person considers appropriate.]

(5) In proceedings for an offence under section 4 or 4A, evidence that payment of a fixed penalty was or was not made before the end of any period may be given by the production of a certificate which—

(a) purports to be signed by or on behalf of the person having responsibility for the financial affairs of the local authority, and

(b) states that payment of a fixed penalty was made on any date or, as the case may be, was not received before the end of that period.

Seizure, etc. of equipment used to make noise unlawfully

10 Powers of entry and seizure etc.

(1) The power conferred by subsection (2) may be exercised where an officer of a local authority has reason to believe that—

(a) a warning notice has been served in respect of noise emitted from a dwelling or other premises, and

(b) at any time in the period specified in the notice, noise emitted from the dwelling or other premises has exceeded the permitted level, as measured from within the complainant's dwelling.

(2) An officer of a local authority, or a person authorised by the authority for the purpose, may enter the dwelling or other premises from which the noise in question is being or has been emitted and may seize and remove any equipment which it appears to him is being or has been used in the emission of the noise.

(3)–(6) . . .

(7) The power of a local authority under section 81(3) of the Environmental Protection Act 1990 to abate any matter, where that matter is a statutory nuisance by virtue of section 79(1)(g) of that Act (noise emitted from premises so as to be prejudicial to health or a nuisance), includes power to seize and remove any equipment which it appears to the authority is being or has been used in the emission of the noise in question.

(8) . . .

(9) The Schedule to this Act (which makes further provision in relation to anything seized and removed by virtue of this section) has effect.

General

11 Interpretation and subordinate legislation

(1) In this Act, 'local authority' means—

(a) in Greater London, a London borough council, the Common Council of the City of London and, as respects the Temples, the Sub-Treasurer of the Inner Temple and the Under-Treasurer of the Middle Temple respectively,

(b) outside Greater London—

(i) any district council,

(ii) the council of any county so far as they are the council for any area for which there are no district councils,

(iii) in Wales, the council of a county borough, and

(c) the Council of the Isles of Scilly.

(2) In this Act—

(a) 'dwelling' means any building, or part of a building, used or intended to be used as a dwelling,

(b) references to noise emitted from any garden, yard, outhouse or other appurtenance belonging to or enjoyed with the dwelling.

(2A) In this Act, 'appropriate person' means—

(a) the Secretary of State, in relation of England;

(b) the National Assembly for Wales, in relation to Wales.

(3) The power to make an order under this Act is exercisable by statutory instrument which (except in the case of an order under section 14 or an order or regulations made solely by the National Assembly for Wales) shall be subject to annulment in pursuance of a resolution of either House of Parliament.

12 Protection from personal liability

(1) A member of a local authority or an officer or other person authorised by a local authority is not personally liable in respect of any act done by him or by the local authority or

any such person if the act was done in good faith for the purpose of executing powers conferred by, or by virtue, of this Act.

(2) Subsection (1) does not apply to liability under section 19 or 20 of the Local Government Finance Act 1982 (powers of district auditor and court).

14 Short title, commencement and extent

(1) This Act may be cited as the Noise Act 1996.

(2) This Act is to come into force on such day as the Secretary of State may by order appoint, and different days may be appointed for different purposes.

(3) ...

(4) ...

Section 10 SCHEDULE

POWERS IN RELATION TO SEIZED EQUIPMENT

Introductory

1 In this Schedule—

(a) a 'noise offence' means—

(i) in relation to equipment seized under section 10(2) of this Act, an offence under section 4 or 4A of this Act, and

(ii) in relation to equipment seized under section 81(3) of the Environmental Protection Act 1990 (as extended by section 10(7) of this Act), an offence under section 80(4) of that Act in respect of a statutory nuisance falling within section 79(1)(g) of that Act,

(b) 'seized equipment' means equipment seized in the exercise of the power of seizure and removal conferred by section 10(2) of this Act or section 81(3) of the Environmental Protection Act 1990 (as so extended),

(c) 'related equipment', in relation to any conviction of or proceedings for a noise offence, means seized equipment used or alleged to have been used in the commission of the offence,

(d) 'responsible local authority', in relation to seized equipment, means the local authority by or on whose behalf the equipment was seized.

Retention

2.—(1) Any seized equipment may be retained—

(a) during the period of twenty-eight days beginning with the seizure, or

(b) if it is related equipment in proceedings for a noise offence instituted within that period against any person, until—

(i) he is sentenced or otherwise dealt with for the offence or acquitted of the offence, or

(ii) the proceedings are discontinued.

(2) Sub-paragraph (1) does not authorise the retention of seized equipment if—

(a) a person has been given a fixed penalty notice under section 8 of this Act in respect of any noise,

(b) the equipment was seized because of its use in the emission of the noise in respect of which the fixed penalty notice was given, and

(c) that person has paid the fixed penalty before the end of the period allowed for its payment.

Forfeiture

3.—(1) Where a person is convicted of a noise offence the court may make an order ('a forfeiture order') for forfeiture of any related equipment.

(2) The court may make a forfeiture order whether or not it also deals with the offender in respect of the offence in any other way and without regard to any restrictions on forfeiture in any enactment.

(3) In considering whether to make a forfeiture order in respect of any equipment a court must have regard—

(a) to the value of the equipment, and

(b) to the likely financial and other effects on the offender of the making of the order (taken together with any other order that the court contemplates making).

(4) A forfeiture order operates to deprive the offender of any rights in the equipment to which it relates.

Consequences of forfeiture

4.—(1) Where any equipment has been forfeited under paragraph 3, a magistrates' court may, on application by a claimant of the equipment (other than the person in whose case the forfeiture order was made) make an order for delivery of the equipment to the applicant if it appears to the court that he is the owner of the equipment.

(2) No application may be made under sub-paragraph (1) by any claimant of the equipment after the expiry of the period of six months beginning with the date on which a forfeiture order was made in respect of the equipment.

(3) Such an application cannot succeed unless the claimant satisfies the court—

(a) that he had not consented to the offender having possession of the equipment, or

(b) that he did not know, and had no reason to suspect, that the equipment was likely to be used in the commission of a noise offence.

(4) Where the responsible local authority is of the opinion that the person in whose case the forfeiture order was made is not the owner of the equipment, it must take reasonable steps to bring to the attention of persons who may be entitled to do so their right to make an application under sub-paragraph (1).

(5) An order under sub-paragraph (1) does not affect the right of any person to take, within the period of six months beginning with the date of the order, proceedings for the recovery of the equipment from the person in possession of it in pursuance of the order, but the right ceases on the expiry of that period.

(6) If on the expiry of the period of six months beginning with the date on which a forfeiture order was made in respect of the equipment no order has been made under sub-paragraph (1), the responsible local authority may dispose of the equipment.

Return etc. of seized equipment

5. If in proceedings for a noise offence no order for forfeiture of related equipment is made, the court (whether or not a person is convicted of the offence) may give such directions as to the return, retention or disposal of the equipment by the responsible local authority as it thinks fit.

6.—(1) Where in the case of any seized equipment no proceedings in which it is related equipment are begun within the period mentioned in paragraph 2(1)(a)—

(a) the responsible local authority must return the equipment to any person who—

(i) appears to them to be the owner of the equipment, and

(ii) makes a claim for the return of the equipment within the period mentioned in sub-paragraph (2), and

(b) if no such person makes such a claim within that period, the responsible local authority may dispose of the equipment.

(2) The period referred to in sub-paragraph (1)(a)(ii) is the period of six months beginning with the expiry of the period mentioned in paragraph 2(1)(a).

(3) The responsible local authority must take reasonable steps to bring to the attention of persons who may be entitled to do so their right to make such a claim.

(4) Subject to sub-paragraph (6), the responsible local authority is not required to return any seized equipment under sub-paragraph (1)(a) until the person making the claim has paid any such reasonable charges for the seizure, removal and retention of the equipment as the authority may demand.

(5) If—

(a) equipment is sold in pursuance of—

(i) paragraph 4(6)

(ii) directions under paragraph 5, or

(iii) this paragraph, and

(b) before the expiration of the period of one year beginning with the date on which the equipment is sold any person satisfies the responsible local authority that at the time of its sale he was the owner of the equipment,

the authority is to pay him any sum by which any proceeds of sale exceed any such reasonable charges for the seizure, removal or retention of the equipment as the authority may demand.

(6) The responsible local authority cannot demand charges from any person under sub-paragraph (4) or (5) who they are satisfied did not know, and had no reason to suspect, that the equipment was likely to be used in the emission of noise exceeding the level determined under section 5.

Human Rights Act 1998

(1998, c. 42)

Introduction

1 The Convention Rights

(1) In this Act 'the Convention rights' means the rights and fundamental freedoms set out in—

(a) Articles 2 to 12 and 14 of the Convention,

(b) Articles 1 to 3 of the First Protocol, and

(c) [Article 1 of the Thirteenth Protocol],

as read with Articles 16 to 18 of the Convention.

(2) Those Articles are to have effect for the purposes of this Act subject to any designated derogation or reservation (as to which see sections 14 and 15).

(3) The Articles are set out in Schedule 1.

(4) The [Secretary of State] may by order make such amendments to this Act as he considers appropriate to reflect the effect, in relation to the United Kingdom, of a protocol.

(5) In subsection (4) 'protocol' means a protocol to the Convention—

(a) which the United Kingdom has ratified; or

(b) which the United Kingdom has signed with a view to ratification.

(6) No amendment may be made by an order under subsection (4) so as to come into force before the protocol concerned is in force in relation to the United Kingdom.

2 Interpretation of Convention rights

(1) A court or tribunal determining a question which has arisen in connection with a Convention right must take into account any—

(a) judgment, decision, declaration or advisory opinion of the European Court of Human Rights,

(b) opinion of the Commission given in a report adopted under Article 31 of the Convention,

(c) decision of the Commission in connection with Article 26 or 27(2) of the Convention, or

(d) decision of the Committee of Ministers taken under Article 46 of the Convention,
whenever made or given, so far as, in the opinion of the court or tribunal, it is relevant to the proceedings in which that question has arisen.

(2) Evidence of any judgment, decision, declaration or opinion of which account may have to be taken under this section is to be given in proceedings before any court or tribunal in such manner as may be provided by rules.

(3) In this section 'rules' means rules of court or, in the case of proceedings before a tribunal, rules made for the purposes of this section—

(a) by... [the Lord Chancellor or] the Secretary of State, in relation to any proceedings outside Scotland;
(b) by the Secretary of State, in relation to proceedings in Scotland; or
(c) by a Northern Ireland department, in relation to proceedings before a tribunal in Northern Ireland—
  (i) which deals with transferred matters; and
  (ii) for which no rules made under paragraph (a) are in force.

Legislation

3 Interpretation of legislation

(1) So far as it is possible to do so, primary legislation and subordinate legislation must be read and given effect in a way which is compatible with the Convention rights.

(2) This section—

(a) applies to primary legislation and subordinate legislation whenever enacted;
(b) does not affect the validity, continuing operation or enforcement of any incompatible primary legislation; and
(c) does not affect the validity, continuing operation or enforcement of any incompatible subordinate legislation if (disregarding any possibility of revocation) primary legislation prevents removal of the incompatibility.

4 Declaration of incompatibility

(1) Subsection (2) applies in any proceedings in which a court determines whether a provision of primary legislation is compatible with a Convention right.

(2) If the court is satisfied that the provision is incompatible with a Convention right, it may make a declaration of that incompatibility.

(3) Subsection (4) applies in any proceedings in which a court determines whether a provision of subordinate legislation, made in the exercise of a power conferred by primary legislation, is compatible with a Convention right.

(4) If the court is satisfied—

(a) that the provision is incompatible with a Convention right, and
(b) that (disregarding any possibility of revocation) the primary legislation concerned prevents removal of the incompatibility,

it may make a declaration of that incompatibility.

(5) In this section 'court' means—

[(a) the Supreme Court;]
(b) the Judicial Committee of the Privy Council;
(c) the Courts-Martial Appeal Court;
(d) ...;
(e) in England and Wales or Northern Ireland, the High Court or the Court of Appeal;
[(f) the Court of Protection, in any matter being dealt with by the President of the Family Division, the Vice-Chancellor or a puisne judge of the High Court].

(6) A declaration under this section ('a declaration of incompatibility')—

(a) does not affect the validity, continuing operation or enforcement of the provision in respect of which it is given; and
(b) is not binding on the parties to the proceedings in which it is made.

Public authorities

6 Acts of public authorities

(1) It is unlawful for a public authority to act in a way which is incompatible with a Convention right.

(2) Subsection (1) does not apply to an act if—

(a) as the result of one or more provisions of primary legislation, the authority could not have acted differently; or

(b) in the case of one or more provisions of, or made under, primary legislation which cannot be read or given effect in a way which is compatible with the Convention rights, the authority was acting so as to give effect to or enforce those provisions.

(3) In this section 'public authority' includes—

(a) a court or tribunal, and

(b) any person certain of whose functions are functions of a public nature,

but does not include either House of Parliament or a person exercising functions in connection with proceedings in Parliament.

(4) [...].

(5) In relation to a particular act, a person is not a public authority by virtue only of subsection (3)(b) if the nature of the act is private.

(6) 'An act' includes a failure to act but does not include a failure to—

(a) introduce in, or lay before, Parliament a proposal for legislation; or

(b) make any primary legislation or remedial order.

7 Proceedings

(1) A person who claims that a public authority has acted (or proposes to act) in a way which is made unlawful by section 6(1) may—

(a) bring proceedings against the authority under this Act in the appropriate court or tribunal, or

(b) rely on the Convention right or rights concerned in any legal proceedings,

but only if he is (or would be) a victim of the unlawful act.

(2) In subsection (1)(a) 'appropriate court or tribunal' means such court or tribunal as may be determined in accordance with rules; and proceedings against an authority include a counterclaim or similar proceeding.

(3) If the proceedings are brought on an application for judicial review, the applicant is to be taken to have a sufficient interest in relation to the unlawful act only if he is, or would be, a victim of that act.

(4) If the proceedings are made by way of a petition for judicial review in Scotland, the applicant shall be taken to have title and interest to sue in relation to the unlawful act only if he is, or would be, a victim of that act.

(5) Proceedings under subsection (1)(a) must be brought before the end of—

(a) the period of one year beginning with the date on which the act complained of took place; or

(b) such longer period as the court or tribunal considers equitable having regard to all the circumstances,

but that is subject to any rule imposing a stricter time limit in relation to the procedure in question.

(6) In subsection (1)(b) 'legal proceedings' includes—

(a) proceedings brought by or at the instigation of a public authority; and

(b) an appeal against the decision of a court or tribunal.

(7) For the purposes of this section, a person is a victim of an unlawful act only if he would be a victim for the purposes of Article 34 of the Convention if proceedings were brought in the European Court of Human Rights in respect of that act.

(8) Nothing in this Act creates a criminal offence.

(9) In this section 'rules' means—

(a) in relation to proceedings before a court or tribunal outside Scotland, rules made by . . . [the Lord Chancellor or] the Secretary of State for the purposes of this section or rules of court, . . .

and includes provision made by order under section 1 of the Courts and Legal Services Act 1990.

(10) In making rules, regard must be had to section 9.

(11) The Minister who has power to make rules in relation to a particular tribunal may, to the extent he considers it necessary to ensure that the tribunal can provide an appropriate remedy in relation to an act (or proposed act) of a public authority which is (or would be) unlawful as a result of section 6(1), by order add to—

(a) the relief or remedies which the tribunal may grant; or

(b) the grounds on which it may grant any of them.

(12) An order made under subsection (11) may contain such incidental, supplemental, consequential or transitional provision as the Minister making it considers appropriate.

8 Judicial remedies

(1) In relation to any act (or proposed act) of a public authority which the court finds is (or would be) unlawful, it may grant such relief or remedy, or make such order, within its powers as it considers just and appropriate.

(2) But damages may be awarded only by a court which has power to award damages, or to order the payment of compensation, in civil proceedings.

(3) No award of damages is to be made unless, taking account of all the circumstances of the case, including—

(a) any other relief or remedy granted, or order made, in relation to the act in question (by that or any other court), and

(b) the consequences of any decision (of that or any other court) in respect of that act,

the court is satisfied that the award is necessary to afford just satisfaction to the person in whose favour it is made.

(4) In determining—

(a) whether to award damages, or

(b) the amount of an award,

the court must take into account the principles applied by the European Court of Human Rights in relation to the award of compensation under Article 41 of the Convention.

(5) A public authority against which damages are awarded is to be treated—

(a) . . . ;

(b) for the purposes of the Civil Liability (Contribution) Act 1978 as liable in respect of damage suffered by the person to whom the award is made.

(6) In this section—

'court' includes a tribunal;

'damages' means damages for an unlawful act of a public authority; and

'unlawful' means unlawful under section 6(1).

Section 1(3)

SCHEDULE 1

THE ARTICLES

PART I THE CONVENTION

Rights and Freedoms

Article 2 Right to life

1. Everyone's right to life shall be protected by law. No one shall be deprived of his life intentionally save in the execution of a sentence of a court following his conviction of a crime for which this penalty is provided by law.

2. Deprivation of life shall not be regarded as inflicted in contravention of this Article when it results from the use of force which is no more than absolutely necessary:

(a) in defence of any person from unlawful violence;

(b) in order to effect a lawful arrest or to prevent the escape of a person lawfully detained;

(c) in action lawfully taken for the purpose of quelling a riot or insurrection.

Article 3 Prohibition of torture

No one shall be subjected to torture or to inhuman or degrading treatment or punishment.

Article 6 Right to a fair trial

1. In the determination of his civil rights and obligations or of any criminal charge against him, everyone is entitled to a fair and public hearing within a reasonable time by an independent and impartial tribunal established by law. Judgment shall be pronounced publicly but the press and public may be excluded from all or part of the trial in the interest of morals, public order or national security in a democratic society, where the interests of juveniles or the protection of the private life of the parties so require, or to the extent strictly necessary in the opinion of the court in special circumstances where publicity would prejudice the interests of justice.

2. Everyone charged with a criminal offence shall be presumed innocent until proved guilty according to law.

3. Everyone charged with a criminal offence has the following minimum rights:

(a) to be informed promptly, in a language which he understands and in detail, of the nature and cause of the accusation against him;

(b) to have adequate time and facilities for the preparation of his defence;

(c) to defend himself in person or through legal assistance of his own choosing or, if he has not sufficient means to pay for legal assistance, to be given it free when the interests of justice so require;

(d) to examine or have examined witnesses against him and to obtain the attendance and examination of witnesses on his behalf under the same conditions as witnesses against him;

(e) to have the free assistance of an interpreter if he cannot understand or speak the language used in court.

Article 7 No punishment without law

1. No one shall be held guilty of any criminal offence on account of any act or omission which did not constitute a criminal offence under national or international law at the time when it was committed. Nor shall a heavier penalty be imposed than the one that was applicable at the time the criminal offence was committed.

2. This Article shall not prejudice the trial and punishment of any person for any act or omission which, at the time when it was committed, was criminal according to the general principles of law recognised by civilised nations.

Article 8 Right to respect for private and family life

1. Everyone has the right to respect for his private and family life, his home and his correspondence.

2. There shall be no interference by a public authority with the exercise of this right except such as is in accordance with the law and is necessary in a democratic society in the interests of national security, public safety or the economic well-being of the country, for the prevention of disorder or crime, for the protection of health or morals, or for the protection of the rights and freedoms of others.

Article 10 Freedom of expression

1. Everyone has the right to freedom of expression. This right shall include freedom to hold opinions and to receive and impart information and ideas without interference by

public authority and regardless of frontiers. This Article shall not prevent States from requiring the licensing of broadcasting, television or cinema enterprises.

2. The exercise of these freedoms, since it carries with it duties and responsibilities, may be subject to such formalities, conditions, restrictions or penalties as are prescribed by law and are necessary in a democratic society, in the interests of national security, territorial integrity or public safety, for the prevention of disorder or crime, for the protection of health or morals, for the protection of the reputation or rights of others, for preventing the disclosure of information received in confidence, or for maintaining the authority and impartiality of the judiciary.

Article 11 Freedom of assembly and association

1. Everyone has the right to freedom of peaceful assembly and to freedom of association with others, including the right to form and to join trade unions for the protection of his interests.

2. No restrictions shall be placed on the exercise of these rights other than such as are prescribed by law and are necessary in a democratic society in the interests of national security or public safety, for the prevention of disorder or crime, for the protection of health or morals or for the protection of the rights and freedoms of others. This Article shall not prevent the imposition of lawful restrictions on the exercise of these rights by members of the armed forces, of the police or of the administration of the State.

Article 14 Prohibition of discrimination

The enjoyment of the rights and freedoms set forth in this Convention shall be secured without discrimination on any ground such as sex, race, colour, language, religion, political or other opinion, national or social origin, association with a national minority, property, birth or other status.

Article 16 Restrictions on political activity of aliens

Nothing in Articles 10, 11 and 14 shall be regarded as preventing the High Contracting Parties from imposing restrictions on the political activity of aliens.

PART II THE FIRST PROTOCOL

Article 1 Protection of property

Every natural or legal person is entitled to the peaceful enjoyment of his possessions. No one shall be deprived of his possessions except in the public interest and subject to the conditions provided for by law and by the general principles of international law.

The preceding provisions shall not, however, in any way impair the right of a State to enforce such laws as it deems necessary to control the use of property in accordance with the general interest or to secure the payment of taxes or other contributions or penalties.

Pollution Prevention and Control Act 1999

(1999, c.24)

1 General purpose of section 2 and definitions

(1) The purpose of section 2 is to enable provision to be made for or in connection with—

(a) implementing Council Directive 96/61/EC concerning integrated pollution prevention and control;

(b) regulating, otherwise than in pursuance of that Directive, activities which are capable of causing any environmental pollution;

(c) otherwise preventing or controlling emissions capable of causing any such pollution.

(2) In this Act—

'activities' means activities of any nature, whether—

(a) industrial or commercial or other activities, or

(b) carried on on particular premises or otherwise,

and includes (with or without other activities) the depositing, keeping or disposal of any substance;

'environmental pollution' means pollution of the air, water or land which may give rise to any harm; and for the purposes of this definition (but without prejudice to its generality)—

(a) 'pollution' includes pollution caused by noise, heat or vibrations or any other kind of release of energy, and

(b) 'air' includes air within buildings and air within other natural or man-made structures above or below ground.

(3) In the definition of 'environmental pollution' in subsection (2), 'harm' means—

(a) harm to the health of human beings or other living organisms;

(b) harm to the quality of the environment, including—

(i) harm to the quality of the environment taken as a whole,

(ii) harm to the quality of the air, water or land, and

(iii) other impairment of, or interference with, the ecological systems of which any living organisms form part;

(c) offence to the senses of human beings;

(d) damage to property; or

(e) impairment of, or interference with, amenities or other legitimate uses of the environment (expressions used in this paragraph having the same meaning as in Council Directive 96/61/EC).

2 Regulation of polluting activities

(1) The Secretary of State may by regulations make provision for any of the purposes listed in Part I of Schedule 1; and Part II of that Schedule has effect for supplementing Part I.

(2) In accordance with subsection (1) of section 1, the provision which may be made by regulations under this section is provision for or in connection with any of the matters mentioned in paragraphs (a) to (c) of that subsection.

(3) Regulations under this section may—

(a) contain such consequential, incidental, supplementary, transitional or saving provisions (including provisions amending, repealing or revoking enactments) as the Secretary of State considers appropriate; and

(b) make different provision for different cases, including different provision in relation to different persons, circumstances, areas or localities.

(4) Before making any regulations under this section, the Secretary of State shall consult—

(a) the Environment Agency if the regulations are to apply in relation to England or Wales;

(b) . . .

(c) such bodies or persons appearing to him to be representative of the interests of local government, industry, agriculture and small businesses respectively as he may consider appropriate; and

(d) such other bodies or persons as he may consider appropriate.

(5) Consultation undertaken before the passing of this Act shall constitute as effective compliance with subsection (4) as if undertaken after that passing.

(6) The power to make regulations under this section shall be exercised by statutory instrument.

(7) A statutory instrument containing regulations under this section, if made without a draft having been laid before, and approved by a resolution of, each House of Parliament, shall be subject to annulment in pursuance of a resolution of either House.

(8) No regulations to which this subsection applies shall be made (whether alone or with other regulations) unless a draft of the statutory instrument containing the regulations has been laid before, and approved by a resolution of, each House of Parliament.

(9) Subsection (8) applies to—

(a) the first regulations to be made under this section which apply in relation to England;

(b) the first regulations to be made under this section which apply in relation to Wales;

(c) . . .

(d) regulations under this section which create an offence or increase a penalty for an existing offence;

(e) regulations under this section which amend or repeal any provision of an Act.

3 Prevention etc. of pollution after accidents involving offshore installations

(1) The Secretary of State may, in relation to offshore installations, by regulations make provision which, subject to any modifications that he considers appropriate, corresponds or is similar to any provision made by, or capable of being made under, sections 137 to 140 of the Merchant Shipping Act 1995 (powers to prevent and reduce pollution, and the risk of pollution, by oil or other substances following an accident) in relation to ships.

(2) In this section—

'offshore installation' means any structure or other thing (but not a ship) in or under—

(a) United Kingdom territorial waters, or

(b) any waters mentioned in section 7(9)(b) or (c),

which is used for the purposes of, or in connection with, the exploration, development or production of petroleum;

'petroleum' has the meaning given by section 1 of the Petroleum Act 1998;

'ship' has the same meaning as in the Merchant Shipping Act 1995.

(3) Regulations under this section may—

(a) contain such consequential, incidental, supplementary, transitional or saving provisions as the Secretary of State considers appropriate; and

(b) make different provision for different cases, including different provision in relation to different persons, circumstances, areas or localities.

(4) Before making any regulations under this section, the Secretary of State shall consult—

(a) the Environment Agency . . .;

(b) such bodies or persons appearing to him to be representative of the interests of owners or operators of offshore installations as he may consider appropriate; and

(c) such other bodies or persons as he may consider appropriate.

(5) The power to make regulations under this section shall be exercised by statutory instrument.

(6) No regulations shall be made under this section (whether alone or with other regulations) unless a draft of the statutory instrument containing the regulations has been laid before, and approved by a resolution of, each House of Parliament.

5 Application to Wales and Scotland

(1) Subsection (2) applies to an Order in Council under section 22 of the Government of Wales Act 1998 (transfer of Ministerial functions) if the Order in Council contains a statement that it makes no provision which is not—

(a) provision about functions under this Act; or

(b) provision in connection with such provision.

(2) An Order in Council to which this subsection applies—

(a) shall not be subject to subsection (4)(a) of that section (affirmative resolution of both Houses of Parliament); but

(b) shall be subject to annulment in pursuance of a resolution of either House of Parliament.

(3) . . .

7 Short title, interpretation, commencement and extent

(1) . . .

(2) In this Act—

'enactment' includes an enactment comprised in subordinate legislation within the meaning of the Interpretation Act 1978;

'modifications' includes additions, alterations and omissions and 'modify' shall be construed accordingly.

(3) . . .

(9) Regulations and orders under this Act may make provision applying in relation to (and to places above and below)—

- (a) the territorial waters adjacent to any part of the United Kingdom,
- (b) the sea in any designated area within the meaning of the Continental Shelf Act 1964, and
- (c) the sea in any area specified under section 10(8) of the Petroleum Act 1998.

SCHEDULE 1

PART I LIST OF PURPOSES

Preliminary

1.—(1) Establishing standards, objectives or requirements in relation to emissions within the meaning of the regulations.

(2) Authorising the making of plans for—

- (a) the setting of overall limits,
- (b) the allocation of quotas, or
- (c) the progressive improvement of standards or objectives, relating to such emissions.

(3) Authorising the making of schemes for the trading or other transfer of quotas so allocated.

2.—(1) Determining the authorities (whether public or local or the Secretary of State) by whom functions conferred by the regulations—

- (a) in relation to permits under the regulations, or
- (b) otherwise for or in connection with the prevention or control of environ-mental pollution,

are to be exercisable (in this Schedule referred to as 'regulators').

(2) Specifying any purposes for which any such functions are to be exercisable by regulators.

3. Enabling the Secretary of State to give directions which regulators are to comply with, or guidance which regulators are to have regard to, in exercising functions under the regulations, including—

- (a) directions providing for any functions exercisable by one regulator to be instead exercisable by another;
- (b) directions given for the purposes of the implementation of any obligations of the United Kingdom under the Community Treaties or under any international agreement to which the United Kingdom is a party;
- (c) directions relating to the exercise of any function in a particular case or class of case.

Permits

4. Prohibiting persons from operating any installation or plant of any specified description, or otherwise carrying on any activities of any specified description, except—

- (a) under a permit in force under the regulations, and
- (b) in accordance with any conditions to which the permit is subject.

5. Specifying restrictions or other requirements in connection with the grant of permits (including provisions for restricting the grant of permits to those who are fit and proper

persons within the meaning of the regulations); and otherwise regulating the procedure to be followed in connection with the grant of permits.

6.—(1) Prescribing the contents of permits.

(2) Authorising permits to be granted subject to conditions imposed by regulators.

(3) Securing that permits have effect subject to—

(a) conditions specified in the regulations; or

(b) rules of general application specified in or made under the regulations.

7.—(1) Requiring permits or the conditions to which permits are subject to be reviewed by regulators (whether periodically or in any specified circumstances).

(2) Authorising or requiring the variation of permits or such conditions by regulators (whether on applications made by holders of permits or otherwise).

(3) Regulating the making of changes—

(a) in the operation of the installations or plant to which permits relate, or

(b) in the case of permits for the carrying on of activities otherwise than in the course of operating any installation or plant, in the carrying on of the activities.

8.—(1) Regulating the transfer or surrender of permits.

(2) Authorising the revocation of permits by regulators.

(3) Authorising the imposition by regulators of requirements with respect to the taking of preventive or remedial action (by holders of permits or other persons) in connection with the surrender or revocation of permits.

9. Authorising the Secretary of State to make schemes for the charging by regulators of fees or other charges in respect of, or in respect of an application for—

(a) the grant of a permit,

(b) the variation of a permit or the conditions to which it is subject, or

(c) the transfer or surrender of a permit, or in respect of the subsistence of a permit.

[9A—(1) Authorising the Secretary of State to make schemes for the charging by regulators of charges, as respects greenhouse gas emissions permits in relation to offshore installations, corresponding to those that may be prescribed under section 41 (read with section 41A) of the Environment Act 1995.

(2) Subsections (2) to (5) of section 41A of that Act apply in relation to the Secretary of State and a charging scheme made by virtue of this paragraph as they apply in relation to the Scottish Environment Protection Agency and a charging scheme made by that Agency under the 1995 Act.

(3) In this paragraph 'greenhouse gas emissions permit' and 'offshore installation' have the same meaning as in the Greenhouse Gas Emissions Trading Scheme Regulations 2005.]

10. Authorising, or authorising a Minister of the Crown to make schemes for, the charging by Ministers of the Crown or public or local authorities of fees or other charges in respect of—

(a) the testing or analysis of substances,

(b) the validating of, or of the results of, any testing or analysis of substances, or

(c) assessing how the environment might be affected by the release into it of any substances,

in cases where the testing, analysis, validating or assessing is in any way in anticipation of, or otherwise in connection with, the making of applications for the grant of permits or is carried out in pursuance of conditions to which any permit is subject.

Information, publicity and consultation

11. Enabling persons of any specified description (whether or not they are holders of permits) to be required—

(a) to compile information—

(i) on emissions within the meaning of the regulations;

(ii) on energy consumption and on the efficiency with which energy is used;

(iii) on waste within the meaning of the regulations and on the destinations of such waste;

(b) to provide such information in such manner as is specified in the regulations.

12. Securing

(a) that publicity is given to specified matters;

(b) that regulators maintain registers of specified matters (but excepting information which under the regulations is, or is determined to be, commercially confidential and subject to any other exceptions specified in the regulations) which are open to public inspection;

(c) that copies of entries in such registers, or of specified documents, may be obtained by members of the public.

13. Requiring or authorising regulators to carry out consultation in connection with the exercise of any of their functions; and providing for them to take into account representations made to them on consultation.

Enforcement and offences

14.—(1) Conferring on regulators functions with respect to the monitoring and inspection of the carrying on of activities to which permits relate, including—

(a) power to take samples or to make copies of information;

(b) power to arrange for preventive or remedial action to be taken at the expense of holders of permits.

(2) Authorising regulators to appoint suitable persons to exercise any such functions and conferring powers (such as those specified in section 108(4) of the Environment Act 1995) on persons so appointed.

15.—(1) Authorising regulators to serve on holders of permits—

(a) notices requiring them to take remedial action in respect of contraventions, actual or potential, of conditions to which their permits are subject;

(b) notices requiring them to provide such financial security as the regulators serving the notices consider appropriate pending the taking of remedial action in respect of any such contraventions;

(c) notices requiring them to take steps to remove imminent risks of serious environmental pollution (whether or not arising from any such contraventions).

(2) Providing for the enforcement of such notices by proceedings in the High Court . . .

16. Authorising regulators to suspend the operation of permits so far as having effect to authorise the carrying on of activities to which they relate.

17. The creation of offences and dealing with matters relating to such offences, including—

(a) the provision of defences; and

(b) evidentiary matters.

18. Enabling, where a person has been convicted of an offence under the regulations—

(a) a court dealing with that person for the offence to order the taking of remedial action (in addition to or instead of imposing any punishment); or

(b) a regulator to arrange for such action to be taken at that person's expense.

Appeals

19. Conferring rights of appeal in respect of decisions made, notices served or other things done (or omitted to be done) under the regulations; and making provision for (or for the determination of) matters relating to the making, considering and determination of such appeals (including provision for or in connection with the holding of inquiries or hearings).

General

20.—(1) Making provision which, subject to any modifications that the Secretary of State considers appropriate, corresponds or is similar to—

(a) any provision made by or under, or capable of being made under, Part I or II of the Environmental Protection Act 1990 or made by any of sections 157, 158 and 160 of that Act; or

(b) any provision made, or capable of being made, under section 2(2) of the European Communities Act 1972 in connection with one of the relevant directives.

(2) In sub-paragraph (1) 'the relevant directives' means—

(a) Council Directive 96/61/EC concerning integrated pollution prevention and control;

(b) Council Directive 75/442/EEC on waste, as amended; and

(c) any other directive of the Council of the European Communities designated by the Secretary of State for the purposes of this paragraph by order made by statutory instrument.

(3) Making provision about the application of the regulations to the Crown.

PART II SUPPLEMENTARY PROVISIONS

Particular types of pollution

21. The regulations may provide for specified provisions of the regulations to have effect in relation only to such environmental pollution as is specified.

[21A. *Emissions quota trading schemes: penalties*

(1) The regulations may authorise the inclusion in a trading scheme of—

(a) provision for penalties in respect of contraventions of provisions of the scheme;

(b) provision for the amount of any penalty under the scheme to be such as may be set out in, or calculated in accordance with-

(i) the scheme, or

(ii) the regulations (including regulations made after the scheme).

(2) In this paragraph 'trading scheme' means a scheme of the kind mentioned in paragraph 1(3).]

Determination of matters by regulators

22. The regulations may make provision for anything which, by virtue of paragraphs 5 to 8, could be provided for by the regulations to be determined under the regulations by regulators.

Imposition of conditions

23. In connection with the determination of conditions as mentioned in paragraph 6(3)(a) the regulations may in particular provide—

(a) for such conditions to be determined in the light of any specified general principles and any directions or guidance given under the regulations;

(b) for such guidance to include guidance sanctioning reliance by a regulator on any arrangements referred to in the guidance to operate to secure a particular result as an alternative to imposing a condition.

Charging schemes

24. The regulations may—

(a) require any such scheme as is mentioned in paragraph 9, 9A or 10 to be so framed that the fees and charges payable under the scheme are sufficient, taking one year with another, to cover such expenditure (whether or not incurred by the regulator or other person to whom they are so payable) as is specified;

(b) authorise any such scheme to make different provision for different cases (and specify particular kinds of such cases).

Offences

25.—(1) The regulations may provide for any such offence as is mentioned in paragraph 17 to be triable—

(a) only summarily; or

(b) either summarily or on indictment.

(2) The regulations may provide for such an offence to be punishable—

(a) on summary conviction by—

(i) imprisonment for a term not exceeding such period as is specified (which may not exceed twelve months), or

(ii) a fine not exceeding such amount as is specified (which may not exceed £50,000),

or both; or

(b) on conviction on indictment by—

(i) imprisonment for a term not exceeding such period as is specified (which may not exceed five years), or

(ii) a fine, or both.

Interpretation

26. In this Schedule—

'functions' includes powers and duties;

'the regulations' means regulations under section 2;

'specified' means specified in regulations under that section.

Freedom of Information Act 2000

(2000, c. 36)

PART II EXEMPT INFORMATION

39 Environmental information

(1) Information is exempt information if the public authority holding it—

(a) is obliged by [environmental information regulations] to make the information available to the public in accordance with the regulations, or

(b) would be so obliged but for any exemption contained in the regulations.

[(1A) In subsection (1) 'environmental information regulations' means—

(a) regulations made under section 74, or

(b) regulations made under section 2(2) of the European Communities Act 1972 for the purpose of implementing any Community obligation relating to public access to, and the dissemination of, information on the environment.]

(2) The duty to confirm or deny does not arise in relation to information which is (or if it were held by the public authority would be) exempt information by virtue of subsection (1).

(3) Subsection (1)(a) does not limit the generality of section 21(1).

PART III GENERAL FUNCTIONS OF SECRETARY OF STATE, LORD CHANCELLOR AND INFORMATION COMMISSIONER

47 General functions of Commissioner

(1) It shall be the duty of the Commissioner to promote the following of good practice by public authorities and, in particular, so to perform his functions under this Act as to promote the observance by public authorities of—

(a) the requirements of this Act, and

(b) the provisions of the codes of practice under sections 45 and 46.

(2) The Commissioner shall arrange for the dissemination in such form and manner as he considers appropriate of such information as it may appear to him expedient to give to the public—

(a) about the operation of this Act,
(b) about good practice, and
(c) about other matters within the scope of his functions under this Act,

and may give advice to any person as to any of those matters.

(3) The Commissioner may, with the consent of any public authority, assess whether that authority is following good practice.

(4) The Commissioner may charge such sums as he may with the consent of the Secretary of State determine for any services provided by the Commissioner under this section.

(5) The Commissioner shall from time to time as he considers appropriate—

(a) consult the Keeper of Public Records about the promotion by the Commissioner of the observance by public authorities of the provisions of the code of practice under section 46 in relation to records which are public records for the purposes of the Public Records Act 1958, and

(b) ...

(6) In this section 'good practice', in relation to a public authority, means such practice in the discharge of its functions under this Act as appears to the Commissioner to be desirable, and includes (but is not limited to) compliance with the requirements of this Act and the provisions of the codes of practice under sections 45 and 46.

48 Recommendations as to good practice

(1) If it appears to the Commissioner that the practice of a public authority in relation to the exercise of its functions under this Act does not conform with that proposed in the codes of practice under sections 45 and 46, he may give to the authority a recommendation (in this section referred to as a 'practice recommendation') specifying the steps which ought in his opinion to be taken for promoting such conformity.

(2) A practice recommendation must be given in writing and must refer to the particular provisions of the code of practice with which, in the Commissioner's opinion, the public authority's practice does not conform.

(3) Before giving to a public authority other than the Public Record Office a practice recommendation which relates to conformity with the code of practice under section 46 in respect of records which are public records for the purposes of the Public Records Act 1958, the Commissioner shall consult the Keeper of Public Records.

(4) ...

PART IV ENFORCEMENT

50 Application for decision by Commissioner

(1) Any person (in this section referred to as 'the complainant') may apply to the Commissioner for a decision whether, in any specified respect, a request for information made by the complainant to a public authority has been dealt with in accordance with the requirements of Part I.

(2) On receiving an application under this section, the Commissioner shall make a decision unless it appears to him—

(a) that the complainant has not exhausted any complaints procedure which is provided by the public authority in conformity with the code of practice under section 45,
(b) that there has been undue delay in making the application,
(c) that the application is frivolous or vexatious, or
(d) that the application has been withdrawn or abandoned.

(3) Where the Commissioner has received an application under this section, he shall either—

(a) notify the complainant that he has not made any decision under this section as a result of the application and of his grounds for not doing so, or

(b) serve notice of his decision (in this Act referred to as a 'decision notice') on the complainant and the public authority.

(4) Where the Commissioner decides that a public authority—

(a) has failed to communicate information, or to provide confirmation or denial, in a case where it is required to do so by section 1(1), or

(b) has failed to comply with any of the requirements of sections 11 and 17,

the decision notice must specify the steps which must be taken by the authority for complying with that requirement and the period within which they must be taken.

(5) A decision notice must contain particulars of the right of appeal conferred by section 57.

(6) Where a decision notice requires steps to be taken by the public authority within a specified period, the time specified in the notice must not expire before the end of the period within which an appeal can be brought against the notice and, if such an appeal is brought, no step which is affected by the appeal need be taken pending the determination or withdrawal of the appeal.

(7) This section has effect subject to section 53.

51 Information notices

(1) If the Commissioner—

(a) has received an application under section 50, or

(b) reasonably requires any information—

(i) for the purpose of determining whether a public authority has complied or is complying with any of the requirements of Part I, or

(ii) for the purpose of determining whether the practice of a public authority in relation to the exercise of its functions under this Act conforms with that proposed in the codes of practice under sections 45 and 46,

he may serve the authority with a notice (in this Act referred to as 'an information notice') requiring it, within such time as is specified in the notice, to furnish the Commissioner, in such form as may be so specified, with such information relating to the application, to compliance with Part I or to conformity with the code of practice as is so specified.

(2) An information notice must contain—

(a) in a case falling within subsection (1)(a), a statement that the Commissioner has received an application under section 50, or

(b) in a case falling within subsection (1)(b), a statement—

(i) that the Commissioner regards the specified information as relevant for either of the purposes referred to in subsection (1)(b), and

(ii) of his reasons for regarding that information as relevant for that purpose.

(3) An information notice must also contain particulars of the right of appeal conferred by section 57.

(4) The time specified in an information notice must not expire before the end of the period within which an appeal can be brought against the notice and, if such an appeal is brought, the information need not be furnished pending the determination or withdrawal of the appeal.

(5) An authority shall not be required by virtue of this section to furnish the Commissioner with any information in respect of—

(a) any communication between a professional legal adviser and his client in connection with the giving of legal advice to the client with respect to his obligations, liabilities or rights under this Act, or

(b) any communication between a professional legal adviser and his client, or between such an adviser or his client and any other person, made in connection with or in contemplation of proceedings under or arising out of this Act (including proceedings before the Tribunal) and for the purposes of such proceedings.

(6) In subsection (5) references to the client of a professional legal adviser include references to any person representing such a client.

(7) The Commissioner may cancel an information notice by written notice to the authority on which it was served.

(8) In this section 'information' includes unrecorded information.

52 Enforcement notices

(1) If the Commissioner is satisfied that a public authority has failed to comply with any of the requirements of Part I, the Commissioner may serve the authority with a notice (in this Act referred to as 'an enforcement notice') requiring the authority to take, within such time as may be specified in the notice, such steps as may be so specified for complying with those requirements.

(2) An enforcement notice must contain—

(a) a statement of the requirement or requirements of Part I with which the Commissioner is satisfied that the public authority has failed to comply and his reasons for reaching that conclusion, and

(b) particulars of the right of appeal conferred by section 57.

(3) An enforcement notice must not require any of the provisions of the notice to be complied with before the end of the period within which an appeal can be brought against the notice and, if such an appeal is brought, the notice need not be complied with pending the determination or withdrawal of the appeal.

(4) The Commissioner may cancel an enforcement notice by written notice to the authority on which it was served.

(5) This section has effect subject to section 53.

53 Exception from duty to comply with decision notice or enforcement notice

(1) This section applies to a decision notice or enforcement notice which—

(a) is served on—

(i) a government department,

(ii) the National Assembly for Wales, or

(iii) any public authority designated for the purposes of this section by an order made by the [Secretary of State], and

(b) relates to a failure, in respect of one or more requests for information—

(i) to comply with section 1(1)(a) in respect of information which falls within any provision of Part II stating that the duty to confirm or deny does not arise, or

(ii) to comply with section 1(1)(b) in respect of exempt information.

(2) A decision notice or enforcement notice to which this section applies shall cease to have effect if, not later than the twentieth working day following the effective date, the accountable person in relation to that authority gives the Commissioner a certificate signed by him stating that he has on reasonable grounds formed the opinion that, in respect of the request or requests concerned, there was no failure falling within subsection (1)(b).

(3) Where the accountable person gives a certificate to the Commissioner under subsection (2) he shall as soon as practicable thereafter lay a copy of the certificate before—

(a) each House of Parliament,

(b) the Northern Ireland Assembly, in any case where the certificate relates to a decision notice or enforcement notice which has been served on a Northern Ireland department or any Northern Ireland public authority, or

(c) the National Assembly for Wales, in any case where the certificate relates to a decision notice or enforcement notice which has been served on the National Assembly for Wales or any Welsh public authority.

(4) In subsection (2) 'the effective date', in relation to a decision notice or enforcement notice, means—

(a) the day on which the notice was given to the public authority, or

(b) where an appeal under section 57 is brought, the day on which that appeal (or any further appeal arising out of it) is determined or withdrawn.

(5) Before making an order under subsection (1)(a)(iii), the [Secretary of State] shall—

(a) if the order relates to a Welsh public authority, consult the National Assembly for Wales,

(b) if the order relates to the Northern Ireland Assembly, consult the Presiding Officer of that Assembly, and

(c) if the order relates to a Northern Ireland public authority, consult the First Minister and deputy First Minister in Northern Ireland.

(6) Where the accountable person gives a certificate to the Commissioner under subsection (2) in relation to a decision notice, the accountable person shall, on doing so or as soon as reasonably practicable after doing so, inform the person who is the complainant for the purposes of section 50 of the reasons for his opinion.

(7) The accountable person is not obliged to provide information under subsection (6) if, or to the extent that, compliance with that subsection would involve the disclosure of exempt information.

(8) In this section 'the accountable person'—

(a) in relation to a Northern Ireland department or any Northern Ireland public authority, means the First Minister and deputy First Minister in Northern Ireland acting jointly,

(b) in relation to the National Assembly for Wales or any Welsh public authority, means the Assembly First Secretary, and

(c) in relation to any other public authority, means—

(i) a Minister of the Crown who is a member of the Cabinet, or

(ii) the Attorney General, the Advocate General for Scotland or the Attorney General for Northern Ireland.

(9) In this section 'working day' has the same meaning as in section 10.

54 Failure to comply with notice

(1) If a public authority has failed to comply with—

(a) so much of a decision notice as requires steps to be taken,

(b) an information notice, or

(c) an enforcement notice,

the Commissioner may certify in writing to the court that the public authority has failed to comply with that notice.

(2) For the purposes of this section, a public authority which, in purported compliance with an information notice—

(a) makes a statement which it knows to be false in a material respect, or

(b) recklessly makes a statement which is false in a material respect,

is to be taken to have failed to comply with the notice.

(3) Where a failure to comply is certified under subsection (1), the court may inquire into the matter and, after hearing any witness who may be produced against or on behalf of the public authority, and after hearing any statement that may be offered in defence, deal with the authority as if it had committed a contempt of court.

(4) In this section 'the court' means the High Court . . .

56 No action against public authority

(1) This Act does not confer any right of action in civil proceedings in respect of any failure to comply with any duty imposed by or under this Act.

(2) Subsection (1) does not affect the powers of the Commissioner under section 54.

PART V APPEALS

57 Appeal against notices served under Part IV

(1) Where a decision notice has been served, the complainant or the public authority may appeal to the Tribunal against the notice.

(2) A public authority on which an information notice or an enforcement notice has been served by the Commissioner may appeal to the Tribunal against the notice.

(3) In relation to a decision notice or enforcement notice which relates—

(a) to information to which section 66 applies, and

(b) to a matter which by virtue of subsection (3) or (4) of that section falls to be determined by the responsible authority instead of the appropriate records authority,

subsections (1) and (2) shall have effect as if the reference to the public authority were a reference to the public authority or the responsible authority.

58 Determination of appeals

(1) If on an appeal under section 57 the Tribunal considers—

(a) that the notice against which the appeal is brought is not in accordance with the law, or

(b) to the extent that the notice involved an exercise of discretion by the Commissioner, that he ought to have exercised his discretion differently,

the Tribunal shall allow the appeal or substitute such other notice as could have been served by the Commissioner; and in any other case the Tribunal shall dismiss the appeal.

(2) On such an appeal, the Tribunal may review any finding of fact on which the notice in question was based.

59 Appeals from decision of Tribunal

Any party to an appeal to the Tribunal under section 57 may appeal from the decision of the Tribunal on a point of law to the appropriate court; and that court shall be—

(a) the High Court of Justice in England if the address of the public authority is in England or Wales, . . .

60 Appeals against national security certificate

(1) Where a certificate under section 23(2) or 24(3) has been issued—

(a) the Commissioner, or

(b) any applicant whose request for information is affected by the issue of the certificate,

may appeal to the Tribunal against the certificate.

(2) If on an appeal under subsection (1) relating to a certificate under section 23(2), the Tribunal finds that the information referred to in the certificate was not exempt information by virtue of section 23(1), the Tribunal may allow the appeal and quash the certificate.

(3) If on an appeal under subsection (1) relating to a certificate under section 24(3), the Tribunal finds that, applying the principles applied by the court on an application for judicial review, the Minister did not have reasonable grounds for issuing the certificate, the Tribunal may allow the appeal and quash the certificate.

(4) Where in any proceedings under this Act it is claimed by a public authority that a certificate under section 24(3) which identifies the information to which it applies by means of a general description applies to particular information, any other party to the proceedings may appeal to the Tribunal on the ground that the certificate does not apply to the information in question and, subject to any determination under subsection (5), the certificate shall be conclusively presumed so to apply.

(5) On any appeal under subsection (4), the Tribunal may determine that the certificate does not so apply.

61 Appeal proceedings

(1) Schedule 4 (which contains amendments of Schedule 6 to the Data Protection Act 1998 relating to appeal proceedings) has effect.

(2) Accordingly, the provisions of Schedule 6 to the Data Protection Act 1998 have effect (so far as applicable) in relation to appeals under this Part.

PART VIII MISCELLANEOUS AND SUPPLEMENTAL

74 Power to make provision relating to environmental information

(1) In this section 'the Aarhus Convention' means the Convention on Access to Information, Public Participation in Decision-making and Access to Justice in Environmental Matters signed at Aarhus on 25th June 1998.

(2) For the purposes of this section 'the information provisions' of the Aarhus Convention are Article 4, together with Articles 3 and 9 so far as relating to that Article.

(3) The Secretary of State may be regulations make such provision as he considers appropriate—

(a) for the purpose of implementing the information provisions of the Aarhus Convention or any amendment of those provisions made in accordance with Article 14 of the Convention, and

(b) for the purpose of dealing with matters arising out of or related to the implementation of those provisions or of any such amendment.

(4) Regulations under subsection (3) may in particular—

(a) enable charges to be made for making information available in accordance with the regulations,

(b) provide that any obligation imposed by the regulations in relation to the disclosure of information is to have effect notwithstanding any enactment or rule of law,

(c) make provision for the issue by the Secretary of State of a code of practice,

(d) provide for sections 47 and 48 to apply in relation to such a code with such modifications as may be specified,

(e) provide for any of the provisions of Parts IV and V to apply, with such modifications as may be specified in the regulations, in relation to compliance with any requirement of the regulations, and

(f) contain such transitional or consequential provision (including provision modifying any enactment) as the Secretary of State considers appropriate.

(5) . . .

Utilities Act 2000

(2000, c. 27)

PART I NEW REGULATORY ARRANGEMENTS

1 Gas and Electricity Markets Authority

(1) There shall be a body corporate to be known as the Gas and Electricity Markets Authority (in this Act referred to as 'the Authority') for the purpose of carrying out—

(a) functions transferred to the Authority from the Director General of Gas Supply and the Director General of Electricity Supply; and

(b) the other functions of the Authority under this Act.

. . .

[5A Duty of Authority to carry out impact assessment

(1) This section applies where—

(a) the Authority is proposing to do anything for the purposes of, or in connection with, the carrying out of any function exercisable by it under or by virtue of Part 1 of the 1986 Act or Part 1 of the 1989 Act; and

(b) it appears to it that the proposal is important;

but this section does not apply if it appears to the Authority that the urgency of the matter makes it impracticable or inappropriate for the Authority to comply with the requirements of this section.

(2) A proposal is important for the purposes of this section only if its implementation would be likely to do one or more of the following—

(a) involve a major change in the activities carried on by the Authority;

(b) have a significant impact on persons engaged in the shipping, transportation or supply of gas conveyed through pipes or in the generation, transmission, distribution or supply of electricity;

(c) have a significant impact on persons engaged in commercial activities connected with the shipping, transportation or supply of gas conveyed through pipes or with the generation, transmission, distribution or supply of electricity;
(d) have a significant impact on the general public in Great Britain or in a part of Great Britain; or
(e) have significant effects on the environment.

(3) Before implementing its proposal, the Authority must either—
(a) carry out and publish an assessment of the likely impact of implementing the proposal; or
(b) publish a statement setting out its reasons for thinking that it is unnecessary for it to carry out an assessment.

(4) An assessment carried out under this section must—
(a) include an assessment of the likely effects on the environment of implementing the proposal; and
(b) relate to such other matters as the Authority considers appropriate.

(5) In determining the matters to which an assessment under this section should relate, the Authority must have regard to such general guidance relating to the carrying out of impact assessments as it considers appropriate.

(6) An assessment carried out under this section may take such form as the Authority considers appropriate.

(7) Where the Authority publishes an assessment under this section—
(a) it must provide an opportunity of making representations to the Authority about its proposal to members of the public and other persons who, in the Authority's opinion, are likely to be affected to a significant extent by the proposal's implementation;
(b) the published assessment must be accompanied by a statement setting out how representations may be made; and
(c) the Authority must not implement its proposal unless the period for making representations about the proposal has expired and it has considered all the representations that were made in that period.

(8) Where the Authority is required (apart from this section)—
(a) to consult about a proposal to which this section applies, or
(b) to give a person an opportunity of making representations about it,
the requirements of this section are in addition to, but may be performed contemporaneously with, the other requirements.

(9) Every report under section 5(1) must set out—
(a) a list of the assessments under this section carried out during the financial year to which the report relates; and
(b) a summary of the decisions taken during that year in relation to proposals to which assessments carried out in that year or previous financial years relate.

(10) The publication of anything under this section must be in such manner as the Authority considers appropriate for bringing it to the attention of the persons who, in the Authority's opinion, are likely to be affected if its proposal is implemented.

(11) References in sections 4AA, 4AB and 4A of the 1986 Act to functions of the Authority under Part 1 of that Act include references to any functions of the Authority under this section that are exercisable in relation to a proposal to do anything for the purposes of, or in connection with, the carrying out of any function of the Authority under Part 1 of the 1986 Act.

(12) References in sections 3A, 3B and 3C of the 1989 Act to functions of the Authority under Part 1 of that Act include references to any functions of the Authority under this section that are exercisable in relation to a proposal to do anything for the purposes of, or in connection with, the carrying out of any function of the Authority under Part 1 of the 1989 Act.]

Sustainable Energy Act 2003

(2003, c. 30)

1 Annual reports on progress towards sustainable energy aims

(1) The Secretary of State must in each calendar year, beginning with 2004, publish a report ('a sustainable energy report') on the progress made in the reporting period towards—

(a) cutting the United Kingdom's carbon emissions;

(b) maintaining the reliability of the United Kingdom's energy supplies;

(c) promoting competitive energy markets in the United Kingdom; and

(d) reducing the number of people living in fuel poverty in the United Kingdom.

[(1A) The report must include, in particular, all such information as the Secretary of State considers appropriate about—

(a) things done during the reporting period for the purposes of the development or the bringing into use of any of the energy sources or technologies mentioned in subsection (1B);

(b) things done during that period for the purpose of ensuring the maintenance of the scientific and engineering expertise available in the United Kingdom that is necessary for the development of potential energy sources (including sources of nuclear energy); and

(c) things done during that period for the purpose of achieving the energy efficiency aims designated under sections 2 and 3.

(1B) The energy sources and technologies referred to in subsection (1A)(a) are—

(a) clean coal technology;

(b) coal mine methane;

(c) biomass;

(d) biofuels;

(e) fuel cells;

(f) photovoltaics;

(g) wave and tidal generation;

(h) hydrogeneration;

(i) microgeneration;

(j) geothermal sources; and

(k) other sources of energy, and technologies for the production of energy, the use of which would, in the opinion of the Secretary of State, cut the United Kingdom's carbon emissions.

(1C) The references in subsection (1A) to things done during the reporting period include references to proposals of the Secretary of State published during that period.]

(2) 'The reporting period', for the purposes of subsections (1)–(1c), means the year ending with 23 February in the calendar year in question.

(3) Accordingly, the report must be published in that calendar year within the period beginning with 24 February and ending with 31 December ('the publication period').

(4) A sustainable energy report may either be published as a single report or published in a number of parts during the publication period, and any such report or part may be contained in a document containing other material.

(5) A sustainable energy report must be based on such information as is available to the Secretary of State when the report is completed (except that if it is published in parts, each of those parts must be based on such information as is so available when that part is completed).

(6) For the purposes of this section a person is to be regarded as living in fuel poverty if he is a member of a household living on a lower income in a home which cannot be kept warm at a reasonable cost.

2 Energy efficiency of residential accommodation: Secretary of State

(1) The Secretary of State must within one week beginning with the coming into force of this section designate under this subsection at least one energy efficiency aim.

(2) For the purposes of this section an 'energy efficiency aim' is an aim which—
(a) is contained in a published document;
(b) relates to the energy efficiency of residential accommodation in England; and
(c) is compatible with Community obligations and any other international obligations of the United Kingdom.

(3) The Secretary of State may, at any time after designation under subsection (1), designate under this subsection a further energy efficiency aim or aims.

(4) Where an energy efficiency aim is for the time being designated under this section, the Secretary of State must take reasonable steps to achieve the aim.

(5) In deciding which steps to take for the purposes of subsection (4), the Secretary of State must consider steps relating to the heating, cooling, ventilation, lighting and insulation of residential accommodation.

(6) A designation under this section may be withdrawn, but not if its withdrawal would result in there being no energy efficiency aim designated under this section.

(7) If an energy efficiency aim designated under this section ceases to meet the condition in subsection (2)(c) it ceases to be designated under this section, but if this results in there being no energy efficiency aim so designated the Secretary of State must without delay designate a new energy efficiency aim.

(8) A designation of an aim under this section, or a withdrawal or cessation of such a designation, must be published in such way as the Secretary of State considers appropriate: a designation may be contained in the same published document as the aim itself.

(9) In this section 'residential accommodation' has the meaning given by section 1 of the Home Energy Conservation Act 1995 (*c.* 10).

3 Energy efficiency of residential accommodation: National Assembly for Wales

. . .

4 Energy efficiency of residential accommodation: energy conservation authorities

(1) In this section an 'energy efficiency direction' means a direction requiring each energy conservation authority to which it applies to take such energy conservation measures as that authority considers to be—
(a) likely to result in achieving, by a date specified in the direction, an improvement so specified (which may be expressed as a percentage) in the energy efficiency of residential accommodation in that authority's area; and
(b) practicable and cost-effective.

(2) For the purposes of this section, 'the energy efficiency' of residential accommodation in an energy conservation authority's area has such meaning as may be specified in an order made by the Secretary of State.

(3) The Secretary of State may, after consulting the Local Government Association, give an energy efficiency direction which applies—
(a) to one or more named energy conservation authorities in England;
(b) to all energy conservation authorities in England; or
(c) to a particular description of energy conservation authority in England.

(4) . . .

(5) With effect from the giving of an energy efficiency direction—
(a) each energy conservation authority to which the direction applies must comply with the direction, using the powers it has apart from this section; and
(b) the Home Energy Conservation Act 1995 (c. 10) ('HECA') shall cease to apply in relation to each such authority.

(6) In deciding which measures to take for the purposes of complying with an energy efficiency direction, an authority must give preference to measures which it considers would also contribute to—
(a) achieving the objective mentioned in paragraph (d) of section 2(2) of the Warm Homes and Energy Conservation Act 2000 (*c.* 31) by the target date for the time being specified under that paragraph;

(b) achieving any interim objectives for the time being specified under paragraph (c) of section 2(2) of that Act by the target date so specified.

(7) Different energy efficiency directions may be given in relation to different energy conservation authorities or different descriptions of such authority.

(8) The Secretary of State may after consulting the Local Government Association, . . . alter the date or the improvement (or both) for the time being specified in an energy efficiency direction given by the Secretary of State or (as the case may be) by the Assembly.

(9) An energy efficiency direction may be revoked, but only if each authority to which it applies either—

(a) is subject to a new energy efficiency direction taking effect immediately on the revocation; or

(b) no longer exists at the time of the revocation.

(10) The Secretary of State may give to energy conservation authorities in England . . ., such guidance as he or it considers appropriate in relation to the exercise of an energy conservation authority's functions under this section.

(11) An energy conservation authority must have regard to any such guidance.

(12) The Secretary of State may by order—

(a) amend this section so as to alter the body which must be consulted by him;

(b) make transitional provision in relation to HECA's ceasing to apply in relation to an energy conservation authority in England.

(13) . . .

(14) Any power to make an order under this section is exercisable by statutory instrument which, in the case of an order made by the Secretary of State, shall be subject to annulment in pursuance of a resolution of either House of Parliament.

(15) In this section the following expressions have the meaning given by section 1 of HECA—

'energy conservation authority';

'residential accommodation';

'area', in relation to an energy conservation authority;

'energy conservation measures'.

5 CHP targets

(1) Before the end of 2003, the Secretary of State must make a statement—

(a) specifying one or more CHP targets; and

(b) specifying the period that each CHP target is for.

(2) At any time after making the statement mentioned in subsection (1), the Secretary of State may make a further statement doing either or both of the following—

(a) specifying as mentioned in that subsection;

(b) revoking a CHP target contained in an earlier statement under this section.

(3) A CHP target is the percentage of the amount of electricity for government use in the period the target is for that the Secretary of State considers will be capable, at a reasonable cost to the government, of being supplied from CHP electricity.

(4) For the purposes of this section—

'amount of electricity for government use in the period the target is for' means the amount of electricity that the Secretary of State estimates that the government will use in that period;

'CHP electricity' means electricity that—

(a) is generated by a generating station which is operated for the purposes of producing heat, or a cooling effect, in association with electricity; and

(b) satisfies any other requirements specified in an order made by the Secretary of State.

(5) The Secretary of State may by order—

(a) specify the departments and other bodies which (taken together) are to constitute 'the government' for the purposes of this section;

(b) provide for the exclusion from any estimation of the amount of electricity that the government will use in a period of—
(i) the use of electricity for purposes specified in the order or in circumstances so specified;
(ii) the use of electricity by any part of the government specified in the order.

(6) One of the periods specified under subsection (1)(b) must—
(a) begin with 1 January 2010; and
(b) end with 31 December 2010.

(7) The Secretary of State must lay any statement made under this section before Parliament.

(8) Any power to make an order under this section is exercisable by statutory instrument which shall be subject to annulment in pursuance of a resolution of either House of Parliament.

(9) No proceedings may be brought to enforce any CHP target contained in a statement made under this section or otherwise to review any act done, or any failure to act, in relation to any such CHP target.

7 Use of certain money held by gas and electricity markets authority

(1) If the Secretary of State so directs, the person prescribed under section 33(1)(b) of the Electricity Act (collection of fossil fuel levy) must pay an amount into the Consolidated Fund out of money that has been paid under section 33(5A) of that Act.

(2) The total of the amounts directed to be paid under this section must not exceed £60,000,000.

(3) At any time which falls after the giving of a direction under this section, the Secretary of State is under a duty to spend the required amount for the purpose of promoting the use of energy from renewable sources.

(4) 'The required amount', for the purposes of subsection (3), is an amount of money equal to the total of the amounts that at the time in question have been paid into the Consolidated Fund under subsection (1), less the total of any amounts that the Secretary of State has already spent under subsection (3).

(5) In subsection (3) 'renewable sources' means sources of energy other than fossil fuel or nuclear fuel.

(6) In subsection (5) 'fossil fuel' means coal, substances produced directly or indirectly from coal, lignite, natural gas, crude liquid petroleum, or petroleum products (and 'natural gas' and 'petroleum products' have the same meanings as in the Energy Act 1976 (c. 76)).

(7) The Secretary of State's duty under subsection (3) is without prejudice to any power or duty of his apart from this section to spend money for the purpose mentioned in that subsection.

(8) In this section—
(a) 'the Electricity Act' means the Electricity Act 1989 (c. 29); and
(b) the references to section 33 of that Act are to that section as it has effect in England and Wales.

8 Financial provision

There shall be paid out of money provided by Parliament—
(a) any expenditure of the Secretary of State under this Act; and
(b) any increase attributable to this Act in the sums which under any other Act are payable out of money so provided.

9 Citation, extent and commencement

(1) This Act may be cited as the Sustainable Energy Act 2003.

(2) Except as provided in subsections (3) and (4), this Act extends to England and Wales...

(3) Sections 2, 3, 4, 5 and 7 extend to England and Wales only.

(4) Section 6 extends to England and Wales...

(5) Sections 2, 4 (so far as it relates to England) and 5 shall come into force on such day as the Secretary of State may be order made by statutory instrument appoint.

(6) Sections 3 and 4 (so far as it relates to Wales) shall come into force on such day as the National Assembly for Wales may by order made by statutory instrument appoint.

(7) The other provisions of this Act shall come into force at the end of two months beginning with the day on which it is passed.

(8) An order under subsection (5) or (6) may appoint different days for different purposes.

Waste and Emissions Trading Act 2003

(2003, c. 33)

PART I WASTE

CHAPTER 1 WASTE SENT TO LANDFILLS

Landfill targets

1 Target years

(1) The Secretary of State must by regulations specify the maximum amount by weight of biodegradable municipal waste allowed, in each scheme year that is a target year, to be sent to landfills from each of—

- (a) the United Kingdom,
- (b) England,
- (c) Scotland,
- (d) Wales, and
- (e) Northern Ireland.

(2) Amounts specified under subsection (1)(a) must be consistent with the obligations of the United Kingdom under Article 5(2) of Council Directive 1999/31/EC.

(3) The total of the amounts specified under subsection (1)(b) to (e) for a year must not exceed the amount specified under subsection (1)(a) for that year.

(4) The Secretary of State must consult—

- (a) The Scottish Ministers before specifying amounts under subsection (1)(c);
- (b) the National Assembly for Wales before specifying amounts under subsection (1)(d);
- (c) the Department of the Environment before specifying amounts under subsection (1)(e).

(5) Subsection (4) may be satisfied by consultation before, as well as by consultation after, the coming into force of this section.

2 Non-target years

(1) The Secretary of State may by regulations specify the maximum amount by weight of biodegradable municipal waste allowed, in a scheme year that is not a target year, to be sent to landfills from—

- (a) England;
- (b) Scotland;
- (c) Wales;
- (d) Northern Ireland.

(2) The power under subsection (1)(b) is exercisable only with the agreement of the Scottish Ministers.

(3) The power under subsection (1)(c) is exercisable only with the agreement of the National Assembly for Wales.

(4) The power under subsection (1)(d) is exercisable only with the agreement of the Department of the Environment.

3 Non-target years: default rules

(1) If—

(a) for England, Scotland, Wales or Northern Ireland no amount is specified under subsection (1) of section 2 for a year to which that subsection applies, and

(b) the year is followed (whether or not immediately) by a target year,

the following sections of this Chapter shall have effect as if for that year ('the default-rule year') there had been specified under section 2(1) for that area the amount given by the formula set out in subsection (2).

(2) The formula is—

$$L - \frac{(L - N)(B + 1)}{(G + 1)}$$

(3) The formula shall be applied in accordance with subsection (4) if there is no scheme year falling between—

(a) the last target year before the default-rule year, and

(b) the default-rule year,

for which an amount has been specified under section 2(1) for the area; otherwise the formula shall be applied in accordance with subsection (5).

(4) Where the formula is to be applied in accordance with this subsection—

L is the amount specified under section 1 for the area for the year that is the last target year before the default-rule year,

N is the amount specified under section 1 for the area for the year that is the first target year after the default-rule year,

G is the number (if any) of scheme years falling between those target years, and

B is the number (if any) of scheme years falling between—

(a) the earlier of those target years, and

(b) the default-rule year.

(5) Where the formula is to be applied in accordance with this subsection—

L is the amount specified under section 2(1) for the area for the year that is the last scheme year before the default-rule year for which an amount has been specified for the area under section 2(1) ('the last fixed year'),

N is the amount specified under section 1 for the area for the year that is the first target year after the default-rule year,

G is the number (if any) of scheme years falling between the last fixed year and that target year, and

B is the number (if any) of scheme years falling between the last fixed year and the default-rule year.

(6) For the purposes of subsections (3) and (4), the year ending with 16th July in 2004 shall be taken to be a target year for-which the amount specified under section 1 for England, Scotland, Wales or Northern Ireland is such amount as may be specified in regulations made by the Secretary of State.

(7) The Secretary of State shall secure that an amount specified under subsection (6) is, or is a fair estimate of, the amount of biodegradable municipal waste sent to landfills from the area concerned in the year ending with 31st March 2001.

(8) Before making regulations under subsection (6), the Secretary of State shall consult the Scottish Ministers, the National Assembly for Wales and the Department of the Environment.

(9) Subsection (8) may be satisfied by consultation before, as well as by consultation after, the coming into force of this section.

Landfill allowances scheme

4 Allocation of landfill allowances

(1) Each allocating authority must—

(a) for each scheme year that is a target year, and

(b) for each other scheme year for which an amount is specified under section 2 for its area, make among waste disposal authorities in its area an allocation of allowances authorising the sending in that year of amounts of biodegradable municipal waste to landfills.

(2) In performing the duty under subsection (1), an allocating authority must ensure that the total amount of biodegradable municipal waste authorised to be sent to landfills by the allowances it allocates for a year does not exceed the amount for the year specified under section 1 or 2 for its area.

(3) An allocation under subsection (1) must be made before the beginning of the year to which it relates.

(4) As soon as an authority has made an allocation under subsection (1), it must publish a statement—

(a) detailing, in relation to each waste disposal authority in its area, what allowances have been allocated to it, and
(b) explaining the basis of the allocation.

(5) Nothing in this section shall be taken as requiring any allowances to be allocated to any particular waste disposal authority.

5 Alteration of allocations under section 4

(1) An authority that has made an allocation under section 4 may at any time alter the allocation, subject to subsections (2) and (3).

(2) The power under subsection (1) does not extend to withdrawing an allowance that has already been utilised.

(3) In exercising the power under subsection (1), an authority must ensure that the total amount of biodegradable municipal waste authorised to be sent to landfills by allowances allocated by it for a year does not exceed the amount for the year specified under section 1 or 2 for its area.

(4) As soon as an authority has exercised the power under subsection (1), it must publish a statement—

(a) detailing the alteration, and
(b) explaining the basis of it.

6 Borrowing and banking of landfill allowances

(1) An allocating authority may be regulations make provision for a waste disposal authority in its area to utilise for a scheme year landfill allowances allocated to it for a different scheme year.

(2) Regulations under subsection (1) may not provide for—

(a) the utilisation for a target year of allowances not allocated for that year;
(b) the utilisation for a scheme year later than a target year of allowances allocated for a scheme year earlier than that target year;
(c) the utilisation for a scheme year earlier than a target year of allowances allocated for a scheme year later than that target year.

(3) Regulations under subsection (1) may (in particular)—

(a) make provision relating only to allowances allocated for specified scheme years;
(b) make provision for allowances allocated for a scheme year to be utilised for a different scheme year only if—
  (i) that different scheme year is a specified scheme year;
  (ii) specified conditions are satisfied;
(c) make provision for quantitative limits on inter-year utilisation of allowances;
(d) make provision authorising the allocating authority to suspend inter-year utilisation of allowances—
  (i) whether indefinitely or for a fixed period, and
  (ii) whether generally or to a limited extent;
(e) make provision for a person to carry out, in relation to inter-year utilisation of allowances, all or any of the functions of registrar and overseer;
(f) make provision imposing, or enabling the imposition of, requirements on waste disposal authorities to provide information in relation to their inter-year utilisation of allowances;

(g) make provision for an authority to be liable to a penalty if it fails to comply with a requirement imposed on it by or under provision of the kind mentioned in paragraph (f);
(h) make provision generally in connection with the administration or regulation of inter-year utilisation of allowances;
(i) make provision for the levying of fees and charges on persons engaged in inter-year utilisation of allowances;
(j) make provision creating offences for breaches of provisions of regulations under subsection (1).

(4) In subsection (3) 'specified' means specified by, or determined in accordance with, regulations under subsection (1).

7 Trading and other transfer of landfill allowances

(1) An allocating authority may by regulations make provision for waste disposal authorities in its area to transfer, whether by way of trade or otherwise, landfill allowances allocated by that or any other allocating authority.

(2) Regulations under subsection (1) may not authorise—
(a) the acquisition of landfill allowances by a person who is not a waste disposal authority;
(b) the utilisation for a target year of allowances not allocated for that year;
(c) the utilisation for a scheme year later than a target year of allowances allocated for a scheme year earlier than that target year;
(d) the utilisation for a scheme year earlier than a target year of allowances allocated for a scheme year later than that target year.

(3) Regulations under subsection (1) may (in 'particular)—
(a) make provision for allowances to be a acquired, or disposed of, only if—
(i) allocated by the allocating authority or by specified allocating authorities;
(ii) allocated for specified scheme years;
(iii) specified conditions are satisfied;
(b) make provision for quantitative limits on the transfer of allowances;
(c) make provision for controlling prices or values put on allowances for the purpose of transferring them;
(d) make provision authorising the allocating authority to suspend the transfer of allowances—
(i) whether indefinitely or for a fixed period, and
(ii) whether generally or to a limited extent;
(e) make provision for allowances acquired by a waste disposal authority to be utilised by the authority for a scheme year only if allocated for that scheme year or for specified scheme years;
(f) make provision for licensing and regulating persons engaged as brokers in the transfer of allowances;
(g) make provision for a person to carry out, in relation to the transfer of allowances, all or any of the functions of registrar, clearing house and overseer;
(h) make provision imposing, or enabling the imposition of, requirements on waste disposal authorities to provide information in relation to their acquisition and disposal of allowances;
(i) make provision for an authority to be liable to a penalty if it fails to comply with a requirement imposed on it by or under provision of the kind mentioned in paragraph (h);
(j) make provision generally in connection with the administration or regulation of the trading of allowances;
(k) make provision for the levying of fees and charges on persons engaged (in any capacity) in the trading of allowances;

(l) make provision creating offences for breaches of provisions of regulations under subsection (1) or of conditions of a broker's licence.

(4) In subsection (3) 'specified' means specified by, or determined in accordance with, regulations under subsection (1).

8 Offences under regulations under sections 6 and 7

(1) This section applies where—

(a) regulations under section 6(1) are making provision of the kind mentioned in section 6(3)(j), or

(b) regulations under section 7(1) are making provision of the kind mentioned in section 7(3)(l).

(2) The regulations may provide for an offence to be triable—

(a) only summarily, or

(b) either summarily or on indictment.

(3) Where the regulations provide for an offence to be triable only summarily, they may provide for the offence to be punishable—

(a) by imprisonment for a term not exceeding such period as is stated in the regulations(which may not exceed three months), or

(b) by a fine—

(i) not exceeding such amount as is so stated (which may not exceed level 5 on the standard scale), or

(ii) not exceeding such level on the standard scale as is so stated, or

(c) by both.

(4) Subsections (5) and (6) apply where the regulations provide for an offence to be triable either summarily or on indictment.

(5) They may provide for the offence to be punishable on summary conviction—

(a) by imprisonment for a term not exceeding such period as is stated in the regulations (which may not exceed three months), or

(b) by a fine—

(i) not exceeding such amount as is so stated (which may not exceed the statutory maximum), or

(ii) expressed as a fine not exceeding the statutory maximum, or

(c) by both.

(6) They may provide for the offence to be punishable on conviction on indictment—

(a) by imprisonment for a term not exceeding such period as is stated in the regulations(which may not exceed two years), or

(b) by a fine, or

(c) by both.

9 Duty not to exceed allowances

(1) If the allocating authority for an area has made an allocation under section 4 for a scheme year, each waste disposal authority in the area owes a duty to the allocating authority to secure that the amount of biodegradable municipal waste sent to landfills in that year in pursuance of arrangements made by the waste disposal authority does not exceed the amount authorised by the landfill allowances available to that authority for the year.

(2) A waste disposal authority that fails to comply with a duty imposed on it by subsection (1) is liable to a penalty.

(3) If—

(a) a waste disposal authority is liable under subsection (2) to a penalty in respect of a target year, and

(b) the total amount of biodegradable municipal waste sent in the year to landfills in pursuance of arrangements made by waste disposal authorities in the United Kingdom exceeds the amount specified for the year under section 1(1)(a), the authority is also liable to a supplementary penalty.

(4) If—

(a) a waste disposal authority is liable under subsection (2) to a penalty in respect of a scheme year that is not a target year,

(b) that scheme year ('the penalty year') is later than the first target years, and

(c) the total amount of biodegradable municipal waste sent in the penalty year to landfills in pursuance of arrangements made by waste disposal authorities in the United Kingdom exceeds the amount specified under section 1(1)(a) for the last target year before the penalty year,

the authority is also liable to a supplementary penalty.

(5) For the purposes of this section, the landfill allowances available to a waste disposal authority for a scheme year are the landfill allowances held by the authority at the end of the year that have not been utilised for an earlier scheme year and that, in the case of—

(a) allowances allocated to the authority for an earlier or later scheme year, or

(b) allowances originally allocated to another waste disposal authority,

are allowed by regulations under section 6 or 7 to be utilised by the authority for the year.

10 Monitoring authorities

(1) Each allocating authority must by regulations appoint a person to be the monitoring authority for its area.

(2) The monitoring authority for an area shall—

(a) monitor the operation in the area of the provisions of this Chapter relating to landfill allowances and, in particular, monitor how much biodegradable municipal waste is sent to landfills in pursuance of arrangements made by waste disposal authorities in the area;

(b) audit the performance of waste disposal authorities in the area in complying with their obligations under this Chapter;

(c) comply with any directions by the allocating authority for the area as to the supply to the allocating authority of information acquired by the monitoring authority in carrying out any of its functions under this Chapter;

(d) without delay notify the allocating authority for the area of any case where it appears to the monitoring authority that a waste disposal authority in the area is or may be liable to a penalty under this Chapter;

(e) comply with any directions by the allocating authority for the area as to the supply to the allocating authority of information or evidence in connection with any case where it appears to the allocating authority or the monitoring authority that a waste disposal authority in the area is or may be liable to a penalty under this Chapter;

(f) co-operate with the monitoring authority for any other area.

11 Scheme regulations

(1) An allocating authority may by regulations make provision for the purpose of carrying into effect, in relation to its area, the provisions of this Chapter relating to landfill allowances.

(2) Regulations under subsection (1) may (in particular)—

(a) make provision about the manner of allocation of, or evidence of entitlement to, landfill allowances;

(b) make provision for the maintaining of registers of matters relating to landfill allowances;

(c) make provision about what amounts to the utilisation of landfill allowances;

(d) make provision for determining the amount of biodegradable municipal waste in an amount of waste;

(e) make provision imposing, or enabling the imposition of, requirements on waste disposal authorities in the area to produce evidence as to amounts of waste, or of waste of any description, sent to landfills in pursuance of arrangements made by them;

(f) make provision requiring waste disposal authorities in the area, in exercising functions in relation to waste that is or contains biodegradable municipal waste, to have regard to guidance specified in the regulations (including future guidance);

(g) make provision imposing or conferring additional functions on the monitoring authority for the area.

(3) Regulations under subsection (1) may provide for a waste disposal authority that fails to comply with a requirement of the regulations to be liable to a penalty.

12 Powers in relation to waste disposal authorities

(1) An allocating authority may, for purposes connected with the sending of biodegradable municipal waste to landfills, by regulations make provision for requiring waste disposal authorities in its area to—

(a) maintain prescribed records;

(b) gather prescribed information by carrying out prescribed operations on prescribed waste;

(c) make prescribed returns to the monitoring authority for the area.

(2) An allocating authority may by regulations make provision for enabling the monitoring authority for its area, or persons authorised by the monitoring authority—

(a) to require waste disposal authorities in the area to produce, for inspection or for removal for inspection elsewhere, records they are required to maintain by provision made under subsection (1);

(b) to require waste disposal authorities in the area to supply the monitoring authority with—

(i) information about matters connected with the sending of biodegradable municipal waste to landfills;

(ii) evidence to substantiate information supplied for the purpose of complying with requirements imposed under sub-paragraph (i);

(iii) evidence to substantiate entries in records maintained for the purpose of complying with provision made under subsection (1);

(c) to specify the form in which, the place at which and the time at or by which records are to be produced or information or evidence is to be supplied;

(d) to copy records that are produced.

(3) A waste disposal authority that fails to comply with a requirement imposed on it under this section is liable to a penalty.

(4) In subsection (1) 'prescribed' means prescribed by or under regulations under that subsection.

13 Powers in relation to landfill operators

(1) An allocating authority may, for purposes connected with the sending of biodegradable municipal waste to landfills, by regulations make provision for requiring a person concerned in the operation of a landfill to—

(a) maintain prescribed records;

(b) gather prescribed information by carrying out prescribed operations on prescribed waste;

(c) make prescribed returns, or provide prescribed information or prescribed evidence, to prescribed persons.

(2) A person commits an offence if he fails to comply with a requirement imposed on him under subsection (1).

(3) An allocating authority may by regulations make provision enabling the monitoring authority for its area, or persons authorised by the monitoring authority—

(a) to require persons concerned in the operation of a landfill to produce records related to the operation of the landfill for inspection or for removal for inspection elsewhere;

(b) to specify the form in which, the place at which and the time at or by which records are to be produced;
(c) to copy records that are produced;
(d) to enter premises (with or without a constable, with any necessary equipment or material and, if need be, by force) for the purposes of—
  (i) finding records relating to the operation of a landfill,
  (ii) inspecting them or removing them for inspection elsewhere, and
  (iii) copying them;
(e) to require persons to afford, to a person exercising any power conferred under paragraphs (a) to (d), such facilities and assistance within their control or in relation to which they have responsibilities as are necessary to enable the person to exercise the power.

(4) A person commits an offence if—
(a) he intentionally obstructs a person exercising a power conferred under subsection (3), or
(b) he fails to comply with a requirement imposed on him under that subsection.

(5) A person guilty of an offence under subsection (2) or (4)(a) is liable—
(a) on summary conviction, to a fine not exceeding the statutory maximum;
(b) on conviction on indictment, to imprisonment for a term not exceeding 2 years or to a fine, or to both.

(6) A person guilty of an offence under subsection (4)(b) is liable on summary conviction to a fine not exceeding level 5 on the standard scale.

(7) In subsection (1) 'prescribed' means prescribed by or under regulations under that subsection.

14 Disclosure of information by monitoring and allocating authorities

(1) A monitoring authority may disclose any of its monitoring information to any other monitoring authority, or to any allocating authority, for the purpose of facilitating the carrying out by the recipient of any of its functions under this Chapter.

(2) An allocating authority may disclose any of its monitoring information to any other allocating authority for the purpose of facilitating the carrying out by the recipient of any of its functions under this Chapter.

(3) For the purposes of this section, a monitoring authority's 'monitoring information' is information or evidence—
(a) acquired by it in carrying out any of its functions under this Chapter, or
(b) disclosed to it after having been acquired by another monitoring authority in carrying out any of its functions under this Chapter.

(4) For the purposes of this section, an allocating authority's 'monitoring information' is information or evidence—
(a) acquired by it in carrying out any of its functions under this Chapter, or
(b) disclosed to it after having been acquired by a monitoring authority, or another allocating authority, in carrying out any of its functions under this Chapter.

(5) Subsections (1) and (2) shall be treated as additional to, and as not prejudicing the generality of, section 113 of the Environment Act 1995 (c.25) (disclosure of information).

15 Monitoring information: registers

(1) An allocating authority may by regulations make provision requiring the monitoring authority for its area to maintain a register containing such of its monitoring information as is of a description specified by the regulations.

(2) For the purposes of subsection (1), a monitoring authority's 'monitoring information' is information or evidence—
(a) acquired by it in carrying out any of its functions under this Chapter, or
(b) disclosed to it after having been acquired by another monitoring authority in carrying out any of its functions under this Chapter.

16 Registers: public access

An allocating authority may, in relation to a register that a person is required to maintain by regulations under this Chapter made by the authority, by regulations—

(a) make provision for public inspection of such of the information contained in the register as is of a description specified by the regulations;

(b) make provision for members of the public to obtain copies of information in the register that is open to public inspection under paragraph (a), including provision for the payment of reasonable charges.

Strategies for reducing landfilling of biodegradable waste

17 Strategy for England

(1) The Secretary of State must have a strategy for reducing—

(a) the amount of biodegradable waste from England that goes to landfills, and

(b) the amount of biodegradable waste from outside England that goes to landfills in England.

(2) The strategy required by subsection (1) must (in particular) include measures to achieve the targets specified for England under sections 1 and 2.

(3) The measures mentioned in subsection (2) include (in particular) measures to achieve the targets by recycling, composting, biogas production, materials recovery or energy recovery.

(4) Before formulating policy for the purposes of subsection (1), the Secretary of State must—

(a) consult the Scottish Ministers, the National Assembly for Wales, the Department of the Environment, the Environment Agency and the Mayor of London,

(b) consult such bodies or persons appearing to him to be representative of the interests of local government as he considers appropriate,

(c) consult such bodies or persons appearing to him to be representative of the interests of industry as he considers appropriate, and

(d) carry out such public consultation as he considers appropriate.

(5) The Secretary of State must set out in a statement any policy formulated for the purposes of subsection (1).

(6) The Secretary of State must, as soon as a statement is prepared for the purposes of subsection (5), send a copy of it to—

(a) the Scottish Ministers,

(b) the National Assembly for Wales, and

(c) the Department of the Environment.

(7) Where subsection (1) is satisfied by policies set out in a statement under section 44A of the Environmental Protection Act 1990 (c. 43) (national waste strategy), if the statement was prepared before the coming into force of that subsection it does not matter that the policies were not formulated for the purposes of that subsection.

(8) . . .

(9) . . .

19 Strategy for Wales

. . .

Interpretation of Chapter 1

21 'Biodegradable waste' and 'municipal waste'

(1) In this Chapter 'biodegradable waste' means any waste that is capable of undergoing anaerobic or aerobic decomposition, such as—

food and garden waste, and

paper and paperboard.

(2) In this Chapter 'biodegradable municipal waste' means waste that is both biodegradable waste and municipal waste.

(3) In subsection (2) 'municipal waste' means—

(a) waste from households, and

(b) other waste that, because of its nature or composition, is similar to waste from households.

22 'Landfill'

(1) In this Chapter 'landfill' means a site for the deposit of waste onto or into land where the site is—

(a) a waste disposal site, or

(b) used for the storage of waste.

(2) In determining whether a site is a landfill for the purposes of this Chapter, the following activities at the site are to be ignored—

(a) the temporary storage of waste if the site is used for such storage for less than one year;

(b) the unloading of waste in order to permit the waste to be prepared for further transport for recovery, treatment or disposal elsewhere;

(c) the storage of waste, prior to recovery or treatment, for a period of less than three years as a general rule;

(d) the storage of waste, prior to disposal, for a period of less than one year.

(3) The fact that a site for the deposit of waste is at the place of production of the waste does not prevent the site from being a landfill for the purposes of this Chapter.

(4) In subsection (2) 'treatment' means the physical, thermal, chemical or biological processes, including sorting, that change the characteristics of waste in order to—

(a) reduce its volume,

(b) reduce its hazardous nature,

(c) facilitate its handling, or

(d) enhance its recoverability.

23 'Scheme year' and 'target year'

[(1) In this Chapter—

'scheme year' means—

(a) for England, Scotland and Northern Ireland, a year beginning with 1st April in any of 2005 to 2019; and

(b) for Wales—

(i) the period of six months beginning with 1st October 2004, or

(ii) a year beginning with 1st April in any of 2005 to 2019;

'target year' means a scheme year ending with 31st March in 2010, 2013 or 2020.]

(2) The Secretary of State may by regulations amend subsection (1) for the purpose of—

(a) providing for a different day to be the first day of a scheme year;

(b) adding or omitting one or more scheme years;

(c) providing for a scheme year to be a period shorter or longer than a year;

(d) changing the target years or any of them;

(e) adding or omitting one or more target years.

(3) Before making regulations under subsection (2), the Secretary of State shall consult the Scottish Ministers, the National Assembly for Wales and the Department of the Environment.

24 Other definitions

(1) For the purposes of this Chapter, the 'allocating authority'—

(a) for England is the Secretary of State,

(b) . . .

(c) . . . for Wales is the National Assembly for Wales

(d) . . .

(2) In this Chapter, any reference to an allocating authority's 'area' is to the area for which it is the allocating authority for the purposes of this Chapter.

(3) In this Chapter 'landfill allowances' means allowances allocated under section 4(1).

(4) References in this Chapter to the monitoring authority for an area are to the monitoring authority designated for the area by regulations under section 10(1).

(5) In this Chapter 'waste disposal authority'—

(a) in relation to England, Wales...has the same meaning as in Part 2 of the Environmental Protection Act 1990 (c. 43);

(b) ...

Supplementary

25 Activities to which Chapter 1 does not apply

(1) References in this Chapter to sending biodegradable waste, or biodegradable municipal waste, to landfills do not include—

(a) the spreading of sludges (including sewage sludges and sludges resulting from dredging operations), or similar matter, on the soil for the purposes of fertilisation or improvement,

(b) the deposit of non-hazardous dredging sludges alongside small waterways from out of which they have been dredged,

(c) the deposit of non-hazardous sludges in surface water or in the bed or subsoil of surface water, or

(d) the deposit of unpolluted soil resulting from—

(i) prospecting for, or the extraction, treatment or storage of, mineral resources, or

(ii) the operation of quarries.

(2) For the purposes of this section, sludge is 'non-hazardous' if it is not hazardous waste within the meaning of regulation 6 of the Hazardous Waste (England and Wales) Regulations 2005.

26 Penalties under Chapter 1: general

(1) Where a waste disposal authority in an allocating authority's area is liable to a penalty under this Chapter—

(a) the amount of the penalty is that specified by, or calculated under, regulations made by the allocating authority under subsection (3);

(b) the penalty, and any interest on it, is to be paid to the allocating athority; and

(c) the allocating authority may—

(i) extend the time for paying the whole or part of the penalty or any interest on it;

(ii) relieve the waste disposal authority, in whole or in part, from liability to the penalty or any interest on it.

(2) Relief under subsection (1)(c) may be given—

(a) in respect of an amount after (as well as before) it becomes due;

(b) in a particular case or in cases of a particular description;

(c) unconditionally or subject to conditions.

(3) An allocating authority may, as regards penalties under this Chapter to which waste disposal authorities in its area are liable, by regulations—

(a) make provision specifying the amounts of penalties or rules for calculating their amounts;

(b) make provision as to when payments in respect of penalties are due;

(c) make provision for interest where payments in respect of penalties are due but unmade;

(d) make provision for recovering or setting off, and securing, unpaid amounts in respect of penalties or interest.

(4) Provision under subsection (3) relating to supplementary penalties under section 9(3) or (4) in respect of waste sent to landfills in a scheme year may be made after the end of that year.

27 Regulations under Chapter 1: consultation

(1) This section applies to regulations under this Chapter, other than regulations under section 1, 2, 3 or 23.

(2) Before making regulations to which this section applies, an allocating authority shall (subject to subsection (4))—

(a) consult such bodies or persons appearing to it to be representative of the interests of waste disposal authorities in its area as it considers appropriate,

(b) consult such bodies or persons appearing to it to be representative of the interests of persons concerned in the operation of landfills in its area as it considers appropriate, and

(c) consult such bodies or persons appearing to it to be representative of any other affected persons as it considers appropriate.

(3) In subsection (2)(c) 'affected person' means a person appearing to the allocating authority to be a person who will or may be affected by the regulations.

(4) The allocating authority need not consult as mentioned in paragraph (a) or (b) of subsection (2) if it appears to the authority that the interests mentioned in that paragraph will not be affected by the regulations.

(5) Subsection (2) may be satisfied by consultation before, as well as by consultation after, the coming into force of this section.

28 Regulations under Chapter 1: procedural provisions

(1) A statutory instrument that—

(a) contains regulations under this Chapter made by the Secretary of State, and

(b) is not subject to any requirement that a draft of the instrument be laid before, and approved by a resolution of, each House of Parliament,

shall be subject to annulment in pursuance of a resolution of either House of Parliament.

(2) No affirmative-procedure regulations shall be made by the Secretary of State unless a draft of the statutory instrument containing the regulations (whether containing them alone or with other provisions) has been laid before, and approved by a resolution of, each House of Parliament.

(3)–(6) . . .

(7) In this section—

'affirmative-procedure regulations' means—

(a) regulations under section 1 or 2 and

(b) the first regulations to be made under each of sections 6,7 and 11 by each of the Secretary of State, . . .

CHAPTER 2 WASTE MANAGEMENT IN WALES

29 Municipal waste management strategies

(1) The National Assembly for Wales may by regulations make provision for requiring a local authority to have for its area a strategy for the management of waste.

(2) Regulations under subsection (1) may (in particular)—

(a) specify matters to be addressed by a strategy;

(b) specify wastes to which a strategy is to relate;

(c) make provision about policies to be included in a strategy;

(d) make provision in connection with review or revision of a strategy;

(e) make provision for consultation, or about other procedural matters, in connection with the formulation of policy for the purposes of a strategy;

(f) make provision for requiring the preparation of statements setting out policies formulated for the purposes of a strategy;

(g) make provision about the contents of such statements;

(h) make provision about the form of such statements;

(i) make provision for publicising such statements once prepared, for publishing them, for sending copies of them to persons specified in the regulations and for public inspection of them;

(j) make provision for the supply of copies of such statements, including provision for the payment of reasonable charges;

(k) make provision for requiring a local authority, when formulating policy for the purposes of a strategy or preparing such a statement, to have regard to guidance (including future guidance);

(l) make provision about when duties imposed by the regulations are to be performed, including provision for duties to be performed by times specified in directions given by the Assembly.

(3) In this section 'local authority' means a county council, or county borough council, in Wales.

30 Provision of information about waste by local authorities

(1) The National Assembly for Wales may by regulations make provision requiring a local authority to provide the Assembly with information—

(a) of a description specified by the regulations, and

(b) relating to, or to a description of, waste that is or has been in, or may or will come into, the authority's area.

(2) Regulations under subsection (1) may—

(a) make provision in connection with the collection, verification or certification of information whose provision is required by such regulations;

(b) make provision about the form in which, and the means by which, information is to be provided;

(c) make provision about when duties imposed by the regulations are to be performed, including provision for duties to be performed by times specified in directions given by the Assembly.

(3) In this section 'local authority' means a county council, or county borough council, in Wales.

CHAPTER 3 WASTE MANAGEMENT IN ENGLAND

32 Joint municipal waste management strategies: England

(1) The waste authorities for a two-tier area must, at all times after the end of the period of 18 months beginning with the day on which this Act is passed, have for the area a joint strategy for the management of—

(a) waste from households, and

(b) other waste that, because of its nature or composition, is similar to waste from households.

(2) The waste authorities for a two-tier area must keep under review the policies formulated by them for the purposes of subsection (1).

(3) The waste authorities for a two-tier area must, before formulating policy for the purposes of subsection (1), carry out such consultation as they consider appropriate.

(4) The waste authorities for a two-tier area must set out in a statement any policy formulated by them for the purposes of subsection (1).

(5) The waste authorities for a two-tier area must—

(a) when formulating policy for the purposes of subsection (1), and

(b) when preparing a statement under subsection (4),

have regard to any guidance given by the Secretary of State.

(6) The waste authorities for a two-tier area in Greater London must, when formulating policy for the purposes of subsection (1), have regard to the Mayor of London's municipal waste management strategy or, where that strategy has been revised, to that strategy as revised.

(7) Where the waste authorities for a two-tier area prepare a statement under subsection (4)—

(a) they must take such steps as in their opinion will give adequate publicity in the area to the statement;

(b) they must send a copy of the statement—

(i) to each of the Secretary of State and the Environment Agency, and

(ii) if the area is in Greater London, to the Mayor of London;

(c) each of the authorities must keep a copy of the statement available at all reasonable times at one of its offices for inspection by the public free of charge; and

(d) each of the authorities must supply a copy of the statement to any person who requests one, on payment by the person of such reasonable charge as the authority requires.

(8) Where subsection (1) is satisfied in relation to a two-tier area by policies set out in a statement prepared before the coming into force of that subsection—

(a) it does not matter that the policies were not formulated for the purposes of subsection (1), but

(b) subsection (2) shall apply as though the policies were formulated for the purposes of subsection (1).

(9) Subsection (3) may be satisfied by consultation before, as well as by consultation after, the coming into force of that subsection.

(10) The Secretary of State may by regulations make provision for subsection (1) to apply, in relation to a two-tier area specified or described in the regulations, with the substitution for '18 months' of some longer period.

(11) A statutory instrument that contains regulations under subsection (10) shall be subject to annulment in pursuance of a resolution of either House of Parliament.

33 Power to disapply duties under section 32

(1) The Secretary of State may by regulations make provision for a duty under section 32(1) to (7)—

(a) not to apply to an authority if conditions specified in the regulations are met;

(b) not to apply to an authority if, on an application made in accordance with the regulations, the Secretary of State is satisfied that conditions specified in the regulations are met;

(c) not to apply to the waste authorities for a two-tier area if, by reason of provision under paragraph (a) and (b), it applies to one or more, but not all, of them;

(d) not to apply to the waste authorities for a two-tier area if, on an application made in accordance with the regulations, the Secretary of State is satisfied that conditions specified in the regulations are met.

(2) The power under paragraph (a) or (b) of subsection (1) must be exercised so that provision under that paragraph will cause a duty under section 32(1) to (7) not to apply to an authority only if—

(a) the standard of the authority's performance in carrying out functions of its has been at, or above, a particular level, and

(b) that level is—

(i) the level that, in the Secretary of State's opinion, counts as satisfactory performance, or

(ii) a level that, in his opinion, is higher than that level.

(3) The power under paragraph (d) of subsection (1) must be exercised so that provision under that paragraph will cause a duty under section 32(1) to (7) not to apply to the waste authorities for a two-tier area only if—

(a) as respects at least one of the authorities, the standard of its performance in carrying out functions of its has been at, or above, a particular level, or

(b) as respects at least two of the authorities, each has so carried out functions of its that the overall standard of their performance in carrying out those functions has been at, or above, a particular level, and (in either case) that level is one mentioned in subsection (2)(b).

(4) Subject to subsection (2), the conditions that may be specified under subsection (1)(a) include (in particular) conditions that may be met only in the case of authorities that from time to time are, by reason of provision made by or under an enactment, of a particular category.

(5) Regulations under subsection (1) may include—

(a) provision about the duration of any disapplication under that subsection of a duty;

(b) provision postponing the application of a duty on the coming to an end of a disapplication under that subsection of the duty;

(c) provision modifying the application of subsections (1) to (7) of section 32 in relation to a two-tier area where a duty under those subsections applies to one or more, but not all, of the waste authorities for the area.

(6) A statutory instrument that contains regulations under this section shall be subject to annulment in pursuance of a resolution of either House of Parliament.

(7) A reference in subsection (2)(a) or (3)(a) or (b) to functions of an authority is to functions of the authority in any capacity (and not only to functions of its in its capacity as a waste disposal authority or waste collection authority).

34 Interpretation of Chapter 3

In this Chapter—

(a) 'two-tier area' means the area of a waste disposal authority in England which is not also a waste collection authority;

(b) 'the waste authorities' for a two-tier area are—

(i) the waste disposal authority for the area, and

(ii) the waste collection authorities within the area; and

(c) 'waste disposal authority' and 'waste collection authority' have the same meaning as in Part 2 of the Environmental Protection Act 1990 (c. 43).

36 Regulations under Part 1

(1) Any power to make regulations under this Part includes—

(a) power to make different provision for different cases, and

(b) power to make incidental, supplementary, consequential or transitional provision or savings.

(2) Power to make regulations under section 23(2)(a), (b) or (c) also includes—

(a) power to make different provision in relation to England, Scotland, Wales and Northern Ireland respectively, and

(b) power to make consequential provision amending section 3(6).

(3) Any power to make regulations under this Part is exercisable by statutory instrument, subject to subsection (4).

(4) . . .

37 Meaning of 'waste' in Part 1

(1) In this Part 'waste' means anything that—

(a) is waste for the purposes of the Waste Directive, and

(b) is not excluded from the scope of that Directive by Article 2 of that Directive.

(2) For the purposes of this section 'the Waste Directive' means Council Directive 75/442/EEC as amended by—

(a) Council Directives 91/156/EEC and 91/692/EEC, and

(b) Commission Decision 96/350/EC.

39 Penalty provisions of UK Greenhouse Gas Emissions Trading Scheme 2002

(1) If incorporated in a participation agreement, the penalty provisions of the Scheme shall have statutory effect between the parties to the agreement.

(2) Subsection (1) applies in relation to agreements entered into before, as well as in relation to agreements entered into after, this section comes into force.

(3) In that subsection—

'participation agreement' means an agreement that has the effect that a person is a participant in the Scheme;

'penalty provisions' means provisions for penalties for non-compliance with the Scheme;

'the Scheme' means the UK Greenhouse Gas Emissions Trading Scheme 2002 (which was made on behalf of the Secretary of State on 8th March 2002) as amended from time to time (whether before or after this section comes into force).

Anti-Social Behaviour Act 2003

(2003, c. 38)

PART VI THE ENVIRONMENT

Noise

40 Closure of noisy premises

(1) The chief executive officer of the relevant local authority may make a closure order in relation to premises to which this section applies if he reasonably believes that—

(a) a public nuisance is being caused by noise coming from the premises, and

(b) the closure of the premises is necessary to prevent that nuisance.

(2) This section applies to premises if—

(a) a premises licence has effect in respect of them, or

(b) a temporary event notice has effect in respect of them.

(3) In this section 'closure order' means an order which requires specified premises to be kept closed during a specified period which—

(a) does not exceed 24 hours, and

(b) begins when a manager of the premises receives written notice of the order.

(4) A person commits an offence if without reasonable excuse he permits premises to be open in contravention of a closure order.

(5) A person guilty of an offence under this section shall be liable on summary conviction to—

(a) imprisonment for a term not exceeding [51 weeks],

(b) a fine not exceeding £20,000, or

(c) both.

41 Closure of noisy premises: supplemental

(1) Where a closure order is made in relation to premises, the chief executive officer of the relevant local authority—

(a) may cancel the closure order by notice in writing to a manager of the premises,

(b) shall cancel the order as soon as is reasonably practicable if he believes that it is no longer necessary in order to prevent a public nuisance being caused by noise coming from the premises, and

(c) shall give notice of the order as soon as is reasonably practicable to the licensing authority for the area in which the premises are situated.

(2) The chief executive officer of a local authority may authorise an environmental health officer of the authority to exercise a power or duty of the chief executive officer under section 40(1) or under subsection (1) above; and—

(a) authority under this subsection may be general or specific, and

(b) a reference in section 40(1) or subsection (1) above to a belief of the chief executive officer includes a reference to a belief of a person authorised under this subsection.

(3) In section 40 and this section—

'chief executive officer' of an authority means the head of the paid service of the authority designated under section 4 of the Local Government and Housing Act 1989 (c 42), 'environmental health officer' of an authority means an officer authorised by the authority for the purpose of exercising a statutory function in relation to pollution of the environment or harm to human health,

'licensing authority' has the same meaning as in the Licensing Act 2003,

'manager' in relation to premises means—

(a) a person who holds a premises licence in respect of the premises,

(b) a designated premises supervisor under a premises licence in respect of the premises,

(c) the premises user in relation to a temporary event notice which has effect in respect of the premises, and

(d) any other person who works at the premises in a capacity (paid or unpaid) which enables him to close them,

'premises licence' has the same meaning as in the Licensing Act 2003,

'relevant local authority' in relation to premises means an authority which has statutory functions, for the area in which the premises are situated, in relation to minimising or preventing the risk of pollution of the environment or of harm to human health, and

'temporary event notice' has the same meaning as in the Licensing Act 2003 (and is to be treated as having effect in accordance with [section 171(6)] of that Act).

Planning and Compulsory Purchase Act 2004

(2004, c. 5)

PART I REGIONAL FUNCTIONS

Spatial strategy

1 Regional spatial strategy

(1) For each region there is to be a regional spatial strategy (in this Part referred to as the 'RSS').

(2) The RSS must set out the Secretary of State's policies (however expressed) in relation to the development and use of land within the region.

(3) In subsection (2) the references to a region include references to any area within a region which includes the area or part of the area of more than one local planning authority.

(4) If to any extent a policy set out in the RSS conflicts with any other statement or information in the RSS the conflict must be resolved in favour of the policy.

(5) With effect from the appointed day the RSS for a region is so much of the regional planning guidance relating to the region as the Secretary of State prescribes.

(6) The appointed day is the day appointed for the commencement of this section.

Planning bodies

2 Regional planning bodies

(1) The Secretary of State may give a direction recognising a body to which subsection (2) applies as the regional planning body for a region (in this Part referred to as the 'RPB').

(2) This subsection applies to a body (whether or not incorporated) which satisfies such criteria as are prescribed.

(3) The Secretary of State must not give a direction under subsection (1) in relation to a body unless not less than 60% of the persons who are members of the body fall within subsection (4).

(4) A person falls within this subsection if he is a member of any of the following councils or authorities and any part of the area of the council or authority (as the case may be) falls within the region to which the direction (if given) will relate—

(a) a district council;

(b) a county council;

(c) a metropolitan district council;
(d) a National Park authority;
(e) the Broads authority.

(5) The Secretary of State may give a direction withdrawing recognition of a body.

(6) Subsection (7) applies if the Secretary of State—
(a) does not give a direction under subsection (1) recognising a body, or
(b) gives a direction under subsection (5) withdrawing recognition of a body and does not give a direction under subsection (1) recognising any other body.

(7) In such a case the Secretary of State may exercise such of the functions of the RPB as he thinks appropriate.

(8) A change in the membership of a body which is not incorporated does not (by itself) affect the validity of the recognition of the body.

3 RPB: general functions

(1) The RPB must keep under review the RSS.

(2) The RPB must keep under review the matters which may be expected to affect—
(a) development in its region or any part of the region;
(b) the planning of that development.

(3) The RPB must—
(a) monitor the implementation of the RSS throughout the region;
(b) consider whether the implementation is achieving the purposes of the RSS.

(4) The RPB must for each year prepare a report on the implementation of the RSS in the region.

(5) The report—
(a) must be in respect of such period of 12 months as is prescribed;
(b) must be in such form and contain such information as is prescribed;
(c) must be submitted to the Secretary of State on such date as is prescribed.

(6) The RPB must give advice to any other body or person if it thinks that to do so will help to achieve implementation of the RSS.

4 Assistance from certain local authorities

(1) For the purpose of the exercise of its functions under sections 3(1) and (3)(a) and 5(1) the RPB must seek the advice of each authority in its region which is an authority falling within subsection (4).

(2) The authority must give the RPB advice as to the exercise of the function to the extent that the exercise of the function is capable of affecting (directly or indirectly) the exercise by the authority of any function it has.

(3) The advice mentioned in subsection (1) includes advice relating to the inclusion in the RSS of specific policies relating to any part of the region.

(4) Each of the following authorities fall within this subsection if their area or any part of their area is in the RPB's region—
(a) a county council;
(b) a metropolitan district council;
(c) a district council for an area for which there is no county council;
(d) a National Park authority.

(5) The RPB may make arrangements with an authority falling within subsection (4) or with any district council the whole or part of whose area is in the region for the discharge by the authority or council of a function of the RPB.

(6) The RPB may reimburse an authority or council which exercises functions by virtue of such arrangements for any expenditure incurred by the authority or council in doing so.

(7) Subsection (5) does not apply to a function of the RPB under section 5(8).

(8) Any arrangements made for the purposes of subsection (5) must be taken to be arrangements between local authorities for the purposes of section 101 of the Local Government Act 1972 (c. 70).

(9) Nothing in this section affects any power which a body which is recognised as an RPB has apart from this section.

RSS revision

5 RSS: revision

(1) The RPB must prepare a draft revision of the RSS—
(a) when it appears to it necessary or expedient to do so;
(b) at such time as is prescribed;
(c) if it is directed to do so under section 10(1).

(2) But the RPB must give notice to the Secretary of State of its intention to prepare a draft revision under subsection (1)(a).

(3) In preparing a draft revision the RPB must have regard to—
(a) national policies and advice contained in guidance issued by the Secretary of State;
(b) the RSS for each adjoining region;
(c) the spatial development strategy if any part of its region adjoins Greater London;
(d) the Wales Spatial Plan if any part of its region adjoins Wales;
(e) the resources likely to be available for implementation of the RSS;
(f) the desirability of making different provision in relation to different parts of the region;
(g) such other matters as are prescribed.

(4) In preparing a draft revision the RPB must also—
(a) carry out an appraisal of the sustainability of the proposals in the draft, and
(b) prepare a report of the findings of the appraisal.

(5) If the RPB decides to make different provision for different parts of the region the detailed proposals for such different provision must first be made by an authority which falls within section 4(4).

(6) But if the RPB and the authority agree, the detailed proposals may first be made—
(a) by a district council which is not such an authority, or
(b) by the RPB.

(7) The Secretary of State may by regulations make provision as to
(a) the subject matter of a draft revision prepared in pursuance of subsection (1)(b);
(b) any further documents which must be prepared by the RPB in connection with the preparation of a draft revision;
(c) the form and content of any draft, report or other document prepared under this section.

(8) When the RPB has prepared a draft revision, the report to be prepared under subsection (4)(b) and any other document to be prepared in pursuance of subsection (7)(b) it must—
(a) publish the draft revision, report and other document;
(b) submit them to the Secretary of State.

(9) But the RPB may withdraw a draft revision at any time before it submits the draft to the Secretary of State under subsection (8)(b).

6 RSS: community involvement

(1) For the purposes of the exercise of its functions under section 5, the RPB must prepare and publish a statement of its policies as to the involvement of persons who appear to the RPB to have an interest in the exercise of those functions.

(2) The RPB must keep the policies under review and from time to time must—
(a) revise the statement;
(b) publish the revised statement.

(3) The RPB must comply with the statement or revised statement (as the case may be) in the exercise of its functions under section 5.

(4) The documents mentioned in section 5(7)(b) and (c) include the statement and revised statement.

7 RSS: Secretary of State's functions

(1) This section applies when the Secretary of State receives a draft revision of the RSS.

(2) Any person may make representations on the draft.

(3) The Secretary of State may arrange for an examination in public to be held into the draft.

(4) In deciding whether an examination in public is held the Secretary of State must have regard to—

(a) the extent of the revisions proposed by the draft;

(b) the extent and nature of the consultation on the draft before it was published;

(c) the level of interest shown in the draft;

(d) such other matters as he thinks appropriate.

8 RSS: examination in public

(1) This section applies if the Secretary of State decides that an examination in public is to be held of a draft revision of the RSS.

(2) The examination must be held before a person appointed by the Secretary of State.

(3) No person has a right to be heard at an examination in public.

(4) The Secretary of State may, after consultation with the Lord Chancellor, make regulations with respect to the procedure to be followed at an examination in public.

(5) The person appointed under subsection (2) must make a report of the examination to the Secretary of State.

(6) The Secretary of State may by regulations make provision as to the procedure to be followed in connection with the recommendations of the person appointed under subsection (2).

(7) An examination in public—

(a) is a statutory inquiry for the purposes of section 1(1)(c) of the Tribunals and Inquiries Act 1992 (c. 53) (report on administrative procedures);

(b) is not a statutory inquiry for any other purpose of that Act.

9 RSS: further procedure

(1) If no examination in public is held the Secretary of State must consider any representations made on the draft revision of the RSS under section 7(2).

(2) If an examination in public is held the Secretary of State must consider—

(a) the report of the person appointed to hold the examination;

(b) any representations which are not considered by the person appointed to hold the examination.

(3) If after proceeding under subsection (1) or (2) the Secretary of State proposes to make any changes to the draft he must publish—

(a) the changes he proposes to make;

(b) his reasons for doing so.

(4) Any person may make representations on the proposed changes.

(5) The Secretary of State must consider any such representations.

(6) The Secretary of State must then publish—

(a) the revision of the RSS incorporating such changes as he thinks fit;

(b) his reasons for making the changes.

(7) But the Secretary of State may withdraw a draft revision of an RSS at any time before he publishes the revision of the RSS under subsection (6).

10 Secretary of State: additional powers

(1) If the Secretary of State thinks it is necessary or expedient to do so he may direct an RPB to prepare a draft revision of the RSS.

(2) Such a direction may require the RPB to prepare the draft revision—

(a) in relation to such aspects of the RSS as are specified;

(b) in accordance with such timetable as is specified.

(3) The Secretary of State may prepare a draft revision of the RSS if the RPB fails to comply with—
(a) a direction under subsection (1),
(b) section 5(1)(b), or
(c) regulations under section 5(7) or 11.

(4) If the Secretary of State prepares a draft revision under subsection (3)—
(a) section 7 applies as it does if the Secretary of State receives a draft revision from the RPB, and
(b) sections 8 and 9 apply.

(5) If the Secretary of State thinks it necessary or expedient to do so he may at any time revoke—
(a) an RSS;
(b) such parts of an RSS as he thinks appropriate.

(6) The Secretary of State may by regulations make provision as to the procedure to be followed for the purposes of subsection (3).

(7) Subsection (8) applies if—
(a) any step has been taken in connection with the preparation of any part of regional planning guidance, and
(b) the Secretary of State thinks that the step corresponds to a step which must be taken under this Part in connection with the preparation and publication of a revision of the RSS.

(8) The Secretary of State may by order provide for the part of the regional planning guidance to have effect as a revision of the RSS.

Supplementary

11 Regulations

(1) The Secretary of State may by regulations make provision in connection with the exercise by any person of functions under this Part.

(2) The regulations may in particular make provision as to—
(a) the procedure to be followed for the purposes of section 5;
(b) the procedure to be followed by the RPB in connection with its functions under section 6;
(c) requirements about the giving of notice and publicity;
(d) requirements about inspection by the public of a draft revision or any other document;
(e) the nature and extent of consultation with and participation by the public in anything done under this Part;
(f) the making of representations about any matter to be included in an RSS;
(g) consideration of any such representations;
(h) the remuneration and allowances payable to a person appointed to carry out an examination in public under section 8;
(i) the determination of the time at which anything must be done for the purposes of this Part;
(j) the manner of publication of any draft, report or other document published under this Part;
(k) monitoring the exercise by RPBs of their functions under this Part;
(l) the making of reasonable charges for the provision of copies of documents required by or under this Part.

12 Supplementary

(1) A region is a region (except London) specified in Schedule 1 to the Regional Development Agencies Act 1998 (c. 45).

(2) But the Secretary of State may by order direct that if the area of a National Park falls within more than one region it is treated as falling wholly within such region as is specified in the order.

(3) Regional planning guidance for a region is a document issued by the Secretary of State setting out his policies (however expressed) in relation to the development and use of land within the region.

(4) The Secretary of State is the Secretary of State for the time being having general responsibility for policy in relation to the development and use of land.

(5) Subsection (4) does not apply for the purposes of section 5(3) (a).

(6) References to a revision or draft revision of an RSS include references to a revision or draft revision—

(a) of any part of an RSS;

(b) of the RSS as it relates to any part of a region.

(7) This section has effect for the purposes of this Part.

PART II LOCAL DEVELOPMENT

Survey

13 Survey of area

(1) The local planning authority must keep under review the matters which may be expected to affect the development of their area or the planning of its development.

(2) These matters include—

(a) the principal physical, economic, social and environmental characteristics of the area of the authority;

(b) the principal purposes for which land is used in the area;

(c) the size, composition and distribution of the population of the area;

(d) the communications, transport system and traffic of the area;

(e) any other considerations which may be expected to affect those matters;

(f) such other matters as may be prescribed or as the Secretary of State (in a particular case) may direct.

(3) The matters also include—

(a) any changes which the authority think may occur in relation to any other matter;

(b) the effect such changes are likely to have on the development of the authority's area or on the planning of such development.

(4) The local planning authority may also keep under review and examine the matters mentioned in subsections (2) and (3) in relation to any neighbouring area to the extent that those matters may be expected to affect the area of the authority.

(5) In exercising a function under subsection (4) a local planning authority must consult with the local planning authority for the neighbouring area in question.

(6) If a neighbouring area is in Wales references to the local planning authority for that area must be construed in accordance with Part 6.

14 Survey of area: county councils

(1) A county council in respect of so much of their area for which there is a district council must keep under review the matters which may be expected to affect development of that area or the planning of its development insofar as the development relates to a county matter.

(2) Subsections (2) to (6) of section 13 apply for the purposes of subsection (1) as they apply for the purposes of that section; and references to the local planning authority must be construed as references to the county council.

(3) The Secretary of State may be regulations require or (in a particular case) may direct a county council to keep under review in relation to so much of their area as is mentioned in subsection (1) such of the matters mentioned in section 13(1) to (4) as he prescribes or directs (as the case may be).

(4) For the purposes of subsection (3)—

(a) it is immaterial whether any development relates to a county matter;

(b) if a matter which is prescribed or in respect of which the Secretary of State gives a direction falls within section 13(4) the county council must consult the local planning authority for the area in question.

(5) The county council must make available the results of their review under subsection (3) to such persons as the Secretary of State prescribes or directs (as the case may be).

(6) References to a county matter must be construed in accordance with paragraph 1 of Schedule 1 to the principal Act (ignoring sub-paragraph (1)(i)).

Development schemes

15 Local development scheme

(1) The local planning authority must prepare and maintain a scheme to be known as their local development scheme.

(2) The scheme must specify—

(a) the documents which are to be local development documents;

(b) the subject matter and geographical area to which each document is to relate;

(c) which documents are to be development plan documents;

(d) which documents (if any) are to be prepared jointly with one or more other local planning authorities;

(e) any matter or area in respect of which the authority have agreed (or propose to agree) to the constitution of a joint committee under section 29;

(f) the timetable for the preparation and revision of the documents;

(g) such other matters as are prescribed.

(3) The local planning authority must—

(a) prepare the scheme in accordance with such other requirements as are prescribed;

(b) submit the scheme to the Secretary of State at such time as is prescribed or as the Secretary of State (in a particular case) directs;

(c) at that time send a copy of the scheme to the RPB or (if the authority are a London borough) to the Mayor of London.

(4) The Secretary of State may direct the local planning authority to make such amendments to the scheme as he thinks appropriate.

(5) Such a direction must contain the Secretary of State's reasons for giving it.

(6) The local planning authority must comply with a direction given under subsection (4).

(7) The Secretary of State may make regulations as to the following matters—

(a) publicity about the scheme;

(b) making the scheme available for inspection by the public;

(c) requirements to be met for the purpose of bringing the scheme into effect.

(8) The local planning authority must revise their local development scheme—

(a) at such time as they consider appropriate;

(b) when directed to do so by the Secretary of State.

(9) Subsections (2) to (7) apply to the revision of a scheme as they apply to the preparation of the scheme.

16 Minerals and waste development scheme

(1) A county council in respect of any part of their area for which there is a district council must prepare and maintain a scheme to be known as their minerals and waste development scheme.

(2) Section 15 (ignoring subsections (1) and (2)(e)) applies in relation to a minerals and waste development scheme as it applies in relation to a local development scheme.

(3) This Part applies to a minerals and waste development scheme as it applies to a local development scheme and for that purpose—

(a) references to a local development scheme include references to a minerals and waste development scheme;

(b) references to a local planning authority include references to a county council.

(4) But subsection (3) does not apply to—
(a) section 17(3);
(b) section 24(1)(b), (4) and (7);
(c) the references in section 24(5) to subsection (4) and the Mayor;
(d) sections 29 to 31.

Documents

17 Local development documents

(1) Documents which must be specified in the local development scheme as local development documents are—
(a) documents of such descriptions as are prescribed;
(b) the local planning authority's statement of community involvement.

(2) The local planning authority may also specify in the scheme such other documents as they think are appropriate.

(3) The local development documents must (taken as a whole) set out the authority's policies (however expressed) relating to the development and use of land in their area.

(4) In the case of the documents which are included in a minerals and waste development scheme they must also (taken as a whole) set out the authority's policies (however expressed) in relation to development which is a county matter within the meaning of paragraph 1 of Schedule 1 to the principal Act (ignoring sub-paragraph (1)(i)).

(5) If to any extent a policy set out in a local development document conflicts with any other statement or information in the document the conflict must be resolved in favour of the policy.

(6) The authority must keep under review their local development documents having regard to the results of any review carried out under section 13 or 14.

(7) Regulations under this section may prescribe—
(a) which descriptions of local development documents are development plan documents;
(b) the form and content of the local development documents;
(c) the time at which any step in the preparation of any such document must be taken.

(8) A document is a local development document only in so far as it or any part of it—
(a) is adopted by resolution of the local planning authority as a local development document;
(b) is approved by the Secretary of State under section 21 or 27.

18 Statement of community involvement

(1) The local planning authority must prepare a statement of community involvement.

(2) The statement of community involvement is a statement of the authority's policy as to the involvement in the exercise of the authority's functions under sections 19, 26 and 28 of this Act and Part 3 of the principal Act of persons who appear to the authority to have an interest in matters relating to development in their area.

(3) For the purposes of sections 19(2) and 24 the statement of community involvement is not a local development document.

(4) Section 20 applies to the statement of community involvement as if it were a development plan document.

(5) But in section 20(5)(a)—
(a) the reference to section 19 must be construed as if it does not include a reference to subsection (2) of that section;
(b) the reference to section 24(1) must be ignored.

(6) In the following provisions of this Part references to a development plan document include references to the statement of community involvement—

(a) section 22;
(b) section 23(2) to (5).

19 Preparation of local development documents

(1) Local development documents must be prepared in accordance with the local development scheme.

(2) In preparing a local development document the local planning authority must have regard to—

(a) national policies and advice contained in guidance issued by the Secretary of State;
(b) the RSS for the region in which the area of the authority is situated, if the area is outside Greater London;
(c) the spatial development strategy if the authority are a London borough or if any part of the authority's area adjoins Greater London;
(d) the RSS for any region which adjoins the area of the authority;
(e) the Wales Spatial Plan if any part of the authority's area adjoins Wales;
(f) the community strategy prepared by the authority;
(g) the community strategy for any other authority whose area comprises any part of the area of the local planning authority;
(h) any other local development document which has been adopted by the authority;
(i) the resources likely to be available for implementing the proposals in the document;
(j) such other matters as the Secretary of State prescribes.

(3) In preparing the other local development documents the authority must also comply with their statement of community involvement.

(4) But subsection (3) does not apply at any time before the authority have adopted their statement of community involvement.

(5) The local planning authority must also—

(a) carry out an appraisal of the sustainability of the proposals in each document;
(b) prepare a report of the findings of the appraisal.

(6) The Secretary of State may by regulations make provision—

(a) as to any further documents which must be prepared by the authority in connection with the preparation of a local development document;
(b) as to the form and content of such documents.

(7) The community strategy is the strategy prepared by an authority under section 4 of the Local Government Act 2000 (c. 22).

20 Independent examination

(1) The local planning authority must submit every development plan document to the Secretary of State for independent examination.

(2) But the authority must not submit such a document unless—

(a) they have complied with any relevant requirements contained in regulations under this Part, and
(b) they think the document is ready for independent examination.

(3) The authority must also send to the Secretary of State (in addition to the development plan document) such other documents (or copies of documents) and such information as is prescribed.

(4) The examination must be carried out by a person appointed by the Secretary of State.

(5) The purpose of an independent examination is to determine in respect of the development plan document—

(a) whether it satisfies the requirements of sections 19 and 24 (1), regulations under section 17(7) and any regulations under section 36 relating to the preparation of development plan documents;

(b) whether it is sound.

(6) Any person who makes representations seeking to change a development plan document must (if he so requests) be given the opportunity to appear before and be heard by the person carrying out the examination.

(7) The person appointed to carry out the examination must—

(a) make recommendations;

(b) give reasons for the recommendations.

(8) The local planning authority must publish the recommendations and the reasons.

21 Intervention by Secretary of State

(1) If the Secretary of State thinks that a local development document is unsatisfactory—

(a) he may at any time before the document is adopted under section 23 direct the local planning authority to modify the document in accordance with the direction;

(b) if he gives such a direction he must state his reasons for doing so.

(2) The authority—

(a) must comply with the direction;

(b) must not adopt the document unless the Secretary of State gives notice that he is satisfied that they have complied with the direction.

(3) But subsection (2) does not apply if the Secretary of State withdraws the direction.

(4) At any time before a development plan document is adopted by a local planning authority the Secretary of State may direct that the document (or any part of it) is submitted to him for his approval.

(5) The following paragraphs apply if the Secretary of State gives a direction under subsection (4)—

(a) the authority must not take any step in connection with the adoption of the document until the Secretary of State gives his decision;

(b) if the direction is given before the authority have submitted the document under section 20(1) the Secretary of State must hold an independent examination and section 20(4) to (7) applies accordingly;

(c) if the direction is given after the authority have submitted the document but before the person appointed to carry out the examination has made his recommendations he must make his recommendations to the Secretary of State;

(d) the document has no effect unless it or (if the direction relates to only part of a document) the part has been approved by the Secretary of State.

(6) The Secretary of State must publish the recommendations made to him by virtue of subsection (5)(b) or (c) and the reasons of the person making the recommendations.

(7) In considering a document or part of a document submitted under subsection (4) the Secretary of State may take account of any matter which he thinks is relevant.

(8) It is immaterial whether any such matter was taken account of by the authority.

(9) In relation to a document or part of a document submitted to him under subsection (4) the Secretary of State—

(a) may approve, approve subject to specified modifications or reject the document or part;

(b) must give reasons for his decision under paragraph (a).

(10) In the exercise of any function under this section the Secretary of State must have regard to the local development scheme.

22 Withdrawal of local development documents

(1) A local planning authority may at any time before a local development document is adopted under section 23 withdraw the document.

(2) But subsection (1) does not apply to a development plan document at any time after the document has been submitted for independent examination under section 20 unless—

(a) the person carrying out the examination recommends that the document is withdrawn and that recommendation is not overruled by a direction given by the Secretary of State, or

(b) the Secretary of State directs that the document must be withdrawn.

23 Adoption of local development documents

(1) The local planning authority may adopt a local development document (other than a development plan document) either as originally prepared or as modified to take account of—

(a) any representations made in relation to the document;

(b) any other matter they think is relevant.

(2) The authority may adopt a development plan document as originally prepared if the person appointed to carry out the independent examination of the document recommends that the document as originally prepared is adopted.

(3) The authority may adopt a development plan document with modifications if the person appointed to carry out the independent examination of the document recommends the modifications.

(4) The authority must not adopt a development plan document unless they do so in accordance with subsection (2) or (3).

(5) A document is adopted for the purposes of this section if it is adopted by resolution of the authority.

24 Conformity with regional strategy

(1) The local development documents must be in general conformity with—

(a) the RSS (if the area of the local planning authority is in a region other than London);

(b) the spatial development strategy (if the local planning authority are a London borough).

(2) A local planning authority whose area is in a region other than London—

(a) must request the opinion in writing of the RPB as to the general conformity of a development plan document with the RSS;

(b) may request the opinion in writing of the RPB as to the general conformity of any other local development document with the RSS.

(3) Not later than the end of the period prescribed for the purposes of this section the RPB must send its opinion to—

(a) the Secretary of State;

(b) the local planning authority.

(4) A local planning authority which are a London borough—

(a) must request the opinion in writing of the Mayor of London as to the general conformity of a development plan document with the spatial development strategy;

(b) may request the opinion in writing of the Mayor as to the general conformity of any other local development document with the spatial development strategy.

(5) Whether or not the local planning authority make a request mentioned in subsection (2) or (4) the RPB or the Mayor (as the case may be) may give an opinion as to the general conformity of a local development document with the RSS or the spatial development strategy (as the case may be).

(6) If in the opinion of the RPB a document is not in general conformity with the RSS the RPB must be taken to have made representations seeking a change to the document.

(7) If in the opinion of the Mayor a document is not in general conformity with the spatial development strategy the Mayor must be taken to have made representations seeking a change to the document.

(8) But the Secretary of State may in any case direct that subsection (6) must be ignored.

(9) If at any time no body is recognised as the RPB under section 2 the functions of the RPB under this section must be exercised by the Secretary of State and subsections (3)(a), (6) and (8) of this section must be ignored.

25 Revocation of local development documents

The Secretary of State—

(a) may at any time revoke a local development document at the request of the local planning authority;

(b) may prescribe descriptions of local development document which may be revoked by the authority themselves.

26 Revision of local development documents

(1) The local planning authority may at any time prepare a revision of a local development document.

(2) The authority must prepare a revision of a local development document—

(a) if the Secretary of State directs them to do so, and

(b) in accordance with such timetable as he directs.

(3) This Part applies to the revision of a local development document as it applies to the preparation of the document.

(4) Subsection (5) applies if any part of the area of the local planning authority is an area to which an enterprise zone scheme relates.

(5) As soon as practicable after the occurrence of a relevant event—

(a) the authority must review every local development document in the light of the enterprise zone scheme;

(b) if they think that any modifications of the document are required in consequence of the scheme they must prepare a revised document containing the modifications.

(6) The following are relevant events—

(a) the making of an order under paragraph 5 of Schedule 32 to the Local Government, Planning and Land Act 1980 (c. 65) (designation of enterprise zone);

(b) the giving of notification under paragraph 11(1) of that Schedule (approval of modification of enterprise zone scheme).

(7) References to an enterprise zone and an enterprise zone scheme must be construed in accordance with that Act.

27 Secretary of State's default power

(1) This section applies if the Secretary of State thinks that a local planning authority are failing or omitting to do anything it is necessary for them to do in connection with the preparation, revision or adoption of a development plan document.

(2) The Secretary of State must hold an independent examination and section 20(4) to (7) applies accordingly.

(3) The Secretary of State must publish the recommendations and reasons of the person appointed to hold the examination.

(4) The Secretary of State may—

(a) prepare or revise (as the case may be) the document, and

(b) approve the document as a local development document.

(5) The Secretary of State must give reasons for anything he does in pursuance of subsection (4).

(6) The authority must reimburse the Secretary of State for any expenditure he incurs in connection with anything—

(a) which is done by him under subsection (4), and

(b) which the authority failed or omitted to do as mentioned in subsection (1).

28 Joint local development documents

(1) Two or more local planning authorities may agree to prepare one or more joint local development documents.

(2) This Part applies for the purposes of any step which may be or is required to be taken in relation to a joint local development document as it applies for the purposes of any step which may be or is required to be taken in relation to a local development document.

(3) For the purposes of subsection (2) anything which must be done by or in relation to a local planning authority in connection with a local development document must be done by or in relation to each of the authorities mentioned in subsection (1) in connection with a joint local development document.

(4) Any requirement of this Part in relation to the RSS is a requirement in relation to the RSS for the region in which each authority mentioned in subsection (1) is situated.

(5) If the authorities mentioned in subsection (1) include one or more London boroughs the requirements of this Part in relation to the spatial development strategy also apply.

(6) Subsections (7) to (9) apply if a local planning authority withdraw from an agreement mentioned in subsection (1).

(7) Any step taken in relation to the document must be treated as a step taken by—

(a) an authority which were a party to the agreement for the purposes of any corresponding document prepared by them;

(b) two or more other authorities who were parties to the agreement for the purposes of any corresponding joint local development document.

(8) Any independent examination of a local development document to which the agreement relates must be suspended.

(9) If before the end of the period prescribed for the purposes of this subsection an authority which were a party to the agreement request the Secretary of State to do so he may direct that—

(a) the examination is resumed in relation to the corresponding document;

(b) any step taken for the purposes of the suspended examination has effect for the purposes of the resumed examination.

(10) A joint local development document is a local development document prepared jointly by two or more local planning authorities.

(11) The Secretary of State may by regulations make provision as to what is a corresponding document.

Joint committees

29 Joint committees

(1) This section applies if one or more local planning authorities agree with one or more country councils in relation to any area of such a council for which there is also a district council to establish a joint committee to be, for the purposes of this Part, the local planning authority—

(a) for the area specified in the agreement;

(b) in respect of such matters as are so specified.

(2) The Secretary of State may by order constitute a joint committee to be the local planning authority—

(a) for the area;

(b) in respect of those matters.

(3)–(10) ...

Miscellaneous

32 Exclusion of certain representations

(1) This section applies to any representation or objection in respect of anything which is done or is proposed to be done in pursuance of—

(a) an order or scheme under section 10, 14, 16, 18, 106(1) or (3) or 108(1) of the Highways Act 1980 (c. 66);

(b) an order or scheme under section 7, 9, 11, 13 or 20 of the Highways Act 1959 (c. 25), section 3 of the Highways (Miscellaneous Provisions) Act 1961 (c. 63) or section 1 or 10 of the Highways Act 1971 (c. 41) (which provisions were replaced by the provisions mentioned in paragraph (a));

(c) an order under section 1 of the New Towns Act 1981 (c. 64).

(2) If the Secretary of State or a local planning authority thinks that a representation made in relation to a local development document is in substance a representation or objection to which this section applies he or they (as the case may be) may disregard it.

33 Urban development corporations

The Secretary of State may direct that this Part does not apply to the area of an urban development corporation.

34 Guidance

In the exercise of any function conferred under or by virtue of this Part the local planning authority must have regard to any guidance issued by the Secretary of State.

35 Annual monitoring report

(1) Every local planning authority must make an annual report to the Secretary of State.

(2) The annual report must contain such information as is prescribed as to—

(a) the implementation of the local development scheme;

(b) the extent to which the policies set out in the local development documents are being achieved.

(3) The annual report must—

(a) be in respect of such period of 12 months as is prescribed;

(b) be made at such time as is prescribed;

(c) be in such form as is prescribed;

(d) contain such other matter as is prescribed.

General

36 Regulations

(1) The Secretary of State may be regulations make provision in connection with the exercise by any person of functions under this Part.

(2) The regulations may in particular make provision as to—

(a) the procedure to be followed by the local planning authority in carrying out the appraisal under section 19;

(b) the procedure to be followed in the preparation of local development documents;

(c) requirements about the giving of notice and publicity;

(d) requirements about inspection by the public of a local development document or any other document;

(e) the nature and extent of consultation with and participation by the public in anything done under this Part;

(f) the making of representations about any matter to be included in a local development document;

(g) consideration of any such representations;

(h) the remuneration and allowances payable to a person appointed to carry out an independent examination under section 20;

(i) the determination of the time at which anything must be done for the purposes of this Part;

(j) the manner of publication of any draft, report or other document published under this Part;

(k) monitoring the exercise by local planning authorities of their functions under this Part;

(l) the making of reasonable charges for the provision of copies of documents required by or under this Part.

37 Interpretation

(1) Local development scheme must be construed in accordance with section 15.

(2) Local development document must be construed in accordance with section 17.

(3) A development plan document is a document which—

(a) is a local development document, and

(b) forms part of the development plan.

(4) Local planning authorities are—

(a) district councils;

(b) London borough councils;

(c) metropolitan district councils;

(d) county councils in relation to any area in England for which there is no district council;

(e) the Broads Authority.

(5) A National Park authority is the local planning authority for the whole of its area and subsection (4) must be construed subject to that.

(6) RSS and RPB must be construed in accordance with Part 1.

(7) This section applies for the purposes of this Part.

PART III DEVELOPMENT

Development plan

38 Development plan

(1) A reference to the development plan in any enactment mentioned in subsection (7) must be construed in accordance with subsections (2) to (5).

(2) For the purposes of any area in Greater London the development plan is—

(a) the spatial development strategy, and

(b) the development plan documents (taken as a whole) which have been adopted or approved in relation to that area.

(3) For the purposes of any other area in England the development plan is—

(a) the regional spatial strategy for the region in which the area is situated, and

(b) the development plan documents (taken as a whole) which have been adopted or approved in relation to that area.

(4) For the purposes of any area in Wales the development plan is the local development plan adopted or approved in relation to that area.

(5) If to any extent a policy contained in a development plan for an area conflicts with another policy in the development plan the conflict must be resolved in favour of the policy which is contained in the last document to be adopted, approved or published (as the case may be).

(6) If regard is to be had to the development plan for the purpose of any determination to be made under the planning Acts the determination must be made in accordance with the plan unless material considerations indicate otherwise.

(7) The enactments are—

(a) this Act;

(b) the planning Acts;

(c) any other enactment relating to town and country planning;

(d) the Land Compensation Act 1961 (c. 33);

(e) the Highways Act 1980 (c. 66).

(8) In subsection (5) references to a development plan include a development plan for the purposes of paragraph 1 of Schedule 8.

Sustainable development

39 Sustainable development

(1) This section applies to any person who or body which exercises any function—

(a) under Part 1 in relation to a regional spatial strategy;

(b) under Part 2 in relation to local development documents;

(c) under Part 6 in relation to the Wales Spatial Plan or a local development plan.

(2) The person or body must exercise the function with the objective of contributing to the achievement of sustainable development.

(3) For the purposes of subsection (2) the person or body must have regard to national policies and advice contained in guidance issued by—

(a) the Secretary of State for the purposes of subsection (1)(a) and (b);

(b) the National Assembly for Wales for the purposes of subsection (1)(c).

PART IV DEVELOPMENT CONTROL

Planning contribution

46 Planning contribution

(1) The Secretary of State may, by regulations, make provision for the making of a planning contribution in relation to the development or use of land in the area of a local planning authority.

(2) The contribution may be made—

(a) by the prescribed means,

(b) by compliance with the relevant requirements, or

(c) by a combination of such means and compliance.

(3) The regulations may require the local planning authority to include in a development plan document (or in such other document as is prescribed)—

(a) a statement of the developments or uses or descriptions of development or use in relation to which they will consider accepting a planning contribution;

(b) a statement of the matters relating to development or use in relation to which they will not consider accepting a contribution by the prescribed means;

(c) the purposes to which receipts from payments made in respect of contributions are (in whole or in part) to be put;

(d) the criteria by reference to which the value of a contribution made by the prescribed means is to be determined.

(4) The regulations may make provision as to circumstances in which—

(a) except in the case of a contribution to which subsection (3) (b) applies, the person making the contribution (the contributor) must state the form in which he will make the contribution;

(b) the contribution may not be made by compliance with the relevant requirements if it is made by the prescribed means;

(c) the contribution may not be made by the prescribed means if it is made by compliance with the relevant requirements;

(d) a contribution must not be made.

(5) The prescribed means are—

(a) the payment of a sum the amount and terms of payment of which are determined in accordance with criteria published by the local planning authority for the purposes of subsection (3) (d),

(b) the provision of a benefit in kind the value of which is so determined, or

(c) a combination of such payment and provision.

(6) The relevant requirements are such requirements relating to the development or use as are—

(a) prescribed for the purposes of this section, and
(b) included as part of the terms of the contribution,

and may include a requirement to make a payment of a sum.

(7) Development plan document must be construed in accordance with section 37(3).

47 Planning contribution: regulations

(1) This section applies for the purpose of regulations made under section 46.

(2) Maximum and minimum amounts may be prescribed in relation to a payment falling within section 46(5)(a).

(3) Provision may be made to enable periodic adjustment of the criteria mentioned in section 46(3)(d).

(4) The local planning authority may be required to publish an annual report containing such information in relation to the planning contribution as is prescribed.

(5) If a document is prescribed for the purposes of section 46(3) the regulations may prescribe—

(a) the procedure for its preparation and the time at which it must be published;
(b) the circumstances in which and the procedure by which the Secretary of State may take steps in relation to the preparation of the document.

(6) Provision may be made for the enforcement by the local planning authority of the terms of a planning contribution including provision—

(a) for a person obstructing the taking of such steps as are prescribed to be guilty of an offence punishable by a fine not exceeding level 3 on the standard scale;
(b) for a person deriving title to the land from the contributor to be bound by the terms of the contribution;
(c) for a condition to be attached to any planning permission relating to the land requiring the contribution to be made before any development is started;
(d) for the enforcement of a planning contribution in respect of land which is Crown land within the meaning of section 293(1) of the principal Act.

(7) The regulations may—

(a) require the local planning authority to apply receipts from planning contributions made by the prescribed means only to purposes mentioned in section 46(3)(c);
(b) make provision for setting out in writing the terms of the planning contribution;
(c) make provision in relation to the modification or discharge of a planning contribution.

(8) The regulations may—

(a) make different provision in relation to the areas of different local planning authorities or different descriptions of local planning authority;
(b) exclude their application (in whole or in part) in relation to the area of one or more local planning authorities or descriptions of local planning authority.

48 Planning contribution: Wales

In relation to land in Wales, sections 46 and 47 apply subject to the following modifications—

(a) references to the Secretary of State must be construed as references to the National Assembly for Wales;
(b) the reference to a development plan document must be construed as a reference to a local development plan (within the meaning of section 62).

54 Duty to respond to consultation

(1) This section applies to a prescribed requirement to consult any person or body (the consultee) which exercises functions for the purposes of any enactment.

(2) A prescribed requirement to consult is a requirement—

(a) with which the appropriate authority or a local planning authority must comply before granting any permission, approval or consent under or by virtue of the planning Acts;

(b) which is prescribed for the purposes of this subsection.

(3) At any time before an application is made for any permission, approval or consent mentioned in subsection (2) any person may in relation to a proposed development consult the consultee on any matter in respect of which the appropriate authority is or the local planning authority are required to consult the consultee.

(4) The consultee must give a substantive response to any consultation mentioned in subsection (2) or by virtue of subsection (3) before the end of—

(a) the period prescribed for the purposes of this subsection, or

(b) such other period as is agreed in writing between the consultee and the appropriate authority or the local planning authority (as the case may be).

(5) The appropriate authority may also prescribe—

(a) the procedure to be followed for the purposes of this section;

(b) the information to be provided to the consultee for the purposes of the consultation;

(c) the requirements of a substantive response.

(6) Anything prescribed for the purposes of subsections (1) to (5) must be prescribed by development order.

(7) A development order may—

(a) require consultees to give the appropriate authority a report as to their compliance with subsection (4);

(b) prescribe the form and content of the report;

(c) prescribe the times at which the report is to be made.

(8) The appropriate authority is—

(a) the Secretary of State in relation to England;

(b) the National Assembly for Wales in relation to Wales.

PART VI WALES

...

PART IX MISCELLANEOUS AND GENERAL

Crown

111 Crown

(1) This Act (except Part 8) binds the Crown.

(2) The amendment of an enactment by or by virtue of Part 8 applies to the Crown to the extent that the enactment amended so applies.

Parliament

112 Parliament

The planning Acts and this Act have effect despite any rule of law relating to Parliament or the law and practice of Parliament.

Miscellaneous

113 Validity of strategies, plans and documents

(1) This section applies to—

(a) a revision of the regional spatial strategy;

(b) the Wales Spatial Plan;

(c) a development plan document;

(d) a local development plan;
(e) a revision of a document mentioned in paragraph (b), (c) or (d);
(f) the Mayor of London's spatial development strategy;
(g) an alteration or replacement of the spatial development strategy,

and anything falling within paragraphs (a) to (g) is referred to in this section as a relevant document.

(2) A relevant document must not be questioned in any legal proceedings except in so far as is provided by the following provisions of this section.

(3) A person aggrieved by a relevant document may make an application to the High Court on the ground that—

(a) the document is not within the appropriate power;
(b) a procedural requirement has not been complied with.

(4) But the application must be made not later than the end of the period of six weeks starting with the relevant date.

(5) The High Court may make an interim order suspending the operation of the relevant document—

(a) wholly or in part;
(b) generally or as it affects the property of the applicant.

(6) Subsection (7) applies if the High Court is satisfied—

(a) that a relevant document is to any extent outside the appropriate power;
(b) that the interests of the applicant have been substantially prejudiced by a failure to comply with a procedural requirement.

(7) The High Court may quash the relevant document—

(a) wholly or in part;
(b) generally or as it affects the property of the applicant.

(8) An interim order has effect until the proceedings are finally determined.

(9) The appropriate power is—

(a) Part 1 of this Act in the case of a revision of the regional spatial strategy;
(b) section 60 above in the case of the Wales Spatial Plan or any revision of it;
(c) Part 2 of this Act in the case of a development plan document or any revision of it;
(d) section 62 to 78 above in the case of a local development plan or any revision of it;
(e) sections 334 to 343 of the Greater London Authority Act 1999 (c. 29) in the case of the spatial development strategy or any alteration or replacement of it.

(10) A procedural requirement is a requirement under the appropriate power or contained in regulations or an order made under that power which relates to the adoption, publication or approval of a relevant document.

(11) References to the relevant date must be construed as follows—

(a) for the purposes of a revision of the regional spatial strategy, the date when the Secretary of State publishes the revised strategy under section 9(6) above;
(b) for the purposes of the Wales Spatial Plan (or a revision of it), the date when it is approved by the National Assembly for Wales;
(c) for the purposes of a development plan document (or a revision of it), the date when it is adopted by the local planning authority or approved by the Secretary of State (as the case may be);
(d) for the purposes of a local development plan (or a revision of it), the date when it is adopted by a local planning authority in Wales or approved by the National Assembly for Wales (as the case may be);
(e) for the purposes of the spatial development strategy (or an alteration or replacement of it), the date when the Mayor of London publishes it.

117 Interpretation

(1) Expressions used in this Act and in the principal Act have the same meaning in this Act as in that Act.

. . .

(4) The planning Acts are—

(a) the principal Act;

(b) the listed buildings Act;

(c) the hazardous substances Act;

(d) the Planning (Consequential Provisions) Act 1990.

(5) The principal Act is the Town and Country Planning Act 1990.

(6) The listed buildings Act is the Planning (Listed Buildings and Conservation Areas) Act 1990.

(7) The hazardous substances Act is the Planning (Hazardous Substances) Act 1990.

. . .

121 Commencement

(1) The preceding provisions of this Act (except section 115 and the provisions specified in subsections (4), (5) and (6)) come into force on such day as the Secretary of State may by order appoint.

. . .

Energy Act 2004

(2004, c. 20)

PART 2 SUSTAINABILITY AND RENEWABLE ENERGY SOURCES

CHAPTER 1 SUSTAINABLE ENERGY

82 Microgeneration

(1) The Secretary of State—

(a) must prepare a strategy for the promotion of microgeneration in Great Britain; and

(b) may from time to time revise it.

(2) The Secretary of State—

(a) must publish the strategy within 18 months after the commencement of this section; and

(b) if he revises it, must publish the revised strategy.

(3) In preparing or revising the strategy, the Secretary of State must consider the contribution that is capable of being made by microgeneration to—

(a) cutting emissions of greenhouse gases in Great Britain;

(b) reducing the number of people living in fuel poverty in Great Britain;

(c) reducing the demands on transmission systems and distribution systems situated in Great Britain;

(d) reducing the need for those systems to be modified;

(e) enhancing the availability of electricity and heat for consumers in Great Britain.

(4) Before preparing or revising the strategy, the Secretary of State must consult such persons appearing to him to represent the producers and suppliers of plant used for microgeneration, and such other persons, as he considers appropriate.

(5) The Secretary of State must take reasonable steps to secure the implementation of the strategy in the form in which it has most recently been published.

(6) For the purposes of this section 'microgeneration' means the use for the generation of electricity or the production of heat of any plant—

(a) which in generating electricity or (as the case may be) producing heat, relies wholly or mainly on a source of energy or a technology mentioned in subsection (7); and

(b) the capacity of which to generate electricity or (as the case may be) to produce heat does not exceed the capacity mentioned in subsection (8).

(7) Those sources of energy and technologies are—

(a) biomass;

(b) biofuels;

(c) fuel cells;

(d) photovoltaics;

(e) water (including waves and tides);

(f) wind;

(g) solar power;

(h) geothermal sources;

(i) combined heat and power systems;

(j) other sources of energy and technologies for the generation of electricity or the production of heat, the use of which would, in the opinion of the Secretary of State, cut emissions of greenhouse gases in Great Britain.

(8) That capacity is—

(a) in relation to the generation of electricity, 50 kilowatts;

(b) in relation to the production of heat, 45 kilowatts thermal.

(9) In this section—

'consumers' includes both existing and future consumers;

'distribution system' and 'transmission system' have the same meanings as in Part 1 of the 1989 Act;

'fuel poverty' has the same meaning as in section 1 of the Sustainable Energy Act 2003 (c 30);

'greenhouse gases' means—

(a) carbon dioxide;

(b) methane;

(c) nitrous oxide;

(d) hydrofluorocarbons;

(e) perfluorocarbons;

(f) sulphur hexafluoride;

'plant' includes any equipment, apparatus or appliance.

Sustainable and Secure Buildings Act 2004

(2004, c. 22)

...

6 Secretary of State to report on building stock

(1) The Secretary of State must—

(a) for the period of two years beginning with the commencement of this section, and

(b) for each succeeding period of two years,

prepare a report on progress during the period in connection with the purposes mentioned in section 1(1)(b) to (e) of the Building Act 1984 in the context of the building stock in England and Wales.

(2) A report under this section must (in particular) deal with—

(a) building regulations made during the period for any of those purposes;

(b) proposals current at the end of the period to make building regulations for any of those purposes;

(c) effects or likely effects of regulations or proposals dealt with in the report under paragraphs (a) and (b);

(d) proposals considered by the Secretary of State during the period for the setting of targets for any of those purposes in relation to—
(i) buildings in England and Wales; or
(ii) services, fittings or equipment provided in or in connection with such buildings;
(e) overall changes during the period in—
(i) the efficiency with which energy is used in buildings in England and Wales;
(ii) levels of emissions from such buildings that are emissions considered by the Secretary of State to contribute to climate change;
(iii) the extent to which such buildings have their own facilities for generating energy;
(iv) the extent to which materials used in constructing, or carrying out works in relation to, such buildings are recycled or re-used materials.

(3) A report under this section must contain an estimate, as at the end of the period, of the number of dwellings in England and Wales.

(4) The Secretary of State must lay before Parliament each report he prepares under this section.

...

11 Short title, repeals, commencement and extent

(1) This Act may be cited as the Sustainable and Secure Buildings Act 2004.

...

(3) This Act, apart from the provisions coming into force in accordance with subsection (4), shall come into force on such day as the Secretary of State may by order made by statutory instrument appoint; and different days may be appointed for different purposes.

(4) This section (apart from subsection (2)) and sections 1, 3(1) to (7), 4(1) to (3) and (5), 6 and 10 shall come into force at the end of the period of two months beginning with the day on which this Act is passed.

(5) This Act extends to England and Wales only.

Clean Neighbourhoods and Environment Act 2005

(2005, c. 16)

PART V WASTE

CHAPTER III SITE WASTE

54 Site waste management plans

(1) The appropriate person may by regulations make provision requiring persons of a specified description—
(a) to prepare plans for the management and disposal of waste created in the course of specified descriptions of works involving construction or demolition;
(b) to comply with such plans.

(2) Descriptions of works that may be specified under subsection (1)(a) include in particular description by reference to the cost or likely cost of such works.

(3) Regulations under this section may make supplementary and incidental provision, including in particular provision as to—
(a) the circumstances in which plans must be prepared;
(b) the contents of plans;
(c) enforcement authorities in relation to plans and the powers of such authorities;
(d) the keeping of plans and their production to enforcement authorities;

(e) offences in relation to a failure to comply with a requirement under the regulations;
(f) penalties for those offences;
(g) the discharging of liability for an offence under the regulations by the payment of a fixed penalty to an enforcement authority;
(h) the uses to which such payments may be put by enforcement authorities.

(4) Regulations under this section may make different provision for different purposes.

(5) Regulations under this section making provision under subsection (3)(h) may in particular make different provision relating to different enforcement authorities or different descriptions of enforcement authority (including provision framed by reference to performance categories under section 99(4) of the Local Government Act 2003).

(6) Regulations under this section are to be made by statutory instrument.

...

(8) The appropriate person may give guidance to persons who are enforcement authorities under subsection (3)(c) in relation to the powers conferred on them under that provision.

(9) In this section—
'appropriate person' means—
(a) in relation to works in England, the Secretary of State;
(b) in relation to works in Wales, the National Assembly for Wales;
'specified' means specified in regulations under this section.

Natural Environment and Rural Communities Act 2006

(2006, c. 16)

PART 1 NATURAL ENGLAND AND THE COMMISSION FOR RURAL COMMUNITIES

CHAPTER I NATURAL ENGLAND

Constitution and general purpose

1 Constitution

(1) There is to be a body known as Natural England.

(2) Natural England is to have the functions conferred on it by or under this Act or any other enactment.

(3) Except where otherwise expressly provided, Natural England's functions are exercisable in relation to England only.

(4) English Nature and the Countryside Agency are dissolved and their functions are (subject to the provisions of this Act) transferred to Natural England.

(5) Schedule 1 contains provisions about the constitution of Natural England and related matters.

2 General purpose

(1) Natural England's general purpose is to ensure that the natural environment is conserved, enhanced and managed for the benefit of present and future generations, thereby contributing to sustainable development.

(2) Natural England's general purpose includes—
(a) promoting nature conservation and protecting biodiversity,
(b) conserving and enhancing the landscape,
(c) securing the provision and improvement of facilities for the study, understanding and enjoyment of the natural environment,

(d) promoting access to the countryside and open spaces and encouraging open-air recreation, and

(e) contributing in other ways to social and economic well-being through management of the natural environment.

(3) The purpose in subsection (2)(e) may, in particular, be carried out by working with local communities.

General implementation powers

5 Carrying out proposals etc.

Natural England may—

(a) carry out proposals which appear to it to further its general purpose, or

(b) assist in, coordinate or promote the carrying out of such proposals by others.

6 Financial and other assistance

(1) Natural England may give financial assistance to any person, if doing so appears to it to further its general purpose.

(2) Financial assistance under this section may be given in any form, and may in particular be given by way of a grant, a loan or a guarantee.

(3) Financial assistance under this section may be given subject to conditions, including (in the case of a grant) conditions for repayment in specified circumstances.

(4)....

7 Management agreements

(1) Natural England may make an agreement (a 'management agreement') with a person who has an interest in land about the management or use of the land, if doing so appears to it to further its general purpose.

(2) A management agreement may, in particular—

(a) impose on the person who has an interest in the land obligations in respect of the use of the land;

(b) impose on the person who has an interest in the land restrictions on the exercise of rights over the land;

(c) provide for the carrying out of such work as may be expedient for the purposes of the agreement by any person or persons;

(d) provide for any matter for which a management scheme relating to a site of special scientific interest provides (or could provide);

(e) provide for the making of payments by either party to the other party or to any other person;

(f) contain incidental and consequential provision.

(3) A management agreement is, unless the agreement otherwise provides—

(a) binding on persons deriving title under or from the person with whom Natural England makes the agreement, and

(b) enforceable by Natural England against those persons.

(4)...

(5)...

(6) 'Interest in land' has the same meaning as in the National Parks and Access to the Countryside Act 1949.

(7) 'Management scheme' and 'site of special scientific interest' have the same meaning as in Part 2 of the Wildlife and Countryside Act 1981.

8 Experimental schemes

(1) Natural England may—

(a) make and carry out experimental schemes designed to establish ways in which its general purpose might be furthered, or

(b) promote the making and carrying out of such schemes.

(2) A scheme is experimental if it involves—

(a) the development or application of new methods, concepts or techniques, or

(b) the testing or further development of existing methods, concepts or techniques.

(3) Before making an experimental scheme, Natural England must consult such persons as appear to it to have an interest in the subject matter of the scheme.

Other functions

12 Power to bring criminal proceedings

(1) Natural England may institute criminal proceedings.

(2) A person who is authorised by Natural England to prosecute on its behalf in proceedings before a magistrates' court is entitled to prosecute in such proceedings even though he is not a barrister or solicitor.

Powers of Secretary of State

14 Grants

(1) The Secretary of State may make grants to Natural England of such amounts as the Secretary of State thinks fit.

(2) A grant under this section may be made subject to such conditions as the Secretary of State thinks fit.

15 Guidance

(1) The Secretary of State must give Natural England guidance as to the exercise of any functions of Natural England that relate to or affect regional planning and associated matters.

(2) The Secretary of State may give Natural England guidance as to the exercise of its other functions.

(3) Before giving guidance under this section the Secretary of State must consult—

(a) Natural England,

(b) the Environment Agency, and

(c) such other persons as the Secretary of State thinks appropriate.

(4) The Secretary of State must publish any guidance given under this section as soon as is reasonably practicable after giving the guidance.

(5) The power to give guidance under this section includes power to vary or revoke it.

(6) In discharging its functions, Natural England must have regard to guidance given under this section.

16 Directions

(1) The Secretary of State may give Natural England general or specific directions as to the exercise of its functions.

(2) Subsection (1) does not apply to functions of Natural England that are exercisable through the Joint Nature Conservation Committee.

(3) The Secretary of State must publish any directions given under this section as soon as is reasonably practicable after giving the directions.

(4) The power to give directions under this section includes power to vary or revoke the directions.

(5) Natural England must comply with any directions given under this section.

. . .

Interpretation

30 Interpretation

(1) In this Part—

...

'nature conservation' means the conservation of flora, fauna or geological or physiographical features;

...

PART 2 NATURE CONSERVATION IN THE UK

Joint Nature Conservation Committee etc.

31 Joint Nature Conservation Committee

The Joint Nature Conservation Committee—

(a) is to continue in existence, but

(b) is to be re-constituted in accordance with Schedule 4.

32 UK conservation bodies

(1) In this Part 'the UK conservation bodies' means—

(a) for England, Natural England;

(b) for Wales, the Countryside Council for Wales;

(c) for Scotland, Scottish Natural Heritage;

(d) for Northern Ireland, the Council for Nature Conservation and the Countryside.

(2) In this Part 'the GB conservation bodies' means the bodies mentioned in subsection (1)(a) to (c).

33 Purpose of functions under this Part

(1) The UK conservation bodies and the joint committee have the functions conferred on them by this Part for the purposes of—

(a) nature conservation, and

(b) fostering the understanding of nature conservation.

(2) Each of them must, in discharging their functions under this Part, have regard to—

(a) actual or possible ecological changes, and

(b) the desirability of contributing to sustainable development.

Coordinated functions

34 Functions of national or international significance

(1) The UK conservation bodies have the functions described in subsection (2), but those functions may be discharged only through the joint committee.

(2) The functions are—

(a) providing advice to the appropriate authorities on the development and implementation of policies for or affecting any nature conservation matter which—

(i) arises throughout the United Kingdom and raises issues common to England, Wales, Scotland and Northern Ireland,

(ii) arises in one or more (but not all) of those places and affects the interests of the United Kingdom as a whole, or

(iii) arises outside the United Kingdom;

(b) providing advice to any persons and disseminating knowledge about any matter falling within paragraph (a)(i), (ii) or (iii);

(c) establishing common standards throughout the United Kingdom for the monitoring of nature conservation and for research into nature conservation and the analysis of the resulting information;

(d) commissioning or supporting (whether by financial means or otherwise) research which the joint committee thinks is relevant to any matter mentioned in paragraphs (a) to (c).

(3) 'The appropriate authorities' means—

(a) the Secretary of State (or any other Minister of the Crown),
(b) the National Assembly for Wales,
(c) the Scottish Ministers, and
(d) the relevant Northern Ireland department.

35 Advice from joint committee to UK conservation body

(1) The joint committee may give advice or information to any of the UK conservation bodies on any matter which—

(a) is connected with the functions of that UK conservation body, and
(b) in the opinion of the joint committee—
(i) arises throughout the United Kingdom and raises issues common to England, Wales, Scotland and Northern Ireland,
(ii) arises in one or more (but not all) of those places and affects the interests of the United Kingdom as a whole, or
(iii) arises outside the United Kingdom.

(2) In discharging their functions relating to nature conservation, the UK conservation bodies must have regard to any advice given to them under subsection (1).

36 GB functions with respect to wildlife

(1) The GB conservation bodies have the functions described in subsection (2), but those functions may be discharged only through the joint committee.

(2) The functions are—

(a) those under sections 22(3) and 24(1) of the 1981 Act (listing of protected animals and plants);
(b) commissioning or supporting (whether by financial means or otherwise) research which the joint committee thinks is relevant to those functions.

(3) 'The 1981 Act' means the Wildlife and Countryside Act 1981.

37 UK conservation bodies: incidental powers for UK purposes, etc.

(1) Each of the UK conservation bodies may do anything that appears to it to be conducive or incidental to its functions under this Part.

(2) In particular each of them may for the purposes of its functions under this Part—

(a) acquire or dispose of property;
(b) accept gifts;
(c) undertake research directly related to those functions if it appears appropriate to do so.

(3) Nothing in any of the enactments concerning the functions of the UK conservation bodies prevents any of them—

(a) if requested to do so by any of the others, from giving advice or information to the other, or
(b) from giving advice or information to the joint committee.

(4) 'Enactment' includes an Act of the Scottish Parliament and Northern Ireland legislation.

Directions

38 Directions

(1) The Secretary of State may give the joint committee general or specific directions as to the discharge of any function under section 34 or 35 (but not as to the discharge of a function under section 36).

(2) Before giving any directions under this section, the Secretary of State must consult the National Assembly for Wales, the Scottish Ministers and the relevant Northern Ireland department.

(3) The Secretary of State must publish any directions given under this section as soon as is reasonably practicable after giving the directions.

(4) The power to give directions under this section includes power to vary or revoke the directions.

(5) The joint committee must comply with any directions given under this section.

Interpretation

39 Interpretation

In this Part—

'the joint committee' means the Joint Nature Conservation Committee;

...

'nature conservation' means the conservation of flora, fauna or geological or physiographical features;

...

'research' includes inquiries and investigations.

PART 3 WILDLIFE ETC.

Biodiversity

40 Duty to conserve biodiversity

(1) Every public authority must, in exercising its functions, have regard, so far as is consistent with the proper exercise of those functions, to the purpose of conserving biodiversity.

(2) In complying with subsection (1), a Minister of the Crown, government department or the National Assembly for Wales must in particular have regard to the United Nations Environmental Programme Convention on Biological Diversity of 1992.

(3) Conserving biodiversity includes, in relation to a living organism or type of habitat, restoring or enhancing a population or habitat.

(4) 'Public authority' means any of the following—

(a) a Minister of the Crown;

(b) the National Assembly for Wales;

(c) a public body (including a government department, a local authority and a local planning authority);

(d) a person holding an office—

(i) under the Crown,

(ii) created or continued in existence by a public general Act, or

(iii) the remuneration in respect of which is paid out of money provided by Parliament;

(e) a statutory undertaker.

(5) In this section—

'local authority' means—

(a) in relation to England, a county council, a district council, a parish council, a London borough council, the Common Council of the City of London or the Council of the Isles of Scilly;

(b) in relation to Wales, a county council, a county borough council or a community council;

'local planning authority' has the same meaning as in the Town and Country Planning Act 1990;

...

'statutory undertaker' means a person who is or is deemed to be a statutory undertaker for the purposes of any provision of Part 11 of the Town and Country Planning Act 1990.

41 Biodiversity lists and action (England)

(1) The Secretary of State must, as respects England, publish a list of the living organisms and types of habitat which in the Secretary of State's opinion are of principal importance for the purpose of conserving biodiversity.

(2) Before publishing any list the Secretary of State must consult Natural England as to the living organisms or types of habitat to be included in the list.

(3) Without prejudice to section 40(1) and (2), the Secretary of State must—

(a) take such steps as appear to the Secretary of State to be reasonably practicable to further the conservation of the living organisms and types of habitat included in any list published under this section, or

(b) promote the taking by others of such steps.

(4) The Secretary of State must, in consultation with Natural England—

(a) keep under review any list published under this section,

(b) make such revisions of any such list as appear to the Secretary of State appropriate, and

(c) publish any list so revised as soon as is reasonably practicable after revising it.

42 Biodiversity lists and action (Wales)

(1) The National Assembly for Wales must, as respects Wales, publish a list of the living organisms and types of habitat which in the Assembly's opinion are of principal importance for the purpose of conserving biodiversity.

(2) Before publishing any list the Assembly must consult the Countryside Council for Wales as to the living organisms or types of habitat to be included in the list.

(3) Without prejudice to section 40(1) and (2), the Assembly must—

(a) take such steps as appear to the Assembly to be reasonably practicable to further the conservation of the living organisms and types of habitat included in any list published under this section, or

(b) promote the taking by others of such steps.

(4) The Assembly must, in consultation with the Countryside Council for Wales—

(a) keep under review any list published under this section,

(b) make such revisions of any such list as appear to the Assembly appropriate, and

(c) publish any list so revised as soon as is reasonably practicable after revising it.

PART 8 FLEXIBLE ADMINISTRATIVE ARRANGEMENTS

CHAPTER I AGREEMENTS WITH DESIGNATED BODIES

Powers to enter into agreements

78 Agreement between Secretary of State and designated body

(1) The Secretary of State may enter into an agreement with a designated body authorising that body to perform a DEFRA function—

(a) either in relation to the whole of England or in relation to specified areas in England;

(b) subject to paragraph (a), either generally or in specified cases.

'Specified' means specified in the agreement.

(2) An agreement under this section—

(a) may be cancelled by the Secretary of State at any time, and

(b) does not prevent the Secretary of State from performing a function to which the agreement relates.

(3) This section is subject to sections 81 and 82 (reserved functions and maximum duration of agreement).

79 Agreement between designated bodies

(1) A designated body ('A') may, with the approval of the Secretary of State, enter into an agreement with another designated body ('B') authorising B to perform a function of A that is related to or connected with a DEFRA function—

(a) either in relation to the whole of England or in relation to specified areas in England;

(b) subject to paragraph (a), either generally or in specified cases.

'Specified' means specified in the agreement.

(2) The Secretary of State's approval may be given—

(a) in relation to a particular agreement or in relation to a description of agreements;

(b) unconditionally or subject to conditions specified in the approval.

(3) Subject to subsection (5), the Secretary of State—

(a) must review an agreement under this section no later than the end of the period of 5 years beginning with the date on which the agreement was entered into or was last reviewed by the Secretary of State, and

(b) if it appears appropriate to do so in the light of the review, may cancel the agreement.

(4) Subject to subsection (5), an agreement under this section may not be varied except—

(a) by agreement between A and B, and

(b) with the approval of the Secretary of State.

(5) An approval given under subsection (1) may provide that subsection (3) or (4) does not apply (or that both of them do not apply).

(6) This section is subject to sections 81 and 82 (reserved functions and maximum duration of agreement).

80 Designated bodies

(1) In this Chapter 'designated body' means a body listed in Schedule 7.

(2) The Secretary of State may by order amend Schedule 7 so as to—

(a) add a body to the list, or

(b) remove a body from it.

(3) But the Secretary of State may not exercise the power conferred by subsection (2)(a) unless satisfied that at least one of the purposes or functions of the body to be added to the list is related to or connected with a DEFRA function.

(4) A body to be added to the list need not be a public body.

(5) The power to make an order under subsection (2) is exercisable by statutory instrument.

(6) A statutory instrument containing an order under subsection (2) is subject to annulment in pursuance of a resolution of either House of Parliament.

81 Reserved functions

(1) An agreement may not authorise a designated body to perform a reserved function.

(2) The reserved functions are—

(a) any function whose performance by the designated body would be incompatible with the purposes for which the body was established;

(b) any power of a Minister of the Crown to make or terminate appointments or lay reports or accounts;

(c) any power to make subordinate legislation, give directions or guidance or issue codes of practice (or to vary or revoke any of those things);

(d) any power to fix fees or charges other than a power prescribed for the purposes of this section by an order made by the Secretary of State;

(e) any function of an accounting officer in his capacity as such;

(f) except in relation to an agreement authorising a public body to perform functions—

(i) any power to enter, inspect, take samples or seize anything, and

(ii) any other power exercisable in connection with suspected offences;

(g) any function of the Secretary of State under the Water Industry Act 1991 or under any subordinate legislation made under that Act.

(3) The power to make an order under subsection (2)(d) is exercisable by statutory instrument.

(4) A statutory instrument containing an order under subsection (2)(d) is subject to annulment in pursuance of a resolution of either House of Parliament.

82 Maximum duration of agreement

The maximum period for which an agreement may authorise a designated body to perform—

(a) a DEFRA function, or

(b) a function that is related to or connected with a DEFRA function, is 20 years.

Supplementary

83 Particular powers

(1) The fact that a function is conferred by or under this Act or an Act passed after the passing of this Act does not prevent it from being the subject of an agreement.

(2) The Secretary of State or a designated body ('A') may, under an agreement, authorise a designated body ('B') to perform a function even though under the relevant enactments or subordinate legislation—

(a) the function is conferred on A by reference to specified circumstances or cases and the same type of function is conferred on B in different specified circumstances or cases,

(b) the function is exercisable by A and B jointly,

(c) B is required to be, or may be, consulted about the function (whether generally or in specified circumstances), or

(d) B is required to consent to the exercise of the function (whether generally or in specified circumstances).

(3) An agreement may provide—

(a) for the performance of a function to be subject to the fulfilment of conditions;

(b) for payments to be made in respect of the performance of the function.

(4) A designated body which is authorised under an agreement to perform a function—

(a) is to be treated as having power to do so;

(b) may, unless (or except to the extent that) the agreement provides for this paragraph not to apply—

(i) authorise a committee, sub-committee, member, officer or employee of the body to perform the function on its behalf;

(ii) form a body corporate and authorise that body to perform the function on its behalf.

(5) However, where the designated body is a local authority—

(a) subsection (4)(a) is subject to section 84(5)(a), and

(b) section 84 applies in place of subsection (4)(b).

(6) Subject to subsection (4)(b) and section 84, a designated body which is authorised under an agreement to perform a function may not authorise any other body or other person to perform that function.

85 Supplementary provisions with respect to agreements

(1) An agreement, and any approval given by the Secretary of State under section 79, must be in writing.

(2) The Secretary of State must arrange for a copy of an agreement to be published in a way that the Secretary of State thinks is suitable for bringing it to the attention of persons likely to be affected by it.

(3) No power of a Minister of the Crown under any enactment to give directions to a statutory body extends to giving a direction—

(a) requiring it to enter into an agreement;

(b) prohibiting it from entering into an agreement;

(c) requiring it to include, or prohibiting it from including, particular terms;

(d) requiring it to negotiate, or prohibiting it from negotiating, a variation or termination of an agreement.

...

86 Interpretation

(1) In sections 81 to 85 'agreement' means an agreement under section 78 or 79.

(2) In this Chapter 'DEFRA function' means a function which at the material time falls to be performed by or through the Department for Environment, Food and Rural Affairs.

(3) A certificate issued by the Secretary of State that a function falls to be performed as mentioned in subsection (2) is conclusive evidence of that fact.

...

PART 9 MISCELLANEOUS

99 Natural beauty in the countryside

The fact that an area in England or Wales consists of or includes—

(a) land used for agriculture or woodlands,

(b) land used as a park, or

(c) any other area whose flora, fauna or physiographical features are partly the product of human intervention in the landscape,

does not prevent it from being treated, for the purposes of any enactment (whenever passed), as being an area of natural beauty (or of outstanding natural beauty).

PART 10 FINAL PROVISIONS

107 Commencement

(1) Part 1 (Natural England and the Commission for Rural Communities) comes into force in accordance with provision made by order by the Secretary of State.

(2) Part 2 (nature conservation in the UK) comes into force in accordance with provision made by order by the Secretary of State, after consulting the Scottish Ministers and the Department of Agriculture and Rural Development in Northern Ireland.

(3) In Parts 3 to 5 (wildlife etc., SSSIs, National Parks and the Broads)—

(a) section 59 comes into force at the end of the period of two months beginning with the day on which this Act is passed, and

(b) the other provisions come into force in accordance with provision made by order by the Secretary of State.

...

(6) In Part 8 (flexible administrative arrangements)—

(a) Chapter 1 comes into force in accordance with provision made by order by the Secretary of State,

(b) ...,

(c) ....

(7) In Part 9 (miscellaneous)—

(a) section 99 (natural beauty in the countryside) comes into force at the end of the period of two months beginning with the day on which this Act is passed, and

...

(8) In this Part—

(a) section 105 and Schedules 11 and 12... comes into force in accordance with provision made by order by the Secretary of State,...

...

108 Extent

(1) Except as provided by this section, this Act extends to England and Wales only...

SCHEDULE 1 NATURAL ENGLAND

Status

1 Natural England is to be a body corporate.

2 Subject to paragraph 22 (nature reserves), Natural England is not to be regarded—

(a) as a servant or agent of the Crown, or

(b) as enjoying any status, privilege or immunity of the Crown, and Natural England's property is not to be regarded as property of, or held on behalf of, the Crown.

Membership

3—(1) Natural England is to consist of—

(a) a chairman appointed by the Secretary of State, and

(b) not less than 8 nor more than 15 other members appointed by the Secretary of State.

(2) The Secretary of State must consult the chairman before appointing the other members.

(3) In appointing a person to be a member, the Secretary of State must have regard to the desirability of appointing a person who has experience of, and has shown some capacity in, some matter relevant to the exercise of Natural England's functions.

(4) The Secretary of State may by order amend sub-paragraph (1)(b) so as to substitute a different number for a number specified there.

(5) The power to make an order under sub-paragraph (4) is exercisable by statutory instrument....

PART II

Statutory Instruments

Town and Country Planning (Use Classes) Order 1987

(SI 1987, No. 764) (as amended)

1 Citation and commencement

This Order may be cited as the Town and Country Planning (Use Classes) Order 1987 and shall come into force in June 1987.

2 Interpretation

In this Order, unless the context otherwise requires:—

'care' means personal care for people in need of such care by reason of old age, disablement, past or present dependence on alcohol or drugs or past or present mental disorder, and in class C2 also includes the personal care of children and medical care and treatment;

'day centre' means premises which are visited during the day for social or recreational purposes or for the purposes of rehabilitation or occupational training, at which care is also provided;

'industrial process' means a process for or incidental to any of the following purposes:—

(a) the making of any article or part of any article (including a ship or vessel, or a film, video or sound recording);

(b) the altering, repairing, maintaining, ornamenting, finishing, cleaning, washing, packing, canning, adapting for sale, breaking up or demolition of any article; or

(c) the getting, dressing or treatment of minerals;

in the course of any trade or business other than agriculture, and other than a use carried out in or adjacent to a mine or quarry;

'Schedule' means the Schedule to this Order;

'site' means the whole area of land within a single unit of occupation.

3 Use classes

(1) Subject to the provisions of this Order, where a building or other land is used for a purpose of any class specified in the Schedule, the use of that building or that other land for any other purpose of the same class shall not be taken to involve development of the land.

(2) References in paragraph (1) to a building include references to land occupied with the building and used for the same purposes.

(3) A use which is included in and ordinarily incidental to any use in a class specified in the Schedule is not excluded from the use to which it is incidental merely because it is specified in the Schedule as a separate use.

(4) Where land on a single site or on adjacent sites used as parts of a single undertaking is used for purposes consisting of or including purposes falling [within classes B1 and B2] in the Schedule, those classes may be treated as a single class in considering the use of that land for the purposes of this Order, so long as the area used for a purpose falling [within class B2] is not substantially increased as a result.

(5) [. . .]

(6) No class specified in the Schedule includes use—

(a) as a theatre,

(b) as an amusement arcade or centre, or a funfair,

[(c) as a launderette,]
(d) for the sale of fuel for motor vehicles,
(e) for the sale or display for sale of motor vehicles,
(f) for a taxi business or business for the hire of motor vehicles,
(g) as a scrapyard, or a yard for the storage or distribution of minerals or the breaking of motor vehicles.
[(h) for any work registrable under the Alkali, etc. Works Regulation Act 1906]
[(i) as a hostel]
[(j) as a waste disposal installation for the incineration, chemical treatment (as defined in Annex IIA to Directive 75/442/EEC under heading D9) or landfill of waste to which Directive 91/689/EEC applies.]
[(k) as a retail warehouse club being a retail club where goods are sold, or displayed for sale, only to persons who are members of that club;
(l) as a night-club],
[(m) as a casino].

[(7) Where a building or other land is situated in Wales, class B8 (storage or distribution) does not include use of that building or land for the storage of, or as a distribution centre for, radioactive material or radioactive waste.

(8) For the purpose of paragraph (7), 'radioactive material' and 'radioactive waste' have the meanings assigned to those terms in the Radioactive Substances Act 1993.]

4 Change of use of part of building or land

In the case of a building used for a purpose within class C3 (dwelling-houses) in the Schedule, the use as a separate dwelling-house of any part of the building or of any land occupied with and used for the same purposes as the building is not, by virtue of this Order, to be taken as not amounting to development.

SCHEDULE

PART A

Class A1 Shops

Use for all or any of the following purposes—
(a) for the retail sale of goods other than hot food,
(b) as a post office,
(c) for the sale of tickets or as a travel agency,
(d) for the sale of sandwiches or other cold food for consumption off the premises,
(e) for hairdressing,
(f) for the direction of funerals,
(g) for the display of goods for sale,
(h) for the hiring out of domestic or personal goods or articles,
[(i) for the washing or cleaning of clothes or fabrics on the premises,]
[(j) for the reception of goods to be washed, cleaned or repaired,]
[(k) as an internet café; where the primary purpose of the premises is to provide facilities for enabling members of the public to access the internet,]
where the sale, display or services is to visiting members of the public.

Class A2 Financial and professional services

Use for the provision of—
(a) financial services, or
(b) professional services (other than health or medical services), or
(c) any other services (including use as a betting office) which it is appropriate to provide in a shopping area,
where the services are provided principally to visiting members of the public.

[Class A3. Restaurants and cafes

Use for the sale of food and drink for consumption on the premises.

Class A4. Drinking establishments

Use as a public house, wine-bar or other drinking establishment.

Class A5. Hot food takeaways

Use for the sale of hot food for consumption off the premises.]

PART B

Class B1 Business

Use for all or any of the following purposes—

(a) as an office other than a use within class A2 (financial and professional services),
(b) for research and development of products or processes, or
(c) for any industrial process,

being a use which can be carried out in any residential area without detriment to the amenity of that area by reason of noise, vibration, smell, fumes, smoke, soot, ash, dust or grit.

Class B2 General industrial

Use for the carrying on of an industrial process other than one falling within class B1 above [. . .]

Class B3–B7 [. . .]

Class B8 Use for storage or distribution

Use for storage or as a distribution centre.

PART C

[Class C1 Hotels

Use as a hotel or as a boarding or guest house where, in each case, no significant element of care is provided.]

Class C2 Residential institutions

Use for the provision of residential accommodation and care to people in need of care (other than a use within class C3 (dwelling houses)).

Use as a hospital or nursing home.

Use as a residential school, college or training centre.

Class C3 Dwellinghouses

Use as a dwellinghouse (whether or not as a sole or main residence)—

(a) by a single person or by people living together as a family, or
(b) by not more than six residents living together as a single household (including a household where care is provided for residents).

PART D

Class D1 Non-residential institutions

Any use not including a residential use—

(a) for the provision of any medical or health services except the use of premises attached to the residence of the consultant or practitioner,
(b) as a crêche, day nursery or day centre,
(c) for the provision of education,
(d) for the display of works of art (otherwise than for sale or hire),

(e) as a museum,
(f) as a public library or public reading room,
(g) as a public hall or exhibition hall,
(h) for, or in connection with, public worship or religious instruction.

Class D2 Assembly and leisure
Use as—

(a) a cinema,
(b) a concert hall,
(c) a bingo hall [. . .],
(d) a dance hall,
(e) a swimming bath, skating rink, gymnasium or area for other indoor or outdoor sports or recreations, not involving motorised vehicles or firearms.

Controlled Waste Regulations 1992

(SI 1992, No. 588) (as amended)

1 Citation, commencement and interpretation

(1) . . .

(2) In these Regulations—

'the Act' means the Environmental Protection Act 1990;

'the 1989 Regulations' means the Sludge (Use in Agriculture) Regulations 1989;

'camp site' means land on which tents are pitched for the purposes of human habitation and land the use of which is incidental to land on which tents are so pitched;

'charity' means any body of persons or trust established for charitable purposes only;

'clinical waste' means

(a) any waste which consists wholly or partly of human or animal tissue, blood or other body fluids, excretions, drugs or other pharmaceutical products, swabs or dressings, or syringes, needles or other sharp instruments, being waste which unless rendered safe may prove hazardous to any person coming into contact with it; and
(b) any other waste arising from medical, nursing, dental, veterinary, pharmaceutical or similar practice, investigation, treatment, care, teaching or research, or the collection of blood for transfusion, being waste which may cause infection to any person coming into contact with it;

'composite hereditament' has the same meaning as in section 64(9) of the Local Government Finance Act 1988;

'construction' includes improvement, repair or alteration;

['Directive waste' has the meaning given by regulation 1(3) of the Waste Management Licensing Regulations 1994;]

. . .

'scrap metal' has the same meaning as in section 9(2) of the Scrap Metal Dealers Act 1964;

'septic tank sludge' and 'sludge' have the same meaning as in regulation 2(1) of the 1989 Regulations; and

'vessel' includes a hovercraft within the meaning of section 4(1) of the Hovercraft Act 1968.

(3) Any reference in these Regulations to a section is, except where the context otherwise requires, a reference to a section of the Act.

(4) References in these Regulations to waste—

(a) do not include waste from any mine or quarry or waste from premises used for agriculture within the meaning of the Agriculture Act 1947 . . .
(b) except so far as otherwise provided, do not include sewage (including matter in or from a privy).

2 Waste to be treated as household waste

(1) [Subject to paragraph (2) and regulations 3 and 7A,] waste of the descriptions set out in Schedule 1 shall be treated as household waste for the purposes of Part II of the Act.

(2) Waste of the following descriptions shall be treated as household waste for the purposes only of section 34(2) (household waste produced on domestic property) [and section 34(2A) (duty of occupiers of domestic property in England [or Wales] when transferring household waste).]—

(a) waste arising from works of construction or demolition, including waste arising from work preparatory thereto; and

(b) septic tank sludge.

3 Waste not to be treated as household waste

(1) Waste of the following descriptions shall not be treated as household waste for the purposes of section 33(2) (treatment, keeping or disposal of household waste within the curtilage of a dwelling)—

(a) any mineral or synthetic oil or grease;

(b) asbestos; and

(c) clinical waste.

(2) Scrap metal shall not be treated as household waste for the purposes of section 34 [at any time before [1st October 1995]].

4 Charges for the collection of household waste

The collection of any of the types of household waste set out in Schedule 2 is prescribed for the purposes of section 45(3) as a case in respect of which a charge for collection may be made.

5 Waste to be treated as industrial waste

(1) Subject to paragraph (2) and [regulations 7 and 7A] waste of the descriptions set out in Schedule 3 shall be treated as industrial waste for the purposes of Part II of the Act.

(2) Waste of the following descriptions shall be treated as industrial waste for the purposes of Part II of the Act (except sections 34(2) and 34(2A))—

(a) waste arising from works of construction or demolition, including waste arising from work preparatory thereto;

(b) septic tank sludge not falling within [regulation 7(1)(a) or (c)].

6 Waste to be treated as commercial waste

Subject to [regulations 7 and 7A] waste of the descriptions set out in Schedule 4 shall be treated as commercial waste for the purposes of Part II of the Act.

7 Waste not to be treated as industrial or commercial waste

(1) Waste of the following descriptions shall not be treated as industrial waste or commercial waste for the purposes of Part II of the Act—

(a) sewage, sludge or septic tank sludge which is treated, kept or disposed of (otherwise than by means of mobile plant) within the curtilage of a sewage treatment works as an integral part of the operation of those works;

(b) sludge which is supplied or used in accordance with the 1989 Regulations;

(c) septic tank sludge which is used [on agricultural land within the meaning of] the 1989 Regulations.

(2) Scrap metal shall not be treated as industrial waste or commercial waste for the purposes of section 34 at any time before [1st October 1995]].

[(3) Animal by-products which are collected and transported in accordance with Schedule 2 to the Animal By-Products Order 1992 shall not be treated as industrial waste or commercial waste for the purposes of section 34 (duty of care etc. as respects waste).

(4) In this regulation, 'animal by-products' has the same meaning as in article 3(1) of the Animal By-Products Order 1992.]

[7A Waste not to be treated as household, industrial or commercial waste

For the purposes of Part II of the Act, waste which is not Directive waste shall not be treated as household waste, industrial waste or commercial waste.]

8 Application of Part II of the Act to litter and refuse

Part II of the Act shall have effect as if—

(a) references to controlled waste included references to litter and refuse to which section 96 applies;

(b) references to controlled waste of a description set out in the first column of Table A below included references to litter and refuse of a description set out in the second column thereof;

(c) references to controlled waste collected under section 45 included references to litter and refuse collected under sections 89(1)(a) and (c) and 92(9); and

(d) references to controlled waste collected under section 45 which is waste of a description set out in the first column of Table B below included references to litter and refuse of a description set out in the second column thereof.

Table A

Description of waste	Description of litter and refuse
Household waste.	Litter and refuse collected under section 89(1)(a), (c) and (f).
Industrial waste.	Litter and refuse collected under section 89(1)(b) and (e).
Commercial waste.	Litter and refuse collected under sections 89(1)(d) and (g), 92(9) and 93.

Table B

Description of waste	Description of litter and refuse
Household waste.	Litter and refuse collected under section 89(1)(a) and (c).
Commercial waste.	Litter and refuse collected under section 92(9).

Regulation 2(1)

SCHEDULE 1

WASTE TO BE TREATED AS HOUSEHOLD WASTE

1. Waste from a hereditament or premises exempted from local non-domestic rating by virtue of—

(a) in England and Wales, paragraph 11 of Schedule 5 to the Local Government Finance Act 1988 (places of religious worship etc.);

(b) . . .

2. Waste from premises occupied by a charity and wholly or mainly used for charitable purposes.

3. Waste from any land belonging to or used in connection with domestic property, a caravan or a residential home.

4. Waste from a private garage which either has a floor area of 25 square metres or less or is used wholly or mainly for the accommodation of a private motor vehicle.

5. Waste from private storage premises used wholly or mainly for the storage of articles of domestic use.

6. Waste from a moored vessel used wholly for the purposes of living accommodation.
7. Waste from a camp site.
8. Waste from a prison or other penal institution.
9. Waste from a hall or other premises used wholly or mainly for public meetings.
10. Waste from a royal palace.
11. Waste arising from the discharge by a local authority of its duty under section 89(2).

Regulation 4 SCHEDULE 2

TYPES OF HOUSEHOLD WASTE FOR WHICH A CHARGE FOR COLLECTION MAY BE MADE

1. Any article of waste which exceeds 25 kilograms in weight.

2. Any article of waste which does not fit, or cannot be fitted into—
   (a) a receptacle for household waste provided in accordance with section 46; or
   (b) where no such receptacle is provided, a cylindrical container 750 millimetres in diameter and 1 metre in length.

3. Garden waste.

4. Clinical waste from a domestic property, a caravan or from a moored vessel used wholly for the purposes of living accommodation.

5. Waste from a residential hostel, a residential home or from premises forming part of a university, school or other educational establishment or forming part of a hospital or nursing home.

6. Waste from domestic property or a caravan used in the course of a business for the provision of self-catering holiday accommodation.

7. Dead domestic pets.

8. Any substances or articles which, by virtue of a notice served by a collection authority under section 46, the occupier of the premises may not put into a receptacle for household waste provided in accordance with that section.

9. Litter and refuse collected under section 89(1)(f).

10. Waste from—
   (a) in England and Wales, domestic property forming part of a composite hereditament;
   (b) . . .

11. Any mineral or synthetic oil or grease.

12. Asbestos.

13. Waste from a caravan which in accordance with any licence or planning permission regulating the use of the caravan site on which the caravan is stationed is not allowed to be used for human habitation throughout the year.

14. Waste from a camp site, other than from any domestic property on that site.

15. Waste from premises occupied by a charity and wholly or mainly used for charitable purposes, unless it is waste falling within paragraph 1 of Schedule 1.

16. Waste from a prison or other penal institution.

17. Waste from a hall or other premises used wholly or mainly for public meetings.

18. Waste from a royal palace.

Regulation 5(1) SCHEDULE 3

WASTE TO BE TREATED AS INDUSTRIAL WASTE

1. Waste from premises used for maintaining vehicles, vessels or aircraft, not being waste from a private garage to which paragraph 4 of Schedule 1 applies.

2. Waste from a laboratory.

3.—(1) Waste from a workshop or similar premises not being a factory within the meaning of section 175 of the Factories Act 1961 because the people working there are not employees or because the work there is not carried on by way of trade or for purposes of gain.

(2) In this paragraph, 'workshop' does not include premises at which the principal activities are computer operations or the copying of documents by photographic or lithographic means

4. Waste from premises occupied by a scientific research association approved by the Secretary of State under section 508 of the Income and Corporation Taxes Act 1988.

5. Waste from dredging operations.

6. Waste arising from tunnelling or from any other excavation.

7. Sewage not falling within a description in regulation 7 which—

(a) is treated, kept or disposed of in or on land, other than by means of a privy, cesspool or septic tank;

(b) is treated, kept or disposed of by means of mobile plant; or

(c) has been removed from a privy or cesspool.

8. Clinical waste other than—

(a) clinical waste from a domestic property, caravan, residential home or from a moored vessel used wholly for the purposes of living accommodation;

(b) ...

(c) waste collected under sections 89, 92(9) or 93.

9. Waste arising from any aircraft, vehicle or vessel which is not occupied for domestic purposes.

10. Waste which has previously formed part of any aircraft, vehicle or vessel and which is not household waste.

11. Waste removed from land on which it has previously been deposited and any soil with which such waste has been in contact, other than—

(a) ...

(b) waste collected under sections 89, 92(9) or 93.

12. Leachate from a deposit of waste.

13. Poisonous or noxious waste arising from any of the following processes under-taken on premises used for the purposes of a trade or business—

(a) mixing or selling paints;

(b) sign writing;

(c) laundering or dry cleaning;

(d) developing photographic film or making photographic prints;

(e) selling petrol, diesel fuel, paraffin, kerosene, heating oil or similar substances; or

(f) selling pesticides, herbicides or fungicides.

14. Waste from premises used for the purposes of breeding, boarding, stabling or exhibiting animals.

15.—(1) Waste oil, waste solvent or (subject to regulation 7(2)) scrap metal, other than—

(a) waste from a domestic property, caravan or residential home;

(b) waste falling within paragraphs 3 to 6 of Schedule 1.

(2) in this paragraph—'waste oil' means mineral or synthetic oil which is contaminated, spoiled or otherwise unfit for its original purpose; and

'waste solvent' means solvent which is contaminated, spoiled or otherwise unfit for its original purpose.

16. Waste arising from the discharge by the Secretary of State of his duty under section 89(2).

17. Waste imported into Great Britain.

18.—(1) Tank washings or garbage landed in Great Britain.

(2) In this paragraph—

['tank washings' has the same meaning as in paragraph 36 of Schedule 3 to the Waste Management Licensing Regulations 1994;] and 'garbage' has the same meaning as in regulation 1(2) of the Merchant Shipping (Reception Facilities for Garbage) Regulations 1988.

Regulation 6 SCHEDULE 4

WASTE TO BE TREATED AS COMMERCIAL WASTE

1. Waste from an office or showroom.

2. Waste from a hotel within the meaning of—
   (a) in England and Wales, section 1(3) of the Hotel Proprietors Act 1956; and
   (b) ...

3. Waste from any part of a composite hereditament, ... which is used for the purposes of a trade or business.

4. Waste from a private garage which either has a floor area exceeding 25 square metres or is not used wholly or mainly for the accommodation of a private motor vehicle.

5. Waste from premises occupied by a club, society or any association of persons (whether incorporated or not) in which activities are conducted for the benefit of the members.

6. Waste from premises (not being premises from which waste is by virtue of the Act or of any other provision of these Regulations to be treated as household waste or industrial waste) occupied by—
   (a) a court;
   (b) a government department;
   (c) a local authority;
   (d) a body corporate or an individual appointed by or under any enactment to discharge any public functions; or
   (e) a body incorporated by a Royal Charter.

7. Waste from a tent pitched on land other than a camp site.

8. Waste from a market or fair.

9. ...

Waste Management Licensing Regulations 1994

(SI 1994, No. 1056) (as amended)

1 Citation, commencement, interpretation and extent

(1) ...

(2) ...

(3) In these Regulations, unless the context otherwise requires—

'the 1990 Act' means the Environmental Protection Act 1990;

'the 1991 Regulations' means the Environmental Protection (Prescribed Processes and Substances) Regulations 1991;

['the 2000 Regulations' means the Pollution Prevention and Control (England and Wales) Regulations 2000;]

'construction work' includes the repair, alteration or improvement of existing works;

'the Directive' means Council Directive 75/442/EEC on waste as amended by Council Directives 91/156/EEC and 91/692/EEC;

'Directive waste' means any substance or object in the categories set out in Part II of Schedule 4 which the producer or the person in possession of it discards or intends or is required to discard but with the exception of anything excluded from the scope of the Directive by Article 2 of the Directive, 'discard' has the same meaning as in the Directive, and 'producer' means anyone whose activities produce Directive waste or who carries out pre-processing, mixing or other operations resulting in a change in its nature or composition;

'disposal' means any of the operations listed in Part III of Schedule 4, and any reference to waste being disposed of is a reference to its being submitted to any of those operations;

'disposal licence' and 'disposal authority' have the meaning given by sections 3(1) and 30(2) to (2D) respectively of the Control of Pollution Act 1974;

'enforcing authority' and 'local enforcing authority' have the meaning given by section 1(7) and (8) of the 1990 Act;

'exempt activity' means any of the activities set out in Schedule 3;

'inland waters'—

(a) in England and Wales, has the meaning given by section 221(1) of the Water Resources Act 1991;

(b) ...

['hazardous waste' has the meaning given by regulation 6 of the Hazardous Waste (England and Wales) Regulations 2005]

['internal drainage board' has the meaning given by section 1(1) of the Land Drainage Act 1991;]

['notifiable exempt activity' means an exempt activity falling within paragraph 7A, 8A, 9A, 10A, 19A or 46A of Schedule 3 to these Regulations;]

'operational land' has the meaning given by sections 263 and 264 of the Town and Country Planning Act 1990...

'recovery' means any of the operations listed in Part IV of Schedule 4, and any reference to waste being recovered is a reference to its being submitted to any of those operations;

['scrap metal dealer' has the meaning given by section 9(1), and 'scrap metal' has the meaning given by section 9(2), of the Scrap Metal Dealers Act 1964;]

'waste' means Directive waste;

'waste management licence' has the meaning given by section 35(1) of the 1990 Act, and 'site licence' has the meaning given by section 35(12) of the 1990 Act;

'waste oil' means any mineral-based lubricating or industrial oil which has become unfit for the use for which it was originally intended and, in particular, used combustion engine oil, gearbox oil, mineral lubricating oil, oil for turbines and hydraulic oil;

'waste regulation authority', 'waste disposal authority' and 'waste collection authority' have the meaning given by section 30 of the 1990 Act; and

'work' includes preparatory work.

(4) Any reference in these Regulations to carrying on business as a scrap metal dealer has the meaning given by section 9(1) of the Scrap Metal Dealers Act 1964, ...

(5) ...

(6) ...

[(7) The provisions of section 160 of the 1990 Act shall apply to—

(a) the service or giving of any notice required or authorised by these Regulations to be served on or given to a person; or

(b) the sending or giving of any document required or authorised by these Regulations to be sent or given to a person,

as if the service or giving of any such notice or, as the case may be, the sending or giving of any such document, was required or authorised by or under that Act.]

2 Application for a waste management licence or for the surrender or transfer of a waste management licence

(1) An application for a waste management licence shall be made in writing.

(2) An application for the surrender of a site licence shall be made in writing and shall, subject to paragraphs (3) and (4) below, include the information and be accompanied by the evidence prescribed by Schedule 1.

(3) Nothing in paragraph (2) above shall require the information prescribed by paragraphs 3 to 6 of Schedule 1 to be provided to the waste regulation authority if the information has previously been provided by the applicant to the authority or a predecessor of the

authority in connection with a waste management licence, or a disposal licence under section 5 of the Control of Pollution Act 1974, in respect of the site in question or any part of it.

(4) Insofar as the information prescribed by paragraphs 4, 5(a) and 6(a) of Schedule 1 relates to activities carried on, or works carried out, at the site at a time prior to the applicant's first involvement with the site, paragraph (2) above only requires that information to be included in the application so far as it is known to either the applicant or, where the applicant is a partnership or body corporate, to any of the partners or, as the case may be, to any director, manager, secretary or other similar officer of the body corporate.

(5) An application for the transfer of a waste management licence shall be made in writing and shall include the information prescribed by Schedule 2.

3 Relevant offences

An offence is relevant for the purposes of section 74(3)(a) of the 1990 Act if it is an offence under any of the following enactments—

(a) section 22 of the Public Health (Scotland) Act 1897;
(b) section 95(1) of the Public Health Act 1936;
(c) section 3, 5(6), 16(4), 18(2), 31(1), 32(1), 34(5), 78, 92(6) or 93(3) of the Control of Pollution Act 1974;
(d) section 2 of the Refuse Disposal (Amenity) Act 1978;
(e) the Control of Pollution (Special Waste) Regulations 1980;
(f) section 9(1) of the Food and Environment Protection Act 1985;
(g) the Transfrontier Shipment of Hazardous Waste Regulations 1988;
(h) the Merchant Shipping (Prevention of Pollution by Garbage) Regulations 1988;
(i) section 1, 5, 6(9) or 7(3) of the Control of Pollution (Amendment) Act 1989;
(j) section 107, 118(4) or 175(1) of the Water Act 1989;
(k) section 23(1), 33, 34(6), 44, 47(6), 57(5), 59(5), 63(2), 69(9), 70(4), 71(3) or 80(4) of the 1990 Act;
(l) section 85, 202 or 206 of the Water Resources Act 1991;
(m) section 33 of the Clean Air Act 1993. [(n) the Transfrontier Shipment of Waste Regulations 1994]
[(n) the Special Waste Regulations 1996.]
[(o) regulation 32(1) of the 2000 Regulations.]
[(p) regulation 17(1) of the Landfill (England and Wales) Regulations 2002.]
[(q) the Hazardous Waste (England and Wales) Regulations 2005.]

4 Technical competence

(1) Subject to paragraph (2) of this regulation and regulation 5 below, and without prejudice to the European Communities (Recognition of Professional Qualifications) (Second General System) Regulations 2002, Schedule 1A has effect to prescribe for the purposes of section 74(3)(b) of the 1990 Act (management of activities to be in the hands of a technically competent person) the qualifications required of a person if that person is to be considered technically competent in relation to a facility of a type listed in Table 1 of that Schedule.

(2) Paragraph (1) does not apply in relation to a facility which is used exclusively for the purpose of—

(a) carrying on business as a scrap metal dealer;
(b) dismantling motor vehicles; or
(c) the burial of dead domestic pets.]

6 Notice of appeal

(1) A person who wishes to appeal to the Secretary of State under section 43 or 66(5) of the 1990 Act (appeals to the Secretary of State from decisions with respect to waste management licences or from determinations that information is not commercially confidential) shall do so by notice in writing.

(2) The notice shall be accompanied by—

(a) a statement of the grounds of appeal;

(b) where the appeal relates to an application for a waste management licence or for the modification, surrender or transfer of a waste management licence, a copy of the appellant's application and any supporting documents;

(c) where the appeal relates to a determination under section 66(2) or (4) of the 1990 Act that information is not commercially confidential, the information in question;

(d) where the appeal relates to an existing waste management licence (including a waste management licence which has been suspended or revoked), a copy of that waste management licence;

(e) a copy of any correspondence relevant to the appeal;

(f) a copy of any other document relevant to the appeal including, in particular, any relevant consent, determination, notice, planning permission, established use certificate or certificate of lawful use or development; and

(g) a statement indicating whether the appellant wishes the appeal to be in the form of a hearing or to be determined on the basis of written representations.

(3) The appellant shall serve a copy of his notice of appeal on the waste regulation authority together with copies of the documents mentioned in paragraph (2) above.

(4) If the appellant wishes to withdraw an appeal, he shall do so by notifying the Secretary of State in writing and shall send a copy of that notification to the waste regulation authority.

7 Time limit for making an appeal

(1) Subject to paragraph (2) below, notice of appeal shall be given—

(a) in the case of an appeal under section 43 of the 1990 Act, before the expiry of the period of 6 months beginning with—

(i) the date of the decision which is the subject of the appeal; or

(ii) the date on which the waste regulation authority is deemed by section 36(9), 37(6), 39(10) or 40(6) of the 1990 Act to have rejected the application;

(b) in the case of an appeal under section 66(5) of the 1990 Act, before the expiry of the period of 21 days beginning with the date on which the determination which is the subject of the appeal is notified to the person concerned.

(2) The Secretary of State may in relation to an appeal under section 43 of the 1990 Act at any time allow notice of appeal to be given after the expiry of the period mentioned in paragraph (1)(a) above.

8 Reports of hearings

The person hearing an appeal under section 43(2)(c) of the 1990 Act shall, unless he has been appointed to determine the appeal under [section 114(1)(a) of the Environment Act 1995], make a written report to the Secretary of State which shall include his conclusions and recommendations or his reasons for not making any recommendations.

9 Notification of determination

(1) The Secretary of State or other person determining an appeal shall notify the appellant in writing of his decision and of his reasons.

(2) If the Secretary of State determines an appeal after a hearing under section 43(2)(c) of the 1990 Act, he shall provide the appellant with a copy of any report made to him under regulation 8.

(3) The Secretary of State or other person determining an appeal shall, at the same time as notifying the appellant of his decision, send the waste regulation authority a copy of any document sent to the appellant under this regulation.

10 Particulars to be entered in public registers

(1) Subject to sections 65 and 66 of the 1990 Act and regulation 11, a register maintained by a waste regulation authority under section 64(1) of the 1990 Act shall contain full particulars of—

(a) current or recently current waste management licences ('licences') granted by the authority and any associated working plans;

(b) current or recently current applications to the authority for licences, or for the transfer or modification of licences, including details of—

(i) documents submitted by applicants containing supporting information;

(ii) written representations considered by the authority under section 36(4)(b), (6)(b) or (7)(b) or 37(5) of the 1990 Act;

(iii) decisions of the Secretary of State under section 36(5)... of the 1990

(iv) notices by the authority rejecting applications;

(v) emergencies resulting in the postponement of references under section 37(5)(a) of the 1990 Act;

(c) notices issued by the authority under section 37 of the 1990 Act effecting the modification of licences;

(d) notices issued by the authority under section 38 of the 1990 Act effecting the revocation or suspension of licences or imposing requirements on the holders of licences;

(e) notices of appeal under section 43 of the 1990 Act relating to decisions of the authority and other documents relating to such appeals served on or sent to the authority under regulation 6(3) or (4) or 9(3);

(f) convictions of holders of licences granted by the authority for any offence under Part II of the 1990 Act (whether or not in relation to a licence) [or regulation 17(1) of the Landfill (England and Wales) Regulations 2002] including the name of the offender, the date of conviction, the penalty imposed and the name of the Court;

(g) reports produced by the authority in discharge of any functions under section 42 of the 1990 Act, including details of—

(i) [...]

(ii) remedial or preventive action taken by the authority under section 42(3) of the 1990 Act;

(iii) notices issued by the authority under section 42(5) of the 1990 Act;

(iv) the scores which result from any risk appraisal relating to a site which is the subject of a waste management licence.

(h) any monitoring information relating to the carrying on of any activity under a licence granted by the authority which was obtained by the authority as a result of its own monitoring or was furnished to the authority in writing by virtue of any condition of the licence or section 71(2) of the 1990 Act;

(i) directions given by the Secretary of State to the authority under section 35(7), 37(3), 38(7), 42(8), 50(9), 54(11) or (15), 58 or 66(7) of the 1990 Act;

(j) any summary prepared by the authority of the amount of hazardous waste produced or disposed of in their area;

(k) registers and records provided to the authority under regulation 13(5) or 14(1) of the Control of Pollution (Special Waste) Regulations 1980 [or regulation 15(5) or 16(1) of the Special Waste Regulations 1996] [or regulation 47(5) and 48(6) of the Hazardous Waste (England and Wales) Regulations 2005];

(l) applications to the authority under section 39 of the 1990 Act for the surrender of licences, including details of—

(i) documents submitted by applicants containing supporting information and evidence;

(ii) information and evidence obtained under section 39(4) of the 1990 Act;

(iii) written representations considered by the authority under section 39(7)(b) or (8)(b) of the 1990 Act;

(iv) decisions by the Secretary of State under section 39(7) or (8) of the 1990 Act; and

(v) notices of determination and certificates of completion issued under section 39(9) of the 1990 Act;

(m) written reports under section 70(3) of the 1990 Act by inspectors appointed by the authority [or written reports under section 109(2) of the Environment Act 1995 by persons authorised by the authority under section 108(1) or (2) of that Act where the articles or substances seized and rendered harmless are waste];

(n) . . .

(o) . . .

[(p) all particulars of any site conditioning plan or notice submitted to the authority under paragraph 1(3) or (5) of Schedule 4 to the Landfill (England and Wales) Regulations 2002;

(q) all particulars of any notice of a decision under paragraph 1(6) of Schedule 4 to the Landfill (England and Wales) Regulations 2002;

(r) all particulars of any notification or report required before definitive closure of a landfill under regulation 15(4) of the Landfill (England and Wales) Regulations 2002.]

(2) The register shall also contain the following—

(a) where an inspector appointed by the authority exercises any power under section 69(3) of the 1990 Act, a record showing when the power was exercised and indicating what information was obtained, and what action was taken, on that occasion;

[(aa) where a person authorised by the authority exercises any power under section 108(4) of the Environment Act 1995 in connection with the authority's functions under Part II of the Environmental Protection Act 1990, a record showing when the power was exercised and indicating what information was obtained, and what action was taken, on that occasion;]

(b) where any information is excluded from the register by virtue of section 66 of the 1990 Act and the information shows whether or not there is compliance with any condition of a waste management licence, a statement based on that information indicating whether or not there is compliance with that condition.

(3) A register maintained under section 64(4) of the 1990 Act by a waste collection authority in England [or Wales] . . . shall contain full particulars of the following information contained in any register maintained under section 64(1) of the 1990 Act, to the extent that it relates to the treatment, keeping or disposal of controlled waste in the area of the authority—

(a) current or recently current waste management licences;

(b) notices issued under section 37 of the 1990 Act effecting the modification of waste management licences;

(c) notices issued under section 38 of the 1990 Act effecting the revocation or suspension of waste management licences;

(d) certificates of completion issued under section 39(9) of the 1990 Act.

[(3A) A register maintained under section 64(4) of the 1990 Act by a waste collection authority in England and Wales shall also contain full particulars of the following information contained in any register maintained by the Environment Agency under regulation 29 of the 2000 Regulations to the extent that it relates to a specified waste management activity (within the meaning of those Regulations) carried out in the area of the authority—

(a) current or recently current permits granted under the 2000 Regulations;

(b) variation notices under regulation 17 of the 2000 Regulations varying such permits;

(c) revocation notices under regulation 21 of those Regulations and suspension notices under regulation 25 of those Regulations issued in relation to such permits;

(d) notices of determination issued under regulation 19 of those Regulations in relation to applications made to surrender such permits.]

(4) For the purposes of this regulation, waste management licences [and permits granted under the 2000 Regulations] are 'recently' current for the period of twelve months after they cease to be in force, and applications for waste management licences, or for the transfer or modification of such licences, are 'recently' current if they relate to a waste management licence which is current or recently current or, in the case of an application which is rejected, for the period of twelve months beginning with the date on which the waste regulation authority gives notice of rejection or, as the case may be, on which the application is deemed by section 36(9), 37(6) or 40(6) of the 1990 Act to have been rejected.

[(5) The Environment Agency shall furnish waste collection authorities with the particulars necessary to enable them to discharge their duty under paragraph (3A).]

11 Information to be excluded or removed from a register

(1) Nothing in regulation 10(1)(g) or (m) or (2) shall require a register maintained by a waste regulation authority under section 64(1) of the 1990 Act to contain information relating to, or to anything which is the subject-matter of, any criminal proceedings (including prospective proceedings) at any time before those proceedings are finally disposed of.

(2) Nothing in regulation 10 shall require a register maintained by a waste regulation authority or waste collection authority under section 64 of the 1990 Act to contain—

(a) any such monitoring information as is mentioned in regulation 10(1)(h) after 4 years have elapsed from that information being entered in the register; or

(b) any information which has been superseded by later information after 4 years have elapsed from that later information being entered in the register.

[(3) Nothing in regulation 10(3A) shall require a register maintained by a waste collection authority under that regulation to contain any information which has been superseded by later information after 4 years have elapsed from that later information being entered in the register.]

[12 Mobile plant

(1) Plant of the following descriptions, if it is designed to move or be moved by any means from place to place with a view to being used at each such place or, if not so designed, is readily capable of so moving or being so moved, but no other plant, shall be treated as being mobile plant for the purposes of Part II of the 1990 Act—

(a) an incinerator which is an exempt incinerator for the purposes of Section 5.1 of Schedule 1 to the 1991 Regulations;

(b) plant for—

(i) the recovery, by filtration or heat treatment, of waste oil from electrical equipment; [...]

(ii) the destruction by dechlorination of waste polychlorinated biphenyls or terphenyls (PCBs or PCTs);

[(iii) the collection or storage of a controlled substance from any waste product, installation or equipment.]

(c) plant for the vitrification of waste;

(d) plant for the treatment by microwave of clinical waste.

[(e) plant for the treatment of waste soil.]

[(f) plant for the dewatering of muds, sludges, soils and dredgings;

(g) plant for the treatment by lime stabilisation of sludge;

(h) plant for the treatment of contaminated material, substances or products, for the purpose of remedial action with respect to land or controlled waters.]

[(1A) For the purposes of paragraph (1)(b)(iii) above, 'controlled substance' means any one of the following:

chlorofluorocarbons, other fully halogenated chlorofluorocarbons, halons, carbon tetrachloride, 1,1,1-trichloroethane, methyl bromide, hydrobromofluorocarbons, hydrochlorofluorocarbons.]

(2) For the purposes of paragraph (1)(d) above, 'clinical waste' has the meaning given by regulation 1(2) of the Controlled Waste Regulations 1992.]

[(3) For the purposes of paragraph (1)(h), 'controlled waters' has the meaning given by section 104 of the Water Resources Act 1991.]

13 Health at work

No conditions shall be imposed in any waste management licence for the purpose only of securing the health of persons at work (within the meaning of Part I of the Health and Safety at Work etc. Act 1974).

14 Waste oils

(1) Where a waste management licence or disposal licence authorises the regeneration of waste oil, it shall include conditions which ensure that base oils derived from regeneration do not constitute a hazardous waste and do not contain PCBs or PCTs at all or do not contain them in concentrations beyond a specified maximum limit which in no case is to exceed 50 parts per million.

(2) Where a waste management licence or disposal licence authorises the keeping of waste oil, it shall include conditions which ensure that it is not mixed with hazardous waste or PCBs or PCTs.

(3) In this regulation—

'PCBs or PCTs' means polychlorinated biphenyls, polychlorinated terphenyls and mixtures containing one or both of such substances; and

['hazardous waste' has the meaning given by regulation 6 of the Hazardous Waste (England and Wales) Regulations 2005].

15 Groundwater

(1) Where a waste regulation authority proposes to issue a waste management licence authorising—

(a) any disposal or tipping for the purpose of disposal of a substance in list I which might lead to an indirect discharge into groundwater of such a substance;

(b) any disposal or tipping for the purpose of disposal of a substance in list II which might lead to an indirect discharge into groundwater of such a substance;

(c) a direct discharge into groundwater of a substance in list I; or

(d) a direct discharge into groundwater of a substance in list II, the authority shall ensure that the proposed activities are subjected to prior investigation.

(2) The prior investigation referred to in paragraph (1) above shall include examination of the hydrogeological conditions of the area concerned, the possible purifying powers of the soil and sub-soil and the risk of pollution and alteration of the quality of the groundwater from the discharge and shall establish whether the discharge of substances into groundwater is a satisfactory solution from the point of view of the environment.

(3) A waste management licence shall not be issued in any case within paragraph (1) above until the waste regulation authority has checked that the groundwater, and in particular its quality, will undergo the requisite surveillance.

(4) In a case within paragraph (1)(a) or (c) above—

(a) where the waste regulation authority is satisfied, in the light of the investigation, that the groundwater which may be affected by a direct or indirect discharge of a substance in list I is permanently unsuitable for other uses, especially domestic and agricultural, the waste management licence may only be issued if the authority is also satisfied that—

(i) the presence of that substance once discharged into groundwater will not impede exploitation of ground resources; and

(ii) all technical precautions will be taken to ensure that no substance in list I can reach other aquatic systems or harm other ecosystems; and

(b) where the waste regulation authority is not satisfied, in the light of the investigation, that the groundwater which may be affected by such a discharge is permanently unsuitable for other uses, especially domestic and agricultural, a waste management licence may only be issued if it is made subject to such conditions as the authority, in the light of the investigations, is satisfied will ensure the observance of all technical precautions necessary to prevent any discharges into groundwater of substances in list I.

(5) In a case within paragraph (1)(b) or (d) above, if a waste management licence is issued, it shall be issued subject to such conditions as the waste regulation authority, in the light of the investigation, is satisfied will ensure the observance of all technical precautions for preventing groundwater pollution by substances in list II.

(6) Where a waste management licence is granted in any case within paragraph (1)(a) or (b) above, the licence shall be granted on such terms and subject to such conditions as specify—

(a) the place where any disposal or tipping which might lead to a discharge into groundwater of any substances in list I or II is to be done;

(b) the methods of disposal or tipping which may be used;

(c) the essential precautions which must be taken, paying particular attention to the nature and concentration of the substances present in the matter to be disposed of or tipped, the characteristics of the receiving environment and the proximity of the water catchment areas, in particular those for drinking, thermal and mineral water;

(d) the maximum quantity permissible, during one or more specified periods of time, of matter containing substances in list I or II and, where possible, of those substances themselves, to be disposed of or tipped and the appropriate requirements as to the concentration of those substances;

(e) the technical precautions required by paragraph (4)(b) or (5) above;

(f) if necessary, the measures for monitoring the groundwater, and in particular its quality.

(7) Where a waste management licence is granted in any case within paragraph (1)(c) or (d) above, the licence shall be granted on such terms and subject to such conditions as specify—

(a) the place where any substances in list I or II are to be discharged into groundwater;

(b) the method of discharge which may be used;

(c) the essential precautions which must be taken, paying particular attention to the nature and concentration of the substances present in the effluents, the characteristics of the receiving environment and the proximity of the water catchment areas, in particular those for drinking, thermal and mineral water;

(d) the maximum quantity of a substance in list I or II permissible in an effluent during one or more specified periods of time and the appropriate requirements as to the concentration of those substances;

(e) the arrangements enabling effluents discharged into groundwater to be monitored;

(f) if necessary, the measures for monitoring the groundwater, and in particular its quality.

(8) Any authorisation granted by a waste management licence for an activity within paragraph (1) above shall be granted for a limited period only.

(9) Any authorisation granted by a waste management licence for an activity within paragraph (1) above shall be reviewed at least every 4 years.

(10) Waste regulation authorities shall review all waste management licences current on 1st May 1994 which authorise any activity within paragraph (1) above and shall, so far as may be necessary to give effect to Council Directive 80/68/EEC, exercise their powers under sections 37 and 38 of the 1990 Act (variation and revocation etc. of waste management licences) in relation to any such authorisation.

(11) . . .

(12) Expressions used both in this regulation and in Council Directive 80/68/EEC have for the purposes of this regulation the same meaning as in that Directive.

16 Exclusion of activities under other control regimes from waste management licensing

(1) Subject to paragraph (2) below, section 33(1)(a), (b) and (c) of the 1990 Act shall not apply in relation to the carrying on of any of the following activities—

(a) the [deposit in or on land,] recovery or disposal of waste under an authorisation granted under Part I of the 1990 Act where the activity is or forms part of a process designated for central control under section 2(4) of the 1990 Act;

(b) the disposal of waste under an authorisation granted under Part I of the 1990 Act where the activity is or forms part of a process within paragraph (a) of Part B of Section 5.1 (incineration) of Schedule 1 to the 1991 Regulations insofar as the activity results in releases of substances into the air;

[(ba) the deposit in or on land, recovery or disposal of waste under a permit granted under the 2000 Regulations to operate a [Part A installation] [or a Part A(2) installation which is a waste incineration installation within the meaning of the 2000 Regulations];

(bb) the disposal of waste under a permit granted under the 2000 Regulations where the activity is or forms part of an activity within paragraph (a) or (b) of Part B of Section 5.1 (incineration) of Part 1 of Schedule 1 to those Regulations in so far as the activity results in the release of substances into the air;]

(c) the disposal of liquid waste under a consent under Chapter II of Part III of the Water Resources Act 1991 or under Part II of the Control of Pollution Act 1974;

(d) the recovery or disposal of waste where the activity is or forms part of an operation which is for the time being either—

(i) the subject of a licence under Part II of the Food and Environment Protection Act 1985; or

(ii) carried on in circumstances where such a licence would be required but for an order under section 7 of that Act; and

[(e) the disposal of agricultural waste under an authorisation granted under regulation 18 of the Groundwater Regulations 1998].

(2) Paragraph (1)(a) [, (b) and (bb)] above does not apply insofar as the activity involves the final disposal of waste by deposit in or on land.

[(3) In paragraph (1)(ba) 'Part A(1) installation' has the meaning given by regulation 2(1) of the 2000 Regulations.]

17 Exemptions from waste management licensing

(1) Subject to the following provisions of this regulation and to any conditions or limitations in Schedule 3, section 33(1)(a) and (b) of the 1990 Act shall not apply in relation to the carrying on of any exempt activity set out in that Schedule.

[(1A) Paragraph (1) above does not apply to the carrying on of an exempt activity falling within paragraph 45(1), (2) or (5) of Schedule 3 where the carrying on of that activity is authorised by a waste management licence granted upon an application made after 31st March 1995 under section 36 of the 1990 Act.]

(2) In the case of an exempt activity set out in paragraph 4, 7, 8, 9, 11, 12, 12A, 13, 14, 15, 17, 18, 19, 25, 37, 40, 41, 45, or 46 of Schedule 3, paragraph (1) above only applies if—

(a) the exempt activity is carried on by or with the consent of the occupier of the land where the activity is carried on; or

(b) the person carrying on the exempt activity is otherwise entitled to do so on that land.

(3) Unless otherwise indicated in Schedule 3, paragraph (1) above does not apply to the carrying on of an exempt activity insofar as it involves hazardous waste.

[(3A) Paragraph (1) does not apply to the carrying on of an exempt activity insofar as it involves the carrying out, by an establishment or undertaking, of their own waste disposal at the place of production if the waste being disposed of is hazardous waste.]

(4) Paragraph (1) above only applies in relation to an exempt activity involving the disposal or recovery of waste by an establishment or undertaking if the type and quantity of waste submitted to the activity, and the method of disposal or recovery, are consistent with the need to attain the objectives mentioned in paragraph 4(1)(a) of Part I of Schedule 4.

(5) For the purposes of Schedule 3, a container, lagoon or place is secure in relation to waste kept in it if all reasonable precautions are taken to ensure that the waste cannot escape from it and members of the public are unable to gain access to the waste, and any reference to secure storage means storage in a secure container, lagoon or place.

[(5A) It shall be the duty of each appropriate registration authority (as defined in regulation 18(10)) to have regard to any guidance issued to it by the Secretary of State with respect to the discharge of its functions in relation to any exempt activity.]

18 Registration in connection with exempt activities

(1) Subject to [paragraphs (1A), (1B) and (7)] below, it shall be an offence for an establishment or undertaking to carry on, after 31st December 1994, an exempt activity involving the recovery or disposal of waste without being registered with the appropriate registration authority.

[(1A) In the case of an exempt activity falling within paragraph 45(1) or (2) of Schedule 3, paragraph (1) above shall have effect as if '30th September 1995' were substituted for '31st December 1994'.

(1B) Paragraph (1) above shall not apply in the case of an exempt activity to which a resolution under section 54 of the 1990 Act relates and which is carried on in accordance with the conditions, specified in the resolution, which relate to it.]

(2) It shall be the duty of each appropriate registration authority to establish and maintain a register for the purposes of paragraph (1) above of establishments and undertakings carrying on exempt activities involving the recovery or disposal of waste in respect of which it is the appropriate registration authority.

(3) Subject to paragraph (4) below, the register shall contain the following particulars in relation to each such establishment or undertaking—

(a) the name and address of the establishment or undertaking;

(b) the activity which constitutes the exempt activity; and

(c) the place where the activity is carried on.

(4) [Subject to paragraphs (4A) and (4B) below,] the appropriate registration authority shall enter the relevant particulars in the register in relation to an establishment or undertaking if it receives notice of them in writing or otherwise becomes aware of those particulars.

[(4A) Paragraph (4) above shall not apply in the case of an exempt activity falling within paragraph 45(1) or (2) of Schedule 3 and, in such a case, the appropriate registration authority shall enter the relevant particulars in the register in relation to an establishment or undertaking only if—

(a) it receives notice of them in writing;

(b) that notice is provided to it by that establishment or undertaking;

(c) that notice is accompanied by a plan of each place at which any such exempt activity is carried on showing—

(i) the boundaries of that place;

(ii) the locations within that place at which the exempt activity is to be carried on;

(iii) the location and specifiations of any such impermeable pavements, drainage systems or hardstandings as are mentioned in paragraph 45(1)(c) or (2)(f) or (g) of Schedule 3; and

(iv) the location of any such secure containers as are mentioned in paragraph 45(2)(e) of Schedule 3;

[(cc) in the case of waste motor vehicles, it has first verified, further to its inspection of each such place—

(i) the type of waste to be treated;

(ii) the quantities of waste to be treated;

(iii) the general technical requirements to be complied with; and

(iv) the safety precautions that are to be taken,

in order to achieve the objectives referred to in Article 4 of the Directive, and a registration further to such verification shall continue subject to the requirement that verification upon inspection be made annually in respect of it.]

and

(d) that notice is also accompanied by payment of [the charge prescribed for the purpose by a charging scheme under section 41 of the Environment Act 1995] in respect of each place where any such exempt activity is carried on.

(4B) Where any fee payable under paragraph 45(3)(d) of Schedule 3 is not received by the appropriate registration authority within 2 months of the due date for its payment as ascertained in accordance with paragraph 45(4) of Schedule 3—

(a) in a case where the establishment or undertaking is registered for exempt activities falling within paragraph 45(1) or (2) in respect of only one place, or where it is so registered in respect of more than one place and the fee in respect of each such place is then unpaid, the registration of the establishment or undertaking shall be cancelled and the authority shall remove from its register the relevant entry in respect of the establishment or undertaking;

(b) in any other case, the registration of the establishment or undertaking in respect of those activities shall be cancelled insofar as it relates to any place in respect of which the fee is then unpaid and the authority shall amend the relevant entry in its register accordingly,

and where the authority removes or amends an entry from or in its register by virtue of this paragraph it shall notify the establishment or undertaking in writing of the removal or amendment.]

(5) For the purposes of paragraph (4) above, the appropriate registration authority shall be taken to be aware of the relevant particulars in relation to an exempt activity mentioned in paragraph (10)(a), (b) or (c) below.

[(5A) The duty to maintain a register in paragraph (2) above includes the duty to remove an entry in relation to an establishment or undertaking if—

(a) the appropriate registration authority has become aware that the undertaking or establishment has ceased to carry on the relevant activity;

(b) the activity is not being carried on in compliance with the conditions or limitations of the relevant paragraph in Schedule 3; or

(c) regulation 17(1) is disapplied in relation to the activity by virtue of any of the provisions in regulation 17(1A) to (4).]

[(6) A person guilty of an offence under paragraph (1) above shall be liable on summary conviction to a fine not exceeding—

(a) in the case of an exempt activity falling within paragraphs 7, 8, 9, 10, 12, 12A, 19 or 46 of Schedule 3, level 3 on the standard scale; and

(b) in any other case, level 2 on the standard scale.]

(7) [...]

(8) Each appropriate registration authority shall secure that any register maintained by it under this regulation is open to inspection ... by members of the public free of charge at all reasonable hours and shall afford to members of the public reasonable facilities for obtaining, on payment of reasonable charges, copies of entries in the register.

(9) Registers under this regulation may be kept in any form.

(10) For the purposes of this regulation, the appropriate registration authority is—

(a) in the case of an exempt activity falling within—

(i) paragraph 1, 2, 3 or 24 of Schedule 3 [and carried out under an authorisation granted under Part I of the 1990 Act];

(ii) paragraph 4 of Schedule 3 if it involves the coating or spraying of metal containers as or as part of a process within Part B of Section 6.5 (coating processes and printing) of Schedule 1 to the 1991 Regulations and the process is for the time being the subject of an authorisation granted under Part I of the 1990 Act, or if it involves storage related to that process; or

(iii) paragraph 12 of Schedule 3 if it involves the composting of biodegradable waste as or as part of a process within paragraph (a) of Part B of Section 6.9 (treatment or processing of animal or vegetable matter) of Schedule 1 to the 1991 Regulations, the compost is to be used for the purpose of cultivating mushrooms and the process is for the time being the subject of an authorisation granted under Part I of the 1990 Act, or if it involves storage related to that process,

the local enforcing authority responsible for granting the authorisation under Part I of the 1990 Act for the prescribed process involving the exempt activity, or to which the exempt activity relates;

[(aa) in the case of an exempt activity falling within—

(i) paragraph 1A, 2A, 3 or 24 of Schedule 3 and carried out under a permit under the 2000 Regulations;

(ii) paragraph 4 of Schedule 3 if it involves the coating or spraying of metal containers as or as part of an activity within Part B of Section 6.4 (coating activities and printing) of Part 1 of Schedule 1 to the 2000 Regulations and the activity is for the time being the subject of a permit granted under those Regulations, or if it involves storage related to that activity; or

(iii) paragraph 12 of Schedule 3 if it involves the composting of biodegradable waste as or as part of an activity within paragraph (a) of Part B of Section 6.8 (treatment of animal and vegetable matter) of Part 1 of Schedule 1 to the 2000 Regulations, the compost is to be used for the purpose of cultivating mushrooms and the activity is for the time being the subject of a permit granted under those Regulations, or if it involves storage related to that activity,

the local authority regulator responsible for granting the permit under the 2000 Regulations authorising the exempt activity;]

(b) in a case falling within paragraph 16 of Schedule 3, the issuing authority responsible for granting the licence under article 7 or 8 of the Diseases of Animals (Waste Food) Order 1973 under which the exempt activity is carried on;b

(c) in a case falling within paragraph 23 of Schedule 3—

(i) where the exempt activity is carried on by virtue of a licence under article 5(2)(c) or 6(2)(d), or an approval under article 8, of the Animal By-Products Order 1992, the Minister;

(ii) where the exempt activity is carried on by virtue of a registration under article 9 or 10 of that Order, the appropriate Minister;

(iii) where the exempt activity is carried on at a knacker's yard in respect of which the occupier holds a licence under section 1 of the Slaughterhouses Act 1974 authorising the use of that yard as a knacker's yard . . . the local authority; and in this sub-paragraph 'the Minister' and 'the appropriate Minister' have the meaning given by section 86(1) of the Animal Health Act 1981, and 'knacker's yard' and 'local authority' have the meaning given by section 34 of the Slaughterhouses Act 1974 . . . ;

(d) in any other case, the waste regulation authority for the area in which the exempt activity is carried on.

[18AA Supervision of exempt activities

(1) An establishment or undertaking which wishes to be registered as carrying on a notifiable exempt activity must provide to the appropriate registration authority—

(a) a notice of its relevant particulars and such other information as the authority reasonably requires in relation to the activity as indicated on a form provided for the purpose by the authority;

(b) such plans and other documents as the authority reasonably requires;

(c) the quantity of waste to be disposed of or recovered; and

(d) any applicable charge prescribed for the purpose by a charging scheme under section 41 of the Environment Act 1995.

(2) For the purposes of paragraph (1), the total area covered by a notice in relation to any exempt activity falling within paragraph 7A of Schedule 3 shall not exceed 50 hectares.

(3) The information required under paragraph (1) above shall include a certificate prepared by a person with appropriate technical expertise containing such evidence as can reasonably be expected to demonstrate that, in relation to an exempt activity falling within paragraphs 7A, 8A or 9A(1)(b) of Schedule 3, the activity will result in benefit to agriculture or ecological improvement and will be consistent with the need to attain the objectives mentioned in paragraph 4(1)(a) of Part 1 of Schedule 4.

(4) Where it receives notification pursuant to paragraph (1), the appropriate registration authority shall—

(a) enter the relevant particulars in the register; or

(b) before the end of the relevant period refuse to enter the relevant particulars in the register (such decision, and the reasons for it, to be set out in writing and served on the establishment or undertaking).

(5) An establishment or undertaking which carries on a notifiable exempt activity and wishes to maintain its entry on the register must, within 12 months of the date that the particulars were entered or last renewed, provide to the appropriate registration authority a renewal notice including—

(a) a notice confirming that it continues to carry on the exempt activity together with such other information as the authority reasonably requires in relation to the activity as indicated on a form provided for that purpose by the authority;

(b) such plans or other documents as the authority may reasonably require;

(c) the quantity of waste to be disposed of or recovered; and

(d) any applicable charge prescribed for the purpose by a charging scheme under section 41 of the Environment Act 1995.

(6) An establishment or undertaking which wishes to dispose of or recover a quantity of waste which exceeds the amount notified by it to the appropriate registration authority shall provide a revised notification under paragraph (1) (including any applicable charge prescribed for the purpose by a charging scheme under section 41 of the Environment Act 1995).

(7) The appropriate registration authority shall remove from the register an entry in relation to an establishment or undertaking which carries on a notifiable exempt activity if—

(a) it has not received a renewal notice in accordance with paragraph (5) within 12 months of the date on which the particulars were entered into the register or were last renewed; or

(b) it has decided to refuse to renew a registration in response to such a notice within the relevant period (such decision, and the reasons for it, to be set out in writing and served on the establishment or undertaking).

(8) Subject to paragraph (9), an establishment or undertaking carrying on a notifiable exempt activity shall keep records of the quantity, nature, origin, and where relevant destination and treatment method of all waste disposed of or recovered in the course of that activity.

(9) Paragraph (8) does not apply in relation to the carrying on of an exempt activity under—

(a) paragraph 9A of Schedule 3 at any place where the quantity of waste recovered in reliance on the exemption at that place is less than 2,500 cubic metres; or

(b) paragraph 19A of Schedule 3 at any place where the quantity of waste recovered in reliance on the exemption at that place is less than 2,500 tonnes.

(10) Records kept under paragraph (8) shall be kept for a period of at least two years in such form as to show for each month the total quantity of waste disposed of or recovered at that place during that month, and during those two years shall be made available to the appropriate registration authority on request.

(11) An establishment or undertaking which carries on an exempt activity in breach of paragraph (6), (8) or (10) shall be guilty of an offence and liable on summary conviction to a fine not exceeding level 2 on the standard scale.

(12) In this regulation, 'the relevant period' means the period of 35 days beginning with the date of receipt of the notice by the authority (or such longer period as the appropriate registration authority and establishment or undertaking may agree in writing).]

19 Waste framework directive

Schedule 4 (which implements certain provisions of Council Directive 75/442/EEC on waste) shall have effect.

20 Registration of brokers

(1) Subject to paragraphs (2) to (4) below, it shall be an offence for an establishment or undertaking after 31st December 1994 to arrange (as dealer or broker) for the disposal or recovery of controlled waste on behalf of another person unless it is a registered broker of controlled waste.

(2) Paragraph (1) above shall not apply in relation to an arrangement under which an establishment or undertaking will itself carry out the disposal or recovery of the waste and either—

(a) it is authorised to carry out the disposal or recovery of the waste by a waste management licence, an authorisation under Part I of the 1990 Act, [a permit under the 2000 Regulations,] a consent under Chapter II of Part III of the Water Resources Act 1991 or under Part II of the Control of Pollution Act 1974 or a licence under Part II of the Food and Environment Protection Act 1985; or

(b) the recovery of the waste is covered by an exemption conferred by—

(i) regulation 17(1) of, and Schedule 3 to, these Regulations; or

(ii) article 3 of the Deposits in the Sea (Exemptions) Order 1985.

(3) Paragraph (1) above shall not apply in relation to an arrangement for the disposal or recovery of controlled waste made by a person who is registered as a carrier of controlled waste, or who is registered for the purposes of paragraph 12(1) of Part I of Schedule 4, if as part of the arrangement he transports the waste to or from any place in Great Britain.

(4) Paragraph (1) above shall not apply to an establishment or undertaking which—

(a) is a charity;

(b) is a voluntary organisation within the meaning of section 48(11) of the Local Government Act 1985 or section 83(2D) of the Local Government (Scotland) Act 1973;

(c) is an authority which is a waste collection authority, waste disposal authority or waste regulation authority; or

(d) applies before 1st January 1995 in accordance with Schedule 5 for registration as a broker of controlled waste but only whilst its application is pending (and paragraph 1(4) and (5) of Part I of Schedule 5 shall apply for the purpose of determining whether an application is pending).

(5) A person guilty of an offence under this section shall be liable on summary conviction to a fine not exceeding level 5 on the standard scale.

(6) Section 157 of the 1990 Act shall apply in relation to an offence under this section as it applies in relation to an offence under that Act.

(7) Schedule 5 (which makes provision for the registration of brokers of controlled waste) shall have effect.

(8) Sections 68(3) to (5), 69 and 71(2) and (3) of the 1990 Act (power to appoint inspectors, powers of entry and power to obtain information) shall have effect as if the provisions of this regulation and Schedule 5 were provisions of Part II of that Act.

Regulation 2(2), (3) and (4) SCHEDULE 1

INFORMATION AND EVIDENCE REQUIRED IN RELATION TO AN APPLICATION FOR THE SURRENDER OF A SITE LICENCE

1. The full name, address and daytime telephone, fax and telex number (if any) of the holder of the site licence and, where the holder employs an agent in relation to the application, of that agent.

2. The number (if any) of the site licence, and the address or a description of the location of the site.

3. A map or plan—

(a) showing the location of the site;

(b) indicating whereabouts on the site the different activities mentioned in paragraph 4 were carried on; and

(c) indicating relevant National Grid references.

4. A description of the different activities involving the treatment, keeping or disposal of controlled waste which were carried on at the site (whether or not in pursuance of the licence), an indication of when those activities were carried on and an estimate of the total quantities of the different types of waste which were dealt with at the site.

5. Where the site is a landfill or lagoon—

(a) particulars of all significant engineering works carried out for the purpose of preventing or minimising pollution of the environment or harm to human health as a result of activities carried on at the site, including—

(i) an indication of when those works were carried out and a copy of all relevant plans or specifications; and

(ii) details of works of restoration carried out after completion of operations at the site;

(b) geological, hydrological and hydrogeological information relating to the site and its surrounds, including information about the flows of groundwater;

(c) monitoring data on the quality of surface water or groundwater which could be affected by the site and on the production of any landfill gas or leachate at the site and information about the physical stability of the site; and

[(d) every record made relating to the site pursuant to regulation 14 of the Control of Pollution (Special Waste) Regulations 1980, regulation 16 of the 1996 Regulations, or regulation 47 of the Hazardous Waste (England and Wales) Regulations 2005;]

and any estimate under paragraph 4 of the total quantities of the different types of waste dealt with at the site shall, in particular, differentiate between biodegradable waste, non-biodegradable waste and hazardous waste.

6. Where the site is not a landfill or lagoon—

(a) details of the contaminants likely to be present at the site having regard to—

(i) the different activities involving the treatment, keeping or disposal of controlled waste carried on at the site (whether or not in pursuance of the licence); and

(ii) the nature of the different types of waste dealt with at the site; and

(b) a report which—

(i) records the results of the analysis of samples taken in such numbers, and at such locations at the site, that they provide a reliable indication of the locations where contaminants are likely to be present in high concentrations; and

(ii) shows how many (and from where) samples were taken.

7. Any other information which the applicant wishes the waste regulation authority to take into account.

[Regulation 4 SCHEDULE 1A

CERTIFICATES OF TECHNICAL COMPETENCE

1 The qualifications required of a person if he is to be regarded as technically competent for the purposes of section 74(3)(b) of the 1990 Act to manage a facility of a description listed in Table 1 are that that person must hold one of the certificates awarded by the Waste Management Industry Training and Advisory Board the codes of which are specified in relation to that description of facility in that Table; and the certificates to which the codes refer are set out in Table 2.

. . .

SCHEDULE 3
ACTIVITIES EXEMPT FROM WASTE MANAGEMENT LICENSING

. . .

Regulations 1(3) and 19 SCHEDULE 4

WASTE FRAMEWORK DIRECTIVE ETC.

PART I GENERAL

1 Interpretation of Schedule 4

In this Schedule, unless the context otherwise requires—

'competent authority' has the meaning given by paragraph 3;

'development', 'development plan', 'government department' and 'planning permission' have the same meaning as in the Town and Country Planning Act 1990 . . .;

'licensing authority' and 'the Ministers' have the meaning given by section 24(1) of the Food and Environment Protection Act 1985;

'local planning authority' and 'the planning Acts' have the same meaning as in the Town and Country Planning Act 1990;

'permit' means a waste management licence, a disposal licence, an authorisation under Part I of the 1990 Act, [a permit under the 2000 Regulations,] a resolution under section 54 of the 1990 Act, a licence under Part II of the Food and Environment Protection Act 1985 or a consent under Chapter II of Part III of the Water Resources Act 1991 or under Part II of the Control of Pollution Act 1974 (and, in relation to a permit, 'grant' includes give, issue or pass, 'modify' includes vary, and cognate expressions shall be construed accordingly);

'plan-making provisions' means paragraph 5 below, section 50 of the 1990 Act . . . Part II of the Town and Country Planning Act 1990 [and section 44A of the Environmental Protection Act 1990 . . .];

'planning authority' means the local planning authority, the person appointed under paragraph 1 of Schedule 6 to the Town and Country Planning Act 1990 or, as the case may be, the government department responsible for discharging a function under the planning Acts . . . and the Secretary of State shall be treated as a planning authority in respect of his functions under the planning Acts . . .;

'pollution control authority' means any competent authority other than a planning authority;

. . .

'specified action' means any of the following—

(a) determining—

(i) an application for planning permission; or

(ii) an appeal made under section 78 of the Town and Country Planning Act 1990 . . . in respect of such an application;

(b) deciding whether to take any action under section 141(2) or (3) or 177(1)(a) or (b) of the Town and Country Planning Act 1990, or under section 196(5) of that Act as originally enacted, or under section 35(5) of the Planning (Listed Buildings and Conservation Areas) Act 1990 . . . ;

(c) deciding whether to direct under section 90(1), (2) or (2A) of the Town and Country Planning Act 1990 or . . . or paragraph 7(1) of Schedule 8 to the Electricity Act 1989, that planning permission shall be deemed to be granted;

(d) deciding whether—

(i) in making or confirming a discontinuance order, to include in the order any grant of planning permission; or

(ii) to confirm (with or without modifications) a discontinuance order insofar as it grants planning permission,

and, for the purposes of this sub-paragraph, 'discontinuance order' means an order under section 102 of the Town and Country Planning Act 1990 (including an order made under that section by virtue of section 104 of that Act), or under paragraph 1 of Schedule 9 to that Act (including an order made under that paragraph by virtue of paragraph 11 of that Schedule) . . .

(e) discharging functions under Part II of the Town and Country Planning Act 1990 . . .

2 Duties of competent authorities

(1) Subject to the following provisions of this paragraph, the competent authorities shall discharge their specified functions, insofar as they relate to the recovery or disposal of waste, with the relevant objectives.

(2) Nothing in sub-paragraph (1) above requires a planning authority to deal with any matter which the relevant pollution control authority has power to deal with.

(3) In a case where the recovery or disposal of waste is or forms part of a prescribed process designated for local control under Part I of the 1990 Act, and either requires a waste management licence or is covered by an exemption conferred by regulation 17(1) of, and Schedule 3 to, these Regulations, nothing in sub-paragraph (1) above shall require a competent authority to discharge its functions under—

(a) Part I of the 1990 Act in order to control pollution of the environment due to the release of substances into any environmental medium other than the air; or

(b) Part II of the 1990 Act in order to control pollution of the environment due to the release of substances into the air resulting from the carrying on of the prescribed process.

(4) In sub-paragraph (3) above, 'prescribed process', 'designated for local control', 'pollution of the environment due to the release of substances into the air' and 'pollution of the environment due to the release of substances into any environmental medium other than the air' have the meaning which they have in Part I of the 1990 Act.

[(5) In a case where the recovery or disposal of waste is or forms part of an activity carried out at a Part B installation and requires a waste management licence, nothing in sub-paragraph (1) shall require a competent authority to discharge its functions under—

(a) the 2000 Regulations for any purpose other than preventing or, where that is not practicable, reducing emissions into the air;

(b) Part II of the 1990 Act for the purpose of preventing or reducing emissions into the air.

(6) In sub-paragraph (5), 'Part B installation' has the meaning given by regulation 2(1) of the 2000 Regulations.]

3 Meaning of 'competent authority' etc.

(1) For the purposes of this Schedule, 'competent authority' means any of the persons or bodies listed in column (1) of Table 5 below and, subject to sub-paragraph (2) below, in

relation to a competent authority 'specified function' means any function of that authority listed in column (2) of that Table opposite the entry for that authority.

Table 5

Competent authorities (1)	Specified functions (2)
Any planning authority.	The taking of any specified action.
A waste regulation authority, the Secretary of State or a person appointed under [section 114(1)(a) of the Environment Act 1995].	Their respective functions under Part II of the 1990 Act in relation to waste management licences, including preparing plans or modifications of them under section 50 of the 1990 Act [and preparing the strategy, or any modification of it, under section 44A... of that Act].
...	...
A licensing authority or the Ministers.	Their respective functions under Part II of the Food and Environment Protection Act 1985, or under paragraph 5 below.
An enforcing authority, the Secretary of State or a person appointed under [section 114(1)(a) of the Environment Act 1995].	Their respective functions under Part I of the 1990 Act in relation to prescribed processes except when— (a) the process is designated for local control; and (b) it is an exempt activity carried out subject to the conditions and limitations specified in Schedule 3.
[The Environment Agency] or the Secretary of State.]	Their respective functions in relation to [— (a) consents under Chapter II of Part III of the Water Resources Act 1991 (offences in relation to pollution of water resources) for any discharge of waste in liquid form other than waste waters; (b) authorisations under regulation 18 of the Groundwater Regulations 1998 (disposal or tipping of substances in list I or II); and (c) notices under regulation 19 of the Groundwater Regulations 1998 (prohibition or authorisation of activities which may result in indirect discharges of substances in list I or II).]
...	...
[A regulator (within the meaning of regulation 2(1) of the 2000 Regulations), the Secretary of State or a person appointed under section 114(1)(a) of the Environment Act 1995.	Their respective functions in relation to permits under the 2000 Regulations except in relation to the carrying out of an exempt activity under such permits.]

(2) In Table 5 above, references to functions do not include functions of making, revoking, amending, revising or re-enacting orders, regulations or schemes where those functions are required to be discharged by statutory instrument.

4 Relevant objectives

(1) For the purposes of this Schedule, the following objectives are relevant objectives in relation to the disposal or recovery of waste—

(a) ensuring that waste is recovered or disposed of without endangering human health and without using processes or methods which could harm the environment and in particular without—

(i) risk to water, air, soil, plants or animals; or

(ii) causing nuisance through noise or odours; or

(iii) adversely affecting the countryside or places of special interest;

(b) implementing, so far as material, any plan made under the plan-making provisions.

(2) The following additional objectives are relevant objectives in relation to the disposal of waste—

(a) establishing an integrated and adequate network of waste disposal installations, taking account of the best available technology not involving excessive costs; and

(b) ensuring that the network referred to at paragraph (a) above enables—

(i) the European Community as a whole to become self-sufficient in waste disposal, and the Member States individually to move towards that aim, taking into account geographical circumstances or the need for specialized installations for certain types of waste; and

(ii) waste to be disposed of in one of the nearest appropriate installations, by means of the most appropriate methods and technologies in order to ensure a high level of protection for the environment and public health.

(3) The following further objectives are relevant objectives in relation to functions under the plan-making provisions—

(a) encouraging the prevention or reduction of waste production and its harmfulness, in particular by—

(i) the development of clean technologies more sparing in their use of natural resources;

(ii) the technical development and marketing of products designed so as to make no contribution or to make the smallest possible contribution, by the nature of their manufacture, use or final disposal, to increasing the amount or harmfulness of waste and pollution hazards; and

(iii) the development of appropriate techniques for the final disposal of dangerous substances contained in waste destined for recovery; and

(b) encouraging—

(i) the recovery of waste by means of recycling, reuse or reclamation or any other process with a view to extracting secondary raw materials; and

(ii) the use of waste as a source of energy.

5 Preparation of offshore waste management plan

(1) Subject to sub-paragraph (2) below, it shall be the duty of a licensing authority to prepare a statement ('the plan') containing the authority's policies in relation to the recovery or disposal of waste for attaining the relevant objectives in those parts of United Kingdom waters and United Kingdom controlled waters for which the authority is the licensing authority.

(2) Two or more licensing authorities may join together to prepare a single statement covering the several parts of United Kingdom waters and United Kingdom controlled waters for which they are the licensing authorities.

(3) The plan shall relate in particular to—

(a) the type, quantity and origin of waste to be recovered or disposed of;

(b) general technical requirements;

(c) any special arrangements for particular wastes; and

(d) suitable disposal sites or installations.

(4) The licensing authority shall make copies of the plan available to the public on payment of reasonable charges.

(5) In this paragraph, 'United Kingdom waters' and 'United Kingdom controlled waters' have the meaning given by section 24(1) of the Food and Environment Protection Act 1985.

6 Matters to be covered by permits

When a pollution control authority grants or modifies a permit, and the activities authorised by the permit include the disposal of waste, the pollution control authority shall ensure that the permit covers—

(a) the types and quantities of waste,

(b) the technical requirements,

(c) the security precautions to be taken,

(d) the disposal site, and

(e) the treatment method.

7 Modifications of provisions relating to development plans

(1) Subject to sub-paragraph (2) below, sections 12(3A), 31(3) and 36(3) of the Town and Country Planning Act 1990 . . . shall have effect as if the policies referred to in those sections also included policies in respect of suitable waste disposal sites or installations.

(2) In the case of the policies referred to in section 36(3) of the Town and Country Planning Act 1990, sub-paragraph (1) above shall have effect subject to the provisions of section 36(5) of that Act.

(3) Section 38(1) of the Town and Country Planning Act 1990 shall have effect as if the definition of waste policies included detailed policies in respect of suitable disposal sites or installations for the carrying on of such development as is referred to in that definition.

9 Modifications of Part II of the Environmental Protection Act 1990

(1) Part II of the 1990 Act shall have effect subject to the following modifications.

(2) Any reference to waste shall include a reference to Directive waste.

(3) In sections 33(1)(a) and (5), 54(1)(a), (2), (3) and (4)(d) and 69(2), any reference to the deposit of waste in or on land shall include a reference to any operation listed in Part III or IV of this Schedule involving such a deposit.

(4) In sections 33(1)(b), 54(1)(b), (2), (3) and (4)(d) and 69(2), any reference to the treatment or disposal, or to the treatment, keeping or disposal, of controlled waste shall be taken to be a reference to submitting controlled waste to any of the operations listed in Part III or IV of this Schedule other than an operation mentioned in sub-paragraph (3) above.

(5) In sections 33(1)(c) and 35, any reference to the treatment or disposal, or to the treatment, keeping or disposal, of controlled waste shall include a reference to submitting controlled waste to any of the operations listed in Part III or Part IV of this Schedule.

(6) Section 33(2) shall not apply to the treatment, keeping or disposal of household waste by an establishment or undertaking.

(7) In section 36(3), the reference to planning permission shall be taken to be a reference to planning permission resulting from the taking of a specified action by a planning authority after 30th April 1994.

(8) In section 50(3), any reference to the disposal of waste shall include a reference to the recovery of waste.

10 . . .

11 References to 'waste' in Planning and Water legislation

In the Town and Country Planning Act 1990, . . . and Chapter II of Part III of the Water Resources Act 1991, any reference to 'waste' shall include a reference to Directive waste.

12 Registration by professional collectors and transporters of waste, and by dealers and brokers

(1) Subject to sub-paragraph (3) below, it shall be an offence for an establishment or undertaking falling within sub-paragraph (a), (c), (f) or (g) of regulation 2(1) of the Controlled

Waste (Registration of Carriers and Seizure of Vehicles) Regulations 1991 after 31st December 1994 to collect or transport waste on a professional basis unless it is registered in accordance with the provisions of this paragraph.

(2) Subject to sub-paragraph (3) below, it shall be an offence for an establishment or undertaking falling within sub-paragraph (a), (b) or (c) of regulation 20(4) after 31st December 1994 to arrange for the recovery or disposal of waste on behalf of another person unless it is registered in accordance with the provisions of this paragraph.

(3) Sub-paragraphs (1) and (2) above do not apply in cases where the establishment or undertaking is carrying on the activities therein mentioned pursuant to, and in accordance with the terms and conditions of, a permit.

(4) An establishment or undertaking shall register with the waste regulation authority in whose area its principal place of business in Great Britain is located or, where it has no place of business in Great Britain, with any waste regulation authority.

(5) Each waste regulation authority shall establish and maintain a register of establishments and undertakings registering with it under the provisions of this paragraph.

(6) The register shall contain the following particulars in relation to each such establishment or undertaking—

(a) the name of the establishment or undertaking;
(b) the address of its principal place of business; and
(c) the address of any place at or from which it carries on its business.

(7) The waste regulation authority shall enter the relevant particulars in the register in relation to an establishment or undertaking if it receives notice of them in writing or otherwise becomes aware of those particulars.

(8) A person guilty of an offence under sub-paragraph (1) or (2) above shall be liable on summary conviction to a fine not exceeding level 2 on the standard scale.

(9) Each waste regulation authority shall secure that any register maintained by it under this paragraph is open to inspection . . . by members of the public free of charge at all reasonable hours and shall afford to members of the public reasonable facilities for obtaining, on payment of reasonable charges, copies of entries in the register.

(10) Registers under this paragraph may be kept in any form.

(11) In this paragraph, 'registered carrier' and 'controlled waste' have the same meaning as they have in the Control of Pollution (Amendment) Act 1989, 'registered broker' has the same meaning as in regulation 20 and Schedule 5, and 'collect' and 'transport' have the same meaning as they have in Article 12 of the Directive.

13 Duty to carry out appropriate periodic inspections

(1) [Subject to sub-paragraphs (3) to (5) below,] any establishment or undertaking which carries out the recovery or disposal of controlled waste, or which collects or transports controlled waste on a professional basis, or which arranges for the recovery or disposal of controlled waste on behalf of others (dealers or brokers), shall be subject to appropriate periodic inspections by the competent authorities.

(2) [Section] 71(2) and (3) of the 1990 Act (. . . power to obtain information) shall have effect as if the provisions of this paragraph were provisions of Part II of that Act and as if, in those sections, references to a waste regulation authority were references to a competent authority.

[(2A) Section 108 of the Environment Act 1995 (powers of entry) shall apply as if the competent authority was an enforcing authority and its functions under this paragraph were pollution control functions.]

[(3) Subject to sub-paragraph (4) below, in a case where an establishment or undertaking is carrying on an exempt activity in reliance upon an exemption conferred by regulation 17(1) of, and paragraph 45(1) or (2) of Schedule 3 to, these Regulations, a competent authority which is a waste regulation authority shall discharge its duty under sub-paragraph (1) in respect of any place where such an activity is so carried on by—

(a) carrying out an initial inspection of that place within two months of having received in respect of that place the notice, plan and fee referred to in regulation 18(4A); and

(b) thereafter carrying out periodic inspections of that place at intervals not exceeding 12 months.

(4) Where the notice, plan and fee referred to in paragraph (a) of sub-paragraph (3) above are received by the authority before 1st October 1995, that paragraph shall have effect as if for the reference to carrying out an initial inspection within two months of the receipt of such notice, plan and fee there were substituted a reference to carrying out such an inspection within nine months of their receipt.

(5) In the case of any such place as is mentioned in sub-paragraph (3) above, but without prejudice to any duties of waste regulation authorities imposed otherwise than by this paragraph, sub-paragraph (1) above does not require (but does permit) a competent authority which is a waste regulation authority to carry out the periodic inspections referred to in sub-paragraph (3)(b) above at intervals of less than 10 months.]

14 Record keeping

(1) Subject to [paragraph 45(3)(b) of Schedule 3 and] sub-paragraph (2) below, an establishment or undertaking which carries out the disposal or recovery of controlled waste shall—

(a) keep a record of the quantity, nature, origin and, where relevant, the destination, frequency of collection, mode of transport and treatment method of any waste which is disposed of or recovered; and

(b) make that information available, on request, to the competent authorities [or, in the case of hazardous waste, to a previous holder; and for this purpose 'holder', in respect of any such waste, means the producer or the person in possession of it].

[(1A) Where hazardous waste is recovered or disposed of by an establishment or undertaking, it shall keep a record of the carrying out and supervision of the operation and, in the case of a disposal operation, of the after-care of the disposal site.]

(2) [Subject to sub-paragraph (3) below,] sub-paragraph (1) above does not apply where the disposal or recovery of the waste is covered by an exemption conferred by—

(a) regulation 17(1) of, and Schedule 3 to, these Regulations; or

(b) article 3 of the Deposits in the Sea (Exemptions) Order 1985

[(3) Sub-paragraph (1) above does apply to an activity subject to an exemption conferred by regulation 17(1) of, and paragraph 45(1) or (2) of Schedule 3 to, these Regulations.]

[(4) Subject to sub-paragraph (5) below, it shall be an offence for an establishment or undertaking to fail to comply with any of the foregoing provisions of this paragraph insofar as that provision imposes any requirement or obligation upon it.

[(5) Paragraph (a) of regulation 66 of the Hazardous Waste (England and Wales) Regulations 2005 (defence in case of emergency) shall apply to a person charged with an offence under paragraph (4) above as it applies to a person charged with an offence under regulation 65 of those Regulations.]

(6) A person who, in purported compliance with a requirement to furnish any information imposed by or under any of the provisions of this paragraph, makes a statement which he knows to be false or misleading in a material particular, commits an offence.

(7) A person who intentionally makes a false entry in any record required to be kept by virtue of any of the provisions of this paragraph commits an offence.

[(8) Regulations 67 and 69(2) of the Hazardous Waste (England and Wales) Regulations 2005 shall apply to an offence under this paragraph as they apply to an offence under regulation 65 of those Regulations.]]

PART II SUBSTANCES OR OBJECTS WHICH ARE WASTE WHEN DISCARDED ETC.

1. Production or consumption residues not otherwise specified in this Part of this Schedule (Q1).

2. Off-specification products (Q2).

3. Products whose date for appropriate use has expired (Q3).

4. Materials spilled, lost or having undergone other mishap, including any materials, equipment, etc., contaminated as a result of the mishap (Q4).

5. Materials contaminated or soiled as a result of planned actions (e.g. residues from cleaning operations, packing materials, containers, etc.) (Q5).

6. Unusable parts (e.g. reject batteries, exhausted catalysts, etc.) (Q6).

7. Substances which no longer perform satisfactorily (e.g. contaminated acids, contaminated solvents, exhausted tempering salts, etc.) (Q7).

8. Residues of industrial processes (e.g. slags, still bottoms, etc.) (Q8).

9. Residues from pollution abatement processes (e.g. scrubber sludges, baghouse dusts, spent filters, etc.) (Q9).

10. Machining or finishing residues (e.g. lathe turnings, mill scales, etc.) (Q10).

11. Residues from raw materials extraction and processing (e.g. mining residues, oil field slops, etc.) (Q11).

12. Adulterated materials (e.g. oils contaminated with PCBs, etc.) (Q12).

13. Any materials, substances or products whose use has been banned by law (Q13).

14. Products for which the holder has no further use (e.g. agricultural, household, office, commercial and shop discards, etc.) (Q14).

15. Contaminated materials, substances or products resulting from remedial action with respect to land (Q15).

16. Any materials, substances or products which are not contained in the above categories (Q16).

(Note:—the reference in brackets at the end of each paragraph of this Part of this Schedule is the number of the corresponding paragraph in Annex I to the Directive.)

PART III WASTE DISPOSAL OPERATIONS

1. Tipping of waste above or underground (e.g. landfill, etc.) (D1).

2. Land treatment of waste (e.g. biodegradation of liquid or sludge discards in soils, etc.) (D2).

3. Deep injection of waste (e.g. injection of pumpable discards into wells, salt domes or naturally occurring repositories, etc.) (D3).

4. Surface impoundment of waste (e.g. placement of liquid or sludge discards into pits, ponds or lagoons, etc.) (D4).

5. Specially engineered landfill of waste (e.g. placement of waste into lined discrete cells which are capped and isolated from one another and the environment, etc.) (D5).

6. Release of solid waste into a water body except seas or oceans (D6).

7. Release of waste into seas or oceans including seabed insertion (D7).

8. Biological treatment of waste not listed elsewhere in this Part of this Schedule which results in final compounds or mixtures which are disposed of by means of any of the operations listed in this Part of this Schedule (D8).

9. Physico-chemical treatment of waste not listed elsewhere in this Part of this Schedule which results in final compounds or mixtures which are disposed of by means of any of the operations listed in this Part of this Schedule (e.g. evaporation, drying, calcination, etc.) (D9).

10. Incineration of waste on land (D10).

11. Incineration of waste at sea (D11).

12. Permanent storage of waste (e.g. emplacement of containers in a mine, etc.) (D12).

13. Blending or mixture of waste prior to the waste being submitted to any of the operations listed in this Part of this Schedule (D13).

14. Repackaging of waste prior to the waste being submitted to any of the operations listed in this Part of this Schedule (D14).

15. Storage of waste pending any of the operations listed in this Part of this Schedule, but excluding temporary storage, pending collection, on the site where the waste is produced (D15).

(Note:—the reference in brackets at the end of each paragraph of this Part of this Schedule is the number of the corresponding paragraph in Annex IIA to the Directive.)

PART IV WASTE RECOVERY OPERATIONS

1. Reclamation or regeneration of solvents (R1).
2. Recycling or reclamation of organic substances which are not used as solvents (R2).
3. Recycling or reclamation of metals and metal compounds (R3).
4. Recycling or reclamation of other inorganic materials (R4).
5. Regeneration of acids or bases (R5).
6. Recovery of components used for pollution abatement (R6).
7. Recovery of components from catalysts (R7).
8. Re-refining, or other reuses, of oil which is waste (R8).
9. Use of waste principally as a fuel or for other means of generating energy (R9).
10. Spreading of waste on land resulting in benefit to agriculture or ecological improvement, including composting and other biological transformation processes, except in the case of waste excluded under Article 2(1)(b)(iii) of the Directive (R10).
11. Use of wastes obtained from any of the operations listed in paragraphs 1 to 10 of this Part of this Schedule (R11).
12. Exchange of wastes for submission to any of the operations listed in paragraphs 1 to 11 of this Part of this Schedule (R12).
13. Storage of waste consisting of materials intended for submission to any operation listed in this Part of this Schedule, but excluding temporary storage, pending collection, on the site where it is produced (R13).

(Note:—the reference in brackets at the end of each paragraph of this Part of this Schedule is the number of the corresponding paragraph in Annex IIB to the Directive.)

Conservation (Natural Habitats, etc.) Regulations 1994

(SI 1994, No. 2716) (as amended)

PART I INTRODUCTORY PROVISIONS

1 Citation and commencement

(1) ...

(2) These Regulations shall come into force on the tenth day after that on which they are made.

2 Interpretation and application

(1) In these Regulations—

'agriculture Minister' means the Minister of Agriculture, Fisheries and Food or the Secretary of State;

'competent authority' shall be construed in accordance with regulation 6;

'destroy', in relation to an egg, includes doing anything to the egg which is calculated to prevent it from hatching, and 'destruction' shall be construed accordingly;

'enactment' includes a local enactment and an enactment contained in subordinate legislation within the meaning of the Interpretation Act 1978;

'European site' has the meaning given by regulation 10 and 'European marine site' means a European site which consists of, or so far as it consists of, marine areas;

'functions' includes powers and duties;

['the Habitats Directive' means Council Directive 92/43/EEC on the conservation of natural habitats and of wild fauna and flora as amended by the Act of Accession to the European Union of Austria, Finland and Sweden and by Council Directive 97/62/EC);]

'land' includes land covered by water and as respects Scotland includes salmon fishings;

'livestock' includes any animal which is kept—

(a) for the provision of food, skins or fur,

(b) for the purpose of its use in the carrying on of any agricultural activity, or

(c) for the provision or improvement of shooting or fishing;

'local planning authority' means—

(a) in England and Wales, except as otherwise provided, any authority having any function as a local planning authority or mineral planning authority under the Town and Country Planning Act 1990, and

(b) . . .

'management agreement' means an agreement entered into, or having effect as if entered into, under regulation 16;

'marine area' means any land covered (continuously or intermittently) by tidal waters or any part of the sea in or adjacent to Great Britain up to the seaward limit of territorial waters;

'Natura 2000' means the European network of special areas of conservation, and special protection areas under the Wild Birds Directive, provided for by Article 3(1) of the Habitats Directive;

'nature conservation body', and 'appropriate nature conservation body' in relation to England, Wales or Scotland, have the meaning given by regulation 4;

'occupier', for the purposes of Part III (protection of species), includes, in relation to any land other than the foreshore, any person having any right of hunting, shooting, fishing or taking game or fish;

. . .

'the register' means the register of European sites in Great Britain provided for by regulation 11;

'relevant authorities', in relation to marine areas and European marine sites, shall be construed in accordance with regulation 5;

'statutory undertaker' has the same meaning as in the National Parks and Access to the Countryside Act 1949;

'the Wild Birds Directive' means Council Directive 79/409/EEC on the conservation of wild birds.

(2) Unless the context otherwise requires, expressions used in these Regulations and in the Habitats Directive have the same meaning as in that Directive.

The following expressions, in particular, are defined in Article 1 of that Directive—

'priority natural habitat types' and 'priority species';

'site' and 'site of Community importance'; and

'special area of conservation'.

(3) In these Regulations, unless otherwise indicated—

(a) any reference to a numbered regulation or Schedule is to the regulation or Schedule in these Regulations which bears that number, and

(b) any reference in a regulation or Schedule to a numbered paragraph is to the paragraph of that regulation or Schedule which bears that number.

(4) . . .

(5) For the purposes of these Regulations the territorial waters of the United Kingdom adjacent to Great Britain shall be treated as part of Great Britain and references to England,

Wales and Scotland shall be construed as including the adjacent territorial waters.

For the purposes of this paragraph—

(a) territorial waters include any waters landward of the baselines from which the breadth of the territorial sea is measured; and

(b) any question as to whether territorial waters are to be treated as adjacent to England, Wales or Scotland shall be determined by the Secretary of State or, for any purpose in relation to which the Minister of Agriculture, Fisheries and Food has responsibility, by the Secretary of State and that Minister acting jointly.

3 Implementation of Directive

(1) These Regulations make provision for the purpose of implementing, for Great Britain, ['the Habitats Directive'].

(2) The Secretary of State, the Minister of Agriculture, Fisheries and Food and the nature conservation bodies shall exercise their functions under the enactments relating to nature conservation so as to secure compliance with the requirements of the Habitats Directive.

Those enactments include—

Part III of the National Parks and Access to the Countryside Act 1949, section 49A of the Countryside (Scotland) Act 1967 (management agreements), section 15 of the Countryside Act 1968 (areas of special scientific interest), Part I and sections 28 to 38 of the Wildlife and Countryside Act 1981, sections 131 to 134 of the Environmental Protection Act 1990, sections 2, 3, 5, 6, 7 and 11 of the Natural Heritage (Scotland) Act 1991, [Part 1 of the Land Reform (Scotland) Act 2003 (asp2) (access rights)] and these Regulations.

(3) In relation to marine areas any competent authority having functions relevant to marine conservation shall exercise those functions so as to secure compliance with the requirements of the Habitats Directive.

This applies, in particular, to functions under the following enactments—

the Sea Fisheries Acts within the meaning of section 1 of the Sea Fisheries (Wildlife Conservation) Act 1992,

the Dockyard Ports Regulation Act 1865,

section 2(2) of the Military Lands Act 1900 (provisions as to use of sea, tidal water or shore),

the Harbours Act 1964,

Part II of the Control of Pollution Act 1974,

sections 36 and 37 of the Wildlife and Countryside Act 1981 (marine nature reserves),

sections 120 to 122 of the Civic Government (Scotland) Act 1982 (control of the seashore, adjacent waters and inland waters),

the Water Resources Act 1991,

the Land Drainage Act 1991, and

these Regulations.

(4) Without prejudice to the preceding provisions, every competent authority in the exercise of any of their functions, shall have regard to the requirements of the Habitats Directive so far as they may be affected by the exercise of those functions.

4 Nature conservation bodies

In these Regulations 'nature conservation body' means [Natural England], the Countryside Council for Wales or Scottish Natural Heritage; and references to 'the appropriate nature conservation body', in relation to England, Wales or Scotland, shall be construed accordingly.

5 Relevant authorities in relation to marine areas and European marine sites

For the purposes of these Regulations the relevant authorities, in relation to a marine area or European marine site, are such of the following as have functions in relation to land or waters within or adjacent to that area or site—

(a) a nature conservation body;

(b) a county council, [county council borough], district council, London borough council or, in Scotland, a regional, islands or district council;

(c) the [Environment Agency,] a water undertaker or sewerage undertaker, or an internal drainage board;
(d) a navigation authority within the meaning of the Water Resources Act 1991;
(e) a harbour authority within the meaning of the Harbours Act 1964;
(f) a lighthouse authority;
(g) a river purification board or a district salmon fishery board;
(h) a local fisheries committee constituted under the Sea Fisheries Regulation Act 1966 or any authority exercising the powers of such a committee.

6 Competent authorities generally

(1) For the purposes of these Regulations the expression 'competent authority' includes any Minister, government department, public or statutory undertaker, public body of any description or person holding a public office.

The expression also includes any person exercising any function of a competent authority in the United Kingdom.

(2) In paragraph (1)—
(a) 'public body' includes any local authority, joint board or joint committee; and
(b) 'public office' means—
(a) an office under Her Majesty,
(b) an office created or continued in existence by a public general Act of Parliament, or
(c) an office the remuneration in respect of which is paid out of money provided by Parliament [or money paid out of the Scottish Consolidated Fund].

(3) In paragraph (2)(a)—
'local authority'—
(a) in relation to England, means a county council, district council or London borough council, the Common Council of the City of London, the sub-treasurer of the Inner Temple, the under-treasurer of the Middle Temple or a parish council,
(b) in relation to Wales, means a county council, [county borough] council or community council, and
(c) in relation to Scotland, means a regional, islands or district council;
'joint board' and 'joint committee' in relation to England and Wales mean—
(a) a joint or special planning board constituted for a National Park by order under paragraph 1 or 3 of Schedule 17 to the Local Government Act 1972 or a joint planning board within the meaning of section 2 of the Town and Country Planning Act 1990, and
(b) a joint committee appointed under section 102(1)(b) of the Local Government Act 1972,

and in relation to Scotland have the same meaning as in the Local Government (Scotland) Act 1973.

PART II CONSERVATION OF NATURAL HABITATS AND HABITATS OF SPECIES

European sites

7 Selection of sites eligible for identification as of Community importance

(1) On the basis of the criteria set out in Annex III (Stage 1) to the Habitats Directive, and relevant scientific information, the Secretary of State shall propose a list of sites indicating with respect to each site—
(a) which natural habitat types in Annex I to the Directive the site hosts, and
(b) which species in Annex II to the Directive that are native to Great Britain the site hosts.

(2) For animal species ranging over wide areas these sites shall correspond to the places within the natural range of such species which present the physical or biological factors essential to their life and reproduction.

For aquatic species which range over wide areas, such sites shall be proposed only where there is a clearly identifiable area representing the physical and biological factors essential to their life and reproduction.

(3) Where appropriate the Secretary of State may propose modification of the list in the light of the results of the surveillance referred to in Article 11 of the Habitats Directive.

(4) The list shall be transmitted to the Commission on or before 5th June 1995, together with information on each site including—

(a) a map of the site,

(b) its name, location and extent, and

(c) the data resulting from application of the criteria specified in Annex III (Stage 1), provided in a format established by the Commission.

8 Adoption of list of sites: designation of special areas of conservation

(1) Once a site of Community importance in Great Britain has been adopted in accordance with the procedure laid down in paragraph 2 of Article 4 of the Habitats Directive, the Secretary of State shall designate that site as a special area of conservation as soon as possible and within six years at most.

(2) The Secretary of State shall establish priorities for the designation of sites in the light of—

(a) the importance of the sites for the maintenance or restoration at a favourable conservation status of—

(i) a natural habitat type in Annex I to the Habitats Directive, or

(ii) a species in Annex II to the Directive, and for the coherence of Natura 2000; and

(b) the threats of degradation or destruction to which those sites are exposed.

9 Consultation as to inclusion of site omitted from the list

If consultation is initiated by the Commission in accordance with Article 5(1) of the Habitats Directive with respect to a site in Great Britain hosting a priority natural habitat type or priority species and—

(a) the Secretary of State agrees that the site should be added to the list transmitted in accordance with regulation 7, or

(b) the Council, acting on a proposal from the Commission in pursuance of paragraph 2 of Article 5 of the Habitats Directive, so decides,

the site shall be treated as added to the list as from the date of that agreement or decision.

10 Meaning of 'European site' in these Regulations

(1) In these Regulations a 'European site' means—

(a) a special area of conservation,

(b) a site of Community importance which has been placed on the list referred to in the third sub-paragraph of Article 4(2) of the Habitats Directive,

(c) a site hosting a priority natural habitat type or priority species in respect of which consultation has been initiated under Article 5(1) of the Habitats Directive, during the consultation period or pending a decision of the Council under Article 5(3),

(d) an area classified pursuant to Article 4(1) or (2) of the Wild Birds Directive, [or

(e) a site in England included in the list of sites which has been proposed by the Secretary of State and transmitted to the Commission under regulation 7 until such time as—

(i) the draft list of sites of Community importance is established under the first sub-paragraph of Article 4(2) of the Habitats Directive where in any case the site is not included in that list, or

(ii) the list of sites referred to in the third sub-paragraph of Article 4(2) of the Habitats Directive is adopted by the Commission in accordance with that sub-paragraph].

(2) Sites which are European sites by virtue only of paragraph (1)(c) are not within regulations 20(1) and (2), 24 and 48 (which relate to the approval of certain plans and projects); but this is without prejudice to their protection under other provisions of these Regulations.

Register of European sites

11 Duty to compile and maintain register of European sites

(1) The Secretary of State shall compile and maintain, in such form as he thinks fit, a register of European sites in Great Britain.

(2) He shall include in the register—

(a) special areas of conservation, as soon as they are designated by him;

(b) sites of Community importance as soon as they are placed on the list referred to in the third sub-paragraph of Article 4(2) of the Habitats Directive, until they are designated as special areas of conservation;

(c) any site hosting a priority natural habitat type or priority species in respect of which consultation is initiated under Article 5(1) of the Habitats Directive, during the consultation period or pending a Council decision under Article 5(3);

(d) areas classified by him pursuant to Article 4(1) or (2) of the Wild Birds Directive, as soon as they are so classified or, if they have been classified before the commencement of these Regulations, as soon as practicable after commencement [; and

(e) any site in England included in the list of sites which has been proposed by the Secretary of State and transmitted to the Commission under regulation 7 until such time as paragraph (i) or paragraph (ii) of regulation 10(1)(e) applies.]

(3) He may, if appropriate, amend the entry in the register relating to a European site.

(4) He shall remove the relevant entry—

(a) if a special area of conservation is declassified by the Commission under Article 9 of the Habitats Directive; or

(b) if a site otherwise ceases to fall within any of the categories listed in paragraph (2) above.

(5) He shall keep a copy of the register available for public inspection at all reasonable hours and free of charge.

12 Notification to appropriate nature conservation body

(1) The Secretary of State shall notify the appropriate nature conservation body as soon as may be after including a site in the register, amending an entry in the register or removing an entry from the register.

(2) Notification of the inclusion of a site in the register shall be accompanied by a copy of the register entry.

(3) Notification of the amendment of an entry in the register shall be accompanied by a copy of the amended entry.

(4) Each nature conservation body shall keep copies of the register entries relating to European sites in their area available for public inspection at all reasonable hours and free of charge.

13 Notice to landowners, relevant authorities, &c.

(1) As soon as practicable after a nature conservation body receive notification under regulation 12 they shall give notice to—

(a) every owner or occupier of land within the site,

(b) every local planning authority in whose area the site, or any part of it, is situated, and

(c) such other persons or bodies as the Secretary of State may direct.

(2) Notice of the inclusion of a site in the register, or of the amendment of an entry in the register, shall be accompanied by a copy of so much of the relevant register entry as relates to land owned or occupied by or, as the case may be, to land within the area of, the person or authority to whom the notice is given.

(3) The Secretary of State may give directions as to the form and content of notices to be given under this regulation.

14 Local registration: England and Wales

An entry in the register relating to a European site in England and Wales is a local land charge.

. . .

Management agreements

16 Management agreements

(1) The appropriate nature conservation body may enter into an agreement (a 'management agreement') with every owner, lessee and occupier of land forming part of a European site, or land adjacent to such a site, for the management, conservation, restoration or protection of the site, or any part of it.

(2) A management agreement may impose such restrictions as may be expedient for the purposes of the agreement on the exercise of rights over the land by the persons who can be bound by the agreement.

(3) A management agreement—

(a) may provide for the management of the land in such manner, the carrying out thereon of such work and the doing thereon of such other things as may be expedient for the purposes of the agreement;

(b) may provide for any of the matters mentioned in sub-paragraph (a) being carried out, or for the costs thereof being defrayed, either by the said owner or other persons or by the appropriate nature conservation body, or partly in one way and partly in another;

(c) may contain such other provisions as to the making of payments by the appropriate nature conservation body, and in particular for the payment by them of compensation for the effect of the restrictions mentioned in paragraph (2), as may be specified in the agreement.

(4) Where land in England and Wales is subject to a management agreement, the appropriate nature conservation body shall, as respects the enforcement of the agreement against persons other than the original contracting party, have the like rights as if—

(a) they had at all material times been the absolute owners in possession of ascertained land adjacent to the land subject to the agreement and capable of being benefited by the agreement, and

(b) the management agreement had been expressed to be for the benefit of that adjacent land;

and section 84 of the Law of Property Act 1925 (which enables the Lands Tribunal to discharge or modify restrictive covenants) shall not apply to the agreement.

(5) . . .

17 Continuation in force of existing agreement, etc.

(1) Any agreement previously entered into under—

(a) section 16 of the National Parks and Access to the Countryside Act 1949 (nature reserves),

(b) section 15 of the Countryside Act 1968 (areas of special scientific interest),

(c) section 49A of the Countryside (Scotland) Act 1967 (management agreements),

in relation to land which on or after the commencement of these Regulations becomes land within a European site or adjacent to such a site, shall have effect as if entered into under regulation 16 above.

Regulation 32(1)(b) (power of compulsory acquisition in case of breach of agreement) shall apply accordingly.

(2) Any other thing done or deemed to have been done under any provision of Part III or VI of the National Parks and Access to the Countryside Act 1949, or under section 49A of the Countryside (Scotland) Act 1967, in respect of any land prior to that land becoming land within a European site, or adjacent to such a site, shall continue to have effect as if done under the corresponding provision of these Regulations.

For the purposes of this paragraph Part III of the 1949 Act shall be deemed to include section 15 of the Countryside Act 1968 and anything done or deemed to be done under that section and to which this paragraph applies shall have effect as if done or deemed to be done under section 16 of the 1949 Act.

(3) Any reference in an outlying enactment to a nature reserve within the meaning of section 15 of the National Parks and Access to the Countryside Act 1949 shall be construed as including a European site.

For this purpose an 'outlying enactment' means an enactment not contained in, or in an instrument made under, the National Parks and Access to the Countryside Act 1949 or the Wildlife and Countryside Act 1981.

Control of potentially damaging operations

18 Notification of potentially damaging operations

(1) Any notification in force in relation to a European site under section 28 of the Wildlife and Countryside Act 1981 (areas of special scientific interest) specifying—

(a) the flora, fauna, or geological or physiographical features by reason of which the land is of special interest, and

(b) any operations appearing to the appropriate nature conservation body to be likely to damage that flora or fauna or those features,

shall have effect for the purposes of these Regulations.

(2) The appropriate nature conservation body may, for the purpose of securing compliance with the requirements of the Habitats Directive, at any time amend the notification with respect to any of the matters mentioned in paragraph (1)(a) or (b).

(3) Notice of any amendment shall be given—

(a) to every owner and occupier of land within the site who in the opinion of the appropriate nature conservation body may be affected by the amendment, and

(b) to the local planning authority; and the amendment shall come into force in relation to an owner or occupier upon such notice being given to him.

(4) The provisions of—

(a) section 28(11) of the Wildlife and Countryside Act 1981 (notification to be local land charge in England and Wales), and

(b) section 28(12) to (12B) of that Act (local registration of notification in Scotland),

apply, with the necessary modifications, in relation to an amendment of a notification under this regulation as in relation to the original notification.

19 Restriction on carrying out operations specified in notification

(1) The owner or occupier of any land within a European site shall not carry out, or cause or permit to be carried out, on that land any operation specified in a notification in force in relation to the site under regulation 18, unless—

(a) one of them has given the appropriate nature conservation body written notice of a proposal to carry out the operation, specifying its nature and the land on which it is proposed to carry it out, and

(b) one of the conditions specified in paragraph (2) is fulfilled.

(2) Those conditions are—

(a) that the operation is carried out with the written consent of the appropriate nature conservation body;

(b) that the operation is carried out in accordance with the terms of a management agreement;

(c) that four months have expired from the giving of the notice under paragraph (1)(a).

(3) A person who, without reasonable excuse, contravenes paragraph (1) commits an offence and is liable on summary conviction to a fine not exceeding level 4 on the standard scale.

(4) For the purposes of paragraph (3) it is a reasonable excuse for a person to carry out an operation—

(a) that the operation was an emergency operation particulars of which (including details of the emergency) were notified to the appropriate nature conservation body as soon as practicable after the commencement of the operation; or

(b) that the operation was authorised by a planning permission granted on an application under Part III of the Town and Country Planning Act 1990 or Part III of the Town and Country Planning (Scotland) Act 1972.

(5) The appropriate nature conservation body has power to enforce this regulation; but nothing in this paragraph shall be construed as authorising the institution of proceedings in Scotland for an offence.

(6) Proceedings in England and Wales for an offence under this regulation shall not, without the consent of the Director of Public Prosecutions, be taken by a person other than the appropriate nature conservation body.

20 Supplementary provisions as to consents

(1) Where it appears to the appropriate nature conservation body that an application for consent under regulation 19(2)(a) relates to an operation which is or forms part of a plan or project which—

(a) is not directly connected with or necessary to the management of the site, and

(b) is likely to have a significant effect on the site (either alone or in combination with other plans or projects),

they shall make an appropriate assessment of the implications for the site in view of that site's conservation objectives.

(2) In the light of the conclusions of the assessment, they may give consent for the operation only after having ascertained that the plan or project will not adversely affect the integrity of the site.

(3) The above provisions do not apply in relation to a site which is a European site by reason only of regulation 10(1)(c) (site protected in accordance with Article 5(4)).

(4) Where in any case, whether in pursuance of this regulation or otherwise, the appropriate nature conservation body have not given consent for an operation, but they consider that there is a risk that the operation may nevertheless be carried out, they shall notify the Secretary of State.

(5) They shall take such steps as are requisite to secure that any such notification is given at least one month before the expiry of the period mentioned in regulation 19(2)(c) (period after which operation may be carried out in absence of consent).

21 Provision as to existing notices and consents

(1) Any notice or consent previously given under section 28(5)(a) or (6)(a) of the Wildlife and Countryside Act 1981 in relation to land which on or after the commencement of these Regulations becomes land within a European site shall have effect, subject as follows, as if given under regulation 19(1)(a) or (2)(a) above.

(2) The appropriate nature conservation body shall review any such consent as regards its compatibility with the conservation objectives of the site, and may modify or withdraw it.

(3) Notice of any such modification or withdrawal of consent shall be given to every owner and occupier of land within the site who in the opinion of the appropriate nature conservation body may be affected by it; and the modification or withdrawal shall come into force in relation to an owner or occupier upon such notice being given to him.

(4) The modification or withdrawal of a consent shall not affect anything done in reliance on the consent before the modification or withdrawal takes effect.

(5) Where or to the extent that an operation ceases to be covered by a consent by reason of the consent being modified or withdrawn, the period after which in accordance with regulation 19(2)(c) the operation may be carried out in the absence of consent shall be four months from the giving of notice of the modification or withdrawal under paragraph (3) above.

(6) Regulation 20(4) and (5) (provisions as to notification of Secretary of State) apply in such a case, with the following modifications—

(a) for the reference to consent not having been given substitute a reference to consent being modified or withdrawn;

(b) for the reference to the period specified in regulation 19(2)(c) substitute a reference to the period specified in paragraph (5) above.

Special nature conservation orders

22 Power to make special nature conservation order

(1) The Secretary of State may, after consultation with the appropriate nature conservation body, make in respect of any land within a European site an order (a 'special nature conservation order') specifying operations which appear to him to be likely to destroy or damage the flora, fauna, or geological or physiographical features by reason of which the land is a European site.

(2) A special nature conservation order may be amended or revoked by a further order.

(3) Schedule 1 has effect with respect to the making, confirmation and coming into operation of special nature conservation orders and amending or revoking orders.

(4) A special nature conservation order in relation to land in England and Wales is a local land charge.

(5) ...

(6) A report submitted by a nature conservation body to the Secretary of State under paragraph 20 of Schedule 6 to the Environmental Protection Act 1990... shall set out particulars of any land in their area as respects which a special nature conservation order has come into operation during the year to which the report relates.

23 Restriction on carrying out operations specified in order

(1) No person shall carry out on any land within a European site in respect of which a special nature conservation order is in force any operation specified in the order unless the operation is carried out, or caused or permitted to be carried out, by the owner or occupier of the land and—

(a) one of them has, after the making of the order, given the appropriate nature conservation body written notice of a proposal to carry out the operation specifying its nature and the land on which it is proposed to carry it out, and

(b) one of the conditions specified in paragraph (2) is fulfilled.

(2) Those conditions are—

(a) that the operation is carried out with the written consent of the appropriate nature conservation body;

(b) that the operation is carried out in accordance with the terms of a management agreement.

(3) A person who, without reasonable excuse, contravenes paragraph (1) commits an offence and is liable—

(a) on summary conviction, to a fine not exceeding the statutory maximum;

(b) on conviction on indictment, to a fine.

(4) For the purposes of paragraph (3) it is a reasonable excuse for a person to carry out an operation—

(a) that the operation was an emergency operation particulars of which (including details of the emergency) were notified to the appropriate nature conservation body as soon as practicable after the commencement of the operation; or

(b) that the operation was authorised by a planning permission granted on an application under Part III of the Town and Country Planning Act 1990...

24 Supplementary provisions as to consents

(1) Where it appears to the appropriate nature conservation body that an application for consent under regulation 23(2)(a) relates to an operation which is or forms part of a plan or project which—

(a) is not directly connected with or necessary to the management of the site, and

(b) is likely to have a significant effect on the site (either alone or in combination with other plans or projects),

they shall make an appropriate assessment of the implications for the site in view of that site's conservation objectives.

(2) In the light of the conclusions of the assessment, they may give consent for the operation only after having ascertained that the plan or project will not adversely affect the integrity of the site.

(3) Where the appropriate nature conservation body refuse consent in accordance with paragraph (2) they shall give reasons for their decision.

(4) The owner or occupier of the land in question may—

(a) within two months of receiving notice of the refusal of consent, or

(b) if no notice of a decision is received by him within three months of an application for consent being made,

by notice in writing to the appropriate nature conservation body require them to refer the matter forthwith to the Secretary of State.

(5) If on the matter being referred to the Secretary of State he is satisfied that, there being no alternative solutions, the plan or project must be carried out for imperative reasons of overriding public interest (which, subject to paragraph (6), may be of a social or economic nature), he may direct the appropriate nature conservation body to give consent to the operation.

(6) Where the site concerned hosts a priority natural habitat type or a priority species, the reasons referred to in paragraph (5) must be either—

(a) reasons relating to human health, public safety or beneficial consequences of primary importance to the environment, or

(b) other reasons which in the opinion of the European Commission are imperative reasons of overriding public interest.

(7) Where the Secretary of State directs the appropriate nature conservation body to give consent under this regulation, he shall secure that such compensatory measures are taken as are necessary to ensure that the overall coherence of Natura 2000 is protected.

(8) This regulation does not apply in relation to a site which is a European site by reason only of regulation 10(1)(c) (site protected in accordance with Article 5(4)).

25 Compensation for effect of order

(1) Where a special nature conservation order is made, the appropriate nature conservation body shall pay compensation to any person having at the time of the making of the order an interest in land comprised in an agricultural unit comprising land to which the order relates who, on a claim made to the appropriate nature conservation body within the time and in the manner prescribed by regulations, shows that the value of his interest is less than it would have been if the order had not been made.

(2) For this purpose an 'agricultural unit' means land which is occupied as a unit for agricultural purposes, including any dwelling-house or other building occupied by the same person for the purpose of farming the land.

(3) No claim for compensation shall be made under this regulation in respect of an order unless the Secretary of State has given notice under paragraph 6(1) or (2) of Schedule 1 of his decision in respect of the order.

26 Restoration where order contravened

(1) Where a person is convicted of an offence under regulation 23, the court by which he is convicted may, in addition to dealing with him in any other way, make an order requiring him to carry out, within such period as may be specified in the order, such operations for the purpose of restoring the land to its former condition as may be so specified.

(2) An order under this regulation made on conviction on indictment shall be treated for the purposes of section 30 of the Criminal Appeal Act 1968; (effect of appeals on orders for the restitution of property) as an order for the restitution of property.

(3) In the case of an order under this regulation made by a magistrates' court the period specified in the order shall not begin to run—

(a) in any case until the expiration of the period for the time being prescribed by law for the giving of notice of appeal against a decision of a magistrates' court;

(b) where notice of appeal is given within the period so prescribed, until determination of the appeal.

(4) At any time before an order under this regulation has been complied with or fully complied with, the court by which it was made may, on the application of the person against whom it was made, discharge or vary the order if it appears to the court that a change in circumstances has made compliance or full compliance with the order impracticable or unnecessary.

(5) If a person fails without reasonable excuse to comply with an order under this regulation, he commits an offence and is liable on summary conviction to a fine not exceeding level 5 on the standard scale; and if the failure continues after conviction, he may be proceeded against for a further offence from time to time until the order is complied with.

(6) If, within the period specified in an order under this regulation, any operations specified in the order have not been carried out, the appropriate nature conservation body may enter the land and carry out those operations and recover from the person against whom the order was made any expenses reasonably incurred by them in doing so.

(7) . . .

27 Continuation in force of existing orders, etc.

(1) Where an order is in force under section 29 of the Wildlife and Countryside Act 1981 (special protection for certain areas of special scientific interest) in relation to land which on or after the commencement of these Regulations becomes land within a European site, the order shall have effect as if made under regulation 22 above.

(2) Any notice previously given under section 29(4)(a) (notice by owner or occupier of proposal to carry out operation) shall have effect as if given under regulation 23(1)(a) and, if the appropriate nature conservation body have neither given nor refused consent, shall be dealt with under these Regulations.

(3) Any consent previously given under section 29(5)(a) shall be reviewed by the appropriate nature conservation body as regards its compatibility with the conservation objectives of the site, and may be modified or withdrawn.

(4) Notice of any such modification or withdrawal of consent shall be given to every owner and occupier of land within the site who in the opinion of the appropriate nature conservation body may be affected by it; and the modification or withdrawal shall come into force in relation to an owner or occupier upon such notice being given to him.

(5) The modification or withdrawal of a consent shall not affect anything done in reliance on the consent before the modification or withdrawal takes effect.

(6) Section 29(5)(c), (6) and (7) shall cease to apply and the carrying out, or continuation, of any operation on land within a European site which is not otherwise authorised in accordance with these Regulations shall be subject to the prohibition in regulation 23(1).

Byelaws

28 Power to make byelaws

(1) The appropriate nature conservation body may make byelaws for the protection of a European site under section 20 of the National Parks and Access to the Countryside Act 1949 (byelaws for protection of nature reserves).

(2) Without prejudice to the generality of paragraph (1), byelaws under that section as it applies by virtue of this regulation may make provision of any of the following kinds.

(3) They may—

(a) provide for prohibiting or restricting the entry into, or movement within, the site of persons, vehicles, boats and animals;

(b) prohibit or restrict the killing, taking, molesting or disturbance of living creatures of any description in the site, the taking, destruction or disturbance of eggs of any such creature, the taking of, or interference with, vegetation of any description in the site, or the doing of anything in the site which will interfere with the soil or damage any object in the site;

(c) contain provisions prohibiting the depositing of rubbish and the leaving of litter in the site;

(d) prohibit or restrict, or provide for prohibiting or restricting, the lighting of fires in the site or the doing of anything likely to cause a fire in the site.

(4) They may prohibit or restrict any activity referred to in paragraph (3) within such area surrounding or adjoining the site as appears to the appropriate nature conservation body requisite for the protection of the site.

(5) They may provide for the issue, on such terms and subject to such conditions as may be specified in the byelaws, of permits authorising—

(a) entry into the site or any such surrounding or adjoining area as mentioned in paragraph (4), or

(b) the doing of anything within the site, or any such surrounding or adjoining area, where such entry, or doing that thing, would otherwise be unlawful under the byelaws.

(6) They may be made so as to relate either to the whole or to any part of the site, or of any such surrounding or adjoining area as is mentioned in paragraph (4), and may make different provision for different parts thereof.

(7) This regulation does not apply in relation to a European marine site (but see regulation 36).

29 Byelaws: limitation on effect

Byelaws under section 20 of the National Parks and Access to the Countryside Act 1949 as it applies by virtue of regulation 28 shall not interfere with—

(a) the exercise by any person of a right vested in him as owner, lessee or occupier of land in the European site, or in any such surrounding or adjoining area as is mentioned in paragraph (4) of that regulation;

(b) the exercise of any public right of way;

(c) the exercise of any functions of statutory undertakers;

(d) the exercise of any functions of an internal drainage board, a district salmon fishery board or the Commissioners appointed under the Tweed Fisheries Act 1969; or

[(e) the provision of an electronic communications code network or the exercise of any right conferred by or in accordance with the electronic communications code on the provider of any such network.]

30 Compensation for effect of byelaws

Where the exercise of any right vested in a person, whether by reason of his being entitled to any interest in land or by virtue of a licence or agreement, is prevented or hindered by the coming into operation of byelaws under section 20 of the National Parks and Access to the Countryside Act 1949 as it applies by virtue of regulation 28, he shall be entitled to receive from the appropriate nature conservation body compensation in respect thereof.

31 Continuation in force of existing byelaws

Any byelaws in force under section 20 of the National Parks and Access to the Countryside Act 1949 in relation to land which on or after the commencement of these Regulations becomes land within a European site, or adjacent to such a site, shall have effect as if made under the said section 20 as it applies by virtue of regulation 28 and shall be construed as if originally so made.

Powers of compulsory acquisition

32 Powers of compulsory acquisition

(1) Where the appropriate nature conservation body are satisfied—

(a) that they are unable, as respects any interest in land within a European site, to conclude a management agreement on terms appearing to them to be reasonable, or

(b) where they have entered into a management agreement as respects such an interest, that a breach of the agreement has occurred which prevents or impairs the satisfactory management of the European site,

they may acquire that interest compulsorily.

(2) Such a breach as is mentioned in paragraph (1)(b) shall not be treated as having occurred by virtue of any act or omission capable of remedy unless there has been default in remedying it within a reasonable time after notice given by the appropriate nature conservation body requiring the remedying thereof.

(3) Any dispute arising whether there has been such a breach of a management agreement shall be determined—

(a) in the case of land in England and Wales, by an arbitrator appointed by the Lord Chancellor;

(b) …

Special provisions as to European marine sites

33 Marking of site and advice by nature conservation bodies

(1) The appropriate nature conservation body may install markers indicating the existence and extent of a European marine site.

This power is exercisable subject to the obtaining of any necessary consent under section 34 of the Coast Protection Act 1949 (restriction of works detrimental to navigation).

(2) As soon as possible after a site becomes a European marine site, the appropriate nature conservation body shall advise other relevant authorities as to—

(a) the conservation objectives for that site, and

(b) any operations which may cause deterioration of natural habitats or the habitats of species, or disturbance of species, for which the site has been designated.

34 Management scheme for European marine site

(1) The relevant authorities, or any of them, may establish for a European marine site a management scheme under which their functions (including any power to make byelaws) shall be exercised so as to secure in relation to that site compliance with the requirements of the Habitats Directive.

(2) Only one management scheme may be made for each European marine site.

(3) A management scheme may be amended from time to time.

(4) As soon as a management scheme has been established, or is amended, a copy of it shall be sent by the relevant authority or authorities concerned to the appropriate nature conservation body.

35 Direction to establish or amend management scheme

(1) The relevant Minister may give directions to the relevant authorities, or any of them, as to the establishment of a management scheme for a European marine site.

(2) Directions may, in particular—

(a) require conservation measures specified in the direction to be included in the scheme;

(b) appoint one of the relevant authorities to co-ordinate the establishment of the scheme;

(c) set time limits within which any steps are to be taken;

(d) provide that the approval of the Minister is required before the scheme is established; and

(e) require any relevant authority to supply to the Minister such information concerning the establishment of the scheme as may be specified in the direction.

(3) The relevant Minister may give directions to the relevant authorities, or any of them, as to the amendment of a management scheme for a European marine site, either generally or in any particular respect.

(4) Any direction under this regulation shall be in writing and may be varied or revoked by a further direction.

(5) In this regulation 'the relevant Minister' means, in relation to a site in England, the Secretary of State and the Minister of Agriculture, Fisheries and Food acting jointly and in any other case the Secretary of State.

36 Byelaws for protection of European marine site

(1) The appropriate nature conservation body may make byelaws for the protection of a European marine site under section 37 of the Wildlife and Countryside Act 1981 (byelaws for protection of marine nature reserves).

(2) The provisions of subsections (2) to (11) of that section apply in relation to byelaws made by virtue of this regulation with the substitution for the references to marine nature reserves of references to European marine sites.

(3) Nothing in byelaws made by virtue of this regulation shall interfere with the exercise of any functions of a relevant authority, any functions conferred by or under an enactment (whenever passed) or any right of any person (whenever vested).

Miscellaneous

37 Nature conservation policy in planning contexts

(1) For the purposes of the planning enactments mentioned below, policies in respect of the conservation of the natural beauty and amenity of the land shall be taken to include policies encouraging the management of features of the landscape which are of major importance for wild flora and fauna.

Such features are those which, by virtue of their linear and continuous structure (such as rivers with their banks or the traditional systems of marking field boundaries) or their function as stepping stones (such as ponds or small woods), are essential for the migration, dispersal and genetic exchange of wild species.

(2) The enactments referred to in paragraph (1) are—

(a) in the Town and Country Planning Act 1990, section 12(3A) (unitary development plans), section 31(3) (structure plans) and section 36(3) (local plans);

(b) . . .

PART III PROTECTION OF SPECIES

Protection of animals

38 European protected species of animals

The species of animals listed in Annex IV(a) to the Habitats Directive whose natural range includes any area in Great Britain are listed in Schedule 2 to these Regulations.

References in these Regulations to a 'European protected species' of animal are to any of those species.

39 Protection of wild animals of European protected species

(1) It is an offence—

(a) deliberately to capture or kill a wild animal of a European protected species;

(b) deliberately to disturb any such animal;

(c) deliberately to take or destroy the eggs of such an animal; or

(d) to damage or destroy a breeding site or resting place of such an animal.

(2) It is an offence to keep, transport, sell or exchange, or offer for sale or exchange, any live or dead wild animal of a European protected species, or any part of, or anything derived from, such an animal.

(3) Paragraphs (1) and (2) apply to all stages of the life of the animals to which they apply.

(4) A person shall not be guilty of an offence under paragraph (2) if he shows—

(a) that the animal had not been taken or killed, or had been lawfully taken or killed, or

(b) that the animal or other thing in question had been lawfully sold (whether to him or any other person).

For this purpose 'lawfully' means without any contravention of these Regulations or Part I of the Widlife and Countryside Act 1981.

(5) In any proceedings for an offence under this regulation, the animal in question shall be presumed to have been a wild animal unless the contrary is shown.

(6) A person guilty of an offence under this regulation is liable on summary conviction to a fine not exceeding level 5 on the standard scale.

40 Exceptions from regulation 39

(1) Nothing in regulation 39 shall make unlawful—

(a) anything done in pursuance of a requirement by the agriculture Minister under section 98 of the Agriculture Act 1947 or section 39 of the Agriculture (Scotland) Act 1948 (prevention of damage by pests); or

(b) anything done under, or in pursuance of an order made under, the Animal Health Act 1981.

(2) Nothing in regulation 39(1)(b) or (d) shall make unlawful anything done within a dwelling-house.

(3) Notwithstanding anything in regulation 39, a person shall not be guilty of an offence by reason of—

(a) the taking of a wild animal of a European protected species if he shows that the animal had been disabled otherwise than by his unlawful act and was taken solely for the purpose of tending it and releasing it when no longer disabled;

(b) the killing of such an animal if he shows that the animal has been so seriously disabled otherwise than by his unlawful act that there was no reasonable chance of its recovering; or

(c) any act made unlawful by that regulation if he shows that the act was the incidental result of a lawful operation and could not reasonably have been avoided.

(4) A person shall not be entitled to rely on the defence provided by paragraph (2) or (3)(c) as respects anything done in relation to a bat otherwise than in the living area of a dwelling-house unless he had notified the appropriate nature conservation body of the proposed action or operation and allowed them a reasonable time to advise him as to whether it should be carried out and, if so, the method to be used.

(5) Notwithstanding anything in regulation 39 a person—

(a) being the owner or occupier, or any person authorised by the owner or occupier, of the land on which the action authorised is taken, or

(b) authorised by the local authority for the area within which the action authorised is taken, shall not be guilty of an offence by reason of the killing or disturbing of an animal of a European protected species if he shows that his action was necessary for the purpose of preventing, serious damage to livestock, foodstuffs, crops, vegetables, fruit, growing timber or any other form of property or fisheries.

(6) A person may not rely on the defence provided by paragraph (5) as respects action taken at any time if it had become apparent before that time that the action would prove necessary for the purpose mentioned in that paragraph and either—

(a) a licence under regulation 44 authorising that action had not been applied for as soon as reasonably practicable after that fact had become apparent, or

(b) an application for such a licence had been determined.

(7) In paragraph (5) 'local authority' means—

(a) in relation to England and Wales, a county [county borough] district or London borough council and includes the Common Council of the City of London, and

(b) . . .

41 Prohibition of certain methods of taking or killing wild animals

(1) This regulation applies in relation to the taking or killing of a wild animal—

(a) of any of the species listed in Schedule 3 to these Regulations (which shows the species listed in Annex V(a) to the Habitats Directive, and to which Article 15 applies, whose natural range includes any area of Great Britain), or

(b) of a European protected species, where the taking or killing of such animals is permitted in accordance with these Regulations.

(2) It is an offence to use for the purpose of taking or killing any such wild animal—

(a) any of the means listed in paragraph (3) or (4) below, or

(b) any form of taking or killing from the modes of transport listed in paragraph (5) below.

(3) The prohibited means of taking or killing of mammals are—

(a) blind or mutilated animals used as live decoys;

(b) tape recorders;

(c) electrical and electronic devices capable of killing or stunning;

(d) artificial light sources;

(e) mirrors and other dazzling devices;

(f) devices for illuminating targets;

(g) sighting devices for night shooting comprising an electronic image magnifier or image converter;

(h) explosives;

(i) nets which are non-selective according to their principle or their conditions of use;

(j) traps which are non-selective according to their principle or their conditions of use;

(k) crossbows;

(l) poisons and poisoned or anaesthetic bait;

(m) gassing or smoking out;

(n) semi-automatic or automatic weapons with a magazine capable of holding more than two rounds of ammunition.

(4) The prohibited means of taking or killing fish are—

(a) poison;

(b) explosives.

(5) The prohibited modes of transport are—

(a) aircraft;

(b) moving motor vehicles

(6) A person guilty of an offence under this regulation is liable on summary conviction to a fine not exceeding level 5 on the standard scale.

Protection of plants

42 European protected species of plants

The species of plants listed in Annex IV(b) to the Habitats Directive whose natural range includes any area in Great Britain are listed in Schedule 4 to these Regulations.

References in these Regulations to a 'European protected species' of plant are to any of those species.

43 Protection of wild plants of European protected species

(1) It is an offence deliberately to pick, collect, cut, uproot or destroy a wild plant of a European protected species.

(2) It is an offence to keep, transport, sell or exchange, or offer for sale or exchange, any live or dead wild plant of a European protected species, or any part of, or anything derived from, such a plant.

(3) Paragraphs (1) and (2) apply to all stages of the biological cycle of the plants to which they apply.

(4) A person shall not be guilty of an offence under paragraph (1), by reason of any act made unlawful by that paragraph if he shows that the act was an incidental result of a lawful operation and could not reasonably have been avoided.

(5) A person shall not be guilty of an offence under paragraph (2) if he shows that the plant or other thing in question had been lawfully sold (whether to him or any other person).

For this purpose 'lawfully' means without any contravention of these Regulations or Part I of the Wildlife and Countryside Act 1981.

(6) In any proceedings for an offence under this regulation, the plant in question shall be presumed to have been a wild plant unless the contrary is shown.

(7) A person guilty of an offence under this section is liable on summary conviction to a fine not exceeding level 4 on the standard scale.

Power to grant licences

44 Grant of licences for certain purposes

(1) Regulations 39, 41 and 43 do not apply to anything done for any of the following purposes under and in accordance with the terms of a licence granted by the appropriate authority.

(2) The purposes referred to in paragraph (1) are—

(a) scientific or educational purposes;
(b) ringing or marking, or examining any ring or mark on, wild animals;
(c) conserving wild animals or wild plants or introducing them to particular areas;
(d) protecting any zoological or botanical collection;
(e) preserving public health or public safety or other imperative reasons of overriding public interest including those of a social or economic nature and beneficial consequences of primary importance for the environment;
(f) preventing the spread of disease; or
(g) preventing serious damage to livestock, foodstuffs for livestock, crops, vegetables, fruit, growing timber or any other form of property or to fisheries.

(3) The appropriate authority shall not grant a licence under this regulation unless they are satisfied—

(a) that there is no satisfactory alternative, and
(b) that the action authorised will not be detrimental to the maintenance of the population of the species concerned at a favourable conservation status in their natural range.

(4) For the purposes of this regulation 'the appropriate authority' means—

(a) in the case of a licence under any of sub-paragraphs (a) to (d) of paragraph (2), the appropriate nature conservation body; and

(b) in the case of a licence under any of sub-paragraphs (e) to (g) of that paragraph, the agriculture Minister.

(5) The agriculture Minister shall from time to time consult with the nature conservation bodies as to the exercise of his functions under this regulation; and he shall not grant a licence of any description unless he has been advised by the appropriate nature conservation body as to the circumstances in which, in their opinion, licences of that description should be granted.

45 Licences: supplementary provisions

(1) A licence under regulation 44—

(a) may be, to any degree, general or specific;

(b) may be granted either to persons of a class or to a particular person; and

(c) may be subject to compliance with any specified conditions.

(2) For the purposes of a licence under regulation 44 the definition of a class of persons may be framed by reference to any circumstances whatever including, in particular, their being authorised by any other person.

(3) A licence under regulation 44 may be modified or revoked at any time by the appropriate authority; but otherwise shall be valid for the period stated in the licence.

(4) A licence under regulation 44 which authorises any person to kill wild animals shall specify the area within which and the methods by which the wild animals may be killed and shall not be granted for a period of more than two years.

(5) It shall be a defence in proceedings for an offence under section 8(b) of the Protection of Animals Act 1911 or section 7(b) of the Protection of Animals (Scotland) Act 1912 (which restrict the placing on land of poison and poisonous substances) to show that—

(a) the act alleged to constitute the offence was done under and in accordance with the terms of a licence under regulation 44, and

(b) any conditions specified in the licence were complied with.

(6) The appropriate authority may charge for a licence under regulation 44 such reasonable sum (if any) as they may determine.

46 False statements made for obtaining licence

(1) A person commits an offence who, for the purposes of obtaining, whether for himself or another, the grant of a licence under regulation 44—

(a) makes a statement or representation, or furnishes a document or information, which he knows to be false in a material particular, or

(b) recklessly makes a statement or representation, or furnishes a document or information, which is false in a material particular.

(2) A person guilty of an offence under this regulation is liable on summary conviction to a fine not exceeding level 4 on the standard scale.

PART IV ADAPTATION OF PLANNING AND OTHER CONTROLS

Introductory

47 Application of provisions of this Part

(1) The requirements of—

(a) regulations 48 and 49 (requirement to consider effect on European sites), and

(b) regulations 50 and 51 (requirement to review certain existing decisions and consents, etc.),

apply, subject to and in accordance with the provisions of regulations 54 to 85, in relation to the matters specified in those provisions.

(2) Supplementary provision is made by—

(a) regulation 52 (co-ordination where more than one competent authority involved), and

(b) regulation 53 (compensatory measures where plan or project is agreed to notwithstanding a negative assessment of the implications for a European site).

General provisions for protection of European sites

48 Assessment of implications for European site

(1) A competent authority, before deciding to undertake, or give any consent, permission or other authorisation for, a plan or project which—

(a) is likely to have a significant effect on a European site in Great Britain (either alone or in combination with other plans or projects), and

(b) is not directly connected with or necessary to the management of the site, shall make an appropriate assessment of the implications for the site in view of that site's conservation objectives.

(2) A person applying for any such consent, permission or other authorisation shall provide such information as the competent authority may reasonably require for the purposes of the assessment.

(3) The competent authority shall for the purposes of the assessment consult the appropriate nature conservation body and have regard to any representations made by that body within such reasonable time as the authority may specify.

(4) They shall also, if they consider it appropriate, take the opinion of the general public; and if they do so, they shall take such steps for that purpose as they consider appropriate.

(5) In the light of the conclusions of the assessment, and subject to regulation 49, the authority shall agree to the plan or project only after having ascertained that it will not adversely affect the integrity of the European site.

(6) In considering whether a plan or project will adversely affect the integrity of the site, the authority shall have regard to the manner in which it is proposed to be carried out or to any conditions or restrictions subject to which they propose that the consent, permission or other authorisation should be given.

(7) This regulation does not apply in relation to a site which is a European site by reason only of regulation 10(1)(c) (site protected in accordance with Article 5(4)).

49 Considerations of overriding public interest

(1) If they are satisfied that, there being no alternative solutions, the plan or project must be carried out for imperative reasons of overriding public interest (which, subject to paragraph (2), may be of a social or economic nature), the competent authority may agree to the plan or project notwithstanding a negative assessment of the implications for the site.

(2) Where the site concerned hosts a priority natural habitat type or a priority species, the reasons referred to in paragraph (1) must be either—

(a) reasons relating to human health, public safety or beneficial consequences of primary importance to the environment, or

(b) other reasons which in the opinion of the European Commission are imperative reasons of overriding public interest.

(3) Where a competent authority other than the Secretary of State desire to obtain the opinion of the European Commission as to whether reasons are to be considered imperative reasons of overriding public interest, they shall submit a written request to the Secretary of State—

(a) identifying the matter on which an opinion is sought, and

(b) accompanied by any documents or information which may be required.

(4) The Secretary of State may thereupon, if he thinks fit, seek the opinion of the Commission; and if he does so, he shall upon receiving the Commission's opinion transmit it to the authority.

(5) Where an authority other than the Secretary of State propose to agree to a plan or project under this regulation notwithstanding a negative assessment of the implications for a European site, they shall notify the Secretary of State.

Having notified the Secretary of State, they shall not agree to the plan or project before the end of the period of 21 days beginning with the day notified to them by the Secretary of State as that on which their notification was received by him, unless the Secretary of State notifies them that they may do so.

(6) In any such case the Secretary of State may give directions to the authority prohibiting them from agreeing to the plan or project, either indefinitely or during such period as may be specified in the direction.

This power is without prejudice to any other power of the Secretary of State in relation to the decision in question.

50 Review of existing decisions and consents, etc.

(1) Where before the date on which a site becomes a European site or, if later, the commencement of these Regulations, a competent authority have decided to under-take, or have given any consent, permission or other authorisation for, a plan or project to which regulation 48(1) would apply if it were to be reconsidered as of that date, the authority shall as soon as reasonably practicable, review their decision or, as the case may be, the consent, permission or other authorisation, and shall affirm, modify or revoke it.

(2) They shall for that purpose make an appropriate assessment of the implications for the site in view of that site's conservation objectives; and the provisions of regulation 48(2) to (4) shall apply, with the appropriate modifications, in relation to such a review.

(3) Subject to the following provisions of this Part, any review required by this regulation shall be carried out under existing statutory procedures where such procedures exist, and if none exist the Secretary of State may give directions as to the procedure to be followed.

(4) Nothing in this regulation shall affect anything done in pursuance of the decision, or the consent, permission or other authorisation, before the date mentioned in paragraph (1).

51 Consideration on review

(1) The following provisions apply where a decision, or a consent, permission or other authorisation, falls to be reviewed under regulation 50.

(2) Subject as follows, the provisions of regulation 48(5) and (6) and regulation 49 shall apply, with the appropriate modifications, in relation to the decision on the review.

(3) The decision, or the consent, permission or other authorisation, may be affirmed if it appears to the authority reviewing it that other action taken or to be taken by them, or by another authority, will secure that the plan or project does not adversely affect the integrity of the site.

Where that object may be attained in a number of ways, the authority or authorities concerned shall seek to secure that the action taken is the least onerous to those affected.

(4) The Secretary of State may issue guidance to authorities for the purposes of paragraph (3) as to the manner of determining which of different ways should be adopted for securing that the plan or project does not have any such effect, and in particular—

(a) the order of application of different controls, and

(b) the extent to which account should be taken of the possible exercise of other powers;

and the authorities concerned shall have regard to any guidance so issued in discharging their functions under that paragraph.

(5) Any modification or revocation effected in pursuance of this regulation shall be carried out under existing statutory procedures where such procedures exist.

If none exist, the Secretary of State may give directions as to the procedure to be followed.

52 Co-ordination where more than one competent authority involved

(1) The following provisions apply where a plan or project—

(a) is undertaken by more than one competent authority,

(b) requires the consent, permission or other authorisation of more than one competent authority, or

(c) is undertaken by one or more competent authorities and requires the consent, permission or other authorisation of one or more other competent authorities.

(2) Nothing in regulation 48(1) or 50(2) requires a competent authority to assess any implications of a plan or project which would be more appropriately assessed under that provision by another competent authority.

(3) The Secretary of State may issue guidance to authorities for the purposes of regulations 48 to 51 as to the circumstances in which an authority may or should adopt the reasoning or conclusions of another competent authority as to whether a plan or project—

(a) is likely to have a significant effect on a European site, or

(b) will adversely affect the integrity of a European site;

and the authorities involved shall have regard to any guidance so issued in discharging their functions under those regulations.

(4) In determining whether a plan or project should be agreed to under regulation 49(1) (considerations of overriding public interest) a competent authority other than the Secretary of State shall seek and have regard to the views of the other competent authority or authorities involved.

53 Compensatory measures

Where in accordance with regulation 49 (considerations of overriding public interest)—

(a) a plan or project is agreed to, notwithstanding a negative assessment of the implications for a European site, or

(b) a decision, or a consent, permission or other authorisation, is affirmed on review, notwithstanding such an assessment,

the Secretary of State shall secure that any necessary compensatory measures are taken to ensure that the overall coherence of Natura 2000 is protected.

Planning

54 Grant of planning permission

(1) Regulations 48 and 49 (requirement to consider effect on European site) apply, in England and Wales, in relation to—

(a) granting planning permission on an application under Part III of the Town and Country Planning Act 1990;

(b) granting planning permission, or upholding a decision of the local planning authority to grant planning permission (whether or not subject to the same conditions and limitations as those imposed by the local planning authority), on determining an appeal under section 78 of that Act in respect of such an application;

(c) granting planning permission under—

(i) section 141(2)(a) of that Act (action by Secretary of State in relation to purchase notice),

(ii) section 177(1)(a) of that Act (powers of Secretary of State on appeal against enforcement notice), or

(iii) section 196(5) of that Act as originally enacted (powers of Secretary of State on reference or appeal as to established use certificate);

(d) directing under section 90(1), (2) or (2A) of that Act (development with government authorisation), or under section 5(1) of the Pipe-lines Act 1962, that planning permission shall be deemed to be granted;

(e) making—

(i) an order under section 102 of that Act (order requiring discontinuance of use or removal of buildings or works), including an order made under that section by virtue of section 104 (powers of Secretary of State), which grants planning permission, or

(ii) an order under paragraph 1 of Schedule 9 to that Act (order requiring discontinuance of mineral working), including an order made under that paragraph by virtue of paragraph 11 of that Schedule (default powers of Secretary of State), which grants planning permission,

or confirming any such order under section 103 of that Act;

(f) directing under—

(i) section 141(3) of that Act (action by Secretary of State in relation to purchase notice), or

(ii) section 35(5) of the Planning (Listed Buildings and Conservation Areas) Act 1990 (action by Secretary of State in relation to listed building purchase notice), that if an application is made for planning permission it shall be granted.

(2) ...

(3) Where regulations 48 and 49 apply, the competent authority may, if they consider that any adverse effects of the plan or project on the integrity of a European site would be avoided if the planning permission were subject to conditions or limitations, grant planning permission or, as the case may be, take action which results in planning permission being granted or deemed to be granted subject to those conditions or limitations.

(4) Where regulations 48 and 49 apply, outline planning permission shall not be granted unless the competent authority are satisfied (whether by reason of the conditions and limitations to which the outline planning permission is to be made subject, or otherwise) that no development likely adversely to affect the integrity of a European site could be carried out under the permission, whether before or after obtaining approval of any reserved matters.

In this paragraph 'outline planning permission' and 'reserved matters' have the same meaning as in section 92 of the Town and Country Planning Act 1990....

55 Planning permission: duty to review

(1) Subject to the following provisions of this regulation, regulations 50 and 51 (requirement to review certain decisions and consents, &c.) apply to any planning permission or deemed planning permission, unless—

(a) the development to which it related has been completed, or

(b) it was granted subject to a condition as to the time within which the development to which it related was to be begun and that time has expired without the development having been begun, or

(c) it was granted for a limited period and that period has expired.

(2) Regulations 50 and 51 do not apply to planning permission granted or deemed to have been granted—

(a) by a development order (but see regulations 60 to 64 below);

(b) ...

(c) ...

(3) Planning permission deemed to be granted by virtue of—

(a) a direction under section 90(1) of the Town and Country Planning Act 1990... in respect of development for which an authorisation has been granted under section 1 or 3 of the Pipe-lines Act 1962,

(b) a direction under section 5(1) of the Pipe-lines Act 1962,

(c) a direction under section 90(1) of the Town and Country Planning Act 1990... in respect of development for which a consent has been given under section 36 or 37 of the Electricity Act 1989,

(d) a direction under section 90(2) of the Town and Country Planning Act 1990 or paragraph 7 of Schedule 8 to the Electricity Act 1989, or

(e) a direction under section 90(2A) of the Town and Country Planning Act 1990 (which relates to development in pursuance of an order under section 1 or 3 of the Transport and Works Act 1992),

shall be reviewed in accordance with the following provisions of this Part in conjunction with the review of the underlying authorisation, consent or order.

(4) In the case of planning permission deemed to have been granted in any other case by a direction under section 90(1) of the Town and Country Planning Act 1990..., the local planning authority shall—

(a) identify any such permission which they consider falls to be reviewed under regulations 50 and 51, and

(b) refer the matter to the government department which made the direction;

and the department shall, if it agrees that the planning permission does fall to be so reviewed, thereupon review the direction in accordance with those regulations.

(5) Save as otherwise expressly provided, regulations 50 and 51 do not apply to planning permission granted or deemed to be granted by a public general Act of Parliament.

(6) Subject to paragraphs (3) and (4), where planning permission granted by the Secretary of State falls to be reviewed under regulations 50 and 51—

(a) it shall be reviewed by the local planning authority, and

(b) the power conferred by section 97 of the Town and Country Planning Act 1990... (revocation or modification of planning permission) shall be exercisable by that authority as in relation to planning permission granted on an application under Part III of that Act.

In a non-metropolitan county in England [...] the function of reviewing any such planning permission shall be exercised by the district planning authority unless it relates to a county matter (within the meaning of Schedule 1 to the Town and Country Planning Act 1990) in which case it shall be exercised by the county planning authority.

56 Planning permission: consideration on review

(1) In reviewing any planning permission or deemed planning permission in pursuance of regulations 50 and 51, the competent authority shall, in England and Wales—

(a) consider whether any adverse effects could be overcome by planning obligations under section 106 of the Town and Country Planning Act 1990 being entered into, and

(b) if they consider that those effects could be so overcome, invite those concerned to enter into such obligations;

and so far as the adverse effects are not thus overcome the authority shall make such order under section 97 of that Act (power to revoke or modify planning permission), or under section 102 of or paragraph 1 of Schedule 9 to that Act (order requiring discontinuance of use, etc.), as may be required.

(2) ...

(3) Where the authority ascertain that the carrying out or, as the case may be, the continuation of the development would adversely affect the integrity of a European site, they nevertheless need not proceed under regulations 50 and 51 if and so long as they consider that there is no likelihood of the development being carried out or continued.

57 Effect of orders made on review: England and Wales

(1) An order under section 97 of the Town and Country Planning Act 1990 (power to revoke or modify planning permission) made pursuant to regulation 55 shall take effect upon service of the notices required by section 98(2) of that Act or, where there is more than one such notice and those notices are served at different times, upon the service of the last such notice to be served.

(2) Where the Secretary of State determines not to confirm such an order, the order shall cease to have effect from the time of that determination, and the permission revoked or modified by the order shall thereafter have effect as if the order had never been made, and—

(a) any period specified in the permission for the taking of any action, being a period which had not expired prior to the date upon which the order took effect under paragraph (1) above, shall be extended by a period equal to that during which the order had effect; and

(b) there shall be substituted for any date specified in the permission as being a date by which any action should be taken, not being a date falling prior to the date upon which the order took effect under paragraph (1) above, such date as post-dates the specified date by a period equal to that during which the order had effect.

(3) An order under section 102 of, or under paragraph 1 of Schedule 9 to, the Town and Country Planning Act 1990 (order requiring discontinuance of use, etc.) made pursuant to regulation 55 shall insofar as it requires the discontinuance of a use of land or imposes conditions upon the continuance of a use of land, take effect upon service of the notices required by section 103(3) or, where there is more than one such notice and those notices are served at different times, upon service of the last such notice to be served.

(4) Where the Secretary of State determines not to confirm any such order, the order shall cease to have effect from the time of that determination and the use which by the order was discontinued or upon whose continuance conditions were imposed—

(a) may thereafter be continued as if the order had never been made, and

(b) shall be treated for the purposes of the Town and Country Planning Act 1990 as if it had continued without interruption or modification throughout the period during which the order had effect.

(5) An order under section 97 of that Act (power to revoke or modify planning permission) made in pursuance of regulation 55 shall not affect so much of the development authorised by the permission as was carried out prior to the order taking effect.

(6) An order under section 102 of, or under paragraph 1 of Schedule 9 to, that Act (order requiring discontinuance of use, etc.) made in pursuance of regulation 55 shall not affect anything done prior to the site becoming a European site or, if later, the commencement of these Regulations.

...

59 Planning permission: supplementary provisions as to compensation

(1) Where the Secretary of State determines not to confirm—

(a) an order under section 97 of the Town and Country Planning Act 1990 (revocation or modification of planning permission) which has taken effect under regulation 57(1), or

(b) ...

any claim for compensation under section 107 of the Act of 1990... shall be limited to any loss or damage directly attributable to the permission being suspended or temporarily modified for the duration of the period between the order so taking effect and the Secretary of State determining not to confirm the order.

(2) Where the Secretary of State determines not to confirm—

(a) an order under section 102 of the Town and Country Planning Act 1990 (order requiring discontinuance of use, etc.) which has taken effect under regulation 57(3) above, or

(b) ...

any claim for compensation under section 115 of the Act of 1990... shall be limited to any loss or damage directly attributable to any right to continue a use of the land being, by virtue of the order, suspended or subject to conditions for the duration of the period between the order so taking effect and the Secretary of State determining not to confirm the order.

(3) Where compensation is payable in respect of—

(a) an order under section 97 of the Town and Country Planning Act 1990, or

(b) any order mentioned in section 115(1) of that Act (compensation in respect of orders under s.102, etc.), or to which that section applies by virtue of section 115(5), and the order has been made pursuant to regulation 50, the question as to the amount of the compensation shall be referred, by the authority liable to pay the compensation, to and be determined by the Lands Tribunal unless and to the extent that in any particular case the Secretary of State has indicated in writing that such a reference and determination may be dispensed with.

(4) . . .

60 General development orders

(1) It shall be a condition of any planning permission granted by a general development order, whether made before or after the commencement of these Regulations, that development which—

(a) is likely to have a significant effect on a European site in Great Britain (either alone or in combination with other plans or projects), and

(b) is not directly connected with or necessary to the management of the site,

shall not be begun until the developer has received written notification of the approval of the local planning authority under regulation 62.

(2) It shall be a condition of any planning permission granted by a general development order made before the commencement of these Regulations that development which—

(a) is likely to have a significant effect on a European site in Great Britain (either alone or in combination with other plans or projects), and

(b) is not directly connected with or necessary to the management of the site, and which was begun but not completed before the commencement of these Regulations,

shall not be continued until the developer has received written notification of the approval of the local planning authority under regulation 62.

(3) Nothing in this regulation shall affect anything done before the commencement of these Regulations.

61 General development orders: opinion of appropriate nature conservation body

(1) Where it is intended to carry out development in reliance on the permission granted by a general development order, application may be made in writing to the appropriate nature conservation body for their opinion whether the development is likely to have such an effect as is mentioned in regulation 60(1)(a) or (2)(a).

The application shall give details of the development which is intended to be carried out.

(2) On receiving such an application, the appropriate nature conservation body shall consider whether the development is likely to have such an effect.

(3) Where they consider that they have sufficient information to conclude that the development will, or will not, have such an effect, they shall in writing notify the applicant and the local planning authority of their opinion.

(4) If they consider that they have insufficient information to reach either of those conclusions, they shall notify the applicant in writing indicating in what respects they consider the information insufficient; and the applicant may supply further information with a view to enabling them to reach a decision on the application.

(5) The opinion of the appropriate nature conservation body, notified in accordance with paragraph (3), that the development is not likely to have such an effect as is mentioned in regulation 60(1)(a) or (2)(a) shall be conclusive of that question for the purpose of reliance on the planning permission granted by a general development order.

62 General development orders: approval of local planning authority

(1) Where it is intended to carry out development in reliance upon the permission granted by a general development order, application may be made in writing to the local planning authority for their approval.

(2) The application shall—

(a) give details of the development which is intended to be carried out; and

(b) be accompanied by—

(i) a copy of any relevant notification by the appropriate nature conservation body under regulation 61, and

(ii) any fee required to be paid.

(3) For the purposes of their consideration of the application the local planning authority shall assume that the development is likely to have such an effect as mentioned in regulation 60(1)(a) or (2)(a).

(4) The authority shall send a copy of the application to the appropriate nature conservation body and shall take account of any representations made by them.

(5) If in their representations the appropriate nature conservation body state their opinion that the development is not likely to have such an effect as is mentioned in regulation 60(1)(a) or (2)(a), the local planning authority shall send a copy of the representations to the applicant; and the sending of that copy shall have the same effect as a notification by the appropriate nature conservation body of its opinion under regulation 61(3).

(6) In any other case the local planning authority shall, taking account of any representations made by the appropriate nature conservation body, make an appropriate assessment of the implications of the development for the European site in view of that site's conservation objectives.

In the light of the conclusions of the assessment the authority shall approve the development only after having ascertained that it will not adversely affect the integrity of the site.

63 General development orders: supplementary

(1) The local planning authority for the purposes of regulations 60 to 62 shall be the authority to whom an application for approval under regulation 62 would fall to be made if it were an application for planning permission.

(2) The fee payable in connection with an application for such approval is—

(a) £25 in the case of applications made before 3rd January 1995, and

(b) £30 in the case of applications made on or after that date.

(3) Approval required by regulation 60 shall be treated—

(a) for the purposes of the provisions of the Town and Country Planning Act 1990, . . . relating to appeals, as approval required by a condition imposed on a grant of planning permission; and

(b) for the purposes of the provisions of any general development order relating to the time within which notice of a decision should be made, as approval required by a condition attached to a grant of planning permission.

68 Construction as one with planning legislation

Regulations 54 to 67 shall be construed as one—

(a) in England and Wales, with the Town and Country Planning Act 1990; and

(b) . . .

Electricity

71 Consents under Electricity Act 1989: application of general requirements

(1) Regulations 48 and 49 (requirement to consider effect on European site) apply in relation to the granting of—

(a) consent under section 36 of the Electricity Act 1989 to construct, extend or operate a generating station, or

(b) consent under section 37 of that Act to install an electric line above ground.

(2) Where in such a case the Secretary of State considers that any adverse effects of the plan or project on the integrity of a European site would be avoided if the consent were subject to conditions, he may grant consent subject to those conditions.

(3) Regulations 50 and 51 (requirement to review existing decisions and consents, &c) apply to such a consent as is mentioned in paragraph (1) unless—

(a) the works to which the consent relates have been completed before the site became a European site or, if later, the commencement of these Regulations, or

(b) the consent was granted subject to a condition as to the time within which the works to which it relates were to be begun and that time has expired without them having been begun, or

(c) it was granted for a limited period and that period has expired.

Where the consent is for, or includes, the operation of a generating station, the works shall be treated as completed when, in reliance on the consent, the generating station is first operated.

(4) Where on the review of such a consent the Secretary of State considers that any adverse effects on the integrity of a European site of the carrying out or, as the case may be, the continuation of the plan or project would be avoided by a variation of the consent, he may vary the consent accordingly.

(5) In conjunction with the review of any such consent the Secretary of State shall review any direction deeming planning permission to be granted for the plan or project and may vary or revoke it.

. . .

Environmental controls

84 Licences under Part II of the Environmental Protection Act 1990

(1) Regulations 48 and 49 (requirement to consider effect on European site) apply in relation to—

(a) the granting of a waste management licence under Part II of the Environmental Protection Act 1990,

(b) the passing of a resolution under section 54 of that Act (provisions as to land occupied by disposal authorities themselves), and

(c) the granting of a disposal licence under Part I of the Control of Pollution Act 1974 and the passing of a resolution under section 11 of that Act.

(2) Where in such a case the competent authority consider that any adverse effects of the plan or project on the integrity of a European site would be avoided by making any licence subject to conditions, they may grant a licence, or cause a licence to be granted, or, as the case may be, pass a resolution, subject to those conditions.

(3) Regulations 50 and 51 (requirement to review existing decisions and consents, &c.) apply to any such licence or resolution as is mentioned in paragraph (1).

(4) Where on the review of such a licence or resolution the competent authority consider that any adverse effects on the integrity of a European site of the carrying out or, as the case may be, the continuation of the activities authorised by it would be avoided by a variation of the licence or resolution, they may vary it, or cause it to be varied, accordingly.

[84A Permits under the Pollution Prevention and Control (England and Wales) Regulations 2000

(1) Regulations 48 and 49 (requirement to consider effect on European site) apply in relation to the granting of a permit under the Pollution Prevention and Control (England and Wales) Regulations 2000.

(2) Where in such a case the competent authority consider that any adverse effects of the plan or project on the integrity of a European site would be avoided if the permit were subject to conditions, they may grant a permit, or cause a permit to be granted, subject to those conditions.

(3) Regulations 50 and 51 (requirement to review existing decisions and consents, etc.) apply to any such permit as is mentioned in paragraph (1).

(4) Where on the review of such a permit the competent authority consider that any adverse effects on the integrity of a European site of the carrying out or, as the case may be, the continuation of activities authorised by it would be avoided by a variation of the permit, they may vary it, or cause it to be varied, accordingly.

(5) Where any question arises as to agreeing to a plan or project, or affirming a permit on review, under regulation 49 (considerations of overriding public interest), the competent authority shall refer the matter to the Secretary of State who shall determine the matter in accordance with that regulation and give directions to the authority accordingly.]

85 Discharge consents under water pollution legislation

(1) Regulations 48 and 49 (requirement to consider effect on European site) apply in relation to the giving of consent under—

(a) Chapter II of Part III to the Water Resources Act 1991 (control of pollution of water resources), or

(b) . . .

(2) Where in such a case the competent authority consider that any adverse effects of the plan or project on the integrity of a European site would be avoided by making any consent subject to conditions, they may give consent, or cause it to be given, subject to those conditions.

(3) Regulations 50 and 51 (requirement to review existing decisions and consents, &c.) apply to any such consent as is mentioned in paragraph (1).

(4) Where on the review of such a consent the competent authority consider that any adverse effects on the integrity of a European site of the carrying out or, as the case may be, the continuation of the activities authorised by it would be avoided by a variation of the consent, they may vary it, or cause it to be varied, accordingly.

. . .

PART V SUPPLEMENTARY PROVISIONS

Supplementary provisions as to protection of species

100 Attempts and possession of means of committing offence

(1) A person who attempts to commit an offence under Part III of these Regulations is guilty of an offence and punishable in like manner as for that offence.

(2) A person who, for the purposes of committing an offence under Part III of these Regulations, has in his possession anything capable of being used for committing the offence is guilty of an offence and punishable in like manner as for that offence.

(3) References below to an offence under Part III include an offence under this regulation.

SCHEDULE 1 PROCEDURE IN CONNECTION WITH ORDERS UNDER REGULATION 22

Coming into operation

1.—(1) An original order or a restrictive amending order takes effect on its being made.

(2) The Secretary of State shall consider every such order, and the order shall cease to have effect nine months after it is made unless he has previously given notice under paragraph 6 that he has considered it and does not propose to amend or revoke it, or has revoked it.

(3) Subject to paragraphs 3(1) and 4(4), a revoking order, or an amending order which is not restrictive, does not take effect until confirmed by the Secretary of State.

(4) An amending or revoking order requiring confirmation shall stand revoked if the Secretary of State gives notice under paragraph 6 below that it is not to be confirmed.

Publicity for orders

2.—(1) The Secretary of State shall, where an order has been made, give notice setting out the order (or describing its general effect) and stating that it has taken effect or, as the case may be, that it has been made and requires confirmation.

(2) The notice shall—

(a) name a place in the area in which the land to which the order relates is situated where a copy of the order may be inspected free of charge at all reasonable hours; and

(b) specify the time (not being less than 28 days from the date of the first publication of the notice) within which, and the manner in which, representations or objections with respect to the order may be made.

(3) The notice shall be given—

(a) by publication in the Gazette and also at least one local newspaper circulating in the area in which the land to which the order relates is situated;

(b) by serving a like notice—

(i) on every owner and occupier of that land (subject to sub-paragraph (4) below); and

(ii) on the local planning authority within whose area the land is situated.

(4) The Secretary of State may, in any particular case, direct that it shall not be necessary to comply with sub-paragraph (3)(b)(i); but if he so directs in the case of any land, then in addition to publication the notice shall be addressed to 'The owners and any occupiers' of the land (describing it) and a copy or copies of the notice shall be affixed to some conspicuous object or objects on the land.

Unopposed orders

3.—(1) Where an order has taken effect immediately and no representations or objections are duly made in respect of it or any so made are withdrawn, the Secretary of State shall, as soon as practicable after considering the order, decide either to take no action on it or to make an order amending or revoking it.

An amending or revoking order under this sub-paragraph takes effect immediately and does not require confirmation nor shall any representation or objection with respect to it be entertained.

(2) Where an order requiring confirmation is made and no representations or objections are duly made in respect of it, or any so made are withdrawn, the Secretary of State may confirm the order (with or without modification).

Opposed orders

4.—(1) If any representation or objection duly made with respect to an order is not withdrawn, then, as soon as practicable in the case of an order having immediate effect and before confirming an order requiring confirmation, the Secretary of State shall either—

(a) cause a local inquiry to be held; or

(b) afford any person by whom a representation or objection has been duly made and not withdrawn an opportunity of being heard by a person appointed by the Secretary of State for the purpose.

(2) On considering any representations or objections duly made and the report of any person appointed to hold the inquiry or to hear representations or objections, the Secretary of State—

(a) if the order has already taken effect, shall decide either to take no action on the order, or to make an order amending or revoking it as he thinks appropriate in the light of the report, representations or objections; and

(b) if the order requires confirmation, may confirm it (with or without modifications).

(3) The provisions of section 250(2) to (5) of the Local Government Act 1972 or section 210(4) to (8) of the Local Government (Scotland) Act 1973 (local inquiries: evidence and costs) apply in relation to an inquiry held under this paragraph:

(4) An amending or revoking order made by virtue of sub-paragraph (2) above takes effect immediately and does not require confirmation nor shall any representation or objection with respect to it be entertained.

Restriction on power to amend orders or confirm them with modifications

5. The Secretary of State shall not by virtue of paragraphs 3(1) or 4(2) amend an order which has taken effect, or confirm any other order with modifications, so as to extend the area to which the order applies.

Notice of final decision on order

6.—(1) The Secretary of State shall as soon as practicable after making an order by virtue of paragraphs 3(1) or 4(2) give notice—

(a) setting out the order (or describing its effect) and stating that it has taken effect; and

(b) naming a place in the area in which the land to which the order relates is situated where a copy of the order may be inspected free of charge at all reasonable hours.

(2) The Secretary of State shall give notice of any of the following decisions of his as soon as practicable after making the decision—

(a) a decision under paragraph 3(1) or 4(2) to take no action on an order which has already taken effect;

(b) a decision to confirm or not to confirm an order requiring confirmation under this Schedule.

(3) A notice under this paragraph of a decision to confirm an order shall—

(a) set out the order as confirmed (or describe its general effect) and state the day on which the order took effect; and

(b) name a place in the area in which the land to which the order relates is situated where a copy of the order as confirmed may be inspected free of charge at all reasonable hours.

(4) Notice under this paragraph shall be given by publishing it in accordance with paragraph 2(3) and serving a copy of it on any person on whom a notice was required to be served under paragraph 2(3) or (4).

Proceedings for questioning validity of orders

7.—(1) This paragraph applies to any order which has taken effect and as to which the Secretary of State has given notice under paragraph 6 of a decision of his to take no action or to amend the order in accordance with paragraph 4; and in this paragraph 'the relevant notice' means that notice.

(2) If any person is aggrieved by an order to which this paragraph applies and desires to question its validity on the ground that it is not within the powers of regulation 22 or that any of the requirements of this Schedule have not been complied with in relation to it, he may within six weeks from the date of the relevant notice make an application to the court under this paragraph.

(3) On any such application the court may, if satisfied that the order is not within those powers or that the interests of the applicant have been substantially prejudiced by a failure to comply with any of those requirements—

(a) in England and Wales, quash the order, or any provision of the order, either generally or in so far as it affects the interests of the applicant; or

(b) in Scotland, make such declarator as seems to the court to be appropriate.

(4) Except as provided by this paragraph, the validity of an order shall not be questioned in any legal proceedings whatsoever.

(5) In this paragraph 'the court' means the High Court in relation to England and Wales and the Court of Session in relation to Scotland.

Interpretation

In this Schedule—

'amending order' and 'revoking order' mean an order which amends or, as the case may be, revokes a previous order;

'the Gazette' means—

(a) if the order relates in whole or in part to land in England and Wales, the London Gazette; and

(b) if the order relates in whole or in part to land in Scotland, the Edinburgh Gazette;

'order' means an order under regulation 22;

'original order' means an order other than an amending or revoking order; and

'restrictive amending order' means an amending order which extends the area to which a previous order applies.

SCHEDULE 2 EUROPEAN PROTECTED SPECIES OF ANIMALS

Common name	*Scientific name*
Bats, Horseshoe (all species)	Rhinolophidae
Bats, Typical (all species)	Vespertilionidae
Butterfly, Large Blue	Maculinea arion
Cat, Wild	Felis silvestris
Dolphins, porpoises and whales (all species)	Cetacea
Dormouse	Muscardinus avellanarius
Lizard, Sand	Lacerta agilis
Newt, Great Crested (or Warty)	Triturus cristatus
Otter, Common	Lutra lutra
Snake, Smooth	Coronella austriaca
Sturgeon	Acipenser sturio
Toad, Natterjack	Bufo calamita
Turtles, Marine	Caretta caretta
	Chelonia mydas
	Lepidochelys kempii
	Eretmochelys imbricata
	Dermochelys coriacea

NOTE: The common name or names given in the first column of this Schedule are included by way of guidance only; in the event of any dispute or proceedings, the common name or names shall not be taken into account.

SCHEDULE 3 ANIMALS WHICH MAY NOT BE TAKEN OR KILLED IN CERTAIN WAYS

Common name	*Scientific name*
Barbel	Barbus barbus
Grayling	Thymallus thymallus
Hare, Mountain	Lepus timidus
Lamprey, River	Lampetra fluviatilis
Marten, Pine	Martes martes
Polecat	Mustela putorius (otherwise known as Putorius putorius)
Salmon, Atlantic	Salmo salar (only in fresh water)
Seal, Bearded	Erignathus barbatus
Seal, Common	Phoca vitulina
Seal, Grey	Halichoerus grypus
Seal, Harp	Phoca groenlandica (otherwise known as Pagophilus groenlandicus)
Seal, Hooded	Cystophora cristata
Seal, Ringed	Phoca hispida (otherwise known as Pusa hispida)
Shad, Allis	Alosa alosa
Shad, Twaite	Alosa fallax
Vendace	Coregonus albula
Whitefish	Coregonus lavaretus

NOTE: The common name or names given in the first column of this Schedule are included by way of guidance only; in the event of any dispute or proceedings, the common name or names shall not be taken into account.

SCHEDULE 4 EUROPEAN PROTECTED SPECIES OF PLANTS

Common name	*Scientific name*
Dock, Shore	Rumex rupestris
Fern, Killarney	Trichomanes speciosum
Gentian, Early	Gentianella anglica
Lady's-slipper	Cypripedium calceolus
Marshwort, Creeping	Apium repens
Naiad, slender	Najas flexilis
Orchid, Fen	Liparis loeselii
Plantain, Floating-leaved water	Luronium natans
Saxifrage, Yellow Marsh	Saxifraga hirculus

NOTE: The common name or names given in the first column of this Schedule are included by way of guidance only; in the event of any dispute or proceedings, the common name or names shall not be taken into account.

Town and Country Planning (General Permitted Development) Order 1995

(SI 1995, No. 418) (as amended)

SCHEDULE 2

PART 3 CHANGES OF USE

[Class A
Permitted development

A. Development consisting of a change of the use of a building to a use falling within Class A1 (shops) of the Schedule to the Use Classes Order from a use falling within Class A3 (restaurants and cafes), A4 (drinking establishments) or A5 (hot food takeaways) of the Schedule.

Class AA
Permitted development

AA. Development consisting of a change of use of a building to a use falling within Class A3 (restaurants and cafes) of the Schedule to the Use Classes Order from a use falling within Class A4 (drinking establishments) or Class A5 (hot food takeaways) of that Schedule.]

Class B
Permitted development

B. Development consisting of a change of the use of a building—

(a) to a use for any purpose falling within Class B1 (business) of the Schedule to the Use Classes Order from any use falling within Class B2 (general industrial) or B8 (storage and distribution) of that Schedule;

(b) to a use for any purpose falling within Class B8 (storage and distribution) of that Schedule from any use falling within Class B1 (business) or B2 (general industrial).

Development not permitted

Development is not permitted by Class B where the change is to or from a use falling within Class B8 of that Schedule, if the change of use relates to more than 235 square metres of floor space in the building.

Class C

Permitted development

[C. Development consisting of a change of use to a use falling within Class A2 (financial and professional services) of the Schedule to the Use Classes Order from a use falling within Class A3 [(restaurants and cafes), Class A4 (drinking establishments) or Class A5 (hot food takeaways)] of that Schedule.]

Class D

Permitted development

D. Development consisting of a change of use of any premises with a display window at ground floor level to a use falling within Class A1 (shops) of the Schedule to the Use Classes Order from a use falling within Class A2 (financial and professional services) of that Schedule.

Class E

Permitted development

E. Development consisting of a change of the use of a building or other land from a use permitted by planning permission granted on an application, to another use which that permission would have specifically authorised when it was granted.

Development not permitted

E.1 Development is not permitted by Class E if—

(a) the application for planning permission referred to was made before the 5th December 1988;

(b) it would be carried out more than 10 years after the grant of planning permission; or

(c) it would result in the breach of any condition, limitation or specification contained in that planning permission in relation to the use in question.

Class F

Permitted development

F. Development consisting of a change of the use of a building—

(a) to a mixed use for any purpose within Class A1 (shops) of the Schedule to the Use Classes Order and as a single flat, from a use for any purpose within Class A1 of that Schedule;

(b) to a mixed use for any purpose within Class A2 (financial and professional services) of the Schedule to the Use Classes Order and as a single flat, from a use for any purpose within Class A2 of that Schedule;

(c) where that building has a display window at ground floor level, to a mixed use for any purpose within Class A1 (shops) of the Schedule to the Use Classes Order and as a single flat, from a use for any purpose within Class A2 (financial and professional services) of that Schedule.

Conditions

F.1 Development permitted by Class F is subject to the following conditions—

(a) some or all of the parts of the building used for any purposes within Class A1 or Class A2, as the case may be, of the Schedule to the Use Classes Order shall be situated on a floor below the part of the building used as a single flat;

(b) where the development consists of a change of use of any building with a display window at ground floor level, the ground floor shall not be used in whole or in part as the single flat;

(c) the single flat shall not be used otherwise than as a dwelling (whether or not as a sole or main residence)—

(i) by a single person or by people living together as a family, or

(ii) by not more than six residents living together as a single household (including a household where care is provided for residents).

Interpretation of Class F

F.2 For the purposes of Class F—'care' means personal care for people in need of such care by reason of old age, disablement, past or present dependence on alcohol or drugs or past or present mental disorder.

Class G

Permitted development

G. Development consisting of a change of the use of a building—

(a) to a use for any purpose within Class A1 (shops) of the Schedule to the Use Classes Order from a mixed use for any purpose within Class A1 of that Schedule and as a single flat;

(b) to a use for any purpose within Class A2 (financial and professional services) of the Schedule to the Use Classes Order from a mixed use for any purpose within Class A2 of that Schedule and as a single flat;

(c) where that building has a display window at ground floor level, to a use for any purpose within Class A1 (shops) of the Schedule to the Use Classes Order from a mixed use for any purpose within Class A2 (financial and professional services) of that Schedule and as a single flat.

Development not permitted

G.1 Development is not permitted by Class G unless the part of the building used as a single flat was immediately prior to being so used used for any purpose within Class A1 or Class A2 of the Schedule to the Use Classes Order.

[Class H

Permitted Development

H. Development consisting of a change of use of a building from use as a casino to a use falling within Class D2 (Assembly and leisure) of the Schedule to the Use Classes Order.]

Statutory Nuisance (Appeals) Regulations 1995

(SI 1995, No. 2644) (as amended)

1 Citation, commencement and interpretation

(1) . . .

(2) In these Regulations—

'the 1974 Act' means the Control of Pollution Act 1974;

'the 1990 Act' means the Environmental Protection Act 1990; and

'the 1993 Act' means the Noise and Statutory Nuisance Act 1993.

2 Appeals under section 80(3) of the 1990 Act

(1) The provisions of this regulation apply in relation to an appeal brought by any person under section 80(3) of the 1990 Act (appeals to magistrates) against an abatement notice served upon him by a local authority.

(2) The grounds on which a person served with such a notice may appeal under section 80(3) are any one or more of the following grounds that are appropriate in the circumstances of the particular case—

(a) that the abatement notice is not justified by section 80 of the 1990 Act (summary proceedings for statutory nuisances);
(b) that there has been some informality, defect or error in, or in connection with, the abatement notice, or in, or in connection with, any copy of the abatement notice served under section 80A(3) (certain notices in respect of vehicles, machinery or equipment);
(c) that the authority have refused unreasonably to accept compliance with alternative requirements, or that the requirements of the abatement notice are otherwise unreasonable in character or extent, or are unnecessary;
(d) that the time, or where more than one time is specified, any of the times, within which the requirements of the abatement notice are to be complied with is not reasonably sufficient for the purpose;
(e) where the nuisance to which the notice relates—
  (i) is a nuisance falling within section 79(1)(a), (d), (e), (f), (fa) or (g) of the 1990 Act and arises on industrial, trade, or business premises, or
  (ii) is a nuisance falling within section 79(1)(b) of the 1990 Act and the smoke is emitted from a chimney, or
  (iii) is a nuisance falling within section 79(1)(ga) of the 1990 Act and is noise emitted from or caused by a vehicle, machinery or equipment being used for industrial, trade or business purposes, [or
  (iv) is a nuisance falling within section 79(1)(fb) of the 1990 Act and—
    (aa) the artificial light is emitted from industrial, trade or business premises, or
    (bb) the artificial light (not being light to which sub-paragraph (aa) applies) is emitted by lights used for the purpose only of illuminating an outdoor relevant sports facility (within the meaning given by section 80(8A) of the 1990 Act).]

  that the best practicable means were used to prevent, or to counteract the effects of, the nuisance;
(f) that, in the case of a nuisance under section 79(1)(g) or (ga) of the 1990 Act (noise emitted from premises), the requirements imposed by the abatement notice by virtue of section 80(1)(a) of the Act are more onerous than the requirements for the time being in force, in relation to the noise to which the notice relates, of—
  (i) any notice served under section 60 or 66 of the 1974 Act (control of noise on construction sites and from certain premises), or
  (ii) any consent given under section 61 or 65 of the 1974 Act (consent for work on construction sites and consent for noise to exceed registered level in a noise abatement zone), or
  (iii) any determination made under section 67 of the 1974 Act (noise control of new buildings);
(g) that, in the case of a nuisance under section 79(1)(ga) of the 1990 Act (noise emitted from or caused by vehicles, machinery or equipment), the requirements imposed by the abatement notice by virtue of section 80(1)(a) of the Act are more onerous than the requirements for the time being in force, in relation to the noise to which the notice relates, of any condition of a consent given under paragraph 1 of Schedule 2 to the 1993 Act (loudspeakers in streets or roads);
(h) that the abatement notice should have been served on some person instead of the appellant, being—
  (i) the person responsible for the nuisance, or
  (ii) the person responsible for the vehicle, machinery or equipment, or
  (iii) in the case of a nuisance arising from any defect of a structural character, the owner of the premises, or
  (iv) in the case where the person responsible for the nuisance cannot be found or the nuisance has not yet occurred, the owner or occupier of the premises;
(i) that the abatement notice might lawfully have been served on some person instead of the appellant being—

(i) in the case where the appellant is the owner of the premises, the occupier of the premises, or
(ii) in the case where the appellant is the occupier of the premises, the owner of the premises,

and that it would have been equitable for it to have been so served;

(j) that the abatement notice might lawfully have been served on some person in addition to the appellant, being—
(i) a person also responsible for the nuisance, or
(ii) a person who is also owner of the premises, or
(iii) a person who is also an occupier of the premises, or
(iv) a person who is also the person responsible for the vehicle, machinery or equipment,

and that it would have been equitable for it to have been so served.

(3) If and so far as an appeal is based on the ground of some informality, defect or error in, or in connection with, the abatement notice, or in, or in connection with, any copy of the notice served under section 80A(3), the court shall dismiss the appeal if it is satisfied that the informality, defect or error was not a material one.

(4) Where the grounds upon which an appeal is brought include a ground specified in paragraph (2)(i) or (j) above, the appellant shall serve a copy of his notice of appeal on any other person referred to, and in the case of any appeal to which these regulations apply he may serve a copy of his notice of appeal on any other person having an estate or interest in the premises, vehicle, machinery or equipment in question.

(5) On the hearing of the appeal the court may—
(a) quash the abatement notice to which the appeal relates, or
(b) vary the abatement notice in favour of the appellant in such manner as it thinks fit, or
(c) dismiss the appeal; and an abatement notice that is varied under sub-paragraph (b) above shall be final and shall otherwise have effect, as so varied, as if it had been so made by the local authority.

(6) Subject to paragraph (7) below, on the hearing of an appeal the court may make such order as it thinks fit—
(a) with respect to the person by whom any work is to be executed and the contribution to be made by any person towards the cost of the work, or
(b) as to the proportions in which any expenses which may become recoverable by the authority under Part III of the 1990 Act are to be borne by the appellant and by any other person.

(7) In exercising its powers under paragraph (6) above the court—
(a) shall have regard, as between an owner and an occupier, to the terms and conditions, whether contractual or statutory, of any relevant tenancy and to the nature of the works required, and
(b) shall be satisfied before it imposes any requirement thereunder on any person other than the appellant, that that person has received a copy of the notice of appeal in pursuance of paragraph (4) above.

3 Suspension of notice

(1) Where—
(a) an appeal is brought against an abatement notice served under section 80 or section 80A of the 1990 Act, and—
(b) either—
(i) compliance with the abatement notice would involve any person in expenditure on the carrying out of works before the hearing of the appeal, or
(ii) in the case of a nuisance under section 79(1)(g) or (ga) of the 1990 Act, the noise to which the abatement notice relates is noise necessarily caused in the course of the performance of some duty imposed by law on the appellant, and
(c) either paragraph (2) does not apply, or it does apply but the requirements of paragraph (3) have not been met,

the abatement notice shall be suspended until the appeal has been abandoned or decided by the court.

(2) This paragraph applies where—

(a) the nuisance to which the abatement notice relates—

(i) is injurious to health, or

(ii) is likely to be of a limited duration such that suspension of the notice would render it of no practical effect, or

(b) the expenditure which would be incurred by any person in the carrying out of works in compliance with the abatement notice before any appeal has been decided would not be disproportionate to the public benefit to be expected in that period from such compliance.

(3) Where paragraph (2) applies the abatement notice—

(a) shall include a statement that paragraph (2) applies, and that as a consequence it shall have effect notwithstanding any appeal to a magistrates' court which has not been decided by the court, and

(b) shall include a statement as to which of the grounds set out in paragraph (2) apply.

Control of Pollution (Applications, Appeals and Registers) Regulations 1996

(SI 1996, No. 2971) (as amended)

1 Citation, commencement and interpretation

(1) These Regulations may be cited as the Control of Pollution (Applications, Appeals and Registers) Regulations 1996 and shall come into force on 31st December 1996.

(2) In these Regulations—

'discharge consent' has the same meaning as in section 91(8) of the Water Resources Act 1991;

'register' means a register maintained by the Agency under section 190 of that Act (pollution control registers).

2 Advertisements

(1) Subject to regulation 4, an application for—

(a) a discharge consent or the variation of a discharge consent;

(b) a consent for the purposes of section 89(4)(a) of the Water Resources Act 1991 (consents for the deposit of solid refuse from mines or quarries on land near inland freshwaters); or

(c) a consent for the purposes of section 90(1) or (2) of that Act (consents for the removal of deposits or for the cutting or uprooting of vegetation in or near inland freshwaters),

shall be advertised in accordance with the following provisions of this regulation and regulation 3.

(2) Notice of the application shall be published—

(a) in one or more newspapers circulating in—

(i) the locality in which the activities which are the subject matter of the application are proposed to be carried on; and

(ii) the locality in which the controlled waters which may be affected by the proposed activities are situated; and

(b) in the London Gazette.

(3) Subject to paragraph (4) below, the notice shall—

(a) state the name of the applicant;

(b) specify where the activities which are the subject matter of the application are proposed to be carried on;

(c) describe briefly the nature of the proposed activities;

(d) state where the register containing information about the application may be inspected, the times at which the register is open for inspection and that the register may be inspected free of charge; and

(e) explain that any person may make representations in writing to the Agency, specify when the period allowed for making representations ends and give the address of the Agency to which representations are to be sent.

(4) Nothing in paragraph (3) above shall require the disclosure of any information which is not to be included in a register by virtue of section 191A or 191B of the Water Resources Act 1991 (exclusion from registers of information affecting national security and of certain confidential information).

3 Timing of advertisements

(1) An application to which regulation 2 applies shall be advertised in accordance with paragraph (2) of that regulation within the period of 28 days beginning 14 days after the relevant date.

(2) Subject to paragraphs (3) to (5) below, the relevant date in relation to an application shall be the date on which the application is received by the Agency.

(3) In a case where the Agency has notified the applicant within 14 days of the receipt of the application that it refuses to proceed with the application until information required by section 90A(4) of, or paragraph 1(3) or (4) of Schedule 10 to, the Water Resources Act 1991 (duty to provide Agency with information) is provided, the relevant date shall be the date on which the Agency is finally provided with the information required.

(4) In a case where a matter falls to be determined under section 191A of the Water Resources Act 1991 (exclusion from registers of information affecting national security), the relevant date shall be the date on which the Secretary of State notifies the applicant of his determination.

(5) In a case where a matter falls to be determined under section 191B of the Water Resources Act 1991 (exclusion from registers of certain confidential information), the relevant date shall be—

(a) if the Agency is treated by virtue of section 191B(3) of that Act as having determined that the information in question is commercially confidential, the date on which the period of 14 days mentioned in section 191B(3) expires;

(b) if the Agency determines under section 191B(2) or (4) of that Act that the information in question is commercially confidential, the date on which the Agency notifies the applicant of its determination;

(c) if the Agency determines under section 191B(2) or (4) of that Act that the information in question is not commercially confidential—

(i) the date on which the period for appealing expires without an appeal having been made;

(ii) the date on which the Secretary of State notifies the applicant of his final determination of the appeal; or

(iii) the date on which the appeal is withdrawn.

(6) Where the relevant date for the purposes of this regulation in relation to an application is later than the date on which the application is received, a period of four months beginning with the relevant date shall be substituted for the period of four months specified in paragraph 3(2) of Schedule 10 to the Water Resources Act 1991 (failure to determine application within four months or longer period agreed with applicant).

4 Exemption from advertising requirements

The Agency may determine that an application is not required to be advertised if it appears to the Agency that it is appropriate to dispense with advertising the application because—

(a) section 191A of the Water Resources Act 1991 (exclusion from registers of information affecting national security) applies; or

(b) the Agency considers that the activities which are the subject matter of the application are unlikely to have an appreciable effect on controlled waters in the locality in which those activities are proposed to be carried on; or

(c) ...

and, in any case where the Agency so determines, the application shall be exempt from the requirements of section 90A(1)(b) of, or, as the case may be, paragraph 1(1)(b) of Schedule 10 to, the Water Resources Act 1991 (requirement to advertise applications).

5 Consultation

(1) Subject to paragraph (3) below, the persons to be consulted under paragraph 2 of Schedule 10 to the Water Resources Act 1991 (consultation in connection with applications) in relation to an application for, or for the variation of, a discharge consent are—

(a) every local authority or water undertaker within whose area any of the proposed discharges are to be made;

(b) each of the Ministers if any of the proposed discharges are to be made into coastal waters, relevant territorial waters or waters outside the seaward limits of relevant territorial waters;

(c) the harbour authority within the meaning of section 57(1) of the Harbours Act 1964 if any of the proposed discharges are to be made into a harbour managed by the authority; and

(d) the local fisheries committee, if any of the proposed discharges are to be made into relevant territorial waters or coastal waters within the sea fisheries district of that committee.

(2) The specified period for notification of those persons under paragraph 2 of Schedule 10 to the Water Resources Act 1991 (consultation in connection with applications) is the period of 14 days beginning with the relevant date and, for this purpose, 'relevant date' has the same meaning as in regulation 3.

(3) The requirements of paragraph 2 of Schedule 10 to the Water Resources Act 1991 (consultation in connection with applications) shall not apply in relation to any of the bodies mentioned in paragraph (1)(a), (c) or (d) above—

(a) in so far as they would require the disclosure of any information which is not to be included in a register by virtue of section 191A or 191B of the Water Resources Act 1991 (exclusion from registers of information affecting national security and of certain confidential information);

(b) in relation to an application for, or for the variation of, a discharge consent which need not be advertised as a result of an exemption under regulation 4.

(4) A period of six weeks beginning with the last date on which the making of the application was advertised in pursuance of paragraph 1(1)(b) of Schedule 10 to the Water Resources Act 1991 shall be substituted for the period specified in paragraph 2(6)(b) of that Schedule (period allowed for making representations).

6 Transmitted applications

(1) The following provisions of this regulation shall apply where an application for, or for the variation of, a discharge consent is transmitted to the Secretary of State under paragraph 5(1) of Schedule 10 to the Water Resources Act 1991 (reference to the Secretary of State of certain applications for consent).

(2) Paragraph 2 of Schedule 10 to the Water Resources Act 1991 (consultation in connection with applications) shall apply subject to the modification that representations made to the Agency within the period allowed for making representations shall, instead of being considered by the Agency, be sent by the Agency to the Secretary of State and shall be considered by him along with any representations made by the Agency.

(3) Any request to be heard by the applicant or the Agency with respect to the application shall be made in writing to the Secretary of State within the period of 28 days beginning with the day on which the applicant is informed by the Agency of the transmission of his application to the Secretary of State.

7 Discharge consents without applications

The provisions of Schedule 1 to these Regulations shall apply where the Agency gives a discharge consent under paragraph 6 of Schedule 10 to the Water Resources Act 1991 (discharge consents without applications).

8 Appeals

(1) A person who wishes to appeal to the Secretary of State under section 91 or 191B(5) of the Water Resources Act 1991 (appeals in respect of consents under Chapter II of Part III and appeals in relation to information which the Agency has determined is not commercially confidential) shall give the Secretary of State notice of the appeal.

(2) The notice of appeal shall—

(a) specify the grounds of appeal; and

(b) indicate whether the appellant wishes the appeal to be determined on the basis of a hearing or written representations.

(3) The notice of appeal shall be accompanied by copies of any application, consent, correspondence, decision, notice or other document relevant to the appeal.

(4) At the same time as the appellant gives notice of the appeal to the Secretary of State, the appellant shall send the Agency a copy of his notice of appeal, together with a list of the documents provided to the Secretary of State under paragraph (3) above.

(5) If the appellant wishes at any time to withdraw his appeal he shall do so by notice informing the Secretary of State and shall send a copy of the notice to the Agency.

9 Time limit for bringing appeal

(1) Subject to the following provisions of this regulation, notice of appeal in accordance with regulation 8(1) shall be given—

(a) in the case of an appeal against the revocation of a consent, before the revocation takes effect;

(b) in the case of an appeal against an enforcement notice, before the expiry of the period of 21 days beginning with the date on which the enforcement notice is received;

(c) in the case of an appeal against a determination under section 191B(2) or (4) of the Water Resources Act 1991 (exclusion from registers of certain confidential information) that information is not commercially confidential, before the expiry of the period of 21 days beginning with the date on which the appellant is notified of the determination; and

(d) in any other case, before the expiry of the period of three months beginning with—

(i) the date on which the appellant is notified of the decision which is the subject matter of the appeal; or

(ii) if paragraph 3(2) of Schedule 10 to the Water Resources Act 1991 (failure to determine application within 4 months or longer period agreed with applicant) applies, the date on which the applicable period under paragraph 3(2) expires.

(2) Subject to paragraph (3) below, the Secretary of State may allow notice of appeal to be given after the expiry of the relevant period mentioned in paragraph (1) above.

(3) Paragraph (2) above shall not apply in the case of an appeal against—

(a) a decision to revoke a discharge consent;

(b) a decision to modify the conditions of any such consent;

(c) a decision to provide that any such consent which was unconditional shall be subject to conditions;

(d) a determination under section 191B(2) or (4) of the Water Resources Act 1991 (exclusion from registers of certain confidential information) that information is not commercially confidential.

10 Action upon receipt of notice of appeal

(1) Subject to paragraph (5) below, the Agency shall, within 14 days of receipt of the copy of the notice of appeal in accordance with regulation 8(4)—

(a) in the case of an appeal against a decision—

(i) to revoke a discharge consent; or

(ii) to modify the conditions of any such consent, or to provide that any such consent which was unconditional shall be subject to conditions, unless in either case the decision was made in response to an application for a variation,

give notice of the appeal to any person who appears to the Agency likely to have a particular interest in its subject matter; and

(b) in any other case give notice of the appeal—
  (i) to any person who made representations or objections to the Agency with respect to the grant or variation of the consent; and
  (ii) to any person who was required to be consulted in relation to the grant or variation of the consent under paragraph 2(1) or 6(4) of Schedule 10 to the Water Resources Act 1991 pursuant to regulation 5(1) or paragraph 3(1) of Schedule 1 to these Regulations.

(2) A notice under paragraph (1) above shall—

(a) inform the person on whom it is served that an appeal to the Secretary of State has been made; and

(b) state—
  (i) that any representations made to the Secretary of State in writing by the recipient of the notice will be considered by the Secretary of State if they are made within the period of 21 days beginning with the date of receipt of the notice;
  (ii) that copies of the representations will be sent to the appellant and the Agency;
  (iii) that copies of the representations will be placed on registers maintained under section 190 of the Water Resources Act 1991 (pollution control registers);
  (iv) that any person who makes any such representations will be informed about the hearing of the appeal if there is to be a hearing held wholly or partly in public, and shall be accompanied by a copy of the notice of appeal.

(3) The Agency shall, within 14 days of sending a notice under paragraph (1) above, notify the Secretary of State of the name and address of every person who was sent such a notice in relation to the appeal and the date on which it was sent.

(4) Where an appeal is withdrawn after a notice under paragraph (1) above has been sent, the Agency shall inform every person who was sent such a notice in relation to the appeal.

(5) This regulation shall not apply in relation to an appeal under section 91(1)(h) or 191B(5) of the Water Resources Act 1991 (appeals against enforcement notices and appeals against determinations that information is not commercially confidential).

11 Written representations

...

12 Hearings

...

13 Notification of determination

(1) The Secretary of State shall notify the appellant in writing of his determination of the appeal and shall provide him with a copy of any report mentioned in regulation 12(8).

(2) The Secretary of State shall at the same time send—

(a) a copy of the documents mentioned in paragraph (1) above to the Agency and to any persons required under regulation 10(1)(b)(ii) to be notified of the appeal; and

(b) a copy of his determination of the appeal to any other person who made representations to the Secretary of State under regulation 10 and, if a hearing was held, to any other person who made representations in relation to the appeal at the hearing.

14 Consents for discharges by the Agency

(1) Section 88 of the Water Resources Act 1991 (defence to principal offences in respect of authorised discharges) shall have effect in relation to cases in which consents for the

purposes of subsection (1)(a) of that section are required by the Agency as if for subsection (2) there were substituted—

'(2) Schedule 2 to the Control of Pollution (Applications, Appeals and Registers) Regulations 1996 shall apply with respect to the making of applications by the Agency for consents under this Chapter for the purposes of subsection (1)(a) above and with respect to the giving, revocation and modification of such consents.'

(2) Schedule 2 to these Regulations (which deals with consents for discharges by the Agency) shall have effect.

15 Pollution control registers

Subject to sections 191A and 191B of the Water Resources Act 1991 and regulations 16 and 17, registers maintained by the Agency under section 190 of that Act (pollution control registers) shall contain full particulars of—

(a) notices of water quality objectives and other notices served under section 83 of that Act;

(b) applications made for consents, or for the variation of consents, under Chapter II of Part III of that Act, together with information provided in connection with such applications;

(c) consents given under that Chapter, the conditions to which the consents are subject and any variation of the consents;

(d) the date and time of each sample of water or effluent taken by the Agency for the purposes of the water pollution provisions of that Act (including details of the place where it was taken) and the result of the analysis of each sample and the steps, if any, taken in consequence by the Agency;

(e) information corresponding to that mentioned in paragraph (d) above with respect to samples of water or effluent taken by any other person, and the analysis of those samples, acquired by the Agency from that person under arrangements made by the Agency for the purposes of any of the water pollution provisions of that Act, including any steps taken by that person in consequence of the results of the analysis of any sample;

(f) prohibition notices served under section 86(1) of that Act;

(g) enforcement notices served under section 90B of that Act;

(h) revocations of discharge consents under paragraph 7 of Schedule 10 to that Act;

(i) notices of appeal under section 91 of that Act, correspondence provided to the Secretary of State under regulation 8(3), the decisions or notices which are the subject matter of the appeals, representations made under regulation 10, written notifications of the Secretary of State's determination of appeals and reports accompanying any such notification;

(j) directions given by the Secretary of State in relation to the Agency's functions under the water pollution provisions of that Act, with the exception of directions under section 191A(2) of that Act (directions in relation to information affecting national security);

(k) convictions, for offences under Part III of that Act, of persons who have the benefit of discharge consents, including the name of the offender, the date of conviction, the penalty imposed, the costs, if any, awarded against the offender and the name of the Court;

(l) returns and other information about the nature, origin, composition, temperature, volume and rate of discharges provided to the Agency in pursuance of conditions of discharge consents; and

(m) information which was entered on the registers under the Control of Pollution (Registers) Regulations 1989.

[(n) works notices under section 161A of the Act;

(o) notices of appeal under section 161C of the Act, documents provided to the Secretary of State in connection with appeals under that section, written notifications of the determinations of such appeals and any report accompanying any such written notification; and

(p) any conviction of any person for any offence under section 161D of the Act, including the name of the offender, the date of conviction, the penalty imposed, the costs, if any, awarded against the offender, and the name of the court.]

16 Entry of particulars on register, removal of certain particulars and indexing of registers

(1) Subject to sections 191A and 191B of the Water Resources Act 1991 and paragraph (2) below, where registers are by virtue of regulation 15 to contain any particulars, those particulars shall be entered on the registers—

(a) if they relate to an application or notice which is to be advertised under regulation 2(2), paragraph 1(1) of Schedule 1 or paragraph 1(2) of Schedule 2, before the beginning of the period of 28 days during which the application or notice is required to be advertised;

(b) if they relate to an enforcement notice served under section 90B of that Act, not later than 7 days after it is served;

[(ba) if they relate to a works notice under section 161A of the Act, not later than 7 days after the notice is served;

(bb) if they relate to any matters mentioned in regulation 15(o), not later than 14 days after those particulars become available to the Agency;]

(c) in all other cases, not later than 28 days after those particulars become available to the Agency.

(2) Where an application for a consent, or for the variation of a consent, is withdrawn at any time before it is determined—

(a) no further particulars relating to the application shall be entered on the registers after the application is withdrawn; and

(b) all particulars relating to the application shall be removed from the registers not less than 2 months, and not more than 3 months, after the application is withdrawn.

(3) The Agency shall keep records in each register showing the dates on which particulars are entered on that register.

(4) Each register shall be indexed in a way which facilitates access to particulars entered on it.

17 Period after which information may be removed from pollution control registers

(1) Nothing in regulation 15 shall require the Agency to keep on a register—

(a) monitoring information more than four years after that information was entered on the register; or

(b) other information which has been superseded by later information more than four years after that later information was entered on the register.

(2) In this regulation 'monitoring information' means information entered on the register by virtue of regulation 15(d), (e) or (1).

Waste Management (Miscellaneous Provisions) Regulations 1997

(SI 1997, No. 351)

1 Citation and commencement

(1) These Regulations may be cited as the Waste Management (Miscellaneous Provisions) Regulations 1997 and, except for regulation 2, shall come into force on 1st April 1997.

(2) Regulation 2 shall come into force on 14th March 1997.

2 Relevant offences

An offence shall be a relevant offence for the purposes of section 74(3)(a) of the Environmental Protection Act 1990 (in addition to the offences prescribed by regulation 3 of the Waste Management Licensing Regulations 1994) if it is an offence under paragraph 15(1), (3), (4) or (5) of Schedule 5 to the Finance Act 1996 (landfill tax).

3 ...

Groundwater Regulations 1998

(SI 1998, No. 2746) (as amended)

1 Citation, extent, commencement and interpretation

(1) These Regulations may be cited as the Groundwater Regulations.

(2) ...

(3) In these Regulations—

'the Groundwater Directive' means Council Directive 80/68/EEC;

'the Agency'—

(a) in relation to England and Wales, means the Environment Agency;

(b) ...

'authorisation' means—

(a) an authorisation under regulation 18 or 19;

(b) a discharge consent within the meaning of section 91(8) of the Water Resources Act 1991;

(c) ...; [...]

(d) an authorisation under Part I of the Environmental Protection Act 1990 in relation to a process designated for central control under section 2 of that Act; 'direct discharge' means the introduction into groundwater of any substance in list I or II without percolation through the ground or subsoil; [and

(e) a permit under the Pollution Prevention and Control (England and Wales) Regulations 2000 in so far as it authorises the operation of a Part A installation or Part A mobile plant within the meaning of those Regulations;]

'groundwater' means all water which is below the surface of the ground in the saturation zone and in direct contact with the ground or subsoil;

'highway drain' means a drain which a highway authority or other person is entitled to keep open by virtue of section 100 of the Highways Act 1980;

'indirect discharge' means the introduction into groundwater of any substance in list I or II after percolation through the ground or subsoil;

'pollution' means the discharge by man, directly or indirectly, of substances or energy into groundwater, the results of which are such as to endanger human health or water supplies, harm living resources and the aquatic ecosystem or interfere with other legitimate uses of water;

...

'substance in list I' and 'substance in list II' shall have the meaning given by paragraphs 1 and 2 of the Schedule to these Regulations (and paragraphs 3 and 4 of that Schedule shall have effect);

and other expressions used in these Regulations which are also used in the Groundwater Directive shall have the same meaning as in that Directive.

2 Exclusions from these Regulations

(1) Nothing in these Regulations shall apply in relation to—

(a) any discharge of matter containing radioactive substances;

(b) any discharge of domestic effluent from an isolated dwelling which is not connected to a sewerage system and which is situated outside any area protected for the abstraction of water for human consumption;

(c) any discharge found by the Agency to contain substances in list I or II in a quantity and concentration so small as to obviate any present or future danger of deterioration in the quality of the receiving groundwater; or

(d) any activity for which a waste management licence (within the meaning of Part II of the Environmental Protection Act 1990) is required.

(2) The Agency shall from time to time publish a summary of its findings under paragraph (1)(c) above in such manner as it considers appropriate and shall make copies of any such summary available to the public free of charge.

3 Discharge of functions

The Agency and the Secretary of State shall for the purposes of implementing the Groundwater Directive discharge their respective functions under these Regulations,... Part III of the Water Resources Act 1991 (control of water pollution—England and Wales) and Part I of the Environmental Protection Act 1990 (integrated pollution control) [and the Pollution Prevention and Control (England and Wales) Regulations 2000] in accordance with the following provisions of these Regulations.

4 Measures to prevent the introduction into groundwater of list I substances

(1) An authorisation shall not be granted if it would permit the direct discharge of any substance in list I.

(2) An authorisation shall not be granted in relation to—

(a) the disposal, or tipping for the purpose of disposal, of any substance in list I which might lead to an indirect discharge of that substance; or

(b) any other activity on or in the ground which might lead to an indirect discharge of any substance in list I,

unless that activity has been subjected to prior investigation.

(3) In the light of any such investigation—

(a) an authorisation shall not be granted if it would permit the indirect discharge of any substance in list I; and

(b) any authorisation granted must include conditions which require that all necessary technical precautions are observed to prevent an indirect discharge of any substance in list I.

(4) The following powers shall be exercised if it is necessary to do so for the purpose of preventing the introduction into groundwater of substances in list I—

(a) in the case of any discharge from a highway drain... which contains any such substance, the powers conferred by section 86(1) of the Water Resources Act 1991... (prohibition of certain discharges by notice);

(b) in the case of any activity falling within paragraph (2)(b) above and not falling within sub-paragraph (a) above, the powers conferred by regulation 19.

(5) However, a discharge of any substance in list I into groundwater may be authorised after prior investigation if—

(a) the investigation reveals that the groundwater is permanently unsuitable for other uses (especially domestic or agricultural uses), presence of that substance does not impede exploitation of ground resources and conditions are imposed which require that all technical precautions are observed to prevent that substance from reaching other aquatic systems or harming other ecosystems; or

(b) the discharge is due to the re-injection into the same aquifer of water used for geothermal purposes, water pumped out of mines and quarries or water pumped out for civil engineering works.

5 Measures to limit the introduction into groundwater of list II substances to avoid pollution

(1) An authorisation shall not be granted in relation to—

(a) any direct discharge of any substance in list II;

(b) any disposal or tipping for the purpose of disposal of any substance in list II which might lead to an indirect discharge of that substance;

(c) any other activity on or in the ground which might lead to an indirect discharge of any substance in list II,

unless that activity has been subjected to prior investigation.

(2) An authorisation may only be granted if, in the light of any such investigation, it includes conditions which require that all necessary technical precautions are observed to prevent groundwater pollution by any substance in list II.

(3) The following powers shall be exercised if it is necessary to do so for the purpose of avoiding pollution of groundwater by substances in list II—

(a) in the case of any discharge from a highway drain . . . which contains such substances, the powers conferred by section 86(1) of the Water Resources Act 1991 . . . (prohibition of certain discharges by notice);

(b) in the case of any activity falling within paragraph (1)(c) above and not falling within sub-paragraph (a) above, the powers conferred by regulation 19.

6 Artificial recharges for the purposes of groundwater management

Artificial recharges may be authorised on a case by case basis for the purpose of groundwater management notwithstanding regulations 4 and 5, but such authorisation shall only be granted if there is no risk of polluting groundwater.

7 Examination required in prior investigation

Any prior investigation required by regulation 4 or 5 shall include examination of—

(a) the hydrogeological conditions of the area concerned;

(b) the possible purifying powers of the soil and subsoil; and

(c) the risk of pollution and alteration of the quality of the groundwater from the discharge,

and shall establish whether the discharge of substances into groundwater is a satisfactory solution from the point of view of the environment.

8 Surveillance of groundwater

An authorisation which is subject to any of the provisions of regulation 4, 5 or 6 may only be granted if the Agency has checked that the groundwater (and, in particular, its quality) will undergo the requisite surveillance.

9 Terms of authorisation of discharge of substances in list I or II

(1) This regulation applies where—

(a) a direct discharge of any substance in list I or II is authorised in accordance with regulation 4(5) or 5; or

(b) waste water disposal which inevitably causes an indirect discharge of any substance in list II is authorised in accordance with regulation 5.

(2) In a case where this regulation applies the authorisation shall specify in particular—

(a) the place where the discharge may be made;

(b) the method of discharge which may be used;

(c) the essential precautions which must be taken, paying particular attention to the nature and concentration of any substance in list I or II present in the effluent, the characteristics of the receiving environment and the proximity of water catchment areas, in particular those for drinking, thermal and mineral water;

(d) the maximum quantity of any such substance permissible in the effluent during one or more specified periods of time and the appropriate requirements as to the concentration of any such substance;

(e) the arrangements for monitoring effluents discharged into groundwater;

(f) if necessary, measures for monitoring groundwater, and in particular its quality.

10 Terms of authorisation for disposal or tipping for the purpose of disposal

(1) This regulation applies where—

(a) any disposal, or tipping for the purpose of disposal, of any matter which might lead to an indirect discharge of any substance in list I or II is authorised in accordance with regulation 4 or 5; and

(b) in the case of a disposal, it is not a disposal of waste water to which regulation 9(1)(b) applies.

(2) In a case where this regulation applies the authorisation shall specify in particular—

(a) the place where the disposal or tipping may be done;

(b) the methods of disposal or tipping which may be used;

(c) the essential precautions which must be taken, paying particular attention to the nature and concentration of any substance in list I or II present in the matter to be disposed of or tipped, the characteristics of the receiving environment and the proximity of water catchment areas, in particular those for drinking, thermal and mineral water;

(d) the maximum quantity permissible, during one or more specified periods of time, of the matter containing any such substance and, where possible, of any such substance, to be tipped or disposed of and the appropriate requirements as to the concentration of any such substance;

(e) the technical precautions to be implemented to prevent any discharge into groundwater of any substance in list I and any pollution of such water by any substance in list II,

(f) if necessary, the measures for monitoring the groundwater, and in particular its quality.

11 Period and conditions of authorisation

(1) An authorisation of—

(a) a discharge of any substance in list I or II; or

(b) any disposal, or tipping for the purpose of disposal, of any matter which might lead to an indirect discharge of any substance in list I or II,

may be granted for a limited period only, and must be reviewed at least once in every four years when it may be renewed, amended or revoked.

(2) If the applicant for any such authorisation states, or it is otherwise evident, that he will be unable to comply with the conditions of the proposed authorisation, the authorisation shall not be granted.

(3) The Agency shall monitor compliance with the conditions of any such authorisation and the effects of discharges on groundwater.

(4) If the conditions of any such authorisation are not complied with, the appropriate steps shall be taken to ensure compliance and, if necessary, the revocation of the authorisation.

12 Inventory of authorisations

The Agency shall keep an inventory of authorisations of—

(a) direct or indirect discharges of any substance in list I;

(b) direct discharges of any substance in list II; and

(c) artificial recharges for the purposes of groundwater management.

13 Application of measures not to lead to pollution of groundwater

The application of the measures taken pursuant to these Regulations may on no account lead, either directly or indirectly, to pollution of groundwater.

14 Application of provisions of water pollution legislation

(1) A person shall be treated as contravening section 85 of the Water Resources Act 1991 . . . (water pollution offences) if—

(a) he causes or knowingly permits—

(i) the disposal or tipping for the purposes of disposal of any substance in list I or II in circumstances which might lead to an indirect discharge of that substance into groundwater unless it is carried on under and in accordance with an authorisation granted under regulation 18; or

(ii) any activity to be carried on in contravention of a prohibition imposed under regulation 19 or any authorisation granted under that regulation; or

(b) he contravenes the conditions of any authorisation under regulation 18 or 19.

(2) Section 88(1) of the Water Resources Act 1991 . . . (defences to water pollution offences in respect of authorised discharges) shall apply in relation to an authorisation under regulation 18 or 19 as if the reference—

(a) in section 88(1)(a) to a consent under Chapter II of Part III of the Water Resources Act 1991;

(b) . . . included a reference to such an authorisation.

(3) Sections 191A and 191B of the Water Resources Act 1991 . . . (exclusion from registers of information affecting national security and certain confidential information) shall apply in relation to the particulars mentioned in regulation 22(1) as if information furnished for the purposes mentioned in paragraphs (a) to (c) of subsection (2) of section 191A . . . included information furnished to the Agency for the purposes of regulation 18 or 19.

(4) Paragraph 11 of Schedule 10 to the Water Resources Act 1991 (transfer of discharge consents) shall apply in relation to an authorisation under regulation 18—

(a) as if any reference to a consent included a reference to such authorisation;

(b) as if references to paragraphs 3 and 6 of that Schedule were references to regulation 18; and

(c) as if references to carrying on or making discharges were references to carrying on the activities regulated by the authorisation.

15 Application of section 71 of the Environmental Protection Act 1990

Section 71 of the Environmental Protection Act 1990 (obtaining of information) shall apply for the purposes of these Regulations as if any reference to functions under Part II of that Act included a reference to functions under these regulations.

16 Application of sections 41, 42 and 123 of the Environment Act 1995

(1) Sections 41 and 42 of the Environment Act 1995 (charging schemes) shall apply in relation to an authorisation under regulation 18 or 19 as if any reference to an environmental licence included a reference to such an authorisation.

(2) Section 123 of the Environment Act 1995 (provisions relating to the service of documents) shall apply to the service of notices under regulation 18 or 19 as it applies to the service of documents under that Act.

. . .

18 Authorisation of disposal or tipping of substances in list I or II

(1) An application for an authorisation for the purposes of regulation 14(1)(a)(i) shall be made in writing to the Agency.

(2) If in any case the Agency considers that there are special reasons why the application should be advertised, it may by notice in writing served on the applicant require him to advertise the application in such manner as may be specified in the notice.

(3) The Agency may either—

(a) grant an authorisation in writing subject to such conditions as it thinks fit; or

(b) by notice in writing served on the applicant, refuse the application and the notice shall state the Agency's reasons for refusal.

(4) The Agency may, by notice in writing served on the person holding an authorisation under this regulation, at any time vary or revoke the authorisation and a notice of variation or revocation shall state the Agency's reasons.

19 Notice to prevent or control indirect discharges of substances in list I or II

(1) Subject to paragraph (2), where—

(a) any person is carrying on, or proposing to carry on, any activity on or in the ground; and

(b) that activity might lead to an indirect discharge of any substance in list I or pollution of groundwater as a result of an indirect discharge of any substance in list II, the Agency may serve notice in writing on that person prohibiting him from carrying on that activity or authorising him to carry on that activity subject to such conditions as are specified in the notice and which are necessary to prevent an indirect discharge of any substance in list I or pollution of groundwater as a result of an indirect discharge of any substance in list II.

(2) This regulation shall not apply to the disposal, or tipping for the purpose of disposal, of any substance in list I or II except in a case falling within regulation 23(3) during the period whilst the application in question is pending.

(3) The Agency may at any time, by notice in writing served on the person on whom a notice under paragraph (1) was served, vary or revoke that notice and a notice of variation or revocation shall state the Agency's reasons.

20 Appeals

(1) A person may appeal by notice in writing to the Secretary of State against any decision of the Agency under regulation 18 or 19—

(a) in the case of a decision under regulation 18, within a period of three months; or

(b) in the case of a decision under regulation 19, within a period of 21 days, beginning in either case with the date on which he was notified of the Agency's decision, or within such longer period as the Secretary of State may allow.

(2) Where—

(a) an application has been made to the Agency in accordance with regulation 18 above; and

(b) the Agency has not notified the applicant of its decision in relation to that application within—

(i) a period of four months beginning with the date on which it received the application (or, if the application must be advertised, the date on which advertising is completed); or

(ii) if the Agency and the applicant agree in writing to a longer period, that period, the applicant may for the purposes of this regulation treat this as a refusal by the Agency of the application and appeal to the Secretary of State.

(3) An appeal under this regulation shall be made by the appellant serving notice in writing on the Secretary of State and the notice shall state the appellant's grounds of appeal.

(4) Before determining an appeal under this regulation the Secretary of State shall—

(a) take into account any written representations of the appellant and of the Agency; and

(b) if requested to do so by the appellant or the Agency, afford them an opportunity of appearing before and being heard by a person appointed by the Secretary of State for the purpose.

(5) On determining an appeal under this regulation the Secretary of State shall have power to dismiss the appeal or to direct the Agency to take such steps in exercise of its powers under regulation 18 or 19 as the Secretary of State considers appropriate to give effect to his decision on the appeal.

21 Codes of practice

(1) The Ministers may from time to time approve for the purposes of these Regulations (or withdraw their approval of) codes of practice issued for the purpose of giving practical guidance to persons engaged in any activity falling within regulation 4(2)(b) or 5(1)(c) about the steps they should take to prevent substances in list I from entering groundwater or to avoid pollution of such water by substances in list II.

(2) In deciding whether or not it is necessary to exercise the Agency's powers under regulation 19, the Agency shall consider whether or not any guidance, which is contained in a relevant code of practice for the time being approved under paragraph (1) above, has been, or is likely to be, followed.

(3) When the Ministers exercise their powers under paragraph (1) above they shall—

(a) notify the Agency of their approval (or withdrawal of their approval) of the relevant code of practice; and

(b) make such arrangements as they consider appropriate for publicising their approval or, as the case may be, its withdrawal.

(4) The Agency shall make appropriate arrangements for bringing each code of practice for the time being approved under paragraph (1) above to the attention of persons engaged in the relevant activity.

(5) In this regulation 'the Ministers' means any Minister of the Crown within the meaning of the Ministers of the Crown Act 1975 acting either alone or jointly with one or more such Ministers.

22 Particulars to be included in registers

(1) Subject to regulation 14(3) and paragraph (2) below, the Agency shall, as soon as reasonably practicable, enter on registers maintained by it under section 190 of the Water Resources Act 1991 or... (pollution control registers) full particulars of—

(a) any authorisation under regulation 18;
(b) any application for such an authorisation;
(c) any variation or revocation of such an authorisation;
(d) any notice under regulation 19;
(e) any variation or revocation of any such notice;
(f) any information furnished to the Agency for the purposes of regulation 18 or 19;
(g) any monitoring information provided in connection with any authorisation under regulation 18 or 19;
(h) any conviction for an offence under section 85 of the Water Resources Act 1991 or... by virtue of regulation 14(1);
(i) any finding of the Agency under regulation 2(1)(c), any determination of the Agency under paragraph 1(2) or 2(2) of the Schedule to these Regulations, any notification by the Secretary of State under paragraph 3(2) of that Schedule and any summary published under regulation 2(2) or paragraph 4 of that Schedule; and
(j) any code of practice for the time being approved under regulation 21 above.

(2) Nothing in paragraph (1) above shall require the Agency to keep on a register—

(a) monitoring information more than four years after that information was entered on the register;
(b) other information which has been superseded by later information more than four years after that later information was entered on the register; or
(c) information relating to an application for an authorisation under regulation 18 after the application has been withdrawn.

Regulation 1(3)

SCHEDULE

LIST 1

1.—(1) Subject to sub-paragraph (2) below, a substance is in list I if it belongs to one of the following families or groups of substances—

(a) organohalogen compounds and substances which may form such compounds in the aquatic environment;
(b) organophosphorus compounds;
(c) organotin compounds;
(d) substances which possess carcinogenic, mutagenic or teratogenic properties in or via the aquatic environment (including substances which have those properties which would otherwise be in list II);
(e) mercury and its compounds;
(f) cadmium and its compounds;
(g) mineral oils and hydrocarbons;
(h) cyanides.

(2) A substance is not in list I if it has been determined by the Agency to be inappropriate to list I on the basis of a low risk of toxicity, persistence and bioaccumulation.

LIST II

2.—(1) A substance is in list II if it could have a harmful effect on groundwater and it belongs to one of the following families or groups of substances—

(a) the following metalloids and metals and their compounds:

Zinc	Tin
Copper	Barium
Nickel	Beryllium
Chromium	Boron
Lead	Uranium
Selenium	Vanadium
Arsenic	Cobalt
Antimony	Thallium
Molybdenum	Tellurium
Titanium	Siiver.

(b) biocides and their derivatives not appearing in list I;
(c) substances which have a deleterious effect on the taste or odour of ground-water, and compounds liable to cause the formation of such substances in such water and to render it unfit for human consumption;
(d) toxic or persistent organic compounds of silicon, and substances which may cause the formation of such compounds in water, excluding those which are biologically harmless or are rapidly converted in water into harmless substances;
(e) inorganic compounds of phosphorus and elemental phosphorus;
(f) fluorides;
(g) ammonia and nitrites.

(2) A substance is also in list II if—

(a) it belongs to one of the families or groups of substances set out in paragraph 1(1) above;
(b) it has been determined by the Agency to be inappropriate to list I under paragraph 1(2); and
(c) it has been determined by the Agency to be appropriate to list II having regard to toxicity, persistence and bioaccumulation.

3.—(1) The Secretary of State may review any decision of the Agency in relation to the exercise of its powers under paragraph 1(2) or 2(2).

(2) The Secretary of State shall notify the Agency of his decision following a review under sub-paragraph (1) above and it shall b' the duty of the Agency to give effect to that decision.

4. The Agency shall from time to time publish a summary of the effect of its determinations under this Schedule in such manner as it considers appropriate and shall make copies of any such summary available to the public free of charge.

Town and Country Planning (Environmental Impact Assessment) (England and Wales) Regulations 1999

(SI 1999, No. 293) (as amended)

PART I GENERAL

1 Citation, commencement and application

(1) These Regulations may be cited as the Town and Country Planning (Environmental Impact Assessment) (England and Wales) Regulations 1999 and shall come into force on 14th March 1999.

(2) Subject to paragraph (3), these Regulations shall apply throughout England and Wales.

(3) . . .

2 Interpretation

(1) In these Regulations—

'the Act' means the Town and Country Planning Act 1990 and references to sections are references to sections of that Act;

['the 1991 Act' means the Planning and Compensation Act 1991;]

['the 1995 Act' means the Environment Act 1995;]

'the consulation bodies' means—

(a) any body which the relevant planning authority is required to consult, or would, if an application for planning permission for the development in question were before them, be required to consult by virtue of article 10 (consultations before the grant of permission) of the Order or of any direction under that article; and

(b) the following bodies if not referred to in sub-paragraph (a)—

(i) any principal council for the area where the land is situated, if not the relevant planning authority;

(ii) where the land is situated in England, Natural England;

(iii) where the land is situated in Wales, the Countryside Council for Wales; and

(iv) the Environment Agency;

'the Directive' means Council Directive 85/337/EEC;

['EEA State' means a State party to the Agreement on the European Economic Area;]

'EIA application' means an application for planning permission for EIA development;

'EIA development' means development which is either—

(a) Schedule 1 development; or

(b) Schedule 2 development likely to have significant effects on the environment by virtue of factors such as its nature, size or location;

'environmental information' means the environmental statement, including any further information, any representations made by any body required by these Regulations to be invited to make representations, and any representations duly made by any other person about the environmental effects of the development;

'environmental statement' means a statement—

(a) that includes such of the information referred to in Part I of Schedule 4 as is reasonably required to assess the environmental effects of the development and which the applicant can, having regard in particular to current knowledge and methods of assessment, reasonably be required to compile, but

(b) that includes at least the information referred to in Part II of Schedule 4;

'exempt development' means development which comprises or forms part of a project serving national defence purposes or in respect of which the Secretary of State has made a direction under regulation 4(4);

'further information' has the meaning given in regulation 19(1);

'General Regulations' means the Town and Country Planning General Regulations 1992;

'inspector' means a person appointed by the Secretary of State pursuant to Schedule 6 to the Act to determine an appeal;

'the land' means the land on which the development would be carried out or, in relation to development already carried out, has been carried out;

'the Order' means the Town and Country Planning (General Development Procedure) Order 1995;

'principal council' has the meaning given by sub-section (1) of section 270 (general provisions as to interpretation) of the Local Government Act 1972;

'register' means a register kept pursuant to section 69 (registers of applications etc.) and 'appropriate register' means the register on which particulars of an application for planning permission for the relevant development have been placed or would fall to be placed if such an application were made;

['relevant mineral planning authority' means the body to whom it falls, fell, or would, but for a direction under paragraph—

(a) 7 of Schedule 2 to the 1991 Act;

(b) 13 of Schedule 13 to the 1995 Act; or

(c) 8 of Schedule 14 to the 1995 Act,

fall to determine the ROMP application in question;]

'relevant planning authority' means the body to whom it falls, fell, or would, but for a direction under section 77 (reference of applications to Secretary of State), fall to determine an application for planning permission for the development in question;

['ROMP application' means an application to a relevant mineral planning authority to determine the conditions to which a planning permission is to be subject under paragraph—

(a) 2(2) of Schedule 2 to the 1991 Act (registration of old mining permissions);

(b) 9(1) of Schedule 13 to the 1995 Act (review of old mineral planning permissions); or

(c) 6(1) of Schedule 14 to the 1995 Act (periodic review of mineral planning permissions);

'ROMP development' means development which has yet to be carried out and which is authorised by a planning permission in respect of which a ROMP application has been or is to be made;]

'Schedule 1 application' and 'Schedule 2 application' mean an application for planning permission for Schedule 1 development and Schedule 2 development respectively;

'Schedule 1 development' means development, other than exempt development, of a description mentioned in Schedule 1;

'Schedule 2 development' means development, other than exempt development, of a description mentioned in Column 1 of the table in Schedule 2 where—

(a) any part of that development is to be carried out in a sensitive area; or

(b) any applicable threshold or criterion in the corresponding part of Column 2 of that table is respectively exceeded or met in relation to that development;

'scoping direction' and 'scoping opinion' have the meanings given in regulation 10;

'screening direction' means a direction made by the Secretary of State as to whether development is EIA development;

'screening opinion' means a written statement of the opinion of the relevant planning authority as to whether development is EIA development;

'sensitive area' means any of the following—

(a) land notified under sub-section (1) of section 28 (areas of special scientific interest) of the Wildlife and Countryside Act 1981;

(b) land to which sub-section (3) of section 29 (nature conservation orders) of the Wildlife and Countryside Act 1981 applies;
(c) an area to which paragraph (u)(ii) in the table in article 10 of the Order applies;
(d) a National Park within the meaning of the National Parks and Access to the Countryside Act 1949;
(e) the Broads;
(f) a property appearing on the World Heritage List kept under article 11 (2) of the 1972 UNESCO Convention for the Protection of the World Cultural and Natural Heritage;
(g) a scheduled monument within the meaning of the Ancient Monuments and Archaeological Areas Act 1979;
(h) an area of outstanding natural beauty designated as such by an order made by the Countryside Commission, as respects England, or the Countryside Council for Wales, as respects Wales, under section 87 (designation of areas of outstanding natural beauty) of the National Parks and Access to the Countryside Act 1949 as confirmed by the Secretary of State;
(i) a European site within the meaning of regulation 10 of the Conservation (Natural Habitats etc.) Regulations 1994;

(2) Subject to paragraph (3), expressions used both in these Regulations and in the Act have the same meaning for the purposes of these Regulations as they have for the purposes of the Act.

(3) Expressions used both in these Regulations and in the Directive (whether or not also used in the Act) have the same meaning for the purposes of these Regulations as they have for the purposes of the Directive.

(4) In these Regulations any reference to a Council Directive is a reference to that Directive as amended at the date these Regulations were made.

(5) In these Regulations references to the Secretary of State shall not be construed as references to an inspector.

[(6) In its application to Wales, these Regulations shall have effect, with any necessary amendments, as if each reference to 'the Secretary of State' were a reference to 'the National Assembly for Wales.']

3 Prohibition on granting planning permission without consideration of environmental information

(1) This regulation applies—
(a) to every EIA application received by the authority with whom it is lodged on or after the commencement of these Regulations; and
(b) to every EIA application lodged by an authority pursuant to regulation 3 or 4 (applications for planning permission) of the General Regulations on or after that date;

and for the purposes of this paragraph, the date of receipt of an application by an authority shall be determined in accordance with paragraph (3) of article 20 (time periods for decision) of the Order.

(2) The relevant planning authority or the Secretary of State or an inspector shall not grant planning permission pursuant to an application to which this regulation applies unless they have first taken the environmental information into consideration, and they shall state in their decision that they have done so.

PART II SCREENING

4 General provisions relating to screening

(1) Subject to paragraphs (3) and (4), the occurrence of an event mentioned in paragraph (2) shall determine for the purpose of these Regulations that development is EIA development.

(2) The events referred to in paragraph (1) are—

(a) the submission by the applicant or appellant in relation to that development of a statement referred to by the applicant or appellant as an environmental statement for the purposes of these Regulations; or

(b) the adoption by the relevant planning authority of a screening opinion to the effect that the development is EIA development.

(3) A direction of the Secretary of State shall determine for the purpose of these Regulations whether development is or is not EIA development.

(4) The Secretary of State may direct that particular proposed development is exempted from the application of these Regulations in accordance with Article 2(3) of the Directive (but without prejudice to Article 7 of the Directive) and shall send a copy of any such direction to the relevant planning authority.

(5) Where a local planning authority or the Secretary of State has to decide under these Regulations whether Schedule 2 development is EIA development the authority or Secretary of State shall take into account in making that decision such of the selection criteria set out in Schedule 3 as are relevant to the development.

(6) Where—

(a) a local planning authority adopt a screening opinion; or

(b) the Secretary of State makes a screening direction under these Regulations;

to the effect that development is EIA development—

(i) that opinion or direction shall be accompanied by a written statement giving clearly and precisely the full reasons for that conclusion; and

(ii) the authority or the Secretary of State, as the case may be, shall send a copy of the opinion or direction and a copy of the written statement required by sub-paragraph (i) to the person who proposes to carry out, or who has carried out, the development in question.

(7) The Secretary of State may make a screening direction irrespective of whether he has received a request to do so.

(8) The Secretary of State may direct that particular development of a description mentioned in Column 1 of the table in Schedule 2 is EIA development in spite of the fact that none of the conditions contained in sub-paragraphs (a) and (b) of the definition of 'Schedule 2 development' is satisfied in relation to that development.

(9) The Secretary of State shall send a copy of any screening direction to the relevant planning authority.

5 Requests for screening opinions of the local planning authority

(1) A person who is minded to carry out development may request the relevant planning authority to adopt a screening opinion.

(2) A request for a screening opinion shall be accompanied by—

(a) a plan sufficient to identify the land;

(b) a brief description of the nature and purpose of the development and of its possible effects on the environment; and

(c) such other information or representations as the person making the request may wish to provide or make.

(3) An authority receiving a request for a screening opinion shall, if they consider that they have not been provided with sufficient information to adopt an opinion, notify in writing the person making the request of the points on which they require additional information.

(4) An authority shall adopt a screening opinion within three weeks beginning with the date of receipt of a request made pursuant to paragraph (1) or such longer period as may be agreed in writing with the person making the request.

(5) An authority which adopts a screening opinion pursuant to paragraph (4) shall forthwith send a copy to the person who made the request.

(6) Where an authority—

(a) fail to adopt a screening opinion within the relevant period mentioned in paragraph (4); or

(b) adopt an opinion to the effect that the development is EIA development;

the person who requested the opinion may request the Secretary of State to make a screening direction.

(7) The person may make a request pursuant to paragraph (6) even if the authority has not received additional information which it has sought under paragraph (3).

6 Requests for screening directions of the Secretary of State

(1) A person who pursuant to regulation 5(6) requests the Secretary of State to make a screening direction shall submit with his request—

(a) a copy of this request to the relevant planning authority under regulation 5(1) and the documents which accompanied it;

(b) a copy of any notification under regulation 5(3) which he has received and of any response;

(c) a copy of any screening opinion he has received from the authority and of any accompanying statement of reasons; and

(d) any representations that he wishes to make.

(2) When a person makes a request pursuant to regulation 5(6) he shall send to the relevant planning authority a copy of that request and of any representations he makes to the Secretary of State.

(3) The Secretary of State shall, if he considers that he has not been provided with sufficient information to make a screening direction, notify in writing the person making the request pursuant to regulation 5(6) of the points on which he requires additional information, and may request the relevant planning authority to provide such information as they can on any of those points.

(4) The Secretary of State shall make a screening direction within three weeks beginning with the date of receipt of a request pursuant to regulation 5 (6) or such longer period as he may reasonably require.

(5) The Secretary of State shall send a copy of any screening direction made pursuant to paragraph (4) forthwith to the person who made the request.

PART III PROCEDURES CONCERNING APPLICATIONS FOR PLANNING PERMISSION

7 Application made to a local planning authority without an environmental statement

(1) Where it appears to the relevant planning authority that—

(a) an application for planning permission which is before them for determination is a Schedule 1 application or Schedule 2 application; and

(b) the development in question has not been the subject of a screening opinion or screening direction; and

(c) the application is not accompanied by a statement referred to by the applicant as an environmental statement for the purposes of these Regulations,

paragraphs (3) and (4) of regulation 5 shall apply as if the receipt or lodging of the application were a request made under regulation 5(1).

(2) Where an EIA application which is before a local planning authority for determination is not accompanied by a statement referred to by the applicant as an environmental statement for the purposes of these Regulations, the authority shall notify the applicant in writing that the submission of an environmental statement is required.

(3) An authority shall notify the applicant in accordance with paragraph (2) within three weeks beginning with the date of receipt of the application or such longer period as may be

agreed in writing with the applicant; but where the Secretary of State, after the expiry of that period of three weeks or of any longer period so agreed, makes a screening direction to the effect that the development is EIA development, the authority shall so notify the applicant within seven days beginning with the date the authority received a copy of that screening direction.

(4) An applicant receiving a notification pursuant to paragraph (2) may, within three weeks beginning with the date of the notification, write to the authority stating—

(a) that he accepts their view and is providing an environmental statement; or

(b) unless the Secretary of State has made a screening direction in respect of the development, that he is writing to the Secretary of State to request a screening direction.

(5) If the applicant does not write to the authority in accordance with paragraph (4), the permission sought shall, unless the Secretary of State has made a screening direction to the effect that the development is not EIA development, be deemed to be refused at the end of the relevant three week period, and the deemed refusal—

(a) shall be treated as a decision of the authority for the purposes of paragraph (4)(c) of article 25 (register of applications) of the Order; but

(b) shall not give rise to an appeal to the Secretary of State by virtue of section 78 (right to appeal against planning decisions and failure to take such decisions).

(6) An authority which has given a notification in accordance with paragraph (2) shall, unless the Secretary of State makes a screening direction to the effect that the development is not EIA development, determine the relevant application only by refusing planning permission if the applicant does not submit an environmental statement and comply with regulation 14(5).

(7) A person who requests a screening direction pursuant to sub-paragraph (4)(b) shall send to the Secretary of State with his request copies of—

(a) his application for planning permission;

(b) all documents sent to the authority as part of the application; and

(c) all correspondence between the applicant and the authority relating to the proposed development,

and paragraphs (2) to (5) of regulation 6 shall apply to a request under this regulation as they apply to a request made pursuant to regulation 5(6).

8 Application referred to the Secretary of State without an environmental statement

(1) Where it appears to the Secretary of State that an application for planning permission which has been referred to him for determination—

(a) is a Schedule 1 application or Schedule 2 application; and

(b) the development in question has not been the subject of a screening opinion or screening direction; and

(c) the application is not accompanied by a statement referred to by the applicant as an environmental statement for the purposes of these Regulations,

paragraphs (3) and (4) of regulation 6 shall apply as if the referral of the application were a request made by the applicant pursuant to regulation 5(6).

(2) Where it appears to the Secretary of State that an application which has been referred to him for determination is an EIA application and is not accompanied by a statement referred to by the applicant as an environmental statement for the purposes of these Regulations, he shall notify the applicant in writing that the submission of an environmental statement is required and shall send a copy of that notification to the relevant planning authority.

(3) The Secretary of State shall notify the applicant in accordance with paragraph (2) within three weeks beginning with the date he received the application or such longer period as he may reasonably require.

(4) An applicant who receives a notification under paragraph (2) may within three weeks beginning with the date of the notification write to the Secretary of State stating that he proposes to provide an environmental statement.

(5) If the applicant does not write in accordance with paragraph (4), the Secretary of State shall be under no duty to deal with the application; and at the end of the three week period he shall inform the applicant in writing that no further action is being taken on the application.

(6) Where the Secretary of State has given a notification under paragraph (2), he shall determine the relevant application only by refusing planning permission if the applicant does not submit an environmental statement and comply with regulation 14(5).

9 Appeal to the Secretary of State without an environmental statement

(1) Where on consideration of an appeal under section 78 (right to appeal against planning decisions and failure to take such decisions) it appears to the Secretary of State that—

(a) the relevant application is a Schedule 1 application or Schedule 2 application; and

(b) the development in question has not been the subject of a screening opinion or screening direction; and

(c) the relevant application is not accompanied by a statement referred to by the appellant as an environmental statement for the purposes of these Regulations,

paragraphs (3) and (4) of regulation 6 shall apply as if the appeal were a request made by the appellant pursuant to regulation 5(6).

(2) Where an inspector is dealing with an appeal and a question arises as to whether the relevant application is an EIA application and it appears to the inspector that it may be such an application, the inspector shall refer that question to the Secretary of State and shall not determine the appeal, except by refusing planning permission, before he receives a screening direction.

(3) Paragraphs (3) and (4) of regulation 6 shall apply to a question referred under paragraph (2) as if the referral of that question were a request made by the appellant pursuant to regulation 5(6).

(4) Where it appears to the Secretary of State that the relevant application is an EIA application and is not accompanied by a statement referred to by the appellant as an environmental statement for the purposes of these Regulations, he shall notify the appellant in writing that the submission of an environmental statement is required and shall send a copy of that notification to the relevant planning authority.

(5) An appellant who receives a notification under paragraph (4) may within three weeks beginning with the date of the notification write to the Secretary of State stating that he proposes to provide an environmental statement.

(6) If the appellant does not write in accordance with paragraph (5), the Secretary of State or, where relevant, the inspector shall be under no duty to deal with the appeal; and at the end of the three week period he shall inform the appellant that no further action is being taken on the appeal.

(7) Where the Secretary of State has given a notification under paragraph (4), the Secretary of State or, where relevant, the inspector shall determine the appeal only by refusing planning permission if the appellant does not submit an environmental statement and comply with regulation 14(5).

PART IV PREPARATION OF ENVIRONMENTAL STATEMENTS

10 Scoping opinions of the local planning authority

(1) A person who is minded to make an EIA application may ask the relevant planning authority to state in writing their opinion as to the information to be provided in the environmental statement (a 'scoping opinion').

(2) A request under paragraph (1) shall include—

(a) a plan sufficient to identify the land;

(b) a brief description of the nature and purpose of the development and of its possible effects on the environment; and

(c) such other information or representations as the person making the request may wish to provide or make.

(3) An authority receiving a request under paragraph (1) shall, if they consider that they have not been provided with sufficient information to adopt a scoping opinion, notify the person making the request of the points on which they require additional information.

(4) An authority shall not adopt a scoping opinion in response to a request under paragraph (1) until they have consulted the person who made the request and the consultation bodies, but shall, subject to paragraph (5), within five weeks beginning with the date of receipt of that request or such longer period as may be agreed in writing with the person making the request, adopt a scoping opinion and send a copy to the person who made the request.

(5) Where a person has, at the same time as making a request for a screening opinion under regulation 5(1), asked the authority for an opinion under paragraph (1) above, and the authority have adopted a screening opinion to the effect that the development is EIA development, the authority shall, within five weeks beginning with the date on which that screening opinion was adopted or such longer period as may be agreed in writing with the person making the request, adopt a scoping opinion and send a copy to the person who made the request.

(6) Before adopting a scoping opinion the authority shall take into account—

(a) the specific characteristics of the particular development;

(b) the specific characteristics of development of the type concerned; and

(c) the environmental features likely to be affected by the development.

(7) Where an authority fail to adopt a scoping opinion within the relevant period mentioned in paragraph (4) or (5), the person who requested the opinion may under regulation 11(1) ask the Secretary of State to make a direction as to the information to be provided in the environmental statement (a 'scoping direction').

(8) Paragraph (7) applies notwithstanding that the authority may not have received additional information which they have sought under paragraph (3).

(9) An authority which has adopted a scoping opinion in response to a request under paragraph (1) shall not be precluded from requiring of the person who made the request additional information in connection with any statement that may be submitted by that person as an environmental statement in connection with an application for planning permission for the same development as was referred to in the request.

11 Scoping directions of the Secretary of State

(1) A request made under this paragraph pursuant to regulation 10(7) shall include—

(a) a copy of the relevant request to the relevant planning authority under regulation 10(1);

(b) a copy of any relevant notification under regulation 10(3) and of any response;

(c) a copy of any relevant screening opinion received by the person making the request and of any accompanying statement of reasons; and

(d) any representations that the person making the request wishes to make.

(2) When a person makes a request under paragraph (1) he shall send to the relevant planning authority a copy of that request, but that copy need not include the matters mentioned in sub-paragraphs (a) to (c) of that paragraph.

(3) The Secretary of State shall notify in writing the person making the request of any points on which he considers the information provided pursuant to paragraph (1) is insufficient to enable him to make a scoping direction; and may request the relevant planning authority to provide such information as they can on any of those points.

(4) The Secretary of State shall not make a scoping direction in response to a request under paragraph (1) until he has consulted the person making the request and the consultation bodies, but shall, within five weeks beginning with the date of receipt of that request or such longer period as he may reasonably require, make a direction and send a copy to the person who made the request and to the relevant planning authority.

(5) Before making a scoping direction the Secretary of State shall take into account the matters specified in regulation 10(6).

(6) Where the Secretary of State has made a scoping direction in response to a request under paragraph (1) neither he nor the relevant planning authority shall be precluded from requiring of the person who made the request additional information in connection with any statement that may be submitted by that person as an environmental statement in connection with an application for planning permission for the same development as was referred to in the request.

12 Procedure to facilitate preparation of environmental statements

(1) Any person who intends to submit an environmental statement to the relevant planning authority or the Secretary of State under these Regulations may give notice in writing to that authority or the Secretary of State under this paragraph.

(2) A notice under paragraph (1) shall include the information necessary to identify the land and the nature and purpose of the development, and shall indicate the main environmental consequences to which the person giving the notice proposes to refer in his environmental statement.

(3) The recipient of—

(a) such notice as is mentioned in paragraph (1); or

(b) a written statement made pursuant to regulation 7(4)(a), or 8(4) or 9(5)

shall—

(i) notify the consultation bodies in writing of the name and address of the person who intends to submit an environmental statement and of the duty imposed on the consultation bodies by paragraph (4) to make information available to that person; and

(ii) inform in writing the person who intends to submit an environmental statement of the names and addresses of the bodies so notified.

(4) Subject to paragraph (5), the relevant planning authority and any body notified in accordance with paragraph (3) shall, if requested by the person who intends to submit an environmental statement enter into consultation with that person to determine whether the [authority or] body has in its possession any information which he or they consider relevant to the preparation of the environmental statement and, if they have, the [authority or] body shall make that information available to that person.

(5) Paragraph (4) shall not require the disclosure of information which is capable of being treated as confidential, or must be so treated, under regulation 4 of the Environmental Information Regulations 1992.

(6) A reasonable charge reflecting the cost of making the relevant information available may be made by [an authority or body], which makes information available in accordance with paragraph (4).

PART V PUBLICITY AND PROCEDURES ON SUBMISSION OF ENVIRONMENTAL STATEMENTS

13 Procedure where an environmental statement is submitted to a local planning authority

(1) When an applicant making an EIA application submits to the relevant planning authority a statement which he refers to as an environmental statement for the purposes of

these Regulations he shall provide the authority with three additional copies of the statement for transmission to the Secretary of State and, if at the same time he serves a copy of the statement on any other body, he shall—

(a) serve with it a copy of the application and any plan submitted with the application (unless he has already served these documents on the body in question);

(b) inform the body that representations may be made to the relevant planning authority; and

(c) inform the authority of the name of every body whom he has so served and of the date of service.

(2) When a relevant planning authority receive in connection with an EIA application such a statement as is first mentioned in paragraph (1) the authority shall—

(a) send to the Secretary of State, within 14 days of receipt of the statement, three copies of the statement and a copy of the relevant application and of any documents submitted with the application;

(b) inform the applicant of the number of copies required to enable the authority to comply with sub-paragraph (c) below; and

(c) forward to any consultation body which has not received a copy direct from the applicant a copy of the statement and inform any such consultation body that they may make representations.

(3) The applicant shall send the copies required for the purposes of paragraph (2)(c) to the relevant planning authority.

(4) The relevant planning authority shall not determine the application until the expiry of 14 days from the last date on which a copy of the statement was served in accordance with this regulation.

14 Publicity where an environmental statement is submitted after the planning application

(1) Where an application for planning permission has been made without a statement which the applicant refers to as an environmental statement for the purposes of these Regulations and the applicant proposes to submit such a statement, he shall, before submitting it, comply with paragraphs (2) to (4).

(2)–(5) . . .

(6) Where an applicant indicates that he proposes to provide such a statement and in such circumstances as are mentioned in paragraph (1), the relevant planning authority, the Secretary of State or the inspector, as the case may be, shall (unless disposed to refuse the permission sought) suspend consideration of the application or appeal until receipt of the statement and the other documents mentioned in paragraph (5); and shall not determine it during the period of 21 days beginning with the date of receipt of the statement and the other documents so mentioned.

(7)–(8) . . .

16 Procedure where an environmental statement is submitted to the Secretary of State

(1) This regulation applies where an applicant submits to the Secretary of State, in relation to an EIA application which is before the Secretary of State or an inspector for determination or is the subject of an appeal to the Secretary of State, a statement which the applicant or appellant refers to as an environmental statement for the purposes of these Regulations.

(2) The applicant or appellant shall submit four copies of the statement to the Secretary of State who shall send one copy to the relevant planning authority.

(3) If at the same time as he submits a statement to the Secretary of State the applicant or appellant serves a copy of it on any other body, he shall comply with regulations 13(1)(a) and

13(1)(b) as if the reference in regulation 13(1)(b) to the relevant planning authority were a reference to the Secretary of State, and inform the Secretary of State of the matters mentioned in regulation 13(1) (c).

(4) The Secretary of State shall comply with regulation 13(2) (except subparagraph (a) of that regulation) and the applicant or appellant with regulation 13(3) as if—

(a) references in those provisions to the relevant planning authority were references to the Secretary of State; and,

(b) in the case of an appeal, references to the applicant were references to the appellant;

and the Secretary of State or the inspector shall comply with regulation 13(4) as if it referred to him instead of to the relevant planning authority.

17 Availability of copies of environmental statements

An applicant for planning permission or an appellant who submits in connection with his application or appeal a statement which he refers to as an environmental statement for the purposes of these Regulations shall ensure that a reasonable number of copies of the statement are available at the address named in the notices published or posted pursuant to article 8 of the Order or regulation 14 as the address at which such copies may be obtained.

18 Charges for copies of environmental statements

A reasonable charge reflecting printing and distribution costs may be made to a member of the public for a copy of a statement made available in accordance with regulation 17.

19 Further information and evidence respecting environmental statements

(1) Where the relevant planning authority, the Secretary of State or an inspector is dealing with an application or appeal in relation to which the applicant or appellant has submitted a statement which he refers to as an environmental statement for the purposes of these Regulations, and is of the opinion that the statement should contain additional information in order to be an environmental statement, they or he shall notify the applicant or appellant in writing accordingly, and the applicant or appellant shall provide that additional information; and such information provided by the applicant or appellant is referred to in these Regulations as 'further information'.

(2) Paragraphs (3) to (9) shall apply in relation to further information, except in so far as the further information is provided for the purposes of an inquiry held under the Act and the request for that information made pursuant to paragraph (1) stated that it was to be provided for such purposes.

(3) The recipient of further information pursuant to paragraph (1) shall publish in a local newspaper circulating in the locality in which the land is situated a notice...

(4) The recipient of the further information shall send a copy of it to each person to whom, in accordance with these Regulations, the statement to which it relates was sent.

(5) Where the recipient of the further information is the relevant planning authority they shall send to the Secretary of State three copies of the further information.

(6) The recipient of the further information may by notice in writing require the applicant or appellant to provide such number of copies of the further information as is specified in the notice (being the number required for the purposes of paragraph (4) or (5)).

(7) Where information is requested under paragraph (1), the relevant planning authority, the Secretary of State or the inspector, as the case may be, shall suspend determination of the application or appeal, and shall not determine it before the expiry of 14 days after the date on which the further information was sent to all persons to whom the statement to which it relates was sent or the expiry of 21 days after the date that notice of it was published in a local newspaper, whichever is the later.

(8) The applicant or appellant who provides further information in accordance with paragraph (1) shall ensure that a reasonable number of copies of the information is available at the address named in the notice published pursuant to paragraph (3) as the address at which such copies may be obtained.

(9) A reasonable charge reflecting printing and distribution costs may be made to a member of the public for a copy of the further information made available in accordance with paragraph (8).

(10) The relevant planning authority or the Secretary of State or an inspector may in writing require an applicant or appellant to produce such evidence as they may reasonably call for to verify any information in his environmental statement.

PART VI AVAILABILITY OF DIRECTIONS ETC. AND NOTIFICATION OF DECISIONS

20 Availability of opinions, directions etc. for inspection

(1) Where particulars of a planning application are placed on Part I of the register, the relevant planning authority shall take steps to secure that there is also placed on that Part a copy of any relevant—

(a) screening opinion;
(b) screening direction;
(c) scoping opinion;
(d) scoping direction;
(e) notification given under regulation 7(2), 8(2) or 9(4);
(f) direction under regulation 4(4);
(g) environmental statement, including any further information;
(h) statement of reasons accompanying any of the above.

(2) Where the relevant planning authority adopt a screening opinion or scoping opinion, or receive a request under regulation 10(1) or 11(2), a copy of a screening direction, scoping direction, or direction under regulation 4(4) before an application is made for planning permission for the development in question, the authority shall take steps to secure that a copy of the opinion, request, or direction and any accompanying statement of reasons is made available for public inspection at all reasonable hours at the place where the appropriate register (or relevant section of that register) is kept. Copies of those documents shall remain so available for a period of two years.

21 Duties to inform the public and the Secretary of State of final decisions

(1) Where an EIA application is determined by a local planning authority, the authority shall—

(a) in writing, inform the Secretary of State of the decision;
(b) inform the public of the decision, by publishing a notice in a newspaper circulating in the locality in which the land is situated, or by such other means as are reasonable in the circumstances; and
(c) make available for public inspection at the place where the appropriate register (or relevant section of that register) is kept a statement containing—
  (i) the content of the decision and any conditions attached thereto;
  (ii) the main reasons and considerations on which the decision is based; and
  (iii) a description, where necessary, of the main measures to avoid, reduce and, if possible, offset the major adverse effects of the development.

(2) Where an EIA application is determined by the Secretary of State or an inspector, the Secretary of State shall—

(a) notify the relevant planning authority of the decision; and
(b) provide the authority with such a statement as is mentioned in sub-paragraph (1)(c).

(3) The relevant planning authority shall, as soon as reasonably practicable after receipt of a notification under sub-paragraph (2)(a), comply with sub-paragraphs (b) and (c) of paragraph (1) in relation to the decision so notified as if it were a decision of the authority.

PART VII SPECIAL CASES

22 Development by a local planning authority

. . .

23 Restriction of grant of permission by old simplified planning zone schemes or enterprise zone orders

(1) Any:

(a) adoption or approval of a simplified planning zone scheme;

(b) order designating an enterprise zone; or

(c) approval of a modified scheme in relation to an enterprise zone,

which has effect immediately before the commencement of these Regulations to grant planning permission shall, on and after that date, cease to have effect to grant planning permission for Schedule 1 development, and cease to have effect to grant planning permission for Schedule 2 development unless either:

(i) the relevant planning authority has adopted a screening opinion; or

(ii) the Secretary of State has made a screening direction,

to the effect that the particular proposed development is not EIA development.

(2) Paragraph (1) shall not affect the completion of any development begun before the commencement of these Regulations.

24 Restriction of grant of permission by new simplified planning zone schemes or enterprise zone orders

No:

(a) adoption or approval of a simplified planning zone scheme;

(b) order designating an enterprise zone made; or

(c) modified scheme in relation to an enterprise zone approved,

after the commencement of these Regulations shall:

(i) grant planning permission for EIA development; or

(ii) grant planning permission for Schedule 2 development unless that grant is made subject to the prior adoption of a screening opinion or prior making of a screening direction that the particular proposed development is not EIA development.

25 Unauthorised development

Prohibition on the grant of planning permission for unauthorised EIA development

(1) The Secretary of State shall not grant planning permission under subsection (1) of section 177 (grant or modification of planning permission on appeals against enforcement notices) in respect of EIA development which is the subject of an enforcement notice under section 172 (issue of enforcement notice) ('unauthorised EIA development') unless he has first taken the environmental information into consideration, and he shall state in his decision that he has done so.

Screening opinions of the local planning authority

(2) Where it appears to the local planning authority by whom or on whose behalf an enforcement notice is to be issued that the matters constituting the breach of planning control comprise or include Schedule 1 development or Schedule 2 development they shall, before the enforcement notice is issued, adopt a screening opinion.

(3) Where it appears to the local planning authority by whom or on whose behalf an enforcement notice is to be issued that the matters constituting the breach of planning

control comprise or include EIA development they shall serve with a copy of the enforcement notice a notice ('regulation 25 notice') which shall—

(a) include the screening opinion required by paragraph (2) and the written statement required by regulation 4(6); and

(b) require a person who gives notice of an appeal under section 174 to submit to the Secretary of State with the notice four copies of an environmental statement relating to that EIA development.

(4) The authority by whom a regulation 25 notice has been served shall send a copy of it to—

(a) the Secretary of State; and

(b) the consultation bodies.

(5) Where an authority provide the Secretary of State with a copy of a regulation 25 notice they shall also provide him with a list of the other persons to whom a copy of the notice has been or is to be sent.

Screening directions of the Secretary of State

(6) Any person on whom a regulation 25 notice is served may apply to the Secretary of State for a screening direction and the following shall apply—

(a) an application under this paragraph shall be accompanied by—

(i) a copy of the regulation 25 notice;

(ii) a copy of the enforcement notice which accompanied it; and

(iii) such other information or representations as the applicant may wish to provide or make;

(b) the applicant shall send to the authority by whom the regulation 25 notice was served, at such time as he applies to the Secretary of State, a copy of the application under this paragraph and of any information or representations provided or made in accordance with sub-paragraph (a)(iii);

(c) if the Secretary of State considers that the information provided in accordance with sub-paragraph (a) is insufficient to enable him to make a direction, he shall notify the applicant and the authority of the matters in respect of which he requires additional information; and the information so requested shall be provided by the applicant within such reasonable period as may be specified in the notice;

(d) the Secretary of State shall send a copy of his direction to the applicant;

(e) without prejudice to sub-paragraph (d), where the Secretary of State directs that the matters which are alleged to constitute the breach of planning control do not comprise or include EIA development, he shall send a copy of the direction to every person to whom a copy of the regulation 25 notice was sent.

Provision of information

(7) The relevant planning authority and any person, other than the Secretary of State, to whom a copy of the regulation 25 notice has been sent ('the consultee') shall, if requested by the person on whom the regulation 25 notice was served, enter into consultation with that person to determine whether the consultee has in his possession any information which that person or the consultee consider relevant to the preparation of an environmental statement and, if they have, the consultee shall make any such information available to that person.

(8) The provisions of regulations 12(5) and 12(6) shall apply to information under paragraph (7) as they apply to any information falling within regulation 12(4).

Appeal to the Secretary of State without a screening opinion or screening direction

(9) Where on consideration of an appeal under section 174 it appears to the Secretary of State that the matters which are alleged to constitute the breach of planning control

comprise or include Schedule 1 development or Schedule 2 development and, in either case, no screening opinion has been adopted and no screening direction has been made in respect of that development, the Secretary of State shall, before any notice is served pursuant to paragraph (12), make such a screening direction.

(10) If the Secretary of State considers that he has not been provided with sufficient information to make a screening direction he shall notify the applicant and the authority by whom the regulation 25 notice was served of the matters in respect of which he requires additional information; and the information so requested shall be provided by the applicant within such reasonable period as may be specified in the notice.

(11) If an appellant to whom notice has been given under paragraph (10) fails to comply with the requirements of that notice:

- (a) the application which is deemed to have been made by virtue of the appeal made under section 174 ('the deemed application'); and
- (b) the appeal in so far as it is brought under the ground mentioned in section 174(2)(a) ('the ground (a) appeal'),

shall lapse at the end of the period specified in the notice.

Appeal to the Secretary of State without an environmental statement

(12) Where the Secretary of State is considering an appeal under section 174 and the matters which are alleged to constitute the breach of planning control comprise or include unauthorised EIA development, and the documents submitted to him for the purposes of the appeal do not include a statement referred to by the appellant as an environmental statement for the purposes of these Regulations, the following procedure shall apply—

- (a) the Secretary of State shall, subject to sub-paragraph (b), within the period of three weeks beginning with the day on which he receives the appeal, or such longer period as he may reasonably require, notify the appellant in writing of the requirements of sub-paragraph (c) below;
- (b) notice need not be given under sub-paragraph (a) where the appellant has submitted a statement which he refers to as an environmental statement for the purposes of these Regulations to the Secretary of State for the purposes of an appeal under section 78 (right to appeal against planning decisions and failure to take such decisions) which—
  - (i) relates to the development to which the appeal under section 174 relates; and
  - (ii) is to be determined at the same time as that appeal under section 174;

  and that statement, any further information, and the representations (if any) made in relation to it shall be treated as the environmental statement and representations for the purpose of paragraph (1) of this regulation;
- (c) the requirements of this sub-paragraph are that the appellant shall, within the period specified in the notice or such longer period as the Secretary of State may allow, submit to the Secretary of State four copies of an environmental statement relating to the unauthorised EIA development in question;
- (d) the Secretary of State shall send to the relevant planning authority a copy of any notice sent to the appellant under sub-paragraph (a);
- (e) if an appellant to whom notice has been given under sub-paragraph (a) fails to comply with the requirements of sub-paragraph (c), the deemed application and the ground (a) appeal (if any) shall lapse at the end of the period specified or allowed (as the case may be);
- (f) as soon as reasonably practicable after the occurence of the event mentioned in sub-paragraph (e), the Secretary of State shall notify the appellant and the local planning authority in writing that the deemed application and the ground (a) appeal (if any) have lapsed.

Procedure where an environmental statement is submitted to the Secretary of State

(13) Where the Secretary of State receives (otherwise than as mentioned in paragraph (12)(b)) in connection with an enforcement appeal a statement which the appellant refers to as an environmental statement for the purposes of these Regulations he shall—

(a) send a copy of that statement to the relevant planning authority, advise the authority that the statement will be taken into consideration in determining the deemed application and the ground (a) appeal (if any), and inform them that they may make representations; and

(b) notify the persons to whom a copy of the relevant regulation 25 notice was sent that the statement will be taken into consideration in determining the deemed application and the ground (a) appeal (if any), and inform them that they may make representations and that, if they wish to receive a copy of the statement or any part of it, they must notify the Secretary of State of their requirements within seven days of the receipt of the Secretary of State's notice; and

(c) respond to requirements notified in accordance with sub-paragraph (b) by providing a copy of the statement or of the part requested (as the case may be).

Further information and evidence respecting environmental statements

(14) Regulations 19(1) and 19(10) shall apply to statements provided in accordance with this regulation with the following modifications—

(a) where the Secretary of State notifies the appellant under regulation 19(1), the appellant shall provide the further information within such period as the Secretary of State may specify in the notice or such longer period as the Secretary of State may allow;

(b) if an appellant to whom a notice has been given under sub-paragraph (a) fails to provide the further information within the period specified or allowed (as the case may be), the deemed application and the ground (a) appeal (if any) shall lapse at the end of that period.

(15) Paragraph (13) shall apply in relation to further information received by the Secretary of State in accordance with paragraph (14) as it applies to such a statement as is referred to in that paragraph.

Publicity for environmental statements or further information

(16) Where an authority receive a copy of a statement or further information by virtue of paragraph (13)(a) they shall publish in a local newspaper circulating in the locality in which the land is situated a notice . . .

(17) The authority shall as soon as practicable after publication of a notice in accordance with paragraph (16) send to the Secretary of State a copy of the notice certified by or on behalf of the authority as having been published in a named newspaper on a date specified in the certificate.

(18) Where the Secretary of State receives a certificate under paragraph (17) he shall not determine the deemed application or the ground (a) appeal in respect of the development to which the certificate relates until the expiry of 14 days from the date stated in the published notice as the last date on which the statement or further information was available for inspection.

Public inspection of documents

(19) The relevant planning authority shall make available for public inspection at all reasonable hours at the place where the appropriate register (or relevant part of that register) is kept a copy of—

(a) every regulation 25 notice given by the authority;

(b) every notice received by the authority under paragraph (12)(d); and

(c) every statement and all further information received by the authority under paragraph (13)(a);

and copies of those documents shall remain so available for a period of two years or until they are entered in Part II of the register in accordance with paragraph (20), whichever is the sooner.

(20) Where particulars of any planning permission granted by the Secretary of State under section 177 are entered in Part II of the register the relevant planning authority shall take steps to secure that that Part also contains a copy of any of the documents referred to in paragraph (19) as are relevant to the development for which planning permission has been granted.

(21) The provisions of regulations 21(2) and 21(3) apply to a deemed application and a grant of planning permission under section 177 as they apply to an application for and grant of planning permission under Part III of the Act.

26 Unauthorised development with significant transboundary effects

(1) Regulation 27 shall apply to unauthorised EIA development as if—

(a) for regulation 27(1)(a) there were substituted—

'(a) on consideration of an appeal under section 174 the Secretary of State is of the opinion that the matters which are alleged to constitute the breach of planning control comprise or include EIA development and that the development has or is likely to have significant effects on the environment in another [EEA State]; or'

(b) in regulation 27(3)(a) the words 'a copy of the application concerned' were replaced by the words 'a description of the development concerned';

(c) in regulation 27(3)(b) the words 'to which that application relates' were omitted; and

(d) in regulation 27(6) the word 'application' was replaced by the word 'appeal'.

[ROMP Applications

General application of the Regulations to ROMP applications

26A—(1) These Regulations shall apply to—

(a) a ROMP application as they apply to an application for planning permission;

(b) ROMP development as they apply to development in respect of which an application for planning permission is, has been or is to be made;

(c) a relevant mineral planning authority as they apply to a relevant planning authority;

(d) a person making a ROMP application as they apply to an applicant for planning permission; and

(e) the determination of a ROMP application as they apply to the granting of a planning permission,

subject to the modifications and additions set out below.

Modification of provisions on prohibition of granting planning permission

(2) In regulation 3(1) (prohibition on granting planning permission without consideration of environmental information)—

(a) in paragraph (a) for the words 'these Regulations' substitute 'the Town and Country Planning (Environmental Impact Assessment) (England and Wales) (Amendment) Regulations 2000';

(b) in paragraph (b) for the words '3 or 4 (applications for planning permission)' substitute '11 (other consents)';

(c) for the words 'determined in accordance with paragraph (3) of article 20 (time periods for decision) of the Order' substitute 'the date on which a ROMP application has been made which complies with the provisions of paragraphs 2(3) to (5) and 4(1) of Schedule 2 to the 1991 Act, 9(2) of Schedule 13 to the 1995 Act, or 6(2) of Schedule 14 to the 1995 Act'.

Modification of provisions on application to local planning authority without an environmental statement

(3) In regulation 7(4) (application made to a local planning authority without an environmental statement)—

(a) for the word 'three' substitute 'six'; and

(b) after 'the notification' insert', or within such other period as may be agreed with the authority in writing,'.

Disapplication of Regulations and modification of provisions on application referred to or appealed to the Secretary of State without an environmental statement

(4) Regulations 7(5) and (6), 8(5) and (6), 9(6) and (7), 22, and 32 shall not apply.

(5) In regulation 8(4) (application referred to the Secretary of State without an environmental statement) and 9(5) (appeal to the Secretary of State without an environmental statement)—

(a) for the word 'three' substitute 'six';

(b) after 'the notification' insert', or within such other period as may be agreed with the Secretary of State in writing,'.

Substitution of references to section 78 right of appeal and modification of provisions on appeal to the Secretary of State

(6) In regulations 9(1) and 15(b), for the references to 'section 78 (right to appeal against planning decisions and failure to take such decisions)' substitute—

'paragraph 5(2) of Schedule 2 to the 1991 Act, paragraph 11(1) of Schedule 13 to the 1995 Act or paragraph 9(1) of Schedule 14 to the 1995 Act (right of appeal)'.

(7) In regulation 9(2) (appeal to the Secretary of State without an environmental statement) omit the words', except by refusing planning permission,'.

Modification of provisions on preparation, publicity and procedures on submission of environmental statements

(8) In regulations 10(9) and 11(6) for the words 'an application for planning permission for' substitute 'a ROMP application which relates to another planning permission which authorises'.

(9) In regulation 13 (procedure where an environmental statement is submitted to a local planning authority) after paragraph (3) insert—

'(3A) Where an applicant submits an environmental statement to the authority in accordance with paragraph (1), the provisions of article 8 of and Schedule 3 to the Order (publicity for applications for planning permission) shall apply to a ROMP application under paragraph—

(a) 2(2) of Schedule 2 to the 1991 Act; and

(b) 6(1) of Schedule 14 to the 1995 Act,

as they apply to a planning application falling within paragraph 8 (2) of the Order except that for the references in the notice in Schedule 3 to the Order to 'planning permission' there shall be substituted 'determination of the conditions to which a planning permission is to be subject' and that notice shall refer to the relevant provisions of the 1991 or 1995 Act pursuant to which the application is made.'

(10) In regulation 14 (publicity where an environmental statement is submitted after the planning application)—

(a) . . .

(b) in paragraph (6) for the words—

(i) '(unless disposed to refuse the permission sought) suspend consideration of the application or appeal until receipt of the statement and the other documents mentioned in paragraph (5)' substitute—

'suspend consideration of the application or appeal until the date specified by the authority or the Secretary of State for submission of the environmental statement and compliance with paragraph (5)';

(ii) 'so mentioned' substitute 'mentioned in paragraph (5)'.

(11) . . .

(12) In regulation 17 (availability of copies of environmental statements) after the words 'the Order' insert '(as applied by regulation 13(3A) or by paragraph 9(5) of Schedule 13 to the 1995 Act),'

(13) In regulation 19 (further information and evidence respecting environmental statements)—

(a) . . .

(b) in paragraph (7) after the words 'application or appeal' insert 'until the date specified by them or him for submission of the further information'.

Modification of provisions on application to the High Court and giving of directions

(14) For regulation 30 (application to the High Court) substitute—

'Application to the High Court

30. For the purposes of Part XII of the Act (validity of certain decisions), the reference in section 288, as applied by paragraph 9(3) of Schedule 2 to the 1991 Act, paragraph 16(4) of Schedule 13 to the 1995 Act or paragraph 9(4) of Schedule 14 to the 1995 Act, to action of the Secretary of State which is not within the powers of the Act shall be taken to extend to the determination of a ROMP application by the Secretary of State in contravention of regulation 3.'.

(15) The direction making power substituted by regulation 35(8) shall apply to ROMP development as it applies to development in respect of which a planning application is made.

Suspension of minerals development

(16) Where the authority, the Secretary of State or an inspector notifies the applicant or appellant, as the case may be, that—

(a) the submission of an environmental statement is required under regulation 7(2), 8(2) or 9(4) then such notification shall specify the period within which the environmental statement and compliance with regulation 14(5) is required; or

(b) a statement should contain additional information under regulation 19(1) then such notification shall specify the period within which that information is to be provided.

(17) Subject to paragraph (18), the planning permission to which the ROMP application relates shall not authorise any minerals development (unless the Secretary of State has made a screening direction to the effect that the ROMP development is not EIA development) if the applicant or the appellant does not—

(a) write to the authority or Secretary of State within the six week or other period agreed pursuant to regulations 7(4), 8(4) or 9(5);

(b) submit an environmental statement and comply with regulation 14(5) within the period specified by the authority or the Secretary of State in accordance with paragraph (16) or within such extended period as is agreed in writing; or

(c) provide additional information within the period specified by the authority, the Secretary of State or an inspector in accordance with paragraph (16) or within such extended period as is agreed in writing.

(18) Where paragraph (17) applies, the planning permission shall not authorise any minerals development from the end of—

(a) the relevant six week or other period agreed in writing as referred to in paragraph (17)(a);

(b) the period specified or agreed in writing as referred to in paragraphs (17)(b) and (c), ('suspension of minerals development') until the applicant has complied with all of the provisions referred to in paragraph (17) which are relevant to the application or appeal in question.

(19) Particulars of the suspension of minerals development and the date when that suspension ends must be entered in the appropriate part of the register as soon as reasonably practicable.

(20) Paragraph (17) shall not affect any minerals development carried out under the planning permission before the date of suspension of minerals development.

(21) For the purposes of paragraphs (17) to (20) 'minerals development' means development consisting of the winning and working of minerals, or involving the depositing of mineral waste.

Determination of conditions and right of appeal on non-determination

(22) Where it falls to—

(a) a mineral planning authority to determine a Schedule 1 or a Schedule 2 application, paragraph 2(6)(b) of Schedule 2 to the 1991 Act, paragraph 9(9) of Schedule 13 to the 1995 Act or paragraph 6(8) of Schedule 14 to the 1995 Act shall not have effect to treat the authority as having determined the conditions to which any relevant planning permission is to be subject unless either the mineral planning authority has adopted a screening opinion or the Secretary of State has made a screening direction to the effect that the ROMP development in question is not EIA development;

(b) a mineral planning authority or the Secretary of State to determine a Schedule 1 or a Schedule 2 application—

(i) section 69 (register of applications, etc), and any provisions of the Order made by virtue of that section, shall have effect with any necessary amendments as if references to applications for planning permission included ROMP applications under paragraph 9(1) of Schedule 13 to the 1995 Act and paragraph 6(1) of Schedule 14 to the 1995 Act; and

(ii) where the relevant mineral planning authority is not the authority required to keep the register, the relevant mineral planning authority must provide the authority required to keep it with such information and documents as that authority requires to comply with section 69 as applied by sub-paragraph (i), with regulation 20 as applied by paragraph (1), and with paragraph (19).

(23) Where it falls to the mineral planning authority or the Secretary of State to determine an EIA application which is made under paragraph 2(2) of Schedule 2 to the 1991 Act, paragraph 4(4) of that Schedule shall not apply.

(24) Where it falls to the mineral planning authority to determine an EIA application, the authority shall give written notice of their determination of the ROMP application within 16 weeks beginning with the date of receipt by the authority of the ROMP application or such extended period as may be agreed in writing between the applicant and the authority.

(25) For the purposes of paragraph (24) a ROMP application is not received by the authority until—

(a) a document referred to by the applicant as an environmental statement for the purposes of these Regulations;

(b) any documents required to accompany that statement; and

(c) any additional information which the authority has notified the applicant that the environmental statement should contain,

has been received by the authority.

(26) Where paragraph (22)(a) applies—

(a) paragraph 5(2) of Schedule 2 to the 1991 Act, paragraph 11(1) of Schedule 13 to the 1995 Act and paragraph 9(1) of Schedule 14 to the 1995 Act (right of appeal) shall have effect as if there were also a right of appeal to the Secretary of State where the mineral planning authority have not given written notice of their determination of the ROMP application in accordance with paragraph (24); and

(b) paragraph 5(5) of Schedule 2 to the 1991 Act, paragraph 11(2) of Schedule 13 to the 1995 Act and paragraph 9(2) of Schedule 14 to the 1995 Act (right of appeal) shall have effect as if they also provided for notice of appeal to be made within six months from the expiry of the 16 week or other period agreed pursuant to paragraph (24).

(27) In determining for the purposes of paragraphs—

(a) 2(6)(b) of Schedule 2 to the 1991 Act, 9(9) of Schedule 13 to the 1995 Act and 6(8) of Schedule 14 to the 1995 Act (determination of conditions); or

(b) paragraph 5(5) of Schedule 2 to the 1991 Act, paragraph 11(2) of Schedule 13 to the 1995 Act and paragraph 9(2) of Schedule 14 to the 1995 Act (right of appeal) as applied by paragraph (26)(b),

the time which has elapsed without the mineral planning authority giving the applicant written notice of their determination in a case where the authority have notified an applicant in accordance with regulation 7(2) that the submission of an environmental statement is required and the Secretary of State has given a screening direction in relation to the ROMP development in question no account shall be taken of any period before the issue of the direction.

ROMP application by a mineral planning authority

...

PART VIII DEVELOPMENT WITH SIGNIFICANT TRANSBOUNDARY EFFECTS

27 Development in England and Wales likely to have significant effects in another [EEA State]

(1) Where—

(a) it comes to the attention of the Secretary of State that development proposed to be carried out in England or Wales is the subject of an EIA application and is likely to have significant effects on the environment in another [EEA State]; or

(b) another [EEA State] likely to be significantly affected by such development so requests,

the Secretary of State shall—

(i) send to the [EEA State] as soon as possible and no later than their date of publication in The London Gazette referred to in subparagraph (ii) below, the particulars mentioned in paragraph (2) and, if he thinks fit, the information referred to in paragraph (3); and

(ii) publish the information in sub-paragraph (i) above in a notice placed in The London Gazette indicating the address where additional information is available; and

(iii) give the [EEA State] a reasonable time in which to indicate whether it wishes to participate in the procedure for which these Regulations provide.

(2) The particulars referred to in paragraph (1)(i) are—

(a) a description of the development, together with any available information on its possible significant effect on the environment in another [EEA State]; and

(b) information on the nature of the decision which may be taken.

(3) Where a [EEA State] indicates, in accordance with paragraph (1)(iii), that it wishes to participate in the procedure for which these Regulations provide, the Secretary of State shall as soon as possible send to that [EEA State] the following information—

(a) a copy of the application concerned;

(b) a copy of the environmental statement in respect of the development to which that application relates; and

(c) relevant information regarding the procedure under these Regulations,

but only to the extent that such information has not been provided to the [EEA State] earlier in accordance with paragraph (1)(i).

(4) The Secretary of State, insofar as he is concerned, shall also—

(a) arrange for the particulars and information referred to in paragraphs (2) and (3) to be made available, within a reasonable time, to the authorities referred to in Article 6(1) of the Directive and the public concerned in the territory of the [EEA State] likely to be significantly affected; and

(b) ensure that those authorities and the public concerned are given an opportunity, before planning permission for the development is granted, to forward to the Secretary of State, within a reasonable time, their opinion on the information supplied.

(5) The Secretary of State shall in accordance with Article 7(4) of the Directive—

(a) enter into consultations with the [EEA State] concerned regarding, inter alia, the potential significant effects of the development on the environment of that [EEA State] and the measures envisaged to reduce or eliminate such effects; and

(b) determine in agreement with the other [EEA State] a reasonable period of time for the duration of the consultation period.

(6) Where a [EEA State] has been consulted in accordance with paragraph (5), on the determination of the application concerned the Secretary of State shall inform the [EEA State] of the decision and shall forward to it a statement of—

(a) the content of the decision and any conditions attached thereto;

(b) the main reasons and considerations on which the decision is based; and

(c) a description, where necessary, of the main measures to avoid, reduce and, if possible, offset the major adverse effects of the development.

28 Projects in another EEA State likely to have significant transboundary effects

(1) Where the Secretary of State receives from another [EEA State] pursuant to Article 7(2) of the Directive information which that [EEA State] has gathered from the developer of a proposed project in that [EEA State] which is likely to have significant effects on the environment in England and Wales, the Secretary of State shall, in accordance with Article 7(4) of the Directive:

(a) enter into consultations with that [EEA State] regarding, inter alia, the potential significant effects of the proposed project on the environment in England and Wales and the measures envisaged to reduce or eliminate such effects; and

(b) determine in agreement with that [EEA State] a reasonable period, before development consent for the project is granted, during which members of the public in England and Wales may submit to the competent authority in that [EEA State] representations pursuant to Article 7(3)(b) of the Directive.

(2) The Secretary of State, insofar as he is concerned, shall also—

(a) arrange for the information referred to in paragraph (1) to be made available, within a reasonable time, both to the authorities in England and Wales which he considers are likely to be concerned by the project by reason of their specific environmental responsibilities, and to the public concerned in England and Wales; and

(b) ensure that those authorities and the public concerned in England and Wales are given an opportunity, before development consent for the project is granted, to forward to the competent authority in the relevant [EEA State], within a reasonable time, their opinion on the information supplied.

PART IX MISCELLANEOUS

30 Application to the High Court

For the purposes of Part XII of the Act (validity of certain decisions), the reference in section 288 to action of the Secretary of State which is not within the powers of the Act shall be taken to extend to a grant of planning permission by the Secretary of State in contravention of regulations 3 or 25(1).

31 Hazardous waste and material change of use

A change in the use of land or buildings to a use for a purpose mentioned in paragraph 9 of Schedule I involves a material change in the use of that land or those buildings for the purposes of paragraph (1) of section 55 (meaning of 'development' and 'new development').

32 Extension of the period for an authority's decision on a planning application

(1) In determining for the purposes of section 78 (right to appeal against planning decisions and failure to take such decisions) the time which has elapsed without the relevant planning authority giving notice to the applicant of their decision in a case where—

(a) the authority have notified an applicant in accordance with regulation 7(2) that the submission of an environmental statement is required; and

(b) the Secretary of State has given a screening direction in relation to the development in question,

no account shall be taken of any period before the issue of the direction.

(2) Where it falls to an authority to determine an EIA application, article 20 (time periods for decision) of the Order shall have effect as if—

(a) for the reference in paragraph (2)(a) of that article to a period of 8 weeks there were substituted a reference to a period of 16 weeks;

(b) after paragraph (3)(b) of that article there were inserted—

'(ba) the environmental statement required to be submitted in respect of the application has been submitted, together with the documents required to accompany that statement; and.'

33 Extension of the power to provide in a development order for the giving of directions as respects the manner in which planning applications are dealt with

The provisions enabling the Secretary of State to give directions which may be included in a development order by virtue of section 60 (permission granted by development order) shall include provisions enabling him to direct that development which is both of a description mentioned in Column 1 of the table in Schedule 2, and of a class described in the direction is EIA development for the purposes of these Regulations.

34 Revocation of Statutory Instruments and transitional provisions

(1) The instruments in Schedule 5 are hereby revoked to the extent shown in that Schedule.

(2) Nothing in paragraph (1) shall affect the continued application of the Instruments revoked by that paragraph to any application lodged or received by an authority before the commencement of these Regulations, to any appeal in relation to such an application, or to any matter in relation to which a local planning authority has before that date issued an enforcement notice under section 172; and these Regulations shall not apply to any such application, appeal, or matter.

35 Miscellaneous and consequential amendments [. . .]

Regulation 2(1) SCHEDULE 1

DESCRIPTIONS OF DEVELOPMENT FOR THE PURPOSES OF THE DEFINITION OF 'SCHEDULE 1 DEVELOPMENT'

Interpretation

In this Schedule—

'airport' means an airport which complies with the definition in the 1944 Chicago Convention setting up the International Civil Aviation Organisation (Annex 14);

'express road' means a road which complies with the definition in the European Agreement on Main International Traffic Arteries of 15 November 1975;

'nuclear power station' and 'other nuclear reactor' do not include an installation from the site of which all nuclear fuel and other radioactive contaminated materials have been permanently removed; and development for the purpose of dismantling or decommissioning a nuclear power station or other nuclear reactor shall not be treated as development of the description mentioned in paragraph 2(b) of this Schedule.

Descriptions of development

The carrying out of development to provide any of the following—

1. Crude-oil refineries (excluding undertakings manufacturing only lubricants from crude oil) and installations for the gasification and liquefaction of 500 tonnes or more of coal or bituminous shale per day.

2. (a) Thermal power stations and other combustion installations with a heat output of 300 megawatts or more; and
   (b) Nuclear power stations and other nuclear reactors (except research installations for the production and conversion of fissionable and fertile materials, whose maximum power does not exceed 1 kilowatt continuous thermal load).

3. (a) Installations for the reprocessing of irradiated nuclear fuel. (b) Installations designed—
   (i) for the production or enrichment of nuclear fuel,
   (ii) for the processing of irradiated nuclear fuel or high-level radioactive waste,
   (iii) for the final disposal of irradiated nuclear fuel,
   (iv) solely for the final disposal of radioactive waste,
   (v) solely for the storage (planned for more than 10 years) of irradiated nuclear fuels or radioactive waste in a different site than the production site.

4. (a) Integrated works for the initial smelting of cast-iron and steel;
   (b) Installations for the production of non-ferrous crude metals from ore, concentrates or secondary raw materials by metallurgical, chemical or electrolytic processes.

5. Installations for the extraction of asbestos and for the processing and transformation of asbestos and products containing asbestos—
   (a) for asbestos-cement products, with an annual production of more than 20,000 tonnes of finished products;
   (b) for friction material, with an annual production of more than 50 tonnes of finished products; and
   (c) for other uses of asbestos, utilisation of more than 200 tonnes per year.

6. Integrated chemical installations, that is to say, installations for the manufacture on an industrial scale of substances using chemical conversion processes, in which several units are juxtaposed and are functionally linked to one another and which are—
   (a) for the production of basic organic chemicals;
   (b) for the production of basic inorganic chemicals;
   (c) for the production of phosphorous-, nitrogen- or potassium-based fertilisers (simple or compound fertilisers);
   (d) for the production of basic plant health products and of biocides;
   (e) for the production of basic pharmaceutical products using a chemical or biological process;
   (f) for the production of explosives.

7. (a) Construction of lines for long-distance railway traffic and of airports with a basic runway length of 2,100 metres or more;
   (b) Construction of motorways and express roads;
   (c) Construction of a new road of four or more lanes, or realignment and/or widening of an existing road of two lanes or less so as to provide four or more lanes, where such new road, or realigned and/or widened section of road would be 10 kilometres or more in a continuous length.

8. (a) Inland waterways and ports for inland-waterway traffic which permit the passage of vessels of over 1,350 tonnes;

(b) Trading ports, piers for loading and unloading connected to land and outside ports (excluding ferry piers) which can take vessels of over 1,350 tonnes.

9. Waste disposal installations for the incineration, chemical treatment (as defined in Annex IIA to Council Directive 75/442/EEC under heading D9), or landfill of hazardous waste as defined in regulation 6 of the Hazardous Waste (England and Wales) Regulations 2005.

10. Waste disposal installations for the incineration or chemical treatment (as defined in Annex IIA to Council Directive 75/442/EEC under heading D9) of non-hazardous waste with a capacity exceeding 100 tonnes per day.

11. Goundwater abstraction or artificial groundwater recharge schemes where the annual volume of water abstracted or recharged is equivalent to or exceeds 10 million cubic metres.

12. (a) Works for the transfer of water resources, other than piped drinking water, between river basins where the transfer aims at preventing possible shortages of water and where the amount of water transferred exceeds 100 million cubic metres per year;

(b) In all other cases, works for the transfer of water resources, other than piped drinking water, between river basins where the multi-annual average flow of the basin of abstraction exceeds 2,000 million cubic metres per year and where the amount of water transferred exceeds 5% of this flow.

13. Waste water treatment plants with a capacity exceeding 150,000 population equivalent as defined in Article 2 point (6) of Council Directive 91/271/EEC.

14. Extraction of petroleum and natural gas for commercial purposes where the amount extracted exceeds 500 tonnes per day in the case of petroleum and 500,000 cubic metres per day in the case of gas.

15. Dams and other installations designed for the holding back or permanent storage of water, where a new or additional amount of water held back or stored exceeds 10 million cubic metres.

16. Pipelines for the transport of gas, oil or chemicals with a diameter of more than 800 millimetres and a length of more than 40 kilometres.

17. Installations for the intensive rearing of poultry or pigs with more than—

(a) 85,000 places for broilers or 60,000 places for hens;

(b) 3,000 places for production pigs (over 30 kg); or

(c) 900 places for sows.

18. Industrial plants for—

(a) the production of pulp from timber or similar fibrous materials;

(b) the production of paper and board with a production capacity exceeding 200 tonnes per day.

19. Quarries and open-cast mining where the surface of the site exceeds 25 hectares, or peat extraction where the surface of the site exceeds 150 hectares.

20. Installations for storage of petroleum, petrochemical or chemical products with a capacity of 200,000 tonnes or more.

Regulation 2(1) SCHEDULE 2

DESCRIPTIONS OF DEVELOPMENT AND APPLICABLE THRESHOLDS AND CRITERIA FOR THE PURPOSES OF THE DEFINITION OF 'SCHEDULE 2 DEVELOPMENT'

1. In the table below—

'area of the works' includes any area occupied by apparatus, equipment, machinery, materials, plant, spoil heaps or other facilities or stores required for construction or installation;

'controlled waters' has the same meaning as in the Water Resources Act 1991

'floorspace' means the floorspace in a building or buildings.

2. The table below sets out the descriptions of development and applicable thresholds and criteria for the purpose of classifying development as Schedule 2 development.

Table

Column 1	Column 2
Description of development	**Applicable thresholds and criteria**
The carrying out of development to provide any of the following—	
1. Agriculture and aquaculture (a) Projects for the use of uncultivated land or semi-natural areas for intensive agricultural purposes;	The area of the development exceeds 0.5 hectare.
(b) Water management projects for agriculture, including irrigation and land drainage projects;	The area of the works exceeds 1 hectare.
(c) Intensive livestock installations (unless included in Schedule 1);	The area of new floorspace exceeds 500 square metres.
(d) Intensive fish farming;	The installation resulting from the development is designed to produce more than 10 tonnes of dead weight fish per year.
(e) Reclamation of land from the sea.	All development.
2. Extractive industry (a) Quarries, open-cast mining and peat extraction (unless included in Schedule 1); (b) Underground mining;	All development except the construction of buildings or other ancillary structures where the new floorspace does not exceed 1,000 square meters.
(c) Extraction of minerals by fluvial dredging;	All development.
(d) Deep drillings, in particular— (i) geothermal drilling; (ii) drilling for the storage of nuclear waste material; (iii) drilling for water supplies; with the exception of drillings for investigating the stability of the soil.	(i) In relation to any type of drilling, the area of the works exceeds 1 hectare; or (ii) in relation to geothermal drilling and drilling for the storage of nuclear waste material, the drilling is within 100 metres of any controlled waters.
(e) Surface industrial installations for the extraction of coal, petroleum, natural gas and ores, as well as bituminous shale.	The area of the development exceeds 0.5 hectare.

Table *(Cont.)*

Column 1	Column 2
Description of development	**Applicable thresholds and criteria**
3. Energy industry (a) Industrial installations for the production of electricity, steam and hot water (unless included in Schedule 1);	The area of the development exceeds 0.5 hectare.
(b) Industrial installations for carrying gas, steam and hot water;	The area of the works exceeds 1 hectare.
(c) Surface storage of natural gas; (d) Underground storage of combustible gases; (e) Surface storage of fossil fuels;	(i) The area of any new building, deposit or structure exceeds 500 square metres; or (ii) a new building, deposit or structure is to be sited within 100 metres of any controlled waters.
(f) Industrial briquetting of coal and lignite;	The area of new floorspace exceeds 1,000 square metres.
(g) Installations for the processing and storage of radioactive waste (unless included in Schedule 1);	(i) The area of new floorspace exceeds 1,000 square metres; or (ii) the installation resulting from the development will require an authorisation or the variation of an authorisation under the Radioactive Substances Act 1993.
(h) Installations for hydroelectric energy production; (i) Installations for the harnessing of wind power for energy production (wind farms).	The installation is designed to produce more than 0.5 megawatts. (i) The development involves the installation of more than 2 turbines: or (ii) the hub height of any turbine or height of any other structure exceeds 15 metres.
4. Production and processing of metals (a) Installations for the production of pig iron or steel (primary or secondary fusion) including continuous casting; (b) Installations for the processing of ferrous metals— (i) hot-rolling mills; (ii) smitheries with hammers; (iii) applications of protective fused metal coats.	

Table *(Cont.)*

Column 1	Column 2
Description of development	**Applicable thresholds and criteria**
(c) Ferrous metal foundries; (d) Installations for the smelting, including the alloyage, of non-ferrous metals, excluding precious metals, including recovered products (refining, foundry casting, etc.); (e) Installations for surface treatment of metals and plastic materials using an electrolytic or chemical process; (f) Manufacture and assembly of motor vehicles and manufacture of motor-vehicle engines; (g) Shipyards; (h) Installations for the construction and repair of aircraft; (i) Manufacture of railway equipment; (j) Swaging by explosives; (k) Installations for the roasting and sintering of metallic ores.	The area of new floorspace exceeds 1,000 square metres.
5. Mineral industry (a) Coke ovens (dry coal distillation); (b) Installations for the manufacture of cement; (c) Installations for the production of asbestos and the manufacture of asbestos-based products (unless included in Schedule 1); (d) Installations for the manufacture of glass including glass fibre; (e) Installations for smelting mineral substances including the production of mineral fibres; (f) Manufacture of ceramic products by burning, in particular roofing tiles, bricks, refractory bricks, tiles, stonewear or porcelain.	The area of new floorspace exceeds 1,000 square metres.
6. Chemical industry (unless included in Schedule 1) (a) Treatment of intermediate products and production of chemicals; (b) Production of pesticides and pharmaceutical products, paint and varnishes, elastomers and peroxides;	The area of new floorspace exceeds 1,000 square metres.
(c) Storage facilities for petroleum, petrochemical and chemical products.	(i) The area of any new building or structure exceeds 0.05 hectare; or (ii) more than 200 tonnes of petroleum, petrochemical or chemical products is to be stored at any one time.

Table *(Cont.)*

Column 1	Column 2
Description of development	**Applicable thresholds and criteria**
7. Food industry (a) Manufacture of vegetable and animal oils and fats; (b) Packing and canning of animal and vegetable products; (c) Manufacture of dairy products; (d) Brewing and malting; (e) Confectionery and syrup manufacture; (f) Installations for the slaughter of animals; (g) Industrial starch manufacturing installations; (h) Fish-meal and fish-oil factories; (i) Sugar factories.	The area of new floorspace exceeds 1,000 square metres.
8. Textile, leather, wood and paper industries (a) Industrial plants for the production of paper and board (unless included in Schedule 1); (b) Plants for the pre-treatment (operations such as washing, bleaching, mercerisation) or dyeing of fibres or textiles; (c) Plants for the tanning of hides and skins; (d) Cellulose- processing and production installations.	The area of new floorspace exceeds 1,000 square metres.
9. Rubber industry Manufacture and treatment of elastomer-based products.	The area of new floorspace exceeds 1,000 square metres.
10. Infrastructure projects (a) Industrial estate development projects; (b) Urban development projects, including the construction of shopping centres and car parks, sports stadiums, leisure centres and multiplex cinemas;	The area of the development exceeds 0.5 hectare.
(c) Construction of intermodal transshipment facilities and of intermodal terminals (unless included in Schedule 1);	
(d) Construction of railways (unless included in Schedule 1);	The area of the works exceeds 1 hectare.
(e) Construction of airfields (unless included in Schedule 1);	(i) The development involves an extension to a runway; or (ii) the area of the works exceeds 1 hectare

Table *(Cont.)*

Column 1	Column 2
Description of development	**Applicable thresholds and criteria**
(f) Construction of roads (unless included in Schedule 1);	The area of the works exceeds 1 hectare.
(g) Construction of harbours and port installations including fishing harbours (unless included in Schedule 1);	The area of the works exceeds 1 hectare.
(h) Inland-waterway construction not included in Schedule 1, canalisation and flood-relief works; (i) Dams and other installations designed to hold water or store it on a long-term basis (unless included in Schedule 1); (j) Tramways, elevated and underground railways, suspended lines or similar lines of a particular type, used exclusively or mainly for passenger transport;	The area of the works exceeds 1 hectare.
(k) Oil and gas pipeline installations (unless included in Schedule 1); (l) Installations of long-distance aqueducts;	(i) The area of the works exceeds 1 hectare; or, (ii) in the case of a gas pipeline, the installation has a design operating pressure exceeding 7 bar gauge.
(m) Coastal work to combat erosion and maritime works capable of altering the coast through the construction, for example, of dykes, moles, jetties and other sea defence works, excluding the maintenance and reconstruction of such works;	All development.
(n) Groundwater abstraction and artificial groundwater recharge schemes not included in Schedule 1; (o) Works for the transfer of water resources between river basins not included in Schedule 1;	The area of the works exceeds 1 hectare.
(p) Motorway service areas.	The area of the development exceeds 0.5 hectare.
11. Other projects (a) Permanent racing and test tracks for motorised vehicles;	The area of the development exceeds 1 hectare.
(b) Installations for the disposal of waste (unless included in Schedule 1);	(i) The disposal is by incineration; or (ii) the area of the development exceeds 0.5 hectare; or (iii) the installation is to be sited within 100 metres of any controlled waters.
(c) Waste-water treatment plants (unless included in Schedule 1);	The area of the development exceeds 1,000 square metres.

Table *(Cont.)*

Column 1	Column 2
Description of development	**Applicable thresholds and criteria**
(d) Sludge-deposition sites; (e) Storage of scrap iron, including scrap vehicles;	(i) The area of deposit or storage exceeds 0.5 hectare; or (ii) a deposit is to be made or scrap stored within 100 metres of any controlled waters.
(f) Test benches for engines, turbines or reactors; (g) Installations for the manufacture of artificial mineral fibres; (h) Installations for the recovery or destruction of explosive substances; (i) Knackers' yards.	The area of new floorspace exceeds 1,000 square metres.
12. Tourism and leisure (a) Ski-runs, ski-lifts and cable-cars and associated developments;	(i) The area of the works exceeds 1 hectare; or (ii) the height of any building or other structure exceeds 15 metres.
(b) Marinas;	The area of the enclosed water surface exceeds 1,000 square metres.
(c) Holiday villages and hotel complexes outside urban areas and associated developments; (d) Theme parks;	The area of the development exceeds 1 hectare.
(e) Permanent camp sites and caravan sites;	The area of the development exceeds 1 hectare.
(f) Golf courses and associated developments.	The area of the development exceeds 1 hectare.
13. (a) Any change to or extension of development of a description listed in Schedule 1 or in paragraphs 1 to 12 of Column 1 of this table, where that development is already authorised, executed or in the process of being executed, and the change or extension may have significant adverse effects on the environment;	(i) In relation to development of a description mentioned in Column 1 of this table, the thresholds and criteria in the corresponding part of Column 2 of this table applied to the change or extension (and not to the development as changed or extended). (ii) In relation to development of a description mentioned in a paragraph in Schedule 1 indicated below, the thres olds and criteria in Column 2 of the paragraph of this table indicated below applied to the change or extension (and not to the development as changed or extended):

Table *(Cont.)*

Column 1	Column 2	
Description of development	**Applicable thresholds and criteria**	
	Paragraph in Schedule 1	Paragraph of this table
	1	6(a)
	2(a)	3(a)
	2(b)	3(g)
	3	3(g)
	4	4
	5	5
	6	6(a)
	7(a)	10(a) (in relation to railways)
	1	or 10(e) (in relation to airports)
	7(b) and (c)	10(f)
	8(a)	10(h)
	8(b)	10(g)
	9	11(b)
	10	11(b)
	11	10(n)
	12	10(o)
	13	11(c)
	14	2(e)
	15	10(i)
	16	10(k)
	17	1(c)
	18	8(a)
	19	2(a)
	20	6(c)
(b) Development of a description mentioned in Schedule 1 undertaken exclusively or mainly for the development and testing of new methods or products and not used for more than two years.	All development.	

Regulation 4(5) SCHEDULE 3

SELECTION CRITERIA FOR SCREENING SCHEDULE 2 DEVELOPMENT

1 Characteristics of development

The characteristics of development must be considered having regard, in particular, to—

(a) the size of the development;

(b) the cumulation with other development;

(c) the use of natural resources;

(d) the production of waste;
(e) pollution and nuisances;
(f) the risk of accidents, having regard in particular to substances or technologies used.

2 Location of development

The environmental sensitivity of geographical areas likely to be affected by development must be considered, having regard, in particular, to—

(a) the existing land use;
(b) the relative abundance, quality and regenerative capacity of natural resources in the area;
(c) the absorption capacity of the natural environment, paying particular attention to the following areas—
 (i) wetlands;
 (ii) coastal zones;
 (iii) mountain and forest areas;
 (iv) nature reserves and parks;
 (v) areas classified or protected under Member States' legislation; areas designated by Member States pursuant to Council Directive 79/409/EEC on the conservation of wild birds and Council Directive 92/43/EEC on the conservation of natural habitats and of wild fauna and flora;
 (vi) areas in which the environmental quality standards laid down in Community legislation have already been exceeded;
 (vii) densely populated areas;
 (viii) landscapes of historical, cultural or archaeological significance.

3 Characteristics of the potential impact

The potential significant effects of development must be considered in relation to criteria set out under paragraphs 1 and 2 above, and having regard in particular to—

(a) the extent of the impact (geographical area and size of the affected population);
(b) the transfrontier nature of the impact;
(c) the magnitude and complexity of the impact;
(d) the probability of the impact;
(e) the duration, frequency and reversibility of the impact.

Regulation 2(1)

SCHEDULE 4

INFORMATION FOR INCLUSION IN ENVIRONMENTAL STATEMENTS

PART I

1. Description of the development, including in particular—
 (a) a description of the physical characteristics of the whole development and the land-use requirements during the construction and operational phases;
 (b) a description of the main characteristics of the production processes, for instance, nature and quantity of the materials used;
 (c) an estimate, by type and quantity, of expected residues and emissions (water, air and soil pollution, noise, vibration, light, heat, radiation, etc.) resulting from the operation of the proposed development.

2. An outline of the main alternatives studied by the applicant or appellant and an indication of the main reasons for his choice, taking into account the environmental effects.

3. A description of the aspects of the environment likely to be significantly affected by the development, including, in particular, population, fauna, flora, soil, water, air, climatic

factors, material assets, including the architectural and archaeological heritage, landscape and the inter-relationship between the above factors.

4. A description of the likely significant effects of the development on the environment, which should cover the direct effects and any indirect, secondary, cumulative, short, medium and long-term, permanent and temporary, positive and negative effects of the development, resulting from:

(a) the existence of the development;

(b) the use of natural resources;

(c) the emission of pollutants, the creation of nuisances and the elimination of waste, and the description by the applicant of the forecasting methods used to assess the effects on the environment.

5. A description of the measures envisaged to prevent, reduce and where possible offset any significant adverse effects on the environment.

6. A non-technical summary of the information provided under paragraphs 1 to 5 of this Part.

7. An indication of any difficulties (technical deficiences or lack of know-how) encountered by the applicant in compiling the required information.

PART II

1. A description of the development comprising information on the site, design and size of the development.

2. A description of the measures envisaged in order to avoid, reduce and, if possible, remedy significant adverse effects.

3. The data required to identify and assess the main effects which the development is likely to have on the environment.

4. An outline of the main alternatives studied by the applicant or appellant and an indication of the main reasons for his choice, taking into account the environmental effects.

5. A non-technical summary of the information provided under paragraphs 1 to 4 of this Part.

Regulation 34(1) [...] SCHEDULE 5

Anti-Pollution Works Regulations 1999

(SI 1999, No. 1006)

1 Citation, commencement and interpretation

(1) These Regulations may be cited as the Anti-Pollution Works Regulations 1999 and shall come into force on 29th April 1999.

(2) In these Regulations 'the Act' means the Water Resources Act 1991; and for the purposes of these Regulations the parties to an appeal are the appellant, the Agency and any person who is served with a copy of a notice of an appeal in accordance with regulation 3(4)(b).

2 Content of works notices

A works notice shall—

(a) in the case of a potential pollution incident, describe the nature of the risk to controlled waters, identifying the controlled waters which may be affected and the place from which the matter in question is likely to enter those waters;

(b) in the case of an actual pollution incident, describe the nature and extent of the pollution, identifying the controlled waters affected by it;

(c) specify the works or operations required to be carried out by the person on whom the notice is served, stating his name and address;

(d) give the Agency's reasons for serving the notice on that person and for requiring those works or operations to be carried out;

(e) inform the person on whom the notice is served of his right of appeal under section 161C of the Act (including the time for appealing) and of the requirements imposed by regulation 3 in relation to its exercise;

(f) state that the Agency is entitled (unless the notice is quashed or withdrawn) to recover from the person on whom the notice is served its costs or expenses reasonably incurred in carrying out such investigations as are mentioned in section 161(1) of the Act; and

(g) set out the contents of section 161 D(1) to (4) of the Act (consequences of not complying with a works notice).

3 Appeals against works notices

(1) A person who wishes to appeal to the Secretary of State under section 161C of the Act (appeals against works notices) shall give the Secretary of State notice of the appeal.

(2) The notice of appeal shall state—

(a) the name and address of the appellant and of all persons to be served with a copy of the notice of appeal;

(b) the grounds on which the appeal is made; and

(c) whether the appellant wishes the appeal to be determined on the basis of written representations or a hearing.

(3) The notice of appeal shall be accompanied by copies of any application, consent, correspondence, decision, notice or other document relevant to the appeal.

(4) At the same time as the appellant gives notice of the appeal to the Secretary of State, the appellant shall send to—

(a) the Agency, and

(b) where a ground of appeal is that the notice might lawfully have been served on some other person, that person,

a copy of the notice of appeal, together with a list of the documents provided to the Secretary of State under paragraph (3).

(5) If the appellant wishes at any time to withdraw his appeal he shall do so by notice informing the Secretary of State and shall send a copy of the notice to the Agency and any other person on whom he is required to serve a copy of his notice of appeal.

4 Written representations

. . .

5 Hearings

. . .

6 Notification of determination

(1) The Secretary of State shall notify the appellant in writing of the determination of the appeal and shall provide him with a copy of any report mentioned in regulation 5(8).

(2) The Secretary of State shall at the same time send a copy of the documents mentioned in paragraph (1) to the Agency and to every other party to the appeal.

7 Compensation for grant of rights under section 161B

The Schedule to these Regulations shall have effect—

(a) for prescribing the period within which a person who grants, or joins in granting, any rights pursuant to section 161B(2) of the Act may apply for compensation for the grant of those rights;

(b) for prescribing the manner in which, and the person to whom, such an application may be made; and

(c) for prescribing the manner of determining such compensation, for determining the amount of such compensation and for making supplemental provision relating to such compensation.

. . .

Regulation 7

SCHEDULE

COMPENSATION FOR GRANT OF RIGHTS

1 Interpretation

In this Schedule—

'the grantor' means the person who grants, or joins in granting, any right pursuant to section 161 B(2) of the Act; and

'relevant interest' means an interest in land out of which a right has been granted or which is bound by a right granted.

2 Period for making an application

An application for compensation shall be made before the expiry of a period of 12 months beginning with—

(a) the date of the grant of the rights in respect of which compensation is claimed, or

(b) where there is an appeal against the notice in relation to which those rights were granted, the date on which the appeal is determined or withdrawn; whichever is the later date.

3 Manner of making an application

(1) An application for compensation shall be made in writing and delivered at or sent by pre-paid post to the last known address for correspondence of the person to whom the right was granted.

(2) The application shall contain—

(a) a copy of the grant of rights in respect of which the grantor is applying for compensation and of any plans attached to such grant;

(b) a description of the exact nature of any interest in land in respect of which compensation is applied for; and

(c) a statement of the amount of compensation applied for, distinguishing the amounts applied for under each of sub-paragraphs (a) to (e) of paragraph 4 and showing how the amount applied for under each sub-paragraph has been calculated.

4 Loss and damage for which compensation payable

Compensation shall be payable for loss and damage of the following descriptions—

(a) any depreciation in the value of any relevant interest to which the grantor is entitled which results from the grant of the right;

(b) loss or damage, in relation to any relevant interest to which he is entitled, which—

(i) is attributable to the grant of the right or the exercise of it;

(ii) does not consist of depreciation in the value of that interest; and

(iii) is loss or damage for which he would have been entitled to compensation by way of compensation for disturbance, if that interest had been acquired compulsorily under the Acquisition of Land Act 1981, in pursuance of a notice to treat served on the date on which the grant of the right was made;

(c) damage to, or injurious affection of, any interest in land to which the grantor is entitled which is not a relevant interest and which results from the grant of the right or from the exercise of it;

(d) any loss or damage sustained by the grantor, other than in relation to any interest in land to which he is entitled, which is attributable to the grant of the right or the exercise of it; and

(e) the amount of any valuation and legal expenses reasonably incurred by the grantor in granting the right and in the preparation of the application for and the negotiation of the amount of compensation.

5 Basis on which compensation assessed

(1) The rules set out in section 5 of the Land Compensation Act 1961 (rules for assessing compensation) shall, so far as applicable and subject to any necessary modifications, have effect for the purpose of assessing any compensation under paragraph 4, as they have effect for the purpose of assessing compensation for the compulsory acquisition of an interest in land.

(2) Where the relevant interest in respect of which any compensation is to be assessed is subject to a mortgage—

(a) the compensation shall be assessed as if the interest were not subject to the mortgage;

(b) no compensation shall be payable in respect of the interest of the mortgagee (as distinct from the interest which is subject to the mortgage); and

(c) any compensation which is payable in respect of the interest which is subject to the mortgage shall be paid to the mortgagee or, if there is more than one mortgagee, to the first mortgagee and shall, in either case, be applied by him as if it were proceeds of sale.

6 Determination of disputes

(1) Any question of disputed compensation shall be referred to and determined by the Lands Tribunal.

(2) In relation to the determination of any such question of compensation the provisions of sections 2 and 4 of the Land Compensation Act 1961 (procedure on references to the Lands Tribunal and costs) shall apply as if—

(a) the reference in section 2 of the Land Compensation Act 1961 to section 1 of that Act were a reference to sub-paragraph (1); and

(b) references in section 4 of the Land Compensation Act 1961 to the acquiring authority were references to the person to whom the rights were granted.

Contaminated Land (England) Regulations 2000

(SI 2000, No. 227) (as amended)

1 Citation, commencement, extent and interpretation

(1) These Regulations may be cited as the Contaminated Land (England) Regulations 2000 and shall come into force on 1st April 2000.

(2) These Regulations extend to England only.

(3) In these Regulations, unless otherwise indicated, any reference to a numbered section is to the section of the Environmental Protection Act 1990 which bears that number.

2 Land required to be designated as a special site

(1) Contaminated land of the following descriptions is prescribed for the purposes of section 78C(8) as land required to be designated as a special site—

(a) land to which regulation 3 applies;

(b) land which is contaminated land by reason of waste acid tars in, on or under the land;

(c) land on which any of the following activities have been carried on at any time—

(i) the purification (including refining) of crude petroleum or of oil extracted from petroleum, shale or any other bituminous substance except coal; or

(ii) the manufacture or processing of explosives;

(d) land on which a prescribed process designated for central control has been or is being carried on under an authorisation where the process does not comprise solely things being done which are required by way of remediation;

[(da) land on which an activity has been or is being carried on in a Part A(1) installation or by means of Part A(1) mobile plant under a permit where the activity does not comprise solely things being done which are required by way of remediation;]

(e) land within a nuclear site;

(f) land owned or occupied by or on behalf of—

(i) the Secretary of State for Defence;

(ii) the Defence Council;

(iii) an international headquarters or defence organisation; or

(iv) the service authority of a visiting force, being land used for naval, military or air force purposes;

(g) land on which the manufacture, production or disposal of—

(i) chemical weapons;

(ii) any biological agent or toxin which falls within section 1(l)(a) of the Biological Weapons Act 1974 (restriction on development of biological agents and toxins); or

(iii) any weapon, equipment or means of delivery which falls within section 1(1)(b) of that Act (restriction on development of biological weapons), has been carried on at any time;

(h) land comprising premises which are or were designated by the Secretary of State by an order made under section 1(1) of the Atomic Weapons Establishment Act 1991 (arrangements for development etc of nuclear devices);

(i) land to which section 30 of the Armed Forces Act 1996 (land held for the benefit of Greenwich Hospital) applies; and

(j) land which—

(i) is adjoining or adjacent to land of a description specified in subparagraphs (b) to (i) above; and

(ii) is contaminated land by virtue of substances which appear to have escaped from land of such a description.

(2) For the purposes of paragraph (1)(b) above, 'waste acid tars' are tars which—

(a) contain sulphuric acid;

(b) were produced as a result of the refining of benzole, used lubricants or petroleum; and

(c) are or were stored on land used as a retention basin for the disposal of such tars.

(3) In paragraph (1)(d) above, 'authorisation' and 'prescribed process' have the same meaning as in Part I of the Environmental Protection Act 1990 (integrated pollution control and air pollution control by local authorities) and the reference to designation for central control is a reference to designation under section 2(4) (which provides for processes to be designated for central or local control).

[(3A) In paragraph (1)(da) above, 'Part A(1) installation', 'Part A(1) mobile plant' and 'permit' have the same meaning as in the Pollution Prevention and Control (England and Wales) Regulations 2000.]

(4) In paragraph (1)(e) above, 'nuclear site' means—

(a) any site in respect of which, or part of which, a nuclear site licence is for the time being in force; or

(b) any site in respect of which, or part of which, after the revocation or surrender of a nuclear site licence, the period of responsibility of the licensee has not come to an end;

and 'nuclear site licence', 'licensee' and 'period of responsibility' have the meaning given by the Nuclear Installations Act 1965.

(5) For the purposes of paragraph (1)(f) above, land used for residential purposes or by the Navy, Army and Air Force Institutes shall be treated as land used for naval, military or air force purposes only if the land forms part of a base occupied for naval, military or air force purposes.

(6) In paragraph (1)(f) above—

'international headquarters' and 'defence organisation' mean, respectively, any international headquarters or defence organisation designated for the purposes of the International Headquarters and Defence Organisations Act 1964;

'service authority' and 'visiting force' have the same meaning as in Part I of the Visiting Forces Act 1952.

(7) In paragraph (1)(g) above, 'chemical weapon' has the same meaning as in sub-section (1) of section 1 of the Chemical Weapons Act 1996 disregarding subsection (2) of that section.

3 Pollution of controlled waters

For the purposes of regulation 2(l)(a), this regulation applies to land where—

(a) controlled waters which are, or are intended to be, used for the supply of drinking water for human consumption are being affected by the land and, as a result, require a treatment process or a change in such a process to be applied to those waters before use, so as to be regarded as wholesome within the meaning of Part III of the Water Industry Act 1991 (water supply);

(b) controlled waters are being affected by the land and, as a result, those waters do not meet or are not likely to meet the criterion for classification applying to the relevant description of waters specified in regulations made under section 82 of the Water Resources Act 1991 (classification of quality of waters); or

(c) controlled waters are being affected by the land and—

(i) any of the substances by reason of which the pollution of the waters is being or is likely to be caused falls within any of the families or groups of substances listed in paragraph 1 of Schedule 1 to these Regulations; and

(ii) the waters, or any part of the waters, are contained within underground strata which comprise wholly or partly any of the formations of rocks listed in paragraph 2 of Schedule 1 to these Regulations.

4 Content of remediation notices

(1) A remediation notice shall state (in addition to the matters required by section 78E(1) and (3))—

(a) the name and address of the person on whom the notice is served;

(b) the location and extent of the contaminated land to which the notice relates (in this regulation referred to as the 'contaminated land in question'), sufficient to enable it to be identified whether by reference to a plan or otherwise;

(c) the date of any notice which was given under section 78B to the person on whom the remediation notice is served identifying the contaminated land in question as contaminated land;

(d) whether the enforcing authority considers the person on whom the notice is served is an appropriate person by reason of—

(i) having caused or knowingly permitted the substances, or any of the substances, by reason of which the contaminated land in question is contaminated land, to be in, on or under that land;

(ii) being the owner of the contaminated land in question; or

(iii) being the occupier of the contaminated land in question;

(e) particulars of the significant harm or pollution of controlled waters by reason of which the contaminated land in question is contaminated land;

(f) the substances by reason of which the contaminated land in question is contaminated land and, if any of the substances have escaped from other land, the location of that other land;

(g) the enforcing authority's reasons for its decisions as to the things by way of remediation that the appropriate person is required to do, which shall show how any guidance issued by the Secretary of State under section 78E(5) has been applied;

(h) where two or more persons are appropriate persons in relation to the contaminated land in question—

(i) that this is the case;

(ii) the name and address of each such person; and

(iii) the thing by way of remediation for which each such person bears responsibility;

(i) where two or more persons would, apart from section 78F(6), be appropriate persons in relation to any particular thing which is to be done by way of remediation, the enforcing authority's reasons for its determination as to whether any, and if so which, of them is to be treated as not being an appropriate person in relation to that thing, which shall show how any guidance issued by the Secretary of State under section 78F(6) has been applied;

(j) where the remediation notice is required by section 78E(3) to state the proportion of the cost of a thing which is to be done by way of remediation which each of the appropriate persons in relation to that thing is liable to bear, the enforcing authority's reasons for the proportion which it has determined, which shall show how any guidance issued by the Secretary of State under section 78F(7) has been applied;

(k) where known to the enforcing authority, the name and address of—
   (i) the owner of the contaminated land in question; and
   (ii) any person who appears to the enforcing authority to be in occupation of the whole or any part of the contaminated land in question;

(l) where known to the enforcing authority, the name and address of any person whose consent is required under section 78G(2) before any thing required by the remediation notice may be done;

(m) where the notice is to be served in reliance on section 78H(4), that it appears to the enforcing authority that the contaminated land in question is in such a condition, by reason of substances in, on or under the land, that there is imminent danger of serious harm, or serious pollution of controlled waters, being caused;

(n) that a person on whom a remediation notice is served may be guilty of an offence for failure, without reasonable excuse, to comply with any of the requirements of the notice;

(o) the penalties which may be applied on conviction for such an offence;

(p) the name and address of the enforcing authority serving the notice; and

(q) the date of the notice.

(2) A remediation notice shall explain—

(a) that a person on whom it is served has a right of appeal against the notice under section 78L;

(b) how, within what period and on what grounds an appeal may be made; and

(c) that a notice is suspended, where an appeal is duly made, until the final determination or abandonment of the appeal.

5 Service of copies of remediation notices

(1) Subject to paragraph (2) below, the enforcing authority shall, at the same time as it serves a remediation notice, send a copy of it to each of the following persons, not being a person on whom the notice is to be served—

(a) any person who was required to be consulted under section 78G(3) before service of the notice;

(b) any person who was required to be consulted under section 78H(1) before service of the notice;

(c) where the local authority is the enforcing authority, the Environment Agency; and

(d) where the Environment Agency is the enforcing authority, the local authority in whose area the contaminated land in question is situated.

(2) Where it appears to the enforcing authority that the contaminated land in question is in such a condition by reason of substances in, on or under it that there is imminent danger

of serious harm, or serious pollution of controlled waters, being caused, the enforcing authority shall send any copies of the notice pursuant to paragraph (1) above as soon as practicable after service of the notice.

6 Compensation for rights of entry etc.

Schedule 2 to these Regulations shall have effect—

(a) for prescribing the period within which a person who grants, or joins in granting, any rights pursuant to section 78G(2) may apply for compensation for the grant of those rights;

(b) for prescribing the manner in which, and the person to whom, such an application may be made; and

(c) for prescribing the manner in which the amount of such compensation shall be determined and for making further provision relating to such compensation.

7 Grounds of appeal against a remediation notice

(1) The grounds of appeal against a remediation notice under section 78L(1) are any of the following—

(a) that, in determining whether any land to which the notice relates appears to be contaminated land, the local authority—

(i) failed to act in accordance with guidance issued by the Secretary of State under section 78A(2), (5) or (6); or

(ii) whether by reason of such a failure or otherwise, unreasonably identified all or any of the land to which the notice relates as contaminated land;

(b) that, in determining a requirement of the notice, the enforcing authority—

(i) failed to have regard to guidance issued by the Secretary of State under section 78E(5); or

(ii) whether by reason of such a failure or otherwise, unreasonably required the appellant to do any thing by way of remediation;

(c) that the enforcing authority unreasonably determined the appellant to be the appropriate person who is to bear responsibility for any thing required by the notice to be done by way of remediation;

(d) subject to paragraph (2) below, that the enforcing authority unreasonably failed to determine that some person in addition to the appellant is an appropriate person in relation to any thing required by the notice to be done by way of remediation;

(e) that, in respect of any thing required by the notice to be done by way of remediation, the enforcing authority failed to act in accordance with guidance issued by the Secretary of State under section 78F(6);

(f) that, where two or more persons are appropriate persons in relation to any thing required by the notice to be done by way of remediation, the enforcing authority—

(i) failed to determine the proportion of the cost stated in the notice to be the liability of the appellant in accordance with guidance issued by the Secretary of State under section 78F(7); or

(ii) whether, by reason of such a failure or otherwise, unreasonably determined the proportion of the cost that the appellant is to bear;

(g) that service of the notice contravened a provision of subsection (1) or (3) of section 78H (restrictions and prohibitions on serving remediation notices) other than in circumstances where section 78H(4) applies;

(h) that, where the notice was served in reliance on section 78H(4) without compliance with section 78H(1) or (3), the enforcing authority could not reasonably have taken the view that the contaminated land in question was in such a condition by reason of substances in, on or under the land, that there was imminent danger of serious harm, or serious pollution of controlled waters, being caused;

(i) that the enforcing authority has unreasonably failed to be satisfied, in accordance with section 78H(5)(b), that appropriate things are being, or will be, done by way of remediation without service of a notice;

(j) that any thing required by the notice to be done by way of remediation was required in contravention of a provision of section 78J (restrictions on liability relating to the pollution of controlled waters);

(k) that any thing required by the notice to be done by way of remediation was required in contravention of a provision of section 78K (liability in respect of contaminating substances which escape to other land);

(l) that the enforcing authority itself has power, in a case falling within section 78N(3)(b), to do what is appropriate by way of remediation;

(m) that the enforcing authority itself has power, in a case falling within section 78N(3)(e), to do what is appropriate by way of remediation;

(n) that the enforcing authority, in considering for the purposes of section 78N(3)(e), whether it would seek to recover all or a portion of the cost incurred by it in doing some particular thing by way of remediation—

 (i) failed to have regard to any hardship which the recovery may cause to the person from whom the cost is recoverable or to any guidance issued by the Secretary of State for the purposes of section 78P(2); or

 (ii) whether by reason of such a failure or otherwise, unreasonably determined that it would decide to seek to recover all of the cost;

(o) that, in determining a requirement of the notice, the enforcing authority failed to have regard to guidance issued by the Environment Agency under section 78V(1);

(p) that a period specified in the notice within which the appellant is required to do anything is not reasonably sufficient for the purpose;

(q) that the notice provides for a person acting in a relevant capacity to be personally liable to bear the whole or part of the cost of doing any thing by way of remediation, contrary to the provisions of section 78X(3)(a);

(r) that service of the notice contravened a provision of section 78YB (interaction of Part IIA of the Environmental Protection Act 1990 with other enactments), and

 (i) in a case where subsection (1) of that section is relied on, that it ought reasonably to have appeared to the enforcing authority that the powers of the Environment Agency under section 27 might be exercised;

 (ii) in a case where subsection (3) of section 78YB is relied on, that it ought reasonably to have appeared to the enforcing authority that the powers of a waste regulation authority or waste collection authority under section 59 might be exercised; or

(s) that there has been some informality, defect or error in, or in connection with, the notice, in respect of which there is no right of appeal under the grounds set out in sub-paragraphs (a) to (r) above.

(2) A person may only appeal on the ground specified in paragraph (1)(d) above in a case where—

(a) the enforcing authority has determined that he is an appropriate person by virtue of subsection (2) of section 78F and he claims to have found some other person who is an appropriate person by virtue of that subsection;

(b) the notice is served on him as the owner or occupier for the time being of the contaminated land in question and he claims to have found some other person who is an appropriate person by virtue of that subsection; or

(c) the notice is served on him as the owner or occupier for the time being of the contaminated land in question, and he claims that some other person is also an owner or occupier for the time being of the whole or part of that land.

(3) If and in so far as an appeal against a remediation notice is based on the ground of some informality, defect or error in, or in connection with, the notice, the appellate

authority shall dismiss the appeal if it is satisfied that the informality, defect or error was not a material one.

8 Appeals to a magistrates' court

(1) An appeal under section 78L(1) to a magistrates' court against a remediation notice shall be by way of complaint for an order and, subject to section 78L(2) and (3) and regulations 7(3), 12 and 13, the Magistrates' Courts Act 1980 shall apply to the proceedings.

(2) An appellant shall, at the same time as he makes a complaint,—

- (a) file a notice ('notice of appeal') and serve a copy of it on—
  - (i) the enforcing authority;
  - (ii) any person named in the remediation notice as an appropriate person;
  - (iii) any person named in the notice of appeal as an appropriate person; and
  - (iv) any person named in the remediation notice as the owner or occupier of the whole or any part of the land to which the notice relates;
- (b) file a copy of the remediation notice to which the appeal relates and serve a copy of it on any person named in the notice of appeal as an appropriate person who was not so named in the remediation notice; and
- (c) file a statement of the names and addresses of any persons falling within paragraph (ii), (iii) or (iv) of sub-paragraph (a) above.

(3) The notice of appeal shall state the appellant's name and address and the grounds on which the appeal is made.

(4) On an appeal under section 78L(1) to a magistrates' court—

- (a) the justices' clerk or the court may give, vary or revoke directions for the conduct of proceedings, including—
  - (i) the timetable for the proceedings;
  - (ii) the service of documents;
  - (iii) the submission of evidence; and
  - (iv) the order of speeches;
- (b) any person falling within paragraph (2)(a)(ii), (iii) or (iv) above shall be given notice of, and an opportunity to be heard at, the hearing of the complaint and any hearing for directions, in addition to the appellant and the enforcing authority; and
- (c) the court may refuse to grant a request by the appellant to abandon his appeal against a remediation notice, where the request is made after the court has notified the appellant in accordance with regulation 12(1) of a proposed modification of that notice.

(5) Rule 15 of the Family Proceedings Courts (Matrimonial Proceedings etc.) Rules 1991 (delegation by justices' clerk) shall apply for the purposes of an appeal under section 78L(1) to a magistrates' court as it applies for the purposes of Part II of those Rules.

(6) In this regulation, 'file' means deposit with the [designated officer for the court].

9 Appeals to the Secretary of State

(1) An appeal to the Secretary of State against a remediation notice shall be made to him by a notice ('notice of appeal') which shall state—

- (a) the name and address of the appellant;
- (b) the grounds on which the appeal is made; and
- (c) whether the appellant wishes the appeal to be in the form of a hearing or to be disposed of on the basis of written representations.

(2) The appellant shall, at the same time as he serves a notice of appeal on the Secretary of State,—

- (a) serve a copy of it on—
  - (i) the Environment Agency;
  - (ii) any person named in the remediation notice as an appropriate person;
  - (iii) any person named in the notice of appeal as an appropriate person; and
  - (iv) any person named in the remediation notice as the owner or occupier of the whole or any part of the land to which the notice relates;

and serve on the Secretary of State a statement of the names and addresses of any persons falling within paragraph (ii), (iii) or (iv) above; and

(b) serve a copy of the remediation notice to which the appeal relates on the Secretary of State and on any person named in the notice of appeal as an appropriate person who is not so named in the remediation notice.

(3) Subject to paragraph (5) below, if the appellant wishes to abandon an appeal, he shall do so by notifying the Secretary of State in writing and the appeal shall be treated as abandoned on the date the Secretary of State receives that notification.

(4) The Secretary of State may refuse to permit an appellant to abandon his appeal against a remediation notice where the notification by the appellant in accordance with paragraph (3) above is received by the Secretary of State at any time after the Secretary of State has notified the appellant in accordance with regulation 12(1) of a proposed modification of that notice.

(5) Where an appeal is abandoned, the Secretary of State shall give notice of the abandonment to any person on whom the appellant was required to serve a copy of the notice of appeal.

10 Hearings and local inquiries

(1) Before determining an appeal, the Secretary of State may, if he thinks fit—

(a) cause the appeal to take or continue in the form of a hearing (which may, if the person hearing the appeal so decides, be held, or held to any extent, in private); or

(b) cause a local inquiry to be held, and the Secretary of State shall act as mentioned in sub-paragraph (a) or (b) above if a request is made by either the appellant or the Environment Agency to be heard with respect to the appeal.

(2) The persons entitled to be heard at a hearing are—

(a) the appellant;

(b) the Environment Agency; and

(c) any person (other than the Agency) on whom the appellant was required to serve a copy of the notice of appeal.

(3) Nothing in paragraph (2) above shall prevent the person appointed to conduct the hearing of the appeal from permitting any other person to be heard at the hearing and such permission shall not be unreasonably withheld.

(4) After the conclusion of a hearing, the person appointed to conduct the hearing shall, unless he has been appointed under section 114(1)(a) of the Environment Act 1995 (power of Secretary of State to delegate his functions of determining appeals) to determine the appeal, make a report in writing to the Secretary of State which shall include his conclusions and his recommendations or his reasons for not making any recommendations.

11 Notification of Secretary of State's decision on an appeal

(1) The Secretary of State shall notify the appellant in writing of his decision on an appeal and shall provide him with a copy of any report mentioned in regulation 10(4).

(2) The Secretary of State shall, at the same time as he notifies the appellant, send a copy of the documents mentioned in paragraph (1) above to the Environment Agency and to any other person on whom the appellant was required to serve a copy of the notice of appeal.

12 Modification of a remediation notice

(1) Before modifying a remediation notice under section 78L(2)(b) in any respect which would be less favourable to the appellant or any other person on whom the notice was served, the appellate authority shall—

(a) notify the appellant and any persons on whom the appellant was required to serve a copy of the notice of appeal of the proposed modification;

(b) permit any persons so notified to make representations in relation to the proposed modification; and

(c) permit the appellant or any other person on whom the remediation notice was served to be heard if any such person so requests.

(2) Where, in accordance with paragraph (1) above, the appellant or any other person is heard, the enforcing authority shall also be entitled to be heard.

13 Appeals to the High Court

An appeal against any decision of a magistrates' court in pursuance of an appeal under section 78L(1) shall lie to the High Court at the instance of any party to the proceedings in which the decision was given (including any person who exercised his entitlement under regulation 8(4)(b) to be heard at the hearing of the complaint).

14 Suspension of a remediation notice

(1) Where an appeal is duly made against a remediation notice, the notice shall be of no effect pending the final determination or abandonment of the appeal.

(2) An appeal against a remediation notice is duly made for the purposes of this regulation if it is made within the period specified in section 78L(1) and the requirements of regulation 8(2) and (3) (in the case of an appeal to a magistrates' court) or regulation 9(1) and (2) (in the case of an appeal to the Secretary of State) have been complied with.

15 Registers

(1) Schedule 3 to these Regulations shall have effect for prescribing—

(a) for the purposes of subsection (1) of section 78R, the particulars of or relating to the matters to be contained in a register maintained under that section; and

(b) other matters in respect of which such a register shall contain prescribed particulars pursuant to section 78R(1)(1).

(2) The following descriptions of information are prescribed for the purposes of section 78R(2) as information to be contained in notifications for the purposes of section 78R(1)(h) and (j)

(a) the location and extent of the land sufficient to enable it to be identified;

(b) the name and address of the person who it is claimed has done each of the things by way of remediation;

(c) a description of any thing which it is claimed has been done by way of remediation; and

(d) the period within which it is claimed each such thing was done.

(3) The following places are prescribed for the purposes of subsection (8) of section 78R as places at which any registers or facilities for obtaining copies shall be available or afforded to the public in pursuance of paragraph (a) or (b) of that sub section—

(a) where the enforcing authority is the local authority, its principal office; and

(b) where the enforcing authority is the Environment Agency, its office for the area in which the contaminated land in question is situated.

Regulation 3(c) SCHEDULE 1

SPECIAL SITES

1. The following families and groups of substances are listed for the purposes of regulation 3(c)(i)—

organohalogen compounds and substances which may form such compounds in the aquatic environment;

organophosphorus compounds;

organotin compounds;

substances which possess carcinogenic, mutagenic or teratogenic properties in or via the aquatic environment;

mercury and its compounds;

cadmium and its compounds;

mineral oil and other hydrocarbons;

cyanides.

2. The following formations of rocks are listed for the purposes of regulation 3(c)(ii)—
Pleistocene Norwich Crag;
Upper Cretaceous Chalk;
Lower Cretaceous Sandstones;
Upper Jurassic Corallian;
Middle Jurassic Limestones;
Lower Jurassic Cotteswold Sands;
Permo-Triassic Sherwood Sandstone Group;
Upper Permian Magnesian Limestone;
Lower Permian Penrith Sandstone;
Lower Permian Collyhurst Sandstone;
Lower Permian Basal Breccias, Conglomerates and Sandstones;
Lower Carboniferous Limestones.

Regulation 6 SCHEDULE 2

COMPENSATION FOR RIGHTS OF ENTRY ETC.

1 Interpretation

In this Schedule—

'the 1961 Act' means the Land Compensation Act 1961;

'grantor' means a person who has granted, or joined in the granting of, any rights pursuant to section 78G(2);

'relevant interest' means an interest in land out of which rights have been granted pursuant to section 78G(2).

2 Period for making an application

An application for compensation shall be made within the period beginning with the date of the grant of the rights in respect of which compensation is claimed and ending on whichever is the latest of the following dates—

(a) twelve months after the date of the grant of those rights;

(b) where an appeal is made against a remediation notice in respect of which the rights in question have been granted, and the notice is of no effect by virtue of regulation 14, twelve months after the date of the final determination or abandonment of the appeal; or

(c) six months after the date on which the rights were first exercised.

3 Manner of making an application

(1) An application shall be made in writing and delivered at or sent by pre-paid post to the last known address for correspondence of the appropriate person to whom the rights were granted.

(2) The application shall contain, or be accompanied by—

(a) a copy of the grant of rights in respect of which the grantor is applying for compensation, and of any plans attached to that grant;

(b) a description of the exact nature of any interest in land in respect of which compensation is applied for; and

(c) a statement of the amount of compensation applied for, distinguishing the amounts applied for under each of sub-paragraphs (a) to (e) of paragraph 4 below, and showing how the amount applied for under each sub-paragraph has been calculated.

4 Loss and damage for which compensation payable

Subject to paragraph 5(3) and (5)(b) below, compensation is payable under section 78G for loss and damage of the following descriptions—

(a) depreciation in the value of any relevant interest to which the grantor is entitled which results from the grant of the rights;

(b) depreciation in the value of any other interest in land to which the grantor is entitled which results from the exercise of the rights;

(c) loss or damage, in relation to any relevant interest to which the grantor is entitled, which—

(i) is attributable to the grant of the rights or the exercise of them;

(ii) does not consist of depreciation in the value of that interest; and

(iii) is loss or damage for which he would have been entitled to compensation by way of compensation for disturbance, if that interest had been acquired compulsorily under the Acquisition of Land Act 1981 in pursuance of a notice to treat served on the date on which the rights were granted;

(d) damage to, or injurious affection of, any interest in land to which the grantor is entitled which is not a relevant interest, and which results from the grant of the rights or the exercise of them; and

(e) loss in respect of work carried out by or on behalf of the grantor which is rendered abortive by the grant of the rights or the exercise of them.

5 Basis on which compensation assessed

(1) The following provisions shall have effect for the purpose of assessing the amount to be paid by way of compensation under section 78G.

(2) The rules set out in section 5 of the 1961 Act (rules for assessing compensation) shall, so far as applicable and subject to any necessary modifications, have effect for the purpose of assessing any such compensation as they have effect for the purpose of assessing compensation for the compulsory acquisition of an interest in land.

(3) No account shall be taken of any enhancement of the value of any interest in land, by reason of any building erected, work done or improvement or alteration made on any land in which the grantor is, or was at the time of erection, doing or making, directly or indirectly concerned, if the Lands Tribunal is satisfied that the erection of the building, the doing of the work, the making of the improvement or the alteration was not reasonably necessary and was undertaken with a view to obtaining compensation or increased compensation.

(4) In calculating the amount of any loss under paragraph 4(e) above, expenditure incurred in the preparation of plans or on other similar preparatory matters shall be taken into account.

(5) Where the interest in respect of which compensation is to be assessed is subject to a mortgage—

(a) the compensation shall be assessed as if the interest were not subject to the mortgage; and

(b) no compensation shall be payable in respect of the interest of the mortgagee (as distinct from the interest which is subject to the mortgage).

(6) Compensation under section 78G shall include an amount equal to the grantor's reasonable valuation and legal expenses.

6 Payment of compensation and determination of disputes

(1) Compensation payable under section 78G in respect of an interest which is subject to a mortgage shall be paid to the mortgagee or, if there is more than one mortgagee, to the first mortgagee and shall, in either case, be applied by him as if it were proceeds of sale.

(2) Amounts of compensation determined under this Schedule shall be payable—

(a) where the appropriate person and the grantor or mortgagee agree that a single payment is to be made on a specified date, on that date;

(b) where the appropriate person and the grantor or mortgagee agree that payment is to be made in instalments at different dates, on the date agreed as regards each instalment; and

(c) in any other case, subject to any direction of the Lands Tribunal or the court, as soon as reasonably practicable after the amount of the compensation has been finally determined.

(3) Any question of the application of paragraph 5(3) above or of disputed compensation shall be referred to and determined by the Lands Tribunal.

(4) In relation to the determination of any such question, sections 2 and 4 of the 1961 Act (procedure on reference to the Lands Tribunal and costs) shall apply as if—

(a) the reference in section 2(1) of that Act to section 1 of that Act were a reference to sub-paragraph (3) of this paragraph; and

(b) references in section 4 of that Act to the acquiring authority were references to the appropriate person.

Regulation 15

SCHEDULE 3

REGISTERS

A register maintained by an enforcing authority under section 78R shall contain full particulars of the following matters—

1 Remediation notices

In relation to a remediation notice served by the authority—

(a) the name and address of the person on whom the notice is served;

(b) the location and extent of the contaminated land to which the notice relates (in this paragraph referred to as the 'contaminated land in question'), sufficient to enable it to be identified whether by reference to a plan or otherwise;

(c) the significant harm or pollution of controlled waters by reason of which the contaminated land in question is contaminated land;

(d) the substances by reason of which the contaminated land in question is contaminated land and, if any of the substances have escaped from other land, the location of that other land;

(e) the current use of the contaminated land in question;

(f) what each appropriate person is to do by way of remediation and the periods within which they are required to do each of the things; and

(g) the date of the notice.

2 Appeals against remediation notices

Any appeal against a remediation notice served by the authority.

3 Any decision on such an appeal.

4 Remediation declarations

Any remediation declaration prepared and published by the enforcing authority under section 78H(6).

5 In relation to any such remediation declaration—

(a) the location and extent of the contaminated land in question, sufficient to enable it to be identified whether by reference to a plan or otherwise; and

(b) the matters referred to in sub-paragraphs (c), (d) and (e) of paragraph 1 above.

6 Remediation statements

Any remediation statement prepared and published by the responsible person under section 78H(7) or by the enforcing authority under section 78H(9).

7 In relation to any such remediation statement—

(a) the location and extent of the contaminated land in question, sufficient to enable it to be identified whether by reference to a plan or otherwise; and

(b) the matters referred to in sub-paragraphs (c), (d) and (e) of paragraph 1 above.

8 Appeals against charging notices

In the case of an enforcing authority, any appeal under section 78P(8) against a charging notice served by the authority.

9 Any decision on such an appeal.

10 Designation of special sites

In the case of the Environment Agency, as respects any land in relation to which it is the enforcing authority, and in the case of a local authority, as respects any land in its area,—

(a) any notice given by a local authority under subsection (1)(b) or (5)(a) of section 78C, or by the Secretary of State under section 78D(4)(b), which, by virtue of section 78C(7) or section 78D(6) respectively, has effect as the designation of any land as a special site;

(b) the provisions of regulation 2 or 3 by virtue of which the land is required to be designated as a special site;

(c) any notice given by the Environment Agency under section 78Q(1)(a) of its decision to adopt a remediation notice; and

(d) any notice given by or to the enforcing authority under section 78Q(4) terminating the designation of any land as a special site.

11 Notification of claimed remediation

Any notification given to the authority for the purposes of section 78R(1)(h) or (j).

12 Convictions for offences under section 78M

Any conviction of a person for any offence under section 78M in relation to a remediation notice served by the authority, including the name of the offender, the date of conviction, the penalty imposed and the name of the Court.

13 Guidance issued under section 78V(1)

In the case of the Environment Agency, the date of any guidance issued by it under subsection (1) of section 78V and, in the case of a local authority, the date of any guidance issued by the Agency to it under that subsection.

14 Other environmental controls

Where the authority is precluded by virtue of section 78YB(1) [or 78YB(2B)] from serving a remediation notice—

(a) the location and extent of the contaminated land in question, sufficient to enable it to be identified whether by reference to a plan or otherwise;

(b) the matters referred to in sub-paragraphs (c), (d) and (e) of paragraph 1 above; and

(c) any steps of which the authority has knowledge, carried out under section 27 [or by means of enforcement action (within the meaning of section 78YB(2C)], towards remedying any significant harm or pollution of controlled waters by reason of which the land in question is contaminated land.

15. Where the authority is precluded by virtue of section 78YB(3) from serving a remediation notice in respect of land which is contaminated land by reason of the deposit of controlled waste or any consequences of its deposit—

(a) the location and extent of the contaminated land in question, sufficient to enable it to be identified whether by reference to a plan or otherwise;

(b) the matters referred to in sub-paragraphs (c), (d) and (e) of paragraph 1 above; and

(c) any steps of which the authority has knowledge, carried out under section 59, in relation to that waste or the consequences of its deposit, including in a case where a waste collection authority (within the meaning of section 30(3)) took those steps or required the steps to be taken, the name of that authority.

16. Where, as a result of a consent given under Chapter II of Part III of the Water Resources Act 1991 (pollution offences), the authority is precluded by virtue of section 78YB(4) from specifying in a remediation notice any particular thing by way of remediation which it would otherwise have specified in such a notice—

(a) the consent;

(b) the location and extent of the contaminated land in question, sufficient to enable it to be identified whether by reference to a plan or otherwise; and

(c) the matters referred to in sub-paragraphs (c), (d) and (e) of paragraph 1 above.

Air Quality (England) Regulations 2000

(SI 2000, No. 928) (as amended)

1 Citation, commencement and extent

(1) These Regulations may be cited as the Air Quality (England) Regulations 2000 and shall come into force on the seventh day after the day on which they are made.

(2) These Regulations extend to England only.

2 Interpretation

(1) In these Regulations, 'the 1995 Act' means the Environment Act 1995.

(2) The provisions of the Schedule to these Regulations which follow the Table in that Schedule shall have effect for the purpose of the interpretation of that Schedule.

3 Relevant periods

(1) The relevant period for the purposes of section 86(3) of the 1995 Act shall be, in relation to the preparation of an action plan to which that section applies, the period of 9 months beginning with the date on which the district council preparing the action plan first consults the relevant county council in relation to the plan pursuant to paragraph 1(2)(e) of Schedule 11 to the 1995 Act.

(2) The relevant period for the purposes of any other provision of Part IV of the 1995 Act shall be, in relation to an air quality objective, the period beginning with the date on which these Regulations come into force and ending on the date set out in the third column of the Table in the Schedule which relates to that objective.

4 Air quality objectives

(1) It is an air quality objective for each substance listed in the first column of the Table in the Schedule to these Regulations that the level at which that substance is present in the air is restricted to a level set out in the second column of that Table for that substance by no later than the date set out in the third column of that Table for that substance and level.

(2) The achievement or likely achievement of an air quality objective prescribed by paragraph (1) shall be determined by reference to the quality of air at locations—

(a) which are situated outside of buildings or other natural or man-made structures above or below ground; and

(b) where members of the public are regularly present.

Regulations 2(2), 3(2) and 4 SCHEDULE

AIR QUALITY OBJECTIVES

Table

Substance	**Air quality objective levels**	**Air quality objective dates**
Benzene	16.25 micrograms per cubic metre or less, when expressed as a running annual mean	31st December 2003
	[5 micrograms per cubic metre or less, when expressed as an annual mean	31st December 2010]
1,3-Butadiene	2.25 micrograms per cubic metre or less, when expressed as a running annual mean	31st December 2003
Carbon monoxide	[10] milligrams per cubic metre or less, when expressed as a [maximum daily] running 8 hour mean	31st December 2003
Lead	0.5 micrograms per cubic metre or less, when expressed as an annual mean	31st December 2004
	0.25 micrograms per cubic metre or less, when expressed as an annual mean	31st December 2008
Nitrogen dioxide	200 micrograms per cubic metre, when expressed as an hourly mean, not to be exceeded more than 18 times a year	31st December 2005
	40 micrograms per cubic metre or less, when expressed as an annual mean	31st December 2005
PM_{10}	50 micrograms per cubic metre or less, when expressed as a 24 hour mean, not to be exceeded more than 35 times a year	31st December 2004
	40 micrograms per cubic metre or less, when expressed as an annual mean	31st December 2004
Sulphur dioxide	125 micrograms per cubic metre or less, when expressed as a 24 hour mean, not to be exceeded more than 3 times a year	31st December 2004
	350 micrograms per cubic metre or less, when expressed as an hourly mean, not to be exceeded more than 24 times a year	31st December 2004
	266 micrograms per cubic metre or less, when expressed as a 15 minute mean, not to be exceeded more than 35 times a year	31st December 2005

Interpretation

For the purposes of this Schedule:

1. 'PM_{10}' means particulate matter which passes through a size-selective inlet with a 50% efficiency cut-off at 10μm aerodynamic diameter.

2.—(1) A running annual mean is a mean which is calculated on an hourly basis, yielding one running annual mean per hour. The running annual mean for a particular substance at a particular location for a particular hour is the mean of the hourly levels for that substance at that location for that hour and the preceding 8759 hours.

(2) For the purpose of the calculation of a running annual mean, the hourly level for a particular substance at a particular location is either:

(a) the level at which that substance is recorded as being present in the air at that location during the hour on the basis of a continuous sample of air taken during that hour for at least 30 minutes; or

(b) the mean of the levels recorded at that location on the basis of 2 or more samples of air taken during the hour for an aggregate period of at least 30 minutes.

[3.—(1) A maximum daily running 8 hour mean is calculated on a daily basis. The maximum daily running 8 hour mean for a particular substance at a particular location for a particular day is the maximum of the running 8 hour means ending during that day.

(2) For the purpose of sub-paragraph (1) a 'running 8 hour mean' is a mean which is calculated on an hourly basis, yielding one running 8 hour mean per hour. The running 8 hour mean for the relevant substance at the relevant location for a particular hour is the mean of the hourly means for the substance at the location for the hour and the preceding 7 hours.]

4.—(1) An annual mean is a mean which is calculated on a yearly basis, yielding one annual mean per calendar year. The annual mean for a particular substance at a particular location for a particular calendar year is:

(a) in the case of lead, the mean of the daily levels for that year;

(b) in the case of nitrogen dioxide, the mean of the hourly means for that year;

(c) in the case of PM_{10}, the mean of the 24 hour means for that year.

[(d) in the case of benzene, either the mean of the daily levels for that year or the mean of the hourly means for that year];

(2) For the purpose of the calculation of the annual mean for lead, the daily level for lead at a particular location for a particular day is the level at which lead is recorded as being present in the air at that location during the week in which the day occurs on the basis of a continuous sample of air taken throughout that week (each day in that week therefore being attributed with the same daily level).

(3) For the purpose of sub-paragraph (2) 'week' means a complete week beginning on a Monday, except that it also includes any period of less than seven days from the beginning of the calendar year until the first Monday in that year or from the beginning of the last Monday in the calendar year to the end of that year.

[(4) For the purpose of any calculation of the annual mean for benzene on the basis of the mean of the daily levels, the daily level for benzene at a particular location for a particular day is the level at which benzene is recorded as being present in the air at that location during the fortnight in which the day occurs on the basis of a continuous sample of air taken throughout that fortnight (each day in the fortnight therefore being attributed with the same daily level).

(5) For the purpose of sub-paragraph (4) 'fortnight' means a complete fortnight, that is a period of two weeks beginning on a Monday (no particular week in a calendar year being included in more than one fortnight), except that it also includes—

(a) in any calendar year beginning on a day other than a Monday, the period from the beginning of the year until the first Monday in that year; and

(b) in any year, the period from the end of the last complete fortnight in the year to the end of that year.]

5. An hourly mean is a mean calculated every hour.

[The hourly mean for a particular substance at a particular location for a particular hour is the mean of the levels recorded for that substance at that location:

(a) in the case of benzene, at a frequency of not less than once during the hour; and

(b) in the case of carbon monoxide, nitrogen dioxide and sulphur dioxide, at a frequency of not less than once every 10 seconds during the hour.]

6. A 24 hour mean is a mean calculated every 24 hours. The 24 hour mean for a particular substance at a particular location for a particular 24 hour period is the level at which that substance is recorded as being present in the air at that location on the basis of a continuous sample of air taken throughout the period.

7. A 15 minute mean is a mean calculated every 15 minutes. The 15 minute mean for a particular substance at a particular location for a particular 15 minutes is the mean of the levels recorded, at a frequency of not less than once every 10 seconds, for that substance at that location during that 15 minutes.

8. The reference to a number of micrograms or milligrams per cubic metre of a substance is a reference to the number of micrograms or milligrams per cubic metre of that substance when measured with the volume standardised at a temperature of 293K and at a pressure of 101.3 kPa.

Pollution Prevention and Control (England and Wales) Regulations 2000

(SI 2000, No. 1973) (as amended)

PART I GENERAL

1 Citation, commencement and extent

(1) These Regulations may be cited as the Pollution Prevention and Control (England and Wales) Regulations 2000 and shall come into force on the 1st August 2000.

(2) These Regulations extend to England and Wales only.

(3) For the purpose of paragraph (2), 'England and Wales' includes the territorial waters adjacent to England and Wales.

2 Interpretation: general

(1) In these Regulations, except in so far as the context otherwise requires—

['the 2002 Regulations' means the Landfill (England and Wales) Regulations 2002;]

'change in operation' means, in relation to an installation or mobile plant, a change in the nature or functioning or an extension of the installation or mobile plant which may have consequences for the environment; [and 'substantial change in operation' means, in relation to an installation or mobile plant, a change in operation which, in the opinion of the regulator, may have significant negative effects on human beings or the environment and shall include (except in relation to Part 1 of Schedule 3)—

(i) in relation to a small SED installation which does not fall wholly within the scope of the IPPC Directive, a change of the nominal capacity leading to an increase of emissions of volatile organic compounds of more than 25 per cent;

(ii) in relation to all other SED installations which do not fall wholly within the scope of the IPPC Directive, a change of the nominal capacity leading to an increase of emissions of volatile organic compounds of more than 10 per cent;

'directly associated activity' means—

(i) in relation to an activity carried out in a stationary technical unit and falling within any description in sections 1.1 to 6.9 of Part 1 of Schedule 1, any directly associated activity which has a technical connection with the activity carried out in the stationary technical unit and which could have an effect on pollution; and

(ii) in relation to an SED activity, any directly associated activity which has a technical connection with the SED activity carried out on the same site and which could have an effect on any discharge of volatile organic compounds into the environment;]

[...]

'emission' means—

(i) in relation to Part A installations, the direct or indirect release of substances, vibrations, heat or noise from individual or diffuse sources in an installation into the air, water or land;

(ii) in relation to Part B installations, the direct release of substances or heat from individual or diffuse sources in an installation into the air;

(iii) in relation to Part A mobile plant, the direct or indirect release of substances, vibrations, heat or noise from the mobile plant into the air, water or land;

(iv) in relation to Part B mobile plant, the direct release of substances or heat from the mobile plant into the air;

'emission limit value' means the mass, expressed in terms of specific parameters, concentration or level of an emission, which may not be exceeded during one or more periods of time;

'enforcement notice' has the meaning given by regulation 24(1);

'general binding rules' has the meaning given by regulation 14(1);

['installation' means (except where used in the term SED installation)—

(i) a stationary technical unit where one or more activities listed in Part 1 of Schedule 1 are carried out;

(ii) any other location on the same site where any other directly associated activities are carried out,

and, other than in Schedule 3, references to an installation include references to part of an installation;

'the IPPC Directive' means Council Directive 96/61/EC concerning integrated pollution prevention and control]

['landfill' means a landfill to which the 2002 Regulations apply;]

'mobile plant' means plant which is designed to move or to be moved whether on roads or otherwise and which is used to carry out one or more activities listed in sections 1.1 to 6.9 of Part 1 of Schedule 1;

['new SED installation' and 'existing SED installation' shall be interpreted in accordance with Schedule 3;]

'off-site condition' has the meaning given by regulation 12(12);

'operator', subject to paragraph (2), means, in relation to an installation or mobile plant, the person who has control over its operation;

'Part A installation', 'Part A(1) installation', 'Part A(2) installation' and 'Part B installation' shall be interpreted in accordance with Part 3 of Schedule 1;

'Part A mobile plant', 'Part A(1) mobile plant', 'Part A(2) mobile plant' and 'Part B mobile plant' shall be interpreted in accordance with Part 3 of Schedule 1;

'permit' means a permit granted under regulation 10;

'pollution' means emissions as a result of human activity which may be harmful to human health or the quality of the environment, cause offence to any human senses, result in damage to material property, or impair or interfere with amenities and other legitimate uses of the environment; and 'pollutant' means any substance, vibration, heat or noise released as a result of such an emission which may have such an effect;

['reduction scheme' means a reduction scheme which complies with Annex IIB of the Solvent Emissions Directive;]

'regulator' means, in relation to the exercise of functions under these Regulations, the authority by whom, under regulation 8, the functions are exercisable; and 'local authority regulator' means a regulator which is a local authority as defined in regulation 8(15) and (16);

'revocation notice' has the meaning given by regulation 21(1);

['SED activity' means any activity falling within section 7 of Part 1 of Schedule 1;

'SED installation' means—

(i) a stationary technical unit where one or more SED activities are carried out; and

(ii) any other location on the same site where any other directly associated activities are carried out;

'small SED installation' means an SED installation which falls within the lower threshold band of items 1, 3, 4, 5, 8, 10, 13, 16 or 17 of Annex IIA to the Solvent Emissions Directive or, for the other activities of Annex IIA, which have a solvent consumption of less than 10 tonnes/year;

'the Solvent Emissions Directive' means Council Directive 1999/13/EC on the limitation of emissions of volatile organic compounds due to the use of solvents in certain activities and installations;]

'specified waste management activity' means any one of the following activities—

(a) the disposal of waste in a landfill,falling within Section 5.2 of Part 1 of Schedule 1;

(b) the disposal of waste falling within Section 5.3 of that Part of that Schedule;

(c) the recovery of waste falling within paragraphs (i), (ii), (v) or (vii) of paragraph (c) of Part A(1) of Section 5.4 of that Part of that Schedule;

but does not include any activity specified in sub-paragraphs (b) or (c) above where that activity—

(i) is carried on at the same installation as any activity falling within Part A(1) of any Section in Part 1 of that Schedule, which is not an activity specified in sub-paragraphs (a) to (c) above; and

(ii) is not the primary activity of that installation,

and, for the purpose of this definition the primary activity of an installation is the activity the carrying out of which constitutes the primary purpose for operating the installation.]

'suspension notice' has the meaning given by regulation 25(1);

'variation notice' has the meaning given by regulation 17(5).

['waste incineration installation' means that part of an installation or mobile plant in which any of the following activities is carried out—

(a) the incineration of waste falling within Section 5.1A(1)(a), (b) or (c) or A(2) of Part 1 of Schedule 1; or

(b) any activity falling within any Section of that Part of that Schedule which is carried out in a co-incineration plant as defined in Section 5.1 of that Part of that Schedule; and]

(2) For the purposes of these Regulations—

(a) where an installation or mobile plant has not been put into operation, the person who will have control over the operation of the installation or mobile plant when it is put into operation shall be treated as the operator of the installation or mobile plant;

(b) where an installation or mobile plant has ceased to be in operation, the person who holds the permit which applies to the installation or mobile plant shall be treated as the operator of the installation or mobile plant.

[(2A) For the purposes of these Regulations where—

(a) an installation includes a combustion plant as defined in Article 2(7) of Council Directive 2001/80/EC on the limitation of emissions of certain pollutants into the air from large combustion plants and to which that Directive applies; and

(b) the rated thermal input of the combustion plant is extended by 50 megawatts or more,

the extension shall be treated as a substantial change in operation.]

[(2B) For the purposes of these Regulations a change in the operation of a waste incineration installation which involves incineration or coincineration for the first time of hazardous waste shall be treated as a substantial change in operation, and for the purposes of this paragraph 'co-incineration' and 'hazardous waste' shall have the meanings given in Section 5.1 of Part I of Schedule 1.]

[(2C) For the purposes of these Regulations any change in operation of an installation which in itself meets any of the thresholds specified for a Part A activity under any Section in Part 1 of Schedule 1 shall be treated as a substantial change in operation.]

(3) In these Regulations—

(a) a reference to a release into water includes a release into a sewer (within the meaning of section 219(1) of the Water Industry Act 1991);

(b) a reference to a Council Directive is a reference to that Directive together with any amendment made before the date on which these Regulations are made.

(4) Part 1 of Schedule 1 shall be interpreted in accordance with the provisions as to interpretation in Part 1 and 2 of that Schedule.

(5) Parts 1 and 2 of Schedule 3 shall be interpreted in accordance with Part 3 of that Schedule.

3 Interpretation: 'best available techniques'

(1) For the purpose of these Regulations, 'best available techniques' means the most effective and advanced stage in the development of activities and their methods of operation which indicates the practical suitability of particular techniques for providing in principle the basis for emission limit values designed to prevent and, where that is not practicable, generally to reduce emissions and the impact on the environment as a whole; and for the purpose of this definition—

(a) 'available techniques' means those techniques which have been developed on a scale which allows implementation in the relevant industrial sector, under economically and technically viable conditions, taking into consideration the cost and advantages, whether or not the techniques are used or produced inside the United Kingdom, as long as they are reasonably accessible to the operator;

(b) 'best' means, in relation to techniques, the most effective in achieving a high general level of protection of the environment as a whole;

(c) 'techniques' includes both the technology used and the way in which the installation is designed, built, maintained, operated and decommissioned.

(2) Schedule 2 shall have effect in relation to the determination of best available techniques.

4 Fit and proper person

(1) This regulation applies for the purpose of the discharge of any function under these Regulations which requires the regulator to determine whether a person is or is not a fit and proper person to carry out a specified waste management activity.

(2) Whether a person is or is not a fit and proper person to carry out a specified waste management activity shall be determined by reference to the fulfilment of the conditions of the permit which apply or will apply to the carrying out of that activity.

(3) Subject to paragraph (4), a person shall be treated as not being a fit and proper person if it appears to the regulator that—

(a) he or another relevant person has been convicted of a relevant offence;

[(b) the management of the specified waste management activity which is to be carried out will not be in the hands of a technically competent person;

(c) he has not made, or will not before commencement of any specified waste management activity consisting of the disposal of waste in a landfill falling within Section 5.2 of Part 1 of Schedule 1 make, adequate financial provision (either by way of financial security or its equivalent) to ensure that—

(i) the obligations (including after-care provisions) arising from the permit in relation to that activity are discharged; and

(ii) any closure procedures required by the permit in relation to that activity are followed;

(d) he and all staff engaged in carrying out any specified waste management activity falling within sub-paragraph (c) will not be provided with adequate professional technical development and training; or

(e) for specified waste management activities not falling within sub-paragraph (c), the person who holds or is to hold the permit has not made and either has no intention of making or is in no position to make financial provision adequate to discharge the obligations arising from the permit in relation to the specified waste management activity.]

(4) The regulator may, if it considers it proper to do so in any particular case, treat a person as a fit and proper person notwithstanding that paragraph (3)(a) applies in his case.

(5) For the purposes of paragraph (3)—

(a) 'relevant offence' means an offence prescribed under section 74(6) of the Environmental Protection Act 1990 for the purposes of section 74(3)(a) of that Act; and

(b) the qualifications and experience required of a person for the purposes of section 74(3)(b) of that Act which are prescribed under section 74(6) of that Act shall be treated as the qualifications and experience required of a person for the purposes of [paragraph (3)(b)].

(6) In paragraph (3)(a), 'another relevant person' means, in relation to the holder or proposed holder of a permit—

(a) any person who has been convicted of a relevant offence committed by him in the course of his employment by the holder or proposed holder of the permit or in the course of the carrying on of any business by a partnership one of the members of which was the holder or proposed holder of the permit;

(b) a body corporate which has been convicted of a relevant offence committed when the holder or proposed holder of the permit was a director, manager, secretary or other similar officer of that body corporate; or

(c) where the holder or proposed holder of the permit is a body corporate, a person who is a director, manager, secretary or other similar officer of that body corporate and who—

(i) has been convicted of a relevant offence; or

(ii) was a director, manager, secretary or other similar officer of another body corporate at a time when a relevant offence for which that other body corporate has been convicted was committed.

5 Application to the Crown

(1) Subject to the provisions of this regulation, these Regulations [and the 2002 Regulations] bind the Crown.

(2)–(5) . . .

6 Notices

. . .

7 Applications

. . .

8 Discharge and scope of functions

(1) This regulation determines the authority by whom the functions conferred or imposed by these Regulations on a regulator are exercisable and the purposes for which they are exercisable.

(2) Those functions, in their application to a Part A(1) installation or Part A(1) mobile plant, shall be functions of the Environment Agency and shall be exercisable for the purpose of achieving a high level of protection of the environment taken as a whole by, in particular, preventing or, where that is not practicable, reducing emissions into the air, water and land.

(3) Subject to regulation 13, those functions, in their application to a Part A(2) installation or Part A(2) mobile plant, shall be functions of the local authority in whose area the installation is (or will be) situated or the mobile plant is (or will be) operated and shall be exercisable for the purpose of achieving a high level of protection of the environment taken as a whole by, in particular, preventing or, where that is not practicable, reducing emissions into the air, water and land.

(4) Those functions, in their application to a Part B installation, shall be functions of the local authority in whose area the installation is (or will be) situated and, [subject to paragraph (4A),] shall be exercisable for the purpose of preventing or, where that is not practicable, reducing emissions into the air.

[(4A) The functions conferred or imposed by these Regulations in relation to an SED installation shall be exercisable for the purpose of preventing or reducing emissions of volatile organic compounds into air, soil and water as well as preventing the inclusion of solvents, or reducing the amount of solvents contained, in any products.]

(5) Those functions, in their application to a Part B mobile plant, shall be functions of—

(a) where the operator of the mobile plant has his principal place of business in England and Wales, the local authority in whose area that place of business is;

(b) where the operator of the mobile plant has his principal place of business outside of England and Wales and the mobile plant is not covered by a permit, the local authority in whose area the plant is first operated or, where the plant has not been operated in England and Wales, the local authority in whose area it is intended by the operator that the plant should first be operated;

(c) where the operator has his principal place of business outside of England and Wales and the mobile plant is covered by a permit, the local authority which granted the permit,

and shall be exercisable for the purpose of preventing or, where that is not practicable, reducing emissions into the air.

(6) The Secretary of State may, as respects functions under these Regulations exercisable by a local authority specified in the direction, direct that those functions shall be exercised instead by the Environment Agency while the direction remains in force or during a period specified in the direction.

(7) A transfer of functions under paragraph (6) to the Environment Agency relating to Part B installations or Part B mobile plant does not make them exercisable by the Agency for any other purpose than that mentioned in paragraphs (4)[, (4A)] and (5).

(8) The Secretary of State may, as respects functions under these Regulations exercisable by the Environment Agency specified in the direction, direct that those functions shall be exercised instead by a local authority while the direction remains in force or during a period specified in the direction.

(9) A direction under paragraph (6) may transfer functions exercisable by a local authority in relation to all or any description of installations or mobile plant (a 'general direction') or in relation to a specific installation or mobile plant specified in the direction (a 'specific direction') but a direction under paragraph (8) may only be a specific direction.

(10) A direction under paragraph (6) or (8) may include such saving and transitional provisions as the Secretary of State considers necessary or expedient.

(11) The Secretary of State, on giving or withdrawing a general direction under paragraph (6), shall—

(a) serve notice of it on the Environment Agency and on the local authorities affected by the direction; and

(b) cause notice of it to be published as soon as practicable in the London Gazette and in at least one newspaper circulating in the area of each authority affected by the direction,

and any such notice shall specify the date on which the direction is to take (or took) effect and (where appropriate) its duration.

(12) The Secretary of State, on giving or withdrawing a specific direction under paragraph (6) or (8), shall—

(a) serve notice on the Environment Agency, the local authority and the operator or the person appearing to the Secretary of State to be the operator of the installation or mobile plant affected; and

(b) cause notice of it to be published in the London Gazette and in at least one newspaper circulating in the authority's area,

and any such notice shall specify the date on which the direction is to take (or took) effect and (where appropriate) its duration.

(13) The requirements of sub-paragraph (b) of paragraph (11), or, as the case may be, sub-paragraph (b) of paragraph (12) shall not apply in any case where, in the opinion of the Secretary of State, the publication of the notice in accordance with that sub-paragraph would be contrary to the interests of national security.

(14) It shall be the duty of regulators to follow developments in best available techniques.

(15) In this regulation, 'local authority' means, subject to paragraph (16)—

(a) in Greater London, a London borough council, the Common Council of the City of London, the Sub-Treasurer of the Inner Temple and the Under Treasurer of the Middle Temple;

(b) in England outside Greater London, a district council or, in relation to an area for which there is a county council but no district council, the county council, and the Council of the Isles of Scilly;

(c) in Wales, a county council or county borough council.

(16) Where, by an order under section 2 of the Public Health (Control of Disease) Act 1984, a port health authority has been constituted for any port health district, the port health authority shall have, as respects its district, the functions conferred or imposed by these Regulations in their application to a Part B installation; and 'local authority' and 'area' shall be construed accordingly.

PART II PERMITS

9 Requirement for permit to operate installation and mobile plant

(1) No person shall operate an installation or mobile plant after the prescribed date for that installation or mobile plant except under and to the extent authorised by a permit granted by the regulator.

(2) In paragraph (1), the 'prescribed date' means the appropriate date set out in or determined in accordance with Schedule 3.

10 Permits: general provisions

(1) An application for a permit to operate an installation or mobile plant shall be made to the regulator in accordance with paragraphs 1 to 3 of Part I of Schedule 4 and shall be accompanied by any fee prescribed in respect of the application under section 41 of the Environment Act 1995 or regulation 22.

(2) Subject to paragraphs (3) and (4), where an application is duly made to the regulator, the regulator shall either grant the permit subject to the conditions required or authorised to be imposed by [regulation 12 or 12A] [below (or regulation 8 of the 2002 Regulations)] or refuse the permit.

(3) A permit shall not be granted if the regulator considers that the applicant will not be the person who will have control over the operation of the installation or mobile plant

concerned after the grant of the permit or will not ensure that the installation or mobile plant is operated so as to comply with the conditions which would be included in the permit.

(4) In the case of an application for a permit that will authorise the carrying out of a specified waste management activity at an installation or by means of mobile plant, the permit shall not be granted unless—

(a) the regulator is satisfied that the applicant is a fit and proper person to carry out that activity; and

(b) in the case of an installation where the use of the application site for the carrying out of that activity requires planning permission granted under the Town and Country Planning Act 1990, such planning permission is in force in relation to that use of the land.

(5) For the purpose of paragraph (4)(b), a certificate under section 191 of the Town and Country Planning Act 1990 (certificate of lawful use or development) in relation to the use of the application site for the carrying out of the specified waste management activity, and an established use certificate under section 192 of that Act, as originally enacted, in relation to that use which continues to have effect for the purpose of subsection (4) of that section, shall be treated as if it were a grant of planning permission for that use.

(6) A permit may authorise the operation of—

(a) more than one Part A installation or Part A mobile plant on the same site operated by the same operator;

(b) more than one Part B installation on the same site operated by the same operator; or

(c) more than one Part B mobile plant operated by the same operator, but may not otherwise authorise the operation of more than one installation or mobile plant.

(7) A permit authorising the operation of a Part A mobile plant may only authorise the operation of that plant on a site specified in the permit and only one site may be specified in each such permit (accordingly, the operation of the plant on a different site shall require a distinct permit).

(8) A permit authorising the operation of an installation or Part A mobile plant shall include a map or plan showing the site of the installation or plant covered by the permit and, in the case of an installation, the location of the installation on that site.

(9) A permit shall be transferred only in accordance with regulation 18 and shall cease to have effect only in accordance with regulation 19 or 20 (surrender) or regulation 21 (revocation) or paragraph (10) (consolidation).

(10) Where—

(a) the conditions of a permit have been varied under regulation 17 or affected by a partial transfer, surrender or revocation under regulations 18 to 21; or

(b) there is more than one permit applying to installations on the same site operated by the same operator or to mobile plant operated by the same operator, the regulator may replace the permit or permits, as the case may be, with a consolidated permit applying to the same installations or mobile plant and subject to the same conditions as the permit or permits being replaced.

(11) Paragraphs 4 to 8 of Part 1 of Schedule 4 shall have effect with respect to applications made under paragraph (1).

(12) Part 2 of Schedule 4 shall have effect in relation to the determination of applications for permits.

(13) Parts 1 and 2 of Schedule 4 shall have effect subject to Part 3 of that Schedule (national security).

(14) This regulation is subject to paragraphs 5 and 9 of Schedule 3 (applications for a permit to operate existing installations or mobile plant, as defined in that Schedule).

11 Conditions of permits: general principles

(1) When determining the conditions of a permit, the regulator shall take account of the general principles set out in paragraph (2) and, in the case of a permit authorising the

operation of a Part A installation or Part A mobile plant, the additional general principles set out in paragraph (3).

(2) The general principles referred to in paragraph (1) are that installations and mobile plant should be operated in such a way that—

(a) all the appropriate preventative measures are taken against pollution, in particular through application of the best available techniques; and

(b) no significant pollution is caused.

(3) The additional general principles referred to in paragraph (1) in relation to a permit authorising the operation of a Part A installation or a Part A mobile plant are that the installation or mobile plant should be operated in such a way that—

(a) waste production is avoided in accordance with Council Directive 75/442/ EEC on waste; and where waste is produced, it is recovered or, where that is technically and economically impossible, it is disposed of while avoiding or reducing any impact on the environment;

(b) energy is used efficiently;

(c) the necessary measures are taken to prevent accidents and limit their consequences, and that, upon the definitive cessation of activities, the necessary measures should be taken to avoid any pollution risk and to return the site of the installation or mobile plant to a satisfactory state.

12 Conditions of permits: specific requirements

(1) Subject to paragraphs (15) and (16) and regulations 13 and 14, there shall be included in a permit—

(a) such conditions as the regulator considers appropriate to comply with paragraphs (2) to (8); and

(b) in relation to any Part A installation or Part A mobile plant authorised by the permit—

(i) such other conditions applying in relation to the Part A installation or Part A mobile plant as the regulator considers appropriate to comply with paragraph (9); and

(ii) such other conditions (if any) applying in relation to the Part A installation or Part A mobile plant, in addition to those required by sub-paragraphs (a) and (b)(i), as appear to the regulator to be appropriate, when taken with the condition implied by paragraph (10), for the purpose of ensuring a high level of protection for the environment as a whole, taking into account, in particular, the general principles set out in regulation 11;

(c) in relation to any Part B installation or Part B mobile plant authorised by the permit, such other conditions (if any) applying in relation to the Part B installation or Part B mobile plant as appear to the regulator to be appropriate, when taken with the condition implied by paragraph (10), for the purpose of preventing or, where that is not practicable, reducing emissions into the air, taking into account, in particular, the general principles set out in regulation 11(2).

(2) Subject to paragraph (8), a permit shall include emission limit values for pollutants, in particular those listed in Schedule 5, likely to be emitted from the installation or mobile plant in significant quantities, having regard to their nature and, in the case of emissions from a Part A installation or a Part A mobile plant, their potential to transfer pollution from one environmental medium to another.

(3) Where appropriate, the emission limit values required by paragraph (2) may apply to groups of pollutants rather than to individual pollutants.

(4) The emission limit values required by paragraph (2) shall normally apply at the point at which the emissions leave the installation or mobile plant, any dilution being disregarded when determining them.

(5) The effect of a waste water treatment plant may be taken into account when determining the emission limit values applying in relation to indirect releases into water from a Part A installation or Part A mobile plant provided that an equivalent level of protection of the environment as a whole is guaranteed and taking such treatment into account does not lead to higher levels of pollution.

(6) Subject to paragraph (7), the emission limit values required by paragraph (2) shall be based on the best available techniques for the description of installation or mobile plant concerned but shall take account of the technical characteristics of the particular installation or mobile plant being permitted, and, in the case of an installation or Part A mobile plant, its geographical location and the local environmental conditions.

(7) Where an environmental quality standard requires stricter emission limit values than those that would be imposed pursuant to paragraph (6), paragraph (2) shall require those stricter emission limit values; and for the purpose of this paragraph 'environmental quality standard' means the set of requirements which must be fulfilled at a given time by a given environment or particular part thereof, as set out in Community legislation.

(8) Where appropriate, the emission limit values required by paragraph (2) may be supplemented or replaced by equivalent parameters or technical measures.

(9) A permit authorising the operation of a Part A installation or Part A mobile plant shall also include conditions—

(a) aimed at minimising long distance and transboundary pollution;

(b) ensuring, where necessary, appropriate protection of the soil and ground-water and appropriate management of waste generated by the installation or mobile plant;

(c) relating to the periods when the installation or mobile plant is not operating normally where there is a risk that the environment may be adversely affected during such periods, including, in particular, conditions relating to the start up of operations, leaks, malfunctions and momentary stoppages;

(d) setting out the steps to be taken prior to the operation of the installation or mobile plant and after the definitive cessation of operations;

(e) setting out suitable emission monitoring requirements, specifying the measurement methodology and frequency and the evaluation procedure, and ensuring that the operator supplies the regulator with the data required to check compliance with the permit;

(f) requiring the operator to supply the regulator regularly with the results of the monitoring of emissions and to inform the regulator, without delay, of any incident or accident which is causing or may cause significant pollution.

(10) Subject to paragraph (11), there is implied in every permit a condition that, in operating the installation or mobile plant, the operator shall use the best available techniques for preventing or, where that is not practicable, reducing emissions from the installation or mobile plant.

(11) The obligation implied by virtue of paragraph (10) shall not apply in relation to any aspect of the operation of the installation or mobile plant in question which is regulated by a condition imposed under any other paragraph of this regulation.

(12) A permit authorising the operation of an installation or Part A mobile plant may include a condition (an 'off-site condition') requiring an operator to carry out works or do other things in relation to land not forming part of the site of the installation or mobile plant notwithstanding that he is not entitled to carry out the works or do the things and any person whose consent would be required shall grant, or join in granting, the operator such rights in relation to that land as will enable the operator to comply with any requirements imposed on him by the permit.

(13) Schedule 6 shall have effect in relation to compensation where rights are granted pursuant to paragraph (12).

(14) A permit may, without prejudice to the generality of the previous provisions of this regulation, include conditions—

(a) imposing limits on the amount or composition of any substance produced or utilised during the operation of the installation or mobile plant in any period;

(b) which are supplemental or incidental to other conditions contained in the permit.

(15) The Secretary of State may give directions to regulators—

(a) as to the specific conditions which are, or are not, to be included in all permits, in permits of a specified description or in any particular permit;

(b) as to the objectives which are to be achieved by conditions included in such permits,

and the regulators shall include in such permits such conditions as are specified or required to comply with such directions.

(16) Guidance issued by the Secretary of State under regulation 37 may sanction reliance by a regulator on any arrangements referred to in the guidance to operate to secure a particular result as an alternative to including a condition in the permit pursuant to this regulation [or regulation 8 of the 2002 Regulations].

(17) Where a Part B mobile plant authorised by a permit is used to carry out an activity on the site of an installation which is authorised by a separate permit, then if different requirements are imposed in the permits as respect the carrying out of the activity the requirements in the permit authorising the operation of the installation shall prevail in the event of any inconsistency.

[12A Conditions of permits: solvents

A permit authorising the operation of an SED installation shall contain such conditions as the regulator considers necessary to give effect to the provisions of the Solvent Emissions Directive.]

13 Conditions of permits: Environment Agency notice in relation to emissions into water

(1) In the case of a Part A installation or Part A mobile plant in relation to which a local authority regulator exercises functions under these Regulations, the Environment Agency may, at any time, give notice to the local authority regulator specifying the emission limit values or conditions (not containing emission limit values) which it considers are appropriate in relation to preventing or reducing emissions into water.

(2) Where a notice under paragraph (1) specifies emission limit values, the emission limit values required by paragraph (2) of regulation 12 in relation to emissions into water from the installation or mobile plant concerned shall be those specified in that notice or such stricter emission limit values as may be determined by the local authority regulator in accordance with paragraph (6) of that regulation or required by paragraph (7) of that regulation.

(3) Where a notice under paragraph (1) specifies conditions in relation to emissions into water from an installation or mobile plant, the permit authorising the operation of that installation or mobile plant shall include those conditions or any more onerous conditions dealing with the same matters as the local authority regulator considers to be appropriate.

14 General binding rules

(1) Subject to paragraph (2), the Secretary of State may make rules ('general binding rules') containing requirements applying to certain types of installation or mobile plant.

(2) The Secretary of State shall only make general binding rules under this regulation applying to Part A installations or Part A mobile plant if he is satisfied that the operation of such installations or mobile plant under the rules will result in the same high level of environmental protection and integrated prevention and control of pollution as would result from the operation of the installations or mobile plant under the conditions that would be included in the permits for those installations or mobile plant pursuant to [regulation 12 and

12A] if the rules did not apply.

(3) Where the Secretary of State makes general binding rules a regulator may, at the request of the operator, include in a permit authorising the operation of an installation or mobile plant covered by the rules a condition (a 'general binding rules condition') providing that the aspects of the operation of the installation or mobile plant covered by the requirements in the rules shall be subject to those requirements instead of to conditions included in the permit pursuant to [regulation 12 and 12A.]

(4) Where a permit includes a general binding rules condition the requirements in the general binding rules shall be treated as if they were conditions of the permit for the purpose of regulations 23, 24 and 32(1)(b).

(5) The Secretary of State may vary general binding rules by means of a notice of variation specifying the variations and the date on which the variations are to take effect, which shall be not less than 3 months after the date on which notice of the variation is given in the London Gazette pursuant to paragraph (9)(c).

(6) The Secretary of State may revoke general binding rules by means of a notice of revocation.

(7) Where aspects of the operation of an installation or mobile plant are covered by the requirements in general binding rules which are revoked, the regulator shall vary the permit authorising the operation of the installation or mobile plant under regulation 17 to delete the general binding rules condition and to insert the conditions that will be required by regulations 11 and 12 when the requirements in the general binding rules no longer apply.

(8) Where the Secretary of State revokes general binding rules the requirements in the general binding rules shall continue to be treated under paragraph (4) as if they were conditions of a permit until the variations of the permit required by paragraph (7) take effect.

(9) Where the Secretary of State makes, varies or revokes general binding rules he shall—

- (a) serve a copy of the rules, notice of variation or notice of revocation on the Environment Agency and on all local authority regulators;
- (b) publish the rules, notice of variation or notice of revocation in such manner as he considers appropriate for the purpose of bringing the rules or notice to the attention of operators likely to be affected by them;
- (c) give notice of the making, variation or revocation of the rules in the London Gazette.

15 Review of conditions of permits

(1) Regulators shall periodically review the conditions of permits and may do so at any time.

(2) Without prejudice to paragraph (1), a review of a permit under this regulation shall be carried out where—

- (a) the pollution caused by the installation or mobile plant covered by the permit is of such significance that the existing emission limit values of the permit need to be revised or new emission limit values need to be included in the permit;
- (b) substantial changes in the best available techniques make it possible to reduce emissions from the installation or mobile plant significantly without imposing excessive costs; or
- (c) the operational safety of the activities carried out in the installation or mobile plant requires other techniques to be used.

16 Proposed change in the operation of an installation

(1) Subject to paragraph (4), where an operator of an installation which is permitted under these Regulations proposes to make a change in the operation of that installation he shall, at least 14 days before making the change, notify the regulator.

(2) A notification under paragraph (1) shall be in writing and shall contain a description of the proposed change in the operation of the installation.

(3) A regulator shall, by notice served on the operator, acknowledge receipt of any notification received under paragraph (1).

(4) Paragraph (1) shall not apply where the operator applies under regulation 17(2) for the variation of the conditions of his permit before making the proposed change and the application contains a description of the change.

17 Variation of conditions of permits

(1) The regulator may at any time vary the conditions of a permit and shall do so if it appears to the regulator at that time, whether as a result of a review under regulation 15, a notification under regulation 13 or 16 or otherwise, that [regulations 11, 12 or 12A] [above or regulation 8 of the 2002 Regulations] require conditions to be included which are different from the subsisting conditions.

(2) An operator of an installation or mobile plant which is permitted under these Regulations may apply to the regulator for the variation of the conditions of his permit.

(3) An application under paragraph (2) shall be made in accordance with paragraph 1 of Part 1 of Schedule 7 and shall be accompanied by any fee prescribed in respect of the application under section 41 of the Environment Act 1995 or regulation 22; and paragraphs 2 and 3 of Part 1 of Schedule 7 shall have effect with respect to such applications.

(4) Where an application is duly made to the regulator under paragraph (2), the regulator shall determine, in accordance with [regulations 11, 12 or 12A] [above or regulation 8 of the 2002 Regulations], whether to vary the conditions of the permit.

(5) Where the regulator decides to vary the conditions of the permit, whether on an application under paragraph (2) or otherwise, it shall serve a notice on the operator (a 'variation notice') specifying the variations of the conditions of the permit and the date or dates on which the variations are to take effect and, unless the notice is withdrawn, the variations specified in the notice shall take effect on the date or dates so specified.

(6) A variation notice served under paragraph (5) shall, unless served for the purpose of determining an application under paragraph (2), require the operator to pay, within such period as may be specified in the notice, any fee prescribed in respect of the variation notice under section 41 of the Environment Act 1995 or regulation 22.

(7) Where the regulator decides on an application under paragraph (2) not to vary the conditions of the permit, it shall give notice of its decision to the operator.

(8) Part 2 of Schedule 7 shall have effect in relation to the determination of applications under paragraph (2) and the issuing of variation notices.

(9) Parts 1 and 2 of Schedule 7 shall have effect subject to Part 3 of that Schedule (national security).

(10) This regulation and Schedule 7 apply to the variation of any provision other than a condition which is contained in a permit as they apply to the variation of a condition.

18 Transfer of permits

(1) Where the operator of an installation or mobile plant wishes to transfer, in whole or in part, his permit to another person ('the proposed transferee') the operator and the proposed transferee shall jointly make an application to the regulator to effect the transfer.

(2)–(3) . . .

(4) Subject to paragraph (5), the regulator shall effect the transfer unless the regulator considers that the proposed transferee will not be the person who will have control over the operation of the installation or mobile plant covered by the transfer after the transfer is effected or will not ensure compliance with the conditions of the transferred permit.

(5) In the case of an application to effect the transfer of a permit or part of a permit which authorises the carrying out of a specified waste management activity, the regulator shall only effect the transfer if the regulator is satisfied that the proposed transferee is a fit and proper person to carry out that activity.

(6) . . .

(7) In the case of a partial transfer effected under this regulation, the conditions included in the new permit and original permit after the transfer shall be the same as the conditions included in the original permit immediately before the transfer in so far as they are relevant to any installation, site and mobile plant covered by the new permit or the original permit, as the case may be, but subject to such variations as, in the opinion of the regulator, are necessary to take account of the transfer.

(8) If within the period of two months beginning with the date on which the authority receives an application under paragraph (1), or within such longer period as the regulator and the applicants may agree in writing, the regulator has neither effected the transfer nor given notice to the applicants that it has rejected the application, the application shall, if the applicants notify the regulator in writing that they treat the failure as such, be deemed to have been refused at the end of that period or that longer period, as the case may be.

(9) The regulator may, by notice, require the operator or the proposed transferee to furnish such further information specified in the notice, within the period so specified, as the regulator may require for the purpose of determining an application under this regulation.

(10) Where a notice is served on an operator or proposed transferee under paragraph (9)—

(a) for the purpose of calculating the period of two months mentioned in paragraph (8), no account shall be taken of the period beginning with the date on which notice is served and ending on the date on which the information specified in the notice is furnished; and

(b) if the specified information is not furnished within the period specified, the application shall, if the regulator gives notice to the operator and proposed transferee that it treats the failure as such, be deemed to have been withdrawn at the end of that period.

19 Application to surrender a permit for a Part A installation or Part A mobile plant

(1) [Subject to paragraph (1A) this regulation] applies where an operator of a Part A installation or Part A mobile plant ceases or intends to cease operating the installation (in whole or in part) or the mobile plant.

[(1A) This regulation does not apply in relation to that part of any installation or mobile plant where an activity falling within Part A(2) of Section 5.1 of Part 1 of Schedule 1 is carried out.]

(2) Where this regulation applies, the operator may—

(a) if he has ceased or intends to cease operating all of the installations and mobile plant covered by the permit, apply to the regulator to surrender the whole permit;

(b) in any other case, apply to the regulator to surrender the permit in so far as it authorises the operation of the installation or mobile plant ('the surrender unit') which he has ceased or intends to cease operating (a 'partial surrender').

(3) An application under paragraph (2) shall be accompanied by any fee prescribed in respect of the application under section 41 of the Environment Act 1995 or regulation 22, and shall contain the following information—

(a) the operator's telephone number and address and, if different, any address to which correspondence relating to the application should be sent;

(b) in the case of a partial surrender, a description of the surrender unit and a map or plan identifying the part of the site used for the operation of the surrender unit (the 'identified part of the site');

(c) a site report describing the condition of the site, or the identified part of the site, as the case may be ('the report site'), identifying, in particular, any changes in the condition of the site as described in the site report contained in the application for the permit; and

(d) a description of any steps that have been taken to avoid any pollution risk on the report site resulting from the operation of the installation or mobile plant or to return it to a satisfactory state.

(4) If the regulator is satisfied, in relation to the report site, that such steps (if any) as are appropriate to avoid any pollution risk resulting from the operation of the Part A installation or Part A mobile plant and to return the site to a satisfactory state have been taken by the operator, it shall accept the surrender and give the operator notice of its determination and the permit shall cease to have effect or, in the case of partial surrender, shall cease to have effect to the extent surrendered, on the date specified in the notice of determination.

(5) If, in the case of a partial surrender, the regulator is of the opinion that it is necessary to vary the conditions included in the permit to take account of the surrender, the regulator shall specify the necessary variations in the notice of determination given under paragraph (4) and the variations specified in the notice shall take effect on the date specified in the notice.

(6) If the regulator is not satisfied as mentioned in paragraph (4), it shall give to the operator a notice of its determination stating that the application has been refused.

(7) The regulator shall give notice of its determination of an application under this regulation within the period of three months beginning with the date on which the regulator receives the application or within such longer period as the regulator and the operator may agree in writing.

(8) If the regulator fails to give notice of its determination accepting the surrender or refusing the application within the period allowed by or under paragraph (7) the application shall, if the operator notifies the regulator in writing that he treats the failure as such, be deemed to have been refused at the end of that period.

(9) The regulator may, by notice to the operator, require him to furnish such further information specified in the notice, within the period so specified, as the regulator may require for the purpose of determining an application under this regulation.

(10) Where a notice is served on an operator under paragraph (9)—

(a) for the purpose of calculating the period of three months mentioned in paragraph (7), no account shall be taken of the period beginning with the date on which notice is served and ending on the date on which the information specified in the notice is furnished; and

(b) if the specified information is not furnished within the period specified the application shall, if the regulator gives notice to the operator that it treats the failure as such, be deemed to have been withdrawn at the end of that period.

(11) For the purpose of deciding whether a pollution risk results from the operation of a Part A installation or Part A mobile plant for the purpose of this regulation—

(a) where the operation of the installation or plant involved the carrying out of a specified waste management activity, only risks resulting from carrying out that activity after the relevant date for that activity shall be treated as resulting from the operation of the installation or mobile plant;

(b) where the operation of the installation or mobile plant involved the carrying out of other activities, only risks resulting from the carrying out of those other activities after the date on which the permit applying to the installation or mobile plant was granted shall be treated as resulting from the operation of the installation or mobile plant.

(12) The relevant date for a specified waste management activity for the purpose of paragraph (11)(a) is—

(a) where the activity was carried out on the site of the installation or mobile plant under a waste management licence which, by virtue of section 35(11A) of the Environmental Protection Act 1990, ceased to have effect in relation to the carrying out of that activity on that site on the granting of the permit applying to the installation or mobile plant, the date on which that waste management licence was granted;

(b) in any other case, the date on which the permit applying to the installation or mobile plant was granted.

(13) In paragraph (12)(a), 'waste management licence' has the same meaning as in section 35(12) of the Environmental Protection Act 1990 (and includes a disposal licence which is treated as a site licence by virtue of section 77(2) of that Act).

20 Notification of surrender of a permit for a Part B installation or Part B mobile plant

(1) This regulation applies where an operator of a Part B installation or Part B mobile plant ceases or intends to cease operating the installation (in whole or in part) or the mobile plant.

[(1A) This regulation also applies in relation to that part of any installation or mobile plant where an activity falling within Part A(2) of Section 5.1 of Part 1 of Schedule 1 is carried out.]

(2) Where this regulation applies, the operator may—

(a) if he has ceased or intends to cease operating all of the installations and mobile plant covered by the permit, notify the regulator of the surrender of the whole permit;

(b) in any other case, notify the regulator of the surrender of the permit in so far as it authorises the operation of the installation or mobile plant ('the surrender unit') which he has ceased or intends to cease operating (a 'partial surrender').

(3) A notification under paragraph (2) shall contain the following information—

(a) the operator's telephone number and address and, if different, any address to which correspondence relating to the notification should be sent;

(b) in the case of a partial surrender of a permit applying to Part B installations, a description of the surrender unit and a map or plan identifying the part of the site used for the operation of the surrender unit (the 'identified part of the site');

(c) in the case of a partial surrender of a permit applying to Part B mobile plant, a list of the mobile plant to which it applies;

(d) the date on which the surrender is to take effect, which shall be at least 28 days after the date on which the notice is served on the regulator.

(4) Subject to paragraph (5), where a surrender is notified under this regulation the permit shall cease to have effect on the date specified in the notification or, in the case of partial surrender, shall cease to have effect on that date to the extent surrendered.

(5) If, in the case of a partial surrender, the regulator is of the opinion that it is necessary to vary the conditions of the permit to take account of the surrender, the regulator shall—

(a) notify the operator of its opinion; and

(b) serve a variation notice under regulation 17 on the operator specifying the variations of the conditions necessitated by the surrender,

and the permit shall cease to have effect to the extent surrendered on the date on which the variations specified in the variation notice take effect if that date is after the date specified in the notification of the surrender.

21 Revocation of permits

(1) The regulator may at any time revoke a permit, in whole or in part, by serving a notice ('a revocation notice') on the operator.

(2) Without prejudice to the generality of paragraph (1), the regulator may serve a notice under this regulation in relation to a permit where—

(a) the permit authorises the carrying out of a specified waste management activity and it appears to the regulator that the operator of the installation or mobile plant concerned has ceased to be a fit and proper person to carry out that activity by reason of his having been convicted of a relevant offence within the meaning of regulation 4(5)(a) or by reason of the management of that activity having ceased to be in the hands of a technically competent person;

(b) the holder of the permit has ceased to be the operator of the installation or mobile plant covered by the permit.

(3) A revocation notice may—

(a) revoke a permit entirely;

(b) revoke a permit only in so far as it authorises the operation of some of the installations or mobile plant to which it applies;

(c) revoke a permit only in so far as it authorises the carrying out of some of the activities which may be carried out in an installation or by means of mobile plant to which it applies.

(4) A revocation notice shall specify—

(a) in the case of a revocation mentioned in sub-paragraph (b) or (c) of paragraph (3) (a 'partial revocation'), the extent to which the permit is being revoked;

(b) in all cases, the date on which the revocation shall take effect, which shall be at least 28 days after the date on which the notice is served.

(5) If, in the case of a revocation mentioned in sub-paragraph (a) or (b) of paragraph (3) applying to a Part A installation or Part A mobile plant, the regulator considers that it is appropriate to require the operator to take steps, once the installation or mobile plant is no longer in operation, to—

(a) avoid any pollution risk resulting from the operation of the installation or mobile plant on the site or, in the case of a partial revocation, that part of the site used for the operation of that installation or mobile plant, or

(b) return the site, or that part of the site, to a satisfactory state, the revocation notice shall specify that this is the case and, in so far as those steps are not already required to be taken by the conditions of the permit, the steps to be taken.

(6) Subject to paragraph (7) and regulation 27(6), a permit shall cease to have effect, or, in the case of a partial revocation, shall cease to have effect to the extent specified in the revocation notice, from the date specified in the notice.

(7) Where paragraph (5) applies the permit shall cease to have effect to authorise the operation of the Part A installation or Part A mobile plant from the date specified in the revocation notice but shall continue to have effect in so far as the permit requires steps to be taken once it is no longer in operation until the regulator issues a certificate stating that it is satisfied that all such steps have been taken.

(8) Where a permit continues to have effect as mentioned in paragraph (7), any steps specified in a revocation notice pursuant to paragraph (5) shall be treated as if they were required to be taken by a condition of the permit and regulations 17, 23, 24, and 32(1)(b) shall apply in relation to the requirement to take such steps, and to any other conditions in the permit which require steps to be taken once the installation is no longer in operation, until the regulator issues a certificate as mentioned in paragraph (7).

(9) A regulator which has served a revocation notice may, before the date on which the revocation takes effect, withdraw the notice.

(10) Regulation 19(11) shall apply for the purpose of deciding whether a pollution risk results from the operation of a Part A installation or Part A mobile plant for the purpose of this regulation as it applies for the purpose of regulation 19.

22 Fees and charges in relation to local authority permits

...

PART III ENFORCEMENT

23 Duty of regulator to ensure compliance with conditions

While a permit is in force it shall be the duty of the regulator to take such action under these Regulations as may be necessary for the purpose of ensuring that the conditions of the permit are complied with.

24 Enforcement notices

(1) If the regulator is of the opinion that an operator has contravened, is contravening or is likely to contravene any condition of his permit, the regulator may serve on him a notice (an 'enforcement notice').

(2) An enforcement notice shall—

(a) state that the regulator is of that opinion;

(b) specify the matters constituting the contravention or the matters making it likely that the contravention will arise, as the case may be;

(c) specify the steps that must be taken to remedy the contravention or to remedy the matters making it likely that the contravention will arise, as the case may be; and

(d) specify the period within which those steps must be taken.

(3) The steps that may be specified in an enforcement notice as steps that must be taken to remedy the contravention of any condition of a permit may include both steps that must be taken to make the operation of the installation or mobile plant comply with the conditions of the permit and steps that must be taken to remedy the effects of any pollution caused by the contravention.

(4) The regulator may withdraw an enforcement notice at any time.

25 Suspension notices

(1) If the regulator is of the opinion, as respects an installation or mobile plant authorised under these regulations, that the operation of the installation or mobile plant, or the operation of it in a particular manner, involves an imminent risk of serious pollution, it shall, unless it intends to arrange for steps to be taken under regulation 26(1) in relation to the risk, serve a notice under this regulation (a 'suspension notice') on the operator of the installation or mobile plant.

(2) Paragraph (1) applies whether or not the particular manner of operating the installation or mobile plant in question is regulated by or contravenes a condition of the permit.

(3) If the regulator is of the opinion, as respects the carrying out of specified waste management activities under a permit, that the operator carrying out the activities has ceased to be a fit and proper person in relation to those activities by reason of their management having ceased to be in the hands of a technically competent person, it may serve a suspension notice on that operator.

(4) A suspension notice shall—

(a) state the regulator's opinion, as mentioned in paragraph (1) or (3), as the case may be;

(b) in the case of a notice served under paragraph (1), specify—

(i) the imminent risk involved in the operation of the installation or mobile plant;

(ii) the steps that must be taken to remove it and the period within which they must be taken;

(c) state that the permit shall, until the notice is withdrawn, cease to have effect to authorise the operation of the installation or mobile plant or the carrying out of specified activities in the installation or by means of the mobile plant; and

(d) where the permit is to continue to have effect to authorise the carrying out of activities, state any steps, in addition to those already required to be taken by the conditions of the permit, that are to be taken in carrying out those activities.

(5) Where a suspension notice is served under this regulation the permit shall, on the service of the notice, cease to have effect as stated in the notice.

(6) The regulator may withdraw a suspension notice at any time and shall withdraw a notice when it is satisfied—

(a) in the case of a notice served under paragraph (1), that the steps required by the notice to remove the imminent risk of serious pollution have been taken;

(b) in the case of a notice served under paragraph (3), that the management of the specified waste management activities is in the hands of a technically competent person.

26 Power of regulator to prevent or remedy pollution

(1) If the regulator is of the opinion, as respects the operation of an installation or mobile plant authorised under these regulations, that the operation of the installation or mobile plant, or the operation of it in a particular manner, involves an imminent risk of serious pollution, the regulator may arrange for steps to be taken to remove that risk.

(2) Where the commission of an offence under regulation 32(1)(a), (b) or (d) causes any pollution the regulator may arrange for steps to be taken towards remedying the effects of the pollution.

(3) A regulator which intends to arrange for steps to be taken under paragraph (2) shall, at least seven days before the steps are taken, notify the operator of the steps that are to be taken.

(4) Subject to paragraph (5), where a regulator arranges for steps to be taken under this regulation it may recover the cost of taking those steps from the operator concerned.

(5) No costs shall be recoverable under paragraph (4) where the regulator arranges for steps to be taken under paragraph (1) if the operator shows that there was no imminent risk of serious pollution requiring any such steps to be taken and no other costs shall be recoverable which the operator shows to have been unnecessarily incurred by the regulator.

PART IV APPEALS

27 Appeals to the Secretary of State

(1) Subject to paragraph (3), the following persons, namely—

(a) a person who has been refused the grant of a permit under regulation 10;

(b) a person who has been refused the variation of the conditions of a permit on an application under regulation 17(2);

(c) a person who is aggrieved by the conditions attached to his permit following an application under regulation 10 or by a variation notice following an application under regulation 17(2);

(d) a person whose application under regulation 18(1) for a regulator to effect the transfer of a permit has been refused or who is aggrieved by the conditions attached to his permit to take account of such a transfer;

(e) a person whose application under regulation 19(2) to surrender a permit has been refused, or who is aggrieved by the conditions attached to his permit to take account of the surrender;

[(f) a person whose request to initiate the closure procedure is not approved under regulation 15(3)(b) of the 2002 Regulations;

(g) a person who is aggrieved by a decision under paragraph 1(6) (b) of Schedule 4 to the 2002 Regulations]

may appeal against the decision of the regulator to the Secretary of State.

(2) Subject to paragraph (3), a person on whom a variation notice is served, other than following an application under regulation 17(2), or on whom a revocation notice, an enforcement notice [a suspension notice or a closure notice under regulation 16(1) of the 2002 Regulations] is served may appeal against the notice to the Secretary of State.

(3) Paragraphs (1) and (2) shall not apply where the decision or notice, as the case may be, implements a direction of the Secretary of State given under regulations 12(15) or 36 or paragraph (4) of this regulation or paragraph 14(6) of Schedule 4 or 6(6) of Schedule 7.

(4) On determining an appeal against a decision of a regulator under paragraph (1) the Secretary of State may—

(a) affirm the decision;

(b) where the decision was a refusal to grant a permit or to vary the conditions of a permit, direct the regulator to grant the permit or to vary the conditions of the permit, as the case may be;

(c) where the decision was as to the conditions attached to a permit, quash all or any of the conditions of the permit;

(d) where the decision was a refusal to effect the transfer or accept the surrender of a permit, direct the regulator to effect the transfer or accept the surrender, as the case may be,

and where he exercises any of the powers in paragraph (b) or (c) he may give directions as to the conditions to be attached to the permit.

(5) On the determination of an appeal under paragraph (2) the Secretary of State may either quash or affirm the notice and, if he affirms it, may do so either in its original form or with such modifications as he may in the circumstances think fit.

(6) Where an appeal is brought under paragraph (2) against a revocation notice, the revocation shall not take effect pending the final determination or the withdrawal of the appeal.

(7) Where an appeal is brought under paragraph (1)(c), (d) or (e) in relation to the conditions attached to a permit, the bringing of the appeal shall not have the effect of suspending the operation of the conditions.

(8) Where an appeal is brought under paragraph (2) against a variation notice, an enforcement notice or a suspension notice, the bringing of the appeal shall not have the effect of suspending the operation of the notice.

[(8A) Where an appeal is brought under paragraph (1)(g) in relation to a requirement to initiate the closure procedure or under paragraph (2) in relation to a closure notice, the closure procedure shall not be initiated pending the final determination or the withdrawal of the appeal.]

(9) Regulations 11 and 12 [above or regulation 8 of the 2002 Regulations] shall apply where the Secretary of State, in exercising any of the powers in sub-paragraph (b) or (c) of paragraph (4), gives directions as to the conditions to be attached to a permit as they would apply to the regulator when determining the conditions of the permit.

(10) Schedule 8 shall have effect in relation to the making and determination of appeals under this regulation.

(11) This regulation and Schedule 8 are subject to section 114 of the Environment Act 1995 (delegation of reference of appeals).

[(12) Where an appeal is brought under paragraph (1)(g) in relation to which a waste management licence within the meaning of Part II of the Environmental Protection Act 1990 ('a licence') is in force, this regulation and Schedule 8 shall apply as if:

(a) references to a permit were references to a licence;

(b) references to the operator were references to the licence holder; and

(c) references to an installation or mobile plant were references to a landfill.]

PART V INFORMATION AND PUBLICITY

28 Information

(1) For the purpose of the discharge of his functions under these Regulations [or the 2002 Regulations], the Secretary of State may, by notice served on a regulator, require the regulator to furnish such information about the discharge of its functions as a regulator as he may require.

(2) For the purposes of the discharge of their functions under these Regulations [or the 2002 Regulations], the Secretary of State or a regulator may, by notice served on any person, require that person to furnish such information as is specified in the notice, in such form and within such period following service of the notice or at such time as is so specified.

(3) For the purposes of this regulation, the discharge by the Secretary of State of an obligation of the United Kingdom under the Community Treaties or any international agreement relating to the environment shall be treated as a function of his under these Regulations and the compilation of an inventory of emissions (whether or not from installations or mobile plant) shall be treated as a function of the Environment Agency under these Regulations.

(4) The information which a person may be required to furnish by a notice served under paragraph (2) includes information on emissions which, although it is not in the possession of that person or would not otherwise come into the possession of that person, is information which it is reasonable to require that person to compile for the purpose of complying with the notice.

29 Public registers of information

(1) Subject to regulations 30 and 31 and to paragraphs 2 to 5 of Schedule 9, it shall be the duty of each regulator, as respects installations or mobile plant for which it is the regulator, to maintain a register containing the particulars described in paragraph 1 of that Schedule.

(2) Subject to paragraph (3), the register maintained by a local authority regulator shall also contain any particulars contained in any register maintained by the Environment Agency relating to the operation of an installation or Part A mobile plant in the area of the local authority regulator in relation to which the Environment Agency has functions under these Regulations.

(3) Paragraph (2) does not apply to port health authorities but each local authority regulator whose area adjoins that of a port health authority shall include in its register the information that it would have had to include under paragraph (2) in relation to the operation of installations and Part A mobile plant in the area of the port health authority if the port health authority had not been constituted.

(4) The Environment Agency shall furnish each local authority regulator with the particulars which are necessary to enable it to discharge its duty under paragraphs (2) and (3).

(5) Where information of any description is excluded from any register by virtue of regulation 31, a statement shall be entered in the register indicating the existence of information of that description.

(6) It shall be the duty of each regulator—

(a) to secure that the registers maintained by them under this regulation are available, at all reasonable times, for inspection by the public free of charge; and

(b) to afford to members of the public facilities for obtaining copies of entries, on payment of reasonable charges.

(7) Registers under this regulation may be kept in any form.

30 Exclusion from registers of information affecting national security

(1) No information shall be included in a register maintained under regulation 29 if and so long as, in the opinion of the Secretary of State, the inclusion in the register of that information, or information of that description, would be contrary to the interests of national security.

(2)–(4) . . .

31 Exclusion from registers of certain confidential information

(1) No information relating to the affairs of any individual or business shall be included in a register maintained under regulation 29, without the consent of that individual or the person for the time being carrying on that business, if and so long as the information—

(a) is, in relation to him, commercially confidential; and

(b) is not required to be included in the register in pursuance of a direction under paragraph (9),

but information is not commercially confidential for the purposes of this regulation unless it is determined under this regulation to be so by the regulator or, on appeal, by the Secretary of State.

(2) Where information is furnished to a regulator for the purpose of these Regulations the person furnishing it may apply to the regulator to have the information excluded from the register on the ground that it is commercially confidential (as regards himself or another person) and the regulator shall determine whether the information is or is not commercially confidential.

(3)–(9) ...

(10) Information excluded from a register shall be treated as ceasing to be commercially confidential for the purposes of this regulation at the expiry of the period of four years beginning with the date of the determination by virtue of which it was excluded or at the expiry of such shorter period as may be specified in the notice of that determination for the purpose of this paragraph; but the person who furnished it may apply to the regulator for the information to remain excluded from the register on the ground that it is still commercially confidential and the regulator shall determine whether or not that is the case.

(11)–(12) ...

PART VI PROVISION AS TO OFFENCES

32 Offences

(1) It is an offence for a person—

(a) to contravene regulation 9(1);

(b) to fail to comply with or to contravene a condition of a permit;

(c) to fail to comply with regulation 16(1);

(d) to fail to comply with the requirements of an enforcement notice, [a suspension notice or a closure notice under regulation 16 of the 2002 Regulations;]

(e) to fail, without reasonable excuse, to comply with any requirement imposed by a notice under regulation 28(2);

(f) to make a statement which he knows to be false or misleading in a material particular, or recklessly to make a statement which is false or misleading in a material particular, where the statement is made—

(i) in purported compliance with a requirement to furnish any information imposed by or under any provision of these Regulations [or the 2002 Regulations;]

(ii) for the purpose of obtaining the grant of a permit to himself or any other person, or the variation, transfer or surrender of a permit;

(g) intentionally to make a false entry in any record required to be kept under the condition of a permit;

(h) with intent to deceive, to forge or use a document issued or authorised to be issued under a condition of a permit or required for any purpose under a condition of a permit or to make or have in his possession a document so closely resembling any such document as to be likely to deceive;

(i) to fail to comply with an order made by a court under regulation 35.

(2) A person guilty of an offence under sub-paragraph (a), (b), (d) or (i) of paragraph (1) shall be liable—

(a) on summary conviction, to a fine not exceeding £20,000 or to imprisonment for a term not exceeding six months or to both;

(b) on conviction on indictment, to a fine or to imprisonment for a term not exceeding five years or to both.

(3) A person guilty of an offence under sub-paragraph (c), (e) and (f) to (h) of paragraph (1) shall be liable—

(a) on summary conviction, to a fine not exceeding the statutory maximum;

(b) on conviction on indictment, to a fine or to imprisonment for a term not exceeding two years or to both.

(4) Where an offence under this regulation committed by a body corporate is proved to have been committed with the consent or connivance of, or to have been attributable to any neglect on the part of, any director, manager, secretary or other similar officer of the body corporate or a person who was purporting to act in any such capacity, he as well as the body corporate shall be guilty of that offence and shall be liable to be proceeded against and punished accordingly.

(5) Where the affairs of a body corporate are managed by its members, paragraph (4) shall apply in relation to the acts or defaults of a member in connection with his functions of management as if he were a director of the body corporate.

(6) Where the commission by any person of an offence under this regulation is due to the act or default of some other person, that other person may be charged with and convicted of the offence by virtue of this paragraph whether or not proceedings for the offence are taken against the first-mentioned person.

33 Enforcement by High Court

If the regulator is of the opinion that proceedings for an offence under regulation 32(1)(d) would afford an ineffectual remedy against a person who has failed to comply with the requirements of an enforcement notice or a suspension notice, the regulator may take proceedings in the High Court for the purpose of securing compliance with the notice.

34 Admissibility of evidence

Where—

(a) by virtue of a condition of a permit granted by a local authority regulator an entry is required to be made in any record as to the observance of any condition of the permit; and

(b) the entry has not been made, that fact shall be admissible as evidence that that condition has not been observed.

35 Power of court to order cause of offence to be remedied

(1) Where a person is convicted of an offence under regulation 32(1)(a), (b) or (d) in respect of any matters which appear to the court to be matters which it is in his power to remedy, the court may, in addition to or instead of imposing any punishment, order him, within such time as may be fixed by the order, to take such steps as may be specified in the order for remedying those matters.

(2) The time fixed by an order under paragraph (1) may be extended or further extended by order of the court on an application made before the end of the time as originally fixed or extended under this paragraph, as the case may be.

(3) Where a person is ordered under paragraph (1) to remedy any matters, that person shall not be liable under regulation 32 in respect of those matters in so far as they continue during the time fixed by the order or any further time allowed under paragraph (2).

PART VII SECRETARY OF STATE'S POWERS

36 Directions to regulators

(1) The Secretary of State may give directions to regulators of a general or specific character with respect to the carrying out of any of their functions under these Regulations [or the 2002 Regulations.]

(2) Without prejudice to the generality of the power conferred by paragraph (1), a direction under that paragraph may direct regulators—

(a) to exercise any of their powers under these Regulations [or the 2002 Regulations] or to do so in such circumstances as may be specified in the directions or in such manner as may be so specified; or

(b) not to exercise those powers, or not to do so in such circumstances or such manner as may be specified in the directions.

(3) Where the Secretary of State receives information pursuant to Article 17(1) of the Directive in relation to the operation of an installation outside of the United Kingdom which is likely to have a significant negative effect on the environment of England or Wales, he shall, for the purpose of complying with Article 17(2) of the Directive, direct the Environment Agency to take such steps as he considers appropriate for the purpose of bringing the information to the attention of the persons in England or Wales likely to be affected by the operation of the installation and providing them with an opportunity to comment on that information.

(4) Any direction given under these Regulations shall be in writing and may be varied or revoked by a further direction.

(5) It shall be a duty of a regulator to comply with any direction which is given to it under these Regulations.

37 Guidance to regulators

(1) The Secretary of State may issue guidance to regulators with respect to the carrying out of any of their functions under these Regulations [or the 2002 Regulations.]

(2) A regulator, in carrying out any of its functions under these Regulations [or the 2002 Regulations], shall have regard to any guidance issued by the Secretary of State under this regulation.

38 Plans relating to emissions

(1) The Secretary of State may make plans for—

(a) the setting of limits on the total amount, or the total amount in any period, of emissions from all or any description of source within England and Wales; or

(b) the allocation of quotas relating to such emissions.

(2) Where the Secretary of State allocates a quota in a plan made under paragraph (1) he may also make a scheme for the trading or other transfer of the quota so allocated.

(3) In this regulation, 'emission' means the direct or indirect release of any substance from individual or diffuse sources into the air, water or land.

Regulation 2

SCHEDULE 1

ACTIVITIES, INSTALLATIONS AND MOBILE PLANT

PART 1 ACTIVITIES

CHAPTER 1—ENERGY INDUSTRIES*

SECTION 1.1—COMBUSTION ACTIVITIES

Part A(1)

(a) Burning any fuel in an appliance with a rated thermal input of 50 megawatts or more.

(b) Burning any of the following fuels in an appliance with a rated thermal input of 3 megawatts or more but less than 50 megawatts unless the activity is carried out as part of a Part A(2) or B activity—

(i) waste oil;
(ii) recovered oil;
(iii) any fuel manufactured from, or comprising, any other waste.

*Editor's note: Chapter 1 only is included in full for illustrative purposes.

Interpretation of Part A(1)

1. For the purpose of paragraph (a), where two or more appliances with an aggregate rated thermal input of 50 megawatts or more are operated on the same site by the same operator those appliances shall be treated as a single appliance with a rated thermal input of 50 megawatts or more.

2. Nothing in this Part applies to burning fuels in an appliance installed on an offshore platform situated on, above or below those parts of the sea adjacent to England and Wales from the low water mark to the seaward baseline of the United Kingdom territorial sea.

3. In paragraph 2, 'offshore platform' means any fixed or floating structure which—

(a) is used for the purposes of or in connection with the production of petroleum; and

(b) in the case of a floating structure, is maintained on a station during the course of production,

but does not include any structure where the principal purpose of the use of the structure is the establishment of the existence of petroleum or the appraisal of its characteristics, quality or quantity or the extent of any reservoir in which it occurs.

4. In paragraph 3, 'petroleum' includes any mineral oil or relative hydrocarbon and natural gas existing in its natural condition in strata but does not include coal or bituminous shales or other stratified deposits from which oil can be extracted by destructive distillation.

Part A(2)

Nil.

Part B

Unless falling within paragraph (a) of Part A(1) of this Section—

(a) Burning any fuel, other than a fuel mentioned in paragraph (b) of Part A(1) of this Section, in a boiler or furnace or a gas turbine or compression ignition engine with, in the case of any of these appliances, a net rated thermal input of 20 megawatts or more but less than a rated thermal output of 50 megawatts.

(b) Burning any of the following fuels in an appliance with a rated thermal input of less than 3 megawatts—

(i) waste oil;

(ii) recovered oil;

(iii) a solid fuel which has been manufactured from waste by an activity involving the application of heat.

(c) Burning fuel manufactured from or including waste, other than a fuel mentioned in paragraph (b), in any appliance—

(i) with a rated thermal input of less than 3 megawatts but at least a net rated thermal output of 0.4 megawatts; or

(ii) which is used together with other appliances which each have a rated thermal input of less than 3 megawatts, where the aggregate net rated thermal input of all the appliances is at least 0.4 megawatts.

Interpretation of Part B

1. Nothing in this Part applies to any activity falling within Part A(1) or A(2) of Section 5.1.

2. In paragraph (c), 'fuel' does not include gas produced by biological degradation of waste.

Interpretation of Section 1.1

For the purpose of this Section—

'waste oil' means any mineral based lubricating or industrial oil which has become unfit for the use for which it was intended, such as used combustion engine oil, gearbox oil, mineral lubricating oil, oil for turbines and hydraulic oil;

'recovered oil' means waste oil which has been processed before being used.

SECTION 1.2—GASIFICATION, LIQUEFACTION AND REFINING ACTIVITIES

Part A(1)

(a) Refining gas where this is likely to involve the use of 1,000 tonnes or more of gas in any period of 12 months.
(b) Reforming natural gas.
(c) Operating coke ovens.
(d) Coal or lignite gasification.
(e) Producing gas from oil or other carbonaceous material or from mixtures thereof, other than from sewage, unless the production is carried out as part of an activity which is a combustion activity (whether or not that combustion activity is described in Section 1.1).
(f) Purifying or refining any product of any of the activities falling within paragraphs (a) to (e) or converting it into a different product.
(g) Refining mineral oils.
(h) The loading, unloading or other handling of, the storage of, or the physical, chemical or thermal treatment of—
   (i) crude oil;
   (ii) stabilised crude petroleum;
   (iii) crude shale oil;
   (iv) where related to another activity described in this paragraph, any associated gas or condensate;
   (v) emulsified hydrocarbons intended for use as a fuel.
(i) The further refining, conversion or use (otherwise than as a fuel or solvent) of the product of any activity falling within paragraphs (g) or (h) in the manufacture of a chemical.
(j) Activities involving the pyrolysis, carbonisation, distillation, liquefaction, gasification, partial oxidation, or other heat treatment of coal (other than the drying of coal), lignite, oil, other carbonaceous material or mixtures thereof otherwise than with a view to making charcoal.
(k) Odorising natural gas or liquified petroleum gas where that activity is related to a Part A activity.

Interpretation of Part A(1)

1. Paragraph (j) does not include the use of any substance as a fuel or its incineration as a waste or any activity for the treatment of sewage or sewage sludge.

2. In paragraph (j), the heat treatment of oil, other than distillation, does not include the heat treatment of waste oil or waste emulsions containing oil in order to recover the oil from aqueous emulsions.

3. In this Part, 'carbonaceous material' includes such materials as charcoal, coke, peat, rubber and wood, but does not include wood that has not been chemically treated.

Part A(2)

(a) Refining gas where this activity does not fall within paragraph (a) of Part A(1) of this Section.

Part B

(a) Odorising natural gas or liquefied petroleum gas, except where that activity is related to a Part A activity.
(b) Blending odorant for use with natural gas or liquefied petroleum gas.
(c) The storage of petrol in stationary storage tanks at a terminal, or the loading or unloading at a terminal of petrol into or from road tankers, rail tankers or inland waterway vessels.

(d) The unloading of petrol into stationary storage tanks at a service station, if the total quantity of petrol unloaded into such tanks at the service station in any period of 12 months is likely to be $500m^3$ or more.

Interpretation of Part B

1. In this Part—

'inland waterway vessel' means a vessel, other than a sea-going vessel, having a total dead weight of 15 tonnes or more;

'petrol' means any petroleum derivative (other than liquefied petroleum gas), with or without additives, having a Reid vapour pressure of 27.6 kilopascals or more which is intended for use as a fuel for motor vehicles;

'service station' means any premises where petrol is dispensed to motor vehicle fuel tanks from stationary storage tanks;

'terminal' means any premises which are used for the storage and loading of petrol into road tankers, rail tankers or inland waterway vessels.

2. Any other expressions used in this Part which are also used in Directive 94/63/EC on the control of volatile organic compound (VOC) emissions resulting from the storage of petrol and its distribution from terminals to service stations have the same meaning as in that Directive.

CHAPTER 2—PRODUCTION AND PROCESSING OF METALS

...

CHAPTER 3—MINERAL INDUSTRIES

...

CHAPTER 4—THE CHEMICAL INDUSTRY

...

CHAPTER 5—WASTE MANAGEMENT

...

CHAPTER 6—OTHER ACTIVITIES

...

SECTION 7—SED ACTIVITIES

...

PART 2 INTERPRETATION OF PART 1

1. The following rules apply for the interpretation of Part 1 of this Schedule.

2.—(1). Subject to sub-paragraph (2), an activity shall not be taken to be a Part B activity if it cannot result in the release into the air of a substance listed in paragraph 12 or there is no likelihood that it will result in the release into the air of any such substance except in a quantity which is so trivial that it is incapable of causing pollution or its capacity to cause pollution is insignificant.

[(2) Sub-paragraph (1) shall not apply to—

(i) an SED activity; or

(ii) an activity which may give rise to an offensive smell noticeable outside the site where the activity is carried out.]

3. An activity shall not be taken to be an acitivty falling within [sections 1.1 to 6.9 of] Part 1 if it is carried out in a working museum to demonstrate an industrial activity of historic interest or if it is carried out for educational purposes in a school as defined in section 4(1) of the Education Act 1996,

4. The running on or within an aircraft, hovercraft, mechanically propelled road vehicle, railway locomotive or ship or other vessel of an engine which propels or provides electricity for it shall not be taken to be an activity falling within [sections 1.1 to 6.9 of] Part 1.

5. The running of an engine in order to test it before it is installed or in the course of its development shall not be taken to be an activity falling within [sections 1.1 to 6.9 of] Part 1.

6.—(1) The use of a fume cupboard shall not be taken to be an activity falling within [sections 1.1 to 6.9 of] Part 1 if it is used as a fume cupboard in a laboratory for research or testing and it is not—

(i) a fume cupboard which is an industrial and continuous production activity enclosure; or

(ii) a fume cupboard in which substances or materials are manufactured.

(2) In sub-paragraph (1) 'fume cupboard' has the meaning given by the British Standard 'Laboratory fume cupboards' published by the British Standards Institution numbered BS7258 : Part I : 1990.

7. An activity shall not be taken to fall within [sections 1.1 to 6.9 of] Part 1 if it is carried out as a domestic activity in connection with a private dwelling.

7A. An activity listed in Section 7 of Part 1 shall include the cleaning of equipment but, except for a surface cleaning activity, not the cleaning of products.

8. References in Part 1 to related activities are references to separate activities being carried out by the same person on the same site.

9.—(1) This paragraph applies for the purpose of determining whether an activity carried out in a stationary technical unit falls within a description in Part A(1) or A(2) which refers to capacity, other than design holding capacity.

(2) Where a person carries out several activities falling within the same description in Part A(1) or A(2) in different parts of the same stationary technical unit or in different stationary technical units on the same site, the capacities of each part or unit, as the case may be, shall be added together and the total capacity shall be attributed to each part or unit for the purpose of determining whether the activity carried out in each part or unit falls within a description in Part A(1) or A(2).

(3) For the purpose of sub-paragraph (2), no account shall be taken of capacity when determining whether activities fall within the same description.

(4) Where an activity falls within a description in Part A(1) or A(2) by virtue of this paragraph it shall not be taken to be an activity falling within a description in Part B [(other than a description in Section 7)].

10.—(1) Where an activity falls within a description in Part A(1) and a description in Part A(2) that activity shall be regarded as falling only within that description which fits it most aptly.

(2) Where an activity falls within a description in Part A(1) and a description in Part B [(other than a description in Section 7)] that activity shall be regarded as falling only within the description in Part A(1).

(3) Where an activity falls within a description in Part A(2) and a description in Part B [(other than a description in Section 7)] that activity shall be regarded as falling only within the description in Part A(2).

11. In Part 1 of this Schedule—

'background quantity' means, in relation to the release of a substance resulting from an activity, such quantity of that substance as is present in—

(i) water supplied to the site where the activity is carried out;

(ii) water abstracted for use in the activity; and

(iii) precipitation onto the site on which the activity is carried out;

'Part A activity' means an activity falling within Part A(1) or A(2) of any Section in Part 1 of this Schedule;

'Part A(1) activity' means an activity falling within Part A(1) of any Section in Part 1 of this Schedule;

'Part A(2) activity' means an activity falling within Part A(2) of any Section in Part 1 of this Schedule;

'Part B activity' means an activity falling within Part B of any Section in Part 1 of this Schedule.

12. References to, or to the release into the air of, a substance listed in this paragraph are to any of the following substances—

oxides of sulphur and other sulphur compounds;
oxides of nitrogen and other nitrogen compounds;
oxides of carbon;
organic compounds and partial oxidation products;
metals, metalloids and their compounds;
asbestos (suspended particulate matter and fibres), glass fibres and mineral fibres;
halogens and their compounds;
phosphorus and its compounds;
particulate matter.

13. References to, or to the release into water of, a substance listed in this paragraph or to its release in a quantity which, in any period of 12 months, is greater than the background quantity by an amount specified in this paragraph are to the following substances and amounts—

Substance	**Amount greater than the background quantity (in grammes) in any period of 12 months**
Mercury and its compounds	200 (expressed as metal)
Cadmium and its compounds	1,000 (expressed as metal)
All isomers of hexachlorocyclohexane	20
All isomers of DDT	5
Pentachlorophenol and its compounds	350 (expressed as PCP)
Hexachlorobenzene	5
Hexachlorobutadiene	20
Aldrin	2
Dieldrin	2
Endrin	1
Polychlorinated Biphenyls	1
Dichlorvos	0.2
1,2—Dichloroethane 2,000	2,000
All isomers of trichlorobenzene	75
Atrazine	350*
Simazine	350*
Tributyltin compounds	4 (expressed as TBT)
Triphenyltin compounds	4 (expressed as TPT)

Table *(Cont.)*

Substance	Amount greater than the background quantity (in grammes) in any period of 12 months
Trifluralin	20
Fenitrothion	2
Azinphos-methyl	2
Malathion	2
Endosulfan	0.5

*Where both Altrazine and Simazine are released, the figure for both substances in aggregate is 350 grammes.

14.—(1) References to a substance listed in this paragraph are to any of the following substances—

alkali metals and their oxides and alkaline earth metals and their oxides;
organic solvents;
azides;
halogens and their covalent compounds;
metal carbonyls;
organo-metallic compounds;
oxidising agents;
polychlorinated dibenzofuran and any congener thereof;
polychlorinated dibenzo-p-dioxin and any congener thereof;
polyhalogenated biphenyls, terphenyls and naphthalenes;
phosphorus;
pesticides.

(2) In sub-paragraph (1), 'pesticide' means any chemical substance or preparation prepared or used for destroying any pest, including those used for protecting plants or wood or other plant products from harmful organisms, regulating the growth of plants, giving protection against harmful creatures, rendering such creatures harmless, controlling organisms with harmful or unwanted effects on water systems, buildings or other structures, or on manufactured products, or protecting animals against ectoparasites.

PART 3 INTERPRETATION OF 'PART A INSTALLATION' ETC

15. For the purpose of these Regulations, subject to paragraph 17—

'Part A installation' means a Part A(1) installation or a Part A(2) installation;

'Part A(1) installation' means an installation where a Part A(1) activity is carried out (including such an installation where a Part A(2) or Part B activity is also carried out);

'Part A(2) installation' means an installation, not being a Part A(1) installation, where a Part A(2) activity is carried out (including such an installation where a Part B activity is also carried out);

'Part B installation' means an installation where a Part B activity is carried out, not being a Part A installation.

16. For the purpose of these Regulations—

'Part A mobile plant' means Part A(1) mobile plant or Part A(2) mobile plant;

'Part A(1) mobile plant' means mobile plant used to carry out a Part A(1) activity (including such plant which is also used to carry out a Part A(2) or Part B activity);

'Part A(2) mobile plant' means mobile plant, not being Part A(1) mobile plant, used to carry out a Part A(2) activity (including such mobile plant used to carry out a Part B activity);

'Part B mobile plant' means mobile plant used to carry out a Part B activity, not being Part A mobile plant.

17.—(1) An installation where a Part A(2) activity is carried out (and no Part A(1) activity) shall nevertheless be a Part A(1) installation if any waste activity is also carried out at the installation.

(2) In sub-paragraph (1) 'waste activity' means an activity mentioned in paragraph (a) or (b) of section 33(1) of the Environmental Protection Act 1990 (deposit, keeping, treatment and disposal of waste) other than—

(a) the incineration of waste falling within Part A2 or Part B of Section 5.1 of Part 1 of this Schedule [or the incineration of waste in a waste incineration installation;]

(b) an exempt activity, as defined in regulation 1(3) of and Schedule 3 to the Waste Management Licensing Regulations 1994 or

(c) the disposal or recycling of animal carcasses or animal waste by rendering in a plant with a capacity exceeding 10 tonnes per day of animal carcasses or animal waste, or, in aggregate, of both].

18. [...]

19. A Part B installation where an activity falling within paragraph (e) of Part B of Section 2.2 is carried out does not include any location where the associated storage or handling of scrap which is to be heated as part of that activity is carried out, other than a location where scrap is loaded into a furnace.

20. A Part B installation where an activity falling with paragraph (a) or (b) of Part B of Section 5.1 is carried out does not include any location where the associated storage or handling of wastes and residues which are to be incinerated as part of that activity is carried out, other than a location where the associated storage or handling of animal remains intended for burning in an incinerator used wholly or mainly for the incineration of such remains or residues from the burning of such remains in such an incinerator is carried out.

[21.—(1) A Part B installation where an activity falling within Part B of Section 6.4 is carried out does not include any location where the associated cleaning of used storage drums prior to painting or their incidental handling in connection with such cleaning is carried out.

(2) Sub-paragraph (1) shall not apply where the location referred to in that sub-paragraph forms part of an SED installation.]

22. Where an installation is a Part A(1) installation, a Part A(2) installation or a Part B installation by virtue of the carrying out of an activity which is only carried out during part of a year that installation shall not cease to be such an installation during the parts of the year when that activity is not being carried out.

23. Where an installation is authorised by a permit granted under these Regulations to carry out Part A(1) activities, Part A(2) activities or Part B activities which are described in Part 1 by reference to a threshold (whether in terms of capacity or otherwise), the installation shall not cease to be a Part A(1) installation, a Part A(2) installation, or a Part B installation, as the case may be, by virtue of the installation being operated below the relevant threshold unless the permit ceases to have effect in accordance with these Regulations.

24. In this Part, 'Part A(1) activity', 'Part A(2) activity' and 'Part B activity' have the meaning given by paragraph 11 in Part 2 of this Schedule.

Regulation 3

SCHEDULE 2

BEST AVAILABLE TECHNIQUES

1. Subject to paragraph 2, in determining best available techniques special consideration shall be given to the following matters, bearing in mind the likely costs and benefits of a measure and the principles of precaution and prevention—

(1) the use of low-waste technology;

(2) the use of less hazardous substances;

(3) the furthering of recovery and recycling of substances generated and used in the process and of waste, where appropriate;

(4) comparable processes, facilities or methods of operation which have been tried with success on an industrial scale;

(5) technological advances and changes in scientific knowledge and understanding;

(6) the nature, effects and volume of the emissions concerned;

(7) the commissioning dates for new or existing installations or mobile plant;

(8) the length of time needed to introduce the best available technique;

(9) the consumption and nature of raw materials (including water) used in the process and the energy efficiency of the process;

(10) the need to prevent or reduce to a minimum the overall impact of the emissions on the environment and the risks to it;

(11) the need to prevent accidents and to minimise the consequences for the environment;

(12) the information published by the Commission pursuant to Article 16(2) of the IPPC Directive or by international organisations.

2. Sub-paragraphs (1) to (3) and (9) to (12) shall not apply for the purposes of determining best available techniques in relation to Part B installations and Part B mobile plant.

Regulations 9 and 10(14)

SCHEDULE 3

PRESCRIBED DATE AND TRANSITIONAL ARRANGEMENTS

PART 1—PART A INSTALLATIONS AND MOBILE PLANT

1. The prescribed date for a new Part A installation or new Part A mobile plant is—

(a) where an application for a permit to operate the installation or mobile plant is duly made before 1st April 2001, the determination date for the installation or mobile plant;

(b) where no such application is made, 1st January 2001.

2.—(1) Subject to paragraph 4, the prescribed date for an existing Part A installation or existing Part A mobile plant is—

(a) where an application for a permit to operate the installation or mobile plant is duly made within the relevant period (or before the beginning of the relevant period where allowed under paragraph 5), the determination date for the installation or mobile plant;

(b) where no such application is made, the day after the date on which the relevant period expires.

(2) For the purpose of sub-paragraph (1) the relevant period for an existing Part A installation or existing Part A mobile plant is the period specified for that description of installation or mobile plant in the following table—

Any installation where an activity falling within the following Section of Part 1 of Schedule 1 is carried out or any mobile plant used to carry out such an activity	Relevant Period
Section 1.1	
Part A(1)	1st January to 31st March 2006
Section 1.2	
Part A(1)	
Paragraph (c)	1st June to 31st August 2001
Remaining paragraphs	1st June to 31st August 2006
Part A(2)	[1st June to 31st August 2006]
Section 2.1	
Part A(1)	
Paragraph (c)	1st May to 31st July 2002
Remaining paragraphs	1st June to 31st August 2001
Part A(2)	[1st May to 31st July 2003]
Section 2.2	
Part A(1)	1st October to 31st December 2001
Part A(2)	1st May to 31st July 2003
Section 2.3	
Part A(1)	1st May to 31st July 2004
[Part A(2)	1st May to 31st July 2004]
Section 3.1	
Part A(1)	1st June to 31st August 2001
[Part A(2)	1st April to 30th June 2003]
Section 3.2	
Part A(1)	1st June to 31st August 2006
Section 3.3	
Part A(1)	1st May to 31st July 2002
Part A(2)	[1st May to 31st July 2003]
Section 3.4	
Part A(1)	1st May to 31st July 2002
[Section 3.5	
Part A(2)	1st April to 30th June 2003]
Section 3.6	
Part A(1)	1st January to 31st March 2004
Part A(2)	1st January to 31st March 2004
Section 4.1 Part A(1)	
Paragraphs (a)(i), (v), (vi), (vii), (b), (f), (g)	1st January to 31st March 2003
Paragraphs (a)(ii), (iii), (iv)	1st June to 31st August 2003
Paragraphs (a)(viii), (ix), (c), (d), (e)	1st January to 31st March 2006
Paragraphs (a)(x)–(xi)	1st June to 31st August 2006
Section 4.2 Part A(1)	
Paragraphs (a)(i), (ii), (iii), (vi), (b) to (g), (i) and (j)	1st October to 31st December 2004
Paragraphs (a)(iv), (v) and (h)	1st June to 31st August 2005
Section 4.3	
Part A(1)	1st June to 31st August 2005
Section 4.4	
Part A(1)	1st January to 31st March 2006

Table *(Cont.)*

Any installation where an activity falling within the following Section of Part 1 of Schedule 1 is carried out or any mobile plant used to carry out such an activity	Relevant Period
Section 4.5	
Part A(1)	1st January to 31st March 2006
Section 4.6	
Part A(1)	1st January to 31st March 2006
Section 4.7	
Part A(1)	1st October to 31st December 2004
Section 5.1	
[Part A(1) Paragraphs (a), (b), (c)	1st January to 31st March 2005
Part A(1) Paragraphs (d), (e)	1st June to 31st August 2005
Part A(1) Paragraph (f)	1st June to 31st August 2005
Part A(2)	1st January to 31st March 2005]
[Section 5.2	
Part A(1)	The period specified in the notice served on the operator under paragraph 1(9) of Schedule 4 to the 2002 Regulations.]
Section 5.3 Part A(1)	
Paragraph (a)	1st June to 31st August 2005
Paragraph (b)	[1st November 2006 to 31st January 2007]
Paragraph (c)(i)	[1st April to 30th June 2006]
Paragraph (c)(ii)	[1st September to 30th November 2006]
Section 5.4	
Part A(1)	1st January to 31st March 2005
Section 5.5	
Part A(1)	1st January to 31st March 2004
Section 6.1	
Part A(1)	1st December 2000 to 28th February 2001
[Part A(2)	1st April to 30th June 2003]
Section 6.2	
Part A(1)	1st January to 31st March 2004
Section 6.3 Part A(1)	
Paragraph (a)(i)	1st January to 31st March 2004
Paragraph (a)(ii)	1st October to 31st December 2001
[Section 6.4	
Part A(1)	
Paragraph (a)	1st January to 31st March 2007
Remaining paragraphs	1st May to 31st July 2002]
Part A(2)	1st May to 31st July 2003
Section 6.6	
Part A(1)	1st June to 31st August 2006
[Section 6.7	
Part A(2)	1st April to 30th June 2003]
Section 6.8	
Part A(1)	
Paragraph (a)	1st May to 31st July 2002
Paragraphs (b), (c), (d)(i)	1st June to 31st August 2004

Table *(Cont.)*

Any installation where an activity falling within the following Section of Part 1 of Schedule 1 is carried out or any mobile plant used to carry out such an activity	**Relevant Period**
Paragraphs (d)(ii), (e), (f)	1st January to 31st March 2005
Part A(2)	1st June to 31st August 2004
Section 6.9	
Part A(1)	1st November 2006 to 31st January 2007

(3) For the purpose of sub-paragraph (2), where an activity falls within a description in Part A(1) of more than one Section of Part 1 of Schedule 1 or within a description in Part A(2) of more than one Section of Part 1 of Schedule 1 it shall be regarded as falling only within that description which fits it most aptly.

(4) Subject to sub-paragraph (5), where more than one activity falling within Part A(1) or A(2) of any Section in Part 1 of Schedule 1 is carried out in an existing Part A installation or using an existing Part A mobile plant, the relevant period for that installation or mobile plant shall be the period beginning with the earliest date listed against one of those activities in the table in sub-paragraph (2).

(5) Where more than one activity falling within Part A(1) or A(2) of any Section in Part 1 of Schedule 1 is carried out in an existing Part A installation, the operator of the installation may apply to the regulator to determine that the relevant period for the installation shall not be the period determined by sub-paragraph (4) but the later period listed in the table in [sub-paragraphs (2) and (3)] against the primary activity of the installation.

[(3) An operator may make an application before the beginning of the relevant period in accordance with regulation 3 of the Solvent Emissions (England and Wales) Regulations 2004.]

(6) An application under sub-paragraph (5) shall be in writing and shall—

(a) identify the installation concerned;

(b) list the activities falling within Part A(1) or A(2) of any Section in Part 1 of Schedule 1 which are carried out in the installation;

(c) identify which of those activities the operator considers to be the primary activity,

and shall be submitted at least 3 months before the beginning of the period which would be the relevant period for the installation concerned under sub-paragraph (4).

(7) Where a regulator receives a duly made application under sub-paragraph (5) it shall, if it agrees with the operator that the activity identified pursuant to sub-paragraph (6)(c) is the primary activity, serve notice of this determination on the operator, and the period listed against that activity in sub-paragraph (2) shall be the relevant period for the installation.

(8) Where the regulator does not agree with the operator as mentioned in sub-paragraph (7) it shall serve notice of this determination on the operator and the relevant period for the installation shall be the period determined by sub-paragraph (4).

(9) A regulator shall serve notice of its determination of any application made under sub-paragraph (5) within 2 months of receiving the application.

(10) Where there is more than one operator of an installation, an application under sub-paragraph (5) shall be made by the operators of the installation jointly and the references in sub-paragraphs (6) to (8) to the operator shall be construed as a reference to all of the operators.

(11) For the purpose of sub-paragraphs (5) to (9) the primary activity of an installation is the activity the carrying out of which constitutes the primary purpose for operating the installation.

[(12) Subject to sub-paragraph (12A), if—

(a) an activity falling within Part A(1) of Section 5.2 in Part 1 of Schedule 1 is carried out in an existing Part A installation; and

(b) an activity falling within some other Section in Part 1 of Schedule 1 is also carried out in the same installation ('a transitional landfill installation'),

the preceding provisions of this paragraph shall apply as if there were two separate existing Part A installations one consisting of the part of the installation where the activity falling within Part A(1) of Section 5.2 in Part 1 of Schedule 1 is carried out and the other consisting of the remainder of the installation.

[(12A) Sub-paragraph (12) shall not apply in a case where the regulator has determined in accordance with the preceding provisions of this paragraph that the primary activity of the installation is one which falls within Part A (1) of Section 5.2 in Part 1 of Schedule 1.]

(13) If—

(a) the relevant period has expired for a transitional landfill installation; and

(b) an application for a permit to operate the installation has been duly made but has not been determined at 15th June 2002, then—

(i) the application shall be treated as an application to operate the parts of the installation other than those where the activity falling within Part A(1) of Section 5.2 in Part 1 of Schedule 1 is carried out; and

(ii) the prescribed date for the remaining part of the installation shall be determined as if it were a separate installation.]

3. For the purpose of paragraphs 1 and 2, where separate applications are made to operate different parts of a Part A installation—

(a) the date by which applications have been made in relation to all parts of the installation shall be treated as the date on which an application for a permit to operate the installation is made;

(b) an application for a permit to operate the installation shall only be treated as having been duly made if each of the separate applications are duly made;

(c) the determination date for the installation shall be, in relation to each part of the installation which is covered by a separate application, the determination date for that part of the installation.

4.—[...]

(2) Where there is a substantial change in the operation of an existing Part A installation on or after 1st [April] 2001, the prescribed date for that part of the installation affected by the change shall be the date on which the change is made if earlier than the date which would be the prescribed date for the installation under paragraph 2.

5.—(1) Subject to sub-paragraphs (2) and (3), an application for a permit to operate an existing Part A installation or Part A mobile plant shall not be made before the beginning of the relevant period for that installation or mobile plant without the consent of the regulator.

(2) Where an operator of an existing Part A installation proposes to make a substantial change in the operation of the installation he may make an application before the beginning of the relevant period for a permit to operate that part of the installation that will be affected by the substantial change.

[(3) An operator may make an application before the beginning of the relevant period in accordance with regulation 3 of the Solvent Emissions (England and Wales) Regulations 2004.]

6. In this Part of this Schedule—

'determination date' means—

(a) for an installation, part of an installation or mobile plant in relation to which a permit is granted, the date on which it is granted, whether in pursuance of the application for the permit or, on an appeal, of a direction to grant it;

(b) for an installation, part of an installation or mobile plant in relation to which a permit is refused and the applicant for the permit appeals against the refusal, the date of the affirmation of the refusal;

(c) for an installation, part of an installation or mobile plant in relation to which a permit is refused and no appeal is made against the refusal, the date immediately following the last day, determined in accordance with paragraph 2 of Schedule 8, on which notice of appeal might have been given.

[(d) for an installation, part of an installation or mobile plant in relation to which an application is withdrawn in accordance with regulation 7(6) or deemed to have been withdrawn in accordance with paragraph 4 of Schedule 4, the date the application is withdrawn, or deemed to have been withdrawn;]

['existing' means, in relation to a Part A installation or a Part A mobile plant—

(a) an installation or mobile plant which is put into operation [pursuant to a relevant authorisation granted] before 1st April 2001; or

(b) an installation or mobile plant which is put into operation on or after that date if—

(i) its operation was authorised by the relevant authorisation before that date; or

(ii) an application for such authorisation was duly made before that date;]

'new' means, in relation to a Part A installation or a Part A mobile plant, an installation or plant which is put into operation on or after [1st April 2001] other than an existing Part A installation or Part A mobile plant;

'relevant authorisation' means, in relation to the operation of a Part A installation or Part A mobile plant—

(a) where the operation of the installation or mobile plant immediately before [1st April 2001] requires an authorisation under Part I of the Environmental Protection Act 1990, an authorisation under that Part of that Act;

(b) where the operation of the installation or mobile plant immediately before [1st April 2001] requires a waste management licence under Part II of the Environmental Protection Act 1990, a waste management licence under that Part of that Act;

(c) in any other case, planning permission granted under the Town and Country Planning Act 1990;

'relevant period' shall be interpreted in accordance with paragraph 2.

PART 2 PART B INSTALLATIONS AND MOBILE PLANT

7. The prescribed date for a new Part B installation or a new Part B mobile plant is the relevant date for that installation or mobile plant.

8. The prescribed date for an existing Part B installation or existing Part B mobile plant is the determination date for that installation or mobile plant.

9.—(1) Subject to the following provisions of this paragraph, no application for a permit to operate an existing Part B installation or existing Part B mobile plant shall be made to the regulator.

(2) Where an operator of a Part B installation or a Pert B mobile plant proposes to put the installation or mobile plant into operation during the period of four months ending on the relevant date for the installation or mobile plant, he may make an application for a permit to operate that installation or mobile plant.

(3) The operator of an existing Part B installation or existing Part B mobile plant shall, unless he has made an application to operate the installation or mobile plant under sub-paragraph (2), be deemed to have made an application for a permit to operate that installation or mobile plant on the relevant date for that installation or mobile plant.

(4) Where sub-paragraph (3) applies in relation to an existing Part B installation and different parts of the installation are operated by different operators, each operator shall be

deemed to have been made an application to operate that part of the installation which he operates.

(5) Schedule 4 shall not apply to a deemed application under sub-paragraph (3).

(6) The regulator shall give notice of its determination of a deemed application under sub-paragraph (3) to the applicant within the period of 12 months beginning with the date on which the application is deemed to have been made and if the regulator fails to give notice of its determination within that period the application shall, if the applicant notifies the authority in writing that he treats the failure as such, be deemed to have been refused at the end of that period.

(7) Where sub-paragraph (3) applies the regulator shall, within 2 months of the date on which the application is deemed to have been made, notify the operator of the installation or mobile plant of the deemed application and of the requirements of sub-paragraph (6).

(8) Where separate applications are deemed to have been made under sub-paragraph (4) to operate different parts of a Part B installation the prescribed date for the installation shall be, in relation to each part of the installation covered by a separate application, the determination date for that part of the installation.

10.—(1) For the purpose of this Part of this Schedule the relevant date for a Part B installation or a Part B mobile plant is the date specified for that description of installation or mobile plant in the following table—

[

Any installation where an activity falling within Part B-of the following Sections of Part 1 of Schedule 1 is carried out or any mobile plant used to carry out such an activity	*Relevant Date*
Section 1.1	1st April 2003
Section 1.2	1st April 2005
Section 2.1	1st April 2004
Section 2.2	1st April 2004
Section 2.3	1st April 2004
Section 3.1	1st April 2003
Section 3.2	1st April 2003
Section 3.3	1st April 2005
Section 3.5	1st April 2003
Section 3.6	1st April 2003
Section 4.1	1st April 2005
Section 4.8	1st April 2005
Section 5.1	1st April 2003
Section 6.3	1st April 2005
Section 6.4	1st April 2004
Section 6.5	1st April 2004
Section 6.6	1st April 2003
Section 6.7	1st April 2004
Section 6.8	1st April 2005

]

(2) For the purpose of sub-paragraph (1), where an activity falls within a description in Part B of more than one Section of Part 1 of Schedule 1 it shall be regarded as falling only within that description which fits it most aptly.

(3) Where more than one activity falling within Part B of any Section in Part 1 of Schedule 1 is carried out in an existing Part B installation or using an existing Part B mobile plant, and the activities have different relevant dates, the relevant date for that installation or mobile plant shall be the earliest of those dates.

11. In this Part of this Schedule—

'determination date' means—

(a) for an installation, part of an installation or mobile plant in relation to which a permit is granted, the date on which it is granted, whether in pursuance of the application for the permit or, on an appeal, of a direction to grant it;

(b) for an installation, part of an installation or mobile plant in relation to which a permit is refused and the applicant for the permit appeals against the refusal, the date of the affirmation of the refusal;

(c) for an installation, part of an installation or mobile plant in relation to which a permit is refused and no appeal is made against the refusal, the date immediately following the last day, determined in accordance with paragraph 2 of Schedule 8, on which notice of appeal might have been given.

'existing' means, in relation to a Part B installation or Part B mobile plant, an installation or mobile plant which is put into operation before the relevant date for that installation or mobile plant;

'new' means, in relation to a Part B installation or Part B mobile plant, an installation or mobile plant which is put into operation on or after the relevant date for that installation or mobile plant;

'relevant date' shall be interpreted in accordance with paragraph 10.

Regulation 12(2)

SCHEDULE 5

POLLUTANTS

Indicative list of the main polluting substances to be taken into account if they are relevant for fixing emission limit values

AIR

1. Sulphur dioxide and other sulphur compounds.
2. Oxides of nitrogen and other nitrogen compounds.
3. Carbon monoxide.
4. Volatile organic compounds.
5. Metals and their compounds.
6. Dust.
7. Asbestos (suspended particulates, fibres).
8. Chlorine and its compounds.
9. Fluorine and its compounds.
10. Arsenic and its compounds.
11. Cyanides.
12. Substances and preparations which have been proved to possess carcinogenic or mutagenic properties or properties which may affect reproduction via the air.
13. Polychlorinated dibenzodioxins and polychlorinated dibenzofurans.

WATER

1. Organohalogen compounds and substances which may form such compounds in the aquatic environment.
2. Organophosphorus compounds.
3. Organotin compounds.
4. Substances and preparations which have been proved to possess carcinogenic or mutagenic properties or properties which may affect reproduction in or via the aquatic environment.
5. Persistent hydrocarbons and persistent and bioaccumulable organic toxic substances.

6. Cyanides.
7. Metals and their compounds.
8. Arsenic and its compounds.
9. Biocides and plant health products.
10. Materials in suspension.
11. Substances which contribute to eutrophication (in particular, nitrates and phosphates).
12. Substances which have an unfavourable influence on the oxygen balance (and can be measured using parameters such as BOD, COD, etc.).

Regulation 29

SCHEDULE 9

REGISTERS

1. A register maintained by a regulator under regulation 29 shall contain—
   (a) all particulars of any application made to the regulator for a permit;
   (b) all particulars of any notice to the applicant by the regulator under paragraph 4 of Schedule 4 and paragraph 3 of Schedule 7 and of any information furnished in response to such a notice;
   (c) all particulars of any advertisement published pursuant to paragraph 5 of Schedule 4 or paragraph 4(8) of Schedule 7 and of any representations made by any person in response to such an advertisement, other than representations which the person who made them requested should not be placed in the register;
   (d) in a case where any such representations are omitted from the register at the request of the person who made them, a statement by the regulator that representations have been made which have been the subject of such a request (but such statement shall not identify the person who made the representations in question);
   (e) all particulars of any representations made by any person required to be given notice under paragraph 9 of Schedule 4 or paragraph 4(5)(c) of Schedule 7;
   (f) all particulars of any permit granted by the regulator;
   (g) all particulars of any notification of the regulator given under regulation 16(1);
   (h) all particulars of any application made to the regulator for the variation, transfer or surrender of a permit;
   (i) all particulars of any variation, transfer and surrender of any permit granted by the regulator;
   (j) all particulars of any revocation of a permit granted by the regulator;
   (k) all particulars of any enforcement notice or suspension notice [or closure notice under the 2002 Regulations] issued by the regulator;
   (l) all particulars of any notice issued by the regulator withdrawing an enforcement notice or a suspension notice;
   (m) all particulars of any notice of appeal under regulation 27 against a decision by the regulator or a notice served by the regulator and of the documents relating to the appeal mentioned in paragraph 1(2)(a), (d) and (e) of Schedule 8;
   (n) all particulars of any representations made by any person in response to a notice given under paragraph 3(1) of Schedule 8, other than representations which the person who made them requested should not be placed in the register;
   (o) in a case where any such representations are omitted from the register at the request of the person who made them, a statement by the regulator that representations have been made which have been the subject of such a request (but such statement shall not identify the person who made the representations in question);

(p) all particulars of any written notification of the Secretary of State's determination of such an appeal and any report accompanying any such written notification;

(q) details of any conviction of or formal caution given to any person for any offence under regulation 32(1) [above or regulation 17(1) of the 2002 Regulations] which relates to the operation of an installation or mobile plant under a permit granted by the regulator, or without such a permit in circumstances where one is required by regulation 9, including the name of the person, the date of conviction or formal caution, and, in the case of a conviction, the penalty imposed and the name of the Court;

(r) all particulars of any monitoring information relating to the operation of an installation or mobile plant under a permit granted by the regulator which has been obtained by the regulator as a result of its own monitoring or furnished to the regulator in writing by virtue of a condition of the permit or under regulation 28(2);

(s) in a case where any such monitoring information is omitted from the register by virtue of regulation 31, a statement by the regulator, based on the monitoring information from time to time obtained by or furnished to them, indicating whether or not there has been compliance with any relevant condition of the permit;

(t) all particulars of any other information furnished to the authority in compliance with a condition of the permit, a variation notice, enforcement notice or suspension notice, or regulation 28(2) [or a closure notice under the 2002 Regulations];

(u) where a permit granted by the regulator authorises the carrying out of a specified waste management activity, all particulars of any waste management licence (within the meaning of regulation 19(13)) which ceased to have effect on the granting of the permit in so far as they may be relevant for the purpose of determining under regulation 19 whether any pollution risk results from the carrying out of such an activity on the site covered by the permit;

(v) all particulars of any report published by a regulator relating to an assessment of the environmental consequences of the operation of an installation in the locality of premises where the installation is operated under a permit granted by the regulator; and

(w) all particulars of any direction (other than a direction under regulation 30(2)) given to the regulator by the Secretary of State under any provision of these Regulations.

[(x) all particulars of any site conditioning plan or notice submitted under subparagraph 1(3) or (5) of Schedule 4 to the 2002 Regulations;

(y) all particulars of any notice requiring a landfill to close (in whole or part) issued under paragraph 1(6) of Schedule 4 to the 2002 Regulations;

(z) all particulars of any notification or report required before definitive closure of a landfill under regulation 15(4) of the 2002 Regulations.]

[(aa) a list which identifies all waste incineration installations which have a capacity of less than two tonnes per hour and which are the subject of a permit or an authorisation granted under section 6 of the Environmental Protection Act 1990 containing conditions which give effect to the provisions of European Parliament and Council Directive 2000/76/EC on the incineration of waste.]

[(bb) all particulars of any fees and charges paid to the local authority regulator pursuant to a scheme made by the Secretary of State under regulation 22 and details of the total expenditure incurred by the local authority regulator in exercising their functions under these regulations in relation to local authority permits];

[(cc) all particulars of any advertisement under paragraph 15A of Schedule 4 or paragraph 7A of Schedule 7, the information specified in paragraphs 15B of

Schedule 4 or 6A or 7B of Schedule 7 and all particulars of any representations made by any person in response to such an advertisement, other than representations which the person who made them requested should not be placed in the register].<split

2. Where an application is withdrawn by the applicant at any time before it is determined, all particulars relating to that application which are already in the register shall be removed from the register not less than two months and not more than three months after the date of withdrawal of the application, and no further particulars relating to that application shall be entered in the register.

3. Where, following the amendment of Schedule 1, these Regulations cease to apply to a description of installation or mobile plant, all particulars relating to installations or mobile plant of that description shall be removed from the register not less than two months and not more than three months after the date on which the amendment comes into force.

4. Nothing in paragraph 1 shall require a regulator to keep in a register maintained by it—

(a) monitoring information relating to a particular installation or a mobile plant four years after that information was entered in the register; or

(b) information relating to a particular installation or mobile plant which has been superseded by later information relating to that installation or mobile plant four years after that later information was entered in the register,

but this paragraph shall not apply to any aggregated monitoring data relating to overall emissions of any substance or class of substance from installations or mobile plant generally or from any class of installations or mobile plant.

5. Any details of a formal caution included in a register pursuant to paragraph 1(q) shall be removed from the register after five years have elapsed since the date on which the caution was given.

The Landfill (England and Wales) Regulations 2002

(SI 2002, No. 1559) (as amended)

PART I

PRELIMINARY

1 Citation, commencement and extent

(1) These Regulations may be cited as the Landfill (England and Wales) Regulations 2002.

(2) These Regulations shall come into force on 15th June 2002 except for regulation 19(1) which shall come into force on 31st August 2002.

(3) These Regulations extend to England and Wales only.

2 Interpretation

In these Regulations, unless the context otherwise requires—

'the 2000 Regulations' means the Pollution Prevention and Control (England and Wales) Regulations 2000;

'biodegradable waste' means any waste that is capable of undergoing anaerobic or aerobic decomposition, such as food or garden waste and paper and cardboard;

'hazardous waste' has the meaning given by regulation 7(2);

'holder' means the producer of waste or the person who is in possession of it;

'inert waste' has the meaning given by regulation 7(4);

['L/S = 10 l/kg' means a liquid to solid ratio of 10 litres to one kilogram;]

['relevant waste acceptance criteria' means, in relation to a landfill, the waste acceptance criteria under Parts 1 and 3 of Schedule 1 which apply to the class of landfill to which that landfill belongs;]

'landfill' means a landfill to which these Regulations apply (see regulations 3 and 4);

'landfill gas' means any gas generated from landfilled waste;

'landfill permit' has the meaning given by regulation 6(2);

'leachate' means any liquid percolating through deposited waste and emitted from or contained within a landfill;

'municipal waste' means waste from households as well as other waste which because of its nature or composition is similar to waste from households;

'non-hazardous waste' has the meaning given by regulation 7(3);

'operator' has the meaning given by regulation 2(1) and (2) of the 2000 Regulations;

'relevant authorisation' means, in relation to a landfill, the landfill permit or waste management licence for the time being in force in relation to the landfill;

'relevant waste acceptance criteria' means, in relation to a landfill, the waste acceptance criteria set out in Schedule 1 which apply to the class of landfill to which that landfill belongs;

['SIC Code' means a code included in 'The United Kingdom Standard Industrial Classification of Economic Activities 2003', published by the Office for National Statistics on 31st December 2002 and implemented on 1st January 2003;

'stable, non-reactive hazardous waste' means hazardous waste, the leaching behaviour of which will not change adversely in the long-term, under landfill design conditions or foreseeable accidents—

(a) in the waste alone (for example, by biodegradation);
(b) under the impact of long-term ambient conditions (for example, water, air, temperature, mechanical constraints); or
(c) by the impact of other wastes (including waste products such as leachate and gas);]

'treatment' means physical, thermal, chemical or biological processes (including sorting) that change the characteristics of waste in order to reduce its volume or hazardous nature, facilitate its handling or enhance recovery;

'waste' means controlled waste within the meaning of section 75(4) of the Environmental Protection Act 1990;

'waste management licence' means a waste management licence within the meaning of Part II of the Environmental Protection Act 1990; and

other expressions used in these Regulations which are also used in Directive 99/31/EC on the landfill of waste shall have the same meaning as in that Directive.

3 Application of regulations

(1) Subject to regulation 4, these Regulations apply to landfills.

(2) Subject to paragraphs (3) and (4), for the purposes of this regulation, a landfill is a waste disposal site for the deposit of the waste onto or into land.

(3) Landfills include—

(a) subject to paragraph (4), any site which is used for more than a year for the temporary storage of waste; and
(b) any internal waste disposal site, that is to say a site where a producer of waste is carrying out its own waste disposal at the place of production.

(4) Landfills do not include—

(a) any facility where waste is unloaded in order to permit its preparation for further transport for recovery, treatment or disposal elsewhere;
(b) any site where waste is stored as a general rule for a period of less than three years prior to recovery or treatment; or
(c) any site where waste is stored for a period of less than one year prior to disposal.

4 Cases where regulations do not apply

These Regulations do not apply to—

(a) the spreading of sludges (including sewage sludges and sludges resulting from dredging operations) and similar matter on the soil for the purposes of fertilisation or improvement;

(b) the use of suitable inert waste for redevelopment, restoration and filling-in work or for construction purposes in a land fill;

(c) the deposit of—

[(i) non-hazardous dredging sludges alongside small waterways from where they have been dredged out;]

(ii) non-hazardous sludges in surface waters, including the bed and its sub-soil; or

(d) any landfill which finally ceased to accept waste for disposal before 16th July 2001.

5 Location

A planning permission under the Town and Country Planning Act 1990 may be granted for a landfill only if the requirements of paragraph 1(1) of Schedule 2 to these Regulations have been taken into consideration.

6 Extension of categories of landfill subject to the 2000 Regulations etc.

(1) . . .

(2) In these Regulations 'landfill permit' means the permit which is required by the 2000 Regulations for the carrying out of the disposal of waste in a landfill.

(3) Regulations 11 and 12(1) to (11) and (14) of the 2000 Regulations shall not apply to landfills.

(4) Paragraph 5(b) in Part 1 of Schedule 4, and paragraph 4(8)(b) in Part 2 of Schedule 7 to the 2000 Regulations (requirement to advertise in the London Gazette), shall not apply to landfills falling within paragraph (b) of Part A(1) of Section 5.2 in Part 1 of Schedule 1 to those Regulations.

PART II
LANDFILL PERMITS

7 Classification of landfills

(1) Before granting a landfill permit, the Environment Agency shall classify the landfill—

(a) as a landfill for hazardous waste;

(b) as a landfill for non-hazardous waste; or

(c) as a landfill for inert waste,

and shall ensure that the classification is stated in the landfill permit.

(2) [Hazardous waste means any waste as defined in regulation 6 of the Hazardous Waste (England and Wales) Regulations 2005].

(3) Non-hazardous waste is waste which is not hazardous waste.

(4) Waste is inert waste if—

(a) it does not undergo any significant physical, chemical or biological transformations;

(b) it does not dissolve, burn or otherwise physically or chemically react, biodegrade or adversely affect other matter with which it comes into contact in a way likely to give rise to environmental pollution or harm to human health; and

(c) its total leachability and pollutant content and the ecotoxicity of its leachate are insignificant and, in particular, do not endanger the quality of any surface water or groundwater.

8 Conditions to be included in landfill permits

(1) A landfill permit shall include conditions specifying the list of defined types, and the total quantity, of waste authorised to be deposited in the landfill.

(2) A landfill permit shall also include appropriate conditions—

(a) specifying requirements for—

(i) preparations for, and the carrying out of, landfilling operations;

(ii) monitoring and control procedures, including contingency plans;

(b) ensuring that the financial provision required by regulation 4(3)(b) of the 2000 Regulations is maintained until the permit is surrendered in accordance with those Regulations;

(c) ensuring that the landfill is operated in such a manner that the necessary measures are taken to prevent accidents and to limit their consequences; and

(d) requiring the operator to report at least annually to the Environment Agency on—

(i) the types and quantities of waste disposed of; and

(ii) the results of the monitoring programme required by regulations 14 and 15.

(3) A landfill permit shall also include—

(a) appropriate conditions for ensuring compliance with the requirements of the following provisions of these Regulations—

(i) Schedule 2 (general requirements for all landfills);

(ii) regulation 9 (prohibition of acceptance of certain wastes at landfills);

(iii) regulation 10 (waste which may be accepted in the different classes of landfill);

(iv) regulation 11 (costs of disposal of waste in landfills);

(v) regulation 12 (waste acceptance procedures);

(vi) regulation 13 (initial site inspections by Environment Agency);

(vii) regulation 14 (control and monitoring of operational landfill sites);

(viii) regulation 15 (closure and after-care procedures for landfills); and

(b) such other conditions as appear appropriate to the Environment Agency, including in particular conditions giving effect to—

(i) any requirement imposed by Community or national legislation; and

(ii) in the case of landfills falling within paragraph (a) of Part A (1) of Section 5.2 in Part 1 of Schedule 1 to the 2000 Regulations, the principle that energy should be used efficiently.

(4) The provisions of these Regulations mentioned in paragraph (3)(a) above shall impose obligations directly on an operator of a landfill (rather than through the conditions of a landfill permit) only to the extent specified in paragraph 3(3) to (5) of Schedule 4.

9 Prohibition of acceptance of certain wastes at landfills

(1) The operator of a landfill shall not accept any of the following types of waste at the landfill—

(a) any waste in liquid form (including waste waters but excluding sludge);

(b) waste which, in the conditions of landfill, is explosive, corrosive, oxidising, flammable or highly flammable;

(c) hospital and other clinical wastes which arise from medical or veterinary establishments and which are infectious;

(d) chemical substances arising from research and development or teaching activities, such as laboratory residues, which are not identified or which are new, and whose effects on man or on the environment are not known;

(e) as from 16th July 2003, whole used tyres other than—

(i) tyres used as engineering material;

(ii) bicycle tyres; and

(iii) tyres with an outside diameter above 1400 mm;

(f) as from 16th July 2006, shredded used tyres other than—

(i) bicycle tyres; and

(ii) tyres with an outside diameter above 1400mm; and

(g) any waste which does not fulfil the relevant waste acceptance criteria.

(2) The operator of a landfill shall ensure that the landfill is not used for landfilling waste which has been diluted or mixed solely to meet the relevant waste acceptance criteria.

(3) For the purposes of this regulation, waste is—

'corrosive' if it consists of substances and preparations which may destroy living tissue on contact;

'explosive' if it consists of substances and preparations which may explode under the effect of flame or which are more sensitive to shocks or friction than dinitrobenzene;

'flammable' if it consists of liquid substances and preparations having a flash point equal to or greater than 21°C and less than or equal to 55°C;

'highly flammable' if it consists of—

(a) liquid substances and preparations having a flash point below 21°C (including extremely flammable liquids);
(b) substances and preparations which may become hot and finally catch fire in contact with air at ambient temperature without any application of energy;
(c) solid substances and preparations which may readily catch fire after brief contact with a source of ignition and which continue to burn or to be consumed after removal of the source of ignition;
(d) gaseous substances and preparations which are flammable in air at normal pressure;
(e) substances and preparations which, in contact with water or damp air, evolve highly flammable gases in dangerous quantities;

'infectious' if it consists of substances containing viable micro-organisms or their toxins which are known or reliably believed to cause disease in man or other living organisms; or

'oxidising' if it consists of substances and preparations which exhibit highly exothermic reactions when in contact with other substances, particularly flammable substances.

10 Waste which may be accepted in the different classes of landfill

(1) The operator of a landfill shall ensure that the landfill is only used for landfilling waste which is subject to prior treatment unless—

(a) it is inert waste for which treatment is not technically feasible; or
(b) it is waste other than inert waste and treatment would not reduce its quantity or the hazards which it poses to human health or the environment.

(2)–(5) [...]

11 Costs of disposal of waste in landfills

The operator of a landfill shall ensure that the charges it makes for the disposal of waste in its landfill covers all of the following—

(a) the costs of setting up and operating the landfill;
(b) the costs of the financial provision required by regulation 4(3)(b) of the 2000 Regulations; and
(c) the estimated costs for the closure and after-care of the landfill site for a period of at least 30 years from its closure.

12 Waste acceptance procedures

[(1) The operator of a landfill shall ensure that waste shall only be accepted at the landfill if—

(a) it has been subject to the relevant waste acceptance procedure set out in Part 2 of Schedule 1; and
(b) any sampling or testing required under Parts 2 or 3 of Schedule 1 is carried out in accordance with Part 4 of that Schedule.

(2) Subject to paragraph (2A) the operator shall visually inspect waste at the entrance to the landfill and at the point of deposit and shall satisfy himself that it conforms to the description provided in the documentation submitted by the holder.

(2A) Where the operator is also the producer of the waste, the visual inspection required by paragraph (2) may be made at the point of dispatch.

(2B) The operator shall at appropriate periodic intervals—

(a) test the waste to establish whether it corresponds to the description in the accompanying documents, by checking its appearance, odour and any other relevant, readily determined properties; and

(b) take representative samples for analysis which shall thereafter be retained, together with the results of the analysis for a period of at least one month.]

(3) The operator shall keep a register showing—

(a) the quantities of waste deposited;

(b) its characteristics;

(c) its origin;

(d) the dates of its delivery;

(e) the identity of the producer or, in the case of municipal waste, the collector; and

(f) in the case of hazardous waste, its precise identity and location on the site.

(4) The information required to be kept under paragraph (3) shall be made available to the Environment Agency on request.

(5) The operator on accepting each delivery of waste shall provide a written receipt to the person delivering it.

(6) Where waste is not accepted at a landfill, the operator shall inform the Environment Agency of that fact as soon as reasonably possible.

13 Initial site inspections by Environment Agency

The operator of a landfill shall not commence disposal operations before the Environment Agency has inspected the site in order to ensure that it complies with the relevant conditions of the landfill permit.

14 Control and monitoring of operational landfill sites

(1) The following requirements shall apply to landfill sites from the start of the operational phase until definitive closure.

(2) The operator shall carry out the control and monitoring procedures set out in Schedule 3.

(3) Where the procedures required by paragraph (2) reveal any significant adverse environmental effects, the operator shall notify the Environment Agency as soon as reasonably possible.

(4) When it receives a notification of significant adverse environmental effects in accordance with paragraph (3), the Environment Agency shall determine the nature and timing of corrective measures that are necessary and shall require the operator to carry them out.

(5) The operator shall report at intervals specified by the Environment Agency, on the basis of aggregated data, the results of monitoring and on such other matters which the Environment Agency requires to demonstrate compliance with the conditions of the landfill permit or to increase its knowledge of the behaviour of waste in landfill.

(6) The operator shall ensure that quality control of—

(a) analytical operations of control and monitoring procedures; and

(b) analyses of representative samples taken in accordance with regulation 12(2),

is carried out by competent laboratories.

15 Closure and after-care procedures for landfills

(1) The following closure and after-care procedures shall apply to all landfill sites.

(2) The procedures may relate to the closure of the whole of the landfill or part of it.

(3) The closure procedure shall begin—

(a) when the conditions specified in the landfill permit are satisfied;

(b) when the Environment Agency approves the initiation of the closure procedure following a request from the operator; or

(c) by a reasoned decision of the Environment Agency which shall be set out in a closure notice served on the operator in accordance with regulation 16.

(4) A landfill shall not be definitively closed until—

(a) such reports as may be required by the Environment Agency have been submitted to it by the operator; and

(b) the Environment Agency—

(i) has assessed all the reports submitted by the operator;

(ii) has carried out a final on-site inspection; and

(iii) has notified the operator by notice in writing served on the operator that it approves the closure.

(5) Following definitive closure of a landfill, after-care procedures shall ensure that—

(a) the operator remains responsible for the maintenance, monitoring and control for such period as the Environment Agency determines is reasonable, taking into account the time during which the landfill could present hazards;

(b) the operator notifies the Environment Agency of any significant adverse environmental effects revealed by the control procedures and takes the remedial steps required or approved by the Agency; and

(c) the operator is responsible for monitoring and analysing landfill gas and leachate from the landfill and the groundwater regime in its vicinity in accordance with Schedule 3 for as long as the Environment Agency considers that the landfill is likely to cause a hazard to the environment.

(6) Notwithstanding regulations 19 and 21 of the 2000 Regulations (requirements on surrender or revocation of permits), the Environment Agency shall not accept any complete or partial surrender of the landfill permit, or revoke it in whole or part, for as long as the Environment Agency considers that the landfill (or the relevant part of it) is likely to cause a hazard to the environment.

(7) The operator shall not be relieved from liability under the conditions of the landfill permit by reason of the Environment Agency's approval of closure under paragraph (4)(b)(iii).

16 Closure Notices

(1) Where the Environment Agency has taken a reasoned decision under regulation 15(3)(c), it shall serve a closure notice under this regulation ('a closure notice') on the operator of the landfill.

(2) A closure notice shall—

(a) state the Environment Agency's reasons for requiring initiation of the closure procedure;

(b) specify the steps the operator is required to take to initiate the procedure; and

(c) the period within which they must be taken.

(3) The Environment Agency may withdraw a closure notice at any time.

PART III
MISCELLANEOUS

17 Offences

(1) It shall be an offence for a landfill operator to contravene—

(a) regulation 9 or 12 in each case as applied by paragraph 3(3)(a) of Schedule 4;

(b) regulation 10(1) [. . .] in both cases as applied by paragraph 3(3)(b) of Schedule 4; or

(c) paragraph 3(5) of Schedule 4.

(2) A person who is guilty of an offence under paragraph (1) shall be liable—

(a) on summary conviction, to a fine not exceeding £20,000 or to imprisonment for a term not exceeding six months or to both; and

(b) on conviction on indictment, to a fine or to imprisonment for a term not exceeding five years or both.

(3) Where an offence under this regulation committed by a body corporate is proved to have been committed with the consent or connivance of, or to have been attributable to any neglect on the part of, any director, manager, secretary of other similar officer of the body corporate or a person who was purporting to act in any such capacity, he as well as the body corporate shall be guilty of that offence and shall be liable to be proceeded against and punished accordingly.

(4) Where the affairs of a body corporate are managed by its members, paragraph (3) shall apply in relation to the acts or defaults of a member in connection with his functions of management as if he were a director of the body corporate.

(5) Where the commission by any person of an offence under this regulation is due to the act or default of some other person, that other person may be charged with and convicted of the offence by virtue of this paragraph whether or not proceedings for the offence are taken against the first-mentioned person.

18 Transitional provisions

Schedule 4 (which contains transitional provisions) shall have effect.

Regulations 2 and 10 [SCHEDULE 1

CRITERIA AND PROCEDURES FOR THE ACCEPTANCE OF WASTE AT LANDFILLS]

[PART 1 GENERAL PRINCIPLES FOR THE ACCEPTANCE OF WASTE AT LANDFILLS]

[General principles for the acceptance of waste at all kinds of landfill

1.—(1) The following criteria shall apply to the acceptance of waste at any landfill.

(2) Waste may only be accepted at a landfill where its acceptance would not—

(a) result in unacceptable emissions to groundwater, surface water or the surrounding environment;

(b) jeopardise environment protection systems (such as liners, leachate and gas collection and treatment systems) at the landfill;

(c) put at risk waste stabilisation processes (such as degradation or wash out) within the landfill; or

(d) endanger human health.

Additional general principles for the acceptance of waste at landfills for hazardous waste

2. Waste may only be accepted at a landfill for hazardous waste if—

[(a) it is a hazardous waste as defined in the Hazardous Waste (England and Wales) Regulations 2005; and]

(b) its total content or leachability—

(i) does not present a short term occupational risk or an environmental risk; and

(ii) would not prevent the stabilisation of the landfill within its projected lifetime taking account of its after care period following closure.

Additional general principles for the acceptance of waste at landfills for non-hazardous waste

3. Waste may only be accepted at a landfill for non-hazardous waste if—

[(a) it is a hazardous waste as defined in the Hazardous Waste (England and Wales) Regulations 2005; and]

[(b) it is a non-hazardous waste as defined in the Hazardous Waste (England and Wales) Regulations 2005].]

[PART 2 PROCEDURE FOR THE ACCEPTANCE OF WASTE AT LANDFILLS]

[Interpretation of Part 2

4. In this Part 'waste regularly generated in the same process' shall mean individual and consistent wastes regularly generated in the same process, where—

(a) the installation and the process generating the waste are well known and the input materials to the process and the process itself are well defined;

(b) the operator of the installation provides all necessary information and informs the operator of the landfill of changes to the process (especially changes to the input material);

(c) the waste comes from a single installation or if from different installations, it can be identified as single stream with common characteristics within known boundaries (eg bottom ash from the incineration of municipal waste); and

(d) there is no significant change in the generation processes,

but shall not include wastes which do not require testing in accordance with paragraph 5(4)(a) or (c).

Basic characterisation

5.—(1) Each type of waste to be accepted at a landfill shall be characterised to ensure all information necessary for safe disposal of the waste in the long term is available including at least the following information—

(a) the source and origin of the waste;

(b) the process producing the waste (including a description of the process, its SIC Code and the characteristics of its raw materials and products);

(c) the waste treatment applied in compliance with regulation 10, or a statement of reasons why such treatment is not considered necessary;

(d) the composition of the waste, including where relevant, an assessment of it against the relevant limit values in Part 3 and, where necessary and available, its other characteristic properties;

(e) the appearance of the waste (including its smell, colour, consistency and physical form);

(f) the Code applicable to the waste under the [List of Waste (England) Regulations 2005];

[(g) in the case of hazardous waste, the relevant properties which render it hazardous as listed in Schedule 3 of the Hazardous Waste (England and Wales) Regulations 2005;]

(h) evidence demonstrating that the waste is not prohibited under regulation 9;

(i) the landfill class at which the waste may be accepted;

(j) the likely behaviour (including, where relevant, leaching behaviour) of the waste in a landfill and any additional precautions that need to be taken at the landfill as a consequence; and

(k) whether the waste can be recycled or recovered.

(2) For waste regularly generated in the same process, the following additional information shall be provided—

(a) the compositional range for the individual wastes;

(b) the range and variability of characteristic properties;

(c) if appropriate, the leachability of the wastes determined by a batch leaching test, a percolation test or a pH dependence test;

(d) identification of the key variables to be tested for compliance testing, the frequency of compliance testing and options for simplification of compliance testing;

(e) in the case of waste which is produced in the same process in different installations, the scope of the evaluation which must include a sufficient number of measurements to show the range and variability of the characteristic properties of the waste.

(3) In order to characterise waste, it must be subject to prior tests in accordance with Part 4 of this Schedule to establish its composition and its leaching behaviour.

(4) Testing is not required in the case of any of the following types of waste—

(a) waste which may be accepted without testing under paragraphs 10 or 13 of Part 3 of this Schedule;

(b) waste in respect of which the Environment Agency is satisfied that all the necessary information for the characterisation under sub-paragraph (1) can be provided without testing; or

(c) waste in respect of which the Environment Agency is satisfied by way of a documented justification supplied to it that—

(i) the waste is of a type where testing is impractical or appropriate testing procedures and acceptance criteria are not available; [and]

(ii) the waste is of a type which is acceptable at the landfill class in question.

(5) Records of the information obtained for the purposes of characterisation under this paragraph shall be retained by the operator for at least two years after the date of characterisation.

Compliance testing

6.—(1) Waste regularly generated in the same process shall not require each batch to be tested as part of its basic characterisation but may instead be subject to compliance testing in accordance with this paragraph.

(2) Compliance testing shall consist of one or more of the tests applied in accordance with paragraph 5(3) above and shall include—

(a) testing of the key variables established under paragraph 5 so as to demonstrate that the waste meets the limit values for those variables;

(b) a batch leaching test using the same method as was used for the test undertaken under paragraph 5(3); and

(c) tests which demonstrate that the waste complies with the results of the characterisation carried out under paragraph 5 and the relevant acceptance criteria described in Parts 1 and 3 of this Schedule.

(3) Compliance testing shall be carried out at the times established in the characterisation but shall be no less frequent than once a year.

(4) Records of the compliance testing shall be retained by the operator for a period of not less than two years.

Wastes accepted without testing

7 Any type of waste which may be accepted without testing under paragraph 5(4) shall be subject to checking for compliance with its basic characterisation established under paragraph 5.]

[PART 3 WASTE ACCEPTANCE CRITERIA]

[Interpretation of Part 3

8 In this Part—

(a) granular waste includes all wastes that are not monolithic; and

(b) a mono-fill landfill means a landfill which is authorised to accept only a single waste type;

[(c) 'PAHs (Polycyclic Aromatic Hydrocarbons)' shall mean Naphthalene, Acenaphthylene, Acenaphthene, Anthracene, Benzo(a)anthracene, Benzo(b)fluoranthene, Benzo(k)fluoranthene, Benzo(g,h,i)perylene, Benzo(a)pyrene, Chrysene, Coronene, Dibenzo(a,h)anthracene, Fluorene, Fluoranthene, Indeno(1,2,3-c,d)pyrene, Phenanthrene and Pyrene].

Criteria for landfills for inert waste

9 Waste may only be accepted at a landfill for inert waste if it meets either the requirements of paragraph 10 (wastes acceptable without testing at landfills for inert waste) or paragraph 11 (limit values for waste acceptable at landfills for inert waste).

Wastes acceptable without testing at landfills for inert waste

10.—(1) Subject to sub-paragraph (2), waste of the types set out in Table 1 may be accepted without testing at landfills for inert waste provided the waste is—

(a) from a single stream waste of a single waste type (unless different waste types from the list in Table 1 are accepted together); and

(b) is from a single source.

(2) Waste referred to in sub-paragraph (1) must be tested where there is suspicion of contamination or doubt that the waste meets the definition of inert waste in regulation 2 or the criteria in paragraph 11.

(3) If such testing reveals contamination or the presence of other materials or substances such as metals, asbestos, plastics or chemicals, the waste must not be accepted at a landfill for inert waste if the extent of the contamination is such as to increase the risk associated with the waste sufficiently to justify its disposal in other classes of landfill.

Table 1

EWC Code	*Description*	*Restrictions*
10 11 03	Waste glass based fibrous materials	Only without organic binders
15 01 07	Glass packaging	
17 01 01	Concrete	Selected C&D waste only[(a)]
17 01 02	Bricks	Selected C&D waste only[(a)]
17 01 03	Tiles and ceramics	Selected C&D waste only[(a)]
17 01 07	Mixtures of concrete, bricks, tiles and ceramics	Selected C&D waste only[(a)]
17 02 02	Glass	
17 05 04	Soil and stones	Excluding topsoil, peat; excluding soil and stones from contaminated sites
19 12 05	Glass	
20 01 02	Glass	Separately collected glass only
20 02 02	Soil and stones	Only from garden and parks waste; Excluding top soil, peat

[(a)] Selected construction and demolition waste (C & D waste): with low contents of other types of materials (like metals, plastic, organics, wood, rubber, etc). The origin of the waste must be known.

No C & D waste from constructions, polluted with inorganic or organic dangerous substances, eg because of production processes in the construction, soil pollution, storage and usage of pesticides or other dangerous substances, etc, unless it is made clear that the demolished construction was not significantly polluted.

No C & D waste from constructions, treated, covered or painted with materials, containing dangerous substances in significant amounts.

Limit values for waste acceptable at landfills for inert waste

11 The following limit values shall apply to waste accepted at landfills for inert waste other than waste which may be accepted without testing under paragraph 10—

(a) the limit values for leaching set out in Table 2; and

(b) the limit values for total content of organic parameters set out in Table 3.

Table 2

Component	*Symbol*	*L/S = 10 l/kg mg/kg dry substance*
Arsenic	As	0.5
Barium	Ba	20
Cadmium	Cd	0.04
Total Chromium	Cr_{total}	0.5
Copper	Cu	2
Mercury	Hg	0.01
Molybdenum	Mo	0.5
Nickel	Ni	0.4
Lead	Pb	0.5
Antimony	Sb	0.06
Selenium	Se	0.1
Zinc	Zn	4
Chloride	Cl^-	800
Fluoride	F^-	10
Sulphate[(a)]	SO_4^{2-}	1,000
Phenol index	PI	1
Dissolved Organic Carbon[(b)]	DOC	500
Total Dissolved Solids[(c)]	TDS	4,000

[(a)] This limit value for sulphate may be increased to 6,000 mg/kg, provided that the value of C_0 (the first eluate of a percolation test at L/S = 0.1 l/kg) does not exceed 1,500 mg/l. It will be necessary to use a percolation test to determine the limit value at L/S = 0.1 l/kg under initial equilibrium conditions.
[(b)] If the waste does not meet this value for Dissolved Organic Carbon (DOC) at its own pH value, it may alternatively be tested at L/S = 10 l/kg and a pH between 7.5 and 8.0. The waste may be considered as complying with the acceptance criteria for DOC, if the result of this determination does not exceed 500 mg/kg.
[(c)] The value for Total Dissolved Solids can be used alternatively to the values for Sulphate and Chloride.

Table 3

Parameter	*Value mg/kg*
Total Organic Carbon (TOC)[(a)]	30,000
BTEX compounds (benzene, toluene, ethyl benzene & xylenes)	6
Polychlorinated biphenyls (PCBs) (7 congeners)	1
Mineral oil (C10 to C40)	500
[PAHs (Polycyclic aromatic hydrocarbons) (total of 17)	100]

[(a)] In the case of soils, a higher limit value may be permitted by the Environment Agency, provided a Dissolved Organic Carbon value of 500 mg/kg is achieved at L/S 10 l/kg at the pH of the soil or at a pH value of between 7.5 and 8.0.

Criteria for landfills for non-hazardous waste

12 Waste may only be accepted at a landfill for non-hazardous waste if it meets either the requirements of paragraph 13 (waste acceptable without testing at landfills for non-hazardous waste) or such of the following paragraphs as apply to the waste in question—

- (a) paragraph 14 (criteria for . . . stable non-reactive hazardous waste and non-hazardous waste landfilled in the same cell with such waste);
- (b) paragraph 15 (criteria relating to gypsum based waste);
- (c) paragraph 16 (criteria for asbestos waste).

Wastes acceptable without testing at landfills for non-hazardous waste

13.—(1) Subject to sub-paragraph (2), waste of the following types may be accepted without testing at landfills for non-hazardous waste—

(a) municipal waste that is classified as non-hazardous in Chapter 20 of the European Waste Catalogue; and

(b) separately collected fractions of household wastes and the same non-hazardous materials from other origins.

(2) Waste referred to in sub-paragraph (1) must meet the following criteria—

(a) it must have been subject to prior treatment in accordance with regulation 10;

(b) it must not be contaminated to such an extent as to justify its disposal in other facilities; and

(c) it must not be accepted in cells where stable, non-reactive hazardous waste is accepted in accordance with paragraph 3(a) of Part 1 of this Schedule.

(3) Waste comprising construction materials containing asbestos and other suitable materials may also be accepted at landfills for non-hazardous waste without testing where it meets the criteria in paragraph 3(a) and is landfilled in accordance with paragraph 16.

[Criteria for stable non-reactive hazardous waste and non-hazardous waste deposited in the same cell with such waste

14. Stable, non-reactive hazardous waste and non-hazardous waste which is to be landfilled in the same cell with such waste shall only be accepted if—

(a) in the case of granular waste—

(i) it meets the limit values for leaching set out in Table 4;

(ii) it meets the additional criteria set out in Table 5; and

(iii) it will have either—

(aa) if it is cohesive waste, a mean in situ shear strength of at least 50kPa; or

(bb) if it is non-cohesive waste, an in situ bearing ratio of at least 5%;

(b) in the case of monolithic waste—

(i) it meets either—

(aa) the limit values for leaching set out in Table 4; or

(bb) the limit values for leaching set out in Table 5A;

(ii) it meets the additional criteria set out in Table 5B;

(iii) it has a mean unconfined compressive strength of at least 1MPa after 28 days curing;

(iv) it has either—

(aa) dimensions of greater than 40cm along each side; or

(bb) a depth and fracture spacing when hardened of greater than 40cm; and

(v) where the waste was subjected to treatment to render it monolithic, prior to such treatment it met the following limit values—

(aa) Loss on Ignition of 10%; or

(bb) Total Organic Carbon of 6%.]

Table 4

Component	*Symbol*	*L/S = 10 l/kg[(a)] mg/kg dry substance*
Arsenic	As	2
Barium	Ba	100
Cadmium	Cd	1
Total Chromium	Cr_{total}	10
Copper	Cu	50
Mercury	Hg	0.2
Molybdenum	Mo	10

Table 4 *(Cont.)*

Component	*Symbol*	*L/S = 10 l/kg*[a] *mg/kg dry substance*
Nickel	Ni	10
Lead	Pb	10
Antimony	Sb	0.7
Selenium	Se	0.5
Zinc	Zn	50
Chloride	Cl^-	15,000
Fluoride	F^-	150
Sulphate	$SO_4{}^{2-}$	20,000
Dissolved Organic Carbon	DOC	800[b]
Total Dissolved Solids	TDS	60,000[c]

[a] These values must be determined using EN 12457/1 to 3 (applied, in the case of monolithic waste, to a sample which has been crushed).
[b] If the waste does not meet this value for Dissolved Organic Carbon (DOC) at its own pH, it may alternatively be tested at L/S = 10 l/kg and a pH of between 7.5 and 8.0. The waste shall be considered as complying with the acceptance criterion for DOC if the result of this determination does not exceed 800 mg/kg.
[c] The value for Total Dissolved Solids can be used alternatively to the values for Sulphate and Chloride.

Table 5

Parameter	*Value*
Total Organic Carbon (TOC)	5%[a]
pH	Minimum 6
Acid Neutralisation Capacity (ANC)	Must be evaluated

[a] If this value is not achieved, a higher limit value may be permitted by the Environment Agency, provided that the Dissolved Organic Carbon value of 800 mg/kg is achieved at L/S = 10l/kg, either at the material's own pH or at a pH value between 7.5 and 8.0.

Table 5A

Component	*Symbol*	*mg/m² (a)*
Arsenic	As	1.3
Barium	Ba	45
Cadmium	Cd	0.2
Total Chromium	Cr_{total}	5
Copper	Cu	45
Mercury	Hg	0.1
Molybdenum	Mo	7
Nickel	Ni	6
Lead	Pb	6
Antimony	Sb	0.3
Selenium	Se	0.4
Zinc	Zn	30
Chloride	Cl^-	10,000
Fluoride	F^-	60

Table 5A *(Cont.)*

Component	*Symbol*	*mg/m² (a)*
Sulphate	SO_4^{2-}	10,000
Dissolved Organic Carbon	DOC	Must be evaluated

(a) These values must be determined using EA NEN 7375:2004. Where it is appropriate for compliance testing, the Environment Agency may specify use of a shortened version of the 64-day tank test provided for in EA NEN 7375:2004 comprising only the first four steps, and in such cases, the limit values shall be a quarter of the values in the table.

Table 5B

Parameter	*Value*
pH of the eluate from the monolith or crushed monolith	Must be evaluated
Electrical conductivity (mS.cm-1m-2) of the eluate from the monolith or crushed monolith	Must be evaluated
Acid Neutralisation Capacity (ANC) of the crushed monolith	Must be evaluated.]

Criteria relating to gypsum based waste

15.—(1) Gypsum based and other high sulphate bearing materials may only be disposed of in landfills for non-hazardous waste in cells where no biodegradable waste is accepted.

(2) The limit values for total organic carbon and dissolved organic carbon given in Tables 4 and 5 above shall apply to wastes landfilled with gypsum based materials.

Criteria for asbestos waste

16. The following criteria apply to the landfilling of asbestos waste and to construction materials containing asbestos—

(a) the waste must contain no hazardous substances other than bound asbestos, including fibres bound by a binding agent or packed in plastic;

(b) construction material containing asbestos or other suitable asbestos waste can only be accepted in a landfill dedicated to these wastes or in a separate cell of a non-dedicated landfill, provided it is sufficiently self-contained;

(c) the zone of deposit must be covered daily and before each compacting operation with appropriate material and, if the waste is not packed, it is regularly sprinkled;

(d) a final top cover is put on the landfill or cell in order to avoid the dispersion of fibres;

(e) no works are carried out on the landfill or cell that could lead to a release of fibres (eg the drilling of holes); and

(f) appropriate measures are taken to limit the possible uses of the land after closure of the landfill in order to avoid human contact with the waste.

[Criteria for waste acceptable at landfills for hazardous waste

17. Waste shall only be accepted at a landfill for hazardous waste if—

(a) in the case of granular waste—

(i) it meets the limit values for leaching set out in Table 6;

(ii) it meets the additional criteria set out in Table 7; and

(iii) it will have either—

(aa) if it is cohesive waste, a mean in situ shear strength of at least 50kPa; or

(bb) if it is non-cohesive waste, an in situ bearing ratio of at least 5%;

(b) in the case of monolithic waste—

(i) it meets either—

(aa) the limit values for leaching set out in Table 6; or
(bb) the limit values for leaching set out in Table 8;
(ii) it meets the additional criteria set out in Table 5B;
(iii) it has a mean unconfined compressive strength of at least 1MPa after 28 days curing;
(iv) it has either—
(aa) dimensions of greater than 40cm along each side; or
(bb) a depth and fracture spacing when hardened of greater than 40cm; and
(v) where the waste was subjected to treatment to render it monolithic, prior to such treatment it met the following limit values—
(aa) Loss on Ignition of 10%; or
(bb) Total Organic Carbon of 6%.]

Table 6

Components	*Symbol*	*L/S = 10 l/kg* [(a)] [(b)] *mg/kg dry substance*
Arsenic	As	25
Barium	Ba	300
Cadmium	Cd	5
Total Chromium	Cr_{total}	70
Copper	Cu	100
Mercury	Hg	2
Molybdenum	Mo	30
Nickel	Ni	40
Lead	Pb	50
Antimony	Sb	5
Selenium	Se	7
Zinc	Zn	200
Chloride	Cl^-	25,000
Fluoride	F^-	500
Sulphate	SO_4^{2-}	50,000
Dissolved Organic Carbon[(c)]	DOC	1,000
Total Dissolved Solids[(d)]	TDS	100,000

[(a)] These values must be determined using EN 12457/1 to 3 (applied, in the case of monolithic waste, to a sample which has been crushed).
[(b)] The Environment Agency may include conditions in a permit authorising limit values for specific parameters (other than Dissolved Organic Carbon) up to three times higher for specified wastes accepted in a landfill, taking into account the characteristics of the landfill and its surroundings and provided a risk assessment demonstrates that emissions (including leachate) from the landfill will present no additional risk to the environment.
[(c)] If the waste does not meet this value for Dissolved Organic Carbon (DOC) at its own pH, it may alternatively be tested at L/S = 10 l/kg and a pH of between 7.5 and 8.0. The waste shall be considered as complying with the acceptance criterion for DOC, if the result of this determination does not exceed 1,000 mg/kg.
[(d)] The value for Total Dissolved Solids can be used alternatively to the values for Sulphate and Chloride.

Table 7

Parameter	*Values*
Loss On Ignition (LOI)[(a)]	10%
Total Organic Carbon (TOC)[(b)]	6%
Acid Neutralisation Capacity (ANC)	Must be evaluated

[(a)] Either Loss on Ignition or Total Organic Carbon must be used
[(b)] If this value for Total Organic Carbon is not achieved, a higher limit value may be permitted by the Environment Agency, provided that the Dissolved Organic Carbon value of 1,000 mg/kg is achieved at L/S = 10 l/kg at its own pH or a pH value of between 7.5 and 8.0.

Table 8

Components	*Symbol*	*mg/m² (a) (b)*
Arsenic	As	20
Barium	Ba	150
Cadmium	Cd	1
Total Chromium	Cr_{total}	25
Copper	Cu	60
Mercury	Hg	0.4
Molybdenum	Mo	20
Nickel	Ni	15
Lead	Pb	20
Antimony	Sb	2.5
Selenium	Se	5
Zinc	Zn	100
Chloride	Cl^-	20,000
Fluoride	F^-	200
Sulphate	SO_4^{2-}	20,000
Dissolved Organic Carbon	DOC	Must be evaluated.

[(a)] These values must be determined using EA NEN 7375:2004. Where it is appropriate for compliance testing, the Environment Agency may specify use of a shortened version of the 64-day tank test provided for in EA NEN 7375:2004 comprising only the first four steps, and in such cases, the limit values shall be a quarter of the values in the table.
[(b)] The Environment Agency may include conditions in a permit authorising limit values for specific parameters (other than Dissolved Organic Carbon) up to three times higher for specified wastes accepted in a landfill, taking into account the characteristics of the landfill and its surroundings and provided a risk assessment demonstrates that emissions (including leachate) from the landfill will present no additional risk to the environment.]

Criteria for underground storage

18.—(1) Waste may only be accepted at an underground storage site in accordance with a site specific safety assessment which complies with the provisions of Appendix A of Council Decision 2003/33/EC establishing criteria and procedures for the acceptance of waste at landfills pursuant to Article 16 of and Annex II to Directive 1999/31/EC on the landfill of waste.

(2) At underground storage sites for inert waste, only waste which fulfils the criteria at paragraph 11 may be accepted.

(3) At underground storage sites for non-hazardous waste, only waste which fulfils the criteria at paragraph 12 may be accepted.

(4) At underground storage sites for hazardous waste, the criteria at paragraph 17 do not apply.]

[PART 4 SAMPLING AND TEST METHODS]

[Interpretation

19 In this Schedule—

. . .

[Sampling and testing

20.—(1) All sampling and testing required by this Schedule shall be carried out in accordance with this paragraph.

(2) Subject to sub-paragraph (3), sampling and testing shall be carried out by independent and qualified persons and institutions and only laboratories which have proven experience in waste testing and analysis and an efficient quality assurance system shall be used.

(3) Sampling and testing may be carried out by producers of waste or operators where—

(a) there is sufficient supervision by independent and qualified persons to ensure that the requirements of this Schedule are met; and

(b) it is carried out in accordance with an appropriate quality assurance system which includes periodic independent checking.

(4) All sampling shall be carried out using a sampling plan developed in accordance with PrEN 14899.

(5) The following standards shall be used for the sampling and testing of general waste properties . . .

(6) The following standards shall be used for strength and stability tests . . .

(7) The following standards shall be used for leaching tests . . .

(8) The following standards shall be used for the digestion of raw waste . . .

(9) The following standards shall be used for analyses . . .

(10) For tests and analysis for which CEN standards are not available, the methods used must be approved by the Environment Agency.]

Regulations 5 and 8(3)(a)(i) SCHEDULE 2

GENERAL REQUIREMENTS FOR LANDFILLS

1.—(1) The location of a landfill must take into consideration requirements relating to—

(a) the distances from the boundary of the site to residential and recreational areas, waterways, water bodies and other agricultural or urban sites;

(b) the existence of groundwater, coastal water or nature protection zones in the area;

(c) the geological or hydrogeological conditions in the area;

(d) the risk of flooding, subsidence, landslides or avalanches on the site; and

(e) the protection of the natural or cultural heritage in the area.

(2) A landfill permit may be issued for the landfill only if—

(a) the characteristics of the site with respect to the requirements in sub-paragraph (1); or

(b) the corrective measures to be taken,

indicate that the landfill does not pose a serious environmental risk.

(3) In this paragraph 'nature protection zone' means a site of special scientific interest within the meaning of section 52 of the Wildlife and Countryside Act 1981 or a European site within the meaning of regulation 10(1) of the Conservation (Natural Habitats, &c.) Regulations 1994.

2.—(1) Subject to the following provisions of this paragraph, appropriate arrangements shall be made with regard to the characteristics of the landfill and prevailing meteorological conditions in order to—

(a) control rainwater entering the landfill body;

(b) prevent surface water or groundwater from entering into landfilled waste;

(c) collect contaminated water and leachate and treat it to the appropriate standard so that it can be discharged.

(2) Arrangements need not be made in accordance with sub-paragraph (1)(c) if the Agency decides that the landfill poses no potential hazard to the environment in view of its location and the kinds of waste to be accepted at the landfill.

(3) This paragraph shall not apply to inert landfills.

3.—(1) The landfill must be situated and designed so as to—

(a) provide the conditions for prevention of pollution of the soil, groundwater or surface water; and

(b) ensure efficient collection of leachate as and when required by paragraph 2.

(2) Soil, groundwater and surface water is to be protected by the use of a geological barrier combined with—

(a) a bottom liner during the operational phase of the landfill; and

(b) a top liner following closure and during the after-care phase.

(3) The geological barrier shall comply with the requirements of sub-paragraph (4) and shall also provide sufficient attenuation capacity to prevent a potential risk to soil and groundwater.

(4) The landfill base and sides shall consist of a mineral layer which provides protection of soil, groundwater and surface water at least equivalent to that resulting from the following permeability and thickness requirements—

(a) in a landfill for hazardous waste: $k \leq 1.0 \times 10^{-9}$ metre/second: thickness ≥ 5 metres;

(b) in a landfill for non-hazardous waste: $k \leq 1.0 \times 10^{-9}$ metre/second: thickness ≥ 1 metres;

(c) in a landfill for inert waste: $k \leq 1.0 \times 10^{-7}$ metre/second: thickness ≥ 1 metres.

(5) Where the geological barrier does not meet the requirements of subparagraph (4) naturally, it may be completed artificially and reinforced by other means providing equivalent protection; but in any such case a geological barrier established by artificial means must be at least 0.5 metres thick.

(6) A leachate collection and sealing system to ensure that leachate accumulation at the base of the landfill is kept to a minimum must also be provided in any hazardous or non-hazardous landfill in accordance with the following table—

Leachate collection and bottom sealing

Landfill category	*Non-hazardous*	*Hazardous*
Artifical sealing liner	Required	Required
Drainage layer $\geq$ 0.5 metres	Required	Required

(7) Where the potential hazards to the environment indicate that the prevention of leachate formation is necessary, surface sealing may be prescribed taking account of the following guidelines—

Landfill category	*Non-hazardous*	*Hazardous*
Gas drainage layer	Required	Not required
Artificial sealing liner	Not required	Required
Impermeable mineral	layer Required	Required
Drainage layer < 0.5 metres	Required	Required
Top soil cover < 1 metre	Required	Required

(8) The requirements of sub-paragraphs (3) to (7) may be reduced to an appropriate extent if on the basis of an assessment of environmental risks, having regard in particular to Directive 80/68/EEC—

(a) it has been decided in accordance with paragraph 2 that the collection and treatment of leachate is not necessary; or

(b) it is established that the landfill poses no potential hazard to soil, groundwater or surface water.

4.—(1) Appropriate measures must be taken in order to control the accumulation and migration of landfill gas.

(2) Landfill gas must be collected from all landfills receiving biodegradable waste and the landfill gas must be treated and, to the extent possible, used.

(3) The collection, treatment and use of landfill gas under sub-paragraph (2) must be carried on in a manner which minimises damage to or deterioration of the environment and risk to human health.

(4) Landfill gas which cannot be used to produce energy must be flared.

5.—(1) Measures must be taken to minimise the nuisances arising from the landfill in relation to—

(a) emissions of odours and dust;

(b) wind-blown materials;

(c) noise and traffic;

(d) birds, vermin and insects;

(e) the formation of aerosols; and

(f) fires.

(2) The landfill must be equipped so that dirt originating from the site is not dispersed onto public roads and the surrounding land.

6.—(1) The placement of waste must ensure stability of all the waste on the site and associated structures and in particular must avoid slippages.

(2) Where an artificial barrier is used, the geological substratum must be sufficiently stable, taking into account the morphology of the landfill, to prevent settlement that may cause damage to the barrier.

7.—(1) The landfill must be secured to prevent free access to the site.

(2) The gates of the landfill must be locked outside operating hours.

(3) The system of control and access to each facility must provide systems to detect and discourage illegal dumping in the facility.

Regulations 14(2) and 15(5)(c) SCHEDULE 3

MINIMUM MONITORING PROCEDURES FOR LANDFILLS

1. This Schedule sets out minimum procedures for monitoring to be carried out to check—

(a) that waste has been accepted for disposal only if it fulfils the relevant waste acceptance criteria;

(b) that the processes within the landfill proceed as desired;

(c) that environmental protections systems are functioning fully as intended; and

(d) that the conditions of the landfill permit are fulfilled.

2.—(1) Samples of leachate or surface water (if present) must be collected at representative points.

(2) Sampling and measuring of the volume and composition of any leachate must be performed separately at each point at which leachate is discharged from the site.

(3) Monitoring of surface water (if present) shall take place at at least two points, one upstream from the landfill and one downstream.

(4) Gas monitoring must be carried out for each section of the landfill and representative samples must be collected and analysed in accordance with Table 1.

(5) A representative sample of leachate and water shall be taken for monitoring purposes in accordance with Table 1.

Table 1

	Operational phase	*After-care phase*[1]
Leachate volume[2]	Monthly[1, 3]	Every six months
Leachate composition[2, 4]	Quarterly[1]	Every six months
Volume and composition of surface water[5]	Quarterly[1]	Every six months
Potential gas emissions and atmospheric pressure[6] (CH_4, CO_2, O_2, H_2S, H_2 etc.)	Monthly[1,7]	Every six months[8]

Notes to Table 1

[1] Longer intervals may be allowed if the evaluation of data indicates that they would be equally effective. For leachates, the conductivity must always be measured at least once a year.

[2] These do not apply where leachate collection is not required under paragraph 2(1)(c) of Schedule.

[3] The frequency of sampling may be adapted on the basis of the morphology of the landfill waste (in tumulus, buried, etc) (but only if the Environment Agency considers that the conditions of the landfill permit should allow for it).

[4] The parameters to be measured and substances to be analysed vary according to the composition of the waste deposited. They must be specified in the conditions of the landfill permit and reflect the leaching characteristics of the wastes.

[5] On the basis of the characteristics of the landfill site, the Environment Agency may determine that these measurements are not required.

[6] These measurements are related mainly to the content of the organic material in the waste.

[7] CH_4, CO_2, O_2 regularly, other gases as required, according to the composition of the waste deposited, with a view to reflecting its leaching properties.

[8] Efficiency of the gas extraction system must be checked regularly.

3.—(1) The sampling measurements taken must be sufficient to provide information on groundwater likely to be affected by the discharge from the landfill, with at least one measuring point in the groundwater inflow region and two in the outflow region.

(2) The number of measurements referred to sub-paragraph (1) may be increased on the basis of a specific hydrogeological survey or the need for an early identification of accidental leachate release in the groundwater.

(3) Sampling must be carried out in at least three locations before filling operations in order to establish reference values for future sampling.

4.—(1) The monitoring of groundwater shall be carried out in accordance with Table 2.

(2) The parameters to be analysed in the samples taken must be derived from the expected composition of the leachate and the groundwater quality in the area.

(3) In selecting the parameters for analysis, the mobility in the groundwater zone must be taken into account.

(4) Parameters may include indicator parameters in order to ensure an early recognition of change in water quality (the recommended parameters are pH, TOC, phenols, heavy metals, fluoride, anionic surfactants As, oil/hydrocarbons).

Table 2

	Operational phase	*After-care phase*
Level of groundwater	Every six months[1]	Every six months[1]
Groundwater	Site-specific	Site-specific

Table 2 *(Cont.)*

	Operational phase	*After-care phase*
Composition	frequency[2,3]	frequency[2,3]

Notes to Table 2

[1] If there are fluctuating groundwater levels, the frequency must be increased.

[2] The frequency must be based on the possibility for remedial action between two samplings if a trigger level is reached, i.e. the frequency must be determined on the basis of knowledge and the evaluation of the velocity of groundwater flow.

[3] When a trigger level is reached (see paragraph 5), verification is necessary by repeating the sampling. When the level has been confirmed, a contingency plan set out in the landfill permit conditions must be followed.

5.—(1) Significant adverse environmental effects, as referred to in regulations 14(3) and 15(5)(b), should be considered to have occurred in the case of groundwater when an analysis of a groundwater sample shows a significant change in water quality.

(2) The level at which the effects referred to in sub-paragraph (1) are considered to have occurred ('the trigger level') must be determined taking account of the specific hydrogeological formations in the location of the landfill and groundwater quality.

(3) The trigger level must be set out in the conditions of the landfill permit whenever possible.

(4) The observations must be evaluated by means of control charts with established control rules and levels for each downgradient well.

(5) The control levels must be determined from local variations in groundwater quality.

6.—The topography of the site and settling behaviour of the landfill body shall be monitored in accordance with Table 3.

Table 3

	Operational phase	*After-care phase*
Structure and composition of landfill body[1]	Yearly	
Settling behaviour of the level of the landfill body	Yearly	Yearly reading

Note to Table 3

[1] Data for the status plan of the relevant landfill: surface occupied by waste, volume and composition of waste, methods of depositing, time and duration of depositing, calculation of the remaining capacity still available at the landfill.

Regulations 17(1) and 18 SCHEDULE 4

TRANSITIONAL PROVISIONS

1 Existing landfills: transitional provisions

(1) Subject to paragraph 2(1), this paragraph shall apply to a landfill if—

(a) it is already in operation on 15th June 2002; or

(b) it has not been brought into operation by that date but the relevant authorisation for its operation was granted before that date.

(2) A landfill to which this paragraph applies which falls within paragraph (b) of Part A(1) of Section 5.2 in Part 1 of Schedule 1 to the 2000 Regulations shall be treated as an existing installation for the purposes of Part 1 of Schedule 3 to those Regulations.

(3) If the operator proposes to continue to accept waste after 16th July 2002, the operator shall prepare a conditioning plan for the landfill site and submit it to the Environment Agency by that date.

(4) The conditioning plan required by sub-paragraph (3) must—

(a) be prepared on a form provided for that purpose by the Environment Agency; and

(b) contain details of any corrective measures which the operator considers will be needed in order to comply with the relevant requirements of these Regulations.

(5) If the operator does not propose to continue to accept waste after 16th July 2002, the operator shall notify the Environment Agency in writing by that date.

(6) Subject to sub-paragraph (7), where—

(a) the operator notifies the Environment Agency that he does not propose to accept waste for disposal after 16th July 2002;

(b) the Environment Agency decides, following the submission by the operator of a conditioning plan, that there is no reasonable prospect of the landfill or part of it meeting the relevant requirements of these Regulations (such decision, and the reasons for it, to be set out in a notice served on the operator); or

(c) the operator fails to submit a conditioning plan as required by subparagraphs (3) and (4) or to notify the Agency as required by subparagraph (5),

the Environment Agency shall ensure that closure of the landfill site (in whole or in part) takes place as soon as possible in accordance with regulation 15.

(7) Where the operator proposes to continue to accept waste but fails to submit a conditioning plan in accordance with sub-paragraphs (3) and (4), the relevant authorisation shall cease to have effect so as to authorise the disposal of waste at the landfill, and the Environment Agency shall proceed with the closure of the site under sub-paragraph (6), unless and until a conditioning plan which complies with sub-paragraph (4) is submitted and the Agency has agreed to consider it.

(8) In any case falling within sub-paragraph (6), (9A) or (9B)—

(a) regulation 15 shall apply as if—

(i) references to a landfill permit were references to a relevant authorisation;

(ii) where the relevant authorisation is a waste management licence, references to the operator were references to the licence holder; and

(iii) in paragraph (6) after 'revocation of permits)' there were inserted 'and sections 38, 39 and 42 of the Environmental Protection Act 1990 (revocation, suspension and surrender of waste management licences)'; and

(b) the Environment Agency shall, if necessary, by notice in writing served on the operator or, in the case of a waste management licence, the licence holder, vary the conditions of the relevant authorisation so that—

(i) waste is no longer accepted for disposal on the whole or the relevant part of the landfill site from such date as is specified in the notice; and

(ii) the closure and after-care procedures will operate in accordance with regulation 15.

(9) In any case where the whole of a landfill site is not subject to closure under sub-paragraph (6), the Environment Agency shall by notice served on the operator specify the period (which shall not be less than six months) within which an application must be made (accompanied by a copy of the conditioning plan)—

(a) where no landfill permit is in force, for a landfill permit under regulation 10 of the 2000 Regulations; or

(b) where a landfill permit is in force, for a variation of the permit under regulation 17(2) of the 2000 Regulations,

so that waste may continue to be accepted for disposal at the landfill.

[(9A) Where following receipt of a notice under sub-paragraph (9)(a)—

(a) the operator notifies the Environment Agency that he does not propose to accept waste for disposal after the date specified in the notice as the end of the period within which an application for a landfill permit under regulation 10 of the 2000 Regulations must be made;

(b) no application for a landfill permit is duly made within the period specified in the notice; or

(c) an application for a landfill permit is made within the period specified in the notice but then withdrawn or deemed withdrawn at some time after the end of that period,

the Environment Agency shall ensure closure of the landfill site as soon as possible (in whole or part) in accordance with regulation 15.

(9B) Where a landfill permit is refused pursuant to an application made under sub-paragraph (9), the Agency shall ensure closure of the landfill site (in whole or part) in accordance with regulation 15 as soon as possible after the determination date for that part of the landfill site.]

(10) In any case falling within sub-paragraph (9)(b), if an application is not duly made within the period specified in the notice served on the operator under that provision, the landfill permit shall cease to authorise the disposal of waste at the landfill until the application is duly made.

(11) Where the Environment Agency decides to grant or vary a landfill permit pursuant to an application made in accordance with sub-paragraph (9), the Agency shall specify the date or dates on which the permit conditions authorised or required by these Regulations shall take effect.

[(11A) From 16th July 2006 any relevant authorisation shall be read as containing the following additional condition—

'Waste of the types listed in regulation 9(1)(e) and (f) of the Landfill (England and Wales) Regulations 2002 shall not be accepted.'

(11B) From 30th October 2007 any relevant authorisation shall be read as containing the following additional condition—

'Waste of the types listed in regulation 9(1)(a) to (d) of the Landfill (England and Wales) Regulations 2002 and waste which does not comply with the requirement for prior treatment in regulation 10(1) of those Regulations shall not be accepted.']

(12) The Environment Agency shall exercise its powers under subparagraphs (9) and (11)—

(a) on the basis of an assessment of environmental risks; and

(b) with a view to achieving full compliance with the relevant requirements of these Regulations—

(i) as soon as possible; and

(ii) by 31st March 2007 at the latest.

[(13) In this Schedule—

(a) 'the relevant requirements of these Regulations' do not include the requirements of paragraph 1 of Schedule 2; and

(b) 'determination date' means--

(i) for a landfill (in whole or part) in relation to which a permit is refused and the applicant for the permit appeals against refusal, the date of affirmation of the refusal;

(ii) for a landfill (in whole or part) in relation to which a permit is refused and no appeal is made against the refusal, the date immediately following the last day, determined in accordance with paragraph 2 of Schedule 8 to the 2000 Regulations, on which a notice of appeal might have been given.]

2.—(1) Paragraph 1 does not apply to a landfill if—

(a) a landfill permit for its operation was granted on or after 16th July 2001 and before 15th June 2002;

(b) it falls within paragraph (b) of Part A(1) of Section 5.2 in Part 1 of Schedule 1 to the 2000 Regulations and a waste management licence for its operation was granted on or after 16th July 2001 and before 15th June 2002; or

(c) the prescribed date determined in accordance with Schedule 3 to the 2000 Regulations for the installation at which the landfill activity is carried out is before 15th June 2002 and an application for a landfill permit was duly made (but not determined) before 15th June 2002.

(2) In any case falling within sub-paragraph (1)(b), the waste management licence shall have effect on or after 15th June 2002 as if it were a landfill permit.

(3) In any case falling within sub-paragraph (1) the Environment Agency shall exercise its power to vary the relevant authorisation (or determine the outstanding application) so that the relevant requirements of these Regulations are complied with as soon as possible in relation to the landfill in question.

(4) In any case falling within sub-paragraph (1)(c), where an application for a waste management licence is also outstanding on 15th June 2002, there shall be no obligation on the Agency to determine the application for a waste management licence.

3.—(1) The Environment Agency shall by notice in writing served on the operator no later than 16th July 2002, classify any landfill which appears to the Agency to require classification as a landfill for hazardous waste.

(2) If a landfill classified under sub-paragraph (1) as a landfill for hazardous waste ceases to accept hazardous waste in accordance with the conditioning plan required under paragraph 1(3), the Environment Agency may at any time before 16th July 2004 by notice in writing served on the operator revoke the classification made under sub-paragraph (1).

(3) The following provisions of these Regulations shall impose obligations directly on the operator of any landfill which is for the time being classified under sub-paragraph (1) as a landfill for hazardous waste pending determination of an application made pursuant to paragraph 1(9)—

(a) on or after 16th July 2002—
  (i) regulation 9 (prohibition of acceptance of certain wastes); and
  (ii) regulation 12 (waste acceptance procedures);
(b) on or after 16th July 2004, regulation 10(1)[. . .](waste acceptance requirements).

(4) For the purposes of applying regulation 9(1)(g) under sub-paragraph (3)(a)(i) in relation to the period beginning on 16th July 2002 and ending on 15th July 2004, only the criteria in paragraph 1 of Schedule 1 are to be treated as relevant waste acceptance criteria.

(5) The operator of a landfill which is not classified as a landfill for hazardous waste shall only accept hazardous waste at that landfill on or after 16th July 2002 [if the waste is stable non-reactive hazardous waste and it fulfils the relevant waste acceptance criteria].

4.—(1) This paragraph shall apply to any landfill if—

(a) it falls within paragraph (b) of Part A(1) of Section 5.2 in Part 1 of Schedule 1 to the 2000 Regulations; and
(b) it has not been brought into operation by 15th June 2002 but an application for a waste management licence was duly made before that date.

(2) Paragraph 1 of Part 1 of Schedule 3 to the 2000 Regulations shall apply as if in sub-paragraphs (a) and (b) '15th June 2002' were substituted for '1st January 2001'.

(3) Anything duly done by or in relation to the application for a waste management licence shall be treated as if it had been duly done in relation to an application for a landfill permit.

(4) The Environment Agency may give the applicant notice requiring him—

(a) to provide such further information of any description specified in the notice; or
(b) to take such further steps as it may require for the purpose of determining the application.

The Large Combustion Plants (England and Wales) Regulations 2002

(SI 2002, No. 2688)

Citation, commencement and extent

1.—(1) These Regulations may be cited as the Large Combustion Plants (England and Wales) Regulations 2002 and shall come into force on 27th November 2002.

(2) These Regulations extend to England and Wales only.

Interpretation

2. In these Regulations—

'the 1990 Act' means the Environmental Protection Act 1990;

'the 2000 Regulations' means the Pollution Prevention and Control (England and Wales) Regulations 2000;

'authorisation' means an authorisation granted under section 6 of the 1990 Act;

'combustion plant' means a combustion plant as defined in Article 2(7) of the Directive and to which the Directive applies;

'the Directive' means Council Directive 2001/80/EC on the limitation of emissions of certain pollutants into the air from large combustion plants;

'new plant' has the meaning given in Article 2(9) of the Directive; and

'permit' means a permit granted under regulation 10 of the 2000 Regulations.

Authorisation to operate new plants

4. Where a new plant is subject on 27th November 2002 to a permit but the plant is not put into operation before 28th November 2003, the permit shall cease to authorise the operation of that plant until such time as it is varied by the Environment Agency pursuant to regulation 17 of the 2000 Regulations so as to give effect in relation to the plant to the requirements of the Directive.

Deemed conditions in authorisations and permits

5.—(1) Where on 27th November 2002—

(a) a new plant is subject to an authorisation or a permit; and

(b) the plant benefits from the derogation in Article 5(1) of Council Directive 88/609/EEC on the limitation of emissions of certain pollutants into the air from large combustion plants by virtue of operating between 2000 and 2200 hours a year,

any condition in the authorisation or permit applying that derogation shall, in so far as it applies that derogation, cease to have effect and the relevant emission limit values prescribed in Articles 4(1) and 17(2) of the Directive shall apply to the plant.

(2) Paragraph (1) shall cease to apply in relation to any authorisation or a permit which is varied by the Environment Agency under Part I of the 1990 Act or regulation 17 of the 2000 Regulations so as to give effect in relation to the plant to Article 5(1) of the Directive.

(3) Where a combustion plant is subject to an authorisation or a permit on 27th November 2002, the authorisation or permit shall be read as containing the following additional condition—

'In the event of malfunction or breakdown of the abatement equipment, the operator shall, if a return to normal operation is not achieved within 24 hours, reduce or close down operations or use low polluting fuels, or take such other steps as the Environment Agency requires. The cumulative duration of unabated operation in any twelve month period shall not, unless agreed in advance by the Environment Agency, exceed 120 hours.'

(4) Paragraph (3) shall cease to apply in relation to any authorisation or permit which is varied by the Environment Agency under Part I of the 1990 Act or regulation 17 of the 2000 Regulations so as to give effect in relation to the plant to Article 7(1) of the Directive.

(5) Where a new plant is subject to an authorisation or a permit on 27th November 2002, the authorisation or permit shall be read as containing the following additional condition—

'The values of the 95% confidence intervals of a single measured result shall not exceed the following percentages of the emission limit values:

Sulphur dioxide	20%
Nitrogen oxides	20%
Dust	30%

The validated hourly and daily average values shall be determined from the measured valid hourly average values after having subtracted the value of the confidence interval specified above.

Any day in which more than three hourly average values are invalid due to malfunction or maintenance of the continuous measurement system shall be invalidated'.

(6) Paragraph (5) shall cease to apply in relation to any authorisation or permit which is varied by the Environment Agency under Part I of the 1990 Act or regulation 17 of the 2000 Regulations so as to give effect in relation to the plant to paragraph 6 of part A of Annex VIII to the Directive.

Waste Incineration (England and Wales) Regulations 2002

(SI 2002, No. 2980)

Citation, commencement and extent

1.—(1) These Regulations may be cited as the Waste Incineration (England and Wales) Regulations 2002.

(2) These Regulations shall come into force on 28th December 2002.

(3) These Regulations extend to England and Wales.

Interpretation

2.—(1) In these Regulations—

'the 1990 Act' means the Environmental Protection Act 1990;

'the 2000 Regulations' means the Pollution Prevention and Control (England and Wales) Regulations 2000;

'authorisation' means an authorisation granted under section 6 of the 1990 Act;

'existing waste incineration installation' means a waste incineration installation which—

(a) in the case of an installation which is a co-incineration plant, is put into operation before 28th December 2004 subject to a relevant approval; or

(b) in any other case—

(i) is put into operation before 28th December 2003 subject to a relevant approval granted before 28th December 2002; or

(ii) is put into operation before 28th December 2004 subject to a relevant approval granted on the basis of a duly made application submitted before 28th December 2002;

and where an installation becomes authorised as a waste incineration installation for the first time as a result of a modification or variation pursuant to section 10, 11 or 37 of the 1990 Act or regulation 17 of the 2000 Regulations, references in this definition to a relevant approval shall be construed as references to that modification or variation and not to the original relevant approval, and references to the grant of an approval shall be construed as references to the service of the notice effecting the modification or variation; and 'relevant approval' means any of the following—

(a) a permit;

(b) an authorisation;

(c) a waste management licence granted under section 36 of the 1990 Act; or

(d) an exemption registered under regulation 18 of the Waste Management Licensing Regulations 1994, and the entry of particulars in the register under regulation 18 of those Regulations shall be treated as the grant of a relevant approval for the purposes of the definition of 'existing waste incineration installation'.

(2) In these Regulations, words and expressions which are defined in the 2000 Regulations shall have the same meaning as in those Regulations.

Applications in relation to waste incineration installations

3.—(1) Where an existing waste incineration installation is on 31st December 2004 subject to a permit, the operator shall within the period 1st January to 31st March 2005 make an application under regulation 17 of the 2000 Regulations for a variation of the conditions of that permit.

(2) Where an existing waste incineration installation (not being one falling within Section 5.1 of Part 1 of Schedule 1 of the 2000 Regulations) is on 31st December 2004 subject to an authorisation, the operator shall within the period 1st January to 31st March 2005 either—

(a) apply under section 11 of the 1990 Act for a variation of the conditions of the authorisation; or

(b) make an application for a permit under regulation 10 of the 2000 Regulations.

(3) An application under paragraph (1) or (2) shall contain the information specified in paragraph 1B of Part 1 of Schedule 4 of the 2000 Regulations.

(4) Where a waste incineration installation would have fallen within paragraph (a), (b)(i) or (b)(ii) of the definition of existing waste incineration installation in regulation 2 had it been put into operation before the date specified in the applicable paragraph, it shall not thereafter be put into operation unless—

(a) in the case of an installation which is already subject to a permit, the permit is varied pursuant to an application under regulation 17 of the 2000 Regulations; or

(b) in any other case, a permit is granted in relation to the installation.

(5) Where an operator fails to comply with any of the requirements of this regulation the regulator shall serve a notice on the operator specifying the relevant requirement, requiring him to comply with that requirement and specifying the period within which it must be complied with.

(6) A notice served under paragraph (5) shall be treated as an enforcement notice served under regulation 24(1) of the 2000 Regulations.

Transitional provisions

. . .

The National Emission Ceilings Regulations 2002

(SI 2002, No. 3118)

Citation and commencement

1. These Regulations may be cited as the National Emission Ceilings Regulations 2002 and shall come into force on 10th January 2003.

Interpretation

2.—(1) In these Regulations—

'emission' means the release of a substance from a point or diffuse source into the atmosphere, with the exception of—

(a) emissions from international maritime traffic; and

(b) aircraft emissions beyond the landing and take-off cycle, being a cycle represented by the following time in each operating mode:

(i) 4 minutes for approach;

(ii) 26 minutes for taxi/ground idle;

(iii) 0.7 minutes for take-off; and

(iv) 2.2 minutes for climb;

'nitrogen oxides' means nitric oxide and nitrogen dioxide, expressed as nitrogen dioxide;

'relevant pollutant' means sulphur dioxide (SO2), nitrogen oxides (NOX), volatile organic compounds (VOC) or ammonia (NH3);

'volatile organic' compound means all organic compounds (other than methane) arising from human activities which are capable of producing photochemical oxidants by reactions with nitrogen oxides in the presence of sunlight.

(2) For the purposes of these Regulations, references to the 'United Kingdom' shall include—

(a) the area adjacent to the United Kingdom up to the seaward limits of territorial waters; and

(b) any area for the time being designated under section 1(7) of the Continental Shelf Act 1964 (designation of areas of continental shelf).

(3) For the purpose of regulations 4(4) and 5(4), 'the public' includes any organisation or body representing or having an interest in the environment, health, business or consumers.

National emission ceilings

3. The Secretary of State shall ensure that, in 2010 and each year thereafter, the total emissions within the United Kingdom of each relevant pollutant do not exceed the amount specified in the Schedule for that pollutant.

National programme

4.—(1) The Secretary of State shall as soon as practicable prepare a programme for the progressive reduction in emissions within the United Kingdom of the relevant pollutants in accordance with Article 6(1) and (2) and having regard to Article 5 of European Parliament and Council Directive 2001/81/EC relating to national emission ceilings for certain atmospheric pollutants.

(2) The Secretary of State may review the programme from time to time and shall update and revise it as necessary by 1st October 2006.

(3) Public authorities shall have regard to the programme when exercising any functions which significantly affect the level of emissions within the United Kingdom of the relevant pollutants.

(4) The Secretary of State shall take appropriate steps to ensure that the programme is made available to the public and is clear, comprehensible and easily accessible.

Emissions inventories and projections

5.—(1) The Secretary of State—

(a) shall as soon as practicable prepare—

(i) a final inventory of emissions within the United Kingdom of the relevant pollutants during the year 2000;

(ii) a provisional inventory of emissions within the United Kingdom of the relevant pollutants during the year 2001; and

(iii) a projection of emissions within the United Kingdom of the relevant pollutants during the year 2010; and

(b) shall—

(i) by 31st December in each year prepare a final inventory of emissions within the United Kingdom of the relevant pollutants during the year ending on 31 December 24 months earlier;

(ii) by 31st December in each year prepare a provisional inventory of emissions within the United Kingdom of the relevant pollutants during the year ending on 31 December 12 months earlier; and

(iii) by 31st December in each year up to and including 2009 update the projection referred to in paragraph (1)(a)(iii).

(2) The inventories and projections referred to in paragraph (1) shall be prepared and updated using the methodologies in the Joint EMEP/CORINAIR Atmospheric Emission Inventory Guidebook, third Edition, 2001, published by the European Environment Agency.

(3) The projection referred to in paragraph (1)(a)(iii) shall include information to enable a quantitative understanding of the key socio-economic assumptions used in its preparation.

(4) The Secretary of State shall take appropriate steps to ensure that the inventories and projections referred to in paragraph (1) are made available to the public.

Regulation 3 SCHEDULE

National emission ceilings for SO_2, NO_X, VOC and NH_3

The amount specified for the purpose of regulation 3 is the relevant figure shown in the Table below less the emissions of that pollutant from Gibraltar in the relevant year.

SO_2 Kilotonnes	NO_X Kilotonnes	VOC Kilotonnes	NH_3 Kilotonnes
585	1167	1200	297

The Air Quality Limit Values Regulations 2003

(SI 2003, No. 2121) (as amended)

Citation, commencement and extent

1.—(1) These Regulations may be cited as the Air Quality Limit Values Regulations 2003 and shall come into force on 9th September 2003.

(2) Subject to paragraph (3), these Regulations shall apply to England.

(3) Regulation 13, and the remainder of these Regulations in so far as they relate to regulation 13, shall apply to the United Kingdom.

Definitions

2. In these Regulations—

'agglomeration' means a zone with a population concentration in excess of 250,000 inhabitants, or, where the population concentration is 250,000 inhabitants or less, a population density per km2 for which the Secretary of State considers that the need for ambient air to be assessed or managed is justified;

'alert threshold' has the meaning given in regulations 10(2) and (3);

'ambient air' means outdoor air in the troposphere, excluding work places;

'assessment' means any method used to measure, calculate, predict or estimate the level of a relevant pollutant, ozone or ozone precursor substances in the ambient air;

'fixed measurements' means measurements taken at fixed sites either continuously or by random sampling, the number of measurements being sufficiently large to enable the levels observed to be determined;

'information threshold' has the meaning given in regulation 10(3);

'level' means the concentration of a relevant pollutant, ozone or ozone precursor substances in ambient air;

'limit value' has the meaning given in regulation 4(1);

'long-term objective' has the meaning given in regulation 5(3);

'lower assessment threshold' has the meaning given in regulation 7(8);

'natural events' means volcanic eruptions, seismic activities, geothermal activities, wildland fires, high-wind events or the atmospheric resuspension or transport of natural particles from dry regions;

'oxides of nitrogen' means the sum of nitric oxide and nitrogen dioxide added as parts per billion and expressed as nitrogen dioxide in microgrammes per cubic metre;

'ozone precursor substances' means substances which contribute to the formation of ground level ozone, including those listed in Schedule 6;

'$PM_{2.5}$' means particulate matter which passes through a size-selective inlet with a 50% efficiency cut-off at 2.5 μm aerodynamic diameter;

'PM_{10}' means particulate matter which passes through a size-selective inlet with a 50% efficiency cut-off at 10 μm aerodynamic diameter;

['public' means natural or legal persons, including health care bodies and other organisations having an interest in ambient air quality and representing the interests of sensitive populations, consumers and the environment;]

'relevant pollutants' means sulphur dioxide, nitrogen dioxide and oxides of nitrogen, particulate matter, lead, benzene and carbon monoxide;

'rural background station' shall be interpreted in accordance with Part II of Schedule 4;

'target value' has the meaning given in regulation 5(2);

'upper assessment threshold' has the meaning given in regulation 7(8);

'volatile organic compounds' or 'VOC' means all organic compounds from anthropogenic and biogenic sources, other than methane, that are capable of producing photochemical oxidants by reaction with nitrogen oxides in the presence of sunlight; and

'zone' means a part of the territory of England shown on a map published by the Secretary of State on 19th January 2001, deposited at the offices of the Department for Environment, Food and Rural Affairs, Ashdown House, 123 Victoria Street, London SW 1E 6DE and displayed on the Department's website at [http://www.defra.gov.uk/environment/airquality/article5/pdf/figure1.pdf].

Designation of competent authority

3. The Secretary of State is designated as the competent authority for the purposes of article 3 (implementation and responsibilities) of Council Directive 96/62/EC on ambient air quality assessment and management.

Duty to ensure compliance with limit values

4.—(1) The Secretary of State shall take the measures necessary to ensure that throughout England, in each zone, concentrations of relevant pollutants in ambient air, as assessed in accordance with regulations 6 to 9, do not exceed the limit values set out in Schedule 1 from the dates specified in that Schedule.

(2) The measures taken shall—

(a) take into account an integrated approach to the protection of air, water and soil;

(b) not contravene Community legislation on the protection of safety and health of workers at work; and

(c) have no significant negative effects on the environment in the other Member States.

Target values and long-term objectives for ozone

5.—(1) The definitions and provisions on interpretation in Part 1 of Schedule 2 shall apply in the interpretation of the other parts of that Schedule.

(2) The target values for ozone concentrations in ambient air are set out in Part II of Schedule 2.

(3) The long-term objectives for ozone concentrations in ambient air are set out in Part III of Schedule 2.

Assessment of ambient air quality

6. The Secretary of State shall ensure that ambient air quality is assessed in each zone in relation to each of the relevant pollutants, ozone and ozone precursor substances in accordance with regulations 7 to 9.

Classification of zones

7.—(1) The Secretary of State shall, in accordance with paragraphs (3), (4) and (7), classify each zone in relation to each of the relevant pollutants according to whether ambient air quality in that zone for that pollutant is required to be assessed by—

(a) measurements;

(b) a combination of measurements and modelling techniques; or

(c) by the sole use of modelling or objective estimation techniques.

(2) The Secretary of State shall, in accordance with paragraphs (5) and (6), classify each zone in relation to ozone according to whether ambient air quality for ozone is required to be assessed by—

(a) fixed continuous measurement; or

(b) a combination of measurement campaigns of short duration and results from emission inventories and modelling.

(3) Measurements must be used to assess ambient air quality in relation to a relevant pollutant in a zone if—

(a) the zone is an agglomeration;

(b) the levels of that pollutant in the zone are between the relevant limit value and upper assessment threshold; or

(c) the levels of that pollutant in the zone exceed the limit value for that pollutant.

(4) A combination of measurements and modelling techniques may be used to assess ambient air quality in any zone in relation to a relevant pollutant where the levels of that pollutant over a representative period are below the relevant upper assessment threshold.

(5) Fixed continuous measurement must be used to assess ambient air quality in relation to ozone if within the last five years concentrations of ozone in that zone have exceeded a long-term objective.

(6) A combination of measurement campaigns of short duration and results from emissions inventories and modelling may be used to assess ambient air quality in relation to ozone in a zone if fewer than five years' data are available to determine exceedances.

(7) Where the levels of a relevant pollutant in any zone over a representative period are below the relevant lower assessment threshold, the sole use of modelling or objective estimation techniques for assessing levels of that pollutant is permissible unless—

(a) the zone is an agglomeration; and

(b) the pollutant is sulphur dioxide or nitrogen dioxide.

(8) The upper and lower assessment thresholds for the relevant pollutants are set out in Part I of Schedule 3.

(9) Where a zone is classified in relation to a pollutant under paragraph (1)(a), modelling techniques may be used for supplementing the measurements taken in order to provide an adequate level of information on ambient air quality in relation to a relevant pollutant in the zone.

(10) The Secretary of State may also designate a zone classified under this regulation in relation to a relevant pollutant as follows.

(11) Where the relevant pollutant is sulphur dioxide, the zone may be designated under this paragraph if the limit value is exceeded in the zone owing to concentrations of sulphur dioxide in ambient air due to natural sources.

(12) Where the relevant pollutant is PM10, the zone may be designated—

(a) under this sub-paragraph if, due to natural events, concentrations of PM_{10} in the ambient air are significantly in excess of normal background levels from natural sources;

(b) under this sub-paragraph if, due to the resuspension of particulates following the winter sanding of roads, concentrations of PM_{10} in the ambient air are significantly in excess of normal background levels from natural sources.

Review of classifications

8.—(1) The Secretary of State shall review the classification of each zone under regulation 7 at least once in every five years in accordance with Part II of Schedule 3.

(2) The Secretary of State shall also review the classification of any zone under regulation 7 in the event of significant changes in activities affecting ambient concentrations in that zone of any of the relevant pollutants.

Method of assessment of ambient air quality

9.—(1) The Secretary of State shall ensure that ambient air quality is assessed in each zone by following the appropriate method for each relevant pollutant and for ozone in accordance with its current classification.

(2) Where a zone is classified under regulation 7(1)(a) or (b) in relation to a relevant pollutant—

(a) measurements of that pollutant must be taken at fixed sites either continuously or by random sampling; and

(b) the number of measurements must be sufficiently large to enable the levels of that pollutant to be properly determined.

(3) Schedule 4 shall have effect for the purposes of determining the location of sampling points for the relevant pollutants.

(4) For each zone classified under regulation 7(1)(a) in relation to a relevant pollutant, the Secretary of State shall ensure that the minimum number of fixed sampling points determined in accordance with Schedule 5 is used for sampling the concentrations of that pollutant in that zone.

(5) For each zone classified under regulation 7(1)(b) in relation to a relevant pollutant, the Secretary of State shall ensure that the number of fixed sampling points used for sampling that pollutant in that zone, and the spatial resolution of other techniques, shall be sufficient for the concentrations of that pollutant to be established in accordance with Part I of Schedule 4 and Part I of Schedule 7.

(6) For each zone classified under regulation 7(2)(a) in relation to ozone, the Secretary of State shall ensure that the minimum number of fixed sampling points determined in accordance with Part III of Schedule 5 is used for sampling the concentrations of ozone in that zone.

(7) For zones to which paragraph (6) applies, the Secretary of State shall ensure that measurements of nitrogen dioxide are made at a minimum of 50 per cent. of the ozone sampling points required by Part III of Schedule 5.

(8) The measurements of nitrogen dioxide required by paragraph (7) shall be continuous, except at rural background stations, where other measurement methods may be used.

(9) For zones within which information from sampling points for fixed measurement is supplemented by information from modelling or indicative measurement, the number of fixed sampling points required by Part III of Schedule 5 may be reduced, provided that—

(a) the modelling techniques adopted pursuant to regulation 7(9) provide an adequate level of information for the assessment of air quality with regard to target values, information and alert thresholds;

(b) the number of sampling points to be installed and the spatial resolution of other techniques are sufficient for the concentration of ozone to be established in accordance with the data quality objectives specified in Part III of Schedule 7 and lead to assessment results as specified in Part IV of Schedule 7;

(c) the number of sampling points in each zone amounts to at least one sampling point per two million inhabitants, or one sampling point per 50,000 km^2, whichever produces the greater number of sampling points;

(d) each zone contains at least one sampling point; and

(e) nitrogen dioxide is measured at all remaining sampling points except rural background stations.

(10) The results of modelling and indicative measurements carried out in zones to which paragraph (9) applies shall be taken into account for the assessment of air quality with respect to target values.

(11) For zones where five years of measurement have been carried out and, during each of the previous five years of measurement, concentrations are below the long-term objectives, the number of continuous measurement stations shall be determined in accordance with Part IV of Schedule 5.

(12) Part II of Schedule 4 shall have effect for determining the classification and location of sampling points for the measurement of ozone.

(13) Reference methods for—

(a) the analysis of sulphur dioxide, nitrogen dioxide and oxides of nitrogen;

(b) the sampling and analysis of lead;

(c) the sampling and measurement of PM_{10};

(d) the sampling and analysis of benzene;

(e) the analysis of carbon monoxide; and

(f) the analysis of ozone and the calibration of ozone instruments

are set out in Schedule 8 and these methods must be used unless other methods are used which the Secretary of State considers can be demonstrated to give equivalent results [or, in relation to the sampling and measurement of PM_{10}, which the Secretary of State considers can be demonstrated to display a consistent relationship to the reference method].

(14) The Secretary of State shall ensure that—

(a) measuring stations to supply representative data on concentrations of $PM_{2.5}$ are installed and operated using methods for the sampling and measurement of $PM_{2.5}$ that she considers suitable; and

(b) sampling points for $PM_{2.5}$ are, where possible, co-located with sampling points for PM_{10}.

(15) For ozone precursor substances, the Secretary of State shall ensure that—

(a) at least one measuring station to supply data on concentrations of the ozone precursor substances listed in Schedule 6 is installed and operated within England; and

(b) in choosing the number and siting of measuring stations for ozone precursor substances, account is taken of the provisions of Schedule 6.

(16) For zones which are classified under regulation 7(1)(b) or (c), the Secretary of State shall ensure that the information set out in Part II of Schedule 7 is compiled.

(17) For sulphur dioxide, nitrogen dioxide, oxides of nitrogen, benzene, carbon monoxide and ozone measurements of volume must be standardised at a temperature of 293K and a pressure of 101,3 kPa.

Action plans

10.—(1) The Secretary of State shall draw up action plans indicating the measures to be taken in the short term where there is any risk of the limit values for any of the relevant pollutants, or the alert thresholds for sulphur dioxide or nitrogen dioxide, being exceeded, in order to reduce that risk and to limit the duration of such an occurrence.

(2) The alert threshold for sulphur dioxide is set out in paragraph 1.2 of Part I of Schedule 1 and the alert threshold for nitrogen dioxide is set out in paragraph 1.2 of Part II of Schedule 1.

(3) The information threshold and alert threshold for ozone are set out in paragraph 1.1 of Part VII of Schedule 1.

(4) The Secretary of State shall draw up action plans indicating the measures to be taken in the short term where there is any risk of the alert threshold for ozone being exceeded if there is in her opinion significant potential to—

(a) reduce such a risk; or

(b) reduce the duration or severity of such an occurrence.

(5) In making the assessment required by paragraph (4), the Secretary of State shall take account of national geographical, meteorological and economic conditions.

(6) The Secretary of State shall make available to the public—

(a) the results of investigations undertaken in the preparation of action plans under paragraph (4);

(b) the action plans; and

(c) information on the implementation of the action plans.

Action to be taken where limit values are exceeded

11.—(1) The Secretary of State shall draw up a list of zones in which the levels of one or more of the relevant pollutants are higher than—

(a) in a case where there is no margin of tolerance shown in Schedule 1 in relation to a limit value, the limit value;

(b) in any other case, the limit value plus the margin of tolerance shown in Schedule 1.

(2) The Secretary of State shall draw up a list of zones in which the levels of one or more of the relevant pollutants are between the limit value and the limit value plus any margin of tolerance.

(3) Subject to paragraphs (6), (8) and (9), the Secretary of State shall draw up for each zone listed under paragraph (1) a plan or programme for attaining the limit values for the pollutants in question within the time limits specified in Schedule 1 and shall ensure that the plan or programme is implemented.

(4) The plan or programme shall at least include the information listed in Schedule 9.

(5) Where in any zone the level of more than one pollutant is higher than the limit value, an integrated plan covering all the pollutants in question shall be prepared.

(6) For any zone designated under regulation 7(11), the Secretary of State may determine that plans or programmes shall be required under this regulation only where the limit values are exceeded owing to man-made emissions.

(7) Plans or programmes for PM_{10} which are prepared in accordance with this regulation shall also have the aim of reducing concentrations of $PM_{2.5}$.

(8) For any zone designated under regulation 7(12)(a), the Secretary of State may determine that plans or programmes shall be required only where the limit values are exceeded owing to causes other than natural events.

(9) For any zone designated under regulation 7(12)(b), the Secretary of State may determine that plans or programmes shall be required only where the limit values are exceeded owing to PM_{10} levels other than those caused by winter road sanding.

[(10) The Secretary of State shall, in accordance with paragraphs (11) and (12), ensure that the public is given early and effective opportunities to participate in the preparation and modification or review of the plans or programmes required to be drawn up under paragraph (3).

(11) The Secretary of State shall—

(a) ensure that the public is informed, whether by public notices or other appropriate means such as electronic media, about any proposals for such plans or programmes or for their modification or review;

(b) ensure that relevant information about the proposals referred to in sub-paragraph (a) is made available to the public, including information about the right to participate in decision-making;

(c) ensure that the public is entitled to make comments before decisions on the plans and programmes are made;

(d) in making those decisions, take due account of the results of the public participation; and

(e) having examined the comments made by the public, make reasonable efforts to inform the public about—

(i) the decisions taken and the reasons and considerations on which those decisions are based; and

(ii) the public participation process.

(12) The Secretary of State shall publish any information required to carry out her functions under paragraphs 10 and 11 in such manner as she considers appropriate for the purpose of bringing it to the attention of the public and shall—

(a) make copies of such information accessible to the public free of charge through the website of the Department for Environment, Food and Rural Affairs; and

(b) specify in a notice on the website the detailed arrangements made to enable participation in the preparation, modification or review of the plans or programmes, including—

(i) the address to which comments may be submitted; and

(ii) the time-frame for any such comments allowing sufficient time for each of the different stages of public participation required by paragraphs 10 and 11.]

Programmes and measures to address ozone levels

12.—(1) The Secretary of State shall draw up three lists of zones, namely zones in which—

(a) levels of ozone in ambient air, as assessed in accordance with regulations 7 and 9, are higher than target values;

(b) levels of ozone in ambient air, as assessed in accordance with regulations 7 and 9, are higher than the long-term objectives, but equal to or below the target levels;
(c) ozone levels meet the long-term objectives.

(2) The Secretary of State shall draw up and implement for each zone listed under paragraph (1)(a) a plan or programme for attaining the target values from the date specified in Part II of Schedule 2.

(3) The obligation in paragraph (2) will not apply if the Secretary of State considers that attaining the target values would not be achievable through proportionate measures.

(4) The Secretary of State shall, in drawing up and implementing plans or programmes under paragraph (2) ensure that, where appropriate, these are integrated with plans drawn up under regulation 10.

(5) Plans or programmes drawn up under paragraph (2) shall contain at least the information specified in Schedule 9, and shall be made available to the public.

(6) The Secretary of State shall prepare and implement for each zone listed under paragraph (1)(b) measures which she considers to be cost-effective with the aim of achieving the long-term objectives.

(7) The Secretary of State shall ensure that the measures described in paragraph (6) are, at least, consistent with the plans or programmes drawn up under paragraph (2).

(8) The Secretary of State shall, for zones to which paragraph (1)(c) applies—
(a) as far as factors including the transboundary nature of ozone pollution and meteorological conditions permit, ensure that ozone levels are kept below long-term objectives; and
(b) preserve through proportionate measures the best ambient air quality which she considers to be compatible with sustainable development and a high level of protection for the environment and human health.

Consultations with other Member States of the European Union

13.—(1) For the purpose of this regulation, a transboundary pollution issue arises when—
(a) in any part of the United Kingdom the level of a relevant pollutant exceeds, or is likely to exceed, the limit value plus the margin of tolerance or, as the case may be, the alert threshold following significant pollution in another Member State of the European Union;
(b) ozone concentrations in any part of the United Kingdom exceed target values or long-term objectives and a significant part of the cause of such exceedance is the emission of ozone precursor substances in another Member State of the European Union; or
(c) ozone concentrations in another Member State of the European Union exceed target values or long-term objectives and a significant part of the cause of such exceedances is the emission of ozone precursor substances in the United Kingdom.

(2) It shall be the duty of the relevant administration to notify the Secretary of State of any transboundary pollution issue affecting Wales, Scotland or Northern Ireland as applicable.

(3) The Secretary of State shall consult any other Member State directly concerned with a view to finding a solution—
(a) when she considers that a transboundary pollution issue has arisen affecting England;
(b) on receiving a notification under paragraph (2); or
(c) on being notified by any other Member State that the limit value or alert threshold for any relevant pollutant may be exceeded in that Member State as a result of pollution originating in any part of the United Kingdom.

(4) In the case of a transboundary pollution issue to which paragraph (1)(b) or (c) applies, where the Secretary of State considers that attaining the target values or long-term objectives in the United Kingdom or the Member State concerned, as the case may be, is reasonably achievable through proportionate measures, she shall take the action prescribed in paragraph (5).

(5) Where paragraph (4) applies, the Secretary of State shall, in consultation with any relevant administration directly concerned, ensure co-operation with the Member State concerned in drawing up joint plans or programmes in order to attain the target values or long-term objectives in the United Kingdom or the other Member State as the case may be.

(6) The Secretary of State shall ensure that where paragraph (4) applies, action plans prepared under regulation 10(4) for England cover neighbouring zones affected in both the United Kingdom and any other Member State concerned, and shall take such steps as she considers appropriate to ensure that action plans prepared by any relevant administration under any equivalent provision cover such neighbouring zones.

(7) The Secretary of State shall ensure that where paragraph (6) applies, any other Member State concerned is provided with the information specified in regulation 10(6).

(8) The Secretary of State shall ensure that where ozone concentrations exceed the information threshold or alert threshold in any zone close to the borders with another Member State, full information of this occurrence is provided promptly to the competent authorities of the other Member State concerned, in order to facilitate the provision of information to the public in that Member State.

(9) In discharging her obligations under this regulation, the Secretary of State shall, where appropriate, seek to ensure full co-operation with any other countries concerned, not being Member States.

(10) In any case which appears to her to affect Wales, Scotland or Northern Ireland, the Secretary of State shall—

(a) inform the relevant administration of any notification made under paragraph (3)(c); and

(b) consult the relevant administration about any action which she proposes to take.

(11) The European Commission may be present at any consultations conducted under paragraph (3) which concern relevant pollutants.

(12) In this regulation, 'relevant administration' means—

(a) the National Assembly for Wales for matters affecting Wales;

(b) Scottish Ministers for matters affecting Scotland; and

(c) Northern Ireland Ministers for matters affecting Northern Ireland.

Extension of power to give directions relating to air quality

14.—(1) For the purposes of the implementation of any obligations of the United Kingdom under Council Directive 96/62/EC on ambient air quality assessment and management; Council Directive 99/30/EC relating to limit values for sulphur dioxide, nitrogen dioxide and oxides of nitrogen, particulate matter and lead in ambient air and of European Parliament and Council Directive 2000/69/EC relating to the limit values for benzene and carbon monoxide in ambient air—

(a) the Secretary of State shall have the same power to give directions to local authorities in Greater London and to the Mayor of London; and

(b) the Mayor of London shall have the same power to give directions to local authorities in Greater London,

as the Secretary of State has under section 85(5) of the Environment Act 1995 in relation to local authorities in England outside Greater London.

(2) The provisions of subsections (6), (6A) and (7) of section 85 of the Environment Act 1995 shall apply to directions given under this regulation as they apply to directions given under that section, and in the case of subsections (6) and (7) as if the Mayor of London were a local authority.

Zones where the levels are lower than the limit value

15.—(1) The Secretary of State shall draw up a list of zones in which the levels of the relevant pollutants are below the limit values.

(2) The Secretary of State shall ensure that the levels of the relevant pollutants in these zones are maintained below the limit values and shall endeavour to preserve the best ambient air quality compatible with sustainable development.

Public information

16.—(1) The Secretary of State shall ensure that up-to-date information on ambient concentrations of each of the relevant pollutants and of ozone is routinely made available to the public in accordance with the following paragraphs.

(2) Information on ambient concentrations of sulphur dioxide, nitrogen dioxide and particulate matter shall be updated—

(a) in the case of hourly values for sulphur dioxide and nitrogen dioxide, where practicable on an hourly basis;

(b) in all other cases, as a minimum on a daily basis.

(3) Information on ambient concentrations of lead shall be updated on a three-monthly basis.

(4) Information on ambient concentrations of benzene, as an average value over the last 12 months, shall be updated—

(a) where practicable, on a monthly basis;

(b) in all other cases, as a minimum on a three-monthly basis.

(5) Information on ambient concentrations of carbon monoxide, as a maximum running average over eight hours, shall be updated—

(a) where practicable, on an hourly basis;

(b) in all other cases, as a minimum on a daily basis.

(6) The information on concentrations of ozone shall be updated—

(a) where appropriate and practicable, on an hourly basis; and

(b) in all other cases, as a minimum on a daily basis.

(7) Information made available with respect to each of the relevant pollutants shall include—

(a) an indication of the extent to which limit values and alert thresholds for relevant pollutants have been exceeded over the averaging periods specified in Schedule 1; and

(b) a short assessment of those exceedances and their effects on health.

(8) Information with respect to ozone made available shall include—

(a) an indication of each time and the extent to which ozone concentrations exceeded—

(i) the long-term objectives for the protection of human health;

(ii) the information threshold; or

(iii) the alert threshold

for the relevant averaging period; and

(b) a short assessment of those exceedances and their effects on health;

(c) comprehensive annual reports; and

(d) timely information about actual or predicted exceedances of the alert threshold.

(9) The annual reports referred to in paragraph (8)(c) shall, at least, contain—

(a) for human health, an indication of all exceedances of the target value, long-term objective or alert threshold for the relevant averaging period; and

(b) for vegetation—

(i) an indication of any exceedance of the target value or long-term objective; and

(ii) where appropriate, a short assessment of the effects of any such exceedance.

(10) The information referred to in paragraph (9)(b) may include, where appropriate—

(a) further information and assessments on forest protection, which set out for suburban, rural and rural background stations, based on one hour averaging, accumulated from May to July for a report of value for each year, whether levels of ozone concentrations in ambient air exceed 6,000 $\mu g/m^3$ per hour; and

(b) information on ozone precursor substances insofar as these are not covered by existing European Community legislation.

(11) Information and reports required to be made available by this regulation shall be published by appropriate means including, as appropriate, broadcast media, press, publications, information screens, the internet or other computer network services.

(12) The Secretary of State shall ensure that where information is provided to the public under paragraphs (7) and (13)—

(a) where there has been an exceedance of the information and alert threshold for ozone it includes the information specified in paragraph 1.2 of Part VII of Schedule 1; and

(b) where practicable, the information specified in paragraph 1.2 of Part VII of Schedule 1 is provided where an exceedance of the information threshold or alert threshold for ozone is predicted.

(13) When an alert threshold for sulphur dioxide or nitrogen dioxide is exceeded, the Secretary of State shall ensure that the necessary steps are taken to inform the public, and the information made available shall as a minimum include the information specified in paragraphs 1.3 of Part I and 1.3 of Part II, as applicable, of Schedule 1.

(14) Information to be made available to the public under this regulation shall include the map mentioned in the definition of 'zone' in regulation 2 and action plans, plans and programmes prepared under regulations 10 and 11 respectively.

(15) [...]

(16) Information made available under this regulation shall be clear, comprehensible and accessible.

Information requirements

18.—(1) The Secretary of State shall ensure that the information specified in Part I of Schedule 11 is obtained and collated.

(2) The criteria for aggregating data and calculating statistical parameters specified in Part II of Schedule 11 shall apply.

Regulation 4(1), 10(2), (3), 11(1), (3), 16 (7), (12), (13)

SCHEDULE 1

LIMIT VALUES, MARGINS OF TOLERANCE, INFORMATION AND ALERT THRESHOLDS

PART I SULPHUR DIOXIDE*

1.1 Limit values for sulphur dioxide

	Averaging period	Limit value	Margin of tolerance [9]	Date by which limit value is to be met
1. Hourly limit value for the protection of human health	1 hour	350 μg/m^3, not to be exceeded more than 24 times a calendar year	60 μg/m^3, reducing to 30 μg/ m^3 on 1st January 2004 and to 0 μg/m^3 on 1st January 2005	

*Editor's note: Part I only included in full for illustrative purposes.

(Cont.)

	Averaging period	Limit value	Margin of tolerance [9]	Date by which limit value is to be met
2. Daily limit value for the protection of human health	24 hours	125 μg/m^3, not to be exceeded more than 3 times a calendar year	None	1st January 2005
3. Limit value for the protection of ecosystems	Calendar year and winter (1st October to 31st March)	20 μg/m^3	None	19th July 2001

1.2 Alert threshold for sulphur dioxide

500 μg/m^3 measured over three consecutive hours at locations representative of air quality over at least 100 km^2 or an entire zone, whichever is the smaller.

1.3 Minimum details to be made available to the public when the alert threshold for sulphur dioxide is exceeded

Details to be made available to the public should include at least:

— the date, hour and place of the occurrence and the reasons for the occurrence, where known;

— any forecasts of:

  — changes in concentration (improvement, stabilisation, or deterioration), together with the reasons for those changes,

  — the geographical area concerned, and

  — the duration of the occurrence;

  — the type of population potentially sensitive to the occurrence;

— the precautions to be taken by the sensitive population concerned.

PART II NITROGEN DIOXIDE (NO_2) AND OXIDES OF NITROGEN (NOx)

...

PART III PARTICULATE MATTER (PM_{10})

...

PART IV LEAD

...

PART V BENZENE

...

PART VI CARBON MONOXIDE

...

PART VII OZONE

...

Regulation 5, 12(2)

SCHEDULE 2

TARGET VALUES AND LONG-TERM OBJECTIVES FOR OZONE CONCENTRATIONS IN AMBIENT AIR

PART I DEFINITIONS AND INTERPRETATION

In this Schedule—

(a) all values shall be expressed in μg/m^3;

(b) the volume shall be standardised at the following conditions of temperature and pressure: 293K and 101,3kPa;

(c) the time shall be specified in Central European Time;

(d) 'AOT40' (expressed in (μg/m^3)-hours) means the sum of the difference between hourly concentrations greater than 80 μg/m^3 (which equals 40 parts per billion) and 80 μg/m^3 over a given period using only the 1 hour values measured between 8:00 and 20:00 Central European Time each day;

(e) in order to be valid, the annual data on exceedances used to check compliance with the target values and long-term objectives below must meet the criteria set out in Part II of Schedule 8.

PART II TARGET VALUES FOR OZONE

	Parameter	Target value for 2010(a)
1. Target value for the protection of human health	Maximum daily 8-hour mean (b)	120 μg/m^3 not to be exceeded on more than 25 days per calendar year averaged over three years(c)
2. Target value for the protection of human health	AOT 40, calculated from 1 h values from May to July	18,000 μg/m^3 h averaged over five years(c)

(a) Compliance with target values will be assessed as of this value. That is, 2010 will be the first year the data for which is used in calculating compliance over three or five years, as appropriate.

(b) The maximum daily 8-hour mean concentration shall be selected by examining 8-hour running averages, calculated from hourly data and updated each hour. Each 8-hour average so calculated shall be assigned to the day on which it ends, that is, the first calculation period for any one day shall be the period from 17:00 on the previous day to 01:00 on that day; the last calculation period for any one day will be the period from 16:00 to 24:00 on the day.

(c) If the three or five year averages cannot be determined on the basis of a full and consecutive set of annual data, the minimum annual data required for checking compliance with the target values shall be as follows—

(i) for the target value for the protection of human health, valid data for one year; and

(ii) for the target value for the protection of vegetation, valid data for three years.

PART III LONG-TERM OBJECTIVES FOR OZONE

	Parameter	Long-term objective
1. Long-term objective for the protection of human health	Maximum daily 8-hour mean within a calendar year	120 μg/m^3
2. Long-term objective for the protection of vegetation	AOT40, calculated from 1 h values from May to July	6,000 μg/m^3.h

Regulation 7(8), 8(1)

SCHEDULE 3

UPPER AND LOWER ASSESSMENT THRESHOLDS AND EXCEEDANCES

PART I UPPER AND LOWER ASSESSMENT THRESHOLDS

The following upper and lower assessment thresholds will apply:

(a) Sulphur dioxide*

	Health protection	Ecosystem protection
Upper assessment threshold	60% of 24-hour limit value (75 μg/m^3), not to be exceeded more than 3 times in any calendar year	60% of winter limit value (12 μg/m^3)
Lower assessment threshold	40% of 24-hour limit value (50 μg/m^3), not to be exceeded more than 3 times in any calendar year	40% of winter limit value (8 μg/m^3)

(b) Nitrogen dioxide and oxides of nitrogen

. . .

(c) Particulate matter

. . .

(d) Lead

. . .

(e) Benzene

. . .

(f) Carbon monoxide

. . .

PART II DETERMINATION OF EXCEEDANCES OF UPPER AND LOWER ASSESSMENT THRESHOLDS

Exceedances of upper and lower assessment thresholds must be determined on the basis of concentrations during the previous five years where sufficient data are available. An assessment threshold will be deemed to have been exceeded if it has been exceeded during at least three separate years out of the previous five years.

*Editor's note: (a) only included in full for illustrate purposes.

Where fewer than five years' data are available, measurement campaigns of short duration during the period of the year and at locations likely to be typical of the highest pollution levels may be combined with results obtained from emission inventories and modelling to determine exceedances of the upper and lower assessment thresholds.

Regulation 9(3), (5), (12)

SCHEDULE 4

LOCATION OF SAMPLING POINTS FOR THE MEASUREMENT OF RELEVANT POLLUTANTS AND OZONE IN AMBIENT AIR

The following considerations will apply to fixed measurement.

PART I MACROSCALE SITING

(a) Protection of human health

Sampling points directed at the protection of human health should be sited:

(i) to provide data on the areas within zones where the highest concentrations occur to which the population is likely to be directly or indirectly exposed for a period which is significant in relation to the averaging period of the limit value;

(ii) to provide data on levels in other areas within the zones which are representative of the exposure of the general population.

Sampling points should in general be sited to avoid measuring very small micro-environments in their immediate vicinity. As a guideline, a sampling point should be sited to be representative of air quality in a surrounding area of no less than 200 m^2 at traffic-orientated sites and of several square kilometres at urban-background sites.

Sampling points should also, where possible, be representative of similar locations not in their immediate vicinity.

Account should be taken of the need to locate sampling points on islands, where that is necessary for the protection of human health.

(b) Protection of ecosystems and vegetation

Sampling points targeted at the protection of ecosystems or vegetation should be sited more than 20 km from agglomerations or more than 5 km from other built-up areas, industrial installations or motorways. As a guideline, a sampling point should be sited to be representative of air quality in a surrounding area of at least 1000 km^2. A sampling point may be sited at a lesser distance or to be representative of air quality in a less extended area, taking account of geographical conditions.

Account should be taken of the need to assess air quality on islands.

PART II MACROSCALE SITING: OZONE

Type of station	Objective of measurement	Representativeness (a)	Macroscale siting criteria
Urban	Protection of human health: To assess the exposure of the urban population to ozone, i.e. where the population density and ozone	A few km^2	Away from the influence of local emissions such as traffic, petrol stations etc.; Vented locations where well mixed levels

(Cont.)

Type of station	Objective of measurement	Representativeness (a)	Macroscale siting criteria
	concentration are relatively high and representative of the exposure of the general population		can be measured; Locations such as residential and commercial areas of cities, parks (away from the trees), big streets or squares with very little or no traffic, open areas characteristic of education, sports or recreation facilities
Suburban	Protection of human health and vegetation: To assess the exposure of the population and vegetation located in the outskirts of the agglomeration, where the highest ozone levels, to which the population and vegetation is likely to be directly or indirectly exposed, occur	Some tens of km^2	At a certain distance from the area of maximum emissions, downwind following the main wind direction during conditions favourable to ozone formation; Where population, sensitive crops or natural ecosystems located in the outer fringe of an agglomeration are exposed to high ozone levels; Where appropriate, some suburban stations also upwind of the area of maximum emissions, in order to determine the regional background levels of ozone.
Rural	Protection of human health and vegetation: To assess the exposure of population, crops and natural ecosystems to subregional scale ozone concentrations	Sub-regional levels (a few km^2)	Stations can be located in small settlements and/or areas with natural ecosystems, forests or crops; Representative for ozone away from the influence of immediate local emissions such as industrial installations and roads; At open area sites, but not on higher mountain-tops.

(Cont.)

Type of station	Objective of measurement	Representa-tiveness (a)	Macroscale siting criteria
Rural background	Protection of vegetation and human health: To assess the exposure of crops and natural ecosystems to regional-scale ozone concentrations as well as exposure of the populations	Regional/ national/ continental levels (1,000 to 10,000 km^2)	Station located in areas with lower population density, e.g. with natural ecosystems, forests, far removed from urban and industrial areas and away from local emissions; Avoid locations which are subject to locally enhanced formation of near-ground inversion conditions, also summits of higher mountains; Coastal sites with pronounced diurnal wind cycles of local character are not recommended.

(a) Sampling points should also, where possible, be representative of similar locations not in their immediate vicinity.

For rural and background stations, consideration should be given, where appropriate, to co-ordination with the monitoring requirements of Commission Regulation 1091/94[*10*] concerning protection of the Community's forests against atmospheric pollution.

PART III MICROSCALE SITING

The following guidelines should be met as far as practicable:

- the flow around the inlet sampling probe should be unrestricted, (and, for ozone sampling, free in an arc of at least 270°) without any obstructions affecting the airflow in the vicinity of the sampler (normally some metres away from buildings, balconies, trees and other obstacles by more than twice the height the obstacle protrudes above the sampler and at least 0.5 m from the nearest building in the case of sampling points representing air quality at the building line);
- in general, the inlet sampling point should be between 1.5 m (the breathing zone) and 4 m above the ground. Higher positions (up to 8 m) may be necessary in some circumstances and in wooded areas. Higher siting may also be appropriate if the station is representative of a large area;
- the inlet probe should not be positioned in the immediate vicinity of sources in order to avoid the direct intake of emissions unmixed with ambient air;
- the sampler's exhaust outlet should be positioned so that recirculation of exhaust air to the sampler inlet is avoided;
- location of traffic-orientated samplers;
  - for all pollutants, such sampling points should be at least 25 m from the edge of major junctions and at least 4 m from the centre of the nearest traffic lane;
  - for nitrogen dioxide and carbon monoxide, inlets should be no more than 5 m from the kerbside;
  - for particulate matter, lead and benzene, inlets should be sited so as to be representative of air quality near to the building line;

— for ozone, the inlet probe should be positioned well away from such sources as furnaces and incineration flues and more than 10m from the nearest road, with distance increasing as a function of traffic intensity.

The following factors may also be taken into account:

- — interfering sources;
- — security;
- — access;
- — availability of electrical power and telephone communications;
- — visibility of the site in relation to its surroundings;
- — safety of public and operators;
- — the desirability of co-locating sampling points for different pollutants;
- — lanning requirements.

PART IV DOCUMENTATION AND REVIEW OF SITE SELECTION

The site-selection procedures should be fully documented at the classification stage by such means as compass-point photographs of the surrounding area and a detailed map. Sites should be reviewed at regular intervals with repeated documentation to ensure that selection criteria remain valid over time.

For ozone, this requires screening and monitoring of the monitoring data in the context of the meteorological and photochemical processes affecting the ozone concentrations measured at the respective site.

Regulation 9(4), (6), (7), (9), (11) SCHEDULE 5

CRITERIA FOR DETERMINING MINIMUM NUMBERS OF SAMPLING POINTS FOR FIXED MEASUREMENT OF CONCENTRATIONS OF RELEVANT POLLUTANTS AND OZONE IN AMBIENT AIR

PART I RELEVANT POLLUTANTS: MINIMUM NUMBER OF SAMPLING POINTS FOR FIXED MEASUREMENT TO ASSESS COMPLIANCE WITH LIMIT VALUES FOR THE PROTECTION OF HUMAN HEALTH AND ALERT THRESHOLDS IN ZONES WHERE FIXED MEASUREMENT IS THE SOLE SOURCE OF INFORMATION

(a) Diffuse sources

Population of zone (thousands)	If concentrations exceed the upper assessment threshold	If maximum concentrations are between the upper and lower assessment thresholds	For SO_2 and NO_2 in agglomerations where maximum concentrations are below the lower assessment thresholds
0–250	1	1	not applicable
250–499	2	1	1
500–749	2	1	1

(Cont.)

Population of zone (thousands)	If concentrations exceed the upper assessment threshold	If maximum concentrations are between the upper and lower assessment thresholds	For SO_2 and NO_2 in agglomerations where maximum concentrations are below the lower assessment thresholds
750–999	3	1	1
1,000–1,499	4	2	1
1,500–1,999	5	2	1
2,000–2,749	6	3	2
2,750–3,749	7	3	2
3,750–4,749	8	4	2
4,750–5,999	9	4	2
>6,000	10 For NO_2 and particulate matter: to include at least one urban-background station and one traffic-orientated station–this requirement shall also apply to benzene and carbon monoxide provided that it does not increase the number of sampling points	5	3

(b) Point sources

For the assessment of pollution in the vicinity of point sources, the number of sampling points for fixed measurement should be calculated taking into account emission densities, the likely distribution patterns of ambient-air pollution and the potential exposure of the population.

PART II RELEVANT POLLUTANTS: MINIMUM NUMBER OF SAMPLING POINTS FOR FIXED MEASUREMENTS TO ASSESS COMPLIANCE WITH LIMIT VALUES FOR THE PROTECTION OF ECOSYSTEMS OR VEGETATION IN ZONES OTHER THAN AGGLOMERATIONS

If maximum concentrations exceed the upper assessment threshold	If maximum concentrations are between the upper and lower assessment thresholds
1 station every 20,000 km^2	1 station every 40,000 km^2

In island zones the number of sampling points for fixed measurement should be calculated taking into account the likely distribution patterns of ambient-air pollution and the potential exposure of ecosystems or vegetation.

PART III OZONE: MINIMUM NUMBER OF SAMPLING POINTS FOR FIXED CONTINUOUS MEASUREMENT TO ASSESS AIR QUALITY IN VIEW OF COMPLIANCE WITH THE TARGET VALUES, LONG-TERM OBJECTIVES AND INFORMATION AND ALERT THRESHOLDS WHERE CONTINUOUS MEASUREMENT IS THE SOLE SOURCE OF INFORMATION

Population (× 1,000)	**Agglomerations (urban and suburban** (a)	**Other zones (suburban and rural)** (a)	**Rural background**
0–250		1	1 station/50,000 km^2 as an average density over all zones in England (b)
251–500	1	2	'
501–1,000	2	2	'
1,001–1,500	3	3	'
1,501–2,000	3	4	'
2,001–2,750	4	5	'
2,751–3,750	5	6	'
>3,750	1 additional station per 2 million inhabitants	1 additional station per 2 million inhabitants	

(a) At least 1 station in suburban areas, where the highest exposure of the population is likely to occur. In agglomerations at least 50% of the stations should be located in suburban areas.
(b) 1 station per 25,000 km^2 for complex terrain is recommended.

PART IV OZONE: MINIMUM NUMBER OF SAMPLING POINTS FOR FIXED MEASUREMENTS FOR ZONES ATTAINING THE LONG-TERM OBJECTIVES

The number of sampling points for ozone must, in combination with other means of supplementary assessment such as air quality modelling and co-located nitrogen dioxide measurements, be sufficient to examine the trend of ozone pollution and check compliance with the long-term objectives. The number of stations located in agglomerations and other zones may be reduced to one-third of the number specified in Part III. Where information from fixed measurement stations is the sole source of information, at least one monitoring station should be kept. If, in zones where there is supplementary assessment, the result of this is that a zone has no remaining station, coordination with the number of stations in neighbouring zones must ensure adequate assessment of ozone concentrations against long-term objectives. The number of rural background stations should be 1 per 100,000 km^2.

Regulation 9(15) SCHEDULE 6

MEASUREMENTS OF OZONE PRECURSOR SUBSTANCES

(a) Objectives

The main objectives of measurements of ozone precursor substances are to analyse any trend in ozone precursors, to check the efficiency of emission reduction strategies, to check the consistency of emission inventories and to help attribute emission sources to pollution concentration.

An additional aim is to support the understanding of ozone formation and precursor dispersion processes, as well as the application of photochemical models.

Substances

Measurements of ozone precursor substances must include at least nitrogen oxides, and appropriate volatile organic compounds (VOC). A list of volatile organic compounds recommended for measurement is given below.

Ethane	1-Butene	Isoprene	Ethyl benzene
Ethylene	trans-2-Butene	n-Hexane	m + p-Xylene
Acetylene	cis-2-Butene	i-Hexane	o-Xylene
Propane	1.3-Butadiene	n-Heptane	1,2,4-Trimeth. benzene
Propene	n-Pentane	n-Octane	1,2,3-Trimeth. benzene
n-Butane	i-Pentane	i-Octane	1,3,5-Trimeth. benzene
i-Butane	1-Pentene	Benzene	Formaldehyde
	2-Pentene	Toluene	Total non-methane hydrocarbons

Reference methods

The reference method for the analysis of oxides of nitrogen shall be ISO 7996: 1985, Ambient air—determination of the mass concentrations of nitrogen oxides—chemiluminescence method: *see* footnote (a) to Part I of Schedule 7.

(b) Siting

Measurements should be taken in particular in urban and suburban areas at any monitoring site set up in accordance with the requirements of the Air Quality Limit Values Regulations 2001 and considered appropriate with regard to the monitoring objectives in this Schedule.

Regulation 9(5), (6), (9), (15), (16) SCHEDULE 7

DATA-QUALITY OBJECTIVES AND COMPLILATION OF RESULTS OF AIR-QUALITY ASSESSMENT

PART I RELEVANT POLLUTANTS: DATA-QUALITY OBJECTIVES

The following data-quality objectives for the required accuracy of assessment methods, of minimum time coverage and of data capture of measurement are laid down to guide quality-assurance programmes.

	Sulphur dioxide, nitrogen dioxide and oxides of nitrogen	Particulate matter and lead
Continuous measurement		
Accuracy	15%	25%
Minimum data capture	90%	90%
Indicative measurement		
Accuracy	25%	50%
Minimum data capture	90%	90%

(Cont.)

	Sulphur dioxide, nitrogen dioxide and oxides of nitrogen	Particulate matter and lead
Minimum time coverage	14% (One measurement a week at random, evenly distributed over the year, or eight weeks evenly distributed over the year.)	14% (One measurement a week at random, evenly distributed over the year, or eight weeks evenly distributed over the year.)
Modelling		
Accuracy:		
Hourly averages	50%–60%	
Daily averages	50%	
Annual averages	30%	50%
Objective estimation		
Accuracy:	75%	100%

The accuracy of the measurement is defined as laid down in the 'Guide to the Expression of Uncertainty of Measurements' (ISO 1993) or in ISO 5725–1 'Accuracy (trueness and precision) of measurement methods and results' (ISO 1994). The percentages in the table are given for individual measurements averaged, over the period considered, by the limit value, for a 95% confidence interval (bias + two times the standard deviation). The accuracy for continuous measurements should be interpreted as being applicable in the region of the appropriate limit value.

The accuracy for modelling and objective estimation is defined as the maximum deviation of the measured and calculated concentration levels, over the period considered by the limit value, without taking account the timing of the events.

The requirements for minimum data capture and time coverage do not include losses of data due to the regular calibration or the normal maintenance of the instrumentation.

The Secretary of State may allow for random measurements to be made instead of continuous measurements for particulate matter and lead by methods for which accuracy within the 95% confidence interval with respect to continuous monitoring has been demonstrated to be within 10%. Random sampling must be spread evenly over the year.

The following data quality objectives, for allowed uncertainty of assessment methods, of minimum time coverage and of data capture of measurement are provided to guide quality assurance programmes.

	Benzene	Carbon monoxide
Fixed measurements		
Uncertainty	25%	15%
Minimum data capture	90%	90%
Minimum time coverage	35% urban background and traffic sites (distributed over the year to be representative of various conditions for climate and traffic) 90% industrial sites	

(Cont.)

	Benzene	Carbon monoxide
Indicative measurements		
Uncertainty	30%	25%
Minimum data capture	90%	90%
Minimum time coverage	14% (one day's measurement a week at random, evenly distributed over the year, or 8 weeks evenly distributed over the year)	14% (one measurement a week at random, evenly distributed over the year, or 8 weeks evenly distributed over the year)
Modelling		
Uncertainty:	—	50%
Eight-hour averages	50%	—
Annual averages		
Objective estimation		
Uncertainty	100%	75%

The uncertainty (on a 95% confidence interval) of the assessment methods shall be evaluated in accordance with the 'Guide to the Expression of Uncertainty of Measurements' (ISO 1993) or the methodology of ISO 5725:1994. The percentages for uncertainty in the above table are given for individual measurements averaged over the period considered by the limit value, for a 95% confidence interval. The uncertainty for the fixed measurements should be interpreted as being applicable in the region of the appropriate limit value.

The uncertainty for modelling and objective estimation is defined as the maximum deviation of the measured and calculated concentration levels, over the period considered by the limit value, without taking into account the timing of the events.

The requirements for minimum data capture and time coverage do not include losses of data due to the regular calibration or the normal maintenance of the instrumentation.

The Secretary of State may allow for random measurements to be made instead of continuous measurements for benzene if the uncertainty, including the uncertainty due to random sampling, meets the quality objective of 25%. Random sampling must be spread evenly over the year.

PART II RELEVANT POLLUTANTS: RESULTS OF AIR QUALITY ASSESSMENT

The following information should be compiled for zones within which sources other than measurement are employed to supplement information from measurement or as the sole means of air quality assessment:

— a description of assessment activities carried out;
— the specific methods used, with references to descriptions of the method;
— the sources of data and information;
— a description of results, including accuracies and, in particular, the extent of any area or, if relevant, the length of road within the zone over which concentrations exceed the limit value or, as may be, the limit value plus applicable margin of tolerance and of any area within which concentrations exceed the upper assessment threshold or the lower assessment threshold;

— for limit values the object of which is the protection of human health, the population potentially exposed to concentrations in excess of the limit value.

Where possible maps shall be compiled showing concentration distributions within each zone.

PART III OZONE AND OZONE PRECURSORS: DATA QUALITY OBJECTIVES

The following data quality objectives, for allowed uncertainty of assessment methods, and of minimum time coverage and of data capture of measurement, are provided to guide quality-assurance programmes.

	For ozone, NO and NO_2
Continuous fixed measurement	
Uncertainty of individual measurements	15%
Minimum data capture	90% during summer 75% during winter
Indicative measurement	
Uncertainty of individual measurements	30%
Minimum data capture	90%
Minimum time coverage	>10% during summer
Modelling	
Uncertainty	
1 hour averages (daytime)	50%
8 hours daily maximum	50%
Objective estimation	
Uncertainty	75%

The uncertainty (on a 95% confidence interval) of the measurement methods shall be evaluated in accordance with the principles laid down in the 'Guide to the Expression of Uncertainty of Measurements' (ISO 1993) of the methodology in ISO 5725–1 'Accuracy (trueness and precision) of measurement methods and results' (ISO 1994) or equivalent. The percentages for uncertainty in the table are given for individual measurements, averaged over the period for calculating target values and long-term objectives, for a 95% confidence interval. The uncertainty for continuous fixed measurements should be interpreted as being applicable in the region of the concentration used for the appropriate threshold.

The uncertainty for modelling and objective estimation means the maximum deviation of the measured and calculated concentration levels, over the period for calculating the appropriate threshold, without taking into account the timing of events.

'Time coverage' means the percentage of time considered for settling the threshold value during which the pollutant is measured.

'Data capture' means the ratio of the time for which the instrument produces valid data, to the time for which the statistical parameter or aggregated value is to be calculated.

The requirements for minimum data capture and time coverage do not include losses of data due to the regular calibration or normal maintenance of the instrumentation.

PART IV OZONE AND OZONE PRECURSORS: RESULTS OF AIR QUALITY ASSESSMENT

The following information should be compiled for zones within which sources other than measurements are employed to supplement information from measurement:

— a description of the assessment activities carried out;
— specific methods used, with references to descriptions of the method;
— sources of data and information;
— a description of results, including uncertainties and, in particular, the extent of any area within the zone over which concentrations exceed long-term objectives or target values;
— for long-term objectives or target values whose object is the protection of human health, the population potentially exposed to concentrations in excess of the threshold.

The Secretary of State shall ensure that maps are compiled showing concentration distributions within each zone.

Regulation 9(13) SCHEDULE 8

REFERENCE METHODS FOR ASSESSMENT OF CONCENTRATIONS OF RELEVANT POLLUTANTS AND OZONE

PART I REFERENCE METHOD FOR THE ANALYSIS OF SULPHUR DIOXIDE*

ISO/FDIS 10498 (Standard in draft) Ambient air - determination of sulphur dioxide—ultraviolet fluorescence method.

Regulation 11(4),12(5) SCHEDULE 9

INFORMATION TO BE INCLUDED IN THE PLAN OR PROGRAMME FOR IMPROVEMENT OF AIR QUALITY

1 Localisation of excess pollution

— region
— city (map)
— measuring station (map, geographical coordinates).

2 General information

— type of zone (city, industrial or rural area)
— estimate of the polluted area (km2) and of the population exposed to the pollution
— useful climatic data
— relevant data on topography
— sufficient information on the type of targets requiring protection in the zone.

3 Responsible authorities

Names and addresses of persons responsible for the development and implementation of improvement plans.

*Editors' note: Part I only included in full for illustrative purposes.

4 Nature and assessment of pollution

— concentrations observed over previous years (before the implementation of the improvement measures)
— concentrations measured since the beginning of the project
— techniques used for the assessment.
— list of the main emission sources responsible for pollution (map)
— total quantity of emissions from these sources (tonnes/year)
— information on pollution imported from other regions.

6 Analysis of the situation

— details of those factors responsible for the excess (transport, including cross-border transport, formation)
— details of possible measures for improvement of air quality.

7 Details of those measures or projects for improvement which existed prior to 21st November 1996

— local, regional, national, international measures
— observed effects of these measures.

8 Details of those measures or projects adopted with a view to reducing pollution following 21st November 1996

— listing and description of all the measures set out in the project
— timetable for implementation
— estimate of the improvement of air quality planned and of the expected time required to attain these objectives.

9 Details of the measures or projects planned or being researched for the long term.

10 List of the publications, documents, work etc used to supplement information requested in this Schedule.

Regulation 18

SCHEDULE II

INFORMATION TO BE OBTAINED AND COLLATED ON OZONE CONCENTRATIONS, AND CRITERIA FOR AGGREGATING DATA AND CALCULATING STATISTICAL PARAMETERS

PART II INFORMATION ON OZONE CONCENTRATIONS

The following information on ozone concentrations shall be obtained and collated—

	Type of station	Level	Averaging/ accumulation time	Provisional data for each month from April to September	Report for each year
Information threshold	Any	180 μg/m^3	1 hour	—for each day with any exceedance: date, total hours of exceedance, maximum 1 hour ozone and related NO_2 values when required—monthly 1 hour maximum ozone	—for each day with any exceedance: date, total hours of exceedance, maximum 1 hour ozone and related NO_2 values, when required
Alert threshold	Any	240 μg/m^3	1 hour	—for each day with any exceedance: date, total hours of exceedance, maximum 1 hour ozone and related NO_2 values, when required	—for each day with any exceedance: date, total hours of exceedance, maximum 1 hour ozone and related NO_2 values, when required
Health protection	Any	120 μg/m^3	8 hours	—for each day with any exceedance: date, 8 hours maximum (b)	—for each day with any exceedance: date, 8 hours maximum (b)
Vegetation protection	Suburban, rural, rural background	AOT40 (a) =6,000 μg/m^3.h	1 hour, accumulated from May to June		Value
Forest protection	Suburban, rural, rural background	AOT40 (a) =20,000 μg/ m^3.h	1 hour, accumulated from April to September		Value
Materials	Any	40 μg/m^3	1 year		Value

(a) In this Schedule, 'AOT40' has the same meaning as in paragraph (d) of Part I to Schedule 2.
(b) Maximum daily 8-hour mean.

Where they do not do so already, annual reports must also contain—(a) for ozone, nitrogen dioxide, oxides of nitrogen and the sums of ozone and nitrogen dioxide (added as parts per billion and expressed in μ/m^3 ozone) the maximum, 99.9th, 98th and 50th percentiles and annual average and number of valid data from hourly series; and

(b) the maximum, 98th and 50th percentile and annual average from a series of daily 8-hour ozone maxima. Data submitted in monthly reports are considered provisional and shall be updated where necessary in subsequent submissions.

PART II CRITERIA FOR AGGREGATING DATA AND CALCULATING STATISTICAL PARAMETERS

In this Part, percentiles are to be calculated using the method specified in Council Decision 97/101/EC establishing a reciprocal exchange of information and data from networks and individual stations measuring ambient air pollution within Member States.

The following criteria are to be used for checking validity when aggregating data and calculating statistical parameters—

Parameter	Required proportion of valid data
1 hour values	75% (45 minutes)
8 hour values	75% of values (6 hours)
Maximum daily 8 hours mean from hourly running 8 hours averages	75% of the hourly running 8 hour averages (8 hours per day)
AOT40	90% of the 1 hour values over the time period defined for calculating the AOT40 value (a)
Annual mean	75% of the 1 hour values over summer (April to September) and winter (January to March, October to December) seasons separately
Number of exceedances and maximum values per month	90% of the daily maximum 8 hours mean value (27 available daily values per month) 90% of the 1 hour values between 8:00 and 20:00 Central European Time
Number of exceedances and maximum values per year	Five out of six summer months over the summer season (April to September)

(a) In cases where all possible measured data are not available, the following factor shall be used to calculate AOT40 values:

$$\text{AOT40 (estimate)} = \text{AOT40 measured} \times \frac{\text{total possible number of hours}^*}{\text{number of measured hourly values}}$$

*being the number of hours within the time period of AOT40 definition (that is, 8:00 to 20:00 Central European Time from 1 May to 31 July each year, for vegetation protection and from 1 April to 30 September each year for forest protection).

The Water Environment (Water Framework Directive) (England and Wales) Regulations 2003

(SI 2003, No. 3242)

Title, commencement, extent and application

1. These Regulations—

(a) may be cited as the Water Environment (Water Framework Directive) (England and Wales) Regulations 2003 and shall come into force on 2nd January 2004;

(b) extend to England and Wales; and

(c) apply only in relation to river basins districts identified by regulation 4(1).

Interpretation

2.—(1) In these Regulations—

'the Agency' means the Environment Agency;

'the appropriate authority' means—

(a) in relation to a river basin district that is wholly in England, the Secretary of State;
(b) in relation to a river basin district that is wholly in Wales, the Assembly; and
(c) in relation to a river basin district that is partly in England and partly in Wales, the Secretary of State and the Assembly acting jointly;

'the Assembly' means the National Assembly for Wales;

'body of water' means a body of groundwater or a body of surface water;

'the Directive' means Directive 2000/60/EC of the European Parliament and of the Council of 23rd October 2000 establishing a framework for Community action in the field of water policy, as amended;

'England' includes the territorial sea adjacent to England not forming any part of Wales;

'environmental objectives', in relation to a river basin district, means the objectives required to comply with Article 4 of the Directive (environmental objectives) including any objectives required to comply with Article 7 (2) and (3) of the Directive (waters used for the abstraction of drinking water);

'programme of measures', in relation to a river basin district, means the programme of measures required to comply with Article 11(2) to (6) of the Directive (programme of measures);

'public body' does not include a Minister of the Crown within the meaning of the Ministers of the Crown Act 1975 or the Assembly, but it does include—

(a) a person otherwise holding an office—
  (i) under the Crown;
  (ii) created or continued in existence by public general Act of Parliament; or
  (iii) the remuneration in respect of which is paid out of money provided by Parliament; and
(b) a statutory undertaker (being a person who by virtue of section 262 of the Town and Country Planning Act 1990 is, or is deemed to be, a statutory undertaker for any purpose);

'river basin district' means an area identified by regulation 4 (1), being the main unit for the management of river basins for the purposes of the Directive and being made up of a river basin or neighbouring river basins, together with associated groundwater, transitional waters and coastal water; and

'Wales' has the meaning given by section 155 of the Government of Wales Act 1998;

(2) Any expression used in both these Regulations and the Directive and not otherwise defined in these Regulations has the same meaning for the purposes of these Regulations as it has for the purposes of the Directive, and the definitions contained in the Directive of expressions used in these Regulations are set out in Schedule 1 (references in those definitions to an Annex or an Article being to an Annex to, or an Article of, the Directive).

The general duties

3.—(1) The Secretary of State, the Assembly and the Agency must exercise their relevant functions so as to secure compliance with the requirements of the Directive.

(2) The Secretary of State and the Assembly must exercise their relevant functions in relation to each river basin district so as best to secure that the requirements of the Directive for the achievement of its environmental objectives, and in particular programmes of measures, are coordinated for the whole of that district.

(3) In this regulation, 'relevant functions' means functions under these Regulations and, so far as material, the enactments listed in Parts 1 and 2 of Schedule 2 (which relate to statutes and subordinate instruments respectively).

River basin districts

4.—(1) The areas shown on the deposited map are identified as river basin districts for the purposes of these Regulations.

(2) The Secretary of State, the Assembly and the Agency must ensure that the deposited map is made available to the public through their respective websites and at the relevant places.

(3) The relevant places are—

(a) in the case of the Secretary of State, the principal library of the Department for Environment, Food and Rural Affairs;

(b) in the case of the Assembly, the library of the Assembly in Cardiff; and

(c) in the case of the Agency, its principal office and its principal regional offices.

(4) In this regulation, 'the deposited map' means the map and related information recorded on the CD-ROM which is—

(a) entitled 'River Basin Districts (England and Wales) 2003'; and

(b) deposited in the principal library of the Department for Environment, Food and Rural Affairs.

Characterisation of river basin districts

5.—(1) The Agency must in accordance with Annex II to the Directive (characterisation, etc. of waters) by 22nd December 2004—

(a) carry out an analysis of the characteristics of each river basin district; and

(b) conduct a review of the impact of human activity on the status of surface water and groundwater in each river basin district.

(2) The results of the work required by paragraph (1) must be periodically reviewed and updated by the Agency, initially by 22nd December 2013 and thereafter by each sixth anniversary of that date.

Economic analysis of water use in river basin districts

6.—(1) The appropriate authority must ensure that an economic analysis of water use in each river basin district is carried out by 22nd December 2004 in accordance with Annex III to the Directive (economic analysis).

(2) The appropriate authority must ensure that the analysis required by paragraph (1) is periodically reviewed and updated, initially by 22nd December 2013 and thereafter by each sixth anniversary of that date.

Bodies of water used for the abstraction of drinking water

7.—(1) The Agency must identify any bodies of water within each river basin district which—

(a) are used for the abstraction of water intended for human consumption and either—

(i) provide more than 10 cubic metres of such water per day as an average; or

(ii) serve more than 50 persons; or

(b) are intended to be used for the abstraction of water intended for human consumption to the extent referred to in sub-paragraph (a)(i) or (ii).

(2) In this regulation, 'water intended for human consumption' has the same meaning as in Council Directive 80/778/EC of 15th July 1980 relating to the quality of water intended for human consumption, as amended.

Register of protected areas

8.—(1) The Agency must for each river basin district—

(a) by 22nd December 2004 prepare, and

(b) thereafter keep under review and up to date, a register of the protected areas lying (whether wholly or partly) within the district.

(2) In this regulation, 'protected area' means—

(a) a body of water which has been identified under regulation 7; and

(b) the areas and bodies of water for the time being designated or otherwise identified as requiring special protection under any Community instrument providing for the protection of surface water and groundwater or for the conservation of habitats or species directly depending on water, or any enactment implementing such a Community instrument, including, in particular—

(i) areas designated for the protection of economically significant aquatic species;
(ii) bodies of water designated as recreational waters;
(iii) nutrient-sensitive areas; and
(iv) areas designated for the protection of habitats or species where the maintenance or improvement of the status of water is an important factor in the protection of the habitats or species.

Monitoring

9.—(1) The Agency must—

(a) establish programmes for monitoring water status in order to establish a coherent and comprehensive overview of water status within each river basin district; and
(b) take such other action as is necessary to give effect to the relevant monitoring provisions of the Directive.

(2) The monitoring programmes must cover—

(a) in relation to surface water—
   (i) the volume and level or rate of flow to the extent relevant to ecological and chemical status and ecological potential; and
   (ii) ecological and chemical status and ecological potential; and
(b) in relation to groundwater, chemical and quantitative status.

(3) The monitoring programmes must be made operational by 22nd December 2006.

(4) The relevant monitoring provisions of the Directive referred to in paragraph (1) are set out in the following provisions of Annex V to the Directive—

(a) points 1.3 to 1.3.6 (monitoring of ecological status, chemical status and ecological potential for surface waters);
(b) points 1.4 to 1.4.3 (classification and presentation of ecological status, chemical status and ecological potential);
(c) points 2.2 to 2.2.4 (monitoring of groundwater quantitative status);
(d) points 2.4 to 2.4.4 (monitoring of groundwater chemical status); and
(e) points 2.4.5 and 2.5 (interpretation and presentation of groundwater status).

Environmental objectives and programmes of measures

10.—(1) For the purposes of the river basin management plan for a river basin district which is required by regulation 11, the Agency must by such date as the appropriate authority may direct prepare and submit to the authority proposals for—

(a) environmental objectives for the district; and
(b) a programme of measures to be applied in order to achieve those objectives.

(2) In preparing proposals under paragraph (1), the Agency must—

(a) take account of the characterisation of, and economic analysis of water use in, the relevant river basin district (and any review of the same) carried out under regulations 5 and 6; and
(b) take such steps as it thinks fit, or the appropriate authority may direct, to—
   (i) provide opportunities for the general public and those persons likely to be interested in or affected by its proposals to participate in discussion and the exchange of information or views in relation to the preparation of those proposals;
   (ii) publicise its draft proposals to those persons; and
   (iii) consult those persons in respect of those proposals.

(3) The appropriate authority may, having considered any proposals for environmental objectives or for a programme of measures submitted to it and any representations received by the authority in relation to those proposals—

(a) approve them, or any of them, in the form submitted;
(b) approve them, or any of them, either with modifications or subject to such modifications as the authority may direct the Agency to make; or

(c) reject them, or any of them;

and, in any case falling within sub-paragraph (b) or (c), must state its reasons for doing so.

(4) Where the appropriate authority rejects any proposals, it must direct the Agency to resubmit proposals, by such time, if any, as the direction may specify with—

(a) modifications of such nature as the direction may specify; and

(b) any further modifications which the Agency considers appropriate.

(5) The appropriate authority must ensure that—

(a) for each river basin district a programme of measures is—

(i) established by 22nd December 2009;

(ii) made operational by 22nd December 2012; and

(iii) periodically reviewed and where appropriate updated, initially by 22nd December 2015 and thereafter by each sixth anniversary of that date; and

(b) in relation to a programme of measures that is updated under sub-paragraph (a)(iii), any new or revised measures are made operational within three years of that updating.

River basin management plans

11.—(1) The Agency must by such date as the appropriate authority may direct prepare and submit to the appropriate authority a river basin management plan for each river basin district.

(2) A river basin management plan must—

(a) relate to such period as the appropriate authority directs; and

(b) include the information specified in the relevant provisions of the Directive.

(3) The relevant provisions of the Directive for the purposes of this regulation are—

(a) Article 9(2) and (4) (recovery of the costs of water services);

(b) Annex II, point 1.3(vi) (exclusion of elements from the assessment of ecological status);

(c) the following provisions of Annex V—

(i) points 1.3 and 1.3.4 (confidence and precision in monitoring surface water);

(ii) point 2.4.1 (confidence and precision in monitoring groundwater); and

(iii) points 2.4.5 and 2.5 (presentation of monitoring results for groundwater); and

(d) Annex VII, Part A (elements to be covered in river basin management plans).

(4) The appropriate authority must ensure that each river basin management plan is—

(a) published by 22nd December 2009; and

(b) periodically reviewed and where appropriate updated, initially by 22nd December 2015 and thereafter by each sixth anniversary of that date.

River basin management plans: public participation

12.—(1) The Agency must in respect of the production of a river basin management plan—

(a) not less than three years before the beginning of the plan period, publish a statement of—

(i) the steps and consultation measures it is to take in connection with the preparation of the plan; and

(ii) the dates by which those steps and measures are to be taken;

(b) not less than two years before the beginning of the plan period, publish a summary of the significant water management matters which it considers arise for consideration in relation to the river basin district; and

(c) not less than one year before the beginning of the plan period, publish a draft plan.

(2) The Agency must publish any matter required by paragraph (1) to be published in such manner as the Agency considers appropriate for the purpose of bringing it to the attention of persons likely to be affected by it and must—

(a) make copies of the statement, summary or draft plan accessible to the public free of charge through its website and at its principal office and each of its principal regional offices;

(b) publish a notice—

(i) stating the fact of publication;

(ii) specifying the arrangements made for making copies of the statement, summary or draft plan available for public inspection; and

(iii) stating that any person may make representations to the Agency in relation to the statement, summary or draft plan;

(c) consult the person referred to in paragraph (4);

(d) take such steps as it thinks fit, or the appropriate authority may direct, to provide opportunities for the general public and the persons referred to in paragraph (4) to participate in discussion and the exchange of information or views in relation to the preparation of the draft plan; and

(e) invite the public and the persons referred to in paragraph (4) to make representations in relation to the draft plan.

(3) A notice required by paragraph (2)(b) must be published—

(a) in the London Gazette; and

(b) at least once in each of two successive weeks, in one or more newspapers circulating in the river basin district to which the plan relates.

(4) The persons to be consulted are—

(a) the appropriate authority;

(b) the Water Services Regulation Authority;

(c) the appropriate nature conservation bodies;

(d) every local authority any part of whose area is within the river basin district;

(e) every local planning authority any part of whose area is within the river basin district;

(f) where any part of the river basin district has been designated as a National Park, the National Park authority for that National Park;

(g) the harbour authority for each harbour in the river basin district;

(h) every navigation authority having functions in relation to any part of the river basin district;

(i) every water undertaker or sewerage undertaker any part of whose area is within the river basin district;

(j) any local fisheries committee for a sea fisheries district any part of which lies within the river basin district;

(k) such persons as appear to the Agency, in relation to the river basin district—

(i) to be representative of the interests of those carrying on any business which relies upon the water environment;

(ii) to have an interest in the protection of the water environment; or

(iii) to have an interest in the promotion of flood management; and

(l) such other persons as—

(i) the Agency thinks fit; or

(ii) the appropriate authority may direct.

(5) In this regulation—

(a) 'appropriate nature conservation bodies' means the Joint Nature Conservation Committee and—

(i) in relation to a river basin district that is wholly in England, English Nature;

(ii) in relation to a river basin district that is wholly in Wales, the Countryside Council for Wales; and

(iii) in relation to a river basin district that is partly in England and partly in Wales, English Nature and the Countryside Council for Wales;

(b) 'harbour' and 'harbour authority' have the meanings given by section 57 of the Harbours Act 1964;

(c) 'local authority' means the council of any county, county borough, district or London borough, the Common Council of the City of London or the Greater London Authority;

(d) 'local fisheries committee' and 'sea fisheries district' mean a local fisheries committee constituted, and a sea fisheries committee created, by an order under section 1 of the Sea Fisheries Regulation Act 1966;

(e) 'local planning authority' has the meaning given by section 1 of the Town and Country Planning Act 1990[12];

(f) 'navigation authority' has the meaning given by section 221(1) of the Water Resources Act 1991; and

(g) 'the plan period', in relation to a plan, means the period to which a direction under regulation 11(2)(a) requires it to relate.

(6) The Agency must take into account any representations relating to a statement, summary or draft plan published in accordance with paragraph (1) which are received by the Agency within the period of six months beginning with the date of publication or such longer period as the appropriate authority may direct.

River basin management plans: submission for approval

13.—(1) As soon as a river basin management plan is submitted to the appropriate authority, the Agency must—

(a) make copies of the plan accessible to the public free of charge through its website and at its principal office and each of its principal regional offices; and

(b) publish a notice—

(i) stating the fact of submission; and

(ii) specifying the arrangements made for making copies of the plan accessible to the public.

(2) The Agency must ensure that a plan submitted to the appropriate authority is accompanied by—

(a) a statement of the steps taken by the Agency to comply with regulation 12(1) and (so far as relating to the draft plan) regulation 12(2) to (4); and

(b) a summary of the representations referred to in regulation 12(6) and of any changes made to the plan in light of those representations.

(3) If the appropriate authority considers in relation to a plan that further action should be taken by the Agency under regulation 12(2) to (4), the appropriate authority may direct the Agency—

(a) to take such further steps under those provisions as the appropriate authority may specify in the direction; and

(b) to resubmit the plan within such period, if any, as the appropriate authority may specify in the direction.

(4) Where the appropriate authority gives a direction to the Agency under paragraph (3), it must state its reasons for doing so.

(5) This regulation applies in relation to a river basin management plan resubmitted to the appropriate authority in accordance with a direction under paragraph (3) as it applies to the plan as originally submitted, with the modification that, for the reference in paragraph (3) to regulation 12(2) to (4), there is substituted a reference to this regulation.

River basin management plans: approval

14.—(1) The appropriate authority may, having considered a river basin management plan submitted to it and any representations received by the authority in relation to that plan—

(a) approve it, in whole or in part, in the form submitted;

(b) approve it, in whole or in part, either with modifications or subject to such modifications as the appropriate authority may direct the Agency to make; or

(c) reject it;

and, in any case falling within sub-paragraph (b) or (c), must state its reasons for doing so.

(2) Where the appropriate authority rejects a plan, it must direct the Agency to resubmit the plan, by such time, if any, as the direction may specify, with—

(a) modifications of such nature as the direction may specify; and

(b) any further modifications which the Agency considers appropriate.

(3) Where the appropriate authority approves a plan, the Agency must publish the approved plan in such manner as the Agency thinks fit for the purpose of bringing the plan to the attention of the general public and of those persons likely to be interested in or affected by it and, in particular, must—

(a) make copies of the approved plan accessible to the public free of charge through its website and at its principal office and each of its principal regional offices; and

(b) publish a notice—

(i) stating that the plan has been approved; and

(ii) specifying the arrangements made for making copies of the plan accessible to the general public.

River basin management plans: review

15.—(1) The Agency must review and update each river basin management plan (including a revised river basin management plan)—

(a) by no later than six years from the date on which it was approved under regulation 14; or

(b) by such earlier date as the appropriate authority may direct.

(2) Following such a review, the Agency must prepare and submit to the appropriate authority a revised river basin management plan by such date as the appropriate authority may direct.

(3) Regulations 11(2) and (3) and 12 to 14 apply in relation to the preparation, submission and approval of a revised river basin management plan.

(4) The revised plan must include the information specified in Part B of Annex VII to the Directive (additional information for inclusion in updated river basin management plans) in addition to the matters required to be included by regulation 11(2)(b) and (3).

Supplementary plans

16.—(1) The Agency may prepare supplementary plans for the purposes of supplementing the river basin management plan for a river basin district.

(2) A plan prepared under paragraph (1) may, for example, relate to—

(a) a particular description of body of water;

(b) a particular catchment or geographical area;

(c) a particular matter relating to, or aspect of, the water environment; or

(d) a particular description of user of water resources.

(3) The Agency must, in relation to the preparation of a supplementary plan, consult such of the persons referred to in regulation 12(4) and such other persons likely to be interested in or affected by that plan as it thinks fit, and must take into account any views expressed by those consulted.

Duty to have regard to river basin management plans and supplementary plans

17. The Secretary of State, the Assembly, the Agency and each public body must, in exercising their functions so far as affecting a river basin district, have regard to—

(a) the river basin management plan for that district as approved under regulation 14; and

(b) any supplementary plan prepared under regulation 16.

Publication of information

18.—(1) The Agency must make accessible to the public at its principal office—

(a) the results of the work required by regulation 5 (characterisation of river basin districts);

(b) maps showing bodies of water identified under regulation 7 (bodies of water used for the abstraction of drinking water);

(c) the registers prepared under regulation 8 (register of protected areas);

(d) the results of the programmes established under regulation 9 (monitoring);

(e) the environmental objectives and programmes of measures proposed or approved under regulation 10 (environmental objectives and programmes of measures); and

(f) any supplementary plan prepared under regulation 16 (supplementary plans).

(2) Where the appropriate authority approves (with or without modifications) proposals made by the Agency under regulation 10 (1), the Agency must publish a notice—

(a) stating that the proposals have been approved; and

(b) specifying the arrangements made for making the approved objectives and programme of measures accessible to the public.

(3) The appropriate authority must make accessible to the public through its website and at its principal office the results of the analysis conducted under regulation 6 (economic analysis of water use in river basin districts).

Provision of information and assistance

19.—(1) A public body must, on being requested to do so by the Agency, provide the Agency with such information in its possession or under its control and such assistance as the Agency may reasonably seek in connection with the exercise of any of the Agency's functions under these Regulations.

(2) Section 202 of the Water Resources Act 1991 (information and assistance in connection with the control of pollution) shall have effect as if functions under these Regulations were functions under the water pollution provisions of that Act.

Directions and guidance to public bodies

20.—(1) Section 40 of the Environment Act 1995 (directions to the new Agencies) shall have effect as if the power in subsection (2) to give directions included a power for the appropriate authority to give directions to any public body for the purposes of giving effect to the Directive.

(2) Section 122 of the Environment Act 1995 (directions) shall apply in relation to any direction given by virtue of paragraph (1).

(3) The appropriate authority may give guidance to the Agency or to any other public body with respect to the practical implementation of the Directive, and the body to whom guidance is issued shall have regard to it.

Regulation 2(2) SCHEDULE 1

DIRECTIVE DEFINITIONS

[Editor's note: see the Water Framework Directive, Article 2, page 606.]

Regulation 3(3) SCHEDULE 2

ENACTMENTS IN RELATION TO WHICH DUTIES IN REGULATION 3 APPLY

PART I STATUTES

1. Section 2(2) of the European Communities Act 1972.
2. The Salmon and Freshwater Fisheries Act 1975.

3. Part 2 of the Food and Environment Protection Act 1985 (deposits in the sea).

4. Parts 1, 2 and 2A of the Environmental Protection Act 1990 (integrated pollution control and air pollution control by local authorities; waste on land; contaminated land).

5. Part 4 of the Water Industry Act 1991 (sewerage services).

6. Parts 2 to 5 and 7 to 9 of the Water Resources Act 1991[*21*] (water resources management; control of pollution of water resources; flood defence; general control of fisheries; land and works powers; information provisions; miscellaneous and supplemental).

7. The Environment Act 1995.

PART II SUBORDINATE INSTRUMENTS

8. The Sludge (Use in Agriculture) Regulations 1989.

9. The Surface Waters (Dangerous Substances) (Classification) Regulations 1989.

10. The Control of Pollution (Silage, Slurry and Agricultural Fuel Oil) Regulations 1991.

11. The Bathing Waters (Classification) Regulations 1991 and the National Rivers Authority (Bathing Waters) Directions 1992.

12. The Surface Waters (Dangerous Substances) (Classification) Regulations 1992.

13. The Waste Management Licensing Regulations 1994.

14. The Urban Waste Water Treatment (England and Wales) Regulations 1994.

15. The Protection of Water Against Agricultural Nitrate Pollution (England and Wales) Regulations 1996.

16. Surface Waters (Abstraction for Drinking Water) (Classification) Regulations 1996 and the Surface Waters (Abstraction for Drinking Water) Directions 1996.

17. The Surface Waters (Fishlife) (Classification) Regulations 1997 and the Surface Waters (Fishlife) Directions 1997.

18. The Surface Waters (Shellfish) (Classification) Regulations 1997 and the Surface Waters (Shellfish) Directions 1997.

19. The Surface Waters (Dangerous Substances) (Classification) Regulations 1997.

20. The Surface Waters (Dangerous Substances) (Classification) Regulations 1998.

21. Action Programme for Nitrate Vulnerable Zones (England and Wales) Regulations 1998.

22. The Groundwater Regulations 1998.

23. The Pollution Prevention and Control (England and Wales) Regulations 2000.

24. The Landfill (England and Wales) Regulations 2002.

25. The Nitrate Vulnerable Zones (Additional Designations) (England) (No. 2) Regulations 2002.

26. The Bathing Waters (Classification) (England) Regulations 2003.

27. The Urban Waste Water Treatment (England and Wales) (Amendment) Regulations 2003.

Environmental Assessment of Plans and Programmes Regulations 2004

(SI 2004, No. 1633)

PART 1 INTRODUCTORY PROVISIONS

1 Citation and commencement

These Regulations may be cited as the Environmental Assessment of Plans and Programmes Regulations 2004 and shall come into force on 20th July 2004.

2 Interpretation

(1) In these Regulations—

'consultation body' has the meaning given by regulation 4;

'England' includes the territorial waters of the United Kingdom that are not part of Northern Ireland, Scotland or Wales, and waters in any area for the time being designated under section 17(1) of the Continental Shelf Act 1964;

'the Environmental Assessment of Plans and Programmes Directive' means Directive 2001/42/EC of the European Parliament and of the Council on the assessment of the effects of certain plans and programmes on the environment;

'the Habitats Directive' means Council Directive 92/43/EEC on the conservation of natural habitats and of wild flora and fauna, as last amended by Council Directive 97/62/EC;

...

'plans and programmes' means plans and programmes, including those co-financed by the European Community, as well as any modifications to them, which—

(a) are subject to preparation or adoption by an authority at national, regional or local level; or

(b) are prepared by an authority for adoption, through a legislative procedure by Parliament or Government; and, in either case,

(c) are required by legislative, regulatory or administrative provisions; and

'responsible authority', in relation to a plan or programme, means—

(a) the authority by which or on whose behalf it is prepared; and

(b) where, at any particular time, that authority ceases to be responsible, or solely responsible, for taking steps in relation to the plan or programme, the person who, at that time, is responsible (solely or jointly with the authority) for taking those steps;

...

'Wales' has the meaning given by section 155 of the Government of Wales Act 1998.

(2) Other expressions used both in these Regulations and in the Environmental Assessment of Plans and Programmes Directive have the same meaning in these Regulations as they have in that Directive.

3 Application of Regulations

(1) With the exception of regulations 14 and 15, these Regulations apply as follows.

(2) These Regulations apply to a plan or programme relating—

(a) solely to the whole or any part of England; or

(b) to England (whether as to the whole or part) and any other part of the United Kingdom.

...

(4) These Regulations do not apply to a plan or programme relating solely—

(a)–(b) ...

(c) to the whole or any part of Wales.

4 Consultation bodies

(1) Subject to paragraph (5), in relation to every plan or programme to which these Regulations apply, each of the following bodies shall be a consultation body—

(a) the Countryside Agency;

(b) the Historic Buildings and Monuments Commission for England (English Heritage);

(c) English Nature; and

(d) the Environment Agency,

but where paragraph (2), (3) or (4) applies, the functions of those bodies under these Regulations shall be exercisable only in relation to so much of the plan or programme as relates to England.

...

(4) In relation to such part of a plan or programme to which these Regulations apply as relates to Wales, each of the following shall be a consultation body for the purposes of these Regulations—

(a) the National Assembly for Wales; and

(b) the Countryside Council for Wales.

(5) Where a body mentioned in paragraph (1) is at any time the responsible authority as regards a plan or programme, it shall not at that time exercise the functions under these Regulations of a consultation body in relation to that plan or programme; and references to the consultation bodies in the following provisions of these Regulations shall be construed accordingly.

PART 2 ENVIRONMENTAL ASSESSMENT FOR PLANS AND PROGRAMMES

5 Environmental assessment for plans and programmes: first formal preparatory act on or after 21st July 2004

(1) Subject to paragraphs (5) and (6) and regulation 7, where—

(a) the first formal preparatory act of a plan or programme is on or after 21st July 2004; and

(b) the plan or programme is of the description set out in either paragraph (2) or paragraph (3),

the responsible authority shall carry out, or secure the carrying out of, an environmental assessment, in accordance with Part 3 of these Regulations, during the preparation of that plan or programme and before its adoption or submission to the legislative procedure.

(2) The description is a plan or programme which—

(a) is prepared for agriculture, forestry, fisheries, energy, industry, transport, waste management, water management, telecommunications, tourism, town and country planning or land use, and

(b) sets the framework for future development consent of projects listed in Annex I or II to Council Directive 85/337/EEC on the assessment of the effects of certain public and private projects on the environment, as amended by Council Directive 97/11/EC.

(3) The description is a plan or programme which, in view of the likely effect on sites, has been determined to require an assessment pursuant to Article 6 or 7 of the Habitats Directive.

(4) Subject to paragraph (5) and regulation 7, where—

(a) the first formal preparatory act of a plan or programme, other than a plan or programme of the description set out in paragraph (2) or (3), is on or after 21st July 2004;

(b) the plan or programme sets the framework for future development consent of projects; and

(c) the plan or programme is the subject of a determination under regulation 9(1) or a direction under regulation 10(3) that it is likely to have significant environmental effects,

the responsible authority shall carry out, or secure the carrying out of, an environmental assessment, in accordance with Part 3 of these Regulations, during the preparation of that plan or programme and before its adoption or submission to the legislative procedure.

(5) Nothing in paragraph (1) or (4) requires the carrying out of an environmental assessment for—

(a) a plan or programme the sole purpose of which is to serve national defence or civil emergency;

(b) a financial or budget plan or programme; or

(c) a plan or programme co-financed under—

(i) the 2000–2006 programming period for Council Regulation (EC) No 1260/1999; or

(ii) the 2000–2006 or 2000–2007 programming period for Council Regulation (EC) No 1257/1999.

(6) An environmental assessment need not be carried out—

(a) for a plan or programme of the description set out in paragraph (2) or (3) which determines the use of a small area at local level; or

(b) for a minor modification to a plan or programme of the description set out in either of those paragraphs,

unless it has been determined under regulation 9(1) that the plan, programme or modification, as the case may be, is likely to have significant environmental effects, or it is the subject of a direction under regulation 10(3).

6 Environmental assessment for plans and programmes: first formal preparatory act before 21st July 2004

(1) Subject to paragraph (2) and regulation 7, where—

(a) a plan or programme of which the first formal preparatory act is before 21st July 2004 has not been adopted or submitted to the legislative procedure for adoption before 22nd July 2006; and

(b) the plan or programme is such that, had the first act in its preparation occurred on 21st July 2004, the plan or programme would have required an environmental assessment by virtue of regulation 5(1); or

(c) the responsible authority is of the opinion that, if a determination under regulation 9(1) in respect of the plan or programme had been made on 21st July 2004, it would have determined that the plan or programme was likely to have significant environmental effects,

the responsible authority shall carry out, or secure the carrying out of, an environmental assessment, in accordance with Part 3 of these Regulations, during the preparation of that plan or programme and before its adoption or submission to the legislative procedure.

(2) Nothing in paragraph (1) shall require the environmental assessment of a particular plan or programme if the responsible authority—

(a) decides that such assessment is not feasible; and

(b) informs the public of its decision.

7 Environmental assessment for plans and programmes co-financed by the European Community

The environmental assessment required by any provision of this Part for a plan or programme co-financed by the European Community shall be carried out by the responsible authority in conformity with the specific provisions in relevant Community legislation.

8 Restriction on adoption or submission of plans, programmes and modifications

(1) A plan, programme or modification in respect of which a determination under regulation 9(1) is required shall not be adopted or submitted to the legislative procedure for the purpose of its adoption—

(a) where an environmental assessment is required in consequence of the determination or of a direction under regulation 10(3), before the requirements of paragraph (3) below have been met;

(b) in any other case, before the determination has been made under regulation 9(1).

(2) A plan or programme for which an environmental assessment is required by any provision of this Part shall not be adopted or submitted to the legislative procedure for the purpose of its adoption before—

(a) if it is a plan or programme co-financed by the European Community, the environmental assessment has been carried out as mentioned in regulation 7;

(b) in any other case, the requirements of paragraph (3) below, and such requirements of Part 3 as apply in relation to the plan or programme, have been met.

(3) The requirements of this paragraph are that account shall be taken of—

(a) the environmental report for the plan or programme;

(b) opinions expressed in response to the invitation referred to in regulation 13(2)(d);
(c) opinions expressed in response to action taken by the responsible authority in accordance with regulation 13(4); and
(d) the outcome of any consultations under regulation 14(4).

9 Determinations of the responsible authority

(1) The responsible authority shall determine whether or not a plan, programme or modification of a description referred to in—

(a) paragraph (4)(a) and (b) of regulation 5;
(b) paragraph (6)(a) of that regulation; or
(c) paragraph (6)(b) of that regulation,

is likely to have significant environmental effects.

(2) Before making a determination under paragraph (1) the responsible authority shall—

(a) take into account the criteria specified in Schedule 1 to these Regulations; and
(b) consult the consultation bodies.

(3) Where the responsible authority determines that the plan, programme or modification is unlikely to have significant environmental effects (and, accordingly, does not require an environmental assessment), it shall prepare a statement of its reasons for the determination.

10 Powers of the Secretary of State

(1) The Secretary of State may at any time require the responsible authority to send him a copy of—

(a) any determination under paragraph (1) of regulation 9 with respect to the plan, programme or modification;
(b) the plan, programme or modification to which the determination relates; and
(c) where paragraph (3) of that regulation applies, the statement prepared in accordance with that paragraph.

(2) The responsible authority shall comply with a requirement under paragraph (1) within 7 days.

(3) The Secretary of State may direct that a plan, programme or modification is likely to have significant environmental effects (whether or not a copy of it has been sent to him in response to a requirement under paragraph (1)).

(4) Before giving a direction under paragraph (3) the Secretary of State shall—

(a) take into account the criteria specified in Schedule 1 to these Regulations; and
(b) consult the consultation bodies.

(5) The Secretary of State shall, as soon as reasonably practicable after the giving of the direction, send to the responsible authority and to each consultation body—

(a) a copy of the direction; and
(b) a statement of his reasons for giving the direction.

(6) In relation to a plan, programme or modification in respect of which a direction has been given—

(a) any determination under regulation 9(1) with respect to the plan, programme or modification shall cease to have effect on the giving of the direction; and.
(b) if no determination has been made under regulation 9(1) with respect to the plan, programme or modification, the responsible authority shall cease to be under any duty imposed by that regulation.

11 Publicity for determinations and directions

(1) Within 28 days of making a determination under regulation 9(1), the responsible authority shall send to each consultation body—

(a) a copy of the determination; and
(b) where the responsible authority has determined that the plan or programme does not require an environmental assessment, a statement of its reasons for the determination.

(2) The responsible authority shall—

(a) keep a copy of the determination, and any accompanying statement of reasons, available at its principal office for inspection by the public at all reasonable times and free of charge; and

(b) within 28 days of the making of the determination, take such steps as it considers appropriate to bring to the attention of the public—

(i) the title of the plan, programme or modification to which the determination relates;

(ii) that the responsible authority has determined that the plan, programme or modification is or is not likely to have significant environmental effects (as the case may be) and, accordingly, that an environmental assessment is or is not required in respect of the plan, programme or modification; and

(iii) the address (which may include a website) at which a copy of the determination and any accompanying statement of reasons may be inspected or from which a copy may be obtained.

(3) Where the responsible authority receives a direction under regulation 10(3), it shall—

(a) keep a copy of the direction and of the Secretary of State's statement of his reasons for giving it available at its principal office for inspection by the public at all reasonable times and free of charge; and

(b) within 28 days of the receipt of such a direction, take such steps as it considers appropriate to bring to the attention of the public—

(i) the title of the plan, programme or modification to which the direction relates;

(ii) that the Secretary of State has directed that the plan, programme or modification is likely to have significant environmental effects and, accordingly, that an environmental assessment is required in respect of the plan, programme or modification; and

(iii) the address (which may include a website) at which a copy of the direction and of the Secretary of State's statement of his reasons for giving it may be inspected or from which a copy may be obtained.

(4) The responsible authority shall provide a copy of any document referred to in paragraph (2)(b)(iii) or (3)(b)(iii) free of charge.

PART 3 ENVIRONMENTAL REPORTS AND CONSULTATION PROCEDURES

12 Preparation of environmental report

(1) Where an environmental assessment is required by any provision of Part 2 of these Regulations, the responsible authority shall prepare, or secure the preparation of, an environmental report in accordance with paragraphs (2) and (3) of this regulation.

(2) The report shall identify, describe and evaluate the likely significant effects on the environment of—

(a) implementing the plan or programme; and

(b) reasonable alternatives taking into account the objectives and the geographical scope of the plan or programme.

(3) The report shall include such of the information referred to in Schedule 2 to these Regulations as may reasonably be required, taking account of—

(a) current knowledge and methods of assessment;

(b) the contents and level of detail in the plan or programme;

(c) the stage of the plan or programme in the decision-making process; and

(d) the extent to which certain matters are more appropriately assessed at different levels in that process in order to avoid duplication of the assessment.

(4) Information referred to in Schedule 2 may be provided by reference to relevant information obtained at other levels of decision-making or through other Community legislation.

(5) When deciding on the scope and level of detail of the information that must be included in the report, the responsible authority shall consult the consultation bodies.

(6) Where a consultation body wishes to respond to a consultation under paragraph (5), it shall do so within the period of 5 weeks beginning with the date on which it receives the responsible authority's invitation to engage in the consultation.

13 Consultation procedures

(1) Every draft plan or programme for which an environmental report has been prepared in accordance with regulation 12 and its accompanying environmental report ('the relevant documents') shall be made available for the purposes of consultation in accordance with the following provisions of this regulation.

(2) As soon as reasonably practicable after the preparation of the relevant documents, the responsible authority shall—

(a) send a copy of those documents to each consultation body;

(b) take such steps as it considers appropriate to bring the preparation of the relevant documents to the attention of the persons who, in the authority's opinion, are affected or likely to be affected by, or have an interest in the decisions involved in the assessment and adoption of the plan or programme concerned, required under the Environmental Assessment of Plans and Programmes Directive ('the public consultees');

(c) inform the public consultees of the address (which may include a website) at which a copy of the relevant documents may be viewed, or from which a copy may be obtained; and

(d) invite the consultation bodies and the public consultees to express their opinion on the relevant documents, specifying the address to which, and the period within which, opinions must be sent.

(3) The period referred to in paragraph (2)(d) must be of such length as will ensure that the consultation bodies and the public consultees are given an effective opportunity to express their opinion on the relevant documents.

(4) The responsible authority shall keep a copy of the relevant documents available at its principal office for inspection by the public at all reasonable times and free of charge.

(5) Nothing in paragraph (2)(c) shall require the responsible authority to provide copies free of charge; but where a charge is made, it shall be of a reasonable amount.

14 Transboundary consultations

(1) Where a responsible authority, other than the Secretary of State, is of the opinion that a plan or programme for which it is the responsible authority is likely to have significant effects on the environment of another Member State, it shall, as soon as reasonably practicable after forming that opinion—

(a) notify the Secretary of State of its opinion and of the reasons for it; and

(b) supply the Secretary of State with a copy of the plan or programme concerned, and of the accompanying environmental report.

(2) Where the Secretary of State has been notified under paragraph (1)(a), the responsible authority shall, within such period as the Secretary of State may specify by notice in writing to the authority, provide the Secretary of State with such other information about the plan or programme or its accompanying environmental report as he may reasonably require.

(3) Where—

(a) the Secretary of State, whether in consequence of a notice under paragraph (1)(a) or otherwise, considers that the implementation of a plan or programme in any part of the United Kingdom is likely to have significant effects on the environment of another Member State); or

(b) a Member State that is likely to be significantly affected by the implementation of a plan or programme so requests,

the Secretary of State shall, before the adoption of the plan or programme or its submission to the legislative procedure for adoption, forward a copy of it and of its accompanying environmental report to the Member State concerned.

(4) Where the Secretary of State receives from a Member State an indication that it wishes to enter into consultations before the adoption, or submission to the legislative procedure for adoption, of a plan or programme forwarded to it in accordance with paragraph (3), the Secretary of State shall—

(a) agree with the Member State—

(i) detailed arrangements to ensure that the authorities referred to in paragraph 3 of Article 6 of the Environmental Assessment of Plans and Programmes Directive and the public referred to in paragraph 4 of that Article in the Member State likely to be significantly affected are informed and given an opportunity to forward their opinion within a reasonable time; and

(ii) a reasonable time for the duration of the consultations;

(b) enter into consultations with the Member State concerning—

(i) the likely transboundary environmental effects of implementing the plan or programme; and

(ii) the measures envisaged to reduce or eliminate such effects; and

(c) where he is not the responsible authority, direct the responsible authority that it shall not adopt the plan or programme, or submit it to the legislative procedure for adoption, until the consultations with the Member State have been concluded.

(5) Where consultations take place pursuant to paragraph (4), the Secretary of State shall—

(a) as soon as reasonably practicable after those consultations begin, notify the consultation bodies of that fact; and

(b) notify the consultation bodies and, where he is not the responsible authority, the responsible authority, of the outcome of the consultations.

15 Plans and programmes of other Member States

(1) This regulation applies where the Secretary of State receives from a Member State (whether or not in response to a request made by the United Kingdom in that behalf under the Environmental Assessment of Plans and Programmes Directive) a copy of a draft plan or programme—

(a) that is being prepared in relation to any part of that Member State; and

(b) whose implementation is likely to have significant effects on the environment of any part of the United Kingdom.

(2) The Secretary of State shall indicate to the Member State whether, before the adoption of the plan or programme or its submission to the legislative procedure for adoption, the United Kingdom wishes to enter into consultations in respect of that plan or programme concerning—

(a) the likely transboundary environmental effects of implementing the plan or programme; and

(b) the measures envisaged to reduce or eliminate such effects.

(3) Where the Secretary of State so indicates, he shall agree with the Member State concerned—

(a) detailed arrangements to ensure that the consultation bodies and the public in the United Kingdom or, as the case may be, the part of the United Kingdom that is likely to be significantly affected by the implementation of the plan or programme, are informed and given an opportunity to forward their opinion within a reasonable time; and

(b) a reasonable time for the duration of the consultations.

(4) Where such consultations take place under this regulation, the Secretary of State shall—

(a) inform the consultation bodies of the receipt of the draft plan or programme;
(b) provide them with a copy of the draft plan or programme and the relevant environmental report provided under Article 7.1 of the Environmental Assessment of Plans and Programmes Directive or specify the address (which may include a website) at which those documents may be inspected;
(c) take such steps as he considers appropriate to bring the receipt of the draft plan or programme to the attention of such persons as, in his opinion, are affected or likely to be affected by, or have an interest in the decisions involved in the assessment and adoption of the plan or programme concerned, required under the Environmental Assessment of Plans and Programmes Directive ('the transboundary consultees');
(d) inform the transboundary consultees of the address (which may include a website) at which a copy of the draft plan or programme and the relevant environmental report provided under Article 7.1 of the Environmental Assessment of Plans and Programmes Directive may be inspected, or from which a copy may be obtained; and
(e) invite the consultation bodies and the transboundary consultees to forward to him their opinions within such period as he may specify.

(5) The period specified under paragraph (4)(e) shall end not later than 28 days before the end of the period that the Secretary of State has agreed with the Member State concerned, pursuant to paragraph (3)(b), as reasonable for the duration of their consultations.

(6) Nothing in paragraph (4)(d) shall require the Secretary of State to provide copies free of charge; but where a charge is made, it shall be of a reasonable amount.

PART 4 POST-ADOPTION PROCEDURES

16 Information as to adoption of plan or programme

(1) As soon as reasonably practicable after the adoption of a plan or programme for which an environmental assessment has been carried out under these Regulations, the responsible authority shall—

(a) make a copy of the plan or programme and its accompanying environmental report available at its principal office for inspection by the public at all reasonable times and free of charge; and
(b) take such steps as it considers appropriate to bring to the attention of the public—
    (i) the title of the plan or programme;
    (ii) the date on which it was adopted;
    (iii) the address (which may include a website) at which a copy of it and of its accompanying environmental report, and of a statement containing the particulars specified in paragraph (4), may be viewed or from which a copy may be obtained;
    (iv) the times at which inspection may be made; and
    (v) that inspection may be made free of charge.

(2) As soon as reasonably practicable after the adoption of a plan or programme—

(a) the responsible authority shall inform—
    (i) the consultation bodies;
    (ii) the persons who, in relation to the plan or programme, were public consultees for the purposes of regulation 13; and
    (iii) where the responsible authority is not the Secretary of State, the Secretary of State; and
(b) the Secretary of State shall inform the Member State with which consultations in relation to the plan or programme have taken place under regulation 14(4),

of the matters referred to in paragraph (3).

(3) The matters are—

(a) that the plan or programme has been adopted;

(b) the date on which it was adopted; and

(c) the address (which may include a website) at which a copy of—

(i) the plan or programme, as adopted,

(ii) its accompanying environmental report, and

(iii) a statement containing the particulars specified in paragraph (4),

may be viewed, or from which a copy may be obtained.

(4) The particulars referred to in paragraphs (1)(b)(iii) and (3)(c)(iii) are—

(a) how environmental considerations have been integrated into the plan or programme;

(b) how the environmental report has been taken into account;

(c) how opinions expressed in response to—

(i) the invitation referred to in regulation 13(2)(d);

(ii) action taken by the responsible authority in accordance with regulation 13(4),

have been taken into account;

(d) how the results of any consultations entered into under regulation 14(4) have been taken into account;

(e) the reasons for choosing the plan or programme as adopted, in the light of the other reasonable alternatives dealt with; and

(f) the measures that are to be taken to monitor the significant environmental effects of the implementation of the plan or programme.

17 Monitoring of implementation of plans and programmes

(1) The responsible authority shall monitor the significant environmental effects of the implementation of each plan or programme with the purpose of identifying unforeseen adverse effects at an early stage and being able to undertake appropriate remedial action.

(2) The responsible authority's monitoring arrangements may comprise or include arrangements established otherwise than for the express purpose of complying with paragraph (1).

Regulations 9(2)(a) and 10(4)(a) SCHEDULE 1

CRITERIA FOR DETERMINING THE LIKELY SIGNIFICANCE OF EFFECTS ON THE ENVIRONMENT

1 The characteristics of plans and programmes, having regard, in particular, to—

(a) the degree to which the plan or programme sets a framework for projects and other activities, either with regard to the location, nature, size and operating conditions or by allocating resources;

(b) the degree to which the plan or programme influences other plans and programmes including those in a hierarchy;

(c) the relevance of the plan or programme for the integration of environmental considerations in particular with a view to promoting sustainable development;

(d) environmental problems relevant to the plan or programme; and

(e) the relevance of the plan or programme for the implementation of Community legislation on the environment (for example, plans and programmes linked to waste management or water protection).

2 Characteristics of the effects and of the area likely to be affected, having regard, in particular, to—

(a) the probability, duration, frequency and reversibility of the effects;
(b) the cumulative nature of the effects;
(c) the transboundary nature of the effects;
(d) the risks to human health or the environment (for example, due to accidents);
(e) the magnitude and spatial extent of the effects (geographical area and size of the population likely to be affected);
(f) the value and vulnerability of the area likely to be affected due to—
  (i) special natural characteristics or cultural heritage;
  (ii) exceeded environmental quality standards or limit values; or
  (iii) intensive land-use; and
(g) the effects on areas or landscapes which have a recognised national, Community or international protection status.

Regulation 12(3) SCHEDULE 2

INFORMATION FOR ENVIRONMENTAL REPORTS

1 An outline of the contents and main objectives of the plan or programme, and of its relationship with other relevant plans and programmes.

2 The relevant aspects of the current state of the environment and the likely evolution thereof without implementation of the plan or programme.

3 The environmental characteristics of areas likely to be significantly affected.

4 Any existing environmental problems which are relevant to the plan or programme including, in particular, those relating to any areas of a particular environmental importance, such as areas designated pursuant to Council Directive 79/409/EEC on the conservation of wild birds and the Habitats Directive.

5 The environmental protection objectives, established at international, Community or Member State level, which are relevant to the plan or programme and the way those objectives and any environmental considerations have been taken into account during its preparation.

6 The likely significant effects on the environment, including short, medium and long-term effects, permanent and temporary effects, positive and negative effects, and secondary, cumulative and synergistic effects, on issues such as—

(a) biodiversity;
(b) population;
(c) human health;
(d) fauna;
(e) flora;
(f) soil;
(g) water;
(h) air;
(i) climatic factors;
(j) material assets;
(k) cultural heritage, including architectural and archaeological heritage;
(l) landscape; and
(m) the inter-relationship between the issues referred to in sub-paragraphs (a) to (l).

7 The measures envisaged to prevent, reduce and as fully as possible offset any significant adverse effects on the environment of implementing the plan or programme.

8 An outline of the reasons for selecting the alternatives dealt with, and a description of how the assessment was undertaken including any difficulties (such as technical deficiencies or lack of know-how) encountered in compiling the required information.

9 A description of the measures envisaged concerning monitoring in accordance with regulation 17.

10 A non-technical summary of the information provided under paragraphs 1 to 9.

Environmental Information Regulations 2004

(SI 2004, No. 3391)

1 Citation and commencement

These Regulations may be cited as the Environmental Information Regulations 2004 and shall come into force on 1st January 2005.

2 Interpretation

(1) In these Regulations—

'the Act' means the Freedom of Information Act 2000;

'applicant', in relation to a request for environmental information, means the person who made the request;

'appropriate records authority', in relation to a transferred public record, has the same meaning as in section 15(5) of the Act;

'the Commissioner' means the Information Commissioner;

'the Directive' means Council Directive 2003/4/EC on public access to environmental information and repealing Council Directive 90/313/EEC;

'environmental information' has the same meaning as in Article 2(1) of the Directive, namely any information in written, visual, aural, electronic or any other material form on—

(a) the state of the elements of the environment, such as air and atmosphere, water, soil, land, landscape and natural sites including wetlands, coastal and marine areas, biological diversity and its components, including genetically modified organisms, and the interaction among these elements;

(b) factors, such as substances, energy, noise, radiation or waste, including radioactive waste, emissions, discharges and other releases into the environment, affecting or likely to affect the elements of the environment referred to in (a);

(c) measures (including administrative measures), such as policies, legislation, plans, programmes, environmental agreements, and activities affecting or likely to affect the elements and factors referred to in (a) and (b) as well as measures or activities designed to protect those elements;

(d) reports on the implementation of environmental legislation;

(e) cost-benefit and other economic analyses and assumptions used within the framework of the measures and activities referred to in (c); and

(f) the state of human health and safety, including the contamination of the food chain, where relevant, conditions of human life, cultural sites and built structures inasmuch as they are or may be affected by the state of the elements of the environment referred to in (a) or, through those elements, by any of the matters referred to in (b) and (c);

'historical record' has the same meaning as in section 62(1) of the Act;

'public authority' has the meaning given by paragraph (2);

'public record' has the same meaning as in section 84 of the Act;

'responsible authority', in relation to a transferred public record, has the same meaning as in section 15(5) of the Act;

. . .

'transferred public record' has the same meaning as in section 15(4) of the Act; and 'working day' has the same meaning as in section 10(6) of the Act.

(2) Subject to paragraph (3), 'public authority' means—

(a) government departments;

(b) any other public authority as defined in section 3(1) of the Act, disregarding for this purpose the exceptions in paragraph 6 of Schedule 1 to the Act, but excluding—

(i) any body or office-holder listed in Schedule 1 to the Act only in relation to information of a specified description; or

(ii) any person designated by Order under section 5 of the Act;

(c) any other body or other person, that carries out functions of public administration; or

(d) any other body or other person, that is under the control of a person falling within sub-paragraphs (a), (b) or (c) and—

(i) has public responsibilities relating to the environment;

(ii) exercises functions of a public nature relating to the environment; or

(iii) provides public services relating to the environment.

(3) Except as provided by regulation 12(10) a Scottish public authority is not a 'public authority' for the purpose of these Regulations.

(4) The following expressions have the same meaning in these Regulations as they have in the Date Protection Act 1998 namely—

(a) 'data' except that for the purposes of regulation 12(3) and regulation 13 a public authority referred to in the definition of data in paragraph (e) of section 1(1) of that Act means a public authority within the meaning of these Regulations;

(b) 'the data protection principles';

(c) 'data subject'; and

(d) 'personal data'.

(5) Except as provided by this regulation, expressions in these Regulations which appear in the Directive have the same meaning in these Regulations as they have in the Directive.

3 Application

(1) Subject to paragraphs (3) and (4), these Regulations apply to public authorities.

(2) For the purposes of these Regulations, environmental information is held by a public authority if the information—

(a) is in the authority's possession and has been produced or received by the authority; or

(b) is held by another person on behalf of the authority.

(3) These Regulations shall not apply to any public authority to the extent that it is acting in a judicial or legislative capacity.

(4) These Regulations shall not apply to either House of Parliament to the extent required for the purpose of avoiding an infringement of the privileges of either House.

(5) Each government department is to be treated as a person separate from any other government department for the purposes of Parts 2, 4 and 5 of these Regulations.

PART 2 ACCESS TO ENVIRONMENTAL INFORMATION HELD BY PUBLIC AUTHORITIES

4 Dissemination of environmental information

(1) Subject to paragraph (3), a public authority shall in respect of environmental information that it holds—

(a) progressively make the information available to the public by electronic means which are easily accessible; and

(b) take reasonable steps to organize the information relevant to its functions with a view to the active and systematic dissemination to the public of the information.

(2) For the purposes of paragraph (1) the use of electronic means to make information available or to organize information shall not be required in relation to information collected before 1st January 2005 in non-electronic form.

(3) Paragraph (1) shall not extend to making available or disseminating information which a public authority would be entitled to refuse to disclose under regulation 12.

(4) The information under paragraph (1) shall include at least—

(a) the information referred to in Article 7(2) of the Directive; and

(b) facts and analyses of facts which the public authority considers relevant and important in framing major environmental policy proposals.

5 Duty to make available environmental information on request

(1) Subject to paragraph (3) and in accordance with paragraphs (2), (4), (5) and (6) and the remaining provisions of this Part and Part 3 of these Regulations, a public authority that holds environmental information shall make it available on request.

(2) Information shall be made available under paragraph (1) as soon as possible and no later than 20 working days after the date of receipt of the request.

(3) To the extent that the information requested includes personal data of which the applicant is the data subject, paragraph (1) shall not apply to those personal data.

(4) For the purposes of paragraph (1), where the information made available is compiled by or on behalf of the public authority it shall be up to date, accurate and comparable, so far as the public authority reasonably believes.

(5) Where a public authority makes available information in paragraph (b) of the definition of environmental information, and the applicant so requests, the public authority shall, insofar as it is able to do so, either inform the applicant of the place where information, if available, can be found on the measurement procedures, including methods of analysis, sampling and pre-treatment of samples, used in compiling the information, or refer the applicant to a standardised procedure used.

(6) Any enactment or rule of law that would prevent the disclosure of information in accordance with these Regulations shall not apply.

6 Form and format of information

(1) Where an applicant requests that the information be made available in a particular form or format, a public authority shall make it so available, unless—

(a) it is reasonable for it to make the information available in another form or format; or

(b) the information is already publicly available and easily accessible to the applicant in another form or format.

(2) If the information is not made available in the form or format requested, the public authority shall—

(a) explain the reason for its decision as soon as possible and no later than 20 working days after the date of receipt of the request for the information;

(b) provide the explanation in writing if the applicant so requests; and

(c) inform the applicant of the provisions of regulation 11 and of the enforcement and appeal provisions of the Act applied by regulation 18.

7 Extension of time

(1) Where a request is made under regulation 5, the public authority may extend the period of 20 working days referred to in the provisions in paragraph (2) to 40 working days if it reasonably believes that the complexity and volume of the information requested means that it is impracticable either to comply with the request within the earlier period or to make a decision to refuse to do so.

(2) The provisions referred to in paragraph (1) are—

(a) regulation 5(2);

(b) regulation 6(2)(a); and

(c) regulation 14(2).

(3) Where paragraph (1) applies the public authority shall notify the applicant accordingly as soon as possible and no later than 20 working days after the date of receipt of the request.

8 Charging

(1) Subject to paragraphs (2) to (8), where a public authority makes environmental information available in accordance with regulation 5(1) the authority may charge the applicant for making the information available.

(2) A public authority shall not make any charge for allowing an applicant—

(a) to access any public registers or lists of environmental information held by the public authority; or

(b) to examine the information requested at the place which the public authority makes available for that examination.

(3) A charge under paragraph (1) shall not exceed an amount which the public authority is satisfied is a reasonable amount.

(4) A public authority may require advance payment of a charge for making environmental information available and if it does it shall, no later than 20 working days after the date of receipt of the request for the information, notify the applicant of this requirement and of the amount of the advance payment.

(5) Where a public authority has notified an applicant under paragraph (4) that advance payment is required, the public authority is not required—

(a) to make available the information requested; or

(b) to comply with regulations 6 or 14,

unless the charge is paid no later than 60 working days after the date on which it gave the notification.

(6) The period beginning with the day on which the notification of a requirement for an advance payment is made and ending on the day on which that payment is received by the public authority is to be disregarded for the purposes of determining the period of 20 working days referred to in the provisions in paragraph (7), including any extension to those periods under regulation 7(1).

(7) The provisions referred to in paragraph (6) are—

(a) regulation 5(2);

(b) regulation 6(2)(a); and

(c) regulation 14(2).

(8) A public authority shall publish and make available to applicants—

(a) a schedule of its charges; and

(b) information on the circumstances in which a charge may be made or waived.

9 Advice and assistance

(1) A public authority shall provide advice and assistance, so far as it would be reasonable to expect the authority to do so, to applicants and prospective applicants.

(2) Where a public authority decides that an applicant has formulated a request in too general a manner, it shall--

(a) ask the applicant as soon as possible and in any event no later than 20 working days after the date of receipt of the request, to provide more particulars in relation to the request; and

(b) assist the applicant in providing those particulars.

(3) Where a code of practice has been made under regulation 16, and to the extent that a public authority conforms to that code in relation to the provision of advice and assistance in a particular case, it shall be taken to have complied with paragraph (1) in relation to that case.

(4) Where paragraph (2) applies, in respect of the provisions in paragraph (5), the date on which the further particulars are received by the public authority shall be treated as the date after which the period of 20 working days referred to in those provisions shall be calculated.

(5) The provisions referred to in paragraph (4) are—

(a) regulation 5(2);

(b) regulation 6(2)(a); and
(c) regulation 14(2).

10 Transfer of a request

(1) Where a public authority that receives a request for environmental information does not hold the information requested but believes that another public authority or a Scottish public authority holds the information, the public authority shall either—

(a) transfer the request to the other public authority or Scottish public authority; or
(b) supply the applicant with the name and address of that authority,

and inform the applicant accordingly with the refusal sent under regulation 14(1).

(2) Where a request is transferred to a public authority, for the purposes of the provisions referred to in paragraph (3) the request is received by that public authority on the date on which it receives the transferred request.

(3) The provisions referred to in paragraph (2) are—

(a) regulation 5(2);
(b) regulation 6(2)(a); and
(c) regulation 14(2).

11 Representations and reconsideration

(1) Subject to paragraph (2), an applicant may make representations to a public authority in relation to the applicant's request for environmental information if it appears to the applicant that the authority has failed to comply with a requirement of these Regulations in relation to the request.

(2) Representations under paragraph (1) shall be made in writing to the public authority no later than 40 working days after the date on which the applicant believes that the public authority has failed to comply with the requirement.

(3) The public authority shall on receipt of the representations and free of charge—

(a) consider them and any supporting evidence produced by the applicant; and
(b) decide if it has complied with the requirement.

(4) A public authority shall notify the applicant of its decision under paragraph (3) as soon as possible and no later than 40 working days after the date of receipt of the representations.

(5) Where the public authority decides that it has failed to comply with these Regulations in relation to the request, the notification under paragraph (4) shall include a statement of—

(a) the failure to comply;
(b) the action the authority has decided to take to comply with the requirement; and
(c) the period within which that action is to be taken.

PART 3 EXCEPTIONS TO THE DUTY TO DISCLOSE ENVIRONMENTAL INFORMATION

12 Exceptions to the duty to disclose environmental information

(1) Subject to paragraphs (2), (3) and (9), a public authority may refuse to disclose environmental information requested if—

(a) an exception to disclosure applies under paragraphs (4) or (5); and
(b) in all the circumstances of the case, the public interest in maintaining the exception outweighs the public interest in disclosing the information.

(2) A public authority shall apply a presumption in favour of disclosure.

(3) To the extent that the information requested includes personal data of which the applicant is not the data subject, the personal data shall not be disclosed otherwise than in accordance with regulation 13.

(4) For the purposes of paragraph (1)(a), a public authority may refuse to disclose information to the extent that—

(a) it does not hold that information when an applicant's request is received;

(b) the request for information is manifestly unreasonable;
(c) the request for information is formulated in too general a manner and the public authority has complied with regulation 9;
(d) the request relates to material which is still in the course of completion, to unfinished documents or to incomplete data; or
(e) the request involves the disclosure of internal communications.

(5) For the purposes of paragraph (1)(a), a public authority may refuse to disclose information to the extent that its disclosure would adversely affect—

(a) international relations, defence, national security or public safety;
(b) the course of justice, the ability of a person to receive a fair trial or the ability of a public authority to conduct an inquiry of a criminal or disciplinary nature;
(c) intellectual property rights;
(d) the confidentiality of the proceedings of that or any other public authority where such confidentiality is provided by law;
(e) the confidentiality of commercial or industrial information where such confidentiality is provided by law to protect a legitimate economic interest;
(f) the interests of the person who provided the information where that person—
    (i) was not under, and could not have been put under, any legal obligation to supply it to that or any other public authority;
    (ii) did not supply it in circumstances such that that or any other public authority is entitled apart from these Regulations to disclose it; and
    (iii) has not consented to its disclosure; or
(g) the protection of the environment to which the information relates.

(6) For the purposes of paragraph (1), a public authority may respond to a request by neither confirming nor denying whether such information exists and is held by the public authority, whether or not it holds such information, if that confirmation or denial would involve the disclosure of information which would adversely affect any of the interests referred to in paragraph (5)(a) and would not be in the public interest under paragraph (1)(b).

(7) For the purposes of a response under paragraph (6), whether information exists and is held by the public authority is itself the disclosure of information.

(8) For the purposes of paragraph (4)(e), internal communications includes communications between government departments.

(9) To the extent that the environmental information to be disclosed relates to information on emissions, a public authority shall not be entitled to refuse to disclose that information under an exception referred to in paragraphs (5)(d) to (g).

(10) For the purposes of paragraphs (5)(b), (d) and (f), references to a public authority shall include references to a Scottish public authority.

(11) Nothing in these Regulations shall authorise a refusal to make available any environmental information contained in or otherwise held with other information which is withheld by virtue of these Regulations unless it is not reasonably capable of being separated from the other information for the purpose of making available that information.

13 Personal data

(1) To the extent that the information requested includes personal data of which the applicant is not the data subject and as respects which either the first or second condition below is satisfied, a public authority shall not disclose the personal data.

(2) The first condition is—

(a) in a case where the information falls within any of paragraphs (a) to (d) of the definition of 'data' in section 1(1) of the Data Protection Act 1998, that the disclosure of the information to a member of the public otherwise than under these Regulations would contravene—
    (i) any of the data protection principles; or

(ii) section 10 of that Act (right to prevent processing likely to cause damage or distress) and in all the circumstances of the case, the public interest in not disclosing the information outweighs the public interest in disclosing it; and

(b) in any other case, that the disclosure of the information to a member of the public otherwise than under these Regulations would contravene any of the data protection principles if the exemptions in section 33A(1) of the Data Protection Act 1998 (which relate to manual data held by public authorities) were disregarded.

(3) The second condition is that by virtue of any provision of Part IV of the Data Protection Act 1998 the information is exempt from section 7(1) of that Act and, in all the circumstances of the case, the public interest in not disclosing the information outweighs the public interest in disclosing it.

(4) In determining whether anything done before 24th October 2007 would contravene any of the data protection principles, the exemptions in Part III of Schedule 8 to the Data Protection Act 1998 shall be disregarded.

(5) For the purposes of this regulation a public authority may respond to a request by neither confirming nor denying whether such information exists and is held by the public authority, whether or not it holds such information, to the extent that—

(a) the giving to a member of the public of the confirmation or denial would contravene any of the data protection principles or section 10 of the Data Protection Act 1998 or would do so if the exemptions in section 33A(1) of that Act were disregarded; or

(b) by virtue of any provision of Part IV of the Data Protection Act 1998, the information is exempt from section 7(1)(a) of that Act.

14 Refusal to disclose information

(1) If a request for environmental information is refused by a public authority under regulations 12(1) or 13(1), the refusal shall be made in writing and comply with the following provisions of this regulation.

(2) The refusal shall be made as soon as possible and no later than 20 working days after the date of receipt of the request.

(3) The refusal shall specify the reasons not to disclose the information requested, including—

(a) any exception relied on under regulations 12(4), 12(5) or 13; and

(b) the matters the public authority considered in reaching its decision with respect to the public interest under regulation 12(1)(b) or, where these apply, regulations 13(2)(a)(ii) or 13(3).

(4) If the exception in regulation 12(4)(d) is specified in the refusal, the authority shall also specify, if known to the public authority, the name of any other public authority preparing the information and the estimated time in which the information will be finished or completed.

(5) The refusal shall inform the applicant—

(a) that he may make representations to the public authority under regulation 11; and

(b) of the enforcement and appeal provisions of the Act applied by regulation 18.

15 Ministerial certificates

(1) A Minister of the Crown may certify that a refusal to disclose information under regulation 12(1) is because the disclosure—

(a) would adversely affect national security; and

(b) would not be in the public interest under regulation 12(1)(b).

(2) For the purposes of paragraph (1)—

(a) a Minister of the Crown may designate a person to certify the matters in that paragraph on his behalf; and

(b) a refusal to disclose information under regulation 12(1) includes a response under regulation 12(6).

(3) A certificate issued in accordance with paragraph (1)—

(a) shall be conclusive evidence of the matters in that paragraph; and

(b) may identify the information to which it relates in general terms.

(4) A document purporting to be a certificate under paragraph (1) shall be received in evidence and deemed to be such a certificate unless the contrary is proved.

(5) A document which purports to be certified by or on behalf of a Minister of the Crown as a true copy of a certificate issued by that Minister under paragraph (1) shall in any legal proceedings be evidence (or, in Scotland, sufficient evidence) of that certificate.

(6) In paragraphs (1), (2) and (5), a 'Minister of the Crown' has the same meaning as in section 25(3) of the Act.

PART 4 CODE OF PRACTICE AND HISTORICAL RECORDS

16 Issue of a code of practice and functions of the Commissioner

(1) The Secretary of State may issue, and may from time to time revise, a code of practice providing guidance to public authorities as to the practice which it would, in the Secretary of State's opinion, be desirable for them to follow in connection with the discharge of their functions under these Regulations.

(2) The code may make different provision for different public authorities.

(3) Before issuing or revising any code under this regulation, the Secretary of State shall consult the Commissioner.

(4) The Secretary of State shall lay before each House of Parliament any code issued or revised under this regulation.

(5) The general functions of the Commissioner under section 47 of the Act and the power of the Commissioner to give a practice recommendation under section 48 of the Act shall apply for the purposes of these Regulations as they apply for the purposes of the Act but with the modifications specified in paragraph (6).

(6) For the purposes of the application of sections 47 and 48 of the Act to these Regulations, any reference to—

(a) a public authority is a reference to a public authority within the meaning of these Regulations;

(b) the requirements or operation of the Act, or functions under the Act, includes a reference to the requirements or operation of these Regulations, or functions under these Regulations; and

(c) a code of practice made under section 45 of the Act includes a reference to a code of practice made under this regulation.

17 Historical and transferred public records

(1) Where a request relates to information contained in a historical record other than one to which paragraph (2) applies and the public authority considers that it may be in the public interest to refuse to disclose that information under regulation 12(1)(b), the public authority shall consult—

(a) the Lord Chancellor, if it is a public record within the meaning of the Public Records Act 1958; . . .

before it decides whether the information may or may not be disclosed.

(2) Where a request relates to information contained in a transferred public record, other than information which the responsible authority has designated as open information for the purposes of this regulation, the appropriate records authority shall consult the responsible authority on whether there may be an exception to disclosure of that information under regulation 12(5).

(3) If the appropriate records authority decides that such an exception applies—

(a) subject to paragraph (4), a determination on whether it may be in the public interest to refuse to disclose that information under regulation 12(1)(b) shall be made by the responsible authority;

(b) the responsible authority shall communicate its determination to the appropriate records authority within such time as is reasonable in all the circumstances; and

(c) the appropriate records authority shall comply with regulation 5 in accordance with that determination.

(4) Where a responsible authority is required to make a determination under paragraph (3), it shall consult—

(a) the Lord Chancellor, if the transferred public record is a public record within the meaning of the Public Records Act 1958; ...

before it determines whether the information may or may not be disclosed.

(5) A responsible authority which is not a public authority under these Regulations shall be treated as a public authority for the purposes of—

(a) the obligations of a responsible authority under paragraphs (3)(a) and (b) and (4); and

(b) the imposition of any requirement to furnish information relating to compliance with regulation 5.

PART 5 ENFORCEMENT AND APPEALS, OFFENCES, AMENDMENT AND REVOCATION

18 Enforcement and appeal provisions

(1) The enforcement and appeals provisions of the Act shall apply for the purposes of these Regulations as they apply for the purposes of the Act but with the modifications specified in this regulation.

(2) In this regulation, 'the enforcement and appeals provisions of the Act' means—

(a) Part IV of the Act (enforcement), including Schedule 3 (powers of entry and inspection) which has effect by virtue of section 55 of the Act; and

(b) Part V of the Act (appeals).

(3) Part IV of the Act shall not apply in any case where a certificate has been issued in accordance with regulation 15(1).

(4) For the purposes of the application of the enforcement and appeals provisions of the Act—

(a) for any reference to—

(i) 'this Act' there shall be substituted a reference to 'these Regulations'; and

(ii) 'Part I' there shall be substituted a reference to 'Parts 2 and 3 of these Regulations';

(b) any reference to a public authority is a reference to a public authority within the meaning of these Regulations;

(c) for any reference to the code of practice under section 45 of the Act (issue of a code of practice by the Secretary of State) there shall be substituted a reference to any code of practice issued under regulation 16(1);

(d) in section 50(4) of the Act (contents of decision notice)—

(i) in paragraph (a) for the reference to 'section 1(1)' there shall be substituted a reference to 'regulation 5(1)'; and

(ii) in paragraph (b) for the references to 'sections 11 and 17' there shall be substituted references to 'regulations 6, 11 or 14';

(e) in section 56(1) of the Act (no action against public authority) for the words 'This Act does not confer' there shall be substituted the words 'These Regulations do not confer';

(f) in section 57(3)(a) of the Act (appeal against notices served under Part IV) for the reference to 'section 66' of the Act (decisions relating to certain transferred public records) there shall be substituted a reference to 'regulations 17(2) to (5)';

(g) in paragraph 1 of Schedule 3 to the Act (issue of warrants) for the reference to 'section 77' (offence of altering etc records with intent to prevent disclosure) there shall be substituted a reference to 'regulation 19'; and

(h) in paragraph 8 of Schedule 3 to the Act (matters exempt from inspection and seizure) for the reference to 'information which is exempt information by virtue of section 23(1) or 24(1)' (bodies and information relating to national security) there shall be substituted a reference to 'information whose disclosure would adversely affect national security'.

(5) In section 50(4)(a) of the Act (contents of decision notice) the reference to confirmation or denial applies to a response given by a public authority under regulation 12(6) or regulation 13(5).

(6) Section 53 of the Act (exception from duty to comply with decision notice or enforcement notice) applies to a decision notice or enforcement notice served under Part IV of the Act as applied to these Regulations on any of the public authorities referred to in section 53(1)(a); and in section 53(7) for the reference to 'exempt information' there shall be substituted a reference to 'information which may be refused under these Regulations'.

(7) Section 60 of the Act (appeals against national security certificate) shall apply with the following modifications—

(a) for the reference to a certificate under section 24(3) of the Act (national security) there shall be substituted a reference to a certificate issued in accordance with regulation 15(1);

(b) subsection (2) shall be omitted; and

(c) in subsection (3), for the words, 'the Minister did not have reasonable grounds for issuing the certificate' there shall be substituted the words 'the Minister or person designated by him did not have reasonable grounds for issuing the certificate under regulation 15(1)'.

(8) A person found guilty of an offence under paragraph 12 of Schedule 3 to the Act (offences relating to obstruction of the execution of a warrant) is liable on summary conviction to a fine not exceeding level 5 on the standard scale.

(9) A government department is not liable to prosecution in relation to an offence under paragraph 12 of Schedule 3 to the Act but that offence shall apply to a person in the public service of the Crown and to a person acting on behalf of either House of Parliament or on behalf of the Northern Ireland Assembly as it applies to any other person.

(10) Section 76(1) of the Act (disclosure of information between Commissioner and ombudsmen) shall apply to any information obtained by, or furnished to, the Commissioner under or for the purposes of these Regulations.

19 Offence of altering records with intent to prevent disclosure

(1) Where—

(a) a request for environmental information has been made to a public authority under regulation 5; and

(b) the applicant would have been entitled (subject to payment of any charge) to that information in accordance with that regulation,

any person to whom this paragraph applies is guilty of an offence if he alters, defaces, blocks, erases, destroys or conceals any record held by the public authority, with the intention of preventing the disclosure by that authority of all, or any part, of the information to which the applicant would have been entitled.

(2) Subject to paragraph (5), paragraph (1) applies to the public authority and to any person who is employed by, is an officer of, or is subject to the direction of, the public authority.

(3) A person guilty of an offence under this regulation is liable on summary conviction to a fine not exceeding level 5 on the standard scale.

(4) No proceedings for an offence under this regulation shall be instituted—

(a) in England and Wales, except by the Commissioner or by or with the consent of the Director of Public Prosecutions; . . .

(5) A government department is not liable to prosecution in relation to an offence under paragraph (1) but that offence shall apply to a person in the public service of the Crown and to a person acting on behalf of either House of Parliament or on behalf of the Northern Ireland Assembly as it applies to any other person.

21 Revocation

The following are revoked—

(a) The Environmental Information Regulations 1992 and the Environmental Information (Amendment) Regulations 1998 . . .;

Local Authorities' Plans and Strategies (Disapplication) (England) Order 2005

(SI 2005, No. 157)

1 Citation and commencement

This Order may be cited as the Local Authorities' Plans and Strategies (Disapplication) (England) Order 2005 and shall come into force on the day after the day on which it is made.

2 Interpretation

In this Order—

'English local authority' has the meaning given by section 99(7) of the Local Government Act 2003; and

'excellent authority' means an English local authority categorised as excellent by reason of an order made by the Secretary of State under section 99(4) of the Local Government Act 2003.

4 Disapplication of duty to submit home energy conservation reports

(1) Section 2 of the Home Energy Conservation Act 1995 (in this article, 'the Act'), and the power of the Secretary of State to give directions under section 5 of the Act, shall not apply to energy conservation authorities which are excellent authorities.

(2) Where, at the date on which this Order comes into force, an excellent authority have prepared a report and published and sent it to the Secretary of State in accordance with section 2(6) of the Act, section 3(2) of the Act shall not apply in relation to that authority.

(3) Paragraph (4) applies where an energy conservation authority cease, by reason of an order made by the Secretary of State under section 99(4) of the Local Government Act 2003, to be categorised as excellent.

(4) Where this paragraph applies the authority shall be treated as an excellent authority for the purposes of paragraph (1), for a period of one year beginning with the date on which the order mentioned in paragraph (3) comes into force.

. . .

8 Disapplication of duty to prepare action plans in relation to air quality

(1) Section 84(2)(b) of the Environment Act 1995 (duty to prepare an action plan) shall not apply to local authorities which are excellent authorities.

(2) Notwithstanding paragraph (1)—

(a) an excellent authority may prepare an action plan and, if they do so, the provisions of Part 4 of the Environment Act 1995 shall apply in relation to the authority as though unmodified by this Order; and

(b) an excellent authority who do not prepare an action plan shall remain under a duty to exercise their powers in pursuit of the achievement of air quality standards and objectives in the designated area.

(3) In consequence of paragraph (1), section 85 of the Environment Act 1995 shall apply in relation to excellent authorities with the modifications shown in paragraph (4).

(4) In section 85 (reserve powers)—

(a) in subsection (4)—

(i) after the word 'above' in the first place in which it occurs, insert 'and subject to subsection (5B) below';

(ii) for the words 'that subsection' substitute the words 'subsection (3) above';

(b) in subsection (5), at the beginning insert 'Subject to subsection (5B) below,';

(c) after subsection (5A), insert—

'(5B) The powers to give directions under subsections (3), (5) and (5A) above may not be exercised so as to require a local authority which is an excellent authority to prepare an action plan for a designated area.

(5C) But directions given to an excellent authority by the Secretary of State under subsections (5) or (5A) above may require the authority to exercise its powers in pursuit of the achievement of air quality standards and objectives in a designated area.

(5D) In subsections (5B) and (5C) above, 'excellent authority' has the meaning given to that term by the Local Authorities' Plans and Strategies (Disapplication) (England) Order 2005.'.

(5) Paragraph (6) applies where a local authority cease, by reason of an order made by the Secretary of State under section 99(4) of the Local Government Act 2003, to be categorised as excellent.

(6) Where this paragraph applies the authority shall be treated as an excellent authority for the purposes of paragraph (1), for a period of one year beginning with the date on which the order mentioned in paragraph (5) comes into force.

Hazardous Waste (England and Wales) Regulations 2005

(SI 2005, No. 1806)

PART 1 GENERAL

1 Citation, commencement, extent and territorial application

(1) These Regulations may be cited as the Hazardous Waste (England and Wales) Regulations 2005 and come into force as follows—

(a) Parts 1, 2, paragraph 1 of Part 1 of Schedule 12 and, for the purposes of that paragraph only, Part 5, regulation 59(3) and Schedule 9 and regulation 78 on 16th April 2005; and

(b) the remainder, on 16th July 2005.

(2) These Regulations extend to England and Wales only.[1]

(3) Nothing in these Regulations applies to Wales except this regulation, Part 11, and regulation 5 so far as relating to that Part.

2 The Waste Directive and the meaning of waste

(1) For the purposes of these Regulations—

(a) 'the Waste Directive' means Council Directive 75/442/EEC on waste as amended by—

(i) Council Directives 91/156/EEC and 91/692/EEC;

(ii) Commission Decision 96/350/EC; and

(iii) Regulation (EC) No 1882/2003; and

[1] Editor's note: for Wales see now the Hazardous Waste (Wales) Regulations 2005 (SI 2005, No. 1806).

(b) 'waste' means anything that—
(i) is waste for the purposes of the Waste Directive; and
(ii) subject to regulation 15, is not excluded from the scope of that Directive by Article 2 of that Directive.

(2) In these Regulations, a reference to the Waste Directive conditions is a reference to the conditions laid down in Article 4 of that Directive, that is to say, to ensure that waste is recovered or disposed of without endangering human health and without using processes or methods which could harm the environment and in particular—
(a) without risk to water, air, soil and plants and animals;
(b) without causing a nuisance through noise or odours; and
(c) without adversely affecting the countryside or places of special interest.

3 The Hazardous Waste Directive

(1) In these Regulations, 'the Hazardous Waste Directive' means Council Directive 91/689/EEC on hazardous waste, as amended by Council Directive 94/31/EC.

(2) A reference in these Regulations to—
(a) Annex I, Annex II or Annex III is a reference to the annex to the Hazardous Waste Directive so numbered, as that annex is set out in these Regulations as follows—
(i) Schedule 1, which sets out Annex I (Categories or generic types of hazardous waste listed according to their nature or the activity which generated them);
(ii) Schedule 2, which sets out Annex II (Constituents of the wastes in Annex I.B which render them hazardous when they have the properties described in Annex III); and
(iii) Schedule 3, which sets out Annex III (Properties of wastes which render them hazardous);
(b) hazardous properties is a reference to the properties in Annex III as so set out.

4 The List of Wastes

(1) In these Regulations—

'the List of Wastes Decision' means Commission Decision 2000/532/EC of 3rd May 2000 replacing Decision 94/3/EC establishing a list of wastes pursuant to Article 1(a) of Council Directive 75/442/EEC on waste and Council Decision 94/904/EC establishing a list of hazardous waste pursuant to Article 1(4) of Council Directive 91/689/EEC on hazardous waste, as amended by amendments thereto which have effect from time to time in relation to England pursuant to the List of Wastes Regulations;

'the List of Wastes Regulations' means the List of Wastes (England) Regulations 2005; and

'the List of Wastes' means the list of wastes set out in the List of Wastes Decision as it is from time to time set out in the List of Wastes Regulations, being the list referred to in the first indent of Article 1(4) of the Hazardous Waste Directive drawn up on the basis of Annexes I and II, having one or more of the properties listed in Annex III, taking account of the origin and composition of the waste and, where necessary, limit values of concentration.

(2) A reference in these Regulations in relation to any waste to—
(a) being 'listed as a waste' and 'listed as a hazardous waste' refers to that waste being listed as a waste, or as a hazardous waste, as the case may be, in the List of Wastes, provided, in the case of a waste to which a limit value of concentration applies, it shall only be considered to be listed as a hazardous waste where the relevant limit value of concentration is satisfied;
(b) being 'not listed as hazardous' refers to that waste being not listed as a hazardous waste in the List of Wastes, whether or not it is listed as a waste, and whether or not it is otherwise a hazardous waste pursuant to these Regulations;

and cognate expressions shall be construed accordingly.

5 General Interpretation

(1) In these Regulations—

'the 1990 Act' means the Environmental Protection Act 1990;

'the 1995 Act' means the Environment Act 1995;
'the 1994 Regulations' means the Waste Management Licensing Regulations 1994;
'the 1996 Regulations' means the Special Waste Regulations 1996);
'the Agency' means the Environment Agency;
'asbestos waste' means waste which contains or is contaminated by asbestos;
'authorised person' has the meaning given by section 108(15) of the 1995 Act;

...

'carrier' in relation to a consignment of hazardous waste, means a person who takes one or more of the following actions, that is to say, collects the consignment from the premises at which it was produced or premises at which it is being held, delivers it to the consignee, or transports it in the course of its transfer from those premises to the consignee;

'consignee', in relation to a consignment of hazardous waste, means the person to whom the waste is or is to be transferred for recovery or disposal;

'consignment code' shall be construed in accordance with regulation 34(1);

'consignment note', in relation to a consignment of hazardous waste, means the identification form which is required to accompany the hazardous waste when it is transferred pursuant to Article 5(3) of the Hazardous Waste Directive;

'consignor', in relation to a consignment of hazardous waste, means the person who causes that waste to be removed from the premises at which it was produced or is being held;

'emergency or grave danger' has the meaning given by regulation 61;

'emergency services' means those police, fire and ambulance services who are liable to be required to respond to an emergency;

'harbour area' has the same meaning as in the Dangerous Substances in Harbour Areas Regulations 1987;

'hazardous waste' has the meaning given by regulation 6; 'mixing' shall be construed in accordance with regulation 18;

'mobile service' means a service operated from premises which consists of any one or more of the following activities, that is to say, the construction, maintenance or repair of any other premises, or of any fixtures, fittings or equipment located on those other premises, being a service in the course of which the operator of the service produces hazardous waste at those other premises;

'multiple collection' has the meaning given by regulation 38;

'multiple collection consignment note' means the form of consignment note set out in Schedule 6 and required to be used in relation to multiple collections;

'non-hazardous waste' has the meaning given by regulation 7;

'premises' includes any ship and any other means of transport from which a mobile service is operated;

'quarter' means any period of three months ending on 31st March, 30th June, 30th September or 31st December;

'registered exemption' means an activity set out in Schedule 3 to the 1994 Regulations which is registered with the appropriate registration authority in accordance with those Regulations;

'schedule of carriers' means the form of schedule set out in Schedule 5 and required to be completed where more than one carrier transports, or is to transport, the consignment;
'SEPA' means the Scottish Environment Protection Agency;

'ship' means a vessel of any type whatsoever including submersible craft, floating craft and any structure which is a fixed or floating platform;

'six digit code' means the six digit code referable to a type of waste in accordance with the List of Wastes, and in relation to hazardous waste, includes the asterisk;

'SIC' means the publication entitled 'the UK Standard Industrial Classification of Economic Activities 2003' prepared by the Office of National Statistics and published by Her Majesty's Stationery Office on 31st December 2002 and implemented on 1st January 2003;

'United Kingdom ship' has the meaning given by section 1 of the Merchant Shipping Act 1995;

'waste management licence' has the meaning given by section 35(1) of the 1990 Act; and

'waste permit' has the same meaning as in Schedule 4 to the 1994 Regulations.

(2) In these Regulations, the following expressions (being the expressions defined in Article 1(b) to (g) of the Waste Directive) have the same meaning as they have in that directive, that is to say—

'producer' means anyone whose activities produce waste ('original producer') or anyone who carries out pre-processing, mixing or other operations resulting in a change in the nature or composition of this waste;

'holder' means the producer of the waste or the person who is in possession of it;

'management' means the collection, transport, recovery and disposal of waste, including the supervision of such operations and after-care of disposal sites;

'disposal' means any of the operations provided for in Annex IIA of the Waste Directive;

'recovery' means any of the operations provided for in Annex IIB of the Waste Directive;

'collection' means the gathering, sorting or mixing of waste or any one or more of those operations, for the purpose of transport,

and expressions cognate to these expressions shall be construed accordingly.

(3) In these Regulations—

(a) any document which is to be provided or given to any person (other than a fixed penalty notice under Part 10) may be provided or given to that person in electronic form if the text is capable of being produced by that person in a visible and legible documentary form;

(b) any requirement to make, keep or retain a record or to maintain a register may be satisfied in electronic form if the text is capable of being produced by that person in a visible and legible documentary form;

(c) any requirement for a signature on a notification, consignment note, schedule of carriers or multiple collection consignment note, may be satisfied by an electronic signature incorporated into the document; and

(d) 'electronic signature' means data in electronic form which are attached to or logically associated with other electronic data and which serve as a method of authentication.

PART 2 HAZARDOUS AND NON-HAZARDOUS WASTE

6 Hazardous waste

Subject to regulation 9, a waste is a hazardous waste if it is—

(a) listed as a hazardous waste in the List of Wastes;

(b) listed in regulations made under section 62A(1) of the 1990 Act; or

(c) a specific batch of waste which is determined pursuant to regulation 49 to be a hazardous waste,

and the term 'hazardous' and cognate expressions shall be construed accordingly.

7 Non-hazardous waste

The following are non-hazardous waste—

(a) a waste which is not a hazardous waste pursuant to regulation 6; or

(b) a specific batch of waste which is determined pursuant to regulation 9 to be a non-hazardous waste,

and the expression 'non-hazardous' and cognate expressions shall be construed accordingly.

8 Specific waste to be treated as hazardous

(1) The Secretary of State, having regard to Annexes I, II and III and the limit values of concentration in the List of Wastes, may determine, in exceptional cases, that a specific batch of waste in England which—

(a) is not listed as a hazardous waste in the List of Wastes;

(b) is not listed in regulations made under section 62A(1) of the 1990 Act; or

(c) though of a type listed as a hazardous waste in the List of Wastes, is treated as non-hazardous pursuant to regulation 9(2),

displays one or more of the hazardous properties, and accordingly that it shall be treated for all purposes as hazardous waste.

(2) A specific batch of waste produced in Wales, Scotland or Northern Ireland and not listed as hazardous in the List of Wastes and which is for the time being determined by the Welsh Assembly Government, the Scottish Executive or the Northern Ireland Department of the Environment, as the case may be, to be hazardous pursuant to Article 3 of the List of Wastes Decision, shall, subject to any determination made under regulation 9, be treated for all purposes as hazardous waste in England.

9 Specific waste to be treated as non-hazardous

(1) The Secretary of State may decide, in exceptional cases, on the basis of documentary evidence provided by the holder, and having regard to Annexes I, II and III and the limit values of concentration in the List of Wastes, that a specific batch of waste in England which—

(a) is listed as hazardous waste in the List of Wastes;

(b) is listed in regulations made under section 62A(1) of the 1990 Act; or

(c) though of a type not listed as a hazardous waste in the List of Wastes, is treated as hazardous pursuant to regulation 8(2),

does not display any of the properties listed in Annex III to the Hazardous Waste Directive and accordingly that it shall be treated for all purposes as non-hazardous in England.

(2) A specific batch of waste produced in Wales, Scotland or Northern Ireland and listed as a hazardous waste in the List of Wastes and which is for the time being determined by the Welsh Assembly Government, the Scottish Executive or the Northern Ireland Department of the Environment, as the case may be, to be non-hazardous pursuant to Article 3 of the List of Wastes Decision, shall, subject to any determination made under regulation 8, be treated for all purposes as non-hazardous in England.

10 Provisions common to regulations 8 and 9

(1) The Secretary of State may revoke a determination made under regulation 8 or 9.

(2) The Secretary of State shall, before making a determination under regulation 8 or 9 or revoking such a determination, except where she considers it inappropriate to do so on account of the nature of any emergency or grave danger, consult—

(a) the requisite bodies;

(b) the holder of the specific batch of waste; and

(c) any other person appearing to her—

(i) to have an interest in the specific waste; or

(ii) to be otherwise directly affected by the determination.

(3) The Secretary of State shall give notice of any determination made under regulation 49 or 50 or revocation of such a determination to—

(a) the requisite bodies;

(b) the holder of the specific batch of waste concerned; and

(c) any person she has consulted pursuant to paragraph (2)(c).

(4) The notice shall give reasons for the determination or revocation, as the case may be.

11 Requisite bodies

For the purposes of this Part, the 'requisite bodies' are—

(a) the Agency;

(b) SEPA;

(c) the National Assembly for Wales;

(d) the Scottish Executive;

(e) the Northern Ireland Department of the Environment;

(f) the Health and Safety Executive; and

(g) any organisation appearing to the Secretary of State to be representative of persons likely to be affected by the relevant determination or revocation of a determination, as the case may be.

PART 3 APPLICATION OF PARTS 4 TO 11

12 General application of Parts 4 to 11

(1) Subject to paragraphs (2) to (4), these Regulations apply to hazardous waste.

(2) Except as provided in regulations 13 (application to asbestos waste) and 14 (application to separately collected fractions), these Regulations do not apply to domestic waste.

(3) Nothing in Part 6 of these Regulations (movement of hazardous waste) shall apply in relation to shipments of waste to which the provisions of Council Regulation 259/93/EEC, other than Title III of that Regulation, apply.

(4) These Regulations apply to hazardous waste in England notwithstanding that the waste—

(a) was produced on or removed from premises in Scotland, Wales, Northern Ireland or Gibraltar; or

(b) is, or is to be, transported from premises in England to premises located in one of those places.

(5) For the avoidance of doubt, in their application to—

(a) ships' waste, these Regulations apply to any ship;

(b) the internal waters and the territorial sea of the United Kingdom adjacent to England, these Regulations apply, without prejudice to paragraph (3), to a consignment of waste transported in any ship,

in each case (whether the ship is a United Kingdom ship or otherwise and, if a United Kingdom ship, whether registered in England or otherwise).

13 Asbestos waste

(1) These Regulations apply to asbestos waste which is domestic waste except in so far as they would, apart from this paragraph, impose obligations on a person to whom paragraph (2) applies.

(2) This paragraph applies to a person who is both the original producer of the domestic waste and either—

(a) a person who resides at the domestic premises at which the asbestos waste arises; or

(b) a person who is acting on behalf of such a person without reward.

(3) These Regulations operate in relation to asbestos waste not being domestic waste which is produced in the course of any of the activities of construction, modification, repair and maintenance (including structural works) or demolition of domestic premises or any part thereof, so as to treat any contractor engaged by a domestic occupier—

(a) as the producer; and

(b) where the contractor does not engage another person as consignor, as the consignor,

of the asbestos waste to the exclusion of the occupier.

14 Separately collected domestic fractions

(1) This regulation applies to separately collected domestic fractions, that is to say, hazardous waste which is—

(a) domestic waste; and

(b) collected from the premises on which it is produced separately from the collection of other waste from those premises.

(2) For the purposes of paragraph (1), hazardous waste may be considered to be collected separately from the collection of other waste notwithstanding that it is collected at the same

time or on the same vehicle or both, provided that the hazardous waste is not mixed with the other waste.

(3) Subject to paragraph (4), these Regulations apply to separately collected fractions.

(4) Nothing in these Regulations shall apply to separately collected fractions until such waste has been removed from the premises at which it was produced and taken to premises for collection, disposal or recovery.

(5) The establishment or undertaking which accepts such waste at those premises shall be treated as producer of the waste for the purposes of these Regulations.

15 Radioactive waste

(1) This regulation applies where radioactive waste within the meaning of section 2 of the Radioactive Substances Act 1993—

(a) is exempt for the time being from the requirements of—

(i) section 13 (disposal of radioactive waste); or

(ii) section 14 (accumulation of radioactive waste),

of that Act by or pursuant to section 15 of that Act; and

(b) has one or more hazardous properties arising other than from its radioactive nature.

(2) Notwithstanding regulation 2(1)(b)(ii), radioactive waste to which this regulation applies is treated as waste for the purposes of these Regulations, and accordingly it is treated as hazardous waste and these Regulations apply to that waste.

16 Agricultural waste

(1) These Regulations do not apply to agricultural waste before 1st September 2006, but apply on and after that date to agricultural waste whenever it became waste.

(2) For the purpose of this regulation, 'agricultural waste' means waste from premises used for agriculture within the meaning of the Agriculture Act 1947.

17 Mines and quarries waste

These Regulations do not apply to waste from a mine or quarry before 1st September 2006, but apply on and after that date to such waste whenever it became waste.

PART 4 MIXING HAZARDOUS WASTE

18 Meaning of mixing hazardous waste

For the purposes of these Regulations, hazardous waste of any description shall be considered to have been mixed if it has been mixed with—

(a) a different category of hazardous waste;

(b) a non-hazardous waste; or

(c) any other substance or material.

19 Prohibition on mixing hazardous waste without a permit

(1) Subject to paragraphs (2) and (3), no establishment or undertaking which carries out the disposal or recovery of hazardous waste, or which produces, collects or transports hazardous waste, shall mix any hazardous waste.

(2) Paragraph (1) does not apply so as to prohibit a process by which waste is produced and which results in the production of mixed wastes, being a process other than one which mixes a waste with any other waste, substance or material, resulting in—

(a) a change in the nature or composition of that waste;

(b) or the production of another waste.

(3) Paragraph (1) does not apply to the extent that the mixing is part of a disposal or recovery operation and is authorised by, and is conducted in accordance with, the requirements (howsoever expressed) of a waste permit or a registered exemption.

20 Duty to separate mixed wastes

(1) This regulation applies to the holder where—

(a) the hazardous waste has been mixed other than under and in accordance with a waste permit or a registered exemption, whether by the holder or a previous holder; and

(b) separation is both—

(i) technically and economically feasible; and

(ii) necessary in order to comply with the Waste Directive conditions.

(2) The holder must make arrangements for separation of the waste to be carried out in accordance with a waste permit or registered exemption as soon as reasonably practicable.

(3) In this Regulation 'separation' means separation of a waste from any other waste, substance or material with which it has been mixed.

PART 5 NOTIFICATION OF PREMISES

21 Requirement to notify premises

(1) Where hazardous waste is produced at, or removed from, any premises other than exempt premises, the premises must be notified to the Agency in accordance with the requirements of this Part.

...

PART 6 MOVEMENT OF HAZARDOUS WASTE

Consignment Codes

33 Coding standard

(1) It is the duty of the Agency from time to time to designate, and at all times to maintain in force a designation of a standard (in these Regulations referred to as a 'coding standard', making provision for the composition of consignment codes for the purposes of this Part.

(2) The coding standard must enable each consignment of hazardous waste to be given a unique consignment code.

...

34 Consignment codes

(1) It is the duty of—

(a) the producer, in relation to—

(i) a consignment of hazardous waste to be removed from premises at which the waste is produced (other than a ship);

(ii) hazardous waste to be removed by pipeline from premises (other than a ship) situated in a case to which regulation 41 applies; or

(iii) hazardous waste to be deposited within the curtilage of premises at which it was produced;

(b) the master of the ship, in relation to any hazardous waste removed from a ship in a harbour area (including waste accidentally spilled on land adjacent to the ship); and

(c) the consignor, in relation to any other consignment of hazardous waste,

to assign to the hazardous waste a unique code in accordance with the coding standard for the time being in force.

(2) The code assigned pursuant to paragraph (1) shall be the consignment code of the hazardous waste concerned for the purposes of these Regulations.

Documents to be Completed for Consignments

35 Completion of consignment notes

(1) Where hazardous waste is removed from any premises—

(a) a consignment note shall be completed in accordance with paragraph (3) of this regulation and the requirements of the relevant regulation if one of the following regulations applies—

(i) regulation 36 (standard procedure);

(ii) regulation 39 (removal of ship's waste to reception facilities);

(iii) regulation 40 (removal of ship's waste other than to reception facilities);

(iv) regulation 41 (removal of waste by pipeline); or

(v) where the consignment or any part thereof is rejected by the consignee, in accordance in each case with regulation 42 and 43;

(b) if regulation 37 (Schedule of carriers) applies, a schedule of carriers shall be completed in accordance with that regulation and paragraph (3) of this regulation; or

(c) if regulation 38 (multiple collection) or regulation 44 (multiple collection procedure for rejected consignments) applies, a multiple collection consignment note shall be completed in accordance with the applicable regulation and paragraph (4) of this regulation.

(2) The form of consignment note set out in Schedule 4, or a form requiring the same information in substantially the same format, shall be used and shall be completed so as to contain (in the place indicated in the form) all the information provided for in that Schedule which is applicable to the case.

(3) The form of the schedule of carriers set out in Schedule 5, or a form requiring the same information in substantially the same format, shall be used and shall be completed so as to contain (in the place indicated in the form) all the information provided for in that Schedule which is applicable to the case.

(4) The form of multiple collection consignment note set out in Schedule 6, or a form requiring the same information in substantially the same format, shall be used and shall be completed so as to contain (in the place indicated in the form) all the information provided for in that Schedule which is applicable to the case.

(5) In this Part, a reference to a part of a consignment note, schedule of carriers or multiple collection consignment note by its number or description is a reference to that part as it is required to be so numbered or described as the case may be in the form in Schedule 4, 5 or 6 as the case may require.

36 Standard procedure

(1) This regulation applies in all cases where a consignment of hazardous waste is to be removed from premises except in cases to which any of regulations 38 to 41 apply.

(2) Before the consignment is removed—

(a) the hazardous waste producer, or holder, as the case may be, shall—

(i) prepare a copy of the consignment note for each of the following: the hazardous waste producer or holder, where different from the consignor; the consignor; the carrier; and the consignee;

(ii) complete Parts A and B on each copy; and

(iii) give every copy to the carrier;

(b) the carrier shall complete Part C on each copy and give every copy to the consignor;

(c) the consignor shall—

(i) complete Part D on each copy;

(ii) where the hazardous waste producer or holder, as the case may be, is not the consignor, give one copy to him;

(iii) retain one copy; and

(iv) give every remaining copy to the carrier.

(3) The carrier shall ensure that every copy which he has received—

(a) travels with the consignment; and

(b) is given to the consignee on delivery of the consignment.

(4) Subject to regulation 42, on receiving the consignment the consignee shall—

(a) complete Part E on both copies; and

(b) give one copy to the carrier.

37 Schedule of carriers

(1) This regulation applies in all cases (whether under regulation 36, or regulation 40) where more than one carrier transports, or is to transport, the consignment.

(2) Before the consignment is removed—

(a) the consignor shall—

(i) prepare a copy of the schedule of carriers for the hazardous waste producer or holder (where different from the consignor), the consignor, every carrier and the consignee; and

(ii) give every copy to the first carrier;

(b) the first carrier shall ensure that every copy he has received travels with the consignment;

(c) on delivery of the consignment to each subsequent carrier—

(i) the previous carrier shall give the subsequent carrier every copy of the schedule which he has received;

(ii) the subsequent carrier shall complete the relevant certificate on each copy, give one to the previous carrier who shall retain it, and ensure that every remaining copy which he has received travels with the consignment; and

(d) when the consignment is delivered to a consignee, the carrier shall retain one copy of the carriers schedule and give every remaining copy to the consignee.

(3) Where—

(a) arrangements for the transport of the consignment have not been made with all carriers intended to be involved before transport commences; or

(b) there is a change in any such arrangements after transport commences for any reason,

paragraph (2) applies as if the carrier in possession of the consignment when further arrangements are made, in the case of paragraph (a), or take effect, in the case of paragraph (b), were the consignor and the next carrier were the first carrier.

(4) Where this regulation applies, other than in the case of a rejected consignment of hazardous waste, regulation 36 has effect as if—

(a) a reference to the hazardous waste being removed includes reference to its possession being transferred to the next carrier;

(b) in paragraph (2)(a)(i), the reference to 'the carrier' were a reference to 'every carrier';

(c) in paragraphs (2)(a)(iii), (2)(b) and (2)(c)(iv), the reference to 'the carrier' were a reference to 'the first carrier';

(d) in paragraph (3)(b), in relation to a carrier who is not the final carrier, the reference to 'the consignee' were a reference to 'the subsequent carrier'; and

(e) in paragraph (4)(b), the reference to 'the carrier' were a reference to 'the final carrier'.

38 Multiple collections

(1) This regulation applies to a journey made by a single carrier which meets the following conditions—

(a) the carrier collects more than one consignment of hazardous waste in the course of the journey;

(b) each consignment is collected from different premises (none of which is a ship);

(c) all the premises from which a collection is made are in England; and

(d) all consignments collected are transported by that carrier in the course of the journey to the same consignee,

and a journey which meets these conditions is referred to in these Regulations as a 'multiple collection'.

(2) Where the carrier elects to apply the multiple collection procedure set out in this regulation to a multiple collection, the requirements of this regulation apply to the carrier, and to the producers, holders and consignors of the consignments collected in the course of the round.

(3) Before the first collection, the carrier shall—

(a) prepare two copies of the multiple consignment collection note, plus one copy for each hazardous waste producer or holder, as the case may be, from whom waste is to be collected during the round, and one copy for each consignor, in cases where the hazardous waste producer, or holder, as the case may be, is not the consignor; and

(b) complete Parts A and B on each copy.

(4) Before the removal of waste from each set of premises from which a collection is made—

(a) the producer, or holder, must complete the annex to the multiple collection consignment note on each copy;

(b) the consignor and carrier must sign their respective declarations to the annex to the multiple collection consignment note on each copy of the note; and

(c) the carrier must pass a completed copy to the producer or holder in each case (and where the producer or holder is not the consignor, the consignor).

(5) After collection of the last consignment but before delivery to the consignee, the carrier must complete the particulars for completion by the carrier in section C on both remaining copies of the consignment note.

(6) Subject to regulation 42, on delivery of the waste—

(a) the carrier must pass to the consignee both remaining copies of the note;

(b) the consignee must complete the particulars for completion by the consignee in Section C and complete the certificate in part D of the note on both copies; and

(c) the consignee must return one copy of the completed note to the carrier.

...

Rejected Consignments

42 Duty of consignee not accepting delivery

(1) This regulation and regulations 43 and 44 apply where the consignee does not accept delivery of a consignment of hazardous waste, whether wholly or in part.

(2) The requirements of regulation 36(4), 38(6)(b) and (c), 39(3) or 40(3) (which relate to the duties of the consignee on acceptance of the consignment) as the case may be, do not apply to the consignee in respect of a consignment, or part thereof, which has been rejected.

(3) If copies of the consignment note relating to a rejected consignment have been given to the consignee he shall—

(a) indicate on Part E of each copy that he receives that he does not accept the consignment, or part of the consignment, as the case may be, and the reasons why he does not accept the consignment or part;

(b) retain one copy;

(c) give one copy to the carrier; and

(d) as soon as reasonably practicable, send a copy to the consignor, and (if different from the consignor, the producer or holder, where known).

(4) If no copy of the consignment note has been given to the consignee he shall—

(a) prepare a written explanation of his reasons for not accepting delivery, including such details of the consignment, the hazardous waste producer or holder, the consignor and the carrier as are known to him;

(b) give such written explanation to the carrier;

(c) as soon as reasonably practicable, send one copy to the consignor, and (if different from the consignor) the producer or holder, where known; and

(d) retain a copy of his written explanation.

(5) On being informed that the consignee will not accept delivery of the consignment or part, the carrier shall—

(a) inform the Agency;

(b) seek instructions from the hazardous waste producer or holder; and

(c) take all reasonable steps to ensure those instructions are fulfilled (including completing any consignment note on their behalf).

(6) It is the duty of the hazardous waste producer or holder identified in the relevant part of the consignment note, as the case may be, to—

(a) make arrangements as soon as reasonably practicable for the transfer of the rejected consignment or part to another specified consignee who holds a waste permit or is registered to carry on an exempt activity for the recovery or disposal of the waste; and

(b) forthwith—

(i) give instructions to the carrier accordingly; and

(ii) inform the Agency of the arrangements and instructions.

(7) If in any case within paragraph (6)(a) no alternative consignee can be found within 5 business days, the hazardous waste producer or holder identified in the relevant part of the consignment note shall make arrangements to return the waste to premises from which it was removed for its storage in accordance with the Waste Directive conditions until a suitable consignee can be found.

43 Further consignment note for rejected consignment

(1) This regulation applies to the removal of any consignment following rejection by the consignee other than a case to which regulation 44 applies.

(2) Before the consignment or part is moved from the original place for delivery, the hazardous waste producer or holder identified in the relevant part of the original consignment note shall ensure that a copy of a new consignment note is prepared in respect of the rejected consignment or part for each of the following—

(a) the hazardous waste producer;

(b) where the hazardous waste producer or holder is not the consignor, the consignor;

(c) the carrier; and

(d) the new consignee.

(3) The producer or holder shall—

(a) complete Parts A and B on each copy of the note as follows—

(i) the information required to complete Part A should be copied from the original consignment note, including the relevant consignment code to which the letter 'R' shall be added to the end;

(ii) the new consignee's name and address (including the postcode) shall be entered in Part A4; and

(iii) subject to paragraph (4), the relevant information from the original consignment note shall (where part of the load is rejected, in so far as it relates to that part) be copied to Part B; and

(b) give every copy to the carrier.

(4) Where the consignee who rejected the consignment or part states in his written explanation that the description of the waste in the original consignment note is incorrect, the producer or holder shall instead include an accurate description of the waste in the new consignment note.

(5) The carrier shall complete Part C on each copy.

(6) The producer or holder identified in the relevant part of the original consignment note shall—

(a) complete Part D on each copy;

(b) where the producer or holder is not the consignor, give one copy to the producer or holder as the case may be; and

(c) give every remaining copy to the carrier.

(7) The carrier shall ensure that every copy of the new consignment note which he has received—

(a) travels with the rejected consignment or part; and

(b) is given to the new consignee on delivery of the consignment or part.

(8) The new consignee shall—

(a) complete Part E on both copies of the new consignment note; and

(b) give one copy to the carrier.

(9) Where there is to be more than one carrier—

(a) in paragraphs (3)(b), (5) and (6)(c), references to the carrier shall be treated as references to the first carrier;

(b) in paragraphs (2)(c) and (7) references to the carrier shall be treated as references to each carrier;

(c) in paragraph (7)(b), in relation to a carrier who is not the final carrier, the reference to 'the new consignee' shall be treated as a reference to 'the subsequent carrier'; and

(d) in paragraph (8)(b) the reference to the carrier shall be treated as a reference to the final carrier.

44 Procedure for rejected multiple collection consignments

(1) Where two or more consignments comprising part of a multiple collection are rejected and are to be delivered to the same consignee, if the carrier elects to apply the multiple collection procedure set out in regulation 38 to such a delivery, the following requirements shall apply—

(a) the carrier shall—

(i) prepare two copies of the multiple consignment collection note, plus one copy for each hazardous waste producer or holder, as the case may be, from whose consignment has been rejected, and one copy for each consignor, in cases where the hazardous waste producer, or holder, as the case may be, is not the consignor; and

(ii) complete Parts A and B on each copy;

(b) before the removal of waste from the original delivery premises—

(i) the producer, or holder, shall complete the annex to the multiple collection consignment note on each copy prepared by the carrier;

(ii) the consignor and carrier must sign their respective declarations to the annex to the multiple consignment note on each copy of the note prepared by the carrier;

(iii) the carrier must pass a completed copy to the producer or holder in each case (and where the producer is not the consignor, to the consignor);

(c) on delivery of the waste to the new consignee—

(i) the carrier must complete the particulars for completion by the carrier in section C on every copy of the consignment note;

(ii) the carrier must pass to the consignee every copy of the note;

(iii) the consignee must complete the particulars for completion by the consignee in Section C and complete the certificate in part D of the note on every copy of the note; and

(iv) the consignee must return one copy of the completed note to the carrier.

Duty to Deliver within Time Limit

45 Duty to deliver consignment promptly

It is the duty of the carrier to deliver the consignment to the consignee promptly and without undue delay.

PART 7 RECORDS AND RETURNS

Site Records

47 Records of tipped (discharged) hazardous waste

(1) Any person who tips (discharges) hazardous waste (whether by way of disposal or storage) in or on any land shall record and identify the waste in accordance with the following requirements of this regulation and regulation 51.

(2) A record shall include either—

(a) a site plan marked with a grid, or

(b) a site plan with overlays on which the deposits of the tipped (discharged) waste are shown in relation to the contours of the site.

(3) Records made under this regulation shall be kept in a register.

(4) Deposits shall be identified by reference to both—

(a) the relevant description and six digit code in the List of Wastes, together with a description of the composition of the waste; and

(b) the consignment note relating to such waste, save that where waste is disposed of within the curtilage of the premises at which it is produced the deposits shall be described by reference to the quarterly return made to the Agency by the hazardous waste producer under regulation 53.

(5) A person who is required to make or retain a register pursuant to this regulation shall—

(a) update the register as soon as reasonably practicable and in any event within 24 hours of the receipt, or deposit, as the case may be, of the waste;

(b) keep the register on the site where the tipping takes place; and

(c) retain the records—

(i) for three years after deposit of the waste; or

(ii) if he has a waste permit pursuant to which the site is operated, until that permit is surrendered or revoked.

(6) In reckoning any period of hours for the purposes of this regulation or regulation 48, only the days or hours of any business day shall be counted.

48 Records of disposal or recovery of hazardous waste by other means

(1) Any person who—

(a) disposes of hazardous waste in or on land (other than any disposal covered by regulation 47);

(b) recovers hazardous waste in or on land; or

(c) receives hazardous waste at a transfer station,

or both shall record and identify any hazardous waste received in accordance with the following requirements of this regulation and regulation 51.

(2) The waste shall be identified in the record by reference to the relevant description in the List of Wastes and six digit code, and the entry shall include a description of the composition of the waste.

(3) The record shall include—

(a) the quantity, nature and origin of any such waste;

(b) the relevant hazardous properties;

(c) where applicable, the recovery method in respect of the waste by reference to the numbering and description applicable in accordance with Annex IIB of the Waste Directive; and

(d) an inventory showing the specific location at which the waste is being held.

(4) Records made under this regulation shall be kept in a register.

(5) The register shall be updated as soon as reasonably practicable and in any event no later than 24 hours after—

(a) a consignment of hazardous waste is received;

(b) any recovery or disposal operations are carried out or any hazardous waste is placed in storage at the transfer station, as the case may be; and

(c) any hazardous waste is removed from the premises.

(6) A person who is required to make or retain records pursuant to this regulation shall—

(a) keep the register of the records on the site where the recovery operations take place or the transfer station is operated, as the case may be; and

(b) retain the records—

(i) where the hazardous waste is fully recovered, or remains at a transfer station, as the case may be, until it leaves the site and for three years thereafter; or

(ii) if he has a waste permit pursuant to which the site is operated, until that permit is surrendered or revoked.

Producer and Transport Records

49 Producers', holders' and consignors' records

(1) A producer or holder of hazardous waste, and where different from the producer, a consignor of hazardous waste, shall keep a record of the quantity, nature, origin and, where relevant, the destination, frequency of collection, mode of transport and treatment method of the waste.

(2) Where the waste is transported, the duty in paragraph (1) includes a requirement to keep a record of particulars sufficient to identify the carrier.

(3) The producer, holder or consignor, as the case may be, shall preserve the records to be made pursuant to this regulation whilst he remains the holder of the waste and for at least three years afterwards commencing on the date on which the waste is transferred to another person.

(4) The information to be recorded pursuant to the foregoing provisions of this regulation shall be recorded in a register kept by the producer, holder or consignor, as the case may be, for the purpose.

(5) The register required to be kept and retained by a producer, holder or consignor under paragraph (4) of this regulation shall be kept—

(a) in relation to the register required to be kept by the producer or holder

(i) at the premises notified pursuant to regulation 24;

(ii) if he no longer occupies those premises, at his principal place of business (or such other address as agreed with the Agency for that purpose); or

(iii) if no premises were notified in relation to the waste, at his principal place of business (or such other address as agreed with the Agency for that purpose).

(b) the register required to be kept by a consignor other than the producer or holder shall be kept at his principal place of business.

(6) If the producer or holder ceases to occupy the notified premises before the period referred to in paragraph (3) expires, he shall inform the Agency forthwith.

50 Carrier's records

(1) An establishment or undertaking which transports hazardous waste shall keep a record of the quantity, nature, origin and, where relevant, the destination, frequency of collection, mode of transport and treatment method of the waste in accordance with the following requirements of this regulation.

(2) The establishment or undertaking shall keep the records made pursuant to this regulation for at least twelve months commencing on the date of delivery of the waste to its destination.

(3) The information required to be recorded pursuant to paragraph (1) shall be entered in a register and the register kept at the carrier's principal place of business.

51 Registers and records: common provisions

(1) The following provisions of this regulation apply in relation to registers required to be kept under regulations 47 to 50.

(2) A person who is required to keep a register shall enter in the register each copy received by them of—

(a) any consignment note (including multiple consignment notes and, where consignments are not accepted, the original note, a copy of any explanation of the reasons for rejection prepared pursuant to regulation 42 and the consignment note prepared pursuant to regulation 43 or 44);

(b) any consignee's return to the producer, holder or consignor received pursuant to regulation 54; and

(c) any carrier's schedule given to him pursuant to regulation 37.

(3) A person who is required to keep a register or retain records until his waste permit is surrendered or revoked shall send those records or that register to the Agency when the permit is surrendered or revoked.

(4) Every register kept or record made pursuant to regulation 15 or 16 of the 1996 Regulations, and every record made pursuant to regulation 13 or 14 of the Control of Pollution (Special Waste) Regulation 1980, shall—

(a) be kept with the register kept pursuant to regulations 47 to 49 by the person required to keep that register for so long as is mentioned in the relevant regulation; and

(b) be sent by that person together with that register if it is sent to the Agency.

. . .

53 Consignee and self-disposal quarterly returns

(1) Every consignee shall make a return, in these Regulations referred to as a consignee quarterly return, to the Agency of information relating to all consignments of hazardous waste received by him in any quarter . . . .

. . . .

54 Consignee's return to the producer, holder or consignor

(1) Without prejudice to any duty under these Regulations on the part of the consignee to send any document or copy thereof to the producer, holder or consignor, a consignee shall send to a producer or holder identified in the relevant part of a consignment note—

(a) a return in a form corresponding to that set out in Schedule 8 or a form substantially to like effect within one month of the end of the quarter in which the waste concerned was accepted; or

(b) a copy of the consignment note together with a description of the method of disposal or recovery undertaken in relation to the waste, within one month of the end of the quarter in which the waste concerned was accepted.

(2) Where hazardous waste was delivered by pipeline in a case to which regulation 41 applies, paragraph (1) shall apply so that the return required under sub-paragraph (a) or the information required under sub-paragraph (b) shall be supplied within one month of the end of the quarter in which the waste concerned was piped.

(3) Where regulation 42 applies, this regulation does not apply to the consignment or part concerned.

55 Duties to supply information

(1) A person who is required to retain any record pursuant to any of the foregoing provisions of this Part shall, at any time during the period in which the record is required to be retained produce that record to the Agency or emergency services on request.

(2) A producer holder, previous holder, consignor, carrier or consignee of hazardous waste shall supply to the Agency on request such information as it may reasonably require for

the purposes of performing its functions in connection with these Regulations and for the purposes of monitoring the production, movement, storage, treatment, recovery and disposal of hazardous waste.

(3) An establishment or undertaking to which hazardous waste is delivered for recovery or disposal, as the case may be, has the duty to supply to the Agency on request documentary evidence that the disposal or recovery operation concerned has been carried out, indicating where applicable, the relevant entry listed in Annex IIA or Annex IIB, as the case may be, of the Waste Directive.

(4) A person who is required to supply information to the Agency pursuant to this regulation shall supply that information in such form as the Agency may reasonably request.

(5) The power conferred by paragraph (4) includes power to require the production in a visible and legible documentary form of any information is held in electronic form.

(6) Any request for information under this regulation shall be in writing and shall specify the period within which the information is to be supplied.

PART 8 THE AGENCY'S FUNCTIONS

56 Inspections of hazardous waste producers

It is the duty of the Agency to carry out appropriate periodic inspections of hazardous waste producers.

57 Inspections of collection and transport operations

(1) In relation to the appropriate periodic inspections of collection and transport operations which are required to be conducted pursuant to Article 13 of the Waste Directive by the Agency, without prejudice to the generality of the requirement to conduct such inspections, it is the duty of the Agency insofar as the inspections relate to hazardous waste to conduct the inspections so that they cover more particularly the origin and destination of the hazardous waste.

(2) In paragraph (1), 'collection and transport operations' includes operations where the hazardous waste is transported following transfer between different carriers.

58 Agency to retain registers etc

The Agency shall retain registers and any accompanying records sent to it pursuant to regulation 51(3) for a period of not less than three years commencing with the receipt thereof by the Agency.

. . .

60 Provision of information to the Secretary of State

(1) The Agency shall inform the Secretary of State each year of any changes in the following information for every establishment or undertaking which carries out disposal or recovery of hazardous waste principally on behalf of third parties and which is likely to form part of the integrated network referred to in Article 5 of the Waste Directive—

(a) name and address;

(b) the method used to treat waste; and

(c) the types and quantities of waste which can be treated.

(2) The Agency shall provide the information required by paragraph (1) in the format provided for pursuant to the fourth paragraph of Article 8(3) of the Hazardous Waste Directive.

PART 9 EMERGENCIES AND GRAVE DANGER

61 General

(1) This Part has effect for the purpose of making provision for an emergency or grave danger.

(2) For the purposes of these Regulations, an 'emergency or grave danger' is a present or threatened situation arising from a substance or object which is, or which there are

reasonable grounds to believe is, hazardous waste, and the situation constitutes a threat to the population or the environment in any place.

62 General duties on the holder in the event of an emergency or grave danger

(1) In cases of emergency or grave danger, a holder of hazardous waste which gives rise to an emergency or grave danger shall—

(a) take all lawful and reasonable steps to avert the emergency or grave danger; or

(b) where it is not reasonably practicable to comply with paragraph (a), take all lawful and reasonable steps to mitigate the emergency or grave danger.

(2) For the purposes of paragraph (1), an act or omission may be considered lawful notwithstanding that it would, apart from this regulation, constitute a breach of these Regulations.

(3) Where the holder of hazardous waste knows or has reasonable grounds to believe that an emergency or grave danger has arisen, he shall notify the Agency as soon as reasonably practicable of the circumstances.

(4) Where the holder takes any step in compliance with paragraph (1), he shall, save where such step has completely averted the emergency or grave danger without breach of these Regulations, notify the Agency as soon as reasonably practicable.

(5) For the purposes of paragraph (4), an emergency or grave danger shall not be considered to have been completely averted if any release has taken place of a substance or object which is, or which there are reasonable grounds to believe is, hazardous waste, whether or not the holder believes he has completely destroyed, retrieved or rendered harmless the substance or object.

(6) In the event of notification pursuant to paragraph (3) or (4) being made orally, the holder shall confirm in writing to the Agency the matters notified within one week of the oral notification.

(7) For the purposes of this regulation a person shall be not be released from any requirement imposed by this regulation merely because he has ceased to be the holder through the waste having left his possession or control due to release.

63 General duties of the Agency

(1) The Agency shall exercise its functions (whether under these Regulations or otherwise) so as to take all reasonably practicable steps necessary or expedient to avert or mitigate an emergency or grave danger.

(2) An authorised person shall in exercising functions in relation to an emergency or grave danger so exercise his powers under sections 108 and 109 of the 1995 Act as to take all reasonably practicable steps to avert or mitigate the emergency or grave danger.

PART 10 ENFORCEMENT

64 Enforcement

(1) Subject to paragraph (2), it is the duty of the Agency to enforce these Regulations.

(2) Paragraph (1) is without prejudice to any right of action which any person may have arising apart from these Regulations, or any other right, power or duty of any person either at law or arising pursuant to any agreement or arrangement (expressly or impliedly) or in consequence of any act or omission.

65 Offences

It is an offence for a person to fail to comply with any requirement imposed on them by or under the following provisions of these Regulations—

(a) Part 4;

(b) regulations 21, 22 and 24 to 26;

(c) regulations 34 to 44;

(d) regulation 46 and Schedule 7;

(e) Part 7 (with the exception of regulation 52); and

(f) Regulation 62.

66 Defences

It shall be a defence for a person charged with an offence under regulation 65 to prove that—

(a) he was not reasonably able to comply with the provision in question by reason of an emergency or grave danger and that he took all steps as were reasonably practicable in the circumstances for—

(i) minimising any threat to the public or the environment; and

(ii) ensuring that the provision in question was complied with as soon as reasonably practicable after the event; or

(b) if there is no emergency or grave danger he took all reasonable precautions and exercised all due diligence to avoid the commission of the offence.

67 Liability of persons other than the principal offender

(1) Where the commission by any person of an offence under this Part is due to the act or default of some other person, that other person may be charged with and convicted of an offence by virtue of this paragraph whether or not proceedings are taken against the first-mentioned person.

(2) Where an offence under this Part which has been committed by a body corporate is proved to have been committed with the consent or connivance of, or to have been attributable to, any neglect on the part of a director, manager, secretary or other similar officer of the body corporate, or any person who was purporting to act in any such capacity, he, as well as the body corporate, shall be liable to be proceeded against and punished accordingly.

(3) Where the affairs of a body corporate are managed by its members, paragraph (2) shall apply in relation to the acts or defaults of a member in connection with his functions of management as if he were a director of the body corporate.

68 False and misleading information

. . .

69 Penalties

(1) A person who commits an offence under regulation 65 in connection with any of the following regulations—

(a) regulation 21 (requirement to notify premises);

(b) regulation 22 (prohibition on removal of waste from premises unless notified or exempt);

(c) regulations 24 to 26 (notifications);

(d) regulation 34 (consignment codes);

(e) regulations 35 to 44 (consignment notes);

(f) regulation 46 and Schedule 7 (cross border consignments);

(g) regulation 53 (consignee and self-disposal quarterly returns);

(h) regulation 54 (consignee's return to the producer, holder or consignor); or

(i) regulation 55 (duties to supply information).

shall be liable on summary conviction, to a fine not exceeding level 5 on the standard scale.

(2) A person who commits an offence under regulation 65 or 68 in connection with any other requirement under these Regulations shall be liable—

(a) on summary conviction, to a fine not exceeding the statutory maximum; or

(b) on conviction on indictment, to a fine or to imprisonment for a term not exceeding two years, or to both.

70 Fixed penalties

(1) Where an authorised person acting on behalf of the Agency has reason to believe that a person has committed an offence under regulation 65 to which this regulation applies, he may give that person a notice offering him the opportunity of discharging any liability to conviction for that offence by payment of a fixed penalty.

(2) This regulation applies to an offence consisting of—

(a) a failure to comply with any requirement of; or

(b) making a false or misleading statement in purported compliance with, any of the regulations listed in regulation 69(1)(a) to (i).

(3) Where a person is given a notice under this regulation in respect of an offence—

(a) no proceedings shall be instituted for that offence before the expiration of twenty eight days following the date of the notice; and

(b) he shall not be convicted of that offence if he pays the fixed penalty before the expiration of that period.

(4) A notice under this regulation shall give such particulars of the circumstances alleged to constitute the offence as are necessary for giving reasonable information of the offence and shall state—

(a) the period during which, by virtue of paragraph (3), proceedings will not be taken for the offence;

(b) the amount of the fixed penalty;

(c) the name of the person to whom and the address at which the fixed penalty may be paid.

(5) Without prejudice to payment by any other method, payment of the fixed penalty may be made by pre-paying and posting to that person at that address a letter containing the amount of the penalty (in cash or otherwise).

(6) Where a letter is sent in accordance with paragraph (5) payment shall be regarded as having been made at the time at which that letter would be delivered in the ordinary course of post.

(7) A fixed penalty notice issued pursuant to this section shall be in the form set out in Schedule 10.

(8) The fixed penalty payable in pursuance of a notice under this regulation shall be £ 300; and as respects the sums received by or on behalf of the Agency, those sums shall be paid to the Secretary of State.

(9) In any proceedings a certificate which—

(a) purports to be signed by or on behalf of the chief finance officer of the Agency;

(b) states that payment of a fixed penalty was or was not received by a date specified in the certificate,

shall be evidence of the facts stated.

(10) In paragraph (8), 'chief finance officer' means the person having responsibility for the financial affairs of the Agency.

PART 12 FINAL PROVISIONS

76 Revocations and savings

(1) Subject to the following paragraphs, the 1996 Regulations are revoked.

...

Regulation 3(2)(a)(i) SCHEDULE 1

ANNEX I TO THE HAZARDOUS WASTE DIRECTIVE

'Annex I
Categories or Generic Types of Hazardous Waste Listed According to their Nature of the Activity which Generated them (*) (Waste may be Liquid, Sludge or Solid in Form)

(*) Certain duplications of entries found in Annex II are intentional.

ANNEX IA

Wastes displaying any of the properties listed in Annex III and which consist of:

1 anatomical substances; hospital and other clinical wastes;

2 pharmaceuticals, medicines and veterinary compounds;
3 wood preservatives;
4 biocides and phyto-pharmaceutical substances;
5 residue from substances employed as solvents;
6 halogenated organic substances not employed as solvents excluding inert polymerized materials;
7 tempering salts containing cyanides;
8 mineral oils and oily substances (eg cutting sludges, etc);
9 oil/water, hydrocarbon/water mixtures, emulsions;
10 substances containing PCBs and/or PCTs (eg dielectrics etc);
11 tarry materials arising from refining, distillation and any pyrolytic treatment (eg still bottoms, etc);
12 inks, dyes, pigments, paints, lacquers, varnishes;
13 resins, latex, plasticizers, glues/adhesives;
14 chemical substances arising from research and development or teaching activities which are not identified and/or are new and whose effects on man and/or the environment are not known (eg laboratory residues, etc);
15 pyrotechnics and other explosive materials;
16 photographic chemicals and processing materials;
17 any material contaminated with any congener of polychlorinated dibenzofuran;
18 any material contaminated with any congener of polychlorinated dibenzo-pdioxin.

ANNEX IB

Wastes which contain any of the constituents listed in Annex II and having any of the properties listed in Annex III and consisting of:
19 animal or vegetable soaps, fats, waxes;
20 non-halogenated organic substances not employed as solvents;
21 inorganic substances without metals or metal compounds;
22 ashes and/or cinders;
23 soil, sand, clay including dredging spoils;
24 non-cyanidic tempering salts;
25 metallic dust, powder;
26 spent catalyst materials;
27 liquids or sludges containing metals or metal compounds;
28 residue from pollution control operations (eg baghouse dusts, etc) except (29), (30) and (33);
29 scrubber sludges;
30 sludges from water purification plants;
31 decarbonization residue;
32 ion-exchange column residue;
33 sewage sludges, untreated or unsuitable for use in agriculture;
34 residue from cleaning of tanks and/or equipment;
35 contaminated equipment;
36 contaminated containers (eg packaging, gas cylinders, etc) whose contents included one or more of the constituents listed in Annex II;
37 batteries and other electrical cells;
38 vegetable oils;
39 materials resulting from selective waste collections from households and which exhibit any of the characteristics listed in Annex III;
40 any other wastes which contain any of the constituents listed in Annex II and any of the properties listed in Annex III.'.

Regulation 3(2)(a)(ii) SCHEDULE 2

ANNEX II TO THE HAZARDOUS WASTE DIRECTIVE

'Annex II
Constituents of the Wastes in Annex IB which Render them Hazardous when they have the Properties Described in Annex III (*)

(*) Certain duplications of generic types of hazardous wastes listed in Annex I are intentional.

Wastes having as constituents:

C1 beryllium; beryllium compounds;
C2 vanadium compounds;
C3 chromium (VI) compounds;
C4 cobalt compounds;
C5 nickel compounds;
C6 copper compounds;
C7 zinc compounds;
C8 arsenic; arsenic compounds;
C9 selenium; selenium compounds;
C10 silver compounds;
C11 cadmium; cadmium compounds;
C12 tin compounds;
C13 antimony; antimony compounds;
C14 tellurium; tellurium compounds;
C15 barium compounds; excluding barium sulfate;
C16 mercury; mercury compounds;
C17 thallium; thallium compounds;
C18 lead; lead compounds;
C19 inorganic sulphides;
C20 inorganic fluorine compounds, excluding calcium fluoride;
C21 inorganic cyanides;
C22 the following alkaline or alkaline earth metals: lithium, sodium, potassium, calcium, magnesium in uncombined form;
C23 acidic solutions or acids in solid form;
C24 basic solutions or bases in solid form;
C25 asbestos (dust and fibres);
C26 phosphorus: phosphorus compounds, excluding mineral phosphates;
C27 metal carbonyls;
C28 peroxides;
C29 chlorates;
C30 perchlorates;
C31 azides;
C32 PCBs and/or PCTs;
C33 pharmaceutical or veterinary coumpounds;
C34 biocides and phyto-pharmaceutical substances (eg pesticides, etc);
C35 infectious substances;
C36 creosotes;
C37 isocyanates; thiocyanates;
C38 organic cyanides (eg nitriles, etc);
C39 phenols; phenol compounds;

C40 halogenated solvents;
C41 organic solvents, excluding halogenated solvents;
C42 organohalogen compounds, excluding inert polymerized materials and other substances referred to in this Annex;
C43 aromatic compounds; polycyclic and heterocyclic organic compounds;
C44 aliphatic amines;
C45 aromatic amines;
C46 ethers;
C47 substances of an explosive character, excluding those listed elsewhere in this Annex;
C48 sulphur organic compounds;
C49 any congener of polychlorinated dibenzo-furan;
C50 any congener of polychlorinated dibenzo-p-dioxin;
C51 hydrocarbons and their oxygen; nitrogen and/or sulphur compounds nototherwise taken into account in this Annex.'.

Regulation 3(2)(a)(iii)

SCHEDULE 3

ANNEX III TO THE HAZARDOUS WASTE DIRECTIVE

'Annex III

Properties of Wastes which Render them Hazardous

H1 'Explosive': substances and preparations which may explode under the effect of flame or which are more sensitive to shocks or friction than dinitrobenzene.

H2 'Oxidizing': substances and preparations which exhibit highly exothermic reactions when in contact with other substances, particularly flammable substances.

H3-A 'Highly flammable':

— liquid substances and preparations having a flash point below 21C (including extremely flammable liquids), or
— substances and preparations which may become hot and finally catch fire in contact with air at ambient temperature without any application of energy, or
— solid substances and preparations which may readily catch fire after brief contact with a source of ignition and which continue to burn or to be consumed after removal of the source of ignition, or
— gaseous substances and preparations which are flammable in air at normal pressure, or
— substances and preparations which, in contact with water or damp air, evolve highly flammable gases in dangerous quantities.

H3-B 'Flammable': liquid substances and preparations having a flash point equal to or greater than 21° C and less than or equal to 55° C

H4 'Irritant': non-corrosive substances and preparations which, through immediate, prolonged or repeated contact with the skin or mucous membrane, can cause inflammation.

H5 'harmful': substances and preparations which, if they are inhaled or ingested or if they penetrate the skin, may involve limited health risks.

H6 'Toxic': substances and preparations (including very toxic substances and preparations) which, if they are inhaled or ingested or if they penetrate the skin, may involve serious, acute or chronic health risks and even death.

H7 'Carcinogenic': substances and preparations which, if they are inhaled or ingested or if they penetrate the skin, may induce cancer or increase its incidence.

H8 'Corrosive': substances and preparations which may destroy living tissue on contacts.

H9 'Infectious': substances containing viable micro-organisms or their toxins which are known or reliably believed to cause disease in man or other living organisms.

H10 'Teratogenic': substances and preparations which, if they are inhaled or ingested or if they penetrate the skin, may induce non-hereditary congenital malformations or increase their incidence.

H11 'Mutagenic': substances and preparations which, if they are inhaled or ingested or if they penetrate the skin, may induce hereditary genetic defects or increase their incidence.

H12 Substances and preparations which release toxic or very toxic gases in contact with water, air or an acid.

H13 Substances and preparations capable by any means, after disposal, of yielding another substance, eg a leachate, which possesses any of the characteristics listed above.

H14 'Ecotoxic': substances and preparations which present or may present immediate or delayed risks for one or more sectors of the environment.'

Notes

1 Attribution of the hazard properties 'toxic' (and 'very toxic'), 'harmful', 'corrosive' and 'irritant' is made on the basis of the criteria laid down by Annex VI, part I A and part II B, of Council Directive 67/548/EEC of 27 June 1967 of the approximation of laws, regulations and administrative provisions relating to the classification, packaging and labelling of dangerous substances, in the version as amended by Council Directive 79/831/EEC.

2 With regard to attribution of the properties 'carcinogenic', 'teratogenic' and 'mutagenic', and reflecting the most recent findings, additional criteria are contained in the Guide to the classification and labelling of dangerous substances and preparations of Annex VI (part II D) to Directive 67/548/EEC in the version as amended by Commission Directive 83/467/EEC.

Test methods

The test methods serve to give specific meaning to the definitions given in Annex III.

The methods to be used are those described in Annex V to Directive 67/548/EEC, in the version as amended by Commission Directive 84/449/EEC, or by subsequent Commission Directives adapting Directive 67/548/EEC to technical progress. These methods are themselves based on the work and recommendations of the competent international bodies, in particular the OECD.

Environmental Offences (Fixed Penalties) (Miscellaneous Provisions) Regulations 2006

(SI 2006, No. 783)

1 Title, commencement and application

These Regulations—

(a) may be cited as the Environmental Offences (Fixed Penalties) (Miscellaneous Provisions) Regulations 2006;

(b) come into force on 6th April 2006;

(c) apply in England only.

2 Prescribed ranges of fixed penalties

. . .

(2) The amount of a fixed penalty capable of being specified by—

(a) a waste collection authority in England under section 47ZB(2)(a) of the Environmental Protection Act 1990;

(b) a principal litter authority in England under section 94A(4)(a) of the Environmental Protection Act 1990;

(c) a local authority in England under section 8A(2)(a) of the Noise Act 1996, shall be not less than £75 and not more than £110.

(3) An authority acting under more than one of the provisions in paragraph (1) or in paragraph (2) may specify a different amount under each such provision.

3 Lesser amounts of fixed penalties

(1) ...

(2) Where—

(a) a waste collection authority in England acting under section 47ZB(3) of the Environmental Protection Act 1990;

(b) ...

(c) a local authority in England acting under section 8A(3) of the Noise Act 1996;

(d) ...,

makes provision for treating a fixed penalty as having been paid if a lesser amount is paid before the end of a period specified by that authority, such lesser amount shall be not less than £60.

(3) ...

(4) Where—

(a) a regulation authority acting under section 5B(11) of the Control of Pollution (Amendment) Act 1989;

(b) an enforcement authority acting under section 34A(11) of the Environmental Protection Act 1990,

makes provision for treating a fixed penalty as having been paid if a lesser amount is paid before the end of a period specified by that authority, such lesser amount shall be not less than £180.

(5) An authority acting under more than one of the sub-paragraphs in paragraph (1), paragraph (2) or paragraph (4) may specify a different lesser amount under each such sub-paragraph.

4 Use of fixed penalty receipts: specification of functions

(1) Where, and for as long as, any authority of a type described in paragraph (2) is categorised as 'excellent' or 'good' in a categorisation Order, any functions of that authority (in addition to those already specified in the section referred to in the relevant description) are hereby specified as functions or, in the case of an authority of a type described in paragraph (2)(d) or (f), as 'qualifying functions', of the authority for the purposes of which it may use its fixed penalty receipts.

(2) The types of authority are—

(a) ...;

(b) a waste collection authority to which section 5C of the Control of Pollution (Amendment) Act 1989 applies;

(c) a waste collection authority to which section 73A of the Environmental Protection Act 1990 applies;

(d) a local authority to which section 9(4), as read with section 9(4A), of the Noise Act 1996 applies;

(e) ...;

(f) ....

(3) In this regulation and in regulation 5 a 'categorisation Order' means an Order made by the Secretary of State under section 99(4) of the Local Government Act 2003.

5 Use of fixed penalty receipts: transitional arrangement

In the event that any authority of a type described in regulation 4(2) is no longer categorised as 'excellent' or 'good' in a categorisation Order, regulation 4(1) will continue to apply for a period of one year from the date on which that cessation comes into effect as though that authority were still categorised as 'excellent' or 'good'.

...

PART III

EC Law*

Consolidated Version of the Treaty Establishing the European Community

PART ONE PRINCIPLES

Article 1

By this Treaty, the High Contracting Parties establish among themselves a European Community.

Article 2

The Community shall have as its task, by establishing a common market and an economic and monetary union and by implementing common policies or activities referred to in Articles 3 and 4, to promote throughout the Community a harmonious, balanced and sustainable development of economic activities, a high level of employment and of social protection, equality between men and women, sustainable and non-inflationary growth, a high degree of competitiveness and convergence of economic performance, a high level of protection and improvement of the quality of the environment, the raising of the standard of living and quality of life, and economic and social cohesion and solidarity among Member States.

Article 3

1. For the purposes set out in Article 2, the activities of the Community shall include, as provided in this Treaty and in accordance with the timetable set out therein:

(a) the prohibition, as between Member States, of customs duties and quantitative restrictions on the import and export of goods, and of all other measures having equivalent effect;

(b) a common commercial policy;

(c) an internal market characterised by the abolition, as between Member States, of obstacles to the free movement of goods, persons, services and capital;

(d) measures concerning the entry and movement of persons as provided for in Title IV;

(e) a common policy in the sphere of agriculture and fisheries;

(f) a common policy in the sphere of transport;

(g) a system ensuring that competition in the internal market is not distorted;

(h) the approximation of the laws of Member States to the extent required for the functioning of the common market;

(i) the promotion of coordination between employment policies of the Member States with a view to enhancing their effectiveness by developing a coordinated strategy for employment;

(j) a policy in the social sphere comprising a European Social Fund;

(k) the strengthening of economic and social cohesion;

*Only European Community official Documents Printed in the Official Journal of the European Union are deemed authentic.

(l) a policy in the sphere of the environment;
(m) the strengthening of the competitiveness of Community industry;
(n) the promotion of research and technological development;
(o) encouragement for the establishment and development of trans-European networks;
(p) a contribution to the attainment of a high level of health protection;
(q) a contribution to education and training of quality and to the flowering of the cultures of the Member States;
(r) a policy in the sphere of development cooperation;
(s) the association of the overseas countries and territories in order to increase trade and promote jointly economic and social development;
(t) a contribution to the strengthening of consumer protection;
(u) measures in the spheres of energy, civil protection and tourism.

2. In all the activities referred to in this Article, the Community shall aim to eliminate inequalities, and to promote equality, between men and women.

Article 5

The Community shall act within the limits of the powers conferred upon it by this Treaty and of the objectives assigned to it therein.

In areas which do not fall within its exclusive competence, the Community shall take action, in accordance with the principle of subsidiarity, only if and insofar as the objectives of the proposed action cannot be sufficiently achieved by the Member States and can therefore, by reason of the scale or effects of the proposed action, be better achieved by the Community.

Any action by the Community shall not go beyond what is necessary to achieve the objectives of this Treaty.

Article 6

Environmental protection requirements must be integrated into the definition and implementation of the Community policies and activities referred to in Article 3, in particular with a view to promoting sustainable development.

Article 10

Member States shall take all appropriate measures, whether general or particular, to ensure fulfilment of the obligations arising out of this Treaty or resulting from action taken by the institutions of the Community. They shall facilitate the achievement of the Community's tasks.

They shall abstain from any measure which could jeopardise the attainment of the objectives of this Treaty.

PART THREE COMMUNITY POLICIES

TITLE I FREE MOVEMENT OF GOODS

CHAPTER 2 PROHIBITION OF QUANTITATIVE RESTRICTIONS BETWEEN MEMBER STATES

Article 28

Quantitative restrictions on imports and all measures having equivalent effect shall be prohibited between Member States.

Article 29

Quantitative restrictions on exports, and all measures having equivalent effect, shall be prohibited between Member States.

Article 30

The provisions of Articles 28 and 29 shall not preclude prohibitions or restrictions on imports, exports or goods in transit justified on grounds of public morality, public policy or public security; the protection of health and life of humans, animals or plants; the protection of national treasures possessing artistic, historic or archaeological value; or the protection of industrial and commercial property. Such prohibitions or restrictions shall not, however, constitute a means of arbitrary discrimination or a disguised restriction on trade between Member States.

TITLE VI COMMON RULES ON COMPETITION, TAXATION AND APPROXIMATION OF LAWS

CHAPTER 3 APPROXIMATION OF LAWS

Article 94

The Council shall, acting unanimously on a proposal from the Commission and after consulting the European Parliament and the Economic and Social Committee, issue directives for the approximation of such laws, regulations or administrative provisions of the Member States as directly affect the establishment or functioning of the common market.

Article 95

1. By way of derogation from Article 94 and save where otherwise provided in this Treaty, the following provisions shall apply for the achievement of the objectives set out in Article 14. The Council shall, acting in accordance with the procedure referred to in Article 251 and after consulting the Economic and Social Committee, adopt the measures for the approximation of the provisions laid down by law, regulation or administrative action in Member States which have as their object the establishment and functioning of the internal market.

2. Paragraph 1 shall not apply to fiscal provisions, to those relating to the free movement of persons nor to those relating to the rights and interests of employed persons.

3. The Commission, in its proposals envisaged in paragraph 1 concerning health, safety, environmental protection and consumer protection, will take as a base a high level of protection, taking account in particular of any new development based on scientific facts. Within their respective powers, the European Parliament and the Council will also seek to achieve this objective.

4. If, after the adoption by the Council or by the Commission of a harmonisation measure, a Member State deems it necessary to maintain national provisions on grounds of major needs referred to in Article 30, or relating to the protection of the environment or the working environment, it shall notify the Commission of these provisions as well as the grounds for maintaining them.

5. Moreover, without prejudice to paragraph 4, if, after the adoption by the Council or by the Commission of a harmonisation measure, a Member State deems it necessary to introduce national provisions based on new scientific evidence relating to the protection of the environment or the working environment on grounds of a problem specific to that Member State arising after the adoption of the harmonisation measure, it shall notify the Commission of the envisaged provisions as well as the grounds for introducing them.

6. The Commission shall, within six months of the notifications as referred to in paragraphs 4 and 5, approve or reject the national provisions involved after having verified whether or not they are a means of arbitrary discrimination or a disguised restriction on trade between Member States and whether or not they shall constitute an obstacle to the functioning of the internal market.

In the absence of a decision by the Commission within this period the national provisions referred to in paragraphs 4 and 5 shall be deemed to have been approved.

When justified by the complexity of the matter and in the absence of danger for human health, the Commission may notify the Member State concerned that the period referred to in this paragraph may be extended for a further period of up to six months.

7. When, pursuant to paragraph 6, a Member State is authorised to maintain or introduce national provisions derogating from a harmonisation measure, the Commission shall immediately examine whether to propose an adaptation to that measure.

8. When a Member State raises a specific problem on public health in a field which has been the subject of prior harmonisation measures, it shall bring it to the attention of the Commission which shall immediately examine whether to propose appropriate measures to the Council.

9. By way of derogation from the procedure laid down in Articles 226 and 227, the Commission and any Member State may bring the matter directly before the Court of Justice if it considers that another Member State is making improper use of the powers provided for in this Article.

10. The harmonisation measures referred to above shall, in appropriate cases, include a safeguard clause authorising the Member States to take, for one or more of the non-economic reasons referred to in Article 30, provisional measures subject to a Community control procedure.

TITLE XIX ENVIRONMENT

Article 174

1. Community policy on the environment shall contribute to pursuit of the following objectives:
   - preserving, protecting and improving the quality of the environment;
   - protecting human health;
   - prudent and rational utilisation of natural resources;
   - promoting measures at international level to deal with regional or worldwide environmental problems.

2. Community policy on the environment shall aim at a high level of protection taking into account the diversity of situations in the various regions of the Community. It shall be based on the precautionary principle and on the principles that preventive action should be taken, that environmental damage should as a priority be rectified at source and that the polluter should pay.

In this context, harmonisation measures answering environmental protection requirements shall include, where appropriate, a safeguard clause allowing Member States to take provisional measures, for non-economic environmental reasons, subject to a Community inspection procedure.

3. In preparing its policy on the environment, the Community shall take account of:
   - available scientific and technical data;
   - environmental conditions in the various regions of the Community;
   - the potential benefits and costs of action or lack of action;
   - the economic and social development of the Community as a whole and the balanced development of its regions.

4. Within their respective spheres of competence, the Community and the Member States shall cooperate with third countries and with the competent international organisations. The arrangements for Community cooperation may be the subject of agreements between the Community and the third parties concerned, which shall be negotiated and concluded in accordance with Article 300.

The previous subparagraph shall be without prejudice to Member States' competence to negotiate in international bodies and to conclude international agreements.

Article 175

1. The Council, acting in accordance with the procedure referred to in Article 251 and after consulting the Economic and Social Committee and the Committee of the Regions, shall decide what action is to be taken by the Community in order to achieve the objectives referred to in Article 174.

2. By way of derogation from the decision-making procedure provided for in paragraph 1 and without prejudice to Article 95, the Council, acting unanimously on a proposal from the Commission and after consulting the European Parliament, the Economic and Social Committee and the Committee of the Regions, shall adopt:

— provisions primarily of a fiscal nature;
— measures concerning town and country planning, land use with the exception of waste management and measures of a general nature, and management of water resources;
— measures significantly affecting a Member State's choice between different energy sources and the general structure of its energy supply.

The Council may, under the conditions laid down in the preceding subparagraph, define those matters referred to in this paragraph on which decisions are to be taken by a qualified majority.

3. In other areas, general action programmes setting out priority objectives to be attained shall be adopted by the Council, acting in accordance with the procedure referred to in Article 251 and after consulting the Economic and Social Committee and the Committee of the Regions.

The Council, acting under the terms of paragraph 1 or paragraph 2 according to the case, shall adopt the measures necessary for the implementation of these programmes.

4. Without prejudice to certain measures of a Community nature, the Member States shall finance and implement the environment policy.

5. Without prejudice to the principle that the polluter should pay, if a measure based on the provisions of paragraph 1 involves costs deemed disproportionate for the public authorities of a Member State, the Council shall, in the act adopting that measure, lay down appropriate provisions in the form of:

— temporary derogations, and/or
— financial support from the Cohesion Fund set up pursuant to Article 161.

Article 176

The protective measures adopted pursuant to Article 175 shall not prevent any Member State from maintaining or introducing more stringent protective measures. Such measures must be compatible with this Treaty. They shall be notified to the Commission.

PART FIVE INSTITUTIONS OF THE COMMUNITY

TITLE I PROVISIONS GOVERNING THE INSTITUTIONS

CHAPTER 1 THE INSTITUTIONS

SECTION 3 COMMISSION

Article 211

In order to ensure the proper functioning and development of the common market, the Commission shall:

— ensure that the provisions of this Treaty and the measures taken by the institutions pursuant thereto are applied;
— formulate recommendations or deliver opinions on matters dealt with in this Treaty, if it expressly so provides or if the Commission considers it necessary;
— have its own power of decision and participate in the shaping of measures taken by the Council and by the European Parliament in the manner provided for in this Treaty;
— exercise the powers conferred on it by the Council for the implementation of the rules laid down by the latter.

SECTION 4 THE COURT OF JUSTICE

Article 220

The Court of Justice and the Court of First Instance, each within its jurisdiction, shall ensure that in the interpretation and application of this Treaty the law is observed. ...

Article 226

If the Commission considers that a Member State has failed to fulfil an obligation under this Treaty, it shall deliver a reasoned opinion on the matter after giving the State concerned the opportunity to submit its observations.

If the State concerned does not comply with the opinion within the period laid down by the Commission, the latter may bring the matter before the Court of Justice.

Article 227

A Member State which considers that another Member State has failed to fulfil an obligation under this Treaty may bring the matter before the Court of Justice.

Before a Member State brings an action against another Member State for an alleged infringement of an obligation under this Treaty, it shall bring the matter before the Commission.

The Commission shall deliver a reasoned opinion after each of the States concerned has been given the opportunity to submit its own case and its observations on the other party's case both orally and in writing.

If the Commission has not delivered an opinion within three months of the date on which the matter was brought before it, the absence of such opinion shall not prevent the matter from being brought before the Court of Justice.

Article 228

1. If the Court of Justice finds that a Member State has failed to fulfil an obligation under this Treaty, the State shall be required to take the necessary measures to comply with the judgment of the Court of Justice.

2. If the Commission considers that the Member State concerned has not taken such measures it shall, after giving that State the opportunity to submit its observations, issue a reasoned opinion specifying the points on which the Member State concerned has not complied with the judgment of the Court of Justice.

If the Member State concerned fails to take the necessary measures to comply with the Court's judgment within the time-limit laid down by the Commission, the latter may bring the case before the Court of Justice. In so doing it shall specify the amount of the lump sum or penalty payment to be paid by the Member State concerned which it considers appropriate in the circumstances.

If the Court of Justice finds that the Member State concerned has not complied with its judgment it may impose a lump sum or penalty payment on it.

This procedure shall be without prejudice to Article 227.

Article 230

The Court of Justice shall review the legality of acts adopted jointly by the European Parliament and the Council, of acts of the Council, of the Commission and of the ECB, other than recommendations and opinions, and of acts of the European Parliament intended to produce legal effects vis-à-vis third parties.

It shall for this purpose have jurisdiction in actions brought by a Member State, the Council or the Commission on grounds of lack of competence, infringement of an essential procedural requirement, infringement of this Treaty or of any rule of law relating to its application, or misuse of powers.

The Court of Justice shall have jurisdiction under the same conditions in actions brought by the European Parliament, by the Court of Auditors and by the ECB for the purpose of protecting their prerogatives.

Any natural or legal person may, under the same conditions, institute proceedings against a decision addressed to that person or against a decision which, although in the form of a regulation or a decision addressed to another person, is of direct and individual concern to the former.

The proceedings provided for in this Article shall be instituted within two months of the publication of the measure, or of its notification to the plaintiff, or, in the absence thereof, of the day on which it came to the knowledge of the latter, as the case may be.

Article 234

The Court of Justice shall have jurisdiction to give preliminary rulings concerning:

(a) the interpretation of this Treaty;

(b) the validity and interpretation of acts of the institutions of the Community and of the ECB;

(c) the interpretation of the statutes of bodies established by an act of the Council, where those statutes so provide.

Where such a question is raised before any court or tribunal of a Member State, that court or tribunal may, if it considers that a decision on the question is necessary to enable it to give judgment, request the Court of Justice to give a ruling thereon.

Where any such question is raised in a case pending before a court or tribunal of a Member State against whose decisions there is no judicial remedy under national law, that court or tribunal shall bring the matter before the Court of Justice.

CHAPTER 2 PROVISIONS COMMON TO SEVERAL INSTITUTIONS

Article 249

In order to carry out their task and in accordance with the provisions of this Treaty, the European Parliament acting jointly with the Council, the Council and the Commission shall make regulations and issue directives, take decisions, make recommendations or deliver opinions.

A regulation shall have general application. It shall be binding in its entirety and directly applicable in all Member States.

A directive shall be binding, as to the result to be achieved, upon each Member State to which it is addressed, but shall leave to the national authorities the choice of form and methods.

A decision shall be binding in its entirety upon those to whom it is addressed. Recommendations and opinions shall have no binding force.

Article 250

1. Where, in pursuance of this Treaty, the Council acts on a proposal front time Commission, unanimity shall be required for an act constituting an amendment to that proposal, subject to Article 251(4) and (5).

2. As long as the Council has not acted, the Commission may alter its proposal at any time during the procedures leading to the adoption of a Community act.

Article 251

1. Where reference is made in this Treaty to this Article for the adoption of an act, the following procedure shall apply.

2. The Commission shall submit a proposal to the European Parliament and the Council. The Council, acting by a qualified majority after obtaining the opinion of the European Parliament,

— if it approves all the amendments contained in the European Parliament's opinion, may adopt the proposed act thus amended;

— if the European Parliament does not propose any amendments, may adopt the proposed act;

— shall otherwise adopt a common position and communicate it to the European Parliament. The Council shall inform the European Parliament fully of the reasons which led it to adopt its common position. The Commission shall inform the European Parliament fully of its position.

If, within three months of such communication, the European Parliament:

(a) approves the common position or has not taken a decision, the act in question shall be deemed to have been adopted in accordance with that common position;

(b) rejects, by an absolute majority of its component members, the common position, the proposed act shall be deemed not to have been adopted;

(c) proposes amendments to the common position by an absolute majority of its component members, the amended text shall be forwarded to the Council and to the Commission, which shall deliver an opinion on those amendments.

3. If, within three months of the matter being referred to it, the Council, acting by a qualified majority, approves all the amendments of the European Parliament, the act in question shall be deemed to have been adopted in the form of the common position thus amended; however, the Council shall act unanimously on the amendments on which the Commission has delivered a negative opinion. If the Council does not approve all the amendments, the President of the Council, in agreement with the President of the European Parliament, shall within six weeks convene a meeting of the Conciliation Committee.

4. The Conciliation Committee, which shall be composed of the members of the Council or their representatives and an equal number of representatives of the European Parliament, shall have the task of reaching agreement on a joint text, by a qualified majority of the members of the Council or their representatives and by a majority of the representatives of the European Parliament. The Commission shall take part in the Conciliation Committee's proceedings and shall take all the necessary initiatives with a view to reconciling the positions of the European Parliament and the Council. In fulfilling this task, time Conciliation Committee shall address the common position on the basis of the amendments proposed by the European Parliament.

5. If, within six weeks of its being convened, the Conciliation Committee approves a joint text, the European Parliament, acting by an absolute majority of the votes cast, and the Council, acting by a qualified majority, shall each have a period of six weeks from that approval in which to adopt the act in question in accordance with the joint text. If either of the two institutions fails to approve the proposed act within that period, it shall be deemed not to have been adopted.

6. Where the Conciliation Committee does not approve a joint text, the proposed act shall be deemed not to have been adopted.

7. The periods of three months and six weeks referred to in this Article shall be extended by a maximum of one month and two weeks respectively at the initiative of the European Parliament or the Council.

Article 252

Where reference is made in this Treaty to this Article for the adoption of an act, the following procedure shall apply:

(a) The Council, acting by a qualified majority on a proposal from the Commission and after obtaining the opinion of the European Parliament, shall adopt a common position.

(b) The Council's common position shall be communicated to the European Parliament. The Council and the Commission shall inform the European Parliament fully of the reasons which led the Council to adopt its common position and also of the Commission's position.

If, within three months of such communication, the European Parliament approves this common position or has not taken a decision within that period, the Council shall definitively adopt the act in question in accordance with the common position.

(c) The European Parliament may, within the period of three months referred to in point (b), by an absolute majority of its component Members, propose amendments to the Council's common position. The European Parliament may also, by the same majority, reject the Council's common position. The result of the proceedings shall be transmitted to the Council and the Commission.

If the European Parliament has rejected the Council's common position, unanimity shall be required for the Council to act on a second reading.

(d) The Commission shall, within a period of one month, re-examine the proposal on the basis of which the Council adopted its common position, by taking into account the amendments proposed by the European Parliament.

The Commission shall forward to the Council, at the same time as its re-examined proposal, the amendments of the European Parliament which it has not accepted, and shall express its opinion on them. The Council may adopt these amendments unanimously.

(e) The Council, acting by a qualified majority, shall adopt the proposal as re-examined by the Commission.

Unanimity shall be required for the Council to amend the proposal as re-examined by the Commission.

(f) In the cases referred to in points (c), (d) and (e), the Council shall be required to act within a period of three months. If no decision is taken within this period, the Commission proposal shall be deemed not to have been adopted.

(g) The periods referred to in points (b) and (f) may be extended by a maximum of one month by common accord between the Council and the European Parliament.

PART SIX GENERAL AND FINAL PROVISIONS

Article 308

If action by the Community should prove necessary to attain, in the course of the operation of the common market, one of the objectives of the Community, and this Treaty has not provided the necessary powers, the Council shall, acting unanimously on a proposal from the Commission and after consulting the European Parliament, take the appropriate measures.

Directive 2000/60/EC of the European Parliament and of the Council

of 23 October 2000

establishing a framework for Community action in the field of water policy (the 'Water Framework Directive')

THE EUROPEAN PARLIAMENT AND THE COUNCIL OF THE EUROPEAN UNION,

Having regard to the Treaty establishing the European Community, and in particular Article 175(1) thereof,

Having regard to the proposal from the Commission,

Having regard to the opinion of the Economic and Social Committee,

Having regard to the opinion of the Committee of the Regions,

Acting in accordance with the procedure laid down in Article 251 of the Treaty(4), and in the light of the joint text approved by the Conciliation Committee on 18 July 2000,

Whereas:

(1) Water is not a commercial product like any other but, rather, a heritage which must be protected, defended and treated as such.

. . .

(18) Community water policy requires a transparent, effective and coherent legislative framework. The Community should provide common principles and the overall framework for action. This Directive should provide for such a framework and coordinate and integrate, and, in a longer perspective, further develop the overall principles and structures for protection and sustainable use of water in the Community in accordance with the principles of subsidiarity.

. . .

(23) Common principles are needed in order to coordinate Member States' efforts to improve the protection of Community waters in terms of quantity and quality, to promote sustainable water use, to contribute to the control of transboundary water problems, to protect aquatic ecosystems, and terrestrial ecosystems and wetlands directly depending on them, and to safeguard and develop the potential uses of Community waters.

. . .

(25) Common definitions of the status of water in terms of quality and, where relevant for the purpose of the environmental protection, quantity should be established. Environmental objectives should be set to ensure that good status of surface water and groundwater is achieved throughout the Community and that deterioration in the status of waters is prevented at Community level.

. . .

(27) The ultimate aim of this Directive is to achieve the elimination of priority hazardous substances and contribute to achieving concentrations in the marine environment near background values for naturally occurring substances.

. . .

(33) The objective of achieving good water status should be pursued for each river basin, so that measures in respect of surface water and groundwaters belonging to the same ecological, hydrological and hydrogeological system are coordinated.

(34) For the purposes of environmental protection there is a need for a greater integration of qualitative and quantitative aspects of both surface waters and groundwaters, taking into account the natural flow conditions of water within the hydrological cycle.

. . .

(40) With regard to pollution prevention and control, Community water policy should be based on a combined approach using control of pollution at source through the setting of emission limit values and of environmental quality standards.

. . .

(44) In identifying priority hazardous substances, account should be taken of the precautionary principle, relying in particular on the determination of any potentially adverse effects of the product and on a scientific assessment of the risk.

. . .

HAVE ADOPTED THIS DIRECTIVE:

Article 1 Purpose

The purpose of this Directive is to establish a framework for the protection of inland surface waters, transitional waters, coastal waters and groundwater which:

(a) prevents further deterioration and protects and enhances the status of aquatic ecosystems and, with regard to their water needs, terrestrial ecosystems and wetlands directly depending on the aquatic ecosystems;

(b) promotes sustainable water use based on a long-term protection of available water resources;

(c) aims at enhanced protection and improvement of the aquatic environment, inter alia, through specific measures for the progressive reduction of discharges, emissions and losses of priority substances and the cessation or phasing-out of discharges, emissions and losses of the priority hazardous substances;

(d) ensures the progressive reduction of pollution of groundwater and prevents its further pollution, and
(e) contributes to mitigating the effects of floods and droughts and thereby contributes to:
— the provision of the sufficient supply of good quality surface water and groundwater as needed for sustainable, balanced and equitable water use,
— a significant reduction in pollution of groundwater,
— the protection of territorial and marine waters, and
— achieving the objectives of relevant international agreements, including those which aim to prevent and eliminate pollution of the marine environment, by Community action under Article 16(3) to cease or phase out discharges, emissions and losses of priority hazardous substances, with the ultimate aim of achieving concentrations in the marine environment near background values for naturally occurring substances and close to zero for man-made synthetic substances.

Article 2 Definitions

For the purposes of this Directive the following definitions shall apply:

1. 'Surface water' means inland waters, except groundwater; transitional waters and coastal waters, except in respect of chemical status for which it shall also include territorial waters.

2. 'Groundwater' means all water which is below the surface of the ground in the saturation zone and in direct contact with the ground or subsoil.

3. 'Inland water' means all standing or flowing water on the surface of the land, and all groundwater on the landward side of the baseline from which the breadth of territorial waters is measured.

4. 'River' means a body of inland water flowing for the most part on the surface of the land but which may flow underground for part of its course.

5. 'Lake' means a body of standing inland surface water.

6. 'Transitional waters' are bodies of surface water in the vicinity of river mouths which are partly saline in character as a result of their proximity to coastal waters but which are substantially influenced by freshwater flows.

7. 'Coastal water' means surface water on the landward side of a line, every point of which is at a distance of one nautical mile on the seaward side from the nearest point of the baseline from which the breadth of territorial waters is measured, extending where appropriate up to the outer limit of transitional waters.

8. 'Artificial water body' means a body of surface water created by human activity.

9. 'Heavily modified water body' means a body of surface water which as a result of physical alterations by human activity is substantially changed in character, as designated by the Member State in accordance with the provisions of Annex II.

10. 'Body of surface water' means a discrete and significant element of surface water such as a lake, a reservoir, a stream, river or canal, part of a stream, river or canal, a transitional water or a stretch of coastal water.

11. 'Aquifer' means a subsurface layer or layers of rock or other geological strata of sufficient porosity and permeability to allow either a significant flow of groundwater or the abstraction of significant quantities of groundwater.

12. 'Body of groundwater' means a distinct volume of groundwater within an aquifer or aquifers.

13. 'River basin' means the area of land from which all surface run-off flows through a sequence of streams, rivers and, possibly, lakes into the sea at a single river mouth, estuary or delta.

14. 'Sub-basin' means the area of land from which all surface run-off flows through a series of streams, rivers and, possibly, lakes to a particular point in a water course (normally a lake or a river confluence).

15. 'River basin district' means the area of land and sea, made up of one or more neighbouring river basins together with their associated groundwaters and coastal waters, which is identified under Article 3(1) as the main unit for management of river basins.

16. 'Competent Authority' means an authority or authorities identified under Article 3(2) or 3(3).

17. 'Surface water status' is the general expression of the status of a body of surface water, determined by the poorer of its ecological status and its chemical status.

18. 'Good surface water status' means the status achieved by a surface water body when both its ecological status and its chemical status are at least 'good'.

19. 'Groundwater status' is the general expression of the status of a body of groundwater, determined by the poorer of its quantitative status and its chemical status.

20. 'Good groundwater status' means the status achieved by a groundwater body when both its quantitative status and its chemical status are at least 'good'.

21. 'Ecological status' is an expression of the quality of the structure and functioning of aquatic ecosystems associated with surface waters, classified in accordance with Annex V.

22. 'Good ecological status' is the status of a body of surface water, so classified in accordance with Annex V.

23. 'Good ecological potential' is the status of a heavily modified or an artificial body of water, so classified in accordance with the relevant provisions of Annex V.

24. 'Good surface water chemical status' means the chemical status required to meet the environmental objectives for surface waters established in Article 4(1)(a), that is the chemical status achieved by a body of surface water in which concentrations of pollutants do not exceed the environmental quality standards established in Annex IX and under Article 16(7), and under other relevant Community legislation setting environmental quality standards at Community level.

25. 'Good groundwater chemical status' is the chemical status of a body of groundwater, which meets all the conditions set out in table 2.3.2 of Annex V.

26. 'Quantitative status' is an expression of the degree to which a body of groundwater is affected by direct and indirect abstractions.

27. 'Available groundwater resource' means the long-term annual average rate of overall recharge of the body of groundwater less the long-term annual rate of flow required to achieve the ecological quality objectives for associated surface waters specified under Article 4, to avoid any significant diminution in the ecological status of such waters and to avoid any significant damage to associated terrestrial ecosystems.

28. 'Good quantitative status' is the status defined in table 2.1.2 of Annex V.

29. 'Hazardous substances' means substances or groups of substances that are toxic, persistent and liable to bio-accumulate, and other substances or groups of substances which give rise to an equivalent level of concern.

30. 'Priority substances' means substances identified in accordance with Article 16(2) and listed in Annex X. Among these substances there are 'priority hazardous substances' which means substances identified in accordance with Article 16(3) and (6) for which measures have to be taken in accordance with Article 16(1) and (8).

31. 'Pollutant' means any substance liable to cause pollution, in particular those listed in Annex VIII.

32. 'Direct discharge to groundwater' means discharge of pollutants into groundwater without percolation throughout the soil or subsoil.

33. 'Pollution' means the direct or indirect introduction, as a result of human activity, of substances or heat into the air, water or land which may be harmful to human health or the quality of aquatic ecosystems or terrestrial ecosystems directly depending on aquatic ecosystems, which result in damage to material property, or which impair or interfere with amenities and other legitimate uses of the environment.

34. 'Environmental objectives' means the objectives set out in Article 4.

35. 'Environmental quality standard' means the concentration of a particular pollutant or group of pollutants in water, sediment or biota which should not be exceeded in order to protect human health and the environment.

36. 'Combined approach' means the control of discharges and emissions into surface waters according to the approach set out in Article 10.

37. 'Water intended for human consumption' has the same meaning as under Directive 80/778/EEC, as amended by Directive 98/83/EC.

38. 'Water services' means all services which provide, for households, public institutions or any economic activity:

(a) abstraction, impoundment, storage, treatment and distribution of surface water or groundwater,

(b) waste-water collection and treatment facilities which subsequently discharge into surface water.

39. 'Water use' means water services together with any other activity identified under Article 5 and Annex II having a significant impact on the status of water.

This concept applies for the purposes of Article 1 and of the economic analysis carried out according to Article 5 and Annex III, point (b).

40. 'Emission limit values' means the mass, expressed in terms of certain specific parameters, concentration and/or level of an emission, which may not be exceeded during any one or more periods of time. Emission limit values may also be laid down for certain groups, families or categories of substances, in particular for those identified under Article 16.

The emission limit values for substances shall normally apply at the point where the emissions leave the installation, dilution being disregarded when determining them. With regard to indirect releases into water, the effect of a waste-water treatment plant may be taken into account when determining the emission limit values of the installations involved, provided that an equivalent level is guaranteed for protection of the environment as a whole and provided that this does not lead to higher levels of pollution in the environment.

41. 'Emission controls' are controls requiring a specific emission limitation, for instance an emission limit value, or otherwise specifying limits or conditions on the effects, nature or other characteristics of an emission or operating conditions which affect emissions. Use of the term 'emission control' in this Directive in respect of the provisions of any other Directive shall not be held as reinterpreting those provisions in any respect.

Article 3 Coordination of administrative arrangements within river basin districts

1. Member States shall identify the individual river basins lying within their national territory and, for the purposes of this Directive, shall assign them to individual river basin districts. Small river basins may be combined with larger river basins or joined with neighbouring small basins to form individual river basin districts where appropriate. Where groundwaters do not fully follow a particular river basin, they shall be identified and assigned to the nearest or most appropriate river basin district. Coastal waters shall be identified and assigned to the nearest or most appropriate river basin district or districts.

2. Member States shall ensure the appropriate administrative arrangements, including the identification of the appropriate competent authority, for the application of the rules of this Directive within each river basin district lying within their territory.

3. Member States shall ensure that a river basin covering the territory of more than one Member State is assigned to an international river basin district. At the request of the Member States involved, the Commission shall act to facilitate the assigning to such international river basin districts.

Each Member State shall ensure the appropriate administrative arrangements, including the identification of the appropriate competent authority, for the application of the rules of this Directive within the portion of any international river basin district lying within its territory.

4. Member States shall ensure that the requirements of this Directive for the achievement of the environmental objectives established under Article 4, and in particular all

programmes of measures are coordinated for the whole of the river basin district. For international river basin districts the Member States concerned shall together ensure this coordination and may, for this purpose, use existing structures stemming from international agreements. At the request of the Member States involved, the Commission shall act to facilitate the establishment of the programmes of measures.

5. Where a river basin district extends beyond the territory of the Community, the Member State or Member States concerned shall endeavour to establish appropriate coordination with the relevant non-Member States, with the aim of achieving the objectives of this Directive throughout the river basin district. Member States shall ensure the application of the rules of this Directive within their territory.

6. Member States may identify an existing national or international body as competent authority for the purposes of this Directive.

7. Member States shall identify the competent authority by the date mentioned in Article 24.

8. Member States shall provide the Commission with a list of their competent authorities and of the competent authorities of all the international bodies in which they participate at the latest six months after the date mentioned in Article 24. For each competent authority the information set out in Annex I shall be provided.

9. Member States shall inform the Commission of any changes to the information provided according to paragraph 8 within three months of the change coming into effect.

Article 4 Environmental objectives

1. In making operational the programmes of measures specified in the river basin management plans:

(a) for surface waters

(i) Member States shall implement the necessary measures to prevent deterioration of the status of all bodies of surface water, subject to the application of paragraphs 6 and 7 and without prejudice to paragraph 8;

(ii) Member States shall protect, enhance and restore all bodies of surface water, subject to the application of subparagraph (iii) for artificial and heavily modified bodies of water, with the aim of achieving good surface water status at the latest 15 years after the date of entry into force of this Directive, in accordance with the provisions laid down in Annex V, subject to the application of extensions determined in accordance with paragraph 4 and to the application of paragraphs 5, 6 and 7 without prejudice to paragraph 8;

(iii) Member States shall protect and enhance all artificial and heavily modified bodies of water, with the aim of achieving good ecological potential and good surface water chemical status at the latest 15 years from the date of entry into force of this Directive, in accordance with the provisions laid down in Annex V, subject to the application of extensions determined in accordance with paragraph 4 and to the application of paragraphs 5, 6 and 7 without prejudice to paragraph 8;

(iv) Member States shall implement the necessary measures in accordance with Article 16(1) and (8), with the aim of progressively reducing pollution from priority substances and ceasing or phasing out emissions, discharges and losses of priority hazardous substances

without prejudice to the relevant international agreements referred to in Article 1 for the parties concerned;

(b) for groundwater

(i) Member States shall implement the measures necessary to prevent or limit the input of pollutants into groundwater and to prevent the deterioration of the status of all bodies of groundwater, subject to the application of paragraphs 6 and 7 and without prejudice to paragraph 8 of this Article and subject to the application of Article 11(3)(j);

(ii) Member States shall protect, enhance and restore all bodies of groundwater, ensure a balance between abstraction and recharge of groundwater, with the aim of achieving good groundwater status at the latest 15 years after the date of entry into force of this Directive, in accordance with the provisions laid down in Annex V, subject to the application of extensions determined in accordance with paragraph 4 and to the application of paragraphs 5, 6 and 7 without prejudice to paragraph 8 of this Article and subject to the application of Article 11(3)(j);

(iii) Member States shall implement the measures necessary to reverse any significant and sustained upward trend in the concentration of any pollutant resulting from the impact of human activity in order progressively to reduce pollution of groundwater.

Measures to achieve trend reversal shall be implemented in accordance with paragraphs 2, 4 and 5 of Article 17, taking into account the applicable standards set out in relevant Community legislation, subject to the application of paragraphs 6 and 7 and without prejudice to paragraph 8;

(c) for protected areas

Member States shall achieve compliance with any standards and objectives at the latest 15 years after the date of entry into force of this Directive, unless otherwise specified in the Community legislation under which the individual protected areas have been established.

2. Where more than one of the objectives under paragraph 1 relates to a given body of water, the most stringent shall apply.

3. Member States may designate a body of surface water as artificial or heavily modified, when:

(a) the changes to the hydromorphological characteristics of that body which would be necessary for achieving good ecological status would have significant adverse effects on:
  (i) the wider environment;
  (ii) navigation, including port facilities, or recreation;
  (iii) activities for the purposes of which water is stored, such as drinking-water supply, power generation or irrigation;
  (iv) water regulation, flood protection, land drainage, or
  (v) other equally important sustainable human development activities;

(b) the beneficial objectives served by the artificial or modified characteristics of the water body cannot, for reasons of technical feasibility or disproportionate costs, reasonably be achieved by other means, which are a significantly better environmental option.

Such designation and the reasons for it shall be specifically mentioned in the river basin management plans required under Article 13 and reviewed every six years.

4. The deadlines established under paragraph 1 may be extended for the purposes of phased achievement of the objectives for bodies of water, provided that no further deterioration occurs in the status of the affected body of water when all of the following conditions are met:

(a) Member States determine that all necessary improvements in the status of bodies of water cannot reasonably be achieved within the timescales set out in that paragraph for at least one of the following reasons:
  (i) the scale of improvements required can only be achieved in phases exceeding the timescale, for reasons of technical feasibility;
  (ii) completing the improvements within the timescale would be disproportionately expensive;
  (iii) natural conditions do not allow timely improvement in the status of the body of water.

(b) Extension of the deadline, and the reasons for it, are specifically set out and explained in the river basin management plan required under Article 13.
(c) Extensions shall be limited to a maximum of two further updates of the river basin management plan except in cases where the natural conditions are such that the objectives cannot be achieved within this period.
(d) A summary of the measures required under Article 11 which are envisaged as necessary to bring the bodies of water progressively to the required status by the extended deadline, the reasons for any significant delay in making these measures operational, and the expected timetable for their implementation are set out in the river basin management plan. A review of the implementation of these measures and a summary of any additional measures shall be included in updates of the river basin management plan.

5. Member States may aim to achieve less stringent environmental objectives than those required under paragraph 1 for specific bodies of water when they are so affected by human activity, as determined in accordance with Article 5(1), or their natural condition is such that the achievement of these objectives would be infeasible or disproportionately expensive, and all the following conditions are met:

(a) the environmental and socioeconomic needs served by such human activity cannot be achieved by other means, which are a significantly better environmental option not entailing disproportionate costs;
(b) Member States ensure,
— for surface water, the highest ecological and chemical status possible is achieved, given impacts that could not reasonably have been avoided due to the nature of the human activity or pollution,
— for groundwater, the least possible changes to good groundwater status, given impacts that could not reasonably have been avoided due to the nature of the human activity or pollution;
(c) no further deterioration occurs in the status of the affected body of water;
(d) the establishment of less stringent environmental objectives, and the reasons for it, are specifically mentioned in the river basin management plan required under Article 13 and those objectives are reviewed every six years.

6. Temporary deterioration in the status of bodies of water shall not be in breach of the requirements of this Directive if this is the result of circumstances of natural cause or force majeure which are exceptional or could not reasonably have been foreseen, in particular extreme floods and prolonged droughts, or the result of circumstances due to accidents which could not reasonably have been foreseen, when all of the following conditions have been met:

(a) all practicable steps are taken to prevent further deterioration in status and in order not to compromise the achievement of the objectives of this Directive in other bodies of water not affected by those circumstances;
(b) the conditions under which circumstances that are exceptional or that could not reasonably have been foreseen may be declared, including the adoption of the appropriate indicators, are stated in the river basin management plan;
(c) the measures to be taken under such exceptional circumstances are included in the programme of measures and will not compromise the recovery of the quality of the body of water once the circumstances are over;
(d) the effects of the circumstances that are exceptional or that could not reasonably have been foreseen are reviewed annually and, subject to the reasons set out in paragraph 4(a), all practicable measures are taken with the aim of restoring the body of water to its status prior to the effects of those circumstances as soon as reasonably practicable, and
(e) a summary of the effects of the circumstances and of such measures taken or to be taken in accordance with paragraphs (a) and (d) are included in the next update of the river basin management plan.

7. Member States will not be in breach of this Directive when:

— failure to achieve good groundwater status, good ecological status or, where relevant, good ecological potential or to prevent deterioration in the status of a body of surface water or groundwater is the result of new modifications to the physical characteristics of a surface water body or alterations to the level of bodies of groundwater, or

— failure to prevent deterioration from high status to good status of a body of surface water is the result of new sustainable human development activities

and all the following conditions are met:

(a) all practicable steps are taken to mitigate the adverse impact on the status of the body of water;

(b) the reasons for those modifications or alterations are specifically set out and explained in the river basin management plan required under Article 13 and the objectives are reviewed every six years;

(c) the reasons for those modifications or alterations are of overriding public interest and/or the benefits to the environment and to society of achieving the objectives set out in paragraph 1 are outweighed by the benefits of the new modifications or alterations to human health, to the maintenance of human safety or to sustainable development, and

(d) the beneficial objectives served by those modifications or alterations of the water body cannot for reasons of technical feasibility or disproportionate cost be achieved by other means, which are a significantly better environmental option.

8. When applying paragraphs 3, 4, 5, 6 and 7, a Member State shall ensure that the application does not permanently exclude or compromise the achievement of the objectives of this Directive in other bodies of water within the same river basin district and is consistent with the implementation of other Community environmental legislation.

9. Steps must be taken to ensure that the application of the new provisions, including the application of paragraphs 3, 4, 5, 6 and 7, guarantees at least the same level of protection as the existing Community legislation.

Article 5 Characteristics of the river basin district, review of the environmental impact of human activity and economic analysis of water use

1. Each Member State shall ensure that for each river basin district or for the portion of an international river basin district falling within its territory:

— an analysis of its characteristics,

— a review of the impact of human activity on the status of surface waters and on groundwater, and

— an economic analysis of water use

is undertaken according to the technical specifications set out in Annexes II and III and that it is completed at the latest four years after the date of entry into force of this Directive.

2. The analyses and reviews mentioned under paragraph 1 shall be reviewed, and if necessary updated at the latest 13 years after the date of entry into force of this Directive and every six years thereafter.

Article 6 Register of protected areas

1. Member States shall ensure the establishment of a register or registers of all areas lying within each river basin district which have been designated as requiring special protection under specific Community legislation for the protection of their surface water and groundwater or for the conservation of habitats and species directly depending on water. They shall ensure that the register is completed at the latest four years after the date of entry into force of this Directive.

2. The register or registers shall include all bodies of water identified under Article 7(1) and all protected areas covered by Annex IV.

3. For each river basin district, the register or registers of protected areas shall be kept under review and up to date.

Article 7 Waters used for the abstraction of drinking water

1. Member States shall identify, within each river basin district:

— all bodies of water used for the abstraction of water intended for human consumption providing more than 10 m3 a day as an average or serving more than 50 persons, and

— those bodies of water intended for such future use.

Member States shall monitor, in accordance with Annex V, those bodies of water which according to Annex V, provide more than 100 m3 a day as an average.

2. For each body of water identified under paragraph 1, in addition to meeting the objectives of Article 4 in accordance with the requirements of this Directive, for surface water bodies including the quality standards established at Community level under Article 16, Member States shall ensure that under the water treatment regime applied, and in accordance with Community legislation, the resulting water will meet the requirements of Directive 80/778/EEC as amended by Directive 98/83/EC.

3. Member States shall ensure the necessary protection for the bodies of water identified with the aim of avoiding deterioration in their quality in order to reduce the level of purification treatment required in the production of drinking water. Member States may establish safeguard zones for those bodies of water.

Article 8 Monitoring of surface water status, groundwater status and protected areas

1. Member States shall ensure the establishment of programmes for the monitoring of water status in order to establish a coherent and comprehensive overview of water status within each river basin district:

— for surface waters such programmes shall cover:

(i) the volume and level or rate of flow to the extent relevant for ecological and chemical status and ecological potential, and

(ii) the ecological and chemical status and ecological potential;

— for groundwaters such programmes shall cover monitoring of the chemical and quantitative status,

— for protected areas the above programmes shall be supplemented by those specifications contained in Community legislation under which the individual protected areas have been established.

2. These programmes shall be operational at the latest six years after the date of entry into force of this Directive unless otherwise specified in the legislation concerned. Such monitoring shall be in accordance with the requirements of Annex V.

3. Technical specifications and standardised methods for analysis and monitoring of water status shall be laid down in accordance with the procedure laid down in Article 21.

Article 9 Recovery of costs for water services

1. Member States shall take account of the principle of recovery of the costs of water services, including environmental and resource costs, having regard to the economic analysis conducted according to Annex III, and in accordance in particular with the polluter pays principle.

Member States shall ensure by 2010

— that water-pricing policies provide adequate incentives for users to use water resources efficiently, and thereby contribute to the environmental objectives of this Directive,

— an adequate contribution of the different water uses, disaggregated into at least industry, households and agriculture, to the recovery of the costs of water services, based on the economic analysis conducted according to Annex III and taking account of the polluter pays principle.

Member States may in so doing have regard to the social, environmental and economic effects of the recovery as well as the geographic and climatic conditions of the region or regions affected.

2. Member States shall report in the river basin management plans on the planned steps towards implementing paragraph 1 which will contribute to achieving the environmental objectives of this Directive and on the contribution made by the various water uses to the recovery of the costs of water services.

3. Nothing in this Article shall prevent the funding of particular preventive or remedial measures in order to achieve the objectives of this Directive.

4. Member States shall not be in breach of this Directive if they decide in accordance with established practices not to apply the provisions of paragraph 1, second sentence, and for that purpose the relevant provisions of paragraph 2, for a given water-use activity, where this does not compromise the purposes and the achievement of the objectives of this Directive. Member States shall report the reasons for not fully applying paragraph 1, second sentence, in the river basin management plans.

Article 10 The combined approach for point and diffuse sources

1. Member States shall ensure that all discharges referred to in paragraph 2 into surface waters are controlled according to the combined approach set out in this Article.

2. Member States shall ensure the establishment and/or implementation of:

(a) the emission controls based on best available techniques, or

(b) the relevant emission limit values, or

(c) in the case of diffuse impacts the controls including, as appropriate, best environmental practices set out in:

— Council Directive 96/61/EC of 24 September 1996 concerning integrated pollution prevention and control(19),

— Council Directive 91/271/EEC of 21 May 1991 concerning urban waste-water treatment(20),

— Council Directive 91/676/EEC of 12 December 1991 concerning the protection of waters against pollution caused by nitrates from agricultural sources(21),

— the Directives adopted pursuant to Article 16 of this Directive,

— the Directives listed in Annex IX,

— any other relevant Community legislation

at the latest 12 years after the date of entry into force of this Directive, unless otherwise specified in the legislation concerned.

3. Where a quality objective or quality standard, whether established pursuant to this Directive, in the Directives listed in Annex IX, or pursuant to any other Community legislation, requires stricter conditions than those which would result from the application of paragraph 2, more stringent emission controls shall be set accordingly.

Article 11 Programme of measures

1. Each Member State shall ensure the establishment for each river basin district, or for the part of an international river basin district within its territory, of a programme of measures, taking account of the results of the analyses required under Article 5, in order to achieve the objectives established under Article 4. Such programmes of measures may make reference to measures following from legislation adopted at national level and covering the whole of the territory of a Member State. Where appropriate, a Member State may adopt measures applicable to all river basin districts and/or the portions of international river basin districts falling within its territory.

2. Each programme of measures shall include the 'basic' measures specified in paragraph 3 and, where necessary, 'supplementary' measures.

3. 'Basic measures' are the minimum requirements to be complied with and shall consist of:

(a) those measures required to implement Community legislation for the protection of water, including measures required under the legislation specified in Article 10 and in part A of Annex VI;
(b) measures deemed appropriate for the purposes of Article 9;
(c) measures to promote an efficient and sustainable water use in order to avoid compromising the achievement of the objectives specified in Article 4;
(d) measures to meet the requirements of Article 7, including measures to safeguard water quality in order to reduce the level of purification treatment required for the production of drinking water;
(e) controls over the abstraction of fresh surface water and groundwater, and impoundment of fresh surface water, including a register or registers of water abstractions and a requirement of prior authorisation for abstraction and impoundment. These controls shall be periodically reviewed and, where necessary, updated. Member States can exempt from these controls, abstractions or impoundments which have no significant impact on water status;
(f) controls, including a requirement for prior authorisation of artificial recharge or augmentation of groundwater bodies. The water used may be derived from any surface water or groundwater, provided that the use of the source does not compromise the achievement of the environmental objectives established for the source or the recharged or augmented body of groundwater. These controls shall be periodically reviewed and, where necessary, updated;
(g) for point source discharges liable to cause pollution, a requirement for prior regulation, such as a prohibition on the entry of pollutants into water, or for prior authorisation, or registration based on general binding rules, laying down emission controls for the pollutants concerned, including controls in accordance with Articles 10 and 16. These controls shall be periodically reviewed and, where necessary, updated;
(h) for diffuse sources liable to cause pollution, measures to prevent or control the input of pollutants. Controls may take the form of a requirement for prior regulation, such as a prohibition on the entry of pollutants into water, prior authorisation or registration based on general binding rules where such a requirement is not otherwise provided for under Community legislation. These controls shall be periodically reviewed and, where necessary, updated;
(i) for any other significant adverse impacts on the status of water identified under Article 5 and Annex II, in particular measures to ensure that the hydromorphological conditions of the bodies of water are consistent with the achievement of the required ecological status or good ecological potential for bodies of water designated as artificial or heavily modified. Controls for this purpose may take the form of a requirement for prior authorisation or registration based on general binding rules where such a requirement is not otherwise provided for under Community legislation. Such controls shall be periodically reviewed and, where necessary, updated;
(j) a prohibition of direct discharges of pollutants into groundwater subject to the following provisions:
Member States may authorise reinjection into the same aquifer of water used for geothermal purposes.
They may also authorise, specifying the conditions for:
— injection of water containing substances resulting from the operations for exploration and extraction of hydrocarbons or mining activities, and injection of water for technical reasons, into geological formations from which hydrocarbons or other substances have been extracted or into geological formations which for natural reasons are permanently unsuitable for other

purposes. Such injections shall not contain substances other than those resulting from the above operations,

— reinjection of pumped groundwater from mines and quarries or associated with the construction or maintenance of civil engineering works,

— injection of natural gas or liquefied petroleum gas (LPG) for storage purposes into geological formations which for natural reasons are permanently unsuitable for other purposes,

— injection of natural gas or liquefied petroleum gas (LPG) for storage purposes into other geological formations where there is an overriding need for security of gas supply, and where the injection is such as to prevent any present or future danger of deterioration in the quality of any receiving groundwater,

— construction, civil engineering and building works and similar activities on, or in the ground which come into contact with groundwater. For these purposes, Member States may determine that such activities are to be treated as having been authorised provided that they are conducted in accordance with general binding rules developed by the Member State in respect of such activities,

— discharges of small quantities of substances for scientific purposes for characterisation, protection or remediation of water bodies limited to the amount strictly necessary for the purposes concerned

provided such discharges do not compromise the achievement of the environmental objectives established for that body of groundwater;

(k) in accordance with action taken pursuant to Article 16, measures to eliminate pollution of surface waters by those substances specified in the list of priority substances agreed pursuant to Article 16(2) and to progressively reduce pollution by other substances which would otherwise prevent Member States from achieving the objectives for the bodies of surface waters as set out in Article 4;

(l) any measures required to prevent significant losses of pollutants from technical installations, and to prevent and/or to reduce the impact of accidental pollution incidents for example as a result of floods, including through systems to detect or give warning of such events including, in the case of accidents which could not reasonably have been foreseen, all appropriate measures to reduce the risk to aquatic ecosystems.

4. 'Supplementary' measures are those measures designed and implemented in addition to the basic measures, with the aim of achieving the objectives established pursuant to Article 4. Part B of Annex VI contains a non-exclusive list of such measures.

Member States may also adopt further supplementary measures in order to provide for additional protection or improvement of the waters covered by this Directive, including in implementation of the relevant international agreements referred to in Article 1.

5. Where monitoring or other data indicate that the objectives set under Article 4 for the body of water are unlikely to be achieved, the Member State shall ensure that:

— the causes of the possible failure are investigated,

— relevant permits and authorisations are examined and reviewed as appropriate,

— the monitoring programmes are reviewed and adjusted as appropriate, and

— additional measures as may be necessary in order to achieve those objectives are established, including, as appropriate, the establishment of stricter environmental quality standards following the procedures laid down in Annex V.

Where those causes are the result of circumstances of natural cause or force majeure which are exceptional and could not reasonably have been foreseen, in particular extreme floods and prolonged droughts, the Member State may determine that additional measures are not practicable, subject to Article 4(6).

6. In implementing measures pursuant to paragraph 3, Member States shall take all appropriate steps not to increase pollution of marine waters. Without prejudice to existing legislation, the application of measures taken pursuant to paragraph 3 may on no account lead, either directly or indirectly to increased pollution of surface waters. This requirement shall not apply where it would result in increased pollution of the environment as a whole.

7. The programmes of measures shall be established at the latest nine years after the date of entry into force of this Directive and all the measures shall be made operational at the latest 12 years after that date.

8. The programmes of measures shall be reviewed, and if necessary updated at the latest 15 years after the date of entry into force of this Directive and every six years thereafter. Any new or revised measures established under an updated programme shall be made operational within three years of their establishment.

Article 12 Issues which can not be dealt with at Member State level

1. Where a Member State identifies an issue which has an impact on the management of its water but cannot be resolved by that Member State, it may report the issue to the Commission and any other Member State concerned and may make recommendations for the resolution of it.

2. The Commission shall respond to any report or recommendations from Member States within a period of six months.

Article 13 River basin management plans

1. Member States shall ensure that a river basin management plan is produced for each river basin district lying entirely within their territory.

2. In the case of an international river basin district falling entirely within the Community, Member States shall ensure coordination with the aim of producing a single international river basin management plan. Where such an international river basin management plan is not produced, Member States shall produce river basin management plans covering at least those parts of the international river basin district falling within their territory to achieve the objectives of this Directive.

3. In the case of an international river basin district extending beyond the boundaries of the Community, Member States shall endeavour to produce a single river basin management plan, and, where this is not possible, the plan shall at least cover the portion of the international river basin district lying within the territory of the Member State concerned.

4. The river basin management plan shall include the information detailed in Annex VII.

5. River basin management plans may be supplemented by the production of more detailed programmes and management plans for sub-basin, sector, issue, or water type, to deal with particular aspects of water management. Implementation of these measures shall not exempt Member States from any of their obligations under the rest of this Directive.

6. River basin management plans shall be published at the latest nine years after the date of entry into force of this Directive.

7. River basin management plans shall be reviewed and updated at the latest 15 years after the date of entry into force of this Directive and every six years thereafter.

Article 14 Public information and consultation

1. Member States shall encourage the active involvement of all interested parties in the implementation of this Directive, in particular in the production, review and updating of the river basin management plans. Member States shall ensure that, for each river basin district, they publish and make available for comments to the public, including users:

(a) a timetable and work programme for the production of the plan, including a statement of the consultation measures to be taken, at least three years before the beginning of the period to which the plan refers;
(b) an interim overview of the significant water management issues identified in the river basin, at least two years before the beginning of the period to which the plan refers;
(c) draft copies of the river basin management plan, at least one year before the beginning of the period to which the plan refers.

On request, access shall be given to background documents and information used for the development of the draft river basin management plan.

2. Member States shall allow at least six months to comment in writing on those documents in order to allow active involvement and consultation.

3. Paragraphs 1 and 2 shall apply equally to updated river basin management plans.

Article 15 Reporting

1. Member States shall send copies of the river basin management plans and all subsequent updates to the Commission and to any other Member State concerned within three months of their publication:

(a) for river basin districts falling entirely within the territory of a Member State, all river management plans covering that national territory and published pursuant to Article 13;
(b) for international river basin districts, at least the part of the river basin management plans covering the territory of the Member State.

2. Member States shall submit summary reports of:

— the analyses required under Article 5, and
— the monitoring programmes designed under Article 8 undertaken for the purposes of the first river basin management plan within three months of their completion.

3. Member States shall, within three years of the publication of each river basin management plan or update under Article 13, submit an interim report describing progress in the implementation of the planned programme of measures.

Article 16 Strategies against pollution of water

1. The European Parliament and the Council shall adopt specific measures against pollution of water by individual pollutants or groups of pollutants presenting a significant risk to or via the aquatic environment, including such risks to waters used for the abstraction of drinking water. For those pollutants measures shall be aimed at the progressive reduction and, for priority hazardous substances, as defined in Article 2(30), at the cessation or phasing-out of discharges, emissions and losses. Such measures shall be adopted acting on the proposals presented by the Commission in accordance with the procedures laid down in the Treaty.

2. The Commission shall submit a proposal setting out a list of priority substances selected amongst those which present a significant risk to or via the aquatic environment. Substances shall be prioritised for action on the basis of risk to or via the aquatic environment, identified by:

(a) risk assessment carried out under Council Regulation (EEC) No 793/93(22), Council Directive 91/414/EEC(23), and Directive 98/8/EC of the European Parliament and of the Council(24), or
(b) targeted risk-based assessment (following the methodology of Regulation (EEC) No 793/93) focusing solely on aquatic ecotoxicity and on human toxicity via the aquatic environment.

When necessary in order to meet the timetable laid down in paragraph 4, substances shall be prioritised for action on the basis of risk to, or via the aquatic environment, identified by a simplified risk-based assessment procedure based on scientific principles taking particular account of:

- evidence regarding the intrinsic hazard of the substance concerned, and in particular its aquatic ecotoxicity and human toxicity via aquatic exposure routes, and
- evidence from monitoring of widespread environmental contamination, and
- other proven factors which may indicate the possibility of widespread environmental contamination, such as production or use volume of the substance concerned, and use patterns.

3. The Commission's proposal shall also identify the priority hazardous substances. In doing so, the Commission shall take into account the selection of substances of concern undertaken in the relevant Community legislation regarding hazardous substances or relevant international agreements.

4. The Commission shall review the adopted list of priority substances at the latest four years after the date of entry into force of this Directive and at least every four years thereafter, and come forward with proposals as appropriate.

5. In preparing its proposal, the Commission shall take account of recommendations from the Scientific Committee on Toxicity, Ecotoxicity and the Environment, Member States, the European Parliament, the European Environment Agency, Community research programmes, international organisations to which the Community is a party, European business organisations including those representing small and medium-sized enterprises, European environmental organisations, and of other relevant information which comes to its attention.

6. For the priority substances, the Commission shall submit proposals of controls for:

- the progressive reduction of discharges, emissions and losses of the substances concerned, and, in particular
- the cessation or phasing-out of discharges, emissions and losses of the substances as identified in accordance with paragraph 3, including an appropriate timetable for doing so. The timetable shall not exceed 20 years after the adoption of these proposals by the European Parliament and the Council in accordance with the provisions of this Article.

In doing so it shall identify the appropriate cost-effective and proportionate level and combination of product and process controls for both point and diffuse sources and take account of Community-wide uniform emission limit values for process controls. Where appropriate, action at Community level for process controls may be established on a sector-by-sector basis. Where product controls include a review of the relevant authorisations issued under Directive 91/414/EEC and Directive 98/8/EC, such reviews shall be carried out in accordance with the provisions of those Directives. Each proposal for controls shall specify arrangements for their review, updating and for assessment of their effectiveness.

7. The Commission shall submit proposals for quality standards applicable to the concentrations of the priority substances in surface water, sediments or biota.

8. The Commission shall submit proposals, in accordance with paragraphs 6 and 7, and at least for emission controls for point sources and environmental quality standards within two years of the inclusion of the substance concerned on the list of priority substances. For substances included in the first list of priority substances, in the absence of agreement at Community level six years after the date of entry into force of this Directive, Member States shall establish environmental quality standards for these substances for all surface waters affected by discharges of those substances, and controls on the principal sources of such

discharges, based, inter alia, on consideration of all technical reduction options. For substances subsequently included in the list of priority substances, in the absence of agreement at Community level, Member States shall take such action five years after the date of inclusion in the list.

9. The Commission may prepare strategies against pollution of water by any other pollutants or groups of pollutants, including any pollution which occurs as a result of accidents.

10. In preparing its proposals under paragraphs 6 and 7, the Commission shall also review all the Directives listed in Annex IX. It shall propose, by the deadline in paragraph 8, a revision of the controls in Annex IX for all those substances which are included in the list of priority substances and shall propose the appropriate measures including the possible repeal of the controls under Annex IX for all other substances.

All the controls in Annex IX for which revisions are proposed shall be repealed by the date of entry into force of those revisions.

11. The list of priority substances of substances mentioned in paragraphs 2 and 3 proposed by the Commission shall, on its adoption by the European Parliament and the Council, become Annex X to this Directive. Its revision mentioned in paragraph 4 shall follow the same procedure.

Article 17 Strategies to prevent and control pollution of groundwater

1. The European Parliament and the Council shall adopt specific measures to prevent and control groundwater pollution. Such measures shall be aimed at achieving the objective of good groundwater chemical status in accordance with Article 4(1)(b) and shall be adopted, acting on the proposal presented within two years after the entry into force of this Directive, by the Commission in accordance with the procedures laid down in the Treaty.

2. In proposing measures the Commission shall have regard to the analysis carried out according to Article 5 and Annex II. Such measures shall be proposed earlier if data are available and shall include:

(a) criteria for assessing good groundwater chemical status, in accordance with Annex II.2.2 and Annex V 2.3.2 and 2.4.5;

(b) criteria for the identification of significant and sustained upward trends and for the definition of starting points for trend reversals to be used in accordance with Annex V 2.4.4.

3. Measures resulting from the application of paragraph 1 shall be included in the programmes of measures required under Article 11.

4. In the absence of criteria adopted under paragraph 2 at Community level, Member States shall establish appropriate criteria at the latest five years after the date of entry into force of this Directive.

5. In the absence of criteria adopted under paragraph 4 at national level, trend reversal shall take as its starting point a maximum of 75 % of the level of the quality standards set out in existing Community legislation applicable to groundwater.

Article 18 Commission report

1. The Commission shall publish a report on the implementation of this Directive at the latest 12 years after the date of entry into force of this Directive and every six years thereafter, and shall submit it to the European Parliament and to the Council.

2. The report shall include the following:

(a) a review of progress in the implementation of the Directive;

(b) a review of the status of surface water and groundwater in the Community undertaken in coordination with the European Environment Agency;

(c) a survey of the river basin management plans submitted in accordance with Article 15, including suggestions for the improvement of future plans;

(d) a summary of the response to each of the reports or recommendations to the Commission made by Member States pursuant to Article 12;

(e) a summary of any proposals, control measures and strategies developed under Article 16;

(f) a summary of the responses to comments made by the European Parliament and the Council on previous implementation reports.

3. The Commission shall also publish a report on progress in implementation based on the summary reports that Member States submit under Article 15(2), and submit it to the European Parliament and the Member States, at the latest two years after the dates referred to in Articles 5 and 8.

4. The Commission shall, within three years of the publication of each report under paragraph 1, publish an interim report describing progress in implementation on the basis of the interim reports of the Member States as mentioned in Article 15(3). This shall be submitted to the European Parliament and to the Council.

5. The Commission shall convene when appropriate, in line with the reporting cycle, a conference of interested parties on Community water policy from each of the Member States, to comment on the Commission's implementation reports and to share experiences.

Participants should include representatives from the competent authorities, the European Parliament, NGOs, the social and economic partners, consumer bodies, academics and other experts.

Article 19 Plans for future Community measures

1. Once a year, the Commission shall for information purposes present to the Committee referred to in Article 21 an indicative plan of measures having an impact on water legislation which it intends to propose in the near future, including any emerging from the proposals, control measures and strategies developed under Article 16. The Commission shall make the first such presentation at the latest two years after the date of entry into force of this Directive.

2. The Commission will review this Directive at the latest 19 years after the date of its entry into force and will propose any necessary amendments to it.

Article 20 Technical adaptations to the Directive

1. Annexes I, III and section 1.3.6 of Annex V may be adapted to scientific and technical progress in accordance with the procedures laid down in Article 21, taking account of the periods for review and updating of the river basin management plans as referred to in Article 13. Where necessary, the Commission may adopt guidelines on the implementation of Annexes II and V in accordance with the procedures laid down in Article 21.

2. For the purpose of transmission and processing of data, including statistical and cartographic data, technical formats for the purpose of paragraph 1 may be adopted in accordance with the procedures laid down in Article 21.

Article 21 Regulatory committee

1. The Commission shall be assisted by a committee (hereinafter referred to as 'the Committee').

2. Where reference is made to this Article, Articles 5 and 7 of Decision 1999/468/EC shall apply, having regard to the provisions of Article 8 thereof.

The period laid down in Article 5(6) of Decision 1999/468/EC shall be set at three months.

3. The Committee shall adopt its rules of procedure.

Article 22 Repeals and transitional provisions

1. The following shall be repealed with effect from seven years after the date of entry into force of this Directive:

— Directive 75/440/EEC of 16 June 1975 concerning the quality required of surface water intended for the abstraction of drinking water in the Member States(25),

— Council Decision 77/795/EEC of 12 December 1977 establishing a common procedure for the exchange of information on the quality of surface freshwater in the Community(26),

— Council Directive 79/869/EEC of 9 October 1979 concerning the methods of measurement and frequencies of sampling and analysis of surface water intended for the abstraction of drinking waters in the Member States(27).

2. The following shall be repealed with effect from 13 years after the date of entry into force of this Directive:

— Council Directive 78/659/EEC of 18 July 1978 on the quality of freshwaters needing protection or improvement in order to support fish life(28),

— Council Directive 79/923/EEC of 30 October 1979 on the quality required of shellfish waters(29),

— Council Directive 80/68/EEC of 17 December 1979 on the protection of groundwater against pollution caused by certain dangerous substances,

— Directive 76/464/EEC, with the exception of Article 6, which shall be repealed with effect from the entry into force of this Directive.

3. The following transitional provisions shall apply for Directive 76/464/EEC:

(a) the list of priority substances adopted under Article 16 of this Directive shall replace the list of substances prioritised in the Commission communication to the Council of 22 June 1982;

(b) for the purposes of Article 7 of Directive 76/464/EEC, Member States may apply the principles for the identification of pollution problems and the substances causing them, the establishment of quality standards, and the adoption of measures, laid down in this Directive.

4. The environmental objectives in Article 4 and environmental quality standards established in Annex IX and pursuant to Article 16(7), and by Member States under Annex V for substances not on the list of priority substances and under Article 16(8) in respect of priority substances for which Community standards have not been set, shall be regarded as environmental quality standards for the purposes of point 7 of Article 2 and Article 10 of Directive 96/61/EC.

5. Where a substance on the list of priority substances adopted under Article 16 is not included in Annex VIII to this Directive or in Annex III to Directive 96/61/EC, it shall be added thereto.

6. For bodies of surface water, environmental objectives established under the first river basin management plan required by this Directive shall, as a minimum, give effect to quality standards at least as stringent as those required to implement Directive 76/464/EEC.

Article 23 Penalties

Member States shall determine penalties applicable to breaches of the national provisions adopted pursuant to this Directive. The penalties thus provided for shall be effective, proportionate and dissuasive.

Article 24 Implementation

1. Member States shall bring into force the laws, regulations and administrative provisions necessary to comply with this Directive at the latest 22 December 2003. They shall forthwith inform the Commission thereof.

When Member States adopt these measures, they shall contain a reference to this

Directive or shall be accompanied by such a reference on the occasion of their official publication. The methods of making such a reference shall be laid down by the Member States.

2. Member States shall communicate to the Commission the texts of the main provisions of national law which they adopt in the field governed by this Directive. The Commission shall inform the other Member States thereof.

Article 25 Entry into force
This Directive shall enter into force on the day of its publication in the Official Journal of the European Communities.

Article 26 Addressees
This Directive is addressed to the Member States.

...

ANNEX III ECONOMIC ANALYSIS

The economic analysis shall contain enough information in sufficient detail (taking account of the costs associated with collection of the relevant data in order to:

(a) make the relevant calculations necessary for taking into account under Article 9 the principle of recovery of the costs of water services, taking account of long term forecasts of supply and demand for water in the river basin district and, where necessary:
 — estimates of the volume, prices and costs associated with water services, and
 — estimates of relevant investment including forecasts of such investments;

(b) make judgements about the most cost-effective combination of measures in respect of water uses to be included in the programme of measures under Article 11 based on estimates of the potential costs of such measures.

ANNEX IV PROTECTED AREAS

1. The register of protected areas required under Article 6 shall include the following types of protected areas:

(i) areas designated for the abstraction of water intended for human consumption under Article 7;

(ii) areas designated for the protection of economically significant aquatic species;

(iii) bodies of water designated as recreational waters, including areas designated as bathing waters under Directive 76/160/EEC;

(iv) nutrient-sensitive areas, including areas designated as vulnerable zones under Directive 91/676/EEC and areas designated as sensitive areas under Directive 91/271/EEC; and

(v) areas designated for the protection of habitats or species where the maintenance or improvement of the status of water is an important factor in their protection, including relevant Natura 2000 sites designated under Directive 92/43/EEC and Directive 79/409/EEC.

2. The summary of the register required as part of the river basin management plan shall include maps indicating the location of each protected area and a description of the Community, national or local legislation under which they have been designated.

ANNEX V*

1.2 Normative definitions of ecological status classifications

* Editor's note: only Table 1.2 included, for illustrative purposes.

Table 1.2. General definition for rivers, lakes, transitional waters and coastal waters

The following text provides a general definition of ecological quality. For the purposes of classification the values for the elements of ecological status for each surface water category are those given in tables 1.2.1 to 1.2.4 below.

Element	High status	Good status	Moderate status
General	There are no, or only very minor, anthropogenic alterations to the values of the physico-chemical and hydromorphological quality element for the surface water body from those normally associated with that type under undisturbed conditions.	The values of the biological quality elements for the surface water body type show low levels of distortion resulting from human activity, but deviate only slightly from those normally associated with the surface water body type under undisturbed conditions.	The values of the biological quality elements for the surface water body type deviate moderately from those normally associated with the surface water body type under undisturbed conditions. The values show moderate signs of distortion resulting from human activity and are significantly more disturbed than under conditions of good status.
	The values of the biological quality element for the surface water body reflect those normally associated with that type under undisturbed conditions, and show no, or only very minor, evidence of distortion. These are the type-specific conditions and communities.		

Waters achieving a status below moderate shall be classified as poor or bad.

Waters showing evidence of major alterations to the values of the biological quality elements for the surface water body type and in which the relevant biological communities deviate substantially from those normally associated with the surface water body type under undisturbed conditions, shall be classified as poor.

Waters showing evidence of severe alterations to the values of the biological quality elements for the surface water body type and in which large portions of the relevant biological communities normally associated with the surface water body under undisturbed conditions are absent, shall be classified as bad.

ANNEX VI LISTS OF MEASURES TO BE INCLUDED WITHIN THE PROGRAMMES OF MEASURES

PART A

Measures required under the following Directives:

(i) The Bathing Water Directive (76/160/EEC);
(ii) The Birds Directive (79/409/EEC);
(iii) The Drinking Water Directive (80/778/EEC) as amended by Directive (98/83/EC);
(iv) The Major Accidents (Seveso) Directive (96/82/EC);
(v) The Environmental Impact Assessment Directive (85/337/EEC);
(vi) The Sewage Sludge Directive (86/278/EEC);
(vii) The Urban Waste-water Treatment Directive (91/271/EEC);
(viii) The Plant Protection Products Directive (91/414/EEC);
(ix) The Nitrates Directive (91/676/EEC);
(x) The Habitats Directive (92/43/EEC);
(xi) The Integrated Pollution Prevention Control Directive (96/61/EC).

PART B

The following is a non-exclusive list of supplementary measures which Member States within each river basin district may choose to adopt as part of the programme of measures required under Article 11(4):

(i) legislative instruments
(ii) administrative instruments
(iii) economic or fiscal instruments
(iv) negotiated environmental agreements
(v) emission controls
(vi) codes of good practice
(vii) recreation and restoration of wetlands areas
(viii) abstraction controls
(ix) demand management measures, inter alia, promotion of adapted agricultural production such as low water requiring crops in areas affected by drought
(x) efficiency and reuse measures, inter alia, promotion of water-efficient technologies in industry and water-saving irrigation techniques
(xi) construction projects
(xii) desalination plants
(xiii) rehabilitation projects
(xiv) artificial recharge of aquifers
(xv) educational projects
(xvi) research, development and demonstration projects
(xvii) other relevant measures

ANNEX VII RIVER BASIN MANAGEMENT PLANS

A. River basin management plans shall cover the following elements:

1. a general description of the characteristics of the river basin district required under Article 5 and Annex II. This shall include:

1.1. for surface waters:

— mapping of the location and boundaries of water bodies,
— mapping of the ecoregions and surface water body types within the river basin,
— identification of reference conditions for the surface water body types;

1.2. for groundwaters:

— mapping of the location and boundaries of groundwater bodies;

2. a summary of significant pressures and impact of human activity on the status of surface water and groundwater, including:

— estimation of point source pollution,
— estimation of diffuse source pollution, including a summary of land use,
— estimation of pressures on the quantitative status of water including abstractions,
— analysis of other impacts of human activity on the status of water;

3. identification and mapping of protected areas as required by Article 6 and Annex IV;

4. a map of the monitoring networks established for the purposes of Article 8 and Annex V, and a presentation in map form of the results of the monitoring programmes carried out under those provisions for the status of:

4.1. surface water (ecological and chemical);

4.2. groundwater (chemical and quantitative);

4.3. protected areas;

5. a list of the environmental objectives established under Article 4 for surface waters, groundwaters and protected areas, including in particular identification of instances where use has been made of Article 4(4), (5), (6) and (7), and the associated information required under that Article;

6. a summary of the economic analysis of water use as required by Article 5 and Annex III;

7. a summary of the programme or programmes of measures adopted under Article 11, including the ways in which the objectives established under Article 4 are thereby to be achieved;

7.1. a summary of the measures required to implement Community legislation for the protection of water;

7.2. a report on the practical steps and measures taken to apply the principle of recovery of the costs of water use in accordance with Article 9;

7.3. a summary of the measures taken to meet the requirements of Article 7;

7.4. a summary of the controls on abstraction and impoundment of water, including reference to the registers and identifications of the cases where exemptions have been made under Article 11(3)(e);

7.5. a summary of the controls adopted for point source discharges and other activities with an impact on the status of water in accordance with the provisions of Article 11(3)(g) and 11(3)(i);

7.6. an identification of the cases where direct discharges to groundwater have been authorised in accordance with the provisions of Article 11(3)(j);

7.7. a summary of the measures taken in accordance with Article 16 on priority substances;

7.8. a summary of the measures taken to prevent or reduce the impact of accidental pollution incidents;

7.9. a summary of the measures taken under Article 11(5) for bodies of water which are unlikely to achieve the objectives set out under Article 4;

7.10. details of the supplementary measures identified as necessary in order to meet the environmental objectives established;

7.11. details of the measures taken to avoid increase in pollution of marine waters in accordance with Article 11(6);

8. a register of any more detailed programmes and management plans for the river basin district dealing with particular sub-basins, sectors, issues or water types, together with a summary of their contents;

9. a summary of the public information and consultation measures taken, their results and the changes to the plan made as a consequence;

10. a list of competent authorities in accordance with Annex I;

11. the contact points and procedures for obtaining the background documentation and information referred to in Article 14(1), and in particular details of the control measures adopted in accordance with Article 11(3)(g) and 11(3)(i) and of the actual monitoring data gathered in accordance with Article 8 and Annex V.

B. The first update of the river basin management plan and all subsequent updates shall also include:

1. a summary of any changes or updates since the publication of the previous version of the river basin management plan, including a summary of the reviews to be carried out under Article 4(4), (5), (6) and (7);

2. an assessment of the progress made towards the achievement of the environmental objectives, including presentation of the monitoring results for the period of the previous plan in map form, and an explanation for any environmental objectives which have not been reached;

3. a summary of, and an explanation for, any measures foreseen in the earlier version of the river basin management plan which have not been undertaken;

4. a summary of any additional interim measures adopted under Article 11(5) since the publication of the previous version of the river basin management plan.

ANNEX VIII INDICATIVE LIST OF THE MAIN POLLUTANTS

1. Organohalogen compounds and substances which may form such compounds in the aquatic environment.

2. Organophosphorous compounds.

3. Organotin compounds.

4. Substances and preparations, or the breakdown products of such, which have been proved to possess carcinogenic or mutagenic properties or properties which may affect steroidogenic, thyroid, reproduction or other endocrine-related functions in or via the aquatic environment.

5. Persistent hydrocarbons and persistent and bioaccumulable organic toxic substances.

6. Cyanides.

7. Metals and their compounds.

8. Arsenic and its compounds.

9. Biocides and plant protection products.

10. Materials in suspension.

11. Substances which contribute to eutrophication (in particular, nitrates and phosphates).

12. Substances which have an unfavourable influence on the oxygen balance (and can be measured using parameters such as BOD, COD, etc.).

ANNEX X LIST OF PRIORITY SUBSTANCES IN THE FIELD OF WATER POLICY(‡)

	CAS number ([1])	EU number ([2])	Name of priority substance	Identified as priority hazardous substance
(1)	15972-60-8	240-110-8	Alachlor	
(2)	120-12-7	204-371-1	Anthracene	(X)(***)
(3)	1912-24-9	217-617-8	Atrazine	(X)(***)
(4)	71-43-2	200-753-7	Benzene	
(5)	not applicable	not applicable	Brominated diphenylethers(**)	X(****)
(6)	7440-43-9	231-152-8	Cadmium and its compounds	X
(7)	85535-84-8	287-476-5	C_{10-13}-chloroalkanes	X
(8)	470-90-6	207-432-0	Chlorfenvinphos	
(9)	2921-88-2	220-864-4	Chlorphyrifos	(X)(***)
(10)	107-06-2	204-458-1	1, 2-Dichloroethane	
(11)	75-09-2	200-838-9	Dichloromethane	
(12)	117-81-7	204-211-0	Di(2-ethylhexyl) phthalate(DEHP)	(X)(***)
(13)	330-54-1	206-354-4	Diuron	(X)(***)
(14)	115-29-7	204-079-4	Endosulfan	(X)(***)
	959-98-8	not applicable	(alpha-endosulfan)	
(15)	206-44-0	205-912-4	Fluoranthene(*****)	
(16)	118-74-1	204-273-9	Hexachlorobenzene	X
(17)	87-68-3	201-765-5	Hexachlorobutadiene	X
(18)	608-73-1	210-158-9	Hexachlorocyclohexane	X
	58-89-9	200-401-2	(gamma-isomer, Lindane)	
(19)	34123-59-6	251-835-4	Isoproturon	(X)(***)
(20)	7439-92-1	231-100-4	Lead and its compounds	(X)(***)
(21)	7439-97-6	231-106-7	Mercury and its compounds	X
(22)	91-20-3	202-049-5	Naphthalene	(X)(***)
(23)	7440-02-0	231-111-4	Nickel and its compounds	
(24)	25154-52-3	246-672-0	Nonylpenols	(X)
	104-40-5	203-199-4	(4-(para)-nonylphenol)	
(25)	1806-26-4	217-302-5	Octylphenols	(X)(***)
	140-66-9	not applicable	(para-terr-octylphenol),	
(26)	608-93-5	210-172-5	Pentachlorobenzene	(X)
(27)	87-86-5	201-778-6	Pentachlorophenol	(X)(***)
(28)	not applicable	not applicable	Polyaromatic hydrocarbons	(X)
	50-32-8	200-028-9	(Benzo(a)pyrene),	
	205-99-2	205-911-9	(Benzo(b)fluoranthene),	
	191-24-2	205-883-8	(Benzo(g,h,i)perylene),	
	207-08-9	205-916-6	(Benzo(k)fluoranthene),	
	193-39-5	205-893-2	(Indeno(1, 2, 3-cd) pyrence)	
(29)	122-34-9	204-535-2	Simazine	(X)(***)

‡ Editor's note: added by Decision No. 2455/2001/EC establishing the list of priority substances in the field of water policy and amending Directive 2000/60/EC.

ANNEX X (*Cont.*)

	CAS number ([1])	EU number ([2])	Name of priority substance	Identified as priority hazardous substance
(30)	688-73-3	211-704-4	Tributyltin compounds	(X)
	36643-28-4	not applicable	(Tributyltin-cation)	
(31)	12002-48-1	234-413-4	Trichlorobenzenes	(X)(***)
	102-82-1	204-428-0	(1, 2, 4-Trichlorobenzene)	
(32)	67-66-3	200-663-8	Trichlorobenzene (Chloroform)	
(33)	1582-09-8	216-428-8	Trifluralin	(X)(***)

(*) Where groups of substances have been selected, typical individual representatives are listed as indicative parameters (in brackets and without number). The establishment of controls will be targeted to these individual substances, without prejudicing the inclusion of other individual representatives, where appropriate.
(**) These groups of substances normally include a considerable number of individual compounds. At present appropriate indicative parameters cannot be given.
(***) This priority substance is subject to a review for identification as possible 'priority hazardous substance'. The Commission will make a proposal to the European Parliament and Council for its final classification not later than 12 months after adoption of this list. The timetable laid down in Article 16 of Directive 2000/60/EC for the Commission's proposals of controls is not affected by this review.
(****) Only pentabbromobiphenylether (CAS-number 32534-81-9).
(*****) Fluoranthene is on the list as an indicator of other, more dangerous Polyaromatic Hydrocarbons.
([1]) CAS: Chemical Abstract Service.
([2]) EU-number, European Inventory of Existing Commercial Chemical Substance (EINECS) or European List of Notified Chemical Substances (ELINCS).

Directive 2004/35/EC of the European Parliament and of the Council

of 21 April 2004

on environmental liability with regard to the prevention and remedying of environmental damage

('the Environmental Liability Directive')

THE EUROPEAN PARLIAMENT AND THE COUNCIL OF THE EUROPEAN UNION,

Having regard to the Treaty establishing the European Community, and in particular Article 175(1) thereof,

Having regard to the proposal from the Commission,

Having regard to the Opinion of the European Economic and Social Committee,

After consulting the Committee of the Regions,

Acting in accordance with the procedure laid down in Article 251 of the Treaty, in the light of the joint text approved by the Conciliation Committee on 10 March 2004,

Whereas:

(1) There are currently many contaminated sites in the Community, posing significant health risks, and the loss of biodiversity has dramatically accelerated over the last decades. Failure to act could result in increased site contamination and greater loss of biodiversity in the future. Preventing and remedying, insofar as is possible, environmental damage contributes to implementing the objectives and principles of the Community's environment policy as set out in the Treaty. Local conditions should be taken into account when deciding how to remedy damage.

(2) The prevention and remedying of environmental damage should be implemented through the furtherance of the 'polluter pays' principle, as indicated in the Treaty and in line with the principle of sustainable development. The fundamental principle of this Directive should therefore be that an operator whose activity has caused the environmental damage or the imminent threat of such damage is to be held financially liable, in order to induce operators to adopt measures and develop practices to minimise the risks of environmental damage so that their exposure to financial liabilities is reduced.

(3) Since the objective of this Directive, namely to establish a common framework for the prevention and remedying of environmental damage at a reasonable cost to society, cannot be sufficiently achieved by the Member States and can therefore be better achieved at Community level by reason of the scale of this Directive and its implications in respect of other Community legislation, namely Council Directive 79/409/EEC of 2 April 1979 on the conservation of wild birds, Council Directive 92/43/EEC of 21 May 1992 on the conservation of natural habitats and of wild fauna and flora, and Directive 2000/60/EC of the European Parliament and of the Council of 23 October 2000 establishing a framework for Community action in the field of water policy, the Community may adopt measures in accordance with the principle of subsidiarity as set out in Article 5 of the Treaty. In accordance with the principle of proportionality, as set out in that Article, this Directive does not go beyond what is necessary in order to achieve that objective.

(4) Environmental damage also includes damage caused by airborne elements as far as they cause damage to water, land or protected species or natural habitats.

(5) Concepts instrumental for the correct interpretation and application of the scheme provided for by this Directive should be defined especially as regards the definition of environmental damage. When the concept in question derives from other relevant Community legislation, the same definition should be used so that common criteria can be used and uniform application promoted.

(6) Protected species and natural habitats might also be defined by reference to species and habitats protected in pursuance of national legislation on nature conservation. Account should nevertheless be taken of specific situations where Community, or equivalent national, legislation allows for certain derogations from the level of protection afforded to the environment.

(7) For the purposes of assessing damage to land as defined in this Directive the use of risk assessment procedures to determine to what extent human health is likely to be adversely affected is desirable.

(8) This Directive should apply, as far as environmental damage is concerned, to occupational activities which present a risk for human health or the environment. Those activities should be identified, in principle, by reference to the relevant Community legislation which provides for regulatory requirements in relation to certain activities or practices considered as posing a potential or actual risk for human health or the environment.

(9) This Directive should also apply, as regards damage to protected species and natural habitats, to any occupational activities other than those already directly or indirectly identified by reference to Community legislation as posing an actual or potential risk for human health or the environment. In such cases the operator should only be liable under this Directive whenever he is at fault or negligent.

(10) Express account should be taken of the Euratom Treaty and relevant international conventions and of Community legislation regulating more comprehensively and more stringently the operation of any of the activities falling under the scope of this Directive. This Directive, which does not provide for additional rules of conflict of laws when it specifies the powers of the competent authorities, is without prejudice to the rules on international jurisdiction of courts as provided, inter alia, in Council Regulation (EC) No 44/2001 of 22 December 2000 on jurisdiction and the recognition and enforcement of judgments in civil and commercial matters. This Directive should not apply to activities the main purpose of which is to serve national defence or international security.

(11) This Directive aims at preventing and remedying environmental damage, and does not affect rights of compensation for traditional damage granted under any relevant international agreement regulating civil liability.

(12) Many Member States are party to international agreements dealing with civil liability in relation to specific fields. These Member States should be able to remain so after the entry into force of this Directive, whereas other Member States should not lose their freedom to become parties to these agreements.

(13) Not all forms of environmental damage can be remedied by means of the liability mechanism. For the latter to be effective, there need to be one or more identifiable polluters, the damage should be concrete and quantifiable, and a causal link should be established between the damage and the identified polluter(s). Liability is therefore not a suitable instrument for dealing with pollution of a widespread, diffuse character, where it is impossible to link the negative environmental effects with acts or failure to act of certain individual actors.

(14) This Directive does not apply to cases of personal injury, to damage to private property or to any economic loss and does not affect any right regarding these types of damages.

(15) Since the prevention and remedying of environmental damage is a task directly contributing to the pursuit of the Community's environment policy, public authorities should ensure the proper implementation and enforcement of the scheme provided for by this Directive.

(16) Restoration of the environment should take place in an effective manner ensuring that the relevant restoration objectives are achieved. A common framework should be defined to that end, the proper application of which should be supervised by the competent authority.

(17) Appropriate provision should be made for those situations where several instances of environmental damage have occurred in such a manner that the competent authority cannot ensure that all the necessary remedial measures are taken at the same time. In such a case, the competent authority should be entitled to decide which instance of environmental damage is to be remedied first.

(18) According to the 'polluter-pays' principle, an operator causing environmental damage or creating an imminent threat of such damage should, in principle, bear the cost of the necessary preventive or remedial measures. In cases where a competent authority acts, itself or through a third party, in the place of an operator, that authority should ensure that the cost incurred by it is recovered from the operator. It is also appropriate that the operators should ultimately bear the cost of assessing environmental damage and, as the case may be, assessing an imminent threat of such damage occurring.

(19) Member States may provide for flat-rate calculation of administrative, legal, enforcement and other general costs to be recovered.

(20) An operator should not be required to bear the costs of preventive or remedial actions taken pursuant to this Directive in situations where the damage in question or imminent threat thereof is the result of certain events beyond the operator's control. Member States may allow that operators who are not at fault or negligent shall not bear the cost of remedial measures, in situations where the damage in question is the result of emissions or events explicitly authorised or where the potential for damage could not have been known when the event or emission took place.

(21) Operators should bear the costs relating to preventive measures when those measures should have been taken as a matter of course in order to comply with the legislative, regulatory and administrative provisions regulating their activities or the terms of any permit or authorisation.

(22) Member States may establish national rules covering cost allocation in cases of multiple party causation. Member States may take into account, in particular, the specific situation of users of products who might not be held responsible for environmental damage

in the same conditions as those producing such products. In this case, apportionment of liability should be determined in accordance with national law.

(23) Competent authorities should be entitled to recover the cost of preventive or remedial measures from an operator within a reasonable period of time from the date on which those measures were completed.

(24) It is necessary to ensure that effective means of implementation and enforcement are available, while ensuring that the legitimate interests of the relevant operators and other interested parties are adequately safeguarded. Competent authorities should be in charge of specific tasks entailing appropriate administrative discretion, namely the duty to assess the significance of the damage and to determine which remedial measures should be taken.

(25) Persons adversely affected or likely to be adversely affected by environmental damage should be entitled to ask the competent authority to take action. Environmental protection is, however, a diffuse interest on behalf of which individuals will not always act or will not be in a position to act. Non-governmental organisations promoting environmental protection should therefore also be given the opportunity to properly contribute to the effective implementation of this Directive.

(26) The relevant natural or legal persons concerned should have access to procedures for the review of the competent authority's decisions, acts or failure to act.

(27) Member States should take measures to encourage the use by operators of any appropriate insurance or other forms of financial security and the development of financial security instruments and markets in order to provide effective cover for financial obligations under this Directive.

(28) Where environmental damage affects or is likely to affect several Member States, those Member States should cooperate with a view to ensuring proper and effective preventive or remedial action in respect of any environmental damage. Member States may seek to recover the costs for preventive or remedial actions.

(29) This Directive should not prevent Member States from maintaining or enacting more stringent provisions in relation to the prevention and remedying of environmental damage; nor should it prevent the adoption by Member States of appropriate measures in relation to situations where double recovery of costs could occur as a result of concurrent action by a competent authority under this Directive and by a person whose property is affected by the environmental damage.

(30) Damage caused before the expiry of the deadline for implementation of this Directive should not be covered by its provisions.

(31) Member States should report to the Commission on the experience gained in the application of this Directive so as to enable the Commission to consider, taking into account the impact on sustainable development and future risks to the environment, whether any review of this Directive is appropriate,

HAVE ADOPTED THIS DIRECTIVE:

Article 1 Subject matter

The purpose of this Directive is to establish a framework of environmental liability based on the 'polluter-pays' principle, to prevent and remedy environmental damage.

Article 2 Definitions

For the purpose of this Directive the following definitions shall apply:

1. 'environmental damage' means:
   (a) damage to protected species and natural habitats, which is any damage that has significant adverse effects on reaching or maintaining the favourable conservation status of such habitats or species. The significance of such effects is to be assessed with reference to the baseline condition, taking account of the criteria set out in Annex I; Damage to protected species and natural habitats does not include

previously identified adverse effects which result from an act by an operator which was expressly authorised by the relevant authorities in accordance with provisions implementing Article 6(3) and (4) or Article 16 of Directive 92/43/EEC or Article 9 of Directive 79/409/EEC or, in the case of habitats and species not covered by Community law, in accordance with equivalent provisions of national law on nature conservation.

(b) water damage, which is any damage that significantly adversely affects the ecological, chemical and/or quantitative status and/or ecological potential, as defined in Directive 2000/60/EC, of the waters concerned, with the exception of adverse effects where Article 4(7) of that Directive applies;

(c) land damage, which is any land contamination that creates a significant risk of human health being adversely affected as a result of the direct or indirect introduction, in, on or under land, of substances, preparations, organisms or micro-organisms;

2. 'damage' means a measurable adverse change in a natural resource or measurable impairment of a natural resource service which may occur directly or indirectly;

3. 'protected species and natural habitats' means:

(a) the species mentioned in Article 4(2) of Directive 79/409/EEC or listed in Annex I thereto or listed in Annexes II and IV to Directive 92/43/EEC;

(b) the habitats of species mentioned in Article 4(2) of Directive 79/409/EEC or listed in Annex I thereto or listed in Annex II to Directive 92/43/EEC, and the natural habitats listed in Annex I to Directive 92/43/EEC and the breeding sites or resting places of the species listed in Annex IV to Directive 92/43/EEC; and

(c) where a Member State so determines, any habitat or species, not listed in those Annexes which the Member State designates for equivalent purposes as those laid down in these two Directives;

4. 'conservation status' means:

(a) in respect of a natural habitat, the sum of the influences acting on a natural habitat and its typical species that may affect its long-term natural distribution, structure and functions as well as the long-term survival of its typical species within, as the case may be, the European territory of the Member States to which the Treaty applies or the territory of a Member State or the natural range of that habitat;

The conservation status of a natural habitat will be taken as 'favourable' when:

— its natural range and areas it covers within that range are stable or increasing,

— the specific structure and functions which are necessary for its long-term maintenance exist and are likely to continue to exist for the foreseeable future, and

— the conservation status of its typical species is favourable, as defined in (b);

(b) in respect of a species, the sum of the influences acting on the species concerned that may affect the long-term distribution and abundance of its populations within, as the case may be, the European territory of the Member States to which the Treaty applies or the territory of a Member State or the natural range of that species;

The conservation status of a species will be taken as 'favourable' when:

— population dynamics data on the species concerned indicate that it is maintaining itself on a long-term basis as a viable component of its natural habitats,

— the natural range of the species is neither being reduced nor is likely to be reduced for the foreseeable future, and

— there is, and will probably continue to be, a sufficiently large habitat to maintain its populations on a long-term basis;

5. 'waters' mean all waters covered by Directive 2000/60/EC;

6. 'operator' means any natural or legal, private or public person who operates or controls the occupational activity or, where this is provided for in national legislation, to whom decisive economic power over the technical functioning of such an activity has been delegated, including the holder of a permit or authorisation for such an activity or the person registering or notifying such an activity;

7. 'occupational activity' means any activity carried out in the course of an economic activity, a business or an undertaking, irrespectively of its private or public, profit or non-profit character;

8. 'emission' means the release in the environment, as a result of human activities, of substances, preparations, organisms or micro-organisms;

9. 'imminent threat of damage' means a sufficient likelihood that environmental damage will occur in the near future;

10. 'preventive measures means' any measures taken in response to an event, act or omission that has created an imminent threat of environmental damage, with a view to preventing or minimising that damage;

11. 'remedial measures' means any action, or combination of actions, including mitigating or interim measures to restore, rehabilitate or replace damaged natural resources and/or impaired services, or to provide an equivalent alternative to those resources or services as foreseen in Annex II;

12. 'natural resource' means protected species and natural habitats, water and land;

13. 'services' and 'natural resources services' mean the functions performed by a natural resource for the benefit of another natural resource or the public;

14. 'baseline condition' means the condition at the time of the damage of the natural resources and services that would have existed had the environmental damage not occurred, estimated on the basis of the best information available;

15. 'recovery', including 'natural recovery', means, in the case of water, protected species and natural habitats the return of damaged natural resources and/or impaired services to baseline condition and in the case of land damage, the elimination of any significant risk of adversely affecting human health;

16. 'costs' means costs which are justified by the need to ensure the proper and effective implementation of this Directive including the costs of assessing environmental damage, an imminent threat of such damage, alternatives for action as well as the administrative, legal, and enforcement costs, the costs of data collection and other general costs, monitoring and supervision costs.

Article 3 Scope

1. This Directive shall apply to:
   (a) environmental damage caused by any of the occupational activities listed in Annex III, and to any imminent threat of such damage occurring by reason of any of those activities;
   (b) damage to protected species and natural habitats caused by any occupational activities other than those listed in Annex III, and to any imminent threat of such damage occurring by reason of any of those activities, whenever the operator has been at fault or negligent.

2. This Directive shall apply without prejudice to more stringent Community legislation regulating the operation of any of the activities falling within the scope of this Directive and without prejudice to Community legislation containing rules on conflicts of jurisdiction.

3. Without prejudice to relevant national legislation, this Directive shall not give private parties a right of compensation as a consequence of environmental damage or of an imminent threat of such damage.

Article 4 Exceptions

1. This Directive shall not cover environmental damage or an imminent threat of such damage caused by:
   (a) an act of armed conflict, hostilities, civil war or insurrection;
   (b) a natural phenomenon of exceptional, inevitable and irresistible character.

2. This Directive shall not apply to environmental damage or to any imminent threat of such damage arising from an incident in respect of which liability or compensation falls within the scope of any of the International Conventions listed in Annex IV, including any future amendments thereof, which is in force in the Member State concerned.

3. This Directive shall be without prejudice to the right of the operator to limit his liability in accordance with national legislation implementing the Convention on Limitation of Liability for Maritime Claims (LLMC), 1976, including any future amendment to the Convention, or the Strasbourg Convention on Limitation of Liability in Inland Navigation (CLNI), 1988, including any future amendment to the Convention.

4. This Directive shall not apply to such nuclear risks or environmental damage or imminent threat of such damage as may be caused by the activities covered by the Treaty establishing the European Atomic Energy Community or caused by an incident or activity in respect of which liability or compensation falls within the scope of any of the international instruments listed in Annex V, including any future amendments thereof.

5. This Directive shall only apply to environmental damage or to an imminent threat of such damage caused by pollution of a diffuse character, where it is possible to establish a causal link between the damage and the activities of individual operators.

6. This Directive shall not apply to activities the main purpose of which is to serve national defence or international security nor to activities the sole purpose of which is to protect from natural disasters.

Article 5 Preventive action

1. Where environmental damage has not yet occurred but there is an imminent threat of such damage occurring, the operator shall, without delay, take the necessary preventive measures.

2. Member States shall provide that, where appropriate, and in any case whenever an imminent threat of environmental damage is not dispelled despite the preventive measures taken by the operator, operators are to inform the competent authority of all relevant aspects of the situation, as soon as possible.

3. The competent authority may, at any time:

(a) require the operator to provide information on any imminent threat of environmental damage or in suspected cases of such an imminent threat;

(b) require the operator to take the necessary preventive measures;

(c) give instructions to the operator to be followed on the necessary preventive measures to be taken; or

(d) itself take the necessary preventive measures.

4. The competent authority shall require that the preventive measures are taken by the operator. If the operator fails to comply with the obligations laid down in paragraph 1 or 3(b) or (c), cannot be identified or is not required to bear the costs under this Directive, the competent authority may take these measures itself.

Article 6 Remedial action

1. Where environmental damage has occurred the operator shall, without delay, inform the competent authority of all relevant aspects of the situation and take:

(a) all practicable steps to immediately control, contain, remove or otherwise manage the relevant contaminants and/or any other damage factors in order to limit or to prevent further environmental damage and adverse effects on human health or further impairment of services and

(b) the necessary remedial measures, in accordance with Article 7.

2. The competent authority may, at any time:

(a) require the operator to provide supplementary information on any damage that has occurred;

(b) take, require the operator to take or give instructions to the operator concerning, all practicable steps to immediately control, contain, remove or otherwise manage the relevant contaminants and/or any other damage factors in order to limit or to prevent further environmental damage and adverse effect on human health, or further impairment of services;

(c) require the operator to take the necessary remedial measures;
(d) give instructions to the operator to be followed on the necessary remedial measures to be taken; or
(e) itself take the necessary remedial measures.

3. The competent authority shall require that the remedial measures are taken by the operator. If the operator fails to comply with the obligations laid down in paragraph 1 or 2(b), (c) or (d), cannot be identified or is not required to bear the costs under this Directive, the competent authority may take these measures itself, as a means of last resort.

Article 7 Determination of remedial measures

1. Operators shall identify, in accordance with Annex II, potential remedial measures and submit them to the competent authority for its approval, unless the competent authority has taken action under Article 6(2)(e) and (3).

2. The competent authority shall decide which remedial measures shall be implemented in accordance with Annex II, and with the cooperation of the relevant operator, as required.

3. Where several instances of environmental damage have occurred in such a manner that the competent authority cannot ensure that the necessary remedial measures are taken at the same time, the competent authority shall be entitled to decide which instance of environmental damage must be remedied first.

In making that decision, the competent authority shall have regard, inter alia, to the nature, extent and gravity of the various instances of environmental damage concerned, and to the possibility of natural recovery. Risks to human health shall also be taken into account.

4. The competent authority shall invite the persons referred to in Article 12(1) and in any case the persons on whose land remedial measures would be carried out to submit their observations and shall take them into account.

Article 8 Prevention and remediation costs

1. The operator shall bear the costs for the preventive and remedial actions taken pursuant to this Directive.

2. Subject to paragraphs 3 and 4, the competent authority shall recover, inter alia, via security over property or other appropriate guarantees from the operator who has caused the damage or the imminent threat of damage, the costs it has incurred in relation to the preventive or remedial actions taken under this Directive.

However, the competent authority may decide not to recover the full costs where the expenditure required to do so would be greater than the recoverable sum or where the operator cannot be identified.

3. An operator shall not be required to bear the cost of preventive or remedial actions taken pursuant to this Directive when he can prove that the environmental damage or imminent threat of such damage:

(a) was caused by a third party and occured despite the fact that appropriate safety measures were in place; or
(b) resulted from compliance with a compulsory order or instruction emanating from a public authority other than an order or instruction consequent upon an emission or incident caused by the operator's own activities.

In such cases Member States shall take the appropriate measures to enable the operator to recover the costs incurred.

4. The Member States may allow the operator not to bear the cost of remedial actions taken pursuant to this Directive where he demonstrates that he was not at fault or negligent and that the environmental damage was caused by:

(a) an emission or event expressly authorised by, and fully in accordance with the conditions of, an authorisation conferred by or given under applicable national laws and regulations which implement those legislative measures adopted by the Community specified in Annex III, as applied at the date of the emission or event;

(b) an emission or activity or any manner of using a product in the course of an activity which the operator demonstrates was not considered likely to cause environmental damage according to the state of scientific and technical knowledge at the time when the emission was released or the activity took place.

5. Measures taken by the competent authority in pursuance of Article 5(3) and (4) and Article 6(2) and (3) shall be without prejudice to the liability of the relevant operator under this Directive and without prejudice to Articles 87 and 88 of the Treaty.

Article 9 Cost allocation in cases of multiple party causation

This Directive is without prejudice to any provisions of national regulations concerning cost allocation in cases of multiple party causation especially concerning the apportionment of liability between the producer and the user of a product.

Article 10 Limitation period for recovery of costs

The competent authority shall be entitled to initiate cost recovery proceedings against the operator, or if appropriate, a third party who has caused the damage or the imminent threat of damage in relation to any measures taken in pursuance of this Directive within five years from the date on which those measures have been completed or the liable operator, or third party, has been identified, whichever is the later.

Article 11 Competent authority

1. Member States shall designate the competent authority(ies) responsible for fulfilling the duties provided for in this Directive.

2. The duty to establish which operator has caused the damage or the imminent threat of damage, to assess the significance of the damage and to determine which remedial measures should be taken with reference to Annex II shall rest with the competent authority. To that effect, the competent authority shall be entitled to require the relevant operator to carry out his own assessment and to supply any information and data necessary.

3. Member States shall ensure that the competent authority may empower or require third parties to carry out the necessary preventive or remedial measures.

4. Any decision taken pursuant to this Directive which imposes preventive or remedial measures shall state the exact grounds on which it is based. Such decision shall be notified forthwith to the operator concerned, who shall at the same time be informed of the legal remedies available to him under the laws in force in the Member State concerned and of the time-limits to which such remedies are subject.

Article 12 Request for action

1. Natural or legal persons:

(a) affected or likely to be affected by environmental damage or

(b) having a sufficient interest in environmental decision making relating to the damage or, alternatively,

(c) alleging the impairment of a right, where administrative procedural law of a Member State requires this as a precondition,

shall be entitled to submit to the competent authority any observations relating to instances of environmental damage or an imminent threat of such damage of which they are aware and shall be entitled to request the competent authority to take action under this Directive.

What constitutes a 'sufficient interest' and 'impairment of a right' shall be determined by the Member States.

To this end, the interest of any non-governmental organisation promoting environmental protection and meeting any requirements under national law shall be deemed sufficient for the purpose of subparagraph (b). Such organisations shall also be deemed to have rights capable of being impaired for the purpose of subparagraph (c).

2. The request for action shall be accompanied by the relevant information and data supporting the observations submitted in relation to the environmental damage in question.

3. Where the request for action and the accompanying observations show in a plausible manner that environmental damage exists, the competent authority shall consider any such observations and requests for action. In such circumstances the competent authority shall give the relevant operator an opportunity to make his views known with respect to the request for action and the accompanying observations.

4. The competent authority shall, as soon as possible and in any case in accordance with the relevant provisions of national law, inform the persons referred to in paragraph 1, which submitted observations to the authority, of its decision to accede to or refuse the request for action and shall provide the reasons for it.

5. Member States may decide not to apply paragraphs 1 and 4 to cases of imminent threat of damage.

Article 13 Review procedures

1. The persons referred to in Article 12(1) shall have access to a court or other independent and impartial public body competent to review the procedural and substantive legality of the decisions, acts or failure to act of the competent authority under this Directive.

2. This Directive shall be without prejudice to any provisions of national law which regulate access to justice and those which require that administrative review procedures be exhausted prior to recourse to judicial proceedings.

Article 14 Financial security

1. Member States shall take measures to encourage the development of financial security instruments and markets by the appropriate economic and financial operators, including financial mechanisms in case of insolvency, with the aim of enabling operators to use financial guarantees to cover their responsibilities under this Directive.

2. The Commission, before 30 April 2010 shall present a report on the effectiveness of the Directive in terms of actual remediation of environmental damages, on the availability at reasonable costs and on conditions of insurance and other types of financial security for the activities covered by Annex III. The report shall also consider in relation to financial security the following aspects: a gradual approach, a ceiling for the financial guarantee and the exclusion of low-risk activities. In the light of that report, and of an extended impact assessment, including a cost-benefit analysis, the Commission shall, if appropriate, submit proposals for a system of harmonised mandatory financial security.

Article 15 Cooperation between Member States

1. Where environmental damage affects or is likely to affect several Member States, those Member States shall cooperate, including through the appropriate exchange of information, with a view to ensuring that preventive action and, where necessary, remedial action is taken in respect of any such environmental damage.

2. Where environmental damage has occurred, the Member State in whose territory the damage originates shall provide sufficient information to the potentially affected Member States.

3. Where a Member State identifies damage within its borders which has not been caused within them it may report the issue to the Commission and any other Member State concerned; it may make recommendations for the adoption of preventive or remedial measures and it may seek, in accordance with this Directive, to recover the costs it has incurred in relation to the adoption of preventive or remedial measures.

Article 16 Relationship with national law

1. This Directive shall not prevent Member States from maintaining or adopting more stringent provisions in relation to the prevention and remedying of environmental damage, including the identification of additional activities to be subject to the prevention and remediation requirements of this Directive and the identification of additional responsible parties.

2. This Directive shall not prevent Member States from adopting appropriate measures, such as the prohibition of double recovery of costs, in relation to situations where double

recovery could occur as a result of concurrent action by a competent authority under this Directive and by a person whose property is affected by environmental damage.

Article 17 Temporal application

This Directive shall not apply to:

- damage caused by an emission, event or incident that took place before the date referred to in Article 19(1),
- damage caused by an emission, event or incident which takes place subsequent to the date referred to in Article 19(1) when it derives from a specific activity that took place and finished before the said date,
- damage, if more than 30 years have passed since the emission, event or incident, resulting in the damage, occurred.

Article 18 Reports and review

1. Member States shall report to the Commission on the experience gained in the application of this Directive by 30 April 2013 at the latest. The reports shall include the information and data set out in Annex VI.

2. On that basis, the Commission shall submit a report to the European Parliament and to the Council before 30 April 2014, which shall include any appropriate proposals for amendment.

3. The report, referred to in paragraph 2, shall include a review of:

(a) the application of:

- Article 4(2) and (4) in relation to the exclusion of pollution covered by the international instruments listed in Annexes IV and V from the scope of this Directive, and
- Article 4(3) in relation to the right of an operator to limit his liability in accordance with the international conventions referred to in Article 4(3).

The Commission shall take into account experience gained within the relevant international fora, such as the IMO and Euratom and the relevant international agreements, as well as the extent to which these instruments have entered into force and/or have been implemented by Member States and/or have been modified, taking account of all relevant instances of environmental damage resulting from such activities and the remedial action taken and the differences between the liability levels in Member States, and considering the relationship between shipowners' liability and oil receivers' contributions, having due regard to any relevant study undertaken by the International Oil Pollution Compensation Funds.

(b) the application of this Directive to environmental damage caused by genetically modified organisms (GMOs), particularly in the light of experience gained within relevant international fora and Conventions, such as the Convention on Biological Diversity and the Cartagena Protocol on Biosafety, as well as the results of any incidents of environmental damage caused by GMOs;

(c) the application of this Directive in relation to protected species and natural habitats;

(d) the instruments that may be eligible for incorporation into Annexes III, IV and V.

Article 19 Implementation

1. Member States shall bring into force the laws, regulations and administrative provisions necessary to comply with this Directive by 30 April 2007. They shall forthwith inform the Commission thereof.

When Member States adopt those measures, they shall contain a reference to this Directive or shall be accompanied by such a reference on the occasion of their official publication. The methods of making such reference shall be laid down by Member States.

2. Member States shall communicate to the Commission the text of the main provisions of national law which they adopt in the field covered by this Directive together with a table

showing how the provisions of this Directive correspond to the national provisions adopted.

Article 20 Entry into force

This Directive shall enter into force on the day of its publication in the Official Journal of the European Union.

Article 21 Addressees

This Directive is addressed to the Member States.

Done at Strasbourg, 21 April 2004.

ANNEX I

CRITERIA REFERRED TO IN ARTICLE 2(1)(A)

The significance of any damage that has adverse effects on reaching or maintaining the favourable conservation status of habitats or species has to be assessed by reference to the conservation status at the time of the damage, the services provided by the amenities they produce and their capacity for natural regeneration. Significant adverse changes to the baseline condition should be determined by means of measurable data such as:

- the number of individuals, their density or the area covered,
- the role of the particular individuals or of the damaged area in relation to the species or to the habitat conservation, the rarity of the species or habitat (assessed at local, regional and higher level including at Community level),
- the species' capacity for propagation (according to the dynamics specific to that species or to that population), its viability or the habitat's capacity for natural regeneration (according to the dynamics specific to its characteristic species or to their populations),
- the species' or habitat's capacity, after damage has occurred, to recover within a short time, without any intervention other than increased protection measures, to a condition which leads, solely by virtue of the dynamics of the species or habitat, to a condition deemed equivalent or superior to the baseline condition.

Damage with a proven effect on human health must be classified as significant damage.

The following does not have to be classified as significant damage:

- negative variations that are smaller than natural fluctuations regarded as normal for the species or habitat in question,
- negative variations due to natural causes or resulting from intervention relating to the normal management of sites, as defined in habitat records or target documents or as carried on previously by owners or operators,
- damage to species or habitats for which it is established that they will recover, within a short time and without intervention, either to the baseline condition or to a condition which leads, solely by virtue of the dynamics of the species or habitat, to a condition deemed equivalent or superior to the baseline condition.

ANNEX II REMEDYING OF ENVIRONMENTAL DAMAGE

This Annex sets out a common framework to be followed in order to choose the most appropriate measures to ensure the remedying of environmental damage.

1. *Remediation of damage to water or protected species or natural habitats*

Remedying of environmental damage, in relation to water or protected species or natural habitats, is achieved through the restoration of the environment to its baseline condition by way of primary, complementary and compensatory remediation, where:

(a) 'Primary' remediation is any remedial measure which returns the damaged natural resources and/or impaired services to, or towards, baseline condition;

(b) 'Complementary' remediation is any remedial measure taken in relation to natural resources and/or services to compensate for the fact that primary remediation does not result in fully restoring the damaged natural resources and/or services;
(c) 'Compensatory' remediation is any action taken to compensate for interim losses of natural resources and/or services that occur from the date of damage occurring until primary remediation has achieved its full effect;
(d) 'interim losses' means losses which result from the fact that the damaged natural resources and/or services are not able to perform their ecological functions or provide services to other natural resources or to the public until the primary or complementary measures have taken effect. It does not consist of financial compensation to members of the public.

Where primary remediation does not result in the restoration of the environment to its baseline condition, then complementary remediation will be undertaken. In addition, compensatory remediation will be undertaken to compensate for the interim losses.

Remedying of environmental damage, in terms of damage to water or protected species or natural habitats, also implies that any significant risk of human health being adversely affected be removed.

1.1. Remediation objectives

Purpose of primary remediation

1.1.1. The purpose of primary remediation is to restore the damaged natural resources and/or services to, or towards, baseline condition.

Purpose of complementary remediation

1.1.2. Where the damaged natural resources and/or services do not return to their baseline condition, then complementary remediation will be undertaken. The purpose of complementary remediation is to provide a similar level of natural resources and/or services, including, as appropriate, at an alternative site, as would have been provided if the damaged site had been returned to its baseline condition. Where possible and appropriate the alternative site should be geographically linked to the damaged site, taking into account the interests of the affected population.

Purpose of compensatory remediation

1.1.3. Compensatory remediation shall be undertaken to compensate for the interim loss of natural resources and services pending recovery. This compensation consists of additional improvements to protected natural habitats and species or water at either the damaged site or at an alternative site. It does not consist of financial compensation to members of the public.

1.2. Identification of remedial measures

Identification of primary remedial measures

1.2.1. Options comprised of actions to directly restore the natural resources and services towards baseline condition on an accelerated time frame, or through natural recovery, shall be considered.

Identification of complementary and compensatory remedial measures

1.2.2. When determining the scale of complementary and compensatory remedial measures, the use of resource-to-resource or service-to-service equivalence approaches shall be considered first. Under these approaches, actions that provide natural resources and/or services of the same type, quality and quantity as those damaged shall be considered first. Where this is not possible, then alternative natural resources and/or services shall be provided. For example, a reduction in quality could be offset by an increase in the quantity of remedial measures.

1.2.3. If it is not possible to use the first choice resource-to-resource or service-to-service equivalence approaches, then alternative valuation techniques shall be used. The competent authority may prescribe the method, for example monetary valuation, to determine the extent of the necessary complementary and compensatory remedial measures. If valuation of the lost resources and/or services is practicable, but valuation of the replacement natural resources and/or services cannot be performed within a reasonable time-frame or at a reasonable cost, then the competent authority may choose remedial measures whose cost is equivalent to the estimated monetary value of the lost natural resources and/or services.

The complementary and compensatory remedial measures should be so designed that they provide for additional natural resources and/or services to reflect time preferences and the time profile of the remedial measures. For example, the longer the period of time before the baseline condition is reached, the greater the amount of compensatory remedial measures that will be undertaken (other things being equal).

1.3. Choice of the remedial options

1.3.1. The reasonable remedial options should be evaluated, using best available technologies, based on the following criteria:

- The effect of each option on public health and safety,
- The cost of implementing the option,
- The likelihood of success of each option,
- The extent to which each option will prevent future damage, and avoid collateral damage as a result of implementing the option,
- The extent to which each option benefits to each component of the natural resource and/or service,
- The extent to which each option takes account of relevant social, economic and cultural concerns and other relevant factors specific to the locality,
- The length of time it will take for the restoration of the environmental damage to be effective,
- The extent to which each option achieves the restoration of site of the environmental damage,
- The geographical linkage to the damaged site.

1.3.2. When evaluating the different identified remedial options, primary remedial measures that do not fully restore the damaged water or protected species or natural habitat to baseline or that restore it more slowly can be chosen. This decision can be taken only if the natural resources and/or services foregone at the primary site as a result of the decision are compensated for by increasing complementary or compensatory actions to provide a similar level of natural resources and/or services as were foregone. This will be the case, for example, when the equivalent natural resources and/or services could be provided elsewhere at a lower cost. These additional remedial measures shall be determined in accordance with the rules set out in section 1.2.2.

1.3.2. Notwithstanding the rules set out in section 1.3.2. and in accordance with Article 7(3), the competent authority is entitled to decide that no further remedial measures should be taken if:

(a) the remedial measures already taken secure that there is no longer any significant risk of adversely affecting human health, water or protected species and natural habitats, and

(b) the cost of the remedial measures that should be taken to reach baseline condition or similar level would be disproportionate to the environmental benefits to be obtained.

2. *Remediation of land damage*

The necessary measures shall be taken to ensure, as a minimum, that the relevant contaminants are removed, controlled, contained or diminished so that the contaminated land, taking account of its current use or approved future use at the time of the damage, no longer poses any significant risk of adversely affecting human health. The presence of such risks shall be assessed through risk-assessment procedures taking into account the characteristic and function of the soil, the type and concentration of the harmful substances, preparations, organisms or micro-organisms, their risk and the possibility of their dispersion. Use shall be ascertained on the basis of the land use regulations, or other relevant regulations, in force, if any, when the damage occurred.

If the use of the land is changed, all necessary measures shall be taken to prevent any adverse effects on human health.

If land use regulations, or other relevant regulations, are lacking, the nature of the relevant area where the damage occurred, taking into account its expected development, shall determine the use of the specific area.

A natural recovery option, that is to say an option in which no direct human intervention in the recovery process would be taken, shall be considered.

ANNEX III ACTIVITIES REFERRED TO IN ARTICLE 3(1)

1. The operation of installations subject to permit in pursuance of Council Directive 96/61/EC of 24 September 1996 concerning integrated pollution prevention and control. That means all activities listed in Annex I of Directive 96/61/EC with the exception of installations or parts of installations used for research, development and testing of new products and processes.

2. Waste management operations, including the collection, transport, recovery and disposal of waste and hazardous waste, including the supervision of such operations and after-care of disposal sites, subject to permit or registration in pursuance of Council Directive 75/442/EEC of 15 July 1975 on waste and Council Directive 91/689/EEC of 12 December 1991 on hazardous waste.

Those operations include, inter alia, the operation of landfill sites under Council Directive 1999/31/EC of 26 April 1999 on the landfill of waste and the operation of incineration plants under Directive 2000/76/EC of the European Parliament and of the Council of 4 December 2000 on the incineration of waste.

For the purpose of this Directive, Member States may decide that those operations shall not include the spreading of sewage sludge from urban waste water treatment plants, treated to an approved standard, for agricultural purposes.

3. All discharges into the inland surface water, which require prior authorisation in pursuance of Council Directive 76/464/EEC of 4 May 1976 on pollution caused by certain dangerous substances, discharged into the aquatic environment of the Community.

4. All discharges of substances into groundwater which require prior authorisation in pursuance of Council Directive 80/68/EEC of 17 December 1979 on the protection of groundwater against pollution caused by certain dangerous substances.

5. The discharge or injection of pollutants into surface water or groundwater which require a permit, authorisation or registration in pursuance of Directive 2000/60/EC.

6. Water abstraction and impoundment of water subject to prior authorisation in pursuance of Directive 2000/60/EC.

7. Manufacture, use, storage, processing, filling, release into the environment and onsite transport of

(a) dangerous substances as defined in Article 2(2) of Council Directive 67/548/EEC of 27 June 1967 on the approximation of the laws, regulations and administrative provisions of the Member States relating to the classification, packaging and labelling of dangerous substances;

(b) dangerous preparations as defined in Article 2(2) of Directive 1999/45/EC of the European Parliament and of the Council of 31 May 1999 concerning the approximation of the laws, regulations and administrative provisions of the Member States relating to the classification, packaging and labelling of dangerous preparations;

(c) plant protection products as defined in Article2(1) of Council Directive 91/414/EEC of 15 July 1991 concerning the placing of plant protection products on the market;

(d) biocidal products as defined in Article 2(1)(a) of Directive 98/8/EC of the European Parliament and of the Council of 16 February 1998 concerning the placing of biocidal products on the market.

8. Transport by road, rail, inland waterways, sea or air of dangerous goods or polluting goods as defined either in Annex A to Council Directive 94/55/EC of 21 November 1994 on the approximation of the laws of the Member States with regard to the transport of dangerous goods by road or in the Annex to Council Directive 96/49/EC of 23 July 1996 on the approximation of the laws of the Member States with regard to the transport of dangerous goods by rail or as defined in Council Directive 93/75/EEC of 13 September 1993 concerning minimum requirements for vessels bound for or leaving Community ports and carrying dangerous or polluting goods.

9. The operation of installations subject to authorisation in pursuance of Council Directive 84/360/EEC of 28 June 1984 on the combating of air pollution from industrial plants in relation to the release into air of any of the polluting substances covered by the aforementioned Directive.

10. Any contained use, including transport, involving genetically modified micro-organisms as defined by Council Directive 90/219/EEC of 23 April 1990 on the contained use of genetically modified micro-organisms.

11. Any deliberate release into the environment, transport and placing on the market of genetically modified organisms as defined by Directive 2001/18/EC of the European Parliament and of the Council.

12. Transboundary shipment of waste within, into or out of the European Union, requiring an authorisation or prohibited in the meaning of Council Regulation (EEC) No 259/93 of 1 February 1993 on the supervision and control of shipments of waste within, into and out of the European Community.

ANNEX IV INTERNATIONAL CONVENTIONS REFERRED TO IN ARTICLE 4(2)

(a) the International Convention of 27 November 1992 on Civil Liability for Oil Pollution Damage;

(b) the International Convention of 27 November 1992 on the Establishment of an International Fund for Compensation for Oil Pollution Damage;

(c) the International Convention of 23 March 2001 on Civil Liability for Bunker Oil Pollution Damage;

(d) the International Convention of 3 May 1996 on Liability and Compensation for Damage in Connection with the Carriage of Hazardous and Noxious Substances by Sea;

(e) the Convention of 10 October 1989 on Civil Liability for Damage Caused during Carriage of Dangerous Goods by Road, Rail and Inland Navigation Vessels.

ANNEX V INTERNATIONAL INSTRUMENTS REFERRED TO IN ARTICLE 4(4)

(a) the Paris Convention of 29 July 1960 on Third Party Liability in the Field of Nuclear Energy and the Brussels Supplementary Convention of 31 January 1963;

(b) the Vienna Convention of 21 May 1963 on Civil Liability for Nuclear Damage;

(c) the Convention of 12 September 1997 on Supplementary Compensation for Nuclear Damage;

(d) the Joint Protocol of 21 September 1988 relating to the Application of the Vienna Convention and the Paris Convention;

(e) the Brussels Convention of 17 December 1971 relating to Civil Liability in the Field of Maritime Carriage of Nuclear Material.

...

Commission Declaration on Article 14(2)— Environmental Liability Directive

The Commission takes note of article 14(2). In accordance with this article, the Commission will present a report, six years after the entry into force of the Directive, covering, inter alia, the availability at reasonable costs and conditions of insurance and other types of financial security. The report will in particular take into account the development by the market forces of appropriate financial security products in relation to the aspects referred to. It will also consider a gradual approach according to the type of damage and the nature of the risks. In the light of the report, the Commission will, if appropriate, submit as soon as possible proposals. The Commission will carry out an impact assessment, extended to the economic, social and environmental aspects, in accordance with the relevant existing rules and in particular the inter-institutional agreement on Better Law-Making and its Communication on Impact Assessment [COM(2002) 276 final].

PART IV

International Law

Rio Declaration on Environment and Development (1992)

The United Nations Conference on Environment and Development,

Having met at Rio de Janeiro from 3 to 14 June 1992,

Reaffirming the Declaration of the United Nations Conference on the Human Environment, adopted at Stockholm on 16 June 1972, and seeking to build upon it,

With the goal of establishing a new and equitable global partnership through the creation of new levels of cooperation among States, key sectors of societies and people,

Working towards international agreements which respect the interests of all and protect the integrity of the global environmental and developmental system,

Recognizing the integral and interdependent nature of the Earth, our home,

Proclaims that:

Principle 1

Human beings are at the centre of concerns for sustainable development. They are entitled to a healthy and productive life in harmony with nature.

Principle 2

States have, in accordance with the Charter of the United Nations and the principles of international law, the sovereign right to exploit their own resources pursuant to their own environmental and developmental policies, and the responsibility to ensure that activities within their jurisdiction or control do not cause damage to the environment of other States or of areas beyond the limits of national jurisdiction.

Principle 3

The right to development must be fulfilled so as to equitably meet developmental and environmental needs of present and future generations.

Principle 4

In order to achieve sustainable development, environmental protection shall constitute an integral part of the development process and cannot be considered in isolation from it.

Principle 5

All States and all people shall cooperate in the essential task of eradicating poverty as an indispensable requirement for sustainable development, in order to decrease the disparities in standards of living and better meet the needs of the majority of the people of the world.

Principle 6

The special situation and needs of developing countries, particularly the least developed and those most environmentally vulnerable, shall be given special priority. International actions in the field of environment and development should also address the interests and needs of all countries.

Principle 7

States shall cooperate in a spirit of global partnership to conserve, protect and restore the health and integrity of the Earth's ecosystem. In view of the different contributions to global environmental degradation, States have common but differentiated responsibilities. The developed countries acknowledge the responsibility that they bear in the international pursuit to sustainable development in view of the pressures their societies place on the global environment and of the technologies and financial resources they command.

Principle 8

To achieve sustainable development and a higher quality of life for all people, States should reduce and eliminate unsustainable patterns of production and consumption and promote appropriate demographic policies.

Principle 9

States should cooperate to strengthen endogenous capacity-building for sustainable development by improving scientific understanding through exchanges of scientific and technological knowledge, and by enhancing the development, adaptation, diffusion and transfer of technologies, including new and innovative technologies.

Principle 10

Environmental issues are best handled with participation of all concerned citizens, at the relevant level. At the national level, each individual shall have appropriate access to information concerning the environment that is held by public authorities, including information on hazardous materials and activities in their communities, and the opportunity to participate in decision-making processes. States shall facilitate and encourage public awareness and participation by making information widely available. Effective access to judicial and administrative proceedings, including redress and remedy, shall be provided.

Principle 11

States shall enact effective environmental legislation. Environmental standards, management objectives and priorities should reflect the environmental and development context to which they apply. Standards applied by some countries may be inappropriate and of unwarranted economic and social cost to other countries, in particular developing countries.

Principle 12

States should cooperate to promote a supportive and open international economic system that would lead to economic growth and sustainable development in all countries, to better address the problems of environmental degradation. Trade policy measures for environmental purposes should not constitute a means of arbitrary or unjustifiable discrimination or a disguised restriction on international trade.

Unilateral actions to deal with environmental challenges outside the jurisdiction of the importing country should be avoided. Environmental measures addressing transboundary or global environmental problems should, as far as possible, be based on an international consensus.

Principle 13

States shall develop national law regarding liability and compensation for the victims of pollution and other environmental damage. States shall also cooperate in an expeditious and more determined manner to develop further international law regarding liability and compensation for adverse effects of environmental damage caused by activities within their jurisdiction or control to areas beyond their jurisdiction.

Principle 14

States should effectively cooperate to discourage or prevent the relocation and transfer to other States of any activities and substances that cause severe environmental degradation or are found to be harmful to human health.

Principle 15

In order to protect the environment, the precautionary approach shall be widely applied by States according to their capabilities. Where there are threats of serious or irreversible damage, lack of full scientific certainty shall not be used as a reason for postponing cost-effective measures to prevent environmental degradation.

Principle 16

National authorities should endeavour to promote the internalization of environmental costs and the use of economic instruments, taking into account the approach that the polluter should, in principle, bear the cost of pollution, with due regard to the public interest and without distorting international trade and investment.

Principle 17

Environmental impact assessment, as a national instrument, shall be undertaken for proposed activities that are likely to have a significant adverse impact on the environment and are subject to a decision of a competent national authority.

Principle 18

States shall immediately notify other States of any natural disasters or other emergencies that are likely to produce sudden harmful effects on the environment of those States. Every effort shall be made by the international community to help States so afflicted.

Principle 19

States shall provide prior and timely notification and relevant information to potentially affected States on activities that may have a significant adverse transboundary environmental effect and shall consult with those States at an early stage and in good faith.

Principle 20

Women have a vital role in environmental management and development. Their full participation is therefore essential to achieve sustainable development.

Principle 21

The creativity, ideals and courage of the youth of the world should be mobilized to forge a global partnership in order to achieve sustainable development and ensure a better future for all.

Principle 22

Indigenous people and their communities and other local communities have a vital role in environmental management and development because of their knowledge and traditional practices. States should recognize and duly support their identity, culture and interests and enable their effective participation in the achievement of sustainable development.

Principle 23

The environment and natural resources of people under oppression, domination and occupation shall be protected.

Principle 24

Warfare is inherently destructive of sustainable development. States shall therefore respect international law providing protection for the environment in times of armed conflict and cooperate in its further development, as necessary.

Principle 25

Peace, development and environmental protection are interdependent and indivisible.

Principle 26

States shall resolve all their environmental disputes peacefully and by appropriate means in accordance with the Charter of the United Nations.

Principle 27

States and people shall cooperate in good faith and in a spirit of partnership in the fulfilment of the principles embodied in this Declaration and in the further development of international law in the field of sustainable development.

United Nations Framework Convention on Climate Change (1992)*

The Parties to this Convention,

Acknowledging that change in the Earth's climate and its adverse effects are a common concern of humankind,

Concerned that human activities have been substantially increasing the atmospheric concentrations of greenhouse gases, that these increases enhance the natural greenhouse effect, and that this will result on average in an additional warming of the Earth's surface and atmosphere and may adversely affect natural ecosystems and humankind,

Noting that the largest share of historical and current global emissions of greenhouse gases has originated in developed countries, that per capita emissions in developing countries are still relatively low and that the share of global emissions originating in developing countries will grow to meet their social and development needs,

Aware of the role and importance in terrestrial and marine ecosystems of sinks and reservoirs of greenhouse gases,

Noting that there are many uncertainties in predictions of climate change, particularly with regard to the timing, magnitude and regional patterns thereof,

Acknowledging that the global nature of climate change calls for the widest possible cooperation by all countries and their participation in an effective and appropriate international response, in accordance with their common but differentiated responsibilities and respective capabilities and their social and economic conditions,

* Reproduced by permission of the United Nations (www.un.org/).

Recalling the pertinent provisions of the Declaration of the United Nations Conference on the Human Environment, adopted at Stockholm on 16 June 1972,

Recalling also that States have, in accordance with the Charter of the United Nations and the principles of international law, the sovereign right to exploit their own resources pursuant to their own environmental and developmental policies, and the responsibility to ensure that activities within their jurisdiction or control do not cause damage to the environment of other States or of areas beyond the limits of national jurisdiction,

Reaffirming the principle of sovereignty of States in international cooperation to address climate change,

Recognizing that States should enact effective environmental legislation, that environmental standards, management objectives and priorities should reflect the environmental and developmental context to which they apply, and that standards applied by some countries may be inappropriate and of unwarranted economic and social cost to other countries, in particular developing countries,

Recalling the provisions of General Assembly resolution 44/228 of 22 December 1989 on the United Nations Conference on Environment and Development, and resolutions 43/53 of 6 December 1988, 44/207 of 22 December 1989, 45/212 of 21 December 1990 and 46/169 of 19 December 1991 on protection of global climate for present and future generations of mankind,

Recalling also the provisions of General Assembly resolution 44/206 of 22 December 1989 on the possible adverse effects of sea-level rise on islands and coastal areas, particularly low-lying coastal areas and the pertinent provisions of General Assembly resolution 44/172 of 19 December 1989 on the implementation of the Plan of Action to Combat Desertification,

Recalling further the Vienna Convention for the Protection of the Ozone Layer, 1985, and the Montreal Protocol on Substances that Deplete the Ozone Layer, 1987, as adjusted and amended on 29 June 1990,

Noting the Ministerial Declaration of the Second World Climate Conference adopted on 7 November 1990,

Conscious of the valuable analytical work being conducted by many States on climate change and of the important contributions of the World Meteorological Organization, the United Nations Environment Programme and other organs, organizations and bodies of the United Nations system, as well as other international and intergovernmental bodies, to the exchange of results of scientific research and the coordination of research,

Recognizing that steps required to understand and address climate change will be environmentally, socially and economically most effective if they are based on relevant scientific, technical and economic considerations and continually re-evaluated in the light of new findings in these areas,

Recognizing that various actions to address climate change can be justified economically in their own right and can also help in solving other environmental problems,

Recognizing also the need for developed countries to take immediate action in a flexible manner on the basis of clear priorities, as a first step towards comprehensive response strategies at the global, national and, where agreed, regional levels that take into account all greenhouse gases, with due consideration of their relative contributions to the enhancement of the greenhouse effect,

Recognizing further that low-lying and other small island countries, countries with low-lying coastal, arid and semi-arid areas or areas liable to floods, drought and desertification, and developing countries with fragile mountainous ecosystems are particularly vulnerable to the adverse effects of climate change,

Recognizing the special difficulties of those countries, especially developing countries, whose economies are particularly dependent on fossil fuel production, use and exportation, as a consequence of action taken on limiting greenhouse gas emissions,

Affirming that responses to climate change should be coordinated with social and economic development in an integrated manner with a view to avoiding adverse impacts on the latter, taking into full account the legitimate priority needs of developing countries for the achievement of sustained economic growth and the eradication of poverty,

Recognizing that all countries, especially developing countries, need access to resources required to achieve sustainable social and economic development and that, in order for developing countries to progress towards that goal, their energy consumption will need to grow taking into account the possibilities for achieving greater energy efficiency and for controlling greenhouse gas emissions in general, including through the application of new technologies on terms which make such an application economically and socially beneficial,

Determined to protect the climate system for present and future generations,

Have agreed as follows:

Article 1

For the purposes of this Convention:

1. 'Adverse effects of climate change' means changes in the physical environment or biota resulting from climate change which have significant deleterious effects on the composition, resilience or productivity of natural and managed ecosystems or on the operation of socio-economic systems or on human health and welfare.
2. 'Climate change' means a change of climate which is attributed directly or indirectly to human activity that alters the composition of the global atmosphere and which is in addition to natural climate variability observed over comparable time periods.
3. 'Climate system' means the totality of the atmosphere, hydrosphere, biosphere and geosphere and their interactions.
4. 'Emissions' means the release of greenhouse gases and/or their precursors into the atmosphere over a specified area and period of time.
5. 'Greenhouse gases' means those gaseous constituents of the atmosphere, both natural and anthropogenic, that absorb and re-emit infrared radiation.
6. 'Regional economic integration organization' means an organization constituted by sovereign States of a given region which has competence in respect of matters governed by this Convention or its protocols and has been duly authorized, in accordance with its internal procedures, to sign, ratify, accept, approve or accede to the instruments concerned.
7. 'Reservoir' means a component or components of the climate system where a greenhouse gas or a precursor of a greenhouse gas is stored.
8. 'Sink' means any process, activity or mechanism which removes a greenhouse gas, an aerosol or a precursor of a greenhouse gas from the atmosphere.
9. 'Source' means any process or activity which releases a greenhouse gas, an aerosol or a precursor of a greenhouse gas into the atmosphere.

Article 2

The ultimate objective of this Convention and any related legal instruments that the Conference of the Parties may adopt is to achieve, in accordance with the relevant provisions of the Convention, stabilization of greenhouse gas concentrations in the atmosphere at a level that would prevent dangerous anthropogenic interference with the climate system. Such a level should be achieved within a time-frame sufficient to allow ecosystems to adapt naturally to climate change, to ensure that food production is not threatened and to enable economic development to proceed in a sustainable manner.

Article 3

In their actions to achieve the objective of the Convention and to implement its provisions, the Parties shall be guided, inter alia, by the following:

1. The Parties should protect the climate system for the benefit of present and future generations of humankind, on the basis of equity and in accordance with their common but differentiated responsibilities and respective capabilities. Accordingly, the developed country Parties should take the lead in combating climate change and the adverse effects thereof.

2. The specific needs and special circumstances of developing country Parties, especially those that are particularly vulnerable to the adverse effects of climate change, and of those Parties, especially developing country Parties, that would have to bear a disproportionate or abnormal burden under the Convention, should be given full consideration.

3. The Parties should take precautionary measures to anticipate, prevent or minimize the causes of climate change and mitigate its adverse effects. Where there are threats of serious or irreversible damage, lack of full scientific certainty should not be used as a reason for postponing such measures, taking into account that policies and measures to deal with climate change should be cost-effective so as to ensure global benefits at the lowest possible cost. To achieve this, such policies and measures should take into account different socio-economic contexts, be comprehensive, cover all relevant sources, sinks and reservoirs of greenhouse gases and adaptation, and comprise all economic sectors. Efforts to address climate change may be carried out cooperatively by interested Parties.

4. The Parties have a right to, and should, promote sustainable development. Policies and measures to protect the climate system against human-induced change should be appropriate for the specific conditions of each Party and should be integrated with national development programmes, taking into account that economic development is essential for adopting measures to address climate change.

5. The Parties should cooperate to promote a supportive and open international economic system that would lead to sustainable economic growth and development in all Parties, particularly developing country Parties, thus enabling them better to address the problems of climate change. Measures taken to combat climate change, including unilateral ones, should not constitute a means of arbitrary or unjustifiable discrimination or a disguised restriction on international trade.

Article 4

1. All Parties, taking into account their common but differentiated responsibilities and their specific national and regional development priorities, objectives and circumstances, shall:

(a) Develop, periodically update, publish and make available to the Conference of the Parties, in accordance with Article 12, national inventories of anthropogenic emissions by sources and removals by sinks of all greenhouse gases not controlled by the Montreal Protocol, using comparable methodologies to be agreed upon by the Conference of the Parties;

(b) Formulate, implement, publish and regularly update national and, where appropriate, regional programmes containing measures to mitigate climate change by addressing anthropogenic emissions by sources and removals by sinks of all greenhouse gases not controlled by the Montreal Protocol, and measures to facilitate adequate adaptation to climate change;

(c) Promote and cooperate in the development, application and diffusion, including transfer, of technologies, practices and processes that control, reduce or prevent anthropogenic emissions of greenhouse gases not controlled by the Montreal Protocol in all relevant sectors, including the energy, transport, industry, agriculture, forestry and waste management sectors;

(d) Promote sustainable management, and promote and cooperate in the conservation and enhancement, as appropriate, of sinks and reservoirs of all greenhouse gases not controlled by the Montreal Protocol, including biomass, forests and oceans as well as other terrestrial, coastal and marine ecosystems;

(e) Cooperate in preparing for adaptation to the impacts of climate change; develop and elaborate appropriate and integrated plans for coastal zone management, water resources and agriculture, and for the protection and rehabilitation of areas, particularly in Africa, affected by drought and desertification, as well as floods;

(f) Take climate change considerations into account, to the extent feasible, in their relevant social, economic and environmental policies and actions, and employ appropriate methods, for example impact assessments, formulated and determined nationally, with a view to minimizing adverse effects on the economy, on public health and on the quality of the environment, of projects or measures undertaken by them to mitigate or adapt to climate change;

(g) Promote and cooperate in scientific, technological, technical, socio-economic and other research, systematic observation and development of data archives related to the climate system and intended to further the understanding and to reduce or eliminate the remaining uncertainties regarding the causes, effects, magnitude and timing of climate change and the economic and social consequences of various response strategies;

(h) Promote and cooperate in the full, open and prompt exchange of relevant scientific, technological, technical, socio-economic and legal information related to the climate system and climate change, and to the economic and social consequences of various response strategies;

(i) Promote and cooperate in education, training and public awareness related to climate change and encourage the widest participation in this process, including that of non-governmental organizations; and

(j) Communicate to the Conference of the Parties information related to implementation, in accordance with Article 12.

2. The developed country Parties and other Parties included in Annex I commit themselves specifically as provided for in the following:

(a) Each of these Parties shall adopt national policies and take corresponding measures on the mitigation of climate change, by limiting its anthropogenic emissions of greenhouse gases and protecting and enhancing its greenhouse gas sinks and reservoirs. These policies and measures will demonstrate that developed countries are taking the lead in modifying longer-term trends in anthropogenic emissions consistent with the objective of the Convention, recognizing that the return by the end of the present decade to earlier levels of anthropogenic emissions of carbon dioxide and other greenhouse gases not controlled by the Montreal Protocol would contribute to such modification, and taking into account the differences in these Parties' starting points and approaches, economic structures and resource bases, the need to maintain strong and sustainable economic growth, available technologies and other individual circumstances, as well as the need for equitable and appropriate contributions by each of these Parties to the global effort regarding that objective. These Parties may implement such policies and measures jointly with other Parties and may assist other Parties in contributing to the achievement of the objective of the Convention and, in particular, that of this subparagraph;

(b) In order to promote progress to this end, each of these Parties shall communicate, within six months of the entry into force of the Convention for it and periodically thereafter, and in accordance with Article 12, detailed information on its policies and measures referred to in subparagraph (a) above, as well as on its resulting projected anthropogenic emissions by sources and removals by sinks of greenhouse gases not controlled by the Montreal Protocol for the period referred to in subparagraph (a), with the aim of returning individually or jointly to their 1990 levels these anthropogenic emissions of carbon dioxide and other greenhouse gases not controlled by the Montreal Protocol. This information will be reviewed by the Conference of the Parties, at its first session and periodically thereafter, in accordance with Article 7;

(c) Calculations of emissions by sources and removals by sinks of greenhouse gases for the purposes of subparagraph (b) above should take into account the best available scientific knowledge, including of the effective capacity of sinks and the respective contributions of such gases to climate change. The Conference of the Parties shall consider and agree on methodologies for these calculations at its first session and review them regularly thereafter;

(d) The Conference of the Parties shall, at its first session, review the adequacy of subparagraphs (a) and (b) above. Such review shall be carried out in the light of the best available scientific information and assessment on climate change and its impacts, as well as relevant technical, social and economic information. Based on this review, the Conference of the Parties shall take appropriate action, which may include the adoption of amendments to the commitments in subparagraphs (a) and (b) above. The Conference of the Parties, at its first session, shall also take decisions regarding criteria for joint implementation as indicated in subparagraph (a) above. A second review of subparagraphs (a) and (b) shall take place not later than 31 December 1998, and thereafter at regular intervals determined by the Conference of the Parties, until the objective of the Convention is met;

(e) Each of these Parties shall:

(i) Coordinate as appropriate with other such Parties, relevant economic and administrative instruments developed to achieve the objective of the Convention; and

(ii) Identify and periodically review its own policies and practices which encourage activities that lead to greater levels of anthropogenic emissions of greenhouse gases not controlled by the Montreal Protocol than would otherwise occur;

(f) The Conference of the Parties shall review, not later than 31 December 1998, available information with a view to taking decisions regarding such amendments to the lists in Annexes I and II as may be appropriate, with the approval of the Party concerned;

(g) Any Party not included in Annex I may, in its instrument of ratification, acceptance, approval or accession, or at any time thereafter, notify the Depositary that it intends to be bound by subparagraphs (a) and (b) above. The Depositary shall inform the other signatories and Parties of any such notification.

3. The developed country Parties and other developed Parties included in Annex II shall provide new and additional financial resources to meet the agreed full costs incurred by developing country Parties in complying with their obligations under Article 12, paragraph 1. They shall also provide such financial resources, including for the transfer of technology, needed by the developing country Parties to meet the agreed full incremental costs of implementing measures that are covered by paragraph 1 of this Article and that are agreed between a developing country Party and the international entity or entities referred to in Article 11, in accordance with that Article. The implementation of these commitments shall take into account the need for adequacy and predictability in the flow of funds and the importance of appropriate burden sharing among the developed country Parties.

4. The developed country Parties and other developed Parties included in Annex II shall also assist the developing country Parties that are particularly vulnerable to the adverse effects of climate change in meeting costs of adaptation to those adverse effects.

5. The developed country Parties and other developed Parties included in Annex II shall take all practicable steps to promote, facilitate and finance, as appropriate, the transfer of, or access to, environmentally sound technologies and know-how to other Parties, particularly developing country Parties, to enable them to implement the provisions of the Convention. In this process, the developed country Parties shall support the development and enhancement of endogenous capacities and technologies of developing country Parties. Other Parties and organizations in a position to do so may also assist in facilitating the transfer of such technologies.

6. In the implementation of their commitments under paragraph 2 above, a certain degree of flexibility shall be allowed by the Conference of the Parties to the Parties included in Annex I undergoing the process of transition to a market economy, in order to enhance the ability of these Parties to address climate change, including with regard to the historical level of anthropogenic emissions of greenhouse gases not controlled by the Montreal Protocol chosen as a reference.

7. The extent to which developing country Parties will effectively implement their commitments under the Convention will depend on the effective implementation by developed country Parties of their commitments under the Convention related to financial resources and transfer of technology and will take fully into account that economic and social development and poverty eradication are the first and overriding priorities of the developing country Parties.

8. In the implementation of the commitments in this Article, the Parties shall give full consideration to what actions are necessary under the Convention, including actions related to funding, insurance and the transfer of technology, to meet the specific needs and concerns of developing country Parties arising from the adverse effects of climate change and/or the impact of the implementation of response measures, especially on:

- (a) Small island countries;
- (b) Countries with low-lying coastal areas;
- (c) Countries with arid and semi-arid areas, forested areas and areas liable to forest decay;
- (d) Countries with areas prone to natural disasters;
- (e) Countries with areas liable to drought and desertification;
- (f) Countries with areas of high urban atmospheric pollution;
- (g) Countries with areas with fragile ecosystems, including mountainous ecosystems;
- (h) Countries whose economies are highly dependent on income generated from the production, processing and export, and/or on consumption of fossil fuels and associated energy-intensive products; and
- (i) Land-locked and transit countries.

Further, the Conference of the Parties may take actions, as appropriate, with respect to this paragraph.

9. The Parties shall take full account of the specific needs and special situations of the least developed countries in their actions with regard to funding and transfer of technology.

10. The Parties shall, in accordance with Article 10, take into consideration in the implementation of the commitments of the Convention the situation of Parties, particularly developing country Parties, with economies that are vulnerable to the adverse effects of the implementation of measures to respond to climate change. This applies notably to Parties with economies that are highly dependent on income generated from the production, processing and export, and/or consumption of fossil fuels and associated energy-intensive products and/or the use of fossil fuels for which such Parties have serious difficulties in switching to alternatives.

Article 5

In carrying out their commitments under Article 4, paragraph 1(g), the Parties shall:

- (a) Support and further develop, as appropriate, international and intergovernmental programmes and networks or organizations aimed at defining, conducting, assessing and financing research, data collection and systematic observation, taking into account the need to minimize duplication of effort;
- (b) Support international and intergovernmental efforts to strengthen systematic observation and national scientific and technical research capacities and capabilities, particularly in developing countries, and to promote access to, and the exchange of, data and analyses thereof obtained from areas beyond national jurisdiction; and

(c) Take into account the particular concerns and needs of developing countries and cooperate in improving their endogenous capacities and capabilities to participate in the efforts referred to in subparagraphs (a) and (b) above.

Article 6

In carrying out their commitments under Article 4, paragraph 1(i), the Parties shall:

(a) Promote and facilitate at the national and, as appropriate, subregional and regional levels, and in accordance with national laws and regulations, and within their respective capacities:

(i) The development and implementation of educational and public awareness programmes on climate change and its effects;

(ii) Public access to information on climate change and its effects;

(iii) Public participation in addressing climate change and its effects and developing adequate responses; and

(iv) Training of scientific, technical and managerial personnel.

(b) Cooperate in and promote, at the international level, and, where appropriate, using existing bodies:

(i) The development and exchange of educational and public awareness material on climate change and its effects; and

(ii) The development and implementation of education and training programmes, including the strengthening of national institutions and the exchange or secondment of personnel to train experts in this field, in particular for developing countries.

Article 7

1. A Conference of the Parties is hereby established.

2. The Conference of the Parties, as the supreme body of this Convention, shall keep under regular review the implementation of the Convention and any related legal instruments that the Conference of the Parties may adopt, and shall make, within its mandate, the decisions necessary to promote the effective implementation of the Convention. To this end, it shall:

(a) Periodically examine the obligations of the Parties and the institutional arrangements under the Convention, in the light of the objective of the Convention, the experience gained in its implementation and the evolution of scientific and technological knowledge;

(b) Promote and facilitate the exchange of information on measures adopted by the Parties to address climate change and its effects, taking into account the differing circumstances, responsibilities and capabilities of the Parties and their respective commitments under the Convention;

(c) Facilitate, at the request of two or more Parties, the coordination of measures adopted by them to address climate change and its effects, taking into account the differing circumstances, responsibilities and capabilities of the Parties and their respective commitments under the Convention;

(d) Promote and guide, in accordance with the objective and provisions of the Convention, the development and periodic refinement of comparable methodologies, to be agreed on by the Conference of the Parties, inter alia, for preparing inventories of greenhouse gas emissions by sources and removals by sinks, and for evaluating the effectiveness of measures to limit the emissions and enhance the removals of these gases;

(e) Assess, on the basis of all information made available to it in accordance with the provisions of the Convention, the implementation of the Convention by the Parties, the overall effects of the measures taken pursuant to the Convention, in particular environmental, economic and social effects as well as their cumulative impacts and the extent to which progress towards the objective of the Convention is being achieved;

(f) Consider and adopt regular reports on the implementation of the Convention and ensure their publication;
(g) Make recommendations on any matters necessary for the implementation of the Convention;
(h) Seek to mobilize financial resources in accordance with Article 4, paragraphs 3, 4 and 5, and Article 11;
(i) Establish such subsidiary bodies as are deemed necessary for the implementation of the Convention;
(j) Review reports submitted by its subsidiary bodies and provide guidance to them;
(k) Agree upon and adopt, by consensus, rules of procedure and financial rules for itself and for any subsidiary bodies;
(l) Seek and utilize, where appropriate, the services and cooperation of, and information provided by, competent international organizations and intergovernmental and non-governmental bodies; and
(m) Exercise such other functions as are required for the achievement of the objective of the Convention as well as all other functions assigned to it under the Convention.

3. The Conference of the Parties shall, at its first session, adopt its own rules of procedure as well as those of the subsidiary bodies established by the Convention, which shall include decision-making procedures for matters not already covered by decision- making procedures stipulated in the Convention. Such procedures may include specified majorities required for the adoption of particular decisions.

...

Article 9

1. A subsidiary body for scientific and technological advice is hereby established to provide the Conference of the Parties and, as appropriate, its other subsidiary bodies with timely information and advice on scientific and technological matters relating to the Convention. This body shall be open to participation by all Parties and shall be multidisciplinary. It shall comprise government representatives competent in the relevant field of expertise. It shall report regularly to the Conference of the Parties on all aspects of its work.

2. Under the guidance of the Conference of the Parties, and drawing upon existing competent international bodies, this body shall:
(a) Provide assessments of the state of scientific knowledge relating to climate change and its effects;
(b) Prepare scientific assessments on the effects of measures taken in the implementation of the Convention;
(c) Identify innovative, efficient and state-of-the-art technologies and know-how and advise on the ways and means of promoting development and/or transferring such technologies;
(d) Provide advice on scientific programmes, international cooperation in research and development related to climate change, as well as on ways and means of supporting endogenous capacity-building in developing countries; and
(e) Respond to scientific, technological and methodological questions that the Conference of the Parties and its subsidiary bodies may put to the body.

3. The functions and terms of reference of this body may be further elaborated by the Conference of the Parties.

Article 10

1. A subsidiary body for implementation is hereby established to assist the Conference of the Parties in the assessment and review of the effective implementation of the Convention. This body shall be open to participation by all Parties and comprise government representatives who are experts on matters related to climate change. It shall report regularly to the Conference of the Parties on all aspects of its work.

2. Under the guidance of the Conference of the Parties, this body shall:
   (a) Consider the information communicated in accordance with Article 12, paragraph 1, to assess the overall aggregated effect of the steps taken by the Parties in the light of the latest scientific assessments concerning climate change;
   (b) Consider the information communicated in accordance with Article 12, paragraph 2, in order to assist the Conference of the Parties in carrying out the reviews required by Article 4, paragraph 2(d); and
   (c) Assist the Conference of the Parties, as appropriate, in the preparation and implementation of its decisions.

Article 11

1. A mechanism for the provision of financial resources on a grant or concessional basis, including for the transfer of technology, is hereby defined. It shall function under the guidance of and be accountable to the Conference of the Parties, which shall decide on its policies, programme priorities and eligibility criteria related to this Convention. Its operation shall be entrusted to one or more existing international entities.

. . .

Article 12

1. In accordance with Article 4, paragraph 1, each Party shall communicate to the Conference of the Parties, through the secretariat, the following elements of information:
   (a) A national inventory of anthropogenic emissions by sources and removals by sinks of all greenhouse gases not controlled by the Montreal Protocol, to the extent its capacities permit, using comparable methodologies to be promoted and agreed upon by the Conference of the Parties;
   (b) A general description of steps taken or envisaged by the Party to implement the Convention; and
   (c) Any other information that the Party considers relevant to the achievement of the objective of the Convention and suitable for inclusion in its communication, including, if feasible, material relevant for calculations of global emission trends.

2. Each developed country Party and each other Party included in Annex I shall incorporate in its communication the following elements of information:
   (a) A detailed description of the policies and measures that it has adopted to implement its commitment under Article 4, paragraphs 2(a) and 2(b); and
   (b) A specific estimate of the effects that the policies and measures referred to in subparagraph (a) immediately above will have on anthropogenic emissions by its sources and removals by its sinks of greenhouse gases during the period referred to in Article 4, paragraph 2(a).

3. In addition, each developed country Party and each other developed Party included in Annex II shall incorporate details of measures taken in accordance with Article 4, paragraphs 3, 4 and 5.

4. Developing country Parties may, on a voluntary basis, propose projects for financing, including specific technologies, materials, equipment, techniques or practices that would be needed to implement such projects, along with, if possible, an estimate of all incremental costs, of the reductions of emissions and increments of removals of greenhouse gases, as well as an estimate of the consequent benefits.

5. Each developed country Party and each other Party included in Annex I shall make its initial communication within six months of the entry into force of the Convention for that Party. Each Party not so listed shall make its initial communication within three years of the entry into force of the Convention for that Party, or of the availability of financial resources in accordance with Article 4, paragraph 3. Parties that are least developed countries may make their initial communication at their discretion. The frequency of subsequent communications by all Parties shall be determined by the Conference of the Parties, taking into account the differentiated timetable set by this paragraph.

. . .

Article 16

1. Annexes to the Convention shall form an integral part thereof and, unless otherwise expressly provided, a reference to the Convention constitutes at the same time a reference to any annexes thereto. Without prejudice to the provisions of Article 14, paragraphs 2(b) and 7, such annexes shall be restricted to lists, forms and any other material of a descriptive nature that is of a scientific, technical, procedural or administrative character.

...

Article 17

1. The Conference of the Parties may, at any ordinary session, adopt protocols to the Convention.

2. The text of any proposed protocol shall be communicated to the Parties by the secretariat at least six months before such a session.

3. The requirements for the entry into force of any protocol shall be established by that instrument.

4. Only Parties to the Convention may be Parties to a protocol.

5. Decisions under any protocol shall be taken only by the Parties to the protocol concerned.

Article 18

1. Each Party to the Convention shall have one vote, except as provided for in paragraph 2 below.

2. Regional economic integration organizations, in matters within their competence, shall exercise their right to vote with a number of votes equal to the number of their member States that are Parties to the Convention. Such an organization shall not exercise its right to vote if any of its member States exercises its right, and vice versa.

Article 21

3. The Global Environment Facility of the United Nations Development Programme, the United Nations Environment Programme and the International Bank for Reconstruction and Development shall be the international entity entrusted with the operation of the financial mechanism referred to in Article 11 on an interim basis. In this connection, the Global Environment Facility should be appropriately restructured and its membership made universal to enable it to fulfil the requirements of Article 11.

Article 23

1. The Convention shall enter into force on the ninetieth day after the date of deposit of the fiftieth instrument of ratification, acceptance, approval or accession.

...

DONE at New York this ninth day of May one thousand nine hundred and ninety-two.

ANNEX I AND ANNEX II COUNTRIES

Annex I

- Australia
- Austria
- Belarus*
- Belgium
- Bulgaria*
- Canada
- Czechoslovakia*
- Denmark
- European Economic Community
- Estonia*

- Finland
- France
- Germany
- Greece
- Hungary*
- Iceland
- Ireland
- Italy
- Japan
- Latvia*
- Lithuania*
- Luxembourg
- Netherlands
- New Zealand
- Norway
- Poland*
- Portugal
- Romania*
- Russian Federation*
- Spain
- Sweden
- Switzerland
- Turkey
- Ukraine*
- United Kingdom of Great Britain and Northern Ireland
- United States of America

*Countries that are undergoing the process of transition to a market economy.

Annex II

- Australia
- Austria
- Belgium
- Canada
- Denmark
- European Economic Community
- Finland
- France
- Germany
- Greece
- Iceland
- Ireland
- Italy
- Japan
- Luxembourg
- Netherlands
- New Zealand
- Norway
- Portugal
- Spain
- Sweden
- Switzerland
- Turkey

- United Kingdom of Great Britain and Northern Ireland
- United States of America

Agreement Establishing the World Trade Organization (1994)*

...

Article I Establishment of the Organization

The World Trade Organization (hereinafter referred to as 'the WTO') is hereby established.

Article II Scope of the WTO

1. The WTO shall provide the common institutional framework for the conduct of trade relations among its Members in matters related to the agreements and associated legal instruments included in the Annexes to this Agreement.

2. The agreements and associated legal instruments included in Annexes 1, 2 and 3 (hereinafter referred to as 'Multilateral Trade Agreements') are integral parts of this Agreement, binding on all Members.

...

Article III Functions of the WTO

1. The WTO shall facilitate the implementation, administration and operation, and further the objectives, of this Agreement and of the Multilateral Trade Agreements ....

2. The WTO shall provide the forum for negotiations among its Members concerning their multilateral trade relations in matters dealt with under the agreements in the Annexes to this Agreement. The WTO may also provide a forum for further negotiations among its Members concerning their multilateral trade relations, and a framework for the implementation of the results of such negotiations, as may be decided by the Ministerial Conference.

3. The WTO shall administer the Understanding on Rules and Procedures Governing the Settlement of Disputes (hereinafter referred to as the 'Dispute Settlement Understanding' or 'DSU') in Annex 2 to this Agreement.

...

Article IV Structure of the WTO

...

3. The General Council shall convene as appropriate to discharge the responsibilities of the Dispute Settlement Body provided for in the Dispute Settlement Understanding. The Dispute Settlement Body may have its own chairman and shall establish such rules of procedure as it deems necessary for the fulfilment of those responsibilities.

...

ANNEX 1A

MULTILATERAL AGREEMENTS ON TRADE IN GOODS

THE GENERAL AGREEMENT ON TARIFFS AND TRADE

PART II

Article III National Treatment on Internal Taxation and Regulation

1. The contracting parties recognize that internal taxes and other internal charges, and laws, regulations and requirements affecting the internal sale, offering for sale, purchase,

transportation, distribution or use of products, and internal quantitative regulations requiring the mixture, processing or use of products in specified amounts or proportions, should not be applied to imported or domestic products so as to afford protection to domestic production.

2. The products of the territory of any contracting party imported into the territory of any other contracting party shall not be subject, directly or indirectly, to internal taxes or other internal charges of any kind in excess of those applied, directly or indirectly, to like domestic products. Moreover, no contracting party shall otherwise apply internal taxes or other internal charges to imported or domestic products in a manner contrary to the principles set forth in paragraph 1.

...

4. The products of the territory of any contracting party imported into the territory of any other contracting party shall be accorded treatment no less favourable than that accorded to like products of national origin in respect of all laws, regulations and requirements affecting their internal sale, offering for sale, purchase, transportation, distribution or use. The provisions of this paragraph shall not prevent the application of differential internal transportation charges which are based exclusively on the economic operation of the means of transport and not on the nationality of the product.

...

Article XI General Elimination of Quantitative Restrictions

1. No prohibitions or restrictions other than duties, taxes or other charges, whether made effective through quotas, import or export licences or other measures, shall be instituted or maintained by any contracting party on the importation of any product of the territory of any other contracting party or on the exportation or sale for export of any product destined for the territory of any other contracting party.

...

Article XX General Exceptions

Subject to the requirement that such measures are not applied in a manner which would constitute a means of arbitrary or unjustifiable discrimination between countries where the same conditions prevail, or a disguised restriction on international trade, nothing in this Agreement shall be construed to prevent the adoption or enforcement by any contracting party of measures:

(a) ...
(b) necessary to protect human, animal or plant life or health;
(c) ...
(d) ...
(e) ...
(f) ...
(g) relating to the conservation of exhaustible natural resources if such measures are made effective in conjunction with restrictions on domestic production or consumption;

...

ANNEX 2

UNDERSTANDING ON RULES AND PROCEDURES GOVERNING THE SETTLEMENT OF DISPUTES

Members hereby *agree* as follows:

Article 1 Coverage and Application

1. The rules and procedures of this Understanding shall apply to disputes brought pursuant to the consultation and dispute settlement provisions of the agreements listed in Appendix 1 to this Understanding (referred to in this Understanding as the 'covered agreements'). ...

Article 2 Administration

1. The Dispute Settlement Body is hereby established to administer these rules and procedures and, except as otherwise provided in a covered agreement, the consultation and dispute settlement provisions of the covered agreements. Accordingly, the DSB shall have the authority to establish panels, adopt panel and Appellate Body reports, maintain surveillance of implementation of rulings and recommendations, and authorize suspension of concessions and other obligations under the covered agreements. . . .

4. Where the rules and procedures of this Understanding provide for the DSB to take a decision, it shall do so by consensus.

APPENDIX 1 AGREEMENTS COVERED BY THE UNDERSTANDING

(A) Agreement Establishing the World Trade Organization

(B) Multilateral Trade Agreements
Annex 1A: Multilateral Agreements on Trade in Goods
Annex 1B: General Agreement on Trade in Services
Annex 1C: Agreement on Trade-Related Aspects of Intellectual Property Rights
Annex 2: Understanding on Rules and Procedures Governing the Settlement of Disputes
. . .

Kyoto Protocol to the United Nations Framework Convention on Climate Change (1997)*

The Parties to this Protocol,

Being Parties to the United Nations Framework Convention on Climate Change, hereinafter referred to as 'the Convention',

In pursuit of the ultimate objective of the Convention as stated in its Article 2,

Recalling the provisions of the Convention,

Being guided by Article 3 of the Convention,

Pursuant to the Berlin Mandate adopted by decision 1/CP.1 of the Conference of the Parties to the Convention at its first session,

Have agreed as follows:

Article 1

For the purposes of this Protocol, the definitions contained in Article 1 of the Convention shall apply. In addition:

1. 'Conference of the Parties' means the Conference of the Parties to the Convention.

2. 'Convention' means the United Nations Framework Convention on Climate Change, adopted in New York on 9 May 1992.

3. 'Intergovernmental Panel on Climate Change' means the Intergovernmental Panel on Climate Change established in 1988 jointly by the World Meteorological Organization and the United Nations Environment Programme.

4. 'Montreal Protocol' means the Montreal Protocol on Substances that Deplete the Ozone Layer, adopted in Montreal on 16 September 1987 and as subsequently adjusted and amended.

5. 'Parties present and voting' means Parties present and casting an affirmative or negative vote.

6. 'Party' means, unless the context otherwise indicates, a Party to this Protocol.

7. 'Party included in Annex I' means a Party included in Annex I to the Convention, as may be amended, or a Party which has made a notification under Article 4, paragraph 2(g), of the Convention.

Article 2

1. Each Party included in Annex I, in achieving its quantified emission limitation and reduction commitments under Article 3, in order to promote sustainable development, shall:

*Reproduced by permission of the United Nations (www.un.org/).

(a) Implement and/or further elaborate policies and measures in accordance with its national circumstances, such as:
   (i) Enhancement of energy efficiency in relevant sectors of the national economy;
   (ii) Protection and enhancement of sinks and reservoirs of greenhouse gases not controlled by the Montreal Protocol, taking into account its commitments under relevant international environmental agreements; promotion of sustainable forest management practices, afforestation and reforestation;
   (iii) Promotion of sustainable forms of agriculture in light of climate change considerations;
   (iv) Research on, and promotion, development and increased use of, new and renewable forms of energy, of carbon dioxide sequestration technologies and of advanced and innovative environmentally sound technologies;
   (v) Progressive reduction or phasing out of market imperfections, fiscal incentives, tax and duty exemptions and subsidies in all greenhouse gas emitting sectors that run counter to the objective of the Convention and application of market instruments;
   (vi) Encouragement of appropriate reforms in relevant sectors aimed at promoting policies and measures which limit or reduce emissions of greenhouse gases not controlled by the Montreal Protocol;
   (vii) Measures to limit and/or reduce emissions of greenhouse gases not controlled by the Montreal Protocol in the transport sector;
   (viii) Limitation and/or reduction of methane emissions through recovery and use in waste management, as well as in the production, transport and distribution of energy;

(b) Cooperate with other such Parties to enhance the individual and combined effectiveness of their policies and measures adopted under this Article, pursuant to Article 4, paragraph 2(e)(i), of the Convention. To this end, these Parties shall take steps to share their experience and exchange information on such policies and measures, including developing ways of improving their comparability, transparency and effectiveness. The Conference of the Parties serving as the meeting of the Parties to this Protocol shall, at its first session or as soon as practicable thereafter, consider ways to facilitate such cooperation, taking into account all relevant information.

2. The Parties included in Annex I shall pursue limitation or reduction of emissions of greenhouse gases not controlled by the Montreal Protocol from aviation and marine bunker fuels, working through the International Civil Aviation Organization and the International Maritime Organization, respectively.

3. The Parties included in Annex I shall strive to implement policies and measures under this Article in such a way as to minimize adverse effects, including the adverse effects of climate change, effects on international trade, and social, environmental and economic impacts on other Parties, especially developing country Parties and in particular those identified in Article 4, paragraphs 8 and 9, of the Convention, taking into account Article 3 of the Convention. The Conference of the Parties serving as the meeting of the Parties to this Protocol may take further action, as appropriate, to promote the implementation of the provisions of this paragraph.

4. The Conference of the Parties serving as the meeting of the Parties to this Protocol, if it decides that it would be beneficial to coordinate any of the policies and measures in paragraph 1(a) above, taking into account different national circumstances and potential effects, shall consider ways and means to elaborate the coordination of such policies and measures.

Article 3

1. The Parties included in Annex I shall, individually or jointly, ensure that their aggregate anthropogenic carbon dioxide equivalent emissions of the greenhouse gases listed

in Annex A do not exceed their assigned amounts, calculated pursuant to their quantified emission limitation and reduction commitments inscribed in Annex B and in accordance with the provisions of this Article, with a view to reducing their overall emissions of such gases by at least 5 per cent below 1990 levels in the commitment period 2008 to 2012.

2. Each Party included in Annex I shall, by 2005, have made demonstrable progress in achieving its commitments under this Protocol.

3. The net changes in greenhouse gas emissions by sources and removals by sinks resulting from direct human-induced land-use change and forestry activities, limited to afforestation, reforestation and deforestation since 1990, measured as verifiable changes in carbon stocks in each commitment period, shall be used to meet the commitments under this Article of each Party included in Annex I. The greenhouse gas emissions by sources and removals by sinks associated with those activities shall be reported in a transparent and verifiable manner and reviewed in accordance with Articles 7 and 8.

4. Prior to the first session of the Conference of the Parties serving as the meeting of the Parties to this Protocol, each Party included in Annex I shall provide, for consideration by the Subsidiary Body for Scientific and Technological Advice, data to establish its level of carbon stocks in 1990 and to enable an estimate to be made of its changes in carbon stocks in subsequent years. The Conference of the Parties serving as the meeting of the Parties to this Protocol shall, at its first session or as soon as practicable thereafter, decide upon modalities, rules and guidelines as to how, and which, additional human-induced activities related to changes in greenhouse gas emissions by sources and removals by sinks in the agricultural soils and the land-use change and forestry categories shall be added to, or subtracted from, the assigned amounts for Parties included in Annex I, taking into account uncertainties, transparency in reporting, verifiability, the methodological work of the Intergovernmental Panel on Climate Change, the advice provided by the Subsidiary Body for Scientific and Technological Advice in accordance with Article 5 and the decisions of the Conference of the Parties. Such a decision shall apply in the second and subsequent commitment periods. A Party may choose to apply such a decision on these additional human-induced activities for its first commitment period, provided that these activities have taken place since 1990.

5. The Parties included in Annex I undergoing the process of transition to a market economy whose base year or period was established pursuant to decision 9/CP.2 of the Conference of the Parties at its second session shall use that base year or period for the implementation of their commitments under this Article. Any other Party included in Annex I undergoing the process of transition to a market economy which has not yet submitted its first national communication under Article 12 of the Convention may also notify the Conference of the Parties serving as the meeting of the Parties to this Protocol that it intends to use an historical base year or period other than 1990 for the implementation of its commitments under this Article. The Conference of the Parties serving as the meeting of the Parties to this Protocol shall decide on the acceptance of such notification.

6. Taking into account Article 4, paragraph 6, of the Convention, in the implementation of their commitments under this Protocol other than those under this Article, a certain degree of flexibility shall be allowed by the Conference of the Parties serving as the meeting of the Parties to this Protocol to the Parties included in Annex I undergoing the process of transition to a market economy.

7. In the first quantified emission limitation and reduction commitment period, from 2008 to 2012, the assigned amount for each Party included in Annex I shall be equal to the percentage inscribed for it in Annex B of its aggregate anthropogenic carbon dioxide equivalent emissions of the greenhouse gases listed in Annex A in 1990, or the base year or period determined in accordance with paragraph 5 above, multiplied by five. Those Parties included in Annex I for whom land-use change and forestry constituted a net source of greenhouse gas emissions in 1990 shall include in their 1990 emissions base year or period the aggregate anthropogenic carbon dioxide equivalent emissions by sources minus removals by sinks in 1990 from land-use change for the purposes of calculating their assigned amount.

8. Any Party included in Annex I may use 1995 as its base year for hydrofluorocarbons, perfluorocarbons and sulphur hexafluoride, for the purposes of the calculation referred to in paragraph 7 above.

9. Commitments for subsequent periods for Parties included in Annex I shall be established in amendments to Annex B to this Protocol, which shall be adopted in accordance with the provisions of Article 21, paragraph 7. The Conference of the Parties serving as the meeting of the Parties to this Protocol shall initiate the consideration of such commitments at least seven years before the end of the first commitment period referred to in paragraph 1 above.

10. Any emission reduction units, or any part of an assigned amount, which a Party acquires from another Party in accordance with the provisions of Article 6 or of Article 17 shall be added to the assigned amount for the acquiring Party.

11. Any emission reduction units, or any part of an assigned amount, which a Party transfers to another Party in accordance with the provisions of Article 6 or of Article 17 shall be subtracted from the assigned amount for the transferring Party.

12. Any certified emission reductions which a Party acquires from another Party in accordance with the provisions of Article 12 shall be added to the assigned amount for the acquiring Party.

13. If the emissions of a Party included in Annex I in a commitment period are less than its assigned amount under this Article, this difference shall, on request of that Party, be added to the assigned amount for that Party for subsequent commitment periods.

14. Each Party included in Annex I shall strive to implement the commitments mentioned in paragraph 1 above in such a way as to minimize adverse social, environmental and economic impacts on developing country Parties, particularly those identified in Article 4, paragraphs 8 and 9, of the Convention. In line with relevant decisions of the Conference of the Parties on the implementation of those paragraphs, the Conference of the Parties serving as the meeting of the Parties to this Protocol shall, at its first session, consider what actions are necessary to minimize the adverse effects of climate change and/or the impacts of response measures on Parties referred to in those paragraphs. Among the issues to be considered shall be the establishment of funding, insurance and transfer of technology.

Article 4

1. Any Parties included in Annex I that have reached an agreement to fulfil their commitments under Article 3 jointly, shall be deemed to have met those commitments provided that their total combined aggregate anthropogenic carbon dioxide equivalent emissions of the greenhouse gases listed in Annex A do not exceed their assigned amounts calculated pursuant to their quantified emission limitation and reduction commitments inscribed in Annex B and in accordance with the provisions of Article 3. The respective emission level allocated to each of the Parties to the agreement shall be set out in that agreement.

2. The Parties to any such agreement shall notify the secretariat of the terms of the agreement on the date of deposit of their instruments of ratification, acceptance or approval of this Protocol, or accession thereto. The secretariat shall in turn inform the Parties and signatories to the Convention of the terms of the agreement.

3. Any such agreement shall remain in operation for the duration of the commitment period specified in Article 3, paragraph 7.

4. If Parties acting jointly do so in the framework of, and together with, a regional economic integration organization, any alteration in the composition of the organization after adoption of this Protocol shall not affect existing commitments under this Protocol. Any alteration in the composition of the organization shall only apply for the purposes of those commitments under Article 3 that are adopted subsequent to that alteration.

5. In the event of failure by the Parties to such an agreement to achieve their total combined level of emission reductions, each Party to that agreement shall be responsible for its own level of emissions set out in the agreement.

6. If Parties acting jointly do so in the framework of, and together with, a regional economic integration organization which is itself a Party to this Protocol, each member State of that regional economic integration organization individually, and together with the regional economic integration organization acting in accordance with Article 24, shall, in the event of failure to achieve the total combined level of emission reductions, be responsible for its level of emissions as notified in accordance with this Article.

Article 5

1. Each Party included in Annex I shall have in place, no later than one year prior to the start of the first commitment period, a national system for the estimation of anthropogenic emissions by sources and removals by sinks of all greenhouse gases not controlled by the Montreal Protocol. Guidelines for such national systems, which shall incorporate the methodologies specified in paragraph 2 below, shall be decided upon by the Conference of the Parties serving as the meeting of the Parties to this Protocol at its first session.

2. Methodologies for estimating anthropogenic emissions by sources and removals by sinks of all greenhouse gases not controlled by the Montreal Protocol shall be those accepted by the Intergovernmental Panel on Climate Change and agreed upon by the Conference of the Parties at its third session. Where such methodologies are not used, appropriate adjustments shall be applied according to methodologies agreed upon by the Conference of the Parties serving as the meeting of the Parties to this Protocol at its first session. Based on the work of, *inter alia*, the Intergovernmental Panel on Climate Change and advice provided by the Subsidiary Body for Scientific and Technological Advice, the Conference of the Parties serving as the meeting of the Parties to this Protocol shall regularly review and, as appropriate, revise such methodologies and adjustments, taking fully into account any relevant decisions by the Conference of the Parties. Any revision to methodologies or adjustments shall be used only for the purposes of ascertaining compliance with commitments under Article 3 in respect of any commitment period adopted subsequent to that revision.

3. The global warming potentials used to calculate the carbon dioxide equivalence of anthropogenic emissions by sources and removals by sinks of greenhouse gases listed in Annex A shall be those accepted by the Intergovernmental Panel on Climate Change and agreed upon by the Conference of the Parties at its third session. Based on the work of, *inter alia*, the Intergovernmental Panel on Climate Change and advice provided by the Subsidiary Body for Scientific and Technological Advice, the Conference of the Parties serving as the meeting of the Parties to this Protocol shall regularly review and, as appropriate, revise the global warming potential of each such greenhouse gas, taking fully into account any relevant decisions by the Conference of the Parties. Any revision to a global warming potential shall apply only to commitments under Article 3 in respect of any commitment period adopted subsequent to that revision.

Article 6

1. For the purpose of meeting its commitments under Article 3, any Party included in Annex I may transfer to, or acquire from, any other such Party emission reduction units resulting from projects aimed at reducing anthropogenic emissions by sources or enhancing anthropogenic removals by sinks of greenhouse gases in any sector of the economy, provided that:

(a) Any such project has the approval of the Parties involved;

(b) Any such project provides a reduction in emissions by sources, or an enhancement of removals by sinks, that is additional to any that would otherwise occur;

(c) It does not acquire any emission reduction units if it is not in compliance with its obligations under Articles 5 and 7; and

(d) The acquisition of emission reduction units shall be supplemental to domestic actions for the purposes of meeting commitments under Article 3.

2. The Conference of the Parties serving as the meeting of the Parties to this Protocol may, at its first session or as soon as practicable thereafter, further elaborate guidelines for the implementation of this Article, including for verification and reporting.

3. A Party included in Annex I may authorize legal entities to participate, under its responsibility, in actions leading to the generation, transfer or acquisition under this Article of emission reduction units.

4. If a question of implementation by a Party included in Annex I of the requirements referred to in this Article is identified in accordance with the relevant provisions of Article 8, transfers and acquisitions of emission reduction units may continue to be made after the question has been identified, provided that any such units may not be used by a Party to meet its commitments under Article 3 until any issue of compliance is resolved.

Article 7

1. Each Party included in Annex I shall incorporate in its annual inventory of anthropogenic emissions by sources and removals by sinks of greenhouse gases not controlled by the Montreal Protocol, submitted in accordance with the relevant decisions of the Conference of the Parties, the necessary supplementary information for the purposes of ensuring compliance with Article 3, to be determined in accordance with paragraph 4 below.

2. Each Party included in Annex I shall incorporate in its national communication, submitted under Article 12 of the Convention, the supplementary information necessary to demonstrate compliance with its commitments under this Protocol, to be determined in accordance with paragraph 4 below.

3. Each Party included in Annex I shall submit the information required under paragraph 1 above annually, beginning with the first inventory due under the Convention for the first year of the commitment period after this Protocol has entered into force for that Party. Each such Party shall submit the information required under paragraph 2 above as part of the first national communication due under the Convention after this Protocol has entered into force for it and after the adoption of guidelines as provided for in paragraph 4 below.

The frequency of subsequent submission of information required under this Article shall be determined by the Conference of the Parties serving as the meeting of the Parties to this Protocol, taking into account any timetable for the submission of national communications decided upon by the Conference of the Parties.

4. The Conference of the Parties serving as the meeting of the Parties to this Protocol shall adopt at its first session, and review periodically thereafter, guidelines for the preparation of the information required under this Article, taking into account guidelines for the preparation of national communications by Parties included in Annex I adopted by the Conference of the Parties. The Conference of the Parties serving as the meeting of the Parties to this Protocol shall also, prior to the first commitment period, decide upon modalities for the accounting of assigned amounts.

Article 8

1. The information submitted under Article 7 by each Party included in Annex I shall be reviewed by expert review teams pursuant to the relevant decisions of the Conference of the Parties and in accordance with guidelines adopted for this purpose by the Conference of the Parties serving as the meeting of the Parties to this Protocol under paragraph 4 below. The information submitted under Article 7, paragraph 1, by each Party included in Annex I shall be reviewed as part of the annual compilation and accounting of emissions inventories and assigned amounts. Additionally, the information submitted under Article 7, paragraph 2, by each Party included in Annex I shall be reviewed as part of the review of communications.

2. Expert review teams shall be coordinated by the secretariat and shall be composed of experts selected from those nominated by Parties to the Convention and, as appropriate, by intergovernmental organizations, in accordance with guidance provided for this purpose by the Conference of the Parties.

3. The review process shall provide a thorough and comprehensive technical assessment of all aspects of the implementation by a Party of this Protocol. The expert review teams shall prepare a report to the Conference of the Parties serving as the meeting of the Parties to this Protocol, assessing the implementation of the commitments of the Party and identifying any

potential problems in, and factors influencing, the fulfilment of commitments. Such reports shall be circulated by the secretariat to all Parties to the Convention. The secretariat shall list those questions of implementation indicated in such reports for further consideration by the Conference of the Parties serving as the meeting of the Parties to this Protocol.

4. The Conference of the Parties serving as the meeting of the Parties to this Protocol shall adopt at its first session, and review periodically thereafter, guidelines for the review of implementation of this Protocol by expert review teams taking into account the relevant decisions of the Conference of the Parties.

5. The Conference of the Parties serving as the meeting of the Parties to this Protocol shall, with the assistance of the Subsidiary Body for Implementation and, as appropriate, the Subsidiary Body for Scientific and Technological Advice, consider:

(a) The information submitted by Parties under Article 7 and the reports of the expert reviews thereon conducted under this Article; and

(b) Those questions of implementation listed by the secretariat under paragraph 3 above, as well as any questions raised by Parties.

6. Pursuant to its consideration of the information referred to in paragraph 5 above, the Conference of the Parties serving as the meeting of the Parties to this Protocol shall take decisions on any matter required for the implementation of this Protocol.

. . .

Article 10

All Parties, taking into account their common but differentiated responsibilities and their specific national and regional development priorities, objectives and circumstances, without introducing any new commitments for Parties not included in Annex I, but reaffirming existing commitments under Article 4, paragraph 1, of the Convention, and continuing to advance the implementation of these commitments in order to achieve sustainable development, taking into account Article 4, paragraphs 3, 5 and 7, of the Convention, shall:

(a) Formulate, where relevant and to the extent possible, cost-effective national and, where appropriate, regional programmes to improve the quality of local emission factors, activity data and/or models which reflect the socio-economic conditions of each Party for the preparation and periodic updating of national inventories of anthropogenic emissions by sources and removals by sinks of all greenhouse gases not controlled by the Montreal Protocol, using comparable methodologies to be agreed upon by the Conference of the Parties, and consistent with the guidelines for the preparation of national communications adopted by the Conference of the Parties;

(b) Formulate, implement, publish and regularly update national and, where appropriate, regional programmes containing measures to mitigate climate change and measures to facilitate adequate adaptation to climate change:

(i) Such programmes would, *inter alia,* concern the energy, transport and industry sectors as well as agriculture, forestry and waste management. Furthermore, adaptation technologies and methods for improving spatial planning would improve adaptation to climate change; and

(ii) Parties included in Annex I shall submit information on action under this Protocol, including national programmes, in accordance with Article 7; and other Parties shall seek to include in their national communications, as appropriate, information on programmes which contain measures that the Party believes contribute to addressing climate change and its adverse impacts, including the abatement of increases in greenhouse gas emissions, and enhancement of and removals by sinks, capacity building and adaptation measures;

(c) Cooperate in the promotion of effective modalities for the development, application and diffusion of, and take all practicable steps to promote, facilitate and finance, as appropriate, the transfer of, or access to, environmentally sound technologies, know-how, practices and processes pertinent to climate change, in particular to developing countries, including the formulation of policies and programmes for the effective transfer of environmentally sound technologies that are publicly owned or in the public domain and the creation of an enabling environment for the private sector, to promote and enhance the transfer of, and access to, environmentally sound technologies;

(d) Cooperate in scientific and technical research and promote the maintenance and the development of systematic observation systems and development of data archives to reduce uncertainties related to the climate system, the adverse impacts of climate change and the economic and social consequences of various response strategies, and promote the development and strengthening of endogenous capacities and capabilities to participate in international and intergovernmental efforts, programmes and networks on research and systematic observation, taking into account Article 5 of the Convention;

(e) Cooperate in and promote at the international level, and, where appropriate, using existing bodies, the development and implementation of education and training programmes, including the strengthening of national capacity building, in particular human and institutional capacities and the exchange or secondment of personnel to train experts in this field, in particular for developing countries, and facilitate at the national level public awareness of, and public access to information on, climate change. Suitable modalities should be developed to implement these activities through the relevant bodies of the Convention, taking into account Article 6 of the Convention;

(f) Include in their national communications information on programmes and activities undertaken pursuant to this Article in accordance with relevant decisions of the Conference of the Parties; and

(g) Give full consideration, in implementing the commitments under this Article, to Article 4, paragraph 8, of the Convention.

Article 11

1. In the implementation of Article 10, Parties shall take into account the provisions of Article 4, paragraphs 4, 5, 7, 8 and 9, of the Convention.

2. In the context of the implementation of Article 4, paragraph 1, of the Convention, in accordance with the provisions of Article 4, paragraph 3, and Article 11 of the Convention, and through the entity or entities entrusted with the operation of the financial mechanism of the Convention, the developed country Parties and other developed Parties included in Annex II to the Convention shall:

(a) Provide new and additional financial resources to meet the agreed full costs incurred by developing country Parties in advancing the implementation of existing commitments under Article 4, paragraph 1(a), of the Convention that are covered in Article 10, subparagraph (a); and

(b) Also provide such financial resources, including for the transfer of technology, needed by the developing country Parties to meet the agreed full incremental costs of advancing the implementation of existing commitments under Article 4, paragraph 1, of the Convention that are covered by Article 10 and that are agreed between a developing country Party and the international entity or entities referred to in Article 11 of the Convention, in accordance with that Article.

The implementation of these existing commitments shall take into account the need for adequacy and predictability in the flow of funds and the importance of appropriate burden sharing among developed country Parties. The guidance to the entity or entities entrusted with the operation of the financial mechanism of the Convention in relevant decisions of the Conference of the Parties, including those agreed before the adoption of this Protocol, shall apply *mutatis mutandis* to the provisions of this paragraph.

3. The developed country Parties and other developed Parties in Annex II to the Convention may also provide, and developing country Parties avail themselves of, financial resources for the implementation of Article 10, through bilateral, regional and other multilateral channels.

Article 12

1. A clean development mechanism is hereby defined.

2. The purpose of the clean development mechanism shall be to assist Parties not included in Annex I in achieving sustainable development and in contributing to the ultimate objective of the Convention, and to assist Parties included in Annex I in achieving compliance with their quantified emission limitation and reduction commitments under Article 3.

3. Under the clean development mechanism:

(a) Parties not included in Annex I will benefit from project activities resulting in certified emission reductions; and

(b) Parties included in Annex I may use the certified emission reductions accruing from such project activities to contribute to compliance with part of their quantified emission limitation and reduction commitments under Article 3, as determined by the Conference of the Parties serving as the meeting of the Parties to this Protocol.

4. The clean development mechanism shall be subject to the authority and guidance of the Conference of the Parties serving as the meeting of the Parties to this Protocol and be supervised by an executive board of the clean development mechanism.

5. Emission reductions resulting from each project activity shall be certified by operational entities to be designated by the Conference of the Parties serving as the meeting of the Parties to this Protocol, on the basis of:

(a) Voluntary participation approved by each Party involved;

(b) Real, measurable, and long-term benefits related to the mitigation of climate change; and

(c) Reductions in emissions that are additional to any that would occur in the absence of the certified project activity.

6. The clean development mechanism shall assist in arranging funding of certified project activities as necessary.

7. The Conference of the Parties serving as the meeting of the Parties to this Protocol shall, at its first session, elaborate modalities and procedures with the objective of ensuring transparency, efficiency and accountability through independent auditing and verification of project activities.

8. The Conference of the Parties serving as the meeting of the Parties to this Protocol shall ensure that a share of the proceeds from certified project activities is used to cover administrative expenses as well as to assist developing country Parties that are particularly vulnerable to the adverse effects of climate change to meet the costs of adaptation.

9. Participation under the clean development mechanism, including in activities mentioned in paragraph 3(a) above and in the acquisition of certified emission reductions, may involve private and/or public entities, and is to be subject to whatever guidance may be provided by the executive board of the clean development mechanism.

10. Certified emission reductions obtained during the period from the year 2000 up to the beginning of the first commitment period can be used to assist in achieving compliance in the first commitment period.

Article 13

1. The Conference of the Parties, the supreme body of the Convention, shall serve as the meeting of the Parties to this Protocol.

2. Parties to the Convention that are not Parties to this Protocol may participate as observers in the proceedings of any session of the Conference of the Parties serving as the meeting of the Parties to this Protocol. When the Conference of the Parties serves as the

meeting of the Parties to this Protocol, decisions under this Protocol shall be taken only by those that are Parties to this Protocol.

...

4. The Conference of the Parties serving as the meeting of the Parties to this Protocol shall keep under regular review the implementation of this Protocol and shall make, within its mandate, the decisions necessary to promote its effective implementation. It shall perform the functions assigned to it by this Protocol and shall:

(a) Assess, on the basis of all information made available to it in accordance with the provisions of this Protocol, the implementation of this Protocol by the Parties, the overall effects of the measures taken pursuant to this Protocol, in particular environmental, economic and social effects as well as their cumulative impacts and the extent to which progress towards the objective of the Convention is being achieved;

(b) Periodically examine the obligations of the Parties under this Protocol, giving due consideration to any reviews required by Article 4, paragraph 2(d), and Article 7, paragraph 2, of the Convention, in the light of the objective of the Convention, the experience gained in its implementation and the evolution of scientific and technological knowledge, and in this respect consider and adopt regular reports on the implementation of this Protocol;

(c) Promote and facilitate the exchange of information on measures adopted by the Parties to address climate change and its effects, taking into account the differing circumstances, responsibilities and capabilities of the Parties and their respective commitments under this Protocol;

(d) Facilitate, at the request of two or more Parties, the coordination of measures adopted by them to address climate change and its effects, taking into account the differing circumstances, responsibilities and capabilities of the Parties and their respective commitments under this Protocol;

(e) Promote and guide, in accordance with the objective of the Convention and the provisions of this Protocol, and taking fully into account the relevant decisions by the Conference of the Parties, the development and periodic refinement of comparable methodologies for the effective implementation of this Protocol, to be agreed on by the Conference of the Parties serving as the meeting of the Parties to this Protocol;

(f) Make recommendations on any matters necessary for the implementation of this Protocol;

(g) Seek to mobilize additional financial resources in accordance with Article 11, paragraph 2;

(h) Establish such subsidiary bodies as are deemed necessary for the implementation of this Protocol;

(i) Seek and utilize, where appropriate, the services and cooperation of, and information provided by, competent international organizations and intergovernmental and non-governmental bodies; and

(j) Exercise such other functions as may be required for the implementation of this Protocol, and consider any assignment resulting from a decision by the Conference of the Parties.

...

Article 15

1. The Subsidiary Body for Scientific and Technological Advice and the Subsidiary Body for Implementation established by Articles 9 and 10 of the Convention shall serve as, respectively, the Subsidiary Body for Scientific and Technological Advice and the Subsidiary Body for Implementation of this Protocol. The provisions relating to the functioning of these two bodies under the Convention shall apply *mutatis mutandis* to this Protocol. ...

2. Parties to the Convention that are not Parties to this Protocol may participate as observers in the proceedings of any session of the subsidiary bodies. When the subsidiary bodies serve as the subsidiary bodies of this Protocol, decisions under this Protocol shall be taken only by those that are Parties to this Protocol.

. . .

Article 17

The Conference of the Parties shall define the relevant principles, modalities, rules and guidelines, in particular for verification, reporting and accountability for emissions trading. The Parties included in Annex B may participate in emissions trading for the purposes of fulfilling their commitments under Article 3. Any such trading shall be supplemental to domestic actions for the purpose of meeting quantified emission limitation and reduction commitments under that Article.

Article 18

The Conference of the Parties serving as the meeting of the Parties to this Protocol shall, at its first session, approve appropriate and effective procedures and mechanisms to determine and to address cases of non-compliance with the provisions of this Protocol, including through the development of an indicative list of consequences, taking into account the cause, type, degree and frequency of non-compliance. Any procedures and mechanisms under this Article entailing binding consequences shall be adopted by means of an amendment to this Protocol.

. . .

Article 21

1. Annexes to this Protocol shall form an integral part thereof and, unless otherwise expressly provided, a reference to this Protocol constitutes at the same time a reference to any annexes thereto. Any annexes adopted after the entry into force of this Protocol shall be restricted to lists, forms and any other material of a descriptive nature that is of a scientific, technical, procedural or administrative character.

. . .

Article 25

1. This Protocol shall enter into force on the ninetieth day after the date on which not less than 55 Parties to the Convention, incorporating Parties included in Annex I which accounted in total for at least 55 per cent of the total carbon dioxide emissions for 1990 of the Parties included in Annex I, have deposited their instruments of ratification, acceptance, approval or accession.

2. For the purposes of this Article, 'the total carbon dioxide emissions for 1990 of the Parties included in Annex I' means the amount communicated on or before the date of adoption of this Protocol by the Parties included in Annex I in their first national communications submitted in accordance with Article 12 of the Convention.

. . .

Article 26

No reservations may be made to this Protocol.

. . .

DONE at Kyoto this eleventh day of December one thousand nine hundred and ninety-seven.

Annex A

Greenhouse gases

Carbon dioxide (CO2)
Methane (CH4)
Nitrous oxide (N2O)
Hydrofluorocarbons (HFCs)
Perfluorocarbons (PFCs)

Sulphur hexafluoride (SF6)

Sectors/source categories

Energy
Fuel combustion
Energy industries
Manufacturing industries and construction
Transport
Other sectors
Other
Fugitive emissions from fuels
Solid fuels
Oil and natural gas
Other
Industrial processes
Mineral products
Chemical industry
Metal production
Other production
Production of halocarbons and sulphur hexafluoride
Consumption of halocarbons and sulphur hexafluoride
Other
Solvent and other product use
Agriculture
Enteric fermentation
Manure management
Rice cultivation
Agricultural soils
Prescribed burning of savannas
Field burning of agricultural residues
Other
Waste
Solid waste disposal on land
Wastewater handling
Waste incineration
Other

Annex B

Party/Quantified emission limitation or reduction commitment (percentage of base year or period)

Australia 108
Austria 92
Belgium 92
Bulgaria* 92
Canada 94
Croatia* 95
Czech Republic* 92
Denmark 92
Estonia* 92
European Community 92
Finland 92
France 92

Germany 92
Greece 92
Hungary* 94
Iceland 110
Ireland 92
Italy 92
Japan 94
Latvia* 92
Liechtenstein 92
Lithuania* 92
Luxembourg 92
Monaco 92
Netherlands 92
New Zealand 100
Norway 101
Poland* 94
Portugal 92
Romania* 92
Russian Federation* 100
Slovakia* 92
Slovenia* 92
Spain 92
Sweden 92
Switzerland 92
Ukraine* 100
United Kingdom of Great Britain and Northern Ireland 92
United States of America 93
* Countries that are undergoing the process of transition to a market economy.

Convention on Access to Information, Public Participation in Decision-Making and Access to Justice in Environmental Matters ('the Aarhus Convention') done at Aarhus, Denmark, on 25 June 1998*

The Parties to this Convention,

...

Have agreed as follows:

Article 1 Objective

In order to contribute to the protection of the right of every person of present and future generations to live in an environment adequate to his or her health and well-being, each Party shall guarantee the rights of access to information, public participation in decision-making, and access to justice in environmental matters in accordance with the provisions of this Convention.

Article 2 Definitions

For the purposes of this Convention,

1. 'Party' means, unless the text otherwise indicates, a Contracting Party to this Convention;
2. 'Public authority' means:
   (a) Government at national, regional and other level;
   (b) Natural or legal persons performing public administrative functions under national law, including specific duties, activities or services in relation to the environment;

* Excerpts from text. Full text available at www.unece.org/enu/pp.

(c) Any other natural or legal persons having public responsibilities or functions, or providing public services, in relation to the environment, under the control of a body or person falling within subparagraphs (a) or (b) above;
(d) The institutions of any regional economic integration organization referred to in article 17 which is a Party to this Convention.

This definition does not include bodies or institutions acting in a judicial or legislative capacity;

3. 'Environmental information' means any information in written, visual, aural, electronic or any other material form on:

(a) The state of elements of the environment, such as air and atmosphere, water, soil, land, landscape and natural sites, biological diversity and its components, including genetically modified organisms, and the interaction among these elements;
(b) Factors, such as substances, energy, noise and radiation, and activities or measures, including administrative measures, environmental agreements, policies, legislation, plans and programmes, affecting or likely to affect the elements of the environment within the scope of subparagraph (a) above, and cost-benefit and other economic analyses and assumptions used in environmental decision-making;
(c) The state of human health and safety, conditions of human life, cultural sites and built structures, inasmuch as they are or may be affected by the state of the elements of the environment or, through these elements, by the factors, activities or measures referred to in subparagraph (b) above;

4. 'The public' means one or more natural or legal persons, and, in accordance with national legislation or practice, their associations, organizations or groups;

5. 'The public concerned' means the public affected or likely to be affected by, or having an interest in, the environmental decision-making; for the purposes of this definition, non-governmental organizations promoting environmental protection and meeting any requirements under national law shall be deemed to have an interest.

Article 3 General provisions

1. Each Party shall take the necessary legislative, regulatory and other measures, including measures to achieve compatibility between the provisions implementing the information, public participation and access-to-justice provisions in this Convention, as well as proper enforcement measures, to establish and maintain a clear, transparent and consistent framework to implement the provisions of this Convention.

2. Each Party shall endeavour to ensure that officials and authorities assist and provide guidance to the public in seeking access to information, in facilitating participation in decision-making and in seeking access to justice in environmental matters.

3. Each Party shall promote environmental education and environmental awareness among the public, especially on how to obtain access to information, to participate in decision-making and to obtain access to justice in environmental matters.

4. Each Party shall provide for appropriate recognition of and support to associations, organizations or groups promoting environmental protection and ensure that its national legal system is consistent with this obligation.

5. The provisions of this Convention shall not affect the right of a Party to maintain or introduce measures providing for broader access to information, more extensive public participation in decision-making and wider access to justice in environmental matters than required by this Convention.

6. This Convention shall not require any derogation from existing rights of access to information, public participation in decision-making and access to justice in environmental matters.

7. Each Party shall promote the application of the principles of this Convention in international environmental decision-making processes and within the framework of international organizations in matters relating to the environment.

8. Each Party shall ensure that persons exercising their rights in conformity with the provisions of this Convention shall not be penalized, persecuted or harassed in any way for their involvement. This provision shall not affect the powers of national courts to award reasonable costs in judicial proceedings.

9. Within the scope of the relevant provisions of this Convention, the public shall have access to information, have the possibility to participate in decision-making and have access to justice in environmental matters without discrimination as to citizenship, nationality or domicile and, in the case of a legal person, without discrimination as to where it has its registered seat or an effective centre of its activities.

Article 4 Access to environmental information

1. Each Party shall ensure that, subject to the following paragraphs of this article, public authorities, in response to a request for environmental information, make such information available to the public, within the framework of national legislation, including, where requested and subject to subparagraph (b) below, copies of the actual documentation containing or comprising such information:
   - (a) Without an interest having to be stated;
   - (b) In the form requested unless:
     - (i) It is reasonable for the public authority to make it available in another form, in which case reasons shall be given for making it available in that form; or
     - (ii) The information is already publicly available in another form.

2. The environmental information referred to in paragraph 1 above shall be made available as soon as possible and at the latest within one month after the request has been submitted, unless the volume and the complexity of the information justify an extension of this period up to two months after the request. The applicant shall be informed of any extension and of the reasons justifying it.

3. A request for environmental information may be refused if:
   - (a) The public authority to which the request is addressed does not hold the environmental information requested;
   - (b) The request is manifestly unreasonable or formulated in too general a manner; or
   - (c) The request concerns material in the course of completion or concerns internal communications of public authorities where such an exemption is provided for in national law or customary practice, taking into account the public interest served by disclosure.

4. A request for environmental information may be refused if the disclosure would adversely affect:
   - (a) The confidentiality of the proceedings of public authorities, where such confidentiality is provided for under national law;
   - (b) International relations, national defence or public security;
   - (c) The course of justice, the ability of a person to receive a fair trial or the ability of a public authority to conduct an enquiry of a criminal or disciplinary nature;
   - (d) The confidentiality of commercial and industrial information, where such confidentiality is protected by law in order to protect a legitimate economic interest. Within this framework, information on emissions which is relevant for the protection of the environment shall be disclosed;
   - (e) Intellectual property rights;
   - (f) The confidentiality of personal data and/or files relating to a natural person where that person has not consented to the disclosure of the information to the public, where such confidentiality is provided for in national law;
   - (g) The interests of a third party which has supplied the information requested without that party being under or capable of being put under a legal obligation to do so, and where that party does not consent to the release of the material; or
   - (h) The environment to which the information relates, such as the breeding sites of rare species.

The aforementioned grounds for refusal shall be interpreted in a restrictive way, taking into account the public interest served by disclosure and taking into account whether the information requested relates to emissions into the environment.

5. Where a public authority does not hold the environmental information requested, this public authority shall, as promptly as possible, inform the applicant of the public authority to which it believes it is possible to apply for the information requested or transfer the request to that authority and inform the applicant accordingly.

6. Each Party shall ensure that, if information exempted from disclosure under paragraphs 3 (c) and 4 above can be separated out without prejudice to the confidentiality of the information exempted, public authorities make available the remainder of the environmental information that has been requested.

7. A refusal of a request shall be in writing if the request was in writing or the applicant so requests. A refusal shall state the reasons for the refusal and give information on access to the review procedure provided for in accordance with article 9. The refusal shall be made as soon as possible and at the latest within one month, unless the complexity of the information justifies an extension of this period up to two months after the request. The applicant shall be informed of any extension and of the reasons justifying it.

8. Each Party may allow its public authorities to make a charge for supplying information, but such charge shall not exceed a reasonable amount.
Public authorities intending to make such a charge for supplying information shall make available to applicants a schedule of charges which may be levied, indicating the circumstances in which they may be levied or waived and when the supply of information is conditional on the advance payment of such a charge.

Article 5 Collection and dissemination of environmental information

1. Each Party shall ensure that:
   (a) Public authorities possess and update environmental information which is relevant to their functions;
   (b) Mandatory systems are established so that there is an adequate flow of information to public authorities about proposed and existing activities which may significantly affect the environment;
   (c) In the event of any imminent threat to human health or the environment, whether caused by human activities or due to natural causes, all information which could enable the public to take measures to prevent or mitigate harm arising from the threat and is held by a public authority is disseminated immediately and without delay to members of the public who may be affected.

2. Each Party shall ensure that, within the framework of national legislation, the way in which public authorities make environmental information available to the public is transparent and that environmental information is effectively accessible, inter alia, by:
   (a) Providing sufficient information to the public about the type and scope of environmental information held by the relevant public authorities, the basic terms and conditions under which such information is made available and accessible, and the process by which it can be obtained;
   (b) Establishing and maintaining practical arrangements, such as:
      (i) Publicly accessible lists, registers or files;
      (ii) Requiring officials to support the public in seeking access to information under this Convention; and
      (iii) The identification of points of contact; and
   (c) Providing access to the environmental information contained in lists, registers or files as referred to in subparagraph (b) (i) above free of charge.

3. Each Party shall ensure that environmental information progressively becomes available in electronic databases which are easily accessible to the public through public telecommunications networks. Information accessible in this form should include:

(a) Reports on the state of the environment, as referred to in paragraph 4 below;
(b) Texts of legislation on or relating to the environment;
(c) As appropriate, policies, plans and programmes on or relating to the environment, and environmental agreements; and
(d) Other information, to the extent that the availability of such information in this form would facilitate the application of national law implementing this Convention, provided that such information is already available in electronic form.

4. Each Party shall, at regular intervals not exceeding three or four years, publish and disseminate a national report on the state of the environment, including information on the quality of the environment and information on pressures on the environment.

5. Each Party shall take measures within the framework of its legislation for the purpose of disseminating, inter alia:
(a) Legislation and policy documents such as documents on strategies, policies, programmes and action plans relating to the environment, and progress reports on their implementation, prepared at various levels of government;
(b) International treaties, conventions and agreements on environmental issues; and
(c) Other significant international documents on environmental issues, as appropriate.

6. Each Party shall encourage operators whose activities have a significant impact on the environment to inform the public regularly of the environmental impact of their activities and products, where appropriate within the framework of voluntary eco-labelling or eco-auditing schemes or by other means.

7. Each Party shall:
(a) Publish the facts and analyses of facts which it considers relevant and important in framing major environmental policy proposals;
(b) Publish, or otherwise make accessible, available explanatory material on its dealings with the public in matters falling within the scope of this Convention; and
(c) Provide in an appropriate form information on the performance of public functions or the provision of public services relating to the environment by government at all levels.

8. Each Party shall develop mechanisms with a view to ensuring that sufficient product information is made available to the public in a manner which enables consumers to make informed environmental choices.

9. Each Party shall take steps to establish progressively, taking into account international processes where appropriate, a coherent, nationwide system of pollution inventories or registers on a structured, computerized and publicly accessible database compiled through standardized reporting. Such a system may include inputs, releases and transfers of a specified range of substances and products, including water, energy and resource use, from a specified range of activities to environmental media and to on-site and offsite treatment and disposal sites.

10. Nothing in this article may prejudice the right of Parties to refuse to disclose certain environmental information in accordance with article 4, paragraphs 3 and 4.

Article 6 Public participation in decisions on specific activities

1. Each Party:
(a) Shall apply the provisions of this article with respect to decisions on whether to permit proposed activities listed in annex I;
(b) Shall, in accordance with its national law, also apply the provisions of this article to decisions on proposed activities not listed in annex I which may have a significant effect on the environment. To this end, Parties shall determine whether such a proposed activity is subject to these provisions; and
(c) May decide, on a case-by-case basis if so provided under national law, not to apply the provisions of this article to proposed activities serving national defence purposes, if that Party deems that such application would have an adverse effect on these purposes.

2. The public concerned shall be informed, either by public notice or individually as appropriate, early in an environmental decision-making procedure, and in an adequate, timely and effective manner, inter alia, of:

(a) The proposed activity and the application on which a decision will be taken;
(b) The nature of possible decisions or the draft decision;
(c) The public authority responsible for making the decision;
(d) The envisaged procedure, including, as and when this information can be provided:
  (i) The commencement of the procedure;
  (ii) The opportunities for the public to participate;
  (iii) The time and venue of any envisaged public hearing;
  (iv) An indication of the public authority from which relevant information can be obtained and where the relevant information has been deposited for examination by the public;
  (v) An indication of the relevant public authority or any other official body to which comments or questions can be submitted and of the time schedule for transmittal of comments or questions; and
  (vi) An indication of what environmental information relevant to the proposed activity is available; and
(e) The fact that the activity is subject to a national or transboundary environmental impact assessment procedure.

3. The public participation procedures shall include reasonable time-frames for the different phases, allowing sufficient time for informing the public in accordance with paragraph 2 above and for the public to prepare and participate effectively during the environmental decision-making.

4. Each Party shall provide for early public participation, when all options are open and effective public participation can take place.

5. Each Party should, where appropriate, encourage prospective applicants to identify the public concerned, to enter into discussions, and to provide information regarding the objectives of their application before applying for a permit.

6. Each Party shall require the competent public authorities to give the public concerned access for examination, upon request where so required under national law, free of charge and as soon as it becomes available, to all information relevant to the decision-making referred to in this article that is available at the time of the public participation procedure, without prejudice to the right of Parties to refuse to disclose certain information in accordance with article 4, paragraphs 3 and 4. The relevant information shall include at least, and without prejudice to the provisions of article 4:

(a) A description of the site and the physical and technical characteristics of the proposed activity, including an estimate of the expected residues and emissions;
(b) A description of the significant effects of the proposed activity on the environment;
(c) A description of the measures envisaged to prevent and/or reduce the effects, including emissions;
(d) A non-technical summary of the above;
(e) An outline of the main alternatives studied by the applicant; and
(f) In accordance with national legislation, the main reports and advice issued to the public authority at the time when the public concerned shall be informed in accordance with paragraph 2 above.

7. Procedures for public participation shall allow the public to submit, in writing or, as appropriate, at a public hearing or inquiry with the applicant, any comments, information, analyses or opinions that it considers relevant to the proposed activity.

8. Each Party shall ensure that in the decision due account is taken of the outcome of the public participation.

9. Each Party shall ensure that, when the decision has been taken by the public authority, the public is promptly informed of the decision in accordance with the

appropriate procedures. Each Party shall make accessible to the public the text of the decision along with the reasons and considerations on which the decision is based.

10. Each Party shall ensure that, when a public authority reconsiders or updates the operating conditions for an activity referred to in paragraph 1, the provisions of paragraphs 2 to 9 of this article are applied mutatis mutandis, and where appropriate.

11. Each Party shall, within the framework of its national law, apply, to the extent feasible and appropriate, provisions of this article to decisions on whether to permit the deliberate release of genetically modified organisms into the environment.

Article 7 Public participation concerning plans, programmes and policies relating to the environment

Each Party shall make appropriate practical and/or other provisions for the public to participate during the preparation of plans and programmes relating to the environment, within a transparent and fair framework, having provided the necessary information to the public. Within this framework, article 6, paragraphs 3, 4 and 8, shall be applied. The public which may participate shall be identified by the relevant public authority, taking into account the objectives of this Convention. To the extent appropriate, each Party shall endeavour to provide opportunities for public participation in the preparation of policies relating to the environment.

Article 8 Public participation during the preparation of executive regulations and/ or generally applicable legally binding normative instruments

Each Party shall strive to promote effective public participation at an appropriate stage, and while options are still open, during the preparation by public authorities of executive regulations and other generally applicable legally binding rules that may have a significant effect on the environment. To this end, the following steps should be taken:

(a) Time-frames sufficient for effective participation should be fixed;
(b) Draft rules should be published or otherwise made publicly available; and
(c) The public should be given the opportunity to comment, directly or through representative consultative bodies.

The result of the public participation shall be taken into account as far as possible.

Article 9 Access to justice

1. Each Party shall, within the framework of its national legislation, ensure that any person who considers that his or her request for information under article 4 has been ignored, wrongfully refused, whether in part or in full, inadequately answered, or otherwise not dealt with in accordance with the provisions of that article, has access to a review procedure before a court of law or another independent and impartial body established by law.

In the circumstances where a Party provides for such a review by a court of law, it shall ensure that such a person also has access to an expeditious procedure established by law that is free of charge or inexpensive for reconsideration by a public authority or review by an independent and impartial body other than a court of law.

Final decisions under this paragraph 1 shall be binding on the public authority holding the information. Reasons shall be stated in writing, at least where access to information is refused under this paragraph.

2. Each Party shall, within the framework of its national legislation, ensure that members of the public concerned

(a) Having a sufficient interest or, alternatively,
(b) Maintaining impairment of a right, where the administrative procedural law of a Party requires this as a precondition,

have access to a review procedure before a court of law and/or another independent and impartial body established by law, to challenge the substantive and procedural legality of any decision, act or omission subject to the provisions of article 6 and, where so provided for under national law and without prejudice to paragraph 3 below, of other relevant provisions of this Convention.

What constitutes a sufficient interest and impairment of a right shall be determined in accordance with the requirements of national law and consistently with the objective of giving the public concerned wide access to justice within the scope of this Convention. To this end, the interest of any non-governmental organization meeting the requirements referred to in article 2, paragraph 5, shall be deemed sufficient for the purpose of subparagraph (a) above. Such organizations shall also be deemed to have rights capable of being impaired for the purpose of subparagraph (b) above.

The provisions of this paragraph 2 shall not exclude the possibility of a preliminary review procedure before an administrative authority and shall not affect the requirement of exhaustion of administrative review procedures prior to recourse to judicial review procedures, where such a requirement exists under national law.

3. In addition and without prejudice to the review procedures referred to in paragraphs 1 and 2 above, each Party shall ensure that, where they meet the criteria, if any, laid down in its national law, members of the public have access to administrative or judicial procedures to challenge acts and omissions by private persons and public authorities which contravene provisions of its national law relating to the environment.

4. In addition and without prejudice to paragraph 1 above, the procedures referred to in paragraphs 1, 2 and 3 above shall provide adequate and effective remedies, including injunctive relief as appropriate, and be fair, equitable, timely and not prohibitively expensive. Decisions under this article shall be given or recorded in writing. Decisions of courts, and whenever possible of other bodies, shall be publicly accessible.

5. In order to further the effectiveness of the provisions of this article, each Party shall ensure that information is provided to the public on access to administrative and judicial review procedures and shall consider the establishment of appropriate assistance mechanisms to remove or reduce financial and other barriers to access to justice.

...

Article 13 Annexes

The annexes to this Convention shall constitute an integral part thereof.

Article 15 Review of compliance

The Meeting of the Parties shall establish, on a consensus basis, optional arrangements of a non-confrontational, non-judicial and consultative nature for reviewing compliance with the provisions of this Convention. These arrangements shall allow for appropriate public involvement and may include the option of considering communications from members of the public on matters related to this Convention.

...

Article 20 Entry into force

1. This Convention shall enter into force on the ninetieth day after the date of deposit of the sixteenth instrument of ratification, acceptance, approval or accession.

...

Procedures and mechanisms relating to compliance under the Kyoto Protocol (Decision 24/CP.7) (2006)*

The Conference of the Parties,

Recalling its decisions 8/CP.4, 15/CP.5, and 5/CP.6 containing the Bonn Agreements on the implementation of the Buenos Aires Plan of Action,

Recalling Article 18 of the Kyoto Protocol to the United Nations Framework Convention on Climate Change,

*Reproduced by permission of The United Nations (www.un.org/).

Noting with appreciation the work done by the Joint Working Group on Compliance on the development of procedures and mechanisms relating to compliance under the Kyoto Protocol,

Recognizing the need to prepare for the early entry into force of the Kyoto Protocol,

Also recognizing the need to prepare for the timely operation of the procedures and mechanisms relating to compliance under the Kyoto Protocol,

Recognizing that the present decision respects the agreement reached at the Conference of the Parties, at the second part of its sixth session, as reflected in section VIII of decision 5/CP.6,

Noting that it is the prerogative of the Conference of the Parties serving as the meeting of the Parties to the Kyoto Protocol to decide on the legal form of the procedures and mechanisms relating to compliance,

1. *Decides* to adopt the text containing the procedures and mechanisms relating to compliance under the Kyoto Protocol annexed hereto;

2. *Recommends* that the Conference of the Parties serving as meeting of the Parties to the Kyoto Protocol, at its first session, adopt the procedures and mechanisms relating to compliance annexed hereto in terms of Article 18 of the Kyoto Protocol.

8th plenary meeting
10 November 2001

ANNEX

Procedures and mechanisms relating to compliance under the Kyoto Protocol

In pursuit of the ultimate objective of the United Nations Framework Convention on Climate Change, hereinafter referred to as 'the Convention', as stated in its Article 2,

Recalling the provisions of the United Nations Framework Convention on Climate Change, and the Kyoto Protocol to the Convention, herein after referred to as 'the Protocol',

Being guided by Article 3 of the Convention,

Pursuant to the mandate adopted in decision 8/CP.4 by the Conference of the Parties at its fourth session,

The following procedures and mechanisms *have been adopted*:

I. Objective

The objective of these procedures and mechanisms is to facilitate, promote and enforce compliance with the commitments under the Protocol.

II. Compliance Committee

1. A compliance committee, hereinafter referred to as 'the Committee', is hereby established.

2. The Committee shall function through a plenary, a bureau and two branches, namely, the facilitative branch and the enforcement branch.

3. The Committee shall consist of twenty members elected by the Conference of the Parties serving as the meeting of the Parties to the Protocol, ten of whom are to be elected to serve in the facilitative branch and ten to be elected to serve in the enforcement branch.

4. Each branch shall elect, from among its members and for a term of two years, a chairperson and a vice-chairperson, one of whom shall be from a Party included in Annex I and one from a Party not included in Annex I. These persons shall constitute the bureau of the Committee. The chairing of each branch shall rotate between Parties included in Annex I and Parties not included in Annex I in such a manner that at any time one chairperson shall be from among the Parties included in Annex I and the other chairperson shall be from among the Parties not included in Annex I.

. . .

6. Members of the Committee and their alternates shall serve in their individual capacities.

They shall have recognized competence relating to climate change and in relevant fields such as the scientific, technical, socio-economic or legal fields.

7. The facilitative branch and the enforcement branch shall interact and cooperate in their functioning and, as necessary, on a case-by-case basis, the bureau of the Committee may designate one or more members of one branch to contribute to the work of the other branch on a non-voting basis.

8. The adoption of decisions by the Committee shall require a quorum of at least three fourths of the members to be present.

9. The Committee shall make every effort to reach agreement on any decisions by consensus. If all efforts at reaching consensus have been exhausted, the decisions shall as a last resort be adopted by a majority of at least three fourths of the members present and voting. In addition, the adoption of decisions by the enforcement branch shall require a majority of members from Parties included in Annex I present and voting, as well as a majority of members from Parties not included in Annex I present and voting.

...

11. The Committee shall take into account any degree of flexibility allowed by the Conference of the Parties serving as the meeting of the Parties to the Protocol, pursuant to Article 3, paragraph 6, of the Protocol and taking into account Article 4, paragraph 6, of the Convention, to the Parties included in Annex I undergoing the process of transition to a market economy.

...

IV. Facilitative branch

1. The facilitative branch shall be composed of:

(a) One member from each of the five regional groups of the United Nations and one member from the small island developing States, taking into account the interest groups as reflected by the current practice in the Bureau of the Conference of the Parties;

(b) Two members from Parties included in Annex I; and

(c) Two members from Parties not included in Annex I.

...

4. The facilitative branch shall be responsible for providing advice and facilitation to Parties in implementing the Protocol, and for promoting compliance by Parties with their commitments under the Protocol, taking into account the principle of common but differentiated responsibilities and respective capabilities as contained in Article 3, paragraph 1, of the Convention. It shall also take into account the circumstances pertaining to the questions before it.

5. Within its overall mandate, as specified in paragraph 4 above, and falling outside the mandate of the enforcement branch, as specified in section V, paragraph 4, below, the facilitative branch shall be responsible for addressing questions of implementation:

(a) Relating to Article 3, paragraph 14, of the Protocol, including questions of implementation arising from the consideration of information on how a Party included in

Annex I is striving to implement Article 3, paragraph 14, of the Protocol; and

(b) With respect to the provision of information on the use by a Party included in Annex I of Articles 6, 12 and 17 of the Protocol as supplemental to its domestic action, taking into account any reporting under Article 3, paragraph 2, of the Protocol.

6. With the aim of promoting compliance and providing for early warning of potential noncompliance, the facilitative branch shall be further responsible for providing advice and facilitation for compliance with:

(a) Commitments under Article 3, paragraph 1, of the Protocol, prior to the beginning of the relevant commitment period and during that commitment period;

(b) Commitments under Article 5, paragraphs 1 and 2, of the Protocol, prior to the beginning of the first commitment period; and

(c) Commitments under Article 7, paragraphs 1 and 4, of the Protocol prior to the beginning of the first commitment period.

7. The facilitative branch shall be responsible for applying the consequences set out in section XIV below.

V. Enforcement branch

1. The enforcement branch shall be composed of:

(a) One member from each of the five regional groups of the United Nations and one member from the small island developing States, taking into account the interest groups as reflected by the current practice in the Bureau of the Conference of the Parties;

(b) Two members from Parties included in Annex I; and

(c) Two members from Parties not included in Annex I.

. . .

3. In electing the members of the enforcement branch, the Conference of the Parties serving as the meeting of the Parties to the Protocol shall be satisfied that the members have legal experience.

4. The enforcement branch shall be responsible for determining whether a Party included in Annex I is not in compliance with:

(a) Its quantified emission limitation or reduction commitment under Article 3, paragraph 1, of the Protocol;

(b) The methodological and reporting requirements under Article 5, paragraphs 1 and 2, and Article 7, paragraphs 1 and 4, of the Protocol; and

(c) The eligibility requirements under Articles 6, 12 and 17 of the Protocol.

5. The enforcement branch shall also determine whether to apply:

(a) Adjustments to inventories under Article 5, paragraph 2, of the Protocol, in the event of a disagreement between an expert review team under Article 8 of the Protocol and the Party involved; and

(b) A correction to the compilation and accounting database for the accounting of assigned amounts under Article 7, paragraph 4, of the Protocol, in the event of a disagreement between an expert review team under Article 8 of the Protocol and the Party involved concerning the validity of a transaction or such Party's failure to take corrective action.

6. The enforcement branch shall be responsible for applying the consequences set out in section XV below for the cases of non-compliance mentioned in paragraph 4 above. The consequences of non-compliance with Article 3, paragraph 1, of the Protocol to be applied by the enforcement branch shall be aimed at the restoration of compliance to ensure environmental integrity, and shall provide for an incentive to comply.

XI. Appeals

1. The Party in respect of which a final decision has been taken may appeal to the Conference of the Parties serving as the meeting of the Parties to the Protocol against a decision of the enforcement branch relating to Article 3, paragraph 1, of the Protocol if that Party believes it has been denied due process.

. . .

3. The Conference of the Parties serving as the meeting of the Parties to the Protocol may agree by a three-fourths majority vote of the Parties present and voting at the meeting to override the decision of the enforcement branch, in which event the Conference of the Parties serving as the meeting of the Parties to the Protocol shall refer the matter of the appeal back to the enforcement branch.

4. The decision of the enforcement branch shall stand pending the decision on appeal. It shall become definitive if, after 45 days, no appeal has been made against it.

. . .

XIV. Consequences applied by the facilitative branch

The facilitative branch, taking into account the principle of common but differentiated responsibilities and respective capabilities, shall decide on the application of one or more of the following consequences:

(a) Provision of advice and facilitation of assistance to individual Parties regarding the implementation of the Protocol;

(b) Facilitation of financial and technical assistance to any Party concerned, including technology transfer and capacity building from sources other than those established under the Convention and the Protocol for the developing countries;

(c) Facilitation of financial and technical assistance, including technology transfer and capacity building, taking into account Article 4, paragraphs 3, 4 and 5, of the Convention; and

(d) Formulation of recommendations to the Party concerned, taking into account Article 4, paragraph 7, of the Convention.

XV. Consequences applied by the enforcement branch

1. Where the enforcement branch has determined that a Party is not in compliance with Article 5, paragraph 1 or paragraph 2, or Article 7, paragraph 1 or paragraph 4, of the Protocol, it shall apply the following consequences, taking into account the cause, type, degree and frequency of the non-compliance of that Party:

(a) Declaration of non-compliance; and

(b) Development of a plan in accordance with paragraphs 2 and 3 below.

2. The Party not in compliance under paragraph 1 above, shall, within three months after the determination of non-compliance, or such longer period that the enforcement branch considers appropriate, submit to the enforcement branch for review and assessment a plan that includes:

(a) An analysis of the causes of non-compliance of the Party;

(b) Measures that the Party intends to implement in order to remedy the non-compliance; and

(c) A timetable for implementing such measures within a time frame not exceeding twelve months which enables the assessment of progress in the implementation.

3. The Party not in compliance under paragraph 1 above shall submit to the enforcement branch progress reports on the implementation of the plan on a regular basis.

4. Where the enforcement branch has determined that a Party included in Annex I does not meet one or more of the eligibility requirements under Articles 6, 12 and 17 of the Protocol, it shall suspend the eligibility of that Party in accordance with relevant provisions under those articles. At the request of the Party concerned, eligibility may be reinstated ...

5. Where the enforcement branch has determined that the emissions of a Party have exceeded its assigned amount, calculated pursuant to its quantified emission limitation or reduction commitment inscribed in Annex B to the Protocol and in accordance with the provisions of Article 3 of the Protocol as well as the modalities for the accounting of assigned amounts under Article 7, paragraph 4, of the Protocol, taking into account emission reduction units, certified emission reductions, assigned amount units and removal units the Party has acquired in accordance with section XIII, it shall declare that that Party is not in compliance with its commitments under Article 3, paragraph 1, of the Protocol, and shall apply the following consequences:

(a) Deduction from the Party's assigned amount for the second commitment period of a number of tonnes equal to 1.3 times the amount in tonnes of excess emissions;

(b) Development of a compliance action plan in accordance with paragraphs 6 and 7 below; and

(c) Suspension of the eligibility to make transfers under Article 17 of the Protocol until the Party is reinstated in accordance with section X, paragraph 3 or paragraph 4.

6. The Party not in compliance under paragraph 5 above shall, within three months after the determination of non-compliance or, where the circumstances of an individual case so warrant, such longer period that the enforcement branch considers appropriate, submit to the enforcement branch for review and assessment a compliance action plan that includes:

(a) An analysis of the causes of the non-compliance of the Party;
(b) Action that the Party intends to implement in order to meet its quantified emission limitation or reduction commitment in the subsequent commitment period, giving priority to domestic policies and measures; and
(c) A timetable for implementing such action, which enables the assessment of annual progress in the implementation, within a time frame that does not exceed three years or up to the end of the subsequent commitment period, whichever occurs sooner. At the request of the Party, the enforcement branch may, where the circumstances of an individual case so warrant, extend the time for implementing such action for a period which shall not exceed the maximum period of three years mentioned above.

7. The Party not in compliance under paragraph 5 above shall submit to the enforcement branch a progress report on the implementation of the compliance action plan on an annual basis.

8. For subsequent commitment periods, the rate referred to in paragraph 5 (a) above shall be determined by an amendment.

XVI. Relationship with Articles 16 and 19 of the Protocol

The procedures and mechanisms relating to compliance shall operate without prejudice to Articles 16 and 19 of the Protocol.

INDEX

Blackstone's

Environmental Legislation